INFORMATION RIGHTS

AUSTRALIA
Law Book Co.
Sydney

CANADA
Carswell
Toronto

HONG KONG
Sweet & Maxwell Asia

NEW ZEALAND
Brookers
Auckland

SINGAPORE and MALAYSIA
Sweet & Maxwell Asia
Singapore and Kuala Lumper

INFORMATION RIGHTS

by

Philip Coppel

Contributors

Hodge Malek Q.C.
Richard Spearman Q.C.
Timothy Straker Q.C.
Jonathan Auburn
Lisa Busch
Gillian Carrington
Sarah Jane Davies
Paul Greatorex
Jonathan Moffett
Oliver Sanders
Murray Shanks
Andrew Sharland

LONDON
SWEET & MAXWELL
2004

Published in 2004 by
Sweet & Maxwell Limited of
100 Avenue Road, Swiss Cottage, London NW3 3PF
(*www.sweetandmaxwell.co.uk*)
Typeset by J&L Composition, Filey, North Yorkshire.
Printed in Great Britain by MPG Books Ltd, Bodmin, Cornwall.
No natural forests were destroyed to make this product;
only farmed timber was used and replanted.

A CIP catalogue record for
this book is available
from the British Library

ISBN 0421 774703

ISBN 0-421-77470-3

9 780421 774704

FOREWORD

Freedom of information is a topical but complex subject. There is a widely acknowledged public interest in giving people a right of access to information held about them by public authorities and in increasing the transparency of governmental decision-making. But the public interest also requires limits to be placed on what public authorities can be required to disclose, and there is room for legitimate debate about where those limits should be drawn. Historically, and perhaps understandably, central government in the United Kingdom has been slow to shed the aura of secrecy surrounding its internal processes. Legislation conferring rights of access to information has been piecemeal, sometimes prompted by the requirements of European Union law. Disclosure has otherwise been the subject of voluntary arrangements rather than enforceable rights. And even where the virtues of increased transparency have been acknowledged in principle, a cautious approach has been adopted towards the drawing of limits to disclosure.

The Freedom of Information Act 2000, due to come fully into force in early 2005, marks an important step forward, though it is superimposed upon the earlier legislation rather than providing in itself a complete legislative code. It will not end the debate about the proper limits of disclosure by public authorities, but it will help to shape that debate for the future. It establishes for the first time a general right to disclosure of information held by public authorities. The regime is, however, elaborate and the right to disclosure is subject to numerous exemptions of various kinds. In many cases a balance has to be struck between the public interest in disclosure of the information and the public interest in maintaining an exemption. The whole area of exemptions is redolent of the issues that have arisen over the years where public interest immunity is relied on as a ground for non-disclosure of information or documents in legal proceedings.

The subject calls for detailed guidance of the kind that Philip Coppel and his team of contributors have provided in this excellent book. The book's analysis of the United Kingdom legislation is clear and comprehensive, so well structured in its treatment of the subject that it is relatively easy to find what one wants even without having recourse to the index (which was not available to me on reading the book at the proof stage). Whilst rightly concentrating on the

Freedom of Information Act 2000, it also deals in detail with the earlier legislation – and with the differences between the Act of 2000 and the regime operating in Scotland pursuant to the Freedom of Information (Scotland) Act 2002. It places the legislative provisions in their historical and policy context, which may be important when it comes to questions of interpretation. It takes account of the impact of the European Convention on Human Rights and of European Union law. It provides helpful comparisons with the experience in a number of other jurisdictions.

Altogether the book is an impressive achievement and will, I am sure, quickly establish itself as a leading work in the field.

The Hon. Mr Justice Richards

PREFACE

The enactment of the Freedom of Information Act 2000 represents the most significant step in the development within the United Kingdom of the right of an individual to elicit information from a public authority. Over the 40 preceding years, a patchwork of legislation had provided the individual with limited rights of access to information held by public authorities. Invariably, there rights were confined in scope by reference to the subject matter of the information, to the identity of the public authority holding the information, to the identity of the person seeking the information, or to any combination of these. While Freedom of Information Act 2000 largely dispenses with these limitations, the patchwork of earlier legislation remains in place. To the extent that a right of access to particular information can be grounded in the earlier legislation, the regime operates to require that that right be used over the right that might otherwise exist under the Freedom of Information Act 2000. Both for the individual seeking to secure information from a public authority and for the public authority responding to a request for information, what is of paramount concern is whether there is a right of access to that information: it is not merely whether there is a right of access to that information under the Freedom of Information Act 2000. This work has therefore sought to treat comprehensively rights of access to information held by public authorities, whatever the source of that right. These have been compendiously termed "information rights". It is, in any event, a term that I consider better describes the reality, with its sharply competing considerations, than does "freedom of information".

The work is a practitioner's text. By this I do not just mean legal practitioners, but all those whose occupation involves seeking or handling requests for official information. Its purpose is not evangelical: that is a purpose that is well served by the material already on offer.

The Freedom of Information Act 2000 is at once both complex and subtle. It is to be hoped that this work will assist in resolving its complexities and in revealing its subtleties. The complexities, which may seem needless at times, are in no small part due to its respect for the earlier evolution of information rights. It is only by simultaneously considering these other information rights that its complexities can begin to be unpicked.

Both during its passage through Parliament and afterwards, considerable criticism was levelled at the range of exemptions provided by the Freedom of Information Act 2000. It is enough for present purposes to make the following observation. It is true that the Act has been cast widely, with an extensive range of public authorities being netted; but it is also true that the mesh of that net is wide in parts. And yet, this is to miss the central feature of the Freedom of Information Act 2000: the role of the public interest and of the Information Commissioner. Together, these result in the ultimate "strength" of the Act lying in the hands of the latter through his conceptualisation of the former.

Inevitably, there has within this work been a certain amount of speculation as to the meaning and operation of the provisions of the Freedom of Information Act 2000. I have sought to found that speculation upon a consideration of cognate branches of the law and by reference to the jurisprudence of comparative jurisdictions. The Freedom of Information Act 2000 will, of course, have to be interpreted according to its own terms and having regard to the circumstances and standards of this jurisdiction. However, in asking and answering the right questions on issues involving complex and sensitive concepts, it is illuminating to consider how other democratic jurisdictions enjoying similar legal traditions have addressed these issues. That a comparable jurisdiction has had to wrestle with these issues is comforting; that that jurisdiction has worked out solutions consistent with its constitutional standards is both invaluable and instructive. Given that freely available databases on the Internet enable sedentary access to most of the comparative authorities cited in this work, it would be wilful to ignore this seam of jurisprudence.

In writing this book, I must first extend my gratitude to the contributors. Having been persuaded or cajoled by me into joining an enterprise that I promised would not materially interfere with their practices, I provided each with piles of material and lists of authorities that I feel reasonably confident none expected. The work has been much enhanced by their expertise and their contributions. For any remaining shortcomings in the book, I take full responsibility.

I am grateful to Mr Justice Richards for making the time to read the proofs and to write his generous Foreword. Finally, I thank my father for his unstinting support for me in this project.

I have attempted to state the law in light of the material available to me at January 1, 2004. It is intended to keep the book updated by the issue of cumulative supplements as appropriate. Comments on the work, critical or otherwise, are generally welcomed.

Philip Coppel
4–5 Gray's Inn Square
London
WC1R 5AH

CONTENTS

For foreign legislation please view online at *www.sweetandmaxwell.co.uk/informationrights.*

TABLE OF CASES

United Kingdom

R. (on the application of Holding & Barnes plc) v Secretary of State for the Environment, Transport and the Regions; sub nom. R. v Secretary of State for the Environment, Transport and the Regions Ex p. Holdings & Barnes plc [2001] UKHL 23; [2001] 2 W.L.R. 1389; [2001] 2 All E.R. 929; [2002] Env. L.R. 12; [2001] H.R.L.R. 45; [2001] U.K.H.R.R. 728; 3 L.G.L.R. 38; 82 P. & C.R. 40; [2001] 2 P.L.R. 76; [2001] J.P.L. 920; [2001] 20 E.G.C.S. 228; 98(24) L.S.G. 45; 151 N.L.J. 727; 145 S.J.L.B. 140; [2001] N.P.C. 90, HL 14–041

R. (on the application of Howard) v Secretary of State for Health; sub nom. Howard v Secretary of State for Health [2002] EWHC 396; [2003] Q.B. 830; [2002] 3 W.L.R. 738; 99(18) L.S.G. 37; 146 S.J.L.B. 86, QBD 1–032, 14–043, 17–023

R. (on the application of Lord) v Secretary of State for the Home Department [2003] EWHC 2073, QBD 4–005, 4–052, 4–077, 14–034, 15–014, 17–023, 20–018

R. (on the application of Morgan Grenfell & Co Ltd) v Special Commissioner of Income Tax; sub nom. R. v Inland Revenue Commissioners Ex p. Morgan Grenfell & Co Ltd; R. v Special Commissioners of Income Tax Ex p. Morgan Grenfell & Co Ltd [2002] UKHL 21; [2003] 1 A.C. 563; [2002] 2 W.L.R. 1299; [2002] 3 All E.R. 1; [2002] S.T.C. 786; [2002] H.R.L.R. 42; 74 T.C. 511; [2002] B.T.C. 223; 4 I.T.L. Rep. 809; [2002] S.T.I. 806; 99(25) L.S.G. 35; 146 S.J.L.B. 126; [2002] N.P.C. 70, HL 21–014

R. (on the application of Munjaz) v Mersey Care NHS Trust; sub nom. R. (on the application of Colonel M) v Ashworth Hospital Authority (now Mersey Care NHS Trust) [2003] EWCA Civ 1036; [2003] 3 W.L.R. 1505; (2003) 147 S.J.L.B. 903, CA 9–003

R. (on the application of Paul Da Costa & Co.) v Thames Magistrates' Court [2002] EWHC 40; [2002] S.T.C. 267; [2002] B.T.C. 5605; [2003] B.V.C. 3; [2002] Crim. L.R. 504; [2002] S.T.I. 112; 152 N.L.J. 141, QBD 7–007

R. (on the application of Persey) v Secretary of State for the Environment, Food and Rural Affairs; sub nom. Persey v Secretary of State for the Environment, Food and Rural Affairs [2002] EWHC 371; [2003] Q.B. 794; [2002] 3 W.L.R. 704; 99(18) L.S.G. 37; 146 S.J.L.B. 92; [2002] N.P.C. 44, QBD 1–032, 14–043, 17–023, 22–023

R. (on the application of ProLife Alliance) v BBC; sub nom. ProLife Alliance v BBC; R. (on the application of Quintavalle) v BBC [2003] UKHL 23; [2003] 2 W.L.R. 1403; [2003] 2 All E.R. 977; [2003] E.M.L.R. 23; [2003] H.R.L.R. 26; [2003] U.K.H.R.R. 758; [2003] A.C.D. 65; 100(26) L.S.G. 35; 153 N.L.J. 823; 147 S.J.L.B. 595, HL 17–036

R. (on the application of Rose and another) v Secretary of State for Health [2002] 2 F.L.R. 962; [2002] UKHRR 13 14–024

R. (on the application of S) v Plymouth City Council [2002] EWCA Civ 388; [2002] 1 W.L.R. 2583; [2002] 1 F.L.R. 1177; [2002] B.L.G.R. 565; 5 C.C.L. Rep. 251; 5 C.C.L. Rep. 560; [2002] Fam. Law 513; 146 S.J.L.B. 115, CA 1–035, 1–036

R. (on the application of Spath Holme Ltd) v Secretary of State for the Environment, Transport and the Regions; sub nom. R. v Secretary of State for the Environment, Transport and the Regions Ex p. Spath Holme Ltd [2001] 2 A.C. 349; [2001] 2 W.L.R. 15; [2001] 1 All E.R. 195; 33 H.L.R. 31; [2001] 1 E.G.L.R. 129; [2000] E.G.C.S. 152; 98(8) L.S.G. 44; 150 N.L.J. 1855; 145 S.J.L.B. 39; [2000] N.P.C. 139, HL 1–011, 1–013

R. (on the application of Wirral MBC) v Chief Schools Adjudicator [2001] E.L.R. 574, QBD. 9–003

Australia

Canada

European Union

EFTA Countries

Ireland

New Zealand

South Africa

United States

TABLE OF STATUTES

United Kingdom

Canada

Ireland

New Zealand

United States

TABLE OF STATUTORY INSTRUMENTS

TABLE OF CIVIL PROCEDURE RULES

TABLE OF EU LEGISLATION

Regulations

Directives

Decisions

TABLE OF TREATIES

CHAPTER 1

Eliciting Official Information

1. OVERVIEW OF OFFICIAL INFORMATION ACCESS LEGISLATION

Introduction

1–001 The last four decades have seen in the United Kingdom a gradual increase in the rights of an individual to elicit information from public authorities. The Public Bodies (Admission to Meetings) Act 1960 marked the first step in that process.[1] That Act had been introduced into Parliament as a private Member's Bill with the following statement of purpose:

> "The public has the right . . . to know what its elected representatives are doing . . . . Unless the Press, which is to report to the public, has some idea from the documents before it what is to be discussed, the business of allowing the Press in becomes wholly abortive . . . . The Press must have some

[1] The Act applies to local authorities, education committees, parish meetings of rural parishes, various NHS boards, bodies and executive councils, as well as their committees. It makes the meetings of all such bodies open to the public, except where publicity "would be contrary to the public interest". Section 1(4)(b) provides that where the meeting is required to be open to the public, a newspaper can request, and on payment of postage must be supplied with, the agenda of the meeting ". . . together with such further statements or particulars, if any, as are necessary to indicate the nature of the items included or, if thought fit in the case of any item, with copies of any reports or other documents supplied to members of the body in connection with the item". The Act is considered further at paras 5–012 to 5–017.

idea from the documents what is the true subject to be discussed at a meeting to which its representatives are entitled to be admitted . . . I hope that hon. Members will think fit to give this Bill a Second Reading, and to consider that the paramount function of this distinguished House is to safeguard civil liberties rather than to think that administrative convenience should take first place in law."[2]

The novelty of the Act lay in its bestowal of a right to obtain access to official documents.[3] Although the scope of the right was narrow, to some it made the Act "a very controversial piece of legislation"[4] and its potential for extension, in particular to the ministries of central government, was recognised.[5] Yet, apart from the right of access to documents, there was little in the Act that was new:

> "As the hon. Member for Islington North said, unless the spirit of the Bill is observed, it will do little more than the existing legislation. It will, however, do one thing more, and that is the most important feature to have come out of the Bill. It is not so much the admission of the public, curiously enough, but the provisions relating to the distribution of documents, that may well turn out to be the most important part of the Bill."[6]

The reasoning behind this early legislation and its identification of the competing considerations for and against disclosure of official information anticipated the preoccupations of Parliament 40 years later.

The Freedom of Information Act 2000

The enactment of the Freedom of Information Act 2000 represented a significant step in the process that had begun with the Public Bodies (Admission to Meetings) Act 1960. The FOI Act gives for the first time in the United Kingdom 1–002

[2] *Hansard*, HC, Vol.616, February 5, 1960, cols. 1350–1358 (Margaret Thatcher, Finchley, Second Reading Speech. This was her maiden speech).

[3] The provision of a right for the press to attend meetings of local authorities had been introduced by The Local Authorities (Admission of the Press to Meetings) Act 1908, passed in consequence of the judgment in *Tenby Corp v Mason* [1908] 1 Ch. 457. Section 3 of the 1908 Act provided that it was not to extend to any meeting of a committee of a local authority, other than education committees. The efficacy of the Act was reduced by the Local Government Act 1933, s.85, which empowered local authorities to appoint any committees they chose. As a result of this, many authorities went into committee of the full council in order to be able to exclude the press. Its efficacy was further reduced by the Education Act 1944, which removed education committees from the operation of the Act.

[4] *Hansard*, HC, Vol.616, February 5, 1960, col.1366 (Mr G.W. Reynolds, Islington North).

[5] "How Parliament would get on in those circumstances I really dread to think:" *Hansard*, HC, Vol.616, February 5, 1960, col.1384 (Mr Arthur Skeffington, Hayes and Harlington, quoting from the Official Report of the Standing Committee D on the Local Government Bill in 1958).

[6] *Hansard*, HC, Vol.617, May 13, 1960, col.830 (Mr Peter Kirk, Gravesend).

a right of access to official information that is not confined either by its permissible subject matter or by reference to the persons who may exercise that right. Its starting point is a right, described without reference to a subject-matter, bestowed upon every person to have disclosed all information answering the terms of a request held by the requested public authority. Up until the FOI Act, every right to elicit official information had been limited. The limitation was generally referable to information answering a particular description or emanating from a particular source. But it could also be limited by reference to the persons to whom the right was granted. In some cases, it was limited in both such respects. The access right bestowed by the FOI Act has no such limitation: it is given to every person, irrespective of that person's interest in the information; and it applies to all information, irrespective of its subject-matter. The right is, however, shaped by a series of specific exemptions.[7] Unless the information falls within one or more of those exemptions, the information must be disclosed. There are two types of exemption. If information falls within the terms of a provision conferring "absolute exemption" the right to disclosure is thereby disapplied.[8] If information falls within the terms of a provision conferring exemption, but not "absolute exemption", then only if the public interest in maintaining that exemption outweighs the public interest in disclosure of the information will the right to disclosure be disapplied. The breadth of the FOI Act gives the Act greater significance than the subject-specific rights of access bestowed by the other legislation.

exemptions

Other official information access legislation

1–003 Although the earlier patchwork of rights initiated by one paragraph in the Public Bodies (Admission to Meetings) Act 1960 has been eclipsed by the Freedom of Information Act 2000, it remains intact.[9] From the perspective of an individual seeking to elicit official information, the paramount concern is the existence of a right to obtain that information, rather than the statutory provenance of that right. From the perspective of a public authority responding to a request for information under the Freedom of Information Act 2000, the existence of an alternative statutory right of access to the information results in that

[7] See Freedom of Information Act 2000, s.1(2); Freedom of Information (Scotland) Act 2002, s.1(6). These make the rights or right, respectively, subject to (most importantly) s.2, thereby bringing in the provisions of Pt II of the Act.

[8] The verb "disapply" in relation to the rights is used throughout this work to signify that one or both of the rights do not apply. It is recognised that the creation of express relationships between ss.1(1), 1(2), 2 and Pt II of the Freedom of Information Act 2000 is simply a legislative technique for delineating the bounds of those substantive rights. In other words, these provisions shape the scope of the rights, rather than remove or negate a right already given. For a similar technique used elsewhere, see *Matthews v Ministry of Defence* [2003] 1 A.C. 1163, esp. at [20], in relation to the Crown Proceedings Act 1947.

[9] Some rights have been repealed by the Data Protection Act 1998, namely: the Access to Personal Files Act 1987; parts of the Access to Health Records Act 1990.

information being conferred with absolute exemption under the FOI Act. earlier legislation thus remains significant. In this work, subject-specific of access have been considered thematically in Chapters 4 and 5. This includes a treatment of the right of access given by the Data Protection Act 1998, which is subject-specific in that the requested information must, generally speaking, relate to the person seeking it. The balance of this work is largely, but not exclusively, devoted to the Freedom of Information Act 2000. As many of the exemptions and procedural provisions in the Data Protection Act 1998 resemble those in the Freedom of Information Act 2000, these have been considered together, with minor divergences generally being footnoted.

2. TERMINOLOGY

The basic rights

It is convenient at this point to set out the principal terms that will be used in this work. **1–004**

(1) When this work refers to the "FOI Act", it generally means both the Freedom of Information Act 2000 and the Freedom of Information (Scotland) Act 2002. Footnotes identify the different section numbers, as well as differences between the two Acts. Where those differences are more substantive than can properly be set out in a footnote, they are treated separately in the main text.

(2) When this work refers to the "DP Act", it means the Data Protection Act 1998. The DP Act applies to Scotland.

(3) The FOI Act bestows on every person two distinct but interrelated entitlements:

   (a) First, an entitlement to be informed in writing by a public authority whether it holds information of the description specified in a request.[11] The FOI Act labels the duty of a public authority to comply with this entitlement as the *duty to confirm or deny*.[12] In shorthand, this may be called the *divulgence duty*. From the perspective of the person who made the request for the information, this may be called the *existence right*.

   (b) Secondly, but more importantly, if the public authority does hold information of the description specified in a request, an

[10] Freedom of Information Act 2000, s.21; Freedom of Information (Scotland) Act 2002, s.25.

[11] Freedom of Information Act 2000, s.1(1)(a). This does not exist as a discrete entitlement under the Freedom of Information (Scotland) Act 2002.

[12] Freedom of Information Act 2000, s.1(6).

entitlement to have that information communicated to him.[13] The FOI Act[14] refers to this at various points as *disclosure*. In this work, this duty has been variously called the *disclosure duty* or the *duty to communicate*. From the perspective of the person requesting the information, this may be called the *access right*. Although the FOI Act locates this right after the existence right, it is better considered first: there is little sense troubling about the existence right if a decision has been made to disclose the information.[15]

(4) The DP Act similarly bestows on every person a right to be informed whether personal data of which the applicant is the data subject is being held and a right to have communicated to him that data.[16] The DP Act speaks of *data* rather than of "information," but the definition of "data" makes it clear that data are simply information that has certain routine characteristics.[17] *Personal data* means data that relate to a living individual who can be identified from the data, including any expressions of opinion about the individual.[18]

Exemptions

1–005 Part II of the FOI Act and Pt IV of the DP Act enumerate a series of provisions, which in this work are called *exemptions*.[19] Each of the provisions of Part II of the FOI Act, in describing one or more types of information, renders it *exempt information*.[20] This designation is significant for the disclosure duty: the designation is a requirement for disapplication of that duty and, in relation to some of the provisions, is sufficient for disapplication of that duty. In relation to the duty to confirm or deny, each of the provisions in Pt II (with two exceptions)[20A], after describing a type of exempt information, is followed by a closely corresponding provision preventing that duty from arising. The FOI Act sometimes speaks of the latter as an *exclusion* of the duty to confirm or deny,[21] and that term is used in this work.

13 Freedom of Information Act 2000, s.1(1)(b); Freedom of Information (Scotland) Act 2002, s.1(1).
14 Freedom of Information Act 2000, ss.9(5), 13(3), 17(4), 22, 23(5), 26(1), 27(1) and (4), 28(1), 29(1), 33(2), 35(4), 36(2) and (7), 38(1), 40(3), 41(1), 42(2), 43(1), 44(1), 45(2), 53(7), 77(1), and 81(2); Freedom of Information (Scotland) Act 2002, ss.9(7), 13(4), 16(2), 26, 27, 28, 29(3), 30, 31(4), 32(1), 33(1) and (2), 35(1), 36(2), 38(2), 39(1), 40, 45, 50(7), 52(3), 60(2), 62(4), 64(1), 65(1).
15 As is implicitly recognised by the Freedom of Information Act 2000, s.1(5).
16 Data Protection Act 1998, s.7(1)(a) and (c).
17 Data Protection Act 1998, s.1(1).
18 Data Protection Act 1998, s.1(1).
19 It is only the DP Act that expressly refers to them as being "exemptions".
20 A term recognised throughout the FOI Act: see Freedom of Information Act 2000, s.84; Freedom of Information (Scotland) Act 2002, s.73. There are some specific sections in Pt II that are simply supportive of other provisions in that Part, *e.g.* s.25.
20A Freedom of Information Act 2000, ss.21 and 43(1).
21 *ibid.*, ss.2(1)(a), 15(2)(a) and 17(3)(a).

Absolute exemptions

Some provisions in Pt II of the FOI Act confer what that Act calls *absolute exemption*.[22] The remaining provisions[23] in Pt II of the FOI Act confer what this work terms *qualified exemption*. Where information falls within the terms of a provision that confers absolute exemption, the disclosure right does not apply and the public authority is thereby relieved from the duty to communicate. Similarly, where confirmation or denial of a holding would fall within one of the provisions in Pt II under which the duty to confirm or deny is said not to arise and that provision confers absolute exemption, the right does not apply and the public authority is thereby relieved from the duty to confirm or deny. The Act speaks of an "exclusion" of the duty to confirm or deny and of an "exemption" from the duty to communicate.[24] Those duties may be said to be *disapplied*.[25] Information that falls within the terms of a provision that confers qualified exemption may or may not be relieved from the duty to confirm or deny and from the duty to communicate depending upon a consideration of the public interest.[26] 1–006

Procedural terms

The person who seeks the information under the FOI Act is called the *applicant*.[27] The person who seeks the information under the DP Act is called the *recipient*.[28] Under both Acts, information is sought by a *request*.[29] A request under the FOI Act is addressed to a *public authority*, which may be a government department, one of the Houses of Parliament, any emanation of local government or the National Health Service, any number of specifically-named public bodies or officers, or a publicly-owned company.[30] A request under the DP Act is addressed to a *data controller*, which includes each government department as if it were a separate individual.[31] Under both Acts, once the public authority receives a valid request, it may give the applicant a *fees notice*, in which it sets out the amount it will charge the applicant for complying with the 1–007

[22] Freedom of Information Act 2000, s.2(3); Freedom of Information (Scotland) Act 2002, s.2(2). These provisions are listed at para.14–015.

[23] Excluding the provisions that are purely supportive, such as s.25. The remaining provisions are listed at para.14–016

[24] Freedom of Information Act 2000, s.2(1), (2)(b).

[25] Freedom of Information Act 2000, s.2(1) and (2); Freedom of Information (Scotland) Act 2002, s. 2(1). See n.8.

[26] See paras 15–010 and 15–011.

[27] Freedom of Information Act 2000, s.84; Freedom of Information (Scotland) Act 2002, s.1(2).

[28] Data Protection Act 1998, s.70(1).

[29] In the Freedom of Information Act 2000, called a "request for information": ss.8 and 84. In Scotland, see Freedom of Information (Scotland) Act 2002, s.8. Data Protection Act 1998, s.7(2).

[30] Public authorities are considered in detail at paras 7–016 to 7–028 below.

[31] Data Protection Act 1998, s.63. The Data Protection Act 1998 also applies to non-governmental persons, but this is outside the scope of this work.

request.[32] Where a public authority decides that some or all of the information sought should not be disclosed to the applicant, it must give the applicant notice of this: in this work called a *refusal notice*. A public authority may decide to mask parts of a document disclosed to an applicant on the basis that it is not obliged to disclose those blanked out parts of the document. That blanking out process is called *redaction* and the document is said to be *redacted*.

Review, etc.

1–008 The FOI Act provides for two codes of practice. The *section 45 Code of Practice* is issued by the Secretary of State for Constitutional Affairs and provides guidance on the handling of requests for information.[33] The *section 46 Code of Practice* is issued by the Lord Chancellor and relates to the keeping, management and destruction of records.[34] An applicant who is dissatisfied with the way in which a public authority has dealt with his request under the FOI Act may complain to that authority and seek *internal review* under the *section 45 Code of Practice*. If the applicant remains dissatisfied with the response, he may pursue what in this work is called a *2nd stage appeal* by making an *application* to the *Information Commissioner*.[35] At this point the applicant becomes a *complainant*.[36] If the Information Commissioner needs more information in order to determine an application, he may serve on the public authority an *information notice*.[37] If the Information Commissioner decides that the public authority has not complied with its disclosure duty or the duty to confirm or deny, he must serve a *decision notice* on the public authority and on the complainant.[38] If the Information Commissioner decides that the public authority has not otherwise properly complied with its duties in relation to a request, he may serve an *enforcement notice* on the public authority and on the complainant.[39] Either

[32] Freedom of Information Act 2000, s.9(1); Freedom of Information (Scotland) Act 2002, s.9(1); Data Protection Act 1998, s.7(2)(b) and Data Protection (Subject Access)(Fees and Miscellaneous Provisions) Regulations 2000.

[33] Freedom of Information Act 2000, s.45; Freedom of Information (Scotland) Act 2002, s.60. The Code is reproduced in the Appendix to this work.

[34] Freedom of Information Act 2000, s.46; Freedom of Information (Scotland) Act 2002, s.61. The Code is reproduced in the Appendix to this work.

[35] Referred to in the Freedom of Information Act 2000 as "the Commissioner"—s.84. The Information Commissioner is simply a new name for the Data Protection Commissioner: Freedom of Information Act 2000, s.18(1). In Scotland, the application is made to the Scottish Information Commissioner, who is referred to in the Freedom of Information (Scotland) Act 2002 as "the Commissioner"—s.73. Appeals under the Data Protection Act 1998 are provided for by s.7(9), with jurisdiction vested in the High Court or a county court: s.15.

[36] Freedom of Information Act 2000, s.50(1).

[37] Freedom of Information Act 2000, s.50(1); Freedom of Information (Scotland) Act 2002, s.50(1).

[38] Freedom of Information Act 2000, s.50(3)–(4). In Scotland the function of decision notices is absorbed within enforcement notices: Freedom of Information (Scotland) Act 2002, s.51.

[39] Freedom of Information Act 2000, s.52. In Scotland, an enforcement notice is employed wherever the Information Commissioner decides that the public authority has not properly complied with its duties in relation to a request: Freedom of Information (Scotland) Act 2002, s.51.

the complainant or the public authority may appeal against the Information Commissioner's decision to the *Information Tribunal*.[40] In this work, such an appeal is called a *3rd stage appeal*.

Miscellaneous terms

Both the FOI Act and DP Act enable a *conclusive certificate* to be issued in certain circumstances by a Minister of the Crown or like official.[41] There are two types of conclusive certificate. An *exemption conclusive certificate* certifies either that a particular exemption or that a particular harm required for exemption is applicable, and the certificate stands as conclusive evidence of that "fact," irrespective of what the reality might be.[42] A *compliance conclusive certificate* certifies that the person signing it has on reasonable grounds formed the opinion that the public authority has not failed to comply with the duty to disclose or the duty to confirm or deny,[43] irrespective of what the reality might be. The effect of both types of certificate is to remove altogether or substantially cut down an applicant's rights of appeal, either by express provision[44] or because of the deeming effect of the certificate. Although the FOI Act and DP Act may excuse a public authority from disclosing certain information, the public authority may nevertheless decide to voluntarily disclose that information. In this work such disclosure is called *discretionary disclosure*. Legislation providing for access to official information exists in many other jurisdictions. In this work, where it has been thought enlightening, reference has been made to the jurisprudence of those jurisdictions whose legal systems and official information access legislation bear the closest resemblance to that of the United Kingdom: the United States of America, the Commonwealth of Australia, New Zealand, Canada and the Republic of Ireland. In this work, these are called *the comparative jurisdictions*. 1–009

40 Freedom of Information Act 2000, s.57(1). There is no such right of appeal in Scotland.

41 Freedom of Information Act 2000, ss.23(2), 24(3)–(4), 25, 34(3), 36(7), 53(2)–(3) and (6); Freedom of Information (Scotland) Act 2002, ss.31(2)–(3), and 52(2); Data Protection Act 1998, s.28(2)–(3).

42 Freedom of Information Act 2000, ss.23(2), 24(3)–(4), 25, 34(3) and 36(7); Freedom of Information (Scotland) Act 2002, s.31(2)–(3); Data Protection Act 1998, s. 28(2)–(3).

43 Freedom of Information Act 2000, s.53(2)–(3) and (6); Freedom of Information (Scotland) Act 2002, s.52(2).

44 Freedom of Information Act 2000, s.60.

3. THE RATIONALE FOR OFFICIAL INFORMATION ACCESS LEGISLATION

Introduction

1–010 Just as intelligence-gathering enhances the prospect of successfully engaging an opponent, so too compelling the disclosure of information from a public authority improves the prospect of securing an advantageous outcome in any dealings with it. The Freedom of Information Act 2000 is concerned with a right to secure the disclosure of information and a correlative duty to disclose it. The short title of the FOI Act is apt to mask its compulsive character. The benefits typically attributed to the dissemination of official information, namely:

— increased information in relation to the making of official decisions; and
— an electorate informed as to what its government is or has been doing,

do not, in theory, require compulsion for their efficacy. The Act is not one that merely enables a public authority to do what otherwise it could not lawfully do for lack of statutory authority. Other than in limited circumstances,[45] it is and always has been perfectly open for a public authority to volunteer any information that it holds to anyone who requests it.[46] Such voluntary disclosure would, moreover, be consistent with the spirit and letter of the Code of Practice on Access to Government Information.[47] A public authority owes its life to the public: unlike a private company or an individual, it has no interests that do not ultimately derive from that public. The compulsion that is at the heart of the FOI Act recognises that often a public authority to which a request for information has been made will be disinclined to disclose it. There is no deference in the Act to that disinclination. Disapplication of the duties under the Act only results where one or more of the statutory exemptions apply and, in some cases, the balance of specific facets of the public interest requires it.

---

[45] For example: information received by a public authority from a third party; or information subject to a statutory or contractual proscription on disclosure.

[46] In *Reynolds v Times Newspapers Ltd* [2001] 2 A.C. 127 at 200, a case concerning qualified privilege, Lord Nicholls of Birkenhead said that "the high importance of freedom to impart and receive information and ideas has been stated so often and so eloquently that this point calls for no elaboration in this case." See para.14–006 below.

[47] The Code is considered further at paras 5–001 to 5–009 below. The Code only applies to central government departments and agencies.

The mischief at which the FOI Act is aimed

It is conventional to speak of Parliament intending that an enactment remedy a particular mischief.[48] From that convention, it is presumed that Parliament intends that courts and those administering an enactment should do so in such a manner that promotes the remedy: a purposive construction.[49] The task is of particular significance for a statute such as the FOI Act. The existence of a public authority's obligation to disclose or not to disclose information, as well as its obligation to confirm or deny that the information requested is held, is in many instances made to depend upon a balancing of competing facets of the public interest.[50] Whilst it is not unusual for the operation of a statutory provision to be part dependent upon the public interest,[51] it is unusual to ascribe to it an overriding importance about which an interested party[52] is given the adjudicative role. Identification of the purposes of the Act moderates the ability of the decision-maker to assess the public interest by undue reference to the interests of the public authority or to the idiosyncratic views of the decision-maker. Equally, an identification of purpose guides the exercise of the discretions bestowed by the Act,[53] including that of whether or not a public authority 1–011

48 *Heydon's case* (1584) 3 Co. Rep. 7a. And, more recently: *Malloch v Aberdeen Corp* [1971] 1 WLR 1578 at 1583–1584, *per* Lord Reid; *Black-Clawson International Ltd v Papierwerke Waldhof-Aschaffenburg AG* [1975] A.C. 591 at 614, *per* Lord Reid; *Attorney-General ex rel Yorkshire Derwent Trust Ltd v Brotherton* [1992] 1 A.C. 425 at 442 and 447; *Attorney-General v Association Newspapers Ltd* [1994] 2 A.C. 238 esp. at 259 *per* Lord Lowry; *R. v Secretary of State for the Environment, Transport and the Regions Ex p. Spath Holme Ltd* [2001] 2 A.C. 349 at 362, 376, 391 and 397.

49 *Pepper v Hart* [1993] AC 593 at 617, *per* Lord Griffiths ("The days have long passed when the courts adopted a strict constructionist view of interpretation which required them to adopt the literal meaning of the language. The courts now adopt a purposive approach which seeks to give effect to the true purpose of legislation and are prepared to look at much extraneous material that bears upon the background against which the legislation was enacted.") and 635, *per* Lord Browne-Wilkinson; *Inland Revenue Commissioners v McGuckian* [1997] 1 W.L.R. 991 at 999, *per* Lord Steyn ("During the last 30 years there has been a shift away from literalist to purposive methods of construction."); *Macniven (HM Inspector of Taxes) v Westmoreland Investments Ltd* [2001] UKHL6; [2001] 2 W.L.R. 377 at [6], *per* Lord Nicholls. In relation to those administering the Act: *Padfield v Minister of Agriculture, Fisheries & Food* [1968] A.C. 977 at 1039, *per* Lord Morris ("Where some legal right or entitlement is conferred or enjoyed, and for the purpose of effectuating such right or entitlement a power is conferred upon someone, then words which are permissible in character will sometimes be construed as involving a duty to exercise the power. The purpose and the language of any particular enactment must be considered."); *Crédit Suisse v Allerdale Borough Council* [1995] 1 Lloyd's Rep. 315 at 345; *R. v Secretary of State for the Environment, Transport and the Regions Ex p. Spath Holme Ltd* [2001] 2 A.C. 349 at 362, 376, 397 and 400.

50 Freedom of Information Act 2000, s.2(1) and (2); Freedom of Information (Scotland) Act 2002, s.2(1).

51 Even though enactments may be seen as an expression of the public interest: *Bombay Province v Bombay Municipal Corp* [1947] A.C. 58 at 62–63.

52 Namely, the public authority to whom a request for information has been made.

53 "*Hansard* has frequently been referred to with a view to ascertaining whether a statutory power has been improperly exercised for an alien purpose or in a wholly unreasonable manner..." *Pepper v Hart* [1993] A.C. 593 at 639; *R. v Northumbrian Water Ltd Ex p. Newcastle and North Tyneside Health Authority* [1999] Env. L.R. 715 at 727, *per* Collins J.

should rely on an exemption.[54] The method for discerning the purpose of an Act or group of provisions in a statute is well-known enough:

> "In the absence of [looking at the legislative history and preparatory works] the courts have five principal avenues of approach to the ascertainment of the legislative intention: (1) examination of the social background, as specifically proved if not within common knowledge, in order to identify the social or juristic defect which is the likely subject of remedy; (2) a conspectus of the entire relevant body of the law for the same purpose; (3) particular regard to the long title of the statute to be interpreted (and, where available, the preamble), in which the general legislative objectives will be stated; (4) scrutiny of the actual words to be interpreted in the light of the established canons of interpretation; (5) examination of the other provisions of the statute in question (or of other statutes in pari materia) for the light which they throw on the particular words which are the subject of interpretation."[55]

The background to the introduction of the legislation

1–012 The White Paper[56] that anticipated introduction of an FOI Bill spelled out the purpose of the legislation. In the preface by the Prime Minister it was said:

> "This White Paper explains our proposals for meeting another key pledge—to legislate for freedom of information, bringing about more open Government. The traditional culture of secrecy will only be broken down by giving people in the United Kingdom the legal right to know. This fundamental and vital change in the relationship between government and governed is at the heart of this White Paper."

The Minister in charge of the Bill declared in his foreword:

[54] See Freedom of Information Act 2000, s.17(1); Freedom of Information (Scotland) Act 2002, s.16(1).

[55] *Ealing London Borough Council v Race Relations Board* [1972] A.C. 342 at 361; [1972] 1 All E.R. 105 at 114, HL, *per* Lord Simon of Glaisdale. Similarly: *Black-Clawson International Ltd v Papierwerke Waldhof-Aschaffenburg AG* [1975] A.C. 591 at 647; [1975] 1 All E.R. 810 at 844, HL, *per* Lord Simon of Glaisdale.

[56] Cabinet Office, *Your Right to Know. The Government's Proposals for a Freedom of Information Act* (White Paper), Cm. 3818, December 11, 1997. As to the permissibility of considering a White Paper, etc., for the purpose of ascertaining the mischief and for drawing inferences as to Parliamentary intention, see: *Pepper v Hart* [1993] A.C. 593 at 630 and 635, *per* Lord Browne-Wilkinson; *R. v Northumbrian Water Ltd Ex p. Newcastle and North Tyneside Health Authority* [1999] Env. L.R. 715 at 727, *per* Collins J.; *R. (on the application of Heather) v Leonard Cheshire Foundation* [2002] EWCA Civ 366; [2002] 2 All E.R. 936; [2002] H.R.L.R. 30.

> "Openness is fundamental to the political health of a modern state. This White Paper marks a watershed in the relationship between the government and people of the United Kingdom. At last there is a government ready to trust the people with a legal right to information. This right is central to a mature democracy."

The opening paragraphs gave a straightforward statement of purpose:

> "1.1 Unnecessary secrecy in government leads to arrogance in governance and defective decision-making. The perception of excessive secrecy has become a corrosive influence in the decline of public confidence in government. Moreover, the climate of public opinion has changed: people expect much greater openness and accountability from government than they used to.
>
> 1.2 [......]The purpose of the Act will be to encourage more open and accountable government by establishing a general statutory right of access to official records and information."[57]

The need for the Act

Official information access legislation has been variously considered to serve the following purposes: 1–013

(1) To enable members of the public to be more informed as to the way in which administrative decisions are made and the basis for such decisions. The House of Commons Select Committee considered that this would improve the quality of government decision-making.[58]

(2) To enable the curious to find out what information the instruments of government hold about themselves and others.[59]

(3) To hold government and other bodies to account by drawing out information revealing maladministration.[60]

---

[57] See also para.2.5.

[58] House of Commons, *Public Administration—Third Report* (Cm. 4355), July 29, 1999, para.12. For judicial support, see *London Regional Transport v Mayor of London* [2001] EWCA Civ 1491; [2003] E.M.L.R. 4 at [40], quoting Sullivan J. with approval. In *Kuijer v Council of the European Union (No.2)* [2002] 1 W.L.R. 1941 at [52] the Court of First Instance, dealing with Council Directive 93/731/EC, said: "It is first necessary to point out that the principle of transparency is intended to secure a more significant role for citizens in the decision-making process and to ensure that the administration acts with greater propriety, efficiency and responsibility *vis-à-vis* the citizens in a democratic system. It helps strengthen the principle of democracy and respect for fundamental rights."

[59] House of Commons, *Public Administration—Third Report* (Cm. 4355), July 29, 1999, para.12.

[60] *United States Department of Justice v Reporters Committee for Freedom of the Press*, 489 US 749 at 773.

(4) To impose the discipline of potential revelation upon public authorities in their recording of information.
(5) To counteract undue secrecy in the making of decisions and the formulation of policy.[61]
(6) For any number of commercial ends.
(7) As a form of pre-action disclosure or disclosure in judicial review or in connection with tribunal proceedings and the like.

The US Supreme Court synthesised the most important of these to:

> "The basic purpose of [the Freedom of Information Act] is to ensure an informed citizenry, vital to the functioning of a democratic society, needed to check against corruption and to hold the governors accountable to the governed."[62]

And similarly the Supreme Court of Canada:

> "The [Access to Information] Act is concerned with securing values of participation and accountability in the democratic process. The overarching purpose of access to information legislation is to facilitate democracy by helping to ensure that citizens have the information required to participate meaningfully in the democratic process and that politicians and bureaucrats remain accountable to the citizenry . . . . Rights to state-held information are designed to improve the workings of government; to make it more effective, responsive and accountable."[63]

The "defect" giving rise to the need for the FOI Act was acknowledged as a matter of public record by the Minister in introducing the Bill that became the Act:

> "Unnecessary secrecy in Government and our public services has long been held to undermine good governance and public administration, ... the Bill will not only provide legal rights for the public and place legal duties on Ministers and public authorities, but will help to transform the culture of Government from one of secrecy to one of openness. It will transform the default setting from "this should be kept quiet unless" to "this should be published unless". By doing so, it should raise public confidence in the processes of government, and enhance the quality of decision making by the Government."[64]

[61] House of Commons, *Public Administration—Third Report* (Cm. 4355), July 29, 1999, para.12.
[62] *National Labour Relations Board v Robbins Tire & Rubber Co* (1978) 437 US 214 at 242.
[63] *Dagg v Canada (Minister of Finance)* [1997] 2 S.C.R. 403 at 432–433 and 450. Similarly, *Canada Post Corp v Canada (Minister of Public Works)* [1995] 2 F.C. 110 at 124, FCA.
[64] *Hansard*, HC, Vol.340, December 7, 1999, col.714 (Mr Jack Straw). In the construction of a statute, reference may be made to Parliamentary materials "where (a) legislation is ambiguous,

And, a little later:

"The Bill will lead to cultural change throughout the public sector. There will be more information about how health authorities, local councils and the police deliver services. It will give citizens a right to know and a right to appeal to the commissioner if they do not get the information that they have sought. That is a fundamental change in the relationship between the citizens and the state."[65]

Implicit in the above statements is that the voluntary code to which the same public sector had been subject for the preceding eight years had not effected the "cultural" or "fundamental" change hoped for the FOI Act.[66] The most significant dissimilarity between the Code and the FOI Act is the replacement of voluntariness with compulsion.[67] This dependence upon compulsion to secure the cultural change from the regime which existed under the voluntary Code offers support for the proposition that notions of due deference to a public authority's claims of exemption should play little or no part in the determination of claims of exemption save to the extent that they are substantiated by objective evidence.

obscure or leads to an absurdity; (b) the material relied upon consists of one or more statements by a minister or other promoter of the Bill together if necessary with such other Parliamentary material as is necessary to understand such statements and their effect; (c) the statements relied upon are clear . . ." *Pepper v Hart* [1993] A.C. 593 at 640, *per* Lord Browne-Wilkinson. Satisfaction of these three conditions is critical to the entitlement to refer to the material: *R. v Secretary of State for the Environment, Transport and the Regions Ex p. Spath Holme Ltd* [2001] 2 A.C. 349 at 391–392, *per* Lord Bingham and at 398–399, *per* Lord Nicholls. It has been said that the true purpose in referring to *Hansard* is to "preven[t] the executive from placing a different meaning on the words used in legislation from that which they attributed to those words when promoting the legislation in Parliament . . ." *R. v A (No.2)* [2001] U.K.H.L. 25; [2002] 1 A.C. 45 at [81], *per* Lord Steyn. Similarly stated in Johan Steyn, "*Pepper v Hart*: A re-examination" (2001) 21 *Oxford Journal of Legal Studies* at 59.

65 *Hansard*, HC, Vol.340, December 7, 1999, col.725 (Mr Jack Straw). Similarly, cols 728, 738–739; 744–745 ("the legislation transforming the relationship between citizen and state"); 754–755; 771–772; *Hansard*, HL, Vol.612, April 20, 2000, cols 830, 831, 835, 837, 847, 849, 853, 858–859, 862; *Hansard*, HL, Vol.618, October 25, 2000, col.440.

66 Thus, Lord Phillips in *The BSE Inquiry—The Report* (2000) found that there had been "positive censorship" (Vol.3, para.2.175) in relation to information relating to zoonotic qualities of bovine spongiform encephalopathy (BSE); that there was a "clear policy of restricting the disclosure of information about BSE" (Vol.3, para.2.189); and he spoke of a policy of secrecy rather than one of openness (Vol.3, para.2.191). Similarly, Sir Richard Scott's *Report of the Inquiry into the Export of Defence Equipment and Dual-Use Goods and Related Prosecutions* (1996): "in circumstances where disclosure might be politically or administratively inconvenient, the balance struck by the government came down, time and time again, against full disclosure" (para.D1.165).

67 At any rate, so far as concerns central government departments and agencies.

The long title and the absence of a purpose clause

1–014 It is unusual for an Act of Parliament to have a purpose clause.[68] To the extent permitted by a single sentence, the purpose of an Act is normally only expressly articulated within a statute by its long title. For the reasons noted above, ascertainment of the purpose of the Act is of particular importance in a statute such as the FOI Act.[69] An amendment to the Bill that would have seen a purpose clause included in the Act was defeated.[70] Instead, it was considered that changing the preposition *about* in the long title of the Bill to *for* would adequately articulate the purpose of the Act.[71]

4. BACKGROUND TO THE FREEDOM OF INFORMATION ACT 2000

Access to official information in the United Kingdom

1–015 As noted above,[72] rights of access to official information in the United Kingdom increased in a piecemeal fashion in the 40 years prior to the enactment of the FOI Act. It may fairly be observed that in that period Parliament showed a greater disposition to impose duties of disclosure upon the emanations of local government than it did upon central government departments or agencies. Notable increases in the right of access[73] came with:

— the Local Government Act 1972, Pt VA (ss.100A–100K), s.228, Sch.12A[74];

[68] But not unknown, see for example: Health and Safety at Work, etc., Act 1974, s.1; Proceeds of Crime Act 2002, s.240; Education Act 2002, s.1; Pollution Prevention and Control Act 1999, s.1.
[69] The inclusion of one was recommended by the House of Commons, *Public Administration—Third Report* (Cm. 4355), July 29, 1999, para.59. A purpose clause is to be found in: Freedom of Information Act 1982 (Cth of Australia), s.3; Official Information Act 1982 (NZ), s.4; Access to Information Act (1982) (Canada), s.2. The Freedom of Information Act 1997 (Ireland), although not including a purpose clause, includes a comprehensive statement of purpose in its long title.
[70] *Hansard*, HC, Vol.347, April 4, 2000, col.830 (Amendment No.100). For discussion on the proposed purpose clause, see: *Hansard*, HC, Vol.347, April 4, 2000, cols 830–855; *Hansard*, HL, Vol.617, October 17, 2000, cols 886–888 and 892–900. It was opposed on the basis that it was "pointless" because it would add nothing to what was explained "more comprehensively" in the long title and that it would cause confusion to those minded to compare the long title with the purpose clause: *Hansard*, HC, Vol.347, April 4, 2000, col.844 (Mr Mike O'Brien); *Hansard*, HL, Vol.617, October 17, 2000, col.894 (Lord Brennan).
[71] An amendment proposed by Lord Archer: *Hansard*, HL, Vol.617, October 17, 2000, col.890.
[72] See para.1–001.
[73] There were additional provisions enacted but which have not yet been brought into force, for example: Education (No.2) Act 1986, s.62, which enables the Secretary of State to make regulations requiring the governing body of certain educational institutions to make available to certain persons documents and information relating to the meetings and proceedings of the governing body.
[74] These provisions were inserted by the Local Government (Access to Information) Act 1985. They are considered in greater detail at paras 5–018 to 5–031 below.

— the Data Protection Act 1984[75];
— the Health Service Joint Consultative Committees (Access to Information) Act 1986[76];
— the Access to Personal Files Act 1987[77];
— the Community Health Councils (Access to Information) Act 1988 (which applied over, with modifications, the provisions of Pt VA of the Local Government Act 1972 to community health councils established under s.20 of the National Health Service Act 1977)[78]; and
— the Access to Health\ Records Act 1990.[79]

Where central government departments or agencies found themselves having to disclose information, this was generally the result of outside obligations.[80]

Attempts at a comprehensive right of access

From 1974 onwards, before each General Election the Labour Party stated a commitment to "freedom of information." The first indication of any realisation of that commitment was a directive issued in 1977 by the head of the Civil Service.[81] This promised to release more of the background detail and information behind Ministerial decisions. In March 1979 the Labour Government published a Green Paper on Open Government, which proposed a non-statutory 1–016

[75] Section 21 of the Data Protection Act 1984 introduced the concept of a "subject-access request" in which a person could seek access to information held by an organisation (which included private organisations as well as governmental organisations) about himself. The right was re-enacted and broadened by s.7 of the Data Protection Act 1998. The right is considered in greater detail in Ch.4 below.

[76] Repealed by the Health Act 1999, s.65, Sch.4, para.72 and Sch.5, with effect from April 1, 2000 (in England) and January 1, 2001 (in Wales).

[77] Repealed by the Data Protection Act 1998, s.74(2), Sch.16, Pt I, as from March 1, 2000. Similarly the Access to Personal Files (Social Services) Regulations 1989 and the Access to Personal Files (Housing) Regulations 1989 made under it. The purpose of this Act was to catch personal information that was recorded in "manual files" and which, accordingly, fell outside the ambit of the Data Protection Act 1984. The Act came into force on May 15, 1987 and provided a right of access to personal information (which was defined in the same way as in the Data Protection Act 1984) falling within defined categories and held by "Housing Act local authorities" and by "local social services authorities."

[78] The Act is considered in greater detail at para.5–030 below.

[79] This establishes a right of access to health records held by, *inter alia*, "health service bodies" (*i.e.* a health authority, a health board, a special health authority or a National Health Service trust) for the individuals to whom the record relates and certain other persons. The Act is considered in greater detail at para.5–043 below.

[80] Such as the Environmental Information Regulations 1992, which implemented Council Directive 90/313/EEC on the freedom of access to information on the environment, and the Data Protection Act 1998, which implemented Directive 95/46, adopted by the European Parliament and European Council on October 24, 1998. These are considered in detail in paras 5–050 to 5–051 below.

[81] The Directive was actually a confidential memorandum from the Head of the Civil Service, Sir Douglas Allen, who became Lord Croham. It was published officially after it was leaked to *The Times*. The directive became known as the "Croham directive."

code for the release of official information.[82] At about the same time a private Member's Bill that would have compelled disclosure of official documents was introduced by Sir Clement Freud MP.[83] Both the non-statutory code and private Member's Bill did not survive the General Election of May 1979. In 1981 another freedom of information Bill, also drafted by the Outer Circle Policy Unit, was introduced by Frank Hooley MP. The Bill was opposed by the Conservative government and defeated at second reading.

The Data Protection Act 1984

1–017 In 1981 the Council of Europe opened for signature and ratification its Convention for the Protection of Individuals with regard to the Automatic Processing of Personal Data. This ultimately led to the Data Protection Act 1984. Although this gave an individual a right of access to information relating to himself provided that it was held as part of a data processing system, the focus of the Act was not the extraction of information from governmental bodies: the right given by the Act applied to personal information irrespective of the identity of the body that held it. In 1984 a freedom of information Bill drafted by the Campaign for Freedom of Information was introduced by David Steel MP. At the same time the Campaign for Freedom of Information also pressed for the introduction of subject-specific legislation establishing more limited rights of access to information. Legislation receiving its support included the Local Government (Access to Information) Act 1985,[84] the Access to Personal Files Act 1987,[85] and the Access to Medical Records Act 1988.[86] The Campaign for Freedom of Information made another attempt at a comprehensive information access Bill in January 1991, but it only lasted 45 minutes in Parliament and did not get a second reading.[87] In the following year the Environmental Information Regulations 1992 were adopted to implement the Access to Environmental Information Directive of the European Community. In that same year, Roy Hattersley MP, the then-shadow Home Secretary, promised that a freedom of information act would be the first piece of Home Office legislation if Labour were to win the election. The Conservatives won the election and William Waldegrave was given responsibil-

[82] *Open Government*, Cmnd. 7520.

[83] Then Mr Clement Freud MP, Isle of Ely.

[84] It was introduced as a private member's Bill promoted by the Community Rights Project and introduced by Robin Squire MP. It gave the public wider rights of access to council meetings, reports and papers. See paras 5–018–5–031 below.

[85] This was also the result of a private member's Bill promoted by the Campaign for Freedom of Information and introduced by Archy Kirkwood MP. It gave people the right to see manually held social work and housing records about themselves. The Bill originally also included access to school records, but this was later brought in under existing legislation by agreement with the government.

[86] This was another private member's Bill drafted by the Campaign for Freedom of Information and introduced by Archy Kirkwood MP. It gives people the right to see any report produced by their own doctor for an employer or insurance company. See para.5–040 below.

ity for implementing an 'open government' policy. In early 1993 a private member's Bill entitled The Right to Know Bill was introduced[88] into Parliament. This Bill had its second reading in the House of Commons and completed its Committee stage, but it failed to receive the necessary support.

The Code of Practice

In July 1993 the Conservative Government issued a White Paper which proposed a Code of Practice on Access to Government Information. In 1994 that Government issued a Code of Practice on Access to Government Information.[89] This was the first true attempt at a comprehensive scheme for the release of official information, but it was voluntary in nature, bestowing no enforceable right of access. In 1996 the Select Committee on the Parliamentary Commissioner for Administration published its report on the operation of the voluntary scheme. It recommended that a freedom of information act be introduced. The government rejected the recommendation and instead issued a slightly revised version of the Code in February 1997. In relation to personal information, the Data Protection Act 1998 was enacted to implement the European Community Data Protection Directive.[90] This removed the limitation on subject-access rights to computerised records, extending it to most manual records. 1–018

Parliamentary history of the Freedom of Information Act 2000

Before the May 1997 General Election, both the Labour Party and Liberal Democrat party had promised to introduce freedom of information legislation if elected. The former secured election in May 1997, and in December 1997 a White Paper[91] was published, setting out its proposals for legislation. On May 19, 1998 the House of Commons Select Committee reported on the proposals,[92] stating in its Introduction: 1–019

> "Freedom of Information Act as a major plank in the Government's proposals for constitutional reform, and a radical advance in open and

[87] This was introduced by Archy Kirkwood MP.

[88] This was introduced by Mark Fisher MP.

[89] The Code is considered in detail at paras 5–001 to 5–010 below. The code was revised in 1997 and remains in effect. The revised version is reproduced in the Appendix.

[90] Directive of the European Parliament and of the Council of October 24, 1995 on the Protection of Individuals with Regard to the Processing of Personal Data and on the Free Movement of Such Data (95/46/EC) [1995] O.J. L281/31.

[91] *Your Right to Know—The Government's Proposals for a Freedom of Information Act*, Cm.3818, December 11, 1997. The document was prepared by the Chancellor of the Duchy of Lancaster, Dr David Clark.

[92] *Third Report of the Select Committee on Public Administration: Your Right to Know—The Government's Proposals for a Freedom of Information Act*, HC (1997–1998) 398–I.

accountable government. It will help to begin to change for good the secretive culture of the public service.

Lack of openness and transparency in British government have featured in tribunals and inquiries as a contributory factor in many cases where things have gone seriously wrong . . . . [M]aking government more open is something which should have a serious impact on the daily lives of ordinary people. In other countries with Freedom of Information laws, most requests for information are for 'my own file.' Public authorities keep a vast amount of information about individuals. Some of this they can now get access to, under a patchwork of statutes and codes of practice. Some of it they still cannot get. Many people may want access to their files in order to pursue a dispute with a government department or other public authority. Individuals who are unhappy with the way they have been dealt with by, for example, the Child Support Agency or the Benefits Agency, or local Housing Authorities and Social Services Departments have a strong need to see how the authority concerned has handled their case . . . .

Freedom of Information should change the culture within the public sector so that the sort of obstruction that members of the public experienced in these cases no longer happens. We believe that the proposals, if implemented as presented in the White Paper, will have three purposes and effects. Increased access to information will:

— Make it easier for members of the public to find out what information government holds about themselves.
— Make it easier for politicians, journalists and members of the public to hold the government to account by making government cover-ups more difficult.
— Make it easier for members of the public to participate in an informed way in the discussion of policy issues, and improve the quality of government decision-making because those drafting policy advice know that they must be able, ultimately, to defend their reasoning before public opinion. We believe that Dr Clark's proposals will begin to bring about a significant change in the culture of the UK Government."

The Report made a total of 44 recommendations and observations. In July 1998 responsibility for the Bill was transferred from the Cabinet Office to the Home Office. The Government officially responded to the Report.[93] The Minister then responsible, Dr David Clark, said:

"The Government's commitment to a radical Freedom of Information Act is clear, and has already been set out in *Your Right to Know* . . . . FOI is a

[93] The Government's reply to the Report was the *Fourth Special Report of the Select Committee on Public Administration: Government Response to the Third Report from the Select Committee on Public Administration (Session 1997–1998) on Your Right to Know—the Government's Proposals for a Freedom of Information Act*, HC (1997–1998) 1020.

key part—and in my view a central part—of the Government's programme to modernise British politics through radical constitutional change. The Prime Minister has said that freedom of information is not some isolated constitutional reform, but a change that is absolutely fundamental to how we see politics developing in this country . . . ."

The consultation paper and draft Bill

On May 24, 1999 the Government published a consultation paper with its proposals for freedom of information legislation, including a draft Bill.[94] The consultation paper was followed by a process of pre-legislative scrutiny by committees in both Houses of Parliament and a period of further public consultation. The House of Commons Select Committee on Public Administration reported on July 29, 1999,[95] summarising its conclusions and recommendations: 1–020

" 1. We welcome the fact that the Government has published a draft Freedom of Information Bill. Legislation on the information rights of citizens is a historic moment for our democracy. However, we believe that the present form of the Bill has significant deficiencies which, if not remedied, will undermine the potential. In particular we recommend that:

— There should a purpose clause stating a clear presumption in favour of disclosure as a right of citizenship;
— The public interest in disclosing particular information in each case should be balanced against the prospect of harm in so doing; the information should be released if the public interest is greater; and decisions about where the balance lies in particular cases should be transparent, and reviewable by an Information Commissioner, whose decisions are enforceable;
— The right of access to information should apply as broadly as possible, and exemptions to it should be drawn as narrowly and precisely as possible with a more demanding harm test;
— A statutory freedom of information regime should contain, as much as possible, enforceable rights of access to information; not undertakings to consider the discretionary release of information;

[.........]

We believe that this will make the draft Bill better, our democracy stronger, and the information rights of citizens more effective."

[94] Home Office, *Freedom of Information: Consultation on draft legislation*, May 1999, Cm. 4355.
[95] House of Commons, *Public Administration—Third Report* (Cm. 4355), July 29, 1999.

The House of Lords appointed its own select committee on June 17, 1999, which reported on July 27, 1999.[96] Its recommendations included:

> "63. The draft Bill should provide a framework for transforming the 'culture of secrecy' in British government . . . .
>
> 64. If the draft Bill is to conform to true Freedom of Information principles, the most important single amendment needed is to give the Information Commissioner a public interest override power in clause 44 to overrule a ministerial decision under clause 14, and to order disclosure. [.......]
>
> 82. The draft Bill does not need a purpose clause but the Long Title should be amended by leaving out the words 'make provision about the disclosure of information' and substituting 'facilitate the disclosure of information.' This would clarify the draft Bill's purpose of providing a framework for transforming the 'culture of secrecy' in British government."

The Government's response to the Report of the House of Commons Select Committee was published on October 27, 1999. The document said that it agreed with the bulk of the Select Committee's recommendations. The Government's response to the Report of the House of Lords Select Committee was published on January 17, 2000. That document, too, said that it agreed with the bulk of the Select Committee's recommendations.

The Freedom of Information Bill

1–021 The Freedom of Information Bill was introduced into the House of Commons on November 18, 1999, and received its second reading on December 7, 1999. It enjoyed a close Parliamentary scrutiny before receiving Royal Assent on November 30, 2000.[97]

[96] *Draft Freedom of Information Bill—First Report* (Select Committee Report HL97), Session 1998–1999, July 27, 1999.

[97] The stages and dates of the Act's progress are as follows. In the House of Commons: (1) Introduction, November 18, 1999, *Hansard*, Vol.339, col.124; (2) Second Reading, December 7, 1999, *Hansard*, Vol.340, cols 714–798; Committee, 1st Sitting, December 21, 1999; 2nd Sitting, January 11, 2000; 3rd Sitting, January 11, 2000; 4th Sitting, January 18, 2000; 5th Sitting, January 18, 2000; 6th Sitting, January 20, 2000 [Pt I]; 6th Sitting January 20, 2000 [Pt II]; 7th Sitting, January 25, 2000; 8th Sitting, January 25, 2000; 9th Sitting, January 27, 2000; 10th Sitting, February 1, 2000; 11th Sitting, February 1, 2000; 12th Sitting, February 8, 2000; 13th Sitting, February 8, 2000; 14th Sitting, February 10, 2000; (4) Report and Third Reading, April 4, 2000, *Hansard*, Vol.1857, cols 830–935; April 5, 2000, *Hansard*, Vol.1857, cols 981–1123; (5) Royal Assent, November 30, 2000, Vol.1877, col.1231. In the House of Lords: (1) Introduction, April 6, 2000, Vol.1802, col.1490; (2) Second Reading, April 20, 2000, *Hansard*, Vol.612, cols 823–893; (3) Committee, October 17, 2000, *Hansard*, Vol.617, cols 883–954 and 971–1020; October 19, 2000, *Hansard*, Vol.617, cols 1208–1300; October 24, 2000, *Hansard*, Vol.618, cols 273–314; October 25, 2000, *Hansard*, Vol.618, cols 407–476; (4) Report, November 14, 2000, *Hansard*, Vol.1824, cols 134–158 and 173–266; (5) Third Reading, November 22, 2000, *Hansard*, Vol.1825, cols 817–852; (6) Royal Assent, November 30, 2000, *Hansard*, Vol.1826, col.1492.

Implementation of the Freedom of Information Act 2000

A limited number of provisions came into effect on February 1, 2001[98], a few other provisions two months after that date,[99] but the majority are to come into force within five years of its passage or on an earlier date appointed by the Secretary of State.[1] The Secretary of State is obliged to report annually on his proposals for bringing into force any outstanding provisions of the Act.[2] On November 13, 2001, the Lord Chancellor announced in Parliament the implementation plan for the Act: 1–022

> "The Act will be fully implemented by January 2005, 11 months before the timetable set out in the Act itself. The publication scheme provisions will be implemented first, on a rolling programme, starting with central government in November 2002. I am today placing a full schedule of organisations and dates of implementation in the Libraries of both Houses. This roll-out [*i.e.* of publication scheme provisions] will be completed in June 2004, and the individual right of access to information held by all public authorities, including government departments, will be implemented in January 2005."

Certain other provisions of the Act have been brought into effect but, by and large, at the date of this work, the bulk of the Act is not yet in force.[3]

5. SCOTLAND, WALES AND NORTHERN IRELAND

Scotland: the demarcation

The applicability of the Freedom of Information Act 2000 and of the Data Protection Act 1998 to Scotland, as well as the scope of the Freedom of Information (Scotland) Act 2002, reflect the settlement of legislative powers effected by the devolution in 1998. Section 1(1) of the Scotland Act 1998 established a Scottish Parliament, which has a limited, devolved power to make laws with respect to certain matters in Scotland.[4] It does not have the power to make laws with respect to "reserved matters", which remain the exclusive competence of 1–023

[98] Freedom of Information Act 2000, s.87(1).
[99] *ibid.*, s.87(2).
[1] *ibid.*, s.87(3).
[2] *ibid.*, s.87(5). The first report was provided in November 2001, HC 367.
[3] To date, one commencement order, the Freedom of Information Act 2000 (Commencement No.1) Order 2001 (SI 2001/1637) has been made. It came into force on May 14, 2001 and brought into force certain, for the most part, technical provisions needed in advance of implementation of the Act's main provisions.
[4] Scotland Act 1998, ss.28–29. These are known as Acts of the Scottish Parliament: s.28(1).

Westminster.[5] Moreover, Westminster retains its plenary power to make laws with respect to Scotland,[6] although the understanding is that it will not generally exercise that power in relation to devolved matters.[7] In relation to the right of access to official information, the legislative competence of the Scottish Parliament is limited to public authorities that operate purely in or as regards Scotland.[8]

Background

1–024 In July 1999 the Scottish Executive published a Code of Practice on Access to Scottish Executive Information.[9] The Code stated its aims and purpose as being:

"1. This Code of Practice supports Scottish Ministers' policy of extending access to official information, and responding to reasonable requests for information. The approach to release of information should in all cases be based on the assumption that information should be released except where disclosure would not be in the public interest, as specified in Part II of this Code.

2. The aims of the Code are:

— to facilitate policy-making and the democratic process by providing access to the facts and analyses which form the basis for the consideration of proposed policy;

— to protect the interests of individuals and companies by ensuring that reasons are given for administrative decisions, except where there is statutory authority or established convention to the contrary; and

These aims are balanced by the need:

— to maintain high standards of care in ensuring the privacy of personal and commercially confidential information; and

— to preserve confidentiality where disclosure would not be in the

---

5 Scotland Act 1998, ss.29(2)(b) and 30(1). Reserved matters are listed in Sch.5. Specifically reserved at Pt II, s.B13 is "public access to information held by public bodies or holders of public offices (including government departments and persons acting on behalf of the Crown)". An exception to this reservation is made in relation to information held by the Scottish Parliament, any part of the Scottish Administration, the Scottish Parliamentary corporation and any Scottish public authority with mixed functions or no reserved functions, unless supplied by a Minister of the Crown or government department and held in confidence.

6 *ibid.*, s.28(7).

7 *Memorandum of Understanding and Supplementary Agreements between the United Kingdom Government, the Scottish Ministers, the Cabinet of the National Assembly of Wales and the Northern Ireland Executive Committee*, Cmd. 5240 (December 2001)(UK); SE/2002/54 (Scotland).

8 Scotland Act 1998, s.29(2)(a).

9 A separate Code of Practice on Openness exists in relation to information held by the NHS in Scotland (covering Health Boards, NHS Trusts and other NHS organisations).

public interest or would breach personal privacy or the confidences of a third party, in accordance with statutory requirements and Part II of the Code."

Like the Code for England and Wales issued in 1994 and revised in 1997,[10] it bestows no enforceable rights.

Freedom of Information (Scotland) Act 2002

On April 24, 2002 the Freedom of Information (Scotland) Act 2002 was passed by the Scottish Parliament[11] As noted above, the Act only applies to public authorities that operate purely in or as regards Scotland.[12] Westminster-established bodies, government departments, offices and office-holders when operating in Scotland, including what are termed cross-border public authorities,[13] are in any event not susceptible to coverage by the Freedom of Information (Scotland) Act 2002.[14] Difficult issues arise as to whether some of the exemptions in the Freedom of Information (Scotland) Act 2002 are outside the legislative competence of the Scottish Parliament on the basis that they represent provisions that relate to reserved matters.[15] Although closely modelled on the Freedom of Information Act 2000, the Scottish Act treats a number of matters differently: 1–025

(1) The scheme for responses that neither confirm nor deny that the public authority holds information answering the terms of the request. The Freedom of Information Act 2000 spells out a separate duty on a public authority to inform an applicant whether it holds information of the description specified in the request.[16] In relation to all but one of the heads of exemption, that duty is disapplied where, or to the extent that, confirming or denying that the public authority holds the requested

[10] See para.1–018 above.

[11] It received Royal Assent on May 28, 2002. The Act requires full implementation by December 31, 2005.

[12] These are listed in Sch.1 to the Freedom of Information (Scotland) Act 2002.

[13] Cross-border authorities are listed in the Scotland Act 1998 (Cross-Border Public Authorities)(Specification) Order 1999 (SI 1999/1319). These include the British Waterways Board, the Criminal Injuries Compensation Board and the Meat and Livestock Commission.

[14] See para.1–023 above and, in particular, n.5. When operating in Scotland, these public authorities will be governed by the Freedom of Information Act 2000.

[15] An Act of the Scottish Parliament is not law in so far as any provision of it is outside the legislative competence of the Scottish Parliament: Scotland Act 1998, s.29(1). A provision will be outside the legislative competence of the Scottish Parliament if it relates to "reserved matters": Scotland Act 1998, s.29(2)(b). Reserved matters are defined in Sch.5 to the Scotland Act 1998. Significantly, in light of the exemptions in the Freedom of Information (Scotland) Act 2002, these include: international relations, including relations with territories outside the United Kingdom, the European Communities (and their institutions) and other international organisations; the defence of the realm and the naval, military or air forces of the Crown; data protection; national security, etc.; social security; health and safety.

[16] Freedom of Information Act 2000, s.1(1)(a). This is termed "the duty to confirm or deny," s.1(6).

information would, or would be likely to, prejudice the matter protected by the head of exemption and, if the exemption is a qualified one, to do so would be contrary to the public interest.[17] The Freedom of Information (Scotland) Act 2002 creates no separate duty to confirm or deny that the information requested is held by the public authority. Instead, more elegantly, it provides that a refusal notice must, amongst other things, disclose that the public authority holds the information sought;[18] that requirement in relation to a refusal notice is then disapplied where information answering the terms of the request would be exempt under certain exemptions[19] and the public authority considers that it would be contrary to the public interest to reveal whether such information exists or is so held.[20]

(2) To the extent that there is an onus in engaging the public interest override in relation to the qualified exemptions, it is reversed. Under the Freedom of Information Act 2000, the duty to disclose exempt information is disapplied where, in all the circumstances of the case, the public interest in maintaining the exemption outweighs the public interest in disclosing the information.[21] Under the Freedom of Information (Scotland) Act 2002, the duty to disclose non-absolute exempt information only applies to the extent that, in all the circumstances of the case, the public interest in disclosing the information is not outweighed by the public interest in maintaining the exemption.[22]

(3) The harm level required to engage the prejudice-based exemptions is higher under the Freedom of Information (Scotland) Act 2002 ("would or might substantially prejudice")[23] than it is under the Freedom of Information Act 2000 ("would or might prejudice").[24] In light of the assurances given during the introduction into Parliament of the Freedom of Information Act 2000[25] the differences in practice ought to be less significant than the language might suggest.

(4) Under the Freedom of Information Act 2000, information held by a public authority is absolutely exempt if it was directly or indirectly

17 Freedom of Information Act 2000, ss.2(1), 22(2), 23(5), 24(2), 26(3), 27(4), 28(3), 29(2), 30(3), 31(3), 32(3), 33(3), 34(2), 35(3), 36(3), 37(2), 38(2), 39(3), 40(5), 41(2), 42(2), 43(3) and 44(2). The sole head of exemption that does not have a disapplication of the duty to confirm or deny is s.21.

18 Freedom of Information (Scotland) Act 2002, s.16(1)(a).

19 The exemptions to which the duty to confirm or deny is disapplied are more limited than those under the Freedom of Information Act 2000: namely, ss.28–35, 39 and 41. The Scottish equivalents to the Freedom of Information Act 2000, ss.22, 32, 33, 40, 41, 42 and 44 do not ground a refusal to confirm or deny under the Freedom of Information (Scotland) Act 2002.

20 Freedom of Information (Scotland) Act 2002, s.18.

21 Section 2(2)(b). The effect of this provision is considered further in Ch.15 below.

22 Section 2(1)(b).

23 Freedom of Information (Scotland) Act 2002, ss.27(2), 28(1), 30, 31(4), 32(1), 33(1), 33(2), 35(1) and 40.

24 Freedom of Information Act 2000, ss.26(1), 27(1), 28(1), 29(1), 31(1), 33(2), 36(2), 38(1) and 43(2).

25 See para.5–013.

supplied to the public authority by one of the security bodies or if it relates to one of the security bodies.[26] Moreover, a Minister of the Crown can sign a conclusive certificate certifying that the information to which the certificate applies was directly or indirectly supplied by, or relates to, any of the security bodies.[27] In Scotland, there is no such exemption.[28]

(5) In England, Wales and Northern Ireland, information the disclosure of which would be a breach of parliamentary privilege enjoys an absolute exemption.[29] There is no such exemption under the Scottish Act.

(6) There are fewer grounds for issuing an exemption conclusive certificate under the Freedom of Information (Scotland) Act 2002[30] than there are under the Freedom of Information Act 2000.[31]

(7) The preconditions for the issue of a compliance conclusive certificate are more onerous under the Freedom of Information (Scotland) Act 2002 than they are under the Freedom of Information Act 2000. In both jurisdictions, where the Information Commissioner is satisifed that a public authority has failed to comply with any of the requirements of Part I of the Act, he may serve on that public authority an enforcement notice specifying the steps that the public authority must take.[32] In both jurisdictions, limited provision[33] is made for a high ranking official to give the Information Commissioner within a certain time a certificate that causes the enforcement notice to cease to have effect.[34] Under the Freedom of Information Act 2000, the precondition for the high-ranking official issuing the certificate is that on reasonable grounds he

---

26 Freedom of Information Act 2000, s.23(1). The security bodies are those listed in s.23(3).

27 *ibid.*, s.23(2). The effect of a conclusive certificate is considered in para.14–030 below.

28 This raises a serious issue in relation to the Freedom of Information (Scotland) Act 2002. See n.14 above. The exemption in the Freedom of Information Act 2000, s.23 does not, of course, operate to render exempt information requested under the Freedom of Information (Scotland) Act 2002.

29 Freedom of Information Act 2000, s.34(1).

30 The only ground is national security: s.31(2).

31 The grounds are: security body information, s.23(2); national security, s.24(3); parliamentary privilege, s.34(3); and deliberative or cabinet information held by either House of Parliament, s.36(7).

32 Freedom of Information Act 2000, s.52(1); Freedom of Information (Scotland) Act 2002, s.51(1).

33 Under the Freedom of Information Act 2000, the power to issue a certificate is confined to where the enforcement notice relates to: (a) a failure to inform an applicant that it holds information of the description specified in the request in circumstances where s.2(1) does not operate to disapply the duty to confirm or deny; (b) a failure to communicate information to an applicant in circumstances where s.2(2) does not operate to disapply the duty to disclose: Freedom of Information Act 2000, s.53(1)(b). In Scotland, the power to issue a certificate is confined to where the enforcement notice relates to a failure to give information to an applicant in circumstances where s.2(1) does not operate to disapply the duty to disclose and the information is exempt information by virtue of s.29, 31(1), 32(1)(b), 34, 36(1) or 41(b): Freedom of Information (Scotland) Act 2002, s.52(1)(b).

34 Under the Freedom of Information Act 2000, that high-ranking official is the "accountable person" (itself defined in s.53(8)) and the time allowed is 20 working days: s.53(2). In Scotland that high-ranking official is the First Minister of the Scottish Executive and the time allowed is 30 working days: Freedom of Information (Scotland) Act 2002, s.52(2).

has formed the opinion that, in respect of the request or requests concerned, there was no relevant[35] failure to comply with the Act.[36] In Scotland, the high-ranking official must also form the opinion that the information requested is of exceptional sensitivity.[37]

(8) The Freedom of Information (Scotland) Act 2002 gives no express right of review in relation to the decision to issue a conclusive certificate.[38]

(9) The Freedom of Information (Scotland) Act 2002 has no equivalent to section 81(1) of the Freedom of Information Act 2000, which treats each government department as a person separate from any other government department.

The Freedom of Information (Scotland) Act 2002 establishes the office of the Scottish Information Commissioner.[39] This is independent of the office of the Information Commissioner, who is responsible for policing the Freedom of Information Act 2000. The Scottish Information Commissioner does not have responsibility for the enforcement of the Data Protection Act 1998 in Scotland.

Subject-access requests: Scotland

1–026 Data protection is a reserved matter and responsibility for enforcement of the Data Protection Act 1998 lies with the Information Commissioner: the Scottish Information Commissioner does not have responsibility for enforcing the Data Protection Act 1998. Thus a request by an individual for information about himself will be exempt under the Freedom of Information (Scotland) Act 2002 and is instead to be treated as a subject access request under the Data Protection Act 1998, save to the extent that it also involves the disclosure of personal information about a third party.[40]

Wales

1–027 Although the Government of Wales Act 1998 created a National Assembly for Wales, it is an administrative body rather than a legislative body. It has no power to make laws with respect to the granting of access to official information. Accordingly, the Freedom of Information Act 2000 applies equally to public

[35] In other words, a failure of the sort set out in n.32 above.
[36] Freedom of Information Act 2000, s.53(2).
[37] Freedom of Information (Scotland) Act 2002, s.52(2).
[38] Either on national security or exceptional sensitivity grounds: Freedom of Information (Scotland) Act 2002, ss.31(2) and 52(2).
[39] Freedom of Information (Scotland) Act 2002, s.42(1).
[40] See Ch.4 below.

authorities in Wales as it does to public authorities in England.[41] Schedule 1 to the Act, which lists public authorities for the purposes of the Act, includes the National Assembly for Wales, Welsh county councils, borough councils and community councils, health authorities, maintained schools and other educational institutions, police authorities, and various other bodies ranging from the Ancient Monuments Board for Wales to the Welsh Optometric Committee. The National Assembly for Wales has issued its own Code of Practice,[42] which, like all such codes,[43] does not bestow rights but does state intent.

Northern Ireland

The Freedom of Information Act 2000 extends to Northern Ireland[44] and specifically captures public authorities whose functions are exercisable only or mainly in or as regards Northern Ireland and relate only or mainly to transferred matters.[45] Schedule 1 to the Act includes the Northern Ireland Assembly, district councils, health and social services boards, schools and universities, the police authority, and various other bodies ranging from the Advisory Committee on Pesticides for Northern Ireland to the Northern Ireland Pig Production Development Committee. 1–028

6. THE EUROPEAN CONVENTION ON HUMAN RIGHTS, ETC.

Introduction

The principal human rights instruments do not directly address the right of access to officially-held information. Attempts to ground such a right in the right to freedom of expression as protected by Art.10 of the European Convention on Human Rights [46] or Art.19 of the International Covenant of 1–029

[41] The only difference is that where the Secretary of State for Constitutional Affairs proposes to add a body or office-holder to the list of public authorities in the Act and that body or office-holder is one whose functions are exercisable only or mainly in or as regards Wales, he must consult the National Assembly before doing so: Freedom of Information Act 2000, s.4(7). The Secretary of State for Constitutional Affairs is not required to consult where he intends to add a police authority to the list.

[42] The Code of Practice on Public Access to Information, the second edition of which was adopted in May 2001.

[43] See para.5–001 below.

[44] s.88(2). The specific reference to Northern Ireland is, strictly speaking, superfluous, but simply accords with a drafting convention.

[45] Freedom of Information Act 2000, s.84. "Transferred matters" are defined in the Northern Ireland Act 1998, s.4(1).

[46] Article 10 of the ECHR provides:

"1. Everyone has the right to freedom of expression. This right shall include freedom to hold opinions and to receive and impart information and ideas without interference by public

Human Rights[47] have, by and large, failed. Article 19 of the ICCPR is framed in wider terms than Art.10 of the ECHR. The former right includes the "freedom to seek, receive and impart information" the latter right is merely to "receive and impart information". But in relation to the ICCPR, the limited nature of enforcement mechanisms has curtailed significant development. In the late 1970s a draft additional protocol to the ECHR was discussed which expressly extended the right to freedom of expression protected under Art.10 of the ECHR to include the freedom to seek information. This draft protocol failed to secure widespread support and was abandoned.[48] However, a right of access to official information has, in certain contexts, been recognised under the rubric of other human rights: in particular, the right to respect for private life protected by Art.8 of the ECHR, the right to a fair trial protected by Art.6 of the ECHR and the right to life protected by Art.2 of the ECHR.

Article 10 of the ECHR: Early Strasbourg jurisprudence

1–030 Article 10 of the ECHR expressly includes the right to receive information. Initially, it appeared that the right would be interpreted broadly to include some form of right of access to information held by States. In *X v Federal Republic Germany*[49] the European Commission on Human Rights stated:

> "it follows from the context in which the right to receive information is mentioned . . . that it envisages first of all access to general sources of information . . . the right to receive information may under certain circumstances include a right of access by the interested person to documents which although not generally accessible are of particular importance."[50]

Subsequent case law from the European Court on Human Rights indicated that Art.10 of the ECHR did not form the basis of a generalised right of access

authority and regardless of frontiers. This article shall not prevent States from requiring the licensing of broadcasting, television or cinema enterprises.

2. The exercise of these freedoms, since it carries with it duties and responsibilities, may be subject to such formalities, conditions, restrictions or penalties as are prescribed by law and are necessary in a democratic society, in the interests of national security, territorial integrity or public safety, for the prevention of disorder or crime, for the protection of health or morals, for the protection of the reputation or rights of others, for preventing the disclosure of information received in confidence, or for maintaining the authority or impartiality of the judiciary."

[47] Article 19 of the ICCRP, para.2 provides that:
"Everyone shall have the right to freedom of expression: this right shall include freedom to seek, receive and impart information and ideas of all kinds, regardless of frontiers, either orally, in writing or in print, in the form of art or through any other media of his choice."

[48] See Malinverni, "Freedom of Information in the European Convention on Human Rights and the International Covenant on Civil and Political Rights" (1983) 4 *Human Rights Law Journal*.

[49] Application 8383/78 (1979) 17 D.R. 227.

[50] At pp.228–229.

to information in circumstances where there was no "willing speaker." In *Leander v Sweden*[51] the European Court of Human Rights held, in relation to the State's refusal to reveal secret information:

> "[T]he right to freedom to receive information basically prohibits a Government from restricting a person from receiving information that others wish or may be willing to impart to him. Article 10 does not, in circumstances such as the present case, confer on the individual a right of access to a register containing information on his personal position, nor does it embody an obligation on the Government to impart such information to the individual."[52]

A similar approach was adopted in *Gaskin v United Kingdom*[53] where the applicant complained that he had been refused access to a case record relating to him created when he was a minor and held by a local authority. The Court found that there was no violation of Art.10 of the ECHR.[54] In both *Leander* and *Gaskin*, the information sought related to a specific individual and its disclosure could not be said to be in the public interest.

Article 10 of the ECHR: Later Strasbourg jurisprudence

The disclosure of information that was in the public interest was considered in 1–031
Guerra and others v Italy,[55] which concerned disclosure of information relating to the dangers of a chemical factory. The residents contended that the authorities were obliged under *inter alia* Art.10 of the ECHR to inform them about the hazards of the activity undertaken at the factories and about major accident procedures. The European Commission of Human Rights held that Art.10 of the ECHR not only placed states under an obligation to make environmental information accessible to the public, but also under a positive obligation to collect, process and disseminate information which, by its very nature, is not directly accessible and which cannot be known to the public unless the authorities act accordingly. However, the European Court refused to adopt the same approach and, reiterating its position previously expressed in *Leander*, ruled that Art.10 of the ECHR was not applicable.[56] The Court categorically stated that the right to receive information referred to in Art.10 of the ECHR:

[51] (1987) 9 E.H.R.R. 433.
[52] At para.74.
[53] (1989) 12 E.H.R.R. 36; [1990] 1 F.L.R. 167.
[54] However, the European Court concluded that the applicant was entitled to the information sought under Art.8 of the ECHR, see paras 1–033 to 1–035 below.
[55] (1998) 26 E.H.R.R. 357; 4 B.H.R.C. 63; [1998] H.R.C.D. 277.
[56] However, again, the European Court found a violation under Art.8 ECHR, see paras 1–033 to 1–035 below.

"cannot be construed as imposing on a State, in circumstances such as those of the present case, positive obligations to collect and disseminate information of its own motion."[57]

Article 10 of the ECHR: Domestic jurisprudence

1–032 There has been little domestic case law successfully relying on Art.10 of the ECHR. The only cases considered by the English Courts have related to the nature of government inquiries. Prior to the coming into force of the Human Rights Act 1998, the claimant in *R. (Wagstaff) v Secretary of State for Health*[58] successfully argued, relying on Art.10 of the ECHR, that the inquiry into Dr Shipman's activities should be held in public. More recently the High Court has rejected arguments that the inquiry into the outbreak of foot and mouth disease be held in public.[59] The court concluded that Art.10 of the ECHR was not engaged by a decision to hold a closed public inquiry because:

"Article 10 ECHR imposes no positive obligation on government to provide, in addition to existing means of communication, an open forum to achieve the yet wider dissemination of views."[60]

The court in *Persey* noted that they had had the benefit of fuller submissions than in *Wagstaff* and this decision is probably confined to its facts as it was not a decision supported by the Strasbourg authorities.[61]

Article 8 of the ECHR: Strasbourg jurisprudence

1–033 Whilst Art.8 of the ECHR[62] does not provide for a generalised right of access to official information, in certain circumstances Art.8 of the ECHR imposes on

---

57 Above at para.53 Although the concurring opinion of Mrs Palm joined by five others indicated that in certain circumstances there may be a positive obligation to make available to the public information which by its nature could not otherwise come to the attention of the public.

58 [2001] 1 W.L.R. 292; [2000] H.R.L.R 646; [2000] U.K.H.R.R. 875.

59 *Persey and other v Secretary of State for Environment, Food and Rural Affairs* [2002] E.W.H.C. 371; [2002] 3 W.L.R. 704.

60 At para.53.

61 See *Howard and others v Secretary of State for Health* [2002] E.W.H.C. 396; [2002] 3 W.L.R. 738 at para.99. The court in *Howard* which adopted a similar approach to *Persey*, concluding that Art.10 ECHR was not engaged in a decision not to hold a public inquiry into circumstances surrounding the serious misbehaviour of a doctor.

62 Article 8 of the ECHR provides:

"1. Everyone has the right to respect for his private and family life, his home and his correspondence.

2. There shall be no interference by a public authority with the exercise of this right except such as is in accordance with the law and is necessary in a democratic society in the interests of national security, public safety or the economic well-being of the country, for the

the State authorities a positive obligation to supply information of particular significance to an individual or group of individuals. Early case law focussed on the right of access to personal data. In *Gaskin v United Kingdom*,[63] the Applicant successfully relied upon Art.8 of the ECHR in challenging a local authority's refusal to supply personal data. The applicant had been fostered as a child. He sought access to his own records, which included contributions from a number of professionals, some of whom objected to disclosure. The European Court of Human Rights concluded that the right to access to his file fell within the ambit of Art.8 of the ECHR and that the local authority's blanket refusal to disclose the applicant's records unjustifiably interfered with his right. In response to the judgment in *Gaskin*, the United Kingdom Government enacted legislation providing access to one's own "personal data" which is now embodied within the Data Protection Act 1998. The existence of a right to appeal to an independent authority against the non-disclosure of certain records under the Data Protection Act 1998 was sufficient to discharge the State's positive obligation to supply personal information under Art.8 of the ECHR.[64] The European Court has recently concluded that there is no positive obligation under Art.8 of the ECHR to disclose to an applicant the identity of his or her mother who had, under domestic law, been permitted to give birth anonymously.[65]

Article 8: Strasbourg jurisprudence and public information

Whilst initially it was thought that Art.8 of the ECHR was limited to granting 1–034
a right to "personal data", the European Court has adopted a broader interpretation and extended the right to access to include environmental information that has an impact on an individual's private life or home life. In *Guerra and*

prevention of disorder or crime, for the protection of health or morals, or for the protection of the rights and freedoms of others."

63 (1989) 12 E.H.R.R. 36; [1990] 1 F.L.R. 167.

64 See *MG v United Kingdom* [2002] 3 F.C.R. 289; (2003) 36 E.H.R.R. 3; (2003) 13 B.H.R.C. 179 (however, the European Court found a violation of Art.8 of the ECHR from 1995 to March 1, 2000 prior to the coming into force of the Data Protection Act 1998); cf. *Martin v United Kingdom* (Application No. 27533/95) (1996) 21 E.H.R.R. CD112, where the European Commission of Human Rights declared inadmissible an application under Art.8 of the ECHR for records relating to an intermittent period of mental health treatment for four years. The court in *MG* distinguished *Martin* on the grounds that the records requested related to five significant periods the applicant spent in care when he was relatively young including a period of three years from age three to six.

65 *Odièvre v France* (Application No.42326/98) (Judgment February 13, 2003). The Grand Chamber concluded ten votes to seven that there was no positive obligation under Art.8 of the ECHR in the circumstances. The majority of the court distinguished *Gaskin* on the grounds that unlike *Gaskin* there were competing Art.8 of the ECHR rights in issue: the child had a right pursuant to Art.8 of the ECHR to know where she came from but the mother also had a right pursuant to Art.8 of the ECHR in "remaining anonymous in order to protect her health by giving birth in appropriate medical conditions" (at para.44). The majority concluded that the balance struck between these competing interests by France was within the State's margin of appreciation.

others v Italy,[66] the Court concluded that the state authorities were under a positive obligation to supply information about the dangers of a local chemical factory to local residents so that they could assess the extent of the risk and take steps to reduce that risk.[67]

Article 8 of the ECHR: Domestic jurisprudence

1–035 Article 8 of the ECHR has been relied upon in a number of cases relating to private information although, so far, its impact has been limited. In *Linda Gunn-Russo v Nugent Care Society and The Secretary of State for Health*[68] the Claimant sought disclosure of her adoption records held by a voluntary adoption agency. The High Court concluded that in that context Art.8 of the ECHR added nothing to the common law. The court rejected the Claimant's argument, based on *Gaskin*, that the voluntary adoption agency could not have the last word and there must be some form of appeal to an independent authority: unlike *Gaskin* the information sought included private information relating to others namely the adoptive family rather than just the Claimant.[69]

Other articles of the ECHR

1–036 Article 6 of ECHR, which concerns the right to a fair trial, has been relied upon to require disclosure of documents that may be relevant to litigation.[70] Article 2 of the ECHR, which protects the right to life may in certain circumstances

66 (1998) 26 E.H.R.R. 357; 4 B.H.R.C. 63; [1998] H.R.C.D. 277.

67 See also *Lopez Ostra v Spain* (1995) 20 E.H.R.R. 277 and *McGinley and Egan v United Kingdom* (1999) 27 E.H.R.R. 1; (1999) 4 B.H.R.C. 421; (1998) 42 B.M.L.R. 123 (court concluded, by a majority of five to four that although there was a positive obligation pursuant to Art.8 of the ECHR to supply information about nuclear tests at Christmas Island to individuals present in the area, this obligation was discharged by r.6 of the Pensions Appeals Tribunals (Scotland) Rules).

68 [2001] EWHC Admin 56; [2002] 1 F.L.R. 1, [2001] U.K.H.R.R. 1320.

69 See also *R. on the application of Ann S v Plymouth City Council and C* [2002] EWCA Civ 388; [2002] 1 W.L.R. 2583; [2002] 1 F.L.R. 1177 (concerning the disclosure to the appellant's mother and nearest relative of certain information contained in social service files concerning her adult but mentally incapacitated son, C. The Court of Appeal concluded, relying in part on Art.8 of the ECHR, that disclosure was appropriate.) and *Re B (Disclosure to other Parties)* [2001] 2 F.L.R. 1017; [2002] 2 F.C.R. 32; [2001] Fam. Law 798 (concerning disclosure of documents in care proceedings).

70 See *McGinley and Egan v United Kingdom* (1999) 27 E.H.R.R. 1; (1999) 4 B.H.R.C. 421; (1998) 42 B.M.L.R. 123 (disclosure of documents relating to nuclear tests for the purposes of litigation before the Pensions Appeals Tribunal. Art.6(1) of the ECHR claim rejected as no documents detailing the fact that they had been exposed to dangerous levels of radiation existed). Art.6 of the ECHR was also invoked before the European Court of Human Rights in *Lopez Ostra v Spain* (1995) 20 E.H.R.R. 277 and *Guerra and others v Italy* (1998) 26 E.H.R.R. 357; 4 B.H.R.C. 63; [1998] H.R.C.D. 277. For consideration by domestic courts see: *Re B (Disclosure to other Parties)* [2001] 2 F.L.R. 1017; [2002] 2 F.C.R. 32; [2001] Fam. Law 798; R. (*on the application of Ann S v Plymouth City Council and C* [2002] EWCA Civ 388; [2002] 1 W.L.R. 2583; [2002] 1 F.L.R. 1177.

require provision of information relating to matters concerning health and safety.[71] Article 2 of the ECHR also imposes positive obligations on States to establish effective mechanisms to investigate certain deaths.[72]

Human Rights Act 1998

In introducing the second reading of the Freedom of Information Bill in the House of Commons, Jack Straw (the then Home Secretary), acknowledged that the Bill and the Human Rights Act 1998 were interrelated. He stated: 1–037

> "The 1998 Act sets out the European Convention's statement of basic rights. Some of those rights are absolute, such as that provided in Article 3, guaranteeing freedom from torture or degrading treatment. The rights which we have had to wrestle in the Freedom of Information Bill are not absolutes, but have to be balanced one with another. Article 10 gives a right to freedom of expression, but that has to be set against Article 8 on the right to respect for a private life.
>
> We have therefore sought in the Bill to secure a balance between the right to information needed for the proper exercise of freedom of expression and the- directly conflicting- right of individuals to protection of information about themselves; the rights that institutions, including commercial companies should have to proper confidentiality; and the need for any organisation, including the Government, to be able to formulate its collective policies in private."[73]

All the bodies that are subject to the duties imposed by s.1 of the Freedom of Information Act 2000 are likely to be public authorities within the meaning of s.6 of the Human Rights Act 1998. Equally, the bodies that are responsible for enforcing the Freedom of Information Act 2000, including the Information Commissioner, the Information Tribunal and the Courts, are also public authorities within the meaning of s.6 of the Human Rights Act 1998. All such bodies are required to act compatibly with the provisions of the European Convention of Human Rights. In most cases under the Freedom of Information Act 2000, no issues will arise under the European Convention of Human Rights. However, in cases concerning personal information, and environmental information that may have an impact on an individual's private or home life, Art.8 of the ECHR may well be of some relevance. Article 2 will be relevant to investigations of deaths in custody. Equally, Art.6 of the ECHR may

[71] See *Osman v United Kingdom* (2000) 29 E.H.R.R. 245; [1999] 1 F.L.R. 193; (1999) 11 Admin. L.R. 200. In this context there is likely to be an overlap with Art.8 of the ECHR, see paras 1–033 to 1–035 above.

[72] See R. v Secretary of State for the Home Department, Ex p. Amin [2003] UKHL 5.

[73] *Hansard*, HC, December 7, 1999, cols 719–720.

be of relevance in relation to information required for litigation. Both the public authorities who hold the information and, on appeal, the Information Commissioner must have regard to the European Convention on Human Rights when considering whether to disclose the requested information. Where a conclusive certificate has been issued, special considerations will apply, and these are considered elsewhere in this work.[74]

[74] See paras 14–034 and 14–041 to 14–043 below.

CHAPTER 2

The Comparative Jurisdictions

1. COMPREHENSIVE INFORMATION ACCESS LEGISLATION ELSEWHERE

Introduction

2–001 Along the path leading to the enactment of the FOI Act 2000, extensive reference was made to analogous legislation in Australia, New Zealand, Canada and Ireland:[1] comparative tables of exemption were prepared; the different types of harm that could engage an exemption were considered; the various approaches to the public interest were analysed; and so forth.[2] This is reflected in the final product, whose structure and occasionally language resemble those employed in

[1] Freedom of Information Act 1982 (Cth of Australia); Official Information Act 1982 (NZ); Access to Information Act (1982) (Canada); Freedom of Information Act 1997 (Ireland). Although it has the most developed body of jurisprudence on the topic, reference to the Freedom of Information Act (1966) 5 USC 552 (USA) was significantly more limited.

[2] See: Cabinet Office, *Your Right to Know—The Government's Proposals for a Freedom of Information Act* (White Paper), Cm. 3818, paras 3–12, Annexes A and B; *Background Material*, paras 33, 56–65, 70–71, 78, 108, 116–117, 125–129, 219; *Hansard*, HC, Vol.340, December 7, 1999, cols 722, 728, 741, 746–749, 754, 759–761, 789; *Hansard*, HC, Vol.347, April 4, 2000, cols 832, 837–839, 848–849, 922–926, 934; *Hansard*, HC, Vol.347, April 5, 2000, cols 996, 1009, 1028, 1041, 1097, 1103; *Hansard*, HL Vol.612, April 20, 2000, cols 830, 834, 838–839, 851, 867–868; *Hansard*, HL, Vol.617, October 17, 2000, cols 888, 893, 939, 941, 946, 1010; *Hansard*, HL, Vol.617, October 19, 2000, cols 1215, 1256, 1279; *Hansard*, HL, Vol.618, October 25, 2000, cols 438, 441–442; *Hansard*, HL, Vol.619, November 14, 2000, col 619.

the legislation of the comparative jurisdictions.[3] The divergences are also pointed, with certain features of the comparative regimes having been considered but not adopted. An overview of each of the comparative regimes is given below. After a short history, the principal features of each regime are identified: the scope of the right; the approach to requests and permissible responses; the general treatment of exemptions, including classification by harm and by class; the role of the public interest; the specific heads of exemption; and the system of appeals and enforcement. These reveal certain universal issues, most notably the identification of those legitimate interests of an open, accountable and representative government that have paramountcy over the general right of access to government-held information. Elsewhere in this work, reference is made to authorities in these comparative jurisdictions where it is considered that it sheds light on the Freedom of Information Act 2000 or the Data Protection Act 1998.

2. UNITED STATES OF AMERICA

Introduction

In 1966 the United States Congress passed the Freedom of Information Act.[4] It had evolved after a decade of debate among agency officials, legislators and public interest group representatives. The Act was not, however, entirely novel. The Administrative Procedure Act of 1964[5] had included a public disclosure section, although this was thought to have fallen short of its goals. In 1974 significant amendments to the Freedom of Information Act were made[6] and the Privacy Act was passed.[7] The latter granted individuals enhanced rights of access to agency records maintained about themselves;[8] it restricted the rights 2–002

[3] Most notably New Zealand and, to a slightly lesser extent, Australia.

[4] 5 USC 1002 (1964) (amended in 1966 and now codified at 5 USC 552). The Act took effect on July 4, 1967.

[5] 5 USC 1002. The Freedom of Information Act was in fact a revision of the public disclosure section of this Act.

[6] The 1974 amendments considerably narrowed the overall scope of the Act's law enforcement and national security exemptions. It also broadened many of the Act's procedural provisions, including fees, time limits, segregability, and *in camera* inspection by the courts.

[7] 5 USC 552a. The Act took effect on September 27, 1975.

[8] 5 USC 552a(d)(1). There is an overlap between the right of access bestowed by the Freedom of Information Act and that which is granted by the Privacy Act. The latter only applies to requests for personal information relating to the person making the request. Such a request need not state under which statute it is made. The technique is first to consider whether any exemption under the Privacy Act applies: if it does not, then the information must be released irrespective of the applicability of an exemption under the Freedom of Information Act. If an exemption under the Privacy Act does apply, then exemptions under the Freedom of Information Act must be considered: if none applies, the requested information must be released notwithstanding the applicability of an exemption under the Privacy Act: 5 USC 552a(t)(1); *Martin v Office of Special Counsel*, 819 F.(2d) 1181 (DC Cir. 1987); *Savada v Department of Defense*, 755 F. Supp. 6 (DDC 1991); *Viotti v United States Air Force*, 902 F. Supp. 1131 (D Colo. 1995).

of agencies to disclose personally identifiable records maintained by an agency; and it granted a right to individuals to seek amendment of agency records maintained on themselves. Further amendments to the Freedom of Information Act were made in 1976, 1986 and 1996.[9]

Scope of the right

2–003 Under the Freedom of Information Act, each federal "agency"[10] is required to make its[11] "records"[12] promptly available to any person[13] who makes a proper

[9] The 1976 amendment narrowed the Act's incorporation of the non-disclosure provisions of other statutes. The Freedom of Information Reform Act (1986) provided broader exemption protection for law enforcement information, special law enforcement record exclusions, and created a new fee and fee waiver structure. The Electronic Freedom of Information Act Amendments (1996) dealt with electronic records, electronic reading rooms, agency backlogs of requests, and other procedural provisions. Smaller changes were also made in 1978 and 1984.

[10] This extends to agencies within the executive branch of the federal government, including the Executive Office of the President and independent regulatory agencies: 5 USC 552(f)(1). However, the Act does not apply to entities that are not controlled by the federal government. Thus, organisations which, although having a relationship with the federal government, are autonomous, are outside the ambit of the Act: *Public Citizen Health Research Group v HEW*, 668 F.(2d) 537 (DC Cir. 1981); *Irwin Memorial Blood Bank v American National Red Cross*, 640 F.(2d) 1051 (9th Cir. 1981); *Gilmore v United States Department of Energy*, 4 F. Supp. 2d 912 (ND Cal. 1998). Similarly, state governments, municipal corporations, the courts, Congress and private citizens are not subject to the Act. Offices within the Executive Office of the President whose functions are limited to advising and assisting the President do not fall within the definition of "agency:" *Armstrong v Executive Office of the President*, 90 F.(3d) 553 (DC Cir. 1996)(National Security Council not an agency).

[11] "Agency records" are records that are (1) either created or obtained by an agency, and (2) under agency control at the time of the request: *United States Department of Justice v Tax Analysts*, 492 U.S. 136 (1989). In determining whether an agency has sufficient control over a record in order for it to be an "agency record," there are four factors to be taken into account: (1) the intent of the record's creator to retain or relinquish control over the record; (2) the ability of the agency to use and dispose of the record as it sees fit; (3) the extent to which agency personnel have read or relied upon the record; and (4) the degree to which the record was integrated into the agency's record-keeping system or files: *Lindsey v Bureau of Prisons*, 736 F.(2d) 1462 (11th Cir. 1984); *Tax Analysts v United States Department of Justice*, 845 F.(2d) 1060 (DC Cir. 1988), affirmed, 492 U.S. 136 (1989). Personal records which are maintained by agency employees are not considered to be agency records: *Bureau of National Affairs Inc v United States Department of Justice*, 742 F.(2d) 1484 (DC Cir. 1984); *Spannaus v United States Department of Justice*, 942 F. Supp. 656 (DDC 1996).

[12] The definition of "record" was widened in 1996 by the inclusion of what is now 5 USC 552(f)(2). Before the inclusion of that definition, it had been held that "records" did not include tangible, evidentiary objects: *Nichols v United States*, 325 F. Supp. 130 (D. Kan. 1971) (holding that archival exhibits consisting of guns, bullets, and clothing relating to the assassination of President Kennedy were not "records"). However, "record" had otherwise been given an expansive meaning to include: "machine readable materials...regardless of physical form or characteristics" (*Forsham v Harris* 445 U.S. 169 (1980)); an audiotape of Challenger astronauts on the basis that the Act "makes no distinction between information in lexical and....non-lexical form" (*N.Y. Times Co v NASA*, 920 F.(2d) 1002 (DC Cir. 1990)); and a motion picture film (*Save the Dolphins v United States Department of Commerce*, 404 F. Supp. 407 (ND Cal. 1975)).

[13] "Any person" includes foreign citizens, partnerships, corporations, associations, states and state agencies, and foreign or domestic governments: 5 USC 552(2). Requests may also be made

request for them.[14] The reason for the making of a request has no bearing on the merits of that request.[15] The scope of the right was curtailed by an amendment to the Act in 1986 which introduced the concept of "exclusions."[16] Three provisions create record "exclusions", the effect of which is to expressly authorise federal law enforcement agencies, in relation to especially sensitive records under certain specified circumstances, to treat the records as not subject to the requirements of the Freedom of Information Act 1966.[17] The application of one of the three record exclusions results in a response stating that no records responsive to the request exist, even though they may exist. These exclusions do not provide additional bases for an agency to withhold documents from the public: the exclusions only apply to records that are otherwise exempt from disclosure.

Other rights

The Act does not speak of publication schemes, but contains two analogous provisions giving rise to automatic disclosure of certain agency information. Under the first, each agency is required to publish in the Federal Register certain information relating to itself for "the guidance of the public." This includes a description of the agency's organization, functions and procedures; its substantive rules; and statements of general policy.[18] This requirement provides the public with automatic access to basic information regarding the transaction of 2–004

through an attorney or other representative on behalf of any person: *Constangy, Brooks & Smith v National Labor Relations Board*, 851 F.(2d) 839 (6th Cir. 1988). However, fugitives may be denied access: *Doyle v United States Department of Justice*, 668 F.(2d) 1365 (DC Cir. 1981).

14 5 USC 552(a)(3)(A).

15 *Environmental Protection Agency v Mink*, 410 U.S. 73 (1973); *United States Department of Justice v Reporters Committee for Freedom of the Press*, 489 U.S. 749 (1989).

16 5 USC 552(c)(1), (c)(2), (c)(3).

17 The first exclusion may be used when a request seeks information that is exempt because disclosure could reasonably be expected to interfere with a current law enforcement investigation (*i.e.* exemption (7)(A)). There are three specific prerequisites for the application of this exclusion. First, the investigation in question must involve a possible violation of criminal law. Second, there must be reason to believe that the subject of the investigation is not already aware that the investigation is underway. Third, disclosure of the existence of the records, as distinguished from the contents of the records, could reasonably be expected to interfere with enforcement proceedings. When all these conditions are satisfied, an agency may respond to a request as if the records were not subject to the requirements of the Act. The second exclusion applies to informant records maintained by a criminal law enforcement agency under the informant's name or personal identifier. The agency is not required to confirm the existence of these records unless the informant's status has been officially confirmed. This exclusion helps agencies to protect the identity of confidential informants. The third exclusion only applies to records maintained by the Federal Bureau of Investigation that relate to foreign intelligence, counterintelligence, or international terrorism. When the *existence* of these types of records is classified, the FBI may treat the records as not subject to the requirements of the Act. This exclusion does not apply to all classified records on the specific subjects. It only applies when the records are classified and when the *existence* of the records is also classified.

18 5 USC 552(a)(1).

agency business. Under the second, certain types of internal records, such as final agency opinions and orders rendered in the adjudication of cases, specific policy statements, certain administrative staff manuals, and some records previously processed for disclosure under the Act, must be routinely made "available for public inspection and copying."[19] This is generally referred to as the "reading room" provision of the Act.[20] A failure to comply with these requirements may provide a ground of challenge to an administrative decision that is related to information that ought to have been disclosed.[21] The effect of information falling within either provision is that it cannot be made the proper subject of a request under the Freedom of Information Act.[22] If an agency does not hold any record that answers the terms of a request, that agency is under no obligation to refer that request to any other agency where such records might be located. The Act contains no procedure entitling or enabling a third party to make representations before information relating to that third party is released to an applicant: this is dealt with, in part, by Executive Order.[23]

The request

2–005 A request must reasonably describe the records sought and it must be made in accordance with the agency's published regulations.[24] An agency is not required to create a record in order to respond to a request.[25] Nor is an agency required to answer a request for future information when it comes into existence.[26] However, an agency must undertake a search that is "reasonably calculated to

[19] 5 USC 552(a)(2). The reading rooms must also include information requested under the Act but which the agency considers is likely to be requested by others as well: 5 USC 552(a)(2)(D). The rationale for this is to prevent the development of agency "secret law," known to agency personnel but not to members of the public who deal with agencies. It is for this reason that records that have no precedent value and which do not constitute the working law of an agency are not required to be made available under this part of the Act: *National Labor Relations Board v Sears, Roebuck & Co*, 421 U.S. 132 at 153–154 (1975); *Skelton v United States Postal Service*, 678 F.(2d) 35 at 41 (5th Cir. 1982).

[20] Some of these records must be made available by agencies in "electronic reading rooms".

[21] *Checkosky v US Securities and Exchange Commission*, 23 F.(3d) 452 (DC Cir. 1994); *Kennecott Utah Copper Corp v United States Department of the Interior*, 88 F.(3d) 1191 (DC Cir. 1996).

[22] 5 USC 552(a)(3)(A).

[23] A more detailed comparative treatment of third party rights of consultation and of "reverse FOI" is given at para.11–043 below.

[24] 5 USC 552(a)(3)(A). The request will "reasonably describe" the records sought if it enables a professional agency employee familiar with the subject area to locate the record with a reasonable amount of effort. Each agency must publish in the *Federal Register* its procedural regulations governing access to its records under the Act. These regulations must inform the public of where and how to address requests; its schedule of fees for search, review, and duplication; its fee waiver criteria; and its administrative appeal procedures.

[25] *National Labor Relations Board v Sears, Roebuck & Co*, 421 U.S. 132 (1975).

[26] *Mandel Grunfeld & Herrick v United States Customs Service*, 709 F.(2d) 41 (11th Cir. 1983).

uncover all relevant documents."[27] The Act provides for three levels of fees that may be assessed in response to a request according to categories of applicants.[28]

The response

Each agency is required to determine within 20 working days after the receipt of a proper request whether to comply with the request.[29] In "unusual circumstances" an agency may have up to 10 days extra to answer.[30] The actual disclosure of records answering the terms of the request must follow promptly[31]. The agency can refuse to disclose if the applicant refuses to pay any fees.[33] Disclosure must be in the form requested by the applicant.[33] If a request is denied in whole or in part, the agency must tell the applicant the reasons for the denial.[34] The agency must also tell the applicant that there is a right to appeal.[35] If an agency fails to make a determination within the time limits, that may be treated as a constructive exhaustion of administrative remedies, entitling the applicant immediately thereafter to seek judicial review.[36] Where a record is not wholly comprised of exempt material the agency must, if it is reasonably practicable to do so, release any reasonably segregable portion that is not subject to an exemption.[37] The fact that supplying the records in answer to a properly described 2–006

27 *Weisberg v United States Department of Justice*, 705 F.(2d) 1344 at 1351 (DC Cir. 1983). The adequacy of the search will depend upon the specificity of the request. The courts may review the adequacy of the search, see: *Krikorian v Department of State*, 984 F.(2d) 461 (DC Cir. 1993).

28 5 USC 552(a)(4)(A)(ii)(I), (II), (III).

29 5 USC 552(a)(6)(A)(i).

30 Defined to mean circumstances in which the agency: (1) needs to search for and collect records from separate offices; (2) needs to examine a voluminous amount of records required by the request; or (3) needs to consult with another agency or agency component: 5 USC 552(a)(6)(B)(ii). The agency is supposed to notify the applicant whenever an extension is invoked.

31 5 USC 552(a)(6)(C)(i).

32 *Trueblood v United States Department of the Treasury*, 943 F. Supp. 64 (DDC 1996).

33 Unless it is not readily reproducible in that form or format: 5 USC 552(a)(3)(B).

34 5 USC 552(a)(6)(F).

35 5 USC 552(a)(6)(A)(i), (a)(6)(C)(i).

36 5 USC 552(a)(6)(c)).

37 5 USC 552(b). The courts will scrutinise decisions to ensure that this obligation has been properly performed: *Trans-Pac. Policing Agreement v United States Customs Service*, 177 F.(3d) 1022 at 1028 (DC Cir. 1999). There are limits to the obligation: see, generally: *Petroleum Information Corp v Department of the Interior*, 976 F.(2d) 1429 (DC Cir. 1992); *Krikorian v Department of State*, 984 F.(2d) 461 (DC Cir. 1993); *Solar Sources Inc v United States*, 142 F.(3d) 1033 (7th Cir. 1998); *PHE Inc.v Department of Justice*, 983 F.(2d) 249 (DC Cir. 1993). Thus in *Students Against Genocide v Department of State*, 257 F.(3d) 828 at 837 (DC Cir. 2001) the Court held that an agency is not obliged to segregate and release images from classified photographs by produc[ing] new photographs at a different resolution in order to mask the [classified] capabilities of the reconnaissance systems that took them. If, however, an agency determines that non-exempt material is so "inextricably intertwined" that disclosure of it would leave only essentially meaningless words and phrases, the entire record may be withheld: *Neufeld v IRS*, 646 F.(2d) 661 at 663 (DC Cir. 1981).

request would be burdensome does not of itself provide a basis for non-compliance.[38]

Exemptions generally

2–007 An agency may refuse to disclose an agency record that falls within any of the nine statutory exemptions in the *Freedom of Information Act*. Generally speaking, the exemptions are discretionary in nature, so that it is open to an agency to grant disclosure to a record for which exemption could be claimed.[39] A document that does not qualify as an "agency record" may be denied on the basis that only agency records are available under the Act. Personal notes of agency employees may be denied on this basis. However, most records in the possession of an agency are "agency records" within the meaning of the 1966 Act.

Specific exemptions

2–008 The right of access is disapplied to nine classes of matter:

(1) National security information concerning national defence or foreign policy, provided that that information has been classified in accordance with the requirements of an executive order.[40] This exemption can be

[38] *Yeager v Drug Enforcement Administration*, 678 F.(2d) 315 (DC Cir. 1982); *Ruotolo v Department of Justice*, 53 F.(3d) 4 (2d Cir. 1995); *Nation Magazine v United States Customs Service*, 71 F.(3d) 885 at 892 (DC Cir. 1995)

[39] *Chrysler Corp v Brown*, 441 U.S. 281 (1979); *Mobil Oil Corp v Environmental Protection Agency*, 879 F.(2d) 698 (9th Cir. 1989); *Public Citizen v Department of State*, 11 F.(3d) 198 (DC Cir. 1993); *Bartholdi Cable Co v Federal Communication Commission*, 114 F.(3d) 274 (DC Cir. 1997); *Sherman v Department of the Army*, 244 F.(3d) 357 (5th Cir. 2001).

[40] 5 USC 552(b)(1). With effect from 14 October 1995, the operative order is Executive Order 12,958. This replaced Executive Order 12,356, which had been issued in 1982. The Executive Order recognises three basic classifications according to the damage to the national security that might reasonably be expected to result from disclosure of the information to which the classification relates: top secret; secret; and confidential. Only information relating to certain matters (*e.g.* military plans, weapons systems, or operations; foreign government information, *etc.*) may be classified, and then only by persons at certain designated levels. The classification generally lasts for 10 years. The courts have consistently declined to reject agency assessments of a threat to national security on the basis that they are not equipped to second-guess such assessments: *Halperin v CIA*, 629 F.(2d) 144 (DC Cir. 1980); *Goldberg v Department of State*, 818 F.(2d) 71 (DC Cir. 1987); *Bowers v United States Department of Justice*, 930 F.(2d) 350 (4th Cir. 1991); *Young v CIA*, 972 F.(2d) 536 (4th Cir. 1992); *Students Against Genocide v Department of State*, 257 F.(3d) 828 (DC Cir. 2001). Agencies, it is thought, have unique insights into such matters: *Miller v United States Department of State*, 779 F.(2d) 1378 (8th Cir. 1985). The Executive Order expressly acknowledges the "mosaic" basis for refusal to disclose a record: Executive Order No.12,958, para.1.8(e). This has also been recognised in the Courts: *Halperin v CIA*, 629 F.(2d) 144 (DC Cir. 1980).

used to give a response that neither confirms nor denies the holding of records answering the terms of the request.[41]

(2) Records that are "related solely to the internal personnel rules and practices of an agency".[42] This covers: (a) internal matters of a relatively trivial nature;[43] and (b) more substantial internal matters, the disclosure of which would risk circumvention of a statute or regulation.[44]

(3) Information prohibited from disclosure by another statute, provided that that statute either requires that the information be withheld from the public in such a manner as to leave no discretion on the issue or that that statute establishes particular criteria for withholding or refers to particular types of information to be withheld.[45]

(4) Trade secrets[46] and commercial or financial information[47] obtained from a person that is privileged or confidential.[48] Information may also be withheld if disclosure would be likely to impair the government's ability to obtain similar information in the future. Only information obtained

---

[41] Executive Order No.12,958, para.3.7(a). This, in the United States, is called a "Glomar" response.

[42] 5 USC 552(b)(2). As interpreted by the courts, there are two separate classes of documents that are generally held to fall within the second exemption. First, information relating to personnel rules or internal agency practices is exempt if it is a trivial administrative matter of no genuine public interest. Secondly, an internal administrative manual can be exempt if disclosure would risk circumvention of law or agency regulations. In order to fall into this category, the material will normally have to regulate internal agency conduct rather than public behaviour.

[43] Often referred to as "low 2" information. This covers routine internal personnel matters, such as performance standards and leave practices. The rationale for this part of the exemption is that the very task of processing and releasing these sorts of record would place an administrative burden on the agency that would not be justified by any genuine public benefit. The exemption does not apply where there is a genuine and significant public interest in disclosure of the records requested. In relation to the application of this provision, see: *Department of the Air Force v Rose*, 425 U.S. 352 (1976); *Crooker v Bureau of Alcohol, Tobacco, Firearms and Explosives*, 670 F.(2d) 1051 (DC Cir. 1981); *Dirksen v United States Department of Health and Human Services*, 803 F.(2d) 1456 (9th Cir. 1986); *Maricopa Audubon Society v United States Forest Service*, 108 F.(3d) 1082 (9th Cir. 1997).

[44] Often referred to as "high 2" information. This will extend to guidelines for conducting investigations; information that would reveal the identities of informants or undercover agents; information referring to the security techniques used in prisons; agency testing material; and so forth.

[45] 5 USC 552(b)(3). In relation to this provision, see: *American Jewish Congress v Kreps*, 574 F.(2d) 624 (DC Cir. 1978); *Halperin v CIA*, 629 F.(2d) 144 (DC Cir. 1980); *Gardels v CIA*, 689 F.(2d) 1100 (DC Cir. 1982); *CIA v Sims*, 471 U.S. 159 (1985).

[46] "Trade secrets" has been given a narrower definition than given to it in tort law, so as to be confined to "a secret, commercially valuable plan, formula, process, or device that is used for the making, preparing, compounding, or processing of trade commodities and that can be said to be the end product of either innovation or substantial effort." (*Public Citizen Health Research Group v FDA*) 704 F.(2d) 1280 (DC Cir. 1983). It requires that there be a direct relationship between the trade secret and the productive process.

[47] Provided that the information relates to business or trade, the courts have generally accepted that it is commercial or financial information: *Public Citizen Health Research Group v FDA*, 704 F.(2d) 1280 (DC Cir. 1983); *Merit Energy Co v United States Department of the Interior*, 180 F. Supp. 2d 1184 (D. Colo. 2001). Detailed information on a company's marketing plans, profits, or costs can qualify as confidential business information.

[48] 5 USC 552(b)(4). In relation to confidentiality, a distinction is made between information submitted pursuant to obligation and information voluntarily submitted. In the former case, information is confidential for purposes of the exemption if disclosure of the information is likely to have either of the following effects: (1) to impair the Government's ability to obtain necessary information in the future; or (2) to cause substantial harm to the competitive position of the

from a person other than a government agency qualifies under this exemption: information that an agency created on its own cannot normally be withheld under this exemption. The provision protect the interests of both the government and those who submit information to government.[49]

(5) Inter-agency or intra-agency[50] memoranda or letters "which would not be available by law to a party other than an agency in litigation with the agency."[51] This has been interpreted to mean records that would normally be privileged in civil proceedings[52]. These privileges are broader than those that are enjoyed by a public authority in the United Kingdom, and include: (a) deliberative process privilege, also known as "executive privilege;"[53] (b) attorney work-product privilege;[54] and (c) attorney-client privilege.[55]

---

person from whom the information was obtained: *National Parks & Conservation Association v Morton*, 498 F.(2d) 765 (DC Cir. 1974). In the case of voluntarily submitted information, it is protected from disclosure provided it is not customarily disclosed to the public by the third party: *Critical Mass Energy Project v Nuclear Regulatory Commission*, 975 F.(2d) 871 (DC Cir. 1992).

49 Although there is no formal requirement under the Act to do so, generally agencies will notify the person who submitted the business information that disclosure of the information is being considered.

50 These terms are not rigidly exclusive terms and can include some records generated outside an agency: *Department of the Interior v Klamath Water Users Protective Association*, 532 U.S. 1 (2001).

51 5 USC 552(b)(5).

52 *National Labor Relations Board v Sears, Roebuck & Co*, 421 U.S. 132 (1975); *FTC v Grolier Inc*, 462 U.S. 19 (1983).

53 The protection of records revealing the deliberative policymaking process of government is said to be founded upon three policy considerations: (1) the encouragement of open, frank discussions on matters of policy between subordinates and superiors; (2) the protection against premature disclosure of proposed policies before they are finally adopted; and (3) the protection against public confusion that might result from disclosure of reasons and rationales that were not in fact ultimately the grounds for an agency's action: *Jordan v United States Department of Justice*, 591 F.(2d) 753 (DC Cir. 1978); *Coastal States Gas Corp v Department of Energy*, 617 F.(2d) 854 (DC Cir. 1980); *Russell v Department of the Air Force*, 682 F.(2d) 1045 (DC Cir. 1982); *Heggestad v United States Department of Justice*, 182 F. Supp. (2d) 1 (DDC 2000). In order to rely on the exemption, there are two requirements. First, the record must pre-date the decision to which it relates: *National Labor Relations Board v Sears, Roebuck & Co*, 421 U.S. 132 (1975); *Access Reports v Department of Justice*, 926 F.(2d) 1192 (DC Cir. 1991). Determining this is not always an easy task and there is much authority on the point. Secondly, the record must be a direct part of the deliberative process, in that it makes recommendations and expresses opinions on legal or policy matters: *Vaughn v Rosen*, 523 F.(2d) 1136 (DC Cir. 1975). This second requirement excludes factual material: *Coastal States Gas Corp v Department of Energy*, 617 F.(2d) 854 (DC Cir. 1980). The provision has been generously interpreted: *Coastal States Gas Corp v Department of the Environment*, 617 F.(2d) 854 (DC Cir. 1980); *Skelton v United States Postal Service*, 678 F.(2d) 35 (5th Cir. 1982); *Afshar v Department of State*, 702 F.(2d) 1125 (DC Cir. 1983); *Formaldehyde Institute v United States Department of Health and Human Services*, 889 F.(2d) 1118 (DC Cir. 1989); *Access Reports v Department of Justice*, 926 F.(2d) 1192 (DC Cir. 1991); *Wolfe v United States Department of Health and Human Services*, 839 F.(3d) 768 (DC Cir. 1998). The courts have recognised that there is no straightforward dichotomy between deliberative material and factual material.

54 In other words, material prepared by a lawyer in contemplation of litigation. The privilege arises if litigation is probable: *Schiller v National Labor Relations Board*, 964 F.(2d) 1205 (DC Cir. 1992). Privilege attaches provided that litigation was the primary factor in the decision to create the document: *Maine v United States Department of the Interior*, 285 F.(3d) 126 (1st Cir. 2002).

55 In other words, confidential communications between a lawyer and his client relating to a legal matter for which the client has sought professional advice: *Mead Data Centre Inc v United States Department of the Air Force*, 566 F.(2d) 242 (DC Cir. 1977).

(6) Information about individuals[56] in "personnel and medical files and similar files,"[57] provided that the disclosure of that information "would constitute a clearly unwarranted invasion of personal privacy."[58]

(7) Records or information compiled for law enforcement purposes.[59] In order to engage the exemption it must also be shown that one or more of six types of harm would flow from the disclosure of such records or information:

(A) The production of such records or information could reasonably be expected[60] to interfere with enforcement proceedings.[61]

---

[56] The exemption requires that the record relate to an identifiable specific individual, and not just a large class of unidentified individuals: *Arieff v United States Department of the Navy*, 712 F.(2d) 1462 (DC Cir. 1983). Corporations cannot fall within this exemption unless they are so small that there is no practicable difference between the individual and the corporation run by the individual: *Providence Journal Co v FBI*, 460 F. Supp. 778, 785 (DRI 1978); *Sims v CIA*, 642 F.(2d) 562 (DC Cir. 1980). It would seem that deceased individuals do not have privacy interests: *Hale v United States Department of Justice*, 973 F.(2d) 894, 902 (10th Cir. 1992); *Na Iwi O Na Kupuna v Dalton*, 894 F. Supp. 1397 (D. Haw. 1995).

[57] The words "similar files" has been construed to mean all information that "applies to a particular individual:" *United States Department of State v Washington Post Co*, 456 U.S. 595 (1982); *Sherman v United States Department of the Army*, 244 F.(3d) 357 (5th Cir. 2001).

[58] 5 USC 552(b)(6). The last words import into the exemption a requirement to balance the public's right to disclosure against the individual's right to privacy: *Department of the Air Force v Rose*, 425 U.S. 352 (1976). If it is shown that a protectable privacy interest would be threatened by disclosure of the record, the public interest in disclosure must be weighed against the privacy interest in non-disclosure. As to the manner in which this task is to be carried out, see: *United States Department of Justice v Reporters Committee for Freedom of the Press*, 489 U.S. 749 (1989); *United States Department of State v Ray*, 502 U.S. 164 (1991); *Department of Defense v F.L.R.A*, 510 U.S. 487 (1994) . As to what are protectable privacy interests, see: *Core v United States Postal Service*, 730 F.(2d) 946 (4th Cir. 1984); *Nation Magazine v United States Customs Service*, 71 F.(3d) 885 (DC Cir. 1995). The right to privacy of a public figure is a diluted one: *Fund for Constitutional Government v National Archives & Records Service*, 656 F.(2d) 856 (DC Cir. 1981). The onus is on the applicant to show that disclosure would be in the public interest of shedding light on an agency's performance of its statutory duties.

[59] The exemption has, by amendments in 1974 and 1986, been broadened in its scope. The phrase "law enforcement purposes" has been given a broad interpretation, to include the enforcement of state laws and of foreign laws: *Bevis v Department of State*, 801 F.(2d) 1386 (DC Cir. 1986); *Hopkinson v Shillinger*, 866 F.(2d) 1185 (10th Cir. 1989). Information not initially obtained or generated for law enforcement purposes may still qualify under this exemption if it is subsequently compiled for a valid law enforcement purpose at any time prior to invocation of the exemption: *John Doe Agency v John Doe Corp*, 493 U.S. 146 (1989). A particularly generous application of the provision is allowed for criminal law enforcement agencies, although this tends to vary with circuit.

[60] The 1986 amendment changed the required likelihood of harm from "would interfere with" to "could reasonably be expected to interfere with," thereby widening the scope of the exemption.

[61] The courts have held that the agency must be able to show some distinct harm could reasonably be expected to result if there were disclosure: *City of Chicago v United States Department of Treasury*, 287 F.(3d) 628 (7th Cir. 2002), holding that hypothetical scenarios are not enough. The protection afforded by the exemption only endures for so long as proceedings are pending or prospective: *National Labor Relations Board v Robbins Tire & Rubber Co*, 437 U.S. 214 (1978). The types of harm which the courts have found might result from disclosure sufficient to engage the exemption include witness intimidation, fabrication of evidence, evasion of detection, premature revelation of evidence and revelation of strategies. A "chilling" of witnesses will suffice: *Solar Inc v United States*, 142 F.(3d) 1033 (7th Cir. 1998).

(B) The production of such records or information would deprive a person of a right to a fair trial or an impartial adjudication.[62]

(C) The production of such records or information could reasonably be expected to constitute an unwarranted invasion of personal privacy.[63]

(D) The production of such records or information could reasonably be expected to reveal the identity of a confidential source.[64]

(E) The production of such records or information would reveal techniques and procedures for law enforcement investigations or prosecutions or would disclose guidelines for law enforcement investigations or prosecutions, provided that disclosure of the information could reasonably be expected to risk circumvention of the law.

(F) The production of such records or information could reasonably be expected to endanger the life or physical safety of any individual.[65]

(8) Matters that are contained in or related to examination, operating, or condition reports prepared by, on behalf of, or for the use of an agency responsible for the regulation or supervision of financial institutions.[66]

(9) Geological and geophysical information and data, including maps, concerning wells.[67]

---

62 This exemption is rarely used, with agencies generally relying on (7)(A) instead.

63 Although there is an overlap between this exemption and exemption (6), the standard for engagement is different. Exemption 7(C) protects against an unwarranted invasion of personal privacy, whereas exemption 6 protects against a clearly unwarranted invasion; exemption 7(C) allows the withholding of information that "could reasonably be expected to" invade someone's privacy, whereas under exemption 6 information can be withheld only if disclosure "would" invade someone's privacy. The exemption is given a generous application: *United States Department of Justice v Reporters Committee for Freedom of the Press*, 489 U.S. 749 (1989); *SafeCard Services v US Securities and Exchange Commission*, 926 F.(2d) 1197 (DC Cir. 1991).

64 A confidential source can include a State, local, or foreign agency or authority, or a private institution that furnished information on a confidential basis. In addition, the exemption protects information furnished by a confidential source if the data was compiled by a criminal law enforcement authority during a criminal investigation or by an agency conducting a lawful national security intelligence investigation. The courts have stated that the exemption must be given a "robust" application in order to protect such sources of information: *Brant Construction Co v Environmental Protection* Agency, 778 F.(2d) 1258 (7th Cir. 1985). Thus, what matters is not the nature of the information itself but the source of that information: *United States Department of Justice v Landano*, 508 U.S. 165 (1993).

65 This has been interpreted as giving a very wide protection from disclosure of those involved in law enforcement: *Spirko v United States Postal Service*, 147 F.(3d) 992 (DC Cir. 1998); *Rugiero v United States Department of Justice*, 257 F.(3d) 534 (6th Cir. 2001).

66 5 USC 552(b)(8). This has been given a generous interpretation: *Gregory v Federal Deposit Insurance Commission*, 631 F.(2d) 986 (DC Cir. 1980); *Public Citizen v Farm Credit Administration*, 938 F.(2d) 290 (DC Cir. 1991). The provision has been said to have two purposes underlying it: (1) to protect the security of financial institutions by withholding from the public reports that contain frank evaluations of a bank's stability; and (2) to promote cooperation and communication between employees and examiners: *Berliner, Zisser, Walter & Gallegos v US Securities and Exchange Commission*, 962 F. Supp. 1348 (D. Colo. 1997).

67 5 USC 552(b)(9). This exemption is rarely used.

Appeals and enforcement

2–009 An applicant has the right to an internal appeal on a merit basis against any adverse determination made by an agency.[68] If the agency upholds the decision, it must inform the applicant of its reasons and of the applicant's right of review in the federal courts.[69] Exclusive jurisdiction in relation to decisions under the Freedom of Information Act is vested in the United States district courts.[70] Before a district court will interfere with an agency's decision, the applicant must show that the agency has improperly withheld agency records.[71] In effect this means judges determine the propriety of agency withholdings *de novo*, with agencies bearing the burden of proof in defending the non-disclosure of records.[72] Agencies are required to prepare an index supported by an affidavit that itemises each withheld document (whether in whole or in part), identifying on a document-by-document basis the specific exemption relied upon and the facts and matters relied upon by the agency to justify non-disclosure.[73] Although the index will often comprise the only evidence produced by the agency, it may be supplemented or displaced by the court's *in camera* inspection

[68] 5 USC 552(a)(6)(A). The request must be answered within 20 working days: 5 USC 552(a)(6)(A)(i).

[69] 5 USC 552(a)(6)(A). Unless there has been no response within the 20 working day limit to a properly made request, the internal review (known as the "administrative remedy") must be exhausted before applying to the Court: *Taylor v Appleton*, 30 F.(3d) 1365 at 1367 (11th Cir. 1994); *Pollack v Department of Justice*, 49 F.(3d) 115 at 118 (4th Cir. 1995). If, after the 20 working days but before a District Court suit is filed, the agency responds to the request, then the administrative remedy must be exhausted before applying to the court: *Oglesby v United States Department of the Army*, 920 F.(2d) 57 at 61 (DC Cir. 1990).

[70] 5 USC 552(a)(4)(B).

[71] *Kissinger v Reporters Committee for Freedom of the Press*, 445 U.S. 136 at 150 (1980).

[72] 5 USC 552(a)(4)(B); *Natural Resources Defense. Council v Nuclear Regulatory Commission*, 216 F.(3d) 1180 (DC Cir. 2000). Although normally appeals are determined on a document-by-document basis, under certain circumstances courts have approved withholdings of entire, but discrete, categories of records which encompass all documents having similar contents: *National Labor Relations Board v Robbins Tire & Rubber Co*, 437 U.S. 214 (1978). Before the court, the agency is not precluded from seeking to rely on an exemption that it did not rely upon at the administrative stage: *Young v CIA*, 972 F.(2d) 536 (4th Cir. 1992). As to waiver of exemptions, see: *North Dakota ex rel. Olson v Department of the Interior*, 581 F.(2d) 177 (8th Cir. 1978); *Ryan v Department of Justice*, 617 F.(2d) 781 (DC Cir. 1980); *Mobil Oil Corp v Environmental Protection Agency*, 879 F.(2d) 698 (9th Cir. 1989); *Public Citizen v Department of State*, 11 F.(3d) 198 (DC Cir. 1993); *Maydak v Department of Justice*, 218 F.(3d) 760 (DC Cir. 2000).

[73] This document is generally called the "Vaughn Index" after the judgment of the Court of Appeals for the District of Columbia Circuit in *Vaughn v Rosen* 484 F.(2d) 820 (1973). The index is required to be sufficiently detailed to enable the court to make a reasoned independent assessment of the claim of exemption. It must also be sufficiently specific to justify non-disclosure of the whole document, as opposed to just part of it: *Judicial Watch v United States Department of Health and Human Services*, 27 F. Supp. (2d) 240 (DDC 1998); *Animal Legal Defense Fund Inc. v Department of the Air Force*, 44 F. Supp. (2d) 295 (DDC 1999). Where the documents are voluminous, a Vaughn Index may be prepared on the basis of representative samples: *Fensterwald v CIA*, 443 F. Supp. 667 (DDC 1977); *Weisberg v United States Department of Justice*, 745 F.(2d) 1476 (DC Cir. 1984); *Bonner v United States Department of State*, 928 F.(2d) 1148 at 1151 (DC Cir. 1991); *Campaign for Responsible Transplantation v FDA*, 180 F. Supp. (2d) 29, 34 (DDC 2001).

of the requested documents.[74] If the court finds that an exemption does apply, it has no inherent or equitable power to order disclosure.[75] The court is empowered to consider the adequacy of the search made by an agency.[76] Appeals from the district courts are heard in the Court of Appeals. Third parties may bring proceedings to prevent an agency from disclosing records under the Act.[77]

3. COMMONWEALTH OF AUSTRALIA

Introduction

2–010 In 1982 the Federal Parliament of Australia passed the Freedom of Information Act 1982.[78] It was the first such piece of legislation in a Westminster system of government. The origin of the Act lay in a report of an inter-departmental committee tabled in the Federal Parliament in November 1976. The first Bill was introduced into the Senate by the Attorney-General in June 1978. That was referred to various committees and inquiries before taking its final form. Since its enactment, the Act has been significantly amended on three occasions, with numerous smaller amendments.[79]

[74] Sometimes the Vaughn Index (because it is available to the applicant) will include less detail than is necessary to make good the claim for exemption, with the agency relying instead on an *in camera* inspection of the records sought: *Ingle v Department of Justice*, 698 F.(2d) 259 (6th Cir. 1983); *Simon v United States Department of Justice*, 980 F.(2d) 782 (DC Cir. 1992); *United States Department of Justice v Landano*, 508 U.S. 165 (1993); *Maynard v CIA*, 986 F.(2d) 547 (1st Cir. 1993); *Quninon v FBI*, 86 F.(3d) 198 (DC Cir. 1993); *Fiduccia v United States Department of Justice*, 185 F.(3d) 1035 (9th Cir. 1999).

[75] *Spurlock v FBI*, 69 F.(3d) 1010, 1016–18 (9th Cir. 1995).

[76] The agency must show that it made "a good-faith effort to conduct a search for the requested records, using methods which can be reasonably expected to produce the information requested:" *Weisberg v United States Department of Justice*, 745 F.(2d) 1476 at 1485 (DC Cir. 1984); *Truitt v Department of State*, 897 F.(2d) 540 at 542 (DC Cir. 1990); *Oglesby v United States Department of the Army*, 920 F.(2d) 57 at 61 (DC Cir. 1990); *Campbell v United States Department of Justice*, 164 F.(3d) 20 at 28 (DC Cir. 1998); *Rugiero v United States Department of Justice*, 257 F.(3d) 534 at 547 (6th Cir. 2001). The court may use its powers to order discovery as part of the process: *Weisberg v United States Department of Justice*, 627 F.(2d) 365 (DC Cir. 1980).

[77] These proceedings themselves are not based upon the Freedom of Information Act but upon the *Administrative Procedures Act* (5 USC 701–06): *Chrysler Corp v Brown* 441 U.S. 281 (1979). As to reverse FOI generally, see: *CNA Finance Corp Donovan*, 830 F.(2d) 1132 (DC Cir. 1987); *McDonnell Douglas Corp v NASA*, 180 F.(3d) 303 (DC Cir. 1999); *Campaign for Family Farms v Glickman*, 200 F.(3d) 1180 (8th Cir. 2000).

[78] Since then each of the six states and one of the two internal territories has passed similar legislation: Freedom of Information Act 1982 (Vic); Freedom of Information Act 1989 (ACT); Freedom of Information Act 1989 (NSW); Freedom of Information Act 1991 (SA); Freedom of Information Act 1991 (Tas); Freedom of Information Act 1992 (Qld); Freedom of Information Act 1992 (WA).

[79] By the Freedom of Information Amendment Act 1983, the Freedom of Information Laws Amendment Act 1986 and the Freedom of Information Amendment Act 1991.

Scope of the right

Section 11 of the *Freedom of Information Act 1982* gives every person[80] a legally enforceable[81] right to obtain access in accordance with the Act to a "document"[82] of an "agency"[83] and to an "official document"[84] of a Minister, other than an "exempt document." The phrase "exempt document" is defined[85] to mean: 2–011

(1) A document that falls within one of the specific exemptions in Pt IV of the Act;[86]

(2) A document that is held by or received from one of the bodies that is exempted from the operation of the Act;[87] and

---

80 This has been held to extend to a foreign corporation: *Re Lordsvale Finance Ltd and Department of the Treasury* (1985) 3 A.A.R. 301, AAT. And to convicted felons: *Re Ward and Secretary, Department of Industry and Commerce* (1983) 8 A.L.D. 324. But in Victoria, not to a severely mentally retarded person: *Wallace v Health Commission of Victoria* [1985] V.R. 403.

81 Freedom of Information Act 1982, s.18. It has been suggested that this does not enable an "unconscientious" use of the statute, *e.g.* to ask an agency for documents that would help the applicant in proceedings in an action against the agency: *Johnson Tiles Pty Ltd v Esso Australia Ltd* [2000] F.C.A. 495.

82 A document is defined broadly to include not only paper records but any other information which is capable of being reduced to written or visual form and which is capable of reproduction in that form: Freedom of Information Act 1982, s.4(1). There is a specific provision in relation to computer-based information: Freedom of Information Act 1982, s.17. Apart from this, however, the Act does not require the generation of documents in order to answer a request: *Re Redfern and the University of Canberra* (1995) 38 A.L.D. 457. Documents created more than five years before the commencement of the Act are excluded from its operation: Freedom of Information Act 1982, s.12(2). It has been held that the Act does not extend to permit requests for documents that might be created in the future: *Re Edelsten and Australian Federal Police* (1985) 4 A.A.R. 220 at 225; 9 A.L.N. N65. But the reviewing Tribunal can make a decision with respect to documents that have come into existence after the date of the request for access in certain circumstances: *Murtagh v Federal Commissioner of Taxation* (1984) 54 A.L.R. 313.

83 "Agency" is defined to mean principally a Department of State of the Commonwealth and a prescribed authority (itself defined to mean a body corporate or unincorporated established by statute for a public purpose, a statutory office-holder and other bodies declared to be agencies): Freedom of Information Act 1982, s.4(1). "Document of an agency" is itself defined to mean a document in the possession of the agency, whether created in the agency or received in the agency: Freedom of Information Act 1982, s.4(1) and see: *Loughnan (Principal Registrar, Family Court of Australia) v Altman* (1992) 111 A.L.R. 445; *Re Sullivan and Department of Industry, Science and Technology* (1996) 23 A.A.R. 59 (in relation to custody of a document); *Beesley v Australian Federal Police* [2001] F.C.A. 836 (importing notions of constructive possession). Personal documents can become documents of an agency: *Re Barkhordar and Australian Capital Territory Schools Authority* (1987) 12 A.L.D. 332.

84 Defined to mean a document that is in the possession of a Minister in his capacity as a Minister, being a document that relates to the affairs of an agency or of a Department of State: Freedom of Information Act 1982, s.4(1). The effect of the definition is to exclude from the Act those documents which the Minister holds in a political, party or personal capacity. A document held by a Member of Parliament in his representative capacity does not become an official document of a Minister because the Member is, incidentally, a Minister. In relation to the Victorian equivalent, see *Birrell v Department of Premier and Cabinet* [1988] V.R. 73. The definition expressly excludes library material maintained for reference purposes and Cabinet notebooks.

85 Freedom of Information Act 1982, s.4(1).

86 As to which, see para.2–015 below.

87 Freedom of Information Act 1982, s.7. The bodies listed in Sch.2 to the Act are exempted from the operation of the Act. Documents emanating from security bodies, being the bodies listed in

(3) An official document of a Minister that contains some matter that does not relate to the affairs of an agency.

The right of access does not extend to documents that are publicly available independently of the Act[88] or to certain library, archive or museum collections.[89] An applicant is not required to demonstrate a need to know in order to exercise the general right of access.[90] The Act provides for publication schemes[91] and requires agencies to advise and assist those seeking to use its provisions.[92]

The request

2–012 A request must be in writing and must be sufficiently specific that the agency can identify the documents answering its terms.[93] If the request is made to the wrong agency, the recipient agency must direct the applicant to the correct agency.[94] Where an agency receives a request but does not hold the documents sought but either knows that another agency does or that the subject matter of the request is more closely connected with another agency, then the former agency may transfer the request to the latter agency.[95]

The response

2–013 The agency can refuse a request if dealing with it would involve an unreasonable diversion of the agency's resources.[96] The request must be answered within 30 days, but there is power to extend that by a further 30 days.[97] Provided that it is reasonably practicable, access must be given in the form sought by the appli-

s.7(2A), render the agency holding the documents exempt from the Act so far as those documents are concerned: Freedom of Information Act 1982, s.7(2A).

88 Freedom of Information Act 1982, s.12(1).

89 *ibid.*, s.13. The right of access to information officially held in the archives collection is dealt with under the Archives Act 1983.

90 *ibid.*, s.11(2). The Act can thus be used to achieve the same results as a subpoena duces tecum or discovery: *Johnson Tiles Pty Ltd v Esso Australia Ltd* (2000) 98 F.C.R. 311.

91 *ibid.*, ss.8 and 9.

92 *ibid.*, s.15(3)–(4).

93 *ibid.*, s.15(2). The Tribunal has been reluctant to find that anything purporting to be a request is not a request: *Re Russell Island Development Association Inc and Department of Primary Industries and Energy* (1994) 33 A.L.D. 683 at 692; *Re Redfern and University of Canberra* (1995) 38 A.L.D. 457; *Re Collie and Deputy Commissioner of Taxation* (1997) 45 A.L.D. 556 at 561.

94 *ibid.*, s.15(4).

95 *ibid.*, s.16(1). The Administrative Appeals Tribunal does not have a general power to look behind a decision to transfer a request: *Re Reith and Minister of State for Aboriginal Affairs* (1988) 14 A.L.D. 430.

96 *ibid.*, s.24. In relation to the use of multiple requests to evade this provision, see: *Secretary, Department of Treasury and Finance v Kelly* [2001] V.S.C.A. 246.

97 *ibid.*, s.15(5)–(6).

cant.[98] The agency may charge fees for dealing with the request, which must be paid in order to give rise to the obligation to disclose.[99] In the event of the agency refusing to disclose, whether in whole or in part, it must give reasons for the refusal.[1] In certain cases, the Act permits an agency neither to confirm nor deny the existence of a document.[2] The Act specifically provides for discretionary disclosure[3] and, in relation to certain exemptions, for third parties to be invited to make representations before a decision is made to release documents.[4]

Exemptions generally

Once a valid request has been made and appropriate charges are paid, a document that is subject to the Act must be disclosed: the only legal reason for not complying with this obligation is that the document is exempt.[5] Although the onus of proving that a document is exempt lies with the agency[6] and despite the existence of a purpose clause expressly promoting the disclosure of information,[7] the courts have declined to interpret the exemptions by or subject to any 2–014

98 Freedom of Information Act 1982, s.20.

99 *ibid.*, ss.18(1)(b) and 29. The charges regime is set out in the Freedom of Information (Fees and Charges) Regulations 1982. Charges may be remitted, but there is no right of review of a decision not to remit charges: *Re Waterford and Attorney-General's Department* (1985) 4 A.A.R. 159.

1 *ibid.*, s.26. Global responses can be given: *Day v Collector of Customs* (1995) 130 A.L.R. 106.

2 *ibid.*, s.25. The Act uses the device of a notional document containing information as to the existence of documents answering the terms of the request. If that notional document would itself be an exempt document under s.33 (national security, defence and international relations), s.33A (Commonwealth/State relations) or s.37 (law enforcement), then the agency is not required to confirm or deny the existence of the actual documents. The Tribunal and Courts have not readily accepted agency claims based on this section: *Department of Community Services v Jephcott* (1987) 15 F.C.R. 122.

3 *ibid.*, ss.14 and 18(2). This does not enable the Administrative Appeals Tribunal to grant discretionary disclosure: *Re Waterford and Department of Health* (1983) 5 A.L.N. N139; *Re Waterford and Department of Treasury* (1983) 5 A.L.D. 193. It has been held that a discretionary disclosure cannot give rise to an estoppel in relation to the subsequent invocation of an exemption in relation to like documents: *Re Lordsvale Finance Ltd and Department of Treasury* (1985) 3 A.A.R. 301.

4 *ibid.*, ss.26A (documents containing information that originated from a State), 27 (documents containing business information) and 27A (documents containing personal information). These provisions enable the third party to rely upon an exemption that is not sought to be engaged by the agency: *Re Parisi and Australian Federal Police* (1987) 14 A.L.D. 11 at 15. However, the process need not be gone through if the agency is proposing to refuse access: *Motor Trades Association of Australia v Trade Practices Commission* (1993) A.T.P.R. 41–201 at 40–821. The procedure was considered in *Mitsubishi Motors Australia Ltd v Department of Transport* (1986) 12 F.C.R. 156; 68 A.L.R. 626, where it was held that the reviewing Tribunal could, at the request of a third party, determine that a document treated by the agency as not exempt was exempt under s.43. A more detailed comparative treatment of third party rights of consultation and of "reverse FOI" is given at para.11–043 below.

5 *ibid.*, s.18.

6 *ibid.*, s.61(1).

7 *ibid.*, s.3.

special, restrictive presumptions.[8] In general terms, exemptions in Part IV of the Freedom of Information Act 1982 are of two basic kinds:

(1) Exemptions which protect a document of a particular class or kind without a need to refer to the effects of disclosure; and
(2) Exemptions which depend on demonstrating a certain likelihood that a particular harm would result from disclosure of document.

The measure of likelihood employed for the harm-based exemptions is that disclosure "would, or could reasonably be expected," to cause the identified harm.[9] The level or type of harm required in order to engage the harm-based exemptions varies: "caus[ing] damage"; having "a substantial adverse effect"; "caus[ing] prejudice"; being "unreasonable"; and being "contrary to the public interest." Although the public interest is a necessary element in some of the exemptions,[10] there is no general public interest override. In relation to certain exemptions, a conclusive certificate may be issued where the relevant Minister is satisfied that a document should not be disclosed.[11] The Act provides for severance of exempt material from a document that generally answers the terms of a request.[12] In certain circumstances, third parties are given rights to be informed that a request for access to documents has been made and to make

[8] *News Corp Ltd v National Companies and Securities Commission* (1984) 1 F.C.R. 64; 52 A.L.R. 27; *Arnold v Queensland* (1987) 73 A.L.R. 607; *Searle Australia Pty Ltd v Public Interest Advocacy Centre* (1992) 36 F.C.R. 111; 108 A.L.R. 163. In relation to the Victorian legislation, a contrary view was taken by the High Court: *Public Service Board v Wright* (1986) 160 C.L.R. 145 at 153–154.

[9] Employed in Freedom of Information Act 1982, ss.33(1), 33A(1), 37(1), 37(2), 40(1), 43(1) and 44(1). The Tribunal and Courts have interpreted this as being something more than fanciful but which need not be more likely than not: *News Corp Ltd v National Companies and Securities Commission* (1984) 57 A.L.R. 550; *Attorney-General's Department v Cockroft* (1986) 10 F.C.R. 180 at 190; 64 A.L.R. 97; *Arnold (on behalf of Australians for Animals) v Australian National Parks and Wildlife Service* (1987) 73 A.L.R. 607; *Re Environment Centre NT and Department of the Environment, Sport & Territories* (1994) 35 A.L.D. 765 at 778. The Tribunal and Court have generally been prepared to accept at face-value agency claims of likely harm: *Arnold (on behalf of Australians for Animals) v Australian National Parks and Wildlife Service* (1987) 73 A.L.R. 607.

[10] The Act employs the concept of the public interest in different ways: (1) as a requisite element before an exemption is engaged, as in s.36(1); (2) in order to disengage an otherwise applicable exemption, as in ss.33A(5), 39(2) and 40(2); and (3) in a merely recitative form, as in s.44(1).

[11] The provisions are: s.33 (national security, defence and international relations), s.33A (Commonwealth/State relations), s.34 (Cabinet documents), s.35 (Executive Council documents) and s.36 (deliberative process documents). The role of the Administrative Appeals Tribunal in reviewing such a certificate is limited to asking whether or not reasonable grounds exist at the time of the hearing for the claims made in the certificate. This prevents the Tribunal from weighing public interest factors in favour of disclosure against public interest factors favouring non-disclosure. The power to issue a certificate cannot be delegated: *Re Association of Mouth and Foot Painting Artists Pty Ltd and Commissioner of Taxation* (1987) 7 A.A.R. 384.

[12] Freedom of Information Act 1982, s.22(1). An agency is under a duty to consider whether some form of severed document can be provided: *Day v Collector of Customs* (1995) 57 F.C.R. 176 at 180; 130 A.L.R. 106. The severed document must not be misleading: *Re Carver and Department of the Prime Minister and Cabinet* (1987) 6 A.A.R. 317 at 328; 12 A.L.D. 447.

submissions that access ought to be refused.[13] If, despite the representations of the third party, the agency decides that it will release the documents, the third party may apply to the Administrative Appeals Tribunal for a review of the agency's decision.[14]

Specific exemptions

The exemptions may be grouped into 20 heads. The class-based exemptions are: 2–015

(1) Cabinet documents and records.[15]
(2) Executive Council documents.[16]
(3) Documents and information the disclosure of which is proscribed by other statutes.[17]

---

[13] Thus, where a request is received by an agency for documents that contain information concerning a person's or organisation's commercial affairs, and it appears that the person or organisation might wish to contest the disclosure of the documents, then that person or organisation must be given notice of the request: Freedom of Information Act 1982, s.27. Similar third party provision is made in relation to documents containing personal information relating to a third party (Freedom of Information Act 1982, s.27A) and in relation to documents containing information that originated from a State (Freedom of Information Act 1982, s.26A).

[14] Freedom of Information Act 1982, ss.58F, 59, 59A. The third party is limited to arguing its case only on the particular exemption applicable to it alone: it may not go further and introduce new arguments under other sections to justify non disclosure: *Re Mitsubishi Australia Ltd and Department of Transport* (1986) 9 A.L.D. 281; *cf. Searle Australia Pty Ltd v Public Interest Advocacy Centre* (1992) 36 F.C.R. 111; 108 A.L.R. 163. Where the decision of the agency is to exempt documents under these sections, and the applicant appeals to the Administrative Appeals Tribunal against this decision, the person or organisation affected is merely notified of the application. A more detailed comparative treatment of third party rights of consultation and of "reverse FOI" is given at para.11–043 below.

[15] *ibid.*, s.34. Purely factual material is generally exempted. The exemption applies to documents prepared for submission to Cabinet, even if not actually submitted to Cabinet: *Re Rae and Department of Prime Minister and Cabinet* (1986) 12 A.L.D. 589; *Re Porter and Department of Community Services and Health* (1988) 14 A.L.D. 403; *Re Reith and Minister for Aboriginal Affairs* (1988) 16 A.L.D. 709. In relation to analogous legislation: *Department of Premier and Cabinet v Birrell (No.2)* [1990] V.R. 51. A conclusive certificate may be issued for this exemption and also for the existence of a document answering the terms of the request. Once issued, the Courts and Tribunal have shown themselves reluctant to find that there were no reasonable grounds for the issue of the certificate, with "reasonableness" being held to be directed to whether the document met the description in the section, rather than to the decision to invoke the exemption: *Department of Industrial Relations v Burchill* (1991) 105 A.L.R. 327. The certificate itself must have sufficient certainty: *Department of Industrial Relations v Forrest* (1990) 21 F.C.R. 93; 91 A.L.R. 417.

[16] *ibid.*, s.35. Purely factual material is generally exempted. A conclusive certificate may be issued for this exemption and also for the existence of a document answering the terms of the request.

[17] *ibid.*, s.38. This provision gave rise to considerable litigation prior to its amendment in 1991. The principles were summarised in *Harrigan v Department of Health* (1986) 72 A.L.R. 293 at 294–295. See also: *Kavvadias v Commonwealth Ombudsman* (1984) 52 A.L.R. 728; *News Corp Ltd v National Companies and Securities Commission* (1984) 57 A.L.R. 550; *Federal Commissioner of Taxation v Swiss Aluminium Australia Ltd* (1986) 66 A.L.R. 159; *Harrigan v Department of Health* (1986) 72 A.L.R. 293. In relation to analogous legislation: *Secretary to the Department of Premier and Cabinet v Hulls* [1999] 3 V.R. 331.

(4) Documents subject to legal professional privilege.[18]
(5) Trade secrets.[19]
(6) Documents the disclosure of which would be a contempt of Court or of the Commonwealth or a State Parliament.[20]
(7) Certain documents arising out of companies and securities legislation.[21]
(8) Electoral rolls.[22]

The harm-based exemptions apply to a document whose disclosure would have one or more of the following effects:

(9) It would, or could be reasonably be expected to, cause damage to the national security, defence or international relations of Australia.[23]

---

18 Freedom of Information Act 1982, s.42. It has been held that for the purposes of the Act, legal professional privilege attaches to confidential professional communications between a Government agency and its salaried legal officers provided that it is undertaken for the sole purpose of seeking or giving legal advice or in connection with anticipated or pending litigation: *Waterford v Commonwealth* (1987) 163 C.L.R. 54; see also *Austin v Deputy Secretary, Attorney-General's Department* (1986) 67 A.L.R. 585; *Secretary, Department of Health v Proudfoot* (1993) 114 F.L.R. 384; *Commonwealth of Australia v Dutton* (2000) 102 F.C.R. 168. In relation to analogous legislation: *Director of Public Prosecutions v Smith* [1991] V.R. 63 (documents relating to the sufficiency of evidence). The sole purpose test has since been reduced to a dominant purpose test: *Esso Australia Resources Ltd v Federal Commissioner of Taxation* (1999) 168 A.L.R. 123. It has been held that, for the purposes of the Act, privilege can be waived: *Bennett v Chief Executive Officer of the Australian Customs Service* [2003] F.C.A. 53.

19 *ibid.*, s.43(1)(a). This whole section is designed to protect the interests of third parties: *Harris v Australian Broadcasting Corp* (1983) 78 F.L.R. 236; 50 A.L.R. 551. As to the meaning of this provision, see: *Searle Australia Pty Ltd v Public Interest Advocacy Centre* (1992) 108 A.L.R. 163; 36 F.C.R. 111; *Secretary, Department of Workplace Relations & Small Business v The Staff Development & Training Centre Pty Ltd* [2001] F.C.A. 382, upheld at [2001] F.C.A. 1375.

20 Freedom of Information Act 1982, s.46.

21 *ibid.*, s.47.

22 *ibid.*, s.47A.

23 *ibid.*, s.33. The head of exemption also exempts a document the disclosure of which would divulge any information communicated in confidence by or on behalf of a foreign government, an authority of a foreign government or an international organization to the Australian Government. The Minister may issue a conclusive certificate in relation to this head of exemption and also in relation to confirming or denying the existence of a document answering the terms of the request. The section does not involve a consideration of whether disclosure would be contrary to the public interest: *Commonwealth of Australia v Hittich* (1994) 53 F.C.R. 152 at 154. The section is an expression of the content of the public interest: *Re Mann and Australian Taxation Office* (1985) 3 A.A.R. 261; *Re O'Donovan and Attorney-General's Department* (1985) 4 A.A.R. 151; 8 A.L.D. 528; *Re Edelsten and Australian Federal Police* (1985) 4 A.A.R. 220. The Courts and Tribunal have been generally ready to accept agency assertions that this sort of harm would be caused: *Re Maher and Attorney-General's Department* (1985) 3 A.A.R. 396; *Re Stolpe and Department of Foreign Affairs* (1985) 9 A.L.D. 104; *Re Fewster and Department of Prime Minister and Cabinet (No.2)* (1987) 13 A.L.D. 139; *Re Wang and Department of Employment, Education and Training* (1988) 15 A.L.D. 497; *Re Bayliss and Department of Health and Family Services* (1997) 48 A.L.D. 443; *Gersten v Minister for Immigration & Multicultural Affairs* [2000] F.C.A. 1221; [2001] F.C.A. 159. In this context, the Courts and Tribunal have been prepared to accept the "mosaic theory" (see paras 15–016 to 15–017): *Re McKnight and Australian Archives* (1992) 28 A.L.D. 95. A document already in the public domain can still enjoy exemption under this section: *Commonwealth of Australia v Hittich* (1994) 53 F.C.R. 152.

(10) It would, or could be reasonably be expected to, cause damage to relations between the Commonwealth and a State.[24]

(11) It records the deliberative process of the federal government[25] and its disclosure would be contrary to the public interest.[26]

(12) It would, or could be reasonably be expected to, cause damage to law enforcement, confidential sources of information relating to law enforcement, fair trials, or methods of criminal investigation.[27]

---

[24] Freedom of Information Act 1982, s.33A. The head of exemption also exempts a document the disclosure of which would divulge information communicated in confidence by or on behalf of the Government of an Australian State to the Federal Government. The role of the public interest is to disengage the exemption that would otherwise be applicable: *Arnold (on behalf of Australians for Animals) v Australian National Parks and Wildlife Service* (1987) 73 A.L.R. 607. The Minister may issue a conclusive certificate in relation to this head of exemption and also in relation to confirming or denying the existence of a document answering the terms of the request. The exemption has been given a broad interpretation: *Re Mickelberg and Australian Federal Police* (1984) 6 A.L.N. N176; *Re Anderson and Department of Special Minister of State* (1984) 7 A.L.N. N155; *Re Angel and Department of Art, Heritage and Environment* (1985) 9 A.L.D. 113; *Arnold (on behalf of Australians for Animals) v Australian National Parks and Wildlife Service* (1987) 73 A.L.R. 607; *Re Guy and Department of Transport* (1987) 12 A.L.D. 358; *Re Birch and Attorney-General's Department* (1994) 33 A.L.D. 675; *Re Environment Centre NT Inc and Department of the Environment, Sport and Territories* (1994) 35 A.L.D. 765.

[25] Freedom of Information Act 1982, s.36. The Courts and Tribunal have given the first paragraph of s.36(1) a broad interpretation, capable of encompassing most documents held by an agency recording any form of consideration of a decision: *Harris v Australian Broadcasting Corp* (1983) 78 F.L.R. 236; 50 A.L.R. 551 (interim reports should not be released because they could mislead); *Re James and Australian National University* (1984) 2 A.A.R. 327; *Murtagh v Federal Commissioner of Taxation* (1984) 54 A.L.R. 313 (documents showing process of making an assessment of taxation); *Re Waterford and Department of the Treasury (No.2)* (1984) 1 A.A.R. 1; 5 A.L.D. 588; *Re Toohey and Department of the Prime Minister and Cabinet* (1985) 9 A.L.N. 94; *Re Howard and the Treasurer (Cth)* (1985) 3 A.A.R. 169 at 172–175; *Re Chapman and Minister for Aboriginal and Torres Strait Islander Affairs* (1996) 23 A.A.R. 142; 43 A.L.D. 139; *Re Subramanian and Refugee Review Tribunal* (1997) 44 A.L.D. 435; *Re The Staff Development and Training Centre and Secretary, Department of Employment, Workplace Relations and Small Business* (2000) 30 A.A.R. 330 at 354. In relation to analogous legislation: *Director of Public Prosecutions v Smith* [1991] V.R. 63 (documents considering whether to prosecute). The Minister may issue a conclusive certificate. Purely factual material, reports *etc.* are excluded from the exemption. As to its meaning: *Harris v Australian Broadcasting Corp (No.2)* (1984) 51 A.L.R. 581.

[26] In order for the exemption to engage, the agency must demonstrate that disclosure would be contrary to the public interest. As to the matters which the Courts and Tribunal have taken into account under the rubric of the "public interest," see: *Murtagh v Federal Commissioner of Taxation* (1984) 54 A.L.R. 313; *Burns v Australian National University (No.1)* (1984) 1 A.A.R. 456 at 458; *Re Howard and Treasurer, Commonwealth* (1985) 3 A.A.R. 169; *Re Swiss Aluminium and Department of Trade* (1985) 9 A.L.D. 243; *Ryder v Booth* [1985] V.R. 869 (inability to get further similar information); *Re Reith and the Attorney-General's Department* (1987) 11 A.L.D. 345; *Re Fewster and Department of Prime Minister and Cabinet (No.2)* (1987) 13 A.L.D. 139; *Re Reith and Minister of State for Aboriginal Affairs* (1988) 16 A.L.D. 709; *Re Kamminga and Australian National University* (1992) 15 A.A.R. 297; *Re Chapman and Minister for Aboriginal and Torres Strait Islander Affairs* (1996) 23 A.A.R. 142 at 155–159; *Re Bartle and Secretary, Department of Employment, Education, Training and Youth Affairs* (1998) 28 A.A.R. 140. If this exemption is relied upon, the ground of public interest must be specified.

[27] Freedom of Information Act 1982, s.37. This has been given a broad interpretation, covering: confidential sources of information (*McKenzie v Secretary to the Department of Social Security* (1986) 65 A.L.R. 645); even if the information provided by the source is not in itself confidential (*Re Dale and Australian Federal Police* (1997) 47 A.L.D. 417); policy documents setting out in

(13) It would have a substantial adverse effect on the financial interests of the Commonwealth of Australia or an agency.[28]

(14) It would, or could be reasonably be expected to, prejudice the effectiveness of audits or tests or to have a substantial adverse effect upon the running of an agency.[29]

(15) It would involve the unreasonable disclosure of personal information other than that relating to the applicant.[30]

(16) It could reasonably be expected to destroy or diminish the commercial value of any information.[31]

(17) It is information relating to a business that could reasonably be expected to have an unreasonably adverse effect upon that business or

what circumstances an agency would prosecute for a breach of statute (*Re Murphy and Australian Electoral Commission* (1994) 33 A.L.D. 718); investigation manuals, even where large parts have been previously disclosed (*Re Arnold Bloch Leibler & Co and Australian Taxation Office (No.2)* (1985) 4 A.A.R. 178; 9 A.L.D. 7); any documents relating to public safety in a broad sense of the phrase (*Re Parisi and Australian Federal Police* (1987) 14 A.L.D. 11); documents being used in an investigation (*News Corp Ltd v National Companies and Securities Commission* (1984) 57 A.L.R. 550). But work accident investigation reports have been held not exempt under analogous Victorian legislation: *Accident Compensation Commission v Croom* [1991] 2 V.R. 322; nor is a police brief necessarily exempt: *Sobh v Police Force of Victoria* [1994] 1 V.R. 41.

[28] Freedom of Information Act 1982, s.39. The exemption does not apply where disclosure of the document would, on balance, be in the public interest.

[29] *ibid.*, s.40. The exemption does not apply where disclosure of the document would, on balance, be in the public interest. The Courts and Tribunal have required a substantial degree of gravity before finding a "substantial adverse effect:" *Harris v Australian Broadcasting Corp* (1983) 78 F.L.R. 236; 50 A.L.R. 551; *Re Dyki and Commissioner of Taxation* (1990) 12 A.A.R. 544; 22 A.L.D. 124 (completed job applications not exempt); *Searle Australia Pty Ltd v Public Interest Advocacy Centre* (1992) 36 F.C.R. 111; 108 A.L.R. 163; *Re Kamminga and Australian National University* (1992) 15 A.A.R. 297; 26 A.L.D. 585; *Re Murphy and Australian Electoral Commission* (1994) 33 A.L.D. 718.

[30] Freedom of Information Act 1982, s.41. Detailed provision is made in relation to personal information the disclosure of which might be detrimental to the well-being of the applicant. It has been held that a company does not have "personal affairs" within the meaning of the Act: *News Corp Ltd v National Companies and Securities Commission* (1984) 1 F.C.R. 64; 52 A.L.R. 277; *The University of Melbourne v Robinson* [1993] 2 V.R. 177. In New South Wales it has been held that the release of the name of a person is not necessarily information concerning the personal affairs of a person: *Commissioner of Police v District Court of NSW* (1993) 31 N.S.W.L.R. 606. In Victoria, detailed references to the business affairs of victims of crime not exempt where the victims had earlier disclosed it to the public: *Director of Public Prosecutions v Smith* [1991] V.R. 63. The words "relating to" have been given a very wide interpretation: *Colakovski v Australian Telecommunications Corp* (1991) 29 F.C.R. 429; 100 A.L.R. 111. "Personal affairs" itself has also been given a wide meaning: *Re Williams and Registrar, Federal Court of Australia* (1985) 8 A.L.D. 219; 3 A.A.R. 529; *Young v Wicks* (1986) 13 F.C.R. 85; *Department of Social Security v Dyrenfurth* (1988) 80 A.L.R. 533; *Bleicher v Australian Capital Territory Health Authority* (1990) 12 A.A.R. 246; *Colakovski v Australian Telecommunications Corp* (1991) 29 F.C.R. 429; 100 A.L.R. 111.

[31] *ibid.*, s.43(1)(b). This whole section is designed to protect the interests of third parties: *Harris v Australian Broadcasting Corp* (1983) 78 F.L.R. 236; 50 A.L.R. 551. As to the meaning of information having a commercial value, see: *Gill v Department of Industry Technology and Resources* [1987] V.R. 681; *Secretary, Dept of Workplace Relations & Small Business v The Staff Development & Training Centre Pty Ltd* [2001] F.C.A. 382, upheld at [2001] F.C.A. 1375.

to prejudice the future supply of information to the Commonwealth of Australia.[32]

(18) It would be likely to result in an unreasonable exposure to disadvantage to specified agencies carrying out research that is incomplete.[33]

(19) It would, or could be reasonably be expected to, have a substantial adverse effect on the ability of the Commonwealth to manage the economy.[34]

(20) It would represent a breach of confidence other than that of the Commonwealth.[35]

Appeals and enforcement

Where an agency refuses access to documents, the first right of appeal is one of internal review by the principal officer of the agency.[36] Generally, the applicant is required to lodge a request for an internal review within 30 days of receiving notification of the original decision. The principal officer must review the decision within 30 days. If the applicant either does not receive a response within that time or receives an unfavourable decision, he is entitled to apply to the Administrative Appeals Tribunal for a further review of the decision.[37] An application for review must generally be made within 60 days after the notice of the decision refusing access to a document was given to the applicant. The power given to the Administrative Appeals Tribunal is to review any decision that has been made by an agency or minister with respect to a request for access to a document and to decide the matter on the same basis as the agency or minister could have decided it.[38] Where a conclusive certificate has been issued, 2–016

[32] Freedom of Information Act 1982, s.43(1)(c). This whole section is designed to protect the interests of third parties: *Harris v Australian Broadcasting Corp* (1983) 78 F.L.R. 236; 50 A.L.R. 551. See also: *Accident Compensation Commission v Croom* [1991] 2 V.R. 322.

[33] *ibid.*, s.43A.

[34] *ibid.*, s.44.

[35] *ibid.*, s.45. This had been interpreted to be wide enough to succeed where an action for common law breach of confidence would not succeed: *Baueris v Commonwealth of Australia* (1987) 75 A.L.R. 327; *Corrs Pavey Whiting & Byrne v Collector of Customs* (1987) 14 F.C.R. 434. Section 45 was subsequently amended to remove this possibility.

[36] *ibid.*, s.54(1).

[37] *ibid.*, ss.55(3) and 56(1).

[38] The Tribunal is not restricted to the grounds of exemption relied upon by the agency: *Searle Australia Pty Ltd v Public Interest Advocacy Centre* (1992) 108 A.L.R. 163; *Victorian Casino and Gambling Authority v Hulls* [1998] 4 V.R. 718 (relating to the analogous Victorian scheme). The Appellant's representative may be given access to documents upon appropriate undertakings: *Day v Collector of Customs* (1995) 130 A.L.R. 106; cf *News Corporation Ltd v National Companies and Securities Commission* (1984) 57 A.L.R. 550; *Department of Industrial Relations v Forrest* (1990) 21 F.C.R. 93; 91 A.L.R. 417 (a certificate case).

the role of the Tribunal is restricted to a consideration of its reasonableness.[39] An appeal on a question of law lies from the Administrative Appeals Tribunal to the Federal Court.

4. NEW ZEALAND

Introduction

2–017 In New Zealand, the power to elicit official information originated in a 1962 statute establishing an ombudsman.[40] In May 1978 a Committee on Official Information was established to consider the extent to which official information could be made more readily available to the public. Following the Committee's reports,[41] the Official Information Act 1982 came into force on July 1, 1983. The State-owned Enterprises Act 1986 brought state-owned enterprises within the Official Information Act 1982. In 1987, the Act was amended by replacing the original ministerial veto of Ombudsman's recommendations with a collective veto by Order in Council; by expanding the protection for information about competitive commercial activities; by imposing time limits; and by extending coverage to additional organisations. In that same year, a separate Act was passed providing analogous rights of access to information held by local authorities.[42] In 1993, the right of access to information where it related to a non-corporate applicant was transferred to the Privacy Act 1993. Thus, rights of access to official information are now split between three statutes:

(1) In relation to information relating to the individual requesting it, under the Privacy Act 1993;

(2) In relation to other information held by local authorities, under the Local Government Official Information and Meetings Act 1987; and

[39] *Department of Industrial Relations v Burchill* (1991) 105 A.L.R. 327; *Australian Doctors' Fund Ltd v Commonwealth of Australia* (1994) 126 A.L.R. 273. The express review provisions in relation to a conclusive certificate do not oust the power of the Court to consider the lawfulness of the decision to issue a certificate on ordinary judicial review principles: *Shergold v Tanner* (2002) 188 A.L.R. 302.

[40] The Parliamentary Commissioner (Ombudsman) Act 1962. That statute empowered the Ombudsman to obtain information from governmental agencies and to disclose in any report such matters as in the Ombudsman's opinion needed to be disclosed in order to establish grounds for any conclusions and recommendations made in the report.

[41] Committee on Official Information, *Towards Open Government: General Report* (Vol.1, 1980); *Towards Open Government: Supplementary Report* (Vol.2, 1981). The Committee is commonly referred to as the Danks Committee and the reports as the Danks Report. The Supplementary Report contained a draft Bill that was to become the Official Information Act 1982.

[42] The Local Government Official Information and Meetings Act 1987.

(3) In relation to all other information, under the Official Information Act 1982.[43]

Scope of the right

Section 12(1) of the Official Information Act 1982 enables citizens, residents and persons in New Zealand, as well as companies incorporated in New Zealand, to request a "department or Minister of the Crown" to make available to the applicant any specified "official information."[44] The term "official information" is defined to mean "information"[45] that is "held"[46] by a department,[47] Minister of the Crown or organisation.[48] The right of access to personal information[49] (whether of an individual or a company) is provided separately from the general right to information.[50] The access statutes require departments etc. 2–018

[43] There is a limited inter-relationship between the statutes, so that where the applicant seeks information under the Official Information Act 1982 or under the Local Government Official Information and Meetings Act 1987 for information relating to a third party, the provisions of the Privacy Act 1993 are relevant: Official Information Act 1982, s.9(2)(a); Local Government Official Information and Meetings Act 1987, s.7(2)(a). A more detailed comparative treatment of third party rights of consultation and of "reverse FOI" is given at para.11–043 below.

[44] In relation to information held by a local authority, the provision is the Local Government Official Information and Meetings Act 1987, s.10(1).

[45] There is no definition of "information." As to the meaning given by the courts to "information," see: *Commissioner of Police v Ombudsman* [1985] 1 N.Z.L.R. 578 at 586; [1988] 1 N.Z.L.R. 385 at 402, CA ("information" is "that which informs, instructs, tells or makes aware"); *Ross v Taranaki City Council* [1990] D.C.R. 11 (information under the Local Government Official Information and Meetings Act 1987 must be tangible or retrievable); *Aldous v Auckland City Council* [1990] D.C.R. 385; *R. v Harvey* [1991] 1 N.Z.L.R. 242 at 246; *Herewini v Ministry of Transport* [1992] 3 N.Z.L.R. 482 at 498; *Leach v Ministry of Transport* [1993] 1 N.Z.L.R. 106 at 108. Excluded from "official information" is certain information held by universities and information contained in library or museum material made or acquired and preserved solely for reference or exhibition purposes and certain other information: see Official Information Act 1982, s.2(2).

[46] The Act does not define when information is "held" by a department. See *R. v Harvey* [1991] 1 N.Z.L.R. 242 at 246.

[47] Departments are those listed in Pt I of the First Schedule to the Ombudsmen Act 1975.

[48] Official Information Act 1982, s.4; Local Government Official Information and Meetings Act 1987, s.2(1). "Organisations" are those named in Part II of the First Schedule to the Ombudsmen Act 1975 and those named in the First Schedule to the Official Information Act 1982. Certain organisations are excluded: see Official Information Act 1982, s.2(6).

[49] That is, information that is about the person requesting the information. The distinction between "personal" and "non-personal" information has been described as "both artificial and arbitrary": *Cornelius v Commissioner for Police* [1998] 3 N.Z.L.R. 373 at 379; *cf. Police v Keogh* [2000] 1 N.Z.L.R. 736 at 742.

[50] Requests for personal information by individuals about themselves are governed by the Privacy Act 1993. That Act provides that where an agency holds personal information in such a way that it can be readily retrieved, the individual about whom the information relates has a legal right, enforceable in a Court of law, to obtain confirmation from the agency of whether or not it holds such information and to have access to that information: s.6, principle 6(1) and s.11(i). This right applies to any individual who is a New Zealand citizen, or a permanent resident of New Zealand, or a person who is in New Zealand: Privacy Act 1993, ss.33 and 34. Part IV of the Official Information Act 1982 (ss.24–27) is devoted to access to personal information by a body corporate. Section 24(1) bestows the right upon a body corporate to be given access to any personal information that is about that body corporate, subject to the exemptions in Pt I of the

to give reasonable assistance to anyone using the Act.[51] The two main Acts also provide for publication schemes.[52]

The request

2–019 A request may be made orally or in writing, but it must have due particularity.[53] The department may refuse to answer a request that is frivolous or vexatious;[54] where the information requested is trivial;[55] where making the information available would involve substantial collation or research;[56] or where the information is or will shortly be publicly available.[57] Where a department receives a request but either does not hold the information sought and believes that another department does, or if it considers that the information requested is more closely connected with another department, then the former department may transfer the request to the latter department.[58]

The response

2–020 Within 20 working days of receiving a request, the department must inform the applicant whether access to the requested information is to be given and of the reasons for the decision.[59] The 20 working day period may be extended for

Act. In relation to local authorities, the right of access by a company to information relating to itself is bestowed by the Local Government and Official Information Act 1987, s.23.

[51] Official Information Act 1982, ss.13 and 24(3); Local Government Official Information and Meetings Act 1987, ss.11 and 23(2); Privacy Act 1993, s.38.

[52] Official Information Act 1982, s.20; Local Government Official Information and Meetings Act 1987, s.19. This requires the publication and updating of a document that describes the structure, functions, and responsibilities of all government departments and organisations subject to each of the Acts, as well as a description of the categories of documents held by each body and certain other details. Every person has a right of access to these latest details: Official Information Act 1982, s.21; Local Government Official Information and Meetings Act 1987, s.20.

[53] Official Information Act 1982, s.12(2); Local Government Official Information and Meetings Act 1987, s.10(2). The request may be made by an agent: Official Information Act 1982, s.25(c); Local Government Official Information and Meetings Act 1987, s.24(c); Privacy Act 1993, s.45(c).

[54] Official Information Act 1982, s.18(h); Local Government Official Information and Meetings Act 1987, s.17(h); Privacy Act 1993, s.29(1)(j).

[55] Official Information Act 1982, s.18(h); Local Government Official Information and Meetings Act 1987, s.17(h); Privacy Act 1993, s.29(1)(j).

[56] Official Information Act 1982, s.18(f); Local Government Official Information and Meetings Act 1987, s.17(f); ; Privacy Act 1993, s.29(2)(a).

[57] Official Information Act 1982, s.18(d); Local Government Official Information and Meetings Act 1987, s.17(d).

[58] Official Information Act 1982, s.14; Local Government Official Information and Meetings Act 1987, s.12(b)(I); Privacy Act 1993, s.39.

[59] Official Information Act 1982, ss.15(1) and 24(3); Local Government Official Information and Meetings Act 1987, ss.13 and 23(2); Privacy Act 1993, s.40(1)(a).

a reasonable period of time where the request is for a large quantity of information, requires searching through a large quantity of information, or requires consultations that cannot be completed within the original time limit.[60] If the requested information is not provided within the 20 working days or the extended period, the request is deemed to have been refused.[61] If the decision is to give access, that may take any of a number of forms: giving the applicant an opportunity to examine the document containing the information; providing a copy of it; providing information about a document's contents, etc.[62] If the decision is to refuse access, the department, etc., must give reasons for the refusal and, if requested, the grounds for that refusal.[63] A department, etc., may only refuse to disclose information answering the terms of a proper request if it falls within one of the grounds of exemption.[64] In refusing a request, the department is not required to confirm or deny whether any information answering the terms of the request actually exists if to do so would be likely to damage security, defence, international relations, represent a breach of confidence, endanger individuals, reveal a trade secret or damage the economy.[65] A charge may be imposed for the disclosure of information, depending upon: the statute under which access is sought; whether the information sought is personal information; and whether the body to which the request is made is a public sector agency or a private sector agency.[66] Specific provision for severance is made where the information is contained in a document.[67] Although there is no express power enabling a conditional release of information, there would appear to be an implicit power to do so, as the ombudsman is given power to investigate such conditions.[68] There is nothing

[60] Official Information Act 1982, ss.15A(1)(a) and 24(3); Local Government Official Information and Meetings Act 1987, ss.14(1)(a) and 23(2); Privacy Act 1993, s.41(1)(a).

[61] Official Information Act 1982, s.28(4).

[62] Official Information Act 1982, ss.16(1)(a)–(f) and 24(3); Local Government Official Information and Meetings Act 1987, ss.15(1)(a)–(f) and 23(2); Privacy Act 1993, s.42(2). The form of access must be that preferred by the applicant unless to do so would impair efficient administration and so forth: Official Information Act 1982, s.16(2); Local Government Official Information and Meetings Act 1987, s.15(2); Privacy Act 1993, s. 42(2).

[63] Official Information Act 1982, s.19; Local Government Official Information and Meetings Act 1987, s.18.

[64] Official Information Act 1982, ss.18 and 27(1); Local Government Official Information and Meetings Act 1987, ss.17 and 26; Privacy Act 1993, s.30.

[65] Official Information Act 1982, s.10; Local Government Official Information and Meetings Act 1987, s.8; Privacy Act 1993, s.32.

[66] Official Information Act 1982, ss.15(2) and 24(3); Local Government Official Information and Meetings Act 1987, s.13(1A); Privacy Act 1993, ss.35, 36 and 59.

[67] Official Information Act 1982, ss.17(1) and 24(3); Local Government Official Information and Meetings Act 1987, ss.16(1) and 23(2); Privacy Act 1993, s.43(1).

[68] Official Information Act 1982, s.28(1)(c); Local Government Official Information and Meetings Act 1987, s.27(1)(c); Privacy Act 1993, s.66(2)(a)(iii), where the power is vested in the Privacy Commissioner. Examples of conditions imposed are: (1) where information was released on the condition that the information could only be published together with a statement or explanation from the holder of the information; (2) where information was to be used for Court proceedings on the basis of undertakings by the parties that the information would not be made available to the media.

proscribing the discretionary release of information that is exempt under the Act.[69]

Exemptions generally

2–021 Exemptions under the New Zealand legislation divide into two broad classes: those that are engaged upon their terms being satisfied;[70] and those that will be disengaged if, in the circumstances, the withholding of particular information is outweighed by other considerations which render it desirable in the public interest to make that information available.[71] The exemptions may also be categorised into prejudice-based exemptions, which require that disclosure "be likely to prejudice" an identified interest,[72] and pure class-based exemptions, which do not require that prejudice flow from disclosure of the requested information. The applicability of exemptions varies according to whether the information sought is personal information and, if so, whether the person is a corporate person. In considering exemptions, the overarching principle is that information is to be made available unless there is good reason for withholding it.[73] Certificates may be issued by the Prime Minister or the Attorney-General on the grounds that disclosure of the requested information would be likely to prejudice: the defence or security of New Zealand or one of its dependancies; international relations; or the investigation, etc., of offences.[74] The effect of a certificate is that the Ombudsman may not recommend the disclosure of the information to which the certificate relates.

---

[69] Although where its disclosure breaches the privacy principles set out in the Privacy Act 1993 this may give rise to a complaint either under that Act or to the ombudsman. Discretionary disclosure does not attract the protection given by the Official Information Act 1982, s.48.

[70] Official Information Act 1982, ss.18(c)(i) and 52(3); Local Government Official Information and Meetings Act 1987, ss.17(c)(i) and 44(2); Privacy Act 1993, s.7.

[71] Official Information Act 1982, ss.18(c)(ii) and 52(1); Local Government Official Information and Meetings Act 1987, ss.17(c)(ii) and 44(1); Privacy Act 1993, s.29(1)(i).

[72] The High Court has held that the test to be applied in determining whether withholding the information is necessary to protect one of the specified interests is one of "reasonable" necessity, rather than "strict" necessity: *Television New Zealand Ltd v Ombudsman* [1992] 1 N.Z.L.R. 106 at 118. The "would be likely" test has been held not to mean "more likely than not," but that it involves a lesser threshold, namely: "a serious or real and substantial risk to a protected interest, a risk that might well eventuate": *Commissioner of Police v Ombudsman* [1988] 1 N.Z.L.R. 385, CA.

[73] Official Information Act 1982, s.5. The Courts have rejected the notion that there is a general presumption that exemptions are to be narrowly construed: *Commissioner of Police v Ombudsman* [1988] 1 N.Z.L.R. 385, CA.

[74] *ibid.*, s.31.

The absolute exemptions

Information may be withheld without a consideration of the public interest where: 2–022

(1) Disclosure would be likely to prejudice the security or defence of New Zealand or certain external dependencies or the international relations of the New Zealand Government.[75]

(2) Disclosure would be likely to prejudice the entrusting of information to the government of New Zealand on a basis of confidence by the government of any other country or any agency of such a government, or by any international organisation.[76]

(3) Disclosure would be likely to prejudice the maintenance of the law, including the prevention, investigation, and detection of offences, and the right to a fair trial.[77]

(4) Disclosure would be likely to endanger the safety of any person.[78]

(5) Disclosure would be likely to damage seriously the New Zealand economy by disclosing prematurely decisions to change or continue government economic or financial policies relating to: exchange rates or the control of overseas exchange transactions; the regulation of banking or credit; taxation; the stability, control, and adjustment of prices of goods and services, rents, and other costs, and rates of wages, salaries, and other incomes; the borrowing of money by the New Zealand government; and the entering into of overseas trade agreements.[79]

(6) Disclosure would be contrary to the provisions of another enactment.[80]

(7) Disclosure would be a contempt of court or of the House of Representatives.[81]

The qualified exemptions

The remaining exemptions involve a two-stage process. First, a consideration of whether withholding the requested information is necessary in order to protect 2–023

[75] Official Information Act 1982, ss.6(a), 7 and 27(1)(a); Privacy Act 1993, ss.27(1)(a) and 27(2)(a)–(c).

[76] Official Information Act 1982, ss.6(b) and 27(1)(a); Privacy Act 1993, s.27(1)(b).

[77] Official Information Act 1982, ss.6(c) and 27(1)(a); Local Government Official Information and Meetings Act 1987, ss.6(a) and 26(1)(a); Privacy Act 1993, s.27(1)(c).

[78] Official Information Act 1982, ss.6(d) and 27(1)(a); Local Government Official Information and Meetings Act 1987, ss.6(b) and 26(1)(a); Privacy Act 1993, s.27(1)(d).

[79] Official Information Act 1982, ss.6(e) and 27(1)(a).

[80] Official Information Act 1982, ss.18(c)(i), 27(1)(a) and 52(3)(b); Local Government Official Information and Meetings Act 1987, ss.17(c)(i), 26(1)(a) and 44(2)(b); Privacy Act 1993, s.7(2)–(3).

[81] Official Information Act 1982, ss.18(c)(ii), 27(1)(a) and 52(1); Local Government Official Information and Meetings Act 1987, ss.17(c)(ii), 26(1)(a) and 44(1); Privacy Act 1993, s.29(1)(h).

particular interests or to avoid particular prejudice. Secondly, if it is so necessary, to consider whether the withholding of the information is outweighed by other considerations that nevertheless render it desirable in the public interest to make that information available. So far as the first stage is concerned, this will be satisfied where the withholding of the information is necessary:

(1) To protect the privacy of natural persons, including that of deceased natural persons.[82]
(2) To protect information where the making available of that information would disclose a trade secret, or would be likely to unreasonably prejudice the commercial position of the person who supplied or who is the subject of the information.[83]
(3) To protect information which is subject to an obligation of confidence or which any person has been or could be compelled to provide under the authority of any enactment.[84]
(4) To avoid prejudice to measures protecting the health or safety of members of the public.[85]
(5) To avoid prejudice to the substantial economic interests of New Zealand.[86]
(6) To avoid prejudice to measures that prevent or mitigate material loss to members of the public.[87]
(7) To maintain the constitutional conventions for the time being which protect: the confidentiality of communications by or with the Sovereign or her representative; collective and individual ministerial responsibility; the political neutrality of officials; and the confidentiality of advice tendered by ministers of the Crown and officials (these reasons are not applicable in the case of local authorities).[88]
(8) To maintain the effective conduct of public affairs, through the free and frank expression of opinions by or between or to ministers or members of a specified organisation or officers and employees of any department, organisation, or local authority in the course of their duty; or

[82] Official Information Act 1982, ss.9(2)(a) and 27(1)(b); Local Government Official Information and Meetings Act 1987, ss.7(2)(a) and 26(1)(b); Privacy Act 1993, s.29(1)(a).
[83] Official Information Act 1982, ss.9(2)(b)(i) and 27(1)(a); Local Government Official Information and Meetings Act 1987, ss.7(2)(b)(i) and 26(1)(a); Privacy Act 1993, s.28(1)(a)–(b).
[84] Official Information Act 1982, ss.9(2)(b)(ii) and 27(1)(c); Local Government Official Information and Meetings Act 1987, ss.7(2)(b)(ii) and 26(1)(c); Privacy Act 1993, s.29(1)(b)b. The courts have rejected the notion that the contractual provisions requiring confidentiality to be kept necessarily protected the information from being disclosed under the Act: *Wyatt Co (NZ) Ltd v Queenstown-Lakes District Council* [1991] 2 N.Z.L.R. 180.
[85] Official Information Act 1982, s.9(2)(c); Local Government Official Information and Meetings Act 1987, s.7(2)(d); Privacy Act 1993, s.29(1)(c).
[86] Official Information Act 1982, s.9(2)(d).
[87] Official Information Act 1982, s.9(2)(e); Local Government Official Information and Meetings Act 1987, s.7(2)(e).
[88] Official Information Act 1982, s.9(2)(f).

through the protection of such ministers, members, officers, and employees from improper pressure or harassment.[89]

(9) To maintain legal professional privilege.[90]

(10) To enable a minister, department, specified organisation, or local authority holding the information to carry out, without prejudice or disadvantage, commercial activities.[91]

(11) To enable a minister, department, specified organisation, or local authority holding the information to carry on negotiations without prejudice or disadvantage, including commercial or industrial negotiations.[92]

(12) To prevent the disclosure or use of official information for improper gain or improper advantage.[93]

Appeals and enforcement

The first stage of the appeal system lies with the Ombudsman, who, upon a complaint, may investigate and review any decision to refuse access or to refuse to confirm or deny the existence of requested information.[94] The Ombudsman has all the normal powers under the Ombudsmen Act 1975, including compelling the production of information. After investigation, the Ombudsman must make a report with recommendations, setting out whether it is considered that the original decision was wrong or unreasonable.[95] The Department is obliged to observe a recommendation of the Ombudsman unless the Governor-General, by Order in Council, otherwise directs.[96] Where no Order in Council is made, a person dissatisfied with the Ombudsman's recommendation may judicially review it and the original decision. Where an Order in Council is made, an appeal may be made to the High Court on grounds that it was wrong 2–024

[89] Official Information Act 1982, s.9(2)(g); Local Government Official Information and Meetings Act 1987, s.7(2)(f).

[90] Official Information Act 1982, ss.9(2)(h) and 27(1)(h); Local Government Official Information and Meetings Act 1987, ss.7(2)(g) and 26(1)(h); Privacy Act 1993, s.29(1)(f).

[91] Official Information Act 1982, s.9(2)(i); Local Government Official Information and Meetings Act 1987, s.7(2)(h).

[92] Official Information Act 1982, s.9(2)(j); Local Government Official Information and Meetings Act 1987, s.7(2)(i).

[93] Official Information Act 1982, s.9(2)(k); Local Government Official Information and Meetings Act 1987, s.7(2)(j).

[94] Official Information Act 1982, s.28(1); Local Government Official Information and Meetings Act 1987, s.27(1).

[95] Official Information Act 1982, s.30(1); Local Government Official Information and Meetings Act 1987, s.29(1).

[96] Official Information Act 1982, s.32(1); Local Government Official Information and Meetings Act 1987, s.31(1).

in law[97] and, from there, to the Court of Appeal.[98] There is statutory protection for those who in good faith release official information under the access acts.[99]

5. CANADA

Introduction

2–025 In Canada, legislation giving a general right of access to government-held information originated in the provinces. In 1977 Nova Scotia became the first Canadian jurisdiction to pass such legislation, followed by New Brunswick in 1978, Newfoundland in 1981 and Quebec in 1982.[1] Federal legislation giving a general right of access to government-held information was passed in June 1982. Called the Access to Information Act,[2] it was enacted at the same time as the Privacy Act,[3] and they came into force on July 1, 1983. All of the remaining provincial and territorial jurisdictions subsequently introduced similar legislation.[4] Since its enactment, the Access to Information Act has been amended on three occasions, all of which have been of relatively minor significance.[5]

[97] Official Information Act 1982, s.32B; Local Government Official Information and Meetings Act 1987, s.34.

[98] Official Information Act 1982, s.32C; Local Government Official Information and Meetings Act 1987, s.35.

[99] Official Information Act 1982, s.48(1); Local Government Official Information and Meetings Act 1987, s.41(1); Privacy Act 1993, s.115(1). If the original supplier to the department did so in breach of confidence, that person will not enjoy the statutory protection where that information is disclosed under an access Act: *Attorney-General v Davidson* [1994] 3 N.Z.L.R. 143, CA.

[1] The original Nova Scotia Act was replaced in 1993 by the Freedom of Information and Protection of Privacy Act 1993 (Nova Scotia); Right to Information Act 1978 (New Brunswick); Freedom of Information Act 1990 (Newfoundland); An Act respecting Access to documents held by public bodies and the Protection of personal information 1982 (Quebec).

[2] (R.S. 1985, c. A–1).

[3] The purpose of the Privacy Act is, broadly speaking, to protect the privacy of individuals with respect to personal information about themselves held by a government institution and to provide individuals with a right of access to that information: *Dagg v Canada (Minister of Finance)* [1997] S.C.J. 63 at para.61; *Attorney-General of Canada and Hartley v Information Commissioner of Canada* [2002] F.C.T. 128.

[4] Freedom of Information Act 1998 (Manitoba); Freedom of Information and Protection of Privacy Act 1992 (Saskatchewan); Freedom of Information and Protection of Privacy Act 1988 (Ontario); Freedom of Information and Protection of Privacy Act 1996 (British Columbia); Freedom of Information and Protection of Privacy Act 1994 (Alberta); Freedom of Information and Protection of Privacy Act 2001 (Prince Edward Island); Access to Information and Protection of Privacy Act 1994 (Northwest Territories); Access to Information and Protection of Privacy Act 1996 (Yukon Territory).

[5] In 1992, the Act was amended to deal with the provision of records in alternate formats to individuals with sensory disabilities.In 1999, it was amended to make it a criminal offence to intentionally obstruct the right of access by destroying, altering, hiding or falsifying a record, or directing anyone else to do so. In 2001, it was amended by the Anti-terrorism Act which provides that a certificate by the Attorney General prohibiting the disclosure of information for the purpose of protecting national defence or national security will override the provisions of the Access to Information Act.

Scope of the right

Section 4 of the Act gives Canadian citizens and permanent residents a right of access to records under the control of a government institution, subject only to specific exclusions[6] and exemptions.[7] The Act gives the Governor in Council power to extend this right to others, and in 1989 the access right was extended to include all individuals and incorporated entities present in the country.[8] The unit of disclosure under the *Access to Information Act* is a "record,"[9] as opposed to a "document" or "information." In order for the right to arise, a record must be "under the control"[10] of a "government institution."[11] Decisions granting or refusing access must be made by the "head" of each government institution, with the head of each institution being designated by regulation.[12] 2–026

The request

A request must be made in writing.[13] There is no power to refuse to answer a request that is frivolous, vexatious or abusive. The only control over 2–027

[6] Published, library and museum material are generally excluded from the operation of the Act: Access to Information Act, s.68. So, too, confidences of the Queen's Privy Council for Canada (*i.e.* cabinet material): Access to Information Act, s.69. In relation to cabinet material generally, see: *Canada (Minister of Environment) v Canada (Information Commissioner)* [2003] F.C.A. 68.

[7] Exemptions, which are provided for by Access to Information Act, ss.13–26, are considered below.

[8] Access to Information Act Extension Order No.1 (SOR/89–207).

[9] Access to Information Act, s.3 defines "record" to include any correspondence, memorandum, book, plan, map, drawing, diagram, pictorial or graphic work, photograph, film, microform, sound recording, videotape, machine readable record, and any other documentary material, regardless of physical form or characteristics, and any copy thereof. It has been held that software does not constitute a record: *Yeager v Canada (Correctional Service)* [2003] F.C.A. 30. A record can include something not yet in existence but that can be assembled from data already held, see: *Yeager v Canada (Correctional Service)* [2003] F.C.A. 30.

[10] The Act does not define when a record is "under the control" of an institution. The authorities indicate that any document that happens to be in the custody or in the hands of a government institution, regardless of how or upon what conditions, will be under its control: *Montana Band of Indians v Canada (Minister of Indian and Northern Affairs)* [1989] 1 F.C. 143, TD 51 D.L.R. (4th) 306; *Ottawa Football Club v Canada (Minister of Fitness and Amateur Sports)* [1989] 2 F.C. 480, TD; *Canada Post Corp v Canada (Minister of Public Works)* [1995] 2 F.C. 110, 30 Admin LR (2d) 242, affirming [1993] 3 F.C. 320, 19 Admin LR (2d) 230; *Rubin v Canada (Minister of Foreign Affairs and International Trade)* [2001] F.C.T. 440 (a returned document is not "under the control" of an institution). In relation to documents obtained by the institution from a third party through court disclosure or discovery, see *Andersen Consulting v Canada* [2001] 2 F.C. 324.

[11] Access to Information Act, s.3 simply defines a government institution as any department or ministry, body or office listed in Schedule I of the Act. Schedule I lists 19 departments and ministries and a number of other bodies and offices.As to ministerial offices, see: *Canada (Attorney-General) v Canada (Information Commissioner)* [2000] F.C.A. 26, FCA.

[12] Access to Information Act Heads of Government Institutions Designation Order (SI 1983/113).

[13] Access to Information Regulations (SOR/83–507), r.4.

burdensome requests lies in the fees regime.[14] Where a government institution receives a request but considers that another government institution has a greater interest in the record, the former institution may transfer the request to the latter institution.[15] The Act provides for a publication scheme.[16] There is, however, no statutory requirement upon government institutions to give assistance to those making a request for records.

The response

2–028 Within 30 days of receiving a request, a government institution must inform the applicant whether access to the requested record is to be given and, if so, to provide it.[17] The 30-day period may be extended "for a reasonable period of time" where the request is for a large number of records, requires a search through a large number of records, requires consultations that cannot be completed within the original time limit, or where notice has to be given to third parties.[18] If a record is not provided within the original 30 days or the extended period, the request is deemed to have been refused.[19] If, after processing a request, it is decided to give access, that takes the form of an opportunity to examine the record or the provision of a copy of the record.[20] If the institution decides to refuse access, it must cite the statutory ground for refusing access or what it would be if the record existed.[21] In refusing a request, the institution is not required to confirm whether any record answering the terms of the request actually exists.[22] An institution must so far as practicable sever exempted portions of records and provide access to the rest.[23]

14 Access to Information Act, s.11 and Access to Information Regulations (SOR/83–507), r.7 provide for an applicant to be charged an application fee, not exceeding $25, and also to be charged for: reasonable search and preparation time in excess of five hours; the costs of producing a record in an alternative format; the production of a machine-readable record; and reproduction costs.In all cases, specific amounts are set by regulation. Heads of institutions can require applicants to pay deposits, or to waive or repay a fee. The ability to use the fees regime to control what are considered to be frivolous or vexatious requests would appear to be limited: *Rubin v Canada (Minister of Finance)* (1987) 9 F.T.R. 317, FCTD 35 D.L.R. (4th) 517.

15 Access to Information Act, s.8; Access to Information Regulations (SOR/83–507), r.6.

16 Access to Information Act, s.5.

17 *ibid.*, s.7.

18 *ibid.*, s.9.

19 As to the review by the courts of decisions to extend the time within which to respond to a request, see: *Canada (Information Commissioner) v Canada (Minister of External Affairs)* [1989] 1 F.C. 3, 32 Admin LR 265 TD; *Canada (Information Commissioner) v Canada (Minister of External Affairs)* [1990] 3 F.C. 514, TD; *X v Canada (Minister of National Defence)* [1991] 1 F.C. 670, TD.

20 Access to Information Act, s.12(1); Access to Information Regulations (SOR/83–507), rr.5 and 8.

21 Access to Information Act, s.10(1).

22 *ibid.*, s.10(2).

23 *ibid.*, s.25. See *Sheldon Blank & Gateway Industries v Canada (Minister of Environment)* [2001] F.C.A. 374, FCA.

Exemptions generally

The Access to Information Act divides exemptions into mandatory and discretionary exemptions.[24] Mandatory exemptions must be invoked; discretionary exemptions allow the head of a government institution to decide whether the exemption needs to be invoked. Each exemption is based on either an "injury test" or "class test." Exemptions which incorporate an "injury test" take into consideration whether the disclosure of certain information could "reasonably be expected" to be injurious to a specified interest.[25] "Class test" exemptions are those applying to a record that matches the description given in the statutory provision; in order to engage the exemption there is no need to demonstrate any likelihood of injury resulting from disclosure of the record. Two of the mandatory exemptions include public interest overrides. These allow the head of a government institution to disclose information where this would be in the public interest as defined in the provision.[26] 2–029

Onus, purpose clause and conclusive certificates

Although there is no specific provision in the Act specifying whether it is the institution or the applicant who must demonstrate the applicability or inapplicability of a ground of exemption, the courts have held that where there is a contest between disclosure and non-disclosure of a record, the burden rests upon the party resisting disclosure.[27] This approach is consistent with the Act's purpose clause, which includes a statement of principle that government information should be available to the public and that necessary exceptions to the right of access should be limited and specific.[28] Until late 2001, the Access to 2–030

---

24 There are no mandatory exemptions in the Freedom of Information Act 2000.

25 The courts have interpreted this to mean that there must be a reasonable expectation of probable harm: *Canada Packers Inc. v Canada (Minister of Agriculture)* [1989] 1 F.C. 47, CA. Mere assertions will not suffice: *Jacques Whitford Environment Ltd v Canada (Minister of National Defence)* [2001] F.C.T. 556; *Wyeth-ayerst Canada Inc v Canada (Attorney General)* [2002] F.C.T. 133; *Geophysical Service Inc v Canada-Newfoundland Offshore Petroleum Board* [2003] F.C.T. 507.

26 Access to Information Act, s.20(6) permits the head of an institution to disclose commercial information from a third party if this would be in the public interest as it relates to health, safety or protection of the environment, and the public interest in disclosure clearly outweighs any injury to the third party. Section 19 of the Access to Information Act provides a similar public interest override in relation to the exemption for personal information. The consideration of the public interest only as it concerns the specific exemption, rather than in general, is the model adopted in the Freedom of Information Act 2000.

27 *Maislin Industries Ltd v Minister for Industry, Trade & Commerce* [1984] 1 F.C. 939, TD; *Rubin v Canada (Canada Mortgage and Housing Corp)* [1989] 1 F.C. 265, CA; *Canada (Information Commissioner) v Canada (Minister of External Affairs)* [1990] 3 F.C. 665, TD. This also applies where a third party resists disclosure: *Wyeth-ayerst Canada Inc v Canada (Attorney General)* [2002] F.C.T. 133; *Cistel Technology Inc v Canada (Correctional Service)* [2002] F.C.T. 253. Where proceedings are on foot, the position is governed by Access to Information Act, s.48.

28 Access to Information Act, s.2.

Information Act did not include any mechanism for taking particular documents outside of its operation or for reducing the ability to review a non-disclosure decision. The Anti-terrorism Act (2001) amended the Access to Information Act by adding a provision[29] which provides that a certificate by the Attorney-General prohibiting the disclosure of information for the purpose of protecting national defence or national security will override the provisions of the Access to Information Act. The certificates are subject to review by the Federal Court of Appeal.

Mandatory exemptions

2–031 There are six class-based mandatory exemptions:

(1) Information received in confidence from other governments.[30]
(2) Information obtained or prepared by the Royal Canadian Mounted Police on provincial or municipal policing services.[31]
(3) Personal information.[32]
(4) Trade secrets of a third party.[33]
(5) Financial, commercial, scientific or technical information received in confidence from a third party.[34]

---

[29] Access to Information Act, s.69(1).

[30] *ibid.*, s.13(1). The exemption becomes discretionary if the body from whom the information was obtained either consents to its disclosure or makes it public itself: s.13(1). See *Sherman v Minister of National Revenue* [2003] F.C.A. 202 (tax information exchanged under convention).

[31] *ibid.*, s.16(3).

[32] *ibid.*, s.19. The Act adopts the definition of "personal information" given in the Privacy Act, s.3, which is that it is "information about an identifiable individual that is recorded in any form" and then proceeds to give a series of specific inclusions.Personal information has been held to extend to qualitative evaluations of an employee's performance (*Canada (Information Commissioner) v Canada (Solicitor General)* [1988] 3 F.C. 557, TD and to the remuneration levels of various chairmen, heads, and presiding officials of an agency (*Rubin v Canada (Clerk of the Privy Council)* (1993) 62 F.T.R. 287, FCTD). See also *Canada (Information Commissioner) v Canada (Cultural Property Export Review Board)* [2001] F.C.T. 1054; *Canada (Information Commissioner) v Canada (Royal Canadian Mounted Police)* [2001] 3 F.C. 70; [2001] F.C.A. 56; *Canada (Information Commissioner) v Canada (Minister of Citizenship and Immigration)* [2002] F.C.A. 270. An "identifiable individual" does not include a corporation: *Geophysical Service Inc v Canada-Newfoundland Offshore Petroleum Board* [2003] F.C.T. 507.

[33] Access to Information Act, s.20(1)(a). The Courts have given this exemption a narrow interpretation: *Merck Frosst Canada Inc v Canada (Minister of Health and Welfare)* (1988) 20 F.T.R. 73, FCTD; *Canada Post Corp v Canada (Minister of Public Works)* [1993] 3 F.C. 320, TD, affirmed (1993), 64 F.T.R. 62, FCA; *Matol Botanical International Inc v Canada (Minister of National Health & Welfare)* (1994) 84 F.T.R. 168, FCTD; *Société Gamma Inc v Canada (Secretary of State)* (1994) 79 F.T.R. 42, FCTD; *PricewaterhouseCoopers, LLP v Canada (Minister of Canadian Heritage)* [2001] F.C.T. 1040; *Wyeth-ayerst Canada Inc v Canada (Attorney-General)* [2002] F.C.T. 133; *Cistel Technology Inc v Canada (Correctional Service)* [2002] F.C.T. 253; *St Joseph Corp v Canada (Public Works and Government Services)* [2002] F.C.T. 274.

[34] Access to Information Act, s.20(1)(b). The courts have held that the information must still have its confidentiality at the time of the request in order for the exemption to operate: *Maislin Industries Ltd v Minister for Industry, Trade & Commerce* [1984] 1 F.C. 939, TD. The general

(6) Information the disclosure of which is restricted by or pursuant to any provision set out in Sch.II to the Act.[35]

There are two injury-based mandatory exemptions:

(7) Records the disclosure of which could reasonably be expected to cause loss or gain to a third party or prejudice to competitive position.[36]
(8) Records the disclosure of which could reasonably be expected to cause interference with contractual or other negotiations of a third party.[37]

Discretionary exemptions

There are nine class-based discretionary exemptions. These grant exemption from disclosure for records that contain: 2–032

(1) Information obtained or prepared by listed investigative bodies.[38]
(2) Information on techniques or plans for investigations.[39]
(3) Trade secrets or valuable financial, commercial, scientific or technical information belonging to the Government of Canada.[40]

approach of the courts has been to scrutinise carefully claims of confidentiality, whether these claims are made by the government institution or by the third party that supplied the information: *Noël v Great Lakes Pilotage Authority Ltd* [1988] 2 F.C. 77, TD; *Intercontinental Packers Ltd v Canada (Minister of Agriculture)* (1987) 14 F.T.R. 142, FCTD; *Ottawa Football Club v Canada (Minister of Fitness and Amateur Sports)* [1989] 2 F.C. 480 TD; *Canada Packers Inc v Canada (Minister of Agriculture)* [1989] 1 F.C. 47, CA; *PricewaterhouseCoopers, LLP v Canada (Minister of Canadian Heritage)* [2001] F.C.T 1040; *Jacques Whitford Environment Ltd v Canada (Minister of National Defence)* [2001] F.C.T. 556. As to whether a third party can protect its information by insisting at the time of submission to the institution that it be treated as confidential, see: *Stenotran Services v Canada (Minister of Public Works and Government Services)* [2000] F.C.J. No.747, QL FCTD.

35 Access to Information Act, s.24. The courts have said that it was intended that the invocation of provisions in other statutes to limit disclosure was intended to be as restrictive as possible: *Canada (Information Commissioner) v Canada (Immigration Appeal Board)* [1988] 3 F.C. 477, TD.

36 *ibid.*, s.20(1)(c). The courts have treated claims for this exemption with circumspection, requiring real evidence to support the reasonable expectation and not just surmise: *Burns Meats Ltd v Canada (Minister of Agriculture)* (1987) 14 F.T.R. 137, FCTD; *Glaxo Canada Inc v Canada (Minister of National Health & Welfare)* (1992) 41 C.P.R. (3d) 176, FCTD; *Cyanamid Canada Inc v Canada (Minister of Health and Welfare)* (1992) 45 C.P.R. (3d) 390, FCA; *Prud'homme v Canada (Canadian International Development Agency)* (1994) 85 F.T.R. 302, FCTD; *Matol Botanical International Inc v Canada (Minister of National Health & Welfare)* (1994), 84 F.T.R. 168, FCTD; *Jacques Whitford Environment Ltd v Canada (Minister of National Defence)* [2001] F.C.T 556.

37 Access to Information Act, s.20(1)(d). The courts have required the negotiations to be on foot and for the interference to amount to actual obstruction: *Société Gamma Inc v Canada (Secretary of State)* (1994) 79 F.T.R. 42, FCTD; *Saint John Shipbuilding Ltd v Canada (Minister of Supply and Services)* (1990) 67 D.L.R. (4th) 315, FCA.

38 *ibid.*, s.16(1)(a).

39 *ibid.*, s.16(1)(b). For an example of its application, see *Rubin v Canada (Solicitor General)* (1986) 1 F.T.R. 157, FCTD.

40 *ibid.*, s.18(a).

(4) Advice or recommendations developed by or for a government institution or a minister of the Crown.
(5) Any account of governmental consultations or deliberations.[41]
(6) Government negotiation plans.[42]
(7) Government personnel or organisational plans.[43]
(8) Solicitor-client privileged information.[44]
(9) Information that is likely to be published within 90 days.[45]

There are nine injury-based discretionary exemptions. These apply to records the disclosure of which could "reasonably be expected" to cause:[46]

(10) Injury to the conduct of federal-provincial affairs.[47]
(11) Injury to the conduct of international affairs, or to the defence of Canada or allied states.[48]

---

[41] Access to Information Act, s.21(1)(a). As to the meaning of "advice or recommendations," see: *Canada Inc v Canada (Minister of Industry)* [2002] 1 F.C. 421, CA. There is an exception where the account relates to a decision that is made in the exercise of a discretionary power or an adjudicative function and that affects the rights of a person: Access to Information Act, s.21(2). Factual information falls outside the exemption: *Canadian Council of Christian Charities v Canada (Minister of Finance)* [1999] 4 F.C. 245, TD.

[42] Access to Information Act, s.21(1)(b). There is an exception where the account relates to a decision that is made in the exercise of a discretionary power or an adjudicative function and that affects the rights of a person: Access to Information Act, s.21(2). The courts have not inquired into the reasons for invoking this exemption: provided that the record answers the description, that will suffice: *Canada (Information Commissioner) v Canadian Radio-television and Telecommunications Commission* [1986] 3 F.C. 413, TD; *Re Rubin and President of CMHC* (1987) 36 D.L.R. (4th) 22, FCTD. Factual information falls outside the exemption: *Canadian Council of Christian Charities v Canada (Minister of Finance)* [1999] 4 F.C. 245, TD.

[43] *ibid.*, s.21(1)(c). There is an exception where the account relates to a decision that is made in the exercise of a discretionary power or an adjudicative function and that affects the rights of a person: Access to Information Act, s.21(2).

[44] *ibid.*, s.21(1)(d). There is an exception where the account relates to a decision that is made in the exercise of a discretionary power or an adjudicative function and that affects the rights of a person: Access to Information Act, s.21(2).

[45] *ibid.*, s.23. The common law test of privilege is applied, including concepts of waiver: *Weiler v Canada (Minister of Justice)* [1991] 3 F.C. 617, TD; *Wells v Canada (Minister of Transport)* (1995) 63 C.P.R. (3d) 201, FCTD; *Professional Institute of the Public Service of Canada v Canadian Museum of Nature* (1995) 63 C.P.R. (3d) 449, FCTD; *Canadian Jewish Congress v Canada (Minister of Employment and Immigration)* [1996] 1 F.C. 268, TD; *Stevens v Canada (Prime Minister)* [1998] 4 F.C. 89, FCA; *Sheldon Blank & Gateway Industries v Canada (Minister for Environment)* [2001] F.C.A. 374 (whether privilege applies to documents incorporated by reference); *St Joseph Corp v Canada (Public Works and Government Services)* [2002] F.C.T 274.

[46] Access to Information Act, s.26.

[47] *ibid.*, s.14.

[48] *ibid.*, s.15. The courts have shown themselves comparatively deferential to respondent claims of exemption under defence grounds: *Canada (Information Commissioner) v Canada (Minister of National Defence)* [1990] 3 F.C. 22, TD; *X v Canada (Minister of National Defence)* (1992) 58 F.T.R. 93, FCTD; *X v Canada (Minister of National Defence)* [1992] 1 F.C. 77, TD; *Do-ky v Canada (Minister of Foreign Affairs and International Trade)* [1999] F.C.J. No.673, QL FCA.

(12) Injury to law enforcement or conduct of lawful investigations.[49]
(13) Harm in facilitating the commission of criminal offence.[50]
(14) Threat to an individual's safety.[51]
(15) Prejudice to the competitive position of government.[52]
(16) Harm in depriving a government researcher of priority of publication.[53]
(17) Injury to the financial or economic interests of Canada.[54]
(18) Prejudice to the use of audits or tests.[55]

Appeals and enforcement

There is a two-tiered review process. Applicants have the right to complain to the Information Commissioner about an institution's handling of their request.[56] Following an investigation and report by the Commissioner to the head of the institution, both applicant and Information Commissioner have a right to seek a review of a denial of access in the Federal Court of Canada.[57] Third parties may also apply to the Federal Court in order to prevent disclosure of a record.[58] The appeal to the Federal Court is an appeal on judicial review 2-033

[49] Access to Information Act, s.16(1)(c). The Courts have required that the respondent identify a particular investigation that would be prejudiced, and declined to uphold a refusal to disclose upon a assertion that investigations generally would be prejudiced: *Rubin v Canada (Clerk of the Privy Council)* [1993] 2 F.C. 391, TD; [1994] 2 F.C. 707, CA; (1996) 179 N.R. 320, SCC; *Lavigne v Canada (Commissioner of Official Languages)* [2000] F.C.J. No.1412, QL FCA; *Information Commissioner v Minister of Citizenship and Immigration* [2002] F.C.A. 270 ("chilling effect" argument rejected).

[50] Access to Information Act, s.16(2).

[51] *ibid.*, s.17.

[52] *ibid.*, s.18(b).

[53] *ibid.*, s.18(c).

[54] *ibid.*, s.18(d). This does not extend to information that would result in an increase in legitimate claims for deductions under tax legislation: *Canadian Council of Christian Charities v Canada (Minister of Finance)* [1999]4 F.C. 245, TD.

[55] Access to Information Act, s.22. For an example, see *Bombardier v Canada (Public Service Commission)* (1990) 44 F.T.R. 39, FCTD.

[56] *ibid.*, s.30.

[57] *ibid.*, ss.41 and 42. There must be a denial of access, so that if the institution claims that it has no documents, the applicant has no right of appeal; a court will not intervene where there is mere assertion that documents are held: *Creighton v Canada (Superintendent of Financial Institutions)* [1990] F.C.J. No.353, QL FCTD; *Sheldon Blank & Gateway Industries Ltd v Canada (Minister of Environment)* [2001] F.C.A. 374. The appeal is against the refusal to grant access, not the information commissioner's review: *Bellemare v Canada (Attorney-General)* [2000] F.C.T 429. However, the Court may properly take into account the commissioner's views: *Canadian Council of Christian Charities v Canada (Minister of Finance)* [1999] 4 F.C. 245, TD. As to an institution's ability to invoke for the first time an exemption during the appeal process, see: *Canada (Information Commissioner) v Canada (Minister of National Defence)* [1999] F.C.J. No.522, QL FCA.

[58] *ibid.*, s.44. As to a third party's rights, see *Heinz Company of Canada Ltd v Attorney-General of Canada* [2003] F.C.T 250. A more detailed comparative treatment of third party rights of consultation and of "reverse FOI" is given at para.11–043 below.

grounds.[59] The Court is entitled to examine any record in dispute[60] and it is normally accepted practice to allow counsel for an applicant to see the disputed documents to enable the case to be properly heard, but on an undertaking not to disclose them to the client.[61]

6. REPUBLIC OF IRELAND

Introduction

2–034 The first proposal to provide a right for access to official information came from a private member's Bill in 1985. It received little support and matters remained there until late 1994 when the Fine Gael/Labour Party made a commitment to introduce access legislation as part of their programme for government. The Freedom of Information Act 1997 was passed on April 21, 1997 and came into operation on April 21, 1998.[62] Significant amendments were effected in 2003, which generally increased the ability of public bodies to claim exemption both from disclosing records and from having to confirm or deny the holding of records.[63]

---

[59] *Canadian Jewish Congress v Canada (Minister of Employment and Immigration)* [1996] 1 F.C. 268, TD. The role of the Court is more limited where the exemption relied on turns on where the head of a governmental institution reasonably believes that disclosure will result in an identified harm: *X v Canada (Minister of National Defence)* (1992) 58 F.T.R. 93, FCTD.

[60] Access to Information Act, s.46. The purpose of this provision is to enable the Court to have the information and material necessary to ensure that the discretion given to the administrative head has been exercised within proper limits and on proper principles: *Rubin v Canada (Canada Mortgage and Housing Corp)* [1989] 1 F.C. 265, CA. See also: *Canada (Minister of Environment) v Canada (Information Commissioner)* [2000] F.C.J. No.480, QL FCA. Protection against disclosure by the Court is given in s.47.

[61] *Maislin Industries Ltd v Minister for Industry, Trade & Commerce* [1984] 1 F.C. 939, TD; *Robertson v Canada (Minister of Employment and Immigration)* (1987) 13 F.T.R. 120, FCTD; *Hunter v Canada (Consumer and Corporate Affairs)* [1991] 3 F.C. 186, CA; *Bland v Canada (National Capital Commission)* [1991] 3 F.C. 325, TD; *Sheldon Blank & Gateway Industries Ltd v Canada (Minister of the Environment)* [1999] F.C.J. No.571, QL FCTD. Cross-examination of deponents of affidavits in support of exemptions is not normally allowed: X *v Canada (Minister of National Defence)* (1992) 58 F.T.R. 93, FCTD.

[62] Freedom of Information Act 1997, s.1(2). In relation to local authorities and health boards, the Act came into force on October 21, 1998.

[63] Freedom of Information (Amendment) Act 2003. This Act effected amendments to the definition of "record;" allowed access to personal information that pre-dated the commencement of the Freedom of Information Act 1997; strengthened the provisions relating to the refusal to confirm or deny the existence of a record answering the terms of a request; converted the protection of records relating to meetings of Government from discretionary to mandatory; extended the non-disclosure period of records relating to meetings of Government from 5 to 10 years; generally widened the scope of the exemptions.The net effect of the amendments is to make the Freedom of Information Act 1997 the most restrictive of the comparative jurisdictions so far as a person's right of access to official information is concerned, notwithstanding the words in the long title of the Act. The High Court in *Deely v Information Commissioner* [2001] I.E.H.C. 91 and prior

Scope of the right

Section 6(1) of the Act gives every person[64] a right of access to any "record"[65] "held"[66] by a "public body".[67] Certain records are, however, taken entirely outside the operation of the Act. These are termed[68] "exempt records" and include: 2–035

— most records held by a court or tribunal other than those of an administrative nature;[69]
— records held or created by the Attorney-General or the Director of Public Prosecutions, or their offices, other than those of a general administrative character;[70]
— records of the Ombudsman, relating to audits, to the President, to any private papers of a member of either House of the Oireachtas;[71]
— records revealing the source of information relating to criminal law enforcement;[72] and
— records otherwise available to members of the public.[73]

With two exceptions, the right of access applies only to records created after the commencement of the Act.[74] The Act makes limited provision for the giving

to the amendments, had described the Act as being "on any view, a piece of legislation independent in existence, forceful in its aim and liberal in outlook and philosophy".

64 "Person" is defined in the Interpretation Act 1937 to include a body corporate. The long title of the Freedom of Information Act 1997 suggests that the Act is principally intended to be for "members of the public" rather than companies.

65 "Record" is defined to include any memorandum, book, plan, map, drawing, diagram, pictorial or graphic work or other document, any photograph, film or recording (whether of sound or images or both), any form in which data is held, any other form (including machine-readable form) or thing in which information is held or stored manually, mechanically or electronically: Freedom of Information Act 1997, s.2(1).

66 The phrase "held by a public body" is defined to include a record under the control of a public body: Freedom of Information Act 1997, s.2(5)(a). It also extends to records in the possession of a person who is providing a service for a public body under a contract for services, provided that the records relate to the service: Freedom of Information Act 1997, s.6(9).

67 Public bodies are listed in the First Schedule and include local authorities, health boards, governmental departments, various bodies and organisations.The Act does not cover the police force, schools, universities, voluntary hospitals, nor various government agencies such as the Health and Safety Executive nor commercial State-sponsored bodies such as Aer Lingus.

68 Freedom of Information Act 1997, s.2(1).

69 *ibid.*, s.46(1)(a).

70 *ibid.*, s.46(1)(b).

71 *ibid.*,, s.46(1)(c)–(e). These are also picked up by the second limb of the definition of "exempt record" in s.2(1).

72 *ibid.*, s.46(1)(f).

73 *ibid.*, s.46(2). This does not extend to information available under the Data Protection Act 1988: Freedom of Information Act 1997, s.46(3).

74 *ibid.*, s.6(5). The first exception is where earlier records are needed in order to understand post-commencement records: Freedom of Information Act 1997, s.6(5)(a). The second exception is in relation to records containing personal information relating to the person making the request: Freedom of Information Act 1997, s.6(5)(b). As to the meaning of the latter, see *EH v Information Commissioner* [2001] I.E.H.C. 182.

of assistance to people who seek access to information.[75] Under the Act, each public body must publish a "reference book" setting out its functions and duties, the classes of records held by it, together with certain information in relation to the making of a request for access to records.[76] In addition to these rights, the Act grants individuals the right to require amendment of incorrect government records containing personal information concerning them.[77]

The request

2–036 A request is normally to be made in writing and must be adequately particularised.[78] The reason for the request is irrelevant to the entitlement to obtain access.[79] A request that is frivolous or vexatious or which would cause a substantial and unreasonable interference with or disruption of the other work of the public body concerned need not be answered.[80] A request need not be answered if the required fee has not been paid.[81]

The response

2–037 The public body is required to take reasonable steps to ascertain the location of records answering the terms of the request.[82] If the public body does not hold records answering the terms of the request but actually or constructively knows that another public body does, the request must be transferred to that latter public body within two weeks of the receipt of the request.[83] Within four weeks

75 Freedom of Information Act 1997, ss.7(7) and 10(2).

76 *ibid.*, s.15. In addition, internal guidelines on the making of any decisions by a public body must be published: Freedom of Information Act 1997, s.16. Apart from s.16(3) no express provision is made for any sanction for non-compliance with s.15 or 16. The Information Commissioner is, however, given the power to examine practices and procedures adopted by public bodies for the purposes of compliance with the Act: Freedom of Information Act 1997, s.36(1).

77 Freedom of Information Act 1997, s.17. Personal information can include records relating to a subject matter in which the applicant has a real and substantial interest, such as proceedings before a committee of the medical council: *EH v Information Commissioner* [2001] I.E.H.C. 182.

78 Freedom of Information Act 1997, s.7(1). The request must specify the form of access sought.

79 *ibid.*, s.8(4). Accordingly, the public body cannot impose restrictions on the purpose for which or persons to whom released records may be used or shown: *EH v Information Commissioner* [2001] I.E.H.C. 58; [2001] 2 I.R. 463.

80 *ibid.*, s.10(1).

81 *ibid.*, s.10(1)(f). The amount of the fee is set by Freedom of Information Act 1997, s.47. Fees can be waived: Freedom of Information Act 1997, s.47(5) and (6).

82 *ibid.*, s.10(1). Where it is estimated that the cost of search and retrieval is likely to exceed £50.80, the public body is entitled to seek a deposit and need not commence the search until such time as the deposit is paid: Freedom of Information Act 1997, s.47(7).

83 *ibid.*, s.7(3) and (6). Where the requested body holds some, but not all, of the records answering the terms of the request and the public body actually or constructively knows that another public body holds other records, the first public body must so notify the applicant: Freedom of Information Act 1997, s.7(4) and (6).

of receipt of the request, the public body must notify the applicant of the decision on the application, together with the fees that must be paid in order to obtain access.[84] Failure to notify within the prescribed period is deemed to constitute a refusal.[85] If the decision involves a refusal, reasons must be given together with a statement of appeal rights.[86] If the public body decides to give access to a record, it can do so in any number of ways.[87] Where part of a record contains exempt material but the remainder does not, the public authority must give disclosure to as much of the non-exempt material as is practicable.[88] The public body can, in a wide range of circumstances, refuse to confirm or deny that it holds records answering the terms of a request.[89] The Act specifically provides for discretionary disclosure.[90]

Exemptions generally

Certain exemptions are mandatory, the remainder are discretionary. Some of the exemptions are prejudice-based exemptions, others are purely class-based. The likelihood of harm needed to engage the prejudice-based exemptions varies from "could reasonably be expected" to occasion the identified harm,[91] to "would be likely" to occasion the identified harm,[92] to "could" occasion the identified harm.[93] Approximately half of the exemptions include a provision that disapplies the exemption where, in the opinion of the head of the public body, the public interest would on balance be better served by granted rather than by refusing to grant the request for access.[94] The Act provides for conclusive certificates in relation to: 2–038

[84] Freedom of Information Act 1997, s.8(1). The period can be extended where the records involved are voluminous or there have been other requests for the same records: Freedom of Information Act 1997, s.9(1).
[85] *ibid.*, s.41.
[86] *ibid.*, s.8(2).
[87] *ibid.*, s.12(1). Generally speaking, the public body must give access in the form sought by the applicant: Freedom of Information Act 1997, s.12(2). The public body cannot impose restrictions on the purpose for which or persons to whom released records may be used or shown: *EH v Information Commissioner* [2001] I.E.H.C. 58; [2001] 2 I.R. 463.
[88] *ibid.*, s.13(1). The resultant redacted record must not be misleading: Freedom of Information Act 1997, s.13(2).
[89] Where to do so would be prejudicial to government business, s.19(5); where to do so would be prejudicial to parliamentary or court business, s.22(2); where to do so would be prejudicial to law enforcement, s.23(2); where to do so would be prejudicial to security, defence or international relations, s.24(3); where to do so would reveal confidential information, s.26(4); where to do so would reveal commercially sensitive information, s.27(4); and where to do so would reveal personal information about someone other than the applicant, s.28(5A).
[90] Freedom of Information Act 1997, s.6(8). It is not clear whether a mandatory exemption represents a prohibition of access by law.
[91] *ibid.*, ss.21(1), 23(1), 24(1), 27(1)(b), 30(1)(b), 31(1) and 31(2)(n).
[92] *ibid.*, ss.26(1)(a) and 30(1)(a).
[93] *ibid.*, s.27(1)(b)–(c).
[94] *ibid.*, ss.20(3), 21(2), 23(3)(b), 26(3), 27(3), 28(5) and 31(3). The language of these exemptions suggests that in so far as there may be an onus in relation to the balancing exercise, it may be said nominally to lie on the applicant: if the head of the public body has no particular view

records recording the deliberations of a public body; records whose access could be expected to prejudice law enforcement, investigations, public safety, domestic or national security, defence and international relations; and records containing certain confidential information or that might reveal the identity of certain informants.[95] The effect of a conclusive certificate is to remove the right of merit review in relation to the decision to treat the record as exempt.[96] Where the information included in a record to which access has been sought includes information obtained in confidence, commercially sensitive information or personal information, a third party to whom the information relates is given the opportunity to make submissions on the disclosure of it.[97]

Specific exemptions

2–039 There are 16 heads of exemption, half of which are mandatory and half of which are discretionary. The public body must refuse access where:

(1) the record has been or is proposed to be submitted to the Government for consideration by a Minister and was created for that purpose, or the record contains information for use at a meeting of the Government or consists of a communication between two or more members of the Government relating to the same[98];

(2) the record contains or reveals a statement made at a meeting of the Government[99];

(3) the record would be exempt from production in a court on the grounds of legal professional privilege; disclosure of the record would constitute a contempt of court; or the record consists of the private papers of a member of the European Parliament, a member of a local authority or of a health board, or it consists of the opinions, advice, recommendations or the results of consultations considered by either House of the Oireachtas or its committees[1];

whether the public interest would be better served by granting or refusing the request, the exemption remains engaged.

[95] Freedom of Information Act 1997, ss.20(1A) and 25.

[96] There remains the more limited right to challenge the issue of the certificate on a point of law: Freedom of Information Act 1997, s.42(2). See also the limited right of review under *ibid*., s.25(7) and (8).

[97] Freedom of Information Act 1997, s.29. A more detailed comparative treatment of third party rights of consultation and of "reverse FOI" is given at para.11–043 below.

[98] *ibid*., s.19(1). Factual material is excluded and the exemption becomes inapplicable 10 years after the decision is made to which the record relates. The public body can refuse to confirm or deny the existence of any record falling within the terms of the exemption if it thinks that to do either would be contrary to the public interest: Freedom of Information Act 1997, s.19(5).

[99] *ibid*., s.19(2).

[1] *ibid*., s.22(1). The public body can refuse to confirm or deny the existence of any record falling within the terms of the exemption if it thinks that to do either would be contrary to the public interest: Freedom of Information Act 1997, s.22(2). For the purposes of the contempt provision,

(4) the record contains information: obtained for intelligence purposes; that relates to the security forces; revealing diplomatic communications; or revealing confidential communications from foreign state organisations[2];
(5) the record contains information given to the public body in confidence or the disclosure of which would constitute a breach of confidence[3];
(6) the record contains trade secrets, financial, etc., information or contractual negotiations[4];
(7) disclosure would be of personal information not relating to the applicant[5]; and
(8) disclosure of the information is prohibited by another statute.[6]

The public body may refuse access where:

(9) the record contains matter relating to the deliberative process of the public body[7];
(10) disclosure of the record could reasonably be expected to prejudice the effectiveness of tests, inquiries, audits etc. carried out by a public body or have a significant adverse effect on staff management or disclose a negotiating position[8];
(11) the record relates to the appointment or business or proceedings of a tribunal or an inquiry[9];

any disclosure will suffice: *EH v Information Commissioner* [2001] I.E.H.C. 58; [2001] 2 I.R. 463.

2 Freedom of Information Act 1997, s.24(2). The relevant minister may issue a conclusive certificate if he takes the view that the exemption applies. The public body can refuse to confirm or deny the existence of any record falling within the terms of the exemption if it thinks that to do either would be contrary to the public interest: Freedom of Information Act 1997, s.24(3).

3 *ibid.*, s.26(1). This exemption is disapplied where the public interest is better served by disclosure than by non-disclosure. The public body can refuse to confirm or deny the existence of any record falling within the terms of the exemption if it thinks that to do either would be contrary to the public interest: Freedom of Information Act 1997, s.26(4).

4 *ibid.*, s.27(1). This exemption is disapplied where the public interest is better served by disclosure than by non-disclosure. The public body can refuse to confirm or deny the existence of any record falling within the terms of the exemption if it thinks that to do either would be contrary to the public interest: Freedom of Information Act 1997, s.27(4).

5 *ibid.*, s.28(1). This exemption is disapplied where the public interest is better served by disclosure than by non-disclosure. The public body can refuse to confirm or deny the existence of any record falling within the terms of the exemption if it thinks that to do either would be contrary to the public interest: Freedom of Information Act 1997, s.28(5A).

6 *ibid.*, s.32.

7 *ibid.*, s.20(1). Factual and statistical material is excluded from the scope of the exemption. The exemption is disapplied where the public interest is better served by disclosure than by non-disclosure: Freedom of Information Act 1997, s.20(3). The relevant minister may issue a conclusive certificate if he takes the view that the exemption applies.

8 *ibid.*, s.21(1). This exemption is disapplied where the public interest is better served by disclosure than by non-disclosure. This was considered in *Minister for Education and Science v Information Commissioner* [2001] I.E.H.C. 116 in relation to a request for education league tables.

9 *ibid.*, s.22(1A).

(12) disclosure of the record could reasonably be expected to prejudice law enforcement and investigations or matters of internal security, or to reveal the name of a police informer[10];
(13) disclosure of the record could reasonably be expected to adversely affect the security or defence of the Republic of Ireland or its international relations[11];
(14) disclosure might be prejudicial to the health of the applicant[12];
(15) disclosure would reveal information about research in progress[13]; or
(16) disclosure would have a serious adverse effect upon the financial interests of the state, on the ability to manage the economy, or might disturb business or could result in an unwarranted benefit or loss to a person or to a class of persons.[14]

Appeals and enforcement

2–040 The first stage of appeal is a merit review by the "branch head" of the public body to whom the request is made.[15] The second stage of appeal is a merit review by the Information Commissioner.[16] The onus of proof lies upon the public body to justify the decision not to grant access.[17] An appeal to the High Court on a point of law lies from a decision of the Information Commissioner[18] or from the decision to issue a conclusive certificate.[19] The Act provides for various enforcement provisions,[20] as well as granting immunity from legal proceedings for the disclosure of information pursuant to the Act.[21]

[10] Freedom of Information Act 1997, s.23(1). The public body can refuse to confirm or deny the existence of any record falling within the terms of the exemption if it thinks that to do either would be contrary to the public interest: Freedom of Information Act 1997, s.23(2). A conclusive certificate may be issued in respect of this head of exemption: Freedom of Information Act 1997, s.25. This exemption is disapplied where the public interest is better served by disclosure than by non-disclosure.

[11] *ibid.*, s.24(1). The public body can refuse to confirm or deny the existence of any record falling within the terms of the exemption if it thinks that to do either would be contrary to the public interest: Freedom of Information Act 1997, s.24(3). A conclusive certificate may be issued in respect of this head of exemption: Freedom of Information Act 1997, s.25.

[12] *ibid.*, s.28(3).

[13] *ibid.*, s.30.

[14] *ibid.*, s.31. This exemption is disapplied where the public interest is better served by disclosure than by non-disclosure.

[15] *ibid.*, s.14(1). The review decision must be made within three weeks of the application for review having been received: Freedom of Information Act 1997, s.14(4). Failure to respond in that time is deemed to constitute a refusal: Freedom of Information Act 1997, s.41.

[16] *ibid.*, s.34. The Information Commissioner also has power to review a decision to defer access; a decision to grant access in the face of opposition from a third party under s.29; a decision to give access in one particular form, rather than another. The Information Commissioner has inquisitorial powers: Freedom of Information Act 1997, ss.35 and 37. He can refer questions of law to the High Court: Freedom of Information Act 1997, s.42(5).

[17] *ibid.*, s.34(12).

[18] *ibid.*, s.42(1).

[19] *ibid.*, s.42(2).

[20] *ibid.*, s.37.

[21] *ibid.*, s.45.

CHAPTER 3

Rights of Access Under European Union law

1. BACKGROUND

Introduction

3–001 The institutions of the European Union have neither a strong nor a lengthy tradition of providing access to documents or information held by them. They are thus closer to the British model of government, with a predisposition towards secrecy and non-disclosure,[1] than to the openness favoured by the Scandinavian members of the EU.[2] In the last 10 years there has, however, been a considerable opening up by the EU institutions. This opening up has met with substantial resistance from the European Commission and Council. The main focus of this chapter is the introduction of measures concerning access to documents held by and relating to the operation of EU institutions. This will include a discussion of the Code of Practice, Decisions 93/731 and 94/90 and the case law interpreting these decisions. Whilst the Code of Practice and decisions have now been repealed and replaced by Regulation 1049/2001, the case law under the earlier regime gives some indication as to how the European Court of First Instance and the Court of Justice will interpret Regulation 1049/2001.

The Maastricht Treaty

3–002 The first express recognition of the importance of transparency and openness appeared in Declaration No.17 annexed to the Final Act of the Treaty of the European Union (the Maastricht Treaty), which stated:

> "The Conference considers that transparency of the decision-making process strengthens the democratic nature of the institutions and the public's confidence in the administration. The Conference accordingly recommends that the Commission submit to the Council no later than 1993, a report on measures to improve the public access to the information available to the institutions."[3]

This stated commitment to openness was reiterated by the European Council in their declaration issued at the conclusion of the Birmingham meeting on

[1] See generally, V. Deckmyn and I. Thompson (eds), *Openness and Transparency in the European Union* (European Commission, European Institute of Public Administration, Maastricht, 1998).

[2] For example, Sweden, which is generally credited with having the longest tradition of access to official documents. The Swedish Freedom of the Press Act 1766 introduced a constitutional right for citizens to both access and print official documents: see S. V. Anderson, "Public Access to Government Files in Sweden" in *American Journal of Comparative Law*, Vol.21 (1973), p.419.

[3] Declaration No. 17 annexed to the Final Act of the Treaty of the European Union signed at Maastricht on February 7, 1992.

October 16, 1992 and reaffirmed by the European Council at Edinburgh in December 1992.

Article 255 of the Treaty of Amsterdam

The right of access to documents has now been recognised in the Treaty of Amsterdam. Article 255 (formerly Art.191a) provides: 3–003

> "1. Any citizen of the Union, and any natural or legal person residing or having its registered office in a Member State, shall have a right of access to European Parliament, Council and Commission documents subject to the principles and conditions to be defined in accordance with paragraphs 2 and 3.
>
> 2. General principles and limits on grounds of public or private interest governing this right of access to documents shall be determined by the Council, acting in accordance with the procedure referred to in Article 251 within two years of the entry into force of the Treaty of Amsterdam.
>
> 3. Each institution referred to above shall elaborate in its own Rules of Procedure specific provisions regarding access to its documents."[4]

The European Charter of Fundamental Rights of The European Union

Article 42 of the Charter of Fundamental Rights replicates the first sentence of Art.255 Treaty of Amsterdam and provides: 3–004

> "Any citizen of the Union, and any natural or legal person residing or having its registered office in a Member State, has a right of access to European Parliament, Council and Commission documents."

At present the Charter is merely a statement of intention and has no legal force. However, the present draft of the European Constitution envisages that the provisions of the Charter will be legally enforceable rights. Even if the Constitution is passed in its present form, Art.42 of the Charter does not add to the rights of the individual; it merely rehearses rights already in existence.

---

[4] The Treaty of Amsterdam came into force on May 21, 1999, so that the regulation had to be adopted by May 1, 2001.

Environmental Information

3–005 The directive on Freedom of Access to Information on the Environment was adopted in 1990 and came into force at the end of 1992.[5] The Directive requires public authorities[6] in the Member States to make available "information relating to the environment" which is defined as:

> "Any available information in written, visual, aural or data-base form on the state of water, air, soil, fauna, flora, land and natural sites, and on activities (including those which give rise to nuisance such as noise) or measures adversely affecting, or likely so to effect these, including administrative measures and environmental management programmes."[7]

Responses to requests for information must be supplied as soon as possible but in any event within two months.[8] Access rights are subject to a substantial number of discretionary exceptions. Member States can enact legislation that provides that a request for environmental information be refused if it affects:

(1) the confidentiality of the proceedings of public authorities, international relations and national defence;
(2) public security;
(3) matters which are, or have been, *sub judice*, or under enquiry (including disciplinary enquiries), or which are the subject of preliminary investigation proceedings;
(4) commercial and industrial confidentiality, including intellectual property;
(5) the confidentiality of personal data and/or files;
(6) materials supplied by a third party without that party being under a legal obligations to do so; or
(7) material which, if disclosed, would make it more likely that the environment to which such material related would be damaged.[9]

The United Kingdom has enacted the Directive into domestic law by way of Environmental Information Regulations 1992.[10]

[5] Directive 90/313/EEC on Environmental Information.
[6] "Public authority" is defined in Art.2 of the Directive 90/313/EEC as: "any public administration at national, regional or local level with responsibilities, and possessing information, relating to the environment with the exception of bodies acting in a judicial or legislative capacity." However, the ambit of the Directive is increased by Article 6 which applies the access provisions to "information relating to the environment held by bodies with public responsibilities for the environment and under the control of the public authorities".
[7] Directive 90/313/EEC, Art.2.
[8] *ibid.*, Art.3(4).
[9] *ibid.*, Art.3(2).
[10] These are considered at paras 5–050 to 5–051 below.

2. THE CODE OF PRACTICE AND DECISIONS 93/731 AND 94/90

General principles

The commitment to openness and transparency expressed in Declaration No.17 annexed to the Maastricht Treaty was realised on December 6, 1993 when, with the approval of both the Commission and the Council, a Code of Conduct concerning public access to Council and Commission documents was published.[11] The Council and Commission subsequently adopted this Code of Conduct by decision.[12] The Code of Conduct followed the conventional template for access legislation: a universal right of access, immediately qualified by exemptions, enforceable with a right of review. Thus, the Code of Conduct and decisions established a general right of access to documents subject to certain exceptions. "Document" was defined widely as including "any written text, whatever its medium, which contains existing data and is held by the Council or the Commission".[13] However, "[w]here the requested document was written by a natural or legal person, a Member State, another Community institution or body, or any other national or international body, the application must not be sent to the Council [or Commission][14] but direct to the author".[15] Thus, the right of access to documents was limited to documents produced by the Council or Commission. The Commission and Council were obliged to inform applicants within one month whether the application was approved or rejected. The Code of Practice provided that a failure to reply within the period amounted to a refusal.[16] There was an obligation, if the request was refused, to give reasons for the refusal and set out further avenues of redress available, namely a complaint to the ombudsman under Art.195 and judicial proceedings under Art.230.[17] 3–006

Exceptions

There were two types of exception to the general right of access. First, mandatory exceptions which provided that access to the document should not be granted where its disclosure could undermine: 3–007

[11] 93/730/EC [1993] O.J. L340/41.

[12] The Council adopted the Code of Conduct by Decision 93/731 on December 20, 1993 (93/731/EC, [1993] OJ L340/43). The Decision came into force on January 1, 1994. The Commission, on February 8, 1994, adopted Decision 94/90 which under Art.1 formally adopted the Code of Conduct. Decisions 93/731 and 94/90 have now been repealed and replaced by Regulation No.1049/2001 discussed below at paras 3–010 to 3–017 below.

[13] See Code of Conduct, General Principles 93/730 Council Decision 93/731/EC, Art.1(2).

[14] See Code of Conduct.

[15] Decision 93/731/EC, Art.2(2).

[16] *ibid.*, Art.7(1).

[17] *ibid.*, Art.7(3).

(1) the protection of the public interest (public security, international relations, monetary stability, court proceedings, inspections and investigations);
(2) the protection of the individual and privacy;
(3) the protection of commercial and industrial secrecy;
(4) the protection of the Community's financial interests;
(5) the protection of confidentiality as requested by the natural or legal person who supplied any of the information contained in the document or as required by the legislation of the Member State which supplied any of that information.[18]

Secondly, a discretionary exception that provided that access to a Council or Commission document *may* be refused "in order to protect the confidentiality of the Council's proceedings".[19]

Legal basis, ambit and extension of the right to access to other European bodies

3–008 The Netherlands, which like the Scandinavian countries, has a long history of freedom of information, sought to challenge the legal basis of the Decision permitting access to documents held by the Council.[20] The legal bases for the decision were founded in the rule of procedure and in Art.207(3) of the Treaty (vesting in the Council the power to adopt its own rules of procedure). The Netherlands Government argued that access to documents was a citizen's fundamental right and should therefore have a different legal basis. Advocate General Tesauro has some sympathy with the Dutch Government's arguments. The European Court of Justice was less convinced. The court appeared to refuse to hold that access to information was a general principle of Community law, although it did indicate that the public's right of access to documents could not be deduced from the Council's rules of procedure. Unfortunately, the court did not indicate what the legal basis was.[21] Whilst the Netherlands Government's arguments have been rejected, the Court has since consistently emphasised the importance of openness on the basis that it strengthens the public's confidence in the administration as well as enabling citizens to carry out genuine and efficient monitoring of the exercise of the powers.[22] The Court of

[18] Decision 93/731, Art.4(1) and Code of Conduct exceptions (Commission).
[19] *ibid.*, Art.4(2) and Code of Conduct exceptions (Commission).
[20] *Netherlands v EC Council*, Case C58/94 [1996] E.C.R. I–2169.
[21] Numerous commentators have expressed the view that the only other legal basis for the decision is in a general principle of law, see: M. Broberg, "Access to documents: a general principle of Community law?" in 27(2002) *European Law Review* 194; U. Öberg, "EU Citizen's Right to Know: The Improbable Adoption of a European Freedom of Information Act" in Alan Dashwood and Angela Ward (eds), *Cambridge Yearbook of European Legal Studies*, Vol.2 (Hart Publishing, Oxford, 2000), pp.303–328 at 315.
[22] See for example, *Interporc Im und Export GMBH v Commission* [1998] 2 C.M.L.R. 82.

First Instance has held that the right of access extended to documents in the possession of the Council or Commission that related to both second pillar[23] (common foreign and security policy) and third pillar[24] documents (justice and home affairs). The Court of First Instance has also concluded that the right of access extended to confidential documents.[25] As a result of an inquiry by the European Ombudsman into access of documents held by institutions and bodies other than the Council and the Commission, the Ombudsman concluded that:

> "failure to adopt and make easily available to the public rules governing public access to documents constitutes an issue of maladministration."[26]

As a result of this ruling all of the bodies to which it was addressed, with the exception of the European Court of Justice, adopted rules governing public access to documents.[27]

Interpretation

Both the Commission and Council initially adopted a narrow approach to disclosing documents under Decisions 93/731 and 94/90. In *Carvel and Guardian Newspapers Ltd v EU Council*[28] the newspaper sought access to preparatory reports, minutes and attendance and voting records of the Council of Ministers' meetings relating to social affairs, justice and agriculture. The Council refused disclosure of the documents relating to justice and agriculture on the grounds 3–009

[23] *Heidi Hautala v EU Council*, Case T-14/98 [1999] 3 C.M.L.R. 528 (see below).

[24] *Svenska Journalistforbundet v EU Council*, Case T-174/95 [1998] E.C.R. II–2289 (refusal of various documents relating to the setting up of Europol. An application was made by Svenska to various Swedish bodies under Swedish legislation for twenty documents. The newspaper received eighteen of the twenty documents. An identical application was made to the Council but only four out of the twenty were disclosed. The remaining sixteen documents were refused on grounds of public interest (public security) and confidentiality because they disclosed positions taken by various member states. The Court of First Instance annulled the decision because the Council had failed to give adequate reasons. It was unclear which exception applied to which document. The Court further doubted that the disclosure would prejudice public security as the documents concerned negotiations on the adoption of the Europol Convention. In relation to the confidentiality exception there was no evidence that the Council had engaged in a balancing exercise).

[25] *Rothmans International BV v EC*, Commission Case T-188/97 [1998] E.C.R. II–2463.

[26] Decision of the European Ombudsman in his own initiative inquiry into public access to documents (616/PUBAC/F/IJH), p.7.

[27] Namely, the European Parliament, the Court of Auditors, The European Investment Bank, The Economic and Social Committee, The Committee of the Regions, The European Monetary Institute, The Office for Harmonisation of the Internal Market, The European Training Foundation, The European Foundation fo the Improvement of Living and Working Conditions, The European Environment Agency, The Translation Centre for Bodies of the European Union, The European Monitoring Centre for Drugs and Drug Addiction, and the European Agency for the Evaluation of Medicinal Products.

[28] Case T-194/94 [1995] E.C.R. II–2765.

of confidentiality. This refusal was challenged by the newspaper with the support of the Danish and Dutch Governments and the European Parliament on the grounds that the decision amounted to a blanket refusal to release information. The newspaper contended that the Council had failed to exercise its discretion and balance the interests of the citizen in gaining access to its documents against any interests of its own in maintaining the confidentiality of its deliberations when making its judgment. The Court of First Instance annulled the decision on the grounds that the Council was obliged to balance relevant considerations and had failed to do so. *The Guardian* obtained the documents. The Court of First Instance indicated that the Commission was obliged to give reasons why it considered that the documents detailed in the request were within one of the exceptions.[29] The Court indicated that Decision 94/90 was designed to provide "for the widest public access possible" and as such any exception was to be interpreted strictly.[30] In *Hautala v European Union Council*[31] the appellant, a Finnish Member of the European Parliament, sought disclosure of a report on criteria for conventional arms exports. Disclosure was refused on the grounds that it was necessary for the protection of the public interest (international relations) as disclosure would harm EU relations with third countries. The decision was annulled because the Court of First Instance concluded that the Council was under a duty to consider partial access to the document excluding the parts of the report that risked damaging the EU's relations with third countries. The Council appealed unsuccessfully to the European Court of Justice which reiterated its view that the exceptions were to be interpreted narrowly and laid down the following general principles:

(1) the Code of Practice related not only to access to documents but also information contained in such documents;
(2) natural and legal persons had a right of access to information contained in a document not covered by one of the exceptions; and
(3) the general principle of proportionality required the Council to consider partial disclosure of a document when disclosure of the whole document would fall within one of the exceptions.[32]

---

[29] See also *World Wildlife Fund UK v EU Commission* [1997] E.C.R. II–313, CFI (refusal to disclose documents relating to EU funded visitors' centre to be located in Ireland on grounds of the protection of the public interest as the documents related to possible infringement proceedings and as such were related to inspections and investigations. Decision of Commission annulled because it had failed to give adequate reasons for refusal. CFI also found that the Commission had failed to balance interests adequately in relation to the confidentiality exception).

[30] See also *Van Der Wal v Commission* [1998] E.C.R. II–545, and *Bavarian Lager Company Ltd* Case T-92/98.

[31] Case T-14/98 [1999] 3 C.M.L.R. 528.

[32] Case C-353/99P [2002] 1 W.L.R. 1930 at 1939–1940 at paras 23–27 and 31–32. See also *Kuijer v Council of the European Union*, Case T-211/00 [2002] 1 W.L.R. 1941.

3. REGULATION 1049/2001

Introduction

Regulation 1049/2001 marks a substantial development in access to documents held by the EU Institutions. The Regulation was adopted under the co-decision procedure and approved by the European Parliament on May 3, 2001. It came into force on June 3, 2001 and was applicable from December 3, 2001.[33] Whilst subject to various exemptions its ambit is considerably wider than previous legislative schemes.[34] The Regulations apply to "documents of the institutions",[35] defined to mean the European Parliament, Council and Commission.[36] Unlike the earlier Code of Practice and Decisions 93/731 and 94/90, Regulation 1049/2001 applies not only to documents created by EU institutions but also to other documents held by the institutions, including documents drawn up or received by it and in its possession, in all areas of activity of the European Union.[37] Article 1 states that the purpose of the Regulation is: 3–010

(1) to define the principles, conditions and limits on grounds of public or private interest governing the right of access to institution documents provided for in Art.255 of the EC Treaty in such a way as to ensure the widest possible access to documents;
(2) to establish rules ensuring the easiest possible exercise of this right; and
(3) to promote good administrative practice on access to documents.[38]

Purpose, beneficiaries and scope

By Art.2(1) every citizen of the European Union and every natural or legal person residing or having its registered office in a Member State is given "a right of access to documents of the institutions, subject to the principles, conditions and limits set out elsewhere in [the] Regulation". The institutions have a discretion to grant access to documents, subject to the same principles, conditions and limits, to any natural or legal person not residing in or not having a registered 3–011

[33] See Art.19 of the Regulation 1049/2001.
[34] Recital (17) notes that "Council Decision 93/731/EC of December 20, 1993 on public access to Council documents, Commission Decision 94/90/ECSC, EC, Euratom of February 8, 1994 on public access to Commission documents, European Parliament Decision 97/632/EC, ECSC, Euratom of July 10, 1997 on public access to European Parliament documents ... should therefore, if necessary, be modified or be repealed".
[35] Art.2(1).
[36] Art.1(a).
[37] Art.2(3).
[38] Art.1.

office in a Member State.[39] "Document" is defined widely to mean "any content whatever its medium (written on paper or stored in electronic form or as a sound, visual or audiovisual recording) concerning a matter relating to the policies, activities and decisions falling within the institution's sphere of responsibility".[40] The regime is not limited to documents created by the institutions, but includes all documents held by the institutions whether drawn up by one of the institutions or received by and in the possession of one of the institutions.[41] The Regulation would appear to be fully retrospective: that is to say, it covers documents created before its coming into force.[42] As with all comparative freedom of information regimes, the motive of an applicant in seeking a document is largely irrelevant to the efficacy of the request.[43]

Exceptions

3–012 Article 4 sets out the various exceptions to the general right of access to documents. It divides exceptions into mandatory exceptions[44] and discretionary exceptions. The former are sub-divided into absolute exceptions (in relation to which the public interest need not be considered) and qualified exceptions (which have a public interest "override"). The mandatory absolute exceptions are contained in Art.4(1), which provides that institutions shall refuse access to a document where disclosure would undermine the protection of:

(1) the public interest[45] as regards:

- public security,[46]
- defence and military matters,[47]
- international relations,[48]
- the financial, monetary or economic policy of the Community or a Member State;[49]

---

[39] Art.2(2).
[40] Art.3(a).
[41] Art.2(3). As to the meaning of the term "held" see para.7–008 below.
[42] See further para.7–009 below.
[43] See paras 7–015 and 15–009 below.
[44] This is the model used in Canada and Ireland: see paras 2–025 to 2–040 above. It is always open for a public authority in the United Kingdom to grant a "discretionary disclosure", being disclosure of information to which the applicant has no right of disclosure under the Freedom of Information Act 2000 or the Freedom of Information (Scotland) Act 2002.
[45] The reference here to the "public interest" is a recitation that these sorts of disclosure would not be in the public interest, rather than an invitation to consider whether the public interest is better served by disclosure or non-disclosure.
[46] Public security would appear to embrace both what, in domestic legislation, is termed national security and matters of law enforcement. See paras 17–033 to 17–040 and 20–014 to 20–024.
[47] See paras 17–051 to 17–059 below.
[48] See paras 18–001 to 18–013 below and 18–039 to 18–042.
[49] See paras 19–001 to 19–009 below.

(2) privacy and the integrity of the individual, in particular in accordance with Community legislation regarding the protection of personal data.[50]

The mandatory qualified exemptions are set out in Art.4(2) and (3). The former provides that the institutions shall refuse access to a document where disclosure would undermine the protection of:

— commercial interests of a natural or legal person, including intellectual property,
— court proceedings[51] and legal advice,[52] and
— the purpose of inspections, investigations and audits,[53]

unless there is an overriding public interest in disclosure.[54] Article 4(3) provides for a qualified exception in relation to internal documents:

> "Access to a document, drawn up by an institution for internal use or received by an institution, which relates to a matter where the decision has not been taken by the institution, shall be refused if disclosure of the document would seriously undermine the institutions' decision-making process, unless there is an overriding public interest in disclosure.
>
> Access to a document containing opinions for internal use as part of deliberations and preliminary consultations within the institution concerned shall be refused even after the decision has been taken if disclosure of the document would seriously undermine the institution's decision-making process, unless there is an overriding public interest in disclosure."[55]

Sensitive documents

Certain documents that concern matters in areas covered by the absolute exceptions in Art.4(1) are classified as "Très Secret/Top Secret", "Secret" or "Confidential". Applications for sensitive documents may be handled only by persons who have a right to acquaint themselves with those documents.[56] Sensitive documents shall only be recorded in the register or released only with the consent 3–013

[50] See Ch.24.
[51] See Ch.20.
[52] See Ch.21.
[53] See Ch.20.
[54] Regulation 1049/2001, Art.4.2. For a consideration of the public interest in the disclosure of information, see paras 15–001 to 15–011 below.
[55] For a consideration of the domestic equivalent, see Ch.22.
[56] Art.9(2).

of the originator.[57] Whilst the duty to give reasons if the institution refuses disclosure still exists, the reasons provided shall be in a manner that does not harm the interests protected in Art.4.[58]

Third parties, partial disclosure, etc.

3–014 In relation to documents created by "third parties"[59] the institution must consult the third party to ascertain whether the document falls within Art.4(1) or (2) unless it is clear.[60] A Member State has the power to request that an institution shall not disclose a document originating from that Member State without its prior agreement.[61] If only parts of a document are covered by one of the exceptions the remaining parts of the document must be disclosed.[62] The exceptions laid down in Art.4(1)–(3) shall only apply for as long as necessary to protect the public interest. Article 4(7) provides that the maximum period under which disclosure can be refused is 30 years although this "long stop" period may be extended in documents that are exempted because they relate to privacy, commercial interests or are "sensitive documents".

Procedure

3–015 Applications for access to a document must be made in written form, including electronic form, in one of the languages referred to in Art.314 of the EC Treaty and in a sufficiently precise manner to enable the institution to identify the document.[63] If a Member State receives a request for a document in its possession that originates from an institution, the Member State must consult with the institution concerned prior to disclosure unless it is clear to the Member State whether or not the document should be disclosed.[64] Alternatively, the Member State may refer the request to the institution concerned.[65] With all documents listed in the Register[66] this should not be too onerous a requirement. An institution has 15 working days after registration of the application to either grant access to a document or provide reasons why access has been refused.[67] This

57 Art.9(3).
58 Art.10(4).
59 "Third Party" is defined in Art.3(b) as meaning "any natural or legal person, or any entity outside the institution concerned, including the Member States, other Community or non-Community institutions and bodies and third countries". For consultation with third parties under the domestic regime, see paras 11–042 to 11–049 below.
60 Art.4(4).
61 Art.4(5).
62 Art.4(6).
63 Art.6.
64 Art.5; see also Recital 15.
65 Art.5.
66 See para.3–016 below.
67 Art.7(1).

period can be extended by another 15 working-days if the request is for a very long document or a large number of documents, although the institution must give reasons in advance for this delay. If the institution makes a partial or total refusal of disclosure the applicant may, within 15 working days of receiving the institution's reply, make a confirmatory application asking the institution to reconsider its position.[68] If for whatever reason the institution fails to reply within the prescribed time limit an applicant is also entitled to make a confirmatory application.[69] The confirmatory application must also be decided within 15 working days from registration of the application, subject to the possibility of an extension of 15 working days if the request relates to a very long document or a large number of documents, although the institution must give reasons in advance for this delay.[70] In the event of a partial or total refusal, the institution must write to the applicant setting out the reasons for the refusal and informing him of the remedies open to him namely instituting court proceedings and/or making a complaint to the ombudsman.[71] A failure to reply within the prescribed period will also entitle an applicant to initiate court proceedings and/or complain to the ombudsman.[72] If access to a document is granted, the applicant may either consult it at the institution in question or receive a copy, including, where available, an electronic copy according to his preference. Consultation on the spot, direct access in electronic form or through the register or copies of less than 20 A4 pages are free.[73] If the applicant is sent written documents exceeding 20 A4 pages the institution may charge the applicant although any charge must be limited to the real cost of producing and sending the copies.[74] To assist visually impaired individuals, documents must be supplied either in an existing version and format or in an alternative format such as Braille, large print or tape with full regard to the applicant's preference.[75] Somewhat surprisingly, other than in relation to sensitive documents,[76] the Regulation does not make provision for an institution to give a response that neither confirms nor denies that the requested document is held by it.

The register and publication

To make the citizen's right of access to documents as effective as possible, the institutions are obliged to provide public access in electronic form to a register 3–016

[68] Art.7(3).
[69] Art.7(4).
[70] Art.8(2).
[71] Art.8(1). Article 230 EC lays down the conditions for instituting court proceedings, whilst Art.95 EC lays down the conditions for making an application to the ombudsman.
[72] Art.8(3).
[73] Art.10(1).
[74] *ibid.*
[75] Art.10(3).
[76] Art.9(4).

of documents.[77] The institutions were obliged to have this register operational from June 3, 2002.[78] Each document must have a reference number, details of the subject matter and/or a short description of the content together with the date on which it was received or drawn up and recorded.[79] The institutions are under an obligation to make, as far as possible, documents publicly accessible in electronic form or through the register.[80] There is an obligation to make all legislative documents[81] directly accessible subject to Arts 4 (exemptions) and 9 (sensitive information).[82] In addition to the Register, a number of documents must, subject to Arts 4 and 9, be published in the official journal. Documents that must be so published include:

(1) Commission proposals;
(2) common positions adopted by the Council in accordance with the procedures referred to in Arts 251 and 252 of the EC Treaty and the reasons underlying those common positions, as well as the European Parliament's positions in these procedures;
(3) framework decisions and decisions referred to in Art.34(2) of the EU Treaty;
(4) conventions established by the Council in accordance with Art.34(2) of the EU Treaty;
(5) conventions signed between Member States on the basis of Art.293 of the EC Treaty;
(6) international agreements concluded by the Community or in accordance with Art.24 of the EU Treaty.[83]

In addition, the following documents shall be published so far as possible:

(7) initiatives presented to the Council by a Member State pursuant to Art.67(1) of the EC Treaty or pursuant to Art.34(2) of the EU Treaty;
(8) common positions referred to in Art.34(2) of the EU Treaty;
(9) directives other than those referred to in Art.254(1) and (2) of the EC Treaty, decisions other than those referred to in Art.254(1) of the EC Treaty, recommendations and opinions.[84]

[77] Art.10(2).
[78] Art.11(3).
[79] Art.10(2).
[80] Art.12(2).
[81] "Legislative documents" are defined in Art.12(2) as documents drawn up or received in the course of procedures for the adoption of acts which are legally binding in or for the Member States.
[82] Art.12(2).
[83] Art.13(1).
[84] Art.13(2).

Information, administrative practice, copyright and reports

Article 14 places a duty on each of the institutions to take measures to inform the public of rights under the Regulation. Member States are obliged to co-operate with the institutions in providing this information. Article 15 provides that the institutions must develop good administrative practices. Article 16 provides that the regulations are without prejudice to any existing rules on copyright which may limit a third party's right to reproduce or exploit released documents. Each institution is obliged to publish an annual report which must include the number of cases in which the institution refused to grant access to documents, the reasons for such refusals and the number of sensitive documents not recorded in the register.[85] 3–017

[85] Art.17(1).

CHAPTER 4

Access to Personal Information Under the Data Protection Act 1998

1. GENERAL PRINCIPLES

Introduction

Section 7 of the Data Protection Act 1998 bestows upon an individual a right of access to personal data of which that individual is the subject,[1] together with three associated rights.[2] These rights are collectively referred to as "subject access rights." They form one aspect of the Data Protection Act 1998. Broadly speaking, that Act: 4–001

— controls the processing of personal data by prescribing certain data protection principles and imposing a duty on those who control personal data to comply with those principles;
— confers individual rights of access to and, to a limited extent, control over, personal information; and
— provides for the regulation and enforcement of those rights and duties.[3]

This chapter is concerned with subject access rights in relation to information held by public authorities.[4] The right of access within the subject access rights is qualified by a number of exemptions, as is the case with the right of access to information under the Freedom of Information Act 2000.

The division between the Data Protection Act 1998 and the Freedom of Information Act 2000

In general terms, where an individual seeks information that is held by a public authority relating to himself and no-one else, the right of access to that 4–002

1 The Data Protection Act 1998 applies equally to England, Northern Ireland, Scotland and Wales. Data protection is a reserved matter under the Scotland Act 1998 and, accordingly, is outside the legislative competence of the Scottish Parliament: see Scotland Act 1998, s.27(2)(b) and Sch.5, and para.1–023 above. As a matter of drafting convention rather than necessity, the Data Protection Act 1998 is expressly stated to apply to Northern Ireland: s.75(5) and (6).

2 The four rights are set out at para.4–026.

3 Other than those relating to the subject access rights, the provisions of the Data Protection Act 1998 are beyond the scope of this work. For a general treatment of the Data Protection Act 1998, see: S. Chalton, S. Gaskill, D. Walden and H. Grant, *Encyclopaedia of Data Protection*, (Sweet & Maxwell, looseleaf service); R. Jay and A. Hamilton, *Data Protection Law and Practice*, (2nd ed., Sweet & Maxwell, 2003).

4 The rights of access to personal information conferred by the Data Protection Act 1998, unlike the rights of access to information conferred by the Freedom of Information Act 2000, are not confined to information held by a public authority. To the extent that the Data Protection Act 1998 confers rights of access to personal information held by a person or body other than a public authority, those rights are beyond the scope of this work, although the basic rights, exemptions and procedures are, with the exception of unstructured personal data, the same irrespective of the identity of the person or body holding the personal information.

information will be that bestowed by the Data Protection Act 1998.[5] Where an individual seeks any other sort of information held by a public authority, the right of access to that information will be that bestowed by the Freedom of Information Act 2000. Where a corporate entity seeks any information held by a public authority, including information relating to itself, the right of access to that information will be that bestowed by the Freedom of Information Act 2000. This separate legislative treatment of the right of access to information relating to the applicant is common, but not universal, amongst the comparative jurisdictions. Thus:

(1) In the United States of America, the Privacy Act bestows an additional, enhanced right of access to personal information, in addition to that enjoyed under the general right of access bestowed by the Freedom of Information Act.[6]

(2) In Australia, the right of access to personal information is that given by the Freedom of Information Act 1982, although the Privacy Act 1988 impinges upon the exercise of that right where personal information is sought.[7]

(3) In New Zealand, the right of access to personal information was originally embodied within the general right of access to information in the Official Information Act 1982. In 1993 the right of access to personal information relating to the applicant was transferred to the Privacy Act 1993.[8]

(4) In Canada, the right of access to personal information under the control of a government institution is governed by the Privacy Act, which came into force at the same time as the Access to Information Act[9]

(5) In the Republic of Ireland, the right of access to personal information is embodied in the general right of access to records held by a public body bestowed by the Freedom of Information Act 1997.[10]

The separate treatment of this class of information in the United Kingdom reflects both the provenance of the right and the peculiar considerations which apply to the disclosure of personal information relating to the applicant.[11]

[5] If a request were made for this sort of information under the Freedom of Information Act 2000, the public authority would be entitled to refuse the request without any consideration of the public interest: see s.40 of that Act; Freedom of Information (Scotland) Act 2002, s.38.

[6] See para.2–002 above.

[7] See para.2–015(15) above.

[8] See para.2–017 above.

[9] See para.2–025 above. Personal information is a mandatory exemption under the Access to Information Act: see para.2–031(3) above.

[10] See para.2–035 above. There is an exemption from disclosure where the personal information is not related to the applicant: see para.2–039(7) above.

[11] In practice, access to personal information relating to the applicant generally forms the most common type of request for information held by a public authority: see, for example, Australian Law Reform Commission, *Open Government: A Review of the Federal Freedom of Information Act 1982*, (Australian Law Reform Commission, ALRC 77), para.2.10.

Origins of the access right

The predecessor to the Data Protection Act 1998 was the Data Protection Act 1984. It was more limited in scope than the Data Protection Act 1998, in particular being confined to "automated data."[12] However, it did grant an individual certain rights of access in respect of personal information: 4–003

— a right to be informed whether personal data about him or her were being processed;
— a right to be supplied with a copy of the information constituting any such personal data; and
— an explanation, if one was necessary, to understand the information supplied.[13]

Those rights of access were subject to a number of exemptions. The Data Protection Act 1984 had its origins, in part, in the Convention for the Protection of Individuals with regard to Automatic Processing of Personal Data, adopted by the Council of Europe in 1981.[14] Specific rights of access to personal information were also provided subsequently by a number of individual statutes: for example, the Access to Personal Files Act 1987[15] and the Access to Health Records Act 1990.[16]

The Data Protection Directive

In 1995 the European Council issued what is generally termed the "Data Protection Directive".[17] This Directive applies not only to automated data[18] but also to certain types of manually stored data,[19] and it confers on the data subject a number of rights. These again include rights of access to personal data. Member States are required to guarantee data subjects the right to obtain from a data controller: 4–004

— confirmation whether personal data about them are being processed;
— information at least as to the purposes of such processing and the recipients or categories of recipients to whom the data are disclosed;

[12] As to the meaning of "automated data," see para 4–012.
[13] Data Protection Act 1984, s.21.
[14] Convention for the Protection of Individuals with regard to Automatic Processing of Personal Data, January 28, 1981, ETS No.108.
[15] Since repealed.
[16] Since repealed.
[17] Council Directive 95/46/EC, [1995] O.J. L281/31.
[18] As to the meaning of "automated data," see para.4–012.
[19] Council Directive 95/46/EC, Art.2(c) and 3(1).

- — the data themselves in an intelligible form, together with any available information as to their source; and
- — knowledge of the logic involved in any automatic processing of data in the case of certain automated decisions.[20]

These rights are to be available to individuals without constraint at reasonable intervals and without excessive delay or expense.[21]

Implementation of the Directive

4–005 Member States were required to implement the Data Protection Directive by October 24, 1998. Implementation in the United Kingdom was by the enactment of the Data Protection Act 1998, which was brought fully into force on March 1, 2000. In the light of its origins in Directive 95/46/EC, much of the Data Protection Act 1998 must be construed in a purposive fashion, having regard to the aims of the Directive.[22] Nevertheless, both the Data Protection Directive and the Data Protection Act 1998 were principally directed at automated data: neither applied to certain types of manually stored data. The right of access bestowed by the Freedom of Information Act 2000 is indifferent to the distinctions between manually stored data and automated data. The unit of disclosure and of exemption is "information",[23] with exemptions being based either upon the likelihood of an identified harm resulting from disclosure or on the basis of the information falling within a class description.[24] In order to maintain parity between the scope of the disclosure right bestowed by each Act, it was necessary to amend the Data Protection Act 1998 in order to make it apply to all manually stored data held by a public authority.[25]

[20] Council directive 95/46/EC, Art.12(a).

[21] *ibid.*, Art.12(a)

[22] *Campbell v Mirror Group Newspapers Ltd* [2002] EWCA Civ 1373; [2003] 2 W.L.R. 80; [2003] 1 All E.R. 224 at [97]; *Durant v Financial Services Authority* [2003] EWCA 1746 at [3]; *R (on the application of Lord) v Secretary of State for the Home Department* [2003] EWHC 2073 (Admin) at [90]–[93].

[23] Defined to mean "recorded information": Freedom of Information Act 2000, s.84; Freedom of Information (Scotland) Act 2002, s.73.

[24] See paras 14–014 to 14–022 below.

[25] Thus, the Freedom of Information Act 2000, ss.68–73 effected the following amendments to the Data Protection Act 1998: (1) the definition of "data" was enlarged to include all recorded information held by a public authority; (2) "held" was given the same meaning as in the Freedom of Information Act 2000; (3) "public authority" was given the same meaning as in the Freedom of Information Act 2000; (4) a special provision, s.9A, was introduced to deal with unstructured personal data held by public authorities; (5) a limited ground of exemption, s.33A, was introduced to protect certain types of manual data held by a public authority; and (6) a further exemption, s.35A, was introduced to protect from disclosure where that was required to avoid an infringement of the privileges of either House of Parliament. These provisions are to come into force at the latest by November 30, 2005, with the indication being that they are to come into force at the beginning of that year: Freedom of Information Act 2000, s.87(3).

Personal information about third parties

Where an applicant seeks information that includes personal information about a third party, the request is governed by the Freedom of Information Act 2000 and not the Data Protection Act 1998. The principles relating to the disclosure of such information is considered in greater detail elsewhere in this work.[26] In broad terms, the provisions of the Freedom of Information Act 2000 are designed to ensure that such information is only provided under that Act if it could have been disclosed under the Data Protection Act 1998 both to the data subject and to the person making the request. Thus, information is exempt from disclosure under the Freedom of Information Act 2000 if: 4–006

(a) disclosure to a member of the public would breach any of the data protection principles;[27]
(b) in the case of most types of personal data[28] disclosure would contravene the individual's right under s.10 of the Data Protection Act 1998 to prevent processing likely to cause damage or distress;[29] or
(c) the information is exempt from the subject access rights of the Data Protection Act 1998.[30]

In Scotland, there are also exemptions under the Freedom of Information (Scotland) Act 2002 in respect of personal census information and a deceased person's health record.[31]

Overriding nature of the access rights

Subject access rights enjoy a general paramountcy over rules preventing disclosure of information. Section 27(5) of the Data Protection Act 1998 provides that, subject only to specific exemptions provided by that Act, the subject access rights[32] have effect notwithstanding any legislative provision or rule of law prohibiting or restricting the disclosure, or authorising the withholding, of information.[33] The Secretary of State does have a power to exempt from the subject access rights information the disclosure of which is subject to such a prohibition or restriction under other legislation, provided that he considers it necessary for safeguarding the interests of the data subject or the rights and freedoms 4–007

26 See paras 24–007 to 24–016.
27 Freedom of Information Act 2000, s.40(2), (3)(a)(i), (3)(b).
28 As to which see paras 3–017 to 3–020 above.
29 Freedom of Information Act 2000, s.40(3)(b).
30 *ibid.*, s.40(4).
31 Freedom of Information (Scotland) Act 2002, s.38(1)(c), (d).
32 Together with the first data protection principle, referred to as the "subject information provisions": Data Protection Act 1998, s.27(2), (5).
33 Data Protection Act 1998, s.27(5).

of any other individual that the prohibition or restriction ought to prevail over the subject access provisions.[34] This paramountcy marks a fundamental difference between the right of access bestowed by the Data Protection Act 1998 and the right of access bestowed by the Freedom of Information Act 2000. The latter Act provides an absolute exemption for information the disclosure of which is prohibited by or under any enactment.[35]

Transitional provisions

4–008 Upon the coming into force of the Data Protection Act 1998 on March 1, 2000, its requirements applied in respect of all personal data being processed by a data controller, unless the data controller could take advantage of transitional exemptions. Certain transitional exemptions are available until October 24, 2001, and a further set is available until October 24, 2007. However, none of the remaining exemptions relates to the subject access rights.[36] There are also transitional provisions in respect of rights of data subjects under the Data Protection Act 1984 that were repealed by the Data Protection Act 1998. By virtue of these provisions, the repeals do not affect the application of the relevant provisions in respect of requests made pursuant to the right of access to personal data prior to the date of repeal;[37] compensation in respect of damage or distress suffered by reason of anything done or not done prior to the date of repeal;[38] and applications to the court for orders for rectification or erasure made before the date of repeal.[39]

Extra-territoriality

4–009 The subject access rights are enjoyed by individuals regardless of their nationality or residence: the application of the Data Protection Act 1998 is determined by reference to the data controller and data themselves.[40] The Act applies:

(1) To data controllers established in the United Kingdom[41] in respect of data processed in the context of that establishment.[42] Establishment in the United Kingdom covers:

[34] Data Protection Act 1998, s.38(1). See further at para.4–076.
[35] Freedom of Information Act 2000, s.44(1)(a); Freedom of Information (Scotland) Act 2002, s.26(a). These provisions are considered in detail in paras 26–015 to 26–025.
[36] Data Protection Act 1998, s.39, Sch.8.
[37] *ibid.*, Sch.14, para.3(1).
[38] *ibid.*, s.39, Sch.14, para.3(4).
[39] *ibid.*, Sch.14, para.3(5).
[40] *ibid.*, s.5. See also Information Commmissioner, *Data Protection Act 1998: Legal Guidance*, para.2.4.
[41] *i.e.* England, Wales, Scotland and Northern Ireland: see Interpretation Act 1978, Sch.1.
[42] Data Protection Act 1998, s.5(1)(a).

— individuals ordinarily resident in the United Kingdom;
— bodies incorporated, and partnerships or unincorporated associations formed, under the law of any part of the United Kingdom; and
— persons who maintain offices, branches or agencies in the United Kingdom through which they carry on any activity, or who maintain a regular practice there.[43]

(2) To data controllers established neither in the United Kingdom nor elsewhere in the European Economic Area, but who use equipment in the United Kingdom for processing data, other than for the purposes of transit through the United Kingdom.[44] A transit exemption means that data merely passing through the United Kingdom, for instance e-mails routed through a United Kingdom server, are not caught by the Act. A data controller has to nominate a representative established in the United Kingdom for the purposes of the Data Protection Act 1998.[45]

Where a data subject with rights under the Data Protection Act 1998 is resident abroad in a country which is a party to the 1981 Convention for the Protection of Individuals with regard to Automatic Processing of Personal Data, the Information Commissioner is under certain obligations to assist that person in exercising his or her subject access rights; for instance, by notifying him or her of the data controller's address and of his or her rights in respect of subject access.[46]

2. THE SCOPE OF THE RIGHTS: PERSONAL DATA

Types of information to which the access right applies

4–010 The access related rights given to an individual by the Data Protection Act 1998 are confined to "personal data" of which that individual is the "data subject".[47] The starting point in considering the access rights under the Data Protection Act 1998 is therefore the concepts of "data", "personal data" and "data subject".

[43] Data Protection Act 1998, s.5(3).
[44] *ibid.*, s.5(1)(b).
[45] *ibid.*, s.5(2).
[46] Data Protection (Functions of Designated Authority) Order 2000 (SI 2000/186), art.4; Convention for the Protection of Individuals with regard to Automatic Processing of Personal Data, arts 8, 13 and 14. In relation to duties to give assistance, see Ch.8.
[47] Data Protection Act 1998, s.7.

Meaning of "data"

4–011 Although it employs the term "data", the Data Protection Act 1998 is essentially concerned with "information". The Act defines "data" to mean information that is processed or stored in particular ways, or by particular bodies.[48] Broadly, the categories of information are:

(1) information which is being processed by equipment operating automatically in response to instructions, or which is recorded with the intention that it should be so processed ("automated data");
(2) information recorded as part of a relevant filing system or with the intention that it should form part of such a system;
(3) information forming part of an accessible record; and
(4) recorded information held by a public authority.[49]

The first two categories of data reflect the coverage of the Data Protection Directive.[50]

Automated data

4–012 So far as automated data is concerned, the Data Protection Directive applies to the processing of data "wholly or partly by automatic means". The definition of "data" under the Data Protection Act 1998 covers not only automated data, but also information recorded with the intention that it should be automatically processed. Automated data is sufficiently wide to include e-mails automatically stored electronically, whether in live, archive or back-up systems, or even in a "deleted" form when they can still technically be recovered.[51] The phrase is also wide enough to include information gathered and automatically processed by website operators.

Information within a relevant filing system

4–013 Certain non-automated or manual filing systems were brought within the scope of the data protection legislation by the Data Protection Act 1998 under the second category of data: information recorded as part of a relevant filing system. A "relevant filing system" is a set of information relating to individuals that is structured, either by reference to individuals or by reference to criteria relating

[48] s.1(1). The Act, wisely, does not attempt to define information.
[49] Data Protection Act 1998, s.1(1).
[50] Council Directive 95/46/EC, Art.3(1).
[51] Information Commissioner, *Subject access to personal data contained in e-mails*, Data Protection Act 1998 Compliance advice.

to individuals, in such a way that specific information relating to a particular individual is readily accessible.[52] Under the definition, in order to qualify as a relevant filing system, not only must the information be structured by reference to individuals or criteria relating to individuals, but it must be structured in such a way that specific information relating to a particular individual is readily accessible. The Court of Appeal has held that it is only to the extent that manual filing systems are broadly equivalent to computerised systems in ready accessibility to relevant information capable of constituting personal data that they are within the system of data protection. Accordingly "relevant filing system" is to be restrictively and proportionately interpreted and is limited to a system:

(1) in which the files forming part of it are structured or referenced in such a way as clearly to indicate at the outset of the search whether specific information capable of amounting to personal data about the individual requesting it is held within the system and, if so, in which files; and
(2) which has as part of its own structure or referencing mechanism, a sufficiently sophisticated and detailed means of readily indicating whether and where in an individual file or files specific criteria or information about the applicant can be readily located.

Therefore it is not enough that a filing system leads a searcher to a file containing documents mentioning the data subject. The file must itself be so structured and/or indexed as to enable easy location within it or any sub-files of specific information about the data subject that he has requested.[53] Thus a set of manual personnel files arranged alphabetically by employee name, each of which relates to a particular individual and contains, in no particular order, every document relating to that individual's employment, would not satisfy the definition. This interpretation is consistent with the Government's view, expressed by Lord Williams of Mostyn during the passage of the Data Protection Bill through Parliament.[54] It also appears to reflect the intentions of the Data Protection Directive itself. The Directive defines the equivalent concept—a "personal data filing system"—as "any structured set of personal data which are accessible according to specific criteria . . . ".[55] Recital 27 makes clear that the Directive is to apply only to filing systems, not to unstructured files, and that individual files, not simply the whole filing system, must be structured according to criteria relating to individuals.[56] The Data Protection Directive also makes clear that the structured set of personal data need not be held in one place: they may be centralised, decentralised or dispersed on a functional or geographical basis.[57] Thus, wage records held in one place and sickness records in another would still be covered.

[52] Data Protection Act 1998, s.1(1).
[53] *Durant v Financial Services Authority* [2003] EWCA Civ 1746 at [34], [45]–[50].
[54] *Hansard*, HL, Vol.587, cols 467–468, March 16, 1998.
[55] Council Directive 95/46/EC, Art.2(c).
[56] *ibid.*, recital 27.
[57] *ibid.*, Art.2(c).

Readily accessible information

4–014 The requirement in the definition of "relevant filing system" that the set of information is structured in such a way that specific information relating to a particular individual be "readily" accessible reflects the reference to "easy" access in recital 27. The legal guidance published by the Information Commissioner offers a suggested approach: to assume that a set of manual information referenced to individuals is caught if it is, as a matter of fact, generally accessible at any time to one or more people within the data controller's organisation in connection with the day-to-day operation of that organisation.[58] Because the definition of data includes information recorded with the intention that it should form part of a relevant filing system, it will include documents that will eventually form part of a structured set, but have not yet been filed: for example an employer's note of a conversation with an employee who phones in sick, intended, eventually, for his or her personnel file. Information not falling within either of the preceding categories is data within the meaning of the Data Protection Act 1998 if it forms part of an accessible record as defined by the Act. There are three specific categories of accessible record:

- health records;
- educational records; and
- accessible public records.[59]

Each is defined in some detail in the Act.[60] Broadly speaking, a health record is a record of information relating to an individual's health made by a health professional, and an educational record is a record of specified information relating a present or former pupil at a maintained or special school. The term health professional includes a wide range of professionals, from doctors, dentists and opticians to clinical psychologists and certain therapists.[61] Accessible public records are defined by reference to particular bodies or authorities. In England and Wales they are: a record of information held by a Housing Act local authority for the purpose of any of its tenancies and a record of information held by a local social services authority for any purpose of its social services functions.[62]

[58] *Information Commissioner, Data Protection Act 1998; Legal Guidance.*
[59] Data Protection Act 1998, s.1(1), s.68.
[60] *ibid.*, ss.68(1)(a), (2), 69 (health record); Data Protection Act 1998, s.68(1)(b), Sch.11 (educational record); *Data Protection Act 1998*, s.68(1)(c), Sch.12 (accessible public record).
[61] *ibid.*, s.69.
[62] *ibid.*, s.68(1)(c), Sch.12, paras 1(a) and 2. In Scotland accessible public records are records of information held by a local authority for any purpose of its tenancies and records of information held by a social work authority for any purpose of specified social work functions: Data Protection Act 1998, s 68(1)(c), Sch.12, paras 1(b) and 4.

Accessible record: jurisprudence

This category of data (and the associated exemption and access provisions dealt with below) has its origins in the decision of the European Court of Human Rights in *Gaskin v United Kingdom*.[63] There an individual had been denied access by a local authority in whose care he had been to certain records relating to him, in order to protect the confidence of individuals who had contributed to those records. The European Court upheld the domestic approach of striking a balance between an individual's right to respect for his private life (and access to the records in question) and the public interest in maintaining the confidence of those who contributed to such records, so as to ensure frankness in such contributions. The provisions of the Data Protection Act 1998 were designed to put that balancing process on a statutory footing. 4–015

Recorded information held by a public authority

The final category of information, "any other recorded information held by a public authority", was introduced by the Freedom of Information Act 2000.[64] Its effect will be that for a public authority the definition of data includes any residual recorded information not falling within the preceding categories. For the purposes of the Data Protection Act 1998, "public authority" has the same meaning as it has under the Freedom of Information Act 2000.[65] Likewise, the reference to information "held" by a public authority is to be construed in accordance with s.3(2) of the Freedom of Information Act 2000.[66] The term "recorded" is not defined.[67] In respect of some public authorities, the Freedom of Information Act 2000 has effect only in relation to specified information.[68] Where that is the case, other information held by the public authority is deemed not to fall within the final limb of the definition of data in the Data Protection Act 1998.[69] However, it seems that such information may still fall within the other limbs of the definition. 4–016

[63] (1989) 12 E.H.R.R. 36.

[64] Data Protection Act 1998, s.1(1); Freedom of Information Act 2000, ss. 68(1), (2), 86, Sch.8 Pt III. For the meaning of "public authority" see paras 7–016 to 7–028 below. The final category will have effect from November 30, 2005.

[65] *ibid.*, s.1(1). For detailed consideration of the meaning of "public authority" see paras 7–016 to 7–028 below.

[66] *ibid.*, s.1(5). For detailed consideration of the meaning of "held" see para.7–008 below.

[67] The reference in the Data Protection Act 1998 to "recorded information" mirrors the Freedom of Information Act 2000, which only applies to recorded information: see the definition of "information" in the Freedom of Information Act 2000, s.84 and in the Freedom of Information (Scotland) Act 2002, s.73.

[68] Freedom of Information Act 2000, s.7, Sch.1. See further paras 7–020 and 7–026.

[69] Data Protection Act 1998, s.1(6).

Personal data: introduction

4–017 The subject access rights only arise in relation to "personal data". Under the Data Protection Act 1998, data are "personal data" if they have two attributes. First, the data must relate to a living individual; and, secondly, it must be possible to identify that individual either from the data themselves or from the data and any other information that is in the possession of the data controller or is likely to come into the controller's possession.[70] In a change from the position under the Data Protection Act 1984, personal data now also includes any expression of opinion about the individual and any indication of the intentions of the data controller or any other person in respect of the individual.[71] This would cover, for example, employee appraisals and assessments of their promotion prospects (provided they fell within the definition of data).[72]

Personal data: first attribute

4–018 Whether data relate to a living individual is, according to the Commissioner, a question of fact depending, in part, on whether a data controller can form a connection between the data and the individual. According to the Court of Appeal, mere mention of the data subject in a document is not necessarily enough—whether the data "relate to" him will depend on where they fall in a "continuum of relevance or proximity" to him. In determining where on that spectrum information falls, it may be helpful to consider both whether the information is biographical in a significant sense—whether it does more than record his involvement in a matter or event with no personal connotations—and whether the focus of the information is the data subject rather than some other person, transaction or event. In short, does the information affect the putative data subject's privacy?[73] Information about the business of a sole trader and about a specific individual in a partnership will be personal information, whereas information solely about a legal entity will not.[74]

Personal data: second attribute, first alternative

4–019 In many circumstances, the second attribute (that it be possible to identify the individual from the data) will be readily satisfied: for example, where the data include the individual's name and address. But the reach of the Act is much broader. Article 2 of the Data Protection Directive defines personal data as

[70] Data Protection Act 1998, s.1(1). See also Information Commissioner, *Data Protection Act 1998: Legal Guidance*, para.2.2.2. For the meaning of data controller see para. 4–023.
[71] Data Protection Act 1998, s.1(1). For the meaning of data controller see para. 4–023.
[72] See also Information Commissioner, *Data Protection Act 1998: Legal Guidance*, para.2.2.6.
[73] *Durant v Financial Services Authority* [2003] EWCA Civ 1746 at [27]–[28].
[74] See also Information Commissioner, *Data Protection Act 1998: Legal Guidance*, para.2.2.1.

information relating to an "identified or identifiable" natural person, and provides that an identifiable person is "one who can be identified, directly or indirectly, in particular by reference to an identification number or to one or more factors specific to his physical, physiological, mental, economic, cultural or social identity".[75] It is clear from recital 14 to the Data Protection Directive that this covers sound and image data relating to the individual. The Information Commissioner has expressed the view that an individual is capable of being identified if the data controller is able to process the data so as to distinguish the data subject from any other individual, and that this would be the case if the data subject could be treated differently from other individuals.[76] Thus, personal data would include, for example, closed circuit television recordings of an individual from which he or she could be visually identified by reference to a photograph, physical description or physical person[77] and many e-mail addresses, such as those including the individual's name and workplace.[78] In the context of the internet, personalised user profiles developed by website operators (*e.g.* through the use of "cookies"), which are capable of being linked to an individual, through his or her name, postal address or e-mail address for example, will also amount to personal data.[79] DNA fingerprints or similar information could also be personal data.

Personal data: second attribute, second alternative

An individual may be capable of being identified not just from the data relating to that individual, but from those data and other information in the possession of, or likely to come into the possession of, the data controller. This limb of the definition will capture data that relate to an individual but from which, without additional information, it is not possible to identify that individual. An obvious example arises in relation to data that relate to an individual who, in that data, is only identified by a number: where the data controller possesses information that ties that number to a named individual (or any other identifier of an individual) that will suffice to render those data "personal data". The identifying information need not be in the possession of the data controller: it is enough that it is likely to come into the posession of the data controller. The Information Commissioner's view is that information may be in the possession of a data controller not simply when it is in his physical control but also, for example, when it is in the physical control of his contracted data processor.[80] It is not clear what information may be said to be "likely to come into the possession of [a] data controller". Recital 26 to the Data Protection Directive provides 4–020

[75] Council Directive 95/46/EC, Art.2(a).
[76] Information Commissioner, *Data Protection Act 1998: Legal Guidance*, para.2.2.3.
[77] See also Council Directive 95/46/EC, recital 14.
[78] Information Commissioner, *Data Protection Act 1998: Legal Guidance*, para.2.2.3.
[79] *ibid.*
[80] *ibid.*, para.2.2.4.

that in order to determine whether a person is identifiable, account should be taken of "all the means likely reasonably to be used" either by the data controller or by any other person to identify the individual.[81] This suggests that it is not simply identification by the data controller that is important, but that identification by any other person would also count. On that basis it would not matter whether the data controller took steps to avoid information coming into his possession, if that information was reasonably likely to be used by a third party to identify the individual. This appears to be beyond the scope of the definition in the Data Protection Act 1998, which is concerned only with identification by the data controller.

Anonymised data

4–021 The Data Protection Act 1998 and the Data Protection Directive do not apply to data anonymised in such a way that the data subject is no longer identifiable.[82] However, care must be taken in anonymising the data. If the data controller simply separates the personal identifiers from the rest of the data, they will remain personal data, because the identifying material will be information in the possession of the data controller. The data controller must get rid of the original data set and the separated identifying material, and in such a way that it is not likely to come into his possession.[83]

Data subject

A data subject is an individual who is the subject of personal data.[84] It appears to follow from the definition of personal data that the data subject must be a
4–022 living individual, and this has been confirmed by the Information Commissioner.[85] In the Data Protection Directive, reference is made to "natural persons" rather than to living individuals.[86] There is no age restriction—children of any age enjoy the subject access rights conferred by the Data Protection Act 1998.

81 Council Directive 95/46/EC, recital 26.

82 *R. v The Department of Health Ex p. Source Informatics Ltd* [2000] 1 All E.R. 786, CA; Directive 95/46/EC, recital 26.

83 Guidance on anonymised data is given in Information Commissioner, *Data Protection Act 1998: Legal Guidance*, para.2.2.5.

84 Data Protection Act 1998, s.1(1). For the meaning of data controller see para.4–023.

85 Information Commissioner, *Data Protection Act 1998: Legal Guidance*, para.2.2.6.

86 Council Directive 95/46/EC, art.2(a).

Data controller

The access rights given to an individual by the Data Protection Act 1998 are rights as against the data controller.[87] A data controller is a person who determines the purposes for which and the manner in which personal data are processed.[88] Where personal data are processed pursuant to an obligation imposed by or under an enactment, the person on whom the obligation to process the data is imposed is the data controller.[89] The definition of data controller follows fairly closely that in the Data Protection Directive.[90] The definition in the Data Protection Directive expressly includes public authorities, but covers all other natural or legal persons, agencies and other bodies.[91] This is in contrast to the Freedom of Information Act 2000, which applies only to public authorities. There may be more than one data controller in respect of the same personal data—the Act makes clear that a data controller may act alone, or jointly or in common with others.[92] 4–023

Data controller: guidance

The Information Commissioner has issued advice on the meaning of "data controller". The view expressed is that where one person determines the purposes for which personal data are processed, but that person delegates responsibility for determining the manner in which they are processed to someone else, it is the person who determines the purposes who is the data controller.[93] In the Commissioner's view, a decision as to the manner in which the data are to be processed is implicit in that determination, and thus determination of the purposes of processing takes precedence in identifying the data controller. 4–024

Processing

Processing is an extremely broad concept under the Data Protection Act 1998. It covers simply obtaining, recording or holding information or data, as well as carrying out any operation or set of operations on it.[94] The carrying out of an operation receives a similarly broad (non-exhaustive) definition, including the organisation, adaptation or alteration of the information or data; its retrieval, 4–025

87 Data Protection Act 1998, s.7.
88 *ibid.*, s.1(1). For the meaning of processing see see para.4–025.
89 *ibid.*, s.1(4).
90 Council Directive 95/46/EC, art.2(d).
91 *ibid.*
92 Data Protection Act 1998, s.1(1).
93 Information Commissioner, *Data Protection Act 1998: Legal Guidance*, para.2.5.
94 Data Protection Act 1998, s.1(1).

consultation, use and disclosure; and its alignment, combination, blocking, erasure or destruction.[95] This reflects the definition of processing in the Data Protection Directive.[96] Recital 14 to the Directive makes it clear that the capture, transmission, manipulation, recording, storage and communication of sound and image data are intended to be covered.[97] For the avoidance of doubt, in relation to personal data, obtaining or recording the data includes obtaining or recording the information to be contained in the data; and using or disclosing the data includes using or disclosing the information to be contained in the data.[98] Given the breadth of these definitions, it is difficult to conceive of an interaction with data that would not amount to processing. That is also the view of the Information Commissioner.[99]

3. THE NATURE OF THE RIGHTS

The four access-related rights granted by the Data Protection Act 1998

4–026 Section 7 of the Data Protection Act 1998 gives an individual four access related rights in respect of personal data of which that individual is the data subject. These are:

(1) to be informed by any data controller whether such data are being processed by or on behalf of the data controller[1];
(2) if so, to be given by the data controller a description of the data, the purposes for which they are being or are to be processed, and the recipients or classes of recipients to whom they are or may be disclosed[2];
(3) to have communicated in an intelligible form the information constituting the personal data and any information available to the data controller as to the source of those data[3]; and
(4) where such data are automatically processed in order to evaluate matters relating to the individual, such as the individual's work performance, creditworthiness, reliability or conduct, and such processing has constituted or is likely to constitute the sole basis for any decision significantly affecting the individual, to be informed by the data controller of the logic involved in that decision-taking.[4]

---

95 Data Protection Act 1998, s.1(1).
96 Council Directive 95/46/EC, art.2(b).
97 *ibid.*, recital 14.
98 Data Protection Act 1998, s.1(2).
99 Information Commissioner, *Data Protection Act 1998: Legal Guidance*, para.2.3.
1 Data Protection Act 1998, s.7(1)(a).
2 *ibid.*, s.7(1)(b).
3 *ibid.*, s.7(1)(c).
4 *ibid.*, s.7(1)(d).

These rights reflect the rights conferred by Art.12(a) of the Data Protection Directive.

First right: to be informed whether data are being processed

This right is straightforward. If personal data about the data subject are not being processed, the data controller may simply inform the applicant of that fact, and the remaining rights are inapplicable. 4–027

Second right: description of data, purposes of processing and recipients

The Data Protection Act 1998 does not make clear the level of detail to which a data subject is entitled under the second right. So far as the description of the data is concerned, the data subject's entitlement under the Data Protection Directive is to information as to "the categories of data concerned."[5] This indicates that the description of the data may be confined to a statement of the categories of data being processed, rather than anything more detailed. The data controller does not have to name the recipients of the data; he may simply describe the categories into which they fall. A recipient is anyone to whom the data are disclosed, including employees or agents of the data controller to whom they are disclosed in the course of processing.[6] However, someone to whom the data are (or may be) disclosed as a result of, or with a view to, a particular inquiry made in the exercise of a legal power is not classed as a recipient.[7] So an employer would have to include, for example, the category of payroll employees to whom an individual's personal data were disclosed, but not the Inland Revenue, if those data were disclosed pursuant to a specific inquiry. 4–028

Third right: information itself and information as to source

This is at the heart of the subject access rights: the right of the individual to have the relevant information itself communicated to him. In addition, the data subject is entitled to be provided with any available information as to the source of the data. This latter, new, right is derived directly from the Data Protection Directive, and adopts the same wording.[8] However, neither the Directive nor the Data Protection Act 1998 provides any indication as to the level of detail to be supplied, nor as to what information is to be classed as "available". Presumably 4–029

---

5 Council Directive 95/46/EC, art.12(a).
6 Data Protection Act 1998, s.70(1).
7 *ibid.*, s.70(1).
8 Council Directive 95/46/EC, art.12(a).

it includes any information in the possession of the data controller—there is no qualification that the information must be readily or reasonably available — but it is not clear whether it also covers information available to the data controller from third parties. Data controllers are not obliged to keep records of this type of information, only to provide such information as is available at the time of the request. Requests for information as to the source of personal data may well involve information relating to other identifiable individuals, and as such will be subject to the third party disclosure provisions.[9]

Fourth right: logic involved in automated decision-taking

4–030 This right, which is derived directly from the Data Protection Directive,[10] is linked to rights to object to such automated decisions being taken about oneself on important matters, and is presumably intended to enable the individual to inform himself in order properly to exercise those rights.[11] The Data Protection Act 1998 does not define the term "logic". This right only applies to data processed automatically in order to evaluate matters relating to the individual such as conduct, reliability and the like. So, for example, a system that rejected job applicants under the age of 18 would not be caught, whereas an automated psychometric testing system would. The decision-taker is not required to provide information as to the logic involved in any decision-taking if the information constitutes a trade secret.[12] Again, "trade secret" is not defined.[13] It appears that it need not be a trade secret of the decision-taker, but may be a trade secret, for example, of the supplier of the automated system. This is the view of the Information Commissioner who has indicated, in relation to the employer/employee relationship, that the decision-taker is not required to disclose matters that either he or the system supplier would reasonably want to keep secret from a competitor on the basis that it provides a significant competitive advantage. That view is consistent with the broad and non-technical approach adopted by the courts in recent years.[14]

---

[9] Data Protection Act 1998, s.7(4), (5). See para.4–041 below.
[10] Council Directive 95/46/EC, art.12(a).
[11] Data Protection Act 1998, s.12; Council Directive 95/46/EC, art.15.
[12] Data Protection Act 1998, s.8(5).
[13] As to its meaning under the Freedom of Information Act 2000, see paras 25–028 to 25–032 below.
[14] See, *e.g. Lansing Linde Ltd v Kerr* [1991] 1 All E.R. 418, at 425 and 435, CA.

4. THE REQUEST

Form of request

A data controller is not obliged to supply any of the information identified above unless he has received a written request.[15] A request sent by electronic means, which is received in legible form and is capable of being used for subsequent reference, satisfies the requirement that the request be in writing.[16] This would appear potentially to cover text messages that can be printed or stored as well as e-mails. 4–031

Requests made by an agent on behalf of adult

It appears that a subject access request may be made not only by a data subject but also by someone acting on the applicant's behalf, such as a solicitor or parent. The Information Commissioner advises data controllers that they should comply with subject access requests made by an agent on behalf of an intellectually capable adult individual if satisfied (*e.g.* by a written authority or power of attorney) that the individual has authorised the agent to make the request.[17] 4–032

Requests by children and mentally incapacitated adults

So far as children are concerned, while the Data Protection Act 1998 does not place any age restriction on the right to exercise the subject access requests, the Information Commissioner's advice is that a data controller who receives a subject access request on behalf of a child will need to judge whether the child understands the nature of the request. If so, then the child is entitled to exercise the right and the data controller should reply to the child. If the child does not understand the nature of the request, someone with parental responsibility, or a guardian, is entitled to make the request on the child's behalf, and receive the response.[18] Similarly, where an adult is incapable of making decisions on his own behalf, an agent acting pursuant to an enduring power of attorney or appointed by the Court of Protection may exercise the subject access rights on his behalf.[19] 4–033

[15] Data Protection Act 1998, s.7(2)(a). Query whether the obligation to submit a written request is a "constraint" contrary to Art.12(a) of the Data Protection Directive.

[16] Data Protection Act 1998, s.64. Unless the contrary intention appears, "writing" includes other modes of representing or reproducing words in a visible form: see the Interpretation Act 1978, s.5.

[17] Information Commissioner, *Data Protection Act 1998: Legal Guidance*, para.4.1.5.

[18] *ibid.*, para.4.1.6.

[19] *ibid.*, para.4.1.7.

Scope of request

4–034 The Data Protection Act 1998 expressly allows an individual in prescribed cases to limit his request to personal data of any prescribed description.[20] A request in relation to one of the first three rights is deemed to include a request in relation to the other two such rights.[21] However, the fourth right (information as to the logic involved in automated decision-taking) is treated separately. A general request is not deemed to include a request in respect of the fourth right unless it shows an express intention to that effect.[22] Similarly, a request in respect of the fourth right is not deemed to include a request in respect of the other rights unless it shows an express intention to that effect.[23]

Particularising the request

4–035 A data controller may ask for further information from a person making a subject access request in certain circumstances, and is not obliged to comply with the request unless he is supplied with that further information.[24] The further information must be reasonably required by the data controller to enable him to satisfy himself as to the identity of the person making the request and to locate the information sought, and the data controller must inform the individual of this requirement.[25] The data controller may need to confirm the authenticity of the request, not by virtue of s.7 itself, but by virtue of other obligations imposed by the Data Protection Act 1998, in particular the obligation to comply with the data protection principles. The further information may again be provided by electronic means.[26]

Unstructured personal data: meaning

4–036 Limits are placed on a public authority's obligations to comply with a subject access request where the request relates to what are termed unstructured personal data.[27] As the name suggests, the concept of unstructured personal data is defined so as to exclude personal data forming part of a structured set.[28]

20 Data Protection Act 1998, s.7(7).
21 Data Protection (Subject Access) (Fees and Miscellaneous Provisions) Regulations 2000 (SI 2000/191), reg.2(1).
22 *ibid.*, reg.2(2).
23 *ibid.*, reg.2(3).
24 Data Protection Act 1998, s.7(3).
25 *ibid.*
26 *ibid.*, s.64.
27 *ibid.*, s.9A. These provisions are to come into force at the latest by November 30, 2005, with the indication being that they are to come into force at the beginning of that year: Freedom of Information Act 2000, s.87(3).
28 Data Protection Act 1998, s.9A.

Accordingly, in order to benefit from the limitations, the personal data must be recorded information held by a public authority not falling within any of the other categories of data (*i.e.* automated data, information recorded as part of a relevant filing system or information forming part of an accessible record).[29] Moreover, the definition of unstructured personal data appears to exclude a broader category of data than is contained in the "relevant filing system" category. That is to say, some recorded information held by public authorities does not benefit from the limitations, even though it does not form part of a relevant filing system. This is because all information recorded as part of a set of information relating to individuals to the extent that the set is structured by reference to individuals or to criteria relating to individuals is excluded, regardless of whether the set is structured in such a way that specific information relating to a particular individual is readily accessible.[30] Provided that the set of information is structured by reference to individuals or criteria relating to individuals, it will not amount to unstructured personal data. This is reflected in the examples given in the explanatory notes to the Freedom of Information Act 2000 (which implemented this provision).[31] While incidental personal information on a policy file or in loose papers would amount to unstructured personal data, a case file about an individual containing correspondence about a number of matters relating to that individual and indexed by reference only to correspondence dates would be structured personal data for these purposes.

Unstructured personal data: significance

Where the subject access request relates to unstructured personal data, a public authority is not obliged to comply with the request unless it contains a description of the data.[32] The authority is therefore allowed to look to the data subject for help in identifying the data. Secondly, if the authority estimates that the cost of complying with the request so far as it relates to the unstructured personal data would exceed the relevant prescribed limit, it is not obliged to comply with it.[33] However, the public authority's obligation to comply with the first access related right, *i.e.* to inform the individual whether unstructured personal data in respect of which the applicant is the data subject are being processed by or on behalf of the data controller, must also be considered separately. Only if the estimated cost of complying with that obligation alone would exceed the appropriate limit is the public authority relieved of the requirement of doing so.[34] When estimating the cost of compliance with the request, the public 4–037

29 *ibid.*, s.1(1).
30 *ibid.*, s.9A(1).
31 Explanatory Notes 215 and 216.
32 Data Protection Act 1998, s.9A(2).
33 *ibid.*, s.9A(3). The limit is prescribed by the Secretary of State for Constitutional Affairs by regulations and he may prescribe different amounts in relation to different cases: s.9A(5).
34 *ibid.*, s.9A(4).

authority must comply with regulations made under the Freedom of Information Act 2000.[35]

Fees

4–038 The general position is that a data controller is not obliged to comply with a subject access request unless he has received such fee as he may require, provided that the fee does not exceed the maximum prescribed by the Secretary of State for Constitutional Affairs.[36] The Secretary of State for Constitutional Affairs also has the power to prescribe cases in which no fee is payable.[37] The normal maximum subject access fee prescribed is currently £10, except in the case of certain educational and health records.[38] In the case of educational records, no fee may be charged at all, unless a permanent copy of the information is to be provided, in which case the maximum fee varies from £1 to £50, according to the type and volume of the copies in question.[39] In the case of health records, the maximum that may be charged for a copy of a non-automated record is £50. Where the request is restricted solely to data forming part of a health record that was created, at least in part, within the forty days preceding the request, no fee may be charged, provided that no permanent copy of the information is to be supplied.[40] Requests may be specifically limited to conform to these circumstances.[41] The view of the Information Commissioner is that higher fees are not justified for access to medical records.[42]

Vexatious requests

4–039 There is a tension between the need to deter vexatious requests and the fundamental right to obtain a copy of personal data. There is no specific power to refuse a request on the basis that it is vexatious.[43] The balance, instead, is struck in the Data Protection Directive by the requirement that individuals should be able to gain access to their data "without excessive expense."[44]

[35] Data Protection Act 1998, s.9A(6), Freedom of Information Act 2000, s.12(5). To date no such regulations have been made.
[36] Data Protection (Subject Access) (Fees and Miscellaneous Provisions) Regulations 2000 (SI 2000/191), reg.5, Sch.
[37] Data Protection Act 1998, s.7(2)(b), (10). See the Data Protection (Subject Access) (Fees and Miscellaneous Provisions) Regulations 2000 (SI 2000/191).
[38] For definition of educational and health records see para.4–014.
[39] Data Protection Act 1998, s.7(2)(b), (10). See the *Data Protection (Subject Access) (Fees and* Miscellaneous Provisions) Regulations 2000 (SI 2000/191).
[40] Data Protection (Subject Access) (Fees and Miscellaneous Provisions) Regulations 2000 (SI 2000/191).
[41] *ibid.*
[42] The Information Commissioner, *Medical Records: Subject Access—Fees for Access* (July 30, 2001).
[43] Contrast the position under the Freedom of Information Act 2000: see paras 12–008 to 12–010.
[44] Directive 95/46/EC, art.12.

Limited request

An individual making a subject access request may, in prescribed cases, specify that his request is limited to personal data of any prescribed description.[45] This provision might in principle overcome a difficulty with the subject access provisions of the Data Protection Act 1984, under which an individual was entitled to be supplied with a copy of the information constituting the personal data.[46] To date the only prescribed circumstances in which a limited request may be made relate to requests for access to health records, designed to enable individuals to confine their requests to those for which no fee may be charged.[47] 4–040

5. THE RESPONSE

Information that also relates to a third party

Where a data controller cannot comply with a subject access request without disclosing information relating to another individual[48] who can be identified from that information,[49] he is not obliged to comply with the request unless that other individual has consented to the disclosure or it is reasonable in all the circumstances for him to comply with the request without such consent.[50] The Data Protection Act 1998 specifies a number of factors to be taken into account in determining whether it is reasonable to comply with the request without such consent.[51] These provisions do not relieve the data controller of the obligation to communicate so much of the information sought by the request as can be communicated without disclosing the identity of the other individual concerned.[52] 4–041

[45] Data Protection Act 1998, s.7(7).

[46] In *R. v Chief Constable of B County Constabulary v Director of the National Identification Service Ex p. R.* Laws J. held that this did not allow the data controller to do anything other than supply all of the information in question (in that case, including information as to a spent conviction). Unreported, November 1997.

[47] Data Protection (Subject Access) (Fees and Miscellaneous Provisions) Regulations 2000 (SI 2000/191), reg.6.

[48] This includes information identifying an individual as the source of the information sought by the request: Data Protection Act 1998, s.7(5).

[49] Another individual can be identified from the information being disclosed if he can be identified from that information, or from that and any other information which, in the reasonable belief of the data controller, is likely to be in, or to come into, the possession of the data subject making the request: Data Protection Act 1998, s.8(7).

[50] Data Protection Act 1998, s.7(4).

[51] *ibid.*, s.7(6).

[52] *ibid.*, s.7(5). See further paras 11–047 to 11–049 below.

Time for compliance

4–042 A data controller is required to comply with a subject access request promptly and in any event within a prescribed period from the day on which he receives the request or, if later, the day on which he has both the required fee and any further information required by him pursuant to s.7(3).[53] The time for compliance mirrors the corresponding provision in the Freedom of Information Act 2000.[54]

Manner of compliance: data at time request received

4–043 The information supplied pursuant to a subject access request must be supplied by reference to the data in question at the time when the request was received, except that it may take account of any subsequent amendment or deletion provided that amendment or deletion would have been made regardless of the receipt of the request.[55] This means that data controllers can carry on with their routine processing despite the receipt of a subject access request. What they cannot do is make special deletions or amendments in response to the request.[56]

Manner of compliance: third subject access right

4–044 Specific requirements are imposed as to the manner of compliance for certain of the access-related rights. In particular, in order to comply with the obligation to communicate to the data subject in an intelligible form the information constituting any personal data of which he is the subject, the data controller must supply the data subject with a copy of the information in permanent form, unless that would be impossible or would involve disproportionate effort or the data subject agrees otherwise.[57] A copy of the information in permanent form would plainly embrace a photocopy, printout or video recording. If any of the information is expressed in terms that are not intelligible without explanation, the copy must be accompanied by an explanation of those terms.[58]

---

[53] Data Protection Act 1998, s.7(8), (10). The Information Commissioner suggests that "promptly" means "as quickly as he can": see *Data Protection Act 1998: Legal Guidance*, para.4.1.

[54] See s.10(1) and Freedom of Information (Scotland) Act 2002, s.10(1). The statutory requirement is dealt with at para.11–051 below.

[55] Data Protection Act 1998, s.8(6). In relation to the possibility of making a request for future information, see para.7–009 below.

[56] See also Information Commissioner, *Data Protection Act 1998: Legal Guidance*, para.4.1.

[57] Data Protection Act 1998, ss.7(1)(c)(i), 8(2). See further paras 11–036 to 11–041 below.

[58] *ibid.*, s.8(2).

Use by data subject of information supplied

The Data Protection Act 1998 imposes no restriction on the use that may be made of information supplied to a data subject pursuant to a subject access request.[59] There is nothing to stop the data subject from using the information supplied in support of proceedings, whether civil, criminal or administrative, against the organisation supplying the information or any other organisation. Nor does the Data Protection Act 1998 prevent a data subject from volunteering the information received under a subject access request to a third party. That being said, the underlying purpose of s.7 is not to assist a data subject, for example, to obtain discovery of documents that may assist him in litigation or complaints against third parties and this is reflected in a narrow interpretation of "personal data".[60] 4–045

Proscription against compulsion to share information received

The Data Protection Act 1998 provides safeguards to prevent individuals from being required to exercise their subject access rights in order to provide information to others, such as employers or prospective employers. These safeguards do not have their origin in the Data Protection Directive. The first set of safeguards relates, broadly speaking, to police, criminal and social security contribution records.[61] It is an offence for a person to require an individual or a third party to supply or produce a record obtained by virtue of a subject access request (a "relevant record") in connection with the individual's recruitment, continued employment or engagement under a contract for the provision of services.[62] The protection is broad, applying not only to employees, but also to contractors and office holders.[63] Indeed, it is not confined to an employment situation. Suppliers of goods, facilities or services are similarly prohibited from requiring individuals or third parties to supply or produce a relevant record as a condition of the provision of such goods, facilities or services.[64] This would prevent, for example, an insurance company from requiring an individual to supply his or her criminal record as a condition of providing insurance cover. However, the prohibitions do not apply to a person who shows that the imposition of the requirement to supply or produce a relevant record was required or authorised by an enactment, a rule of law or a court order, or was, in the particular circumstances, justified as being in the public interest.[65] 4–046

[59] As to the ability of a data controller to impose such a condition, see para.15–019 below.

[60] *Durant v Financial Services Authority* [2003] EWCA Civ 1746 at [27].

[61] Data Protection Act 1998, s.56(1), (2), (6). Social security contribution records are included because of the tendency of some employers to rely on a gap in contributions as evidence of time spent in prison.

[62] *ibid.*, s.56(1), (5).

[63] *ibid.*, s.56(1), (10).

[64] *ibid.*, s.56(2).

[65] *ibid.*, s.56(3). As to the meaning of the "public interest," see para.15–003 below.

Certificates under the Police Act 1997

4–047 These safeguards in the Data Protection Act 1998 go hand in hand with the regime under Pt V of the Police Act 1997 for the provision of certificates as to criminal convictions and records by the Criminal Records Agency.[66] Under that Act, such certificates may only be obtained by the individuals to whom they relate and certain other registered persons.[67] In the absence of s.56 of the Data Protection Act 1998, it would be open to employers to seek to circumvent that regime by requiring individuals to exercise their rights under the Data Protection Act 1998. The Secretary of State may by order add to the categories of information and suppliers thereof that constitute a relevant record.[68] This power addresses the concern that employers or others would find different ways of obtaining information as to individuals' criminal records via their subject access rights. In the light of the provision made by the Police Act 1997 for the supply of criminal record and conviction certificates, the Data Protection Act 1998 makes clear that the public interest defence will not be satisfied merely on the ground that the imposition of a requirement to supply a relevant record would assist in the prevention or detection of crime.[69]

Use of information required: health records

4–048 Safeguards also apply in the case of health records. Any contractual term or condition purporting to require an individual to supply or produce any health record obtained by virtue of a subject access request is deemed to be void.[70] This prevents employers from requiring their employees to obtain and disclose their medical records.

6. DISENTITLEMENT

Multiple and repeat requests

4–049 Where a data controller has previously complied with a subject access request, it is not obliged to comply with a subsequent identical or similar request made by the same individual unless a reasonable interval has elapsed between compliance with the previous request and the making of the current request. This "reasonable interval" limitation reflects the wording of the Data Protection

[66] Data Protection Act 1998, s.75(4); Police Act 1997, Pt V.
[67] *ibid.*, Police Act 1997, ss.12, 113, 115, 120.
[68] Data Protection Act 1998, s.56(4).
[69] Data Protection Act 1998.
[70] *ibid.*, s.57. As to the meaning of "health record" see para.4–014.

Directive.[71] In determining whether a reasonable interval has elapsed, regard must be had to the nature of the data, the purpose for which they are processed and the frequency with which they are altered.[72]

Excessive cost of compliance

Insofar as a subject access request relates to unstructured personal data,[73] the public authority is not obliged to comply with it if it estimates that the cost of doing so would exceed the relevant prescribed limit.[74] In this context, the public authority's obligation to comply with the first access related right, *i.e.* to inform the individual whether unstructured personal data in respect of which he or she is the data subject are being processed by or on behalf of the data controller, must be considered separately. Only if the estimated cost of complying with that obligation alone would exceed the appropriate limit is the public authority relieved of the requirement of doing so.[75] When estimating the cost of compliance with the request, the public authority must comply with regulations made under the Freedom of Information Act 2000.[76] 4–050

7. EXEMPTIONS

Introduction

Both the Data Protection Directive and the Data Protection Act 1998 set out a series of exemptions.[77] Where an exemption is engaged, the data controller is relieved of the obligation to meet the rights of access of the data subject. This does not prevent the data controller from voluntarily supplying the data subject with the information sought.[78] The exemptions in the Data Protection Act 1998 are largely, but not entirely, mirrored in the Freedom of Information Act 2000. These are considered in detail in Chapters 14–26 of this work. What follows is a brief outline of each of the heads of exemption existing under the Data Protection Act 1998, cross-referenced to the detailed treatment of that exemption. 4–051

[71] Directive 95/46/EC, art.12(a). There is a corresponding provision in the Freedom of Information Act 2000, s.14(2); Freedom of Information (Scotland) Act 2002, s.14(2). See further paras 12–011 to 12–015 below.

[72] Data Protection Act 1998, s.8(4).

[73] As to the meaning of "unstructured personal data", see para.4–036.

[74] Data Protection Act 1998, s.9A(3). The limit is prescribed by the Secretary of State for Constitutional Affairs by regulations and he may prescribe different amounts in relation to different cases:s.9A(5). There is a parallel provision in the Freedom of Information Act 2000, s.13(1); Freedom of Information (Scotland) Act 2002, s.12.

[75] *ibid*, s.9A(4).

[76] *ibid.*, s.9A(6), Freedom of Information Act 2000, s.12(5). To date no such regulations have been made. See para.12–003 below.

[77] Data Protection Act 1998, Pt IV, ss.27–39.

[78] See paras 14–006 to 14–013 below.

The Directive

4–052 The Directive is deemed not to apply to personal data processed by a natural person in the course of a purely personal or household activity.[79] In addition, it provides for exemptions on a number of broad grounds:

— safeguarding of national security, defence and public security;
— the prevention and prosecution of crime and breaches of professional ethics;
— State economic and financial interests;
— certain regulatory functions;
— the protection of the data subject and the rights and freedoms of others.[80]

It provides for specific exemptions in relation to:

— scientific research and statistics;[81] and
— data processed for journalistic, artistic and literary purposes.[82]

These exemptions are on the whole reflected in the Data Protection Act 1998, although some of the exemptions under the Act appear only loosely related, at best, to the permissible exemptions under the Directive.

National security

4–053 Personal data are exempt from the subject access rights if exemption from those rights is required for the purpose of safeguarding national security.[83] As with the Freedom of Information Act 2000, a claim for exemption on the grounds of safeguarding national security may be the subject of a conclusive certificate signed by a Minister of the Crown.[84] A conclusive certificate stands as conclu-

[79] Directive 95/46/EC, art.3(2).

[80] Directive 95/46/EC, arts 3(2), 13(1). Reference to "the rights and freedoms of others" embraces those rights and freedoms conferred or recognised by the European Convention on Human Rights: see *R. (on the application of Lord) v Secretary of State for the Home Department* [2003] EWHC 2073 (Admin) at [91]–[93].

[81] *ibid.*, art.13(2).

[82] *ibid.*, art.9.

[83] Data Protection Act 1998, s.28(1)(b). Detailed treatment of exemption on the grounds of national security is provided at paras 17–003 to 17–040 below. Equivalent provisions are found in the Freedom of Information Act 2000, s.24, and in the Freedom of Information (Scotland) Act 2002, s.31(1). National security is a qualified exemption under the Freedom of Information Act 2000, so that it may be disengaged upon a consideration of the public interest. There is no such potential public interest override where the national security exemption is engaged under the Data Protection Act 1998.

[84] Data Protection Act 1998, s.28(2). Detailed treatment of the effect of a conclusive certificate is provided at paras 14–030 *et seq*. The only Ministers that may issue a certificate are those who are members of the Cabinet or the Attorney-General or the Lord Advocate: Data Protection Act 1998, s.28(10).

sive evidence of the "fact" that exemption from the subject access rights is or at any time was required for the purpose of safeguarding national security.[85] The certificate may identify the personal data to which it applies by means of a general description; it may also be expressed to have prospective effect.[86] The principal effect of a conclusive certificate is to change the right of appeal against a decision to refuse access from one of independent merit review, in which the Information Tribunal makes a fresh decision unconstrained by the original decision, to one in which the Information Tribunal merely determines whether the Minister was reasonable in his decision to issue a certificate.[87] If a data controller claims that the terms of a conclusive certificate employing a general description applies to particular personal data, the certificate is presumed so to apply.[88] That presumption is itself capable of challenge by any party to proceedings before the Information Tribunal, which may determine that the certificate does not apply to the personal data in question.[89]

Crime detection and tax collection

Personal data are exempt from the subject access rights where they are held for the purpose of: 4–054

— crime prevention or detection;[90]
— the apprehension or prosecution of offenders; or
— the assessment or collection of any tax, duty or similar imposition,

[85] A conclusive certificate may also be issued for purpose of defeating any of the other provisions of the Data Protection Act 1998 mentioned in s.28(1).
[86] Data Protection Act 1998, s.28(3).
[87] Appeals against non-certificated claims of exemption under the Data Protection Act 1998 are considered at paras 28–031 to 28–035 below; appeals against certificated exemptions under the Data Protection Act 1998 are considered at paras 4–078 and 28–036 to 28–037. In *Norman Baker MP v Secretary of State for the Home Department* [2001] U.K.H.R.R. 1275 the Data Protection Tribunal (as the Information Tribunal was then known) held that a national security exemption certificate applying effectively a blanket exemption to files held by MI5 was unreasonably wide. A revised form of the certificate was considered by the High Court in *Re Ewing* [2002] All E.R. (D.) 350 (Dec.), where it was held that the criticisms of the Information Tribunal had been addressed: " . . . a general [neither confirm nor deny] policy, in response to requests for personal data, including as to the existence (or non-existence) of personal data, is in principle justifiable and cannot be criticised as unreasonable or unnecessary" (at [60]).
[88] Data Protection Act 1998, s.28(6).
[89] *ibid.*
[90] In *Re Martin* [2002] N.I.Q.B. 67 the High Court in Northern Ireland held that information held by the Health & Social Services Trust obtained by it when investigating allegations of sexual abuse by the applicant represented data processed for the purposes of the prevention or detection of crime. In *R (on the application of A) v Chief Constable of C* [2001] 1 W.L.R. 461; [2001] 2 F.C.R. 431 it was held that non-conviction information following a police vetting enquiry in respect of the applicant's application for the post of head-teacher represented data processed for the prevention and detection of crime.

but only in any case to the extent that such access would be likely to prejudice any such purpose.[91] In order for the exemption to be engaged, a likelihood of prejudice to the exemption is required.[92] Similarly, personal data are exempt from the subject access rights where they are held for the purpose of discharging any statutory function, provided that those data were obtained for that purpose from a person who had them in his possession for any of the preceding purposes.[93] There is a further specific exemption in the case of personal data that consist of a classification applied to the data subject as part of a system of risk assessment operated for the purpose either of tax assessment or collection, or of the prevention or detection of crime involving unlawful claims for payment out of, or unlawful application of, public funds.[94] The exemption applies where the data controller operating the risk assessment system is a government department, a local authority or an authority administering housing benefit or council tax benefit.[95] The data are exempt to the extent to which exemption is required in the interests of the operation of that risk assessment system.[96]

Health information

4–055 The Data Protection Act 1998 does not by its own terms exempt from the subject access rights information relating to the health of a person.[97] Indeed, certain health records are specifically brought within the definition of an "accessible record".[98] Section 30 of the Act does, however, empower the Secretary of State to exempt or modify the subject access rights in relation to personal data consisting of information as to the physical or mental health of the data subject.[99] The Secretary of State has made an order[1] under this power. The order defines three circumstances in which information as to the physical or mental health of the data subject will be exempt from the subject access rights:

[91] Data Protection Act 1998, s.29(1). Equivalent provisions are found in the Freedom of Information Act 2000, s.31(1)(a), (b) and (d), and in the Freedom of Information (Scotland) Act 2002, s.35. These are considered in detail at paras 20–014 to 20–020 below. Law enforcement is a qualified exemption under the Freedom of Information Act 2000, so that it may be disengaged upon a consideration of the public interest. There is no such potential public interest override where the law enforcement exemption is engaged under the Data Protection Act 1998.

[92] As to the meaning of "would be likely to prejudice," see paras 15–012 to 15–020 below.

[93] Data Protection Act 1998, s.29(2). However, the exemption does not apply to personal data held by the Football Membership Authority for the purposes of the national football membership scheme: see the Football Spectators Act 1989, s.5(6).

[94] Data Protection Act 1998, s.29(4).

[95] *ibid.*, s.29(4), (5).

[96] *ibid.*, s.29(4).

[97] Limited exemptions for certain health information exist under the Freedom of Information Act 2000, ss.31(2)(j) and 38(1)(a) and the Freedom of Information (Scotland) Act 2002, ss.35(2)(i) and 39(1).

[98] Data Protection Act 1998, s.68.

[99] *ibid.*, s.30(1).

[1] The Data Protection (Subject Access Modification) (Health) Order 2000 (SI 2000/413).

(1) Where the information is held by a court and it consists of information supplied to it in a report or other evidence given by certain bodies or individuals.[2]

(2) Where application of the rights would be likely to cause serious harm to the physical or mental health or condition of the data subject or any other person.[3] Where the data controller is not a health professional, the controller must consult (or have consulted) the appropriate health professional before withholding information on this ground.[4] However, the obligation to consult does not arise where the data controller is satisfied that the information requested has previously been seen by the data subject or is known to the data subject.[5]

(3) Where a request is made on behalf of the data subject by the person with parental responsibility for the data subject (if the data subject is a child) or by the person appointed by the court to manage his affairs (if the data subject is incapable of doing so) and granting access would disclose information:

   (i) that the data subject had provided in the expectation that it would not be disclosed to the applicant;
   (ii) that was obtained as a result of an examination or investigation to which the data subject consented in the expectation that the information would not be so disclosed; or
   (iii) that the data subject had expressly indicated should not be so disclosed.[6]

Educational records

The Data Protection Act 1998 does not by its own terms exempt from educational records the subject access rights. Educational records[7] are specifically brought within the definition of an "accessible record".[8] But again, s.30 of the 4–056

[2] *ibid.*, art.4. The bodies and persons are: a local authority; a Health and Social Services Board; a Health and Social Services Trust; a probation officer; and other persons who give evidence in the course of any proceedings to which the Family Proceedings Courts (Children Act 1989) Rules 1991, the Magistrates' Courts (Children and Young Persons) Rules 1992, the Magistrates' Courts (Criminal Justice (Children)) Rules (Northern Ireland) 1999, the Act of Sederunt (Child Care and Maintenance Rules) 1997 or the Children's Hearings (Scotland) Rules 1996 apply provided that under those rules the information may be withheld by the court in whole or in part from the data subject.

[3] The Data Protection (Subject Access Modification) (Health) Order 2000 (SI 2000/413), art.5. This is similar to the exemption granted by the Freedom of Information Act 2000, s.38(1)(a) and the Freedom of Information (Scotland) Act 2002, s.39(1). These are considered at paras 23–001 to 23–006 below.

[4] The Data Protection (Subject Access Modification) (Health) Order 2000 (SI 2000/413), art.5(2), 7.

[5] *ibid.*, art.6(2).

[6] *ibid.*, art.5(3)–(4).

[7] Defined in the Data Protection Act 1998, Sch.11.

[8] Data Protection Act 1998, s.68(1).

Act empowers the Secretary of State to exempt or modify the subject access rights in relation to certain sorts of educational information.[9] The Secretary of State has made an order under this power.[10] The order defines three circumstances in which personal data consisting of information constituting an "educational record"[11] are exempt from the subject access provisions:

(1) where the data have been provided to a court in specified proceedings, information that the court may withhold from the data subject[12];
(2) where the disclosure of the data would be likely to cause serious harm to the physical or mental health or condition of the data subject or any other person.[13]
(3) where the request is made on behalf of the data subject by a person with parental responsibility for the data subject (in the case of a child) or by a person appointed by the court to manage the data subject's affairs (in the case of a person incapable of doing so) and the request relates to information as to whether the data subject has been the subject of or may be at risk of child abuse. In such circumstances, the subject access rights do not apply in any case to the extent to which their application would not be in the best interests of the data subject.[14]

These exemptions do not apply to data to which the health exemption applies.[15]

---

[9] *ibid.*, s.30(2)(a). The exemption is restricted to data in respect of which the data controller is the proprietor of, or a teacher at, a school, and which consist of information relating to persons who are or have been pupils at the school. The proprietor of a school is the person or body responsible for its management, generally the governing body: Data Protection Act 1998, s.30(5) and Education Act 1996, s.579.

[10] The Data Protection (Subject Access Modification) (Education) Order 2000 (SI 2000/414).

[11] As defined in the Data Protection Act 1998, Sch.11, para.1.

[12] The Data Protection (Subject Access Modification) (Education) Order 2000 (SI 2000/414), art.4. The proceedings to which it applies are those under the Family Proceedings Courts (Children Act 1989) Rules 1991, the Magistrates' Courts (Children and Young Persons) Rules 1992, the Magistrates' Courts (Criminal Justice (Children)) Rules (Northern Ireland) 1999, the Act of Sederunt (Child Care and Maintenance Rules) 1997 or the Children's Hearings (Scotland) Rules 1996 apply, provided that under those rules the information may be withheld by the court in whole or in part from the data subject.

[13] The Data Protection (Subject Access Modification) (Education) Order 2000 (SI 2000/414), art.5(1). In Scotland, where an education authority receives a request relating to relevant education information it believes to have originated from the Principal Reporter, it must notify the Principal Reporter of that request and may not communicate the information to the data subject unless the Principal Reporter has given his opinion that this ground of exemption (serious harm to the physical or mental health or condition of the data subject or any person) does not apply: art.6. This is similar to the exemption granted by the Freedom of Information Act 2000, s.38(1)(a) and the Freedom of Information (Scotland) Act 2002, s.39(1). These are considered at paras 23–001 to 23–006 below.

[14] The Data Protection (Subject Access Modification) (Education) Order 2000 (SI 2000/414), art.5(2)–(5). This exemption does not apply in Scotland.

[15] The Data Protection (Subject Access Modification) (Education) Order 2000 (SI 2000/414), art.3(2)(a). As to the health exemption, see para.4–055.

Social work records: the power to exempt

The Secretary of State's power to exempt or modify the subject access rights in relation to social work records applies to a much broader category of personal data than that to which the relevant accessible public record provisions apply (*i.e.* information held by a local social services authority for any purpose of its social services functions).[16] It applies to personal data consisting of information processed by government departments, local authorities, voluntary organisations or other bodies designated by the Secretary of State, where that information appears to him to be processed in the course of, or for the purposes of carrying out, social work in relation to the data subject or other individuals.[17] Social work is not defined. The power to exempt is therefore apt to attach to a broader category of records held by public authorities than simply the relevant accessible public records. The power to exempt or modify the subject access provisions is only exercisable where the Secretary of State considers that the application of those provisions would be likely to prejudice the carrying out of social work.[18] 4–057

Social work records: the exemption orders

The Secretary of State has exercised his power of exemption by the making of an order.[19] The order applies to personal data held by certain bodies in connection with certain social services functions.[20] Where the data is held by any such body in connection with any such social service function, they will be exempt: 4–058

(1) Where the information has been provided to a court in specified proceedings, and is information that the court may withhold from the data subject.[21]

---

[16] Data Protection Act 1998, s.68(1)(c), Sch.12. See further s.2 above.
[17] *ibid.*, s.30(4).
[18] *ibid.*, s.30(3).
[19] The Data Protection (Subject Access Modification) (Social Work) Order 2000 (SI 2000/415).
[20] *ibid.*, art.3(1), 4 and the Schedule. In relation to a local authority, it applies to data held: (i) in connection with its social services functions within the meaning of the Local Authority Social Services Act 1970 or any functions exercised by local authorities under the Social Work (Scotland) Act 1968 or referred to in s.5(1B) of that Act, or (ii) in the exercise of other functions but obtained or consisting of information obtained in connection with any of its social services functions. In relation to a local education authority, it applies to data held in the exercise of its functions under s.36 of the Children Act 1989 or Chapter II of Pt VI of the Education Act 1996 so far as those functions relate to ensuring that children of compulsory school age receive suitable education whether by attendance at school or otherwise. It applies to a health authority and an NHS Trust where they have obtained the data from a local authority or local education authority in the above-mentioned circumstances.
[21] The Data Protection (Subject Access Modification) (Social Work) Order 2000 (SI 2000/415), art.3(1), 4 and Sch., para.2. The proceedings to which it applies are those to which the Family Proceedings Courts (Children Act 1989) Rules 1991, the Magistrates' Courts (Children and Young Persons) Rules 1992, the Magistrates' Courts (Criminal Justice (Children)) Rules

(2) Where disclosure of the information would be likely to prejudice the carrying out of social work by reason of the fact that serious harm to the physical or mental health or condition of the data subject or any other person would be likely to be caused.[22] Further, two elements must be satisfied before the second exemption may be relied upon: not only must application of the relevant access rights be likely to cause serious harm to physical or mental health, but this must, in turn, be likely to prejudice the carrying out of social work.[23]

(3) In the case of requests made on behalf of the data subject, where the information was provided by the data subject in the expectation that it would not be disclosed to the person making the request.[24]

The latter two exemptions apply to information processed by a diverse range of authorities and bodies pursuant to a variety of functions specified in the Data Protection (Subject Access Modification) (Social Work) Order 2000.[5] This includes information processed by local authorities in connection with their social services functions, and also, for example, data processed by probation committees, special health authorities and the National Society for the Prevention of Cruelty to Children in connection with specified functions.[26] The social work exemptions do not apply to data to which the health or education exemptions apply.[27]

(Northern Ireland) 1999, the Act of Sederunt (Child Care and Maintenance Rules) 1997 or the Children's Hearings (Scotland) Rules 1996 apply provided that under those rules the information may be withheld by the court in whole or in part from the data subject.

[22] The Data Protection (Subject Access Modification) (Social Work) Order 2000 (SI 2000/415), arts 3(1), 5(1)–(2) and Sch., para.1. This exemption applies only to the second, third and fourth subject access rights: the data subject remains entitled to be informed whether personal data of which he or she is the subject are being processed by the data controller: The Data Protection (Subject Access Modification) (Social Work) Order 2000 (SI 2000/415), art.5(1); Data Protection Act 1998, s.7(1).

[23] The Data Protection (Subject Access Modification) (Social Work) Order 2000 (SI 2000/415), art.5(1). This reflects the qualification to the Secretary of State's exemption power: see footnote above. In Scotland, where a social work authority receives a request relating to relevant social work information it believes to have originated from the Principal Reporter, it must notify the Principal Reporter of that request and may not communicate the information to the data subject unless the Principal Reporter has given his opinion that this ground of exemption (prejudice to social work because of serious harm to the physical or mental health or condition of the data subject or any other person) does not apply: art.6.

[24] The Data Protection (Subject Access Modification) (Social Work) Order 2000 (SI 2000/415), arts 3(1), 5(3)–(4) and Sch., para.1.

[25] *ibid.*

[26] The Data Protection (Subject Access Modification) (Social Work) Order 2000 (SI 2000/415), Sch., para.1.

[27] *ibid.*, art.3(2)(a). As to the health exemption, see para.4–055. As to educational records, see para.4–056.

Prejudice to regulatory activity

Personal data that are held (or otherwise processed) for certain regulatory functions are exempt from the subject access rights to the extent that application of those subject access rights to the data would be likely to prejudice[28] the proper discharge of the regulatory functions.[29] Broadly, the regulatory functions covered by this exemption are: 4–059

(1) statutory, governmental or public functions designed to protect the public against financial loss at the hands of financial services professionals or corporate management,[30] bankrupts[31] or persons authorised to carry on professions or activities[32];
(2) statutory, governmental or public functions designed for protecting charities against misconduct or mismanagement,[33] or for protecting or recovering their property[34];
(3) statutory, governmental or public functions designed for securing the health, safety and welfare of persons at work[35] or for protecting other persons from risks to their health, safety and welfare arising out of the actions of persons at work[36];
(4) the statutory functions of the various ombudsmen[37] designed for protecting members of the public against maladministration by public bodies and failures in services provided by public bodies[38]; and

---

[28] As to the meaning of the word "prejudice" and the phrase "would be likely to prejudice" see paras 15–009 to 15–020 below.
[29] Data Protection Act 1998, s.31.
[30] Data Protection Act 1998, s.31(1), (2)(a)(i), (3). Analogous provisions are contained in the Freedom of Information Act 2000, s.31(2)(d) and the Freedom of Information (Scotland) Act 2002, s.35(2)(d). These are considered in para.20–025 below.
[31] Data Protection Act 1998, s.31(1), (2)(a)(ii), (3). Analogous provisions are contained in the Freedom of Information Act 2000, s.31(2)(d) and the Freedom of Information (Scotland) Act 2002, s.35(2)(d). These are considered in para.20–025 below.
[32] Data Protection Act 1998, s.31(1), (2)(a)(iii), (3). Analogous provisions are contained in the Freedom of Information Act 2000, s.31(2)(d) and the Freedom of Information (Scotland) Act 2002, s.35(2)(d). These are considered in para.20–025 below.
[33] Data Protection Act 1998, s.31(1), (2)(b), (3). Analogous provisions are contained in the Freedom of Information Act 2000, s.31(2)(f)–(h) and the Freedom of Information (Scotland) Act 2002, s.35(2)(f)–(h). These are considered in para.20–025 below.
[34] Data Protection Act 1998, s.31(1), (2)(c), (2)(d), (3).
[35] *ibid.*, s.31(1), (2)(e), (3). As to the meaning of prejudice to health and safety see further paras 23–002 to 23–003 below. Analogous provision are contained in the Freedom of Information Act 2000, s.31(2)(i)–(j) and the Freedom of Information (Scotland) Act 2002, s.35(2)(i)–(j). These are considered in para.20–025 below.
[36] Data Protection Act 1998, s.31(1), (2)(f), (3).
[37] The Parliamentary Commissioner for Administration, the Commissioners for Local Administration, the Health Service Commissioners, the Welsh Administration Ombudsman, the Assembly Ombudsman for Northern Ireland and the Northern Ireland Commissioner for Complaints: Data Protection Act 1998, s.31(4)(a).
[38] Data Protection Act 1998, s.31(4)(b).

(5) the statutory functions of the Director General of Fair Trading[39] designed for protecting members of the public against conduct that may adversely affect their interests by persons carrying on a business, for regulating anti-competitive agreements and for regulating market abuses.[40]

These heads of exemption are considered more extensively elsewhere in this work.[41]

Journalism, literature and art

4–060 Personal data held (or otherwise processed) only for journalistic, artistic or literary purposes ("the special purposes") are exempt from the subject access rights if:

— they are held (or otherwise processed) with a view to the publication of journalistic, literary or artistic material; and
— the data controller reasonably believes both that publication would be in the public interest and that compliance with the subject access rights would be incompatible with the special purposes.[42]

This exemption, which has its origins in art.9 of the Data Protection Directive, is concerned with the balance between the protection of individual privacy and the right to freedom of expression. Thus, in considering whether publication would be in the public interest, the data controller is required to have particular regard to the special importance of the public interest in freedom of expression.[43] This exemption is unlikely to have much application to information held by public authorities.

Information held only for research purposes

4–061 Personal data held (or otherwise processed) only for "research purposes" are exempt from the subject access rights provided that:

---

[39] The Office of Fair Trading on commencement of s.278(1) of, and Sch.25, para.37 to, the Enterprise Act 2002.

[40] Data Protection Act 1998, s.31(5).

[41] See para.26–025 below.

[42] Data Protection Act 1998, ss.32(1) and 31(2). There is no matching exemption in the Freedom of Information Act 2000 or in the Freedom of Information (Scotland) Act 2002.

[43] Data Protection Act 1998, s.32(1)(b). The public interest is treated in greater detail at paras 15–001 to 15–009. In *Campbell v Mirror Group Newspapers Ltd* [2002] EWCA Civ 1373; [2003] 2 W.L.R. 80; [2003] 1 All E.R. 224 it was held that publications detailing a well-known fashion model's drug addiction and attendance at meetings of Narcotics Anonymous were justified in the public interest.

— the data are not held (or otherwise processed) in order to support measures or decisions with respect to particular individuals;
— they are not processed in such a way that substantial damage or distress is, or is likely to be, caused to any data subject; and
— the results of the research or any resulting statistics are not made available in a form which identifies any data subject.[44]

"Research purposes" includes statistical and historical purposes.[45] Personal data are not treated as held otherwise than for research purposes simply because they are disclosed to a person for research purposes, or are disclosed to the data subject or a person acting on his behalf, or are disclosed at the request or with the consent of the data subject or a person acting on his behalf.[46] Further, they are not treated as being so processed where the person making the disclosure has reasonable grounds for believing that one of those circumstances applies.[47]

Manual data relating to Crown employment

Personal data falling within the final limb of the definition of "data", *i.e.* manual data recorded by a public authority,[48] and which relate to personnel matters concerning Crown employment are exempt from the subject access rights.[49] The types of personnel matters concerned include appointments and removals, pay, discipline and superannuation.[50] The exemption covers service in the armed forces, service in any office or employment under the Crown or a public authority, and service in any other office or employment or under any contract for services where the power to take action in respect of such personnel matters rests with Her Majesty, a Minister of the Crown, the National Assembly for Wales, a Northern Ireland Minister or any public authority.[51] This exemption is designed to achieve parity between those who work for public authorities and those who work in the private sector. The view is taken that the former should not have additional rights of access in the employment context merely because of the identity of their employer. **4–062**

[44] Data Protection Act 1998, s.33(1) and (4). There is no matching exemption in the Freedom of Information Act 2000 or in the Freedom of Information (Scotland) Act 2002. Indeed, under those Acts, statistical and "factual" information is expressly taken out of certain of the exemptions: Freedom of Information Act 2000, ss.35(2), 35(4) and 36(4); Freedom of Information (Scotland) Act 2002, ss.29(2) and 29(3).
[45] Data Protection Act 1998, s.33(1).
[46] *ibid.*, s.33(5)(a)–(c).
[47] *ibid.*, s.33(5)(d).
[48] As to which, see para.4–013.
[49] Data Protection Act 1998, s.33A(2). An applicant cannot circumvent the exemption by arranging for another person to request the information under the Freedom of Information Act 2000: see ss.40(2) and (4) of that Act and Freedom of Information (Scotland) Act 2002, ss.38(1)(b) and 38(3). Both are absolute exemptions under those Acts.
[50] Data Protection Act 1998, s.33A(2).
[51] *ibid.*

Information otherwise available

4–063 Where personal data are available to the public independently of the subject access rights, those data are exempt from the subject access rights.[52] This exemption applies to any personal data comprising information which the data controller is statutorily obliged to make available to the public, whether by publishing it or making it available for inspection or by making it available in some other way, and whether on payment of a fee or otherwise, apart from information the data controller is obliged to make available under the Freedom of Information Act 2000.

Parliamentary privilege

4–064 Personal data are exempt from the subject access rights if the exemption is required for the purpose of avoiding an infringement of the privileges of either House of Parliament, *i.e.* Parliamentary Privilege.[53]

Legal professional privilege

4–065 Personal data are exempt from the subject access rights if the data comprise information in respect of which a claim to legal professional privilege, or, in Scotland, confidentiality of communications, could be maintained in legal proceedings.[54]

Domestic purposes

4–066 Personal data processed by an individual only for the purposes of the individual's personal, family or household affairs, including recreational purposes, are exempt from the subject access rights.[55] This exemption is, or at least should be, unlikely to have much application to information held by public authorities.

[52] Data Protection Act 1998., s.34. The analogous provisions are the Freedom of Information Act 2000, s.21(1) and the Freedom of Information (Scotland) Act 2002, s.25(1). These exemptions are considered further in para.16–001 to 16–005 below.

[53] Data Protection Act 1998, s.35A. The analogous provision is the Freedom of Information Act 2000, s.34. There is no analogous provision in the Freedom of Information (Scotland) Act 2002. These exemptions are considered further in para.21–001 to 21–010 below.

[54] Data Protection Act 1998, s.37, Sch.7, para.10. The analogous provisions are the Freedom of Information Act 2000, s.42(1) and Freedom of Information (Scotland) Act 2002, s.36(1). These exemptions are considered further in para.21–011 to 21–020 below.

[55] Data Protection Act 1998, s.36.

Confidential references

Personal data are exempt from the subject access rights if they consist of a reference given (or to be given) in confidence[56] by the data controller for the purposes of the education, training or employment of the data subject; his or her appointment to any office; or the provision by him or her of any service.[57] It is notable that this exemption applies only to references given or to be given by the data controller. If the data controller has on file references provided by a previous employer, they do not fall within the scope of the exemption. However, the data controller may, for example, decline to reveal the identity of the author of the reference, pursuant to s.7(4) and (5). 4–067

Judicial appointments and honours

Personal data are exempt from the subject access rights where they are held (or otherwise processed) for the purposes of assessing a person's suitability for judicial office or the office of Queen's Counsel, or for the purposes of the conferring by the Crown of any honour or dignity.[58] 4–068

Crown employment and Crown or Ministerial appointments

The Data Protection Act 1998 confers a power on the Secretary of State to exempt from the subject access rights personal data processed for the purposes of assessing a person's suitability for Crown employment or appointment to any office by Her Majesty, a Minister of the Crown or a Northern Ireland department.[59] This power has been exercised in relation to a variety of Crown appointments, including archbishops, bishops and certain other clergy; Lord-Lieutenants; Masters of certain Cambridge colleges; the Provost of Eton; the Poet Laureate and the Astronomer Royal.[60] 4–069

[56] As to the meaning of information given "in confidence," see paras 25–001 to 25–027 below. The Freedom of Information Act 2000, s.41(1) and the Freedom of Information (Scotland) Act 2002, s.36, provide a general exemption for information acquired in confidence. The Freedom of Information Act 2000, s.27(3) and the Freedom of Information (Scotland) Act 2002, s.32(1)(b) also deal with certain other information acquired by a public authority in confidence: see para.18–012 to 18–013 below.

[57] Data Protection Act 1998, s.37; Sch.7, para.1.

[58] *ibid.*, s.37; Sch.7, para.3. An applicant cannot circumvent the exemption by arranging for another person to request the information under the Freedom of Information Act 2000: see ss.40(2) and (4) of that Act and Freedom of Information (Scotland) Act 2002, ss.38(1)(b) and 38(3). Both are absolute exemptions under those Acts.

[59] Data Protection Act 1998, s.37; Sch.7, para.4.

[60] The Data Protection (Crown Appointments) Order 2000, SI 2000/416.

Armed forces

4–070 Personal data are exempt from the subject access rights in any case to the extent to which the application of those provisions would be likely to prejudice the combat effectiveness of any of the armed forces of the Crown.[61]

Management forecasts

4–071 Personal data processed for the purposes of management forecasting or management planning to assist the data controller in the conduct of any business or other activity are exempt from the subject access rights in any case to the extent to which the application of those provisions would be likely to prejudice the conduct of that business or activity.[62]

Corporate finance

4–072 There is an exemption in relation to personal data processed for the purposes of, or in connection with, a corporate finance service.[63] The concept of a "corporate finance service" is derived from the EC Directive on investment services in the securities field.[64] It covers certain activities relating to issues of specified instruments, as well as the provision of advice to undertakings on matters such as capital structure, industrial strategy and mergers.[65] Where personal data are processed for the purposes of, or in connection with, a corporate finance service provided by a relevant person,[66] the data are exempt from the subject access rights to the extent to which the application of those provisions could affect the price of any specified instrument (whether it already exists, or is to be or may be created).[67] This limb of exemption also extends to circumstances in which the data controller reasonably believes that the price of such an instrument could be so affected.[68] Such data are also exempt if exemption is required to

---

[61] Data Protection Act 1998, s.37, Sch.7, para.2. The analogous provisions are the Freedom of Information Act 2000, s.26(1), and the Freedom of Information (Scotland) Act 2002, s.31(4). These are qualified exemptions under the FOI Acts. These exemptions are considered in paras 17–051 to 17–059 below. As to the meaning of the word "prejudice" and the phrase "would be likely to prejudice" see paras 15–009 to 15–020 below.

[62] Data Protection Act 1998, s.37, Sch.7, para.5. There is no analogous provision under either the Freedom of Information Act 2000 or the Freedom of Information (Scotland) Act 2002. As to the meaning of the word "prejudice" and the phrase "would be likely to prejudice" see paras 15–009 to 15–020 below.

[63] Data Protection Act 1998, s.37, Sch.7, para.6.

[64] Council Directive 93/22/EEC. See Data Protection Act 1998, Sch.7, para.6(3).

[65] Data Protection Act 1998, Sch.7, para.6(3).

[66] Defined in Data Protection Act 1998, Sch.7, para.6(3).

[67] Data Protection Act 1998., Sch.7, para.6(1)(a)(i).

[68] *ibid.*, Sch.7, para.6(1)(a)(ii).

safeguard an important economic or financial interest of the United Kingdom.[69] The Secretary of State has a power to specify matters to be taken into account in determining whether exemption on the latter ground is required, or circumstances in which exemption is (or is not) to be taken to be required.[70] This power has been exercised in relation to personal data to which the application of the subject information provisions could affect decisions whether to deal in, subscribe for or issue instruments or decisions which are likely to affect any business activity.[71] In such cases, the matter to be taken into account is the inevitable prejudicial effect on the orderly functioning of financial markets or the efficient allocation of capital within the economy resulting from the application of the subject access rights.[72]

Negotiations

Personal data comprising records of the data controller's intentions in relation to any negotiations with the data subject are exempt from the subject access rights in any case to the extent to which the application of those provisions would be likely to prejudice those negotiations.[73] 4–073

Examination marks and scripts

A group of exemptions and modifications relates to examination marks and scripts. Examination scripts, that is to say personal data consisting of information recorded by candidates during an academic, professional or other examination,[74] are exempt from the subject access rights.[75] Those rights are modified in relation to examination marks or other information processed for the purpose of determining examination results, or of enabling those results to be determined, or in consequence of their determination.[76] The modifications prevent a data subject from using his or her subject access rights to obtain examination results before they are announced. They achieve this by extending the period for compliance with a subject access request.[77] 4–074

---

69 *ibid.*, Sch.7, para.6(1)(b).
70 *ibid.*, Sch.7, para.6(2).
71 Data Protection (Corporate Finance Exemption) Order 2000, SI 2000/184, art.2(3).
72 *ibid.*, art.2.
73 Data Protection Act 1998, s.37, Sch.7, para.7. As to the meaning of the word "prejudice" and the phrase "would be likely to prejudice" see paras 15–009 to 15–020 below.
74 Data Protection Act 1998, Sch.7, para.9(1).
75 *ibid.*, s.37, Sch.7, para.9.
76 *ibid.*, para.8(1), (5).
77 *ibid.*, para.8.

Self-incrimination

4–075 The privilege against self-incrimination is preserved by the Data Protection Act 1998. A person is not required to comply with a subject access request (or order under s.7) to the extent that to do so would, by revealing evidence of the commission of any offence (other than an offence under the Data Protection Act 1998) expose him to proceedings for that offence.[78] Furthermore, information disclosed by a person in compliance with such a request or order is not admissible against him in proceedings for an offence under the Data Protection Act 1998.[79]

Disclosure prohibited by other legislation

4–076 In addition to the exemptions conferred by the Data Protection Act 1998 itself, there are additional exemptions from the subject access rights made pursuant to a further general power of exemption conferred on the Secretary of State by the Act in respect of information the disclosure of which is already prohibited or restricted by other legislation. The Secretary of State may exempt personal data consisting of such information, where he considers it necessary for safeguarding the interests of the data subject or the rights and freedoms of any other individual that the prohibition or restriction should prevail over the subject access rights.[80] Pursuant to this power, there are exemptions in respect of certain information relating to human fertilisation and embryology,[81] adoption records and reports,[82] statements of special educational needs[83] and parental order records and reports.[84]

[78] *ibid.*, s.37, Sch.7, para.11(1).
[79] *ibid.*, para.11(2).
[80] *ibid.*, s.38(1).
[81] The Data Protection (Miscellaneous Subject Access Exemptions) Order 2000, SI 2000/419, art.2, Sch., Pt I.
[82] *ibid.*, art.2, Sch., Pt II(a), III(a), IV(a) as amended by the Data Protection (Miscellaneous Subject Access Exemptions) (Amendment) Order 2000, SI 2000/1865. In Scotland information provided by a Principal Reporter for a children's hearing is also exempted: The Data Protection (Miscellaneous Subject Access Exemptions) Order 2000, SI 2000/419, art.2, Sch., Pt III(b).
[83] The Data Protection (Miscellaneous Subject Access Exemptions) Order 2000, SI 2000/419, art.2, Sch., Pt II(b), III(c) (record of special educational needs in Scotland), IV(b).
[84] *ibid.*, art.2, Sch., Pt II(c), III(d), IV(c).

8. APPEALS

Ordinary appeals

Appeals under the Data Protection Act 1998 are considered in detail in Chapter 28 below.[85] In summary, where no national security certificate has been issued in respect of the data sought, the dissatisfied applicant may appeal to the High Court or a county court or, in Scotland, to the Court of Session or the sheriff against any failure to comply with a subject access request.[86] There is no provision or requirement for the dissatisfied applicant first to seek a re-consideration by the data controller of the decision. The question for the court on such an appeal is whether the data controller has failed to comply with the request in contravention of the provisions of s.7 of the Data Protection Act 1998.[87] In other words, the right of appeal involves the court considering afresh the applicability of any exemption, unfettered by the decision of the data controller: it is not a review of the reasonableness of the data controller's decision or of the methodology applied by the data controller in reaching the appealed decision. However, where the data controller itself is required to make an assessment of reasonableness—*e.g.* the reasonableness of complying with a subject access request without the consent of a third party about whom information will necessarily be disclosed—the court's role is not routinely to "second-guess" the merits of the data controller's decision, rather, ordinarily, to carry out a review of its reasonableness based on anxious scrutiny.[88] To this end, the court is entitled to require the data controller to make available to the court any information held (or otherwise processed) by or on behalf of the data controller.[89] Where the court does require the data controller to make available to it any such information, the court is not permitted to disclose to the applicant or his representive the information made available pending the determination of the appeal 4–077

[85] See paras 28–031 to 28–040 below. Under the Data Protection Directive, Member States are required to provide individuals with a right to a "judicial remedy" for any breach of the rights guaranteed to them: Directive 95/46/EC, art.22. The rights of appeal are compliant with the Human Rights Act 1998: *MG v United Kingdom* [2002] 3 F.C.R. 289; (2003) 36 E.H.R.R. 3; (2003) 13 B.H.R.C. 179/ (However, the European Court found a violation of Art.8 of the ECHR from 1995 to March 1, 2000 prior to the coming into force of the Data Protection Act 1998.) See further paras 1–029 to 1–037 above.

[86] Data Protection Act 1998, s.15(1).

[87] *ibid.*, s.7(9). As the applicant's entitlement under s.7(1) is "subject to the following provisions of [ss.7,] 8, 9 and 9A" of the Act, the court will have jurisdiction to consider whether the procedural requirements set out in those sections have been met in order to determine whether the failure to comply with the applicant's request is, in fact, in contravention of the applicant's entitlement.

[88] *Durant v Financial Services Authority* [2003] EWCA Civ 1746 at [58]–[61].

[89] The information that may be sought is not expressly limited to that answering the terms of the request.

in the applicant's favour.[90] The court has a "general and untrammelled" discretion whether to order compliance with the request.[91]

National security certificate appeals

4–078 Where a national security certificate has been issued certifying in respect of some or all of the data sought that exemption from the subject access rights[92] is, or at any time was, required for the purpose of safeguarding national security, then the certificate will be conclusive evidence of that "fact".[93] A national security certificate effectively removes the right of a merit review to the extent that it relates to the data sought. In its place, there are two rights of appeal to the Information Tribunal:

(1) A person directly affected by the issuing of conclusive certificate may appeal against the reasonableness of the decision to issue the conclusive certificate.
(2) There is a right of appeal as to the applicability of a national security certificate to particular data.

Procedure on appeals

4–079 The procedure on appeals is considered in detail in Chapter 28 below.[94] In brief terms, ordinary appeals are governed by the rules of the court in which the appeal is heard.[95] Both sorts of national security appeals are governed by a special regime, which is shared with national security appeals under the Freedom of Information Act 2000.[96]

---

[90] Data Protection Act 1998, s.15(2).
[91] *Durant v Financial Services Authority* [2003] EWCA Civ 1746 at [74]; *R. (on the application of Lord) v Secretary of State for the Home Department* [2003] EWHC 2073 (Admin) at [160].
[92] Whether specifically or as part of any of the provisions mentioned in s.28(1) of the Data Protection Act 1998.
[93] Data Protection Act 1998, s.28(2). A certificate may identify the personal data to which it applies by means of a general description; and it may be expressed to have prospective effect: Data Protection Act 1998, s.28(3). Conclusive certificates are considered further in paras 14–030 *et seq*.
[94] See paras 28–033 and 28–037 below.
[95] The court has special powers to call for the information that is the subject of the request and certain other information: see para.4–077.
[96] Data Protection Act 1998, s.28(12) and Sch.6. In relation to the Freedom of Information Act 2000, s.60(1) and (4). The Freedom of Information (Scotland) Act 2002 gives no express right of review in relation to the decision to issue a conclusive certificate, whether issued on national security grounds (s.31(2)) or on exceptional sensitivity grounds (s.52(2)).

9. ENFORCEMENT

Introduction

Enforcement under the Data Protection Act 1998 is considered in depth together with enforcement under the Freedom of Information Act 2000 in Chapter 29 below. What follows here is a brief outline of enforcement process under the Data Protection Act 1998. 4–080

Enforcement notice

In addition to a dissatisfied applicant appealing to a court against against any failure to comply with a subject access request,[97] the subject access rights may also be enforced by the Information Commissioner.[98] The Commissioner has power to issue an enforcement notice where she is satisfied that a data controller has contravened any of the data protection principles.[99] The sixth data protection principle requires personal data to be processed in accordance with the rights of data subjects under the Data Protection Act 1998, and it is a breach of that principle to fail to supply information in accordance with s.7.[1] Thus, failure to comply with a subject access request may be the subject of enforcement action by the Commissioner, who may issue a notice requiring the data controller to comply with the request.[2] Failure to comply with an enforcement notice is an offence, subject to a defence of due diligence.[3] The Commissioner's enforcement powers are, however, restricted in the case of processing for journalistic, artistic and literary purposes.[4] 4–081

Request for assessment

A data subject who is, or believes that he is, directly affected by any personal data processing may also request the Information Commissioner for an assessment whether it is likely or unlikely that such processing is being carried out in compliance with the provisions of the Data Protection Act 1998.[5] This, too, will include an assessment of whether it is likely that a data controller is acting in 4–082

---

[97] See para.4–077.

[98] Where a national security certificate has been issued, none of the enforcement provisions in Part V (ss.40–50) of the Act may be exercised: Data Protection Act 1998, s.28(11). This does not contravene the Human Rights Act 1998: *Re Ewing* [2002] All E.R. (D.) 350 (Dec.) [62–67].

[99] Data Protection Act 1998, s.40(1).

[1] *ibid.*, Sch., Pt I and Pt II, para.8(a).

[2] *ibid.*, s.40(1).

[3] *ibid.*, s.47.

[4] *ibid.*, s.46.

[5] *ibid.*, s.42.

breach of the subject access rights, since, if so, he would not be processing personal data in compliance with the sixth data protection principle.[6] Having received such a request, the Information Commissioner may serve an information notice on the data controller where the Commissioner reasonably requires information in order to make the assessment.[7] Failure to comply with an information notice is an offence, subject to a defence of due diligence.[8]

Compensation

4–083 Where a data controller contravenes any of the requirements of the Data Protection Act 1998, an individual who suffers damage or distress as a result is entitled to be compensated by the data controller.[9] The right to compensation for distress only arises if the individual also suffers damage by reason of the contravention, or if the contravention relates to the processing of personal data for journalistic, artistic or literary purposes.[10] It is a defence to a claim for damages for the data controller to prove that he took such care to comply with the requirement concerned as was reasonably required in all of the circumstances.[11] This appears to be somewhat more generous than the defence for which the Data Protection Directive provides, namely that the data controller was not responsible for the event giving rise to the damage.[12] The right to compensation is conferred only on individuals.[13] Compensation is awarded by the courts.

Rectification and destruction

4–084 The court's powers to order the rectification, blocking, erasure or destruction of inaccurate personal data generally are outside the scope of this work. However, the court has a specific power to order such rectification, blocking, erasure or destruction following a contravention of any of the requirements of the Data Protection Act 1998, including the subject access rights, in respect of any personal data.[14] It may, on an application by the data subject, order the data controller to rectify, block, erase or destroy the personal data in question if it is satisfied both that the data subject has suffered damage by reason of the contravention, in circumstances entitling him to compensation under s.13, and that there is a substantial risk of further contravention in respect of those data in

[6] This is consistent with the guidance given by the Information Commissioner: *Data Protection Act 1998: Subject Access Rights and Third Party Information*, (March 2000), para.3.

[7] Data Protection Act 1998, s.43.

[8] *ibid.*, s.47.

[9] *ibid.*, s.13. See also Directive 95/46/EC, art.23.

[10] *ibid.*, ss.3 and 13(2).

[11] *ibid.*, s.13(3).

[12] Directive 95/46/EC, art.23(2).

[13] Data Protection Act 1998, s.13(1) and (2).

[14] *ibid.*, s.14(4).

such circumstances.[15] Moreover, the court may additionally, if it considers it reasonably practicable, order the data controller to notify third parties to whom the data have been disclosed of their rectification, blocking, erasure or destruction.[16] The question of reasonable practicability is to be assessed, in particular, having regard to the number of persons who would have to be notified.[17]

Failure to comply with enforcement or information notice

It is not an offence for a data controller to fail to comply with a subject access request in itself. However, as noted above, it is an offence for him to fail to comply with an enforcement notice that orders him to comply with such a request[18] or to fail to comply with an information notice issued by the Commissioner in relation to such a request.[19] 4–085

Unlawful obtaining of personal data

It is an offence knowingly or recklessly to obtain or disclose personal data, or to procure their disclosure, without the consent of the data controller.[20] It appears that this applies as much to the data subject as to any other person: the data subject must obtain access to his personal data by exercising his rights under s.7. It is not an offence if the obtaining or disclosure was necessary for the prevention or detection of crime; was required or authorised by law or was reasonably believed to be; if the person obtaining or disclosing the data reasonably believed that the data controller would, in the circumstances, have consented; or if the obtaining or disclosure was justified as being in the public interest.[21] 4–086

Disclosure by Commissioner or Commissioner's staff

It is an offence for the Commissioner, or anyone who has worked for her or on her behalf, knowingly or recklessly[22] to disclose any information obtained for the purposes of the Data Protection Act 1998 which relates to an identifiable 4–087

---

15 Data Protection Act 1998.
16 *ibid.*, s.14(5).
17 *ibid.*, s.14(6).
18 *ibid.*, ss.40(1), 47.
19 *ibid.*, s.47.
20 *ibid.*, s.55(1). On "knowingly and recklessly," see n.18.
21 *ibid.*, s.55(2).
22 As to a body vicariously acting "knowingly and recklessly", see *Information Commissioner v London Borough of Islington* [2002] EWHC 1036; [2003] B.L.G.R. 38, where it was held that the London Borough of Islington could properly be convicted of having knowingly and recklessly contravened the proscription against holding personal data without a current registration: it was

individual or business and which is not already within the public domain, unless he or she has lawful authority to make such a disclosure.[23] A disclosure is made with lawful authority if the data subject or person carrying on the business consents; if it was made pursuant to or for the purposes of certain statutory functions or obligations, or of criminal or civil proceedings; or if it was necessary in the public interest, having regard to the rights, freedoms and legitimate interests of others.[24]

Enforced subject access

4-088 As noted above, it is an offence for a person to require someone to supply him with certain records such as police and criminal records in connection with his recruitment, employment or retention under a contract of services.[25] This prevents individuals from being forced to exercise their subject access rights in such circumstances.

Prosecutions and penalties

4-089 Criminal proceedings for an offence under the Data Protection Act 1998 may only be brought by the Commissioner or with the consent of the Director of Public Prosecutions.[26] For all offences under the Data Protection Act 1998 the prescribed punishment, whether on summary conviction or on conviction on indictment, is a fine.[27] There are powers of entry and inspection under the Data Protection Act 1998.[28]

not necessary to show that the individual officer who accessed and used the data had acted recklessly. See also *Data Protection Registrar v Amnesty International* [1995] Crim. L.R. 633.

[23] Data Protection Act 1998, s.59(1), (3).
[24] *ibid.*, s.59(2).
[25] *ibid.*, s.56. See para.4–045.
[26] *ibid.*, s.60(1).
[27] *ibid.*, s.60(2), (3).
[28] *ibid.*, s.50, Sch.9.

CHAPTER 5

Other Domestic Rights of Access

1. THE OPEN GOVERNMENT CODE OF PRACTICE

The Open Government Code of Practice

5–001 The Open Government Code of Practice of Access to Government Information ("the Code") was published in 1993 and revised in 1997 and 1998.[1] The Code applies to bodies falling within the jurisdiction of the Parliamentary Commissioner for Administration, and it is he who enforces the Code.[2] These bodies include almost all central government departments and their agencies, as well as many other public bodes. The Code contains a non-statutory, discretionary regime. It does not itself confer rights of access to information of any kind upon any person or class of person. Nor can it override any statutory prohibitions upon the release of information or documents. Where information that falls, in principle, within the scope of the Code is also available pursuant to a statutory right of access, that right takes precedence and the release of the information in question will be governed thereby.[3] In particular, the Code expressly states that it is not intended to override statutory provisions on access to public records, whether over or under 30 years old. The reason for this lies in the fact that the Ombudsman is not required, under s.12(3) of the Parliamentary Commissioner Act 1967, to question the merits of a decision if it is taken without maladministration by a government department or other body in the exercise of a discretion vested in it; and decisions made in England and Wales with respect to public records by the Lord Chancellor, or in Scotland and Northern Ireland by their Secretary of State are such discretionary decisions.[4]

The Code's five main commitments

5–002 The Code's five main commitments are to supply facts and analysis with major policy decisions; to open up internal guidelines about departments' dealings with the public; to supply reasons with administrative decisions; to provide

[1] The Cabinet Office has also published *Open Government Code of Practice on Access to Government Information: Guidance on Interpretation*, 2nd ed., 1997.
[2] Code of Practice, paras 3 and 6.
[3] Code of Practice, para.8. The bodies in question are listed in Sch.2 to the Parliamentary Commissioner Act 1967.
[4] Code of Practice, para.9.

information about public services, what they cost, targets, performance, complaints and redress; and to respond to requests for information.

The purpose and aims of the Code

The Code is intended to give effect to the government's stated policy of extending access to official information. The approach to the release of information that it embodies rests on an explicit assumption that information should be disclosed, except where its release would not be in the public interest.[5] Cases where the release of information would not be in the public interest are described in Pt II of the Code. Exemptions under the Code may therefore be seen as the articulation of those circumstances where it would not be in the public interest (at least in the view of the Cabinet Office) to disclose information. The Code has three aims, subsidiary to its overall purposes.[6] These are: to improve policy-making and the democratic process by extending access to the facts and analyses which provide the basis for the consideration of proposed policy; to protect the interests of individuals and companies by ensuring that reasons are given for administrative decisions, except where there is statutory authority or established convention to the contrary; and to support and extend the principles of public service established by the Citizen's Charter. 5–003

Protection of privacy and confidentiality under the Code

The Code recognises that its aims must be balanced against the need to keep information private or confidential in certain circumstances. In particular, it expressly recognises that the aims of the Code must be balanced against two countervailing requirements, namely the need to maintain high standards of care in ensuring the privacy of personal and commercially confidential information, and the need to preserve confidentiality where disclosure would not be in the public interest or would breach personal privacy or the confidences of a third party in accordance with statutory requirements and Pt II of the Code.[7] 5–004

Information that the government will release under the Code

Subject to the exemptions contained in Pt II of the Code, the Code commits the departments and public bodies to whom its applies to publishing the facts and analyses of the facts that the government considers relevant and important in framing major policy proposals and decisions, and, in the normal case, to 5–005

[5] Code of Practice, para.1.
[6] Code of Practice, para.2.
[7] Code of Practice, para.2.

making such information available when policies and decisions are announced. The second Code commitment is a commitment to publish, or otherwise make available, "as soon as practicable after the Code becomes operational", explanatory material on departments' dealings with the public (including such rules, procedures, internal guidance to officials, and similar administrative manuals as will assist better understanding of departmental action in dealing with the public) except where publication could prejudice any matter which should properly be kept confidential under Pt II of the Code. Thirdly, the Code enshrines a commitment on behalf of the bodies to whom it applies to give reasons for administrative decisions to those affected, and to publish in accordance with the Citizen's Charter full information about how public services are run, how much they cost, who is in charge, and what complaints and redress procedures are available; and full and (where possible) comparable sets of information about what services are being provided, what targets are set, what standards of service are expected and the results achieved. The final Code commitment is to release, in response to specific requests, information relating to the policies of the bodies covered, as well as information relating to their actions and decisions and other matters related to their areas of responsibility.[8] The Code does not require the release of information that the relevant public bodies do not themselves possess, or to provide information that has already been published, or to provide information which is provided as part of an existing service other than through that service.[9]

Bodies specifically exempted from the Code

5–006 The Security and Intelligence Services are not within the scope of the Code, and information obtained from or relating to them is not covered by it.[10] The Code does not apply to or affect information held by courts or tribunals or inquiries, or information contained in the documents of such bodies.[11]

Information excluded by Part II of the Code

5–007 Part II of the Code excludes fifteen categories of information from the commitment of disclosure set out in Pt I. These categories of information are variously subject to two kinds of exemption from the assumption that information will be disclosed, namely an exemption which applies in cases where a "harm" or "prejudice" test is satisfied, and an exemption that is absolute in the sense that

[8] Code of Practice, para.3.
[9] Code of Practice, para.4.
[10] Code of Practice, para.6. In relation to security bodies, see further paras 17–009 to 17–025. In relation to information supplied by the security bodies, see further paras 17–027.
[11] Code of Practice, para.10. The bodies in question include the Northern Ireland Enforcement of Judgments Office.

no harm or prejudice test applies. "Harm" and "prejudice", for the purposes of Pt II of the Code, include actual harm and prejudice and a risk or reasonable expectation of harm or prejudice. The Code explains that in such cases, consideration should be given to whether any harm or prejudice arising from disclosure is outweighed by the public interest in making the information available.[12] The Ombudsman has interpreted the "harm" test under the Code as allowing for a balancing of public interests, such that information should be disclosed when the public interest is best served thereby.[13] The categories of exempt information that are subject to a "harm" test under Pt II of the Code include information relating to defence,[14] security[15] and international relations[16]; and information whose disclosure would harm the frankness and candour of internal discussion.[17] The Code gives, as examples of the latter kind of information, the proceedings of Cabinet and Cabinet committees; internal opinion, advice, recommendations, consultation and deliberation; projections and assumptions relating to internal policy and analysis, analysis of alternative policy options and information relating to rejected policy options; as well as confidential communications between departments, public bodies and regulatory bodies. The categories of information that are subject to an absolute exemption include information relating to confidential communications with the Royal Household[18]; and information relating to public employment and public appointments and honours.[19] Most of the fifteen categories of excluded information are, however, subject to a "harm" or "prejudice" test of some form or other.

Procedure for obtaining information covered by the Code

Information that is made available by the Code may be obtained simply by writing to the relevant department, agency or body and explaining what information is required. It is not necessary to specify particular files or documents. The Code specifies that departments should reply to most requests within 20 working days, and should inform the maker of the request that they need longer to reply, if that is the case. Most information should be provided free of charge, especially where it is needed to explain such matters as benefits, grants and entitlements; the standards and performances of services; the reasons for administrative decisions made with respect to the person requesting information; the way in which the person requesting information may exercise rights to appeal or 5–008

[12] Code of Practice, Pt II.
[13] Case A8/00 HC 494 (1999–00), Case A31/99 HC 21 (1999–00).
[14] See further paras 17–051 to 17–059.
[15] See further paras 17–033 to 17–040.
[16] See further paras 18–001 to 18–010.
[17] See further paras 22–018 to 22–024.
[18] See further paras 26–001 to 26–007.
[19] See further paras 26–008 to 26–014.

complain about a decision; or regulatory requirements bearing upon the business of the person making the request. If the request does not fall within any one or more of the above categories, however, then a charge may be imposed for supplying it.

Enforcement of the Code

5–009 As noted above, the Code does not confer rights of access to information upon anyone. If a department does not comply with a request for information the matter may be taken up by the Ombudsman, who can, however, only instigate an investigation upon the referral of a complaint from an MP. The Ombudsman can then recommend disclosure or uphold the department's decision not to disclose. His recommendations are not legally binding, although in practice most departments comply with them.

Relationship between the Code and the Freedom of Information Act 2000

5–010 It will be noted from the above outline that the Code bears some resemblance to the Freedom of Information Act 2000 in its structure. It is to be expected that once the Act comes fully into force there will be little scope for the operation of the Code.[20] Nevertheless, the Code will remain significant for two reasons. First, para.8 of the Code provides that it:

> "cannot override provisions contained in statutory rights of access to information or records (nor can it override statutory prohibitions on disclosure). Where the information could be sought under an existing statutory right, the terms of the right of access takes precedence over the Code . . . ."

To the extent that the Freedom of Information Act 2000 gives a right of access to particular information, the Code cannot detract from that right. To the extent that the Freedom of Information Act 2000 does not give a right of access to particular information (*i.e.* because it is exempt information, either under an absolute exemption or under a qualified exemption and the public interest favours maintenance of the exemption), that does not constitute a statutory prohibition on disclosure: it is simply an absence of a right. Thus, it is possible that an applicant who has no right of access under the Freedom of Information Act 2000 to information may still be able to rely on the Code. This is because the exemptions in the Code do not perfectly overlap the exemptions in the Freedom of Information Act 2000. Of course, the Code (unlike the Freedom of

[20] Indeed, para.8 of the Code causes it to be largely eclipsed by the Freedom of Information Act 2000.

Information Act 2000) does not give a direct right to information. Secondly, the Code provides valuable insight into the public interest in disclosure of information held by a public authority and in the public authority maintaining the various exemptions under the Freedom of Information Act 2000. To the extent that the Act provides a qualified exemption in respect of information that the Code does not exempt, it may be that the Code's treatment of that information will be relevant to the consideration of the public interest under s.2 of the Freedom of Information Act 2000.

2. LOCAL GOVERNMENT

Introduction

At common law an individual has no general right of access to information held by a public authority. However, the common law does recognise a limited right for a member of a local authority to see such documents as are reasonably necessary to enable him to carry out his duties.[21] Onto this very limited common law right are grafted a series of statutory rights specifically relating to information held by local authorities and cognate bodies. In each case, the scope of the right is dependent upon: 5–011

— the identity of the applicant;
— the nature of the information sought;
— the body by whom the information is held; and
— the applicability of an exemption to that right.

In very broad terms:

(1) The Public Bodies (Admission to Meetings) Act 1960 gives member of the press an entitlement to be supplied with a copy of the agenda and limited additional information relating to meetings of certain local government bodies that are required to be open to the public.[22]

[21] *R. v Southwold Corporation Ex p. Wrightson* (1907) 5 L.G.R. 888; *R. v Barnes Borough Council Ex p. Conlan* [1938] 3 All E.R. 226; *R. v Lancashire County Council Police Authority Ex p. Hook* [1980] Q.B. 603; *R. v Birmingham City Council Ex p. O* [1983] 1 A.C. 578 (where the House of Lords held that a councillor has the right to have access to all written material in the possession of the local authority of which the councillor is a member provided that the councillor has a good reason for having access. That good reason will exist in relation to all documents held by a committee of which the councillor is a member; but otherwise some need to know will need to be demonstrated); *R. v Hackney London Borough Council Ex p. Gamper* [1985] 1 W.L.R. 1229. This right does not extend to documents that the member is merely curious to see: the member has to be actuated solely by the desire to discharge his public functions: *R. v Hampstead Borough Council Ex p. Woodward* (1917) 15 L.G.R. 309.

[22] See further paras 5–012 to 5–013.

(2) Part VA of the Local Government Act 1972 gives members of the public a right of access to the agenda, reports and certain background papers used at meetings of a wide range of local government bodies.[23]

(3) Section 96 of the Local Government, Planning and Land Act 1980 gives members of the public access to a register of certain land holdings of local authority bodies.[24]

(4) Section 28 of the Local Government Finance Act 1982 gives members of the public access to certain information in local domestic rating lists.[25]

(5) Section 22 of the Local Government Act 2000 and the regulations made under it provide similar rights of access as Pt VA of the Local Government Act 1972, but in relation to informatoin put to meetings of local authority executives.[26]

Public Bodies (Admission to Meetings) Act 1960

5–012 The Public Bodies (Admission to Meetings) Act 1960 was passed at the instigation of Margaret Thatcher MP in 1960.[27] This Act opened up "the meetings of certain bodies exercising public functions" to the press and other members of the public. The Act applies to the bodies listed in Sch.1 to the Act, including parish and community councils, the Welsh Development Agency, the Commission for Health Improvement, Strategic Health Authorities, Primary Care Trusts,[28] regional and local flood defence committees, advisory committees established and maintained under s.12 of the Environment Act 1995, National Health Service Trusts established under s.5(1) of the National Health Service and Community Care Act 1990[29]; and, in Scotland, Health Boards constituted under the National Health Service (Scotland) Act 1978 (but only so far as regards the exercise of their executive functions), and National Health Service Trusts established under s.12A of the National Health Service (Scotland) Act 1978.[30] Section 1(1) of the Act provides that any meeting of a body exercising public functions to which the Act applies shall be open to the public. Section 1(1) is, however, subject to a proviso contained in s.1(2), by virtue of which a public body may, by resolution, exclude the public from a meeting (whether during the whole or a part of the proceedings) whenever publicity would be preju-

[23] See further paras 5–014 to 5–031.
[24] See further paras 5–032 to 5–034.
[25] See further para.5–035.
[26] See further paras 5–036 to 5–042.
[27] See further para.1–001.
[28] Except as regards the exercise of their functions under the National Health Service (Service Committees and Tribunal) Regulations 1992 or any regulations amending or replacing those Regulations: para.1(gg) of Sch 1 to the Public Bodies (Admission to Meetings) Act 1960.
[29] Added by art.2 of the Public Bodies (Admission to Meetings) (National Health Service Trusts) Order 1997.
[30] Added by art.2 of the Public Bodies (Admission to Meetings) (National Health Service Trusts) Order 1997.

dicial to the public interest by reason of the confidential nature of the business to be transacted or for other special reasons stated in the resolution and arising from the nature of the business or of the proceedings. Where such a resolution is passed, the Act does not require the meeting to be open to the public during the proceedings to which the resolution applies. Section 1(3) of the Public Bodies (Admission to Meetings) Act 1960 further provides that a body may, under s.1(2), treat the need to receive or consider recommendations or advice from sources other than members, committees or sub-committees of the body as a special reason why publicity would be prejudicial to the public interest, without regard to the subject or purport of the recommendations or advice, but that the making by s.1(3) of express provision for that case shall not be taken to restrict the generality of s.1(2) in relation to other cases (including, in particular, cases where the report of a committee or sub-committee of the body is of a confidential nature. This provision covers advice from officers.

The right to certain information under the Public Bodies (Admission to Meetings) Act 1960

Section 1(4) of the Public Bodies (Admission to Meetings) Act 1960 provides 5–013
that where a body is required by the Act to be open to the public during the proceedings or any part of them, the following conditions must be satisfied. First, public notice of the time and place of the meeting must be given by posting it at the offices of the body (or, if the body has no offices, then in some central and conspicuous place in the area with which it is concerned) three clear days at least before the meeting, or, if the meeting is convened at shorter notice, then at the time it is convened. Secondly, on request and payment of postage or other necessary charge for transmission, a copy of the agenda for the meeting as supplied to the members of the body must be supplied for the benefit of any newspaper (although the agenda so supplied may, if thought fit, exclude any item during which the meeting is likely not to be open to the public), together with such further statements or particulars, if any, as are necessary to indicate the nature of the items included, or, if thought fit in the case of any item, with copies of any reports or other documents supplied to the members of the body in connection with the item. This provision thus provides a limited class of person with a limited right to information in limited circumstances. To the extent that the Public Bodies (Admission to Meetings) Act 1960 bestows a right to information, that information will be exempt information under the Freedom of Information Act 2000.[31] Section 1(4)(c) of the Public Bodies (Admission to Meetings) Act 1960 provides that, while the meeting is open to the public, the body lacks the power to exclude members of the public from the meeting. Duly accredited representatives of newspapers attending for the purpose of reporting

[31] Freedom of Information Act 2000, s.21(1). See paras 16–001 to 16–004.

the proceedings for those newspapers must, so far as practicable, be afforded reasonable facilities for making their report and, unless the meeting is held in premises not belonging to the body or on the telephone, for telephoning the report at their own expense.

Local Government Act 1972

5–014 The public have a right under Pt VA of the Local Government Act 1972[32] to attend meetings of principal councils and their committees, as well as to be given access to certain documents connected with the proceedings of the latter bodies. Section 100A(1) of the Local Government Act 1972 provides that meetings of principal councils shall be open to the public, except to the extent that they are excluded under s.100A(2) or by resolution under s.100A(4). By s.100A(2), the public must be excluded from a meeting of a principal council during an item of business whenever it is likely, in view of the nature of the business to be transacted or the nature of the proceedings, that, if members of the public were to be present during that item, confidential information[33] would be disclosed to them in breach of the obligation of confidence. Section 100A(2) further provides that nothing in Pt VA can be taken to authorise or require the disclosure of confidential information in breach of the obligation of confidence.

Meaning of "principal council"

5–015 The primary meaning of a "principal council" as the term is used in the Local Government Act 1972 is a council elected for a non-metropolitan county, for a district or for a London Borough and, in relation to Wales, for a county or for a county borough.[34] For the purposes of Pt VA of the Act, the term also includes a joint authority,[35] the London Fire and Emergency Planning Authority,[36] the Common Council of the City of London,[37] the Broads Authority,[38] a National Park Authority,[39] a joint board or joint committee constituted under any enact-

[32] Pt VA of the Local Government Act 1972 comprises ss.100A to 100K and Sch.12. Pt VA was inserted by the Local Government (Access to Information) Act 1985.

[33] The term "information", as it appears in Pt VA of the Local Government Act 1972, includes an expression of opinion, any recommendations and any decision taken: Local Government Act 1972, s.100K(1). The definition of "confidential information" in the Local Government Act 1972 is materially different from its common law meaning: see paras 25–001 to 25–021.

[34] Local Government Act 1972, s.270(1). These are listed in Sch.1 to the Act.

[35] That is, an authority established by Pt IV of the Local Government Act 1985: Local Government Act 1972, s.270(1).

[36] Established under the Local Government Act 1985, s.27 (now repealed) but reconstituted by the Greater London Authority Act 1999, Pt III.

[37] In other words, the mayor, aldermen and commons of the City of London in common council assembled: see City of London (Various Powers) Act 1958, s.5.

[38] As established by the Norfolk and Suffolk Broads Act 1988, s.1.

[39] These are established under the Environment Act 1995, ss.63 and 64 and Sch.7.

ment as a body corporate and discharging the functions of two or more principal councils,[40] a police authority established under s.3 of the Police Act 1996, the Metropolitan Police Authority, and a combined fire authority.[41]

Meaning of "confidential information"

For the purposes of Pt VA of the Local Government Act 1972, "confidential information" is defined to mean: 5–016

— information furnished to a principal council by a government department upon terms (however expressed) that forbid the disclosure of the information to the public; and
— information the disclosure of which to the public is prohibited by or under any enactment or by the order of a court.[42]

As noted above, the definition given to "confidential information" is materially different from its common law meaning.[43]

Power to exclude the public by resolution

Principal councils have a power by resolution to exclude the public from a meeting during an item of business whenever it is likely, in view of the nature of the business to be transacted or the nature of the proceedings, that if members of the public were present during the item there would be disclosure to them of "exempt information."[44] A resolution must identify the proceedings, or the part of the proceedings, to which it applies[45] and it must state the description, in terms of Sch.12A to the Local Government Act 1972, of the exempt information giving rise to the exclusion of the public.[46] Where such a resolution is made, the meeting need not be open to the public during the proceedings to which the resolution relates. 5–017

[40] Local Government Act 1972, s.100J(2).
[41] Meaning a fire authority constituted by a combination scheme under the Fire Service Act 1947: see Local Government Act 1972, s.100J(5).
[42] s.100A(3)(a) of the Local Government Act 1972.
[43] As to which see paras 25–001 to 25–021.
[44] Local Government Act 1972, s.100A(4). For examples of the exercise of this power see *R. v Kensington and Chelsea LBC Ex p. Stoop* [1992] 1 P.L.R. 58 (public excluded during a consideration of an application for the grant of planning permission); and *R. v Wandsworth LBC Ex p. Darker Enterprises Ltd* (1999) 1 L.G.L.R. 601 (public excluded during consideration of an application for a renewal of a licence for a sex establishment).
[45] s.100A(5)(a) of the Local Government Act 1972.
[46] s.100A(5)(b) of the Local Government Act 1972.

Exempt information under the Local Government Act 1972

5–018 Section 100I defines "exempt information" as information described in Pt I of Sch.12A to the Local Government Act 1972, subject to any qualifications contained in Pt II,[47] and as interpreted in the light of Pt III. The items of information specified in Pt I of Sch.12A to the Local Government Act 1972 are:

(1) information relating to a particular employee, a former employee or an applicant to become an employee of the authority concerned,[48] or to a particular office-holder, former office-holder or applicant to become an office-holder under such an authority[49];
(2) information relating to a particular employee, former employee or applicant to become an employee of a magistrates' court committee,[50] a probation committee[51] or a local probation board[52]; or to a particular office-holder, former office-holder or applicant to become an officer-holder in such a committee or board;
(3) information relating to a particular chief officer or applicant to become a chief officer of a local probation board[53];

---

[47] By para.7 of Pt II of Sch.12A to the Local Government Act 1972, information falling within any paragraph of Pt I is not exempt information by virtue of that paragraph if it relates to proposed development for which the local planning authority can grant itself planning permission pursuant to reg.3 of the Town and County Planning General Regulations 1992 (SI 1992/1492).

[48] Para.1(2) of Pt III of Sch.12A provides that any reference in that Sch.to "the authority" is a reference to the principal council, or, as the case may be, the committee or sub-committee in relation to whose proceedings or documents the question whether information is exempt or not falls to be determined; and includes a reference, in the case of a principal council, to any committee or sub-committee of the council, and, in the case of a committee, to any constituent principal council, any other principal council by which appointments are made to the committee or whose functions that committee discharges, and any other committee or sub-committee of a principal council of the abovementioned kinds. In the case of a sub-committee, references to "the authority" include the committee or any committees of which it is a sub-committee and any principal council which falls within the abovementioned kinds in relation to that committee.

[49] Local Government Act 1972, Sch.12A, para.1. By para.1 of Pt II of Sch.12A to the Local Government Act 1972, this information is not exempt information unless it relates to an individual of the description in the relevant paragraph (being a paragraph contained within paras 1 to 5) of Pt I in the capacity indicated by the description.

[50] Local Government Act 1972, Sch.12A, para.2(a). By para.1 of Pt II of Sch.12A to the Local Government Act 1972, this information is not exempt information unless it relates to an individual of the description in the relevant paragraph (being a paragraph contained within paras 1 to 5) of Pt I in the capacity indicated by the description.

[51] Within the meaning of the Probation Service Act 1993: Local Government Act 1972, Sch.12A, para.2(b). By para.1 of Pt II of Sch.12A to the Local Government Act 1972, this information is not exempt information unless it relates to an individual of the description in the relevant paragraph (being a paragraph contained within paras 1 to 5) of Pt I in the capacity indicated by the description.

[52] Within the meaning of the Criminal Justice and Court Services Act 2000: Local Government Act 1972, Sch.12A, para.2(c). By para.1 of Pt II of Sch.12A to the Local Government Act 1972, this information is not exempt information unless it relates to an individual of the description in the relevant paragraph (being a paragraph contained within paras 1 to 5) of Pt I in the capacity indicated by the description.

[53] Within the meaning of the Criminal Justice and Court Services Act 2000: Local Government Act 1972, Sch.12A, para.2A. By para.1 of Pt II of Sch.12A to the Local Government Act 1972, this

(4) information relating to any particular occupier or former occupier of, or applicant for, accommodation provided by or at the expense of the authority[54];
(5) information relating to any particular applicant for, or recipient or former recipient of, any service provided by the authority[55];
(6) information relating to any particular applicant for, or recipient or former recipient of, any financial service provided by the authority[56];
(7) information relating to the adoption, care, fostering or education of any particular child[57];
(8) information relating to the financial or business affairs of any particular person (other than the authority)[58];
(9) the amount of any expenditure proposed to be incurred by the authority under any particular contract for the acquisition of property or the supply of goods or services[59];
(10) any terms proposed or to be proposed by or to the authority in the course of negotiations for a contract for the acquisition or disposal of property or the supply of goods or services[60];

information is not exempt information unless it relates to an individual of the description in the relevant paragraph (being a paragraph contained within paras 1 to 5) of Pt I in the capacity indicated by the description.

[54] Local Government Act 1972, Sch.12A, para.3. By para.1 of Pt II of Sch.12A to the Local Government Act 1972, this information is not exempt information unless it relates to an individual of the description in the relevant paragraph (being a paragraph contained within paras 1 to 5) of Pt I in the capacity indicated by the description.

[55] Local Government Act 1972, Sch.12A, para.4. By para.1 of Pt II of Sch.12A to the Local Government Act 1972, this information is not exempt information unless it relates to an individual of the description in the relevant paragraph (being a paragraph contained within paras 1 to 5) of Pt I in the capacity indicated by the description.

[56] Local Government Act 1972, Sch.12A, para.5. By para.1 of Pt II of Sch.12A to the Local Government Act 1972, this information is not exempt information unless it relates to an individual of the description in the relevant paragraph (being a paragraph contained within paras 1 to 5) of Pt I in the capacity indicated by the description.

[57] Local Government Act 1972, Sch.12A, para.6.

[58] Local Government Act 1972, Sch.12A, para.7. By para.2 of Pt II of Sch.12A to the Local Government Act 1972, information falling within para.7 of Pt I is not exempt information by virtue of that paragraph if it is required to be registered under the Companies Act 1985, the Friendly Societies Act 1974, the Industrial and Provident Societies Acts 1965–1978, the Building Societies Act 1986, or the Charities Act 1960.

[59] Local Government Act 1972, Sch.12A, para.8. By para.3 of Pt II of Sch.12A to the Local Government Act 1972, information falling within para.8 of Pt I is exempt information if and so long as disclosure to the public of the amount there referred to would be likely to give an advantage to a person entering into, or seeking to enter into, a contract with the authority in respect of property, goods or services, whether the advantage would arise as against the authority or as against other such persons.

[60] Local Government Act 1972, Sch.12A, para.9. By para.4 of Pt II of Sch.12A to the Local Government Act 1972, information falling within para.9 of Pt I is exempt information if and so long as disclosure to the public of the terms would prejudice the authority in those or any other negotiations concerning property or goods or services.

(11) the identity of the authority (as well as of any other person by virtue of para.7 of Pt I of Sch.12A) as the person offering any particular tender for a contract for the supply of goods or services[61];

(12) information relating to any consultations or negotiations, or contemplated consultations or negotiations, in connection with any labour relations matter arising between the authority or Minister of the Crown and employees of, or office-holders under, the authority[62];

(13) any instructions to counsel and any opinion of counsel (whether or not in connection with any proceedings) and any advice received, information obtained or action to be taken in connection with any legal proceedings by or against the authority, or the determination of any matter affecting the authority (whether, in either case, proceedings have been commenced or are in contemplation)[63];

(14) information which, if disclosed to the public, would reveal that the authority proposed to give under any enactment a notice under which, or by virtue of which, requirements are imposed on a person, or to make an order or direction under any enactment[64];

(15) any action taken or to be taken in connection with the prevention, investigation or prosecution of crime[65]; and,

(16) the identity of a protected informant.

Access to documents: agendas and reports

5–019 Section 100B of the Local Government Act 1972 confers a right of access upon members of the public to:

— copies of the agenda for a meeting of a principal council; and
— copies of any report for the meeting.[66]

[61] Local Government Act 1972, Sch.12A, para.10.

[62] Local Government Act 1972, Sch.12A, para.11. By para.5 of Pt II of Sch.12A to the Local Government Act 1972, information falling within para.11 of Pt I is exempt information if and so long as disclosure to the public of the information would prejudice the authority in those or any other consultations or negotiations in connection with a labour relations matter arising as mentioned in that paragraph.

[63] Local Government Act 1972, Sch.12A, para.12.

[64] Local Government Act 1972, Sch.12A, para.13. By para.6 of Pt II of Sch.12A to the Local Government Act 1972, information falling within para.13 of Pt I is exempt information if and so long as disclosure to the public might afford an opportunity to a person affected by the notice, order or direction to defeat the purpose of one or other of the purposes for which the notice, order or direction is to be given or made.

[65] Local Government Act 1972, Sch.12A, para.14.

[66] Local Government Act 1972, s.100B(1). By s.100B(6), where a meeting of a principal council is required by s.100A to be open to the public during the proceedings or any Pt of them, a reasonable number of copies of the agenda, and subject to s.100B(8), of the reports for the meeting, must be made available for the use by members of the public present at the meeting. Section 100B(8) provides that s.100B(2) applies in relation to copies of reports provided in pursuance of s.100B(6)

These documents are required to be open to inspection by members of the public at least five clear days before the meeting in question, except that, where the meeting is convened at shorter notice, the copies of the agenda and reports must be open to inspection from the time the meeting is convened.[67] Where an item is added to an agenda, copies of which are open to inspection by the public, copies of the item (or of a revised agenda) and the copies of any report for the meeting relating to the item, must be open to inspection from the time the item is added to the agenda.[68] Copies of any agenda or report that is open to inspection by the public need not be made available to the public until copies have been made available to members of the council.[69] The right of access to copies of reports is subject to the power conferred upon the proper officer by s.100B(2), if he thinks fit, to exclude from such copies the whole or any part of a report which relates only to items during which, in his opinion, the meeting is likely not to be open to the public. Where the officer in question does take the view that the whole or part of any report should be excluded for this reason, every copy of the report, or part of the report, so excluded must be marked "Not for publication",[70] and every copy of the whole or of the part of the report so excluded must state the description, in terms of Sch.12A to the Local Government Act 1972, of the exempt information by virtue of which the council are likely to exclude the public during the item to which the report relates.[71] An item of business may not be considered at a meeting of a principal council unless a copy of the agenda including the item (or a copy of the item) is open to inspection by members of the public for at least five clear days before the meeting or, where the meeting is convened at shorter notice, from the time the meeting is convened[72]; or unless, by reason of special circumstances, which must

or 100B(7) as it applies in relation to copies of reports provided in pursuance of s.100B(1). In order to benefit from the rights of access to information under the Local Government Act 1972, it is sufficient that one is a local government elector, but it is not necessary that one should seek to obtain access to the information in question in that capacity. In *Stirrat v Edinburgh City Council* [1999] S.L.T. 274; [1998] S.C.L.R. 971 the Claimant, who was a partner in a firm providing a property enquiry service and also a council taxpayer in the City of Edinburgh, attended the Council's office in order to inspect documents in the exercise of his right to do so under s.101(1) of the Local Government (Scotland) Act 1973. Some documents were not available, and the Council refused the claimant access to them on the grounds of confidentiality and expense. The claimant presented a petition seeking a declaration that he was entitled to inspect the documents. The Council opposed the petition on the ground that the right to inspect the documents was linked to the right of the council taxpayer to object to the accounts, and did not apply where the inspection was for professional purposes. The Scottish Outer House granted the declaration, holding that the claimant had right and title to inspect the documents as a council taxpayer under s.101(1), and that the motive with which he sought to exercise that right was irrelevant.

67 Local Government Act 1972, s.100B(3)(a). The reference to "five clear days" means five working days: *R. v Swansea City Council Ex p. Elitestone* [1993] 46 E.G. 181.

68 Local Government Act 1972, s.100B(3)(b).

69 *ibid.*, s.100B(3).

70 *ibid.*, s.100B(5)(a).

71 *ibid.*, s.100B(5)(b).

72 *ibid.*, s.100B(4)(a).

be specified in the minutes, the chairman of the meeting is of the opinion that the item should be considered at the meeting as a matter or urgency.[73]

Access to documents: inspection of minutes and other documents after meetings

5–020 Once a meeting of a principal council has been held, members of the public are entitled to inspect at the offices of the council until the expiration of the period of six years beginning with the date of the meeting:

- the minutes of the meeting, or a copy of the minutes, excluding that part of the minutes of proceedings during which the meeting was not open to the public as disclosures of exempt information[74];
- where applicable, a summary of the meeting[75];
- a copy of the agenda for the meeting; and
- a copy of so much of any report for the meeting as relates to any item during which the meeting was open to the public.[76]

5–021 Where, as result of the exclusion of parts of the minutes that disclose exempt information, the minutes of the meeting that are made open to inspection do not provide members of the public with a reasonably fair and coherent record of the whole or part of the proceedings, the proper officer must make a written summary of those (or that part of the) proceedings.[77]

Access to documents: inspection of background papers

If and so long as copies of the whole or part of a report for a meeting of a principal council are required by s.100B(1) or 100C(1) to be open to inspection by members of the public, then:

- those copies must include a copy of a list, compiled by the proper officer, of the background papers for the report or the part of the report,[78] and
- at least one copy of each of the documents included in that list must also be open to inspection at the offices of the council.[79]

73 Local Government Act 1972, s.100B(4)(b).
74 *ibid.*, s.100C(1)(a).
75 *ibid.*, s.100C(1)(b).
76 *ibid.*, s.100C(1)(c).
77 *ibid.*, s.100C(2).
78 *ibid.*, s.100D(1)(a).
79 *ibid.*, s.100D(1)(b). Section 100D(3) further provides that where a copy of any background papers for a report is required by s.100D(1) to be open to inspection by members of the public, the copy

The background papers for a report are those documents relating to the subject-matter of the report that disclose any facts or matters on which, in the opinion of the proper officer, the report or an important part of the report is based, and that have, in that officer's opinion, been relied on to a material extent in preparing the report.[80] The material to be disclosed need not include any confidential information the disclosure of which would be in breach of the obligation of confidence.[81]

Application to committees and sub-committees

The above disclosure provisions apply to committees and sub-committees of principal councils as they apply in relation to principal councils.[82] 5–022

Additional rights of access by members of principal councils

Members of principal councils also have a right to inspect any document that is in the possession or under the control of a principal council and contains material relating to any business to be transacted at a meeting of the council or a committee or sub-committee of the council.[83] This provision does not, however, apply in respect of documents which appear to the proper officer to disclose exempt information of a description falling within any of paras 1 to 6, 9, 11, 12 to 14 of Pt I of Sch.12A to the Local Government Act 1972.[84] 5–023

shall be taken for the purposes of Pt VA of the Local Government Act 1972 to be so open if arrangements exist for its production to members of the public as soon as is reasonably practicable after the making of a request to inspect the copy.

80 Local Government Act 1972, s.100D(5). The background papers for a report do not, however, include any published works.

81 In *Maile v Wigan MBC* (QBD) [2001] Env.L.R. 11, [2001] J.P.L. 193 Eady J. held that a database dealing with potentially contaminated sites in the Council's area did not form part of the committee report for the purposes of s.100C of the Local Government Act 1972, and was not a "background paper" for the purposes of s.100D of that Act, because the Council's environmental health officer had not relied upon the database when drafting his report to committee. Consequently the claimant was not entitled to inspect the database under the provisions of the Local Government Act 1972.

82 Local Government Act 1972, s.100E(1). As to the publication of notices of meetings of committees and sub-committees of principal councils, see s.100E(2) of the Local Government Act 1972.

83 This right is in addition to any other rights that members of principal councils may have apart from s.100F: Local Government Act 1972, s.100F(5).

84 Local Government Act 1972, s.100F(2). These classes of exempt information are listed at para.5–018.

Additional information

5–024 Principal councils are required to maintain a register stating:

— the name and address of every current member of the council and the ward or division which that member represents[85];
— the name and address of every current member of each committee or sub-committee of the council.[86]

Principal councils must also maintain a list specifying those powers of the council which, for the time being, are exercisable from time to time by officers of the council in pursuance of arrangements made under the Local Government Act 1972 or any other enactment for their discharge by those officers and stating the title of the officer by whom each of the powers so specified is for the time being so exercisable.[87] Finally, principal councils are required to keep at their offices a written summary of the rights to attend the meetings of a principal council and of committees and sub-committees of a principal council, and to inspect and copy documents and to be furnished with documents which are conferred by Pt VA of the Local Government Act 1972.[88] The abovementioned register, list and summary must be kept open to inspection by the public at the offices of the council.[89]

Times for inspection, payment and copying of documents

5–025 A document that, under the above provisions, is to be open to inspection must be so open at all reasonable hours[90] and without payment, except in the case of background papers for reports, where payment of a reasonable fee for inspection may be demanded.[91] Where a document is open to inspection by a person under the above provisions, the person may make copies of or extracts from the document,[92] or require the person having custody of the document to supply

[85] Local Government Act 1972, s.100G(1)(a).
[86] *ibid.*, s.100G(1)(b). A substituted version of this paragraph (effected by the Local Government and Housing Act 1989, s.194, Sch.11, para.24), which would require additional information in relation to speaking rights at such committee and sub-committee meetings, has yet to be put in force.
[87] Local Government Act 1972, s.100G(2). This section does not, however, require a power to be specified in the list if the arrangements for its discharge by the officer are made for a specified period not exceeding six months.
[88] Local Government Act 1972, s.100G(3). The same written summary must also set out the rights to attend meetings and inspect, copy and be furnished with documents conferred by Pt XI of the Local Government Act 1972 and such other enactments as the Secretary of State by order specifies: Local Government Act 1972, s.100G(3).
[89] Local Government Act 1972, s.100G(4).
[90] *ibid.*, s.100H(1).
[91] *ibid.*, s.100H(1).
[92] *ibid.*, s.100H(2)(a).

him with a photographic copy of the document or of extracts from it.[93] The rights so conferred are in addition, and without prejudice, to any such rights conferred by or under any other enactment.[94]

Offences

It is a summary offence for a person having custody of a document which is required to be open to inspection under the above provisions to obstruct any person from exercising that right[95] or to refuse to furnish copies to any person entitled to obtain them.[96] 5–026

Publication of defamatory material

Where any accessible document for a meeting to which that section applies is supplied to, or open to inspection by, a member of the public, or is supplied for the benefit of any newspaper in pursuance of s.100B(7), the publication thereby of any defamatory matter contained in the document is privileged, unless the publication is proved to be made with malice.[97] This applies[98] to any meeting of a principal council and any meeting of a committee or sub-committee of a principal council. The "accessible documents" for a meeting are: 5–027

- any copy of the agenda or of any item included in the agenda for the meeting[99];
- any such further statements or particulars for the purpose of indicating the nature of any item included in the agenda[1];
- any copy of a document relating to such an item which is supplied for the benefit of a newspaper in pursuance of s.100B(7)(c)[2];
- any copy of the whole or part of a report for a meeting[3]; and any copy of the whole or part of any background papers for a report for the meeting.[4]

[93] Local Government Act 1972, s.100H(2)(b). S.100H(2) does not require or authorise the doing of any act which infringes the copyright in any work, except that, where the owner of the copyright is a principal council, nothing done in pursuance of s.100H(2) constitutes an infringement of that copyright: Local Government Act 1972, s.100H(3).

[94] Local Government Act 1972, s.100H(7).

[95] Local Government Act 1972, s.100H(4)(a). The offence is punishable on conviction by the imposition of a fine not exceeding level 1 on the standard scale.

[96] Local Government Act 1972, s.100H(4)(b).

[97] Local Government Act 1972, s.100H(5).

[98] By virtue of Local Government Act 1972, s.100H(6).

[99] Local Government Act 1972, s.100H(6)(a).

[1] *ibid.*, s.100H(6)(b).

[2] *ibid.*, s.100H(6)(c).

[3] *ibid.*, s.100H(6)(d).

[4] *ibid.*, s.100H(6)(e).

Parish and community councils, joint authorities, police authorities and Broads authorities

5–028 The Local Government Act 1972 provides for the inspection by local government electors for the area of parish and community councils of the minutes of their proceedings, and such local government electors have the right, in addition, to make a copy of or extract from those minutes.[5] Orders for payments of money made by local authorities are also open to inspection by local electors,[6] while the accounts of local authorities, as well as those of any proper officer of a local authority, are open to inspection by the members of that authority, who may make a copy of or extract from the accounts.[7] These provisions apply to the minutes of proceedings and accounts of a joint authority and police authorities established under s.3 of the Police Act 1996, as well as to the Metropolitan Police Authority and the Broad Authority, as if those authorities were local authorities and as if references to a local government elector for the area of the authority were references to a local government elector for any local government area in the area for which the authority is established.[8]

Application to the Greater London Authority

5–029 Part VA of the Local Government Act 1972 has effect as if the London Assembly were a principal council and any committee or sub-committee of the Assembly were a committee or sub-committee of a principal council, within the meaning of Pt VA, with certain modifications.[9]

---

5 Local Government Act 1972, s.228(1). Section 228 also applies to the minutes of proceedings and accounts of a parish meeting as if that meeting were a parish council: Local Government Act 1972, s.228(8).

6 Local Government Act 1972, s.228(2).

7 Local Government Act 1972, s.228(3). Documents directed by s.228 to be open to inspection must be so open at all reasonable hours and, except where otherwise provided, without payment: Local Government Act 1972, s.228(6). It is an offence punishable upon summary conviction by a fine not exceeding level 1 on the standard scale for a person having custody of a document required by s.228 to be open to the public to obstruct any person entitled to inspect the document or to make a copy or extract, or to refuse to give copies or extracts to any person entitled to obtain copies or extracts: Local Government Act 1972, s.228(7). Local Government Act 1972, s.228(9). The authorities in question are Norfolk County Council, Suffolk County Council, Broadland District Council, Great Yarmouth Borough Council, North Norfolk District Council, Norwich City Council, South Norfolk District Council and Waveney District Council.

8 Local Government Act 1972, s.228(7A). In its application to the Broads Authority, those references in that section to a local government elector are to be construed as references to an elector for the area of any of the local authorities mentioned in s.1(3)(a) of the Norfolk and Suffolk Broads Act 1988.

9 Greater London Authority Act 1999, s. 58(1). By s.58(2) of the Greater London Authority Act 1999, in the application of Pt VA of the Local Government Act 1972 by s.58(1), any information furnished to the Greater London Authority and available to the Assembly must be treated as information furnished to the Assembly; any offices of or belonging to the Authority must be treated as also being offices of or belonging to the Assembly; and the proper officer of the

Application to Community Health Councils

Subject to certain modifications, ss.100A to 100D of the Local Government Act 1972 also apply to Community Health Councils as they apply to principal councils. There are further provisions for access to information relating to members of Community Health Councils and to the right of members of the public to attend meetings of Community Health Councils and community health committees, and to inspect and copy and be furnished with documents relating to such Councils and committees.[10] 5–030

Authority must be taken to be the proper officer in relation to the Assembly. By s.58(3), in the following provisions of the Local Government Act 1972, namely s.100A(2) and 100D(4), any reference to the disclosure (or likelihood of disclosure) of confidential information in breach of the obligation of confidence includes a reference to the disclosure of information of any of the descriptions specified in s.58(4) without the consent of the relevant body concerned. The descriptions in s.58(4) are: any information relating to the financial or business affairs of any particular person which was acquired in consequence of a relationship between that person and a relevant body; the amount of any expenditure proposed to be incurred by a relevant body under any particular contract, if and so long as disclosure would be likely to give an advantage to a person entering into, or seeking to enter into, a contract with the relevant body, whether the advantage would arise against the relevant body or another such person; any terms proposed or to be proposed by or to a relevant body in the course of negotiations for any particular contract, if and so long as disclosure would prejudice the relevant body in those or any other negotiations concerning the subject-matter of the contract; and the identity of any person as the person offering any particular tender for a contract for the supply of goods or services to a relevant body. In s.58(4), the phrase "relevant body" means Transport for London or the London Development Agency. By s.58(5) of the Greater London Authority Act 1999, any reference to the minutes of a meeting in s.100C of the Local Government Act 1972 shall, in the case of a meeting of the Assembly under s.52(3) of the Greater London Authority Act 1999, be taken to include a reference to the text of any question put pursuant to s.52(3) at the meeting and the text of any answer given to any such question, whether the question was put orally or in writing. By s.58(6), nothing in s.100D of the Local Government Act 1972 requires or authorises the inclusion of any such list as is referred to in s.100D(1) of any document which discloses anything which, by virtue of s.45(6) of the Greater London Authority Act 1999, is not required to be disclosed under s.45(3) or s.45(4) of the Greater London Authority Act 1999. By s.58(7) of the Greater London Authority Act 1999, in s.100E of the Local Government Act 1972, s.100E(3)(a) shall have effect as if s.55 of the Greater London Authority Act 1999 were included among the enactments specified in s.101(9) of the Local Government Act 1972. By s.58(8) of the Greater London Authority Act 1999, for the purposes of s.100F of the Local Government Act 1972, any document which is in the possession or under the control of the Authority and is available to the Assembly shall be treated as a document which is in the possession or under the control of the Assembly. By s.58(9) of the Greater London Authority Act 1999, in the case of the Assembly, the register of members required to be maintained under s.100G(1) of the Local Government Act 1972 shall, instead of stating the ward or division which a member represents, state whether the member is a London member or a constituency member, and if he is a constituency member, the Assembly constituency for which he is a member. By s.58(10) of the Greater London Authority Act 1999, for the purposes of s.100H(3) of the Local Government Act 1972, the Authority shall be treated as a principal council. Finally, by s.58(11) of the Greater London Authority Act 1999, in the application in relation to the Assembly of Sch.12A to the Local Government Act 1972, any reference to "the authority" includes a reference to the Authority.

[10] Community Health Councils (Access to Information Act) 1988, s.2.

Relationship between Part VA of the Local Government Act 1972 and the Freedom of Information Act 2000

5–031 To the extent that one or other of the provisions of Pt VA of the Local Government Act 1972 bestows a right to information (whether directly or as extended to another body by a further statutory provision) that information will be exempt information under the Freedom of Information Act 2000.[11] Although not entirely clear, it would seem that s.100H(7) will not operate to preserve the rights of access bestowed by the Freedom of Information Act 2000. This is because once a public authority is obliged by Pt VA of the Local Government Act 1972 to communicate information to members of the public on request, that information becomes exempt information and the duty to communicate under the Freedom of Information Act 2000 does not apply[12]—there is, accordingly, no right remaining for s.100H(7) to add to. It should be noted, however, that the Freedom of Information Act 2000 draws a distinction for the purposes of this exemption between information that is required to be made available for inspection (to which the exemption will not apply) and information that is required to be communicated upon request (to which the exemption will apply).

The Local Government, Planning and Land Act 1980

5–032 Section 96 of the Local Government, Planning and Land Act 1980 provides for registers of land holdings compiled and maintained under s.95 of that Act to be accessible by the public. In very general terms, the aim of the register is to list land holdings of local government bodies which, in the opinion of the Secretary of State, are being under-utilised and to make that list open to the public. Under s.95(1), the Secretary of State is empowered to compile and maintain a register of land which satisfies certain conditions.[13] These conditions are:

- that a freehold or leasehold interest in the land is owned by a body to which Pt X of the Act applies or a subsidiary of that body[14];
- that it is situated in an area in relation to which Pt X of the Act is in operation,[15] or is not so situated, but adjoins other land which is so sit-

[11] Freedom of Information Act 2000, s.21(1). See paras 16–001 to 16–004.

[12] By combination of ss.21(2)(b), 2(2)–(3) and 1(1)–(2), in that order, of the Freedom of Information Act 2000.

[13] These conditions are spelled out in s.95(2).

[14] Local Government, Planning and Land Act 1980, s.95(2)(a).

[15] The areas in relation to which Pt X of the Local Government, Planning and Land Act 1980 is in operation are determined by order made by statutory instrument by the Secretary of State in relation to the area of any district council or London borough council specified in the order: Local Government, Planning and Land Act 1980, s.94(2). See SIs 1980/1871 (in relation to certain specified areas of district and London borough councils); 1981/194 (in relation to certain specified areas of district and London borough councils); 1981/1251 (in relation to certain specified areas of district councils); 1981/1618 (in relation to all other areas of district councils in

uated and in which a freehold or leasehold interest is owned by a body to which Pt X of the Act applies or a subsidiary of that body[16]; and
— that in the opinion of the Secretary of State the land is not being used or not being sufficiently used for the purposes of the body's functions.[17]

The Secretary of State has the power to enter on the register any such land satisfying the above conditions as he thinks fit.[18] He may also enter on the register any Crown land situated in an area in relation to which Pt X of the Act is in operation or not so situated but adjoining other Crown land which is so situated.[19]

Bodies to whom Part X applies

Part X of the Local Government, Planning and Land Act 1980 applies to any body for the time being specified in Sch.16 to the Act.[20] The bodies presently specified in Sch.16 are: 5–033

— a county council, a county borough council, a district council, a London borough council, and the Common Council of the City of London;
— a joint authority established by Pt IV of the Local Government Act 1985;
— the London Fire and Emergency Planning Authority;
— a police authority established under s.3 of the Police Act 1996 and the Metropolitan Police Authority;
— the Commission for the New Towns, a development corporation established under the New Towns Act 1981 and an Urban Development Corporation established under the Local Government, Planning and Land Act 1980;
— a housing trust established under Pt III of the Housing Act 1988;

England, all other London Boroughs and the City of London); 1983/94 (in relation to certain specified areas of district councils); and 1984/1493 (in relation to all other areas of district councils in Wales).

16 Local Government, Planning and Land Act 1980, s.95(2)(b).
17 *ibid.*, s.95(2)(c).
18 *ibid.*, s.95(3).
19 *ibid.*, s.95(4). Section 95(5) further provides that the information to be included in the register in relation to any land entered on it shall be such as the Secretary of State thinks fit.
20 Local Government, Planning and Land Act 1980, s.93(1). The Secretary of State has the power to amend Sch.16 by order made by statutory instrument by adding an entry naming a public body not for the time being specified in that Sch.or by amending or deleting any entry for the time being contained in the Schedule: Local Government, Planning and Land Act 1980, s.93(2). A statutory instrument containing an order under s.93(2) is subject to annulment in pursuance of a resolution of either House of Parliament: Local Government, Planning and Land Act 1980, s.93(3).

— the Housing Corporation;
— British Shipbuilders, the Coal Authority, the British Broadcasting Association and the Environment Agency; and
— statutory undertakers, defined to mean persons authorised by any enactment to carry on any railway, light railway, road transport, water transport, canal, inland navigation, dock or harbour undertaking, or undertaking for the supply of hydraulic power; provided that where any persons carry on a business to the main purpose of which any such undertaking is merely ancillary, those persons shall not be treated as statutory undertakers.

Public access to the register

5–034 The Secretary of State must send to a council in respect of whose area a register is maintained a copy of that register and such amendments to it as he may from time to time consider appropriate.[21] That council has a duty to incorporate any such amendments.[22] A copy of the register must be available at the council's principal office for inspection by any member of the public at all reasonable hours.[23] If any member of the public requires a council to supply him with a copy of any information contained in such a copy of the register, the council must supply him with a copy of that information on payment of such reasonable charge for making it as the council may determine.[24]

The Local Government Finance Act 1992

5–035 The Local Government Finance Act 1992 confers various rights upon members of the public to obtain information with respect to local domestic rating lists. A person may require a listing officer to give him access to such information as will enable him to establish what is the state of a list, or has been its state at any time since it came into force, if that officer is maintaining the list, and the list is in force or has been in force at any time in the preceding five years.[25] A person may also require a billing authority to give him access to such information as will enable him to establish what is the state of a copy of a list, or has been its state at any time since it was deposited if the authority has deposited the copy under the relevant provisions of the Act[26] and the list is in force or has been in force at any time in the preceding five years.[27] A person may also require a billing

[21] Local Government, Planning and Land Act 1980, s.95(1).
[22] *ibid.*, s.95(2).
[23] *ibid.*, s.96(3).
[24] *ibid.*, s.96(4).
[25] Local Government Finance Act 1992, s.28(1).
[26] Namely, ss.22(8), 22A(10) or 22B(1) of the Local Government Finance Act 1982.
[27] Local Government Finance Act 1992, s.28(2).

authority to give him access to such information as will enable him to establish what is the state of a copy of a proposed list if the list has been deposited under the relevant provisions of the Act,[28] and the list itself is not yet in force.[29] A requirement under any of the above provisions must be complied with at a reasonable time and place and without payment being sought; but the information may be in documentary or other form, as the person or authority of whom the requirement is made thinks fit.[30] Where access is given to information in documentary form, the person to whom access is given may make copies of or extracts from the document, or may require a person having custody of the document to supply to him a photographic copy of the document or of extracts from it.[31] Where access is given in a form which is not documentary, the person to whom access is given may make transcripts of or extracts from the information, or require a person having control of access to the information to supply him with a copy in documentary form of the information or of extracts from it.[32] It is an offence[33] for a person having custody of a document containing information, or having control of access to information, access to which is sought under s.28, without reasonable excuse intentionally to obstruct a person in exercising that right of access,[34] or to refuse to comply with a requirement that he should supply the person making the request with a photographic copy of the document or of extracts from it,[35] or with a requirement that he should supply the person making the request with a copy in documentary form of the information or of extracts from it.[36]

The Local Government Act 2000

The Local Government Act 2000 makes provision for access to information held by local authority executives. Section 22(1) of the Local Government Act 2000 provides that meetings of a local authority executive, or a committee of such an executive, are to be open to the public or held in private. It is for a local authority executive to decide which of its meetings, and which of the meetings of any committee of the executive, are to be open to the public and which of those meetings are to be held in private. Written records must be kept of prescribed[37] 5–036

[28] Namely, ss.22(6) or 22B(8) of the Local Government Finance Act 1982.
[29] Local Government Finance Act 1992, s.28(3)
[30] *ibid.*, s.28(4). If, however, a reasonable charge is required for a facility under ss.28(5) or 28(6), then whichever of those two sections is concerned shall not apply unless the person seeking to avail himself of the facility pays the charge: Local Government Finance Act 1982, s.28(7).
[31] Local Government Finance Act 1982, s.28(5).
[32] *ibid.*, s.28(6).
[33] Under Local Government Finance Act 1982, s.28(8).
[34] Specifically, a right of access under s.28(1), 28(2), 28(3), 28(5)(a) or 28(6)(a).
[35] *i.e.* under Local Government Finance Act 1982, s. 5(b).
[36] *i.e.* under Local Government Finance Act 1982, s.6(b).
[37] *i.e.* prescribed by regulations made by the Secretary of State: Local Government Act 2000, s.22(18).

decisions made at meetings of local authority executives or committees of such executives which are held in private,[38] and of prescribed decisions made by individual members of local authority executives.[39] These written records must include the reasons for the decisions to which they relate.[40] Further, the written records, together with such reports, background papers or other documents as may be prescribed, must be made available to members of the public in accordance with regulations made by the Secretary of State.[41] The regulations made by the Secretary of State are the Local Authorities (Executive Arrangements) (Access to Information) (England) Regulations 2000. These apply to county and district councils in England, and to London borough councils that operate executive arrangements under Pt II of the Local Government Act 2000.

Executive decisions made at meetings

5–037 Under the Local Authorities (Executive Arrangements) (Access to Information) (England) Regulations 2000, as soon as reasonably practicable after a private meeting or a public meeting of a decision-making body[42] at which an executive decision[43] has been made, the proper officer, or in the event that the proper officer is not present at the meeting, the person presiding,[44] must

[38] Local Government Act 2000, s.22(3). Executive decisions made by decision-making bodies are prescribed decisions for the purpose of s.22(3) of the Local Government Act 2000: Local Authorities (Executive Arrangements) (Access to Information) (England) Regulations 2000, reg.3(4). A "decision-making body", in relation to an executive decision, means the executive of a local authority; the committee of a local authority executive; a joint committee, where all members of the joint committee are members of the local authority executive; or a sub-committee of a joint committee where all the members of the joint committee are members of a local authority executive, and which is authorised to discharge the function to which the executive decision relates in accordance with the Local Authorities (Arrangements for the Discharge of Functions) (England) Regulations 2000: Local Authorities (Executive Arrangements) (Access to Information) (England) Regulations 2000, reg.2.

[39] Local Government Act 2000, s.22(4). Executive decisions made by individual members of local authority executives are prescribed decisions for the purposes of s.22(4) of the Local Government Act 2000: Local Authorities (Executive Arrangements) (Access to Information) (England) Regulations 2000, reg.4(3).

[40] Local Government Act 2000, s.22(5).

[41] S.22(7) of the Local Government Act 2000 provides that regulations made under s.22(6) may make provision for or in connection with preventing the whole or part of any record or document containing prescribed information from being made available to members of the public. Further powers to make regulations in connection with local authority executive meetings are conferred on the Secretary of State by ss.22(8), 22(9), 22(1), 22(11) and 22(12) of the Local Government Act 2000.

[42] See n.38.

[43] Namely, a decision made or to be made, by a decision-maker, in connection with the discharge of a function which is the responsibility of the executive of a local authority: Local Authorities (Executive Arrangements) (Access to Information) (England) Regulations 2000, reg.2.

[44] Namely, the person actually presiding, or the person nominated to preside at the meeting: Local Authorities (Executive Arrangements) (Access to Information) (England) Regulations 2000, reg.3(3).

ensure that a written statement is produced in respect of every executive decision made at that meeting.[45] This written statement must include the following information:

— a record of the decision;
— a record of the reasons for the decision;
— details of any alternative options considered and rejected by the decision-making body at the meeting at which the decision was made;
— a record of any conflict of interest in relation to the matter decided which is declared by any member of the decision-making body which made the decision; and
— in respect of any declared conflict of interest, a note of any dispensation granted by the local authority's standards committee.[46]

Executive decisions made by individuals

Similar provisions apply in respect of executive decisions made by individual members of local authority executives,[47] and also in respect of "key decisions" made by officers.[48] A key decision is an executive decision which is likely to result in the local authority incurring expenditure which is, or the making of savings which are, significant having regard to the local authority's budget for the service or function to which the decision relates, or to be significant in terms of its effects on communities living or working in an area comprising two or more wards or electoral divisions in the area of the local authority.[49] 5–038

Inspection of documents following executive decisions

After a private meeting or a public meeting of a decision-making body at which an executive decision has been made, after an individual member has made an executive decision, or after an officer has made a key decision, the proper officer is required to ensure that a copy of any records prepared in accordance with regs 3 or 4, or of any report considered at the meeting or, as the case may be, considered by the individual member or officer and relevant to a decision 5–039

[45] Local Authorities (Executive Arrangements) (Access to Information) (England) Regulations 2000, reg.3(1).
[46] *ibid.*, reg.3(2).
[47] *ibid.*, reg.4.
[48] *ibid.*, reg.4(4).
[49] *ibid.*, regs 2 and 8(1). Reg.8(2) further provides that, in accordance with s.38 of the Local Government Act 2000, in determining the meaning of "significant" for the purposes of reg.8(1), regard shall be had to any guidance issued for the time being by the Secretary of State.

recorded in accordance with regs 3 or 4, or of that part, where only a part of the report is relevant to such a decision, shall be available for inspection by members of the public, as soon as is reasonably practicable, at the offices of the relevant local authority.[50] Where a request on behalf of a newspaper is made for a copy of any of the documents available for public inspection under para.5(1), those documents must be supplied for the benefit of the newspaper by the local authority on payment by the newspaper to the local authority of postage, copying or other necessary charge for transmission.[51] When a copy of the whole or part of a report for a private or a public meeting is made available for inspection by members of the public in accordance with reg.5,[52] at the same time a copy of the list compiled by the proper officer of the background papers to the report or part of the report must be included in the report or part of the report, and at least one copy of each of the documents included in that list must be made available for inspection by the public at the offices of the relevant local authority.[53] The above requirements are subject to certain provisions concerning confidential information, exempt information and advice given by political advisers or assistants.[54]

Meetings to be held in public

5–040 Where the executive leader, a s.11(2) mayor,[55] a council manager, or any other person likely to preside at a meeting[56] of a decision-making body, reasonably believes:

— that a decision to be made at that meeting will be a key decision[57]; or

50 Local Authorities (Executive Arrangements) (Access to Information) (England) Regulations 2000, reg.5(1).
51 *ibid.*, reg.5(2).
52 Or reg.11, as to which, see below.
53 *ibid.*, reg.6.
54 *ibid.*, reg.21. See para.5–041.
55 Namely an elected mayor who is a member of a mayor-and-cabinet executive: Local Authorities (Executive Arrangements) (Access to Information) (England) Regulations 2000, reg.2.
56 For the purposes of reg.7(1), "meeting" does not include a meeting to which the circumstances specified in reg.7(2)(b) apply and the principal purpose of which is for an officer of the local authority to brief a decision-maker on matters connected with the making of an executive decision: Local Authorities (Executive Arrangements) (Access to Information) (England) Regulations 2000, reg.7(2A).
57 Local Authorities (Executive Arrangements) (Access to Information) (England) Regulations 2000, reg.7(2)(a). The steps that must be taken to publicise key decisions are set out in reg.12 of the Local Authorities (Executive Arrangements) (Access to Information) (England) Regulations 2000. The steps that must be taken in relation to key decisions taken by individual executive members or officers are set out in reg.9. The procedure to be followed prior to public meetings generally is set out in reg.10.

— that a matter that is included in the forward plan[58] or is the subject of a notice given under reg.15 is likely to be discussed at the meeting, and the decision on that matter is likely to be made within 28 days, and an officer who is not a political adviser, assistant or council manager will be present at the discussion,[59]

the meeting (or that part of it) must be held in public.[60] This requirement is also subject to certain provisions concerning confidential information, exempt information and advice given by political advisers or assistants.[61]

Confidential information, exempt information, and advice

The public may be excluded from a meeting of a decision-making body that is exercising an executive function where it is likely, in view of the nature of the business to be transacted or of the nature of the proceedings, that if members of the public were present during the transaction of an item of business: 5–041

— confidential information would be disclosed to them in breach of the obligation of confidence[62];
— a resolution has been passed by the decision-making body concerned excluding the public during the transaction of an item of business where it is likely, in view of the nature of the item of business, that if members of the public were present during the transaction of that item, exempt information would be disclosed to them[63];
— a resolution has been passed by the decision-making body concerned excluding the public during the transaction of an item of business where it is likely, in view of the nature of the item, that if members of the public were present during the transaction of that item, the advice of a political adviser or assistant would be disclosed to them[64]; or,

58 Forward plans are required to contain details of all the matters likely to be the subject of key decisions, and must be prepared in accordance with regs 13 and 14 of the Local Authorities (Executive Arrangements) (Access to Information) (England) Regulations 2000: Local Authorities (Executive Arrangements) (Access to Information) (England) Regulations 2000, reg.13(1).
59 Local Authorities (Executive Arrangements) (Access to Information) (England) Regulations 2000, reg.7(2)(b).
60 *ibid.*, reg.7(1)).
61 *ibid.*, reg.21. See para.5–041.
62 *ibid.*, reg.21(1)(a).
63 *ibid.*, reg.21(1)(b). A resolution under reg.21(1)(b) must identify the proceedings or part of the proceedings to which it applies, and state by reference to the descriptions in Sch.12A to the Local Government Act 1972 the description of exempt information giving rise to the exclusion of the public: Local Authorities (Executive Arrangements) (Access to Information) (England) Regulations 2000, reg.21(2).
64 *ibid.*, reg.21(1)(c).

— a lawful power is used to exclude a member or members of the public in order to maintain orderly conduct or to prevent misbehaviour at a meeting.[65]

An exclusion of the public on any of the first three of the abovementioned bases may apply only to the part or parts of the meeting during which it is likely that confidential information, exempt information, or the advice of a political adviser or political assistant would be disclosed.[66] A local authority is not authorised by the Regulations to disclose to the public or make available for public inspection any document or part of a document if, in the opinion of the proper officer, that document or part of a document:

— contains or may contain confidential information;
— contains or is likely to contain exempt information or the advice of a political adviser or assistant.[67]

Access to agenda and connected reports

5–042 Copies of the agenda and every report for a public meeting must be available for inspection by the public at the offices of the local authority when they are made available to the members of the executive or decision-making body responsible for making the decision to which they relate.[68] The proper officer is empowered to have excluded from the copy of any report the whole, or any part, of the report which relates only to the transaction of any item of business during which, in his opinion, the meeting is not likely to be open to the public.[69] Any document which is required to be available for inspection by the public must be available for inspection for at least five clear days before the meeting, except

[65] Local Authorities (Executive Arrangements) (Access to Information) (England) Regulations 2000, reg.21(1)(d).

[66] *ibid.*, reg.21(3).

[67] Reg.21(5) makes similar provision in respect of documents relating to executive decisions made in accordance with executive arrangements made by members of local authority executives and officers.

[68] Local Authorities (Executive Arrangements) (Access to Information) (England) Regulations 2000, reg.11(1).

[69] *ibid.*, reg.11(2). Where, by virtue of reg.11(2), the whole or any part of a report for a public meeting is not available for inspection by the public, every copy of the whole report, or the part of the report, as the case may be, must be marked "not for publication". Moreover, there must be stated on every copy of the whole or part of the report either that it contains confidential information; or exempt information and, by reference to the descriptions in Sch.12A to the Local Government Act 1972, the description of the exempt information by virtue of which the decision-making body discharging the executive function is likely to exclude the public during the item to which the report relates; or that the report, or to part of the report, contains the advice of a political adviser or assistant as the case may be: Local Authorities (Executive Arrangements) (Access to Information) (England) Regulations 2000, reg. 11(5).

that, when the meeting if convened at shorter notice,[70] a copy of the agenda and associated reports must be available for inspection at the time when the meeting is convened; and, where an item which would be available for inspection by the public is added to the agenda, a copy of the revised agenda, and of any report relating to the item for consideration at the meeting, must be available for inspection by the public when the item is added to the agenda.[71] The local authority must, except during any part of a public meeting from which the public are excluded, make available for the use of members of the public present at the meeting a reasonable number of copies of the agenda and reports for the meeting.[72] In addition, local authorities must, following any request on behalf of a newspaper and on payment being made of postage charges or other necessary charge for transmission, supply to the newspaper a copy of the agenda for the public meeting and a copy of each of the reports for consideration at the meeting; such further statements or particulars, if any, as are necessary to indicate the nature of the items contained in the agenda; and, if the proper officer thinks fit in the case of any item, a copy of any other document supplied to members of the executive in connection with the item.[73]

3. HEALTH, MEDICAL AND CARE RECORDS

Introduction

Rights of access to medical information are to be found in various legislative provisions. The nature of the information is such that ordinarily the person seeking the information will be the subject of that information. To the extent that medical information relating to the applicant is "data" that is "processed" (which terms will include information that is held) under an automated or computerised system, it will generally be available to the applicant under the Data Protection Act 1998.[74] In addition to this right: 5–043

[70] In accordance with reg.15 or 16 of the Local Authorities (Executive Arrangements) (Access to Information) (England) Regulations 2000: Local Authorities (Executive Arrangements) (Access to Information) (England) Regulations 2000, reg.11(3)(a).

[71] Local Authorities (Executive Arrangements) (Access to Information) (England) Regulations 2000, reg.11(3). Reg.11(3) is subject to reg.11(4), which provides that nothing in reg.11(3) shall require a copy of the agenda, item or report to be available for inspection by the public until a copy is available to members of the decision-making body concerned.

[72] Local Authorities (Executive Arrangements) (Access to Information) (England) Regulations 2000: reg.11(6).

[73] Subject to Local Authorities (Executive Arrangements) (Access to Information) (England) Regulations 2000, reg.21, as to which see para.5–041. The Local Authorities (Executive Arrangements) (Access to Information) (England) Regulations 2000 also contain provisions concerning times for inspection, payment and copying of documents, and provisions concerning offences involving the withholding of information, similar to those that are to be found in the Local Government Act 1972.

[74] See Ch. 4.

(1) Under the Access to Medical Reports Act 1988 a person has specific rights of access to any report relating to himself prepared by a medical practitioner for employment or insurance purposes.[75]

(2) In 1995, the Department of Health published *The Patients' Charter and You: A Charter for England*, setting out every patient's "rights" in dealing with the NHS: this included a statement of a patient's "right" to have access to his own health records. This was later replaced by another Department of Health publication *Your Guide to the NHS*. This describes as one of its "core principles" the provision of open access to information about services, treatment and performance.[76] Neither document bestows any rights of access to medical information.

(3) In 1995 the Department of Health also produced a *Code of Practice on Openness in the NHS*, which applied to Regional Health Authorities, Family Health Service Authorities, District Health Authorities, Special Health Authorities, NHS Trusts, the Mental Health Act Commission and Community Health Councils. Although it spelled out in some detail the procedure that was to be followed, the time within which information was to be provided, a series of nine exemptions, and a complaints procedure, it did not create any enforceable rights.

(4) The Access to Health Records Act 1990 provided a right of access to "manual" health records. This was largely repealed by the Data Protection Act 1998, the scope of which extended to information caught by the 1990 Act.[77]

Rights of access to medical reports under the Access to Medical Reports Act 1988

5–044 An individual has a right of access to any medical report relating to him which is to be or has been supplied by a medical practitioner for employment or insurance purposes.[78] In addition, medical practitioners have a duty to retain a copy of any medical report which they have supplied for employment or insurance purposes for at least six months from the date when it was supplied.[79] A medical practitioner, if so requested, must give an individual access to any medical report relating to him which the practitioner has supplied for employment or insurance purposes in the previous six months.[80]

[75] See paras 5–044 to 5–047.

[76] This is to be found at *www.nhs. uk/nhsguide*.

[77] The Act now applies only to applications for access to records by the personal representative of a patient who has died or by a person who might have a claim arising out of the patient's death: Access to Health Records Act 1990, s.3(1)(f).

[78] Access to Medical Reports Act 1988, s.1.

[79] *ibid*., s.6(1).

[80] *ibid*., s.6(2). By s.6(3), the reference in s.6(2) to giving an individual access to a medical report is a reference to making a copy of the report available for his inspection, or supplying him with a copy of it.

Rights upon an application for a medical report for employment or insurance purposes

No person may apply to a medical practitioner to be supplied with a medical report for employment or insurance purposes and relating to an individual unless that person ("the applicant") has notified the individual that he proposes to make the application and the individual has notified the applicant that he consents to the making of the application.[81] Any such notification given by an applicant to the individual must inform him of his right to withhold consent to the making of the application, and of the following rights that he has under the Access to Medical Reports Act 1988: 5–045

— his rights arising under ss.4(1) to 4(3) and 6(2) with respect to access to the report before or after it is supplied;
— the right to withhold consent under s.5(1); and
— the right to request the amendment of the report under s.5(2).[82]

The notification must also inform the individual concerned of the effect of s.7 of the Access to Medical Reports Act 1988.[83] An individual who gives his consent to the making of an application shall be entitled, when giving his consent, to state that he wishes to have access to the report to be supplied in response to the application before it is so supplied; and that, if he does so, the applicant shall notify the medical practitioner of that fact at the time when the application is made and, at the same time, notify the individual of the making of the application.[84] Further, each such application must contain a statement to the effect of s.4(2).[85] Where a medical practitioner is notified by the applicant that the individual in question wishes to have access to the report before it is supplied, the practitioner must not supply the report unless he has given the individual access to it and any requirements of s.5 have been complied with, or the period of 21 days beginning with the date of the making of the application has elapsed without his having received any communication from the individual concerning arrangements for the individual to have access to it.[86] Where a medical practitioner receives an application for a medical report to be supplied for employment or insurance purposes without being notified by the applicant as mentioned in s.4(1) but, before supplying the report, receives a notification from the individual that he wishes to have access to the report before it is supplied, the practitioner must not supply the report unless the same conditions as are set

[81] Access to Medical Reports Act 1988, s.3(1).
[82] *ibid.*, s.3(2).
[83] *ibid.*, s.3(2).
[84] *ibid.*, s.4(1).
[85] *ibid.*, s.4(1).
[86] *ibid.*, s.4(2).

out in s.4(2) have been satisfied.[87] Where an individual has been given access to a report under s.4, the report may not be supplied in response to the application in question unless the individual has notified the medical practitioner that he consents to its being so supplied.[88] The individual in question is entitled, before giving his consent, to request the medical practitioner to amend any part of the report which the individual considers to be incorrect or misleading. If the individual does so, then the practitioner must amend the report accordingly, if he is to any extent prepared to accede to the individual's request; or, if he is not to any extent prepared to accede to it, but the individual requests him to attach to the report a statement of the individual's views in respect of any part of the report which he is declining to amend, then he must attach such a statement to the report.[89]

Denial of access

5–046 Medical practitioners are not obliged to give an individual access to any part of a medical report whose disclosure would, in the opinion of the practitioner, be likely to cause serious harm to the physical or mental health of the individual or others or would indicate the intentions of the practitioner in respect of the individual.[90] Secondly, medical practitioners are not obliged to give an individual access to any part of a medical report whose disclosure would be likely to reveal information about another person, or to reveal the identity of another person who has supplied information to the practitioner about the individual, unless that person has consented, or that person is a health professional who has been involved in the care of the individual and the information relates to or has been provided by the professional in that capacity.[91] Where it appears to a medical practitioner that either exemption is applicable to any part (but not the whole) of a medical report, he must notify the individual of that fact. Where it appears to the practitioner that either exemption is applicable to the whole of the report, then he must notify the individual of that fact and he may not supply the report unless he is notified by the individual that the individual consents to its being supplied. If he is so notified by the individual, then the restrictions imposed by s.4(2) and 4(3) do not have effect in relation to it.[92]

---

[87] Access to Medical Reports Act 198, s.4(3).
[88] *ibid.*, s. 5(1).
[89] *ibid.*, s. 5(2). Section 5(3) further provides that any request made by an individual under s.5(2) must be made in writing.
[90] Access to Medical Reports Act 1988, s.7(1). A broadly similar exemption is provided by the Freedom of Information Act 2000, s.38: see paras 23–001 to 23–003.
[91] Access to Medical Reports Act 1988, s.7(2).
[92] *ibid.*, s.7(4).

Application to the court

If a court is satisfied on the application of an individual that any person, in connection with a medical report relating to that individual, has failed or is likely to fail to comply with any requirement of the Access to Medical Reports Act 1988, then the court may order that person to comply with that requirement.[93] The jurisdiction is exercisable by a county court or, in Scotland, by the sheriff.[94] 5–047

4. ENVIRONMENTAL INFORMATION

Introduction

Information relating to environmental matters and held by public authorities has for some time been subject to statutory provisions requiring its disclosure to members of the public.[94A] This has in large part been the result of Council Directives. The interaction of these rights of access with those bestowed by the Freedom of Information Act 2000 is particularly complex, with the Act making specific exemption in relation to certain environmental information,[95] in addition to the usual provision rendering material exempt information where a public authority is by another enactment obliged to communicate it to the applicant.[96] In summary, specific rights of access to environmental information are bestowed by: 5–048

(1) the Environment and Safety Information Act 1988;
(2) the Environmental Information Regulations 1992;
(3) Sch.11 to the Environment Act 1995;
(4) s.86 of the National Parks and Access to the Countryside Act 1949;
(5) the information provisions of the Aarhus Convention; and
(6) once passed, the Environmental Information Regulations giving effect to the information provisions of the Aarhus Convention: these will replace the Environmental Information Regulations 1992.

---

93 Access to Medical Reports Act 1988, s.8(1).

94 *ibid.*, s.8(2).

94A That there is a particular public interest in the disclosure of information relating to the environment is reflected in Pt IVA of the Employment Rights Act 1996, as inserted by the Public Interest Disclosure Act 1998, which sanctions as being in the public interest a disclosure by an employee tending to show "that the environment has been, is being or is likely to be damaged." —s.43B(1)(e).

95 Freedom of Information Act 2000, s.39; Freedom of Information (Scotland) Act 2002, s.39(2)(a). See further para.5–059 and paras 16–009 to 16–013.

96 Freedom of Information Act 2000, s.21; Freedom of Information (Scotland) Act 2002, s.25(1). See further paras 16–001 to 16–004.

The Environment and Safety Information Act 1988

5–049 The right of access to information bestowed by this Act is very limited. It requires certain authorities to keep a register of certain notices served by the authority, to ensure that the register is indexed and to ensure that the register and the index are open to inspection by the public free of charge at all reasonable hours.[97] A person inspecting the register can require the authority to provide him with a copy of the entry in the register.[98] The only authorities to which the Act applies and the only notices to which the Act applies are:

(1) notices issued by a fire authority[99] under s.10 of the Fire Precautions Act 1971;
(2) notices issued by an enforcing authority[1] under ss.21 and 22 of the Health and Safety at Work etc. Act 1974,
(3) notices issued by a local authority[2] under s.10 of the Safety of Sports Grounds Act 1975; and
(4) notices issued by the responsible authority[3] under ss.19(5) and 19(6) of the Food and Environment Protection Act 1985.

An exemption is provided where an entry would disclose a trade secret, but the provision requires the person upon whom the notice has been served to claim this exemption within 14 days of service.[4]

The Environmental Information Regulations 1992

5–050 The main legislative provisions currently governing access to environmental information are to be found in the Environmental Information Regulations 1992. These Regulations implement Council Directive 90/313 on Freedom of Access to Information on the Environment. They apply in respect of information relating to the environment,[5] in particular, information relating to the state of any body of water or air, the state of any flora or fauna, the state of any natural site or other land; any activities or measures (including activities giving rise to noise or any other nuisance) which adversely affect any of the above or are likely adversely to affect any of the above; and any activities or administrative

[97] Environment and Safety Information Act 1988, s.1(1). The register can be kept on a computer.
[98] *ibid.*, s.1(2). The authority can require the payment of a reasonable fee: presumably the cost of photocopying the page in the register.
[99] As defined in the Fire Precautions Act 1971, s.43(1).
[1] As defined in the Health and Safety at Work etc Act 1974, s.18(7)(a).
[2] As defined in the Safety of Sports Grounds Act 1975, s.17(1).
[3] As defined in the Food and Environment Protection Act 1985, s.2(2).
[4] Environment and Safety Information Act 1988, s.4(1). As to trade secrets, see paras 25–028 to 25–033.
[5] Environmental Information Regulations 1992, reg.2(1)(a).

or other measures (including any environmental management programmes) which are designed to protect any of the above.[6] "Information" is defined to include anything contained in any records,[7] while "records" includes registers, reports and returns, as well as computer records and other records kept otherwise than in a document. A "relevant person"[8] who holds any information to which the Regulations apply must make that information available to any person who requests it.[9] In addition, every relevant person who holds information to which the Regulations apply has a duty to make arrangements for giving effect to reg.3(1) that secure that every request made for the purposes of reg.3(1) is responded to as soon as possible; that no such request is responded to more than two months after it is made[10]; and that where the response to such a request contains a refusal to make information available, the refusal is in writing and specifies the reasons for the refusal.[11] These arrangements may include provision entitling the relevant person to refuse a request for information in cases where the request is manifestly unreasonable or is formulated in too general a manner.[12] They may also include provision for the imposition of a charge on any person in respect of the costs reasonably attributable to the supply of

6 Environmental Information Regulations 1992, reg.2(2). In *Mecklenburg v Kreis Pinnenberg der Landrat (Case C 321/96)* [1999] All E.R. (EC) 166; [1999] 2 C.M.L.R. 418; [1999] Env.L.R. D6, the European Court of Justice held that the concept of "information relation to the Environment" in Art.2 of Council Directive 90/313 on Freedom of Access to Information on the Environment was intentionally broad, so that a statement of views put forward by a local authority with respect to the planning approval for a road could constitute such information, on the basis that it was capable of adversely affecting, or of protecting, the state of one of the sectors of the environment governed by the Directive.

7 Environmental Information Regulations 1992, reg.2(4).

8 The following are relevant persons for the purposes of the Environmental Information Regulations 1992: by reg.2(3)(a), all such Ministers of the Crown, Government departments, local authorities, and other persons carrying out functions of public administration at a national, regional or local level as, for the purposes of or in connection with their functions, have responsibilities in relation to the environment; and, by reg.2(3)(b), any body with public responsibilities for the environment which does not fall within reg.2(3)(a), but is under the control of a person falling within that regulation.

9 Environmental Information Regulations 1992, reg.3(1). The obligation contained in reg.3(1) does not require the relevant person to make information available except in such form, and at such times and places, as may be reasonable: Environmental Information Regulations 1992, reg.3(5). Reg.3(6) further provides that, without prejudice to any remedies available apartt from reg.3 in respect of a failure by a relevant person to comply with the requirements of the Environmental Information Regulations 1992, the obligation to make information available in pursuance of reg.3(1) is a duty owed to the person who requested the information.

10 Environmental Information Regulations 1992, reg.3(2).

11 The purpose of the duty to give reasons for a refusal to disclose information under reg.3(2)(c) is to enable the individual concerned to know whether the refusal was legally and factually well-founded. A bare assertion to the effect that the information in question falls within one of the exceptions set out in reg.4, *e.g.* that the information is confidential information, will be inadequate for this purpose: *R v Secretary of State for the Environment, Transport and the Regions; Ex p. Alliance Against Birmingham Northern Relief Road (No.1)* [1999] Env.L.R. 447; [1999] J.P.L. 231; [1999] C.O.D. 45 (QBD, per Sullivan J.). Regulation 5 of the Environmental Information Regulations 1992 makes similar provision with respect to information which is not information to which the Regulations apply, but which is required under any statutory provision to be made available to any person.

12 Environmental Information Regulations 1992, reg.3(3).

information to that person in pursuance of reg.3(1); and may make the supply of any information in pursuance of reg.3(1) conditional on the payment of such a charge.[13] Subject to certain exceptions considered in the following paragraph, where any statutory provision or rule of law imposes any restriction or prohibition on the disclosure of information by any person, that restriction or prohibition is inapplicable to any disclosure of information in pursuance of the Environmental Information Regulations 1992.

Exceptions to the right to information under the Environmental Information Regulations 1992

5–051 Information that is capable of being treated as confidential, or authorises or requires the disclosure of any information that must be so treated, is exempted from the obligation to disclose.[14] For the purposes of the Regulations, information is capable of being treated as confidential if and only if it is information the disclosure of which would affect international relations,[15] national defence[16] or public security[17]; would affect matters which are, or have been, an issue in any legal proceedings or in any inquiry (including any disciplinary inquiry), or are the subject-matter of an investigation undertaken with a view to any such proceedings or inquiry[18]; would affect the confidentiality of the deliberations of any relevant person; would involve the supply of a document or other record which is still in the course of completion,[19] or of any internal communication of a relevant person; or would affect the confidentiality of matters to which any commercial or industrial confidentiality attaches, including intellectual

[13] Environmental Information Regulations 1992, reg.3(4). In *Commission of the European Communities v Germany (Case C2 17/97)* [1999] 3 C.M.L.R. 277; [2000] Env.L.R. 141, however, the European Court of Justice held that the imposition of a charge to be made even in cases where requests for information were refused was incompatible with Art.5 of Council Directive 90/313 on Freedom of Access to Information on the Environment.

[14] Environmental Information Regulations 1992, reg.4(1).

[15] See further paras 18–001 to 18–010 for a consideration of the analogous exemption in the Freedom of Information Act 2000.

[16] See further paras 17–051 to 17–059 for a consideration of the analogous exemption in the Freedom of Information Act 2000.

[17] This appears to be concerned with internal public security and might embrace enforcement of the criminal law (as to which, see further paras 20–014 to 20–023 for a consideration of the analogous exemption in the Freedom of Information Act 2000) as well as national security (as to which, see further paras 17–033 to 17–040 for a consideration of the analogous exemption in the Freedom of Information Act 2000).

[18] See further paras 20–004 to 20–007 and 20–019 to 20–034 for a consideration of the analogous exemptions in the Freedom of Information Act 2000.

[19] Thus in *Maile v Wigan MBC* (QBD) [2001] Env.L.R. 11, [2001] J.P.L. 193 Eady J. held that, by virtue of reg.4(2)(d) of the Environmental Information Regulations 1992, the Council was not obliged to disclose to the claimant a database of potentially contaminated sites in its area, because the database was still in the course of completion. In addition, the information came within the confidentiality exception in reg.4(2)(c).

property.[20] Information must be treated as confidential, for the purposes of the Regulations, if and only if:

- in the case of any request made to a relevant person under reg.3, it is capable of being so treated and its disclosure in response to that request would[21] contravene any statutory provision or rule of law or would involve the breach of any agreement;
- the information is personal information contained in records held in relation to an individual who has not given his consent to its disclosure;
- the information is held by the relevant person in consequence of having been supplied by a person who was not under, and could not have been put under, any legal obligation to supply it to the relevant person; did not supply it in circumstances such that the relevant person is entitled apart from the Environmental Information Regulations 1992 to disclose it; and has not consented to its disclosure.[22]
- in the case of a request to a relevant person made under reg.3, the disclosure of the information in response to that request would, in the circumstances, increase the likelihood of damage to the environment affecting anything to which the information relates.[23]

Regulation 4 does not authorise a refusal to make available any information contained in the same record as, or otherwise held with, other information which is withheld by virtue of reg.4, unless it is incapable of being separated from the other information for the purpose of making it available.[24]

The Environment Act 1995 and National Parks and Access to the Countryside Act 1949

The Environment Act 1995 and Access to the Countryside Act 1949 provide two further instances in which access to environmental information may be obtained. Schedule 11 to the Environment Act 1995 sets out a scheme for the provision by a local authority to the public of information concerning air quality in connection with its duties to conduct air quality reviews and air quality 5–052

[20] See further paras 25–001 to 25–042 for a consideration of the analogous exemptions in the Freedom of Information Act 2000.

[21] Apart from reg.3(7) of the Environmental Information Regulations 1992.

[22] Environmental Information Regulations 1992, reg.4(3)(a)–(c).

[23] *ibid.*, reg.4(3)(d). The questions of whether any information relating to the environment is confidential, and whether reg.4(3) applies, are factual questions to be resolved objectively. If the information is "capable of being treated as confidential" for the purposes of reg.4(1), then the relevant person has a discretion as to whether or not to disclose the information: *R. v Secretary of State for the Environment, Transport and the Regions Ex p. Alliance Against Birmingham Northern Relief Road (No.1)* [1999] Env.L.R. 447, [1999] J.P.L. 231, [1999] C.O.D. 45 (QBD, *per* Sullivan J.).

[24] Environmental Information Regulations 1992, reg.4(4).

assessments of the air within its area, to designate air quality management areas, and to conduct assessments of air quality in air quality management areas. Thus, each local authority has a duty to ensure that the reports of air quality reviews and results of air quality assessments which it conducts pursuant to the abovementioned provisions are available for inspection by the public at all reasonable times and free of charge.[25] The Countryside Commission (in relation to England) and the Countryside Council for Wales (in relation to Wales) must take steps[26] for ensuring that persons interested are informed of the situation and extent of, and means of access to, national parks, areas of outstanding national beauty and certain long-distance routes, and of the accommodation and facilities there available for visitors.[27] The above-mentioned bodies must also take steps to ensure that persons interested are able to learn about the history, natural features and flora and fauna of national parks, the objects of architectural, archaeological or historical interest in them and opportunities there available for recreation.[28]

The Aarhus Convention

5–053 The UN Economic Commission for Europe (UNECE) Convention on Access to Information, Public Participation in Decision-Making and Access to Justice on Environmental Matters, commonly known as the Aarhus Convention, was adopted on June 25, 1998 in the Danish city of Aarhus at the Fourth Ministerial Conference in the "Environment for Europe" process. It entered into force on October 30, 2001. The UK is a signatory to the Aarhus Convention, as is the European Community in its own right. The Aarhus Convention establishes a number of rights of the public (citizens and their associations) with respect to the environment. It contains three broad themes or "pillars", namely access to information; public participation; and access to justice.[29] It also refers to the goal of protecting the right of every person of present and future generations to live in an environment which is adequate to health and well-being. The UNECE has described the Aarhus Convention as "a new kind of environmental agreement", which links environmental rights and human rights; and government accountability and environmental protection. Thus, it is not only an environmental agreement, but also an agreement about government accountability,

[25] Environment Act 1995, Sch.11, para.4.
[26] National Parks and Access to the Countryside Act 1949, s.86(3).
[27] *ibid.*, s.86.
[28] *ibid.*, s.86(1)(b).
[29] Thus Art.1 of the Aarhus Convention provides "In order to contribute to the protection of the right of every person of present and future generations to live in an environment adequate to his or her health and well-being, each Party shall guarantee the rights of access to information, public participation in decision-making, and access to justice in environmental matters in accordance with the provisions of this Convention".

transparency and responsiveness.[30] The Secretary of State for the Environment, has stated that the UK government strongly supports the objectives of the Aarhus Convention, adding that the three areas in which it provides additional rights (namely under the three "pillars" referred to above) will allow the public[31] to be better informed and more involved in decision-making, and that "more broadly based discussion can lead to better decisions and so make an important contribution to achieving sustainable development". The Secretary of State has also stated that the UK government intends to ratify the Aarhus Convention as quickly as possible.

The first "pillar" of the Aarhus Convention—access to information

5–054 The Aarhus Convention provides for the right of everyone to receive environmental information that is held by public authorities.[32] The term "environmental information" is defined in Art.2(3)(a) of the Aarhus Convention to mean any information in written, visual, aural, electric or any other material form on the state of elements of the environment, such as air and atmosphere, water,

[30] The Preamble to the Aarhus Convention states, *inter alia*, that the parties thereto agreed to its terms "Affirming the need to protect, preserve and improve the state of the environment and to ensure sustainable and environmentally sound development; Recognising that adequate protection of the environment is essential to human well-being and the enjoyment of basic human rights, including the right to life itself; Recognising also that every person has the right to live in an environment adequate to his or her health and well-being, and the duty, both individually and in association with others, to protect and improve the environment for the benefit of present and future generations; Considering that, to be able to assert this right and observe this duty, citizens must have access to information, be entitled to participate in decision-making and have access to justice in environmental matters, and acknowledging in this regard that citizens may need assistance in order to exercise their rights; Recognising that, in the field of the environment, improved access to information and public participation in decision-making enhance the quality and the implementation of decisions, contribute to public awareness of environmental issues, give the public the opportunity to express its concerns and enable public authorities to take due account of such concerns; Aiming thereby to further the accountability and transparency in decision-making and to strengthen public support for decisions on the environment; Recognising the desirability of transparency in all branches of government and inviting legislative bodies to implement the principles of the Convention in their proceedings; [and] Recognising also that the public needs to be aware of the procedures for participation in environmental decision-making, have free access to them and know how to use them . . .".

[31] "The public" is defined in Art.2(4) of the Aarhus Convention to mean "one or more natural or legal persons, and, in accordance with national legislation or practice, their associations, organisations or groups".

[32] "Public authority" is defined in Art.2(2) of the Aarhus Convention as meaning "(a) Government at national, regional and other level; (b) Natural or legal persons performing public administrative functions under national law, including specific duties, activities or services in relation to the environment; (c) Any other natural or legal persons having public responsibilities or functions, or providing public services, in relation to the environment, under the control of a person falling within subparagraphs (a) or (b) above; (d) the institutions of any regional economic integration organisation referred to in art.17 which is a party to this Convention." Art.2 further states that the above definition of "public authority" does not include bodies or institutions acting in a judicial or legislative capacity.

soil, land, landscape and natural sites, biological diversity and its components, including genetically modified organisms, and the interaction among those elements; and, by Art.2(3)(b), factors, such as substances, energy, noise and radiation, and activities or measures, including administrative measures, environmental agreements, policies, legislation, plans and programmes, affecting or likely to affect the elements of the environment within the scope of Art.2(3)(a), and cost-benefit and other economic analyses and assumptions used in environmental decision-making. "Environmental information" also includes information concerning the state of human health and safety, conditions of human life, cultural sites and built structures, inasmuch as they are or may be affected by the state of the elements of the environment or, through those elements, by the factors, activities or measures referred to in Art.2(3)(b). This information must be provided within one month of a request for it,[33] and without the person making the request having to say why he requires it.[34] A request for environmental information may be refused in the circumstances set out in Art.4(4) of the Aarhus Convention. These include circumstances where disclosure would adversely affect:

- the confidentiality of the proceedings of public authorities, provided that such confidentiality is provided for under national law[35];
- international relations,[36] national defence or public security[37];
- the course of justice[38];
- the confidentiality of commercial and industrial information, where such confidentiality is protected by law in order to protect a legitimate economic interest[39];
- intellectual property rights[40];
- the confidentiality of personal data and/or files relating to a natural person, where that person has not consented to the disclosure of the

33 Art.4(2). This requirement is subject to the proviso that this period may be extended, if the volume and complexity of the information justifies the extension, to up to two months after the request. The applicant for information must be informed of any extension and the reasons for it.

34 Art.4(1)(a).

35 Art.4(4)(a).

36 See paras 18–001 to 18–012 for a consideration of the analogous exemption in the Freedom of Information Act 2000.

37 Art.4(4)(b). See paras 17–033 to 17–059 for a consideration of the analogous exemption in the Freedom of Information Act 2000. The reference to public security will probably embrace enforcement of the criminal law (as to which, see paras 20–014 to 20–023 for a consideration of the analogous exemption in the Freedom of Information Act 2000).

38 Including, in particular, the ability of a person to receive a fair trial or the ability of a public authority to conduct an inquiry of a criminal or disciplinary nature: Art.4(4)(c).

39 Art.4(4)(d). This Art.specifically provides, further, that "Within this framework, information on emissions which is relevant for the protection of the environment shall be disclosed." See paras 25–001 to 25–028 for a consideration of the analogous exemptions in the Freedom of Information Act 2000.

40 Art.4(4)(e).

information to the public and where such confidentiality is provided for in national law[41];
— the interests of a third party which has supplied the information requested without that party being under or capable of being put under a legal obligation to do so, and where that party does not consent to the release of the material[42];
— the environment to which the information relates, such as the breeding sites of rare species.[43]

Article 4 of the Aarhus Convention further provides that "The aforementioned grounds for refusal shall be interpreted in a restrictive way, taking into account the public interest served by the disclosure and taking into account whether the information requested relates to emissions into the environment". Public authorities also have a separate obligation, under the Aarhus Convention, actively to disseminate environmental information in their possession.[44]

The second "pillar" of the Aarhus Convention—public participation

Article 6 of the Aarhus Convention guarantees the right to participate from an early stage in environmental decision-making with respect to certain specified activities,[45] and with respect to activities that are not specified in the Aarhus Convention itself, but which may have a significant effect on the environment. Under Art.6(2), where the provisions of Art.6 are applicable, the public concerned[46] must be informed, either by public notice or individually as appropriate, early in the environmental decision-making procedure, and in an adequate, timely and effective manner, *inter alia*, of the proposed activity and the application on which a decision will be taken; the nature of the possible decisions or draft decision; the public authority responsible for making the decision, the envisaged decision-making procedure; and the fact that the activity is subject to 5–055

41 Art.4(4)(f). See paras 24–007 to 24–016 for a consideration of the analogous exemption in the Freedom of Information Act 2000.
42 Art.4(4)(g).
43 Art.4(4)(h).
44 Art.5.
45 Namely, those listed in Annex I to the Aarhus Convention. These include activities carried out in the energy sector; in the course of the production and processing of materials; in the mineral and chemical industries; in waste management; by water treatment plants with a capacity exceeding 150,000 population equivalent; by industrial plants; in the construction of transport infrastructure such as railways, airports and roads; and other activities; as well as any activities not specifically mentioned where public participation is provided for under an environmental impact assessment procedure in accordance with national legislation.
46 Namely by Art.2(5), the public affected or likely to be affected by, or having an interest in, the environmental decision-making. Article 2(5) further provides that, for the purpose of the latter definition, non-governmental organisations promoting environmental protection and meeting any requirements under national law shall be deemed to have an interest.

a national or transboundary environmental impact assessment procedure. By Art.6(6), each party to the Convention must require the competent public authorities to give the public concerned access for examination, upon request where so required under national law, free of charge and as soon as it becomes available, all information relevant to the decision-making referred to in Art.6 that is available at the time of the public participation procedure, including at least a description of the site and the physical and technical characteristics of the proposed activity; a description of the significant effects of the proposed activity on the environment; a description of the measures envisaged to prevent and/or reduce the effects, including emissions; a non-technical summary of the above; an outline of the main alternatives studied by the applicant; and, in accordance with national legislation, the main reports and advice issued to the public authority at the time when the public concerned shall be informed in accordance with Art.6(2).[47] The procedure for public participation must then allow for the public to submit, in writing or, as appropriate, at a public hearing or inquiry with the applicant, any comments, information, analyses, or opinions that it considers relevant to the proposed activity[48]; and the parties to the Convention must ensure that in the decision due account is taken of the outcome of the public participation.[49]

The third "pillar" of the Aarhus Convention—access to justice

5–056 This pillar of the Aarhus Convention, which is set out in Art.9, aims to provide access to justice in three contexts, namely, review procedures with respect to information requests; review procedures with respect to specific decisions that are subject to the public participation requirements, and challenges to breaches of environmental law in general. So far as access to information appeals are concerned, the Convention provides that a person who considers that his Convention request for information has been ignored, wrongfully refused, inadequately answered, or otherwise not dealt with in accordance with the provisions of that Article, must be provided with access to a review procedure by a court or another independent and impartial body established by law.[50] The Convention further provides that, in the circumstances where a party provides

[47] These provisions are without prejudice to the provisions of Art.4 of the Aarhus Convention: Aarhus Convention, Art.6(6).

[48] Art.6(7).

[49] Further steps in the public participation procedure are provided for in Art.6(8)–(11). In addition, requirements for public participation concerning plans, programmes and policies relating to the environment are set out in Art.7; while Art.8 provides for public participation during the preparation of executive regulations and/or generally applicable legally binding normative instruments. The abovementioned provisions are already largely reflected in the Environmental Impact Assessment procedure that is provided for in UK law under the Town and Country Planning (Environmental Impact Assessment) (England and Wales) Regulations 1999, which were drafted with the Aarhus Convention in mind.

[50] Art.9(1).

for such a review by a court of law, it must ensure that a complainant also has access to an expeditious procedure established by law, that is free of charge or inexpensive, for reconsideration by a public authority or review by an independent and impartial body other than a court of law. Secondly, Art.9(2) provides that each party must, within the framework of its national legislation, ensure that members of the public concerned having a sufficient interest, or, alternatively, maintaining impairment of a right, where the administrative procedural law of a party requires this as a precondition, have access to a review procedure before a court of law and/or another independent and impartial body established by law to challenge the substantive and procedural legality of any decision, act or omission subject to the provisions of Art.6 and, where so provided for under national law, of other relevant provisions of the Aarhus Convention.[51] Article 9(2) further provides that what constitutes a sufficient interest or impairment of a right shall be determined in accordance with the requirements of national law and consistently with the objective of giving the public concerned wide access to justice within the scope of the Convention. To this end, Art.9(2) states, the interest of any non-governmental organisation meeting the requirements referred to in Art.2(5) (namely non-governmental organisations which promote environmental protection and meeting any requirements under national law) shall be deemed sufficient; and that such organisations shall also be deemed to have rights capable of being impaired for the purposes of Art.9(2).

The proposed Directive

The European Commission has produced a proposal for a Directive on Providing for Public Participation in respect of the drawing up of certain plans and programmes relating to the environment and amending Council Directives 85/337 EEC and 96/61 EC, which is aimed at consolidating and enhancing the rights of the public to participate in the decision-making process in environmental matters, so that the Member States of the European Community can ratify the Aarhus Convention. The proposal has two main strands. First, it aims to align existing environmental legislation with Art.7 of the Aarhus Convention by proposing a public participation procedure which should be provided for in certain existing Directives concerning the drawing up of plans and programmes 5–057

[51] This provision is subject to Art.9(3), which provides that in addition and without prejudice to the review procedures referred to in Arts 9(1) and 9(2), each Party shall ensure that, where they meet the criteria, if any, laid down in its national law, members of the public have access to administrative or judicial procedures to challenge acts and omissions by private persons and public authorities which contravene provisions of its national law relating to the environment.

that relate to the environment.[52] Secondly, it amends public participation rights in the EIA Directive (85/337/EEC) and the IPPC Directive (96/61/EC).

The proposed Regulations

5–058 In 2002 the Government published for consultation a draft of the regulations designed to implement the "information provisions" of the Aarhus Convention.[53]

Inter-relationship with the Freedom of Information Act 2000

5–059 Information to which an individual has a right of access pursuant to the regulations made under the Aarhus Convention is exempt information under the Freedom of Information Act 2000.[54] The effect is to attempt to give exclusivity to the access rights provided under those regulations.

5. PERSONAL INFORMATION

Disclosure of birth records of adopted children

5–060 Section 51 of the Adoption Act 1976[55] provides for the disclosure of the birth records of adopted children. By s.51(1) of the Adoption Act 1976, the Registrar General must, on an application made in the prescribed manner by an adopted person a record of whose birth is kept by him and who has attained the age of 18 years, supply that adopted person on payment of a prescribed fee (if any) with such information as is necessary to enable that person to obtain a certified copy of the record of his birth.[56] By s.51(2), on an application made in the

[52] Namely, the 1975 framework waste Directive (75/442), the 1991 batteries Directive (91/157), the 1991 agricultural nitrate Directive (91/676), the 1991 hazardous waste Directive (91/689), the 1994 packaging Directive (94/62), the 1996 ambient air quality Directive (92/62/EEC), and the 1999 waste landfill Directive (99/31).

[53] Called The Environmental Information Regulations 2002. As at the date of writing, these had not yet been brought into force. The "information provisions" of the Aarhus Convention are Art.4, together with Arts 3 and 9 so far as relating to that Article. Power to make the regulations derives from Freedom of Information Act 2000, s.74(3).

[54] Freedom of Information Act 2000, s.39(1)(a); Freedom of Information (Scotland) Act 2002, s.39(2)(a). See further paras 16–009 to 16–013.

[55] s.51 of the Adoption Act 1976 has been repealed by s.139(3) of and Sch.5 to the Adoption and Children Act 2002, which will come into force on a date to be appointed (see ss.148(1) and 148(2) of the Adoption and Children Act 2002).

[56] This requirement is, however, subject to an implied exception in cases where adherence to it would create a serious risk of a crime being committed. *R. v Registrar General Ex p. Smith* [1991] 2 Q.B. 393; [1991] 2 All E.R. 88 concerned an application under s.51 of the Adoption Act

prescribed manner by an adopted person under the age of 18 years, a record of whose birth is kept by the Registrar General and who is intending to be married in England or Wales, and on payment of the prescribed fee (if any), the Registrar General shall inform the applicant whether or not it appears from information contained in the registers of live births or other records that the applicant and the person whom he intends to marry may be within the prohibited degrees of relationship for the purposes of the Marriage Act 1949. Before supplying any information to an applicant under s.51(1), the Registrar General must inform the applicant that counselling services are available to him.

6. ECONOMIC AND BUSINESS INFORMATION

Introduction

A limited number of access rights to what might broadly be termed economic and business information exist in various statutory provisions. In brief these are: 5–061

(1) Under s.39 of the Radioactive Substances Act 1993, a limited amount of information relating to radioactive substances, held by the chief inspector but generally supplied to him by those involved in that industry.
(2) Under s.57 of the Coal Industry Act 1994, a limited amount of information relating to the coal industry, held by the Coal Authority but generally supplied to it by those involved in that industry.
(3) Under s.27 of the Industry Act 1975, certain economic planning information held by the Treasury.
(4) Under s.66 of the Land Registration Act 2002 and the regulations made under it, certain information relating to holdings and ownership of land held by the registrar.

The Radioactive Substances Act 1993

Provision is made under the Radioactive Substances Act 1993 for the public to obtain access to certain information concerning radioactive substances. Thus, 5–062

1976 by a convicted murderer for access to his birth certificate. The applicant suffered from a mental illness and had murdered a man whom he had mistaken for his foster mother. The Court of Appeal upheld the refusal of the Registrar to release the birth certificate, on the basis that an implied exception existed in the enforcement of Acts of Parliament for the court to interpret statutes in such a way as to prevent a serious crime from being committed. In the present case, releasing the applicant's birth certificate would pose a real and serious risk to the life of his mother, and it was right that his application should be refused.

under s.39 of the Act, the chief inspector[57] must keep copies of all applications made to him under any provision of the Radioactive Substances Act 1993[58]; of all documents issued by him under any provision of that Act[59]; of all other documents sent by him to any local authority pursuant to directions of the Secretary of State[60]; and of such records of convictions as may be prescribed in regulations.[61] The chief inspector must make copies of those documents available to the public,[62] except to the extent that this would involve the disclosure of information relating to any relevant process[63] or trade secret,[64] or would involve the disclosure of applications or certificates with respect to which the Secretary of State has directed[65] that knowledge should be restricted on grounds of national security. Every local authority must keep and make available to the public copies of all documents sent to the authority under any provision of that Act, unless directed by the chief inspector, or, as the case may be, the appropriate minister and the chief inspector, that all or any part of such document is not to be available for inspection.[66] It is not necessary for copies made available to the public by the chief inspector or a local authority to be kept in documentary form,[67] but the public nevertheless has the right to inspect such documents at all reasonable times and, on payment of a reasonable fee, to be provided with copies of such documents.[68] Because the right bestowed is one of inspection, the existence of this right does not of itself cause the information to be exempt information under the Freedom of Information Act 2000.[69]

The Coal Industry Act 1994

5–063 Similar provision for public access to information in respect of the coal industry is made under the Coal Industry Act 1994. Thus the Coal Authority is required to establish and maintain arrangements under which every person is entitled, on payment to the Authority of such fee and subject to such other conditions as the Authority may consider appropriate, to be furnished with certain

57 Namely the chief inspector appointed under s.4 of the Radioactive Substances Act 1993.
58 Radioactive Substances Act 1993, s.39(1)(a).
59 *ibid.*, s.39(1)(b).
60 *ibid.*, s.39(1)(c).
61 *ibid.*, s.39(1)(d).
62 *ibid.*, s.39(1).
63 "Relevant process" means any process applied for the purposes of, or in connection with, the production or use of radioactive material: Radioactive Substances Act 1993, s.34(3).
64 See paras 25–028 to 25–034 for a consideration of the analogous exemption in the Freedom of Information Act 2000.
65 Under Radioactive Substances Act 1993, s.25. In relation to what constitutes "national security", see paras 17–033 to 17–040, where it is considered in the context of the Freedom of Information Act 2000.
66 Radioactive Substances Act 1993, s.39.
67 *ibid.*, s.39(4).
68 *ibid.*, s.39(5).
69 See para.5–031.

information[70] and to have so much of the records maintained by the Authority as contain any such information, to be made available to him for inspection at such office of the Authority as it may determine and at such times as may be reasonable[71]; and also to make or be supplied with copies of or extracts from so much of the records maintained by the Authority as contain any such information.[72] For these purposes, "records" includes registers, maps, plans and accounts, as well as computer records and other records kept otherwise than in documentary form.[73] The information that must be made available in this way is that contained in the register of licences and orders[74]; that contained in the register of rights[75]; and any of the following which is for the time being in the possession of the Authority: information about the geological or physiological features or characteristics of any land in which any unworked coal or any coal mine is situated or of any other land[76]; information about the identity of persons in whom interests and rights in any unworked coal or coal mine have been vested[77]; the contents of any plans of any coal mines or coal workings[78]; any other information about proposals for the carrying on by any person of any coal mining operations[79]; information about any subsidence or subsidence damage or about claims made under the Coal Mining Subsidence Act 1991[80]; and information about such other matters as the Secretary of State may prescribe by regulations.[81] In so far as the right of access bestowed is one of inspection (and does not extend to being able to require the supply of a copy of the information), the existence of this right does not of itself cause the information to be exempt information under the Freedom of Information Act 2000.[82]

Excluded information

Certain types of information are excluded from the information that is required to be made available to any person in pursuance of the arrangements under the Coal Industry Act 1994. The Authority is not required or authorised to disclose any information which relates to the affairs of an individual or specifically to 5–064

70 Coal Industry Act 1994, s.57(2)(a).
71 *ibid.*, s.57(2)(b).
72 *ibid.*, s.57(2)(c).
73 *ibid.*, s.57(8). Records of the Coal Authority are public records for the purposes of the Public Records Act 1958: Coal Industry Act 1994, s.10.
74 *i.e.* under Coal Industry Act 1994, s.35.
75 *i.e.* under Coal Industry Act 1994, s.56.
76 Coal Industry Act 1994, s.57(1)(a).
77 *ibid.*, s.57(1)(b).
78 *ibid.*, s.57(1)(c). The Authority must maintain such records of information which comes into its possession and which falls into any of the preceding three heads as it considers appropriate: Coal Industry Act 1994, s.57(6).
79 Coal Industry Act 1994, s.57(1)(d).
80 *ibid.*, s.57(1)(e).
81 *ibid.*, s.57(1)(f).
82 See para.5–031.

the affairs of any body of persons (whether corporate or unincorporated, including the Authority itself), and which is not contained in the register of licences and orders or the register of rights, if the disclosure of that information would or might, in the opinion of the Authority, seriously and prejudicially affect the interests of the individual or body concerned.[83] Secondly, the arrangements do not require or authorise the Authority to disclose, without the consent of the person to whom it owes an obligation of confidence, any information which has been furnished to it under certain provisions,[84] or which, under the provisions of a licence, agreement or undertaking given by the Authority to the applicant for the purpose of that application is to be treated as subject to an obligation of confidence owed by the Authority to any other person.[85] The information that is to be excluded from the information which is to be made available does not include any information that appears to the Authority to relate to matters which are or may be relevant to the safety of members of the public or of any particular individual or individuals other than the person whose consent is required for its disclosure.[86] Excluded information may, of course, be sought under the Freedom of Information Act 2000.

The Industry Act 1975

5–065 Section 27 of the Industry Act 1975 provides for the disclosure of information by Ministers of the Crown and the Treasury. The information in question is described in Sch.5 to the Industry Act 1975, and consists of a macro-economic model, to be kept by the Treasury, which is suitable for demonstrating the likely effects on economic events in the United Kingdom of different assumptions about the following matters, namely government economic policies; economic events outside the UK; and such (if any) other matters as appear to the Treasury from time to time likely to have a substantial effect on economic events in the UK.[87] The model must enable forecasts to be made of any of the following: the level of gross domestic product; unemployment; the balance of payments on current account; the general index of retail prices; and average earnings.[88] The model must also enable forecasts to be made of such (if any) other economic variables as are appropriate in the opinion of the Treasury from time

83 Coal Industry Act 1994, s.57(3).

84 Namely, in pursuance of a licence under Pt II of the Coal Industry Act 1994; in pursuance of any provisions of an agreement entered into or in connection with any proposals for the carrying on of any activities in the course of any exploration for coal or of any activities for which a licence under s.2 of the Petroleum (Production Act) 1934 is required; or for the purposes of any application to the Authority for the grant of a licence under Pt II of the Coal Industry Act 1994, for the making of such an agreement, or for the transfer or creation of any interests or rights in or in relation to any land: Coal Industry Act 1994, s.57(4)(a).

85 Coal Industry Act 1994, s.57(4)(b).

86 *ibid.*, s.57(5).

87 Industry Act 1975, Sch.5, para.1.

88 *ibid.*, Sch.5, para.2(a).

to time.[89] The model must be maintained on a computer,[90] and be available to members of the public to make forecasts based on their own assumptions, using the computer during office hours upon payment of such reasonable fee as the Treasury may determine.[91] The Treasury also have a duty, under para.6 of Sch.5 to the Industry Act 1975, not less than twice in each year commencing with a date not later than one year from the coming into force of that Act,[92] to publish forecasts with the aid of the model as to such matters and based on such alternative assumptions as appear to them to be appropriate[93]; and, under para.8, from time to time to publish an analysis of errors in such forecasts that would have remained even if the assumptions set out in the forecasts and on which they were based had been correct.

The Land Registration Act 2002

The register of title maintained under the Land Registration Act 2002 is open to inspection by any person; and any person may make copies of, or of any part of, the register of title; any document kept by the registrar which is referred to in the register of title; any other document kept by the registrar which relates to an application by him; or the register of cautions against title.[94] This right is subject to rules which may provide for exceptions to the right and impose conditions on its exercise, including conditions requiring the payment of fees.[95] The registrar has a duty to keep an index for the purpose of enabling the following matters to be ascertained in relation to any parcel of land: whether any registered estate relates to the land; how any registered estate which relates to the land is identified for the purposes of the register; whether the land is affected by any, and if so, what, caution against first registration; and such other matters as rules may provide.[96] Rules may also make provision about how the index is to be kept, and may, in particular, make provision about the information to be contained in the index; the form in which information contained in the index is to be kept; and the arrangement of that information. Rules may make provision 5–066

[89] Industry Act 1975, Sch.5, para.2(b). The references to forecasts in para.2 are references to forecasts relating to successive periods of three months, and not to shorter periods: Industry Act 1975, Sch.5, para.3.

[90] *ibid.*, Sch.5, para.4.

[91] *ibid.*, Sch.5, para.5.

[92] Namely November 20, 1975.

[93] Any forecast under Sch.5 must indicate, where possible, the margin of error attaching to it: Industry Act 1975, Sch.5, para.7.

[94] Land Registration Act 2002, s.66(1).

[95] *ibid.*, s.66(2). The relevant rules are contained in the Land Registration Rules 2003 (SI 2003/1417).

[96] Land Registration Act 2002, s.68(1). The relevant rules are contained in the Land Registration Rules 2003 (SI 2003/1417).

about official searches of the index.[97] Under s.69 of the Land Registration Act 2002, the registrar has a power to provide, on application, information about the history of a registered title[98]; and may arrange for the provision of information about the history of registered titles and may authorise anyone who has the function of providing information of the latter sort to have access on such terms as he thinks fit to any relevant information kept by him.

7. EDUCATIONAL RECORDS

Introduction

5–067 The specific right to educational information differs somewhat from the other rights to official information in that it is essentially concerned with providing members of the public with general information relating to educational bodies, rather than information that is specifically addressed to answering the terms of a request. In brief terms, the Education (School Information) (England) Regulations 2002 spell out certain basic information relating to the provision of education that must be provided:

(1) by the governing body of each school; and
(2) by each local education authority.

The Education (No.2) Act 1986

5–068 The Secretary of State is empowered to make regulations requiring the governing body of any institution that is maintained by a local education authority and that provides higher education or further education (or both) to make available to such persons or classes of persons as may be prescribed such documents and information relating to the meetings and proceedings of the governing body as may be prescribed.[99] The regulations currently in force for England are the Education (School Information) (England) Regulations 2002.[1]

[97] Land Registration Act 2002, s.68. The relevant rules are contained in the Land Registration Rules 2003 (SI 2003/1417).

[98] Land Registration Act 2002, s.69(1). Section 69(2) provides that rules may make provision about applications for the exercise of the power conferred on the registrar by section 69(1): see the Land Registration Rules 2003 (SI 2003/1417).

[99] Education (No.2) Act 1986, s.62(1).

[1] SI 2002/2897.

Governing bodies

Part 5 of the Education (School Information) (England) Regulations 2002 deals with the information that governing bodies must publish with respect to maintained schools. The information that must be published includes: 5–069

— the name, address and telephone number of the school and the names of both the head teacher and chairman of the governing body[2];
— the classification of the school[3];
— particulars of the admissions policy determined for the school by the governing body (in the case of a community or voluntary controlled school) or by the relevant local educational authority (in the case of a foundation or voluntary aided school) in relation to each age group at the school, including ages above and below compulsory school age[4];
— where there are specific arrangements for parents who are considering sending their child to the school to visit it, particulars of those arrangements[5];
— in the case of a secondary school, where information is available, the number of places for pupils of the normal age of entry to the school which were available at the start of the school year immediately following the reporting school year[6];
— the number of written applications for places from the start of that school year or preferences expressed for places at the school pursuant to the arrangements made by the local education authority under s.86(1) of the School Standards and Framework Act 1998 or under s.89B(1) or 89B(2) of that Act[7];
— a statement of the ethos and values of the school[8];
— the affiliations, if any, of the school with a particular religion or religious denomination,[9] and particulars of the religious education to be provided at the school, a statement that a pupil shall[10] be excused wholly or partly from attendance at religious worship in the school or

[2] Education (School Information) (England) Regulations 2002, Sch.3, para.1.
[3] *i.e.* as a community, foundation, voluntary controlled or voluntary aided school or a community special or foundation school; a primary, middle or secondary school; a comprehensive, secondary modern or grammar school; a co-educational or single sex school; and as a day or boarding school or (as the case may be) a school taking both day and boarding pupils: Education (School Information) (England) Regulations 2002, Sch.3, para.2.
[4] Education (School Information) (England) Regulations 2002, Sch.3, para.3.
[5] *ibid.*, Sch.3, para.4.
[6] Namely, the school year immediately preceding the publication school year, which is defined as meaning the school year immediately preceding the admission school year, which is itself defined as meaning a school year at the beginning of which pupils are to be admitted to any school: Education (School Information) (England) Regulations 2002, reg.3(1).
[7] *ibid.*, Sch.3, para.6.
[8] *ibid.*, Sch.3, para.7.
[9] *ibid.*, Sch.3, para.8(1).
[10] Pursuant to s.71 of the School Standards and Framework Act 1998.

from receiving religious education given at the school, or both, if the parent or pupil so requests, together with particulars of any arrangements as respects the exercise by the parent of a pupil of rights under s.71 of the School Standards and Framework Act 1998 in relation to the pupil's attendance at religious worship or religious education or both.[11]

The governing body must, in the case of a school with registered pupils in the final year of the first key stage,[12] publish the number of such pupils. Where the number of such pupils is eleven or more, the governing body must publish the percentage who in respect of each level of the National Curriculum level scale were assessed as having reached that level for mathematics, science, spelling and the attainment targets in English (namely, reading, writing and speaking and listening)[13], or were assessed as working towards level 1, or failed to register a level because they missed the assessment by reason of absence. The governing body must also publish the most recent national summary figures in respect of this information.[14] Where the number of pupils referred to in para.9(1) is eleven or more, the governing body must also publish the percentage who were exempted under s.92 or s.93 of the Education Act 2002 from assessment by the administration of the National Curriculum standard tasks administered to pupils in the final year of the first key stage pursuant to art.5 of the Education (National Curriculum) (Key Stage 1 Assessment Arrangements) (England) Order 1999.[15] By para.12 of the Education (School Information) (England) Regulations 2002, governing bodies in respect of schools with registered pupils aged 15 are required to publish specified information concerning those pupils; and, by paras 13 and 14, the specified information must be published by governing bodies of schools with registered pupils aged 16, 17 or 18 which are reporting results for the reporting school year 2002–2003 or any subsequent reporting school year; and by governing bodies of maintained schools with registered pupils aged 15, 16, 17 or 18. Governing bodies are also required, by para.15, to publish the number of pupils of compulsory school age[16] registered at any time on or before the Friday before the last Monday in May during the reporting school year[17]; and the number of authorised and unauthorised

[11] Education (School Information) (England) Regulations 2002, Sch.3, para.8(2). This requirement is stated to be without prejudice to para.7.
[12] As to which, see s.82(1) of the Education Act 2002.
[13] Education (School Information) (England) Regulations 2002, Sch.3, para.9(3).
[14] *ibid.*, Sch.3, para.9(2).
[15] *ibid.*, Sch.3, para.9(5). Different publishing requirements are set out in paras 9(4) and 9(6) as regards cases in which the number of pupils referred to in para.9(1) is fewer than eleven but not fewer than five; and in which the number of such pupils is fewer than five. The Education (School Information) (England) Regulations 2002 also provide for the publication of comparable information with respect to schools with registered pupils in the final year of the second key stage (as to which, see s.82(1) of the Education Act 2002) (para.10); and in the final year of the third key stage (as to which, see s.82(1) of the Education Act 2002) (para.11).
[16] As defined in Education (School Information) (England) Regulations 2002, Sch.3, para.15(3)(c).
[17] Education (School Information) (England) Regulations 2002, Sch.3, para.15(1).

absences[18] of registered pupils of compulsory school age during the reporting year on or before the Friday before the last Monday in May, expressed as a percentage of the total number of possible attendances[19] in that reporting school year.[20] In the case of a maintained school, the information in relation to the school specified in Sch.3 must be published in a single document and be identified as the school prospectus,[21] and copies must be made available at the school for distribution without charge to parents on request and for reference by parents and other persons.[22] In the case of any maintained secondary school, a copy of the school prospectus must also be provided without charge to the offices in the area served by the school of persons providing career services in accordance with arrangements made, or directions given, under s.10 of the Employment and Training Act 1973.

Local education authorities

Local education authorities are also required to publish detailed information concerning schools in their area.[23] This information includes: 5–070

- — the addresses and telephone numbers of the offices of the authority to which enquiries in respect of primary and secondary education in their area should be addressed[24];
- — the arrangements for parents to obtain the information specified in Sch.3 in the case of individual schools other than special schools[25];
- — as respects each school maintained by the authority, other than a special school, the name, address and telephone number of the school and the name of a person to whom enquiries should be addressed, as well as the expected number of pupils at the school and their age range.[26]

Local education authorities must also publish the classification of each school maintained by them[27]; the affiliations, if any, of each such school with a

[18] As defined in Education (School Information) (England) Regulations 2002, Sch.3, para.15(3)(a).
[19] As defined in Education (School Information) (England) Regulations 2002, Sch.3, para.15(3)(b).
[20] Education (School Information) (England) Regulations 2002, Sch.3, para.15(2).
[21] *ibid.*, reg.14(2)(a). That document may be combined with any other document whose preparation by the governing body is required by or under any enactment.
[22] Education (School Information) (England) Regulations 2002, reg.14(2)(b).
[23] *ibid.*, Pt 3 and Sch.1.
[24] *ibid.*, Sch.1, para.1.
[25] As defined in s.337(1) of the Education Act 1996 (Education (School Information) (England) Regulations 2002, reg.3(1)): Education (School Information) (England) Regulations 2002, Sch.1, para.2.
[26] Education (School Information) (England) Regulations 2002, Sch.1, para.3.
[27] *i.e.* as a community, foundation, voluntary controlled or voluntary aided school or a community special or foundation school; a primary, middle or secondary school; a comprehensive, secondary modern or grammar school; a co-educational or single sex school; and as a day or boarding

particular religious denomination[28]; the authority's general arrangements and policies in respect of transport for pupils of compulsory school age and below to and from schools and institutions within the further education sector, including in particular the provision of free transport, the carriage on school buses of pupils for whom free transport is not provided, and the payment in whole or in part of reasonable travel expenses.[29] Local education authorities must publish their general arrangements and policies in respect of the provision of milk, meals and other refreshments including, in particular, the remission in whole or in part of charges. Under para.8, such authorities must also publish details of their general arrangements and policies in respect of the provision of school clothing (including uniform and physical training clothes), and the making of grants to defray expenses in respect of such clothing and, in particular, the address from which parents may obtain detailed information about the assistance which is available and eligibility for it.[30] Local education authorities must also publish further details of their general arrangements and policies, in the case of pupils attending any school maintained by them, in respect of the making of grants to defray other expenses and the granting of allowances in the case of pupils of compulsory school age, including, in particular, the address from which parents may obtain detailed information about the assistance which is available and eligibility for it. Finally, local education authorities must publish: their general policy in respect of the entering of pupils for public examination; their general arrangements and policies in respect of special educational provision[31] for pupils with special educational needs[32] including, in particular, the arrangements for parents to obtain information about the matters referred to in Pt 2 of Sch.1; and the arrangements for parents and others to obtain copies of and to refer to particulars of the charging and remissions policies determined by the authority under s.457 of the Education Act 1996.

Information concerning special educational provision

5–071 Local education authorities have a further duty to publish the information specified in Pt 2 of Sch.1 to the Education (School Information) (England) Regulations 2002 concerning special educational provision.[33] This information

school or (as the case may be) a school taking both day and boarding pupils: Education (School Information) (England) Regulations 2002, Sch.1, para.4.

[28] Education (School Information) (England) Regulations 2002, Sch.1, para.5.

[29] *ibid.*, Sch.1, para.6.

[30] *ibid.*, Sch.1, para.7.

[31] As defined in s.312 of the Education Act 1996: Education (School Information) (England) Regulations 2002, reg.3(1).

[32] As defined in s.312 of the Education Act 1996: Education (School Information) (England) Regulations 2002, reg.3(1).

[33] As defined in s.312 of the Education Act 1996: Education (School Information) (England) Regulations 2002, reg.3(1).

includes the authority's detailed arrangements and policies in respect of the identification and assessment of children with special educational needs and the involvement of parents in that process; the provision made in community, voluntary and special schools maintained by them for pupils with special educational needs and the use made by them of such special schools maintained by other authorities; and special educational provision supplied otherwise than at school.[34] In addition, local education authorities must publish:

— their arrangements and policies in respect of the use of non-maintained special and independent schools[35];
— the arrangements for parents who consider that their child may have special educational needs to obtain advice and further information[36];
— the authority's arrangements and policies in respect of transport for pupils of compulsory school age and below to and from maintained and non-maintained special schools and independent schools[37]; and
— the arrangements for parents to obtain the information particularised in Sch.3 in the case of the special schools used by the authority which are maintained by them or other authorities.[38]

Further provisions concerning the publication of information by local education authorities

The information described in Sch.1 to the Education (School Information) (England) Regulations 2002 must be published by copies being made available for distribution without charge to parents on request, and for reference by parents and other persons at the office of the relevant authority and at every school maintained by the authority (other than nursery schools and special schools).[39] Copies of the abovementioned information must also be distributed without charge to parents of pupils at schools maintained by the relevant authority (other than nursery schools or special schools) who, in the publication school year, are in the final year at such schools and who might transfer to other schools so maintained[40]; and by copies being made available for reference by parents and other persons at the public libraries in the area of the relevant authority.[41] Local authorities also have a duty, with respect to maintained schools,[42] to publish a composite prospectus containing the information 5–072

[34] Education (School Information) (England) Regulations 2002, Sch.1, para.13.
[35] *ibid.*, Sch.1, para.14.
[36] *ibid.*, Sch.1, para.15.
[37] *ibid.*, Sch.1, para.16.
[38] *ibid.*, Sch.1, para.17.
[39] *ibid.*, reg.7(3)(a).
[40] *ibid.*, reg.7(3)(b).
[41] *ibid.*, reg.7(3)(c). These requirements are subject to certain exceptions set out in regs 7(4) to 7(8).
[42] As defined by s.84(6) of the School Standards and Framework Act 1998.

specified in Sch.2 to the Education (School Information) (England) Regulations 2002 concerning those schools.[43]

8. RIGHTS IN CONNECTION WITH CIVIL LITIGATION

Introduction

5–073 Civil litigation generally brings with it an obligation upon the parties, and occasionally non-parties, to disclose information in the form of documents.[44] This obligation is called "disclosure": it was formerly called "discovery". The obligation is not unique to public authorities and a public authority may enjoy a public interest immunity exemption not available to ordinary litigants. While a full treatment of the law of disclosure is beyond the scope of this book,[45] the disclosure obligation may impinge upon a person's rights under the Freedom of Information Act 2000 as well as represent a means of eliciting information from a public authority.

The concept of disclosure

5–074 Court rules[46] provide for a formal procedure, termed "disclosure", by which one party to a civil case obtains the documents and other information relevant to those proceedings in advance of the trial. It is a means of compelling the production of evidence and therefore applies in relation to all material that may constitute evidence, except that for which there is a lawful ground on which to resist compulsion. The obligation of disclosure extends to both documents and real evidence. "Disclosure" is defined as "stating that a document exists or has existed".[47] Section 28 of the Crown Proceedings Act 1947 expressly provides that the general rules relating to (what were previously termed) discovery and interrogatories apply to the Crown. The rule of public interest immunity is preserved.[48]

Court-ordered pre-action disclosure

5–075 Applications for pre-action disclosure are permitted under s.33 of the Supreme Court Act 1981 and s.52 of the County Court Act 1984. These provisions

---

[43] Education (School Information) (England) Regulations 2002, reg.8.

[44] "Document" is defined in CPR, r.31.4 to mean anything in which information of any description is recorded.

[45] For a more comprehensive treatment, see Matthews and Malek, *Disclosure*, 2nd ed. (Sweet & Maxwell, London, 2001).

[46] CPR, Pt 31.

[47] CPR, r.31.2.

[48] Also see RSC, O.77, rr.12 and 14. O.77 still operates under the CPR.

empower the court in preliminary proceedings to order a potential defendant to subsequent proceedings to disclose documents in or likely to be in his possession, custody or power and which are relevant to an issue arising or likely to be so relevant.[49] The court may order disclosure before proceedings have commenced where:

— both the applicant and respondent are likely to be parties to proceedings if proceedings were commenced;
— the respondent's duty by way of standard disclosure would extend to the documents or classes of documents sought; and
— pre-action disclosure is desirable in order to dispose fairly of the anticipated proceedings, to assist in the resolution of the dispute without proceedings, or to save costs.[50]

An order for pre-action disclosure must specify the documents or class of documents to be disclosed.[51] The order may require the respondent to indicate what has happened to any documents which are no longer in his control.[52]

Pre-action disclosure in personal injury and clinical negligence actions

There are specific protocols regulating pre-action disclosure in these types of claims. In respect of personal injury claims the protocol recommends that the claimant's solicitor identify in a letter of claim the particular categories of documents which he considers relevant.[53] If the defendant denies liability, he should enclose with the letter of reply documents in his possession which are material to the issues between the parties and which would be likely to be ordered to be disclosed by the court.[54] Annex B of the pre-action protocol for personal injury claims contains lists of the types of disclosure which should be given for different types of personal injury claims. The pre-action protocol for the resolution of clinical disputes contains detailed guidance on the obtaining of health 5–076

[49] *Burns v Shuttlehurst Ltd* [1999] 1 W.L.R. 1449, CA; *Howe v David Brown Tractors (Retail) Ltd* [1991] 4 All E.R. 30.

[50] CPR, r.31.16(3). *See Bermuda International Securities Ltd v K.PM6* [2001] EWCA Civ 269, [2001] Lloyd's Rep PN392; *Black v Sumitomo Corporation* [2001] EWCA Civ 1819; [2002] 1 W.L.R. 1562; *Central Exchange Ltd v Anaconda Nickel Ltd* [2001] W.A.S.C. 128, Sup. Ct. of W.A; *Arsenal Football Club v Elite Sports Distribution*, *The Times*, December 27, 2002, Ch. D; *Snowster Shipping Co Ltd v Graig Shipping plc* [2003] EWHC 1367 (Comm); *Moresfield v Banners* [2003] EWHC 1602 (Ch).

[51] CPR, r.31.16(4).

[52] CPR, r.31.16(5).

[53] Pre-action Protocols for Personal Injury Claims, Notes of Guidance ("the Protocol"), para.2.10.

[54] Protocol para.3.10.

records.[55] The protocol sets out those matters which the defendant should provide in response to a letter of claim.[56]

Pre-action disclosure in judicial review claims

5–077 Like the other protocols, the pre-action protocol for judicial review claims contains detailed guidance on the matters to be set out in a letter of claim and a response to a letter before claim.[57] The introduction to the protocol states that the protocol does not impose a greater obligation on a public body to disclose documents or give reasons for its decision than that already provided for in statute and common law. However, where the court considers that a public body should have provided other documents or information, particularly where this failure is a breach of a statutory or common law requirement, then it may impose sanctions.[58]

Actions for disclosure—Norwich Pharmacal orders

5–078 At common law[59] courts have power to order that persons mixed up in the wrongful[60] acts of others disclose the identity and address[61] of the wrongdoers and the person into whose hands the subject property has passed, as well as other information.[62] These are often described as "Norwich Pharmacal" orders.[63] The subject of inquiry can be any wrongdoing, whether criminal or civil.[64] Although such orders against a public authority are unlikely, there is no principle precluding their application to such a body. The victim of a crime may seek the identity of the wrongdoer. However, a person is not required to so dis-

[55] See paras 3.7 to 3.13 of that Protocol.

[56] See paras 3.23 to 3.27 and Annex C2 of the Protocol.

[57] See Pre-Action Protocol for Judicial Review, paras 8 to 12 (letter before claim) and 13 to 17 (letter of response).

[58] See para.6 of the introduction to the protocol.

[59] The CPR does not limit the common law powers that courts possess to order disclosure before proceedings have started, or to order disclosure against third parties: CPR, r.31.18.

[60] The rule is no longer restricted to torts: *Ashworth Hospital Authority v MGN Ltd* [2001] 1 W.L.R. 515 at 530; [2002] UKHL 29; [2002] 1 W.L.R. 2033.

[61] *Coca-Cola Company v British Telecommunications plc* [1999] F.S.R. 518.

[62] In theory the action can be used to obtain disclosure of documents from potential defendants, but in practice CPR, r.31.16 will often provide an adequate alternative to the common law action in such cases. See *Taylor v Anderton*, *The Times*, October 21, 1986.

[63] After the leading case, *Norwich Pharmacal Co. v Commissioners of Customs & Excise* [1974] A.C. 133, where a person innocently caught up in a wrongdoing was required to disclose the wrongdoer's identity.

[64] *Ashworth Hospital Authority v MGN Ltd* [2002] UKHL 29; [2002] 1 W.L.R. 2033, disapproving *Interbrew SA v Financial Times* [2002] EWCA Civ 274; [2002] 1 Lloyd's Rep. 542, CA on this aspect. Also see *Mersey Care NHS Trust v Ackroyd* [2003] EWCA Civ 663, *The Times*, May 21, 2003.

close the identity of another person if that first person is a "mere witness" and is not caught up in the wrongdoing.[65] Orders can also be granted for the disclosure of the holding of disputed property and the identity of trustees or the identity of further innocent parties mixed up in the wrongdoing,[66] for example as recipients of property.[67] The information required to be disclosed is not just the identity of a person, but such full information as to enable a practical commercial judgment to be made as to enforcement of remedies against the wrongdoer.[68] The claimant need not show he intends to take legal proceedings against the wrongdoer.[69] An order can be obtained to require the employees or agents of a public authority to give the necessary information.[70] Orders are not made as of right; the court retains a discretion whether to make the order. There are four defences available: (1) disclosure will not be ordered if that would complete a cause of action; (2) the privilege against self-incrimination operates as a defence[71]; (3) s.10 of the Contempt of Court Act 1981 provides another defence for sources of information contained in publications in that a person responsible for a publication will not be required to give discovery of the source of information contained in that publication unless it is necessary in the interests of national security, the interests of justice, or for the prevention of disorder or crime[72]; and (4) an order will not be made if it would infringe the sovereignty of another country.[73] In addition, a public interest defence may be available to the source, and if there is an even arguable public interest defence there may be no wrongdoer for the purpose of a Norwich Pharmacal Order.[73A] Proceedings may be brought under either CPR, Pt 7 or Pt 8. The order may be the sole relief sought or ancillary relief.[74] The order is usually granted following a trial of the action, but can be granted on an interlocutory application, normally with notice but exceptionally without.[75] The claimant must identify the wrongdoing in general terms and identify the purposes for which disclosure will be used when made.[76]

[65] *Ricci v Chow* [1987] 1 W.L.R. 1658.
[66] *Re Murphy's Settlements* [1998] 3 All E.R. 1.
[67] *Bankers Trust v Shapira* [1980] 1 W.L.R. 1274.
[68] *Norwich Pharmacal Co. v Commissioners of Customs & Excise* [1974] A.C. 133 at 175; *Banker's Trust v Shapira* [1980] 1 W.L.R. 1274 at 1281; *AXA Equity and Law Life Assurance Society plc v National Westminster Bank plc* [1998] P.N.L.R. 433.
[69] *Ashworth Hospital Authority v MGN Ltd* [2002] UKHL 29; [2002] 1 W.L.R. 2033, where the claimant intended to dismiss the relevant employee.
[70] *Harrington v North London Polytechnic* [1984] 1 W.L.R. 1293.
[71] *Re Westinghouse Electric Corp.* [1978] A.C. 547.
[72] See, *e.g.*, *X Ltd v Morgan-Grampian (Publishers) Ltd* [1991] 1 A.C. 1; *Secretary of State for Defence v Guardian Newspapers Ltd* [1985] A.C. 339; *Ashworth Hospital Authority v MGN Ltd* [2002] UKHL 29; [2002] 1 W.L.R. 2033.
[73] See, *e.g.*, *McKinnon v Donaldson Lufkin and Jenrette Securities Corp.* [1986] Ch.482.
[73A] *Mersey Care NHS Trust v Ackroyd* [2003] EWCA Civ 663, *The Times*, May 21, 2003.
[74] *Microsoft Corporation v Plato Technology Ltd* [1999] F.S.R. 834.
[75] *Banker's Trust v Shapira* [1980] 1 W.L.R. 1274.
[76] *Ashworth Hospital Authority v MGN Ltd* [2002] UKHL 29 at [60]; [2002] 1 W.L.R. 2033.

Disclosure after commencement of litigation

5–079 Once civil proceedings have commenced all parties are subject to compulsory requirements of disclosure, as provided for in court rules. There are broadly two types of disclosure: standard and specific disclosure. Disclosure during the course of civil litigation will normally be limited to "standard disclosure".

Standard disclosure

5–080 Standard disclosure requires a party to disclose only documents on which he relies, documents adversely affecting one party's case or supporting another party's case, and documents required to be disclosed by reference to a practice direction.[77] This formulation significantly reduces the obligation to disclose from the Peruvian Guano test of relevance, which applied in relation to discovery prior to the introduction of the Civil Procedure Rules in 1999.[78] On the Fast Track the court is likely to direct less than standard disclosure.[79] A party must disclose documents on which it relies.[80] The Civil Procedure Rules contain no definition of "reliance". It probably means "use in court", including use for cross-examination. It probably does not extend to all documents which a party may use in or out of court to advance the case. The concept of documents adversely affecting a party's case is not defined in the CPR. A document is not covered if it merely indicates a line of inquiry which may lead to other information having an adverse effect.[81] Parties need only disclose:

- — documents which are or have been in their control, including those documents in their physical possession;
- — documents over which they have the right to possession; and
- — documents over which they have a right to inspect or take copies.[82]

Specific disclosure

5–081 The court may make an order for specific disclosure, being an order that a party:

- — disclose documents or classes of documents as specified;

[77] CPR, r.31.6. Pt 31 does not apply in relation to cases on the Small Claims Track. The court can give directions as to disclosure in such cases: CPR, rr.27.2(2)(b), 27.4(1).
[78] *Compagnie Financiere du Pacifique v Peruvian Guano* Co. (1882) 11 Q.B.D. 55 at 63.
[79] CPR, Pt 28 Practice Direction, para.3.6(1)(c), (4).
[80] CPR, r.31.6(a).
[81] Matthews and Malek, *Disclosure*, 2nd ed. (Sweet & Maxwell, London, 2001), para.4.16.
[82] CPR, r.31.8.

— carry out a search to the extent stated in the order; and/or
— disclose any documents located as a result of the search.[83]

While the timing of such an application depends on the circumstances, often it will be appropriate to apply when directions are given, namely on allocation to a track and on filing of the listing questionnaire,[84] or at a case management conference.[85] The party seeking the order must normally file an application notice, supported by evidence, specifying the order sought. The application should specify the document or classes of documents sought, using a schedule if appropriate. It is important to keep the materials sought within proper limits, and the application may be refused or amended if cast too broadly.[86] The same applies in relation to a search requested to be ordered. The grounds for seeking the order may be in the application notice or in the accompanying evidence.[87] The usual grounds for seeking the order are that it is alleged that the search carried out was unreasonably limited, and/or that the party believes that there are relevant documents which ought to be disclosed and it is appropriate to require their disclosure. The evidence should describe the material sought and/or extent of search sought, and explain why it is reasonable and proportionate that each aspect of the order be made. This should be done by reference to the issues in the action. If appropriate, the sources and grounds for believing that particular materials exist should be stated. For cases allocated to the Small Claims Track, Pt 31 does not apply, so a party seeking specific disclosure must apply for special directions, and the court may hold a preliminary hearing to determine such an application.[88] Specific disclosure will only be granted if there is at least a prima facie basis for believing that the materials are in the control of the party and are relevant.[89] The court retains a discretion whether to make the order.[90] The court will consider all surrounding circumstances, the importance of the material sought, the nature of the issues, the cost and burden to the disclosing party of compliance and general proportionality.[91] A party opposing such an order should normally file evidence in opposition. The response to an order may be that the respondent party has no materials as sought by the order. Alternatively he may assert that the materials he holds are irrelevant, but only if the court has not already ruled that the particular materials are relevant.

[83] CPR, r.31.12.
[84] As to the Fast Track see CPR, Pt 28 Practice Direction, The Fast Track, para.2.
[85] Although the Queen's Bench Guide para.7.85 discourages this practice for cases to which it relates. On the timing of specific disclosure applications, see Matthews and Malek, *Disclosure*, 2nd ed. (Sweet & Maxwell, London, 2001), paras 5.42, 5.43, 5.47.
[86] *David Kahn Inc. v Conway Stewart & Co.* [1972] F.S.R. 169; [1972] R.P.C. 572; Gotha City v Sotheby's [1998] 1 W.L.R. 114 at 123.
[87] CPR, Pt 31 Practice Direction, Disclosure and Inspection, paras 5.2 and 5.3.
[88] CPR, r.27.6; also see r.27.4(1)(a).
[89] *Portman Building Society v Royal Insurance plc* [1998] P.N.L.R. 672.
[90] *Berkeley Administration Inc. v MacClelland* [1990] FSR 381.
[91] CPR, Pt 31 Practice Direction, Disclosure and Inspection, para.5.4.

Disclosure of copies

5–082 A party need not disclose more than one copy of a document.[92] A copy of a document that contains the modification, obliteration or other marking feature on which the party intends to rely or which adversely effects his own case or another party's case or supports another party's case, is treated as a separate document.[93]

Lists of documents

5–083 The procedure for standard disclosure is by list. Each party must make and serve on the other party or parties a list of documents in the required form identifying the documents in a convenient order and manner and as concisely as possible.[94] The list must indicate those documents in respect of which the party claims a right or duty to withhold inspection and those documents that are no longer in their control and, in relation to them, what has happened to those documents.[95]

Documents referred to in statements of case and experts' reports

5–084 A party also has the right to inspect documents mentioned in a statement of case, witness statement, witness summary, affidavit or expert's report.[96] Documents are probably only "mentioned" for this purpose if the reference to them is specific and direct. Mere reference to a transaction which must have been carried out by a particular written document is probably insufficient.[97]

Third party disclosure

5–085 The court has power to order a person who is not a party to the proceedings to disclose whether documents relevant to an issue in the claim are in that person's possession, custody or power, and to produce those documents.[98] Such an order

92 CPR, r.31.9(1).
93 CPR, r.31.9(2).
94 CPR, r.31.10(1)–(3).
95 CPR, r.31.10(4).
96 CPR, r.31.14.
97 Matthews and Malek, *Disclosure*, 2nd ed. (Sweet & Maxwell, London, 2001), para.7.09.
98 Supreme Court Act 1981, s.34; County Courts Act 1985, s.53. *Burrells Wharf Freeholds Ltd v Galliard Homes Ltd* [1999] 2 E.G.L.R. 81; *Hipwood v Gloucester Health Authority* [1995] I.C.R. 999; *Re Howglen* [2001] 1 All E.R. 376; *Three Rivers District Council v Bank of England (Disclosure) (No.4)* [2002] EWCA Civ 1182; [2002] 4 All E.R. 881; *Rowe v Fryers* [2003] EWCA Civ 655, *Franlison v Home Office* [2003] EWCA Civ 665, [2003] 1 W.L.R. 1952 (CA).

shall not be made if compliance would be likely to be injurious to the public interest.[99] An application for such an order must be supported by evidence.[1] The court may only make such an order where the documents are likely to support the applicant's case or adversely affect another party's case, and if disclosure is necessary to fairly dispose of the claim or save costs.[2] This power applies to all legal proceedings, not just those relating to personal injury or death (as was formerly the case). Disclosure can be ordered to be made to medical or legal advisers only,[3] or on the giving of certain undertakings.[4] Applications for disclosure by persons not a party to the proceedings are made, as with interlocutory applications generally, under Pt 23. The application must be supported by evidence.[5] This can be achieved by simply verifying the application with a statement of truth, if the application covers the requisite matters.[6] The order must specify the documents or class of documents to be disclosed and require the respondent, when making disclosure, to specify which documents are no longer in his control or those in relation to which he claims a right or duty to withhold inspection.[7]

Access to documents used in other litigation

Where civil proceedings are held in open court, the public may attend, take notes and publish or otherwise use information heard during those proceedings.[8] The same generally applies to criminal cases,[9] though there are a number of important statutory exceptions.[10] The public normally are allowed access to witness statements and written submissions used in civil litigation.[11] Material disclosed by the prosecution to the accused in criminal proceedings is now regulated by the provisions of the Criminal Procedure and Investigations Act 1996, Pt I.[12] However, until such time as documents are read to or by the court, or referred to, at a hearing held in public, it is impermissible for a party to the proceedings to use disclosed documents for a collateral or ulterior purpose, without the leave of the court or the consent of the party providing the 5–086

[99] Supreme Court Act 1981, s.35(1).
[1] CPR, r.31.17(2).
[2] CPR, r.31.17(3).
[3] Supreme Court Act 1981, s.34(2)(b).
[4] See, *e.g.*, *Church of Scientology v DHSS* [1979] 1 W.L.R. 723.
[5] CPR, r.31.17(2).
[6] CPR, Pt 31 Practice Direction, para.9.7.
[7] CPR, r.31.17(4).
[8] *Forbes v Smith* [1998] 1 All E.R. 973; *Hodgson v Imperial Tobacco* [1998] 2 All E.R. 673; *cf. Clibbery v Allen* [2002] EWCA Civ 45; [2002] Fam. 261; [2002] 1 All E.R. 865. In relation to proceedings held in private see s.12 of the Administration of Justice Act 1960.
[9] *e.g.* under the Criminal Appeal Rules 1968, r.19 (transcripts).
[10] *e.g.* example under the Children and Young Persons Act 1933, s.37; Official Secrets Act 1920, s.8.
[11] *GIO Personal Investment Services Ltd v Liverpool and London Steamship, etc. Ltd* [1999] 1 W.L.R. 984.
[12] In particular see ss.17 and 18.

documents.[13] This principle is now articulated in the Civil Procedure Rules.[14] The principle applies equally to documents produced under a summons or under the "Norwich Pharmacal" procedure.[15]

Summonses to produce documents

5–087 Prior to the Civil Procedure Rules, a person (including a public authority) could be *subpoenaed* to attend court to produce documents.[16] The procedure is now called a "witness summons," which can be used to require a witness to attend court and produce documents.[17] Permission of the court is not generally required for the issue of a witness summons.[18] It is not entirely clear what limitations there are on the documents that may be required to be produced under a summons.[19]

---

[13] *Alterskye v Scott* [1948] 1 All E.R. 469; *Crest Homes plc v Marks* [1987] 1 A.C. 829; *Taylor v Serious Fraud Office* [1999] 2 A.C. 177. By "collateral or ulterior" is meant any use not reasonably necessary for the proper conduct of the action in which they were disclosed: *Home Office v Harman* [1983] A.C. 280 at 302, 312 and 319. See also: *Woolgar v, Chief Constable of Sussex* [2000] 1 W.L.R. 25; [1999] 3 All E.R. 604; *Preston Borough Council v McGrath,The Times*, May 19, 2000 (CA).

[14] CPR, r.31.22.

[15] *Sybron Corp. v Barclays Bank plc* [1985] 1 Ch.299 at 318–320.

[16] A *subpoena duces tecum* under RSC, O.38, r.14.

[17] CPR, r.34.2(1).

[18] Unless the summons is issued less than seven days before the date of the trial or is returnable other than at trial: CPR, r.34.3. The power to obtain disclosure against non-parties makes the early return date procedure less important than it was previously.

[19] See the discussion in C. Hollander, *Documentary Evidence*, 8th ed. (Sweet & Maxwell, London, 2003), pp.57–59.

CHAPTER 6

Public Records

1. BACKGROUND

Introduction

6–001 A public record may be described as a document created by a government or a department of government in the course of the business of government.[1] Such a description in a historical context necessarily begs a number of questions. The business of government varies over time: at some moments it may be thought to show an undue interest in men's souls; at other moments an indifference bordering on callousness. The historian A.J.P. Taylor reckoned that until August 1914 a sensible, law-abiding Englishman could pass through life and hardly notice the existence of the state, beyond the post office and the policeman.[2] Since 1914 the position has changed dramatically. The extent of government

[1] A specific definition of "public record" is given in the Freedom of Information Act 2000, s.84, which picks up the definition in the *Public Records Act 1958*, s.10 and Sch.1: see para.6–017.

[2] The opening line in English History, 1914–1945, in the Oxford History of England series (rev. ed., Oxford University Press, Oxford, 1976), Vol.15.

business and the quantity of records generated by it have hugely increased. Furthermore, the means by which records can be maintained have also changed dramatically in the last 25 years. Nonetheless, what constitutes government varies in context; for the mass of the population, until comparatively recently, what mattered in government was what occurred locally.

Medieval records

After the Norman Conquest there was, just as before 1066, no separation of records into those which might (according to later lights) have been classified as "personal" to the king and those classified as "public".[3] All records were simply the king's personal records created in the course of his business governing his kingdom.[4] Likewise, such records as were kept by feudal lords derived from their position in feudal society or the maintenance of their estates and were their personal records which simply happened to have been created in the course of governing a feudal society. The king carried on his business in a peripatetic manner, taking with him his exchequer, personal belongings and records. Documents were conveyed in large chests.[5] The Domesday Book[6] (1086) was one such record of the king and is now regarded as the best-known public record in England. It was, in effect, a government survey of William's realm of England.[7] The Domesday Book, as a record of public inquisition or survey, remains admissible as evidence of boundaries.[8] It was compiled by royal commissioners and contains a general survey of most of the counties of England. It specifies the name and local position of every place, its possessor both in the 6–002

3 For a more comprehensive treatment of the history of public records in Great Britain, reference should be made to: C.P. Cooper, *An Account of the Most Important Public Records of Great Britain, and the Publications of the Record Commissioners: Together With Other Miscellaneous, Historical, and Antiquarian Information. Compiled From Various Printed Books and Manuscripts*, (Baldwin & Cradock, London, 1872), 2 Vols; J.D. Cantwell, *The Public Record Office 1838–1958* (The Stationery Office, London, 1991); J.D. Cantwell, *The Public Record Office 1959–1969* (The Public Record Office, Richmond, 2000).

4 Across the Channel, Louis XIV, who later proclaimed "l'Etat, c'est moi", would have had no difficulty with the concept.

5 Some of which are preserved in the Public Record Office in Kew, near Richmond, Surrey TW9 4DU.

6 The document references for Domesday in the Public Record Office are E31/1 and E31/2. It consists of one folio volume of 382 pages and one quarto volume of 450 pages. The name "Domesday" is from Old English "Dom," meaning judgment.

7 However, it is not the oldest document held at the Public Record Office; that is an Anglo-Saxon land deed dated 974. However, if this and other such deeds are regarded as private records, then the Domesday Book is the oldest public record held by the Public Record Office.

8 *Iveagh v Martin* [1961] 1 Q.B. 232 at 238; *Brackenborough v Spalding UDC* [1942] A.C. 310 at 313; *Nicholls v Ely Beet Sugar Factory* [1931] 2 Ch. 84 at 89; *Harris v Earl of Chichester* [1911] A.C. 623 at 629, 632; *Attorney-General v Simpson* [1901] 2 Ch. 671 at 688, 700; *Martens v Hill* [1901] 1 Ch. 842 at 850, 854; *Duke of Beaufort v John Aire & Co* (1904) 20 T.L.R. 602; *Alcock v Cooke* (1829) 5 Bing. 340.

reign of King Edward the Confessor and at the time of the survey with particulars,[9] quantities and descriptions of the land. It is, principally, manors which are described in the Domesday Book, England being at the time of the survey (and for some time thereafter) largely divided into manors.[10] Some northern counties and the cities of London and Winchester, which were not within manors, are not within the Domesday Book.

The development of state records

6–003 Royal administration, which was inseparable from the governance of the state, came to develop and grow in complexity. It also became more centralised, with others (notably the king's justices) travelling on the king's business. Records, by way of copies, came to be necessary so that instructions (for example, by a writ) could be conveyed, but knowledge maintained centrally. In addition, records of the royal income and expenditure were maintained. In this regard it can be observed that the essential purpose of the Domesday Book was the establishment of the terms of a new rating system to protect and enlarge the King's Revenue:[11] information is seldom obtained simply for the sake of obtaining information, no more than books are written simply for the sake of writing. Copies were made on parchment, that is to say on cleaned, dried and smoothed sheepskin. Copies were enrolled, *i.e.* sheets of parchment were sewn together to create rolls,[12] for easy carriage and storage. Departments of State gradually developed. The Exchequer was concerned with the financial side of medieval government and the Chancery was concerned with the administrative side. There was no systematic archiving of these records once their immediate use had passed. In the Tudor period the various secretaries of state retained many important state papers when they left office. In order to prevent this leakage and to make some permanent provision for the custody and arrangement of these papers, in 1578 the State Paper office was established. In the early eighteenth century the House of Lords established an inquiry into domestic records. As was the way, the inquiry proceeded through the reigns of Anne and George I. Before its conclusion, the House of Commons commenced its own inquiry, producing, some 30 years later, a report which observed that there were no indexes to the records and that such catalogues that did exist were incomplete. Another committee was appointed; but little was done over the following 40 years.

---

[9] The Anglo-Saxon Chronicle for 1085 records that no pig was left out. It is a comfort to know that the ancestors to the Empress of Blandings would have been recorded.

[10] C. Jessel, *Law of the Manor*, (Barry Rose Law Publishers, Chichester, 1998).

[11] See Colin Platt, *Medieval England: A Social History and Archaeology from the Conquest to A.D. 1600* (Routledge and Kegan Paul, London 1978). The "Domesday Book" was for some time used as a term to denote any book containing a list of the rateable value of land: see *Lumsden v Inland Revenue Commissioners* [1914] A.C. 877 at 897, 900; *Commissioners of Inland Revenue v Herbert* [1913] A.C. 326 at 348, 351, 356.

[12] Hence, the office of Master of the Rolls.

The establishment of a public record office

In all this time, no measures had been taken for the housing of the increasing mass of records. The casual or adventitious nature of storage created difficulties as to both access and maintenance. The usual places in which these records were stored,[13] such as the Chapter House at Westminster, the Tower of London and the stables in Holborn, were too small to contain the increasing mass of records, as well as being ill-suited to the purpose. That said, the purpose was not as it is today. From time-to-time, records might be consulted to resolve some legal controversy, but: 6–004

> "except for these practical purposes they had hardly ever been consulted. Occasionally, indeed, historians had arisen who refused to base their story upon any but the best evidence. For the majority the study of the records under the then existing conditions was, to use Prynne's expression, too 'heroic'."[14]

The House of Commons committee, which had been appointed some 40 years earlier, produced a report; and the report prompted the appointment of a Record Commission in 1800 to investigate the state of the public records. Its minute book for June 28, 1809 has the following entry:

> "On Wednesday the 28th of June, 1809, and the three following days, Mr Meaking of the Chirographer's Office brought and delivered into the Record Office at the Chapter House ten large cartloads of the transcript of Fines, each load being about one ton weight, and the number of bundles being about fourteen hundred . . . . Some of these bundles were brought from the Temple Church, where, from the dampness of the place, and a constant accumulation of filth and dirt, many of them are rendered almost completely useless, and many half-destroyed through lying in the wet, whereby they are become so fixed together as not to be separated without breaking them in pieces. The smell arising from the sad condition they were in rendered the arrangement of them etc. very disagreeable and unhealthy."[15]

The Commissioners reported in 1819,[16] as did a Select Committee in 1822,[17] and their work led to the passage of the Public Record Office Act 1838. This was the first legislation to protect public records by the creation of an official archive.

---

[13] There were over 60 by the beginning of the nineteenth century.

[14] W. Holdsworth, *A History of English Law in Sixteen Volumes* (4th ed., Methuen, London, 1936) p.601.

[15] Quoted in *ibid.*, n.14 above, p.600.

[16] Reports from the Commissioners Appointed to Execute the Measures Recommended by the Committee of the House of Commons, Respecting the Public Records of the Kingdom with an Account of their Proceedings.

[17] Report from the Select Committee on Public Records of the Kingdom.

The Public Record Office

6–005 Section 8 of the Public Record Office Act 1838 established the Public Record Office under the direction of the Master of the Rolls. The principal concern of the Public Record Office Act 1838 was to make provision for the records of the Exchequer, Chancery and other ancient courts of law. The Record Office when first constituted was supposed to exist for the sake of litigants who wanted copies of documents, rather than for historians.[18] The records were brought together in a single repository, administered by professional staff in a new government department. The site chosen was a place where records had since the thirteenth century been stored and was the redundant chapel of a hostel called Domus Conversarium. Situated in Chancery Lane, it had been a lodging house for Jews who had converted to Christianity. However, all Jews had been expelled from England in 1290 and the Chapel, thereby superfluous, was then converted and used for storage of the rolls of Chancery. The Master of the Rolls came to live on the site, which became known as the Rolls Estate. The Public Record Office Act 1838 created no compulsion for the transfer of records to the Public Record Office. Many records were given to the Public Record Office, but no selection occurred and some material was worthless. The Public Record Office Act 1877 authorised the culling of such documents, provided that they did not pre-date 1715.

The Public Records Act 1958

6–006 As the business of government developed over the next hundred years or so, there was a corresponding growth in the quantity of records. This necessitated a reconsideration of the regime which had been established in 1838. A parliamentary committee was established under Sir James Grigg.[19] The recommendations of that committee in 1954 led to the Public Records Act 1958, which remains the principal piece of legislation governing the operations of the Public Record Office. As its long title records, it was an Act to make new provision with respect to public records and the Public Record Office and for connected purposes. Accordingly, the 1958 Act repealed the Public Record Office Acts 1838 to 1898.[20]

[18] W. Holdsworth, *A History of English Law in Sixteen Volumes* (4th ed., Methuen, London, 1936), pp.601–602.

[19] Later, Lord Altrincham.

[20] That being the collective title for the Public Record Office Act 1838, the Public Record Office Act 1877 and the Public Record Office Act 1898. The 1898 Act enabled worthless documents created between 1660 and 1715 to be destroyed.

The Freedom of Information Act 2000

One of the matters dealt with in the Public Records Act 1958 was public access to public records. In very general terms, the approach taken under the 1958 Act was to refuse access to records that were less than 50 years old (reduced in 1967 to 30 years old) held by the Public Record Office, but to extend the refusal period where disclosure "could or might constitute a breach of good faith on the part of the Government".[21] Whilst having a certain simplicity about it, the vagueness of such a determinant of access does not sit comfortably with a prescriptive scheme of disclosure such as is created by the Freedom of Information Act 2000. For this reason, the rudimentary access regime originally bestowed by s.5 of the Public Records Act 1958 has been replaced by the regime created by s.1 of the Freedom of Information Act 2000. The special characteristics of information held by the Public Record Office, the fact that public records are held by bodies other than the Public Record Office, and the fact that the interest of the Public Record Office in the contents of a record is different from that of the public authority which created that record, have all necessitated important modifications to the regime which ordinarily applies to information held by a public authority under the 2000 Act. These modifications are considered in detail below. What must be also kept in mind is that there is an important legislative distinction between the obligations in relation to the preservation of public records and those in relation to the access to such records. Generally, the framework given by the public records legislation[22] has been retained for the preservation of records, whilst the Freedom of Information Act 2000 controls the ability to access such records. It should also be added that the Public Record Office is itself a "public authority" subject to the Freedom of Information Act 2000. 6–007

2. PUBLIC RECORD BODIES

The Public Record Office

The historical background to the Public Record Office has already been outlined. The Public Record Office Act 1958 sets out the powers and duties of the Keeper of Public Records. These seemingly simple provisions belie the complexity of his functions. The Public Record Office[23] produces a manual, entitled Access to Public Records, which is intended to be a tool for use by those who need to understand the legal basis for the working of the public records system. 6–008

[21] Public Records Act 1958, s.5.

[22] Now the Public Records Act 1958.

[23] On April 2, 2003 the Public Record Office and the Historical Manuscripts Commission joined together to form a new organisation called "The National Archives". The website is *www.pro.gov.uk*.

As is there stated, from the moment of a record's creation to its final archiving in the Public Record Office, a complex web of legislative provisions, government policy instructions and departmental practices govern how it may be treated. It is the stated principal aim of the Public Record Office to assist and promote the study of the past in order to inform the present and the future.[24] Whilst this work is not concerned with the preservation obligations as such, their interrelationship with the rights of access necessitates some understanding of them. Before doing so, however, it is convenient to introduce the protagonists in the archiving of records.

The Keeper of Public Records

6–009 Section 1 of the Public Records Act 1958 provided for the transfer of the direction of the Public Record Office from the Master of the Rolls to the Lord Chancellor. He was made generally responsible for the execution of the Public Records Act 1958 and required to supervise the care and preservation of public records. There was established by s.1(2) an Advisory Council on Public Records to advise the Lord Chancellor on matters concerning public records in general and, in particular, on those aspects of the work of the Public Record Office affecting members of the public who make use of the facilities provided by the Public Record Office. The Advisory Council on Public Records now operates in the context of the Advisory Council on National Records and Archives. The Master of the Rolls is chairman of the Advisory Council on Public Records. The other members of the Council are appointed by the Lord Chancellor on such terms as he specifies. By s.1(2A), introduced by the Freedom of Information Act 2000, the matters on which the Advisory Council on Public Records may advise the Lord Chancellor include matters relating to the application of the Freedom of Information Act 2000 to information contained in public records which are historical records within the meaning of Pt VI of the FOI Act. Every year the Lord Chancellor must lay before Parliament a report of the work of the Public Record Office. The report has to include any report made to him by the Advisory Council on Public Records. Section 2 of the Public Records Act 1958 empowers the Lord Chancellor to appoint a Keeper of Public Records. The Keeper of Public Records takes charge, under the direction of the Lord Chancellor, of the Public Record Office and of the records in it. Further, the Lord Chancellor may with the concurrence of the Treasury as to numbers and conditions of service appoint such other persons to serve in the Public Record Office as he thinks fit. The Keeper of Public Records has, by s.2 of the 1958 Act, power to do all such things as appear to him necessary or expedient for maintaining the utility of the Public Record Office. In particular, he may:

[24] The *Public Record Office Corporate Plan 1995–96 to 1997–98*.

(a) compile and make available indexes and guides to, and calendars and texts of, the records in the Public Record Office;
(b) prepare publications concerning the activities of and facilities provided by the Public Record Office;
(c) regulate the conditions under which members of the public may inspect public and other records or use the other facilities of the Public Record Office;
(d) provide for the making and authentication of copies of and extracts from records required as evidence in legal proceedings or for other purposes;
(e) accept responsibility for the safe keeping of records other than public records;
(f) make arrangements for the separate housing of films and other records which have to be kept under special conditions;
(g) where the Lord Chancellor gives his approval, lend records for display at commemorative exhibitions or for other special purposes; and
(h) acquire records and accept gifts and loans.

The Public Record Office (Fees)(No. 2) Regulations 2001[25] prescribe the fees which may be charged for inspection, authentication of records in the charge of the Keeper of Public Records and other services given by officers of the Public Record Office.

The Historical Manuscripts Commission

The Historical Manuscripts Commission[26] was appointed by Royal Warrant dated April 2, 1869. The Commission's terms of reference were revised and extended by a further Royal Warrant given on December 5, 1959. Since then they have been: 6–010

— To make enquiry as to the existence and location of manuscripts, including records or archives of all kinds, of value for the study of history, other than records which are for the time being public records by virtue of the Public Records Act 1958.
— With the consent of the owners or custodians to inspect and report upon these.
— To record the particulars of such manuscripts and records in a National Register.

[25] SI 2001/3462 made under s.2(5) by the Lord Chancellor with the concurrence of theTreasury.
[26] The Historical Manuscripts Commission has offices in Quality House, Quality Court, Chancery Lane, London WC2A 1HP. It there provides access to the National Register of Archives and to the Manorial Documents Register.

— To promote and assist the proper preservation and storage of such manuscripts and records.
— To assist those wishing to use such manuscripts or records for study or research.
— To consider and advise upon general questions relating to the location, preservation and use of such manuscripts and records.
— To promote the co-ordinated action of all professional and other bodies concerned with the preservation and use of such manuscripts and records.
— To carry out in place of the Public Record Office the statutory duties of the Master of the Rolls in respect of manorial and tithe documents.

Since its inception, the Commission has, in summary, created and maintained:

— The National Register of Archives: a resource for those seeking information on the nature and location of records relating to British history. The National Register of Archives holds over 43,000 unpublished catalogues and listed manuscript collections and has been indexed. The indexes contain 150,000 references, with a further 300,000 connected records and these are available on the Historical Manuscripts Commission website.
— ARCHON: an up to date electronic directory of repositories in the United Kingdom and abroad and a portal to archival resources. ARCHON provides the framework for a virtual UK archival network.
— The Manorial Documents Register: administered by the Historical Manuscripts Commission on behalf of the Master of the Rolls. The Manorial Documents Register is an index to surviving manorial records in England and Wales. Some sections of the Manorial Documents Register have been stored on computer and are available on the Historical Manuscripts Commission website. The Manorial Documents Register records information on the whereabouts of manorial records excluding title deeds. Manorial records survive today in many national and local record offices and in some cases in private hands. The Historical Manuscripts Commission itself holds no manorial records. The Manorial Documents Register is not a register of title to manorial lordships and the Historical Manuscripts Commission does not collect or record information of this nature.
— Archives in Focus: an introduction to archives. It includes information on online archival resources designed for teachers, practical advice on what can be expected and what can be found when visiting a record office and guidance on how archives can be used for family, local and house history.

The National Archives

On April 2, 2003 the Historical Manuscripts Commission informally merged with the Public Record Office to form the National Archives. The National Archives is, in fact, an umbrella term, with the two bodies remaining distinct for legislative purposes. 6–011

The Lord Chancellor

The Lord Chancellor is the government minister responsible for the National Archives. On normal policy matters concerning the National Archives, public and other records and the work of the Public Record Office and the Historical Manuscripts Commission he relies on advice from the Keeper of Public Records[27] and from his officials in the Lord Chancellor's Department. Since 1958, as minister responsible for the Public Record Office, he has had the benefit of independent advice on matters relating to public records from his Advisory Council on Public Records. For the moment he remains responsible for these, despite the transfer of certain functions formerly performed by him to the Secretary of State for Constitutional Affairs.[28] 6–012

The Advisory Council on National Records and Archives

The Advisory Council[29] on National Records and Archives was established by the Lord Chancellor on April 2, 2003. It has advisory functions of its own in relation to strategic and policy matters relating to the National Archives and archival policy. The Advisory Council on National Records and Archives embraces two further bodies, which advise on specific areas: the Advisory Council on Public Records (created by s.1(2) of the Public Records Act 1958) to advise on public records issues; and the Advisory Council on Historical Manuscripts to advise on matters relating to non-public records and manuscripts. All three bodies are chaired by the Master of the Rolls who sits with unpaid members, appointed by the Lord Chancellor, who represent a wide range of different interests, including Parliament, regular users of historical records and owners of private papers. The Council is independent of the Keeper of Public Records. The three Advisory Councils are all advisory Non-Departmental Public Bodies within the remits of the Parliamentary Commissioner for Administration (the Ombudsman), the Commissioner for Public Appointments and the Information Commissioner. None has any executive functions or powers. 6–013

---

[27] Appointed under s.2 of the Public Records Act 1958.

[28] See The Secretary of State for Constitutional Affairs Order 2003, SI 2003/1887.

[29] The Advisory Council's address is: The Advisory Council on National Records and Archives, The National Archives, Kew, near Richmond, Surrey TW9 4DU.

The role of the Advisory Council

6–014 The Advisory Council's task is to advise the Lord Chancellor on any subject concerning archives and manuscripts, on issues relating to public access to the public records, and on the preservation of records, archives and manuscripts. It has no role in the day-to-day running of the National Archives, and no authority over the Keeper. The Council will normally meet four times a year, in February, June, October and December. Its most important task is to consider applications from departments for the extended closure of public records beyond the normal 30 years, or for the retention of public records by departments. The Lord Chancellor's practice is never to sign an instrument approving extended closures or retentions until he has received advice on it from the Advisory Council. The reasons for applications are scrutinised closely, and departments may be asked for further justification. This reconsideration can lead to a document being made available after all. The Advisory Council also considers subjects such as the corporate plan of the National Archives and its performance against its objectives and targets; the acceptance by the nation of papers in lieu of tax; the sale and export of historical manuscripts; public services provided by the National Archives and other UK archives; preservation policy for records and manuscripts of all sorts; and the level and fairness of fees.[30] The Advisory Council reports to the Lord Chancellor every year in an annual report by the Master of the Rolls, which is published with the Keeper's Report. On matters of urgency or of particular importance it asks the Master of the Rolls to write to him directly.

The Master of the Rolls

6–015 Apart from the continuing responsibility in respect of the Chancery of England, the Master of the Rolls does not have charge and superintendence over, or custody of, any public records. Those public records which on the commencement of the 1958 Act were in the custody of the Master of the Rolls were thereafter (save for records of the Chancery of England) in the custody of the Keeper of Public Records or such other officer as the Lord Chancellor might from time to time appoint.

[30] The Government's policy on archives is available at: *www.pro.gov.uk/archives/archivepolicy/introduction.*

3. THE PRESERVATION OF RECORDS

Introduction

The utility of most information, whether official or otherwise, is ephemeral. A public authority will wish to hold information for as long as it appears to have some relevance, or at least potential relevance, to the performance of that public authority's functions. The significance to a public authority of any information held by it will with time generally diminish. If for no other reasons than those of space and management, a public authority will ordinarily wish to cull the "non-current" information held by it, either by destroying it or by archiving it. As will be seen in this section, the public record regime provides an orderly and defined methodology for doing so which recognises that information that has lost its contemporaneity to a public authority may nevertheless hold a different, residual interest for others. As will be seen in the next section, as particular information "ages", the grounds for exempting the information from disclosure, which remain founded in the Freedom of Information Act 2000, are reduced to a series of key exemptions. 6–016

The meaning of "public records"

The Public Records Act 1958 distinguishes between public and other records. Section 10 provides that the phrase "public records" has the meaning given by the first schedule to the Act and that the word "records" includes not merely written records but records conveying information by any other means whatsoever. When records for administrative purposes are kept together in one file they are, in consequence of s.10(2), treated for the purposes of the Act as having been created on the date of the last record. The provisions of Sch.1 of the Public Records Act 1958 have effect for determining what constitute public records. A comprehensive list is set out in the Schedule: 6–017

(1) The first category is administrative and departmental records belonging to Her Majesty, whether in the United Kingdom or overseas, in right of Her Majesty's Government in the United Kingdom.[31] This expressly embraces records of, or held in, any department of Her Majesty's Government in the United Kingdom or records of any office, commission or other body whatsoever under Her Majesty's Government in the United Kingdom. This first broad category is subject to a number of exemptions. These cover:

[31] Public Records Act 1958, Sch.1, para.2.

(a) the records of any government department or body which is wholly or mainly concerned with Scottish affairs, or which carries on its activities wholly or mainly in Scotland;

(b) registers, or certified copies of entries in registers, being registers or certified copies kept or deposited in the General Register Office under or in pursuance of any enactment, whether past or future, which provides for the registration of births, deaths, marriages or adoptions;

(c) except as provided by para.4 of the Schedule (which deals with records of court proceedings) records of the Duchy of Lancaster;

(d) records of the office of Public Trustee relating to individual trusts; and

(e) Welsh public records as defined in the Government of Wales Act 1998. This first category will cover much of what is "information held by a public authority" within the meaning of the Freedom of Information Act 2000.

(2) The second category of public records is given by way of a table set out at the end of para.3 of the Schedule to the Act. This category is without prejudice to the generality of the first category and embraces the administrative and departmental records of the bodies and establishments set out in the table whether or not they are records belonging to Her Majesty. However, the provisions of para.3 of the Schedule are not taken as applying to records in any museum or gallery listed in the table which are part of its records acquired otherwise than by transfer from or under arrangements with a government department. The table (identifying public records), mentioned in the previous paragraph, is divided into two parts. The first is a list of bodies and establishments under government departments and the second is a list of other establishments and organisations. Part I of the table, which has been substantially amended since 1958, includes such bodies as the Agricultural Wages Board and the Legal Services Commission. Part II, likewise much amended since 1958, includes such bodies as the Adult Learning Inspectorate and the War Works Commission. The table in the Act should be consulted as necessary having in mind that by para.3A of the Schedule the table may, by Her Majesty in Council, be amended by adding to either part of the table an entry relating to any body or establishment which is specified in Sch.2 to the Parliamentary Commissioner Act 1967 (*i.e.* departments or other bodies subject to investigation) or a body or establishment which could be added to Sch.2 to the Act of 1967.

(3) Records of courts and tribunals constitute the third category of public records.[32] Excluded from the scope of this category are records of any

[32] Public Records Act 1958, Sch.1, para.4.

court or tribunal whose jurisdiction extends only to Scotland or Northern Ireland. Records for the purposes of this category include records of any proceedings in the court or tribunal in question and includes rolls, writs, books, decrees, bills, warrants and accounts of, or in the custody of, the court or tribunal in question. Paragraph 4 of the Schedule gives a list of courts and tribunals, which has also been amended since 1958. Further, the Lord Chancellor is given power to render public records those records of such other courts and tribunals as hespecifies.[33] The list given by para.4 of Sch.1 to the 1958 Act includes records of, or held in, any department of the Supreme Court (including any court held under a commission of assize); records of county courts; quarter sessions; magistrates' courts; coroners' courts; courts-martial, whether held by any of Her Majesty's Forces in or outside the United Kingdom; naval courts in or outside the United Kingdom under enactments relating to merchant shipping; any court exercising jurisdiction held by Her Majesty within a country outside Her dominions; records of any tribunal having jurisdiction connected with any functions of a department of Her Majesty's Government in the United Kingdom or having jurisdiction in proceedings to which such a Government department; records of the Lands Tribunal or of any Rent Tribunal or Local Valuation Court; of any Conveyancing Appeal Tribunal; of the Industrial Court; of umpires and deputy umpires appointed under the National Service Act 1948 or the Resumption in Civil Employment Act 1944; records of ecclesiastical courts when exercising certain testamentary and matrimonial jurisdictions; and the Information Tribunal. The Lord Chancellor is, by s.8 of the 1958 Act, responsible for the public records of every court of record or magistrates' court which are not in the Public Record Office or a place of deposit appointed by him under the Act. The Lord Chancellor is given power to determine in the case of any such records the officer in whose custody they are for the time being to be placed. Section 124 of the Supreme Court Act 1981 requires all original wills and other documents which are under the control of the High Court in the Principal Registry or in any district probate registry to be deposited and preserved in such places as the Lord Chancellor may direct and, subject to the control of the High Court and probate rules, to be open to inspection. There is a particular saving (by s.8(5)) from the selection and transfer provisions of s.3 of the Act in respect of certain records of ecclesiastical courts but the Lord Chancellor is able, after consulting

33 Public Records Act 1958, Sch.1, para.4(1)(o). The power is exercised by order in a statutory instrument.

the President of the Family Division, to direct their transfer to a place of deposit which he appoints.[34]

(4) Records of the Chancery of England are, other than any which are Welsh public records (as defined in the Government of Wales Act 1998), public records for the purposes of the Public Records Act 1958. Subject to the terms of s.7 of the Act, the Master of the Rolls continues to be responsible for, and to have custody of, the records of the Chancery of England and has power to determine where they should be deposited.[35] Section 3 of the Act, which deals with selection and preservation of public records, does not apply to the records of the Chancery of England; nor does s.6(4) (which deals with consultation by the Lord Chancellor before appointing a place of deposit) apply. However, if records of the Chancery of England are deposited in the Public Record Office then they are in the custody of the Keeper of Public Records and subject to the directions of the Lord Chancellor as in the case of any other records in the Public Record Office.

Extension of the meaning of public records

6–018 Paragraphs 6, 7 and 8 of the First Schedule to the 1958 Act extend what is embraced by the definition of public records. Thus, public records include, other than any which are Welsh public records (as defined in the Government of Wales Act 1998):

— all records within the meaning of the Public Record Office Act 1838 or to which that Act was applied, which, at the commencement of the Public Records Act 1958,[36] were in the custody of the Master of the Rolls in pursuance of that Act;

— all records within the meaning of the Public Record Office Act 1838 or to which that Act was applied which at the commencement of the Public Records Act 1958 were in the Public Record Office and under the charge and superintendence of the Master of the Rolls; and

[34] There are certain public records, in the custody of the University of Oxford, included in an index a copy of which was transmitted to the principal probate registrar under s.2 of the Oxford University Act 1860 which are not required to be transferred. However, the Lord Chancellor has to make arrangements with the University of Oxford as to the conditions under which those records may be inspected by the public.

[35] By s.73(1) of the Courts and Legal Services Act 1990 where the Master of the Rolls expects to be absent at a time when it may be appropriate for any relevant functions of his to be exercised he may appoint a judge of the Supreme Court to exercise those functions on his behalf. Relevant functions include functions under s.144A of the Law of Property Act 1922 (functions relating to manorial documents) and functions under s.7(1) of the Public Records Act 1958 (power to determine where records of the Chancery of England are to be deposited).

[36] January 1, 1959: Public Records Act 1958, s.13(3).

— all records forming part of the same series of documents as any series of documents falling under the previous heads. Paragraph 7 of the Schedule enables Her Majesty by order in Council to direct that any description of records (not being Welsh public records within the meaning of the Government of Wales Act 1998) not falling within the Schedule shall be treated as public records. No recommendation is to be made to Her Majesty for such an order unless a draft has been laid before Parliament and approved by each House.

Paragraph 7(2) provides that a question whether any records or description of records are public records for the purposes of the Act shall be referred to and determined by the Lord Chancellor who has to include his decisions on such questions in his annual report to Parliament. Furthermore, the Lord Chancellor has from time to time to compile and publish lists of the departments, bodies, establishments, courts and tribunals comprised in paras 2, 3 and 4 of the Schedule and lists describing more particularly the categories of records which are, or are not, public records as defined in the Schedule. Paragraph 8 of the Schedule declares that any description of government department, court, tribunal or other body or establishment in the Schedule by reference to which a class of public records is framed extends to a government department, court, tribunal or other body or establishment which has ceased to exist whether before or after the passing of the Public Records Act 1958. Further, by virtue of s.8(4) of the Public Records Act 1958 where private documents have remained in the custody of a court in England and Wales for more than 50 years without being claimed, the Keeper of Public Records may, with the approval of the Master of the Rolls, require their transfer to the Public Record Office, whereupon they become public records. Scotland and Northern Ireland have their own record offices and the National Assembly for Wales has the power to establish one for Wales. If one is established, the Lord Chancellor has power to impose (by statutory instrument) arrangements analogous to those in the Public Records Act 1958. The access regimes in Scotland and Northern Ireland reflect the access arrangements in England.

Welsh public records

By s.116(1) of the Government of Wales Act 1998, Welsh public records are not public records for the purposes of the Public Records Act 1958. However, by subs.(2), the Public Records Act 1958 has effect in relation to Welsh public records until an order under s.117 imposes a duty on the National Assembly for Wales to preserve them. No such order has yet been made. Welsh public records are defined in s.118 of the Government of Wales Act 1998. 6–019

Preservation of records that are not public records

6–020 The Keeper of Public Records is empowered to accept records which are not public records. This is done where the Keeper is of the view that the records merit permanent preservation, and the body generating the records agrees to deposit them.[37] An agreement is entered into between the body and the Public Record Office. The agreement renders the deposit similar in relation to access and copying to that by public record bodies. The organisation making the deposit must carry out the necessary selection and indexing work under the supervision of staff from the Public Record Office. The ownership of the records and their copyright status remain unaffected by the deposit. The Lord Chancellor is also able (in consequence of s.3(5)), if it appears to him in the interests of the proper administration of the Public Record Office, to direct that the transfer of any class of records shall be suspended until arrangements for their reception have been completed. As will be seen, although such records do not metamorphose into public records, they are "historical records" with accompanying rights of access.

Selection of public records for preservation

6–021 The wide definition given to "public records" will plainly pick up the prosaic as well as the principal; and it will do so before any formal decision as to retention has been made by the public authority that brought the record into being. Inevitably, there must be some reduction in this mountain of material. Section 3 of the Public Records Act 1958 imposes a duty on every person responsible for public records of any description which are not in the Public Record Office or a place of deposit appointed by the Lord Chancellor under the 1958 Act to make arrangements for the selection of those records which ought to be permanently preserved and their safekeeping. These duties are to be performed under the guidance of the Keeper of Public Records, who is responsible for the co-ordination and supervision of all action taken under s.3. The obligation imposed by the Public Records Act 1958 is in respect of those which ought to be permanently preserved.[38] Current practice has a two-stage selection process. Each government department has a Departmental Record Officer who is responsible for the management of its records.[39] He carries out the selection process under the guidance of the Public Record Office through the Central

[37] Other records can be visited upon the Public Record Office, for example: records relating to a dissolved company under the Companies Act 1985, s.707A(3); manorial documents, under the Law of Property Act 1922, s.144A; instruments of apportionment, under the Tithes Act 1936, s.36(3); and orders of exchange by the Inclosure Commissioners, under the Inclosure Act 1857, s.5.

[38] s.3(3) of the Act requires that all public records created before 1660, *i.e.* the year of the restoration of the monarchy, be amongst those selected for permanent preservation.

[39] As explained by the Public Record System at: *www.pro.gov.uk/about/access/system*.

Records Management Department. The first review takes place, generally, five years[40] after a departmental file is closed. Records considered to be valueless are destroyed. Those thought possibly necessary in the future for administrative or research purposes are kept for another ten to twenty years. They are then assessed for permanent preservation on second review. Once selected for permanent preservation public records are, subject to a proviso, required to be transferred not later than 30 years after their creation either to the Public Record Office or to such other place of deposit appointed by the Lord Chancellor under the 1958 Act as the Lord Chancellor may direct.[41] Section 4 of the Act gives the Lord Chancellor power to appoint places of deposit. The proviso given by s.3(4) enables any records to be retained after 30 years if, in the opinion of the person responsible for them, they are required for administrative purposes or ought to be retained for any other special reason. If the person responsible is not the Lord Chancellor, then the Lord Chancellor must be informed of the facts and give his approval. The quantity annually transferred to the Public Record Office is about 1,830 metres.

Destruction of public records

Those public records which have been rejected as not required for permanent preservation are destroyed or, in the case of records for which some person other than the Lord Chancellor is responsible, subject to the approval of the Lord Chancellor, are disposed of in any other way. Any question arising under s.3 as to the person whose duty it is to make arrangements under the section with respect to any class of public records is required to be referred to the Lord Chancellor for his decision. If it appears to the Keeper of Public Records that as respects any public records in the Public Record Office or any place of deposit appointed under the Act that they are duplicated by other public records which have been selected for permanent preservation or that there is some other special reason why they should not permanently be preserved, he may, with the approval of the Lord Chancellor and of the minister or other person, appearing to the Lord Chancellor as primarily concerned with public records of the class in question, authorise the destruction of those records or, with the same approval, their disposal in any other way.[42] Section 3 of the 1958 Act, which deals with selection and presentation of public records, does not render it unlawful for the person responsible for any public record to transmit it to the Keeper of the Records of Scotland or to the Public Record Office of Northern Ireland. 6–022

[40] This period of time is consistent with the policy of opening new files after five years of inactivity rather than adding to an existing file. If one merely added to the existing file, s.10(2) of the Public Records Act 1958 would, for the purposes of the Act, treat the record as having been created on the last date.

[41] Public Records Act 1958, s.3(4).

[42] *ibid*., s.6.

Access to public records: regime to November 2005

6–023 Section 5 of the Public Records Act 1958, as originally enacted, kept public records closed to public inspection for 50 years. This was reduced, subject to exceptions, to 30 years by the Public Records Act 1967 which amended s.5 with effect from January 1, 1968. The regime as given by s.5 of the 1958 Act is repealed by the Freedom of Information Act 2000[43] from November 30, 2005 unless the Secretary of State by order[44] appoints an earlier date. At present, *i.e.* until November 30, 2005, access by the public to public records in the Public Record Office (other than those to which the public had access before their transfer to the Public Record Office) is not permitted for a period of 30 years beginning with the first day of January in the year next after that in which they were created.[45] However,[46] if it appears to the person responsible[47] for any public records which have been selected by him for permanent preservation that they contain information which was obtained from members of the public under such conditions that the opening of the records to the public after the 30-year period[48] might constitute a breach of good faith on the part of the Government or on the part of the persons who obtained the information, that person must inform the Lord Chancellor accordingly so that those records are not available for public inspection after the expiration of 30 years or such other period as was determined except in circumstances as the person responsible for selection and the Lord Chancellor approve or after such further period of time as they approve. The 30-year closure period does not apply to records which have been open to the public prior to their transfer; they have to remain open. Further, s.5(1) gives the Lord Chancellor a discretion to open records, with the concurrence of the Minister concerned, earlier than the specified period. This is known as accelerated opening.[49] Where a variation of the normal 30-year period occurs it is effected by a document signed by the Lord Chancellor and known as a Lord Chancellor's Instrument. The duty imposed on the Keeper of Public Records[50] to arrange that reasonable facilities are available to the public for inspecting and obtaining copies of public records in the Public Record Office is subject to the time rule (*i.e.* the 30-year rule) and the good faith restraint, if applicable. It has been seen that the period of 30 years is capable of extension. An illustration is in respect of records relating to the abdication in 1936 of King

43 ss.67 and 86 and Sch.5, Pt I and Sch.8, Pt II.

44 Freedom of Information Act 2000, s.87(3).

45 Or such other period as the Lord Chancellor may, with the approval, or at the request, of the Minister or other person, who appears to him to be principally concerned, prescribe as respects any particular class of public records.

46 In consequence of the Public Records Act 1958, s.5(2).

47 Under the Public Records Act 1958, s.3.

48 Or other period determined under s.5(1).

49 The current policy on access to public records is set out in the White Paper "Open Government" (Cmnd. 2290, 1993). This deals with the policy in respect of accelerated opening, extended closure and retention.

50 By the Public Records Act 1958, s.5(3).

Edward VIII (later HRH the Duke of Windsor). Certain records were closed until after the death in 2002 of Her Majesty Queen Elizabeth, the Queen Mother.

Additional proscriptions against disclosure before November 2005

Furthermore, the access right is subject to those enactments set out in the Second Schedule to the 1958 Act which prohibit the disclosure of certain information obtained from the public except for certain limited purposes.[51] The Second Schedule lists a variety of enactments having the prohibitory effect mentioned in the previous sentence including the Coal Industry Nationalisation Act 1946 (s.56), the Statistics of Trade Act 1947 (s.9), the Industrial Organisation and Development Act 1947 (s.5), the Agricultural Statistics Act 1979 and the Film Levy Finance Act 1981 (s.8). Schedule 2 to the Act is repealed by the Freedom of Information Act 2000, with effect from November 30, 2005.[52] 6–024

Disposition of public records to other places of deposit

The Public Record Office has published a disposition policy providing a principled framework on which decisions are based to offer public records to archival institutions other than the Public Record Office. The power to appoint places of deposit was delegated by the Lord Chancellor to the Keeper of Public Records when, in 1992, the Public Record Office became an executive agency. There are about 235 archives, libraries, museums, galleries and government agencies which have been inspected by the Public Record Office and appointed to hold specified classes of public record. Throughout England and Wales local authority archive services have been appointed as places of deposit for public records of strong local interest. Many of the major national museums and galleries are appointed to hold their own administrative records or specialist material which falls within their collecting policies. Places of deposit are periodically inspected by a member of staff from the Public Record Office. It is usual for a major place of deposit, such as a county record office, to be visited once every five years. All inspections are carried out by professionally qualified archivists with experience of working in a record office. The purpose of these inspections is to determine whether places of deposit offer conditions for the storage of records and facilities for public access meeting the Public Record Office's standards. These standards are largely based on BS 5454 relating to Records in Places of Deposit. From the year 2000 onwards, a checklist based on the Standard for Access to 6–025

[51] The duty is also subject to any other Act or instrument whether passed or made before or after the Public Records Act 1958 containing a similar prohibition.

[52] Unless the Secretary of State by order appoints an earlier date.

Archives, which has been developed by the Public Services Quality Group, will also inform the Public Record Office's inspections of places of deposit, so that access to records by users has the same weight as preservation.

Other places of deposit

6–026 The preceding paragraphs have been substantially concerned with access to material in the Public Record Office. The Lord Chancellor is required, for all public records in places of deposit appointed by him outside the Public Record Office, to arrange that facilities are available for their inspection by the public comparable to those for public records in the Public Record Office. Prior to November 30, 2005 such arrangements are subject to the restrictions corresponding with those contained in s.5 of the 1958 Act. After November 30, 2005, or such earlier date as may be appointed by the Secretary of State, the words having the effect of making such arrangements subject to those restrictions are repealed so as to secure that access is thereafter in accordance with the Freedom of Information Act 2000.

Transfer of public records instead of destruction

6–027 In addition to transfers of public records to places of deposit, s.3(6) of the Public Records Act 1958 allows the Public Record Office, under powers delegated by the Lord Chancellor to the Keeper of Public Records, to present government records which have not been selected for permanent preservation to places of deposit and other bona fide institutions. In this way such records are preserved and made publicly available as an alternative to their destruction. Presented records become the property of the recipient and cease to have public record status.[53] These records are transferred subject to conditions stipulated by the Public Record Office. Normal conditions will be a restriction on the disposal of the records without advance consultation with the Public Record Office and a 30-year closure period.

4. ACCESS TO PUBLIC RECORDS: THE NEW REGIME

Introduction

6–028 From November 2005 the basic principles relating to access to public records will be founded upon the rights to information held by a public authority. It is

[53] Accordingly, they are not "transferred public records" within the meaning of s.15(4) of the Freedom of Information Act 2000.

thus essential to a proper understanding of the new regime to be familiar with the two basic rights bestowed by s.1 of the Freedom of Information Act 2000, together with the distinction between those provisions in Pt II of the Act conferring absolute exemption and those provisions in Pt II of the Act conferring a qualified exemption. These are dealt with elsewhere in this work.[54] But, in brief, by s.1(1) of the Freedom of Information Act 2000, any person making a request for information to a public authority is entitled to be informed in writing by the public authority whether it holds information of the description specified in the request and if that is the case to have that information communicated to him. Those rights are made subject to a number of other provisions in the Act,[55] most notably s.2, which brings in the provisions of Pt II. Thus, the s.1 rights are shaped by the provisions of Pt II. As noted earlier, the special characteristics of information held by the Public Record Office, the fact that public records are held by bodies other than the Public Record Office, and the fact that the interest of the Public Record Office in the contents of a record is different from that of the public authority which created that record, have all necessitated important modifications to the regime which ordinarily applies to information held by a public authority under the 2000 Act. As will be seen, these modifications are secured by s.15 of the Freedom of Information Act 2000, which makes special provision relating to public records transferred to the Public Record Office, and by Pt VI of the Act (ss.62–67), which deals with historical records and records in the Public Record Office or the Public Record Office of Northern Ireland.

Administrative arrangements after 2005

From November 30, 2005, the duty of the Keeper of Public Records[56] becomes one tof arranging that reasonable facilities are available to the public for inspecting and obtaining copies of those public records in the Public Record Office which fall to be disclosed in accordance with the Freedom of Information Act 2000.[57] The new subs.5(3) signifies that after November 2005 the regime, so far as public records are concerned, will be that their selection, deposit and destruction are to be governed by the 1958 Act, whilst their accessibility is to be controlled by the 2000 Act. Hence, the mechanics of maintenance of public records is given by the earlier Act whilst, consistent with the theme that access to information is substantially administered by one Act, securing access to information is given by the Freedom of Information Act 2000. So far as the latter Act is concerned, it is to be kept in mind that the Public Record Office is a 6–029

[54] See, in particular, Chs 1, 14 and 15. There is no distinct existence right under the Freedom of Information (Scotland) Act 2002.

[55] Freedom of Information Act 2000, s.1(2); Freedom of Information (Scotland) Act 2002, s.1(6).

[56] By virtue of a new s.5(3), inserted into the Public Records Act 1958 by the Freedom of Information Act 2000.

[57] The Lord Chancellor is likewise obliged in respect of records held in places of deposit other than at the Public Record Office: Public Records Act 1958, s.5(5).

government department and so, by virtue of para.1 of Sch.1 to the Act, constitutes a "public authority" within the meaning of that Act. In this way, the manifold obligations imposed upon a public authority by the Freedom of Information Act 2000 attach to the Public Record Office.

Summary of changes to the 1958 regime

6–030 The broad nature of the new regime, looking exclusively for the moment at the Public Record Office, is as follows.

(1) First, the Public Record Office is a public authority and subject to the obligations of the Freedom of Information Act 2000.
(2) Second, in any event, the Public Records Act 1958, as amended, obliges access to public records held by the Public Record Office to be provided in accordance with the Freedom of Information Act 2000.
(3) Third, the access right is that given by s.1 of the Freedom of Information Act 2000, as shaped by the provisions in Pt II of that Act.
(4) Fourth, some of those provisions confer absolute exemptions; the remainder confer a qualified exemption, which involves considering whether in all the circumstances the public interest in maintaining the exemption outweighs the public interest in disclosing the information.
(5) Fifth, the range of exemptions available under the Freedom of Information Act 2000 is reduced where the public record is a "historical record".
(6) Sixth, where information contained in a record that has been transferred to the Public Record Office falls within a provision of the Freedom of Information Act 2000 that confers a qualified exemption,[58] then, unless the information has been designated "open information", the weighing of the public interest described in (4) above is determined by the "responsible authority" and not by the Public Record Office.
(7) Finally, the Act enables responsible authorities to designate information as "open".[59] This designation, putting the matter broadly, leaves the decision-making principally with the Public Record Office, but with some involvement by the Lord Chancellor where it is proposed to refuse access on the basis of a qualified exemption.

The regime operates in a similar way for places of deposit other than the Public Record Office.[60]

---

[58] Or a qualified exclusion of the duty to confirm or deny.
[59] Curiously, no definition is given in the Act of open information; nor is it revealed how such information receives such a designation.
[60] Freedom of Information Act 2000, s.15(5).

Exemptions: introduction

The operation of the Public Records Act 1958 and the Freedom of Information Act 2000 contemplates the Keeper of Public Records arranging reasonable facilities for the inspection and copying of those public records in the Public Record Office which fall to be disclosed in accordance with the Freedom of Information Act 2000.[61] That obligation to disclose is framed by the applicability of the exemptions in Pt II of that Act. So far as public records are concerned, the way those exemptions operate is affected by a variety of factors, but principally by the age of the record. It should be observed, parenthetically, that the Public Record Office will hold, just as other public authorities hold, information, for example about its current operating programme, for which access can be sought in the usual way under the Act. However, in this chapter we are concerned principally with the regime as it applies to public records. 6–031

The reduction of exemptions and exclusions

The starting point is that the access right and the existence right apply equally to information held by the Public Record Office as they do to ordinary information held by a public authority: in other words, a person has the rights given by s.1(1) of the Freedom of Information Act 2000 in relation to all information held by the Public Record Office, those rights being shaped by the exemptions and exclusions in Part II of the Freedom of Information Act 2000. The fact that the information is contained in what the Public Records Act 1958 terms a "public record" of itself effects no change to the ambit of the right to obtain access to that information under the Freedom of Information Act 2000 or to the ambit of the existence right. Modification to the ambit of those rights occurs if and only if the information is contained in a "historical record." The modifications then vary according to the age of the historical record in which the information is contained. In very general terms, what Pt VI of the Freedom of Information Act 2000 does is to remove in respect of information contained in a historical record some of the exemptions in Pt II of the Act, thereby extending the scope of the right of access.[62] The exemptions that are removed are those relating to: 6–032

- Relations within the United Kingdom (s.28);
- Criminal investigations and proceedings (s.30(1));
- Court records, etc. (s.32);
- Audit functions (s.33);
- Formulation of government policy, etc. (s.35);
- Prejudice to effective conduct of public affairs (s.36);

[61] See para.6–029.
[62] Freedom of Information Act 2000, s.63(1); Freedom of Information (Scotland) Act 2002, s.58(1).

- — Communications with Her Majesty, etc. (s.37(1)(a));
- — Legal professional privilege (s.42);
- — Commercial interests (s.43).

A similar modification is made to the existence right given by s.1(1)(a) of the 2000 Act.[63] In the following paragraphs of this chapter, the term "Public Record Office" has for ease of understanding been used in place of "the appropriate records authority"; however, it should be remembered that the points made equally apply to the other approved places of deposit and to the Public Record Office of Northern Ireland.

Historical record

6–033 Section 62 of the Freedom of Information Act 2000 introduces the concept of the "historical record." A record, for the purposes of Pt VI of the Act, becomes a historical record at the end of 30 years beginning with the year[64] following that in which it was created. The period of 30 years appears to have been selected in the light of the period presently given by the Public Records Act 1958 for the commencement of access. A historical record is not necessarily a public record.[65] Thus, a record that is not a public record but which has been accepted by the Public Record Office for preservation[66] will constitute a "historical record" provided that the age requirements of s.62 are met. Where records are created at different dates but are kept together in one file or other assembly, all the records are to be treated as having been created when the latest of those records was created.[67]

Historical records at most 60 years old

6–034 Having defined a "historical record", the Freedom of Information Act 2000 removes an increasing number of the provisions in Pt II of the Act according to the age of the record. Where up to 60 years has elapsed since the start of the year following that in which the record was created, information contained in it can only be exempt information under:

[63] Freedom of Information Act 2000, s.63(2). Note, however, that the exclusions of the duty to confirm or deny that information is held granted by ss.30(3), 32(3), 35(3) and 37(2) are not removed in relation to historical records. There is no separate duty to confirm or deny under the Freedom of Information (Scotland) Act 2002.

[64] A year is a calendar year: Freedom of Information Act 2000, s.62(3).

[65] As is recognised by Freedom of Information Act 2000, s.65.

[66] See para.6–020.

[67] Freedom of Information Act 2000, s.62(2); Freedom of Information (Scotland) Act 2002, s.57(2).

— s.21, *i.e.* the information is accessible to the applicant by other means.[68] However, this exemption cannot operate if the historical record is in either the Public Record Office or the Public Record Office of Northern Ireland.[69]
— s.22, *i.e.* the information is intended for future publication.[70] However, this exemption cannot operate if the historical record is in either the Public Record Office or the Public Record Office of Northern Ireland.[71]
— s.23, *i.e.* the information is supplied by or relating to bodies dealing with security matters.[72]
— s.24, *i.e.* the information is required for the purpose of national security.[73]
— s.26, *i.e.* the information is such that its disclosure would prejudice or be likely to prejudice defence.[74]
— s.27, *i.e.* the information is such that its disclosure would or would be likely to prejudice international relations.[75]
— s.29, *i.e.* the information is such that its disclosure would or would be likely to prejudice the economic interests of the United Kingdom or the financial interests of any administration in the United Kingdom.[76]
— s.30(2), *i.e.* the information was obtained or recorded for the purposes of a public authority's functions relating to criminal investigations or proceedings as to impropriety (listed in s.31(2)) or civil proceedings, and it relates to obtaining information from confidential sources.[77]
— s.31, *i.e.* the information relates to law enforcement.[78]
— s.34, *i.e.* the information is required for the purpose of avoiding an infringement of the privileges of either House of Parliament.[79]

[68] Similarly, Freedom of Information (Scotland) Act 2002, s.25. As to which exemption, see paras 16–001 to 16–004 below.
[69] Freedom of Information Act 2000, s.64(1).
[70] Similarly, Freedom of Information (Scotland) Act 2002, s.27. As to which exemption, see para.16–006 to 16–008 below.
[71] Freedom of Information Act 2000, s.64(1).
[72] As to which exemption, see para.17–026 to 17–031 below. There is no analogous exemption under the Freedom of Information (Scotland) Act 2002.
[73] Similarly, Freedom of Information (Scotland) Act 2002, s.31. As to which exemption, see para.17–033 to 17–040 below.
[74] Similarly, Freedom of Information (Scotland) Act 2002, s.31. As to which exemption, see para.17–051 to 17–059 below.
[75] Similarly, Freedom of Information (Scotland) Act 2002, s.32. As to which exemption, see para.18–001 to 18–012 below.
[76] Similarly, Freedom of Information (Scotland) Act 2002, s.33(2). As to which exemption, see para.19–001 to 19–009 below.
[77] Similarly, Freedom of Information (Scotland) Act 2002, s.34. As to which exemption, see para.20–004 *et seq*. below.
[78] Similarly, Freedom of Information (Scotland) Act 2002, s.35. As to which exemption, see para.20–014 *et seq*. below.
[79] As to which exemption, see para.21–001 to 21–009 below.

— s.37(1)(b), *i.e.* the information relates to the conferring by the Crown of any honour or dignity.[80]
— s.38, *i.e.* the information is such that its disclosure would or would be likely to endanger health or safety.[81]
— s.39, *i.e.* the information is environmental information which the holding public authority is obliged by regulations under s.74 to make available or would be obliged but for an exemption under the regulations.[82]
— s.40, *i.e.* the information constitutes personal data of which the applicant is the data subject.[83]
— s.41, *i.e.* the disclosure of the information would constitute an actionable breach of confidence.[84]
— s.44, *i.e.* the disclosure of the information is prohibited by or under another enactment, is incompatible with any European Community obligation or would constitute or be punishable as a contempt of court.[85]

Historical records at most 100 years old

6–035 Where more than 60 years has elapsed since the start of the year following that in which the record containing the information was created, the potential grounds of exemption in respect of information in that record are further reduced by the removal of s.37(1)(b), *i.e.* the information cannot be exempt information by virtue of it relating to the conferring by the Crown of any honour or dignity.[86]

6–036 Historical records more than 100 years old

Where a historical record is more than 60 but less than 100 years old, then the potential grounds of exemption are further reduced by the removal of s.31, *i.e.*

[80] Similarly, Freedom of Information (Scotland) Act 2002, s.41(b). As to which exemption, see paras 26–008 to 26–014 below.
[81] Similarly, Freedom of Information (Scotland) Act 2002, s.39. As to which exemption, see para.23–001 to 23–004 below.
[82] Similarly, Freedom of Information (Scotland) Act 2002, s.39. As to which exemption, see para.16–009 to 16–013 above.
[83] Similarly, Freedom of Information (Scotland) Act 2002, s.38. As to which exemption, see para.24–005 below.
[84] As to which exemption, see para.25–001 to 25–027 below. The position under the Freedom of Information (Scotland) Act 2002 is different.
[85] Similarly, Freedom of Information (Scotland) Act 2002, s.26. As to which exemption, seeparas 26–015 to 26–033 below.
[86] Freedom of Information Act 2000, s.63(3); Freedom of Information (Scotland) Act 2002, s.58(2)(a).

the information cannot be exempt information by virtue of it relating to law enforcement.[87]

The duty to confirm or deny

As has been noted elsewhere in this work, although the Freedom of Information Act 2000 places the duty to confirm or deny before the disclosure duty, the latter is more sensibly considered first. Quite simply, if a decision is made to disclose information then a public authority will not need to exercise itself with the duty to confirm or deny.[88] If, however, a decision is made to refuse disclosure of certain information, then a public authority will need to go on to consider separately the duty to confirm or deny.[89] As with the disclosure duty, the technique employed by the Act is to remove certain of the exclusions from the duty to confirm or deny in relation to a historical record, thereby widening the range of historical records in relation to which the Public Record Office (as a public authority) must discharge the duty to confirm or deny.[90] The result is as follows: 6–037

(1) To the extent that the information held by the Public Record Office that answers, or that would answer, the terms of the request is not in a historical record, the scope of the duty to confirm or deny is the same as it is in relation to information held by any other public authority which is subject to the Freedom of Information Act 2000.[91]

(2) To the extent that the information held by the Public Record Office that answers, or that would answer, the terms of the request is in a historical record that is less than 61 years old, the scope of the duty to confirm or deny is enlarged by the removal of the exclusions relating to:

   — Relations within the United Kingdom (s.28(3));
   — Audit functions (s.33(3));
   — Prejudice to effective conduct of public affairs (s.36(3));

[87] Freedom of Information Act 2000, s.63(4); Freedom of Information (Scotland) Act 2002, s.58(2)(b), with additional exemptions falling away.

[88] Freedom of Information Act 2000, s.1(5).

[89] Note also that if the decision on disclosure is made in two stages because the weighing of the public interest has not been completed within the 20 working day time-limit (see Freedom of Information Act 2000, s.17(2) and para.11–028 below), then it is quite possible that the decision on the duty to confirm or deny will have to be concluded before the second stage of the decision on disclosure. This is both because the exclusions of the duty to confirm or deny given by various provisions in Pt II are not coincidental with the exemptions from disclosure given by that Part (see paras 14–004, 14–015 and 14–016 below) and because, in relation to historical records, the exclusions removed by s.63(2) are not as extensive as the exemptions removed by s.63(1) and (3).

[90] The reference in Freedom of Information Act 2000, s.63(2) to "a historical record" should probably be read as a reference to "information contained in a historical record" as information is the unit of the obligation in s.1(1)(a): see paras 7–001 and 14–005 below.

[91] This is because the reduction in exclusions only applies to historical records: Freedom of Information Act 2000, s.63.

— Legal professional privilege (s.42(2)); and
— Commercial interests (s.43(3)).[92]

(3) To the extent that the information held by the Public Record Office that answers, or that would answer, the terms of the request is in a historical record that is more than 100 years old, the scope of the duty to confirm or deny is further enlarged by the removal of the exclusions relating to law enforcement (s.31(1)).[93]

Practical considerations

6–038 The preceding paragraphs have shown that any information contained in a historical record may fall outside the disclosure obligation and the duty to confirm or deny. Theoretically this means that if access were sought to what is already reasonably accessible, say, the Domesday Book, the Duke of Marlborough's despatches or records relating to Lord Nelson, it would be possible to refuse access on the basis of the residual exemptions that apply to historical records more than 100 years old. From the perspective of the Public Record Office, the removal of s.21 as a ground of exemption[94] may seem odd, as it removes the opportunity for it to refuse requests for such information on the straightforward basis that that information is already reasonably accessible by the general access arrangements provided by the Public Record Office. Nevertheless, it is suggested that a request for information made to the Public Record Office for information which is contained in a historical record that is freely accessible in the Public Record Office will, in some circumstances, be a vexatious request, so that it will not have to be complied with.[95]

5. DECISION-MAKING RESPONSIBILITY IN RELATION TO PUBLIC RECORDS

Introduction

6–039 As noted earlier, whenever a request for information is made of a public authority, it is ordinarily that public authority which makes the disclosure decision in

[92] Freedom of Information Act 2000, s.63(2).
[93] Freedom of Information Act, s.63(5).
[94] *ibid*., s.64(1). This is not so in Scotland with the equivalent Freedom of Information (Scotland) Act 2002, s.25 remaining in place.
[95] Freedom of Information Act 2000, s.14(1); Freedom of Information (Scotland) Act 2002, s.14(1). In relation to vexatious requests, see para.12–009 below. If the person requesting the information expresses a preference for communication by means of a copy and, particularly if the person lives some distance from the Public Record Office, it may be more difficult to characterise the request as "vexatious" unless the information is otherwise freely available.

relation to all information answering the terms of the request which is held by it, irrespective of whether the information originated from another public authority. A request may be transferred by one public authority to another public authority: where this occurs, the receiving public authority will determine the request solely according to the information that it holds.[96] But for s.15 of the Freedom of Information Act 2000, the ordinary position would have had the result that if a request for information were made of the Public Record Office,[97] it would have been the Public Record Office that would have determined the request in relation to all information held by it, including records previously transferred by a public authority to the Public Record Office under the Public Records Act 1958. As will be seen, the Freedom of Information Act 2000, displaces the usual decision-maker for the purposes of weighing the public interest only and allocates decision-making responsibility on that point to the "responsible authority." There is thus a division of decision-making responsibility between the Public Record Office and the "responsible authority". It is first necessary to consider the four terms used by the Freedom of Information Act 2000 to secure this division of responsibility:

— "transferred public record";
— "responsible authority";
— "appropriate records authority"; and
— "open information".

Transferred public record

Section 15(4) of the Freedom of Information Act 2000 introduces the concept of a "transferred public record." This is a public record[98] that has been transferred to the Public Record Office, to another place of deposit appointed by the Lord Chancellor under the Public Records Act 1958 or to the Public Record Office of Northern Ireland. Thus, when a public record is transferred from a public authority to the Public Record Office (or to another place of deposit, etc.) it remains a "public record" for the purposes of the Public Records Act 1958, but is labelled a "transferred public record" for the purposes of the Freedom of Information Act 2000. As noted earlier, not all information held by the Public Record Office is a public record: the Office can accept and hold material that is not a public record;[99] by definition such material will not be a "transferred 6–040

[96] In relation to transfers, see paras 11–032 to 11–033 below.
[97] Or another place of deposit appointed by the Lord Chancellor under the Public Records Act 1958 or the Public Records Office of Northern Ireland.
[98] "Public record" means public record as defined by the Public Records Act 1958: see paras 6–017 to 6–018.
[99] See para.–020.

public record".[1] In relation to this non-public record material held by the Public Record Office (or other place of deposit, etc.), all decision-making for the purposes of the Freedom of Information Act 2000 remains with the Public Record Office (or other place of deposit, etc.).[2] It should also be noted that the division of responsibility is not confined to "historical records:" it applies equally to public records that are not historical records but that have been transferred to the Public Record Office (or other place of deposit, etc.).

"Responsible authority" and "appropriate records authority"

6–041 Section 15(5) of the Freedom of Information Act 2000 defines "responsible authority" by reference both to the party transferring the public record and to the destination of the transferred public record.

(1) In the case of a public record transferred from a government department either to the Public Record Office or to a place of deposit appointed by the Lord Chancellor, the "responsible authority" is the Minister of the Crown who appears to the Lord Chancellor to be primarily concerned.

(2) In the case of a public record transferred from any person other than a government department either to the Public Record Office or to a place of deposit appointed by the Lord Chancellor, the "responsible authority" is the person who appears to the Lord Chancellor to be primarily concerned. Bearing in mind the wide definition given to "public record,"[3] it is readily apparent that that person may not be a public authority within the meaning of the Freedom of Information Act 2000.[4] In this situation, that person is deemed to be a public authority, with certain consequential obligations which are discussed below.[5]

(3) In the case of a record transferred to the Public Record Office of Northern Ireland from a government department in the charge of a Minister of the Crown, the responsible authority is that minister of the Crown who appears to the appropriate Northern Ireland Minister to be primarily concerned. If the transfer is from a Northern Ireland department then the responsible authority is the Northern Ireland Minister who appears to the appropriate Northern Ireland Minister to be pri-

[1] Freedom of Information Act 2000, s.15(4). There is a broadly similar regime in Freedom of Information (Scotland) Act 2002, s.22.

[2] On the basis that it will be treated as "information held by a public authority" (*i.e.* the Public Record Office), but without the modifications effected by the Freedom of Information Act 2000 in relation to transferred public records.

[3] See paras 6–017 to 6–018.

[4] See Freedom of Information Act 2000, ss.3–7.

[5] Freedom of Information Act 2000, s.66(6). As to those obligations, see paras 6–043 to 6–044. The obligations can be lightened by simply designating all the information "open information".

marily concerned. If the record was transferred from any other person then the responsible authority is the person who appears to the appropriate Northern Ireland Minister to be primarily concerned.[6]

Section 15(5) of the Freedom of Information Act 2000 identifies the Public Record Office as "the appropriate records authority" in relation to public records transferred to the Public Record Office. In relation to a transferred public record transferred to a place of deposit appointed by the Lord Chancellor, the "appropriate records authority" is the Lord Chancellor; if the record is in the Public Record Office of Northern Ireland, then "the appropriate records authority" is the Public Record Office of Northern Ireland.

"Open information"

Section 66 of the Freedom of Information Act 2000 contains the only reference in the Act to "open information." The term is not defined, but the operation of ss.15, 65 and 66 allows its meaning to be discerned. Open information is information contained in a transferred public record that the responsible authority has, at some stage prior to the receipt by the Public Record Office of a request relating to that information, designated as "open information". The designation of information as "open information" has the result[7] that the Public Record Office, when it receives a request for information contained in a transferred public record: 6–042

(a) need not consult the responsible authority in relation to a determination of whether that information is "exempt information" (in other words, a determination whether the information falls within one or more of the provisions of Pt II of the Act);
(b) need not consult the responsible authority in relation to a determination of whether the duty to confirm or deny that the information requested is or would be held has been excluded by one or more of the provisions of Pt II of the Act;
(c) retains for itself the task of balancing the public interest where the information is subject to a qualified exemption; and
(d) retains for itself the task of balancing the public interest where the exclusion of the duty to confirm or deny is a qualified exclusion.

It should be borne in mind that the designation of information as "open information" by the responsible authority does not dictate the determination by

6 The same remarks as in (2) apply in relation to a person that is not a "public authority" within the meaning of the Freedom of Information Act 2000.

7 Because the obligations in Freedom of Information Act 2000, s.66(2)–(4) do not arise in relation to information contained in a transferred public record that the responsible authority has designated as open information: Freedom of Information Act 2000, s.66(1).

the Public Record Office of matters (a)–(d). However, where the information has been designated as "open information", then, if the information is contained in a historical record that is a public record, the Public Record Office must first consult the Lord Chancellor before refusing to disclose the information solely on the basis of a qualified exemption.[8]

The first stage of a request

6–043 Where the Public Record Office receives a request under the Freedom of Information Act 2000 that relates to information that is contained in a "transferred public record," then, after satisfying itself as to the usual formalities for a proper request,[9] the Public Record Office must, within the usual time allowed for a public authority to answer a request:[10]

(1) identify the information held by it that answers the terms of the request;
(2) in relation to that information, having consulted the responsible authority,[11] determine whether it is "exempt information" within the meaning of the Freedom of Information Act 2000 (in other words, determine whether it falls within one or more of the provisions of Pt II of the Act, bearing in mind the age of the record in which the information is contained and the removal of certain of those provisions in relation to a public record that is a historical record[12]);
(3) if any of the information that is determined to be exempt information is only so by virtue of a "qualified exemption", send a copy of the request to the responsible authority;[13]
(4) where the information is "exempt information",[14] and again having consulted the responsible authority,[15] further determine whether the duty to confirm or deny that information answering the terms of the request is held by the Public Record Office has been excluded by one or more of the provisions of Pt II of the Freedom of Information Act 2000,

---

8 Freedom of Information Act 2000, s.65(1). Reading ss.65(2) and 66(1) together, it is apparent that s.65 applies to, *inter alia*, information that the responsible authority has not designated as open information.
9 See paras 11–001 to 11–012 below.
10 See paras 11–022 to 11–030 below.
11 Freedom of Information Act 2000, s.66(2)(b). The obligation to consult the responsible authority does not, however, arise if the responsible authority has previously designated the information as "open information".
12 See paras 6–034 to 6–044.
13 Freedom of Information Act 2000, s.15(1)–(2).
14 If it is determined not to be exempt information, it will have to be disclosed and the duty to confirm or deny will be taken to be complied with: Freedom of Information Act 2000, s.1(5).
15 Freedom of Information Act 2000, s.66(2)(a). The obligation to consult the responsible authority does not, however, arise if the responsible authority has previously designated the information as "open information".

again bearing in mind the age of the record in which the information sought is contained and the removal of certain of those provisions in relation to a public record that is (or would be) a historical record;[16]

(5) if the duty to confirm or deny is only excluded by virtue of a "qualified exclusion" and the request has not been sent under (3), send a copy of the request to the "responsible authority";[17]

(6) communicate to the applicant any information that is not "exempt information";[18] and

(7) in relation to any information that is "exempt information":

(i) give the applicant a notice under s.17(1); and

(ii) in relation to any such information in respect of which it is necessary to weigh the public interest, give the applicant a notice as required under s.17(2).[19]

The second stage of the request

By the end of the first stage, the Public Record Office will have dealt with all information answering the terms of the request except that which is exempt information only by virtue of a provision conferring a qualified exemption with such information answering the terms of the request being, or if it existed to be, excluded from the duty to confirm or deny only by virtue of a qualified exclusion. The second stage of a request received by the Public Record Office that relates to information contained in a "transferred public record" is thus concerned with the weighing of the public interest. The way in which this task must be carried out varies according to whether the responsible authority has designated information in question as "open information" and to whether the duty to confirm or deny has prima facie been excluded: 6–044

(1) If the information has been designated as "open information" and it has been determined in the first stage that the information is exempt information (but only by virtue of a "qualified exemption"), then the Public Record Office must determine whether in all the circumstances of the case, the public interest in maintaining the exemption outweighs the public interest in disclosing the information.[20] Insofar as the outcome of this exercise is that the public interest weighs in favour of disclosure, then that information must be communicated to the applicant.[21] Insofar as the outcome of this exercise is that the public

[16] See paras 6–034 to 6–044.
[17] Freedom of Information Act 2000, s.15(1)–(2).
[18] Freedom of Information Act 2000, s.10(1).
[19] See para.13–010 below.
[20] As to the general approach to this task, see paras 15–005 to 15–009 below.
[21] Freedom of Information Act 2000, s.11.

interest weighs in favour of maintaining the exemption, then the Public Record Office must first consult the Lord Chancellor[22] and, if that consultation does not cause it to change its mind, give a notice to the applicant stating the reasons for that decision.[23]

(2) If the information has not been disclosed to the applicant under (1) above, then, if it has been designated as "open information" and it has been determined in the first stage that the duty to confirm or deny does not arise in relation to it (but only by virtue of a "qualified exclusion"), the Public Record Office must determine whether in all the circumstances of the case, the public interest in maintaining the exclusion of the duty to confirm or deny outweighs the public interest in disclosing whether the Public Record Office holds the information.[24] Insofar as the outcome of this exercise is that the public interest weighs in favour of disclosing that the Public Record Office holds the information, then the Public Record Office must so inform the applicant. Insofar as the outcome of this exercise is that the public interest weighs in favour of maintaining the exclusion, then the Public Record Office must give a notice to the applicant stating the reasons for that decision.[25]

(3) If the information has not been designated as "open information" and it has been determined in the first stage that the information is exempt information (but only by virtue of a "qualified exemption"), then the responsible authority[26] must determine whether in all the circumstances of the case, the public interest in maintaining the exemption outweighs the public interest in disclosing the information.[27] Insofar as the outcome of this exercise is that the public interest weighs in favour of disclosure, then that information must be communicated to the applicant.[28] Insofar as the outcome of this exercise is that the public interest weighs in favour of maintaining the exemption, then the responsible authority must first consult the Lord Chancellor[29] and, if

[22] Freedom of Information Act 2000, s.65(1)(a).

[23] Freedom of Information Act 2000, s.17(3): unless, or to the extent that, the statement would involve the disclosure of information which would itself be exempt information (s.17(4)). Plainly, it would be sensible for the notice to record that the Lord Chancellor had been consulted.

[24] As to the general approach to this task, see paras 15–010 to 15–011 below.

[25] Freedom of Information Act 2000, s.17(3): unless, or to the extent that, the statement would involve the disclosure of information which would itself be exempt information (s.17(4)).

[26] By virtue of Freedom of Information Act 2000, s.66(4).

[27] As to the general approach to this task, see paras 15–005 to 15–009 below.

[28] Freedom of Information Act 2000, s.11. It is not entirely clear whether it is the responsible authority, rather than the Public Record Office, that is responsible for informing the applicant of the decision and of communicating the information. Section 66(6) of the Freedom of Information Act 2000 tends to suggest that it is the responsible authority who must do so: if this be correct, presumably it would simply pass over the copy which it had received from the Public Record Office under s.15(1) or a copy of that copy. On the other hand, s.15(3) tends to suggest that the responsible authority simply makes the determination, leaving execution of that determination to the Public Record Office. Either way, the responsible authority must inform the Public Record Office of the determination reached by it in relation to the weighing of the public interest.

[29] Freedom of Information Act 2000, s.66(5)(a).

that consultation does not cause it to change its mind, give a notice to the applicant stating the reasons for that decision.[30]

(4) On the footing that the information has not been disclosed to the applicant under (3) above, then, if the information has not been designated as "open information" and it has been determined in the first stage that the duty to confirm or deny does not arise in relation to it (but only by virtue of a "qualified exclusion"), the responsible authority[31] must determine whether in all the circumstances of the case, the public interest in maintaining the exclusion of the duty to confirm or deny outweighs the public interest in disclosing whether the Public Record Office holds the information.[32] Insofar as the outcome of this exercise is that the public interest weighs in favour of disclosing that the Public Record Office holds the information, then the responsible authority must so inform the applicant.[33] Insofar as the outcome of this exercise is that the public interest weighs in favour of maintaining the exclusion, then the responsible authority must first consult the Lord Chancellor[34] and, if that consultation does not cause it to change its mind, give a notice to the applicanstating the reasons for that decision.[35]

In all cases, the task must be carried out within a reasonable time[36] and, in any event, within the time specified in the notice given in the first stage.[37]

---

30 Freedom of Information Act 2000, s.17(3): unless, or to the extent that, the statement would involve the disclosure of information which would itself be exempt information (s.17(4)). Plainly, it would be sensible for the notice to record that the Lord Chancellor had been consulted. As to whether it is the responsible authority or the Public Record Office that must carry into effect the determination, see n.28.

31 By virtue of Freedom of Information Act 2000, s.66(3).

32 As to the general approach to this task, see paras 15–010 to 15–011 below.

33 As to whether it is the responsible authority or the Public Record Office that must so inform the applicant, see n.28.

34 Freedom of Information Act 2000, s.66(5)(a). The astute reader will have noticed that the obligation to consult the Lord Chancellor in relation to a determination neither to confirm nor deny that the information is held does not apply where the information is open information: see s.65(1).

35 *ibid.*, s.17(3): unless, or to the extent that, the statement would involve the disclosure of information which would itself be exempt information (s.17(4)). Plainly, it would be sensible for the notice to record that the Lord Chancellor had been consulted. As to whether it is the responsible authority or the Public Record Office that must carry into effect the determination, see n.28.

36 *ibid.*, s.10(3).

37 *ibid.*, s.17(2). It would seem that if there were good, objective reasons why the decision-making body could not determine the matter within the time specified in the earlier notice, then, provided that the decision were nevertheless made within a reasonabletime, this would be satisfactory.

CHAPTER 7

The Right to Information

1. THE NATURE OF INFORMATION

Introduction

The access right and the existence right conferred by s.1 of the Freedom of Information Act 2000 are rights conferred in relation to "information".[1] Similarly, engagement of any of the provisions of Pt II, which render information exempt information, turns upon the attributes of the information in question or upon the likely effects of its disclosure: it does not turn upon the attributes of the document or record containing the information sought nor upon the likely effects of disclosure of such a document or record. If a provision in Pt II does apply, the information that caused it to apply will become exempt information: only if the document or record is coincident with that information will it thereby be rendered exempt.[2] The unit of disclosure and of exemption may therefore be said to be "information".[3] Although information is at the heart of the Freedom of Information Act 2000, in relation to the great majority of requests for information it is to be expected that there will be no real question whether that which falls within the terms of a request represents information. The mere ability to consider that a certain matter answers the terms of the request will normally be sufficient indication that that matter constitutes information. Thus, in most cases, the words appearing on the face of a document will represent recorded information capable of being the subject matter of a request: accordingly, no issue on this point will arise. The simplicity of this part of the exercise in the vast majority of cases is deceptive. The word "information" does not enjoy a clearly delineated, universal meaning, but varies 7–001

[1] Freedom of Information Act 2000, s.1; Freedom of Information (Scotland) Act 2002, s.1. The Data Protection Act 1998 employs the term "data," which is defined to mean "information" having certain attributes: see further at para.4–011 above. It is suggested that the analysis below holds true for "data" under that Act. Of the comparative jurisdictions, only New Zealand employs "information" as the unit of the disclosure: see para.2–018 above. In the United States, a person is entitled to access to "records" of an agency: see para.2–003 above. In Australia, the right of access is to "documents" of an agency: see para.2–011. In Canada, a person is given a right of access to "records" under the control of a government institution: see para.2–026. And in the Republic of Ireland, a person is given a right of access to any "record" held by a public institution: see para.2–035.

[2] Subject to Freedom of Information Act 2000, s.2. See para.14–008 below.

[3] That the distinction in the Act between "information" and "record" is both real and intentional is apparent from Freedom of Information Act 2000, s.77 and Freedom of Information (Scotland) Act 2002, s.65.

according to the context in which it is used.[4] Subject to the qualification introduced by the limited definition of information in the Act,[5] it is suggested that so far as the Freedom of Information Act 2000 is concerned "information" is any matter that is capable of being recorded and of being communicated from one person to another. This definition, which is consistent with the ordinary meaning of the word, accommodates the intractable difficulties which attach to any narrower definition of the word.

The meaning of information

7–002 The term "information" is defined in the Act to mean information recorded in any form,[6] implicitly recognising that information may be unrecorded. The *New Shorter Oxford Dictionary* (1993) defines information as:

> "1. [....]
> 2. Communication of the knowledge of some fact or occurrence.
> 3. a. Knowledge or facts communicated about a particular subject, event, etc.; intelligence, news.
> b. [....]
> c. Without necessary relation to a recipient: that which inheres in or is represented by a particular arrangement, sequence, or set, that may be stored in, transferred by, and responded to by inanimate things; MATH. a statistically defined quantity representing the probability of occurrence of a symbol, sequence, message, etc., as against a number of possible alternatives."

The dictionary definition does not turn upon the recipient's state of knowledge. While the extent, if any, to which material is informative will depend upon the knowledge of the recipient, even adopting the narrowest dictionary

4 Other fields of human endeavour have struggled to find a satisfactory definition of "information," with the impetus largely originating with telecommunications and its need to identify the limits of message degradation before that which is received ceases to be information to the recipient. The starting point is generally considered to be found in C.E. Shannon, "A mathematical theory of communication"in (July and October 1948) 27 *Bell System Technical Journal* 379–423 and 623–656. There are many treatments of the subject: see, *e.g.* R. Losee, "A Discipline Independent Definition of Information" in (1997) 48 *Journal of the American Society for Information Science* 254–269.

5 Freedom of Information Act 2000, s.84; Freedom of Information (Scotland) Act 2002, s.73.

6 *ibid*. An exception is made for Freedom of Information Act 2000, s.51(8), empowering the Information Commissioner to require a public authority to furnish him with information, whether recorded or not recorded, for the purpose of determining whether a public authority has complied or is complying with its duties under Part I of the Act, and for Freedom of Information Act 2000, s.75(2), enabling the Secretary of State for Constitutional Affairs to override a statutory proscription on the disclosure of information, whether recorded or unrecorded, in order to give full effect to Freedom of Information Act 2000, s.1. The equivalent provisions in Freedom of Information (Scotland) Act 2002, are ss.50(9) and 64(2), respectively.

definition material will be "information" if it is capable of being informative, irrespective of whether it is to the recipient. This accords with the nature of disclosure under the Freedom of Information Act 2000. As it is effectively disclosure to the world, the fact that certain material is wholly uninformative to the applicant does not cause that material to cease to be information.[7] Whether material constitutes information for the purposes of the Act should not, therefore, depend upon the state of knowledge of the applicant. While the same issue may arise in relation to the state of knowledge of the public authority holding the information,[8] as a matter of practice it is difficult to imagine how a public authority could identify material as being information answering the terms of a request unless the nature of that material were understood by someone within the public authority.

The medium on which information is recorded

The medium on which matter is recorded should not, in principle, impinge upon its characterisation as information: material stored on the hard disk of a computer or on a video tape is just as much capable of being information as words appearing on a document. So, too, the fact that a machine or an instrument may be required to render the matter intelligible or readable is of no greater significance to its being information than are the spectacles of a hypermetropic applicant. This is confirmed by the White Paper that anticipated the introduction of the Act. This indicated that information should extend to computer data, drawings, maps, plans, photographs, images, video and sound recordings.[9] 7–003

Incorrect, etc., information.

On one view, information that is incorrect may be said not to be information at all. The Government appears to have taken the view during the passage of the Freedom of Information Bill through Parliament that issues about the accuracy of information are separate from the rights of access to information under the 7–004

[7] Most people would, for example, recognise that the Rosetta Stone contains information, even if themselves unable to read hieroglyphics, demotic or Greek.

[8] So that the inscriptions on the Rosetta Stone would represent information even if there were no-one in the British Museum who could read hieroglyphics, demotic or Greek. And, it may be added, the hieroglyphs were information even before Champollion completed his work.

[9] See, *e.g.* Home Office, *Your Right to Know* (1997), para.85. These are no more than different means for the *storage* or *conveyance* of information. Information stored on a computer is no more than an array of binary digits, wholly unintelligible to a normal person. Also included would be undeleted voice-box messages.

Act.[10] In terms of sheer practicality, there is much sense in ignoring inaccuracies in material in deciding whether that material constitutes information. This approach has been taken elsewhere when considering whether material represents information. Thus, in *Win v Minister for Immigration and Multicultural Affairs* the Federal Court of Australia pragmatically considered that the term was sufficiently wide to cover material that was completely worthless or that was bare assertion.[11]

The meaning given to information in other contexts

7–005 As noted above,[12] of the comparative jurisdictions, only New Zealand employs "information" as the unit of disclosure. The jurisprudence of that country gives some indication of the scope that has been given to that word and of a general disinclination to refuse a request on the basis that what is sought does not constitute information. In *Commissioner of Police v Ombudsman*,[13] the applicant had been charged with various offences. His solicitors made a request under the Official Information Act 1982 for copies of the briefs of evidence of the witnesses that the police intended to call. This was refused. On appeal to the Ombudsman, he recommended that the information be made available. The police sought judicial review of the Ombudsman's decision. Although the police accepted that the briefs contained "personal information", the High

[10] During the Bill's passage through Parliament, Mr David Lock, The Parliamentary Secretary, Lord Chancellor Department, rejected a proposed amendment that would have required a public authority to make a judgment on whether the information is accurate, saying:

> "The authority may not know whether the information is accurate, and the cost ceiling for charges made under the freedom of information regime is designed only to cover finding and retrieving the information. The public authority should not have to go to further unlimited lengths in verifying the accuracy of information. If information is disclosed by a public authority under the duty and is subsequently found to be inaccurate, the manufacturer could subject the decision to legal proceedings, thereby placing severe burdens on a range of public authorities on whom the duty was placed. I remind hon. Members that the provisions of clause 13 apply, and that those are the better route." (*Hansard*, HC, Vol.347, April 4, 2000, col.909.)

[11] [2001] F.C.A. 56 at [17]–[21]; (2001) 105 F.C.R. 212 at 217–218. The case concerned the Migration Act 1958, s.503A, which provides that information communicated in confidence to a migration officer by particular agencies is to be protected from disclosure, including from disclosure under the Freedom of Information Act 1982. On the other hand, in *WAGP of 2002 v Minister for Immigration & Multicultural & Indigenous Affairs* [2002] F.C.A.F.C. 266 the Full Court of the Federal Court held that mere "observations" did not constitute information. The court there was considering the Migration Act 1958, s.424A, which provides that the Refugee Review Tribunal must give an applicant to that tribunal particulars of any information that it considers would be a reason for affirming a decision, in this case refusing to grant the applicant a protection visa. The Court held that neither of two observations by the Tribunal: (a) that the applicant did not refer to a particular matter in his evidence; and (b) that there was inconsistency between two pieces of information, constituted information. Similarly, *NAIH of 2002 v Minister for Immigration & Multicultural & Indigenous Affairs* [2002] F.C.A. 1010.

[12] See para.7–001, n.1 above.

[13] [1985] 1 N.Z.L.R. 578.

Court,[14] in a general overview of the Act, considered the meaning of the word information:

> "Perhaps the most outstanding feature of the definition is that the word 'information' is used which dramatically broadens the scope of the whole Act. The stuff of what is held by Departments, Ministers, or organizations is not confined to the written word but embraces any knowledge, however gained or held, by the named bodies in their official capacities. The omission, undoubtedly deliberate, not to define the word 'information' serves to emphasise the intention of the Legislature to place few limits on relevant knowledge."[15]

On appeal, the Court of Appeal[16] said:

> "Information is not defined in the Act. From this it may be inferred that the draftsman was prepared to adopt the ordinary dictionary meaning of that word. Information in its ordinary dictionary meaning is that which informs, instructs, tells or makes aware. It is reasonable to suppose that, by their very nature, the police briefs contain information pointing to the commission of offences of the kind charged against the appellant and to the involvement of the appellant in them."[17]

In other legislative contexts, a similarly broad meaning has been given to the word. Thus, in relation to a trade descriptions offence, the mileage shown on the odometer of a car has been treated as information.[18] In relation to a defence of relying upon information supplied by another to a prosecution under the Consumer Credit Advertisements Regulations 1989, the Divisional Court has held that "information" extended to advice as well as factual information.[19] And, in relation to the expenses to be borne by the purchaser of land where he requires verification of information not in the possession of the vendor[20] the

---

14 Which held that the information was exempt on the grounds that substantial disclosure before trial would be likely to prejudice the maintenance of the law.

15 [1985] 1 N.Z.L.R. 578 at 586. See also *Mecklenburg v Kreis Pinneburg der Landrat* [1999] 2 C.M.L.R. 418; [1999] Env. L.R. D6; [1999] All E.R. (EC) 166, where the European Court of Justice had to interpret Council Directive (EEC) 1990/313 on the freedom of access to information on the environment. Article 2(a) of the Directive provides a more detailed definition of information than in the Freedom of Information Act 2000, but the ECJ showed a willingness to find that the Community legislature intended to make the concept of information a broad one: see para.19.

16 Which allowed the appellant's appeal and found that the disclosure would not be likely to prejudice the maintenance of the law, including the prevention, investigation and detection of offences, and the right to a fair trial.

17 [1988] 1 N.Z.L.R. 385 at 402. Considered further in *R. v Harvey* [1991] 1 N.Z.L.R. 242.

18 For the purposes of the Trade Descriptions Act 1968, s.24(1)(a): *Simmons v Potter* [1975] R.T.R. 347; [1975] Crim. L.R. 354.

19 *Coventry City Council v Lazarus* (1996) 160 J.P. 188; [1996] C.C.L.R. 5.

20 Now under the Law of Property Act 1925, s.45(4).

Court of Appeal has said: "[t]he word 'information' is as large as can be."[21] The suggested definition[22] is sufficiently wide to avoid the need to inquire as to the intelligibility of what is sought to the applicant, or to any other person, or to ascertain its worth or reliability, whilst according with the dictionary meaning.[23]

The information must be recorded

7–006 As noted above, the access right and the existence right only apply to information that is "recorded in any form".[24] In practical effect, this qualification to the meaning of "information" makes the regime under the Freedom of Information Act 2000 closer to the comparative regimes that confer rights to "documents" and "records",[25] than to that in New Zealand which requires only that the information be held, not that it be recorded.[26] The Act specifically does not limit or prescribe the medium on which the information must be recorded. The purpose of the requirement that the information be recorded "in any form" is, self-evidently, to remove the need for a public authority to search through, record or communicate information held by it but unrecorded.[27] Matters known to an officer or employee of a public authority but not recorded will thus be outside the scope of the Act.[28] Similarly, information that can be assembled from material held by a public authority but which has not been recorded at the time of the receipt of a request will not be information recorded in any form. By way of example, most public authorities will hold numerous word-processing files, the contents of each of which will fall within the definition of "information", whether or not a paper copy of that word-processing file is held by the public authority. However, the statistics[29] relating to any such word-processing file, which most word-processors derive from data automatically tagged to the file,

[21] *Re Stuart and Seadon* [1896] 2 Ch.328 at 334.
[22] See para.7–001 above.
[23] See definition 3c. at para.7–002 above. That the Freedom of Information Act 2000 recognises that something may be information even though not recorded suggests that, for the purposes of the Act, matter takes on the quality of information before its articulation in one form or another.
[24] Freedom of Information Act 2000, s.84; Freedom of Information (Scotland) Act 2002, s.73. See n.6 above.
[25] These terms are given an expanded definition in each of the Acts to cover non-written material and so forth: see paras 2–003, 2–011, 2–026 and 2–035 above.
[26] See para.7–001 above and, in particular, n.1 and the cross-references therein.
[27] *cf.* House of Commons, Public Administration Third Report (Cm. 4355), July 28, 1999, Annex 6, para.3 where the Freedom of Information Unit, Home Office stated, "we think that it would be unworkable to include information which had not been recorded in any form whatsoever within the scope of the statutory right because of the difficulty of establishing whether such information actually exists. There is a need for absolute clarity when creating statutory rights and obligations."
[28] Except for the purposes of Freedom of Information Act 2000, ss.51(8) and 75(2): see n.6 above.
[29] *i.e.* usually showing the date on which the file was created, how much time has been spent editing the file, who first typed it, who has edited it, when it was last edited, when it was first printed, when it was last printed, etc.

is not recorded as such. It is only when a request for the "properties" or statistics of a word-processing file is made that the information is assembled by the computer, displayed on screen and, if requested, stored or printed.[30]

Information stored in a computer

Computers, which are increasingly used to store the bulk of information held by a public authority, present three particular difficulties so far as the recording of information is concerned. First, any computer will typically store information in a variety of ways, principally according to the manner in which the computer needs to access the information at any given time. Its storage systems are conventionally divided into volatile and non-volatile.[31] Volatile memory may properly be said to lack the requisite degree of permanence to be described as having been "recorded". The position in relation to non-volatile memory is less straightforward, and this leads to the second difficulty. A computer ordinarily generates numerous temporary or working files during any session, without any specific intervention by the user. Some of these temporary files are stored in the volatile memory, but some are also written to the hard disk of the computer. The computer may automatically delete these files at the end of a session, after a set time, by over-writing them, or they may be left on the hard disk indefinitely. Information so stored can include accessed web pages, backup files, unsaved documents, overflow files and so forth. These files are generally capable of being retrieved. The unifying feature of these files is that although they contain information, the information has been created and is stored within the computer without specific user intervention. It is arguable, but perhaps no more, that such information is not "recorded" on the basis that that verb requires an animate subject or at least some conscious decision connected to the process.[32] Thirdly, most computer files, whether word processing and the like or the automatically generated variety, remain accessible for some time after "deletion", whether deleted automatically or by human intervention.[33] On the footing that the file 7–007

[30] Arguably, a properly-worded request could secure all of such a file, including the tagged data, and, if the information were requested to be received as a word-proceeding file, an applicant could assemble the statistical information on his own computer.

[31] Volatile memory is "held" by an electrical charge which requires regular "refreshing" if it is not to be lost. Unless there is some other source of power, shutting down a computer will result in the loss of this memory. Non-volatile memory does not require such refreshing, and will be stored on devices such as the computer's hard disk. Once "written" to the disk, it will remain accessible, unless deleted or over-written.

[32] The *New Shorter Oxford English Dictionary* (1993), gives as the meaning of the verb "record": "4.a. Relate, tell, or narrate in writing; set down in writing or other permanent form; make a written record of. 4.b. Make an official record of (an action, decision, etc.); set down officially or permanently."

[33] Deletion normally only removes the leading character of the filename, so that that file no longer appears in the list of files which is accessible to most programs. Provided that the file has not been overwritten, it is normally a comparatively simple task to restore the totality, or the better part, of the file by assigning a character to replace the missing one.

before its "deletion" was recorded information, if such a file is deleted but remains accessible, it will continue to be subject to the Act.[34]

2. THE HOLDING REQUIREMENT

When information is "held" by a public authority

7–008 For the purposes of the Freedom of Information Act 2000, information is "held" by a public authority if it is held by the authority otherwise than on behalf of another person, or if it is held by another person on behalf of the authority.[35] The Act has avoided the technicalities associated with the law of disclosure, which has conventionally drawn a distinction between a document in the power, custody or possession of a person.[36] Without the effects of s.3(2), the word "held" suggests a relationship between a personal authority and the information akin to that of ownership or bailment of goods. Information:

— that is, without request or arrangement, sent to or deposited with a public authority which does not hold itself out as willing to receive it and which does not subsequently use it;[37]

[34] It may be that the restoration of the file will cause the cost of compliance to exceed the appropriate limit and enable the public authority to avoid answering the request. See Freedom of Information Act 2000, s.13 and paras 12–002 to 12–007 below. It is notable that certain public authorities, relying on their powers to have access to documents and other recorded information of, for example, taxpayers, will in the exercise of that power restore deleted files from a computer hard disk: see, generally, *R. (on the application of Paul da Costa & Co (a firm)) v Thames Magistrates' Court* [2002] EWHC 40; [2002] S.T.C. 267; [2002] Crim. L.R. 504.

[35] Freedom of Information Act 2000, s.3(2). The position is the same under the Freedom of Information (Scotland) Act 2002, s.3(2), except for three differences: information is not held by an authority if it is held by the authority in confidence, having been supplied by a Minister of the Crown or by a department of the Government of the United Kingdom (s.3(2)(a)(ii)); the definition is subject to any qualification set out in Sch.1 (s.3(3)); and there is a particular exception relating to the Keeper of the Records of Scotland (s.3(4)). Differing approaches are taken in the comparative regimes. In the United States, the right attaches to "agency records:" see para.2–003. In Australia, the right attaches to "documents of an agency:" see para.2–011. In New Zealand, the right attaches to information "held" by a department, etc.: see para.2–018. In Canada, the right attaches to a record "under the control" of a government institution: see para.2–026. This phrase, too, is vague and the Federal Court in *Canada Post Corp v Canada (Minister of Public Works)* [1995] 2 F.C. 110, 30 Admin CR (2d) 242 (affirming [1993] 3 F.C. 320, 19 Admin CR (2d) 230) held that the notion of control was not limited to the power to dispose of a record, that there was nothing in the Act that indicated that the word "control" should not be given a broad interpretation, and that a narrow interpretation would deprive citizens of a meaningful right of access under the Act. In the Republic of Ireland, the right attaches to any record "held" by a public body: see para.2–035 above.

[36] See P. Matthews and H. Malek, *Disclosure* (2nd ed., Sweet & Maxwell, 2001), pp.107–114.

[37] By analogy with a gratuitous bailment by deposit: *Howard v Harris* (1884) 1 Cab. & El. 253. In the law of bailment, a slight assumption of control of the chattel so deposited will render the recipient a depositary: *Newman v Bourne and Hollingworth* (1915) 31 T.L.R. 309. For further examples, see N. Palmer, *Bailment* (2nd ed., Sweet & Maxwell, 1991) pp.31–43, 434–435 and 677–680.

— that is accidentally left with a public authority;[38]
— that just passes through a public authority; or
— that "belongs" to an employee or officer of a public authority but which is brought[39] by that employee or officer onto the public authority's premises,[40]

will, it is suggested, lack the requisite assumption by the public authority of responsibility for or dominion over the information that is necessary before it can be said that the public authority can be said to "hold" the information. On the other hand, information sent to a public authority without invitation and knowingly kept for any material length of time can probably be said to be held by the public authority. In short, information will not be "held" by a public authority, it is suggested, where that information neither is nor has been created, sought, used or consciously retained by it. Thus, in the example given by the explanatory notes to the legislation,[41] a Minister's constituency papers would not be held by the department just because the Minister happens to keep them there.[42] Section 3(2) of the Act has two effects. First, to take out of the scope of "documents held by a public authority" those documents which are held by it on behalf[43] of another person.[44] Secondly, to bring within "documents held by a public authority" information held by another person on behalf of that public authority. Thus, where an authority uses a private data storage company to maintain its records,[45] or where information is processed by another on behalf of the authority,[46] that information will be treated as being held by the authority.

[38] Also by analogy with a gratuitous bailment by deposit: *Mills v Brooker* [1919] 1 K.B. 555.

[39] *Quaere* would this be the case if the employee or officer were to place the information on a computer of the public authority?

[40] This is the approach that has been taken in the comparative jurisdictions: *Re Horesh and Ministry of Education* [1986] 1 V.A.R. 143 (departmental inquiry concerning the professional relationship between the applicant and the principal of the school at which he had taught, notes taken by a friend of the principal who was also the secretary of the relevant teachers association and not used by the authority were personal to the principal and not disclosable under Australian legislation); *Re Mann and Capital Territory Health Commission* (1983) 5 A.L.N. N368; *Re O'Sullivan and Family Court of Australia* (1997) 47 A.L.D. 765 (dealing with the meaning of the "documents of a court"); *Loughman v Altman* (1992) 39 F.C.R. 90; 111 A.L.R. 445 (document held to be "of a court" even though possessed by another agency); *Re Barkhordar and Australian Capital Territory Schools Authority* (1987) 12 A.L.D. 332 (personal documents can become documents of an agency); *Bureau of National Affairs, Inc v US Department of Justice* 742 F.(2d) 1484 (DC Cir. 1984); *Canada (Privacy Commissioner) v Canada (Labour Relations Board)* [1996] 3 F.C. 609, (1996) 118 FTR 1, approved on appeal (1996) 180 FTR 313, 25 Admin LR (3d) 305 (notes taken by members of the Canada Labour Relations Board in the course of quasi-judicial proceedings are not under the control of the Board itself).

[41] Stationery Office, *Explanatory Notes, Freedom of Information Act 2000*, para.31.

[42] This has been held to be the case in Australia: *Re Said and Dawkins* (1993) 30 ALD 242.

[43] The phrase "on behalf of" suggests an agency relationship between the public authority and the person for whom the information is held.

[44] Each government department is treated as a separate person: Freedom of Information Act 2000, s.81(1).

[45] See Stationery Office, *Explanatory Notes, Freedom of Information Act 2000*, para.31.

[46] House of Commons, *Public Administration—Third Report* (Cm. 4355), July 29, 1999, Annex 6, para.6.

Information previously and subsequently held

7–009 The information which is to be communicated, or to have its existence disclosed, is the information held at the time when the request is received, irrespective of the date at which the information was recorded or came to be held by the public authority.[47] The Freedom of Information Act 2000 is thus retrospective.[48] The public authority is not obliged when answering a request to consider information that is first held or recorded after the receipt of the request, even though this subsequently-created or -received information answers the terms of the request.[49] It follows that a request which is specifically expressed to apply to information of a particular description that may, after receipt of the request, come to be held or recorded by the public authority, is ineffective.[50] Where an appeal is lodged against a decision of a public authority, the appeal body will be concerned with the information held by the public authority at the time of the request, and not at the time of the appeal. The receipt of a request does not, however, require the public authority to take a "snapshot" of the information held by it at the time of the receipt of the request. The Act specifically contemplates that a public authority might, in the time between receipt of a request and determination of that request, legitimately have sought to amend or delete information answering the terms of the request. Where such amendment or deletion has taken place, the public authority is not obliged to answer, but may answer, the request so far as the deleted or pre-amendment information is concerned. Nevertheless, it is suggested that a public authority would be wise to consider its position very carefully before relying upon s.1(4) in relation to deleted or amended information. Unless the record of information is of very recent vintage or is one that is routinely amended without recording the amendments made, amendment (and even more so deletion) after receipt of a request is bound to engender suspicion. Moreover, the Information Commissioner's powers under s.51 of the Act upon an application by a disgruntled applicant extend to unrecorded information, which will include deleted information (*i.e.* information that is no longer recorded).[51]

---

47 Freedom of Information Act 2000, s.1(4); Freedom of Information (Scotland) Act 2002, s.1(4).

48 This was confirmed by the Home Secretary during the passage of the Bill through the House of Commons: *Hansard*, HC, Vol.340, December 7, 1999, col.728. The position is the same in Canada and New Zealand. Only limited retrospectivity is granted by the Freedom of Information Act 1982 (Cth of Aust), s.12(2) and the Freedom of Information Act 1997 (Ireland), s.6(4).

49 Freedom of Information Act 2000, s.1(4). The wording in the Freedom of Information (Scotland) Act 2002, s.1(4) is slightly different, stating that any such amendment or deletion may be made before the information is given. In addition, the Scottish Act provides that the requested information is not, by virtue of s.1(4), to be destroyed before it can be given unless the circumstances are such that it is not reasonably practicable to prevent such destruction from occurring: s.1(5).

50 As has been held under the Australian Act: *Murtagh v Federal Commissioner of Taxation* (1984) 1 A.A.R. 419; 54 A.L.R. 313; *Re Edelsten and Australian Federal Police* (1985) 4 A.A.R. 220.

51 See n.6 above.

Alteration, destruction, etc., of records

It is a criminal offence to alter, deface, block, erase, destroy or conceal any record[52] held by a public authority with the intention of preventing the disclosure by that authority of all or any part of the information, to the communication of which the applicant would have been entitled.[53] This applies to the public authority itself (but not a government department)[54] as well as to any person who is employed by, is an officer of, or is subject to the direction of that authority.[55] A prosecution for this offence, which is triable summarily only, can only be brought by the Information Commissioner or with the consent of the Director of Public Prosecutions.[56] The maximum fine is level five on the standard scale.[57] 7–010

3. PERSONS ENTITLED TO EXERCISE THE RIGHTS

Individuals, companies, unincorporated associations, etc.

The rights bestowed by s.1 of the Freedom of Information Act 2000 are rights bestowed upon any "person". The term "person" extends to any body of persons corporate or incorporate,[58] so that companies, clubs and associations are able to rely on the Acts. 7–011

Territoriality of the rights

It is a principle of statutory interpretation that Parliament does not assert or assume jurisdiction that goes beyond the limits established by the common consent of nations. Provided that its language admits, an Act of Parliament is to be applied so as not to be inconsistent with the comity of nations or with the 7–012

[52] Note the reference is to a "record" rather than "information".
[53] Freedom of Information Act 2000, s.77; Freedom of Information (Scotland) Act 2002, s.65.
[54] Freedom of Information Act 2000, s.81(3). However, this only applies to the government department itself. Section 77 applies to a person in the public service of the Crown as it does to any other person: s.81(3). In Scotland, the exemption is for the Scottish Parliament, the Parliamentary Corporation and the Scottish Administration although again this immunity does not extend to members of staff of these entities or persons acting on their behalf: Freedom of Information (Scotland) Act 2002, s.68.
[55] Freedom of Information Act 2000, s.77(2).
[56] *ibid.*, s.77(4). In Northern Ireland, it is the consent of the Director of Public Prosecutions for Northern Ireland which is necessary. The Freedom of Information (Scotland) Act 2002 contains no limitation.
[57] Freedom of Information Act 2000, s.77(3); Freedom of Information (Scotland) Act 2002, s.65(3).
[58] "Person" includes a body of persons corporate or unincorporated: Interpretation Act 1978, s.5 and Sch.1. It can include a committee: *Davey v Shawcroft* [1948] 1 All E.R. 827.

established principles of public international law.[59] The principle of comity between nations requires that each sovereign state should be left to govern its own territory.[60] Thus, while words in a statute may be expressed in universally-applicable language, the rebuttable presumption is that Parliament is concerned with the conduct of persons taking place within the territories to which the Act extends, and with no other conduct.[61] In relation to rights bestowed and obligations imposed by a statute, the presumption operates to limit these rights and obligations to those persons within the country at the time at which the right is sought to be exercised.[62] There is little within the Freedom of Information Act 2000 to suggest that the presumption against extra-territoriality was intended to be rebutted.[63] Although the Freedom of Information Act 2000 will certainly extend to bestow rights on a person in Scotland, it is doubtful whether the Freedom of Information (Scotland) Act 2002 extends to bestow rights on a person in England, Wales or Northern Ireland, as the territorial limits of the Acts of the Scottish Parliament are the boundaries of Scotland. Nevertheless, the presumption against extra-territoriality is unlikely to make much practical difference, as a foreign applicant can always engage an undisclosed local agent to make the request. As well, in the case of a natural person, there is nothing to stop such a person coming into the jurisdiction for the purpose of making a request. It follows that a non-resident present in the United Kingdom, however

---

[59] See *Halsbury's Laws of England* (4th ed., 1995 re-issue), Vol.44(1), para.1317.

[60] *Attorney-General v Prince Ernest Augustus of Hanover* [1957] A.C. 436 at 462; *Gaudiya Mission v Brahmachary* [1998] Ch.341.

[61] F. Bennion, *Statutory Interpretation* (4th ed., Butterworths, 2002), ss.102, 105, 106, 128–131; *Halsbury's Laws of England, op. cit.*, no.59 above, para.1319; *Clark (Inspector of Taxes) v Oceanic Contractors Inc* [1983] 2 A.C. 130 at 144–145; *Wanganui-Rangitikei Electric Power Board v AMP Society* (1934) 50 C.L.R. 581 at 601.

[62] *Jefferys v Boosey* (1854) 4 H.L. Cas. 815 (copyright given by the Copyright Act 1709 to "the author of any book" included only authors who were British subjects or were aliens resident in the country); *Tamalin v Perarson & Son Ltd* [1909] 2 K.B. 61 (where it was held that the Workmen's Compensation Act 1906, which provided for compensation to be paid "if in any employment personal injury by accident arising out of and in the course of the employment is caused to any workma", did not apply to an English workman employed by an English company sent to carry out work in Malta); *cf. Howgate v Bagnall* [1951] 1 K.B. 265, dealing with the Personal Injuries (Emergency Provisions) Act 1939.

[63] In the United States, foreign citizens, partnerships, corporations, associations, states and state agencies, and foreign or domestic governments could until very recently apply: 5 USC 551(2): see para.2–003 above. In Australia, the Freedom of Information Act 1982 is expressed to give every person a right of access. This has been held to extend to a foreign corporation: *Re Lordsvale Finance Ltd and Department of the Treasury* (1985) 3 A.A.R. 301, AAT: see para.2–011. Section 12(1) of the Official Information Act 1982 (New Zealand) enables citizens, residents and persons in New Zealand and companies incorporated in New Zealand to make a request for official information see para.2–018. Section 4 of the Access to Information Act (Canada) gives Canadian citizens and permanent residents a right of access to records under the control of a government institution: see para.2–026. The review of the Act recommended that the Act be amended to provide that any person has a right of access: Government of Canada, *Report of the Access to Information Review Task Force* (June 2002), p.19. The Freedom of Information Act 1997 (Ireland) gives every person a right of access to records held by a public body: see para.2–035.

fleetingly, is entitled to make a request under the Freedom of Information Act 2000.[64]

Convicted criminals

On the face of the Act, a convicted criminal is equally entitled to rely on the rights bestowed by the Freedom of Information Act 2000 as is the law-abiding citizen. Depending upon the terms of the request, however, it may be that a request from the former will be more readily characterised as vexatious. The position in the comparative jurisdictions, none of which excepts convicted criminals, varies. In the USA, exceptions to the right of access have sometimes,[65] but not always,[66] been made in the case of criminals. In Australia, it has been held that the fact a person had convictions for rape and armed robbery did not prevent him from applying for access to documents under the legislation.[67] 7–013

Children

The Freedom of Information (Scotland) Act 2002 provides that where a question falls to be determined as to the legal capacity of a person who has not attained the age of sixteen years to exercise any right conferred by any provision of this Act, any such person is to be taken to have that capacity who has a general understanding of what it means to exercise the right.[68] A child over 12 is presumed to have this understanding.[69] The Freedom of Information Act 2000 does not make any mention of applications by children and the Interpretation Act 1978 is silent on the question whether a reference to a "person" is confined to persons of full age and capacity.[70] In both cases, any limitation can readily be circumvented by the application being made by someone on the minor's behalf. 7–014

---

64 Examples of recently-arrived persons enjoying statutory rights include: *R. v Inhabitants of Eastbourne* (1803) 4 East 103; *R. v Hillingdon London Borough Council Ex p. Streeting* [1980] 1 W.L.R. 1425; *Re Islam* [1983] 1 A.C. 688.

65 *Doyle v US Department of Justice*, 668 F.(2d) 1365 (DC Cir. 1981) (fugitive not entitled to enforcement of the Freedom of Information Act access provisions because he could not expect judicial aid in obtaining government records related to the sentence he was evading).

66 *O'Rourke v US Department of Justice*, 684 F. Supp. 716 (DDC 1988) and *Doherty v US Department of Justice*, 596 F. Supp. 423 (SDNY 1984) (convicted criminal and fugitive from his own country and undergoing US deportation proceedings qualified as "any person").

67 *Re Ward and Secretary, Department of Industry and Commerce* (1983) 8 A.L.D. 324.

68 Freedom of Information (Scotland) Act 2002, s.69(1).

69 *ibid*.

70 In *Wallace v Health Commission of Victoria* [1985] V.R. 403 the Supreme Court of Victoria held, in relation to a request made under the Freedom of Information Act 1982 (Vic.) by a person lacking mental capacity, that it was a prerequisite to enforcement of the right of access that an application is made which is the conscious voluntary act of the person making it so that the person making it fully understood the nature and significance of the act and wished it to be done in order to obtain access to documents. Similarly, in a different context, *R. v Oldham Metropolitan Borough Council Ex p. Garlick* [1993] A.C. 509 at 520, although this may be explained on the

Applicant's motives

7–015 An applicant's motives in making a request are irrelevant and so cannot be demanded by a public authority.[71] Nor does the absence of any actual or apparent motive for the request provide any basis for refusing it. The Government considered an amendment to the Bill making this clear, but considered that it was unnecessary:[72]

> "It is perfectly legitimate for an official to have a discussion with the applicant with a view to helping the applicant to refine the request he or she is making so as to use better the provisions of the Bill. That is only for the purpose of assistance, not for examining motive with a view to determining whether to proceed with the request because that is quite irrelevant in the context of the Bill as drafted."[73]

Having said this, the absence of any apparent motive for a request may be relevant in considering whether a request is vexatious or in determining whether the public authority's response has been reasonable.[74] Where it is apparent that the applicant has a legitimate motive for making the request, that may be relevant in balancing the public interest for the purpose of qualified exemptions.

basis that the wider interpretation of "person" would have enabled a circumvention of restricted rights in the Housing Act 1985.

[71] This is conventional in freedom of information legislation. Thus, in the USA, see *United States Department of Justice v Reporters Committee for Freedom of the Press*, 489 U.S. 749 (1989); *Durns v Bureau of Prisons*, 804 F. (2d) 701 (DC Cir. 1986) ("Congress granted the scholar and the scoundrel equal rights of access to agency records"); *Forsham v Califano*, 587 F. (2d) 1128 (DC Cir. 1978). In Australia, see *Re Green and Australian and Overseas Telecommunications Corp* (1992) 28 A.L.D. 655; *Re Russell Island Development Association Inc. and Department of Primary Industry and Energy* (1994) 33 A.L.D. 683; *Re Collie and Deputy Commissioner of Taxation* (1997) 45 A.L.D. 556. And in Canada, see *Intercontinental Packers Ltd v Canada (Minister of Agriculture)* (1987) 14 F.T.R. 142; *Prud'homme v Canada (Canadian International Development Agency)* (1994) 85 F.T.R. 302.

[72] *Hansard*, HL, Vol.617, October 17, 2000, col.921, by the Minister of State, Cabinet Office (Lord Falconer).

[73] *Hansard*, HL, Vol.617, October 17, 2000, col.921, by the Minister of State, Cabinet Office (Lord Falconer). See also the Code of Practice on the Discharge of the Functions of Public Authorities under Pt I of the Freedom of Information Act (November 2002) (issued under s.45 of the Act), para.9 of which states:

> "where the applicant does not describe the information sought in a way which would enable the public authority to identify or locate it, or the request is ambiguous, the authority should, as far as practicable, provide assistance to the applicant to enable him or her to describe more clearly the information requested. Authorities should be aware that the aim of providing assistance is to clarify the nature of the information sought, not to determine the aims or motivation of the applicant. Care should be taken not to give the applicant the impression that he or she is obliged to disclose the nature of his or her interest or that he or she will be treated differently if he or she does."

[74] For example, under the Freedom of Information Act 2000, ss.17(3) and 22(1)(c).

4. BODIES AGAINST WHICH THE RIGHTS MAY BE EXERCISED

Exhaustive definition

The rights bestowed by the Freedom of Information Act 2000 are only exercisable against "public authorities".[75] These are defined to mean: 7–016

(1) any body,[76] person or office holder who or which is listed in Sch.1 of the Act;[77]
(2) any body, person or office holder designated by order of the Secretary of State;[78] or
(3) a publicly-owned company.[79]

These categories are exhaustive[80] and are estimated to cover in excess of 50,000 bodies.[81]

Schedule 1: public authorities under the Freedom of Information Act 2000

Schedule 1 to the Freedom of Information Act 2000[82] provides the core list of those bodies, persons and office-holders who are deemed to be public authorities and against whom the s.1 rights may be exercised. The Schedule is divided into seven numbered parts: 7–017

[75] Those bestowed by the Freedom of Information (Scotland) Act 2002 are exercisable against Scottish public authorities.

[76] Body includes an unincorporated association: Freedom of Information Act 2000, s.84; Freedom of Information (Scotland) Act 2002, s.73.

[77] Freedom of Information Act 2000, s.3(1)(a)(i); Freedom of Information (Scotland) Act 2002, s.3(1)(a)(i). These are considered at paras 7–017 and 7–023 below.

[78] Freedom of Information Act 2000, s.3(1)(a)(ii); Freedom of Information (Scotland) Act 2002, s.3(1)(a)(ii). These are considered at paras 7–021 and 7–027 below.

[79] Freedom of Information Act 2000, s.3(1)(b); Freedom of Information (Scotland) Act 2002, s.3(1)(b). These are considered at paras 7–022 and 7–028.

[80] The Home Office Freedom of Information Unit stated during the passage of the Bill: "Because FOI applications are made direct by a person to an organisation, there needs to be absolute clarity as to whether any particular organisation is covered by the legislation. It is therefore necessary to spell out either in the Bill itself, or in an order, those organisations which are public authorities for the purpose of the legislation": House of Commons, *Public Administration—Third Report* (Cm. 4355), July 29, 1999, Annex 6, para.1.

[81] Government estimates have ranged from 50,000 (*Hansard*, HC, Vol.347, April 4, 2000, col.883, by the Parliamentary Under-Secretary of State for the Home Department, Mr Mike O'Brien) to 88,000 (the Lord Chancellor's Advisory Group on implementation of the Freedom of Information Act).

[82] Which now includes those authorities added by the Freedom of Information (Additional Public Authorities) Order 2002 (SI 2002/2623), adding 22 new public authorities in England, Wales and Northern Ireland.

(I) GENERAL: This includes all government departments,[83] both Houses of Parliament, the Northern Ireland Assembly and the National Assembly for Wales, and most of the armed forces.[84] A government department is defined to include any body or authority exercising statutory functions on behalf of the Crown,[85] so that information held by government agencies (*e.g.* the Child Protection Agency, Benefits Agency, etc.) will be subject to the Act.[86] However, the Security Service, the Secret Intelligence Service and the Government Communication Headquarters are not included in the definition[87] and are therefore exempt from the operation of the Act.[88]

(II) LOCAL GOVERNMENT: This Part contains a list of 29 types of local government bodies in England and Wales, including the Greater London Authority, county councils, London borough councils, district councils, parish councils, county borough councils, community councils, fire authorities, National Parks authorities, Transport for London, magistrates court committees, as well as all Northern Ireland district councils.

(III) THE NATIONAL HEALTH SERVICE: This covers core NHS bodies in England, Wales and Northern Ireland, such as health authorities, special health authorities, NHS and primary care trusts, community health councils and so forth. It also extends to individual GPs, dentists, opticians and pharmacists, but only in respect of information relating to the provision of medical services under the NHS.

---

[83] Each government department is to be treated as a person separate from any other government department: Freedom of Information Act 2000, s.81. However, a government department cannot rely upon this to claim a duty of confidence arising with respect to another government department so as to rely upon the exemption in s.41 (information provided in confidence): Freedom of Information Act 2000, s. 81(2). There is no equivalent provision under the Freedom of Information (Scotland) Act 2002. For information provided in confidence, see Ch.25.

[84] The only exceptions are the special forces (meaning those units of the armed forces of the Crown the maintenance of whose capabilities is the responsibility of the Director of Special Forces or which are for the time being subject to the operational command of that Director: Freedom of Information Act 2000, s.84) and any unit or part of a unit which is for the time being required by the Secretary of State to assist the Government Communications Headquarters in the exercise of its functions: Freedom of Information Act 2000, Sch.1, Pt I, para.6. As to the special exemption granted in relation to information supplied by these, and other, security bodies, to a public authority, see Ch.17.

[85] Freedom of Information Act 2000, s.84.

[86] This was confirmed by the Government during the Bill's passage: *Hansard*, HL, Vol.619, November 14, 2000, col.231 by the Parliamentary Under-Secretary of State, Home Office (Lord Bassam).

[87] Freedom of Information Act 2000, s.84.

[88] The Scottish Parliament, any part of the Scottish Administration, the Scottish Parliamentary Corporate Body, any Scottish public authority with mixed functions or no reserved functions (within the meaning of the Scotland Act 1998) and the National Assembly for Wales are also excluded from the definition of "government department": Freedom of Information Act 2000, s.84. All but the last are, of course, subject instead to the Freedom of Information (Scotland) Act 2002.

(IV) MAINTAINED SCHOOLS AND OTHER EDUCATIONAL INSTITUTIONS: Governing bodies of all maintained schools,[89] as well as further and higher education institutions, are all included in this Part. It was suggested by the Government in Parliament that information about institutions which do not have governing bodies, such as pupil referral units, will be accessible through the local education authority directly responsible for such institutions.[90] The Teacher Training Agency, the Higher Education Funding Council in England and Wales and the Northern Ireland Higher Education Council, Her Majesty's Chief Inspector of Schools in Wales and the School Teachers Review Body are all listed in Pt VI.

(V) POLICE: This Part covers all police authorities in England, Wales and Northern Ireland, the chief officer of police forces (including the Chief Constable of the Royal Ulster Constabulary), the British Transport Police, the Ministry of Defence Police and any person (not otherwise covered by Sch.1) who has the statutory power to nominate individuals for appointment as special constables by magistrates (but only in respect of information relating to this function). The National Crime Squad and the Police Complaints Authority are listed in Pt VI, although the National Criminal Intelligence Service is not.

(VI) OTHER PUBLIC BODIES AND OFFICES: GENERAL: This Part enumerates over 350 miscellaneous public bodies and offices, ranging from the Advisory Committee on Conscientious Objectors and the British Potato Council to the OSO Board and the Zoos Forum. Some are well known, such as the Health and Safety Executive, the Arts Council and the Post Office, whereas others such as the Unlinked Anonymous Serosurveys Steering Group, the Marshall Aid Commemoration Commission and the Place Names Advisory Committee are less so. The BBC, Channel 4 and Sianel Pedwar Cymru (S4C) are included (but only in respect of information held for purposes other than those of journalism, art or literature), as well as the Broadcasting Standards Commission, the Independent Television Commission, the Theatres Trust and most of the country's main museums and galleries. The Bank of England is included, but information relating to its functions with respect to monetary policy, financial operations intended to support financial institutions for the purposes of maintaining stability, and the provision of private banking and related services is all excluded. Bodies omitted include the British Board of Film Classification, those running prisons under contract, the Press Complaints Commission, and those assigned responsibility for running the railways.

[89] Within the meaning of the School Standards and Framework Act 1998: Freedom of Information Act 2000, Sch.1, Pt I, para.52.

[90] *Hansard*, HL, Vol.617, October 17, 2000, col.946, by the Minister of State, Cabinet Office (Lord Falconer).

(VII) OTHER PUBLIC BODIES AND OFFICES: Northern Ireland: This is a very similar list to that in Pt VI above, containing over 80 bodies and offices which relate to Northern Ireland.

Adding public authorities to Schedule 1

7–018 The Secretary of State for Constitutional Affairs[91] has the power[92] to add to Sch.1 any body or holder of any office which satisfies two specified conditions.[93] The first specified condition is that the body or office is either (a) established by virtue of royal prerogative, an enactment or subordinate legislation,[94] or (b) is established in any other way by a Minister of the Crown (in his capacity as such), a government department or the Welsh Assembly.[95] The second condition is (in the case of a body) that the body is wholly or partly constituted by appointment made by the Crown, a Minister of the Crown, a government department or the Welsh Assembly,[96] or (in the case of an office) that appointments to the office are made by one of the same.[97] However, this power may not be exercised to add the Scottish Parliament, any part of the Scottish administration, the Scottish Parliamentary Corporate Body, or any Scottish public authority with mixed functions or no reserved functions (within the meaning of the Scotland Act 1998).[98] An order adding a public authority to Sch.1 in this way may relate to a specified person or office or to persons or offices falling within

[91] The Freedom of Information Act 2000 originally referred to the "Secretary of State" but all his functions under the Act were first transferred to the Lord Chancellor by the Transfer of Functions (Miscellaneous) Order 2001 (SI 2001/3500) and then to the Secretary of State for Constitutional Affairs by the Secretary of State for Constitutional Affairs Order 2003 (SI 2003/1887).

[92] Freedom of Information Act 2000, s.4(1). Where such an order relates to a body or office-holder whose functions are exercisable only or mainly in or as regards Wales, or who would be a Northern Ireland public authority, the Secretary of State must consult either the National Assembly for Wales or the First Minister and deputy First Minister in Northern Ireland respectively: Freedom of Information Act 2000, s.4(7). "Northern Ireland public authority" means any public authority, other than the Northern Ireland Assembly or a Northern Ireland department, whose functions are exercisable only or mainly in or as regards Northern Ireland and relate only or mainly to transferred matters: Freedom of Information Act 2000, s.84. "Transferred matter" has the meaning given by s.4(1) of the Northern Ireland Act 1998: Freedom of Information Act 2000, s.84. Such an order is subject to annulment in pursuance of a resolution of either House of Parliament: Freedom of Information Act 2000, s.82(3).

[93] One such order has been made, adding 22 new authorities in England, Wales and Northern Ireland to Sch.1: Freedom of Information (Additional Public Authorities) Order 2002, (SI 2002/2623).

[94] Freedom of Information Act 2000, s.4(2)(a).

[95] *ibid.*, s.4(2)(b).

[96] *ibid.*, s.4(3)(a).

[97] *ibid.*, s.4(3)(b).

[98] *ibid.*, s.80.

a specified description[99] and may list the new entry only in relation to information of a specified description.[1]

Removing or amending public authorities from or listed in Schedule 1

The Secretary of State for Constitutional Affairs has the power to limit any entry on Sch.1 to information of a specified description, as well as to remove any such limitation.[2] Whilst the removal of a limitation is unlikely to be controversial (at least outside the body in question), the power to introduce limits would allow the government to cut down the Act's scope so far as rights of access to particular information are concerned. Concern about this was expressed during the Bill's passage through Parliament and in response to a proposed amendment removing this power, and a direct question asking what the Government's intention was in conferring this, Lord Bassam, the Parliamentary Under-Secretary of State, Home Office, replied as follows: 7–019

> "The power to amend the entries in Schedule 1 so as to limit them to specific types of information is necessary in order to ensure that the bodies listed at Schedule 1 are covered by the Freedom of Information Act only in respect of those activities which should properly be the subject of the obligations in the Bill. It is not the Government's [intention] to apply the Bill to information held for purposes in respect of which it would be inappropriate and damaging to apply freedom of information principles. Journalistic information held by public sector broadcasters or private banking information held by the Bank of England are two current examples of such information.
>
> Where we have identified information which needs to be protected in this way, we have amended the entry in Schedule 1 accordingly. However, we cannot be certain that any of the bodies listed may not change their functions in the future. For that reason, we need to make provision for a power to amend the entry if this should be deemed necessary. To that extent, clause 7(3) is a just-in-case provision.
>
> The noble Lord asked for an example, hypothetical or otherwise, and I am happy to try to provide one. The entry in Schedule 1 relating to the Bank of England is already limited to certain information. Should the Bank decided to add, say, an insurance provision to the services it provides to its private customers, that private activity which would relate to private

[99] Freedom of Information Act 2000, s.4(6). An example of this is found in Sch. 1, Pt VI, "any housing action trust established under Pt III of the Housing Act 1988".

[1] *ibid.*, s.7(2). For such partly-affected public authorities, see para.7–020 below.

[2] *ibid.*, s.7(3). In other words, a public authority can be turned into a "partly-affected" public authority and vice versa: see para.7–020 below.

> customers would be brought within the scope of the Freedom of Information Act, unless an order was made to limit the entry in Schedule 1 specifically to exclude it.
>
> That is why the power in clause 7(3) is necessary. I hope that the noble Lord will accept the example I have given and feel able to withdraw his amendment."[3]

The Act provides that all such orders must be approved by a resolution of each House of Parliament.[4] A body or office-holder listed in Pts VI and VII of Sch.1 automatically ceases to be a public authority by virtue of its entry in the Schedule if it ceases to satisfy either of the two conditions specified above.[5] Where this happens, or where the body or office ceases to exist, the Secretary of State for Constitutional Affairs has the power to amend Sch.1 to reflect this change,[6] described in Parliament as a "form of housekeeping . . . necessary so that the lists may be routinely updated to remove dead wood".[7] So long as a body or office continues to fulfil the two specified conditions,[8] however, it can only be removed from Sch.1 by means of further primary legislation.

Partly-affected Schedule 1 public authorities

7–020 Some public authorities are listed in Sch.1 only in relation to information of a specified description.[9] In these cases, the rights bestowed by the Freedom of Information Act 2000 do not apply to any other information held by that authority.[10] The Secretary of State for Constitutional Affairs has the power, in

3 *Hansard*, HL, Vol.619, November 14, 2000, cols 182–183. Lord Mackay, who had tabled the amendment and asked the question, replied as follows: "I am reasonably grateful for the answer. [Lord Bassam] set out a clear scenario and I hope that if the Secretary of State decides to go a good deal further a clever lawyer will be able to prevent him by using the courts and quoting what the noble Lord said and the example he gave. I am pleased to beg leave to withdraw my amendment": *Hansard*, HL, Vol.619, November 14, 2000, col.183. See also the debate in the House of Commons, with Government pronouncements on very similar lines: *Hansard*, HC, Vol.347, April 4, 2000, col.871–890, *per* the Parliamentary Under-Secretary of State for the Home Department (Mr Mike O'Brien).

4 Freedom of Information Act 2000, s.82(2).

5 *ibid*., s.4(4). The two conditions are those in s.4(2)–(3), as to which see para.7–018 above.

6 *ibid*., s.4(5). But this is not necessary as the removal occurs automatically under s.4(4).

7 *Hansard*, HL, Vol.617, October 17, 2000, col.952 by the Minister of State, Cabinet Office (Lord Falconer). In contrast to other powers to add to or amend Sch.1 (see paras 7–018, 7–019 and 7–021), the Freedom of Information Act 2000 requires only that such an order be laid before Parliament after being made: s.82(4).

8 *i.e*. those in Freedom of Information Act 2000, s.4(2)–(3): see para.7–018 above.

9 For example, Pt VI includes the entry: "The British Broadcasting Corporation, in respect of information held for purposes other than those of journalism, art or literature."

10 Freedom of Information Act 2000, s.7(1).

relation to any entry in Sch.1, to introduce, remove or amend any such limitation.[11]

Designated public authorities

An entity not listed in Sch.1 nor capable of being added to that list by an order under s.4(1) may be designated by order as a public authority for the purposes of the Act if it appears to the Secretary of State for Constitutional Affairs to exercise functions of a public nature or is providing under a contract made with a public authority any service whose provision is a function of that authority.[12] It is not necessary in this latter case that the contractor itself should be performing functions of a public nature.[13] The determination of what is and is not a "function of a public nature" is a familiar one for the courts, being central to both judicial review and the Human Rights Act 1998.[14] When exercising this power, the Secretary of State for Constitutional Affairs may designate a specified person or office falling within a specified description.[15] Before making such an order the Secretary of State for Constitutional Affairs must consult every person to whom the order relates, or persons appearing to represent them.[16] An order of this type made in relation to a person who appears to exercise functions 7–021

[11] Freedom of Information Act 2000, s.7(3). If such an order relates to the National Assembly for Wales or a Welsh public authority, the Northern Ireland Assembly, or a Northern Ireland department or a Northern Ireland public authority, the Secretary of State for Constitutional Affairs must consult the National Assembly for Wales, the Presiding Officer of the relevant Northern Ireland Assembly, or the First Minister and deputy First Minister in Northern Ireland respectively before making such an order: Freedom of Information Act 2000, s.7(4). As to the meaning of a "Welsh public authority", see Freedom of Information Act 2000, s.83. In any event, a draft of such an order must be laid before and approved by a resolution of each House of Parliament before it is made: Freedom of Information Act 2000, s.82(2).

[12] Freedom of Information Act 2000, s.5(1). A draft of such an order must be laid before and approved by a resolution of each House of Parliament before it is made: Freedom of Information Act 2000, s.82(2). Such a draft is not to be treated for the purposes of the Standing Orders of either House of Parliament as a hybrid instrument: s.82(5). As with orders under s.4(1) (as to which see para.7–018 above) this power cannot be exercised in relation to the Scottish Parliament, any part of the Scottish administration, the Scottish Parliamentary Corporate Body, or any Scottish public authority with mixed functions or no reserved functions (within the meaning of the Scotland Act 1998): ss.5(4) and 80.

[13] House of Commons, *Public Administration—Third Report* (Cm. 4355), July 29, 1999, Annex 6, para.9 (Notes by the Freedom of Information Unit, Home Office).

[14] Human Rights Act 1998, s.6 makes it unlawful for public authorities to act incompatibly with rights under the European Convention on Human Rights and provides that "public authority" includes (a) a court or tribunal and (b) any person certain of whose functions are functions of a public nature.

[15] Freedom of Information Act 2000, s.5(2).

[16] *ibid.*, s.5(3). It was also said by the Home Office that, "as a matter of good administrative practice it is expected that the Secretary of State will consult other persons whom he believes have a legitimate and direct interest in the order": House of Commons, *Public Administration—Third Report* (Cm. 4355), July 29, 1999, Annex 6, para.10 (Notes by the Freedom of Information Unit, Home Office).

of a public nature[17] must specify the functions of the designated public authority with respect to which the order is to have effect. The general right of access under the Act to information held by the public authority does not apply to information held by the authority which does not relate to the exercise of those functions.[18] Similarly, where an order is made in relation to a person who is providing under a contract made with a public authority any service whose provision is a function of that authority,[19] it must specify the services provided under contract with respect to which the order is to have effect. The general right of access under the Act to information held by the public authority does not apply to information held by the authority which does not relate to the provision of those services.[20]

Publicly-owned companies

7–022 A company is a publicly-owned company[21] and therefore a public authority under the Freedom of Information Act 2000 if it is wholly-owned by either (1) the Crown; or (2) any public authority listed in Sch.1 to the Act, other than a government department or any authority listed only in relation to particular information.[22] For these purposes, a company is considered to be wholly-owned by the Crown if it has no members other than Ministers of the Crown,[23] government departments or companies wholly-owned by the Crown, or persons acting on behalf of any of these.[24] A company is considered to be wholly-owned by a public authority listed in Sch.1 other than a government department if it has no members except that public authority or companies wholly-owned by that public authority, or persons acting on behalf of either of these.[25] However, the general right of access to information under the Act does not apply to any information held by a publicly-owned company which is defined by order of the Secretary of State for Constitutional Affairs as "excluded information" in relation to that company.[26]

---

17 *i.e.* under Freedom of Information Act 2000, s.5(1)(a).
18 *ibid.*, s.7(5).
19 *i.e.* under Freedom of Information Act 2000, s.5(1)(b).
20 *ibid.*, s.7(6).
21 "Company" includes any body corporate: Freedom of Information Act 2000, s.6(3).
22 Freedom of Information Act 2000, s.6(1). For public authorities listed in Sch.1 only in relation to particular information see para. 7–020 above.
23 Including a Northern Ireland Minister: Freedom of Information Act 2000, s.6(3).
24 *ibid.*, s.6(2)(a).
25 *ibid.*, s.6(2)(b).
26 *ibid.*, s.7(8).

Schedule 1: public authorities under the Freedom of Information (Scotland) Act 2002

Schedule 1 to the Freedom of Information (Scotland) Act 2002 provides a similarly-divided list to that in Sch.1 to the Westminster Act. It is estimated to cover some 9,000 authorities in total.[27] 7–023

(I) MINISTERS, THE PARLIAMENT: This comprises the Scottish Ministers, the Scottish Parliament and the Scottish Parliamentary Corporate Body.

(II) NON-MINISTERIAL OFFICER HOLDERS IN THE SCOTTISH ADMINISTRATION: This includes such persons as the Chief Dental Officer and Chief Medical Officer of the Scottish Administration, Her Majesty's various Chief Inspectors of Constabulary and of Prisons, Her Inspector of Anatomy, of Fire Services and inspectors of schools for Scotland, the Keepers of the Records and Registers of Scotland, procurators fiscal, the Queen's and Lord Treasurer's Remembrancer, the Queen's Printer for Scotland, the Registrars of Births, Deaths and Marriages and of Independent Schools, rent officers[28] and social work inspectors.[29]

(III) LOCAL GOVERNMENT: This comprises Councils constituted, and assessors appointed, under the Local Government, etc. (Scotland) Act 1994, joint boards within the meaning of s.235(1) of the Local Government (Scotland) Act 1973, licensing boards constituted in accordance with the provisions of s.1 of the Licensing (Scotland) Act 1976 and the Strathclyde Passenger Transport Authority.

(IV) THE NATIONAL HEALTH SERVICE: This Part covers most NHS institutions in Scotland and, as with the Freedom of Information Act 2000, includes individual GPs, dentists, opticians and pharmacists, but only in respect of information relating to their provision of services under the NHS.

(V) EDUCATIONAL INSTITUTIONS: This lists the board of management of colleges of further education, central institutions within the meaning of the Education (Scotland) Act 1980, and institutions in receipt of funding from the Scottish Higher Education Funding Council other than any institution whose activities are principally carried on outside Scotland.

(VI) POLICE: Listed here are the chief constables of police forces in Scotland, joint police boards and the Police Advisory Board for Scotland.

(VII) OTHERS: This is a general list of 53 other public bodies and offices, similar to that contained in Pt VI of Sch.1 to the Freedom of Information Act 2000.

[27] According to the Scottish Information Commissioner at *www.itspublicknowledge.info*.

[28] Appointed under Rent (Scotland) Act 1984, s.43(3): Freedom of Information (Scotland) Act 2002, Sch.1, Pt 2, para.18.

[29] Freedom of Information (Scotland) Act 2002, Sch.1, Pt 2, para.19.

Adding Scottish public authorities from Schedule 1

7–024 The Scottish Ministers have the power[30] to add to Sch.1 any body or holder of any office which is either a part of the Scottish Administration or a Scottish public authority with mixed functions or no reserved functions.[31] The Act imposes no duty to consult before making such an order.[32] An order adding a Scottish public authority to Sch.1 in this way may relate to a specified person or office or to persons or offices falling within a specified description.[33]In addition, the order may list the new entry only in relation to information of a specified description, in which case nothing in the Act applies to any other information held by the authority.[34]

Removing Scottish public authorities from Schedule 1

7–025 The Scottish Ministers have the power to remove from Sch.1 any entry listed there.[35] There is no requirement for approval of such an order by the Scottish Parliament.[36]

Partly-affected Schedule 1: Scottish public authorities

7–026 The Freedom of Information (Scotland) Act 2002 provides that any body listed in Sch.1 is considered a Scottish public authority for the purposes of that Act,[37] subject to any qualification in that Schedule.[38] Therefore, as with the Freedom of Information Act 2000, there is no right of access to information held by such

---

30 Freedom of Information (Scotland) Act 2002, s.4(1). Such an order is subject to annulment in pursuance of a resolution of the Scottish Parliament: Freedom of Information (Scotland) Act 2002, s.72(2)(a). If the order is adding an authority only in relation to information of a specified description then a draft order must be laid before and approved by a resolution of that body before being made: Freedom of Information (Scotland) Act 2002, s.72(2)(b).

31 "Scottish public authority" has the meaning it has in the rest of the Act, as defined in Freedom of Information (Scotland) Act 2002, s.3(1), *i.e.* either a body or office which is listed in Sch.1 (although obviously that could not apply here, since this concerns adding a body or office to Sch.1), designated by the Scottish Ministers or a publicly-owned company. However, this reference to an authority with mixed functions or no reserved functions is to be construed in accordance with paras 1(4) and 2 of Pt III of Sch.5 to the Scotland Act 1998: Freedom of Information (Scotland) Act 2002, s.4(2).

32 Contrast the position under the Freedom of Information Act 2000, s.4(7): see n.92 above.

33 Freedom of Information (Scotland) Act 2002, s.4(3).

34 *ibid.*, s 7(1).

35 *ibid.*, s.4(1)(b).

36 As there is when adding bodies in relation to specified information, or introducing such a limitation to a body on Sch.1: see para.7–027 below.

37 Freedom of Information (Scotland) Act 2002, s.3(1)(a)(i).

38 *ibid.*, s.3(3). For example, Pt 4 (the National Health Service) has the entry, "A person providing general medical services, general ophthalmic services or pharmaceutical services under Pt II of the National Health Service (Scotland) Act 1978, but only in respect of information relating to the provision of those services."

an authority if the information falls outside the description in the Schedule. The difference is really only conceptual: the effect of the Scottish approach is that such a body is not considered by the Act to be a Scottish public authority in such circumstances, whereas under the Freedom of Information Act 2000 such a body remains at all times a public authority under the statute, just not always subject to the Act's main provisions.[39] The Scottish Ministers have the power, in relation to any entry in Sch.1, to introduce, amend or remove any such limitation.[40]

Designated Scottish public authorities

A person who is not listed in Sch.1 nor capable of being added to that list by an order under s.4(1)[41] may be designated by order as a Scottish public authority for the purposes of the Act if he: (a) appears to the Scottish Ministers to exercise functions of a public nature, or (b) is providing under a contract made with a Scottish public authority any service whose provision is a function of that authority.[42] In such cases, the order must specify the functions of a public nature which appear to be exercised or the service being provided.[43]As with orders made under s.4(1) of the Freedom of Information Act 2000,[44] such an order may designate a specified person or office or persons or offices falling within a specified description.[45] In contrast to the position under s.4(1),[46] however, before making this type of order the Scottish Ministers must consult every person to whom the order relates, or persons appearing to represent them.[47] 7–027

Publicly-owned companies

A company is a publicly-owned company[48] and therefore a Scottish public authority under the Freedom of Information (Scotland) Act 2002 if it is wholly-owned by either (1) the Scottish Ministers; or (2) any other Scottish public authority listed in Sch.1 to the Act other than an authority listed only in relation 7–028

[39] *i.e.* those in Pts I to V of the Freedom of Information (Scotland) Act 2002. See para.7–020 above.

[40] Freedom of Information (Scotland) Act 2002, s.7(2). Such an order must be laid before and approved by a resolution of the Scottish Parliament before being made: Freedom of Information (Scotland) Act 2002, s.72(2)(b).

[41] See para. 7–024 above.

[42] Freedom of Information (Scotland) Act 2002, s.5(1)–(2). Such an order must be laid before and approved by a resolution of the Scottish Parliament before being made: Freedom of Information (Scotland) Act 2002, s.72(2)(b).

[43] Freedom of Information (Scotland) Act 2002, s.5(4).

[44] See para.7–021 above.

[45] Freedom of Information (Scotland) Act 2002, s.5(3).

[46] See para.7–024 above.

[47] Freedom of Information (Scotland) Act 2002, s.5(3).

[48] "Company" includes any body corporate: Freedom of Information (Scotland) Act 2002, s.6(3).

to particular information.[49] For these purposes, a company is considered to be wholly-owned by the Scottish Ministers if it has no members other than the Scottish Ministers or companies wholly-owned by the Scottish Ministers, or persons acting on behalf of either of these.[50] A company is considered to be wholly-owned by any other Scottish public authority if it has no members except that authority or companies wholly-owned by that authority, or persons acting on behalf of either of these.[51] However, nothing in the Act applies to any information held by a publicly-owned company which is of a description specified in relation to that company in an order made by the Scottish Ministers.[52]

[49] Freedom of Information (Scotland) Act 2002, s.6(1). For Scottish public authorities listed in Sch.1 only in relation to particular information see para.7–026 above.
[50] *ibid.*, s.6(2)(a).
[51] *ibid.*, s.6(2)(b).
[52] *ibid.*, s.7(4). This is the equivalent of the "excluded information" provision in s.7(7)–(8) of the Freedom of Information Act 2000.

CHAPTER 8

The Duty to Advise and Assist

Introduction

8–001 Section 16(1) of the Freedom of Information Act 2000 imposes a duty upon a public authority to provide advice and assistance to any person who proposes to make, or who has made, a request for information to it.[1] The scope of the duty is not open-ended, but is stated to be a duty to provide advice and assistance "so far as would be reasonable to expect the authority to do".[2] The duty

[1] Similarly, the Freedom of Information (Scotland) Act 2002, s.15(1). A "request for information" is defined in the Freedom of Information Act 2000, s.8(1) and a similar definition is in the Freedom of Information (Scotland) Act 2002, s.8(1). There is no duty to advise and assist in relation to a subject-access request made under s.7 of the Data Protection Act 1998 except in the very narrow circumstances contemplated by s.53 (where data is being processed for any of the special purposes and the matter is one of substantial public importance). The draft European environmental information Directive imposes a duty to provide advice and assistance: see para.5–058 above.

[2] There are similar duties in three of the comparative jurisdictions: Freedom of Information Act 1982 (Cth of Aust), s.15(3); Official Information Act 1982 (NZ), s.13; Freedom of Information Act 1997 (Ireland), long title and ss.6(2), 7(7) and 10(2). There is no provision in either the US or the Canadian Act requiring an agency to give assistance. In the recent review of the Canadian Act, it was recommended that that Act be amended to require that the institution make a reasonable effort to assist an applicant upon request, and offer to help the requester reformulate the request in a way that will avoid negative outcomes: Government of Canada, *Report of the Access to Information Review Task Force* (June 2002), p.86. In its review of the Freedom of Information Act 1982, the Australian Law Reform Commission noted that many agencies did not seem to have an adequate commitment to the obligation to give assistance. The Review declined to prescribe further what assistance had to be given, instead considering that the FOI Commissioner should encourage agencies to do more than the bare statutory minimum. The Commission concluded: "if agencies take care to find out exactly what information an applicant requires they may ultimately save resources and avoid disputes": Australian Law Reform Commission and Administrative Review Council, *Open Government: a review of the Federal Freedom of Information Act 1982* (A.L.R.C. 77, A.R.C. 40, Canberra, 1995), para.7.5; see also paras 7.14, 8.14 and 10.9.

was introduced on the basis that it represented an important step in achieving the cultural change stated to be sought by the legislation.[3] There had been an initial reluctance on the part of the government to impose such a duty, said to be because of difficulties in adequately describing the limits of the duty.[4] The expedient adopted was to leave the detail to one of the codes of practice.[5]

Scope of the duty

8–002 Section 16(2) provides that a public authority that conforms with the code of practice issued under s.45 is to be taken to comply with the duty to advise and assist. That, however, does not mean that nothing less will suffice. To ascertain the minimum requirements of the duty it is necessary to consider the terms of the section before considering the effect of the code of practice. The duty is necessarily shaped by the underlying purpose of the Act, as manifested by its other provisions and its long title. There are a number of notable features about the duty to advise and assist. First, there is no identification of the matters with respect to which the public authority is obliged to provide advice and assistance: it is to a class of person to which the duty is confined. Secondly, there is nothing to suggest that the duty is only engaged where the applicant seeks advice or assistance: the public authority may have to volunteer advice and assistance. Thirdly, the duty relates to both an unformed request and to one already made. The former implies that the duty includes advising and assisting in the formulation of a request that meets the formal requirements of the Act.[6] Fourthly, the fact that the duty is not tied to advice and assistance in relation to the Freedom of Information Act 2000 suggests that a public authority may also be required to advise and assist where the request for information would be better made under other legislation, such as the Data Protection Act 1998 in relation to a request for personal information.[7] Fifthly, it is apparent from the wording of the section that the duty to advise and assist does not end with the receipt by the

[3] See *Hansard*, HL, Vol.617, October 17, 2000, cols 940 and 942.

[4] See House of Commons, *Public Administration—Third Report* (Cm. 4355), July 29, 1999, Annex 6, para.24; House of Commons, *Select Committee on Public Administration, 5th Special Report*, Appendix, October 27, 1999, p.11; *Hansard*, HC, Vol.347, April 4, 2000, cols 856–870; *Hansard*, HL, Vol.617, October 17, 2000, cols 938–945. For the final acceptance by the Government of this, see *Hansard*, HL, Vol.619, November 14, 2000, cols 194–197.

[5] During the passage of the Bill, it had been suggested that rather more detail should be spelled out in the Act itself: House of Commons, *Public Administration–Third Report* (Cm. 4355), July 29, 1999, para.52; House of Commons, *Select Committee on Public Administration 5th Special Report*, Appendix, October 27, 1999, p.5; *Hansard*, HC, Vol.347, April 4, 2000, cols 868–870; *Hansard*, HL, Vol.619, November 14, 2000, cols 250–252.

[6] That is, the requirements set out in the Freedom of Information Act 2000, s.8(1) and the Freedom of Information (Scotland) Act 2002, s.8(1). This may also extend to advising and assisting where the proposed request would be treated as vexatious or repeated under the Freedom of Information Act 2000, s.14 or under the Freedom of Information (Scotland) Act 2002, s.14.

[7] A request for such information made under the Freedom of Information Act 2000 could properly be refused by virtue of Freedom of Information Act 2000, s.21 or Freedom of Information (Scotland) Act 2002, s.25.

public authority of a properly-formulated request. Thus the duty may require the giving of advice and assistance:

— where a public authority apprehends that the request is more likely to retrieve the information requested if directed to another public authority;
— where a public authority estimates that the cost of compliance with the request will exceed the appropriate limit, thereby removing the obligation upon the public authority to comply with the request[8] or, if it choses to do so, to charge for meeting the request;[9]
— where a public authority considers that it requires further information in order to identify and locate the information requested by the applicant;[10]
— where a public authority considers that the request would be more successful if the applicant were to obtain the consent of a third party to disclosure and that could properly be suggested to the applicant without the disclosure of exempt information; and
— in relation to the applicant's appeal and enforcement rights.

And sixthly, the duty is one to give advice and assistance to the extent that it is reasonable to expect of the public authority. This suggests that the size and resources of the public authority will in part determine how much advice and assistance a public authority must give an applicant in the proper discharge of its duty.

The role of the code of practice

Section 45(1) of the Freedom of Information Act 2000 obliges the Secretary of State for Constitutional Affairs to issue a code of practice providing guidance to public authorities as to the practice which it would be desirable for public authorities to follow in connection with the discharge of their functions under Pt I of the Act. The section specifically requires the code of practice to cover the provision of advice and assistance by public authorities to persons who propose to make, or have made, requests for information.[11] The code of practice under s.45 was laid before Parliament on November 20, 2002.[12] As noted above, the Act provides that conformity with the code will constitute compliance with the duty to advise and assist, so that so far as this duty is concerned it may go beyond the minimum that is required of a public authority. Other Acts of 8–003

[8] Freedom of Information Act 2000, s.12(1); Freedom of Information (Scotland) Act 2002, s.12(1).
[9] Freedom of Information Act 2000, s.13(1); Freedom of Information (Scotland) Act 2002, s.13(1).
[10] Freedom of Information Act 2000, s.1(3); Freedom of Information (Scotland) Act 2002, s.1(3).
[11] Freedom of Information Act 2000, s.45(2)(a); Freedom of Information (Scotland) Act 2002, s.60(2)(a).
[12] It is reproduced in the Appendix, see App 3–01 below.

Parliament may also be relevant to the way in which authorities provide advice and assistance to applicants or potential applicants, such as the Disability Discrimination Act 1995.[13] The code's requirements do not, of course, prevent an authority from offering additional assistance if it wishes.[14]

The requirements of the code of practice

8–004 Although paras 5 to 15 of the code of practice are specifically directed to the duty to advise and assist, the full extent to which the code describes the duty requires a consideration of all its provisions. In summary, the requirements of the code so far as the duty is concerned are:

(1) For each public authority to publish its procedures for dealing with a request for information, which may, but need not, include a standard procedure for a transfer of the request from one public authority to another where the public authority does not hold the information requested.[15]
(2) For a public authority to alert a potential applicant that it may need to consult other public authorities or third persons before determining the application.[16]
(3) For a public authority to volunteer the existence of the Act to those who are unaware of it.[17]
(4) For a public authority to assist an applicant in formulating a request that is both proper and that enables it to locate the requested information.[18]
(5) For a public authority to indicate to an applicant which information of the kind sought is available free of charge.[19]
(6) For a public authority to advise an applicant that it does not hold all or part of the requested information.[20] Where the public authority to which the request has been made believes that some or all of that information is held by another public authority, the public authority that has

[13] See the Foreword to the *Code of Practice on the Discharge of the Functions of Public Authorities under Part I of the Freedom of Information Act 2000* (issued by the Lord Chancellor under s.45), para.11, and the Scottish Ministers *Code of Practice on the Discharge of Functions by Public Authorities under the Freedom of Information (Scotland) Act 2002* (Draft revised version, April 2003), Introduction.

[14] See *Hansard*, HL, Vol.619, November 14, 2000, col.196 by Lord Falconer, the then-Minister of State, Cabinet Office.

[15] See para.6 of the *Code of Practice*. Transfers of requests for information is treated at paras 11–032 to 11–033 below.

[16] Para.6 of the *Code of Practice*.

[17] Para.7.

[18] Para.8–12.

[19] Para.13–14.

[20] Para.23.

> received the request is expected to consider the most helpful way of assisting the applicant, which will normally include advising the applicant of the identity of that other public authority and suggesting that application is made to it.[21] If the public authority does not know the identity of another public authority that might hold the requested information, the first-mentioned public authority must at least consider what advice it can give the applicant to assist him with his request.[22]

It is suggested that the line between the minimum duty such as can be discerned from the words of s.45(1) and the duty as described in the code of practice is a fine one.

Enforcement of the duty to advise and assist

There are two principal mechanisms contemplated in the Act for enforcement of the duty to advise and assist. First, a duty is imposed upon the Information Commissioner to promote the following of "good practice", which is defined to include compliance with the requirements of the Act and the provisions of the code of practice.[23] Where it appears to the Information Commissioner that the practice of a particular public authority does not conform with what is laid out in the code of practice, the Information Commissioner can issue a "practice recommendation" that specifies the steps which, in the opinion of the Information Commissioner, ought to be taken in order to promote conformity.[24] The first mechanism, then, does not depend upon the applicant in order for it to be instigated. The second mechanism is applicant-driven. In addition to being able to apply to the Information Commissioner on the basis of non-disclosure of requested information, a person may apply to the Information Commissioner on the grounds that the advice and assistance that he was entitled to receive from the Information Commissioner after having made a request was not provided to him.[25] In order to be able to make the application, the person must have made a request for information that meets all the formal requirements.[26] The latter is probably more hypothetical than real, in that once an applicant makes complaint to the Information Commissioner the applicant will normally be seeking the Commissioner's decision upon a refusal to disclose, irrespective of the level of help that might have been given. 8–005

21 Para.24 of the *Code of Practice*.
22 Para.30.
23 Freedom of Information Act 2000, s.47(1); Freedom of Information (Scotland) Act 2002, s.43(1).
24 Freedom of Information Act 2000, s.48(1); Freedom of Information (Scotland) Act 2002, s.44(1).
25 Freedom of Information Act 2000, s.50(1). The position would appear to be otherwise in Scotland: see Freedom of Information (Scotland) Act 2002, s.47.
26 Freedom of Information Act 2000, ss.8(1) and 50(1).

CHAPTER 9

Codes of Practice

Introduction

9–001 The Freedom of Information Act 2000 requires two codes of practice to be issued: the first, to be issued by the Secretary of State for Constitutional Affairs,[1] providing guidance to public authorities on good practice in dealing with requests for information;[2] the second, to be issued by the Lord Chancellor, providing guidance to relevant authorities[3] on good practice in keeping, managing and destroying records.[4] The Secretary of State for Constitutional Affairs

[1] The Act originally assigned the function to the Secretary of State, but that function was first transferred to the Lord Chancellor by the Transfer of Functions (Miscellaneous) Order 2001 (SI 2001/3500) and then to the Secretary of State for Constitutional Affairs by the Secretary of State for Constitutional Affairs Order 2003 (SI 2003/1887).

[2] Freedom of Information Act 2000, s.45; Freedom of Information (Scotland) Act 2002, s.60. In Scotland, the duty is cast upon the Scottish Ministers. These provisions set out what must be included in the code, and allow for different provisions to be made for different public authorities. The former also provides that before issuing or revising any code under this section, the Secretary of State for Constitutional Affairs must consult the Information Commissioner and then must subsequently lay any code or revised code before each House of Parliament.

[3] "Relevant authority" means: (a) any public authority, and (b) any office or body which is not a public authority but whose administrative and departmental records are public records for the purposes of the Public Records Act 1958 or the Public Records Act (Northern Ireland) 1923: Freedom of Information Act 2000, s.46(7).

[4] Freedom of Information Act 2000, s.46; Freedom of Information (Scotland) Act 2002, s.61. In exercising his functions under this section the Secretary of State for Constitutional Affairs is required to have regard to the public interest in allowing public access to information held by relevant authorities. The code may make different provision for different relevant authorities. Before issuing or revising any code under this section the Secretary of State for Constitutional Affairs must consult the Secretary of State, the Information Commissioner and (in relation to

and the Lord Chancellor may amend the respective codes from time to time.[5] The Information Commissioner is under a duty to promote observance of the codes by public authorities.[6] The Data Protection Act 1998 also provides for codes of practice.[7]

Status of the codes

The codes of practice issued under the Freedom of Information Act 2000 do not have any statutory force.[8] The Act imposes no direct duty on public authorities to follow or even to have regard to them. Instead, where it appears to the Information Commissioner that the practice of a public authority in relation to the exercise of its functions under the Freedom of Information Act 2000 does not conform with that proposed in the codes of practice, the Information Commissioner can give the public authority a written "practice recommendation" specifying the steps which in the opinion of the Information Commissioner ought to be taken for promoting such conformity.[9] In contrast to non-compliance with a decision notice, information notice or enforcement notice issued by the Information Commissioner (which can amount to contempt of 9–002

Northern Ireland), the appropriate Northern Ireland Minister, and then must subsequently lay any code or revised code before each House of Parliament.

[5] The Secretary of State for Constitutional Affairs and the Lord Chancellor must consult the Information Commissioner before revising a code of practice: Freedom of Information Act 2000, ss.45(4) and 46(5). In Scotland, the Scottish Ministers must consult the Information Commissioner before revising a code of practice: Freedom of Information (Scotland) Act 2002, ss.60(4) and 61(5). Any revision to a code of practice must be laid before both Houses of Parliament: Freedom of Information Act 2000, ss.45(5) and 46(6). In Scotland, revisions must be laid before the Parliament: Freedom of Information (Scotland) Act 2002, ss.60(5) and 61(6).

[6] Freedom of Information Act 2000, s.47(1); Freedom of Information (Scotland) Act 2002, s.43(1). The code of practice issued under s.45 of the Freedom of Information Act 2000 provides that authorities are expected to abide by the Code unless there are good reasons, capable of being justified to the Information Commissioner, why it would be inappropriate to do so. Code of Practice on the Discharge of the Functions of Public Authorities under Part I of the Freedom of Information Act (November 2002), para.3.

[7] Data Protection Act 1998, s.51(3). The codes of practice are issued by the Information Commissioner upon direction by the Secretary of State for Constitutional Affairs or where the Commissioner considers it appropriate to do so. There is a consultation process that reflects all the preoccupations of the Data Protection Act 1998, rather than merely the right of access to personal data. Although no specific code of practice relating to subject-access requests has been issued, the Information Commissioner has issued certain documents providing "compliance advice".

[8] See the *Code of Practice on the Discharge of the Functions of Public Authorities under Part I of the Freedom of Information Act* (November 2002), para.3, issued pursuant to Freedom of Information Act 2000, s.45; Scottish Ministers Code of Practice on the Discharge of Functions by Public Authorities under the Freedom of Information (Scotland) Act 2002, Introduction, issued pursuant to Freedom of Information (Scotland) Act 2002, s.60.

[9] Freedom of Information Act 2000, s.48(1); Freedom of Information (Scotland) Act 2002, s.44(1). The Information Commissioner is required to consult the Keeper of the Public Records (or the Deputy Keeper of the Records of Northern Ireland) before giving a practice recommendation relating to conformity with the Lord Chancellor's Code of Practice on record-keeping: Freedom of Information Act 2000, s.48(3) and (4).

court), the Act does not specify the consequences of a failure to comply with a practice recommendation. The Government referred to this during the Bill's passage through Parliament, and commented as follows:

> "[C]ompliance with the published codes of practice would not be enforceable in the courts in the same way that a statutory duty might be. We believe it would be an exceptional authority which ignored a [practice] recommendation, particularly given the commissioner's powers to name and shame in any report that she might make to Parliament. An additional point is that the code of practice could be referred to in any test case which was the subject of judicial review. The power of naming and shaming should not be underestimated in regard to public sector bodies keen to keep the confidence of the public they serve."[10]

Other methods of compelling compliance

9–003 Although it would be open to the Information Commissioner to seek judicial review of a public authority's refusal to follow a practice recommendation, the non-statutory nature of the codes of practice, the fact that the refusal relates to a recommendation rather than a direction, and the absence of any statutory duty to follow or have regard to a practice direction, would materially weaken such a claim.[11] It is suggested that unless non-compliance with a practice recommendation also represents a breach of the Act, a court would rule that the appropriate forum for securing compliance is a political one and not the courts. Similarly, judicial review by any other person based solely on a breach of a code of practice is unlikely to succeed.[12] However, non-compliance with the codes

---

[10] *Hansard*, HL, Vol.617, October 17, 2000, col.944, by Lord Bassam of Brighton, Parliamentary Under-Secretary of State, Home Office. See also the Code of Practice made under the Freedom of Information Act 2000, s.45 which states: "practice recommendation is simply a recommendation and cannot be directly enforced by the Information Commissioner. However, a failure to comply with a practice recommendation may lead to a failure to comply with the Act. Further a failure to take account of a practice recommendation may lead to an adverse comment in a report to Parliament by the Commissioner": *Code of Practice on the Discharge of the Functions of Public Authorities under Part I of the Freedom of Information Act* (November 2002), Foreword, para.6.

[11] Even where there is a duty to have regard to a code of practice, it has been held that this does not mean it has to be applied: *R. (on the application of Wirral MBC) v Chief Schools Adjudicator* [2001] E.L.R. 574; *R. (on the application of Munjaz) v Mersey Care NHS* [2003] EWCA Civ 1036; [2003] 3 W.L.R. 1505 at paras 71–74, concerning a code of practice prepared under s.118(2) of the Mental Health Act 1983, where the Court of Appeal considered that since the code related to matters where a person's human rights were or might be engaged, "the arguments for according the code the greater status [*i.e.* the status of being required to be followed unless there is some good reason to the contrary, as opposed to a code which a public authority is free not to follow unless to do so would be Wednesbury unreasonable] are compelling".

[12] *cf. R. (on the application of Munjaz) v Mersey Care NHS* [2003] EWCA Civ 1036 at para.77 where the Court of Appeal treated a hospital's breach of code as giving rise to the affected individual being able to seek a declaration of illegality, possible damages for tort (unlawful detention) and damages under the Human Rights Act 1998.

could form part of a wider challenge to the discharge by a public authority of its duties under the Act, such as a failure in relation to the duty to advise and assist.[13] In these circumstances, the Information Commissioner could serve an enforcement notice. By itself, however, the failure of a public authority to comply with either of the codes of practice does not provide a basis for a disgruntled applicant to make an application to the Information Commissioner under s.50.[14]

The aims of the section 45 code

The code of practice under s.45 of the Freedom of Information Act 2000[15] was issued by the then-Lord Chancellor in November 2002. It provides guidance to public authorities as to the practice which it would, in his opinion, be desirable for them to follow in connection with the discharge of their functions under Pt I of the Act.[16] The Code sets out its aims as follows:[17] 9–004

(1) to facilitate the disclosure of information under the Act by setting out good administrative practice that it is desirable for public authorities to follow when handling requests for information, including, where appropriate, the transfer of a request to a different authority;
(2) to protect the interests of applicants by setting out standards for the provision of advice which it would be good practice to make available to them and to encourage the development of effective means of complaining about decisions taken under the Act;
(3) to ensure that the interests of third parties who may be affected by any decision to disclose information are considered by the authority by setting standards for consultation; and
(4) to ensure that authorities consider the implications for Freedom of Information before agreeing to confidentiality provisions in contracts and accepting information in confidence from a third party more generally.

---

[13] This is suggested by the Foreword to the current Code of Practice.

[14] This is because compliance with the codes of practice is not a requirement of Pt I of the Act: see Freedom of Information Act 2000, s.50(1). This is confirmed by Freedom of Information Act 2000, s.51(1)(b), which contradistinguishes the requirements of Pt I of the Act from the codes of practice.

[15] Printed in full in the Appendix. The code is also available on the Department for Constituional Affairs Website: *www.dca.gov.uk*. The Scottish equivalent is still in draft form and can be found at: *www.scotland. gov.uk/government/foi/reviseds60.pdf*.

[16] Freedom of Information Act 2000, s.45.

[17] *Code of Practice on the Discharge of the Functions of Public Authorities under Part I of the Freedom of Information Act 2000* (November 2002), para.2.

The contents of the section 45 code

9–005 The code is divided into 12 overlapping topics:

(1) An introduction. Notably, this recites the code's lack of statutory force.

(2) The provision of advice and assistance to persons making requests for information. As noted before, the code goes little beyond what is required by the terms of the Act.[18]

(3) The handling of requests for information that appear to be part of an organised campaign. Section 12(4) of the Freedom of Information Act 2000 and the fees regulations[19] enable aggregation in certain circumstances of the cost of compliance of multiple requests. The code suggests that in these circumstances disclosure by publication on the public authority's website may be appropriate, but otherwise adds little to the scheme established by the Act.

(4) Timeliness in dealing with requests for information. Section 10(1) of the Act provides a basic 20 working day limit for compliance with a request that does not involve a qualified exemption.[20] The code exhorts earlier compliance if possible. In relation to a request involving a qualified exemption, for which the Act provides no time limit for responding to the request, the code encourages a response within the basic 20 working day time limit.

(5) Charging fees. The code does little more than recite the position under the Freedom of Information Act 2000 and the charging regulations made under it.[21]

(6) Transferring requests for information. The code sets out what a public authority should do where it either holds none or just some of the requested information, with the balance being held by some other public authority. The code encourages such transfers to take place as quickly as possible.[22]

(7) Consultation with third parties. Given that the Freedom of Information Act 2000 makes no express provision for third party involvement in the determination of a request for information, this part of the code is of particular importance.[23] Where the absence of consent from a third party would necessarily defeat a request for information (*e.g.* because the requested information was supplied in confidence to the public authority by the third party), the code of practice exhorts the public

---

18 This is considered further at para.8–003 above.

19 Freedom of Information (Fees and Appropriate Limits) Regulations, so far issued in draft only.

20 See further paras 11–022 to 11–030 below.

21 See further paras 11–014 to 11–021 below.

22 See further paras 11–032 to 11–033 below.

23 See para.25–020 below. The Information Commissioner has issued guidance in relation to requests for data under the Data Protection Act 1998 that contain third party information.

authority to seek the consent of the third party unless that third party cannot be located or the cost of doing so is disproportionate. Consultation with a third party is also commended where disclosure would impinge upon the interests of that third party, where it might assist in the determination of the applicability of an exemption, or where it might assist the public authority in determining where the public interest lies. If, however, the information sought will be rendered exempt by another provision of the Act, the code dispenses with the need to consult an interested third party.

(8) Freedom of information and public sector contracts. The code advises public authorities to refuse to enter private sector contracts that include a term that purports to restrict or oust the operation of the Act in relation to the contract and to ensure that only truly confidential information is received on an in-confidence basis from private sector contractors.

(9) Accepting information in confidence from third parties. The code cautions against public authorities receiving information from third parties on an in-confidence basis unless:

   (a) it is necessary to obtain that information in connection with the exercise of any of the authority's functions;
   (b) the information would not otherwise be provided to the public authority by the third party; and
   (c) the information is confidential in nature.

(10) Consultation with devolved administrations. The code builds on s.28 of the Act by suggesting that public authorities should consult with a devolved administration directly concerned with the information proposed to be disclosed irrespective of whether any prejudice to relations with the devolved administration would be caused by a disclosure.

(11) Refusal of request. The code requires public authorities, when refusing a request, to do more than incant the words of the provision relied upon to found the exemption and, where a qualified exemption is relied upon, to enumerate the public interest factors relied upon in the weighing exercise.[24]

(12) Complaints procedure. The code encourages public authorities to have a complaints procedure, which should provide an effective right of internal appeal, and to advise applicants of their statutory rights of appeal.

[24] See further paras 13–006 to 13–010 below.

The section 46 code

9–006 This Code of Practice was issued by the then-Lord Chancellor in November 2002.[25] Its aims are:

(1) To set out practices which public authorities, and bodies subject to the Public Records Act 1958 and the Public Records Act (NI) 1923, should follow in relation to the creation, keeping, management and destruction of their records (including specific provision for management of electronic records) (Pt I of the Code); and
(2) To describe the arrangements which public record bodies should follow in reviewing public records and transferring them to the Public Record Office or to places of deposit or to the Public Record Office of Northern Ireland (Pt II of the Code).

This code is considered in detail in Chapter 4 of this work.

[25] The code is reproduced in the Appendix. It is also available at *www.dca.gov.uk*. The Scottish code is available at *www.scotland.gov.uk*.

CHAPTER 10

Publication Schemes

Introduction

Every public authority must adopt and maintain a scheme, called a "publication scheme", which relates to the publication of information by that authority.[1] In 10–001

[1] Freedom of Information Act 2000, s.19(1); Freedom of Information (Scotland) Act 2002, s.23(1). The freedom of information legislation in each of the comparative jurisdictions includes the equivalent of a publication scheme. Most of the comparative regimes also require their statutory equivalent of a public authority to prepare and make available a statement that sets out the organisation, functions and adopted policies of the public authority. So far as equivalents of the publication scheme are concerned, in the United States, the Freedom of Information Act 1966, s.552(a)(2) requires that certain sorts of records, such as policy statements and certain administrative staff manuals, be routinely made available for public inspection and copying. This is often referred to as the "reading room" provision of the Act, and certain records must also be made available in "electronic reading rooms". In Australia, the Freedom of Information Act 1982, s.8 requires the minister responsible for an agency to publish a statement that includes the categories of publicly-available documents that are maintained in its possession, the facilities for enabling the public to obtain access to its documents, as well as its procedures for handling requests. In Canada, the Access to Information Act 1982, s.5(1) requires the designated Minister to publish at least once a year "a description of all classes of records under the control of each government institution in sufficient detail to facilitate the exercise of the right of access under [the] Act". The Minister must also prepare a bulletin at least twice a year, and both documents must be "made available throughout Canada in conformity with the principle that every person is entitled to reasonable access thereto". In New Zealand, the Official Information Act 1982, s.20 requires the Ministry of Justice to publish for each Department and organisation subject to the Act a general description of the categories of documents held by it, a description of the manuals containing policies by which decisions are made, as well as the officer to whom requests for information should be sent. Under s.21, a person is entitled to access to the latest edition of the publication, and there are various provisions giving a person an absolute right to particular documents. In Ireland, the Freedom of Information Act 1997, ss.15 and 16 require each public body to prepare and publish a "reference book" containing, amongst other things, a general description of the classes of records held by it, giving such particulars as are reasonably necessary to facilitate the

that publication scheme, a public authority must specify the classes of information that it publishes or intends to publish, the manner in which it publishes each class of information, and state whether the material is available to the public free-of-charge or on payment.[2] The publication scheme is not intended to be a list of information held by the authority.[3] The rationale for the scheme is twofold: to spare a public authority from having to deal with conventional requests under the Act which may be anticipated will be sought; and to encourage a culture of openness within public authorities:[4]

> "The Freedom of Information Act must be a catalyst for changes in the way that public authorities approach openness. Experience overseas consistently shows the importance of changing the culture through requiring active disclosure, so that public authorities get used to making information publicly available in the course of their activities. This helps ensure that FOI does not simply become a potentially confrontational arrangement under which nothing is released unless someone has specifically asked for it. We believe it is important that further impetus is given to the pro-active release of information. So, the Act will impose duties upon public authorities to make certain information publicly available, as a matter of course."[5]

There is a particular incentive for authorities to publish information under a publication scheme, as it grounds an absolute exemption under Pt II of the Act[6] or, in the case of information intended to be published, a qualified exemption.[7]

Duties on public authorities

10–002 The publication scheme requirement comprehends three discrete duties upon a public authority:

(1) to adopt and maintain a publication that is approved by the Information Commissioner;

exercise of the right of access as well as the rules, procedures, etc. used by the body for the purposes of any enactment or scheme administered by it.

[2] Freedom of Information Act 2000, s.19(2); Freedom of Information (Scotland) Act 2002, s.23(2).

[3] House of Commons, *Public Administration—Third Report* (Cm. 4355), July 29, 1999, Annex 6, para.18.

[4] *Hansard*, HL, Vol.612, April 20, 2000, col.826 by the Minister of State, Cabinet Office (Lord Falconer).

[5] White Paper, *Cabinet Office Your Right to Know—The Government's Proposals for a FOI Act* (Cm. 3818), December 11, 1997, paras 2.17–2.18.

[6] Freedom of Information Act 2000, s.21(1); Freedom of Information (Scotland) Act 2002, s.25(1).

[7] Freedom of Information Act 2000, s.22(1); Freedom of Information (Scotland) Act 2002, s.27(1).

(2) to publish information in accordance with its publication scheme; and
(3) from time to time to review that publication scheme.[8]

A public authority can comply with the first of these either by creating and adopting its own bespoke scheme or by using a model publication scheme prepared or approved by the Information Commissioner. The timetable for introducing publications schemes is as follows:[9]

(1) Central government (except the Crown Prosecution Service and the Serious Fraud Office), Parliament, the National Assembly for Wales and some non-departmental public bodies:[10] November 30, 2002.
(2) Local government (except police authorities): February 28, 2003.
(3) Police, police authorities, the Crown Prosecution Service, the Serious Fraud Office and the armed forces: June 30, 2003.
(4) Health service: October 30, 2003.
(5) Schools, universities, remaining non-departmental public bodies and publicly owned companies: February 29, 2004
(6) Other public authorities: June 30, 2004.

In Scotland, the deadlines are as follows:[11]

(7) The Scottish Ministers, the Scottish Parliament, the Scottish Parliamentary Corporate Body, non-ministerial office holders in the Scottish Administration, local government and the police: June 1, 2004.
(8) Health service and education: September 1, 2004.
(9) Other public authorities: November 30, 2004.

Public authorities in Northern Ireland are required to apply publication schemes at the same time as their counterparts in England and Wales, unless alternative arrangements are made: the matter is one for discussion with the Northern Ireland Assembly.[12]

[8] Freedom of Information Act 2000, s.19(1); Freedom of Information (Scotland) Act 2002, s.23(1).
[9] The timetable was announced by the Lord Chancellor to the House of Lords and is referred to in his Annual Report on proposals for bringing fully into force those provisions of the Freedom of Information Act 2000 which are not yet fully in force (HC 367, November 2001). Precise details of the timetable, including the deadlines by which schemes must be submitted to the Commissioner for approval, are available on the Commissioner's website at *www.dataprotection.gov.uk*.
[10] Those subject to the 1994 Code of Practice on Access to Government Information.
[11] Scottish Information Commissioner website at *www.itspublicknowledge.info*.
[12] See the Lord Chancellor's Annual report on proposals for bringing fully into force those provisions of the Freedom of Information Act 2000 which are not yet fully in force (HC 367, November 2001). The report was presented to Parliament by the Lord Chancellor pursuant to the Freedom of Information Act 2000, s.87(5).

Model publication schemes

10–003 In order to accommodate the large and diverse number of public authorities which are subject to the legislative regime, the Freedom of Information Act 2000 has provided for the Information Commissioner to approve model publication schemes for public authorities falling within particular classes.[13] These model schemes may be prepared by the Commissioner or by any other person.[14] If a public authority falls within the class to which an approved model scheme relates, it can adopt that scheme. If it does so without modification, then no further approval of the Commissioner is necessary, so long as the model scheme remains approved.[15] A public authority may also choose to adopt an approved model scheme with modifications, in which case approval of the modifications is all that is required.[16] If any of the modifications are not approved, the Commissioner must give the public authority reasons for the refusal.[17] When giving approval to a model publication scheme, the Commissioner can provide that his approval is to expire at the end of a specified period.[18] The Commissioner may revoke his approval for a model publication scheme at any time, but must give six months' notice[19] and must also give reasons for the revocation.[20] If the Commissioner refuses to approve a proposed model publication scheme he must give reasons for the refusal.[21] A public authority which adopts a model scheme is still under a duty to maintain that scheme and to review it from time to time.[22] This means that when conducting its review, the authority must have regard to the same matters as an authority adopting its own bespoke scheme: namely, the public interest in (a) allowing public access to information held by it and (b) in the publication of reasons for decisions it makes.[23] Accordingly, the onus remains with an authority to satisfy itself that its scheme remains appropriate or to make whatever changes it considers necessary.

[13] Freedom of Information Act 2000, s.20(1); Freedom of Information Act (Scotland) 2002, s.24(1).
[14] *ibid.*
[15] Freedom of Information Act 2000, s. 20(2); Freedom of Information Act (Scotland) 2002, s. 24(2).
[16] *ibid.*
[17] Freedom of Information Act 2000, s.20(6); Freedom of Information Act (Scotland) 2002, s.24(4)(a)(ii).
[18] Freedom of Information Act 2000, s.20(3); Freedom of Information (Scotland) Act 2002, s.24(3).
[19] Freedom of Information Act 2000, s.20(4); Freedom of Information Act (Scotland) 2002, s.24(3)(b).
[20] Freedom of Information Act 2000, s.20(7); Freedom of Information Act (Scotland) 2002, s.24(4)(b).
[21] Freedom of Information Act 2000, s.20(5); Freedom of Information Act (Scotland) 2002, s.24(4)(a)(i).
[22] Freedom of Information Act 2000, s.19(1); Freedom of Information (Scotland) Act 2002, s.23(1).
[23] Freedom of Information Act 2000, s.19(3). The same principle applies in Scotland except that the matters to which it has to have regard are different: Freedom of Information (Scotland) Act 2002, s.23(3). See n.25 below.

Bespoke publication schemes

If a public authority does not wish to adopt a model scheme, it must develop its own bespoke scheme and submit that scheme to the Information Commissioner for approval. The requirements of a publication scheme are that it must: 10–004

(1) specify classes of information which the public authority publishes or intends to publish;
(2) specify the manner in which information of each class is, or is intended to be, published; and
(3) specify whether the material is, or is intended to be, available to the public free-of-charge or on payment.[24]

In adopting or reviewing a publication scheme, a public authority must have regard to the public interest in allowing public access to information held by the authority and in the publication of reasons for decisions made by the authority.[25] If the Commissioner refuses to approve a proposed model publication scheme he must give reasons for the refusal.[26] If the Commissioner gives approval to a publication scheme, he can provide that the approval is to expire at the end of a specified period.[27] Once it is approved, the public authority must publish its publication scheme, but can do so in whatever manner it thinks fit.[28] Approval for a publication scheme can be revoked by the Commissioner at any time, but he must give six months' notice[29] and must also give reasons for the revocation.[30] The Commissioner has published advice for public authorities on how to develop their own publication schemes.[31]

24 Freedom of Information Act 2000, s.19(2); Freedom of Information Act (Scotland) 2002, s.23(2).

25 Freedom of Information Act 2000, s.19(3). This is the only point where the Scottish Act differs. In adopting or reviewing its publication scheme a Scottish public authority must have regard to the public interest in: (a) allowing public access to information held by it and in particular to information which relates to the provision of services by it, the cost to it of providing them or the standards attained by services so provided or which consists of facts, or analyses, on the basis of which decisions of importance to the public have been made by it; and (b) the publication of reasons for decisions made by it: Freedom of Information Act (Scotland) 2002, s.23(3).

26 Freedom of Information Act 2000, s.19(7)(a); Freedom of Information Act (Scotland) 2002, s.23(6)(a).

27 Freedom of Information Act 2000, s.19(5); Freedom of Information Act (Scotland) 2002, s.23(5)(a).

28 Freedom of Information Act 2000, s.19(4); Freedom of Information Act (Scotland) 2002, s.23(4).

29 Freedom of Information Act 2000, s.19(6); Freedom of Information Act (Scotland) 2002, s.23(5)(b).

30 Freedom of Information Act 2000, s.19(7)(b); Freedom of Information Act (Scotland) 2002, s.23(6)(b).

31 Available on the Commissioner's website: at *www.dataprotection.gov.uk*.

Enforcing the publication scheme regime

10–005 The initial obligation upon public authorities is to adopt a publication scheme that has been approved by the Information Commissioner. If a public authority does not do this, it is in breach of its statutory duty and the Commissioner can serve an enforcement notice on the authority requiring it to remedy this.[32] Similarly, where a public authority has adopted a model publication scheme and the Commissioner considers that the authority does not fall within the class to which that model scheme relates, he can serve an enforcement notice.[33] The stated intention in relation to publication schemes was that the Information Commissioner would exercise an active supervisory role:

> "Authorities will not be able to get away with weak or self-serving publication schemes. They will all have to be approved by the Commissioner and she will ensure they are strong and meaningful."[34]

On this basis, once the Information Commissioner has concluded that there has been non-compliance with the statutory requirements, the Commissioner is not obliged to be deferential to the views of the public officer before exercising his powers of enforcement. Although the Commissioner can ensure that model codes he prepares are strong and meaningful, he has much less control over publication schemes prepared by others since he cannot rewrite them, only withhold approval.[35] Authorities have no statutory right of appeal against the refusal of the Commissioner to approve a publication scheme or a decision to revoke approval for a scheme. There is, therefore, a theoretical, if unseemly, right in a public authority to seek judicial review of the Information Commissioner's refusal of approval. Once a scheme is approved, the authority is required to publish it in such manner as it thinks fit.[36] The government rejected proposed amendments that would have required authorities to publish their publication schemes in certain forms and free-of-charge, stating as follows:

> "The Government are confident that public authorities will not wish to embarrass themselves by making people pay unreasonably for copies of their publication schemes. We have made it clear all along that we expect public authorities to bear most of the additional cost of freedom of

[32] Under the Freedom of Information Act 2000, s.52(1) or the Freedom of Information (Scotland) Act 2002, s.51(1). See Freedom of Information Act 2000, s.52 and Freedom of Information (Scotland) Act 2002, s.52 discussed in paras 28–011 and 28–014 below.

[33] On the basis that the authority has not adopted a publication scheme in accordance with the statutory provisions and has therefore failed to comply with one of the requirements of Pt I of the Act.

[34] *Hansard*, HL, Vol.612, April 20, 2000, col.826 by the Minister of State, Cabinet Office (Lord Falconer).

[35] House of Commons, *Public Administration—Third Report* (Cm. 4355), July 29, 1999, Annex 6, para.21.

[36] Freedom of Information Act 2000, s.19(4); Freedom of Information (Scotland) Act 2002, s.23(4).

information . . . . All publication schemes will have to have the approval of the information commissioner. She is bound to question any unreasonable proposals with regard to charging. She will also be best placed to judge what is the most appropriate form for the publication of these schemes in individual cases . . . . The Bill offers the best way of ensuring that public authorities will publish their schemes in the manner most appropriate in the circumstances and that they will make them available either free or at minimal cost . . . . The commissioner will not have the power to approve the manner of the publication of the scheme, but she can issue guidance as to how it is done. In any event, we believe that it is in the interests of the authority for the public body to make its scheme known widely, as the aim of such schemes is to minimise the burden on an authority from individual requests for information that it makes available generally."[37]

The authority's only obligation is to comply with the statute: that is, to publish its publication scheme in whatever manner it thinks fit, which can only be supervised by judicial review. Nevertheless, given that the real burden lies in the preparation rather than in the publishing (particularly on the internet) of a publication scheme, given the public interest articulated in s.19(3) of the Act, and given the absence of any provision enabling the imposition of a charge for providing it, it is suggested that a decision by a public authority to charge a person for access to its publications scheme would leave it exposed to such a challenge. Finally, authorities are under a statutory duty to publish information in accordance with their publication scheme.[38] If an authority fails or refuses to do this, the Commissioner can issue an enforcement notice.[39] In these circumstances it would be open to make an application for a conventional request under the Act and the exemptions otherwise open to the public authority on the basis of the information being otherwise available will not be open to the public authority.[40]

---

[37] *Hansard*, HL, Vol.619, November 14, 2000, cols 199–200 (Lord Bach).

[38] Freedom of Information Act 2000, s.19(1)(b), Freedom of Information (Scotland) Act 2002, s.23(1)(b).

[39] On the basis that a request for information has not been dealt with in accordance with Pt I of the Act. For enforcement notices, see Freedom of Information Act 2000, s.52 and Freedom of Information (Scotland) Act 2002, s.52 discussed in paras 28–011 and 28–014 below.

[40] Freedom of Information Act 2000, ss.21 and 22; Freedom of Information (Scotland) Act 2002, ss.25 and 27.

CHAPTER 11

The Request and the Response

1. THE REQUEST FOR INFORMATION

Introduction

11–001 Under the Freedom of Information Act 2000, for a person to exercise his right to information held by a public authority, he must first make a "request for information".[1] A "request for information" is one that:

— is made in writing;[2]
— states the name of the applicant;
— states an address for correspondence; and
— describes the information requested.[3]

For an individual to exercise his corresponding right under the Data Protection Act 1998, all that is required is that he make a request in writing.[4] Quite apart from meeting the formal requirements of each Act, the terms of a request are fundamentally important to the whole disclosure exercise. An applicant's description of the information sought will impinge upon the efficacy of the request, upon the cost of compliance, upon the public authority's obligation to comply with the request on the grounds of particularity, repetitiveness, etc. as well as, of course, upon the information yielded and, thereafter, the applicable exemptions. It is suggested that, save for routine requests, it will generally be in the interests of both the applicant and the public authority for a request to describe the information sought by reference to one or more of the following attributes:

(a) the date or period over which the information was created or first held by the public authority;
(b) the subject matter of the information, with as much precision as possible;
(c) the types of information sought (*e.g.* correspondence, reports, internal documents and so forth);
(d) the authorship or provenance of the information, if needs be by class;
(e) the intended recipient of the information; and

---

1 Freedom of Information Act 2000, s.1(1). The Freedom of Information (Scotland) Act 2002 does not invoke the concept of a defined "request for information" but gives an entitlement to "a person who requests information": Freedom of Information (Scotland) Act 2002, s.1(1). Section 8(1) of the Scottish Act provides that a reference in the Act to "requesting" information is a reference to a request which, save for the requirement that it be in writing, has the same characteristics as a "request for information".

2 "Writing" includes other modes of representing or reproducing words in a visible form: Interpretation Act 1978, s.5 and Sch.1.

3 Freedom of Information Act 2000, s.8(1).

4 Data Protection Act 1998, s.7(2)(a). However, in certain circumstances a data controller need not comply with a request unless the individual provides certain information: see para.11–005 below.

(f) the manner in which the information is recorded (*e.g.* written or stored on a computer, etc.).

This is not to say that an applicant should strive to guess precisely what information is held by a public authority: it is simply a matter of reflecting upon the attributes of the information that is being sought and attempting, so far as is reasonably practicable, to articulate those attributes. Whilst an applicant's motives for requesting information are irrelevant to a request,[5] where an applicant anticipates that some or all of the information may fall within a qualified exemption, it may be in the applicant's interests to set out in the request any facts and matters which may relate to the public interest in disclosing the information.[6] Finally, there will be circumstances in which it will be mutually advantageous for an applicant to take a staged approach to the obtaining of information from a public authority. For example, a properly-drawn first request may be designed to elicit information that will assist in the subsequent identification of the information sought to be disclosed.[7]

Request must be in writing

A request made under the Freedom of Information Act 2000 (or of a data con- 11–002
troller under the Data Protection Act 1998) must be made in writing.[8] A request is deemed to have been made in writing where it has been transmitted by electronic means, it has been received in legible form and it is capable of being used for subsequent reference.[9] Accordingly, a request made by way of a facsimile transmission or e-mail should qualify as a request made in writing.

Request made orally

The requirement that a request be made in writing means that an oral request 11–003
will not be sufficient to give rise to an obligation on a public authority or a data

5 See para.15–009 below.

6 See paras 15–006, 15–007 and 15–011 below.

7 For example, a request for any list (howsoever described) of files relating to a particular topic may, when answered, help the applicant to identify from which of those files a second request for information should be answered. If the second request does not yield the information expected, the applicant can make a third request identifying other files from the list, and so on. Although this may provoke a claim of "fishing," this is to be preferred to "trawling". The *Code of Practice on the Discharge of the Functions of Public Authorities under Part I of the Freedom of Information Act 2000*, para.10, gives support to this sort of approach.

8 Freedom of Information Act 2000, s.8(1)(a); Data Protection Act 1998, s.7(2)(a). The Freedom of Information (Scotland) Act 2002 provides that although such a request may be made in writing, it may also be made in another form which has some permanency: see para.11–004 below.

9 Freedom of Information Act 2000, s.8(2); Freedom of Information (Scotland) Act 2002, s.8(2); Data Protection Act 1998, s.64(2).

controller to communicate information.[10] However, on the basis that an individual who makes a request orally should be regarded as someone who is proposing to make a request for information and that it would normally be reasonable to expect a public authority to inform such an individual of the formal requirements of a request for information, in most such cases a public authority's duty to provide advice and assistance[11] will require it to advise the individual that his request should be made in writing. The *Code of Practice* suggests that where a person is unable to put his request in writing, the public authority should provide appropriate assistance to enable that person to make a request for information, such as pointing them towards another person who could assist him (such as a Citizen's Advice Bureau) or by taking a note of the person's request and then sending it to him for confirmation (in which case receipt of the confirmed note would constitute a written request).[12]

Request in other permanent form

11–004 In Scotland, a request need not be made in writing but may be made in another form which, by reason of it having some permanency, is capable of being used for subsequent reference.[13] The Freedom of Information (Scotland) Act 2002 cites recordings made on audio or video tape as specific examples of such a form,[14] and presumably a request consisting of a word-processor document recorded onto a floppy disc or a CD-ROM would also suffice.

Request must state name of the applicant

11–005 A request made under the Freedom of Information Act 2000 or the Freedom of Information (Scotland) Act 2002 must state the name of the applicant.[15] In this context, "the applicant" is the person who is making the request.[16] As noted

[10] In Scotland, an oral request recorded onto audio tape is likely to be sufficient: see para.11–004 below.

[11] As to the duty to provide advice and assistance, see Ch.8.

[12] *Code of Practice on the Discharge of Public Authorities' Functions under Part I of the Freedom of Information Act 2000*, para.8. This was anticipated by the House of Commons' Public Administration Committee's *Third Report* (Cm.4355), July 29, 1999, Annex 6, para.13.

[13] Freedom of Information (Scotland) Act 2002, s.8(1)(a).

[14] *ibid*. Quite whether and why anyone would wish to make a request by video-tape remains to be seen.

[15] Freedom of Information Act 2000, s.8(1)(b); Freedom of Information (Scotland) Act 2002, s.8(1)(b).

[16] Freedom of Information Act 2000, s.84; Freedom of Information (Scotland) Act 2002, s.1(2). In the House of Lords debate on this provision, it was suggested by the Parliamentary Under-Secretary of State for the Home Office that s.8(1)(b) of the Freedom of Information Act 2000 did not require an applicant to give his real name (*Hansard*, HL, Vol.619, November 14, 2000, col.184). However, the requirement in s.8(1)(b) to give *the* name *of* the applicant rather than *a* name *for* the applicant suggests the contrary.

elsewhere,[17] the identity of the applicant will only be relevant to a public authority's obligation to communicate information in limited circumstances.[18] The fact that "any person" may make a request for information means that there is no reason why one individual cannot apply on behalf of another,[19] there is no need for an applicant to have any particular standing to seek information and an applicant need not be a United Kingdom national or resident.[20] Although there is no requirement on a person making a request under the Data Protection Act 1998 to provide his name, a data controller is not obliged to comply with a request unless he is supplied with such information as he reasonably requires in order to satisfy himself as to the identity of the person making the request.[21] Given that the right bestowed by that Act is to information constituting personal data of which the applicant is the data subject and given the proscriptions against unauthorised processing of data,[22] it would be reasonable for a data controller to require basic confirmation of identity before satisfying himself as to identity.

Request must state address for correspondence

A request made under the Freedom of Information Act 2000 or the Freedom of Information (Scotland) Act 2002 must state an address for correspondence.[23] There is no such requirement under the Data Protection Act 1998. Neither the Freedom of Information Act 2000 nor the Freedom of Information (Scotland) Act 2002 specifies what is meant by "an address for correspondence". In particular, it is not specified whether, in the light of the fact that a request may be made by electronic means,[24] the provision of an electronic address (such as an email address or a fax number) would be sufficient to meet the requirements of the Acts. During debate on the Bill the view expressed was that the provision of an electronic address would not be sufficient.[25] The stated fear was that practical difficulties might ensue if a public authority were obliged to communicate a large volume of information which was recorded in documentary form where **11–006**

[17] See paras 12–009 and 15–009 below.

[18] For example, in the case of vexatious or repeated requests (see para.12–008 below) or if a request relates to information which is personal data (see para.15–009 below).

[19] As was recognised in the House of Commons' Public Administration Committee's *Third Report* (Cm. 4355), July 29, 1999, Annex 6, para.14.

[20] As is recognised in the Explanatory Notes to the Freedom of Information Act 2000, para.49. As to applications made by persons outside the United Kingdom, see paras 7–011 to 7–015 above.

[21] Data Protection Act 1998, s.7(3).

[22] Data Protection Act 1998, s.13(1) and Pt V. "Processing" includes disclosure: Data Protection Act 1998, s.1(1).

[23] Freedom of Information Act 2000, s.8(1)(b); Freedom of Information (Scotland) Act 2002, s.8(1)(b).

[24] See para.11–002 above.

[25] *Hansard*, HL, Vol.619, November 14, 2000, col.184.

the public authority had only been provided with an electronic address.[26] In any event, an individual who makes a request which includes only an electronic address should at the very least be regarded as someone who is proposing to make a request for information and, as it would normally be reasonable to expect a public authority to inform such an individual of the formal requirements of a request for information, a public authority's duty to provide advice and assistance[27] will generally require it to advise the individual that his request should include a postal address.

Request must describe information requested

11–007 A request for information must describe the information requested.[28] There is no formal obligation on an applicant to describe the information sought in a particular way and, in particular, an applicant is not required to describe a particular record.[29] It is questionable whether it would be sufficient for an applicant to request a random sample of information, as this does not identify the information requested but requires the intercession of an act of selection by the public authority.[30] Where a request does not describe the information requested with sufficient particularity, the recipient public authority ought to consider whether it should advise or assist the applicant in relation to the proper particularisation of his request or whether it should inform the applicant that it requires further particulars,[31] or both. The emphasis in the Code of Practice is on the provision of assistance and it suggests possible examples of such assistance as being the provision of an outline of the different types of information which might meet the terms of the request as made, the provision of detailed catalogues or indexes to help the applicant ascertain the nature of the information held by the public authority, or the provision of a general response setting out options for further information which could be provided.[32] Although there is no such requirement under the Data Protection Act 1998, in certain circumstances a data controller is not obliged to comply with a request if he reasonably

[26] As to the means by which information should be communicated, see paras 11–036 to 11–041 below. In fact there may be instances in which electronic communication is easier. In the USA, agencies establish "electronic reading rooms" to deal with disclosure of policy statements, staff manuals, records previously processed for disclosure and other documents routinely sought: see para.2–004 above.

[27] As to the duty to provide advice and assistance, see para.11–010 below.

[28] Freedom of Information Act 2000, s.8(1)(c); Freedom of Information (Scotland) Act 2002, s.8(1)(c).

[29] As is recognised in the Explanatory Notes to the Freedom of Information Act 2000, para.23. But see para.11–001 above.

[30] See *Redfern v University of Canberra* (1995) 38 A.L.D. 457 in relation to the comparable s.15(2)(b) of the Freedom of Information Act 1982 (Cth of Australia).

[31] As to requiring particulars in order to identify and locate requested information, see paras 11–011 to 11–012 below.

[32] *Code of Practice on the Discharge of Public Authorities' Functions under Part I of the Freedom of Information Act 2000*, para.10.

requires further information in order to locate the information sought by the person making the request.[33]

Matters not required

There is no requirement in the Freedom of Information Act 2000 for a request for information to make reference to the fact that it is being made under the Act. Nevertheless, as a public authority has a duty to provide advice and assistance to those who make requests under the Act, it is desirable that a request for information states that it is being made under the Freedom of Information Act 2000. Further, as there is no requirement in the Act that a request for information be sent to a particular individual or department within a public authority, it will be necessary for public authorities to ensure that all staff who might receive such requests are aware of the appropriate procedures for dealing with them.[34] 11–008

Treatment of a request for information under the Data Protection Act 1998

Where a request for information is made under any of paras (a), (b) or (c) of s.7(1) of the Data Protection Act 1998, it is to be treated as also extending to the other two paragraphs of those three.[35] Any such request will only be treated as extending to information under para.(d) of s.7(1) where the request shows an express intention that it should do so.[36] Conversely, unless a request for information made under s.7(1)(d) of the Data Protection Act 1998 shows an express intention that it should extend to information under any of the other three paragraphs in s.7(1), then it is not to be treated as extending to information under any of those other paragraphs.[37] 11–009

Duty to provide advice and assistance

A public authority has a duty to provide advice and assistance, so far as it is reasonable to expect it to do so, to persons who have made or who propose to make requests for information to it pursuant to the Freedom of Information Acts.[38] 11–010

[33] Data Protection Act 1998, s.7(3). As to requesting particulars under the Data Protection Act 1998, see para.11–013 below.
[34] This is recommended by para.14 of the foreword to the *Code of Practice on the Discharge of Public Authorities' Functions under Part I of the Freedom of Information Act 2000*.
[35] Data Protection (Subject Access) (Fees and Miscellaneous Provisions) Regulations 2000 (SI 2000/191), r.2(1).
[36] *ibid.*, r.2(2).
[37] *ibid.*, r.2(3).
[38] Freedom of Information Act 2000, s.16(1); Freedom of Information (Scotland) Act 2002, s.15(1). See generally Ch.8.

Compliance with the relevant provisions of the Code of Practice[39] is deemed to be compliance with the duty to provide advice and assistance.[40] The terms of the Code of Practice indicate that there is a strong emphasis on public authorities providing advice and assistance to applicants and potential applicants and that public authorities will be discouraged from relying upon formal or procedural defects in would-be requests for information to avoid having to comply with requests which would otherwise have been valid requests for information under the Freedom of Information Act 2000.

2. PARTICULARISING THE REQUEST

Introduction

11–011 Although a request for information under the Freedom of Information Act 2000 or the Freedom of Information (Scotland) Act 2002 must describe the information requested,[41] provision is made under these Acts, and also under the Data Protection Act 1998, for the situation where an applicant does not provide sufficient particulars of the information sought to enable the public authority to identify and locate that information.[42]

Insufficient particularity under the Freedom of Information Acts

11–012 Under the Freedom of Information Act 2000, where a public authority reasonably requires further particulars in order to identify and locate the information requested, then, as long as it has informed the applicant of that requirement, the public authority is not obliged to provide the information requested unless it is furnished with the further particulars that it requires to identify and locate that information.[43] In such a case, the time allowed for the public authority to comply with the request for information only starts to run from the date on which it receives the further particulars.[44] A public authority may only seek further particulars which are relevant to identifying the information sought by the applicant and not, for example, to seek information which is relevant to the

---

[39] As to the *Code of Practice on the Discharge of Public Authorities' Functions under Part I of the Freedom of Information Act 2000*, see Ch.9 above.

[40] Freedom of Information Act 2000, s.16(2); Freedom of Information (Scotland) Act 2002, s.15(2).

[41] As to the requirement that a request for information must describe the information requested, see para.11–007 above.

[42] The original version of s.1(3) of the Freedom of Information Act 2000 did not feature the requirement that a public authority must inform an applicant that it requires further particulars before it is absolved of its obligations under s.1(1): Freedom of Information Bill 1999, cl.8(3).

[43] Freedom of Information Act 2000, s.1(3); Freedom of Information (Scotland) Act 2002, s.1(3).

[44] As to the time for compliance generally, see para.11–022 below.

applicant or his motives.[45] Further, a public authority may not seek further particulars which an applicant could not reasonably be expected to have, such as a file number or the exact location of the information sought.[46]

Insufficient particularity under the Data Protection Act 1998

Where a data controller reasonably requires further particulars in order to satisfy himself as to the identity of the person making a request and to locate the information which that person seeks and has informed that person of that requirement, the data controller is not obliged to comply with the request unless it is supplied with those further particulars.[47] The two reasons for requiring further information set out in s.7(3)(a) of the Data Protection Act 1998 need to be read disjunctively in order to give proper effect to that section. Thus a data controller may avail himself of the provisions of s.7(3) if either he requires further particulars in order to satisfy himself as to the identity of the person making the request or he requires further particulars in order to locate the information which that person seeks. 11–013

3. FEES

Introduction

Both the Freedom of Information Act 2000 and the Freedom of Information (Scotland) Act 2002 establish a framework for the charging of fees by any public authority that receives a request for information.[48] Neither Act obliges a public authority to charge fees. In some cases, a public authority will have had the practice of voluntarily providing information pursuant to informal requests: there is nothing in the Freedom of Information Act 2000 to prevent such a practice continuing.[49] Nevertheless, a public authority in exercising its discretion to charge a fee must do so in accordance with normal public law principles. Thus, improper discrimination between different types of requests or a lack of consistency in approach in relation to the imposition of fees may be unlawful. The level of fee is to be determined in accordance with regulations to be made under 11–014

[45] *Code of Practice on the Discharge of Public Authorities' Functions under Part I of the Freedom of Information Act 2000*, para.9. See also the House of Commons' Public Administration Committee's *Third Report* (Cm. 4355), July 29, 1999, Annex 6, para.25. As to the irrelevancy of motives, see para.7–015 above.

[46] *Code of Practice on the Discharge of Public Authorities' Functions under Part I of the Freedom of Information Act 2000*, para.11. See also the House of Commons' Public Administration Committee's *Third Report* (Cm.4355), July 29, 1999, Annex 6, para.25.

[47] Data Protection Act 1998, s.7(3).

[48] Freedom of Information Act 2000, s.9; Freedom of Information (Scotland) Act 2002, s.9.

[49] See paras 14–006 to 14–013 below.

the Acts.[50] To date no such regulations have been made, although draft Freedom of Information (Fees and Appropriate Limit) Regulations have been published. Under the Data Protection Act 1998, except in prescribed cases, a data controller is not required to supply any information unless he has received such fee as he may require (subject to a prescribed maximum).[51]

Fees notice

11–015 Where a public authority receives a request for information, it may, within the period of time allowed for it to comply with its duties under s.1(1) of the Freedom of Information Act 2000, give the applicant a fees notice. A fees notice is a notice in writing which states that a fee of the amount stated in the notice is to be charged by the public authority for complying with its duties under s.1(1).[52] Section 9 gives a public authority a "time window" within which to give an applicant a fees notice. It is to be noted that under s.9(1) the fee that may be charged is one "for complying with s.1(1)"; in other words, for complying with the duty to communicate and with the duty to confirm or deny. The former duty does not crystallise until such time as the information answering the terms of a request has been located and it has been established that the information is not exempt information either by virtue of an absolute exemption or by virtue of a qualified exemption with the public interest being against disclosure.[53] Thus, if there is a decision to disclose certain information, the fee may only relate to the communication of that information.[54] If and to the extent that there is a decision to inform the applicant that the public authority holds information of the description specified in the request but not to disclose that information, the fee may only relate to the cost to the public authority of so informing the applicant.

Fees notice in Scotland

11–016 In Scotland, a fees notice must also comply with the formal requirements prescribed by s.19 of the Freedom of Information (Scotland) Act 2002.[55] A fees notice in Scotland must therefore also contain particulars of the procedure

[50] Freedom of Information Act 2000, s.9(3); Freedom of Information (Scotland) Act 2002, s.9(4). This restriction does not apply where provision is made by or under another enactment for the charging of a fee by a public authority for the disclosure of the information (Freedom of Information Act 2000, s.9(5); Freedom of Information (Scotland) Act 2002, s.9(7)).

[51] Data Protection Act 1998, s.7(2)(b). Fees under the Data Protection Act 1998 are considered at para.4–038 above.

[52] Freedom of Information Act 2000, s.9(1); Freedom of Information (Scotland) Act 2002, s.9(1).

[53] See Freedom of Information Act 2000, s.2(2); Freedom of Information (Scotland) Act 2002, s.2(1).

[54] Which will be taken to be compliance with the duty to confirm or deny: Freedom of Information Act 2000, s.1(5).

[55] Freedom of Information (Scotland) Act 2002, s.9(2).

provided by the public authority for dealing with complaints about the handling by it of requests for information[56] and about the rights of the applicant to apply for a review of the public authority's actions and to apply to the Commissioner for a decision as to whether the public authority has acted in accordance with Pt I of the Act.[57]

Determination of fees

Unless provision is made by or under some other enactment for the charging of fees by a public authority for the disclosure of information,[58] then any fee must be determined in accordance with the relevant regulations.[59] The fees regime thus gives a public authority a discretion whether to give an applicant a fees notice. But if the public authority decides to give a fees notice, the public authority has no discretion in relation to the application of the fees regulations, the calculation of the fee or the time allowed for payment of the fee, unless permitted by the regulations. The Act provides that the regulations may make provision that a fee is not payable in particular cases,[60] that a fee is to be calculated in a particular manner[61] and that a fee is not to exceed a particular maximum.[62] Although to date no such regulations have been made, the draft Freedom of Information (Fees and Appropriate Limit) Regulations indicate that the maximum fee which may be charged by a public authority shall not exceed the sum of the 10 per cent of the "prescribed costs" "disbursements" and that would be incurred by the public authority in complying with the request for information to which the fee relates.[63] 11–017

Prescribed costs

The draft Freedom of Information (Fees and Appropriate Limit) Regulations indicate that the "prescribed costs" are likely to be defined as any costs which would reasonably be incurred by the public authority in determining whether it holds information of the description specified in the request for information, in 11–018

56 Freedom of Information (Scotland) Act 2002, s.19(a).
57 *ibid.*, s.19(b).
58 Freedom of Information Act 2000, s.9(3) and (5); Freedom of Information (Scotland) Act 2002, s.9(4) and (7).
59 Freedom of Information Act 2000, s.9(3); Freedom of Information (Scotland) Act 2002, s.9(4).
60 Freedom of Information Act 2000, s.9(4)(a); Freedom of Information (Scotland) Act 2002, s.9(5)(c).
61 Freedom of Information Act 2000, s.9(4)(c); Freedom of Information (Scotland) Act 2002, s.9(5)(b).
62 Freedom of Information Act 2000, s.9(4)(b); Freedom of Information (Scotland) Act 2002, s.9(5)(a).
63 Draft Freedom of Information (Fees and Appropriate Limit) Regulations, r.4. As to prescribed costs, see para.11–018. As to disbursements, see para.11–019 below.

locating and retrieving any such information and in giving effect to any preference expressed by the applicant as to the means of communication of such information.[64] Although prescribed costs are likely to include the costs of associated staff time, they are unlikely to include the cost of any staff time incurred in determining whether the public authority is obliged to comply with the request for information.[65] Other than in relation to routine requests, this will exclude what may prove to be the most time-consuming part of the exercise—ascertaining whether the information is exempt information and, if so, the public interest balancing exercise. In the Freedom of Information (Fees and Appropriate Limit) Regulations any reference to prescribed costs includes a reference to such costs as the public authority reasonably estimates would be incurred in relation to the request.[66]

Disbursements

11–019 The draft Freedom of Information (Fees and Appropriate Limit) Regulations indicate that the disbursements are likely to be defined as any costs directly and reasonably incurred by a public authority in informing the applicant whether it holds information of the description specified in the request and in communicating any such information to him.[67] As such, disbursements are likely to include the cost of any photocopying or the cost of a floppy disk where the information is provided in that format. In the Freedom of Information (Fees and Appropriate Limit) Regulations any reference to disbursements includes a reference to such disbursements as the public authority reasonably estimates would be incurred in relation to the request.[68]

Effect of fees notice

11–020 Where a public authority gives a fees notice to an applicant, it is not required to comply with s.1(1) of the Freedom of Information Act 2000 unless the applicant pays the fee within the period of three months beginning with the day on which the fees notice is given to the applicant.[69] However, if an applicant indicates that

---

[64] Draft Freedom of Information (Fees and Appropriate Limit) Regulations, r.2(1). This is possibly *ultra vires* the Act: see para.11–015 above.

[65] Draft Freedom of Information (Fees and Appropriate Limit) Regulations, r.2(1).

[66] *ibid.*

[67] *ibid.* To the extent that the regulations purport to permit charging for matters that merely anticipate "the duty to communicate" this is possibly *ultra vires* the Act: see para.11–015 above.

[68] *ibid.*

[69] Freedom of Information Act 2000, s.9(2); Freedom of Information (Scotland) Act 2002, s.9(3). This is a similar formulation to that used in other comparable legislation, such as s.111(2)(a) of the Employment Rights Act 1996. It is suggested that a similar approach to the calculation of the relevant period should be adopted as is adopted under that Act. This would mean that the

he is not prepared to pay the fee, the public authority should consider whether it can provide any of the information free of charge.[70] Where a fees notice has been given to an applicant and he has paid the fee within the requisite period, the time taken for the applicant to pay the fee is to be discounted when calculating the date on which the public authority is required to comply with s.1(1).[71] The combined effect of the provisions is to make it prudent for a public authority to serve a fees notice as soon as possible after receipt of a request. In this way a public authority may lessen the possibility of abortive costs where an applicant indicates that he is not prepared to pay.

Fees in cases where cost of compliance is excessive

In cases where a public authority is not obliged to comply with a request for information because the cost of complying with it is deemed to be excessive,[72] where the communication of the information is not otherwise required by law, and where no provision is made by or under another enactment for the charging of fees, if the public authority nevertheless decides to communicate the information it may charge a fee for doing so.[73] The fee is to be determined by the public authority in accordance with regulations.[74] To date no such regulations have been made. The draft Freedom of Information (Fees and Appropriate Limit) Regulations indicate that the maximum fee which may be charged is likely to be the sum of 10 per cent of the first £550 of prescribed costs,[75] any prescribed costs over £550 and the disbursements.[76] In such a case, it will be good practice for the public authority to provide an indication of what information could be provided within the costs ceiling.[77] 11–021

correct method for determining the final day of the period is to take the day and the date immediately before the date on which the fees notice was given to the applicant and then go forward three months: *Pruden v Cunard Ellerman Ltd* [1993] I.R.L.R. 317, EAT.

70 *Code of Practice on the Discharge of Public Authorities' Functions under Part I of the Freedom of Information Act 2000*, para.13.

71 Freedom of Information Act 2000, s.10(2); Freedom of Information (Scotland) Act, s.10(3).

72 As to the situation where the cost of complying with a request for information would be excessive, see paras 12–001 to 12–007 paras.

73 Freedom of Information Act 2000, s.13(1) and (3); Freedom of Information (Scotland) Act 2002, s.13(1) and (4).

74 Freedom of Information Act 2000, s.13(1); Freedom of Information (Scotland) Act 2002, s.13(1).

75 As to prescribed costs, see para.11–018 above.

76 Draft Freedom of Information (Fees and Appropriate Limit) Regulations, r.5. As to disbursements, see para.11–019 above.

77 *Code of Practice on the Discharge of Public Authorities' Functions under Part I of the Freedom of Information Act 2000*, para.14.

4. TIME FOR COMPLIANCE

Introduction

11–022 A public authority is required to comply with a request for information promptly and in any event not later than the twentieth working day following the "date of receipt".[78] The date of receipt is generally the date on which the public authority receives the request.[79] The date of receipt is effectively postponed in cases where a public authority has sought further particulars of a request.[80] Further, the period for compliance is in effect extended where a public authority has given a fees notice to an applicant.[81] Where a request is made under the Data Protection Act 1998, a data controller is required to comply with a request promptly and in any event before the end of the period which has been prescribed by the relevant regulations.[82]

Legislative history

11–023 The provisions of the Freedom of Information Act 2000 relating to time for compliance[83] are largely the same as those proposed in the Freedom of Information Bill 1999,[84] save in two important respects. First, the original outer time-limit was 40 days rather than 20 working days.[85] The 20th working-day time-limit was introduced in response to suggestions at the Committee stages that as the 40–day time-limit had originated in the Data Protection Act 1984, when information processing technology was less advanced that it is today and as the Code of Practice on Access to Government Information had suggested a time-limit of 20 days, a time-limit of 40 days was overly generous.[86] Secondly, the Freedom of Information Bill did not provide for public authorities to have an additional amount of time to conduct the public interest balancing exercise which is now required where information is subject to a qualified exemption. The introduction of a provision to this effect was the cause of some controversy,

[78] Freedom of Information Act 2000, s.10(1). The Freedom of Information (Scotland) Act 2002, s.10(1) does not invoke a defined concept of "date of receipt", but its effect is the same.

[79] Freedom of Information Act 2000, s.10(6); Freedom of Information (Scotland) Act 2002, s.10(1)(a).

[80] Freedom of Information Act 2000, ss.1(3) and 10(6); Freedom of Information (Scotland) Act 2002, ss.1(3) and 10(1)(b).

[81] Freedom of Information Act 2000, s.10(2); Freedom of Information (Scotland) Act 2002, s.10(3).

[82] Data Protection Act 1998, s.7(8). See para.4–042 above.

[83] Freedom of Information Act 2000, s.10.

[84] Freedom of Information Bill 1999, cl.10.

[85] *ibid.*, cl.10(1).

[86] See the House of Commons' Select Committee on Public Administration, *Fifth Special Report*, October 27, 1999, Appendix. A shortening of the time-limit was also recommended by the House of Lords Select Committee on the Draft Freedom of Information Bill: House of Lords' Select Committee on the Draft Freedom of Information Bill, *First Report*, July 29, 1999, para.56.

as it was feared that the absence of a finite time-limit would result in procrastination on the part of public authorities.[87]

Promptness

The primary obligation on a public authority is that it must promptly comply with s.1(1) of the Act.[88] Accordingly, the requirement that a public authority comply in any event not later than the twentieth working day following the date of receipt is simply an outer, or "long-stop", time-limit:[89] the fact that a public authority complies within 20 working days will not necessarily mean that it has complied promptly.[90] It is implicit[91] in the dual requirement that there will be instances in which compliance in 20 or fewer working days will not constitute prompt compliance. There is no provision in the Freedom of Information Act 2000 to deal with the situation where a request for information is particularly urgent.[92] However, the urgency or otherwise of a request is likely to be one of the factors relevant to an assessment of whether a public authority has promptly complied with its obligations under s.1(1). 11–024

Date of receipt

Ordinarily, the period for compliance with a request for information is calculated from the date of actual receipt, namely the day on which the public authority receives the request for information.[93] However, in a case where a public authority has sought further particulars about a request,[94] then the date of receipt is deemed to be the day on which the public authority receives the further particulars sought by it.[95] 11–025

[87] *Hansard*, HL, Vol.617, October 17, 2000, cols 1000–1006; Vol.619, November 14, 2000, cols 187–190; *Hansard*, HC, Vol.357, November 27, 2000, cols 727–729.

[88] Freedom of Information Act 2000, s.10(1); Freedom of Information (Scotland) Act 2002, s.10(1).

[89] This was the intention of Parliament: see House of Commons, *Hansard*, Vol.347, April 4, 2000, col.858.

[90] This also accords with the approach adopted to similar provisions in the former RSC, Ord.53, r.3(4) (see now CPR, Pt 54, r.54.5(1)): *R. v Independent Television Commission Ex p. TV NI Ltd, The Times*, December 30, 1991, CA.

[91] On the basis that there is a strong presumption that every word in a statute must be given some effective meaning: *McMonagle v Westminster City Council* [1990] 2 A.C. 716 at 727; *Gubay v Kingston* [1984] 1 W.L.R. 163 at 172, HL.

[92] *cf.* the Official Information Act 1982 (New Zealand), s.12(3), which provides that an applicant may inform the body of which he makes his request that the request is urgent and the reasons why it is urgent.

[93] Freedom of Information Act 2000, s.10(6)(a); Freedom of Information (Scotland) Act 2002, s.10(1)(a).

[94] As to requiring particulars in order to identify and locate requested information, see paras 11–011 to 11–013 above.

[95] Freedom of Information Act 2000, s.10(6)(b); Freedom of Information (Scotland) Act 2002, s.10(1)(b).

Meaning of a "working day"

11–026 A "working day" is any day other than a Saturday, a Sunday, Christmas Day, Good Friday or a bank holiday "in any part of the United Kingdom".[96]

Cases where public authority has given a fees notice to the applicant

11–027 Where a public authority has given a fees notice to an applicant and the fee is paid within the specified period,[97] the working days in the period beginning with the day on which the fees notice is given to the applicant and ending on the day on which the fee is received by the public authority are to be discounted when calculating the 20th working day following the date of receipt.[98]

Requests involving information subject to a qualified exemption

11–028 To the extent that the requested information is exempt information by virtue of one of the qualified exemptions[99] in Pt II of the Freedom of Information Act 2000, then the ordinary 20 working day time-limit for compliance is extended, but only for the purpose of determining the public interest balancing exercise. For this exercise, the public authority is allowed "such time as is reasonable in the circumstances".[1] Some idea of what is meant by "reasonable in the circumstances" can be deduced from the fact that where s.10(3) applies, the only addition to the public authority's burden in dealing with the request is the balancing

[96] Freedom of Information Act 2000, s.10(6); Freedom of Information (Scotland) Act 2002, s.73. Good Friday is a working day for the purposes of the Scottish Act. Because bank holidays under the Banking and Financial Dealings Act 1971 differ in the various parts of the United Kingdom, the effect of picking up a bank holiday under the Banking and Financial Dealings Act 1971 "in any part" of the United Kingdom is to exclude each of the following days: New Year's Day (or, if New Year's Day be a Sunday, January 3), January 2 (or if January 2 be a Sunday, January 3), March 17 (or if March 17 be a Sunday, March 18), Easter Monday, the first Monday in May, the last Monday in May, the first Monday in August, the last Monday in August, December 25, December 26 (if it not be a Sunday) and December 27 (in a year in which December 25 or 26 is a Sunday): see Banking and Financial Dealings Act 1971, Sch.1.

[97] As to the period within which fees must be paid, see para.11–020 above.

[98] Freedom of Information Act 2000, s.10(2); Freedom of Information (Scotland) Act 2002, s.10(3).

[99] The qualified exemptions are listed at para.14–016 below.

[1] Freedom of Information Act 2000, s.10(3). There is no comparable provision in the Freedom of Information (Scotland) Act 2002. It is difficult to see what practical difference s.10(3)(a) makes to the operation of s.10(3). The public authority's consideration of whether it is obliged to communicate information logically precedes a discrete consideration of the obligation to confirm or deny: see para.1–004(3)(b) and Freedom of Information Act 2000, s.1(5). Exclusion of the duty to confirm or deny will at most be co-extensive with exemption from the duty to disclose. Accordingly, other than where information is exempt information by virtue of a qualified exemption in Pt II of the Freedom of Information Act 2000, there are no circumstances in which the duty to confirm or deny does not arise or apply, and extension of the ordinary time limit will already have been secured by s.10(3)(b).

exercise set out in s.2(1) and (2) of the Act. On the assumption that Parliament, in specifying the ordinary time limit in s.10(1), was not setting a time limit that it thought was or might be unreasonable in any circumstance, it is to be inferred that, notwithstanding the extension of the ordinary time-limit, the "reasonable time" permitted by s.10(3) can only exceed the time-limit set by s.10(1) to the extent, if any, that is reasonably required to carry out the public interest balancing exercise. This reading is confirmed by the requirements of s.17, relating to the giving of a refusal notice. Section 10(3) expressly retains the obligation to give a refusal notice within the ordinary 20 working-day time-limit, even where a qualified exemption is involved. Where s.10(3) applies, however, if the public interest balancing exercise has not been determined within that ordinary time-limit, the refusal notice must state that an exemption applies and that no decision has been taken on the balancing exercise required by the Act, and must give an estimate of the date on which the public authority expects that such a decision will be taken.[2] Where a request for information relates to information, some of which is exempt information by virtue of one of the qualified exemptions and the balance of which is either not exempt or is exempt information by virtue of one of the absolute exemptions, the public authority must both disclose the non-exempt information and give a refusal notice (dealing with everything save for the public interest balancing exercise) within the ordinary time-limit.

Time-limits for refusal notices

If a public authority is required to give a refusal notice to an applicant,[3] then it must do so within the time allowed for compliance with s.1(1) of the Freedom of Information Act 2000.[4] In other words, the back-stop time for compliance (save for the public interest balancing exercise) is the same whether a public authority is communicating the information to the applicant or whether it is giving the applicant a refusal notice, or a combination of the two. The special provisions that relate to cases where a public authority has sought further particulars of a request for information[5] or where a public authority has given a fees notice to an applicant[6] equally apply to extend the time given to a public authority for giving a refusal notice. 11–029

[2] Freedom of Information Act 2000, s.17(2) and see Ch.13. The *Code of Practice on the Discharge of Public Authorities' Functions under Part I of the Freedom of Information Act 2000*, para.18, states that these estimates should be realistic and reasonable and that in the majority of cases public authorities will be expected to comply with their estimates. The Code of Practice also states that if an estimate is exceeded, the public authority should apologise and provide reasons for the delay.

[3] The requirements of a refusal notice are considered at paras 13–006 to 13–010 below.

[4] Freedom of Information Act 2000, s.17(1); Freedom of Information (Scotland) Act 2002, s.16(1).

[5] As to seeking further particulars of a request for information, see paras 11–011 to 11–012 above.

[6] As to fees notices, see para.11–015 above.

Miscellaneous cases

11–030 There is power to modify by regulations references to the 20th working day to another working day not more than the 60th working day after the date of receipt.[7] To date no such regulations have been made.[8] Under the Freedom of Information (Scotland) Act 2002, where the public authority of whom the request is made is the Keeper of the Records of Scotland and the request is one that relates to information which is contained in a record transferred to him by a public authority and which has not been designated by the public authority as open information,[9] then references to the 20th working day are to be read as references to the 30th working day.[10]

Time-limits under the Data Protection Act 1998

11–031 The primary obligation on a data controller is also to comply promptly with a request.[11] This primary obligation is supplemented by a further obligation to comply with the request within a period which has been prescribed by regulations.[12] The relevant day on which the prescribed period begins is the day on which the data controller receives the request or, where later, the first day on which the data controller receives both the required fee[13] and any further particulars[14] requested by him.[15] In this respect, the Data Protection Act 1998 is similar to the Freedom of Information Act 2000.[16] In a case where the request relates wholly or partly to personal data forming part of an accessible record[17] that is part of an educational record,[18] and where the address of the data controller is in England and Wales, then the prescribed period is 15 school days.[19] These obligations are subject to the provisions relating to the disclosure of

[7] Freedom of Information Act 2000, s.10(4); Freedom of Information (Scotland) Act 2002, s.10(4).
[8] According to the Parliamentary Secretary for the Lord Chancellor's Department, such regulations will only be made in "exceptional circumstances": *Hansard*, HC, Vol.347, April 4, 2000, col.858.
[9] Freedom of Information (Scotland) Act 2002, s.22(1). As to "open information", see para.6–042 above.
[10] *ibid*., s.10(2).
[11] Data Protection Act 1998, s.7(8).
[12] *ibid*. As to the interrelationship between the duty to act promptly and the duty in any event to comply with a request within a specified period, see para.11–024 above.
[13] As to fees under the Data Protection Act 1998, see para.4–038 above.
[14] As to requiring further particulars under the Data Protection Act 1998, see para.11–013 above.
[15] Data Protection Act 1998, s.7(8) and (10).
[16] As to the equivalent position under the Freedom of Information Act 2000, see paras 11–022, 11–024, 11–027 and 11–029 above.
[17] As defined in the Data Protection Act 1998, s.68(1). As to accessible records, see paras 4–014, 4–015 and 4–055 above.
[18] As defined in Sch.11 to the Data Protection Act 1998. As to educational records, see para.4–056 above.
[19] Data Protection (Subject Access) (Fees and Miscellaneous Provisions) Regulations 2000, r.5(2). For these purposes, a "school day" means any day on which at the relevant school there is a school session: Education Act 1996, s.579(1).

information relating to third parties.[20] For example, if a data controller were to take reasonable steps to seek the consent of a third party to the disclosure of the information (and it was not reasonable to comply with the request without obtaining that consent), then any delay in complying with the request occasioned by the taking of those steps would not amount to a lack of promptness contrary to s.7(8) of the Data Protection Act 1998.

5. TRANSFERRING REQUESTS FOR INFORMATION

Introduction

The Freedom of Information Act 2000 does not expressly deal with the situation where a public authority receives a request for information which it itself does not hold, but which it believes is held by a different public authority.[21] This is relegated to the Code of Practice issued under s.45 of the Act.[22] 11–032

Provisions of Code of Practice on transferring requests for information

The Code of Practice states that where a public authority receives a request for information that it does not hold, but which it believes is held by another public authority, then it should consider whether to transfer the request to that other public authority.[23] The Code of Practice states that before transferring a request, the public authority should ascertain whether the other public authority holds the information, consider whether a transfer is appropriate and whether the applicant would have any grounds to object to a transfer.[24] If a public authority reasonably considers that an applicant would not have any grounds to object, then it may transfer a request without further reference to him, but if it reasonably considers that an applicant would object, then it should only transfer with his consent.[25] Furthermore, the public authority's duty to provide advice and assistance may require it to inform the applicant that 11–033

[20] See the Data Protection Act 1998, s.7(4).

[21] This is in contrast to freedom of information legislation in other jurisdictions. See, *e.g.* Freedom of Information Act 1982, s.16 (Commonwealth of Australia); Official Information Act 1982, s.14 (New Zealand); Freedom of Information Act 1997, s.7(3) (Republic of Ireland).

[22] In Scotland, under Freedom of Information (Scotland) Act 2002, s.60. For a general treatment of the Code, see Ch.9.

[23] *Code of Practice on the Discharge of Public Authorities' Functions under Part I of the Freedom of Information Act 2000*, para.25.

[24] *ibid.*, para.26.

[25] *ibid.*, paras 26 to 27.

it believes that the information requested is held by a different public authority.[26] The process of transfer should be conducted as soon as is practicable and it does not relieve the public authority of its normal obligations, which continue to apply whether the public authority holds some or none of the information requested.[27] Where a public authority, with its agreement, receives a transferred request for information, it should treat it in the same way as if it had been received directly from the applicant.[28]

6. FAILURE TO LOCATE INFORMATION

Failure to locate any information

11–034 The Freedom of Information Act 2000 does not deal expressly with what is required of a public authority before it may respond to a request by stating that it does not hold any information of the type requested by an applicant.[29] A failure to locate any information answering the terms of the request does not constitute a "refusal" of that request and, accordingly, none of the notice requirements of s.17 is applicable.[30] The Code of Practice gives no guidance as to the thoroughness of the search that is required before a public authority may properly conclude that it holds no information answering the terms of the request[31] nor of the form of response that must be given to an applicant in those circumstances.[32] Since the duty to confirm or deny applies (subject to Pt II and s.2(1)) irrespective of whether a public authority holds the information

[26] *Code of Practice on the Discharge of Public Authorities' Functions under Part I of the Freedom of Information Act 2000*, para.24. As to the duty to provide advice and assistance, see Ch.8.

[27] *Code of Practice on the Discharge of Public Authorities' Functions under Part I of the Freedom of Information Act 2000*, paras 23 and 29.

[28] *ibid.*, para.28.

[29] In the USA, the yardstick used is that an agency must undertake a search that is "reasonably calculated to uncover all relevant documents": *Weisberg v United States Department of Justice*, 705 F.(2d) 1344 (DC Cir. 1983). This involves a consideration of: (a) how the agency conducted its search in light of the scope of the request; (b) applicant's description of the records sought; (c) the standards the agency used in determining where the records were likely to be found; and (d) whether the agency believes the records sought may exist.

[30] *cf.* the Freedom of Information Act 1982 (Commonwealth of Australia), s.24A, which expressly provides for the refusal of a request for access to a document if all reasonable steps have been taken to find the document and the relevant public authority is satisfied that it cannot be found. See also the similar provision in the Freedom of Information Act 1997 (Republic of Ireland), s.10(1)(a). In Canada, the Federal Court has suggested that a total failure to make a search or an adequate search might, if proven, be tantamount to a refusal to disclose: *X v Canada (Minister of National Defence)* (1992) 58 F.T.R. 93.

[31] Elsewhere the view taken is that the public authority must carry out a search that is reasonable in the circumstances: *Re Anti-Fluoridation Association of Victoria v Secretary to the Department of Health* (1985) 8 A.L.D. 163.

[32] Elsewhere, the view taken is that where documents answering the terms of the request cannot be located, it is not suffient to state merely that no such documents exist, on the basis that this is a bare statement of ultimate fact: *Re Luton and Commissioner of Taxation* (1996) 22 A.A.R. 492 at 496.

requested, it is to be deduced that any search must be completed within 20 working days[33] and that the minimum entitlement of the applicant is to be informed in writing that the public authority does not hold information of the description specified in the request.[34] In contrast, the Freedom of Information (Scotland) Act 2002 does expressly provide for the form which such written notice must take.[35] Where no information is found, the public authority is entitled to give an applicant a fees notice under s.9(1), but the amount required by that notice is, strictly speaking, confined to the costs of complying with s.1(1)(a): in other words, the cost of informing the applicant, and not the cost of the search.

Partial location of information

The Code of Practice states that where a public authority has been able to identify and locate some information, but not other information, then it should provide the information that it has located and explain to the applicant why it has not been able to identify or locate the remainder.[36] Given that the unit of disclosure is "information", this does not take matters much beyond what is required by the terms of the Act: the public authority is required to communicate all the information that it holds answering the terms of the request. 11–035

7. COMMUNICATION OF INFORMATION

Introduction

The primary obligation on a public authority which communicates information pursuant to the Freedom of Information Act 2000 is to communicate that information by any means which are reasonable in the circumstances.[37] It is implicit in the Freedom of Information Act 2000 that the communication of information does not necessarily involve the provision of a copy of that information to an applicant, and that in certain circumstances the provision of a summary or of an opportunity to inspect a record of it will be sufficient.[38] More onerous obligations apply under the Data Protection Act 1998.[39] 11–036

[33] Freedom of Information Act 2000, s.10(1). See paras 1–022 to 11–029 above.
[34] *ibid.*, s.1(1)(a).
[35] Freedom of Information (Scotland) Act 2002, s.17.
[36] *Code of Practice on the Discharge of Public Authorities' Functions under Part I of the Freedom of Information Act 2000*, para.12.
[37] Freedom of Information Act 2000, s.11(4); Freedom of Information (Scotland) Act 2002, s.11(4).
[38] See, *e.g.*, the Freedom of Information Act 2000, s.11(1)(b) and the Freedom of Information (Scotland) Act 2002, s.11(2)(c).
[39] See para.4–044 above.

Obligation to provide information by reasonable means

11–037 Without the expression of a preference by an applicant for a particular means of communication, a public authority may comply with a request for information by communicating that information by any means which are reasonable in the circumstances.[40] The notion of "reasonableness" of communication must be informed by the purpose of the Act, which is to facilitate rather than hinder the disclosure of information held by public authorities.[41] The circumstances which will be relevant for these purposes would normally include the form in which the relevant information is held by a public authority, the volume of the information to be communicated, the cost of different means of communication and the applicant's ability to receive or read different means of communication. There seems no sensible reason why different "pieces" of information answering the terms of a request should not be communicated by different means, if that is what is reasonable in the circumstances.

Preference expressed by the applicant

11–038 The entitlement of a public authority to communicate the information requested by any means that are reasonable in the circumstances is subject to the authority's obligation to communicate in accordance with an applicant's expressed preference, provided that that preference is one of the three enumerated in s.11(1) and to the extent that giving effect to the preference is reasonably practicable. In subordinating subs.(4) to subs.(1), it is implicit that the expressed preference may be for a means that is not reasonable in the circumstances. However, if it is reasonably practicable to comply with expressed preferences, then the public authority must comply with it.[42] The specified means are the provision to the applicant of a copy of the information in a permanent form (or another form acceptable to the applicant),[43] the provision to the applicant of a reasonable opportunity to inspect a record containing the information,[44] and the provision to the applicant of a digest or summary of the information in a permanent form (or another form acceptable to the applicant).[45] The use of the phrase "one or more" indicates that the applicant is not limited to expressing a preference for only one of the specified means. Again, there seems no sensible reason why an applicant should not be able to specify a particular means of

[40] Freedom of Information Act 2000, s.11(4); Freedom of Information (Scotland) Act 2002, s.11(4).

[41] See paras 1–012, 1–014 and 1–019 to 1–021 above.

[42] Freedom of Information Act 2000, s.11(1); Freedom of Information (Scotland) Act 2002, s.11(1).

[43] Freedom of Information Act 2000, s.11(1)(a); Freedom of Information (Scotland) Act 2002, s.11(2)(a).

[44] Freedom of Information Act 2000, s.11(1)(b); Freedom of Information (Scotland) Act 2002, s.11(2)(c).

[45] Freedom of Information Act 2000, s.11(1)(c); Freedom of Information (Scotland) Act 2002, s.11(2)(b). The latter provision does not require that the digest or summary be in any particular form.

communication for certain sorts of information and another means for the remainder. Alternatively, an applicant may express a preference for a particular means if the information answering the terms of the request is less than a particular quantity and for a different means if it is more. Such a course may be sensible having regard to fees, the cost of compliance and copyright issues.

Reasonable practicability

The obligation to give effect to a preference expressed by an applicant for communication by way of one or more specified means only extends as far as it is reasonably practicable for the public authority to give effect to it.[46] In other contexts, the phrase "reasonably practicable" has been equated to "reasonable feasibility".[47] Although this is a somewhat circular explication, it is clear that the test of reasonable practicability falls somewhere between the two extremes of mere reasonableness and physical possibility.[48] A public authority may have regard to all the circumstances when deciding whether it is reasonably practicable to give effect to an applicant's preference, including the cost of doing so.[49] In addition to cost, such circumstances would normally include the form in which the relevant information is held by a public authority, the ease with which it can be converted from its existing form to the preferred form, the volume of the information to be communicated or summarised, and, where copies have been requested, any relevant copyright restrictions. It is suggested that where it is difficult to provide the applicant with information in a particular form without also providing him with information to which he is not entitled (for example, exempt information or information outside the scope of the request), this will be a relevant circumstance for the public authority to take into account.[50] Where a public authority determines that it is not reasonably practicable to comply with an applicant's preference, it must notify the applicant of its reasons for that determination.[51] **11–039**

46 Freedom of Information Act 2000, s.11(1); Freedom of Information (Scotland) Act 2002, s.11(1). Section 11(5) of the Freedom of Information (Scotland) Act 2002 expressly provides that a public authority cannot rely upon the "reasonable practicability" test to side-step any duty to make reasonable adjustments imposed upon it by the Disability Discrimination Act 1995, s.21.

47 *Palmer and Saunders v Southend-on-Sea Borough Council* [1984] 1 W.L.R. 1129; [1984] 1 All E.R. 945, CA.

48 *Edwards v National Coal Board* [1949] 1 K.B. 704 at 712 (a health and safety case); *Marshall v Gotham Co Ltd* [1954] A.C. 360 at 370 (a health and safety case); *Palmer and Saunders v Southend-on-Sea Borough Council* [1984] 1 W.L.R. 1129; [1984] 1 All E.R. 945, CA; *London Underground Ltd v Noel* [2000] I.C.R. 109, CA.

49 Freedom of Information Act 2000, s.11(2); Freedom of Information (Scotland) Act 2002, s.11(3).

50 As to redaction of documents, see para.13–012 below.

51 Freedom of Information Act 2000, s.11(3); Freedom of Information (Scotland) Act 2002, s.11(3).

Effect of communication of information on the duty to confirm or deny

11–040 Where a public authority has complied with any obligation to communicate information to an applicant, then it is deemed to have complied with its duty to confirm or deny under the Freedom of Information Act 2000.[52]

Communication of information pursuant to the Data Protection Act 1998

11–041 The obligations relating to the manner in which information is communicated pursuant to the Data Protection Act 1998 are more onerous than the corresponding duties under the Freedom of Information Act 2000. In particular, the obligation to communicate to an individual information constituting personal data and information as to the source of those data[53] must be complied with by providing the individual with a copy of the information in permanent form.[54] A data controller is only absolved from this obligation if the supply of such a copy is not possible or would involve disproportionate effort[55] or the individual agrees otherwise.[56] Further, where any of the information is expressed in terms which are not intelligible without explanation, the copy must be accompanied by an explanation.[57] The Data Protection Act 1998 also prevents a data controller from deliberately modifying information in response to a request. The information communicated must be supplied by reference to the data in question as they stood at the time when the relevant request was made, and it may only take account of any amendments or deletions made since the time of the request if those amendments or deletions would have been made regardless of the receipt of the request.[58] Where a data controller is obliged to inform an individual of the logic involved in any decision-making process,[59] then that obligation does not extend to informing the individual of any information as to the decision-taking process which is a trade secret.[60]

[52] Freedom of Information Act 2000, s.1(5).
[53] Data Protection Act 1998, s.7(1)(c). As to the obligation to communicate personal data and information as to the source of those data, see paras 4–026 and 4–029 below.
[54] *ibid.*, s.8(2).
[55] *ibid.*, s.8(2)(a).
[56] *ibid.*, s.8(2)(b).
[57] *ibid.*, s.8(2).
[58] *ibid.*, s.8(6). See further para.4–043 above.
[59] *ibid.*, s.7(1)(d).
[60] *ibid.*, s.7(5). As to the meaning of trade secrets, see paras 25–028 to 25–031 below.

8. CONSULTATION WITH THIRD PARTIES

Consultation with third parties: "reverse FOI"

The disclosure of information by a public authority to an applicant will frequently have implications for third parties. Disclosure of information to one person may, for example, impinge upon the commercial interests, confidentiality or privacy of a third party. A third party's statutory entitlement to compel a public authority to refuse access to information held by it is commonly described as "reverse freedom of information". 11–042

Comparative jurisdictions

The differing approaches taken in the comparative jurisdictions is illuminating, showing the importance that has been attached to the rights of third parties.[61] Thus: 11–043

(1) In the USA, the Freedom of Information Act 1966 makes no provision for a third party to attempt to stop disclosure of information. In *Chrysler Corp v Brown*[62] the Supreme Court held that jurisdiction for a reverse FOI action cannot be based on the Freedom of Information Act itself "because Congress did not design the FOIA exemptions to be mandatory bars to disclosure." Instead, the Court found that review of an agency's decision to disclose requested records can be brought under the Administrative Procedure Act.[63] As a result, a third party will ordinarily argue that an agency's contemplated release would violate the Trade Secrets Act and thus would "not be in accordance with law" or would be "arbitrary and capricious" within the meaning of the Administrative Procedure Act. The third party's right of challenge is thus on judicial review grounds, and not one of merit review. On top of this, Executive Order 12,600 requires that notice be given to submitters of confidential commercial information whenever an agency "determines that it may be required to disclose" the requested information. When a third party is given notice, it must be given a reasonable period of time within which to object to disclosure of any of the requested material. If the third party's objection is not upheld by the agency, the third party must be notified in writing and given a brief explanation of the

[61] Given that the Freedom of Information Act 2000 was the last of its comparators and that those comparators were the subject of close scrutiny (see para.2–001 above), it is a little surprising that its treatment of third parties' interests is the most primitive.

[62] (1979) 441 U.S. 281.

[63] 5 USC 701–706 (2000).

agency's decision. The notification must be provided a reasonable number of days before the disclosure date, so as to give the third party an opportunity to seek judicial relief.

(2) In Australia, the Freedom of Information Act 1982 provides that before an agency discloses documents containing information that originated from a State, that contain business information or contain personal information (each of which is an exemption[64]), the agency holding the documents is required to give the potentially-affected third party an opportunity to make representations as to whether the relevant exemption applies. If, despite the representations, the agency decides to release the information, the third party has a right to ask the Administrative Appeals Tribunal for a review of the agency's decision.[65] The third party is entitled to put forward to the Tribunal any of the grounds of exemption, including those not relied upon by the agency holding the documents.[66] The Act is silent as to whether the third party should be advised of the identity of the applicant.[67]

(3) In New Zealand, the Official Information Act 1982 imposes no binding obligation upon an agency to consult with a third party before releasing information relating to that party. Instead, s.30(3) of the Official Information Act 1982 and s.18(3) of the Ombudsmen Act 1975 require an Ombudsman, before making any report or recommendation that may adversely affect any person, to give that person an opportunity to be heard.[68] Limited provision is also made by the Privacy Act 1993 in relation to personal information.

(4) In Canada, the Access to Information Act, deals methodically with the rights of third parties.[69] Section 20 provides a number of exemptions for records specifically relating to third parties: trade secrets; financial, commercial, scientific or technical information supplied by third parties in confidence; information disclosure of which might cause material financial loss or gain to, or prejudice the competitive position of, a third party; information disclosure of which might prejudice negotiations of a third party. Under s.27, where the institution intends to disclose a record that contains, or that the head of the institution has reason to believe might contain, matter specifically exempted by s.20, notice must be given to the third party giving him 20 days within which

---

64 ss.26A, 27 and 27A respectively.

65 Freedom of Information Act 1982, ss.58F, 59 and 59A. The review is a merit review.

66 *Mitsubishi Motors Australia Ltd v Department of Transport* (1986) 12 F.C.R. 156; 68 A.L.R. 626.

67 In its review of the Freedom of Information Act 1982, the Australian Law Reform Commission said that revealing the identity of the applicant to the third party was best left to the discretion of the agency, although it was sensible to consult the applicant before doing so: Australian Law Reform Commission and Administrative Review Council, *Open Government: a Review of the Federal Freedom of Information Act 1982* (1995) A.L.R.C. 77; A.R.C. 40, Canberra, para.10.17.

68 See *Wyatt Co (NZ) Ltd v Queenstown-Lakes District Council* [1991] 2 N.Z.L.R. 180.

69 ss.20, 27, 28, 33, 37, 43 and 44.

to make representations as to whether the record should be disclosed.[70] Section 28 deals with the manner in which a third party is required to make representations. Section 33 provides that a third party is to be given notice of a complaint against a non-disclosure decision, provided that notification under s.27 would have been required had it been intended to disclose. Section 35 gives a third party a right, where necessary, to make representations to the Information Commissioner and the third party will, in those circumstances, receive a copy of his report (s.37(2)). An affected, or potentially-affected, third party is given a right to participate in a review application and is notified of the same (s.43). A third party may also itself apply for a review order to prevent disclosure of a record (s.44). The statutory scheme is said to give a third party a vested right to have its information withheld from unqualified requesters.[71] The courts have taken the view that a third party is not able to invoke exemptions with which it has no connections, such as injury to international relations, if the government institution has chosen not to invoke it.[72]

(5) In Ireland, there are two separate procedures in the Freedom of Information Act 1997 obliging a public body to consult with a third party before deciding to disclose records answering the terms of the request. The first applies where the records stand to fall within the scope of one of three particular exemptions: records obtained in confidence, commercially sensitive information and personal information about third parties.[73] Where a record answering the terms of a request falls within the scope of one or more of these exemptions but the head of the public body is nevertheless of the opinion that the public interest lies in favour of disclosure, that public body is required to inform a third party to whom the record relates of this fact.[74] The third party has a right to make written representations in relation to the access request.[75] The second applies to certain categories of record relating to matters before govenment: the head of a public body may not release the record until he has consulted with the leader of each political party to which a member of the government belonged that made any decision to which the record relates.[76] A person notified under the first procedure must be

[70] Outside the grounds specified in s.27, a third party has no right to be notified of a disclosure and, accordingly, no right of review under s.44: *Twinn v Canada (Minister of Indian Affairs and Northern Development)* [1987] 3 F.C. 368.

[71] *Glaxo Canada Inc v Canada (Minister of National Health and Welfare)* [1990] 1 F.C. 652.

[72] *Saint John Shipbuilding Ltd v Canada (Minister of Supply and Services)* (1988) 24 F.T.R. 32; on app. (1990) 67 D.L.R. (4th) 315.

[73] ss.26, 27 and 28, respectively.

[74] Freedom of Information Act 1997, s.29.

[75] *ibid.*, s.29(3). The third party has three weeks in which to do so. The head is obliged to take the submissions into account before making his decision.

[76] *ibid.*, s.19.

advised in writing of the decision and of his right of appeal.[77] The Act is silent as to whether the third party should be advised of the identity of the applicant.

No statutory right of consultation

11–044 Under the Freedom of Information Act 2000 and the Data Protection Act 1998 there are generally no formal reverse freedom of information procedures: there is no legal obligation to notify or consult a third party whose interests would be affected by the disclosure of information nor do third parties have a statutory right to challenge or seek a review of decisions to disclose information. Thus, although many of the exemptions under the Acts are designed to protect third parties' interests, the Acts themselves do not provide procedural mechanisms for protecting those interests.

Protection of third party interests under the Freedom of Information Act 2000

11–045 The principal means of protecting the interest of a third party who may be affected by disclosure under the Freedom of Information Act 2000 is a non-statutory statement of expectation that such a third party will be consulted before any such disclosure.[78] This aspect of the draft freedom of information legislation drew considerable criticism during its passage through Parliament.[79] Businesses concerned about their commercial interests, as well as others concerned at the possible implications of the release of information about them (a striking example being the Research Defence Society, which expressed concerns about the implications for holders of licences for scientific research involving animals) argued that the protection afforded to third parties by a code of practice was inadequate, and there were recommendations that third parties should be given a legal right to be consulted and to challenge decisions to disclose information about them. However, professed concerns about the administrative burden and lack of flexibility to which such an approach would give rise, its cost to the public purse by comparison with reliance on third parties' existing legal

[77] Freedom of Information Act 1997, s.29(3). If the public body accedes to the third party's representations, the applicant may also appeal: Freedom of Information Act 1997, ss.34(1) and 34(15). There is no internal review in relation to the third party consultation procedure.

[78] See the Secretary of State for Constitutional Affairs' *Code of Practice on the Discharge of Public Authorities' Functions under Part I of the Freedom of Information Act 2000*, November 20, 2002. As to the enforceability of this ersatz protection, see paras 9–002 to 9–003 above.

[79] While the original White Paper (Cabinet Office, *Your Right to Know: The Government's Proposals for a Freedom of Information Act*, Cm. 3818, December 11, 1997) invited views on whether a mechanism for protecting third parties was needed (at para.5.19), the draft bill contained no such mechanism.

rights (*e.g.* by way of action for breach of confidence) and its putative potential to undermine the very principle of access to information, were seized upon to defeat the concerns of third parties.[80]

Effect of the Code of Practice

So far as third party consultation is concerned, the Code of Practice advises that: 11–046

(1) where the third party's consent is required (*e.g.* because otherwise disclosure would be an actionable breach of confidence), public authorities should consult the third party unless that would be impracticable;[81]
(2) where the third party's consent is not required, consultation may be appropriate;[82]
(3) public authorities should consult affected third parties where the third parties' views may assist in determining whether an exemption applies or where the public interest lies;[83]
(4) however, public authorities may consider that consultation would not be appropriate where its cost would be disproportionate;[84]
(5) consultation with third parties is unnecessary where a public authority does not intend to disclose the information, where the third parties' views can have no effect or where no exemption applies so that disclosure is required;[85]
(6) public authorities may consult representative organisations, or even representative samples of numbers of individuals.[86]

Requests involving personal information about third parties

Where compliance with a request for information may entail disclosure of personal information about a third party there are specific provisions to protect the interests of that individual. A distinction is drawn between: 11–047

[80] See, *e.g.* House of Commons *Select Committee on Public Administration—Third Report*, Cm. 4355, July 29, 1999, paras 107–110; *Report from the House of Lords Select Committee appointed to consider the draft Freedom of Information Bill*, July 27, 1999, paras 40–47, 76; House of Commons, *Select Committee on Public Administration—Fifth Special Report*, Appendix, p.10, October 27, 1999; *Hansard*, HC, Vol.347, April 4, 2000, cols 890–915; and *Hansard*, HL, Vol. 617, October 17, 2000, cols 983–991.
[81] Code of Practice, para.32.
[82] *ibid.*, para.34.
[83] *ibid.*, para.35.
[84] *ibid.*, para.36.
[85] *ibid.*, para.37.
[86] *ibid.*, para.38.

(1) requests for access to personal information about the person making the request (*i.e.* subject access requests) but that also entail the disclosure of personal information about a third party; and
(2) requests for the disclosure of personal information about a third party.

The latter are dealt with under the Freedom of Information Act 2000 and are considered in detail in Chapter 24 below. As already noted, the issue of consultation is addressed through the Code of Practice.[87] The former, as with all subject access requests, are channelled through the Data Protection Act 1998.

The Data Protection Act 1998

11–048 Since the Code of Practice is directed at public authorities exercising their functions under Pt I of the Freedom of Information Act 2000, it has no application in the case of requests for access to personal information under the Data Protection Act 1998. Where a data controller cannot comply with a subject access request without disclosing information relating to another individual[88] who can be identified from that information,[89] he is not obliged to comply with the request unless:

(1) the other individual has consented to the disclosure; or
(2) it is reasonable in all the circumstances to comply with the request without such consent.[90]

The balancing process this calls for mirrors that required under Art.8 of the European Convention on Human Rights and it has been suggested that in this context data controllers should have in mind the principles of necessity and proportionality.[91] In determining whether it is reasonable to comply with the request without the third party's consent, particular regard must be paid to any duty of confidentiality owed to the third party, any steps the data controller has taken with a view to seeking the third party's consent, the capacity of the third party to consent and any express refusal of consent by the third party.[92] The requirement, in particular, to have regard to the steps taken with a view to

[87] *Code of Practice*, para.33.
[88] This includes information identifying an individual as the source of the information sought by the request: Data Protection Act 1998, s.7(5). However, the information must necessarily form part of the personal data requested by the data subject, otherwise no question of balancing under s.7(4) arises at all: see *Durant v Financial Services Authority* [2003] EWCA Civ 1746 at [65].
[89] Another individual can be identified from the information being disclosed if he can be identified from that information, or from that and any other information which, in the reasonable belief of the data controller, is likely to be in, or to come into, the possession of the data subject making the request: Data Protection Act 1998, s.8(7).
[90] Data Protection Act 1998, s.7(4).
[91] *Durant v Financial Services Authority* [2003] EWCA Civ 1746 at [54], [60].
[92] Data Protection Act 1998, s.7(6).

seeking the third party's consent may be thought to give rise, at the least, to a pragmatic need to consult the third party or to attempt to do so. This is recognised in guidance issued by the Information Commissioner on this specific aspect of the Data Protection Act 1998.[93] The Commissioner advises that data controllers may at the very least need to take steps to seek consent in order to demonstrate that it was reasonable in the circumstances to make the disclosure without consent.[94] As the Commissioner notes, these provisions may give rise to complex judgments for data controllers, weighing on the one hand the data subject's right of access (and the potential breach of the sixth data protection principle to which non-disclosure might give rise) and on the other hand the third party's right to respect for his private life.[95] While the right to privacy and other legitimate interests of third parties identified in or identifiable from the data subject's personal data will be highly relevant, so too will the question what, if any, legitimate interest the data subject has in the disclosure of that third party's identity.[96] In an application under s.7(9) of the Act concerning this balance, the role of the court is, ordinarily, confined to a review of the reasonableness of the data controller's judgment—albeit on an anxious scrutiny basis—rather than entailing a review of the merits.[97] The Court of Appeal has suggested that the starting point for the data controller is a "presumption" against disclosure of third party information without that third party's consent, but beyond this has expressed reluctance to attempt to devise any generally applicable principles.[98]

Disclosure without revealing identity of third party

Where the data controller can communicate part of the information sought by the data subject without disclosing the third party's identity, for example by omitting the third party's name or other identifying particulars, then he must do so. The prohibition on disclosure applies only to the information from which the third party can be identified.[99] **11–049**

[93] *Data Protection Act 1998: Subject Access Rights and Third Party Information*, March 2, 2000. However, in *Durant v Financial Services Authority* [2003] EWCA Civ 1746 at [56] the Court of Appeal emphasised that s.7(4) leaves the data controllers with a choice whether to do so: it does not oblige him to do so.

[94] *ibid.*, para.7.5.

[95] *ibid.* paras 2–4.

[96] *Durant v Financial Services Authority* [2003] EWCA Civ 1746 at [61].

[97] *ibid.*, at [59]–[60].

[98] *ibid.*, at [55], [66].

[99] Data Protection Act 1998, s.7(5).

CHAPTER 12

Disentitlement

1. EXCESSIVE COST OF COMPLIANCE

Introduction

12–001 One of the risks of a freedom of information regime is that an applicant may make applications for information which would result in a public authority incurring disproportionate cost or in an unreasonable diversion of its resources.[1] The Freedom of Information Act 2000 does not require a public authority to comply with a request for information where the cost of complying with the request would exceed a specified limit.[2] However, where the cost of compliance does exceed the specified limit so that the disclosure duty does not arise, a public authority may nevertheless provide the information and charge for the same.[3] As will be seen, the combined operation of the provisions has the result that:

— a public authority, when determining whether it is not obliged to comply with a request for information on the ground of the excessive cost of compliance, does so on the basis of compliance with the request: that is, the cost of locating the information, of considering whether the information is exempt information, of considering the public interest and of communicating that information to the applicant; but
— where a public authority is not obliged to communicate the information by reason of excessive cost compliance but nevertheless decides to do so, it may only charge for the cost of communication: in other words, not for the earlier parts of the exercise.

The Data Protection Act 1998 also provides that, in certain cases, the obligation on a data controller to comply with s.7(1) of that Act does not arise where the cost of compliance would be excessive.[4]

No obligation to comply with request where cost of compliance is excessive

Where a public authority estimates that the cost of complying with a request for information would exceed the appropriate limit,[5] then it is relieved of its two obligations under s.1(1) of the Freedom of Information Act 2000.[6] However, a public authority is only relieved of its duty to confirm or deny if the estimated **12–002**

[1] This was a potential problem identified in the white paper: Cabinet Office, *Your Right to Know: The Government's Proposals for a Freedom of Information Act* (White Paper), Cm. 3818, December 11, 1997, para.2.26. The concept of a "substantial and unreasonable diversion of resources" is deployed expressly in the Australian legislation (Freedom of Information Act 1982 (Commonwealth of Australia), s.24(1)(a)).

[2] Freedom of Information Act 2000, s.12(1); Freedom of Information (Scotland) Act 2002, s.12(1).

[3] Freedom of Information Act 2000, s.13(1); Freedom of Information (Scotland) Act 2002, s.13(1).

[4] As to the position under the Data Protection Act 1998 where the cost of complying with a request for information would be excessive, see para.4–050.

[5] Freedom of Information Act 2000, s.12(1). Although the Freedom of Information (Scotland) Act 2002 does not invoke the concept of an "appropriate limit", the effect of the relevant provision is broadly the same (see the Freedom of Information (Scotland) Act 2002, s.12(1)). As to the "appropriate limit", see para.12–004 below.

[6] As to a public authority's obligations under s.1(1) of the Freedom of Information Act 2000, see para.1–004(3) above. The position under the Data Protection Act 1998 is considered at para.4–026 above.

cost of complying with that duty alone would exceed the appropriate limit.[7] It is notable that the Acts use the word "would" rather than "might". This is likely to be of particular relevance where a public authority is unable to estimate the costs of compliance with any certainty. In such a case, if the public authority were to estimate that the cost of compliance would fall somewhere between a lower and an upper figure, it is unlikely that it would be able to take advantage of the provisions on excessive cost of compliance where the lower figure was below the appropriate limit. In such a case, it could not be said that the estimated costs would exceed the appropriate limit.

Estimating the cost of compliance

12–003 The Freedom of Information Act 2000 does not itself prescribe the type of costs which a public authority is entitled to take into account, or the manner of estimating those costs, when assessing whether the cost of complying with a request for information would exceed the appropriate limit.[8] However, as noted above, the Act makes provision for such matters to be prescribed by regulations.[9] Although to date no such regulations have been made, the draft Freedom of Information (Fees and Appropriate Limit) Regulations indicate that it is likely that the costs to be taken into account will be those "prescribed costs"[10] which a public authority would incur in complying with a request for information, to be estimated by reference only to the marginal cost of locating and providing the information and associated disbursements.[11] Marginal costs are likely to include the staff costs of locating the information and preparing it for provision to the applicant (for example, preparing a summary or screening for exempt information)[12] and any associated costs such as those of computer processing.[13] Costs that would be incurred in any event, such as office overheads, fall outside the ordinary meaning of the phrase "marginal costs".[14]

---

7 Freedom of Information Act 2000, s.12(2). There is no equivalent provision in the Freedom of Information (Scotland) Act 2002.

8 In Scotland any costs incurred in complying with a duty under or by virtue of the Disability Discrimination Act 1995, s.21, are expressly excluded from the cost of complying with a request (Freedom of Information (Scotland) Act 2002, s.12(6)).

9 Freedom of Information Act 2000, s.12(5); Freedom of Information (Scotland) Act 2002, s.12(4).

10 Draft Freedom of Information (Fees and Appropriate Limit) Regulations, r.6(2). As to prescribed costs, see para.11–018 above.

11 House of Commons, *Public Administration Committee—Third Report* (Cm 4355), July 29, 1999, Annex 6, para.30.

12 In Australia, it was held that the former excessive cost provisions of the Freedom of Information Act 1982, s.24(1)(b) (see now s.24(2)(b) of that Act), which referred to "the work involved in giving access to all the documents to which the request relates" did not extend to cover the work done in deciding whether the documents were exempt (*Re Timmins and National Media Liaison Service* (1986) 4 A.A.R. 311, para.26; *cf. Re Shewcroft and Australian Broadcasting Corporation* (1985) 2 A.A.R. 496).

13 House of Commons, *Public Administration Committee—Third Report* (Cm. 4355), July 29, 1999, Annex 6, para.26.

14 In relation to "marginal costs" see *Pepper v Hart* [1993] A.C. 593.

Disbursements are likely to include the costs of copying, postage and, where information has been requested on a computer disk, the cost of that disk.[15] It is questionable whether the Act permits the regulations to charge for anything other than the communication of any information answering the terms of the request.[16] The Freedom of Information Act 2000 articulates a distinction between:

— "the cost of complying with a request",[17] which will embrace the cost of locating the information, determining whether the information is exempt information,[18] considering (if necessary) the public interest and, if there is accordingly a duty to communicate, the communication of the information; and
— "the cost of communication",[19] which embraces the three sorts of provision of information enumerated in s.11(1)(a)–(c).

The duty to communicate does not arise in relation to information that is either exempt information by virtue of an absolute exemption or exempt information by virtue of a qualified exemption and the public interest is against disclosure.[20]

The "appropriate limit"

The "appropriate limit" for the purposes of the Freedom of Information Act 2000 is to be prescribed by regulations, which may provide that different limits apply in different cases.[21] The draft Freedom of Information (Fees and Appropriate Limit) Regulations indicate that it is likely that the "appropriate limit" will be set at £550.[22] 12–004

15 House of Commons, *Public Administration Committee—Third Report* (Cm. 4355), July 29, 1999, Annex 6, para.26.
16 On the basis of the opening words in Freedom of Information Act 2000, s.13(1).
17 See Freedom of Information Act 2000, s.9(1); Freedom of Information (Scotland) Act 2002, s.9(1).
18 Although perhaps not the cost of considering inapplicable exemptions.
19 Freedom of Information Act 2000, s.13(1); Freedom of Information (Scotland) Act 2002, s.13(1).
20 Freedom of Information Act 2000, s.2(2), to which the duties in s.1 are made subject.
21 Freedom of Information Act 2000, s.12(3). Although the Freedom of Information (Scotland) Act 2002 does not invoke the concept of an "appropriate limit", the Freedom of Information (Scotland) Act 2002, s.12(1) provides that the relevant amount should be prescribed by regulations.
22 Draft Freedom of Information (Fees and Appropriate Limit) Regulations, r.6(1).

Cumulative cost of complying with separate requests

12–005 The Freedom of Information Act 2000 anticipates the possibility that the provisions protecting public authorities from incurring excessive costs in complying with requests could be rendered ineffective in a situation where several separate requests are submitted.[23] Accordingly, the Act makes provision for regulations to prescribe that in certain circumstances, where two or more requests for information are made to a public authority by one person, or by different persons who appear to the public authority to be "acting in concert"[24] or in pursuance of a campaign, the public authority may treat the estimated cost of compliance as being the estimated cost of complying with all of the requests.[25] To date no such regulations have been made. The draft Freedom of Information (Fees and Appropriate Limit) Regulations indicate that it is likely that the prescribed circumstances will be that there be two or more requests for information which is on the same subject matter or is otherwise related, the last of the requests is received by the public authority before the 20th working day following the date of receipt of the first request and it appears to the public authority that the requests have been made in an attempt to ensure that the prescribed costs of complying separately with each request would not exceed the appropriate limit.[26] In Scotland, a public authority is also entitled to treat the estimated cost of compliance as being the estimated cost of complying with all the requests where the requests come from different persons and the public authority considers that it would be reasonable to make the information available to the public at large and it elects to do so.[27] In a case where the cumulative cost of complying with related requests is excessive, the Code suggests that the public authority may wish to consider whether the information could be communicated in a more cost-effective manner, such as by publication on its website.[28]

[23] This was a potential problem identified in the white paper (Cabinet Office, *Your Right to Know: The Government's Proposals for a Freedom of Information Act* (White Paper), Cm. 3818, December 11, 1997, para.2.26).

[24] A phrase normally associated with a criminal enterprise (see *DPP v Merriman* [1973] AC 584), but which has been extended to members of the animal kingdom (see *Arneil v Paterson* [1931] A.C. 560). It generally connotes a joining together of two or more persons to do what is sought to be done.

[25] Freedom of Information Act 2000, s.12(4); Freedom of Information (Scotland) Act 2002, s.12(2). The Freedom of Information (Scotland) Act 2002 differs slightly from the Freedom of Information Act 2000 in this respect, in that it does not refer to different persons who appear to be acting in pursuance of a campaign, but refers to different persons whose requests appear to have been instigated wholly or mainly for a purpose other than the obtaining of the information itself.

[26] Draft Freedom of Information (Fees and Appropriate Limit) Regulations, r.7. As to prescribed costs, see para.11–018 above. As to the appropriate limit, see para.12–004 above.

[27] Freedom of Information (Scotland) Act 2002, s.12(2)(c). In such a case, the Act provides that regulations may make provision as to how and when the information is to be made available as to the public at large (Freedom of Information (Scotland) Act 2002, s.12(3)). To date no such regulations have been made.

[28] Code of Practice On the Discharge of Public Authorities' Functions under Part I of the Freedom of Information Act 2000, para.16.

Notices in cases where cost of compliance is excessive

Where a public authority claims that it is not obliged to comply with its duties under s.1(1) of the Freedom of Information Act 2000 because the cost of complying with it would be excessive, it must within the time for compliance with that section give the applicant a notice stating that fact.[29] 12–006

Fees in cases where cost of compliance is excessive

The Freedom of Information Act 2000 makes provision for public authorities to charge for the provision of information which might not otherwise be provided because of cost considerations.[30] In cases where a public authority is not obliged to comply with a request for information because the cost of complying with it is deemed to be excessive,[31] where the communication of the information is not otherwise required by law, and where no provision is made by or under another enactment for the charging of fees, then the public authority may charge a fee for the communication of that information.[32] Such fees are to be determined by the public authority in accordance with regulations.[33] To date no such regulations have been made. The draft Freedom of Information (Fees and Appropriate Limit) Regulations indicate that it is likely that the maximum fee which may be charged is likely to be the sum of 10 per cent of the first £550 of prescribed costs,[34] any prescribed costs over £550 and the disbursements.[35] In such a case, the Code suggests that the public authority may wish to consider providing an indication of what information could be provided within the costs ceiling.[36] 12–007

[29] Freedom of Information Act 2000, s.17(5); Freedom of Information (Scotland) Act 2002, s.16(4). As to notices in cases where the cost of compliance with a request for information would be excessive, see further para.13–008 below.

[30] Explanatory Notes to the Freedom of Information Act 2000, para.58.

[31] As to cases where the cost of compliance with a request for information would be excessive, see para.12–014 below.

[32] Freedom of Information Act 2000, s.13(1) and (3); Freedom of Information (Scotland) Act 2002, s.13(1) and (4). The charge cannot include an amount in respect of locating the information, determining whether it is exempt information or weighing the public interest: see para.12–001 above.

[33] Freedom of Information Act 2000, s.13(1); Freedom of Information (Scotland) Act 2002, s.13(1).

[34] As to prescribed costs, see para.11–018 above.

[35] Freedom of Information (Fees and Appropriate Limit) Regulations, r.5. As to disbursements, see para.11–019 above.

[36] *Code of Practice On the Discharge of Public Authorities' Functions under Part I of the Freedom of Information Act 2000*, para.14.

2. VEXATIOUS REQUESTS

Introduction

12–008 A public authority is not obliged to comply with a request for information[37] under the Freedom of Information Act 2000 if the request is vexatious.[38] There is no equivalent provision in the Data Protection Act 1998.[39]

Meaning of "vexatious"

12–009 The Freedom of Information Act 2000 does not provide any assistance as to what is meant by "vexatious".[40] It has been suggested that an analogy may be drawn with the concept of vexatious litigants,[41] but that analogy is apt to mislead. The FOI Acts adopt what has been termed an "applicant-blind" approach.[42] Accordingly, it matters not whether an applicant is vexatious: the proper question is whether a particular request is vexatious.[43] The motive of an applicant for making a request cannot transform an otherwise proper request into a vexatious request,[44] unless perhaps it is apparent that the applicant has no interest in receiving the information requested but is bent on creating administrative difficulty for the public authority.[45] Similarly, it is questionable whether the manner in which a request is made will be sufficient to render an otherwise

[37] That is, the public authority is not obliged to comply with its duties under s.1(1) of the Freedom of Information Act 2000 (or of the Freedom of Information (Scotland) Act 2002, as the case may be).

[38] Freedom of Information Act 2000, s.14(1); Freedom of Information (Scotland) Act 2002, s.14(1).

[39] See para.4–039 above.

[40] The Australian Law Reform Commission rejected an amendment to the Australian Freedom of Information Act 1982 which would have allowed requests to be rejected on the basis that they were vexatious, arguing that vexatiousness is a vague concept likely to result in unpredictable implementation (Australian Law Reform Commission and Administrative Review Council, *Open Government: a Review of the Federal Freedom of Information Act* 1982, para.7.18).

[41] This analogy was drawn in the white paper (Cabinet Office, *Your Right to Know: the Government's Proposals for a Freedom of Information Act* (White Paper), Cm. 3818, December 11, 1997, para.2.25).

[42] *Hansard*, HL, Vol.617, October 17, 2000, col.1015.

[43] Accordingly, a better analogy may be with vexatious claims. See, for example, the Employment Tribunals (Constitution and Rules of Procedure) Regulations 2001, Sch.1, para.15(2)(c) and the old RSC, Ord.18, r.19(1)(b). Because a large measure of protection is already given to a public authority from such requests through the "excessive cost of compliance" and "repeat request" mechanisms, it is difficult to see the particular need for this provision. Other comparable jurisdictions, such as Canada, have managed without it, although it is fair to observe that the Report of the Access to Information Review Task Force, June 2002, recommended that such a provision be inserted in the Canadian Act (p.73).

[44] There is nothing in the Freedom of Information Acts which require or preclude anything in terms of motive.

[45] See, by way of analogy, *Attorney-General v Barker* [2000] 2 F.C.R. 1 at 6d–f *per* Lord Bingham of Cornhill C.J.

proper request vexatious,[46] although an abusive or offensively-worded request might be considered vexatious. What will amount to a vexatious request will depend on all the circumstances.[47] Examples of requests which are likely to be vexatious are those which go beyond the point at which no further information can be provided[48] and those which amount to an attempt to interfere with or undermine the integrity of court processes.[49]

Notices in cases of vexatious requests

If a public authority is relying on a claim that it is not obliged to comply with a request for information because the request is vexatious, then it must (subject to one exception)[50] give a notice to that effect to the applicant within the time for compliance with s.1(1) of the Freedom of Information Act 2000.[51] 12–010

3. REPEAT REQUESTS

Introduction

A public authority is not obliged to comply with a request for information where it is a request for information[51A] which is identical or substantially similar to a previous request made by the same applicant, where the public authority has already complied with that previous request and where a reasonable interval has yet to elapse between compliance with the previous request and the making of the current request.[52] Similar provisions apply under the Data Protection Act 1998.[53] 12–011

[46] Explanatory Notes to the Freedom of Information Act 2000, para.59: the fact that an applicant "vents his frustration" in a request will not be sufficient to render that request vexatious.

[47] *Ashmore v British Coal Corporation* [1990] 2 Q.B. 338 CA, 348A–C, *per* Stuart-Smith L.J., dealing with abuse of process as an aspect of frivolous or vexatious claims in the Employment Tribunal.

[48] *Hansard*, HL, Vol.617, October 17, 2000, col.1014.

[49] *Johnson Tiles Pty v Esso Australia Ltd* [2000] F.C.A. 495 at paras 48–54, 56, *per* Merkel J.

[50] As to the exception to the duty to give a notice to the applicant in cases where the request for information is vexatious, see para.13–007 below.

[51] Freedom of Information Act 2000, s.17(5); Freedom of Information (Scotland) Act 2002, s.16(5). As to the time for compliance, see paras 11–022 to 11–030 above. As to the requirement to give a notice in cases where a request for information is vexatious, see para.13–007 below.

[51A] In other words, the public authority is not obliged to comply with its duties under s.1(1) of the Freedom of Information Act 2000 or under s.1 of the Freedom of Information (Scotland) Act 2002.

[52] Freedom of Information Act 2000, s.14(2); Freedom of Information (Scotland) Act 2002, s.14(2).

[53] See para.4–049 above.

Identical or substantially similar request

12–012 The Freedom of Information Act 2000 does not give any guidance as to what is meant by "identical" or "substantially similar". Whilst the former concept should not prove problematic for most public authorities, it is likely that the concept of "substantially similar" will provoke differences of opinion between public authorities and applicants. The provision is unfortunately worded, in that by altering a mere word or two used in a first request it is possible to change completely the information sought in a second request. In particular, an applicant may very properly restrict a request for information by reference to a period within which the information was created or first held by the public authority. Such a temporal restriction will generally be mutually advantageous, limiting the scope of the task for the public authority and helping to ensure that the cost of compliance does not exceed the applicable limit. It may be that this temporally-limited request does not yield the information anticipated or that it yields information that points to further information outside the original limit. Accordingly, a staged approach to the request process is generally to be commended rather than condemned. This reasoning, together with the concatenation of the phrase "substantially similar" with the word "identical," suggests that the mischief to which the provision is directed is the wasting of a public authority's resources through the provision of information to an applicant who has already been provided with that information. It is not intended to preclude a request the words of which may be substantially similar to a previous request but where the information that answers its terms is materially different.[54] It is notable that the provisions on repeat requests only apply where the requests are made by the same person, so that its effect may be side-stepped by the expedient of placing a request through another person. Where identical or substantially similar requests are made by different persons, it may be appropriate to consider whether the later request is vexatious.[55]

A reasonable interval between requests

12–013 Unlike the Data Protection Act 1998,[56] the Freedom of Information Act 2000 does not give any guidance as to what should be taken into account when determining whether a reasonable interval has elapsed. However, it is likely that

[54] The Home Office Freedom of Information Unit suggested that one of the factors which could be taken into account when assessing whether a request was "substantially similar" to an earlier one was whether it was reasonable to expect that fresh information would be disclosed on the new request: House of Commons, *Public Administration Committee—Third Report* (Cm. 4355), July 29, 1999, Annex 6, para.31. However, it would seem that this is a matter which goes to the reasonableness of the interval between the requests (as to which, see para.12–013 below) rather than to the similarity of the requests.

[55] As to vexatious requests, see paras 12–008 to 12–010.

[56] As to the assessment of a "reasonable interval" under the Data Protection Act 1998, see para.4–049 above.

similar considerations will apply, such as the nature of the information, the purpose for which the information is held and the frequency with which the information is altered.[57]

Notices in cases of repeat requests

If a public authority is relying on a claim that it is not obliged to comply with a request for information because the request is a repeat request, then (subject to one exception)[58] it must give a notice to that effect to the applicant within the time for compliance with s.1(1) of the Freedom of Information Act 2000.[59] 12–014

Position under the Data Protection Act 1998

Where a data controller has previously complied with a request made under s.7 of the Data Protection Act 1998, he is not obliged to comply with a subsequent identical or similar request made by the same individual unless a reasonable interval has elapsed between compliance with the previous request and the making of the current request.[60] When deciding what constitutes a reasonable interval for these purposes, regard is to be had to the nature of the data, the purpose for which the data are processed and the frequency with which the data are altered.[61] 12–015

[57] See the Data Protection Act 1998, s.8(4). During the debate in the House of Lords, the latter consideration, the frequency with which the information is altered, was put forward by the government spokesman as one of the factors which would affect the reasonableness of an interval (*Hansard*, HL, Vol.617, October 17, 2000, col.1014).

[58] As to the exception to the duty to give a notice to the applicant in cases where the request for information is a repeat request, see para.13–007 below.

[59] Freedom of Information Act 2000, s.17(5); Freedom of Information (Scotland) Act 2002, s.16(5). As to the requirement to give a notice to the applicant in cases where the request for information is a repeat request, see para.13–007 below.

[60] Data Protection Act 1998, s.8(3).

[61] *ibid.*, s.8(4).

CHAPTER 13

Refusal

1. GROUNDS FOR REFUSAL

Introduction

A person's entitlement to receive information requested and to be informed whether the information requested is held by the public authority[1] is made subject to certain other provisions of the Freedom of Information Act 2000.[2] The bases upon which a public authority may refuse to comply with a request may conveniently be grouped into two broad classes: 13–001

(1) Procedural bases, where the form of the request is defective in a manner that entitles the public authority to treat it as not representing a proper request.
(2) Substantive bases, where the information is exempt information, either by virtue of a provision conferring absolute exemption or where the information is exempt information by virtue of a qualified exemption and the public interest is on balance against disclosure.

The basis for refusal is significant to the form of the refusal notice that must be given to the applicant.

Requests defective in form

There are four types of formal defect that entitle a public authority to refuse or to place in abeyance a request for information: 13–002

(1) Inadequately particularised request: where a public authority reasonably requires further particulars in order to identify and locate the information requested, then, provided that it has informed the applicant of that requirement, it is not obliged to provide the information requested until it is provided with the further particulars that it requires to identify and locate that information.[3]
(2) Vexatious or repeat request: a public authority is not obliged to comply with a request for information if that request is vexatious.[4] Nor is a public authority obliged to comply with a request for information if it is a request which is identical or substantially similar to a previous

---

[1] Termed, in this work, "the access right" and "the existence right", respectively: see para.1–004 above.
[2] Freedom of Information Act 2000, s.1(2); Freedom of Information (Scotland) Act 2002, s.1(6).
[3] Freedom of Information Act 2000, s.1(3); Freedom of Information (Scotland) Act 2002, s.1(3). As to requiring further particulars of a request for information, see paras 11–011 to 11–013 above.
[4] Freedom of Information Act 2000, s.14(1); Freedom of Information (Scotland) Act 2002, s.14(1). As to vexatious requests, see paras 12–008 to 12–010 above.

request made by the same applicant, the public authority has already complied with the previous request, and a reasonable interval has yet to elapse between compliance with the previous request and the making of the current request.[5]

(3) Failure to pay required fee: where a public authority has given a fees notice to an applicant, it is not obliged to comply with the request for information unless the applicant pays the fee within the period of three months beginning with the day on which the fees notice was given to the applicant.[6]

(4) Excessive cost of compliance: where a public authority estimates that the cost of complying with a request for information would exceed the appropriate limit, it is not obliged to comply with that request.[7]

Substantive refusals

13–003 Where a request is made in respect of information which is exempt information by virtue of a provision conferring absolute exemption, a public authority is not obliged to communicate that information to the applicant.[8] Similarly, where a request is made in respect of information which is exempt information (but not by virtue of a provision conferring absolute exemption), a public authority is not obliged to communicate that information to the applicant where the public interest in maintaining the exemption outweighs the public interest in disclosing the information.[9] In either such case, however, the public authority is not automatically relieved of its duty to confirm or deny that it holds the information.

Information excluded from the duty to confirm or deny

13–004 Where a request is made in respect of information in relation to which an absolute exclusion from the duty to confirm or deny applies, a public authority is not obliged to comply with the request.[10] Where a request is made in respect of information in relation to which there is an exclusion (but not an absolute

[5] Freedom of Information Act 2000, s.14(2): Freedom of Information (Scotland) Act 2002, s.14(2). As to repeat requests, see paras 12–011 to 12–014 above.

[6] Freedom of Information Act 2000, s.9(2); Freedom of Information (Scotland) Act 2002, s.9(3). As to fees notices, see paras 11–014 to 11–021 above.

[7] Freedom of Information Act 2000, s.12(1); Freedom of Information (Scotland) Act 2002, s.12(1). As to the situations where the cost of complying with a request for information would be excessive, see paras 12–001 to 12–007 above.

[8] Freedom of Information Act 2000, s.2(2)(a); Freedom of Information (Scotland) Act 2002, s.2(1)(a).

[9] Freedom of Information Act 2000, s.2(1)(b); Freedom of Information (Scotland) Act 2002, s.2(1)(b).

[10] Freedom of Information Act 2000, s.2(1)(a).

exclusion) of the duty to confirm or deny, a public authority is not obliged to comply with the request where the public interest in maintaining the exclusion of the duty to confirm or deny outweighs the public interest in disclosing whether the public authority holds the information.[11]

Deferred decision

Where a request is made in respect of information in relation to which there is an exclusion (but not an absolute exclusion) of the duty to confirm or deny or in respect of information which is exempt information (but not by virtue of a provision conferring absolute exemption), a public authority may defer compliance with the request for such time as is reasonable in the circumstances pending a decision on where the public interest lies.[12] 13–005

2. REFUSAL NOTICE

Introduction

Where a public authority relies on a claim that it is not obliged to comply with a request for information, it is required to give the applicant a notice to that effect.[13] The purpose of a refusal notice is not just to ensure that an applicant is informed of the outcome of a request for information, but also to ensure that an unsuccessful applicant is aware of the reasons why his request has been refused and to provide him with a more informed basis on which to decide whether to take the matter further.[14] It is to be expected that the requirement to give such a notice will make it less likely that a public authority will make an unjustified claim that it is not obliged to comply with a request for information, as it will be required to apply its mind to the justification at the time.[15] The nature of a refusal notice and the time within which it is provided to an applicant depends upon the basis for refusal, as well as upon what it is that is being refused. These may be divided into the following categories: 13–006

11 Freedom of Information Act 2000, s.2(1)(b).
12 *ibid.*, s.10(2).
13 *ibid.*, s.17; Freedom of Information (Scotland) Act 2002, s.16.
14 In some jurisdictions, public authorities are subject to more onerous duties in relation to explaining their decisions. See, *e.g.*, the Freedom of Information Act 1997 (Republic of Ireland), s.10(2), the Freedom of Information Act 1982 (Cth of Australia), s.26(1) and *Re Luton and Commissioner of Taxation* (1996) A.A.R. 492.
15 See, for example, Australian Law Reform Commission and Administrative Review Council, *Open Government: A Review of the Federal Freedom of Information Act 1982* (1995) A.L.R.C. 77; A.R.C. 40, Canberra, para.7.19.

(1) refusal notices where a request is vexatious or is a repeat request;
(2) refusal notices where the cost of compliance is excessive;
(3) refusal notices where the information falls within Pt II of the Act but no public interest balancing exercise is involved; and
(4) refusal notices where information falls within Pt II of the Act and a public interest balancing exercise is involved.

Refusal notice where request is vexatious or is a repeat request

13–007 Where a public authority is relying on a claim that it is not obliged to comply with a request for information because it is a vexatious or repeat request,[16] then (subject to one exception) it must give the applicant a notice stating that fact.[17] The exception is that the public authority need not give such a notice where it has given the applicant a notice in relation to a previous request for information stating that it is relying on such a claim[18] and, in all the circumstances, it would be unreasonable to expect the public authority to serve a further notice in relation to the current request.[19] The Freedom of Information Act 2000 does not impose upon a public authority a duty to state why it considers a request to be a vexatious or repeat request and it must be questionable whether it would be reasonable to expect a public authority which is faced with a vexatious or repeat request to provide advice and assistance in this respect to the applicant.[20] As is the case with other refusal notices, any such notice must contain particulars of the public authority's procedures for dealing with complaints about requests for information (or state that the authority does not have such a procedure)[21] and it must provide details of the right to apply for a decision by the Information

[16] Under the Freedom of Information Act 2000, s.14 or the Freedom of Information (Scotland) Act 2002, s.14. As to vexatious requests, see paras 12–008 to 12–010 above. As to repeat requests, see paras 12–011 to 12–014 above.

[17] Freedom of Information Act 2000, s.17(5); Freedom of Information (Scotland) Act 2002, s.16(5).

[18] The Freedom of Information Act 2000, s.17(6)(b) refers to a previous notice that the public authority is relying on a claim that s.14 applies and not just a previous notice that the public authority is relying on a claim that a request was vexatious. Accordingly, it would seem that a public authority is entitled to rely upon the provisions of s.17(6) where it has previously served either a notice that a request is vexatious or a notice that a request is a repeat request. The Scottish provisions are slightly more restrictive, in that a public authority is only excused from giving a notice if it has previously given a notice in respect of an identical or substantially similar request (Freedom of Information (Scotland) Act 2002, s.16(5)(a)).

[19] Freedom of Information Act 2000, s.17(6); Freedom of Information (Scotland) Act 2002, s.16(5). In Scotland, there is an additional requirement that the previous request was identical or substantially similar to the current request: Freedom of Information (Scotland) Act 2002, s.16(5)(a).

[20] That is, pursuant to the duty imposed by s.16(1) of the Freedom of Information Act 2000 or s.15(1) of the Freedom of Information (Scotland) Act 2002. Para.15 of the Code of Practice On the Discharge of Public Authorities' Functions under Part I of the Freedom of Information Act 2000 suggests that a public authority is not expected to provide assistance to applicants whose requests are vexatious.

[21] Freedom of Information Act 2000, s.17(7)(a); Freedom of Information (Scotland) Act 2002, s.19(a).

Commissioner as to whether the request has been properly dealt with.[22] Any notice must be served within the time for compliance with s.1(1) of the Freedom of Information Act 2000.[23]

Refusal notice where cost of compliance is excessive

Where a public authority is relying on a claim that it is not obliged to comply with a request for information because the cost of compliance would be excessive,[24] then it must give the applicant a notice stating that fact.[25] The Freedom of Information Act 2000 does not impose upon a public authority an express duty to state why it considers that the cost of complying with a request would be excessive, but it may be reasonable to expect a public authority which is faced with such a request to provide advice and assistance in this respect to the applicant.[26] As is the case with other refusal notices, such a notice must contain particulars of the public authority's procedures for dealing with complaints about requests for information (or state that the authority does not have such a procedure)[27] and it must provide details of the right to apply for a decision by the Information Commissioner as to whether the request has been properly dealt with.[28] The notice must be given within the time for compliance with s.1(1) of the Freedom of Information Act 2000.[29] 13–008

[22] That is, the right conferred by the Freedom of Information Act 2000, s.50 or the Freedom of Information (Scotland) Act 2002, s.47: Freedom of Information Act 2000, s.17(1)(b); Freedom of Information (Scotland) Act 2002, s.19(b). In Scotland, the notice must also contain particulars of the right to apply to the public authority for a review of its decision under s.20(1): Freedom of Information (Scotland) Act 2002, s.19(b).

[23] Freedom of Information Act 2000, s.17(5). In Scotland, the notice must be given within the time for compliance laid down by s.10 of the Freedom of Information (Scotland) Act 2002: Freedom of Information (Scotland) Act 2002, s.16(5). As to the time for compliance, see paras 11–022 to 11–030 above.

[24] Under the Freedom of Information Act 2000, s.12 or the Freedom of Information (Scotland) Act 2002, s.12. As to the situation where the cost of complying with a request for information would be excessive, see paras 12–001 to 12–007 above.

[25] Freedom of Information Act 2000, s.17(5); Freedom of Information (Scotland) Act 2002, s.16(4).

[26] Pursuant to the duty imposed by the Freedom of Information Act 2000, s.16(1) or the Freedom of Information (Scotland) Act 2002, s.15(1). Paragraph 14 of the *Code of Practice On the Discharge of Public Authorities' Functions under Part I of the Freedom of Information Act 2000* suggests that in such a case a public authority should give an indication of what information could be provided within the cost ceiling.

[27] Freedom of Information Act 2000, s.17(7)(a); Freedom of Information (Scotland) Act 2002, s.19(a).

[28] In other words, the right conferred by s.50 in the Westminster Act and s.47 in the Scottish Act: Freedom of Information Act 2000, s.17(1)(b); Freedom of Information (Scotland) Act 2002, s.19(b). In Scotland, the notice must also contain particulars of the right to apply to the public authority for a review of its decision under s.20(1): Freedom of Information (Scotland) Act 2002, s.19(b).

[29] Freedom of Information Act 2000, s.17(5). In Scotland, the notice must be given within the time for compliance laid down by s.10: Freedom of Information (Scotland) Act 2002, s.16(4). As to the time for compliance, see paras 11–022 to 11–030 above.

Refusal notice where information is excluded from the duty to confirm or deny or where information is exempt information

13–009 Where a public authority is to any extent relying on a claim that any of the information requested is excluded from the duty to confirm or deny (whether an absolute exclusion or otherwise) or a claim that information is exempt information, then it must give the applicant a notice to that effect.[30] Such a notice must state that the public authority is relying on the relevant claim,[31] it must specify the exclusion or exemption in question[32] and it must state (if it would not otherwise be apparent) why the exclusion or exemption applies.[33] However, the public authority is not required to state why an exemption applies if, and to the extent that, that statement would involve the disclosure of information which would itself be exempt information.[34] As has proven to be the case in other jurisdictions, where a significant number of "pieces" of information are involved with differing exemptions, this is often most conveniently done in tabular form, with a row for each discrete piece of information and a column for each exemption and explanations for the same. As is the case with other refusal notices, such a notice must contain particulars of the public authority's procedures for dealing with complaints about requests for information (or state that the authority does not have such a procedure)[35] and it must provide details of the right to apply for a decision by the Information Commissioner as to whether the request has been properly dealt with.[36] The

[30] Freedom of Information Act 2000, s.17(1); Freedom of Information (Scotland) Act 2002, s.16(1).

[31] Freedom of Information Act 2000, s.17(1)(a); Freedom of Information (Scotland) Act 2002, s.16(1)(b). In Scotland, subject to s.18 of the Freedom of Information (Scotland) Act 2002, the notice must also state that the public authority holds the information: Freedom of Information (Scotland) Act 2002, s.16(1)(a). The difference in treatment presumably arises from the fact that s.16(1) of the Freedom of Information (Scotland) Act 2002 applies only to requests for information which the public authority holds, whereas s.17(1) of the Freedom of Information Act 2000 applies to any request for information. Section 18 of the Freedom of Information (Scotland) Act 2002 disapplies s.16(1)(a) and (2) in a case where the public authority considers that to reveal whether the information exists or is held would be contrary to the public interest.

[32] Freedom of Information Act 2000, s.17(1)(b); Freedom of Information (Scotland) Act 2002, s.16(1)(c).

[33] Freedom of Information Act 2000, s.17(1)(c); Freedom of Information (Scotland) Act 2002, s.16(1)(d). Paragraph 50 of the *Code of Practice On the Discharge of Public Authorities' Functions under Part I of the Freedom of Information Act 2000* states that in this context it will not be sufficient for the public authority merely to paraphrase the wording of the exemption. The addition of this requirement was a departure from the position in the Freedom of Information Bill 1999, cl.15. See also House of Commons, *Public Administration—Third Report* (Cm. 4355), July 29, 1999, Annex 6, para.39B and House of Lords, *Draft Freedom of Information Bill—First Report* (Select Committee Report HL97), Session 1998–1999, July 27, 1999, paras 51 to 54.

[34] Freedom of Information Act 2000, s.17(4); Freedom of Information (Scotland) Act 2002, s.16(3).

[35] Freedom of Information Act 2000, s.17(7)(a); Freedom of Information (Scotland) Act 2002, s.19(a).

[36] In other words, the right conferred by s.50 of the Westminster Act and s.47 of the Scottish Act: Freedom of Information Act 2000, s.17(1)(b); Freedom of Information (Scotland) Act 2002, s.19(b). In Scotland, the notice must also contain particulars of the right to apply to the public authority for a review of its decision under s.20(1): Freedom of Information (Scotland) Act 2002, s.19(b).

notice must be served within the time for compliance with s.1(1) of the Freedom of Information Act 2000.[37]

Refusal notice where disclosure would be contrary to the public interest

Where a public authority is to any extent relying on a claim that any information is exempt information (but not by virtue of a provision conferring absolute exemption) and that the public interest in maintaining the exemption outweighs the public interest in disclosing the information, then it must (subject to one exception)[38] state the reasons why it has so decided.[39] Similarly, where a public authority is to any extent relying on a claim that any information is subject to an exclusion (but not an absolute exclusion) from the duty to confirm or deny (but not by virtue of a provision conferring absolute exclusion) and that the public interest in maintaining the exclusion of the duty to confirm or deny outweighs the public interest in disclosing whether the public authority holds the information, then it must (subject to one exception)[40] state the reasons why it has so decided.[41] The exception in each case is that the public authority need not make such a statement if, and to the extent that, the statement would involve the disclosure of information which would itself be exempt information.[42] The reasons must be stated in the refusal notice or in a separate notice given within such time as is reasonable in the circumstances.[43] The provision for separate notice to be given is to allow for the situation where the public authority has deferred its decision on where the public interest lies.[44] Where a public 13–010

[37] Freedom of Information Act 2000, s.17(1). In Scotland, the notice must be served in accordance with the time allowed for compliance with the request by s.10: Freedom of Information (Scotland) Act 2002, s.16(1).

[38] In Scotland, two exceptions apply: see n.42 below.

[39] Freedom of Information Act 2000, s.17(3); Freedom of Information (Scotland) Act 2002, s.16(2). Paragraph 50 of the *Code of Practice On the Discharge of Public Authorities' Functions under Part I of the Freedom of Information Act 2000* states that in this context the public authority should specify the public interest factors, both for and against disclosure, that it has taken into account.

[40] In Scotland, two exceptions apply: see n.42 below.

[41] Freedom of Information Act 2000, s.17(3); Freedom of Information (Scotland) Act 2002, s.16(2). Paragraph 50 of the *Code of Practice On the Discharge of Public Authorities' Functions under Part I of the Freedom of Information Act 2000* states that in this context the public authority should specify the public interest factors, both for and against disclosure, that it has taken into account.

[42] Freedom of Information Act 2000, s.17(4); Freedom of Information (Scotland) Act 2002, s.16(3). In Scotland, s.18 of the Freedom of Information (Scotland) Act 2002 provides for a further exception in a case where the public authority considers that to reveal whether the information exists or is held would be contrary to the public interest.

[43] As the Freedom of Information (Scotland) Act 2002 does not provide for a public authority to defer a decision on where the public interest lies in such a case, that Act contains no provision for a separate notice to be served at a time after the service of the refusal notice.

[44] See the Freedom of Information Act 2000, s.10(3) and para.11–028 above. As to the position in Scotland, see para.11–028 above.

authority has deferred its decision on where the public interest lies, then the notice given to the applicant[45] must:

(a) state that the public authority has not yet reached a decision as to where the balance of the public interest lies;
(b) contain an estimate of the date by which the public authority expects that it will have reached that decision; and
(c) contain all the usual matters that must be included in a refusal notice where the information is exempt.[46]

3. PARTIAL REFUSAL AND REDACTION

Partial refusal

13–011 It may be the case that a request for information will seek both information which a public authority is required to communicate to the applicant and information which it is not required to communicate, for example, because it is exempt information. In such a case, a public authority must communicate the information which it is required to communicate in the normal way and follow the normal procedures in relation to that information which it refuses to communicate.

Redaction

13–012 The Freedom of Information Act 2000 provides for the communication of information to applicants and not for the provision of documents.[47] Accordingly, where an applicant requests information which forms part of a document and that document also contains other information which the applicant is not entitled to receive (for example, because the information is exempt information or because it is outside the terms of the request), the public authority must decide whether it will:

---

[45] That is, the notice given in accordance with s.17(1) of the Freedom of Information Act 2000.

[46] Freedom of Information Act 2000, s.17(2). As to requirement (c), see para.13–009 above. The *Code of Practice On the Discharge of Public Authorities' Functions under Part I of the Freedom of Information Act 2000*, para.18, states that these estimates should be realistic and reasonable and that in the majority of cases public authorities will be expected to comply with their estimates. The Code of Practice also states that if an estimate is exceeded, the public authority should apologise and provide reasons for the delay. As the Freedom of Information (Scotland) Act 2002 does not provide for a public authority to defer such a decision, that Act contains no similar provisions as to notices.

[47] This is in contrast to freedom of information legislation in all but one of the comparable jurisdictions. Where provision is made for access to documents, provision is also made for the redaction of those documents. See, *e.g.*, the Freedom of Information Act 1982 (Commonwealth of Australia), s.22(1); Access to Information Act 1982 (Canada), s.25; Freedom of Information Act 1997 (Republic of Ireland), s.13.

— provide the applicant with the entire document, thereby effectively waiving the exemption in relation to any exempt information[48] or providing the applicant with information that has not been requested;[49]

— redact the document so that the applicant only receives what he is entitled to and what has been asked for; or

— provide the information by a means other than the provision of a copy of the document (*e.g.* by the provision of a newly-created document containing only those parts of the original document containing information to which the applicant is entitled or of a summary of the document).

Whichever option is adopted, the public authority is not entitled to avoid its obligations in relation to the requested information that is either not exempt information or is exempt information solely by virtue of a qualified exemption for which the public interest weighs in favour of disclosure.[50] Where the second or third option is chosen, a public authority should be careful to ensure that any new or redacted document does not create a misleading impression of the information which is held by the public authority. If there is a risk of such a misleading impression being created, then it might be more appropriate to consider providing the information in an alternative manner, such as by way of a summary.[51]

48 In other words, a discretionary disclosure: see paras 14–006 to 14–013 below.

49 In Australia (where the unit of disclosure and exemption is a "document"), the approach taken where disclosure of a single document would disclose information that would reasonably be regarded as irrelevant to a request, is to ask whether such disclosure would reasonably, as opposed to irrationally or absurdly, be considered or looked on as irrelevant and, if so, not include it in the response: *Re Russell Island Development Association Inc and Deparment of Primary Industries and Energy* (1994) 33 A.L.D. 683.

50 This accords with the view expressed by the government spokesman in the House of Lords: *Hansard*, HL, Vol.617, October 17, 2000, cols 930–931. The House of Commons Public Administration Committee had recommended that an express provision to this effect be included in the Act: House of Commons, *Public Administration—Third Report* (Cm. 4355), July 29, 1999, para.120. This is the approach adopted in the Official Information Act 1982 (New Zealand), s.17.

51 It is likely that the difficulty of redacting information which an applicant is not entitled to see is one of the circumstances which a public authority would be entitled to take into account when deciding whether it is reasonably practicable to give effect to an applicant's preference as to the means of communication of the information: Freedom of Information Act 2000, s.11; Freedom of Information (Scotland) Act 2002, s.11. As to the applicant's preference as to the means of communication of the information, see para.11–038 above.

CHAPTER 14

Exemptions: General Principles

1. THE UNIT OF EXEMPTION UNDER THE FOI ACT

Information, not documents

As noted earlier,[1] both the existence and the access rights attach to "information" rather than to documents or records.[2] Although the distinction is narrowed by "information" being defined to mean "recorded information,"[3] the terms are not synonymous: a document or record may contain any number of discrete pieces of information. Similarly, engagement of each of the exemptions 14–001

[1] See Ch.8.

[2] Freedom of Information Act 2000, s.1(1); Freedom of Information (Scotland) Act 2002, s.1(1). S.1(1) of the Data Protection Act 1998 defines "data" to mean "information" possessing certain characteristics, but does not define "information."

[3] Freedom of Information Act 2000, s.84; Freedom of Information (Scotland) Act 2002, s.73. However, for the Commissioner's purposes in serving an information notice under s.51, information extends to unrecorded information: Freedom of Information Act 2000, s.51(8); Freedom of Information (Scotland) Act 2002, s.50(9). Although "information" is not defined in the Data Protection Act 1998, paras (b) and (c) of the s.1(1) definition require it to be recorded.

and consideration of the public interest both turn upon the quality or characteristics of the particular "information," rather than of the document or record containing that information. It is the information that has that quality or characteristic, rather than the document or record containing it, which becomes exempt from the duty to confirm or deny and from the duty to disclose.[4]

Exempt information

14–002 Information that falls within one or other of the exemptions in Pt II of the FOI Act is termed "exempt information."[5] Only "exempt information" is capable of being excused from the duty to disclose. If information falls within one of the "absolute exemptions"[6] under Pt II, then that will be sufficient to disapply the duty to communicate that information. If it does not fall within one of the absolute exemptions, disapplication of the duty to communicate will depend upon a consideration of the public interest.

Partial disclosure

14–003 A single document or record may contain some information that (or the existence of which) need not be disclosed under the FOI Act and other information that (or the existence of which) must be disclosed. Where the information in a document is segregable then, provided that the information in the remainder of the document or record falls within the terms of a request, a public authority remains under its two duties in relation to that information. The use of "information" as the unit of disclosure and of exemption makes it unnecessary for there to be a specific provision requiring a public authority to redact and disclose a document of which only a part contains information that is excused from disclosure.[7] An amendment to the Freedom of Information Bill that would have compelled a public authority to consider partial disclosure[8] was withdrawn following this explanation:

---

4 Freedom of Information Act 2000, s.2(1) and (2); Freedom of Information (Scotland) Act 2002, ss.2(1) and 18(1).

5 Freedom of Information Act 2000, s.84, referring to ss.21(1), 22(1), 23(1), 24(1), 26(1), 27(1), 28(1), 29(1), 30(1) and (2), 31(1), 32(1) and (2), 33(2), 34(1), 35(1), 36(2), 37(1), 38(1), 39(1), 40(1) and (2), 41(1), 42(1), 43(1) and (2), and 44(1). Freedom of Information (Scotland) Act 2002, s.73, referring to ss.25(1), 26, 27(1) and (2), 28(1), 29(1), 30, 31(1) and (4), 32(1), 33(1) and (2), 34(1)-(4), 35(1), 36(1) and (2), 37(1), 38(1), 39(1) and (2), 40 and 41.

6 Freedom of Information Act 2000, s.2(2); Freedom of Information (Scotland) Act 2002, s.2(1). Absolute exemptions are considered at para.14–015 below.

7 Contrast: Freedom of Information Act 1982 (Cth of Aust), s.22(1); The Official Information Act 1982 (NZ), s.17; Access to Information Act, (1982) (Canada), s.25; Freedom of Information Act 1997 (Ireland), s.13.

8 Amendment no.25, moved by Lord Lucas, *Hansard*, HL, Vol.617, October 17, 2000, col.930; withdrawn, col.932.

> "We have been discussing whether the Bill in effect permits partial disclosure. It will in fact require that when some of the information that is requested is exempt but other information is not. The right of access in Clause 1 involves information that is recorded in any form. That means that the right of access attaches to the content of documents or records rather than to the documents or records themselves. When a document contains a mixture of disclosable and non-disclosable information, the disclosable information must be communicated to the applicant."[9]

2. THE DUTY TO CONFIRM OR DENY

Exemption from the duty to confirm or deny: England, Wales & Northern Ireland

Dispensation from the duty to confirm or deny turns upon the purpose for which the information is held, the nature of the information sought or, most commonly, the effect that confirmation or denial of holding the sought information would have. In the last case, the effect required in order to trigger dispensation varies according to the ground of exemption. In summary: 14–004

(1) Where the information sought:

- (a) has at any time been held for the purposes of a criminal investigation or is confidential information obtained for the purposes of the authority's functions relating to such an investigation;
- (b) has at any time been held as part of court or arbitral proceedings;
- (c) is held by a government department and relates to the formulation of policy or to Ministerial communications;
- (d) relates to communications with the Royal Family or the conferring of honours or dignities;
- (e) is required to be made available under the access to environmental information provisions; or
- (f) constitutes personal data of which the requester is the data subject,

then the public authority is excused from the duty to confirm or deny that such information is held.[10]

(2) Where, or to the extent that, exemption from confirmation or denial of a holding of the information sought is required:

- (a) to safeguard national security;

[9] Lord Falconer of Thoroton, *Hansard*, HL, Vol.617, October 17, 2000, col.931.

[10] Freedom of Information Act 2000, ss.30(3), 32(2), 35(3), 37(2), 39(2) and 40(5)(a), respectively.

(b) to avoid an infringement of the privileges of either House of Parliament;
(c) to avoid an actionable breach of confidence;
(d) to maintain the possibility of a claim of legal professional privilege; or
(e) to avoid contravention of an enactment or of a community obligation, or to avoid a contempt of court,

then the public authority is excused from the duty to confirm or deny that any information answering the request is held.[11]

(3) Where the information sought:

(a) is intended for future publication;
(b) is supplied by, or relates to, bodies dealing with security matters; or
(c) is confidential information obtained from the Government of any State other than the United Kingdom or from an international organisation or court,

then the duty to confirm or deny does not arise if, or to the extent that, confirmation or denial that the requested public authority holds the information sought would itself involve the disclosure of any information so exempted from disclosure.[12]

(4) Where confirmation or denial that the public authority holds the information sought would, or would be likely to, prejudice:

(a) the defence of the nation or the effectiveness of the armed forces;
(b) relations between the United Kingdom and another state or an international organisation or the interests of the United Kingdom abroad;
(c) governmental relations within the United Kingdom;
(d) the economic interests of the United Kingdom or the financial interests of any administration within the United Kingdom;
(e) the efficacy of law enforcement;
(f) the exercise of an auditing body's functions;
(g) cabinet confidentiality, the frank provision of advice or the effective conduct of public affairs;
(h) the physical or mental health or safety of an individual; or
(i) the commercial interests of a person,

then the duty to confirm or deny is, to that extent, disapplied.[13]

(5) Where the information sought constitutes personal data of which the requester is not the data subject and where confirmation or denial that

---

[11] Freedom of Information Act 2000, ss.24(2), 34(2), 41(2), 42(2) and 44(2), respectively.
[12] *ibid*., ss.22(2), 23(5) and 27(4)(b), respectively.
[13] Freedom of Information Act 2000, ss.26(3), 27(4)(a), 28(3), 29(2), 31(1), 33(3), 36(3), 38(2) and 43(3)), respectively.

the public authority holds the information requested would contravene one of the data protection principles or s.10 of the Data Protection Act 1998 or the information is exempt from s.7(1)(a) of that Act, then the duty to confirm or deny is, to that extent, disapplied.[14]

(6) In relation to:

(a) information accessible to a requester by other means; or
(b) information that constitutes a trade secret,

there is no disapplication of the duty to confirm or deny the existence of such information.[15]

Exemption from the duty to confirm or deny: Scotland

There is no discrete duty in the Scottish FOI Act to confirm or deny the existence of information answering the terms of a request. A public authority nevertheless can, in certain circumstances, reply to a request for information by neither confirming or denying the existence of the information, or some of the information, sought.[16] The ability to do so does not, of course, depend upon the existence of the information sought: to so confine it would rob the provision of its efficacy. The exercise involves assuming that the sought information exists (irrespective of whether or not it does). If, on that assumed basis, the public authority could give a refusal notice on the basis that that information would be exempt by virtue of: 14–005

- its disclosure substantially prejudicing relations between United Kingdom administrations;
- it relating to the formulation of Scottish Administration policy;
- its disclosure substantially prejudicing the effective conduct of public affairs;
- its exemption being required to safeguard national security;
- its disclosure being substantially prejudicial to the defence of the country;
- its disclosure being substantially prejudicial to international relations;
- it constituting a trade secret;
- its disclosure being substantially prejudicial to commercial interests or the economic or financial interest of the country;
- it having been held for the purposes of a criminal investigation;
- its disclosure being substantially prejudicial to a criminal investigation, prosecution, the administration of justice, tax collection, immigration controls and so forth;

[14] Freedom of Information Act 2000, s.40(4)(b).
[15] *ibid.*, ss.21 and 43(1), respectively.
[16] Freedom of Information (Scotland) Act 2002, s.18(1).

— its disclosure endangering the health or safety of an individual; or
— it relating to communications with Her Majesty or other members of the Royal Family,[17]

then the public authority may proceed to consider whether confirming or denying the existence of the information would be contrary to the public interest.[18] If confirmation or denial would be so contrary to the public interest, the public authority is permitted to give the applicant a refusal notice that neither discloses that it holds the sought information nor sets out its reasoning in relation to the public interest.[19]

3. THE DISCRETION TO MAINTAIN AN EXEMPTION

Introduction

14–006 The scheme of the FOI Act starts by describing an unrestricted entitlement to be informed as to the existence of, and to have communicated, information held by a public authority. These broadly-described entitlements are cut down by a series of exemptions, some of which involve a consideration of the public interest. The applicability of an exemption, whether an absolute one or a qualified one, does not preclude the public authority from otherwise disclosing the information: a "discretionary disclosure." It simply means that the applicant has no entitlement under the FOI Act to the disclosure of that information. The Act expressly affirms this position.[20] In relation to central government departments it has occasionally been suggested that they may disclose and disseminate information under a prerogative power of the Crown.[21] Alternatively, the power to disclose and disseminate information may be seen as a common law power possessed by the Crown by virtue of its legal personality as a corporation sole.[22]

[17] Freedom of Information (Scotland) Act 2002, ss.28, 29, 30, 31(1), 31(4), 32, 33(1)(a), 33(1)(b) and 33(2), 34, 35, 39(1) and 41 respectively.

[18] Freedom of Information (Scotland) Act 2002, s.18(1).

[19] *ibid.*, s.18(2).

[20] Freedom of Information Act 2000, s.78; Freedom of Information (Scotland) Act 2002, s.65. See also Freedom of Information Act 2000, s.17 and Freedom of Information (Scotland) Act 2002, s.16(1) which speak of "relying" on a "claim" that information is exempt information, that the duty to confirm or deny does not arise and that the public interest is against disclosure. In this respect, the scheme of the FOI Act resembles those in the Freedom of Information Act 1982 (Cth of Aust) and Official Information Act 1982 (New Zealand), differing from those in the Access to Information Act, (1982) (Canada) and the Freedom of Information Act 1997 (Ireland) which spell out circumstances in which a request may be refused and circumstances in which a request must be refused.

[21] *Jenkins v Attorney-General* (1971) *The Times*, August 14 (issue of a pamphlet on the common market); *R. v Secretary of State for the Environment, Ex p. Greenwich London Borough Council* [1989] C.O.D. 530, DC (publication of a leaflet about the Community Charge or "Poll Tax").

[22] *Malone v Metropolitan Police Commissioner* [1979] Ch.344, *sub nom Malone v Metropolitan Police Commissioner (No 2)* [1979] 2 All E.R. 620; *R. v Secretary of State for Health, Ex p. C* [2000] 1 F.L.R. 627, CA.

Regardless of Crown status, all public authorities will also have power to disclose information where this is expressly provided for by statute or it is necessarily incidental or conducive to the exercise of another statutory, prerogative or common law function: subject, of course, to any countervailing restrictions on disclosure under statute or the general law. In this latter regard, the power to make a voluntary disclosure may be precluded by a statutory bar or a comprehensive statutory regime which provides for similar disclosures subject to specific requirements and which must be read as displacing any more general power to act outside that regime.[23]

The nature of the discretion

Other than perhaps through its long title, the Act does not expressly encourage the discretionary disclosure of information.[24] Some encouragement is to be found in the *Code of Practice on Access to Government Information*[25] and in the statutory recognition of a public interest in disclosing exempt information, at least in relation to qualified exemptions.[26] The decision to provide discretionary disclosure of information is distinct from the conclusion that results from weighing the public interest in maintaining a qualified exemption against the public interest in disclosing the information.[27] Other than in relation to 14–007

[23] *R. v Liverpool City Council, Ex p. Baby Products Association* [2000] B.L.G.R. 171; 2 L.G.R. 689; *Attorney-General v De Keyser's Royal Hotel Ltd* [1920] A.C. 508; *R. v Secretary of State for the Home Department, Ex p. Fire Brigades Union* [1995] 2 A.C. 513.

[24] Contrast Freedom of Information Act 1982, s.14 (Cth of Aust): "Nothing in this Act is intended to prevent or discourage Ministers and agencies from publishing or giving access to documents (including exempt documents), otherwise than as required by this Act, where they can properly do so or are required by law to do so."

[25] Second edition, 1997. See paras 5–001 to 5–010. That document opens: "1. This Code of Practice supports the Government's policy under the Citizen's Charter of extending access to official information, and responding to reasonable requests for information. The approach to release of information should in all cases be based on the assumption that information should be released except where disclosure would not be in the public interest, as specified in Part II of this Code." It should be noted that the Code only applies to central government, and not to many in the wide range of public authorities that are subject to the Freedom of Information Act 2000. The Code is, of course, a document of the Executive, rather than an articulation of Parliament's will.

[26] Freedom of Information Act 2000, s.2(2); Freedom of Information (Scotland) Act 2002, s.2(1). Amendments to the Bill that would have recorded that the purpose of the Act was to encourage the provision of information by public authorities to the public were unsuccessful: *Hansard*, HL, Vol.617, October 17, 2000, cols 886–888. Lord Falconer of Thoroton (the Minister of State, Cabinet Office) said that a purpose clause was not "appropriate:" *Hansard*, HL, Vol.617, October 17, 2000, col.898. He later said: "We make it clear, and made it clear in Committee, that what we are interested in seeking to achieve is a change of culture in relation to freedom of information. . ..[the Government's amendments] put beyond doubt the Government's resolve that information must be disclosed except where there is an overriding public interest in keeping specific information confidential. Perhaps I may repeat that: information must be disclosed except where there is an overriding public interest in keeping specific information confidential" — *Hansard*, HL, Vol.619, November 14, 2000, col.143. See para.1–014.

[27] See Freedom of Information Act 2000, ss.17 and 18; Freedom of Information (Scotland) Act 2002, s.16(1). It is tolerably clear from s.17 (in Scotland, s.16(1)) that a public authority makes a

information the disclosure of which is proscribed or that has emanated from a third party, a public authority does not require a statutory mandate to disclose information held by it.[28] It is an ordinary incident of holding information that the person holding it may choose to disclose it to others. A public authority may, however, be constrained by other considerations, most notably the effect of any disclosure upon either the public generally or specific individuals.[29]

Scope for discretionary disclosure

14–008 It is nevertheless difficult to see much scope for discretionary disclosure, certainly in relation to information that is not required to be disclosed on the basis of a qualified exemption: the public authority will necessarily already have concluded that the public interest in maintaining the exemption outweighs the public interest in disclosing the information.[30] In the United States, discretionary disclosure is generally confined to:

— where the administrative burden of dealing with the request affords a ground of exemption[31];
— where the information in question is a portion of a document not otherwise exempt in its entirety;
— deliberative process documents[32];
— documents that are litigation-related.[33]

decision whether to rely both on the applicability of a provision in Pt II and on the result of the public interest weighing exercise.

[28] *Attorney-General v Guardian Newspapers Ltd (No. 2)* [1990] 1 A.C. 109 at 256: "The general rule is that anyone is entitled to communicate anything he pleases to anyone else, by speech or in writing or in any other way . . . ."

[29] In *R. v Chief Constable North Wales Police, Ex p. AB* [1999] Q.B. 396; [1998] 3 All E.R. 310 (which involved applications for judicial review of the decision of the police to reveal the identity of two former sex offenders) the Court held that where a public authority (in that case, the defendant police authority) acquired information in the course of its duties, relating to a member of the public and potentially damaging to that member of the public, that public authority "ought not to disclose such information save for the purpose of and to the extent necessary for performance of its public duty or enabling some other public body to perform its public duty" (at 410). It was said that "this principle does not . . . rest on the existence of a duty of confidence owed by the public body to the member of the public, although it might well be that such a duty of confidence might in certain circumstances arise. The principle . . . rests on a fundamental rule of good public administration, which the law must recognise and if necessary enforce" (at 410). The applications for judicial review were dismissed on the basis that the balance struck between the competing interests served by disclosure and non-disclosure could not be said to have been unlawfully wrong. On appeal the Court of Appeal, upholding that decision, held that "disclosure should only be made when there is a pressing need for that disclosure" (at 428).

[30] The House of Commons Select Committee appeared to consider that there was scope for discretionary disclosure in relation to purely class-based exemptions: House of Commons, *Public Administration–Third Report*, (Cm 4355), July 29, 1999, para.60.

[31] 5 USC 552(b)(2), "Exemption 2".

[32] 5 USC 552(b)(5), "Exemption 5".

[33] 5 USC 552(b)(5), "Exemption 5".

Waiver by discretionary disclosure

A discretionary disclosure of information may impinge upon the subsequent ability of a public authority to rely on a claim[34] of exemption or exclusion in relation to similar requests for information. Elsewhere it has been held that a decision not to maintain any of the available grounds of exemption and to release information that could properly be withheld does not prevent a subsequent maintenance of grounds of exemption.[35] In the United States, the starting point is that an agency may make a discretionary disclosure of material that is exempt under the FOI Act without undue concern that it will be impairing its ability subsequently to invoke applicable exemptions in relation to like information. Notions of waiver have usually been resisted on the basis that they would tend to thwart the purpose of the Act: 14–009

> "Implying such a waiver could tend to inhibit agencies from making any disclosures other than those explicitly required by law because voluntary release of documents exempt from disclosure requirements would expose other documents [of a related nature] to risk of disclosure. An agency would have an incentive to refuse to release all exempt documents if it wished to retain an exemption for any documents . . . [R]eadily finding waiver of confidentiality for exempt documents would tend to thwart the [FOI Act's] underlying statutory purpose, which is to implement a policy of broad disclosure of government records."[36]

Although it is possible for a claim of waiver to meet with success, such claims have been met with a preliminary requirement that the applicant establish that the exempt information sought duplicates or sufficiently matches the information that previously has been voluntarily disclosed.[37] Moreover, in order to

---

34 See Freedom of Information Act 2000, s.17 and Freedom of Information (Scotland) Act 2002, s.16(1).

35 *Re Lordsvale Finance Ltd v Department of Treasury* (1985) 9 A.L.D. 16; 3 A.A.R. 301 (Australia).

36 *Mobil Oil Corp v Environmental Protection Agency*, 879 F.(2d) 698 (9th Cir. 1989), where the applicant argued that by making a discretionary disclosure of certain records that could have been withheld under the FOI Act, the agency had waived its right to invoke that exemption for a group of related records.The Court did hold that the release of the documents amounted to a waiver of the exemptions for those documents so released. Similarly: *Nationwide Building Maintenance Inc v Sampson*, 559 F.(2d) 704 at 712 (D.C. Cir. 1977)("The FOI Act should not be construed so as to put the federal bureaucracy in a defensive or hostile position with respect to the Act's spirit of open government and liberal disclosure of information."); *Mehl v Environmental Protection Agency*, 797 F. Supp 43 at 47 (D.D.C. 1992)("A contrary rule would create an incentive against voluntary disclosure of information."); *Greenberg v United States Department of Treasury*, 10 F. Supp.(2d) at 23–24 (D.D.C. 1998).

37 *Public Citizen v Department of State*, 276 F.3d 634 at 645 (D.C. Cir. 2002); *Afshar v Department of State*, 702 F.(2d) 1125 at 1132 (D.C. Cir. 1983).

found a waiver, the previous disclosure must have been an authorised one[38] and it must have been made voluntarily.[39]

Effect of discretionary disclosure upon prejudiced-based exemptions

14–010 A distinction needs to be drawn between the effect of discretionary disclosure upon the subsequent invocation of a purely class-based exemption and the subsequent invocation of a prejudice-based exemption. In the former case, previous disclosure of like information does not impede subsequent information from falling within the terms of the exemption. In the latter case, the exemption requires that disclosure "would or would be likely to" cause some prejudice. The requirement that it "cause" or "be likely to cause" prejudice may be lost by the earlier disclosure of like information. Similarly, discretionary disclosure may impinge upon a subsequent weighing of the public interest in maintaining an exemption in respect of like information.

Other consequences of discretionary disclosure

14–011 In granting discretionary disclosure, a public authority will not enjoy any protection should that disclosure represent a publication of defamatory matter. That protection only applies to publication effected by a communication of information under the FOI Act.[40] Where a public authority decides to give discretionary disclosure it may charge for the cost of the communication of that information.[41]

Review of discretionary disclosure

14–012 A decision not to disclose information in circumstances where there is no right of access under the FOI Act will not engage the appeal structure set out in the

[38] *Public Citizen Health Research Group v FDA*, 953 F. Supp. 400 (D.D.C. 1996) (no waiver where material accidently released); *Simmons v United States Department of Justice*, 796 F.(2d) 709 (4th Cir. 1986) (unauthorised disclosure does not constitute waiver); similarly *Medina-Hincapie v Department of State*, 700 F.(2d) 73 (D.C. Cir. 1983).

[39] *Lead Industry Association v OSHA*, 610 F.(2d) 70 (2d Cir. 1979).

[40] Freedom of Information Act 2000, s.79; Freedom of Information (Scotland) Act 2002, s.67.

[41] Freedom of Information Act 2000, s.13(1)(b); Freedom of Information (Scotland) Act 2002, s.13(1)(b). The provisions do not enable the public authority to charge for the cost of locating the information, determining whether the information is exempt information or considering the public interest: see paras 11–017 to 11–019.

FOI Act.[42] Such a decision is theoretically justiciable by judicial review, but other than in relation to an unjustifiably selective discretionary disclosure of exempt information, it is questionable whether there is much scope for judicial review of a refusal to provide discretionary disclosure.

Non-reliance upon an exemption

Where there is more than one ground upon which a public authority can rely for the disapplication of its duty to confirm or deny or of its duty to disclose information, it may when giving a refusal notice choose not to rely on one or more of those grounds of exemption.[42A] The distinction between this and discretionary disclosure is that here the public authority maintains that confirmation or denial, or that disclosure, of the information should be resisted. The public authority, in choosing not to rely on a particular exemption, makes no concession other than as to its assessment of the focus of the public interest. Moreover, by having not disclosed the information, it will remain open for the disclosure of the information to have, or to be likely to have, a prescribed prejudicial effect. Accordingly, the decision of a public authority not to invoke a potential ground of exemption does not preclude a subsequent invocation of that ground of exemption, either in relation to a subsequent like request or in the enforcement or appeal procedure. 14–013

4. CLASSIFICATION OF EXEMPTIONS UNDER THE FOI ACT

Introduction

Part II of the FOI Act enumerates discrete grounds upon which a public authority is excused both from its duty to confirm or deny that it holds the information sought and from its duty to disclose that information.[43] A classification of the different grounds for dispensation from the duty to confirm or deny has been considered above.[44] More generally and in relation to both duties, the FOI Act divides each of the exemptions into absolute exemptions and qualified 14–014

[42] So held in Australia in relation to the analogous s.14 Freedom of Information Act 1982: *Re Waterford and Department of Treasury* (1983) 5 A.L.D. 193, *Re Waterford and Department of Health* (1983) 5 A.L.N. N139.

[42A] Freedom of Information Act 2000, s.17(1); Freedom of Information (Scotland) Act 2002, s.16(1)

[43] Freedom of Information Act 2000, ss.21–44; Freedom of Information (Scotland) Act 2002, ss.25–41. Pt 2 of the latter Act relates only to exemption from the duty to disclose information. In relation to the circumstances in which a Scottish public authority is excused from revealing in a refusal notice whether the information sought exists, see para.4–005.

[44] See para.14–004.

exemptions. Each exemption can also be characterised as either being a purely class-based exemption or being a prejudice-based exemption.

Absolute exemptions

14–015 Absolute exemptions are defined in the FOI[45] Act to be those conferred in respect of:

- information that is reasonably accessible to the applicant otherwise than under the FOI Act[46];
- information held by the requested public authority that was directly or indirectly supplied to it by, or that relates to, any of the defined security bodies[47];
- information held by the requested public authority only by virtue of that information being contained in a formal document filed with a court or tribunal, in a formal document served for the purposes of court or tribunal proceedings, or in a formal document created by a court or by staff of a court[48];
- information held by the requested public authority only by virtue of it being contained in a document placed in the custody of a person conducting an inquiry or arbitration, or in a document created by a person conducting an inquiry or arbitration, for the purposes of the inquiry or arbitration[49];
- information for which exemption is required for the purpose of avoiding an infringement of the privileges of either House of Parliament[50];
- information held by the House of Commons or the House of Lords that, in the reasonable opinion of the Speaker of the House of Commons or the Clerk of the Parliaments respectively, if disclosed under the FOI Act, would or would be likely to:
    - prejudice the convention of the collective responsibility of Ministers of the Crown, etc.;
    - inhibit the free and frank provision of advice or exchange of views for the purposes of deliberation; or
    - otherwise prejudice the effective conduct of public affairs[51];

[45] Freedom of Information Act 2000, s.2(3); Freedom of Information (Scotland) Act 2002, s.2(2).
[46] Freedom of Information Act 2000, s.21(1); Freedom of Information (Scotland) Act 2002, s.25(1).
[47] Freedom of Information Act 2000, s.23(1). This does not constitute an absolute exemption in Scotland.
[48] *ibid.*, s.32(1); Freedom of Information (Scotland) Act 2002, s.37(1)(a).
[49] *ibid.*, s.32(2); Freedom of Information (Scotland) Act 2002, s.37(1)(b).
[50] *ibid.*, s.34(1). This does not constitute an absolute exemption in Scotland.
[51] Freedom of Information Act 2000, s.36(2). This does not constitute an absolute exemption in Scotland.

— information that constitutes personal data of which the applicant is the data subject[52];
— information that constitutes personal data of which the applicant is not the data subject, that is not manual data and the disclosure of which would contravene one of the data protection principles[53];
— information that constitutes personal data of which the applicant is not the data subject and the disclosure of which would contravene one of the data protection principles (in the case of manual data, disregarding the exemptions from the data protection principles granted by s.33A of the Data Protection Act 1998)[54];
— information obtained by the public authority from any other person (including another public authority) the disclosure of which would constitute an actionable breach of confidence by the public authority;[55] and
— information the disclosure of which is prohibited by or under an enactment, is incompatible with any Community obligation or would constitute a contempt of court.[56]

Where information satisfies a provision conferring absolute exemption, that will be sufficient to disapply both the duty to confirm or deny the existence of that information and the duty to disclose that information.[57] Subject to any proscription against disclosure, a public authority may, in its discretion, nevertheless decide to disclose the information.[58]

Qualified exemptions

The remaining exemptions, which may for convenience be termed "qualified exemptions," are those conferred in respect of: 14–016

— information intended for future publication[59];
— information for which exemption from the duties is required for the purpose of safeguarding national security[60];

---

[52] Freedom of Information Act 2000, s.40(1); Freedom of Information (Scotland) Act 2002, s.38(1)(a). In Scotland, personal census information and a deceased person's health record are also absolute exemptions: s.38(1)(c) and (d).
[53] *ibid.*, s.40(3)(a)(i); Freedom of Information (Scotland) Act 2002, s.38(1)(a).
[54] *ibid.*, s.40(3)(b); Freedom of Information (Scotland) Act 2002, s.38(1)(b).
[55] *ibid.*, s.41(1); Freedom of Information (Scotland) Act 2002, s.36(2).
[56] *ibid.*, s.44(1); Freedom of Information (Scotland) Act 2002, s.26.
[57] Freedom of Information Act 2000, ss.2(1)(a) and 2(1)(b); Freedom of Information (Scotland) Act 2002, s.2(1)(a). In Scotland it will not automatically lead to a public authority being excused from revealing in a refusal notice whether the information sought exists: see para.14–005.
[58] See para.14–006.
[59] Freedom of Information Act 2000, s.22(1); Freedom of Information (Scotland) Act 2002, s.27(1).
[60] Freedom of Information Act 2000, s.24(1); Freedom of Information (Scotland) Act 2002, s.31(1).

— information whose disclosure would or would be likely to prejudice the defence of the British Isles[61];
— information whose disclosure would or would be likely to prejudice relations between the United Kingdom and any other State or international organisation or to prejudice the interests of the United Kingdom abroad[62];
— confidential information obtained from a foreign state or from an international organisation or court[63];
— information whose disclosure would or would be likely to prejudice relations between administrations within the United Kingdom[64];
— information the disclosure of which would or would be likely to prejudice the economic or financial interests of the United Kingdom or any part of it[65];
— information held by a public authority for the purposes of a criminal investigation or proceedings[66];
— information the disclosure of which would or would be likely to prejudice the prevention or detection of crime, etc.[67];
— information that would or would be likely to prejudice an auditing body's audit functions[68];
— policy information[69];
— information, other than that held by the House of Commons or the House of Lords that, in the reasonable opinion of a qualified person, if disclosed under the FOI Act, would or would be likely to:
    — prejudice the convention of the collective responsibility of Ministers of the Crown, etc.;
    — inhibit the free and frank provision of advice or exchange of views for the purposes of deliberation; or
    — otherwise prejudice the effective conduct of public affairs[70];
— communications with Her Majesty or the Royal Household[71];
— information the disclosure of which would or would be likely to endanger the physical or mental health of an individual or endanger an individual's safety[72];

61 Freedom of Information Act 2000, s.26(1); Freedom of Information (Scotland) Act 2002, s.31(4).
62 Freedom of Information Act 2000, s.27(1); Freedom of Information (Scotland) Act 2002, s.32(1)(a).
63 Freedom of Information Act 2000, s.27(2); Freedom of Information (Scotland) Act 2002, s.32(1)(b).
64 Freedom of Information Act 2000, s.28(1); Freedom of Information (Scotland) Act 2002, s.28(1).
65 Freedom of Information Act 2000, s.29(1); Freedom of Information (Scotland) Act 2002, s.33(2).
66 Freedom of Information Act 2000, s.30(1); Freedom of Information (Scotland) Act 2002, s.34(1).
67 Freedom of Information Act 2000, s.31(1); Freedom of Information (Scotland) Act 2002, s.35(1).
68 Freedom of Information Act 2000, s.33(2); Freedom of Information (Scotland) Act 2002, s.40.
69 Freedom of Information Act 2000, s.35(1); Freedom of Information (Scotland) Act 2002, s.29(1).
70 Freedom of Information Act 2000, s.36(2). Freedom of Information (Scotland) Act 2002, s.30.
71 Freedom of Information Act 2000, s.37(1); Freedom of Information (Scotland) Act 2002, s.41.
72 Freedom of Information Act 2000, s.38(1); Freedom of Information (Scotland) Act 2002, s.39(1).

— environmental information[73];
— information in respect of which a claim to legal professional privilege could be maintained[74];
— information that constitutes a trade secret or the disclosure of which would or would be likely to prejudice the commercial interests of any person.[75]

Principal significance of the division between absolute and qualified exemptions

As noted above, where information satisfies a provision conferring absolute exemption, that will be sufficient to disapply the duty to disclose that information.[76] And similarly a provision conferring absolute exclusion from the duty to confirm or deny the existence of information. Where information satisfies a provision conferring qualified exemption then: 14–017

(a) the duty to confirm or deny will be disapplied where, in all the circumstances of the cases, the public interest in maintaining the exclusion of the duty to confirm or deny outweighs the public interest in disclosing whether the public authority holds the information; and
(b) the duty to disclose will be disapplied where, in all the circumstances of the case, the public interest in maintaining the exemption outweighs the public interest in disclosing the information.

That which is being balanced thus differs according to the duty being disapplied. Although the public interest in "maintaining the exclusion of the duty to confirm or deny" may be thought to be less pressing than the public interest in "maintaining the exemption," the counterbalancing public interest in "disclosing whether the public authority holds the information" may be thought to be correspondingly less compelling than the public interest in "disclosing the information." The public interest in maintaining the exclusion of the duty to confirm or deny will involve a consideration of the terms of the request. A highly specific request is more likely than a general request to result in the public interest in maintaining the exclusion of the duty to confirm or deny outweighing the public interest in disclosing whether the public authority holds the information: answering a highly specific request can effectively amount to a disclosure of the information sought. The public interest in maintaining the exemption from

[73] Freedom of Information Act 2000, s.39(1); Freedom of Information (Scotland) Act 2002, s.39(2).
[74] Freedom of Information Act 2000, s.42(1); Freedom of Information (Scotland) Act 2002, s.36(1).
[75] Freedom of Information Act 2000, s.43(1) and (2); Freedom of Information (Scotland) Act 2002, s.33(1).
[76] Freedom of Information Act 2000, ss.2(1) and (2); Freedom of Information (Scotland) Act 2002, s.2(1): in Scotland there is no separate duty to confirm or deny the existence of information sought.

disclosure will, on the other hand, involve a greater emphasis on the information itself, rather than on the terms of the request.

Significance of distinction for time-limits

14–018 The distinction between the two categories of exemption has significance for the time within which a public authority must reply to a request. The time-limit for complete compliance with a request under the FOI Act varies according to whether there are any qualified grounds of exemption applicable to the information sought. To the extent that a public authority, in claiming a disapplication of the duty to confirm or deny or to communicate particular information, relies exclusively upon one or more absolute exemptions, the public authority must give notice of its refusal within 20 working days.[77] To the extent that a public authority, in claiming a disapplication of the duty to confirm or deny or to communicate particular information, relies upon one or more qualified exemptions, the public authority must first, within 20 working days, give notice specifying the exemption relied upon and the reason it applies, but advising the applicant that no decision in relation to the weighing of the public interest has yet been reached and giving an estimate of when it expects that exercise to be completed.[78] The public authority then has a reasonable time within which to carry out the exercise of weighing the public interest[79] and a further reasonable time to give the applicant notice of that decision.[80]

Significance of distinction for enforcement

14–019 The distinction between the two categories of exemption also has significance for the ability of certain public authorities to shield themselves from decision notices and enforcement notices. Certain core, central government public authorities, when served with a decision notice or an enforcement notice, may give the Information Commissioner a certificate under s.53(2).[81] In general terms, the effect of the certificate is to shield that public authority from its duty to comply with a decision notice or an enforcement notice.[82] In relation to the communication obligation, the ability to serve such a notice is confined to where there has been a failure to comply with the duty to communicate in respect of exempt information. In relation to the duty to confirm or deny, the

[77] Freedom of Information Act 2000, ss.17(1) and 10(1)); Freedom of Information (Scotland) Act 2002, ss.17(1) and 10(1).

[78] Freedom of Information Act 2000, ss.17 and 10(1). No additional time for responding is provided under the Freedom of Information (Scotland) Act 2002. See further paras 11–022 to 11–031.

[79] Freedom of Information Act 2000, s.10(3); Freedom of Information (Scotland) Act 2002, s.33(1).

[80] Freedom of Information Act 2000, s.17(3); Freedom of Information (Scotland) Act 2002, s.33(1).

[81] In Scotland, s.52(2).

[82] See para.14–030.

ability to serve such a notice is confined to where there has been a failure to comply with the duty to confirm or deny in respect of information falling within any provision of Pt II stating that that duty does not arise. In those circumstances, the "accountable person" of the public authority can give the Information Commissioner a certificate stating that he has on reasonable grounds formed the opinion that, in respect of the request, there has been no failure to comply with the s.1 duty. Because certification can only apply to a decision notice or an enforcement notice that relates to a failure to comply with the s.1 duty, the issue of whether the information falls within any provision of Pt II is outwith the certification process under s.53. The s.53(2) certificate is directed to the accountable person's opinion in relation to the weighing of the public interest: it is only that weighing which can reasonably induce an accountable person to form the opinion that there has been no failure to comply with the s.1(1) duties where the information is exempt information. In short, the effect of a s.53(2) certificate is confined to shielding certain central government public authorities from the Information Commissioner's determination that information falling within a qualified exemption ought to be disclosed in the public interest.[83]

Implicit significance of the statutory distinction

Underlying each of the exemptions in Pt II of the FOI Act is a public interest 14–020
against the disclosure of information falling within the terms of the exemption. It is implicit in the creation of the qualified exemptions that the public interest in a public authority confirming or denying that it holds certain information and in it communicating that information are each capable of outweighing the underlying public interest in maintaining each of the exemptions. Approximately half of the qualified exemptions, in order to be engaged, expressly require that disclosure of the information under the Act cause, or be likely to cause, some form of prejudice.[84] The existence of that prejudice or of the

[83] As is confirmed in *Explanatory Notes* to the Freedom of Information Act 2000, para.180. This was also confirmed to Parliament by Lord Falconer of Thoroton (the Minister of State, Cabinet Office) who said: "Contrary to what my noble friend Lord Brennan said, it is worth noting that the effect of this provision is not that any decision of the information commissioner can be overridden: the only decision of the information commissioner that can be overridden is one on the balance of the public interest under Cl.13. If, for example, the information commissioner determined that something was not covered by an exemption, then the ministerial override would never apply. Once it is not exempt, disclosure is automatic. The ministerial override under Clause 13 applies only where something is exempt and the Minister or the public authority concerned has refused to override the exemption in the public interest"—*Hansard*, HL, Vol.618, October 25, 2000, cols 445–446. See also: *Hansard*, HL, Vol.619, November 14, 2000, col.258, Lord Falconer of Thoroton.

[84] Freedom of Information Act 2000, ss.26(1), 27(1), 28(1), 29(1), 31(1), 33(2) and (3), 36(2), 38(1) and 43(2); Freedom of Information (Scotland) Act 2002, ss.28(1), 30, 31(4), 32(1)(a), 33(1)(b), 33(2), 35(1), 39(1) and 40. The requirement in Scotland is that the prejudice be a "substantial" one before the exemption is engaged and before considering whether nevertheless the public

likelihood of that prejudice will not automatically represent an adequate counterbalancing public interest against disclosure, as that would effectively elevate the exemption into an absolute exemption.[85] The FOI Act recognises that where a qualified exemption is engaged, the public interest in the maintenance of that exemption is not of fixed weight, but that it will vary according to "all the circumstances of the case." Similarly, the FOI Act recognises that whilst there always exists a public interest in disclosing whether a public authority holds information and in disclosing that information, the weight to be afforded to these will vary according to "all the circumstances of the case."[86]

Purely class-based exemptions

14–021 Independently of the statutory distinction between absolute and qualified exemptions, it is possible to characterise some of the exemptions as purely class-based,[87] whereas others require some form of prejudice before the exemption is engaged. Purely class-based exemptions are those conferred in respect of:

— information that is reasonably accessible to the applicant otherwise than under the FOI Act[88];
— information intended for future publication[89];

interest in disclosing the information is not outweighed by the public interest in maintaining the exemption.

[85] See generally *Hansard*, HL, Vol.617, October 17, 2000, cols 901–905, 912–913, and 923–924 Lord Falconer of Thoroton, the Minister of State at the Cabinet Office, during Committee Stage of the FOI Bill in the House of Lords and introducing the amendment that resulted in s.2. Questioned as to what a public official was to do when required to weigh the competing public interests, he said (col.921): "As far as public interest between disclosure on the one hand and the maintenance of exemption on the other is concerned, it has to be looked at objectively. One looks at the impact of disclosure, that is, making it public. What is the impact of the exemption being maintained? That should be looked at objectively rather than in terms of whatever the motive may be of the person applying. That does not mean that the motive of the person applying may not coincide with factors that could be relevant to what damage may be done and what assistance could be served by making the matter public. But individual motives will not be relevant to that." The FOI Bill as originally introduced (cl.14, later cl.13) required a public authority to consider "discretionary disclosure" of exempt information: see House of Commons, *Public Administration—Third Report*, (Cm.4355), July 29, 1999, para.60.

[86] The necessity of carrying out this exercise on a case-by-case basis was acknowledged by Lord Falconer of Thoroton: *Hansard*, HL, Vol.619, November 22, 2000, col.831.

[87] Although the term "class-based exemption" is not used in the Act, they were so described in the *Explanatory Notes,* FOI Act 2000 (see paras 12 and 85) and in House of Commons, *Public Administration—Third Report*, (Cm 4355), July 29, 1999, para.60. The following categorisation is consistent with that given in the *Explanatory Notes,* FOI Act 2000 and in the *Public Administration—Third Report*.

[88] Freedom of Information Act 2000, s.21(1); Freedom of Information (Scotland) Act 2002, s.25(1).

[89] Freedom of Information Act 2000, s.22(1); Freedom of Information (Scotland) Act 2002, s.27(1).

- information held by the requested public authority that was directly or indirectly supplied to it by, or that relates to, any of the defined security bodies[90];
- confidential information obtained from a foreign state or from an international organisation or court[91];
- information held by a public authority for the purposes of a criminal investigation or proceedings[92];
- information held by the requested public authority only by virtue of that information being contained in a formal document filed with a court or tribunal, in a formal document served for the purposes of court or tribunal proceedings, or in a formal document created by a court or by staff of a court[93];
- information held by the requested public authority only by virtue of it being contained in a document placed in the custody of a person conducting an inquiry or arbitration, or in a document created by a person conducting an inquiry or arbitration, for the purposes of the inquiry or arbitration[94];
- information for which exemption is required for the purpose of avoiding an infringement of the privileges of either House of Parliament[95];
- policy information[96];
- communications with Her Majesty or the Royal Household[97];
- environmental information[98];
- information that constitutes personal data[99];
- information obtained by the public authority from any other person (including another public authority) the disclosure of which would constitute an actionable breach of confidence by the public authority[1];
- information in respect of which a claim to legal professional privilege could be maintained[2];
- information that constitutes a trade secret[3]; and

[90] Freedom of Information Act 2000, s.23(1). This does not constitute an absolute exemption in Scotland.
[91] *ibid.*, s.27(2); Freedom of Information (Scotland) Act 2002, s.32(1)(b).
[92] *ibid.*, s.30(1); Freedom of Information (Scotland) Act 2002, s.34(1).
[93] *ibid.*, s.32(1); Freedom of Information (Scotland) Act 2002, s.37(1)(a).
[94] *ibid.*, s.32(2); Freedom of Information (Scotland) Act 2002, s.37(1)(b).
[95] *ibid.*, s.34(1). This does not constitute an absolute exemption in Scotland.
[96] *ibid.*, s.35(1); Freedom of Information (Scotland) Act 2002, s.29(1).
[97] Freedom of Information Act 2000, s.37(1); Freedom of Information (Scotland) Act 2002, s.41.
[98] Freedom of Information Act 2000, s.39(1); Freedom of Information (Scotland) Act 2002, s.39(2).
[99] Freedom of Information Act 2000, s.40(1); Freedom of Information (Scotland) Act 2002, s.38(1)(a). In Scotland, personal census information and a deceased person's health record are also absolute exemptions: s.38(1)(c) and (d).
[1] Freedom of Information Act 2000, s.41(1); Freedom of Information (Scotland) Act 2002, s.36(2).
[2] Freedom of Information Act 2000, s.42(1); Freedom of Information (Scotland) Act 2002, s.36(1).
[3] Freedom of Information Act 2000, s.43(1); Freedom of Information (Scotland) Act 2002, s.33(1).

— information the disclosure of which is prohibited by or under an enactment, is incompatible with any Community obligation or would constitute a contempt of court.[4]

In relation to each of these, the fact that the disclosure of the information would be demonstrably harmless will not detract from it being "exempt information." Where the exemption is a qualified exemption, that harmlessness may, however, impinge upon the public interest in maintaining the exemption.

Prejudice-based exemptions

14–022 The remaining exemptions all require "prejudice" in order for the exemption to be engaged; or, in the case of Scotland, "substantial prejudice." Prejudice-based exemptions are those conferred in respect of:

- information for which exemption from the duties is required for the purpose of safeguarding national security[5];
- information whose disclosure would or would be likely to prejudice the defence of the British Isles[6];
- information whose disclosure would or would be likely to prejudice relations between the United Kingdom and any other State or international organisation or to prejudice the interests of the United Kingdom abroad[7];
- information whose disclosure would or would be likely to prejudice relations between administrations within the United Kingdom[8];
- information the disclosure of which would or would be likely to prejudice the economic or financial interests of the United Kingdom or any part of it[9];
- information the disclosure of which would or would be likely to prejudice the prevention or detection of crime, etc.[10];
- information that would or would be likely to prejudice an auditing body's audit functions[11];
- information held by the House of Commons or the House of Lords that, in the reasonable opinion of the Speaker of the House of

[4] Freedom of Information Act 2000, s.44(1); Freedom of Information (Scotland) Act 2002, s.26.
[5] Freedom of Information Act 2000, s.24(1); Freedom of Information (Scotland) Act 2002, s.31(1).
[6] Freedom of Information Act 2000, s.26(1); Freedom of Information (Scotland) Act 2002, s.31(4).
[7] Freedom of Information Act 2000, s.27(1); Freedom of Information (Scotland) Act 2002, s.32(1)(a).
[8] Freedom of Information Act 2000, s.28(1); Freedom of Information (Scotland) Act 2002, s.28(1).
[9] Freedom of Information Act 2000, s.29(1); Freedom of Information (Scotland) Act 2002, s.33(2).
[10] Freedom of Information Act 2000, s.31(1); Freedom of Information (Scotland) Act 2002, s.35(1).
[11] Freedom of Information Act 2000, s.33(2); Freedom of Information (Scotland) Act 2002, s.40.

Commons or the Clerk of the Parliaments respectively, if disclosed under the FOI Act, would or would be likely to:

- prejudice the convention of the collective responsibility of Ministers of the Crown, etc.;
- inhibit the free and frank provision of advice or exchange of views for the purposes of deliberation; or
- otherwise prejudice the effective conduct of public affairs[12];

- information the disclosure of which would or would be likely to endanger the physical or mental health of an individual or endanger an individual's safety;[13] and
- information the disclosure of which would or would be likely to prejudice the commercial interests of any person.[14]

5. INTERPRETATION OF EXEMPTIONS AND ONUS

Introduction

The FOI Act does not explicitly specify whether it is for the applicant to show that he has a right to the information requested or for the public authority to show that it is excused from disclosing the information requested; or whether there is a shifting "onus" of some sort.[15] In this, the FOI Act is no different from most statutes that bestow upon an individual a right against a public authority.[16] It has been held in the context of a confidentiality claim: 14–023

[12] Freedom of Information Act 2000, s.36(2); Freedom of Information (Scotland) Act 2002, s.30. This does not constitute an absolute exemption in Scotland.

[13] Freedom of Information Act 2000, s.38(1); Freedom of Information (Scotland) Act 2002, s.39(1).

[14] Freedom of Information Act 2000, s.43(1) and (2); Freedom of Information (Scotland) Act 2002, s.33(1).

[15] However, Freedom of Information Act 2000, s.10(3), in speaking of "if the condition in section 2(1)(b) were satisfied" implies some sort of a burden. Similarly, Freedom of Information Act 2000, s.17 and Freedom of Information (Scotland) Act 2002, s.16(1), in referring to "relying on a claim" that any of the provisions in Pt II.

[16] The freedom of information legislation of most comparative jurisdictions does specifically state that the onus of establishing an exemption lies upon the recipient public authority or agency: Freedom of Information Act 1982, ss.3 and 61 (Cth of Australia); Access to Information Act, (1982) (Canada), s.48; Freedom of Information Act 1997 (Ireland), s.34(12). In New Zealand there is a general statement of principle: Official Information Act 1982 (NZ), s.5. This has been held not to create an onus upon the agency seeking to rely upon an exemption: *Commissioner of Police v Ombudsman* [1988] 1 N.Z.L.R. 385, CA, on appeal from [1985] 1 N.Z.L.R. 578. In debate on the FOI Bill, it was thought to be "seriously defective" in not having a clear presumption in favour of disclosure, with most debate as to presumption concerned with the presumption in relation to the weighing of the aspects of the public interest, rather than the presumption in relation to whether information falls within one or other of the provisions of Pt II of the FOI Act: *Hansard*, HL, Vol.619, November 14, 2000, col.136, Lord Lester of Herne Hill.

> "it is incumbent upon the Crown, in order to restrain disclosure of Government secrets, not only to show that the information is confidential, but also to show that it is in the public interest that it should not be published . . . . The reason for this additional requirement in cases concerned with Government secrets appears to be that, although in the case of private citizens there is a public interest that confidential information should as such be protected, in the case of Government secrets the mere fact of confidentiality does not alone support such a conclusion, because in a free society there is a continuing public interest that the workings of government should be open to scrutiny and criticism. From this it follows that, in such cases, there must be demonstrated some other public interest which requires that publication should be restrained."[17]

And, in relation to adoption information held by a local authority:

> "the bias, if any, should be in favour of allowing access to information rather than concealing information."[18]

These statements pre-date the FOI Act. It may be thought that their sentiments are sufficiently embodied within the FOI Act as not to require the application of any gloss to its provisions.

Onus or burden of proof: exempt information

14–024 The scope of the rights given by s.1(1) of the Freedom of Information Act 2000 is materially shaped by whether the information to which a request relates is or is not "exempt information." To be exempt information, the information must fit within one or more of the descriptions of exempt information given by the provisions of Pt II of the Act. Some of these descriptions involve an identification of some specific sort of prejudice or likely prejudice: matters on which there will often be legitimate differences of view. It is generally considered inappropriate to speak of a formal "onus of proof" in the exercise of an administrative duty or discretion.[19] The convention is that a public authority is presumed to have properly and duly performed its statutory duties[20]:

[17] *Attorney-General v Guardian Newspapers (No. 2)* [1990] 1 A.C. 109 at 283 *per* Lord Goff. See also the quotation at para.25–018 from *A-G (UK) v Heinemann Publishers Pty Ltd* (1987) 10 N.S.W.L.R. 86 at 191; 75 A.L.R. 353 at 454.

[18] *Birmingham City District Council v O* [1983] 1 A.C. 578 at 596.

[19] *Pye (Oxford) Estates Ltd v Secretary of State for the Environment* [1982] J.P.L. 575 (in relation to a planning appeal).

[20] *Point of Ayr Collieries Ltd v Lloyd-George* [1943] 2 All E.R. 546; *Wilover Nominees Ltd v Inland Revenue Commissioners* [1973] 1 W.L.R. 1393 at 1389; *R. v Inland Revenue Commissioners, Ex p. Rossminster* [1980] A.C. 952 at 1009, 1013; *R. v Inland Revenue Commissioners, Ex p. TC Coombs & Co* [1991] 2 A.C. 283 at 300.

"The legal, as contrasted with the evidential, burden being on the applicant to establish his entitlement to relief, [the courts] are entitled and are very willing to assume that the authority has acted in accordance with law, until the contrary is shown. But authorities assist neither themselves nor the courts, if their response is a blanket assertion of having acted in accordance with law or one which begs the question. If the issue is whether an authority took a particular factor into account, it will be a sufficient response to show that it did. But if the allegation is that a decision is prima facie irrational and that there are grounds for inquiring whether something immaterial may have been considered or something material omitted from consideration, it really does not help to assert baldly that all relevant matters and no irrelevant matters were taken into consideration without condescending to mention some at least of the principal factors on which the decision was based."[21]

Where a public authority is required to be satisfied of something or to form some opinion, then, absent evidence to the contrary, its say-so that it was satisfied or formed that opinion will suffice.[22] Although official material leading to the passage of the Act spoke of "a presumption of openness," there is no such presumption expressed in the Act itself.[23] The short title of the FOI Act might suggest some sort of presumption of openness, although as an interpretative tool it is of limited use.[24] Nevertheless, the basic scheme of the FOI Act and the language employed suggest that it is for a public authority to demonstrate the applicability of a provision in Pt II of the Act before it may avail itself of that provision. The specifying of "exemptions" from "a general right of access" carries within itself a requirement that the operative words of any of those exemptions must be satisfied in order for it to be triggered[25] on the basis of:

---

21 *R. v Lancashire County Council, Ex p. Huddleston* [1986] 2 All E.R. 941 at 945–946, *per* Donaldson M.R.

22 *Wilover Nominees Ltd v Inland Revenue Commissioners* [1973] 1 W.L.R. 1393 at 1389; *Stoke-on-Trent City Council v B&Q (Retail) Ltd* [1984] Ch.1; *R. v Inland Revenue Commissioners, Ex p. TC Coombs & Co* [1991] 2 A.C. 283 at 299–302.

23 Cabinet Office, *Your Right to Know. The Government's Proposals for a FOI Act*, (White Paper), Cm.3818, December 11, 1997, para.3.1. In *R. (on the application of Rose and another) v Secretary of State for Health* [2002] 2 F.L.R. 962; [2002] UKHRR 13 at [47] Scott Baker J. (in the context of an application by an individual conceived through artificial insemination for information about the donor) said: "We live in a much more open society than even 20 years ago. Secrecy nowadays has to be justified where previously it did not."

24 *Re Vexatious Actions Act 1886, Re Boaler* [1915] 1 K.B. 21 at 40; *R. v Wheatley* [1979] 1 W.L.R. 144 at 147; *Lonrho Ltd v Shell Petroleum Co Ltd (No 2)* [1982] A.C. 173 at 187.

25 Similarly, when refusing a request, it is for the public authority to rely upon a claim that one of the provisions of Pt II applies: Freedom of Information Act 2000, s.17(2); Freedom of Information (Scotland) Act 2002, s.16(2). In Canada, the view taken is that since the basic principle of the statute is to codify the right of public access to government information two things follow: first, that such public access ought not to be frustrated by the Courts except upon the clearest grounds so that doubt ought to be resolved in favour of disclosure; secondly, the burden of persuasion must rest upon the party resisting disclosure whether it be a private corporation,

> "the orthodox principle (common to both the criminal and the civil law) that exceptions, etc., are to be set up by those who rely on them."[26]

Onus of proof elsewhere

14–025 In the analogous regime in New Zealand, the courts have held[27] that the ombudsman, to whom an appeal against an agency's decision lies, has no predetermined starting point and that the agency withholding the information is under no obligation to establish affirmatively each element of the exemption. Nevertheless, despite avoiding use of terms such as "onus," the courts there have held that the withholding agency bears an obligation:

> "to justify its refusal to disclose . . . with sufficient particularity for the ombudsman to make his or her decision and recommendation."[28]

Onus of proof: public interest

14–026 Having established that information answering the terms of the request falls within one of the provisions of Pt II, if those provisions do not confer absolute exemption it will be necessary to weigh the competing aspects of the public interest to determine if the duty to acknowledge and the duty to communicate are disapplied.[29] When the public interest override was first introduced in the FOI Bill, it provided that, if information fell within one of the qualified exemptions, then it would only be required to be communicated to the applicant if:

> "in all the circumstances of the case, the public interest in disclosing the information outweighs the public interest in maintaining the exemption."[30]

citizen or the Government: *Maislin Industries Limited v Minister for Industry, Trade & Commerce* [1984] 1 F.C. 939; *Rubin v Canada (Canada Mortgage and Housing Corp.)* [1989] 1 F.C. 265, CA ("the general rule is disclosure, the exception is exemption and the onus of proving the entitlement to the benefit of the exception rests upon those who claim it."); *Canada (Information Commissioner) v Canada (Minister of External Affairs)* [1990] 3 F.C. 665; *Rubin v Canada (Solicitor General)* (2000) 187 D.L.R. (4th) 675. Note, however, that the Access to Official Information Act, (1982) (Canada) has both a purpose clause (s.2) and an onus provision in relation to appeals (s.48).

[26] *Nimmo v Alexander Cowan & Sons Ltd* [1968] A.C. 107 at 130 *per* Lord Wilberforce. Similarly: *R. v Hunt* [1987] A.C. 352 at 373–375 *per* Lord Griffiths.

[27] *Commissioner of Police v Ombudsman* [1988] 1 N.Z.L.R. 385, CA, on appeal from [1985] 1 N.Z.L.R. 578.

[28] *Commissioner of Police v Ombudsman* [1988] 1 N.Z.L.R. 385 at 406.

[29] Freedom of Information Act 2000, s.2(1)(b) and 2(2)(c); Freedom of Information (Scotland) Act 2002, s.2(1)(b). In Canada the two-stage burden, i.e. that the information falls within the exemption and that the public interest is against disclosure, is recognised: *Rubin v Canada (Solicitor General)* (2000) 187 D.L.R. (4th) 675.

[30] Under this, it was recognised that if evenly-balanced, there should be no disclosure *Hansard*, HL, Vol.617, October 17, 2000, col.914, Lord Falconer of Thoroton.

In the face of criticism,[31] the section was modified to its present form, which reversed the order. In moving the amendments, it was specifically stated:

> "the starting point is the public right of access and the public interest in disclosure, and it is for the public authority to justify non-disclosure on the basis that public disclosure is outweighed in the circumstances of the case by the public interest in non-disclosure .... The burden of proof, as lawyers would say, is placed upon the public authority to show that there is some pressing need for non-disclosure and that the restriction on the public right of access is necessary in the sense of being a proportionate way of meeting that need."[32]

The suggested amendments were accepted by the Minister in charge of the Bill in the House of Lords, saying they:

> "will result in an important and significant shift towards greater openness. They will put beyond doubt the Government's resolve that information must be disclosed except where there is an overriding public interest in keeping specific information confidential. Perhaps I may repeat that: information must be disclosed except where there is an overriding public interest in keeping specific information confidential .... They significantly contribute to the change in culture. They contribute significantly to ensuring that the public authority must make out the case for non-disclosure before there is non-disclosure. That is why we have agreed to accept them."[33]

Section 2, in speaking of the acknowledgement and communication duties being disapplied where "the public interest in maintaining the exemption outweighs the public interest in disclosing the information," posits a starting position of disclosure.[34] Accordingly, it is for a public authority which does not wish to communicate or acknowledge the existence of information that falls within

---

[31] Described as turning the burden the wrong way round: *Hansard*, HL, Vol.617, October 17, 2000, col.907, Lord Goodhart. And, later on, as making the balance to be in favour of concealment: *Hansard*, HL, Vol.619, November 14, 2000, col.134, Lord Archer.

[32] *Hansard*, HL, Vol.619, November 14, 2000, col.137, Lord Lester of Herne Hill.

[33] *ibid.*, cols.143–144, Lord Falconer of Thoroton (the Minister of State, Cabinet Office). See also *Hansard*, HC, Vol.357, November 27, 2000, cols 719, 721–72, where, in introducing the amendment that led to s.2, the Parliamentary Under-Secretary of State for the Home Department (Mr O'Brien), said: "the amendment also reverses the way in which the test works, so that the public interest in disclosing the information must be outweighed by the public interest in maintaining an exemption before any information can be withheld."

[34] The position under the Freedom of Information (Scotland) Act 2002 is slightly different. The duty to disclose non-absolute exempt information only applies to the extent that, in all the circumstances of the case, the public interest in disclosing the information is not outweighed by the public interest in maintaining the exemption: s.2(1)(b). The provision is couched as part of the circumscription of the parameters of the right of access, rather than as an exception to be invoked in order to disapply the right of access.

one of the provisions of Pt II, other than one conferring absolute exemption, to demonstrate that in all the circumstances that stance is supported by a weighing of the relevant aspects of the public interest.

Standard of proof

14–027 In administrative matters, to the extent that there is any standard of proof, the civil standard of proof applies.[35] In other spheres where the courts have had to consider the public interest in disclosing and in not disclosing information, a mere say-so of harm, other than in cases involving national security, has not sufficed.[36]

Principles of interpretation: special characteristics

14–028 Applying the ordinary principles of administrative law, a public authority must exercise its discretion to promote the policy and objects of the FOI Act, and not so as to frustrate that policy and those objects.[37] In the comparative jurisdictions, it has sometimes been argued that the nature of freedom of information legislation calls for any ambiguity to be decided in favour of wider disclosure. Underlying this argument is the notion that legislation providing for access to official information is akin to a constitutional instrument and that special principles of interpretation apply.[38] Whilst support can be found in judgments from comparative jurisdictions for the idea that official information access legislation may rank as a constitutional measure, those same judgments have not taken the additional step of giving the legislation a benevolent interpretation as a result of it.[39]

---

[35] *R. v Secretary of State for the Home Department, Ex p. Khawaja* [1984] A.C. 74.

[36] *Attorney-General v Guardian Newspapers (No. 2)* [1990] 1 A.C. 109 at 263 and 283.

[37] *Padfield v Minister of Agriculture, Fisheries and Food* [1968] A.C. 997 at 1030; *London Boroughs Transport Committee v Freight Transport Assocn Ltd* [1991] 1 W.L.R. 828 at 836.

[38] In relation to the principles of construction of a true constitutional instrument, see *Minister of Home Affairs v Fisher* [1980] A.C. 319 at 329; *Riley v Attorney-General of Jamaica* [1983] 1 A.C. 719. Most recently, in *Thoburn v Sunderland City Council* [2002] EWHC 195 Admin at [62] Laws L.J. spoke of a hierarchy of "ordinary" and "constitutional" statutes, with the former being amenable to implied repeal and the latter not: "In my opinion a constitutional statute is one which (a) conditions the legal relationship between citizen and State in some general, overarching manner, or (b) enlarges or diminishes the scope of what we would now regard as fundamental constitutional rights."

[39] *Commissioner of Police v Ombudsman* [1988] 1 N.Z.L.R. 385 at 391, 402 and 411, CA; *Wyatt Co ltd v Queenstown Lakes District Council* [1991] 2 N.Z.L.R. 180.

Principles of interpretation: general

Independently of their characterisation as a constitutional measure or not, an issue that has arisen elsewhere is whether ambiguities in freedom of information legislation should as a rule be resolved so as to favour disclosure. In Australia, the High Court has said: 14–029

> "In the light of [s.3 and s.16] it is proper to give to the relevant provisions of the Act a construction which would further, rather than hinder, free access to information."[40]

In Canada, the view taken is that public access ought not to be frustrated by the Courts except upon the clearest grounds, so that doubt ought to be resolved in favour of disclosure.[41] European case law in relation to Decision 93/731, art.4, has consistently stated that exceptions must be construed and applied restrictively so as not to defeat the general principle enshrined in that decision.[42]

Most recently, the European Court of Justice has said: "The aim pursued by Decision 93/731, as well as being to ensure the internal operation of the Council in conformity with the interests of good administration . . . is to provide the public with the widest possible access to documents held by the Council, so that any exception to that right of . . . access must be interpreted and applied strictly."[42A]

---

[40] *Victorian Public Service Board v Wright* (1986) 160 C.L.R. 145 at 153, considering the FOI Act of the State of Victoria. Similarly: *Accident Compensation Commission v Croom* [1991] 2 V.R. 322; *Sobh v Police Force of Victoria* [1994] 1 V.R. 41, although these decisions are in part based on an objects section in the legislation. See also: *Commissioner of Police v District Court of NSW and Perrin* (1993) 31 N.S.W.L.R. 606; *Re Eccleston and Dept of Family Services and Aboriginal and Islander Affairs* (1993) 1 Q.A.R. 60. Contrast decisions of the Federal Court, considering the Commonwealth Act: *Kavvaadias v Commonwealth Ombudsman* (1984) 1 F.C.R. 80 at 85; *News Corporation Ltd v National Companies & Securities Commission* (1984) 1 F.C.R. 64; *Attorney-General's Department v Cockcroft* (1986) 10 F.C.R. 180 at 195; *Commissioner of Taxation v Swiss Aluminium Australia Ltd* (1986) 10 F.C.R. 321 at 327; *Searle Australia Pty Ltd v Public Interest Advocacy Centre* (1992) 36 F.C.R. 111 at 114–115; *cf. Arnold v Queensland* (1987) 13 A.L.D. 195 at 205.

[41] *Maislin Industries Limited v Minister for Industry, Trade & Commerce* [1984] 1 F.C. 939.

[42] *World Wide Fund for Nature v Commission of the European Communities* [1997] E.C.R. II–313; [1997] All E.R. (E.C.) 300, [1997] Env. L.R. 242, para.5; *Svenska Journalistförbundet v Council of the European Union* [1998] E.C.R. II–2289, [1998] All E.R. (E.C.) 545, para.110; *Hautala v Council of the European Union* [1999] 3 C.M.L.R. 528 at para.84; *Denkavit Nederland BV v Commission of the European Communities* [2000] 3 C.M.L.R. 1014 at para. 45; *Kuijer v Council of the European Union* [2002] 1 W.L.R. 1941, paras 55 and 57 ("Decision 93/731 must be interpreted in the light of the principle of the right to information and the principle of proportionality"). In relation to Decision 93/731 [1993] O.J. L340/43 generally, see Ch.6.

[42A] *Hautala v Council of the European Union* [2002] 1 W.L.R. 1930 at [25].

6. CONCLUSIVE CERTIFICATES

Introduction

14–030 Both the Freedom of Information Act 2000 and the Data Protection Act 1998 provide for the signing and issuing of "conclusive certificates." The effect of a conclusive certificate is evidential: the certificate stands as conclusive evidence of the "facts" certified in it, irrespective of the reality. The "facts" that may be so certified are:

(1) that particular information was directly or indirectly supplied by, or relates to, any of the security bodies specified in section 23(3)[43];
(2) that exemption from s.1(1)(b) (in other words the disclosure duty), or from s.1(1)(a) and (b) (in other words the existence duty and the disclosure duty), is, or at any time was, required for the purpose of safeguarding national security[44];
(3) that exemption from the disclosure duty, or from the existence duty and the disclosure duty, is required for the purpose of avoiding an infringement of the privileges of either House of Parliament[45];
(4) that disclosure of information held by either House of Parliament would, or would be likely to, have any of the effects mentioned in s.36(2) (in other words, it would be prejudicial to the maintenance of the convention of the collective responsibility of the Ministers of the Crown; it would inhibit the free and frank provision of advice or of the exchange of views for the purposes of deliberation; or it would otherwise prejudice the effective conduct of public affairs).[46]

Section 53 of the Freedom of Information Act 2000[47] also sets out circumstances in which the duty to comply with a decision notice or enforcement notice may be excepted through the issue of a certificate. A certificate under s.53 has a prescribed statutory effect: it is not a conclusive evidential certificate as such. Certificates under s.53 are considered elsewhere in this work.[48]

[43] Freedom of Information Act 2000, s.23(2). Neither the certificate provision nor the underlying exemption exist in the Freedom of Information (Scotland) Act 2002.
[44] Freedom of Information Act 2000, s.24(3); Data Protection Act 1998, s.28 and Sch.6; Freedom of Information (Scotland) Act 2002, s.31(2).
[45] Freedom of Information Act 2000, s.34(2). Neither the certificate provision nor the underlying exemption exist in the Freedom of Information (Scotland) Act 2002.
[46] Freedom of Information Act 2000, s.36(7). Although the underlying exemption is provided for by the Freedom of Information (Scotland) Act 2002, s.30, it does not provide for conclusive certificates to facilitate its engagement.
[47] Freedom of Information (Scotland) Act 2002, s.52(2).
[48] See para.28–012.

General effect of a conclusive certificate

14–031 Each of the four types of conclusive certificate effectively deems that a prerequisite to the application of a particular exemption is satisfied, thereby facilitating the application of that exemption for the purposes of the relevant Act.[49] These conclusive evidential certificates fall into two categories: appealable ministerial "national security certificates" under ss.23(2) and 24(3) of the Freedom of Information Act 2000 and s.28(2) of the Data Protection Act 1998; and non-appealable "Parliamentary certificates" under ss.34(3) and 36(7) of the Freedom of Information Act 2000. The former may be signed by certain Ministers of the Crown[50] and the latter may be signed by the Speaker of the House of Commons or the Clerk of the Parliaments ("the House Authorities").[51] Each of the underlying exemptions can nevertheless operate independently of conclusive certificates: the issue of an appropriate certificate is a sufficient but not a necessary condition for the engagement of each one.

Types of ouster clause

14–032 Statutory provisions which seek to confer finality on determinations of the executive by excluding judicial review of those determinations are often referred to as "preclusive clauses" or "ouster clauses" because they seek to preclude or oust the supervisory jurisdiction of the courts over the executive.[52] Such clauses can take the form of "finality" clauses, "no certiorari" clauses, "as if enacted" clauses, "shall not be questioned" clauses and "conclusive evidence" clauses.[53] An ouster clause which seeks to preclude judicial review other than by way of an exclusive statutory appeal or a review mechanism is known as a "partial" ouster clause and, where the prescribed mechanism must be invoked within a particular limitation period, as a "time-limited" clause.[54] The provisions in the Freedom of Information Act 2000 and the Data Protection Act 1998 allowing for the issue of conclusive certificates thus contain a species of conclusive evidence

[49] Both Acts confer power to "sign" such certificates but talk in terms of their being "issued" in relation to appeals.See also the Freedom of Information (Scotland) Act 2002, s.31(2)–(3).

[50] Freedom of Information Act 2000, s.25(3); Data Protection Act 1998, s.28(10).

[51] Freedom of Information Act 2000, ss.34(4) and 36(5)(d)–(e) and (7).

[52] De Smith, Woolf and Jowell, *Judicial Review of Administrative Action* (5th ed., Sweet & Maxwell, London, 1995), paras 5–015 to 5–040; Wade and Forsyth, *Administrative Law* (8th ed., Oxford University Press, Oxford, 2000), pp.700–720.

[53] De Smith, Woolf and Jowell, *Judicial Review of Administrative Action*, (5th ed., Sweet & Maxwell, London, 1995), paras 5–020 to 5–023; Wade and Forsyth, *Administrative Law*, (8th ed., Oxford University Press, Oxford, 2000), pp.700–707; M. Fordham, *Judicial Review Handbook*, (3rd ed., Hart Publishing, Oxford, 2001), Ch.P28.

[54] De Smith, Woolf and Jowell, *Judicial Review of Administrative Action*, (5th ed., Sweet & Maxwell, London, 1995), paras 5–024 to 5–026 and 5–040; Wade and Forsyth, *Administrative Law*, (8th ed., Oxford University Press, Oxford, 2000), pp.698, 711–712 and 714–720; M. Fordham, *Judicial Review Handbook*, (3rd ed., Hart Publishing, Oxford, 2001), Ch.P36.

clause[55]: in relation to ss.23(2) and 24(3) of the Freedom of Information Act 2000 and s.28(2) of the Data Protection Act 1998 these are partial ouster clauses because national security certificates signed thereunder are appealable. In relation to ss.34(3) and 36(7) of the Freedom of Information Act 2000, they are absolute as there is no scope for challenging Parliamentary certificates.

Judicial approach to ouster clauses

14–033 In very general terms, the courts have been prepared to enforce partial and time-limited ouster clauses on the basis that they do not altogether preclude judicial oversight.[56] By contrast, the courts have had a long-standing reluctance to give full literal effect to absolute ouster clauses in general, eventually leading to a complete unwillingness to read "shall-not-be-questioned" clauses as ousting their supervisory jurisdiction over subordinate authorities in particular.[57] In recent times, the domestic courts have upheld conclusive evidence clauses[58] and accepted that they cannot go behind or scrutinise non-appealable national security certificates unless and insofar as obtained or issued in bad faith.[59] However,

---

[55] For examples of traditional certificate-based conclusive evidence clauses see: the Race Relations Act 1976, ss.42 and 69 as originally enacted (subsequently amended by the Employment Rights Act 1996 and the Race Relations (Amendment) Act 2000); and the Fair Employment (Northern Ireland) Act 1976, s.42 (subsequently repealed and replaced by the Fair Employment and Treatment (Northern Ireland) Order 1998, SI 1998/3162 (NI 21)). Both sets of provisions were amended or replaced so as to allow, *inter alia*, for appeals to be brought against the relevant type of ministerial national security certificate following the decision of the European Court of Human Rights in *Tinnelly and Sons Ltd v United Kingdom* (1999) 27 E.H.R.R. 249. For further examples see: the Parliamentary Commissioner Act 1967, s.8(4) allowing the Secretary to the Cabinet to issue a certificate with the approval of the Prime Minister certifying conclusively that any information, question, document or part of a document relates to proceedings of the Cabinet or any committee of the Cabinet and is thus immune from compulsory disclosure or production under that Act (such a certificate was issued in the Court Line case: HC 498, 1974–1975, para.9: Wade and Forsyth, *Administrative Law*, (8th ed., Oxford University Press, Oxford, 2000), p. 820); and the International Criminal Court Act 2001, s.39.

[56] *Smith v East Elloe RDC* [1956] A.C. 736; *R. v Secretary of State for the Environment, Ex p. Ostler* [1977] Q.B. 122; *R. v Cornwall CC, Ex p. Huntington* [1992] 3 All E.R. 566; *R. v Dacorum DC, Ex p. Cannon* [1996] 2 P.L.R. 45; *cf. Anisminic Ltd v Foreign Compensation Commission* [1969] 2 A.C. 147 at 171 (*per* Lord Reid), 200 (*per* Lord Pearce), 210 (*per* Lord Wilberforce).

[57] *Anisminic Ltd v Foreign Compensation Commission* [1969] 2 A.C. 147; *R. v Hull University Visitor, Ex p. Page* [1993] A.C. 682; *Boddington v British Transport Police* [1999] 2 A.C. 143; *R. v Secretary of State for the Home Department, Ex p. Fayed* [1998] 1 W.L.R. 763.

[58] *R. v Registrar of Companies, Ex p. Central Bank of India* [1986] Q.B. 1114; *cf. R. v Preston Supplementary Benefits Appeal Tribunal, Ex p. Moore* [1975] 1 W.L.R. 624. See also the Tribunals and Inquiries Act 1958, s.11, Tribunals and Inquiries Act 1971, s.14 and Tribunals and Inquiries Act 1992, s.12.

[59] See the references to the various unreported judicial review proceedings in the Northern Ireland High Court before Nicholson and McCollum JJ which preceded *Tinnelly and Sons Ltd v United Kingdom* (1999) 27 E.H.R.R. 249 at paras 18–32, 64, 66–67 and 74–75 and before Kerr J. which preceded *Devlin v United Kingdom* (2002) 34 E.H.R.R. 43 at paras 12–14. See also: *R. v Secretary of State for Foreign and Commonwealth Affairs, Ex p. Vidler* [1993] C.O.D. 305 (national security certificate under the Employment Protection (Consolidation) Act 1978, Sch.9, para.2); *R. v Secretary of State for Transport, Ex p. Evans and Commission for Racial Equality* [1992]

recent decisions of the European Court of Justice and the European Court of Human Rights founded on human rights principles have, in effect, declared certain conclusive evidence clauses precluding any judicial oversight to be incompatible with fundamental rights.[60]

Human rights

Human rights issues[61] are therefore potentially important to the application and effectiveness of the conclusive evidence clauses in the Freedom of Information Act 2000 and the Data Protection Act 1998. If it can be shown that a conclusive certificate issued under one of these Acts has interfered with the enjoyment or exercise of a "Convention right" within the meaning of the Human Rights Act 1998[62] or a right under European Community law that can be relied upon before the domestic courts,[63] this will have two important consequences. First, the 14–034

C.O.D. 196 (national security certificate under the Race Relations Act 1976, ss.42 and 69); and *R. v Secretary of State for Northern Ireland, ex p. Gilmore* (unreported, April 10, 1987) referred to in White, "Security Vetting, discrimination and the right to a fair trial" [1999] P.L. 406.

[60] Case 222/84 *Johnston v Chief Constable of the Royal Ulster Constabulary* [1987] Q.B. 129, ECJ; *Tinnelly and Sons Ltd v United Kingdom* (1999) 27 E.H.R.R. 249; *Devlin v United Kingdom* (2002) 34 E.H.R.R. 43; *Devenney v United Kingdom* (2002) 35 E.H.R.R. 24. See further para.14–034 below.

[61] For the role of the ECHR in relation to the Freedom of Information Act 2000 generally, see paras 1–029 to 1–037.

[62] Human Rights Act 1998, s.1(1)–(3), Sch.1 define "the Convention rights" for the purposes of that Act as the rights and fundamental freedoms set out in Arts 2–12 and 14 of the Convention for the Protection of Human Rights and Fundamental Freedoms (Cmd 8969, 1953), Arts 1–3 of the First Protocol and Arts 1–2 of the Sixth Protocol. The ECHR, Arts 1 and 13 are notable omissions from "the Convention rights". Primary and subordinate legislation must, so far as possible, be read and given effect in a way which is compatible with the Convention rights (s.3) and it is unlawful for public authorities (including courts) to act in a way which is incompatible with them unless left with no alternative by primary legislation (s.6).

[63] In this regard, reliance can be placed on Community law in accordance with the doctrine of direct effect including the subsidiary or related doctrines of vertical, indirect and incidental direct effect: P. Craig and G. De Búrca, *EU Law: Text, Cases and Materials*, (3rd ed., Oxford University Press, London, 2003),Chs 5–6. In particular, the doctrine of indirect direct effect requires that national law implementing Directives is interpreted and applied in accordance with Community law and norms and is therefore relevant to the Data Protection Act 1998 which implements the European Community Data Protection Directive 95/46: Case 14/83 *Von Colson v Land Nordrhein-Westfalen* [1984] E.C.R. 1891; Case C-106/89 *Marleasing SA v La Comercial Internacional de Alimentacion SA* [1990] E.C.R. I-4135; Cases C-240–244/98 *Océano Grupo Editorial v Rocio Murciano Quintero* [2000] E.C.R. I-4491; Craig "Directives: Direct Effect, Indirect Effect and the Construction of National Legislation" (1997) 22 E.L.Rev. 519. In relation to the interpretation of the Data Protection Act 1998 see in particular: *Campbell v MGN Ltd* [2002] EWCA Civ 1373; [2003] Q.B. 633, para.[96] (*per* Phillips MR); *Durant v Financial Services Authority* [2003] EWCA Civ 1746, paras [3]–[4] (*per* Auld L.J.); *R. (Alan Lord) v Secretary of State for the Home Department* [2003] EWHC 2073 (Admin), para. [83] (*per* Munby J.). Where Community law can be relied upon, the legality of acts done by European Community member states in the exercise of powers conferred or reserved by Community law falls to be determined by reference to the "general principles of Community law" which include principles of administrative or procedural fairness: J. Usher, *General Principles of EC Law*, (Longmans, London, 1998); T. Tridimas, *The General Principles of EC Law* (Oxford University Press, Oxford, 1999);

Information Tribunal and the courts will need to be persuaded that there is sufficient judicial control over the operation of the relevant provisions when reading and giving effect to them generally and when considering whether it is possible and appropriate to intervene in relation to decisions taken thereunder.[64] Secondly, the Information Tribunal and the courts will apply a more intensive proportionality-based standard of scrutiny if and when called upon to review any such decisions.[65] Whether any relevant Convention or Community rights

P. Craig and G. De Búrca, *EU Law: Text, Cases and Materials*, (3rd ed., Oxford University Press, Oxford, 2003), Chs 8–9; European Community Treaty, Art.288 (ex 215); Treaty on European Union, Art.6(2). In relation to procedural fairness, these principles can confer a right to a fair hearing (Case 17/74 *Transocean Marine Paint Association v EC Commission* [1974] E.C.R. 1063 at 1080) and to judicial oversight and control (Case 222/84 *Johnston v Chief Constable of the Royal Ulster Constabulary* [1987] Q.B. 129, ECJ at 147 (although note that the decision itself rested on "the principle of effective judicial control laid down in article 6 of Council Directive (76/207/EEC) of 9 February 1976": see p.155)).

64 The scope for appealing national security certificates issued under the Freedom of Information Act 2000, ss.23(2) and 24(3) and the Data Protection Act 1998, s.28(2) should suffice for these purposes but questions may nevertheless arise as to the grounds and intensity of the review thereby allowed and as to the absence of any provision allowing for a further appeal to the High Court on a point of law (*cf.* the non-appealability of Parliamentary certificates issued under the Freedom of Information Act 2000, ss.34(3) and 36(7) and the scope for further appeals under the Freedom of Information Act 2000, s.59 and Data Protection Act 1998, s.49(6)). In *Tinnelly and Sons Ltd v United Kingdom* (1999) 27 E.H.R.R. 249 two non-appealable certificates had been signed by the Secretary of State under the Fair Employment (Northern Ireland) Act 1976, s.42 certifying conclusively that certain decisions were acts done for the purpose of safeguarding national security, etc. The European Court of Human Rights held that: civil rights under the ECHR, Art.6(1) were engaged (paras 61–63); the scope for judicial review of the certificates was limited to a review of whether they had been obtained or issued in bad faith and could not entail "full scrutiny" of their factual basis (paras 74–75); and the exclusion of a judicial determination of the merits of the complaints constituted a disproportionate interference with the applicants' rights under the ECHR, Art. 6(1) (paras 77 and 79). In Case 222/84 *Johnston v Chief Constable of the Royal Ulster Constabulary* [1987] Q.B. 129, ECJ a non-appealable certificate had been signed by the Secretary of State under the Sex Discrimination (Northern Ireland) Order 1976 (SI 1976/1042 (NI 15)), art.53(2) certifying conclusively that Mrs Johnston had been refused employment on the grounds of national security, etc. The ECJ held that the exclusion of judicial review was contrary to Community law: "The requirement of judicial control stipulated by [Article 6 of the Equal Treatment Directive] reflects a general principle of law which underlies the constitutional traditions common to the member states.That principle is also laid down in articles 6 and 13 of the [ECHR]" (at 147); and "The principle of effective judicial control laid down in article 6 of Council Directive (76/207/EEC) of February 9, 1976 does not allow a [national security certificate] . . . to exclude the exercise of any power of review by the courts" (at 155).

65 The traditional standard of review for reasonableness is that enunciated in *Associated Provincial Picture Houses Ltd v Wednesbury Corpn* [1948] 1 K.B. 223 and *Council of Civil Service Unions v Minister for the Civil Service* [1985] A.C. 374 at 410 (*per* Lord Diplock). As a matter of common law principle, a heightened standard of review will be applied where "fundamental rights" are engaged (*R. v Ministry of Defence, Ex p. Smith* [1996] Q.B. 517 at 554 (*per* Sir Thomas Bingham M.R.)) and where "Convention rights" are engaged for the purposes of the Human Rights Act 1998 a yet more intensive proportionality-based standard of review is appropriate (*R. (Daly) v Secretary of State for the Home Department* [2001] UKHL 26; [2001] 2 A.C. 532 at [26]–[27] (*per* Lord Steyn)). In the light of these principles, the Information Tribunal adopted a proportionality-based standard of review in *Baker v Secretary of State for the Home Department* [2001] U.K.H.R.R. 1275 in an appeal under the Data Protection Act 1998, s.28(4) against a certificate issued by the Home Secretary which effectively conferred a blanket exemption allowing the Security Service to respond with a "neither confirm nor deny" reply to every request made to it under the Data Protection Act 1998, s.7(1)(a) without considering each request on its

will be engaged by the issue of conclusive certificates for these purposes is another matter[66] but the rights which are most likely to be relied upon in this regard are: rights to procedural fairness and judicial oversight under Art.6 of the ECHR and the general principles of Community law;[67] rights to privacy and data protection rights under Art.8 of the ECHR and the European Community Data Protection Directive 95/46/EC;[68] and rights to freedom of expression under Art.10 of the ECHR.[69]

Legislative history

The policy and consultation documents which preceded and underlay the Freedom of Information Act 2000 contain very little discussion of its conclusive evidence clauses.[70] Section 28 of the Data Protection Act 1998 was plainly the model for s.24 of the Freedom of Information Act 2000[71] and thus provided a template for adopting a certification procedure in relation to the national security exemption.[72] So far as Parliamentary debate is concerned, Mr O'Brien, the 14–035

individual merits (para.83). Having referred in general terms to the Council of Europe Convention for the Protection of Individuals with Regard to Automatic Processing of Personal Data dated January 28, 1981, the European Community Data Protection Directive 95/46 dated October 24, 1995 and the Human Rights Act 1998, ss.1, 3 and 6, the Tribunal asked itself whether the issue of the certificate was "reasonable in the extended sense of proportionate by reference to the precepts of the ECHR" (para.63) and concluded that the certificate had an "unnecessarily wide effect" and should be quashed accordingly (summary, para.14). See also *Gosling v Secretary of State for the Home Department* (unreported, decision of the Information Tribunal dated August 1, 2003) and *Hitchens v Secretary of State for the Home Department* (unreported, decision of the Information Tribunal dated August 4, 2003). Whether or not human rights are engaged for these purposes, it remains the case that the courts will show "considerable deference" to the executive's assessment of national security matters whilst bearing in mind that they must do so "in a manner appropriate to the national security context": *Baker v Secretary of State for the Home Department* [2001] U.K.H.R.R. 1275, para.76; *Gosling v Secretary of State for the Home Department* (unreported, decision of the Information Tribunal dated August 1, 2003), paras 44 and 48; *A, X and Y v Secretary of State for the Home Department* [2002] EWCA Civ 1502; [2003] 2 W.L.R. 564 at [40] (*per* Lord Woolf C.J.) and at [66] and [81] (*per* Brooke L.J.); *Secretary of State for the Home Department v Rehman* [2001] UKHL 47; [2003] 1 AC 153 at [50] and [62] (*per* Lord Hoffman) and at [16] (*per* Lord Slynn).

66 See paras 14–041 to 14–043.

67 See para.14–041. See, generally, para.1–036.

68 See para.14–042. See, generally, paras 1–033 to 1–035.

69 See para.14–043. See, generally, paras 1–030 to 1–032.

70 As already mentioned, the use of conclusive certificate provisions is by no means unprecedented, particularly in the national security context, and once an exemption has been settled on as a matter of principle, the technicalities of its application are much less likely to generate political or public interest or debate.

71 "The clause [which became the Freedom of Information Act 2000, s.24] is drafted in similar terms to section 28 of the Data Protection Act 1998. The two provisions have the same purpose. It is therefore sensible for them to be drafted in similar language. Any difference of approach between the provisions could lead to them being interpreted differently. Clearly, that is not the intention" (Mr O'Brien, the Home Office Minister, Report and Third Reading debate on the Freedom of Information Bill in the House of Commons, *Hansard*, HC, Vol.347, col. 1060, April 5, 2000).

72 Data Protection Act 1998, s.28 was itself preceded by the national security exemption in the Data Protection Act 1984, s.27 which provided that, "Any question whether the exemption mentioned

Home Office Minister, made the following points during the Report and Third Reading debate in the House of Commons in relation to the clauses which became ss.23–24 of the Freedom of Information Act 2000:

— information covered by certificates signed under these provisions will be "extremely sensitive" and should not therefore be seen by the Information Commissioner or his staff;
— such certificates can only be signed "at the highest level"; and
— they will not operate as "ministerial vetoes" because they are "nothing more than evidential certificates" subject to challenge before the Information Tribunal.[73]

During Committee Stage in the House of Lords, Lord Falconer of Thoroton, the Cabinet Office Minister, said he could not conceive that a conclusive certificate issued under the clause which became s.23 of the Freedom of Information Act 2000 could ever be subject to an exemption itself or be anything other than a public document.[74]

The comparative jurisdictions

14–036 The Freedom of Information Act 1982 (Cth of Aust) and the Freedom of Information Act 1997 (Ireland) both[75] provide for the issue of conclusive certificates as a means of activating certain exemptions:[76]

in subsection (1) above is or at any time was required for the purpose there mentioned [*i.e.* the purpose of safeguarding national security] in respect of any personal data shall be determined by a Minister of the Crown; and a certificate signed by a Minister of the Crown certifying that the exemption is or at any time was so required shall be conclusive evidence of that fact" (Data Protection Act 1984, s.27(2), see also s.27(3)). The "required for the purpose of safeguarding national security" test was therefore the same under both Acts, the key difference being the addition of an appeal mechanism in the Data Protection Act 1998, s.28. This was explained during the Parliamentary passage of the 1998 Data Protection Bill as follows: "This is broadly familiar from the 1984 provision, but it contains two important changes.First, it allows a certificate confirming the need for the exemption to be expressed in general terms and to be prospective, and, secondly, it allows a limited right of appeal to the Data Protection Tribunal for individuals who are affected by such a certificate" (Lord Williams, the Home Office Minister, Second Reading in the House of Lords, *Hansard*, HL, Vol.585, col.441, February 2, 1998); and "The right of appeal against a national security certificate is an important new safeguard. It represents an advance on the 1984 Act, which offered no appeal rights" (Mr Howarth, the Home Office Minister, Report and Third Reading in the House of Commons, *Hansard*, HC, Vol.315, col.586, July 2, 1998).

[73] *Hansard*, HC, Vol.347, col.1060, April 5, 2000.

[74] *Hansard*, HL, Vol.617, col.1259, October 19, 2000. See also J. Wadham, J. Griffiths and B. Rigby, *Blackstone's Guide to the Freedom of Information Act 2000*, (Blackstone Press, London, 2001), para.7.3.2 contending that the minister's assertion is "open to question."

[75] As to the position under the Access to Information Act (1982) (Canada) see paras 2–025 to 2–030.

[76] Official Information Act 1982, s.31 (NZ) allows for certificates to be issued preventing an Ombudsman from recommending the disclosure of information where this would be likely to prejudice: (a) security, defence or international relations (power conferred on Prime Minister); or (b) the prevention, investigation or detection of offences (power conferred on Attorney-General).

(1) Under the Freedom of Information Act 1982 (Cth of Aust), conclusive certificates can be issued by ministers under s.33(2) and (4) (documents affecting national security, defence or international relations), s.33A(2) and (4) (documents affecting relations with States) and s.36(3) (internal working documents),[77] by the Secretary to the Department of the Prime Minister and Cabinet under s.34(2) and (4) (Cabinet documents) and by the Secretary to the Executive Council (or a person performing his or her duties) under s.35(2) and (4) (Executive Council documents). Such certificates must, where appropriate, identify the part or parts of the document covered by the relevant exemption[78] and they must make clear the particular kind of document in respect of which the exemption has been claimed.[79] While they remain in force,[80] such certificates are conclusive in their effect subject to the relevant review procedures in Pt VI of the Freedom of Information Act 1982 (Cth of Aust). In this latter regard, the Administrative Appeals Tribunal, on an application under s.55, may not review the decision to give the certificate but may review "whether there exist reasonable grounds" for claiming that the relevant exemption applies.[81] It has been held "that it is a heavy thing for the Tribunal to reject a certified claim."[82]

(2) In relation to the Freedom of Information Act 1997 (Ireland), conclusive certificates can be issued by ministers under s.25 in order to declare that a record is exempt by virtue of s.23 (law enforcement and public

These are not "conclusive certificates" as such but they operate in a similar way and demonstrate a common approach in relation to the provision of executive override mechanisms in areas generally regarded as being particularly sensitive. See para.2–021.

[77] Ministerial certificates must specify the relevant ground of exemption: Freedom of Information Act 1982 , ss.33(2) and (4), 33A(2) and (4) and 36(3) (Cth of Aust).

[78] Freedom of Information Act 1982, ss.33(3), 33A(3), 34(3), 35(3) and 36(4) (Cth of Aust).

[79] Department of Industrial Relations v Forrest (1990) 21 F.C.R. 93; 11 A.A.R. 256; 91 A.L.R. 417 (certificate under Freedom of Information Act 1982, s.34 (Cth of Aust) invalid for uncertainty).

[80] Freedom of Information Act 1982, s.36A (Cth of Aust).

[81] Freedom of Information Act 1982, s.58(3), (4), (5) and (5A) (Cth of Aust). The issue for the Tribunal under s.58(4) is whether the view expressed in the certificate is reasonably open and not whether it is reasonable to release the document: *Re Bracken and Minister of State for Education and Youth Affairs* (1984) 2 A.A.R. 406; (1985) 7 A.L.D. 243; *Re Waterford and the Treasurer of the Commonwealth* (No.2) (1985) 8 A.L.N. N37; *Re Porter and Department of Community Services* (1988) 8 A.A.R. 335; 14 A.L.D. 403; *Department of Industrial Relations v Burchill* (1991) 33 F.C.R. 122, 14 A.A.R. 408; 105 A.L.R. 327; Re Cleary and Department of the Treasury (1993) 18 A.A.R. 83; *Australian Doctors Fund Ltd v Commonwealth* (1994) 49 F.C.R. 478; 34 A.L.D. 451. Specific provision is made regarding the constitution of the Tribunal and its hearings in cases where a conclusive certificate has been issued: Freedom of Information Act 1982 , ss.58B, 58C and 58E (Cth of Aust). Where the Tribunal determines that there do not exist reasonable grounds for claiming that an exemption applies, the appropriate minister has 28 days either to revoke the certificate or follow the special procedure for deciding not to do so: Freedom of Information Act 1982, s.58A (Cth of Aust). The existence of these review procedures does not oust the scope for judicial review of the issue of conclusive certificates: *Shergold v Tanner* [2002] H.C.A. 19; (2002) 188 A.L.R. 302, HCA.

[82] *Re Porter and Department of Community Services and Health* (1988) 14 A.L.D. 403 at 405–406.

safety) or s.24 (security, defence and international relations).[83] Such certificates can only be issued where access to a record has been refused in reliance on one of these exemptions and the minister is satisfied that the record is of "sufficient sensitivity or seriousness" to "justify" the issue of a certificate.[84] While they remain in force,[85] such certificates are conclusive in their effect[86] subject to appeal to the High Court on a point of law under s.42(2) of the Freedom of Information Act 1997 (Ireland). The Act also establishes various mechanisms for monitoring, controlling and publicising the use of such certificates.[87]

National security certificates

14–037 Appealable ministerial national security certificates may be issued under the Freedom of Information Act 2000 and the Data Protection Act 1998 as follows:

(1) Under s.23(2) of the Freedom of Information Act 2000 a Minister of the Crown may sign a certificate certifying that the information to which it applies was directly or indirectly supplied by, or relates to, any of the "security bodies" specified in s.23(3). Such a certificate will then stand as conclusive evidence of that fact, thus facilitating the applicability of the s.23 exemption, unless and until withdrawn or revoked[88] or quashed on an appeal under s.60 of the Freedom of Information Act 2000. The coincidence between what is certified by a s.23(2) certificate and what is

---

83 M. McDonagh *Freedom of Information Law in Ireland* (Round Hall, Sweet & Maxwell, Dublin, 1998), pp. 115–119.

84 Freedom of Information Act 1997, s.25(1)(a) (Ireland).

85 Freedom of Information Act 1997, s.25(9), (10) and (13) (Ireland).

86 Freedom of Information Act 1997, s.25(3) (Ireland). The issue of a certificate cannot therefore be subject to internal review or review by the Information Commissioner: Freedom of Information Act 2000, s.25(3)(b) (Ireland).

87 Under the Freedom of Information Act 1997, s.25(6)(b) (Ireland) the Taoiseach (and prescribed ministers) must be provided with a copy of every certificate and a statement explaining why it was issued and, under s.25(7), they must in turn carry out periodic reviews of the operation of s.25(1). The Taoiseach also has power under s.25(8) to conduct specific reviews of the operation of s.25(1) in relation to particular ministers or certificates.In accordance with s.25(9), both periodic and specific reviews can result in requests that a certificate be revoked which must be complied with. Each minister must also provide the Information Commissioner with a written annual return detailing the number of conclusive certificates issued by him or her in the preceding year and these are then appended to the Commissioner's annual report to the Houses of the Oireachtas: ss.25(11) and 40(1)(b).

88 There is no obvious reason for construing the Freedom of Information Act 2000, ss.23(2), 24(3), 34(3) or 36(7) or Data Protection Act 1998, s.28(2) as preventing the withdrawal or revocation of certificates or rendering the signatories *functus officio*. Changes in circumstances may very well make the withdrawal or revocation of a certificate appropriate without the need (where this route is open) for an appeal to the Information Tribunal. See: *Al Fayed v Secretary of State for the Home Department and Secretary of State for Foreign and Commonwealth Affairs* (unreported decision of the Information Tribunal, February 28, 2002) paras 9 and 15–16; Wade and Forsyth, *Administrative Law* (8th ed., Oxford University Press, Oxford, 2000), pp.235–238; and the Interpretation Act 1978, s.12.

required to engage the s.23(1) exemption is not perfect. The certificate will not certify whether the information was directly or indirectly supplied *to* the public authority *by* any of the s.23(3) bodies. It is possible that a public authority's holding of information to which a certificate applies does not result, directly or indirectly, from a supply by any of the bodies specified in s.23(3). For example, where a public authority has acquired the information independently or where it has acquired it from a third party that has itself acquired it independently.[89] There is no provision allowing such a certificate to identify the information to which it applies by means of a general description or to be expressed to have prospective effect.[90] Such a certificate may only be signed by a Minister of the Crown who is a member of the Cabinet or by the Attorney General, the Advocate General for Scotland or the Attorney General for Northern Ireland.[91] It is to be noted that while a certificate facilitates the rendering of information as exempt information (and therefore disapplication of the disclosure duty), it is not determinative of the separate question of whether the duty to confirm or deny arises, although that exercise will be undoubtedly affected by the certificate.

(2) Under s.24(3) of the Freedom of Information Act 2000 a Minister of the Crown may sign a certificate certifying that exemption from the disclosure duty in s.1(1)(b), or from the divulgence and disclosure duties in s.1(1)(a) and (b), is, or at any time was, required for the purpose of safeguarding national security.[92] Such a certificate will then stand as conclusive evidence of that fact, thus confirming the engagement of the s.24 exemption, unless and until withdrawn or revoked or quashed on an appeal under s.60 of the Freedom of Information Act 2000. If a s.24(3) certificate is confined to exemption from s.1(1)(b), determination of the existence duty will be decided on the ordinary basis, unaffected by the certificate. A s.24(3) certificate may not deem that the public interest in maintaining the exemption outweighs the public interest in divulgence or disclosure but may identify the information to which it applies by means of a general description and may be expressed to have prospective effect.[93] Such a certificate may only be

89 Always assuming, of course, that it does not relate to any of the s.23(3) bodies.

90 *cf.* Freedom of Information Act 2000, s.24(4) and Data Protection Act 1998, s.28(3).

91 Freedom of Information Act 2000, s.25(3).

92 Freedom of Information (Scotland) Act 2002, s.31(2)–(3). Under the Freedom of Information (Scotland) Act 2002, s.31(2) a certificate may be signed by a member of the Scottish Executive and will stand as being conclusive of the fact certified (*i.e.* exemption from s.1(1) is required for the purpose of safeguarding national security): the Freedom of Information (Scotland) Act 2002 does not expressly provide or allow for any appeal or review. Under the Freedom of Information (Scotland) Act 2002, s.31(3), such a certificate may identify the information to which it applies by means of a general description and may be expressed to have prospective effect.

93 Freedom of Information Act 2000, s.24(4). Pursuant to the Freedom of Information Act 2000, s.60(4) a public authority may claim in proceedings under or by virtue of that Act that a certificate issued under s.24(3) which identifies the information to which it applies by means of a

signed by a Minister of the Crown who is a member of the Cabinet or by the Attorney General, the Advocate General for Scotland or the Attorney General for Northern Ireland.[94]

(3) Under s.28(2) of the Data Protection Act 1998 a Minister of the Crown may sign a certificate certifying that exemption from all or any of the provisions of the data protection principles or Pts II (which includes the access rights bestowed by s.7), III or V or s.55 of the Data Protection Act 1998 is, or at any time was, required for the purpose of safeguarding national security in respect of any personal data. Such a certificate will then stand as conclusive evidence of that fact, thus confirming the engagement of the s.28 exemption, unless and until withdrawn or revoked or quashed on an appeal under Sch.6 to the Data Protection Act 1998. Such a certificate may identify the personal data to which it applies by means of a general description and may be expressed to have prospective effect.[95] Such a certificate may only be signed by a Minister of the Crown who is a member of the Cabinet or by the Attorney General, the Advocate General for Scotland or the Attorney General for Northern Ireland.[96]

Appeals against national security certificates

14–038 The appeals procedure is considered in detail later in this work.[97] In summary, certificates issued under ss.23(2) and 24(3) of the Freedom of Information Act 2000 and s.28(2) of the Data Protection Act 1998 may be appealed to the Information Tribunal under a common appeal mechanism provided for by ss.60–61 of the Freedom of Information Act 2000 and s.28 of, and Sch.6 to, the Data Protection Act 1998. In relation to certificates issued under ss.23(2) and 24(3) of the Freedom of Information Act 2000, such an appeal may be brought by the Information Commissioner or any applicant whose request for information is affected and, in relation to certificates issued under s.28(2) of the Data Protection Act 1998, such an appeal may be brought by any person directly affected.[98] The Tribunal may allow the appeal and quash the certificate if it finds: in relation to a certificate under s.23(2) of the Freedom of Information

general description applies to particular information and, subject to any contrary determination by the Information Tribunal on appeal, the certificate will be conclusively presumed so to apply.

94 Freedom of Information Act 2000, s.25(3).

95 Data Protection Act 1998, s.28(3). Pursuant to the Data Protection Act 1998, s.28(6) a data controller may claim in proceedings under or by virtue of that Act that a certificate issued under s.28(2) which identifies the personal data to which it applies by means of a general description applies to any personal data and, subject to any contrary determination by the Information Tribunal on appeal, the certificate will be conclusively presumed so to apply.

96 Data Protection Act 1998, s.28(10).

97 See paras 28–018 to 28–020 and 28–036 to 28–037.

98 Freedom of Information Act 2000, s.60(1); Data Protection Act 1998, s.28(4).

Act 2000, that the information referred to in the certificate was not exempt information by virtue of s.23(1)[99]; or, in relation to a certificate under s.24(3) of the Freedom of Information Act 2000 or s.28(2) of the Data Protection Act 1998, that, applying the principles applied by the court on an application for judicial review, the minister did not have reasonable grounds for issuing the certificate.[1]

Parliamentary certificates

Non-appealable Parliamentary certificates may be issued under the Freedom of Information Act 2000 as follows: 14–039

(1) Under s.34(3) of the Freedom of Information Act 2000, the "appropriate authority" may sign a certificate certifying that exemption from the disclosure duty in s.1(1)(b), or from the divulgence and disclosure

[99] Freedom of Information Act 2000, s.60(2). The Tribunal is thus given full appellate jurisdiction to review the matter unconstrained by any caveat that it "apply the principles applied by the court on an application for judicial review" and assess only whether the minister had "reasonable grounds for issuing the certificate" (*cf.* Freedom of Information Act 2000, s.60(3) and Data Protection Act 1998, s.28(5)).

[1] Freedom of Information Act 2000, s.60(3); Data Protection Act 1998, s.28(5). In determining whether the minister did or did not have reasonable grounds for issuing the certificate, the Tribunal will inevitably have to assess whether the minister did or did not have reasonable grounds for concluding that exemption from the relevant provision is, or at any time was, required for the purpose of safeguarding national security. It would appear that the Tribunal is thus confined to applying only one of the three heads of judicial review identified in *Council of Civil Service Unions v Minister for the Civil Service* [1985] A.C. 374 at 410 (*per* Lord Diplock) (*i.e.* irrationality but not illegality or procedural impropriety): if the minister took into account an irrelevant consideration or failed to take into account a relevant consideration, made an error of law or failed to act fairly in a procedural sense this will only be relevant if and in so far as it led or contributed to him not having reasonable grounds for issuing the certificate. So far as concerns "the principles applied by the court on an application for judicial review" in relation to "reasonable grounds", the Tribunal will review whether the minister's decision was reasonable or so unreasonable that no reasonable minister could have taken it (*Associated Provincial Picture Houses Ltd v Wednesbury Corpn* [1948] 1 K.B. 223) and the intensity of its scrutiny will increase if it can be shown that "fundamental rights" are engaged (*R. v Ministry of Defence, Ex p. Smith* [1996] Q.B. 517 at 554 (*per* Sir Thomas Bingham M.R.). If satisfied that a "Convention right" as defined by the Human Rights Act 1998 has also been affected by the minister's decision and the appellant may have been the "victim" of this for the purposes of that Act, the Tribunal will also need to go further and determine whether the decision to issue a certificate was compatible with that Convention right and would thus have to apply a more intensive proportionality-based standard of review: *R. (Daly) v Secretary of State for the Home Department* [2001] UKHL 26; [2001] 2 A.C. 532 at [26]–[27] (*per* Lord Steyn); *Baker v Secretary of State for the Home Department* [2001] U.K.H.R.R. 1275, para.63; *Gosling v Secretary of State for the Home Department* (unreported decision of the Information Tribunal, August 1, 2003), para.48. The language used in the Freedom of Information Act 2000, s.60(3) and Data Protection Act 1998, s.28(5) might also be thought to suggest that the Tribunal must focus solely on the grounds which the minister had in his mind at the time he issued the certificate (to the exclusion of other grounds which he might now wish to rely upon). However, this will not affect the eventual outcome because there is nothing to prevent a minister from issuing a fresh certificate on new grounds to replace one that has been quashed.

duties in s.1(1)(a) and (b), is, or at any time was, required for the purpose of avoiding an infringement of the privileges of either House of Parliament.[2] Such a certificate will then stand as conclusive evidence of that fact, thus confirming the engagement of the s.34 exemption, unless and until withdrawn or revoked or (in so far as this is possible given that Parliamentary privilege should be in play and there is no scope for an appeal under the Freedom of Information Act 2000) quashed on an application for judicial review.[3] The "appropriate authority" for these purposes is, in relation to the House of Commons, the Speaker of that House, and in relation to the House of Lords, the Clerk of the Parliaments.[4] If a s.34(3) certificate is confined to exemption from s.1(1)(b), determination of the existence duty will be decided on the ordinary basis, unaffected by the certificate.

(2) Under s.36(7) of the Freedom of Information Act 2000, the "qualified person" may sign a certificate certifying that, in his reasonable opinion, disclosure of information held by either House of Parliament or compliance with the divulgence duty in s.1(1)(a) by either House would, or would be likely to, have any of the effects mentioned in s.36(2) of the Freedom of Information Act 2000 (in other words, it would be prejudicial to the maintenance of the convention of the collective responsibility of the Ministers of the Crown; it would inhibit the free and frank provision of advice or of the exchange of views for the purposes of deliberation; or it would otherwise prejudice the effective conduct of public affairs). Such a certificate will then stand as conclusive evidence of the "fact" that disclosure or divulgence would, or would be likely to, produce any of those effects, thus facilitating application of the s.36 exemption. The certificate is not determinative of the application of the exemption, as it will also be necessary to demonstrate that the information satisfies the description in s.36(1). The certificate stands unless and until withdrawn or revoked or (in so far as this is possible given that Parliamentary privilege may be in play and there is no scope for an appeal under the Freedom of Information Act 2000) quashed on an application for judicial review.[5] The "qualified person" for these purposes is, in relation to information held by the House of Commons, the Speaker of that House, and in relation to information held by the House of Lords, the Clerk of the Parliaments.[6] If a s.36(7) certificate is

[2] See also the Data Protection Act 1998, s.35A exempting personal data from certain data protection principles and provisions of that Act if required for the purpose of avoiding an infringement of the privileges of either House of Parliament. Provision inserted by the Freedom of Information Act 2000, s.73, Sch.6, para.2 from November 30, 2005 or such day before then as the Lord Chancellor may by order appoint (Freedom of Information Act 2000, s.87(3)).

[3] Freedom of Information Act 2000, ss.2(3) and 34 confer an "absolute exemption."

[4] Freedom of Information Act 2000, s.34(4).

[5] Freedom of Information Act 2000, ss.2(3) and 36 (so far as relates to information held by the House of Commons or the House of Lords) confer an "absolute exemption."

[6] Freedom of Information Act 2000, s.36(5)(d)–(e) and (7).

confined to exemption from s.1(1)(b), determination of the existence duty will be decided on the ordinary basis, unaffected by the certificate.

Challenges to Parliamentary certificates

As mentioned above, certificates issued by the House Authorities under ss.34(3) and 36(7) of the Freedom of Information Act 2000 are not subject to any express appeal procedure. The following factors tend to suggest that the courts would probably be disinclined to intervene if an attempt were made to challenge such a certificate by way of judicial review: the wording of the relevant conclusive evidence clauses follows a format which has previously been given full effect as a matter of statutory construction without any consideration of human rights[7]; the clear intention not to provide for any oversight by way of an appeal to the Information Tribunal[8]; and the fact that considerations of Parliamentary privilege will inevitably be engaged in circumstances where the courts will not as a matter of principle interfere with the affairs of Parliament.[9] As already explained, were it possible to establish that a Parliamentary certificate had interfered with the enjoyment or exercise of a Convention or Community right, the courts might be more inclined to intervene.[10] The scope for relying on such arguments is limited in this context, however, and the very strong constitutional and policy reasons which inhibit the courts from interfering with the affairs of Parliament would probably be enough to establish that any infringement of rights was necessary and proportionate in any event. 14–040

[7] See: para.14–033; *Tinnelly and Sons Ltd v United Kingdom* (1999) 27 E.H.R.R. 249 at paras 18–32, 64, 66–67 and 74–75; *Devlin v United Kingdom* (2002) 34 E.H.R.R. 43 at paras 12–14; *R. v Secretary of State for Foreign and Commonwealth Affairs, Ex p. Vidler* [1993] C.O.D. 305; *R. v Secretary of State for Transport, Ex p. Evans and Commission for Racial Equality* [1992] C.O.D. 196.

[8] *cf.* Freedom of Information Act 2000, ss.23(2), 24(3) and 60(1) and (4) and Data Protection Act 1998, s.28(4) and (6).

[9] *Prebble v Television New Zealand Ltd* [1995] 1 A.C. 321 at 332 "wider principle . . . that the courts and Parliament are both astute to recognise their respective constitutional roles.So far as the courts are concerned they will not allow any challenge to be made to what is said or done within the walls of Parliament in performance of its legislative functions and protection of its established privileges" (*per* Lord Browne-Wilkinson). See also: *Bradlaugh v Gossett* (1884) 12 Q.B.D. 271; *Pickin v British Railways Board* [1974] A.C. 765; *Hamilton v Al Fayed* [2001] 1 A.C. 395; *R. v Parliamentary Commissioner for Standards, Ex p. Al Fayed* [1998] 1 W.L.R. 669. Support for this can also be found in De Smith, Woolf and Jowell, *Judicial Review of Administrative Action*, (5th ed., Sweet & Maxwell, London, 1995), para.5–027 where it is suggested, in relation to statutory formulae purporting to exclude judicial review by general but comprehensive language, that in the context of the working of the Parliamentary system there is a much stronger probability that the courts will give the words prohibiting judicial review a literal interpretation (referring to the Parliament Act 1911, s.3). See also the Ministerial and other Salaries Act 1975, s.2(2).

[10] See para.14–034.

Rights to procedural fairness and judicial supervision of conclusive certificates

14–041 Article 6(1) of the ECHR confers a right of access to a fair and effective hearing before an independent and impartial tribunal in relation to "the determination of civil rights and obligations" and Community law can also require a similar level of judicial oversight and effective judicial protection in relation to the exercise, enjoyment and implementation of Community rights. Such rights only guarantee a certain level of procedural protection, however, and they cannot confer, or alter the substantive extent of, any freestanding rights of access to information or personal data.[11] Having said this, the relevance of such rights to procedural fairness and judicial oversight in relation to conclusive certificates issued under the Freedom of Information Act 2000 and Data Protection Act 1998 is somewhat debatable. It may be difficult to argue that Art.6 of the ECHR can be relied upon in this context in relation to either Act but there is a reasonable case for invoking Community rights in relation to the Data Protection Act 1998:

(1) So far as concerns Art.6 of the ECHR, it is doubtful that the rights of access to information and personal data conferred by the Freedom of Information Act 2000 and the Data Protection Act 1998 have the requisite "private law" character to count as "civil rights" for the purposes of Art.6(1). In this regard: "article 6(1) is engaged where the decision which is to be given is of an administrative character, that is to say one given in an exercise of a discretionary power, as well as a dispute in a court of law regarding the private rights of the citizen, provided that it directly affects civil rights and obligations and is of a genuine and serious nature."[12] If it were possible to show that Art.6(1) is *prima facie*

---

[11] ECHR, Art.6 can itself confer a subsidiary right of access to information but only where it has already been established that Art.6 is engaged and it is then shown that access to the information in question is essential to the exercise of the right to a fair trial: *McGinley and Egan v United Kingdom* (1998) 27 E.H.R.R. 1, 4 E.H.R.C. 421. In general terms, the rules and procedures on disclosure and witness, summonses in domestic civil and criminal proceedings (*e.g.* Civil Procedure Rules 1998, SI (1998/3132) (L.17), Pts 31 and 34, Employment Tribunals Rules of Procedure, r. 4(5) at Employment Tribunals (Constitution and Rules of Procedure) Regulations 2001, (SI 2001 1171), Sch.1, para.4(5) and Criminal Procedure and Investigations Act 1996) can be seen as satisfying Art.6 for these purposes and the Freedom of Information Act 2000 need not be seen as contributing to this: *McGinley and Egan v United Kingdom* (1998) 27 E.H.R.R. 1, 4 E.H.R.C. 421 at [86] and [90].

[12] *R.(Alconbury Developments Ltd) v Secretary of State for the Environment, Transport and the Regions* [2001] UKHL 23; [2001] 2 W.L.R. 1389 at [150] (*per* Lord Clyde); see also [79]–[80] (*per* Lord Hoffmann); *Ringeisen v Austria (No 1)* (1979–80) 1 E.H.R.R. 455, para.94; *König v Germany* (1978) 2 E.H.R.R. 170; *Le Compte, Van Leuven and De Meyere v Belgium* (1981) 4 E.H.R.R. 1, paras 46 and 49; *H v France* (1990) 12 E.H.R.R. 74, para.47. The right must be a private law right or it must be "decisive for private rights and obligations". In *Tinnelly and Sons Ltd v United Kingdom* (1999) 27 E.H.R.R. 249 it was held that the right not to be discriminated against conferred by the Fair Employment (Northern Ireland) Act 1976 was a "civil right" for the purposes of the ECHR, Art.6(1) "having regard to the context in which it applied and to its

engaged through the presence of a relevant "civil right", it would next be necessary to show that the issue of a conclusive certificate or the operation of the relevant exemption has interfered with the exercise or enjoyment of that right.[13] In other words, it would have to be shown that the certificate or the exemption has operated to "defeat" or "cut off" an otherwise enforceable entitlement to the information or personal data in question rather than having acted simply to define and confirm the substantive bounds of a right which never extended further.[14] If these hurdles can be overcome, non-appealable national security certificates have been found to operate as procedural bars to the judicial resolution of disputes in contravention of Art.6(1), unless justified by reference to principles of proportionality.[15] However, the context and structure of the Freedom of Information Act 2000 and the Data Protection Act 1998 are very different and it is arguable that the relevant exemptions (whether or not engaged via the issue of a conclusive certificate) do not infringe rights to information or personal data whose non-disclosure is required for the purpose of safeguarding national security but rather confirm the total absence of any such right.[16]

(2) Community law has no bearing on the application or enforcement of the Freedom of Information Act 2000 but it is relevant to the Data Protection Act 1998 which implements the European Community Data Protection Directive 95/46 and which must therefore be construed and given effect in accordance with the terms of that Directive and the

pecuniary nature" and that s.42 of that Act did not define the scope of that substantive right *in limine* but provided a respondent with a defence to a complaint of unlawful discrimination (at paras 61–63). The same reasoning was applied and the same conclusion was reached in the employment context in *Devlin v United Kingdom* (2002) 34 E.H.R.R. 43 at para.26 and *Devenney v United Kingdom* (2002) 35 E.H.R.R. 24.

13 *Matthews v Ministry of Defence* [2003] UKHL 4; [2003] 1 A.C. 1163 at [3] (*per* Lord Bingham); *Wilson v First County Trust Ltd (No. 2)* [2003] UKHL 40; [2003] 3 W.L.R. 568 at [32]–[35] (*per* Lord Nicholls), [103]–[105] (*per* Lord Hope), [132] (*per* Lord Hobhouse), [165] (*per* Lord Scott); *Golder v United Kingdom* (1979–80) 1 E.H.R.R. 524; *König v Germany* (1978) 2 E.H.R.R. 170; *Fayed v United Kingdom* (1994) 18 E.H.R.R. 393 at 429–430, paras 65–67; *Tinnelly and Sons Ltd v United Kingdom* (1999) 27 E.H.R.R. 249 at 288–292, paras 72–79; *Z v United Kingdom* [2001] 2 F.L.R. 612 at 634, para.87.

14 *Matthews v Ministry of Defence* [2003] UKHL 4; [2003] 1 A.C. 1163 at [141] (*per* Lord Walker).

15 *Tinnelly and Sons Ltd v United Kingdom* (1999) 27 E.H.R.R. 249; *Devlin v United Kingdom* (2002) 34 E.H.R.R. 43; *Devenney v United Kingdom* (2002) 35 E.H.R.R. 24. However, note the emphasis on the context and the pecuniary nature of the right not to be discriminated against.

16 While the Freedom of Information Act 2000, s.1(1) does enact what is described in the side-note as a "general right of access to information held by public authorities" this is immediately qualified by s.1(2) which brings in the remainder of s.1, ss.2, 9, 12 and 14 and, in turn, Pt II. It is made clear in s.1(2) that s.1(1) "has effect" throughout and at all times "subject to" these provisions (see also the language of "section 1(1)(a) does not apply" and "section 1(1)(b) does not apply" (in s.2) and "the duty to confirm or deny does not arise" (throughout)). See especially the ultimate conclusion reached by the House of Lords on whether the ECHR, Art. 6(1) was engaged in *Matthews v Ministry of Defence* [2003] UKHL 4; [2003] 1 A.C. 1163.

general principles of Community law.[17] As a consequence, there may be scope for relying on Community rights to effective judicial protection by this route in relation to s.28 of the Data Protection Act 1998.

It is in any event important to appreciate the practical consequences that would flow from being able to show that rights to procedural fairness and judicial oversight are engaged and arguably infringed in relation to the issue of conclusive certificates under the Freedom of Information Act 2000 or the Data Protection Act 1998. In this regard, the scope for appealing national security certificates issued under ss.23(2) and 24(3) of the Freedom of Information Act 2000 and s.28(2) of the Data Protection Act 1998 arguably provides a respectable measure of judicial oversight[18] that should justify the restrictions entailed, bearing in mind the importance of national security matters and the fact that the executive is better qualified and equipped to judge related issues.[19] As a consequence, the successful invocation of such rights would probably have most effect in encouraging the Information Tribunal to apply a more intensive proportionality-based standard of scrutiny when considering this type of appeal.

Rights to privacy and data protection rights

14–042 The right to respect for private and family life contained in Art.8 of the ECHR can confer a right of access to personal information where this is essential to the exercise and enjoyment of that right.[20] Although it is not inconceivable that information falling within this category might be sought under the Freedom of Information Act 2000, it is much more likely that requests under the Data Protection Act 1998 will seek such information. So far as concerns conclusive certificates issued under s.28 of the Data Protection Act 1998, Convention rights under Art.8 may therefore be engaged in a very direct way and Community rights may also come into play by virtue of the fact that the Data Protection Act

[17] See para.14–034.

[18] Questions may nevertheless arise as to the grounds and intensity of the review thereby allowed and as to the absence of any provision allowing for a further appeal to the High Court on a point of law (*cf.* the non-appealability of Parliamentary certificates issued under the Freedom of Information Act 2000, ss.34(3) and 36(7) and the scope for further appeals under the Freedom of Information Act 2000, s.59 and Data Protection Act 1998, s.49(6)).

[19] It is important to note that the right of access to the courts secured by the ECHR, Art.6(1) is not absolute and may be subject to limitations provided they do not restrict or reduce the access left to the individual in such a way or to such an extent that the very essence of the right is impaired, provided that they pursue a legitimate aim and provided that there is a reasonable relationship of proportionality between the means employed and the aim sought to be achieved: *Fayed v United Kingdom* (1994) 18 E.H.R.R. 393 at 429–430, paras 65–67; *Tinnelly and Sons Ltd v United Kingdom* (1999) 27 E.H.R.R. 249, at 271, para. 74; *Lithgow v United Kingdom* (1986) 8 E.H.R.R. 329, at 393, para.194.

[20] *Gaskin v United Kingdom* (1990) 12 E.H.R.R. 36; *Guerra v Italy* (1998) 26 E.H.R.R. 357; *McGinley and Egan v United Kingdom* (1998) 27 E.H.R.R. 1, 4 E.H.R.C. 421 at paras 101 and 103.

1998 implements the European Community Data Protection Directive 95/46.[21] Of course, Art.8 of the ECHR, the Data Protection Directive and the Data Protection Act 1998 do not confer absolute rights and all three expressly and quite consistently allow, where necessary and proportionate, for the curtailment and denial of these rights in the interests of national security.[22] The rights of appeal under ss.28(4) and (6) of the Data Protection Act 1998 and the adequacy of the judicial oversight they provide will therefore be crucial if it is to be demonstrated that the use of national security certificates thereunder, and the application of the exemption therein, is compatible with Convention rights and Community law. In this regard, it is notable that in relation to the first substantive decision taken by the Information Tribunal under s.28(4) of the Data Protection Act 1998, a more intensive proportionality-based standard of review was applied and the certificate in question was quashed for having an "unnecessarily wide effect."[23]

Rights to freedom of expression

Although expressed to include "the right to receive and impart information and ideas without interference" the right to freedom of expression guaranteed by Art.10 to the ECHR has been consistently held not to confer or entail a general right of access to information.[24] For this reason, and in the absence of some development in the jurisprudence on this,[25] it will not be possible to invoke 14–043

[21] Indeed, the connection between rights to privacy (including under the ECHR, Art.8) and data protection is strongly emphasised throughout the recitals to the European Community Data Protection Directive 95/46 (see especially recitals (1)–(3), (7) and (9)–(11)) and in Art.1. See paras 14–034 to 14–041 and on the way in which the Community law connection can engage rights to effective judicial oversight.

[22] ECHR, Art.8(2); European Community Data Protection Directive 95/46, recital (16) and Art.13(1); Data Protection Act 1998, s.28.

[23] *Baker v Secretary of State for the Home Department* [2001] U.K.H.R.R. 1275. Note the emphasis on Convention and Community rights at paras 50–64 and, more generally, see para.14–034 above. In *Gosling v Secretary of State for the Home Department* (unreported, decision of the Information Tribunal dated August 1, 2003) a replacement certificate whose application depends upon a consideration of the requirements of national security in relation to the need for particular exemptions in each individual case was subsequently upheld by the Information Tribunal albeit upon limited grounds (para.28) and the Tribunal again emphasised the relevance of Convention and Community rights when considering the appropriate intensity of its review (para.48). This decision was followed in *Hitchens v Secretary of State for the Home Department* (unreported, decision of the Information Tribunal dated August 4, 2003).

[24] *R. (Persey) v Secretary of State for the Environment, Food and Rural Affairs* [2002] EWHC 371 (Admin); [2003] Q.B. 794 at [52]–[53] (*per* Simon Brown LJ); *R. (Howard) v Secretary of State for Health (Note)* [2002] EWHC 396 (Admin) at [103] (*per* Scott Baker J.); *Leander v Sweden* (1987) 9 E.H.R.R. 433; *Gaskin v United Kingdom* (1989) 12 E.H.R.R. 36; *Guerra v Italy* (1998) 26 E.H.R.R. 357; *BBC, Petitioners (No. 2)* 2000 J.C. 521; *cf. R.(Wagstaff) v Secretary of State for Health* [2001] 1 W.L.R. 292.

[25] See, *e.g.* Sir Stephen Sedley, "Information as a Human Right" in *Freedom of Expression and Freedom of Information: Essays in Honour of Sir David Williams*, (J. Beatson and Y. Cripps (eds), Oxford University Press, Oxford, 2000).

Art.10 rights in order to bring or enhance a challenge to the issue of a conclusive certificate under ss.23–24, 34 or 36 of the Freedom of Information Act 2000 or s.28 of the Data Protection Act 1998 or to the application of one of the exemptions contained in these provisions. The practical significance of this should not be overstated, however, particularly in the national security context, as Art.10(2) of the ECHR expressly recognises that the right to freedom of expression may be restricted, where necessary and proportionate, in the interests of national security.

CHAPTER 15

Prejudice and the Public Interest

1. THE PUBLIC INTEREST

Introduction

15–001 The Freedom of Information Act 2000 implicitly recognises a public interest underlying each of the grounds of exemption, as well as a public interest in divulging whether information is held and in disclosing that information.[1] Indeed, most of the exemptions simply articulate a public interest in non-disclosure that has been well-recognised in other contexts, most notably public interest immunity and confidentiality. Where information falls within one of the qualified exemptions within Part II of the Act, the competition between the relevant aspects of the public interest is determinative of whether the duty to confirm or deny and the duty to communicate are disapplied or not. In requiring such a balancing exercise, the FOI Act also recognises that the force of an aspect of the public interest will vary according to the information sought and "all the circumstances of the case." In relation to the disclosure of exempt information under a qualified exemption, the task under s.2 is not to "weigh"[2] the public interest in non-disclosure against the public interest in disclosure: the task is to weigh the public interest "in maintaining the exemption[3]" afforded by the provision rendering it exempt information against the public interest in disclosing the information.[3A] Only if the weighing process favours maintenance of the exemption is the duty to communicate disapplied. Accordingly, the balancing exercise does not involve a consideration of all aspects of the public interest that weigh against disclosure. The consideration of the public interest, so far as it weighs against disclosure, is focussed upon the public interest embodied in the exemption by which the information sought is rendered exempt information.[4]

[1] Freedom of Information Act 2000, s.2(1) and (2); Freedom of Information (Scotland) Act 2002, s.2(1).

[2] The FOI Act employs the term "outweigh," although as has been observed in relation to public interest immunity it is "a rough metaphor" and "a more complex process than merely using the scales"—at *Science Research Council v Nassé* [1980] A.C. 1028 at 1067 *per* Lord Wilberforce.

[3] "Exemption" here cannot mean exemption from the duty to communicate, as that only arises after the weighing process: it cannot, at this stage, be said to be being "maintained." See, also, Pt IV of the Data Protection Act 1998, which terms the provisions analogous to those in Pt II of the FOI Act as "exemptions."

[3A] In order for the absolute exemption that applies to information provided in confidence to arise, it is necessary to consider the public interest: see para.25–014.

[4] In this respect, the treatment of the public interest in the FOI Act differs markedly from that which had originally been proposed in cl.14(3) of the original FOI Bill. Some indication of this change appears from *Hansard*, HL, Vol.617, October 17, 2000, cols 901–902, Lord Falconer of Thoroton (the Minister of State, Cabinet Office), when introducing the amendment that led to s.2 and in *Hansard*, HL, Vol.617, October 19, 2002, col.1265, where Lord Falconer of Thoroton gave an example of how it should work in practice.

The public interest in comparative official information access legislation

This focused approach to the public interest in the FOI Act distinguishes it from the freedom of information legislation of comparative jurisdictions. The FOI Acts of Australia, New Zealand and Ireland all require the decision-maker, if he is to rely on certain exemptions, to be satisfied that the disclosure of the document would be contrary to "the public interest."[5] This generalised reference to the public interest enables a broad range of matters to be taken into account as part of the balancing exercise.[6] But it also means that despite a superficial similarity with the UK Act, their jurisprudence on this issue is limited in its comparative value. 15–002

The nature of the public interest

The "public interest", whether unlimited in its scope or focussed upon a particular matter, is not a reference to something that is of interest to the public: it signifies something that is in the interests of the public; that is, for the common welfare.[7] Thus: 15–003

> "The public are interested in many private matters which are no real concern of theirs and which the public have no pressing need to know."[8]

[5] Freedom of Information Act 1982 (Cth of Australia), ss.21(1)(c), 33A, 36(1), 39(2), 40(2), 58 and 58C; *cf.* ss.33(1) and 44(1), which, although declaring certain disclosures to be contrary to the public interest, do not require a general or focused weighing of it; Official Information Act 1982 (NZ), s.9(1); Freedom of Information Act 1997 (Ireland), ss.20(1), 21(2), 22(3), 23(3), 26(3), 27(3), 30(3) and 31(3), *cf.* 28(5)(a). The Access to Information Act (1982) (Canada) does not involve consideration of the public interest, except where the request relates to "third party information," in which case the decision-making involves a focussed treatment of the public interest: s.20(6). Within the terms of the Freedom of Information Act 1966 (USA) itself, the role of the public interest is confined to considering whether the information requested should be provided free of charge: 5 U.S.C. 552(a)(4)(A)(i). In relation to declassification decisions, Executive Order 12,958 3.2(b) authorises agencies to apply a balancing test: namely, to determine "whether the public interest in disclosure outweighs the damage to national security that might reasonably be expected from disclosure."

[6] See, for example: *Re Howard and the Treasurer* (1985) 7 A.L.D. 626, 3 A.A.R. 169; *Director of Public Prosecutions v Smith* [1991] 1 V.R. 63. The absence of any such focus led the Australian Law Reform Commission and the Administrative Review Council in their joint review of the operation of the Freedom of Information Act 1982 to recommend that the FOI Commissioner issue guidelines listing the factors that are relevant and that are irrelevant when weighing the public interest: Australian Law Reform Commission and Administrative Review Council, "Open Government: a review of the Federal Freedom of Information Act 1982", A.L.R.C. 77, A.R.C. 40, Canberra, 1995, para.8.14, recommendation 37.

[7] The definition given to it in the *Shorter Oxford English Dictionary*, (2nd ed.) (OUP, Oxford, 1993).

[8] *Lion Laboratories Ltd v Evans* [1985] Q.B. 526 at 537, [1984] 2 All E.R. 417, CA. In *Francome v Mirror Group Newspapers Ltd.* [1984] 1 W.L.R. 892 (at 898) the Court of Appeal spoke of the newspapers as being "peculiarly vulnerable to the error of confusing the public interest with their own interest".

And:

> "There is a wide difference between what is interesting to the public and what it is in the public interest to make known."[9]

Where a statute speaks of a decision-maker being able to do something when that is in the public interest, that operates as a device by which the discretion vested in the decision-maker is directed away from matters of narrower or immediate concern to the decision-maker and to matters which are not necessarily of direct interest to the decision-maker. The public interest is not immutable.[10] The balancing of the competing facets of the public interest must be carried out by reference to the circumstances that exist at the time that the exercise is performed. Any change in those circumstances may influence the outcome of the balancing exercise. Accordingly, while a public authority may properly refuse to disclose information subject to a qualified exemption, where a subsequent request is made for the same information a change in the surrounding circumstances may result in the public authority being obliged to disclose that information.

The two balancing exercises

15–004 The FOI Act distinguishes the public interest in disclosing whether a public authority holds certain information from the public interest in disclosing that information. Although the FOI Act places the balancing exercise for the purpose of disclosure after the balancing exercise for the purpose of the duty to confirm or deny,[11] the former is better considered before the latter. If it is in the public interest for a public authority to disclose certain information, it follows that it will be in the public interest for that public authority to disclose that it holds that information. Logically, then, the need to carry out the weighing exercise set out in subs.2(1) of the FOI Act will only arise if the result of carrying out the separate weighing exercise in subs.2(2) is a decision not to disclose the information.

[9] *Hyde Park Residences Ltd v Yelland* [2001] Ch.143 at 164; *Reynolds v Times Newspapers Ltd* [2001] 2 A.C. 127 at 202; *Douglas v Hello!* [2001] Q.B. 967 at 997–998; *British Steel Corporation v Granada Television Ltd* [1981] A.C. 1096 at 1168 *per* Lord Wilberforce. Similarly: *R. v Inhabitants of the County of Bedfordshire* (1855) 24 L.J.Q.B. 81 at 84; *Sinclair v Mining Warden at Maryborough* (1975) 132 C.L.R. 473 at 480; *Director of Public Prosecutions v Smith* [1991] 1 V.R. 63 at 75. Similarly in *Attorney General for the United Kingdom v Wellington Newspapers Limited* [1988] 1 N.Z.L.R. 129 at 178–179, McMullin J. said: "By public interest is meant something more than that which catches one's curiosity or merely raises the interest of the gossip. It is something which may be of real concern to the public."

[10] *Attorney-General v Times Newspapers Ltd* [1974] A.C. 273 at 320.

[11] *i.e.* Freedom of Information Act 2000, ss.2(2) and 2(1), respectively. In Scotland, Freedom of Information (Scotland) Act 2002, ss.18(1) and 2(1) respectively.

2. WEIGHING THE PUBLIC INTEREST: DISCLOSURE

The public interest in maintaining the exemption

15–005 As noted above,[12] disapplication of the duty to communicate information rendered exempt information by virtue of a provision conferring a qualified exemption involves weighing "the public interest in maintaining the exemption," rather than all facets of the public interest that are against disclosure of the information. Where information is rendered exempt information by more than one qualified exemption, it would seem that the public interest in maintaining the exemption must be balanced one exemption at a time against the public interest in disclosure. It will never be enough for a public authority simply to rely upon the public interest against disclosure that is inherent in the particular qualified exemption that applies to the information sought without a consideration of the particular circumstances relating to the information. To allow this would effectively be to elevate a qualified exemption into an absolute exemption. Sub-section 2(2) contemplates instances in which information rendered exempt information by a qualified exemption will be required to be disclosed. The specific aspect of the public interest that underlies each of the qualified exemptions is considered in more detail in the chapters that deal with particular exemptions. The only "internal" indication of the public interest in maintaining the exemptions comes from the provisions reducing the exemptions and exclusions in relation to historical records.[13] Implicit in the taking out of those exemptions is that if the information is without contemporaneity there is no significant public interest served by the exemption.

The public interest in disclosure

15–006 The FOI Act describes at various points a public interest in disclosing information.[14] In introducing the Bill and in commending its provisions, the objectives and aspirations for it were said to be:

> "... the Bill will not only provide legal rights for the public and place legal duties on Ministers and public authorities, but will help to transform the culture of Government from one of secrecy to one of openness. It will transform the default setting from 'this should be kept quiet unless' to 'this should be published unless'. By doing so, it should raise public confidence

[12] para.15–001.

[13] Freedom of Information Act 2000, s.63; Freedom of Information (Scotland) Act 2002, s.58. See paras 6–031 to 6–037.

[14] Freedom of Information Act 2000, ss.2(2)(b), 17(3)(b), 19(3), 35(4) and 46(3); Freedom of -Information (Scotland) Act 2002, ss.2(1)(b), 16(2), 23(3), 29(3) and 61(3). See also para.14–024 in relation to the presumption of openness in the FOI Act.

> in the processes of government, and enhance the quality of decision making by the Government."[15]

It may be thought that the public interest in disclosure lies partly in the attainment of those stated objectives. The significance of the public interest was described by those supporting the Bill in these terms:

> "The duty to disclose information in the public interest is one of the most important aspects of the Bill. It is the key to creating the new culture of openness in the public sector with which the Government intend to replace the secrecy that, as everyone accepts, permeates Whitehall and too much of the public sector. We are introducing the Bill because we want to change that. The question is how to achieve the necessary balance between opening up the public sector and recognising that openness does not always have a monopoly on righteousness. It needs to be balanced against the need for personal privacy, commercial confidentiality and effective government."[16]

A consideration of the provisions and structure of the Act reveals that it is the disclosure of information that animates it. The purposes of the FOI Act, although not recited within its provisions, guide the public interest in disclosure.[17] To the extent that discernment of the public interest in disclosure is left in the hands of the Courts, it may be thought that some guidance may be found in this underlying philosophy of the Act:

> "Where over a period of years there can be discerned a steady trend in legislation which reflects the view of successive Parliaments as to what the public interest demands in a particular field of law, development of the common law in that part of the same field which has been left to it ought to proceed upon a parallel rather than a diverging course"[18]

External indications of the public interest in disclosure

15–007 The precursor to the FOI Act, the Code of Practice on Access to Government Information,[19] stated that its aims were:

[15] *Hansard*, HC, Vol.340, December 7, 1999, Mr J. Straw, second reading speech.

[16] *Hansard*, HC, Vol.357, November 27, 2000, col.719, Mr O'Brien (Parliamentary Under-Secretary of State for the Home Department) introducing amendments to the public interest provisions of the Bill.

[17] The purposes of the FOI Act are considered in Ch.1.

[18] *Erven Warnink Besloten Vennootschap v J. Townend & Sons (Hull) Ltd.* [1979] A.C. 731 at 743 *per* Lord Diplock. See also the quotation at para.25–018 from *A-G (UK) v Heinemann Publishers Pty Ltd* (1987) 10 N.S.W.L.R. 86 at 191, 75 A.L.R. 353 at 454.

[19] In relation to Scotland, see paras 1–023–1–026.

— "to improve policy-making and the democratic process by extending access to the facts and analyses which provide the basis for the consideration of proposed policy;
— to protect the interests of individuals and companies by ensuring that reasons are given for administrative decisions, except where there is statutory authority or established convention to the contrary; and
— to support and extend the principles of public service established under the Citizen's Charter."[20]

The FOI Act was intended to represent a development from the Code of Practice, but there is nothing to suggest that its core purpose was materially different from that of the Code.[21]

The public interest in disclosing information in other contexts

The balancing of competing interests for and against the disclosure of information has arisen in other contexts, such as claims for confidentiality and public interest immunity[22] from the disclosure of documents in civil and criminal litigation.[23] Although the interests on the non-disclosure side of the balance do not always wholly coincide with the public interest in maintaining an exemption under the FOI Act, so far as the other side of the balance is concerned they provide a useful articulation of the grounds on which it may be said that there is a public interest in the disclosure of information. Thus, it has been held to be in the public interest to disclose: 15–008

— information that raised serious doubts about the reliability of an instrument which was providing the sole evidence on which members of the public had been or were being prosecuted (an instrument to assess the level of alcohol in a motorist's blood).[24] The court held

[20] 2nd ed. 1997, para.2.

[21] See para.14–007 for the important distinctions between the Act and the Code.

[22] The government's current approach to public interest immunity is set out in statements made in the House of Lords and the House of Commons on December 18, 1996 by the then-Lord Chancellor and the then-Attorney General respectively (*Hansard*, HC, Vol.287, cols 949–950). These statements were made following the House of Lords' decision in *R. v Chief Constable of the West Midlands Police, Ex p. Wiley* [1995] 1 A.C. 274 and a wide consultation on public interest immunity generally. The December 1996 statements were accompanied by a detailed paper put in the Libraries of both Houses of Parliament and endorsed on July 11, 1997 (*Hansard*, HC, Vol.297, cols 616–617).

[23] See further para.25–014.

[24] *Lion Laboratories Ltd v Evans* [1985] Q.B. 526; [1984] 2 All E.R. 417, CA, where the Court spoke of "the countervailing interest of the public in being kept informed of matters which are of real public concern" (at 536). The case involved an injunction by a private company to restrain former employees from engaging in a breach of confidence. Similarly in the United States *Teich v FDA*, 751 F. Supp. 243 (D.D.C. 1990) where disclosure of certain safety and effectiveness data relating to a medical device was held "unquestionably in the public interest."

that it was not necessary to show "iniquity" on the part of a public official[25];

— information that is of public concern and of which the public ought to know.[26] There is, however, no public interest in disseminating information that is untrue such that the public is misinformed[27];
— information that results in citizens being informed of the processes of their government and its agencies[28];
— information that discloses corruption or illegality on the part of officials[29];
— information that discloses possible breaches of a regulatory system or fiscal irregularities[30];
— information that discloses mismanagement of public enterprises or financial resources[31];
— information that is needed to disclose the full picture: in other words, where there has been a partial disclosure of information upon a particular matter the selection of which is unrepresentative of the whole, the public interest is served by disclosure of information that renders representative the totality of material disclosed[32];

---

25 *Lion Laboratories Ltd v Evans* [1985] Q.B. 526 at 537–538, 550, following *Fraser v Evans* [1969] 1 Q.B. 349 at 362.

26 *British Steel Corporation v Granada Television Ltd* [1981] A.C. 1096 at 1129, *per* Lord Denning. Similarly: *X v Morgan-Grampian (Publishers) Ltd* [1991] 1 A.C. 1 at 40 ("The courts have always recognised an important public interest in the free flow of information"); *Camelot Group plc v Centaur Communications Ltd* [1999] Q.B. 124 at 139 (the "general public interest in access to information"); *Hyde Park Residence Ltd v Yelland* [2001] Ch. 143 at 170 ("the public interest in knowing the truth" per Mance L.J.).

27 *Reynolds v Times Newspapers Ltd* [2001] 2 A.C. 127, [1999] 3 W.L.R. 1010; [1999] 4 All E.R. 609 *per* Lord Hobhouse.

28 *Harris v Australian Broadcasting Corporation* (1983) 78 F.L.R. 236, 50 A.L.R. 551.

29 *Beloff v Pressdram Ltd.* [1973] 1 All E.R. 241 at 260 ("disclosure justified in the public interest, of matters carried out or contemplated, in breach of the country's security, or in breach of law, including statutory duty, fraud, or otherwise destructive of the country or its people, including matters medically dangerous to the public; and doubtless other misdeeds of similar gravity"); *Attorney-General v Guardian Newspapers (No. 2)* [1990] 1 A.C. 109 ("possibly—the public interest in the exposure of iniquity in the Security Service" *per* Dillon L.J. at 212; and see Lord Griffiths at 268–269 and Lord Goff at 282–283); *Sankey v Whitlam* (1978) 142 C.L.R. 1; *Director of Public Prosecutions v Smith* [1991] 1 V.R. 63; *Cochran v United States*, 770 F.2d 949 (11th Cir. 1985); *Columbia Packing Co. v USDA*, 563 F.2d 495. See also the Public Interest Disclosure Act 1998, which inserted Pt IVA (ss.43A–43L) into the Employment Rights Act 1996. One of the classes of "qualifying disclosure" which are said to be in the public interest is a disclosure tending to show "that a criminal offence has been committed, is being committed or is likely to be committed"—s.43B(1)(a).

30 *In a Company's Application* [1989] Ch. 477. Under the Employment Rights Act 1996, as amended by the Public Interest Disclosure Act 1998, one of the classes of "qualifying disclosure" which are said to be in the public interest is one tending to show "that a person has failed, is failing or is likely to fail to comply with any legal obligation to which he is subject"—s.43B(1)(b).

31 Based on the dissenting views of Lord Salmon in *British Steel Corporation v Granada Television Ltd* [1981] A.C. 1096 at 1185.

32 *Woodward v Hutchins* [1977] 1 W.L.R. 760 at 764 ("If the image which they fostered was not a true image, it is in the public interest that it should be corrected. In these cases of confidential information it is a question of balancing the public interest in knowing the truth," *per* Lord

— information that will enable a fair trial to take place[33] and that will permit an administrative tribunal to be appraised of all the facts[34];
— information that corrects a misleading public pronouncement.[35]
— information that shows that the health and safety of any individual has been, is being or is likely to be endangered.[35A]
— information that shows that the environment has been, is being or is likely to be endangered.[35B]

If there is to be a transposition of these to the FOI Act, that cannot properly be done without a consideration of the context in which they arose. In particular, in confidentiality cases, the courts are not performing a straightforward balancing exercise: they are drawing the line at the point where equity or the common law will no longer protect a confidence for reasons of public policy or for reasons affecting the conscience of the claimant.[36] Moreover, it is often the case in confidentiality cases that the information will already be in the hands of someone other than the confider; whereas in the freedom of information context the public authority is being asked to disclose the information for the first time. And even where some sort of disclosure is required in the public interest, the courts recognise that this does not necessarily extend to publication to the

Denning). Significant doubts have been expressed about this authority: it was said to be "framed in astonishingly wide terms" in *Douglas v Hello! Ltd* [2001] Q.B. 967 at [96], p.995; and it was doubted by Lightman J. at first instance in *Campbell v Frisbee* [2002] EWHC 328 (Ch); [2002] E.M.L.R. 656, paras [40]–[41] and the Court of Appeal (reversing his decision) said his doubts "may well be right," [2002] EWCA Civ 1374; [2003] I.C.R. 141 at [34]. Moreover, Australian courts have expressly departed from it in favour of a narrower approach: *Castrol Australia Pty Ltd v Emtech Associates Pty Ltd* (1980) 33 A.L.R. 31 *per* Rath J. at 56. Less controversially, in *Attorney-General v Guardian Newspapers (No. 2)* [1990] 1 A.C. 109 at 196 Lord Donaldson M.R. spoke of "the legitimate public interest in being fully informed."

33 *Marcel v Commissioner for Police* [1992] Ch. 225 at 265; *Hasselblad (G.B.) Ltd v Orbinson* [1985] Q.B. 475 (" the public interest in requiring the full disclosure of documents for the proper conduct of litigation" at 505 *per* May L.J.); *Air Canada v Secretary of State for Trade* [1983] 2 A.C. 394 ("the public interest in the due administration of justice" at 442 *per* Edmund Davies L.J.; and similarly at 445 *per* Lord Scarman and at 448–449 *per* Lord Templeman).

34 *W v Edgell* [1990] Ch. 359, CA. Under the Employment Rights Act 1996, as amended by the Public Interest Disclosure Act 1998, one of the classes of "qualifying disclosure" which are said to be in the public interest is a disclosure finding to show "that a miscarriage of justice has occured, is occuring or is likely to occur"—s.43(1)(c).

35 *Campbell v MGN Ltd* [2002] EWCA Civ 1373; [2003] Q.B. 633 at [43]; *Theakston v MGN Ltd* [2002] EWHC 137, QB; [2002] E.M.L.R. 398 at [68].

35A Under the Employment Rights Act 1996, as amended by the Public Interest Disclosure Act 1998, this is one of the classes of "qualifying disclosure" which are said to be in the public interest—s.43B(1)(d)

35B Under the Employment Rights Act 1996, as amended by the Public Interest Disclosure Act 1998, this is one of the classes of "qualifying disclosure" which are said to be in the public interest—s.43B(1)(e).

36 See *Venables v News Group Newspapers Ltd* [2001] Fam. 430 at[33]; *London Regional Transport v Mayor for London* [2001] EWCA Civ 1491 *per* Sedley L.J.; *Jockey Club v Buffham* [2002] EWHC 1866; [2003] Q.B. 462 at [46]–[51] and [57]; *Douglas v Hello! Ltd* [2003] EWHC 786 (Ch) at [193].

world at large and may be limited to the police or regulators.[37] Crucially, Art.10 Convention rights are always engaged in breach of confidence injunction cases, whilst they are not engaged in relation to freedom of information; producing a very different balancing exercise.

The significance of the identity and motive of the applicant

15–009 Although the identity of and motive for the applicant seeking access to information provide no separate grounds for declining to answer a request,[38] these can impinge upon the public interest in disclosing the information. Case law in most comparative jurisdictions recognises that the public interest in disclosure embraces the right of an individual to have disclosed documents that relate to him or that may affect his interests.[39] Under the FOI Act, where what is requested amounts to personal information relating to the applicant, the information enjoys absolute exemption under the FOI Act,[40] so that the public interest in its disclosure need not be considered. The issue may, nevertheless, arise in other circumstances. Information, although not personal information, may be of especial interest to or significance for the applicant: for example, information relating to an institution with which the applicant is associated.[41]

---

[37] *Francome v MGN Ltd* [1984] 1 W.L.R. 892; *In re A Company's Application* [1989] Ch. 477. The public interest may equally allow publication to the public at large: *Initial Services Ltd v Putterill* [1968] 1 Q.B. 396 at 405–406; *Lion Laboratories Ltd v Evans* [1985] Q.B. 526; *London Regional Transport v Mayor for London* [2001] EWCA Civ 1491.

[38] As was stated in *Durns v Bureau of Prisons*, 804 F.2d 701 at 706 (D.C. Cir. 1986), "Congress granted the scholar and the scoundrel equal rights of access to agency records."

[39] *Burns v Australian National University (No. 1)* (1984) 6 A.L.D. 193, 1 A.A.R. 456; *Burns v Australian National University (no. 2)* (1985) 7 A.L.D. 425. The courts in the USA have been generally less receptive to this notion, taking the view that although the public interest may affect the priority of processing requests, it has no bearing on an individual's rights of access under the FOI Act: *EPA v Mink*, 410 US 73 (1973) (the FOI Act "is largely indifferent to the intensity of a particular requester's need"); *United States Department of Justice v Reporters Committee for Freedom of the Press*, 489 U.S. 749 (1989); *Forsham v Califano*, 587 F.(2d) 1128 (D.C. Cir. 1978). Thus, it has been held that a convicted criminal's wish to establish his own innocence through the requested documents does not create a FOI Act-recognised public interest: *Landano v United States Department of Justice*, 956 F.(2d) 422 (3d Cir. 1991); *Hale v United States Department of Justice*, 973 F.(2d) 894 (10th Cir. 1992); *Neely v FBI*, 208 F.(3d) 461 (4th Cir. 2000).

[40] Freedom of Information Act 2000, s.40(1); Freedom of Information (Scotland) Act 2002, s.38(1). It is instead normally accessible under the Data Protection Act 1998, s.7. The ability of the data subject to rectify, etc., such information under s.14 would serve to enhance the public interest in that individual being granted access to it.

[41] As in *Burns v Australian National University (No. 1)* (1984) 6 A.L.D. 193, 1 A.A.R. 456.

3. WEIGHING THE PUBLIC INTEREST: CONFIRMATION AND DENIAL

The public interest in maintaining the exclusion of the duty to confirm or deny

As noted above,[42] the need to undertake the weighing exercise set out in subs.2(1)[43] will only arise if the result of carrying out the separate weighing exercise in subs.2(2)[44] is a decision not to disclose the information. Unlike the weighing exercise in relation to the duty to communicate, under subs.2(1) there is no focussing of the public interest upon the particular provision of Pt II by which the duty to confirm or deny does not arise. The identified public interest is the maintenance of "the exclusion of the duty to confirm or deny." The public interest in maintaining the exclusion of the duty to confirm or deny will vary with the specificity of the request: the more specifically the request identifies the information sought, the more readily will the public interest in maintaining the exclusion of the duty to confirm or deny outweigh the public interest in disclosing whether the public authority holds the information. Authorities from the USA illustrate the types of request that have been there held entitle a public authority in the name of the public interest neither to confirm nor deny holding any documents of the sort requested.[45] 15–010

The public interest in disclosing whether the public authority holds the information

This public interest is analogous to the public interest in disclosing the information. However, as the applicant is not receiving the information requested but only an acknowledgment that it is or is not held by a particular public authority, 15–011

[42] See para.15–004.
[43] In Scotland, s.18(1).
[44] In Scotland, s.2(1). The exemptions to which the duty to confirm or deny is disapplied are more limited than those under the Freedom of Information Act 2000: namely, ss.28–35, 39 and 41. The Scottish equivalents to the Freedom of Information Act 2000, ss.22, 32, 33, 40, 41, 42 and 44 do not ground a refusal to confirm or deny under the Freedom of Information (Scotland) Act 2002. In relation to the differences between the approach taken to the duty to confirm or deny in the Freedom of Information Act 2000 and that which is taken in the Freedom of Information (Scotland) Act 2002, see para.1–025.
[45] *Frugone v CIA*, 169 F.(3d) 772 (D.C. Cir. 1999) (where it was upheld that the CIA's refusal to confirm or deny whether plaintiff was ever employed by CIA on the basis that disclosure could cause "diplomatic tension between Chile and the United States" or could "lessen the burden facing a foreign intelligence agency attempting to track the CIA's covert activities abroad"); *Miller v Casey*, 730 F.(2d) 773 (D.C. Cir. 1984) (upholding a refusal to confirm or deny holding any record reflecting any attempt by western countries to overthrow the Albanian government); *Gardels v CIA*, 689 F.(2d) 1100 (D.C. Cir. 1982) (upholding a refusal to confirm or deny holding any record revealing any covert CIA connection with the University of California). In the United States, this is often called a "Glomar response."

it may be thought that the public interest in it is generally less compelling than the public interest in communicating the information requested. The analogy, moreover, has its limitations. In order to be effective, disapplication of the duty to confirm or deny must be invoked consistently to requests of a particular type, whether or not the public authority holds information of the precise sort requested. Unless this is done, a response neither confirming or denying that the sought information is held by the public authority will be understood to represent an acknowledgment that that information is in fact held. The public interest in disclosing whether an authority holds the information sought thus involves a consideration of the public interest in generally disclosing whether that authority holds information of the type requested. For example[46]: an applicant may request all information received by a public authority from X that contributed to the public authority's decision to discontinue benefits to the applicant; the public authority holds no such information received from X; the public authority nevertheless declines to disclose whether it holds the information sought on the basis that unless it uniformly so declines all requests for information on informants, irrespective of the identity or existence of the informant, its ability to conceal the identity of its informants will be prejudiced. The public interest here is that of protecting the anonymity of informants.

4. ASCERTAINING AND WEIGHING PREJUDICE

Introduction

15–012 With the exception of the national security and health and safety exemptions, under each of the prejudice-based exemptions[47] information only becomes exempt information if its disclosure under the FOI Act "would, or would be likely to, prejudice" that which the particular exemption seeks to protect.[48] If a public authority is to refuse a request for information, it must specify the exemption relied on and the reason it applies.[49] Where a prejudice-based exemption is specified in the refusal notice, that will involve, if it is not otherwise apparent, stating the basis upon which disclosure "would, or would be likely to, prejudice" that which the particular exemption seeks to protect.

[46] The example is loosely based on the Australian case of *Department of Community Services v Jephcott* (1987) 15 F.C.R. 122, 73 A.L.R. 493 (Federal Court on appeal from the Administrative Appeals Tribunal to which the matter had previously been remitted by the Federal Court—see (1985) 8 F.C.R. 85, 62 A.L.R. 421).

[47] Freedom of Information Act 2000, ss.26(1), 27(1), 28(1), 29(1), 31(1), 33(2), 36(2), 38(1) and 43(2); Freedom of Information Act (Scotland) Act 2002, ss.27(2), 28(1), 30, 31(4), 32(1), 33(1), 33(2), 35(1) and 40.

[48] In Scotland the requirement is to show "serious prejudice."

[49] Freedom of Information Act 2000, s.17(1); Freedom of Information (Scotland) Act 2002, s.16(1).

The meaning of "prejudice"

Some indication of what was said to be intended by the word "prejudice" appears from the Second Reading speech in the House of Lords: 15–013

> "I want to emphasise the strength of the prejudice test. Prejudice is a term used in other legislation relating to the disclosure of information. It is a term well understood by the courts and the public. It is not a weak test. The commissioner will have the power to overrule an authority if she feels that any prejudice caused by a disclosure would be trivial or insignificant. She will ensure that an authority must point to prejudice which is 'real, actual or of substance.' We do not think that reliance on undefined terms such as 'substantial' or 'significant' is a sensible way forward. We do not know how they will be interpreted by the commissioner or the courts. We can never deliver absolute certainty, but we can avoid making uncertainty worse by adding ill-defined terminology into the Bill."[50]

In rejecting a proposed amendment that would have required a similar requirement in England and Wales, it was said:

> ". . .qualification of the term is unnecessary. The Government have consistently stated their views that prejudice means prejudice that is actual, real or of substance."[51]

And similarly in the House of Lords:

> "There were also complaints about the 'harm' test. A number of noble Lords said that the reference should be to 'substantial harm.' That was the kind of test they were looking for. The word that was chosen where we are dealing with a harm test is 'prejudice.' To all lawyers present—there are depressingly few—'prejudice' will mean some real harm to government, or whatever the reference is in a particular part of the Bill. It is something real, and it is harm. Should it be 'substantial harm,' or should it be

[50] *Hansard*, HL, Vol.162, April 20, 2000, col.827, Lord Falconer of Thoroton (the Minister of State, Cabinet Office). When the Lord Chancellor (Lord Irvine) announced in the House of Lords the publication of the White Paper, *Your Right to Know*, (Cm. 3818), *Hansard*, HL, Vol.584 December 11, 1997, col.245, he identified as one of the key features of the proposed FOI regime: "Thirdly, fewer exemptions. . . . Significantly, in most cases information could only be withheld if its disclosure would cause 'substantial' harm—a further important advance on the Code." The House of Lords, *Draft FOI Bill—First Report*, (Select Committee Report HL97), Session 1998–99, July 29, 1999, had recommended that prejudice be qualified by "substantial:" para.32.

[51] *Hansard*, HC, Vol.347, April 5, 2000, col.1067, Mr Mike O'Brien. The Government advised the House of Commons Select Committee that the formula required "probable prejudice, not just possible prejudice"—House of Commons, *Public Administration—Third Report*, (Cm. 4355), July 29, 1999, para 65–71; Annex 6, para.47–48. The Home Secretary specifically invited reliance upon his explanation in Parliament as a tool of interpretation in the Courts: *ibid.*, para.68.

> 'prejudice'? That sounds like the kind of discussion that a lawyer would like to enter into, but it does not cut to the heart of the debate. It sounds much more theological, if I may use that word in this context, rather than cutting to the fundament of the Bill."[52]

The required degree of likelihood

15–014 With the exception of the national security exemption, each of the prejudice-based exemptions employs the formula "would, or would be likely to" prejudice (or "endanger", in the case of the health and safety exemption). The range of meaning that might be given to the phrase was noted by the House of Commons Select Committee, which quoted one witness before it:

> "I think the words 'likely to prejudice' are ones which are not the most desirable to have in this field because there is a very considerable risk of conflict as to what the word 'likely' means. Does it mean 'likely to rain,' as in the possibility that it is going to rain, or does it mean 'it is more likely than that,' in other words that it is more probable than that. . . . If 'prejudice' is the appropriate word, surely the issue is whether some interest would be prejudiced, and the word 'likely' can be somewhat weasel."[53]

In *R. (on the application of Lord) v Secretary of State for the Home Department*[54] Munby J. had cause to consider the meaning of the phrase "would be likely to prejudice" for the purpose of considering certain exemptions under the Data Protection Act 1998. In the course of judgment, he said:

> "I accept that 'likely' in section 29(1) [of the Data Protection Act 1998] does not mean more probable than not. But on the other hand, it must connote a significantly greater degree of probability than merely 'more than fanciful'. A 'real risk' is not enough. I cannot accept that the important rights intended to be conferred by section 7 are intended to be set at nought by something which measures up only to the minimal requirement of being real, tangible or identifiable rather than merely fanciful. Something much

52 *Hansard*, HL, Vol.612, April 20, 2000, col.889, Lord Falconer of Thoroton (the Minister of State, Cabinet Office). See also *Hansard*, HL, Vol.617, October 19, 2000, col.1267—the harm must be "real." The House of Commons, *Public Administration—Third Report*, (Cm. 4355), July 29, 1999, para.65, although considering them to be synonymous, preferred the word "prejudice" to "harm" on the basis that it was "more common in other legislation," citing the Local Government Act 1972, Sch.12A, para.4, Taxes Management Act 1970, s.20(8H), Drug Trafficking Act 1994, s.53(2)(b), and Data Protection Act 1998, ss.29, 30 and 31.

53 Lord Woolf, quoted in House of Commons, *Public Administration—Third Report*, (Cm. 4355), July 29, 1999, para.66. The Government had argued before the Committee that the phrase required the prejudice to be at least "likely" or "probable," rather than merely "possible": *Public Administration—Third Report*, (Cm. 4355), July 29, 1999, para.68.

54 [2003] EWHC 2073 (Admin) at [106].

more signficant and weighty than that is required.... In my judgment 'likely' in section 29(1) connotes a degree of probability where there is a very significant and weighty chance of prejudice to the identified public interests. The degree of risk must be such that there 'may very well' be prejudice to those interests, even if the risk falls short of being more probable than not."

When considering s.12(3) of the Human Rights Act 1998, the Court of Appeal concluded that, in that context, "likely" meant having "a real prospect of success, convincingly established"[55] or "a realistic possibility of eventual success in preventing publication."[56] One possibility, therefore, is that in order to satisfy the "would be likely" standard it is sufficient for the public authority to establish that there is "a realistic possibility" or "a more than fanciful prospect" of harm resulting from disclosure. As against that, it may be said that to ascribe such meanings to the words "would be likely" has the effect of including within those words that which, although it cannot be ruled out, "would be unlikely," and that this cannot be right on the basis that the synonym for "likely" is "not unlikely" rather than "unlikely."[57] In any event, it does not appear possible to interpret "would be likely to" as meaning "would be more probable than not to" for the purposes of this provision, having regard to the contrast made by the draftsman between, on the one hand, "would" and, on the other, "would be likely to."

Approach elsewhere

Similar formulae of likelihood of harm are used in the prejudice-based exemptions of other FOI Acts. In Australia, the phrase "would or could reasonably be expected to" has been consistently been held to mean that the decision-maker must have real and substantial grounds for the expectation that harm will occur: it requires more than a possibility, risk or chance of the event occurring.[58] In New Zealand, the phrase "likely to prejudice" has been held to mean no more than a distinct or significant possibility, and that it is enough if there is a 15–015

[55] *Cream Holdings Ltd v Banerjee* [2003] EWCA Civ 103; [2003] 2 All E.R. 318, para.12(i).

[56] *ibid.* para.83.

[57] See Professor John Smith's commentary that is quoted in *ibid.* para.34 as part of a detailed discussion by the Court of Appeal of the range of definitions of the word "likely" in various contexts.

[58] *News Corporation v National Companies and Securities Commission* (1984) 5 F.C.R. 88, 57 A.L.R. 550, where (at A.L.R. 561) a distinction was drawn between the two phrases "would or could reasonably be expected to prejudice" and "would or might prejudice," with the former requiring more than the latter; *Attorney-General's Department v Cockcroft* (1986) 10 F.C.R. 180, 64 A.L.R. 97; *Arnold v Queensland* (1987) 13 A.L.D. 195 at 215; *Re Binnie and Department of Agriculture and Rural Affairs* [1989] V.R. 836; *Searle Australia Pty Ltd v Public Interest Advocacy Centre and Department of Community Services and Health* (1992) 108 A.L.R. 163; *George v Rocket* (1990) 170 C.L.R. 104. See Freedom of Information Act 1982 (Cth of Australia), ss.33, 33A, 37, 40, 43, 43A and 44.

serious or real and substantial risk to a protected interest or that a risk might well eventuate.[59] In Canada, in order to rely on a prejudice-based exemption,[60] it has been held that the agency need not prove direct causation between disclosure and harm: indirect causality will suffice.[61] However, in order to uphold non-disclosure on an appeal, the Courts have required evidence to justify the apprehension of prejudice: evidence that describes in a most general way certain consequences that could ensue from disclosure has been held to fall short of meeting the burden of proving the harm that disclosure would cause.[62] Similarly, mere affirmations that the disclosure would cause the harm required by the section will not suffice where the expectation of the harm is not self-evident.[63] European case law in relation to Decision 93/731, Art.4, requires that "the risk of the public interest being undermined must . . . be reasonably foreseeable and not purely hypothetical."[64]

"Mosaic" or cumulative prejudice

15–016 Although disclosure of particular information, when considered in isolation, may fail to satisfy the prejudice requirement, consideration of the prejudice caused by the disclosure of that information together with that caused by the disclosure of other similarly non-prejudicial information may yield a different result. This is variously termed "jigsaw," "mosaic" or "cumulative" prejudice. There is nothing in the FOI Acts requiring such an exercise to be carried out. A provision in the FOI Bill specifically enabling such an exercise was criticised by

[59] *Commissioner of Police v Ombudsman* [1988] 1 N.Z.L.R. 385 at 391, 404 and 411, which considered the various possible shades of meaning that could be given to the word "likely." The Official Information Act 1983 ss.6 and 7 render information exempt from disclosure where that disclosure "would be likely to prejudice/endanger/damage seriously" one of the protected interests. Exemption is also granted where that "is necessary to protect/avoid prejudice/maintain the constitutional conventions which would protect/maintain the effective conduct of public affairs/enable a Minister to carry out/prevent the disclosure of use of official information for improper gain "(s.9).

[60] s.20(1)(c) of the Access to Information Act creates a mandatory exemption for "information the disclosure of which could reasonably be expected to result in material financial loss or gain to, or could reasonably be expected to prejudice the competitive position of, a third party." See also: ss.14, 15 and 16, which use "could reasonably be expected to be injurious"; s.16, "could reasonably be expected to facilitate the commission of an offence"; s.17, "could reasonably be expected to threaten"; s.18, "could reasonably be expected to prejudice"; s.18, "could reasonably be expected to result in an undue benefit".

[61] *Canada Packers Inc. v Canada (Minister of Agriculture)* [1989] 1 F.C. 47.

[62] *Ottawa Football Club v Canada (Minister of Fitness and Amateur Sports)* [1989] 2 F.C. 480; *Merck Frosst Canada Inc. v Canada (Minister of Health and Welfare)* (1988), 20 F.T.R. 73, 30 C.P.R. (3d) 473; *Canada Post Corp. v Canada (Minister of Public Works)* [1993] 3 F.C. 320, affd (1993), 64 F.T.R. 62.

[63] *Canadian Broadcasting Commission v National Capital Commission* (1998) 147 F.T.R. 264.

[64] *Kuijer v Council of the European Union* [2002] 1 W.L.R. 1941 at para.56

both the House of Commons Select Committee and the House of Lords Select Committee, and did not find its way into the statute.[65]

"Mosaic" or cumulative prejudice elsewhere

Freedom of information legislation in comparative jurisdictions invariably prescribes certain exemptions on the basis of anticipated prejudice or harm resulting from disclosure. The concept of "mosaic" or cumulative prejudice has been accepted as capable of constituting that prejudice or harm, albeit only in particular spheres of governmental activity. In the United States, mosaic prejudice is well-recognised in relation to intelligence gathering activities,[66] with it now being explicitly recognised by Executive Order.[67] In Australia, security and criminal investigation agencies have usually been able to sustain claims of exemption founded upon prejudice to the integrity of their intelligence from incremental disclosure.[68] In Canada, there is less authority on the point: it has on one occasion received passing acceptance in relation to police information.[69] 15–017

Information already in the public domain

Each of the prejudice-based exemptions requires that disclosure "would, or would be likely to, prejudice" a particular protected interest. If that anticipated prejudice has already resulted from an earlier disclosure, it will be difficult to attribute any material prejudice[70] to a later disclosure of the same or like information. The fact that there has been an earlier disclosure of the same or like information does not, however, necessarily mean that the anticipated prejudice 15–018

---

[65] House of Commons, *Public Administration—Third Report*, (Cm. 4355), July 29, 1999, paras 113–116; Annex 6, paras 70–72; House of Lords, *Draft FOI Bill—First Report*, (Select Committee Report HL97), Session 1998–99, July 29, 1999, paras 36–37, referring to cl.37. In relation to mosaic prejudice and intelligence and national secrity matters, see para.17–023(1).

[66] *Halperin v CIA*, 629 F.(2d) 144 (D.C. Cir. 1980), "each individual piece of intelligence information, much like a piece of a jigsaw puzzle, may aid in piecing together other bits of information even when the individual piece is not of obvious importance in itself"; *Salisbury v United States*, 690 F.(2d) 966; *Taylor v Department of the Army*, 684 F.(2d) 99.

[67] Executive Order 12,958, 1.8(e).

[68] *Re Low and Department of Defence* (1984) 2 A.A.R. 142 at 149; *Re Actors' Equity Association of Australia and Australian Broadcasting Tribunal (No. 2)* (1985) 7 A.L.D. 584 (information sought relating to commercial television licensees); *Re Robinson and Department of Foreign Affairs* (1986) 11 A.L.N. N48; *Re Throssell and Australian Archives* (1986) 10 A.L.D. 403 at 406 and 407; *Re Throssell and Department of Foreign Affairs* (1987) 14 A.L.D. 296; *Re Slater and Cox (Director-General, Australian Archives)* (1988) 15 A.L.D. 20 at 27; *Re McKnight v Australian Archives* (1992) 28 A.L.D. 95 at 112; *Re Ewer and Australian Archives* (1995) 38 A.L.D. 789.

[69] *Ruby v Canada (Royal Canadian Mounted Police)* [1998] 2 F.C. 351, TD. The Court of Appeal appeared less enthusiastic about it: *Ruby v Canada (Solicitor General)*, [2000] 3 F.C. 589, CA at paras 89 *et seq.*

[70] See para.15–013 for the meaning of "prejudice."

has already occurred. The manner in which information is disclosed can impinge upon the prejudice resulting from that disclosure. In particular, the prejudice resulting from an unintentional or unauthorised disclosure of information may, in some circumstances, be different from that resulting from an official disclosure of the same information.[71] Official confirmation carries with it secondary information as to the accuracy of the earlier disclosure: this secondary information can turn theory into fact and render others more likely to act upon it. In the United States the courts have held that, in asserting a claim of prior public disclosure, the applicant bears the initial burden of pointing to specific information in the public domain that appears to duplicate that being withheld.[72] If the public authority has made the information available to certain quarters of the public, it will be difficult to sustain a prejudice-based exemption.[73]

The nature of disclosure under the FOI Act

15–019 Once the access right is engaged, it not having been disapplied by any provision in the Act, the duty on a public authority is to communicate the requested information in one of the ways specified in the Act. There is nothing in the FOI Act enabling a public authority when communicating information to place restrictions on the use of that information. The unqualified nature of any disclosure required under the Act is shared by the FOI legislation in comparative jurisdictions. Attempts in the USA and Australia to impose restrictions on the use of disclosed information have been held unlawful.[74]

[71] In Australia, in *Ascic v Australian Federal Police* (1986) 11 A.L.N. N184, it was held that the mere fact that information in respect of which an agency claimed exemption may have been "leaked" did not necessarily prejudice the merits of the exemption claimed: disclosure by order under the Act being considered a very different thing with very different consequences to unauthorised access. In Canada the jurisprudence indicates that once information is public from another source the release of the same information by the Government will be less likely to cause harm; the Courts have required the Government to show specific reasons why its release of the same information would cause harm: *Canada (Information Commissioner) v Canada (Prime Minister)* [1993] 1 F.C. 427, TD; *Cyanamid Canada Inc. v Canada (Minister of Health and Welfare)* (1992). 45 C.P.R. (3d) 390, FCA.

[72] *Afshar v Department of State*, 702 F.(2d) 1125 (D.C. Cir. 1983); *Assassination Archives & Research Centre v CIA*, 177 F. Supp. (2d) 1 (D.D.C. 2001) (holding that CIA's prior disclosure of some intelligence methods employed in Cuba does not oblige it to disclose all forms of intelligence gathering in Cuba); *Billington v Department of Justice*, 11 F. Supp. (2d) 45 (D.D.C. 1998) (holding that because FBI may have released similar types of information in one case does not warrant disclosure in this case); *Hunt v CIA*, 981 F.(2d) 1116 (9th Cir. 1992) (held that although some information about subject of request may have been made public by other governmental agencies, CIA's "neither confirm nor deny" response was warranted).

[73] *Kuijer v Council of the European Union (No.2)* [2002] 1 W.L.R. 1941 at paras 73–74 (Court of First Instance of the European Communities).

[74] *Schiffer v FBI* 78 F 3rd 1405 (9th Cir. 1996). The FOI Act (US) does not provide for limited disclosure; rather, it "speaks in terms of disclosure and nondisclosure [and] ordinarily does not recognize degrees of disclosure, such as permitting viewing, but not copying, of documents": *Julian v United States Department of Justice*, 806 F.(2d) 1411 at 1419 n.7 (9th Cir. 1986). In Australia, *Re Dwyer and Department of Finance* (1985) 8 A.L.D. 474.

Significance of the nature of disclosure

The inability of a public authority to restrict the use made of information disclosed under the Act is of particular significance in the determination of the prejudice-based exemptions. The prejudice that is to be measured is that resulting from an unrestricted disclosure, and not just a disclosure to the applicant. There is nothing in the FOI Act to prevent a person when requesting information and who anticipates that the public authority may claim that disclosure would prejudice a protected interest, to reduce the scope for prejudice by offering to limit use of the information so disclosed. Such undertakings have, however, been rejected in the US.[75] 15–020

[75] *Maricopa Audobon Society v United States Forest Service*, 108 F.(3d) 1082 at 1088–89 (9th Cir. 1997) on the basis that the "FOI Act does not permit selective disclosure of information to only certain parties, and that once the information is disclosed to [the plaintiff], it must be made available to all members of the public who request it."

CHAPTER 16

Information Otherwise Accessible

1. INFORMATION OTHERWISE ACCESSIBLE

Introduction

16–001 Information that is reasonably accessible to the applicant otherwise than under the Freedom of Information Act 2000 is exempt information.[1] The exemption is absolute, so that if information falls within s.21(1) it is not necessary to consider the public interest. The underlying rationale for the exemption would appear

[1] Freedom of Information Act 2000, s.21(1); Freedom of Information (Scotland) Act 2002, s.25(1).

to be two-fold. First, where an applicant has a right under a specific legislative regime to obtain access to particular information, then that specific legislative regime should normally be used rather than the Freedom of Information Act 2000. In particular, the exemption ensures that an applicant does not circumvent the fees regime of a specific legislative regime by using the Freedom of Information Act 2000. Where there is no such fees regime, the exemption is not so rigid in its application. Secondly, where information is made available by a public authority under a publication scheme, then a public authority cannot be required to communicate that information to a person making a request under the Act. A broadly equivalent exemption is to be found in the freedom of information legislation of most of the comparative jurisdictions.[2] A similar exemption is also found in the Code of Practice.[3] The exemption had a relatively uneventful passage through Parliament.[4]

2 There is no directly comparable exemption in the Freedom of Information Act, 1966 (USA). Although the Federal Court had suggested that an agency was not required to make requested records available by giving copies of them to a requester if the agency preferred to make the records available in one central location for examination (*i.e.* the reading room system)(*Oglesby v United States Department of the Army*, 920 F.(2d) 57, 70 (D.C. Cir. 1990)), the Department of Justice recommends that such documents be copied to the requester: Freedom of Information Act Update, Vol. XII, No.2, at p.5. The Freedom of Information Act 1982 (Cth of Australia), s.12(1) removes the right of access to a document where "(a) a document, or a copy of a document, which is, under the Archives Act 1983, within the open access period within the meaning of that Act unless the document contains personal information (including personal information about a deceased person); or (b) a document that is open to public access, as part of a public register or otherwise, in accordance with another enactment, where that access is subject to a fee or other charge; or (ba) a document that is open to public access, as part of a land title register, in accordance with a law of a State or Territory where that access is subject to a fee or other charge; or (c) a document that is available for purchase by the public in accordance with arrangements made by an agency:" see para.2–011. The Official Information Act 1982 (New Zealand), s.18(d), provides a discretionary exemption for information that "is or will soon be publicly available:" see para.2–019. The Access to Information Act (Canada), s.68, provides that the Act does not apply to published material or material available for purchase by the public nor to library material: see para.2–032(9). However, ss.2(2) and 19(2)(b) appear to specifically enable the Act to be used notwithstanding that the same material is available under other legislation or another source: see *Cyanamid Canada Inc v Canada (Minister of Health and Welfare)* (1992) 41 C.P.R. (3d) 512 (FCTD). The Freedom of Information Act 1997 (Ireland), s.46(2), provides that the Act does not apply to a record that is available for inspection by members of the public, whether upon payment or free of charge, nor to a record where a copy is available for purchase or removal free of charge by members of the public, whether under an enactment or otherwise: see para.2–035.

3 *Open Government Code of Practice on Access to Government Information* (2nd ed., 1997), Pt II, para.10 provides an exemption for "information which is ... published." The *Open Government Code of Practice on Access to Government Information: Guidance on Interpretation* (2nd ed., 1997), Pt II, paras 10.1 to 10.3 explains: "The Code of Practice commits the Government to provide more information on its own account, without waiting for access requests. The general purpose of this exemption is to avoid damaging the existing mechanisms for providing information, which are often the most cost-effective way of meeting a regular demand for particular types of information .... If an applicant's information request can be answered by reference to an existing publication, the response need only be to refer the applicant to it, with full details of title, price and availability. If a particular query can be answered by reference to a few pages of a published document, and the holder of the copyright is the Crown, departments may provide photocopies of those pages." See further paras 5–001 to 5–010.

4 The provision (cl.19) originally referred to information that was reasonably accessible to members of the public, but this was amended early on in its passage: see *Hansard*, HC, Vol.347, April

Scope of the exemption

16–002 The sole criterion for exemption is that the information be "reasonably accessible to the applicant" otherwise than under the Freedom of Information Act 2000. Section 21 gives some guidance as to when information is "reasonably accessible to the applicant":

(1) Information is deemed to be reasonably accessible to the applicant if it is information which the public authority or any other person is obliged by or under any enactment[5] to communicate to members of the public on request, whether free of charge or on payment.[6] An obligation to communicate in this context does not include an obligation to make information available for inspection.[7]

(2) Information may be reasonably accessible to the applicant even though payment is required to access the information.[8]

(3) Subject to (4), information is not to be regarded as reasonably accessible to the applicant merely because the information is available from the public authority on request.[9] Thus, information that is available under the Code of Practice will not by that reason alone fall within the s.21 exemption. This is because the Code, while exhorting certain public authorities to make certain information available, does not oblige the public authority to do so.[10] Similarly, any other regime to which a public authority may be subject that merely encourages or recommends

5, 2000, col.1053. Another amendment that would have taken information reasonably accessible in one format (*e.g.* paper) but not in another format (*e.g.* electronic) out of the exemption was withdrawn: *Hansard*, HL, Vol.617, October 17, 2000, cols 1011–1012.

[5] As to the meaning of "enactment" see para.26–017.

[6] Freedom of Information Act 2000, s.21(2)(b); Freedom of Information (Scotland) Act 2002, s.25(2)(b). Examples would include: documents available under the Radioactive Substances Act 1993, s.39; the register kept under the Local Government, Planning and Land Act 1980, s.95.

[7] Freedom of Information Act 2000, s.21(2)(b); Freedom of Information (Scotland) Act 2002, s.25(2)(b). By way of example, the following rights to consult will not render the information "reasonably accessible" for the purposes of s.21: the building notice register kept by each local authority under the Building Act 1984, s.56; the minutes of a magistrates' court committee kept under the Justices of the Peace Act 1997, s.30; the register kept by the General Chiropractic Council under the Chiropractors Act 1994, s.9; the register of persons to whom the electronic communications code applies, which is kept by OFCOM under the Communications Act 2003, s.108; the registers kept by waste regulation authorities and waste collection authorities under the Control of Pollution Act 1974, s.64; a local authority's summary of its housing allocation rules, kept under the Housing Act 1985, s.106 (but cf the Housing Act 1996, s.168, which gives an entitlement to receive a copy of the rules); the register of hazardous substances, kept under the Planning (Hazardous Substances) Act 1990, s.28; the registers of planning applications and of enforcement and stop notices kept by every local planning authority under the Town and Country Planning Act 1990, ss.69 and 188; sewer maps and so forth prepared by sewerage undertakers and provided to each local authority under the Water Industry Act 1991, ss.199 and 200.

[8] Freedom of Information Act 2000, s.21(2)(a); Freedom of Information (Scotland) Act 2002, s.25(2)(a).

[9] Freedom of Information Act 2000, s.21(3); Freedom of Information (Scotland) Act 2002, s.25(3). In relation to publication schemes, see Ch.10.

[10] See paras 5–001 to 5–010.

disclosure of particular information, or indicates that disclosure of particular information should be forthcoming, will not result in that information being captured by s.21. This, of course, does not mean that such information is not reasonably accessible to the applicant: it simply means that the existence of a voluntary code or scheme is not determinative of the issue.

(4) Information that is made available by a public authority in accordance with its publication scheme and any payment required for that access specified in, or determined in accordance with, the scheme is to be regarded as being reasonably accessible.[11] It is to be noted that for these purposes the information must be made available by the public authority to which the applicant has made his request: for the purposes of s.21(3) it is not enough that another public authority has made the information requested available through its publication scheme.[12]

The information must be reasonably accessible to the applicant

The exemption applies only where the information is reasonably accessible to the applicant. The fact that information may be reasonably accessible to another person is insufficient to render it exempt information under s.21. There are two aspects to this requirement: 16–003

(1) Some legislation gives a right of access to certain information only to a particular class of person.[13] In order for information under such an alternative right to fall within s.21, the applicant must belong to the class of person who is entitled to exercise that right.

(2) Where the information is available (but not as of right) to the applicant, the public authority must consider the personal circumstances of the applicant in determining whether that information is reasonably accessible. Factors affecting an individual applicant's ability to access information include the form in which the information is accessible (for example, digitally or otherwise), geographical restrictions or financial means. Thus, if the applicant's means are particularly limited or the fee payable for access to the information is excessively high, the information may not be reasonably accessible. Conversely, information may be significantly more accessible to a well-resourced applicant with access to all forms of information dissemination so that reliance on the exemption is justified. A public authority seeking to rely on the exemp-

[11] Freedom of Information Act 2000, s.21(3); Freedom of Information (Scotland) Act 2002, s.25(3).
[12] Assuming, of course, that the requested information is held by both public authorities.
[13] See Ch.5.

tion will be required to address the applicant's individual circumstances in its response to the request.[14]

Information available from a source other than the requested public authority

16–004 In order for s.21 to apply it is not necessary that the information be reasonably accessible to the applicant from the public authority to which the request under the Freedom of Information Act 2000 has been made. Section 21 is capable of applying irrespective of the identity of the alternative source of the information. Thus, information available from a public library or from a readily-available newspaper will generally fall within the terms of the exemption. It should be noted that information contained in a historical record in the Public Record Office or the Public Record Office of Northern Ireland cannot be exempt information by virtue of s.21.[15]

The Data Protection Act 1998

16–005 Section 34 of the Data Protection Act 1998 deals with information available to the public by or under an enactment. It provides that personal data[16] are exempt from, *inter alia*, the access rights[17] in s.7 of the Data Protection Act 1998 if the data consist of information which the data controller[18] is obliged by or under any enactment[19] to make available to the public, whether by publishing it,[20] making it available for inspection or otherwise and whether gratuitously or on payment of a fee. Three differences between this exemption and the corresponding exemption in the Freedom of Information Act 2000 are evident. First, under the Data Protection Act 1998 the exemption applies only where the data are in the hands of a given data controller and does not extend to information in the hands of third parties. Secondly, under the 1998 Act data are exempted when they are made available for inspection by or under any enactment. Thus, for example, information contained in the Register of Births, Marriages and Deaths is available within the meaning of the 1998 Act and will fall within the exemption: under the Freedom of Information Act 2000 such information is not

[14] Freedom of Information Act 2000, s.17(1)(c); Freedom of Information (Scotland) Act 2002, s.16(1)(d).

[15] Freedom of Information Act 2000, s.64. There is no comparable provision in the Freedom of Information (Scotland) Act 2002. In relation to historical records, see Ch.6.

[16] As to the meaning of which, see paras. 4–017 to 4–020.

[17] As to the meaning of which, see paras 4–026 to 4–030. Section 7 is one of "the subject information provisions": see Data Protection Act 1998, s.27(2).

[18] As to the meaning of which, see para.4–023.

[19] Including one passed after the Data Protection Act 1998: see s.70(1).

[20] In relation to journalistic, literary or artistic material, "publish" means make available to the public or any section of the public: Data Protection Act 1998, s.32(6).

deemed to be reasonably accessible. Thirdly, the data controller under the 1998 Act is not required to consider whether the information is reasonably accessible to the public, merely whether it is available. Thus, the personal circumstances of the applicant and the form in which the data are available are not relevant considerations.

2. INFORMATION INTENDED FOR FUTURE PUBLICATION

Introduction

Under s.22(1) of the Freedom of Information Act 2000[21] information held by a public authority is exempt information if held by it with a view to its future publication (whether by the public authority to which the request is made or any other persons), whether or not the date for publication has been determined. The information is exempt information if: 16–006

(a) the information is held by it with a view to its future publication (whether by the public authority to which the request is made or any other person), whether or not the date for publication has been determined;
(b) at the time of the request, the information was already being held with a view to such publication; and
(c) it is reasonable in all the circumstances that the information should not be disclosed until the future date.

Section 22(2) provides that the duty to confirm or deny does not arise if, or to the extent that, compliance with that duty would involve the disclosure of any information (whether or not already recorded) that falls within s.22(1).[22] Both exemption from the disclosure duty and exclusion from the duty to divulge are non-absolute. Thus, the duty to communicate information that falls within s.22(1) does not apply only if, or to the extent that, in all the circumstances of the case, the public interest in maintaining the exemption outweighs the public interest in disclosing the information.[23] Similarly, the duty to confirm or deny that such information is held remains excluded only if, in all the circumstances of the case, the public interest in maintaining the exclusion of that duty outweighs the public interest in divulging whether the public authority holds the information.[24] An equivalent exemption is to be found in the freedom of

[21] Freedom of Information (Scotland) Act 2002, s.27(1).
[22] There is no corresponding provision in the Freedom of Information (Scotland) Act 2002.
[23] Freedom of Information Act 2000, s.2(2)(b).
[24] *ibid.*, s.2(1)(b).

information legislation of two of the comparative jurisdictions.[25] A similar exemption can also be found in the *Code of Practice*.[26] There is no corresponding exemption in the Data Protection Act 1998.

Scope of the exemption

16–007 The principal purpose of the exemption is to spare a public authority that is, at the time of a request for information, engaged in the collation of information intended for future publication from being disrupted in that task by having to retrieve, edit and copy parts or all of that information in order to answer the request. The exemption is not concerned to protect a public authority from harm resulting from the premature release of information.[27] In relation to this sort of harm, the information will be exempt under one or more of the other provisions of Pt II of the Freedom of Information Act 2000: it will be a matter for an applicant to re-submit his request for information at a later time when the harm resulting from disclosure will have diminished or disappeared. In order to rely on the exemption, the public authority must show that the three conditions set out in paras (a)–(c) are met. The information must be held by the public authority with a "view" to its publication at a future date. This connotes more than a mere hope or aspiration that the information will be published and

[25] There is no directly comparable exemption in the Freedom of Information Act, 1966 (USA), the Freedom of Information Act 1982 (Cth of Australia) or the Freedom of Information Act 1997 (Ireland). Both the Freedom of Information Act 1982 (Cth of Australia), s.43A, and the Freedom of Information Act 1997 (Ireland), s.30(1)(a), contain a very narrow exemption for documents or records (respectively) containing information in relation to research being carried out that has not been completed the disclosure of which would expose the person carrying out the research or the subject matter of the research to serious disadvantage. The Official Information Act 1982 (New Zealand), s.18(d), provides a discretionary exemption for information that "is or will soon be publicly available:" see para.2–019. The Access to Information Act (Canada), s.26, provides a discretionary exemption for a record where the head of the institution believes on reasonable grounds that the material in the record or part thereof will be published by a government institution, agent of the Government of Canada or minister of the Crown within ninety days after the request is made: see para.2–032(9).

[26] *Open Government Code of Practice on Access to Government Information* (2nd ed., 1997), Pt II, para.10 provides: "Information which is or will soon be published, or whose disclosure, where the material relates to a planned or potential announcement or publication, could cause harm (for example, of a physical or financial nature)." *Open Government Code of Practice on Access to Government Information: Guidance on Interpretation* (2nd ed., 1997), Pt II, paras 10.1 to 10.4 explains: "[This exemption] recognises that premature release of information can cause harm, for example by creating unnecessary planning blight . . . Information which is soon to be published need not be provided under the Code of Practice. The applicant should be informed of the position, and given an indication of the expected publication date. Pointers supporting the use of the exemption would be a planned publication date and evidence that release of certain information before that date would damage the impact of the planned publication and would not therefore be in the public interest. How far ahead a publication is planned should not be decisive." The third limb of para.10 of the Code (Information whose disclosure, where the material relates to a planned or potential announcement or publication, could cause harm) has not been carried over to the Freedom of Information Act 2000.

[27] Contrast para.10 of the *Code of Practice*: see n.26.

suggests rather a concluded intention that the information will be published. The point at which the public authority must assess whether it holds the information with a view to future publication is the point at which the request is received. The public authority is not entitled to decide on receipt of a request that it will avoid disclosure by publishing the information. The intention must pre-date the request for the exemption to be relied on. The information may be published by the public authority or a third party such as a commercial publisher or an internet service provider. Section 22 (1)(a) does not require that a date is fixed for publication in order to allow reliance on the exemption, although the more uncertain the timetable for future publication, the less likely it is that the information is held with a view to its eventual publication and the less likely it is that it would be reasonable to withhold the information. Finally, it must be reasonable in "all the circumstances" for the information to be withheld until the proposed future publication. The test of reasonableness must be applied to the withholding of the information, not, for example, to some aspect of a public authority's policy on the early release of information. Whether or not it is reasonable to withhold the information must be assessed objectively, having regard to a wide range of factors. These will include the extent of the information requested, the imminence or otherwise of the future publication date, the significance of the information to the applicant, whether undue disturbance would be caused to any person or persons by the early release of information, and the time and resources which must be devoted to answering the request. If a commercial price is to be obtained for the published information, it is thought that loss of revenue could affect whether or not it is reasonable in all the circumstances for the information to be withheld although this will also depend on other factors. It is difficult to see why a single limited piece of information should be withheld, merely because it will at some point in the future form a small part of an expensive book.[28]

The public interest

Even if information is exempt because it falls within the scope of s.22(1), an applicant will still be entitled to have the information communicated to him unless, in all the circumstances of the case, the public interest in maintaining the exemption outweighs the public interest in disclosing the information.[29] Similarly, even if the duty to confirm or deny does not arise as a result of the operation of s.22(2), an applicant will still be entitled to be informed that the public authority holds the information requested unless, in all the circumstances of the 16–008

[28] In relation to the analogous exemption in *The Code of Practice*, the *Guidance* suggests that the information should be released in such circumstances: see n.26. Moreover, it would seem that this would be an instance when the public interest in maintaining the exemption will be modest and fairly readily outweighed by the public interest in disclosure.
[29] Freedom of Information Act 2000, s.2(2)(b).

case, the public interest in maintaining the exclusion outweighs the public interest in divulging its existence.[30] The decision of the Legislature not to make exemption under s.22 absolute contemplates some situations in which information falling within s.22(1) will have to be disclosed. This decision cannot properly be undone by giving the public interest in maintaining the exemption such weight as to make the public interest in disclosure unable to outweigh it. The interplay between para.22(1)(c) and the public interest may be problematic. On the one hand it is difficult to see how it is possible for the public authority to determine that it is not reasonable in all the circumstances for the information to be withheld, but to determine that nonetheless it is in the public interest not to disclose the information. Nonetheless the Freedom of Information Act 2000 appears to contemplate this possibility. On the other hand, it is possible to envisage situations where it is thought reasonable to withhold information because of time and resources considerations but those considerations are outweighed by the public interest in a significant piece of information being aired in public as soon as possible.

3. ENVIRONMENTAL INFORMATION

Introduction

16–009 The UN Economic Commission for Europe Convention on Access to Information, Public Participation in Decision-Making and Access to Justice on Environmental Matters, commonly known as the "Aarhus Convention", has already been introduced.[31] In very general terms, the approach taken by the Freedom of Information Act 2000 to environmental information is to remove the s.1 rights[32] in relation to any information for which there is a right of access under the regulations that implement the Aarhus Convention.

The enabling provision

16–010 Section 74(3) of the Freedom of Information Act 2000 confers on the Secretary of State the power to make by regulations such provisions as he considers appropriate for the purpose of implementing the "information provisions"[33] of the Aarhus Convention and for the purpose of dealing with matters arising out of or related to the implementation of those provisions ("Aarhus regulations").

---

[30] Freedom of Information Act 2000, s.2(1)(b).

[31] See paras 5–052 to 5–056.

[32] In other words, the right to have the requested information communicated and the right to know whether the requested information is held by the public authority.

[33] S.74(2) of the Freedom of Information Act 2000 defines these as Art.4, together with Arts 3 and 9 so far as relating to Art.4.

The Aarhus regulations cannot extend to information held by the Scottish Parliament, any part of the Scottish Administration, the Scottish Parliamentary Corporate Body or any Scottish public authority with mixed functions or reserved functions (within the meaning of the Scotland Act 1998).[34] At the time of writing, draft Aarhus regulations have been suggested but not yet formally drafted or passed.[35] The suggested regulations attempt to dovetail the rights given by the Aarhus Convention with the access regime created by the Freedom of Information Act 2000. Thus, while the Convention definition of "public authorities" is broad, the suggested regulations would extend the definition to those authorities within the meaning of s.3 of the Freedom of Information Act 2000. The suggested Aarhus regulations are expected to introduce a proper system of review and enforcement by applying the enforcement and appeal provisions of the Freedom of Information Act 2000 to requests for environmental information.

The exemption

Under s.39(1) of the Freedom of Information Act 2000 information is exempt information if the public authority holding it: 16–011

(a) is obliged by the Aarhus regulations to make the information available to the public in accordance with the regulations[36]; or
(b) would be so obliged but for any exemption contained in the regulations.[37]

Section 39(2) provides that the duty to confirm or deny does not arise if, or to the extent that, compliance with that duty would involve the disclosure of any information (whether or not already recorded) that falls within s.39(1).[38] Both exemption from the disclosure duty and exclusion from the duty to divulge are non-absolute. Thus, the duty to communicate information that falls within s.39(1) does not apply only if, or to the extent that, in all the circumstances of the case, the public interest in maintaining the exemption outweighs the public interest in disclosing the information.[39] Similarly, the duty to confirm or deny that such information is held remains excluded only if, in all the circumstances

[34] Freedom of Information Act 2000, ss.74(5) and 80. See further para.1–023.
[35] Directive 2003/4 ([2003] O.J. L41 p.26) purports to implement the provisions of the Aarhus Convention and repeals Directive 90/313. As the United Kingdom has yet to pass the Aarhus regulations, the Directive will have direct effect until such Regulations are passed. The Directive does not, however, cause s.39 to be engaged.
[36] Freedom of Information Act 2000, s.39(1)(a); Freedom of Information (Scotland) Act 2002, s.39(2)(a).
[37] Freedom of Information Act 2000, s.39(1)(b); Freedom of Information (Scotland) Act 2002, s.39(2)(b).
[38] There is no corresponding provision in the Freedom of Information (Scotland) Act 2002.
[39] Freedom of Information Act 2000, s.2(2)(b).

of the case, the public interest in maintaining the exclusion of that duty outweighs the public interest in divulging whether the public authority holds the information.[40] There is no corresponding exemption in the Data Protection Act 1998.

Scope of the exemption

16–012 The purpose of the exemption is not to prevent or impede access to environmental information.[41] Rather, its purpose is to give exclusivity to the Aarhus regulations insofar as they cover a particular field of information. Unlike the system of precedence established by s.21 of the Freedom of Information Act 2000 (which does not disapply an applicant's s.1 rights where the information is exempted under the other access regime), s.39(1) also gives the Aarhus regulations paramountcy in relation to its exemptions. Thus, if information falls within the scope of the Aarhus regulations but is rendered exempt by those regulations, that information will be also exempt information for the purposes of the Freedom of Information Act 2000.[42] Information is exempt under s.39 only if there is an obligation on the public authority holding it to make the information available to the public in accordance with the Aarhus regulations. Thus information available at discretion is not rendered exempt information by s.39.

The public interest

16–013 Even if information is exempt because it falls within the scope of s.39(1), an applicant will still be entitled to have the information communicated to him unless, in all the circumstances of the case, the public interest in maintaining the exemption outweighs the public interest in disclosing the information.[43] Similarly, even if the duty to confirm or deny does not arise as a result of the operation of s.39(2), an applicant will still be entitled to be informed that the public authority holds the information requested unless, in all the circumstances of the case, the public interest in maintaining the exclusion outweighs the public interest in divulging its existence.[44] As with all other qualified exemptions, the decision of the Legislature not to make exemption under s.39 absolute contemplates some situations in which information falling within s.39(1) will have to be disclosed. Given that: (a) the only public interest in maintaining the exemption created by s.39(1) is the upholding of an exclusive, as opposed to a parallel,

[40] Freedom of Information Act 2000, s.2(1)(b).

[41] Indeed, in certain circumstances the right of access to environmental information is guaranteed by the European Convention on Human Rights; see *Guerra v Italy* (1998) 26 E.H.R.R. 357.

[42] Freedom of Information Act 2000, s.39(1)(b); Freedom of Information (Scotland) Act 2002, s.39(2)(b).

[43] Freedom of Information Act 2000, s.2(2)(b).

[44] Freedom of Information Act 2000, s.2(1)(b).

regime of access to environmental information; (b) that the Freedom of Information Act 2000 is itself an articulation of the public interest in the disclosure of information that is not exempt information under its own terms; and (c) that there is a particular public interest in the disclosure of environmental information, it may well be that information exempted under the Aarhus regulations will be accessible under the Freedom of Information Act 2000, provided of course that none of the other exemptions in the Act applies. In practice, this would mean that the rigour of s.39(1)(b) would be softened, enabling an applicant unsuccessful under the Aarhus regulations to obtain the information under the Freedom of Information Act 2000.

CHAPTER 17

Security Bodies, National Security and Defence

1. INTRODUCTION

Outline of the security and defence provisions in the Freedom of Information Act 2000

17–001 Sections 23 to 26 of the Freedom of Information Act 2000 provide a series of exemptions and exclusions for information that, broadly speaking, relates to national security or defence matters.[1] Collectively, these provisions operate to

[1] See para.17–007 in relation to the Freedom of Information (Scotland) Act 2002, s.31.

exclude certain security bodies from the Freedom of Information Act 2000 regime and to describe three overlapping classes of exempt information.[2] Thus:

(1) Certain bodies dealing with security matters ("security bodies") are excluded from the definition of a "public authority" in s.3 of, and Sch.1 to, the Freedom of Information Act 2000 and are thus institutionally excluded from the regime of the Act altogether. As a result, an effective request for information cannot be made to these bodies and they are not subject to any of the provisions or duties which otherwise apply to those listed or designated as public authorities by or under the Freedom of Information Act 2000.[3]

(2) Information held by a public authority which was directly or indirectly supplied to it by, or which relates to, a security body is subject to an absolute exemption under s.23 of the Freedom of Information Act 2000. In respect of such information, the duty to confirm or deny and the duty to communicate do not arise.[4]

(3) Information held by a public authority which was not directly or indirectly supplied to it by, and which does not relate to, any of the security bodies is subject to a qualified exemption under s.24 of the Freedom of Information Act 2000 if this is required for the purpose of safeguarding national security. In respect of such information, the duty to communicate does not arise, if the public interest in maintaining the exemption outweighs the public interest in disclosing the information. Similarly, the duty to confirm or deny is excluded where or to the extent that the public interest in maintaining the exclusion outweighs the public interest in divulging whether the public authority holds the information.[5]

(4) Information whose disclosure under the Freedom of Information Act 2000 would, or would be likely to, prejudice the defence of the British Islands or of any colony or the capability, effectiveness or security of the armed forces of the Crown or of any forces co-operating with those forces is also subject to a qualified exemption under s.26 of the Freedom of Information Act 2000. The duty to communicate does not arise in relation to such information if or to the extent that the public interest in maintaining the exemption outweighs the public interest in its disclosure. Similarly, the duty to confirm or deny does not arise in relation to such information if divulging whether the public authority holds it

---

[2] The government document *Factual and Background Material* published under *Your Right to Know: The Government's Proposals for a Freedom of Information Act* (Cm.3818) 1997, para.3.13 drew a distinction between "two basic ways" of protecting specific bodies and types of information from the disclosure requirements of Freedom of Information legislation, namely, "exclusions" (for bodies) and "exemptions" (for types of information) (paras 24–30). Later parts of the document blurred the clarity of this distinction somewhat by referring to the "exclusion" as well as the "exemption" of types of information (paras 93–99).

[3] See paras 17–009 to 17–025.

[4] See paras 17–026 to 17–032, 17–041, 17–043 to 17–046 and 17–050.

[5] See paras 17–033 to 17–040, 17–042 to 17–044, 17–047 to 17–050 and 17–053.

would, or would be likely to, prejudice the same defence interests and if the public interest in maintaining the exclusion of that duty outweighs the public interest in disclosure.[6]

The institutional exclusion of the security bodies outlined at (1) above and the exemptions outlined at (2)–(4) above potentially provide four layers of protection for sensitive security and defence information. While it will often be impossible to peel away all of these layers in order to gain access to such information, this will not always be the case. The institutional exclusion of the security bodies is insurmountable and will conceal information regardless of its sensitivity, but other public authorities do hold security and defence information and this will be accessible unless one or more of the three exemptions is applicable.

Outline of the security and defence provisions in the Data Protection Act 1998

17–002 Section 28 of the Data Protection Act 1998 exempts personal data from the provisions of the data protection principles and Pts II–III and V and s.55 of the Data Protection Act 1998 if exemption from the relevant provision is required for the purpose of safeguarding national security.[7] Personal data may therefore be exempt from the right of access under s.7 of the Data Protection Act 1998, other related rights and the regulatory requirements of the regime of that Act if this is required for the purpose of safeguarding national security. Schedule 7 to the Data Protection Act 1998 further exempts personal data from the subject information provisions in any case to the extent to which the application of those provisions would be likely to prejudice the combat effectiveness of any of the armed forces of the Crown.[8]

Policy background

17–003 The *Code of Practice on Access to Government Information* contained an exemption for "information whose disclosure would harm national security or defence."[9] The accompanying *Guidance on Interpretation* stated that the

[6] See paras 17–051 to 17–052 and 17–054 to 17–059.

[7] See paras 17–034 to 17–040, 17–042 to 17–044, 17–047 to 17–050 and 17–053.

[8] Data Protection Act 1998, s.37, Sch.7, para.2.

[9] *Open Government Code of Practice on Access to Government Information* (2nd ed., 1997), Pt II, para.1(a). As the exemption referred to "harm" there was nevertheless a presumption that such information should be disclosed unless the harm likely to arise from disclosure would outweigh the public interest in making the information available: *ibid*., Pt II. See also: the *White Paper on Open Government* (Cm.2290) 1993, paras 3.5–3.7 and Annex A, Pt II, para.i; the Scottish Executive's *Code of Practice on Access to Scottish Executive Information* (2nd ed., 2003), Pt II, para.1(a); and the National Assembly for Wales' *Code of Practice on Public Access to Information* (2nd ed., 2001), Annex B.

purpose of this exemption encompassed, so far as national security was concerned, the protection of "information which could be of assistance to those engaged in espionage, sabotage, subversion or terrorism", "individuals and sites which may be at risk" and "the operations, sources and methods of the security and intelligence services" and, so far as defence was concerned, the protection of "the operational effectiveness of the armed forces and their capacity to protect the country from external aggression" and "servicemen and their civilian support staff, including those of friendly forces, and those under their protection."[10] The White Paper, *Your Right to Know: The Government's Proposals for a Freedom of Information Act*, described "national security, defence and international relations" as one of seven key "specified interests" which could require non-disclosure if liable to be harmed by disclosure.[11] Both the White Paper[12] and the accompanying *Factual and Background Material*[13] went on to propose that a number of security bodies be excluded from the scope of any Act in order to preserve their effectiveness. When reporting on these proposals the House of Commons Public Administration Select Committee recommended against the institutional exclusion of the security bodies after noting that the comparable statutes in the USA, New Zealand and Canada contained exemptions for security and defence information but did not altogether exclude security bodies from the scope of their access regimes.[14]

The Freedom of Information Bill: drafting

The provisions containing the security and defence exemptions in the draft Freedom of Information Bill published on May 24, 1999[15] underwent only minor revision before being included in the Freedom of Information Bill introduced in the House of Commons on November 18, 1999.[16] When reporting on the draft Bill, the House of Commons Public Administration Select Committee referred to arguments opposing the blanket exclusion of the security bodies put forward by a former Legal Adviser to the security and intelligence services[17] but ultimately 17–004

[10] *Open Government Code of Practice on Access to Government Information: Guidance on Interpretation* (2nd ed., 1997), Pt II, para.1.3.
[11] (Cm.3818) 1997, paras 3.8–3.11.
[12] (Cm.3818), 1997, para.2.3.
[13] Published under (Cm.3818) 1997, para.3.13. See para.96.
[14] House of Commons Public Administration Select Committee Third Report Session 1997–1998 *Your Right to Know: the Government's Proposals for a Freedom of Information Act*, (HC 398-I), 1998, paras 38–39. See also House of Lords Draft Freedom of Information Bill Select Committee First Report Session 1998–1999 *Report from the Select Committee Appointed to Consider the Draft Freedom of Information Bill* (HL 97) 1999, para.39.
[15] *Freedom of Information: Consultation on Draft Legislation* (Cm. 4355) 1999, Pt II, cll. 18 (information supplied by, or relating to, bodies dealing with security matters), 19 (national security), 20 (certificates under ss.18 and 19: supplementary provisions) and 21 (defence).
[16] cll.21 (information supplied by, or relating to, bodies dealing with security matters), 22 (national security), 23 (certificates under ss.21 and 22: supplementary provisions) and 24 (defence).
[17] *i.e.* Mr David Bickford. See M. Urban, *UK Eyes Alpha: The Inside Story of British Intelligence* (Faber & Faber, London, 1996), pp.85–86.

accepted that the approach adopted was reasonable.[18] In relation to the security and defence exemptions, the introduction print of the Bill only differed from the draft version in two respects: cll.21(5), 22(2) and 24(3) of the introduction print took a textually different approach to the engagement of the relevant exemptions and the non-application of the duty to confirm or deny[19]; and cl.22 on national security did not feature a "jigsaw puzzle" exemption expressly ensuring the non-disclosure of apparently harmless information which might be harmful when looked at in conjunction with other pieces of a wider jigsaw puzzle.[20] Section 28 of the Data Protection Act 1998 was plainly the model for the clauses which became s.24 of the Freedom of Information Act 2000.[21]

The Freedom of Information Bill: passage

17–005 The relevant clauses in the introduction print of the Freedom of Information Bill did not thereafter change on their way to enactment as ss.23–26 of the Freedom of Information Act 2000, save for the inclusion in the list of security bodies of the Tribunal newly established under s.65 of the Regulation of Investigatory Powers Act 2000.[22] Indeed the security and defence exemptions in the

[18] House of Commons Public Administration Select Committee Third Report Session 1998–1999 *Freedom of Information Draft Bill* (HC 570-I) 1999, paras 74–77 and Annex 6, paras 43–48.

[19] *cf.* draft Freedom of Information Bill published on May 24, 1999, cll.18(5), 19(2), 21(3).

[20] *cf.* draft Freedom of Information Bill published on May 24, 1999, cl.19(3) which provided as follows "Where, in relation to any information ("the information requested"), exemption from section 8(1)(b)–(a) is not required for the purpose of safeguarding national security, but (b) would be required for that purpose if any other information (whether or not held by the public authority and whether or not accessible, or likely to become accessible, to members of the public) became available at the same time or subsequently, the exemption shall be taken for the purposes of this section to be required for that purpose in relation to the information requested." See House of Lords Draft Freedom of Information Bill Select Committee First Report Session 1998–1999 *Report from the Select Committee Appointed to Consider the Draft Freedom of Information Bill* (HL 97) 1999, paras 36–37. See also para.17–023(1).

[21] See Mr O'Brien, the Home Office Minister, Report and Third Reading debate on the Freedom of Information Bill in the House of Commons, *Hansard*, HC, Vol.347, April 5, 2000 col.1060: "The clause [which became the Freedom of Information Act 2000, s.24] is drafted in similar terms to s.28 of the Data Protection Act 1998. The two provisions have the same purpose. It is therefore sensible for them to be drafted in similar language. Any difference of approach between the provisions could lead to them being interpreted differently. Clearly, that is not the intention." Section 28 of the Data Protection Act 1998 replaced the national security exemption in the Data Protection Act 1984, s.27 which provided that, "[A]ny question whether the exemption mentioned in subsection (1) above is or at any time was required for the purpose there mentioned [*i.e.* the purpose of safeguarding national security] in respect of any personal data shall be determined by a Minister of the Crown; and a certificate signed by a Minister of the Crown certifying that the exemption is or at any time was so required shall be conclusive evidence of that fact" (*ibid.*, s.27(2), see also s.27(3)). The "required for the purpose of safeguarding national security" test was therefore the same under both Acts, the key difference being the addition of an appeal mechanism in the Data Protection Act 1998, s.28: "The right of appeal against a national security certificate is an important new safeguard. It represents an advance on the 1984 Act, which offered no appeal rights" (Mr Howarth, the Home Office Minister, Report and Third Reading debate on the Data Protection Bill in the House of Commons, *Hansard*, HC, Vol.315, July 2, 1998, col.586).

[22] Freedom of Information Act 2000, s.23(3)(e) (inserted pursuant to a government amendment; see *Hansard*, HL, Vol.619, November 14, 2000, cols 205–207).

Freedom of Information Act 2000 passed through Parliament with very little controversy. Amendments were put forward, but later withdrawn, which would have omitted the (s.23) exemption for information supplied by, or relating to, the security bodies altogether and made the operation of both that exemption and the (s.24) national security exemption dependent on the satisfaction of a prejudice or harm test.[23] These proposals were all partly justified by reference to the broader crime-related functions of some of the security bodies such as the Security Service[24] and the National Criminal Intelligence Service.[25] Amendments were also put forward which would have made the operation of the defence exemption dependent on the satisfaction of a "substantial" prejudice requirement but these were defeated on a vote.[26]

Scotland

Under the Scotland Act 1998, the Scottish Parliament cannot make legislation which relates to or modifies the law on "reserved matters."[27] Corresponding restrictions apply in relation to the exercise of certain functions by the Scottish Ministers.[28] The following are in turn defined as "reserved matters" for the purposes of the Scotland Act 1998: the functions of the Security Service, the Secret Intelligence Service and the Government Communications Headquarters[29]; the defence of the realm, the naval, military or air forces of the Crown (including reserve forces), visiting forces, international headquarters and defence organisations[30]; national security, the interception of communications, official secrets and terrorism[31]; and public access to information held by public bodies or holders of public offices other than certain Scottish public authorities.[32] In terms of the Scottish devolution settlement, it therefore follows that the Scottish Parliament had limited scope for creating access rights in relation to security and 17–006

[23] In relation to the proposed omission of cl.21 (information supplied by, or relating to, bodies dealing with security matters) and the amendment of cl.22 (national security) see: *Hansard*, HC, Vol.347, April 5, 2000, cols 1054–1062 (House of Commons Report and Third Reading). In relation to the proposed amendment of cl.21 (information supplied by, or relating to, bodies dealing with security matters) see: *Hansard*, HL, Vol.617, October 19, 2000, cols 1256–1259, (House of Lords Committee Stage).

[24] Including under the Security Service Act 1996 and the Security Service's "management consultancy" type work advising other public bodies on matters such as security systems and controls.

[25] Including, *e.g.* in relation to football hooliganism.

[26] *Hansard*, HC, Vol.347, April 5, 2000, cols 1062–1071 (House of Commons Report and Third Reading).

[27] Scotland Act 1998, ss.28–30, Sch. 4, Pt I, paras 2, 3, Sch.5 (on "legislative competence").

[28] Scotland Act 1998, ss.53–54 (on "devolved competence").

[29] Scotland Act 1998, s.30, Sch.5, Pt I, paras 1, 2(4).

[30] Scotland Act 1998, s.30, Sch.5, Pt I, para.9(1)(a)–(d).

[31] Scotland Act 1998, s.30, Sch.5, Pt II, s.B8.

[32] Scotland Act 1998, s.30, Sch.5, Pt II, s.B13. The subject matter of the Data Protection Act 1998 and the European Community Data Protection Directive 95/46 ([1995] O.J. L281/31) is also a "reserved matter" under Scotland Act 1998, s.30, Sch.5, Pt II, s.B2.

defence information in the Freedom of Information (Scotland) Act 2002.[33] More generally, the reservation of these matters in the Scottish devolution settlement (and their similar treatment in the Northern Ireland[34] and Wales[35] devolution settlements) derives from and reflects their national importance and may thus help to explain the cautious approach taken to them in the Freedom of Information Act 2000.

Outline of the security and defence provisions in the Freedom of Information (Scotland) Act 2002

17–007 The Freedom of Information (Scotland) Act 2002 follows the Freedom of Information Act 2000 fairly closely in its approach to security and defence matters. Given the limitations on the legislative competence of the Scottish Parliament referred to above, the security bodies are inevitably excluded from the definition of a "Scottish public authority" in s.3 of, and Sch.1 to, the Freedom of Information (Scotland) Act 2002.[36] Information held by a Scottish public authority is subject to a qualified exemption under s.31 of the Freedom of Information (Scotland) Act 2002 if this is required for the purpose of safeguarding national security or if its disclosure under that Act would, or would be likely to, prejudice substantially the defence of the British Islands or of any colony or the capability, effectiveness or security of the armed forces of the Crown or of any forces co-operating with those forces. These exemptions closely follow those in ss.24 and 26 of the Freedom of Information Act 2000 and both exclude the operation of the general entitlement to information in s.1 of the Freedom of Information (Scotland) Act 2002 if or to the extent that the public interest in disclosing the information is outweighed by the public interest in maintaining the exemption.[37] The Freedom of Information (Scotland) Act 2002 departs from the Freedom of Information Act 2000 model in relation to security and defence matters in two main respects: first, there is no express exemption for information held by a Scottish public authority which was directly or indirectly supplied

[33] This is not to say that the Freedom of Information (Scotland) Act 2002 as enacted is necessarily outside the legislative competence of the Scottish Parliament: it does not obviously contain any provisions which "relate to" any "reserved" security or defence "matters" when the expression "relates to" is read in accordance with the Scotland Act 1998, s.29(3); and the proviso to the Scotland Act 1998, Sch.5, Pt II, s.B13 would also appear to envisage legislation along the lines of the Freedom of Information (Scotland) Act 2002. See further footnote 38.

[34] Northern Ireland Act 1998, ss.4(1), 6(2), 14(5), Sch.2, paras 1, 4, 17. Devolution in Northern Ireland was suspended for the time being on October 15, 2002 pursuant to the Northern Ireland Act 2000, ss.1 and 4 and the Northern Ireland Act 2000 (Suspension of Devolved Government) Order 2002, (SI 2002/2574), art.2.

[35] Government of Wales Act 1998, s.22, Sch.2; National Assembly for Wales (Transfer of Functions) Order 1999, (SI 1999/672); National Assembly for Wales (Transfer of Functions) Order 2000, (SI 2000/253); National Assembly for Wales (Transfer of Functions) (No.2) Order 2000, (SI 2000/1830).

[36] See also Scotland Act 1998, ss.29–30, Sch.5, Pt II, s.B13.

[37] Freedom of Information (Scotland) Act 2002, s.2(1)(b).

to it by, or which relates to, a security body[38]; and, secondly, the exemption for defence information operates by reference to the "substantial prejudice" test adopted elsewhere in the Freedom of Information (Scotland) Act 2002.[39]

The comparative jurisdictions

National security exemptions are common to the freedom of information legislation of each of the comparative jurisdictions[40]: 17–008

(1) *United States of America*. "Exemption 1" of the federal Freedom of Information Act 1966 (USA) exempts matters that are specifically authorised to be kept secret in the interest of national defence or foreign policy under criteria established by a Presidential Executive Order and are in fact properly classified pursuant to such an Order.[41] The Presidential Order for these purposes is currently Executive Order 12,958 which was issued by President Clinton in 1995.[42] This Order provides that information may not be classified unless "its disclosure reasonably could be expected to cause damage to the national security."[43] The Order further

[38] *cf.* Freedom of Information Act 2000, ss.2, 23. Given the limitations on the legislative competence of the Scottish Parliament referred to above, it may have been felt unnecessary or even inappropriate to include an equivalent exemption in the Freedom of Information (Scotland) Act 2002 and/or the omission may simply reflect the narrower responsibilities and competences of the Scottish public authorities and the limited extent to which they are likely to hold information supplied by or relating to the security bodies in practice. Having said this, a number of the Scottish public authorities (*e.g.* the Scottish Ministers and other authorities with criminal justice functions in relation to policing, prisons and parole) presumably hold some information within the terms of the Freedom of Information Act 2000, s.23(1). See further para.1–025.

[39] Freedom of Information (Scotland) Act 2002, s.31(4); *cf.* Freedom of Information Act 2000, s.26(1). See further para.1–025(3).

[40] Freedom of Information Act 1966 5 USC 552(b)(1) (1994 & Supp. IV 1998) (USA); Freedom of Information Act 1982, s.33(1)(a)(i) (Cth of Aust); Official Information Act 1982, ss.6(a), 31 (NZ); Access to Information Act (1982), ss.15(1), 16 (Canada); Freedom of Information Act 1997, s.24(1) (Ireland).

[41] Freedom of Information Act 1966 5 USC 552(b)(1), s.6F(b) (USA). See also 5 USC 552(a)(3)(E), (b)(7)(D), (c)(3). See further para.2–008(1).

[42] Executive Order 12,958 replaced Executive Order 12,356, which was issued in 1982. According to its preamble the Order "prescribes a uniform system for classifying, safeguarding, and declassifying national security information." On March 19, 2002, the White House Chief of Staff issued a directive to the heads of all federal departments and agencies tightening the approach to be taken to the classification of information regarding weapons of mass destruction and other sensitive homeland security-related information: *White House Memorandum for Heads of Executive Departments and Agencies Concerning Safeguarding Information Regarding Weapons of Mass Destruction and Other Sensitive Documents Related to Homeland Security* (March 19, 2002).

[43] Under Executive Order 12,958: "damage to the national security" means "harm to the national defense or foreign relations of the United States from the unauthorized disclosure of information, to include the sensitivity, value, and utility of that information" (Pt 1, s.1.1(l)); there are three basic classifications, *i.e.* Top Secret, Secret and Confidential (Pt 1, s.1.3(a)); and these are applied according to the damage to national security that might reasonably be expected to result from disclosure, *i.e.* exceptionally grave damage (Top Secret), serious damage (Secret) and damage (Confidential).

provides that documents may only be classified by persons at certain designated levels[44] and that information may not be considered for classification unless it concerns at least one of the following matters: (a) military plans, weapons systems or operations; (b) foreign government information; (c) intelligence activities (including special activities), intelligence sources or methods or cryptology; (d) foreign relations or foreign activities of the United States, including confidential sources; (e) scientific, technological or economic matters relating to the national security; (f) United States Government programs for safeguarding nuclear materials or facilities; or (g) vulnerabilities or capabilities of systems, installations, projects or plans relating to the national security.[45] Classification generally lasts for 10 years but is subject to various provisions regarding review and declassification.[46] There is no institutional exclusion for security, intelligence or defence bodies.

(2) *Commonwealth of Australia.* Section 33 of the Freedom of Information Act 1982 (Cth of Aust) exempts documents if their disclosure under the Act would, or could reasonably be expected to, cause damage to the security or defence of the Commonwealth.[47] The expression "security of the Commonwealth" is in turn defined to extend to: (a) matters relating to the detection, prevention or suppression of activities, whether within or outside Australia, subversive of, or hostile to, the interests of the Commonwealth or of any country allied or associated with the Commonwealth; and (b) the security of any communications system or cryptographic system of the Commonwealth or of another country used for the defence of the Commonwealth or of any country allied or associated with the Commonwealth or the conduct of the international relations of the Commonwealth.[48] The Freedom of

---

[44] Executive Order 12,958, Pt 1, s.1.4.

[45] Executive Order 12,958, Pt 1, s.1.5.

[46] Executive Order 12,958, Pt 1, s.1.6.

[47] Freedom of Information Act 1982, s.33(1)(a)(i)–(ii) (Cth of Aust). See further para.2–015(9). The section does not involve a consideration of whether disclosure would be contrary to the public interest: *Commonwealth of Australia v Hittich* (1994) 53 F.C.R. 152 at 154. Rather, the section is an expression of the content of the public interest: *Re Mann and Australian Taxation Office* (1985) 3 A.A.R. 261; *Re O'Donovan and Attorney-General's Department* (1985) 4 A.A.R. 151 8 A.L.D. 528; *Re Edelsten and Australian Federal Police* (1985) 4 A.A.R. 220. See also the Archives Act 1983, s.33(1)(a) (Cth of Aust). Ministers can issue conclusive certificates specifying the relevant ground of exemption, the part or parts of the document covered and the particular kind of document in respect of which the exemption has been claimed: Freedom of Information Act 1982, s.33(2)–(4) (Cth of Aust). Such certificates are conclusive in their effect subject to the relevant review procedures in Freedom of Information Act 1982, Pt VI (Cth of Aust). See para.14–036(1).

[48] Freedom of Information Act 1982, s.4(5) (Cth of Aust). In *Re Slater and Cox* (1988) 15 A.L.D. 20 it was held that damage to the security of the country would be found where disclosure would enable those engaged in espionage, sabotage, subversion, terrorism or similar activities to resist attempts by official security organisations to obtain information about their activities. In *Re Aarons and Australian Archives* (1986) 12 A.L.D. 155 disclosure of symbols and expressions used by the security service ASIO was held to be contrary to national security.

Information Act 1982 (Cth of Aust) also contains provisions which produce a similar effect to s.23 of the Freedom of Information Act 2000 and the institutional exclusion of the security bodies under that Act: the Australian Secret Intelligence Service, the Australian Security Intelligence Organisation and the Inspector-General of Intelligence and Security are exempt agencies which are deemed not to be "prescribed authorities" for the purposes of the Freedom of Information Act 1982 (Cth of Aust)[49]; the Department of Defence is also an exempt agency in relation to documents in respect of activities of the Defence Intelligence Organisation and the Defence Signals Directorate[50]; and all agencies which are "prescribed authorities" are exempt from the operation of the Freedom of Information Act 1982 (Cth of Aust) in relation to documents that have originated with, or have been received from, the Australian Secret Intelligence Service, the Australian Security Intelligence Organisation, the Inspector-General of Intelligence and Security, the Office of National Assessments, the Defence Intelligence Organisation or the Defence Signals Directorate of the Department of Defence.[51]

(3) *New Zealand*. Sections 6 and 31 of the Official Information Act 1982 (NZ) provide that information may be withheld from disclosure under the Act if making it available would be likely to prejudice the security or defence of New Zealand.[52] There is no institutional exclusion for security, intelligence or defence bodies: the New Zealand Security Intelligence Service is expressly subject to the provisions of the Official Information Act 1982 (NZ).[53]

(4) *Canada*. Sections 15–16 of the federal Access to Information Act (1982) (Canada) contain exemptions for information relating to international relations and defence (s.15) and law enforcement and investigations (s.16).[54] Under s.15 of the Access to Information Act (1982) (Canada) the head of a government institution has a discretion to refuse to disclose any record requested under the Act that contains information the disclosure of which could reasonably be expected to be injurious to the conduct of international affairs, the defence of Canada or any state allied or associated with Canada or the detection, prevention or suppression of subversive or hostile activities (including information relating to various specific defence and intelligence matters).[55] Section 16 of

---

[49] Freedom of Information Act 1982, s.7, Sch.2, Pt I (Cth of Aust).

[50] Freedom of Information Act 1982, s.7, Sch.2, Pt II (Cth of Aust).

[51] Freedom of Information Act 1982, s.7(2A) (Cth of Aust).

[52] Official Information Act 1982, ss.6(a), 31 (NZ). See para.2–022(1). The Prime Minister may certify that disclosure would be likely to have this effect. Requests for personal information under Official Information Act 1982, s.24 (NZ) may also be refused if disclosure would be likely to prejudice the security or defence of New Zealand: s.27(1)(a).

[53] Official Information Act 1982, s.2, Sch.1 (NZ).

[54] Access to Information Act 1982, ss.15(1) and 16 (Canada). See para.2–032(1) and (11).

[55] On appeal, the court must form its own opinion in determining whether the explanations provided by the head of the government institution for refusing to disclose the requested records are

the Access to Information Act (1982) (Canada) confers a similar discretion to withhold information obtained or prepared by certain investigative bodies in the course of lawful investigations pertaining to criminal and law enforcement matters and activities suspected of constituting threats to the security of Canada. There is no institutional exclusion for security, intelligence or defence bodies: the Canadian Security Intelligence Service, the Office of the Inspector General of the Canadian Security Intelligence Service, the Security Intelligence Review Committee and the Department of National Defence are all listed in Sch.1 to the Access to Information Act (1982) (Canada) as "government institutions" subject to the requirements of the Act.

(5) *Republic of Ireland*. Section 24 of the Freedom of Information Act 1997 (Ireland) provides that the head of a public body may refuse to grant a request under s.7 in relation to a record if, in the opinion of the head, access to it could reasonably be expected to affect adversely the security, defence or international relations of the State or matters relating to Northern Ireland.[56] Such a refusal must be issued in relation to records which contain information that was obtained or prepared for the purpose of intelligence in respect of the security or defence of the State or relate to specified security or defence interests.[57] The head of the public body must also refuse to confirm or deny the existence of any such records if satisfied that this would prejudice any of these matters.[58] While the main departments of state and the defence forces are listed as "public bodies" for the purposes of the Freedom of Information Act 1997 (Ireland),[59] no security or intelligence bodies are listed as such.

---

reasonable but it is not entitled to order disclosure simply because it would have reached a different conclusion: *X v Canada (Minister of National Defence)* [1992] 1 F.C. 77, TD; *X v Canada (Minister of National Defence)* (1992) 58 F.T.R. 93, FCTD. In this regard, the Canadian courts have shown themselves comparatively deferential to respondent claims of exemption based on defence grounds: *Canada (Information Commissioner) v Canada (Minister of National Defence)* [1990] 3 F.C. 22, TD; *X v Canada (Minister of National Defence)* (1992) 58 F.T.R. 93, FCTD; *X v Canada (Minister of National Defence)* [1992] 1 F.C. 77, TD; *Do-ky v Canada (Minister of Foreign Affairs and International Trade)* [1999] F.C.J. No. 673, QL, FCA.

[56] Freedom of Information Act 1997, s.24(1) (Ireland); as amended by Freedom of Information (Amendment) Act 2003, s.19 (Ireland). See para.2–039(4) and (13). Ministers can issue conclusive certificates in order to declare that a record is exempt by virtue of Freedom of Information Act 1997, s.24 (Ireland) provided that access to a record has been refused in reliance on this exemption and the minister is satisfied that the record is of "sufficient sensitivity or seriousness" to "justify" the issue of a certificate. While they remain in force, such certificates are conclusive in their effect subject to appeal to the High Court on a point of law under the Freedom of Information Act 1997, s.42(2) (Ireland). See: Freedom of Information Act 1997, s.25 (Ireland); M. McDonagh, *Freedom of Information Law in Ireland* (Round Hall, Dublin, 1998), pp.115–119; and see further para.14–036(1).

[57] Freedom of Information Act 1997, s.24(1)–(2) (Ireland).

[58] Freedom of Information Act 1997, s.24(3) (Ireland).

[59] Freedom of Information Act 1997, s.2, Sch.1 (Ireland).

2. THE SECURITY BODIES

The specified security bodies

As mentioned above, certain security bodies are excluded from the Freedom of Information Act 2000 regime altogether and information held by other public authorities is subject to an absolute exemption if it was directly or indirectly supplied to them by, or relates to, any of those bodies. The twelve security bodies are themselves specified in s.23(3) of the Freedom of Information Act 2000 as: 17–009

(a) the Security Service;
(b) the Secret Intelligence Service ("SIS");
(c) the Government Communications Headquarters ("GCHQ");
(d) the special forces;
(e) the Regulation of Investigatory Powers Act 2000 Tribunal ("the RIPA Tribunal")[60];
(f) the Interception of Communications Act 1985 Tribunal ("the IOCA Tribunal")[61];
(g) the Security Service Act 1989 Tribunal ("the SSA Tribunal")[62];
(h) the Intelligence Services Act 1994 Tribunal ("the ISA Tribunal")[63];
(i) the Security Vetting Appeals Panel;
(j) the Security Commission;
(k) the National Criminal Intelligence Service ("NCIS"); and
(l) the Service Authority for NCIS.

This section deals with the institutional exclusion of the security bodies from the Freedom of Information Act 2000 regime, describes the identity and functions of each body and provides contextual information on the legal and constitutional framework within which they operate and the extent to which this ensures both secrecy and accountability.[64]

---

[60] Established under the Regulation of Investigatory Powers Act 2000, s.65.
[61] Established under the Interception of Communications Act 1985, s.7.
[62] Established under the Security Service Act 1989, s.5.
[63] Established under the Intelligence Services Act 1994, s.9.
[64] The Intelligence Services Commissioner, Interception of Communications Commissioner and Intelligence and Security Committee (which have close links with the security bodies) are also institutionally excluded from the Freedom of Information Act 2000 in the sense that they are not listed as "public authorities" in Sch.1 but they are not then specified as security bodies in s.23(3) and are therefore treated as distinct from the security bodies in this chapter: see para.17–024(2), (3) and (6).

The security bodies: exclusion

17–010 The twelve security bodies are not expressly excluded from the Freedom of Information Act 2000 regime by reference to the list in s.23(3) of the Freedom of Information Act 2000 or any other list. Their exclusion is instead achieved through their omission from the list of "public authorities" in Sch.1 to the Freedom of Information Act 2000.[65] In this regard, s.1(1) only confers a general right of access to information held by a "public authority" and in relation to requests for information made to a "public authority." The expression "public authority" is in turn defined for present purposes by s.3(1)(a)(i) as "any body which, any other person who, or the holder of any office which is listed in Sch.1."[66] None of the security bodies specified in s.23(3) is "listed in Schedule 1" and it follows that none of them is a "public authority" for the purposes of the Act.[67] By contrast, none of the security bodies is excluded or exempted from the provisions of the Data Protection Act 1998: in so far as each security body is a data controller or data processor for the purposes of that Act,[68] it is obliged to

[65] Furthermore, the Freedom of Information Act 2000 does not expressly bind the Crown and therefore only binds the Crown to the extent required by necessary implication: *Province of Bombay v Municipal Corporation of Bombay* [1947] A.C. 58, PC; *Attorney-General of Ceylon v A D Silva* [1953] A.C. 461, PC; *Madras Electric Supply Corp Ltd v Boarland* [1955] A.C. 667, HL; *Ministry of Agriculture v Jenkins* [1963] 2 Q.B. 317, CA; *Wood v Leeds Area Health Authority* [1974] I.C.R. 535; and *Lord Advocate v Strathclyde Regional Council* [1990] 2 A.C. 580, HL. This "doctrine of Crown immunity" is expressly saved and recognised by the Crown Proceedings Act 1947, ss.31(1), 40(2)(f). Following *BBC v Johns (Inspector of Taxes)* [1965] Ch.32, CA at 81 (*per* Diplock L.J.) the Crown's "immunity" from the Freedom of Information Act 2000 regime will also be enjoyed by the Crown's servants and agents to the extent that they are not brought under that regime by express provision or necessary implication (see also F. Bennion, *Statutory Interpretation* (4th ed., Butterworths, London, 2002), p.164, and Wade and Forsyth, *Administrative Law* (8th ed., Oxford University Press, Oxford 2000), p.820). As the Freedom of Information Act 2000 does not expressly bind the Crown it therefore follows that the Crown's servants and agents are only bound to the extent that they are expressly listed as "public authorities" in the Freedom of Information Act 2000, Sch.1 or to the extent that their being bound is required by necessary implication. See also s.81(3) and, in relation to the intelligence services, see the definition of "government department" in s.84 at sub-para.(b). The exclusion of those security bodies which are servants or agents of the Crown is thus doubly-ensured through the operation of the presumption that statutes do not bind the Crown. The criminal offence provisions in the Freedom of Information Act 2000, s.77 and Sch.3, para.12 are nevertheless applied to all persons in the public service of the Crown as they apply to any other person: Freedom of Information Act 2000, s.81(3).

[66] For these purposes, "body" includes an unincorporated association (Freedom of Information Act 2000, s.84; Freedom of Information (Scotland) Act 2002, s.73) and "person" includes a body of persons corporate or unincorporate (Interpretation Act 1978, s.5, Sch.1).

[67] None of the security bodies is a "Scottish public authority" for the purposes of the Freedom of Information (Scotland) Act 2002, s.3, Sch.1. See also the Scotland Act 1998, ss.29–30, Sch.5, Pt II, s.B13.

[68] Data Protection Act 1998, ss.1(1) and (4), 5. Each of the intelligence services is a data controller for these purposes: *Baker v Secretary of State for the Home Department* [2001] U.K.H.R.R. 1275, paras 4 and 9; *Al Fayed v Secretary of State for the Home Department & Secretary of State for Foreign and Commonwealth Affairs*, (unreported, decision of the Information Tribunal dated February 28, 2002) para.3; *Gosling v Secretary of State for the Home Department*, (unreported, decision of the Information Tribunal dated August 1, 2003) para.2; *Hitchens v Secretary of State for the Home Department*, (unreported, decision of the Information Tribunal dated August 4, 2003) para.2.

comply with its provisions and the obligations conferred thereunder subject, of course, to any relevant exemptions in Pt IV.[69]

The security bodies: order

The order in which the security bodies are listed in s.23(3) of the Freedom of Information Act 2000 would appear to be intentional. The security bodies are not listed in alphabetical order and they have not been ordered simply according to their size or practical importance, otherwise NCIS and its Service Authority would not have been listed last after the Security Vetting Appeals Panel and the Security Commission.[70] Rather, the appearance of the Security Service, SIS, GCHQ and the special forces at the head of the list appears to reflect a certain primacy in terms of the nature and quality of the type of information which these bodies may supply to public authorities or which may relate to them: these four would certainly appear to be the most important of the security bodies. Whether or not the final order was intended to convey a particular message or came about simply because the later entries were, in policy or drafting terms, just that,[71] the final order can be said to reflect a division between principal and ancillary security bodies as follows: 17–011

(1) The principal security bodies:

(a) the three "intelligence services", that is to say, the Security Service, SIS and GCHQ,[72] come first as the key operational bodies

---

69 *e.g.* Data Protection Act 1998, s.28 (on national security).

70 The Freedom of Information Act 2000 adopts an alphabetical approach to the straightforward lists of "other public bodies and offices" in Sch.1, Pts VI–VII but a more hierarchical approach in other areas where bodies are ordered according to their relative size or importance, with national bodies coming before devolved or regional bodies and with bodies from Scotland, Northern Ireland and Wales appearing in that order (*e.g.* Freedom of Information Act 2000, ss.28(2), 59, 76, Sch.1, Pts I–III).

71 See para.17–012.

72 The compendious expression "the intelligence services" is used in this chapter to refer to the Security Service, SIS and GCHQ in the same way as in the Regulation of Investigatory Powers Act 2000, s.81(1). The alternative expression "the security and intelligence services" appears in the Official Secrets Act 1989, s.1 without further definition but there is no reason to think it goes any further than the three intelligence services. At the time the Official Secrets Act 1989 was enacted the Security Service Act 1989 (which would place the Security Service on a statutory basis upon coming into force) had only just been enacted and SIS and GCHQ still had no legal status: the Official Secrets Act 1989 received Royal Assent on May 11, 1989 and came into force on March 1, 1990 (see Official Secrets Act 1989, s.16(6) and Official Secrets Act 1989 (Commencement) Order 1990, (SI 1990/199)) while the Security Service Act 1989 received Royal Assent a fortnight before on April 27, 1989 and came into force on December 18, 1989 (see Security Service Act 1989, s.7(2) and Security Service Act 1989 (Commencement) Order 1989, (SI 1989/2093)). Although the Intelligence Services Act 1994 treated SIS as "the Intelligence Service" (*ibid.*, s.1(1)) its short title, coupled with its provisions relating to the Security Service, could be read as suggesting that it regarded all three services as "intelligence services" (*cf. ibid.*, ss.8 and 10 in relation to the Intelligence Services Commissioner (originally distinct from the Security Service Commissioner) and the naming of the Intelligence and Security Committee with "intelligence and security" in alphabetical order).

whose exclusion from the Freedom of Information Act 2000 regime is most important and most easily explained in policy terms[73];

(b) the special forces come next as something akin to a fourth security and intelligence service who are also operational and whose exclusion from the Freedom of Information Act 2000 regime is seen as being equally important.[74]

(2) The ancillary security bodies:

(a) the RIPA, IOCA, SSA and ISA Tribunals, the Security Vetting Appeals Panel and the Security Commission come next as a collection of non-operational oversight bodies whose exemption is, presumably, required by reason of their close connections with the principal security bodies or security and intelligence matters generally[75];

(b) the NCIS and its Service Authority come last and, while NCIS has an operational role, these would appear to be the most borderline of the security bodies whose exemption presumably came about by reason of their close connections with the Security Service.[76]

The security bodies: selection

17–012 The criteria by which the security bodies were selected for designation as such were never fully articulated prior to the enactment of the Freedom of Information Act 2000. The exclusion of the principal security bodies, the intelligence services and the special forces, was proposed at the outset but the selection of the ancillary security bodies and the non-selection of other apparently similar bodies were not the subject of much scrutiny or debate. The White Paper, *Your Right to Know: The Government's Proposals for a Freedom of Information Act*, stated that the four principal security bodies would be excluded because they "could not carry out their duties effectively in the interests of the nation if their operations and activities were subject to freedom of information legislation."[77] Continuing this theme, the accompanying *Factual and Background Material*[78] referred again to the principal security bodies as candidates for exclusion "requiring careful consideration" together with "support provided to

[73] Freedom of Information Act 2000, s.23(3)(a)–(c).
[74] Freedom of Information Act 2000, s.23(3)(d).
[75] Freedom of Information Act 2000, s.23(3)(e)–(j).
[76] Freedom of Information Act 2000, s.23(3)(k)–(l).
[77] (Cm.3818) 1997, para.2.3. This passage goes on to state, "These organisations, and the information they provide, will be excluded from the Act, as will information about these organisations held by other public authorities."
[78] Published under (Cm.3818) 1997, para.3.13.

them by other bodies and information originating from them but held by other bodies."[79] The government consultation paper *Freedom of Information: Consultation on Draft Legislation* first mentioned NCIS as a likely candidate for exclusion on the basis that its work is "closely analogous" to that of the intelligence services.[80] The proposed exclusion of the IOCA, SSA and ISA Tribunals[81] was similarly explained on the grounds that "their work is wholly concerned with security and intelligence matters" and "they would not be able to carry out their work effectively if their activities, or even their administrative functions, were subject to freedom of information legislation."[82] The designation of the Security Vetting Appeals Panel and the Security Commission as security bodies was not discussed at all in the policy and consultation documents which preceded and underlay the Freedom of Information Act 2000.

The intelligence services

The Security Service, SIS and GCHQ are specifically excluded from the Freedom of Information Act 2000 regime by s.84 which provides that they are not "government departments" for the purposes of the Act.[83] Their identities and functions are prescribed and regulated primarily by the Security Service Act 1989, the Intelligence Services Act 1994 and the Regulation of Investigatory Powers Act 2000.[84] Taking each service in turn: 17–013

(1) *The Security Service.* The Security Service (more commonly known as "MI5") was "placed on a statutory basis" by the Security Service Act

[79] para.96. This passage goes on to state, "It is argued that reliance solely on a harm tested exemption would lead to the cumulative disclosure of a significant quantity of the agencies' records or of operational information. This would undermine confidence among those individuals and bodies on whose co-operation the effective functioning of the agencies relies, and would have a deleterious impact on the effectiveness of the Special Forces."

[80] (Cm.4355) 1999, para.26.

[81] The explanation is to be found in notes produced by the Home Office Freedom of Information Unit for the House of Commons Public Administration Select Committee on the clause in the draft Freedom of Information Bill published on May 24, 1999 which eventually formed the basis for the Freedom of Information Act 2000, s.23 (see *Freedom of Information: Consultation on Draft Legislation* (Cm.4355) 1999 Pt II, cl.18).

[82] House of Commons Public Administration Select Committee Third Report Session 1998–1999 *Freedom of Information Draft Bill* (HC 570-I) 1999, Annex 6, para.43.

[83] The intelligence services are not otherwise listed as "public authorities" in the Freedom of Information Act 2000, Sch.1. Each one on the face of it satisfies the test of being a "body or authority exercising statutory functions on behalf of the Crown," which would make it a "government department" for the purposes of the Freedom of Information Act 2000, s.84, Sch.1, Pt I, para.1 but for the fact that each one is expressly excluded from the definition of "government department" in s.84.

[84] See generally: *Halsbury's Laws of England* (4th ed.), Vol.8(2), title "Constitutional Law and Human Rights", paras 471–476; I. Leigh and L. Lustgarten, "The Security Service Act 1989" (1989) 52 M.L.R. 801; L. Lustgarten and I. Leigh, *In From the Cold: National Security and Parliamentary Democracy* (Oxford University Press, Oxford, 1994); J. Wadham, "The Intelligence Services Act 1994" (1994) 57 M.L.R. 916; M. Urban, *UK Eyes Alpha: The Inside Story of British*

1989 which provides that "there shall continue to be a Security Service."[85] The Security Service is under the authority of the Home Secretary who appoints a Director-General to control its operations and be responsible for its efficiency.[86] The Director-General in turn makes an annual report on the work of the Security Service to the Prime Minister and Home Secretary and may at any time report to either of them on any matter relating to this work.[87] The Security Service has the following functions[88]: the protection of national security and, in particular,

---

Intelligence (Faber & Faber, London, 1996); A. Bradley and K. Ewing, *Constitutional and Administrative Law* (13th ed., Longman, London, 2003), pp. 577–585; P. Jackson, *Hood Phillips and Jackson: Constitutional and Administrative Law* (8th ed., Sweet & Maxwell, London, 2001), paras 19–038—19–040. See also the official government publications: Cabinet Office, *National Intelligence Machinery* (2nd ed., HMSO, London, 2001); Intelligence and Security Committee, *Intelligence Oversight* (London, 2002); Home Office, *MI5: The Security Service*, (4th ed., 2002). Further information about the Security Service can also be found on its website *www.mi5.gov.uk* and further information about GCHQ can be found on its website *www.gchq.gov.uk*.

85 Security Service Act 1989, s.1(1). This Act was passed against a background which had seen Lord Donaldson M.R. call for the Security Service to be placed on a statutory basis (comments made in the Court of Appeal on February 10, 1988 during the course of *Attorney-General v Guardian Newspapers Ltd (No.2)* [1990] 1 A.C. 109, HL) and the commencement of *Hewitt and Harman v United Kingdom* (1992) 14 E.H.R.R. 657, ECtHR. In ECHR terms, it had already been held in *Leander v Sweden* (1987) 9 E.H.R.R. 433, ECtHR that it is legitimate for member states to establish security or secret services to gather and disclose information about their citizens provided that such services are placed on a clear legal basis and made subject to adequate and effective safeguards against abuse (see also *Klass v Germany* (1979–80) 2 E.H.R.R. 214, ECtHR). The Security Service Act 1989 was itself modelled on the Interception of Communications Act 1985 which had been passed following *Malone v United Kingdom* (1985) 7 E.H.R.R. 14, ECtHR. Prior to this the operation of the Security Service was governed by a directive issued by the Home Secretary, Sir David Maxwell Fyffe, to the Director-General in 1952 as publicised by Lord Denning M.R. in his *Report on the Profumo Affair* (Cmnd.2152) 1963 and in his judgment in *R. v Secretary of State for the Home Department, Ex p. Hosenball* [1977] 3 All E.R. 452, CA. A great deal of the Maxwell Fyffe Directive found expression in the Security Service Act 1989 (Cabinet Office, *National Intelligence Machinery* (2nd ed., HMSO, London, 2001), p.9). See also the House of Commons Home Affairs Select Committee Third Report Session 1998–1999 *Accountability of the Security Service* (HC 291) 1999.

86 Security Service Act 1989, ss.1(1), 2(1).

87 Security Service Act 1989, s.2(4).

88 According to Home Office, *MI5: The Security Service* (4th ed., 2002), the Security Service fulfils its functions by: "collecting and disseminating intelligence, investigating and assessing threats and working with others to counter them, advising on protection and providing effective support for those tasks" (p.5); working "closely" with SIS, GCHQ, the Home Office, the Foreign and Commonwealth Office, the Cabinet Office, the Northern Ireland Office, the Department of Trade and Industry, the Ministry of Defence and its Defence Intelligence Staff, law enforcement agencies (*i.e.* the United Kingdom's 56 police forces, the National Crime Squad, NCIS and HM Customs and Excise), the armed forces and various foreign security and intelligence services (pp.20 and 25–26); and by gathering intelligence through covert human intelligence sources, the interception of communications and directed and intrusive surveillance (p.22). See also Cabinet Office, *National Intelligence Machinery* (2nd ed., HMSO, London, 2001), p.10. The Security Service has very close working relationships with the 53 police Special Branches in the United Kingdom, so much so that the Special Branches have been described as an executive partner of the Security Service and a major extension to its intelligence collection capability (*Intelligence and Security Committee Annual Report 2002–2003* (Cm.5837) 2003, paras 68–71).

its protection against threats from espionage, terrorism[89] and sabotage, from the activities of agents of foreign powers and from actions intended to overthrow or undermine Parliamentary democracy by political, industrial or violent means[90]; to safeguard the economic well-being of the United Kingdom against threats posed by the actions or intentions of persons outside the British Islands[91]; and to act in support of the activities of police forces, NCIS, the National Crime Squad and other law enforcement agencies in the prevention and detection of serious crime.[92]

(2) *The Secret Intelligence Service.* SIS (more commonly known as "MI6") was placed on a statutory basis by the Intelligence Services Act 1994 which provided that "there shall continue to be a Secret Intelligence Service."[93] SIS is under the authority of the Foreign Secretary who appoints a Chief of the Intelligence Service to control its operations.[94] The Chief makes an annual report on the work of SIS to the Prime Minister and Foreign Secretary and may at any time report to either of them on any matter relating to this work.[95] The functions of SIS are to obtain and provide information relating to the actions or intentions of persons outside the British Islands and to perform other tasks relating to the actions or intentions of such persons.[96] These functions are exercisable

[89] In May 1992, following the end of the Cold War, the Security Service acquired from the police responsibility for the collection of intelligence regarding Irish Republican terrorism in Great Britain: *Hansard*, HC, Vol.207, May 8, 1992, cols 297–306; *Intelligence and Security Committee Report on Security Service Work Against Organised Crime* (Cm.3065) 1995; M. Urban, *UK Eyes Alpha: The Inside Story of British Intelligence* (Faber & Faber, London, 1996), Chs 15 and 21; A. Bradley and K. Ewing, *Constitutional and Administrative Law* (13th ed., Longman, London, 2003), pp.578–579. In October 2001 the Security Service established a Counter-Terrorist Analysis Centre and in June 2003 this was expanded into a single Joint Terrorism Analysis Centre with responsibility for the detailed and long-term study of the threat from terrorism and the production of immediate assessments of day-to-day developments and current threats: *Government Response to the Intelligence and Security Committee Inquiry into Intelligence, Assessments and Advice Prior to the Terrorist Bombings on Bali 12 October 2002* (Cm.5765) 2003, para.11; *Intelligence and Security Committee Annual Report 2002–2003* (Cm.5837) 2003, para.62; *Government Response to the Intelligence and Security Committee's Annual Report 2002–2003* (Cm.5838) 2003, para.13.

[90] Security Service Act 1989, s.1(2).

[91] Security Service Act 1989, s.1(3). See para.17–054.

[92] Security Service Act 1989, s.1(4) as inserted by the Security Service Act 1996, s.1(1) and amended by the Police Act 1997, s.134(1), Sch.9, para.60. The Director-General must also ensure that there are arrangements, agreed with the Director General of NCIS, for co-ordinating the activities of the Security Service in pursuance of the Security Service Act 1989, s.1(4) with the activities of police forces, NCIS, the National Crime Squad and other law enforcement agencies: Security Service Act 1989, s.2(2)(c) as inserted by the Security Service Act 1996, s.1(1) and (3) and amended by the Police Act 1997, ss.12 and 134(1), Sch.9, para.61.

[93] Intelligence Services Act 1994, s.1(1). The Intelligence Services Act 1994 was modelled on the Security Service Act 1989 and the Interception of Communications Act 1985 on which the Security Service Act 1989 was itself modelled.

[94] Intelligence Services Act 1994, ss.1(1) and 2(1).

[95] Intelligence Services Act 1994, s.2(4).

[96] Intelligence Services Act 1994, s.1(1). According to Cabinet Office, *National Intelligence Machinery* (2nd ed., HMSO, London, 2001), SIS "uses human and technical sources" and "liaison with a wide range of foreign intelligence and security services" to fulfil its functions (p.6).

only in the interests of national security, with particular reference to the defence and foreign policies of Her Majesty's Government in the United Kingdom, in the interests of the economic well-being of the United Kingdom or in support of the prevention or detection of serious crime.[97]

(3) *GCHQ*. GCHQ was also placed on a statutory basis by the Intelligence Services Act 1994 which provided that "there shall continue to be a Government Communications Headquarters."[98] GCHQ is under the authority of the Foreign Secretary who appoints a Director of GCHQ to control its operations.[99] The Director makes an annual report on the work of GCHQ to the Prime Minister and Foreign Secretary and may at any time report to either of them on any matter relating to this work.[1] GCHQ has two main functions under the Intelligence Services Act 1994: first, to monitor or interfere with electromagnetic, acoustic and other emissions and any equipment producing such emissions and to obtain and provide information derived from or related to such emissions or equipment and from encrypted material[2]; and, secondly, to provide advice and assistance about languages (including terminology used for technical matters) and cryptography and other matters relating to the protection of information and other material to the armed forces of the Crown, Her Majesty's Government in the United Kingdom, Northern Ireland departments and any other organisation determined in such manner as may be specified by the Prime Minister.[3] The first (monitoring) function is exercisable only in the interests of national security, with particular reference to the defence and foreign policies of Her Majesty's Government in the United Kingdom, in the interests of the economic well-being of the United Kingdom in relation to the actions or intentions of persons outside the British Islands or in support of the prevention or detection of serious crime.[4] The second (advisory) function is not subject to a specific purpose condition.

The special forces: identity

17–014 The special forces are not themselves a "public authority" for the purposes of the Freedom of Information Act 2000 and they are not a part of the wider

[97] Intelligence Services Act 1994, s.1(2).
[98] Intelligence Services Act 1994, s.3(1).
[99] Intelligence Services Act 1994, ss.3(1), 4(1).
[1] Intelligence Services Act 1994, s.4(4).
[2] Intelligence Services Act 1994, s.3(1)(a).
[3] Intelligence Services Act 1994, s.3(1)(b).
[4] Intelligence Services Act 1994, s.3(2).

"public authority" comprising the armed forces of the Crown.[5] Section 84 of the Freedom of Information Act 2000 defines "the special forces" to mean "those units of the armed forces of the Crown the maintenance of whose capabilities is the responsibility of the Director of Special Forces or which are for the time being subject to the operational command of that Director." The identities of the Director of Special Forces and of the units under his responsibility or command are not clarified further in the Freedom of Information Act 2000. The only official statements made by the government on this topic in connection with the Freedom of Information Bill linked the special forces to the Special Air Service and the Special Boat Service.[6] More generally, the government has elsewhere confirmed that the special forces include seven "major joint units", namely, three Special Air Service Regiments (including two Territorial Army Reserve Regiments) and four Special Boat Service Squadrons.[7]

The special forces: functions

There is very little publicly available official information about the special forces to explain their exclusion from the Freedom of Information Act 2000 regime.[8] This is largely attributable to the longstanding government policy of not commenting publicly on special forces matters.[9] However, a small number of public 17–015

[5] The "armed forces of the Crown" are listed as a "public authority" by the Freedom of Information Act 2000, Sch.1, Pt I, para.6 but the special forces and units of the armed forces which are for the time being required by the Secretary of State to assist GCHQ in the exercise of its functions are expressly excepted from this provision by Sch.1, Pt I, para.6(a)–(b).

[6] *Your Right to Know: The Government's Proposals for a Freedom of Information Act* (Cm.3818) 1997, para.2.3 and the *Factual and Background Material* (1997), para.96 (published under *Your Right to Know*, para.3.13), both contain explanatory references to the "SAS" and "SBS," after references to the special forces and a written answer to a Parliamentary Question about the clause in the Freedom of Information Bill which became the Freedom of Information Act 2000, s.4 confirmed that these initials stand for "Special Air Service" and "Special Boat Service" (*Hansard*, HL, Vol.612, April 20, 2000, col.124).

[7] *Ministry of Defence Performance Report* 2001/2002 (Cm.5661) 2002, Annex E, table 43. It is also apparent from published Ministry of Defence documents that the Special Air Service Regiments are a part of the Army (*www.mod.uk/aboutus/factfiles/army.htm*) and the Special Boat Service Squadrons are a part of the Royal Marines (*www.rnjobs.co.uk/static/pages/1907.html*). Under the Army Act 1955, s.210 the Royal Marines are a separate corps of the regular forces and all members of the marine forces (*i.e.* members of the Royal Marines and members of the Royal Marines Reserve and Royal Fleet Reserve who have served with the Royal Marines or enlisted as marines) are subject to military law under the Army Act 1955, notwithstanding that they may also be subject to the Naval Discipline Act 1957 and therefore members of the naval forces: Naval Discipline Act 1957, s.132(7)–(8); *Halsbury's Laws of England*, Vol.8(2), title "Constitutional Law and Human Rights", para.887.

[8] Indeed, the exclusion of the special forces from the Freedom of Information Act 2000 regime can itself be seen as a telling public pronouncement on the nature of their functions: "*R*" *v Attorney-General for England and Wales* [2003] UKPC 22; [2003] E.M.L.R. 499, PC at para.36 (*per* Lord Hoffmann).

[9] *The Threat from Terrorism: Government Response*, para.39 at House of Commons Defence Select Committee, *Fourth Special Report of 2001–02* (HC 667), Appendix: "The Government has in the past made it known that the UK has Special Forces which, as well as their war-fighting

statements have been made. In 1996 the government stated that the special forces have four primary roles, namely, reconnaissance, offensive action, the provision of support to indigenous forces and counter-terrorism.[10] During the course of the Strategic Defence Review begun in 1997, the government further stated that the special forces are involved in warfighting operations and counter-terrorism work[11] and that they are a "Spearhead" component of the "First Echelon" of the United Kingdom's "Joint Rapid Reaction Forces."[12] And, in 2002, the government also confirmed that it was planning to enhance the capabilities of the special forces and their "enablers" in order to maximise their utility and flexibility.[13] Further information about the role of the special forces can be derived from: the introduction in 1996 of a Defence Council Instruction making the signing of a confidentiality contract a pre-requisite to all service with the special forces[14]; and the issue in 2000 of an amended "DA-Notice" reiterating the counter-terrorist role of the special forces and suggesting that they are "involved with" covert operations, sources and methods of the intelligence services.[15]

roles, are used in support of its counter-terrorist policy, and to provide assistance in this area to the law enforcement agencies. However, successive governments have adopted a policy of not commenting, save in exceptional circumstances, on Special Forces matters. The effectiveness of the Special Forces in the counter-terrorist role depends on maintaining secrecy about their operations, methods, capabilities (including numbers) and equipment. Moreover, we need to protect their identities because they and their families are at risk from terrorist groups. This therefore constrains what we can say in public about our plans for Special Forces." See also *Statement on the Defence Estimates 1996* (Cm.3223) 1996, para.731, "as a general rule, the government will not comment on matters which are judged to have an unacceptable impact on the successful conduct of operations or on the best interests of special forces personnel."

10 *Statement on the Defence Estimates 1996* (Cm.3223) 1996, para.727. See also the remainder of the section headed "disclosure of information on the special forces" at paras 727–731.

11 *Strategic Defence Review* (Cm.3999) 1998. The conclusions of the *Strategic Defence Review* were approved by the House of Commons: *Hansard*, HC, Vol. 317, October 20, 1998, cols 1097–1177.

12 *Strategic Defence Review* (Cm.3999) 1998.

13 *Strategic Defence Review: A New Chapter* (Cm.5566) 2002, para.45.

14 *Attorney-General for England and Wales v Television New Zealand Ltd* (1999) 44 I.P.R. 123, CA (NZ) at pp.124–126 (*per* Henry J.); *"R" v Attorney-General for England and Wales* [2003] UKPC 22; [2003] E.M.L.R. 499, PC at paras [2]–[10] (*per* Lord Hoffmann) on appeal from *Attorney-General for England and Wales v "R"* [2002] 2 N.Z.L.R. 91, CA (NZ) (see at paras [16]–[19] and [24] (*per* Tipping J.)). The Defence Council Instruction ("DCI") was issued on October 4, 1996 and provided, "From the date of this DCI all Armed Forces personnel serving currently or in future on the establishment of units under the operational or administrative command of the Director Special Forces will be required to sign a contract binding the signatory to a lifelong commitment not to disclose, without prior permission of the [Ministry of Defence], any information gained during service with Special Forces" (*Attorney-General for England and Wales v "R"* [2002] 2 N.Z.L.R. 91, CA (NZ) (see at para.[19] (per Tipping J.)).

15 Standing Defence Advisory Notice 5, "United Kingdom Security and Intelligence Services and Special Forces" (DA-Notice 5) issued by the Defence, Press and Broadcasting Advisory Committee ("DPBAC") on May 24, 2000. The DPBAC is a non-statutory advisory body which provides "advice and guidance to the media about defence and counter-terrorist information the publication of which would be damaging to national security" on a voluntary and confidential basis (see *www.dnotice.org.uk*). The DPBAC itself comprises senior civil servants and editors from national and regional newspapers, periodicals, news agencies, television and radio and is chaired by the Permanent Under Secretary of State for Defence. The DA-Notices cannot therefore be regarded as government statements as such but they are drafted within government and reviewed by the Secretary to the DPBAC before being agreed and issued by the DPBAC as a whole. See:

The RIPA, IOCA, SSA and ISA Tribunals

The RIPA Tribunal established under s.65 of the Regulation of Investigatory Powers Act 2000 deals with proceedings and complaints relating to the intelligence services and the use of investigatory powers under the Intelligence Services Act 1994 and the Regulation of Investigatory Powers Act 2000.[16] In this regard, the Intelligence Services Act 1994 makes provision for warrants to be issued by a relevant Secretary of State authorising the intelligence services to enter on or interfere with property or wireless telegraphy or to do certain acts outside the British Islands.[17] The Regulation of Investigatory Powers Act 2000 makes similar provision for interception warrants to be issued by a relevant Secretary of State authorising, amongst others, the intelligence services and NCIS, to intercept communications.[18] The Regulation of Investigatory Powers Act 2000 also makes provision in relation to the authorisation of the acquisition and disclosure of communications data[19] and the authorisation of directed surveillance (*e.g.* the covert monitoring of a target's activities, conversations and movements), intrusive surveillance (*e.g.* sound or video eavesdropping in a target's residential premises or private vehicle) and the conduct and use of covert human intelligence sources (*i.e.* under-cover officers and agents).[20] Any member of the 17–016

Jaconelli, "The D Notice System" [1982] P.L. 37; H.C. 773 (1979–1980); *The Protection of Military Information* (Cmnd.9112), 1983; Fairley, "D Notices, Official Secrets and the Law" (1990) 10 O.J.L.S. 430; A. Bradley and K. Ewing, *Constitutional and Administrative Law* (13th ed., Longman, London, 2003), pp.596–597; P. Jackson, *Hood Phillips and Jackson: Constitutional and Administrative Law*, (8th ed., Sweet & Maxwell, London, 2001), para.26–011.

[16] Regulation of Investigatory Powers Act 2000, ss.65–69, Sch.3; Investigatory Powers Tribunal Rules 2000 (SI 2000/2665); *Interception of Communications in the United Kingdom: A Consultation Paper* (Cm.4368) 1999.

[17] Intelligence Services Act 1994, ss.5–7 (ss.5–6 replacing Security Service Act 1989, s.3). See also Regulation of Investigatory Powers Act 2000, ss.42, 44, 74.

[18] Regulation of Investigatory Powers Act 2000, Pt I, c.I (see esp. ss.5–11). Interception warrants under s.5 may be issued to, *inter alia*, the Director-General of the Security Service, Chief of the Secret Intelligence Service, Director of GCHQ, Director General of NCIS and Chief of Defence Intelligence (ss. 6(2)(a)–(d) and (i) and 7(3)(a)).

[19] Regulation of Investigatory Powers Act 2000, Pt I, c.II (acquisition and disclosure of communications data). The intelligence services and NCIS are "relevant public authorities" for the purposes of these provisions and certain of their members can therefore grant authorisations and engage in certain conduct in relation to communications data (s. 25(1)).

[20] Regulation of Investigatory Powers Act 2000, Pt II (surveillance and covert human intelligence sources). The intelligence services, NCIS and any of Her Majesty's forces are "relevant public authorities" for the purposes of ss.28–29 and certain of their members can therefore authorise directed surveillance and the conduct and use of covert human intelligence sources (s.30, Sch.1, paras 2 and 5–6 and Regulation of Investigatory Powers (Prescription of Offices, Ranks and Positions) Order 2000 (SI 2000/2417)). A relevant Secretary of State and the Director General of NCIS are among those who can authorise intrusive surveillance on the application of the intelligence services, the Ministry of Defence and the armed forces (in the case of a Secretary of State) and NCIS (in the case of the Director General of NCIS) under the Regulation of Investigatory Powers Act 2000, s.32. See also: ss.33–40 (which are modelled on the Police Act 1997, Pt III) in relation to police authorisations granted and applied for by members of NCIS and the additional requirements regarding Surveillance Commissioner approval, etc., that apply in relation to intrusive surveillance authorisations granted and applied for by members of NCIS; s.41 in relation to Secretary of State intrusive surveillance authorisations; and ss.42 and 44 in relation to the grant by the Secretary of State of authorisations to the intelligence services.

public who is aggrieved by any conduct which they believe to have been carried out in relation to them by or on behalf of the intelligence services or who wishes to bring proceedings against them under s.7 of the Human Rights Act 1998 may make a complaint to or bring such proceedings before the RIPA Tribunal. The RIPA Tribunal has effectively replaced the IOCA, SSA, and ISA Tribunals which are now defunct except in relation to complaints made before October 2, 2000.[21] None of these Tribunals is listed as a "public authority" in Sch.1 to the Freedom of Information Act 2000.

The Security Vetting Appeals Panel

17–017 The creation of the Security Vetting Appeals Panel was formally announced in both Houses of Parliament on June 19, 1997 in written answers to two Parliamentary Questions asking "what are the arrangements for hearing appeals from those who need to have access to protectively marked Government assets and have been refused security clearance or have had that clearance withdrawn?" These written answers read as follows[22]:

> "An independent Security Vetting Appeals Panel, chaired by Sir Anthony May, will be established on July 1 to hear appeals against the refusal or withdrawal of clearance at Security Check (SC) or Developed Vetting (DV) levels and to advise the head of the organisation concerned. The Panel will be available to all those, other than recruits, in the public and private sectors and in the Armed Forces who are subject to security vetting at these levels, have exhausted existing appeals mechanisms within their own organisations and remain dissatisfied with the result. Separate arrangements are available

---

[21] Interception of Communications Act 1985, s.7 and Sch.1 (establishing the IOCA Tribunal), Security Service Act 1989, s.5 and Schs 1–2 (establishing the SSA Tribunal) and Intelligence Services Act 1994, s.9 and Schs 1–2 (establishing the ISA Tribunal) were repealed except in relation to complaints made to those Tribunals before October 2, 2000 by the Regulation of Investigatory Powers Act 2000, ss.70, 82(2), Sch.5 and the Regulation of Investigatory Powers Act 2000 (Commencement No. 1 and Transitional Provisions) Order 2000 (SI 2000/2543).

[22] *Hansard*, HC, Vol.296, June 19, 1997, cols 245–246 (question by Mr Rooney MP, answer by the Prime Minister, Mr Blair); *Hansard*, HL, Vol.580, June 19, 1997, col.123 (question by Lord Graham of Edmonton, answer by the Lord Privy Seal, Lord Richards). In March 1948 the Prime Minister, Mr Attlee, announced that all Communists and Fascists would be excluded from work "vital to the security of the state" via a vetting system (*Hansard*, HC, Vol.448 March 25, 1948, cols 3417–3426). This system evolved into the current Security Vetting Scheme which was last re-announced in a statement made by the Prime Minister, Mr Major (*Hansard*, HC, Vol.251 December 15, 1994, cols 764–766), and which operates in conjunction with the government's Protective Marking Scheme whereby documents and other "assets" are classified "RESTRICTED", "CONFIDENTIAL", "SECRET", "TOP SECRET" etc. See: Hennessy and Brownfield "Britain's Coldwar Security Purge: the Origins of Positive Vetting" (1982) 25 *The Historical Journal* 4, pp.965–973; Joelson, "The Dismissal of Civil Servants in the Interests of National Security" [1963] P.L. 51; A. Bradley and K. Ewing, *Constitutional and Administrative Law* (13th ed., Longman, London, 2003), pp.587–588; White, "Security vetting, discrimination and the right to a fair trial" [1999] P.L. 406.

> to staff of the security and intelligence agencies. The establishment of the Panel therefore brings to an end the role of the Three Advisers who, since 1948, have been available to consider cases where security clearance was refused or withdrawn on the grounds of subversion."

The Security Vetting Appeals Panel is not listed as a "public authority" in Sch.1 to the Freedom of Information Act 2000 and is not a "government department" for the purposes of para.1 of that Schedule.[23] In formal terms, the Panel is an advisory non-departmental public body sponsored by the Cabinet Office.[24]

The Security Commission

The creation of the Security Commission was formally announced by the Prime Minister, Sir Alec Douglas-Home, on January 23, 1964 in the wake of the Profumo Affair.[25] The Commission's original terms of reference, which have since been slightly modified, were[26]: 17–018

> "If so requested by the Prime Minister, to investigate and report upon the circumstances in which a breach of security is known to have occurred in the public service, and upon any related failure in departmental security arrangements or neglect of duty; and, in the light of any such investigations, to advise whether any change in security arrangements is desirable."

The Security Commission is not listed as a "public authority" in Sch.1 to the Freedom of Information Act 2000 and is not a "government department" for the purposes of para.1 of that Schedule.[27] In formal terms, the Commission is an advisory non-departmental public body sponsored by the Cabinet Office.[28]

[23] Freedom of Information Act 2000, s.84.

[24] See the Cabinet Office publication *Public Bodies 2003* (2003), p.3. On non-departmental public bodies generally see also *Halsbury's Laws of England* (4th ed.), Vol.8(2), title "Constitutional Law and Human Rights", paras 951–954.

[25] I. Leigh and L. Lustgarten, "The Security Commission: Constitutional Achievement or Curiosity" [1991] P.L. 215; L. Lustgarten and I. Leigh, *In From the Cold: National Security and Parliamentary Democracy* (Oxford University Press, Oxford, 1994), pp.476–492; A. Bradley and K. Ewing, *Constitutional and Administrative Law* (13th ed., Longman, London, 2003), pp.598–599.

[26] *Hansard*, HC, Vol.687, January 23, 1964, cols 1271–1275. The Security Commission has been unflatteringly described as a "lightning conductor" for security crises (*The Times*, January 24, 1964 cited in D. Williams, *Not in the Public Interest: the Problem of Security in Democracy* (Hutchinson, London, 1965), pp.167–169) and a "stable door operation" (*Hansard*, HC, Vol.145, January 16, 1989, cols 64–65). The terms of reference were twice expanded by the Prime Minister, Mr Wilson: *Hansard*, HC, Vol.712, May 10, 1965, col.34, and *Hansard*, HC, Vol.780, March 26, 1969, col.311.

[27] Freedom of Information Act 2000, s.84.

[28] See the Cabinet Office publication *Public Bodies 2003* (2003), p.2. On non-departmental public bodies generally see also *Halsbury's Laws of England* (4th ed.), Vol.8(2), title "Constitutional Law and Human Rights", paras 951–954. Since its creation in 1964, the Security Commission has conducted 17 separate inquiries to date including: (Cmnd.2722) 1965 on Bossard and Allen;

There is some overlap between the respective remits of the Security Commission and the Intelligence and Security Committee established under the Intelligence Services Act 1994.[29] It remains to be seen whether this will eventually result in the decline or even demise of the Security Commission, but early statements made by the Intelligence and Security Committee appeared to suggest a desire to take primacy in cases of overlap.[30] As mentioned above, the basis for the Security Commission's specification as a security body was not explained prior to the passage of the Freedom of Information Act 2000, but it can be observed that some of its reports have never been published, or at least not wholly.[31]

NCIS and its Service Authority: identities

17–019 NCIS was established in 1992 on a non-statutory basis as a common police service under the aegis of the Home Office before being placed on a statutory footing by the Police Act 1997 and becoming an executive non-departmental public body sponsored by the Home Office under the Criminal Justice and Police Act 2001.[32] The Police Act 1997 provides for the establishment of NCIS and its Service Authority (neither of which is listed as a "public authority" in Sch.1 to the Freedom of Information Act 2000)[33] as well as the National Crime Squad and

(Cmnd.3151) 1966 on Squadron Leader Reen; (Cmnd.3365) 1967 on Helen Keenan; (Cmnd.3856) 1968 on Chief Technician Britten; (Cmnd.3892) 1969 on Clive Bland; (Cmnd.5367) 1973 on Earl Jellicoe and Lord Lambton; (Cmnd.8235) 1981 on John Wagstaff; (Cmnd.8540) 1982 on civil service security procedures; (Cmnd.8876) 1983 on Geoffrey Prime; (Cmnd.9212) 1984 on Lance Corporal Aldridge; (Cmnd.9514) 1985 on Michael Bettaney; (Cmnd.9923) 1986 on security in Static Signals Units; (Cm.2930) 1995 on Michael Smith; (Cm.4578) 2000 on Steven Hayden.

29 See para.(6).

30 *Intelligence and Security Committee Annual Report 1997–1998* (Cm.4073) 1998, para.59; *Intelligence and Security Committee Annual Report 1998–1999* (Cm.4532) 1999, para.75.

31 *e.g.* the report on Sir Roger Hollis (see *Hansard*, HC, Vol.1, March 26, 1981, cols 1079–1085). In lieu of the report's publication (Cmnd.8540) 1982 was issued containing a summary of certain action taken in response to some of the recommendations contained in the report. A large part of the report on Michael Bettaney also remains unpublished (see (Cmnd.9514) 1985).

32 See the Cabinet Office publication *Public Bodies 2003* (2003), p.67. In relation to NCIS and its Service Authority see: Police Act 1997, Pt I; Criminal Justice and Police Act 2001, Pt V; *Halsbury's Laws of England* (4th ed.), vol. 36(1), title "Police", paras 218–260. Further information about NCIS and its Service Authority can be found on its website *www.ncis.gov.uk*.

33 It is plain that neither NCIS nor its Service Authority is meant to be a "public authority" for the purposes of the Freedom of Information Act 2000 and this is particularly apparent when one compares the approach taken to the similarly constituted National Crime Squad and its Service Authority which are both listed in the Freedom of Information Act 2000, Sch.1, Pt VI. A contrary argument might nevertheless be constructed to the effect that NCIS is a "government department" and thus a "public authority" for the purposes of the Freedom of Information Act 2000, s.84, Sch.1, Pt I, para.1 on the basis that it is a "body or authority exercising statutory functions on behalf of the Crown." In this regard, reliance could be placed on the fact that NCIS partly comprises police members who are attested constables and who are therefore officers of the Crown: *Halsbury's Laws of England* (4th ed.), Vol.36(1), title "Police", paras 202–205 ("A member of a police force, of whatever rank, when carrying out his duties as a constable acts as an officer of the Crown and a public servant" at para.204); *Mackalley's Case* (1611) 9 Co. Rep. 65b at 68b; *Enever v R.* (1906) 3 C.L.R. 969 at 977 (*per* Griffiths C.J.); *Lewis v Cattle* [1938] 2 K.B.

its Service Authority (which are both listed as "public authorities" for these purposes).[34] Since it became a non-departmental public body on April 1, 2002, NCIS has been funded by direct government grant, as opposed to a levy on police authorities, and it has thus been required to make budget submissions to the Home Secretary who now decides the level of grant for the forthcoming year.[35] The NCIS Service Authority has legal personality as a body corporate consisting of 11 members,[36] whilst NCIS itself is a body consisting of its Director General together with police and civilian members.[37]

NCIS and its Service Authority: functions

The NCIS Service Authority operates under a Chairman and is charged with maintaining NCIS which in turn has the following functions: (1) to gather, store and analyse information in order to provide criminal intelligence; (2) to provide criminal intelligence to police forces in Great Britain, the Police Service for Northern Ireland, the National Crime Squad and other law enforcement agencies; and (3) to act in support of those bodies carrying out their criminal 17–020

454, DC at 457 (*per* Hewart C.J.); *Coomber v Justices of the County of Berks.* (1883) 9 App. Cas. 61, HL at 67 (*per* Lord Blackburn); *Fisher v Oldham Corporation* [1930] 2 K.B. 364 at 369–371 and 377 (*per* MacCardie J.); *Attorney-General for New South Wales v Perpetual Trustee Co Ltd* [1955] A.C. 457, PC at 480–481 and 489–490; *R. v Rasool* [1997] 1 W.L.R. 1092, CA; Crown Proceedings Act 1947, s.2(5) and (6); Police Act 1996, s.88; Police Act 1997, ss.42 and 86. Interesting though such an argument might be, it clearly asks too much of the definition of "government department" in Freedom of Information Act 2000, s.84 and flies in the face of the overall scheme of the Act, which did not intend NCIS to be treated as a "public authority." Establishing that NCIS is a "public authority" would have little practical effect given the nature of the exemption in Freedom of Information Act 2000, s.23, but it would engage duties to provide advice and assistance and adopt and maintain publication schemes under ss.16 and 19.

[34] In relation to the National Crime Squad and its Service Authority see: Police Act 1997, Pt II; Criminal Justice and Police Act 2001, Pt V; Freedom of Information Act 2000, Sch.1, Pt VI; *Halsbury's Laws of England*, (4th ed.), Vol.36(1), title "Police", paras 261–300. The original proposal that a National Crime Squad be established in place of the previous Regional Crime Squads was made in House of Commons Home Affairs Select Committee Third Report Session 1994–1995 *Organised Crime* (HC 18–11) 1995. The National Crime Squad thereafter came into being under the Police Act 1997 on April 1, 1998, its principal function being to prevent and detect serious crime which is of relevance to more than one police area. Like NCIS, the National Crime Squad is also an executive non-departmental public body sponsored by the Home Office: see the Cabinet Office publication *Public Bodies 2003* (2003), p.67. The National Crime Squad also has a website *www.nationalcrimesquad.police.uk*.

[35] *NCIS Annual Report 2001–2002* prepared under the Police Act 1997, ss.5, 11.

[36] Police Act 1997, ss.1, 46 and 90. The NCIS Service Authority and the National Crime Squad Service Authority have a common membership with eight "core members," one of whom is appointed Chairman of both, and one of whom is appointed Vice-Chairman of both, by the Secretary of State: Police Act 1997, ss.1(7), 47(7), Sch.1, Pt I, paras 1, 2(3), 6B(1). One member of the NCIS Service Authority is also a member of the Security Service appointed by the Secretary of State: Police Act 1997, s.1(7) and Sch.1, Pt II, para.7(c). The membership of the NCIS Service Authority and National Crime Squad Service Authority may in practice be identical: Police Act 1997, ss.1(7), 47(7) and Sch.1, Pt IV, para.11.

[37] Police Act 1997, ss.2, 9, 46, 90.

intelligence activities.[38] In discharging its functions, the NCIS Service Authority must have regard to various objectives, targets, service plans, codes of practice and directions, must ensure that NCIS is efficient and effective and must produce service plans and reports on an annual basis.[39] NCIS is itself under the direction and control of a Director General with the rank of chief constable who is appointed by the Home Secretary and who must have regard to the Service Authority's service plan in discharging his functions and produce an annual report.[40]

The security bodies: importance of secrecy

17–021 In *Attorney-General v Guardian Newspapers Ltd (No.2)* Lord Griffiths advanced the following basic proposition: "The security and intelligence services are necessary for our national security. They are, and must remain, secret services if they are to operate efficiently."[41] This proposition has three limbs: first, the implicit and unquestionable point that national security is itself a fundamentally important public interest objective[42]; secondly, the recognition that operationally effective intelligence services (and other security bodies) are essential to the achievement and maintenance of this objective; and, thirdly, the more practical point that their effectiveness is in turn dependent upon secrecy.[43]

---

[38] Police Act 1997, ss.1, 2, 46 and 90. "Law enforcement agency" includes any government department, the Jersey, Guernsey and Isle of Man police and other national and overseas bodies charged with investigating offenders and charging offenders (s.2(2)(b)). See also the National Criminal Intelligence Service (Secretary of State's Objectives) Order 2002 (SI 2002/778) (made under the Police Act 1997, s.26), art.3: "The objectives for the National Criminal Intelligence Service are: (a) to provide high quality assessments and actionable intelligence, where appropriate in partnership with other law enforcement agencies, in support of: (i) the Government's interagency strategy for reducing the supply of class A controlled drugs in the United Kingdom; and (ii) the Government's interagency strategy for combating organised immigration crime (people smuggling and human trafficking) affecting the United Kingdom; (b) to provide high quality assessments and actionable intelligence in order to increase disruption of criminal enterprises engaged in other forms of serious and organised crime within or affecting the United Kingdom, according to agreed priorities, and maximising mutual support and co-operation with law enforcement agencies at local, national and international levels."

[39] Police Act 1997, ss.2–5.

[40] Police Act 1997, ss.6 and 10–11. As mentioned above, the Security Service Act 1989, s.2(2)(c) places a duty on the Director-General of the Security Service to ensure that there are arrangements, agreed with the Director General of NCIS, for co-ordinating the activities of the Security Service in pursuance of the Security Service Act 1989, s.1(4) with the activities of police forces, NCIS, the National Crime Squad and other law enforcement agencies.

[41] [1990] 1 A.C. 109, HL at 269. See also the reference to the Security Service needing to "operate under and be protected by a cloak of secrecy" in order to carry out its functions effectively in *R. v Shayler* [2002] UKHL 11; [2003] 1 A.C. 247, HL at para.[98] (*per* Lord Hutton).

[42] This is, of course, partly because national security in turn provides part of the foundation for a stable and democratic society in which human rights are protected and may be enjoyed.

[43] It is important not to lose sight of the first of these limbs because the effectiveness and secrecy of the intelligence services are not simply ends in themselves, they are also means to the greater end of national security.

This secrecy is said to be necessary because of the "special nature"[44] of the functions of the principal security bodies outlined above. In this regard, the principal security bodies deal in intelligence and surveillance and counter-intelligence and counter-surveillance and they undertake covert and clandestine operations: their activities, methods, operations, sources and techniques must therefore remain secret, otherwise their targets will be able to adopt evasive or counter-active measures.[45]

The security bodies: maintenance of secrecy

For information to remain secret it must be accessible to only a limited number of people. Once information becomes "generally accessible"[46] it loses the quality of confidence and ceases to be secret. At a very basic level, information supplied by, or relating to, the security bodies only needs to be kept secret to prevent its being exploited to the disadvantage of national security. However, despite the fact that the vast majority of the general public would have neither the desire nor the ability to exploit information of this kind in such a way, it must nevertheless be kept secret from them in order to prevent it becoming accessible to those who might. Apart from the Freedom of Information Act 2000 and the Data Protection Act 1998, various other statutory and non-statutory legal rules regulate the accessibility and disclosure of information supplied by, or relating to, the security bodies. These at least demonstrate a consistent approach by the courts, Parliament and the government to such issues and form the legal and policy background into which the relevant exemptions in the Freedom of Information Act 2000 and Data Protection Act 1998 fit and must be understood. The most significant of these rules are mentioned in outline below: 17–022

[44] *R. v Shayler* [2002] UKHL 11; [2003] 1 AC 247, HL at para.[36] (*per* Lord Bingham).

[45] *ibid.* at para.[25] "There is much domestic authority pointing to the need for a security or intelligence service to be secure. The commodity in which such a service deals is secret and confidential information. If the service is not secure those working against the interests of the state, whether terrorists, other criminals or foreign agents, will be alerted, and able to take evasive action; its own agents may be unmasked; members of the service will feel unable to rely on each other; those upon whom the service relies as sources of information will feel unable to rely on their identity remaining secret; and foreign countries will decline to entrust their own secrets to an insecure recipient" (*per* Lord Bingham). See also the references in the same speech at paras [25]–[26] to: *Attorney-General v Guardian Newspapers Ltd (No.2)* [1990] 1 A.C. 109, HL at 118, 213–214, 259, 265 and 269; *Attorney-General v Blake* [2001] 1 A.C. 268, HL at 287; *Engel v The Netherlands (No.1)* (1979–80) 1 E.H.R.R. 647, ECtHR at paras 100–103; *Klass v Federal Republic of Germany* (1979–80) 2 E.H.R.R. 214, ECtHR at para.48; *Leander v Sweden* (1987) 9 E.H.R.R. 433, ECtHR at para.59; *Hadjianastassiou v Greece* (1993) 16 E.H.R.R. 219, ECtHR at paras 45–47; *Esbester v United Kingdom* (1994) 18 E.H.R.R. CD 72, ECommHR at para.74; *Brind v United Kingdom* (1994) 18 E.H.R.R. CD 76, ECommHR at paras 83–84; *Murray v United Kingdom* (1995) 19 E.H.R.R. 193, ECtHR at para.58; *Vereniging Weekblad Bluf! v The Netherlands* (1995) 20 E.H.R.R. 189, ECtHR at paras 35 and 40.

[46] *Attorney-General v Guardian Newspapers Ltd (No.2)* [1990] 1 A.C. 109, HL at 282 (*per* Lord Goff).

(1) *Criminal law*. In criminal terms, the Official Secrets Act 1989 makes it an offence for serving or former members of the security and intelligence services,[47] other Crown servants,[48] and government contractors to disclose certain types of information, documents or other articles without lawful authority.[49] Members of the security and intelligence services are thus prohibited from making any unauthorised disclosures of information, etc. relating to security or intelligence.[50] Furthermore, all Crown servants and government contractors are prohibited from making "damaging" unauthorised disclosures of information, etc. relating to security or intelligence,[51] defence[52] or international rela-

[47] As discussed above, it is not thought that "the security and intelligence services" means anything other than the three intelligence services: para.17–011, n.72.

[48] The expression "Crown Servant" includes Ministers of the Crown, civil servants, members of the naval, military or air forces of the Crown and any constable and any other person employed or appointed in or for the purposes of NCIS (Official Secrets Act 1989, s.12(1)(a) and (c)–(e)). It also includes the Comptroller and Auditor General, the staff of the National Audit Office and the Parliamentary Commissioner for Administration (Official Secrets Act 1989, s.12(1)(g); Official Secrets Act 1989 (Prescription) Order 1990 (SI 1990/200), Sch.2).

[49] See generally: *Departmental Committee on Section 2 of the Official Secrets Act 1911, vols 1–4* (Cmd.5104) 1972 (The Franks Report); the Home Office White Paper *Reform of Section 2 of the Official Secrets Act 1911* (Cm. 408) 1988; R. Thomas, *Espionage and Secrecy: the Official Secrets Acts 1911–1989 of the United Kingdom* (Routledge, London, 1991); Palmer, "The Government Proposals for Reforming Section 2 of the Official Secrets Act 1911" [1988] P.L. 523; Palmer, "Tightening Secrecy Law: the Official Secrets Act 1989" [1990] P.L. 243. The ancillary offences provided for by the Official Secrets Act 1989, ss.5–6 and 8 are not dealt with further in this chapter. The RIPA Tribunal can give "official authorisations" and impose "official restrictions" for the purposes of the Official Secrets Act 1989 (Official Secrets Act 1989, s.7(5); Official Secrets Act 1989 (Prescription) Order 1990 (SI 1990/200), Sch.3). The IOCA, SSA and ISA Tribunals were formerly prescribed for the same purposes but replaced by the RIPA Tribunal under the Official Secrets Act 1989 (Prescription) (Amendment) Order 2003 (SI 2003/1918), art.2(3), Sch.2.

[50] Official Secrets Act 1989, s.1(1)–(2), (5) and (9). The information, document or article must be or have been in the person's possession by virtue of their position as a member of any of the security or intelligence services (s.1(1)). "Security or intelligence" is defined to mean the work of, or in support of, the security and intelligence services or any part of them and references to information relating to security or intelligence are defined to include references to information held or transmitted by those services or by persons in support of them, or any part of them (s. 1(9)). See *R. v Shayler* [2002] UKHL 11; [2003] 1 A.C. 247, HL confirming Official Secrets Act 1989, s.1 is not incompatible with Convention rights.

[51] Official Secrets Act 1989, s.1(3)–(5) and (9). The information, document or article must be or have been in the person's possession by virtue of their position as a Crown servant or government contractor (s.1(3)). "Security or intelligence" and references to information relating to security or intelligence have the same meaning as in s.1(1)–(2) (s.1(9)). For the purposes of s.1(3) a disclosure is damaging if it causes damage to the work of, or any part of, the security and intelligence services or would be likely to cause such damage (s.1(4)).

[52] Official Secrets Act 1989, s.2. The information, document or article must be or have been in the person's possession by virtue of their position as a Crown servant or government contractor (s.2(1)). "Defence" is defined to mean (a) the size, shape, organisation, logistics, order of battle, deployment, operations, state of readiness and training of the armed forces of the Crown, (b) the weapons, stores or other equipment of those forces and the invention, development, production and operation of such equipment and research relating to it, (c) defence policy and strategy and military planning and intelligence and (d) plans and measures for the maintenance of essential supplies and services that are or would be needed in time of war (s.2(4)). For the purposes of s.2(1) a disclosure is damaging if it (a) damages the capability of, or any part of, the armed forces of the Crown to carry out their tasks or leads to loss of life or injury to members of those

tions.[53] There are also offences prohibiting all Crown servants and government contractors from making unauthorised disclosures of information, etc. which have or would be likely to have certain effects in relation to the commission, prevention or detection of offences or the apprehension, prosecution or detention of offenders[54] or which are connected with interceptions of communications under, or other actions authorised by, warrants under various statutes.[55]

(2) *Civil law*. In civil law terms, actionable private law obligations not to disclose, without authority, information which is confidential to the Crown or which was acquired during the course of Crown service can arise at equity or common law under the general law of confidence,[56]

forces or serious damage to the equipment or installations of those forces, (b) endangers the interests of the United Kingdom abroad, seriously obstructs the promotion or protection by the United Kingdom of those interests or endangers the safety of British citizens abroad or (c) would be likely to have any of those effects (s.2(2), see also s.3(2)). Serving members of the armed forces of the Crown are also subject to service discipline under the Naval Discipline Act 1957, Army Act 1955 and Air Force Act 1955, the Queen's Regulations for the Royal Navy, Army and Royal Air Force and the Manuals of Naval, Military and Air Force Law which themselves restrict unauthorised disclosures of information.

53 Official Secrets Act 1989, s.3. The offence covers information, etc., relating to international relations (s.3(1)(a)) and confidential information, etc., obtained from a State other than the United Kingdom or an international organisation (s.3(1)(b)). The information, document or article must be or have been in the person's possession by virtue of their position as a Crown servant or government contractor (s.3(1)). "International relations" are defined to mean the relations between States, between international organisations or between one or more States and one or more such organisations and includes any matter relating to a state other than the United Kingdom or to an international organisation which is capable of affecting the relations of the United Kingdom with another State or with an international organisation (s.3(5)). For the purposes of s.3(1) a disclosure is damaging if it (a) endangers the interests of the United Kingdom abroad, seriously obstructs the promotion or protection by the United Kingdom of those interests or endangers the safety of British citizens abroad or (b) would be likely to have any of those effects (s.3(2), see also s.2(2)(b)–(c)). In relation to the exemption under the Freedom of Information Act 2000 for international relations, see paras 18–001 to 18–012.

54 Official Secrets Act 1989, s.4(1)–(2) and (4)–(6).

55 Official Secrets Act 1989, s.4(1) and (3)–(6). The statutes in question are the Interception of Communications Act 1985, the Security Service Act 1989, the Intelligence Services Act 1994 and the Regulation of Investigatory Powers Act 2000. See also the Regulation of Investigatory Powers Act 2000, s.19 which makes it an offence for the heads of the intelligence services and NCIS, every person holding office under the Crown and every member of NCIS to disclose certain information about the interception of communications.

56 e.g. *Attorney-General v Guardian Newspapers Ltd (No.2)* [1990] 1 A.C. 109, HL. It is also notable that the conventions governing the publication by former ministers of memoirs and other works relating to their experience as ministers (known as the "Radcliffe Rules") provide that the consent of the Cabinet Secretary (with a right of appeal to the Prime Minister) is always required in relation to the publication of two categories of information, namely, information whose revelation would contravene the requirements of national security and information whose disclosure would be injurious to the United Kingdom's relations with other nations. See: the statement made to the House of Commons on behalf of the Prime Minister, Mr Attlee, by the Lord President of the Council, Mr Morrison, at *Hansard*, HC, Vol.426, August 1, 1946, cols 1207–1208; the *Report of the Committee of Privy Counsellors [chaired by Lord Radcliffe] on Ministerial Memoirs* (Cmnd.6386) 1976, paras 79 and 91–92 produced following the "Crossman Affair" and *Attorney-General v Jonathan Cape Ltd* [1976] Q.B. 752; A. Bradley and K. Ewing, *Constitutional and Administrative Law* (13th ed., Longman, London, 2003), p.266; the reference to the Radcliffe Report in *Open Government Code of Practice on Access to Government Information: Guidance*

contract[57] or fiduciary duties.[58] The government can and does seek to enforce or vindicate such obligations through the pursuit of civil proceedings seeking any combination of injunctive relief, an account of profits, damages, the delivery up or destruction of material and costs. Proceedings with similar objectives may also be brought to prevent or remedy infringements of intellectual property rights[59] or tortious interferences with other civil law rights and obligations.[60] Lastly, the government can and does bring ancillary proceedings for contempt of court against those who have breached or undermined the purpose of related court orders.[61]

(3) *Public law*. In public law terms, the Security Service Act 1989 and Intelligence Services Act 1994 put the head of each intelligence service under a duty to ensure that there are arrangements for securing that no information is obtained by his service except so far as necessary for the proper discharge of its functions or disclosed by it except so far as necessary for that purpose, in the interests of national security, for the prevention or detection of serious crime or for the purpose of any criminal proceedings.[62] The relevant provisions thus establish a statutory bar to the onward disclosure of security and defence information held by the

on Interpretation (2nd ed., 1997), Pt II, para.2.3 in relation to the "internal discussion and advice" exemption under that Code. The same restrictions apply, in relation to these two categories of information, to similar publications by former members of the Civil Service and Diplomatic Service under their respective Management Codes.

57 *e.g. "R" v Attorney-General for England and Wales* [2003] UKPC 22; [2003] E.M.L.R. 499, PC.

58 *e.g. IDC Ltd v Cooley* [1972] 1 W.L.R. 443; *Island Export Finance Ltd v Umunna* [1986] B.C.L.C. 460; *cf. Attorney-General v Blake* [1998] Ch.439, CA at 453–455 (*per* Lord Woolf M.R.) (in relation to existence of fiduciary duties after service; a point not considered on appeal in *Attorney-General v Blake* [2001] 1 A.C. 268, HL).

59 *e.g.* under Copyright, Designs and Patents Act 1988, s.163; or on the grounds suggested in *Attorney-General v Guardian Newspapers Ltd (No.2)* [1990] 1 A.C. 109, Ch at 139–140 (*per* Scott J.) and HL at 263 (*per* Lord Keith), 266 (*per* Lord Brightman) and 275–276 (*per* Lord Griffiths) and *Paragon Finance Plc v Thakerar & Co* [1999] 1 All E.R. 400, CA at 409 (*per* Millett L.J.).

60 *e.g.* A. Dugdale (ed.), *Clerk and Lindsell On Torts* (18th ed., Sweet & Maxwell, London), 2000, Ch. 24; Sales and Stilitz, "Intentional Infliction of Harm by Unlawful Means" (1999) 115 L.Q.R. 411.

61 *Attorney-General v Newspaper Publishing Plc.* [1988] Ch. 333, CA; *Attorney-General v Times Newspapers Ltd* [1992] 1 A.C. 191, HL; *Attorney-General v Punch Ltd* [2002] UKHL 50; [2003] 1 A.C. 1046, HL.

62 Security Service Act 1989, s.2(2)(a) (in relation to the Security Service); Intelligence Services Act 1994, ss.2(2)(a) and 4(2)(a) (in relation to SIS and GCHQ respectively). See the *Second Report to Parliament on the Review of Legislation Governing the Disclosure of Information* (November 2002) referring to the Security Service Act 1989, s.2(2)(a) and the Intelligence Services Act 1994, ss.2(2)(a), 4(2)(a), 5(2)(c), 7(3)(c), 10(7). In relation to the latter set of provisions the report records that, "[T]he Foreign and Commonwealth Office, in consultation with the Home Office, considers that these provisions form an essential and integral part of the statutory governance of the Agencies and it is right that the provisions are retained within the primary legislation for that purpose. The Agencies are not covered by the Freedom of Information Act 2000 and therefore these items will be retained." This report is in turn referred to in the report published under the Freedom of Information Act 2000, s.87(5) by the Lord Chancellor, *Freedom of Information Annual Report* (HC 6) 2002, s.5.

intelligence services.[63] If and in so far as these provisions or the arrangements arrived at thereunder "prohibit" other public authorities from disclosing the same information, s.44(1)(a) of the Freedom of Information Act 2000 confers a further absolute exemption on such information.[64]

(4) *Employment law*. In employment law terms, the "whistle-blower" provisions inserted into the Employment Rights Act 1996[65] by the Public Interest Disclosure Act 1998 do not apply to employment for the purposes of the intelligence services or operate to protect disclosures which entail the commission of an offence under the Official Secrets Act 1989.[66] Section 202 of the Employment Rights Act 1996 also imposes more general restrictions on certain disclosures of information in the employment rights context which "in the opinion of any Minister of the Crown" would be "contrary to the interests of national security."

(5) *Evidence, procedure and public interest immunity*. In evidential and procedural terms, it has long been recognised that public interest immunity[67] may be claimed to prevent the disclosure and inspection of

---

[63] The Interception of Communications Act 1985, s.6 provided, in similar terms, that the Secretary of State should make arrangements minimising the disclosure and use of intercepted material. In *R. v Preston* [1994] 2 A.C. 130, HL it was held that the Interception of Communications Act 1985, ss.2 and 6 entirely prevented the disclosure of such material in criminal proceedings despite the fact that they did not impose prohibitions or criminal sanctions in connection with the making or observance of the relevant arrangements. See at 143 (*per* Lord Jauncey) and 166, 168–169 and 172 (*per* Lord Mustill).

[64] Freedom of Information Act 2000, ss.2(3)(h), 44(1)(a). The wording of the absolute exemption in the Freedom of Information Act 2000, s.23 means that this point is unlikely to have any practical significance in relation to that Act. However, it could have a potentially greater significance in relation to the Freedom of Information (Scotland) Act 2002 which does not contain an exemption for information supplied by, or relating to, the security bodies equivalent to the Freedom of Information Act 2000, s.23 but which does confer an absolute exemption on information whose disclosure by a Scottish public authority is prohibited by or under an enactment (Freedom of Information (Scotland) Act 2002, ss.2(2)(b) and 26(a)). See further para.17–007.

[65] Employment Rights Act 1996, Pt IVA, ss.47B, 103A, 105(6A) and other provisions added by the Public Interest Disclosure Act 1998. These provisions protect workers from victimisation, dismissal and redundancy in the event that they make specified types of "protected disclosures" relating to specified types of misconduct and malpractice.

[66] Employment Rights Act 1996, ss.43B(3), 193. Those in Crown employment (including members of the intelligence services and the armed forces) are otherwise able to rely on the bulk of the employment rights conferred under that Act: see Employment Rights Act 1996, ss.191–193.

[67] See generally: *Conway v Rimmer* [1968] A.C. 910, HL; *Balfour v Foreign Office* [1994] 1 W.L.R. 681, CA; *R. v Chief Constable of the West Midlands Police, Ex p. Wiley* [1995] 1 A.C. 274, HL; Crown Proceedings Act 1947, s.28; Criminal Procedure and Investigations Act 1996, ss.14–16; Crown Court (Criminal Procedure and Investigations Act 1996) (Disclosure) Rules 1997 (SI 1997/698); Civil Procedure Rules 1998 (SI 1998/3132), Pt 31.19; De Smith, Woolf and Jowell, *Judicial Review of Administrative Action* (5th ed., Sweet & Maxwell, London, 1995), paras 1–130—1–159 and 10–006—10–011; Wade and Forsyth, *Administrative Law* (8th ed., Oxford University Press, Oxford, 2000), pp. 825–836; P. Jackson, *Hood Phillips and Jackson: Constitutional and Administrative Law* (8th ed., Sweet & Maxwell, London, 2001), paras 33–022—33–028; *Halsbury's Laws of England* (4th ed.), Vol.17(1), title "Evidence", paras 436–440. Central government's current approach to public interest immunity issues is set out in identical statements made in both Houses of Parliament by the Lord Chancellor, Lord Mackay, and the Attorney General, Sir Nicholas Lyell, on December 18, 1996 (*Hansard*, HC, Vol.287, December

documents, the asking of written and oral questions and the admission of evidence in criminal and civil proceedings and inquests and inquiries before courts and tribunals[68] where this would cause harm or damage to, *inter alia*, national security and defence interests.[69] The European Court of Human Rights has held that the exclusion of similar material from public law proceedings regarding the validity of certain decisions taken on national security grounds can constitute an unjustifiable interference with Convention rights including the right of effective access to justice under Art.6 of the ECHR.[70] For this reason, a number of instruments now provide that documents and hearings dealing with sensitive material which must remain closed to parties in such proceedings should instead be handled by "special advocates" who will act in the interests of those parties but who will not disclose that material to them.[71] It has further been suggested that the courts have an inherent

18, 1996, cols 949–950 and *Hansard*, HL, Vol.576, December 18, 1996, cols 1507–1508). These statements were made following a wide-ranging consultation exercise which itself followed the publication of the Scott Report (*Inquiry into the Export of Defence Equipment and Dual Use Goods to Iraq and Related Prosecutions* (HC 115) 1995–1996 and *R. v Chief Constable of the West Midlands Police, Ex p. Wiley* [1995] 1 A.C. 274, HL. The statements were accompanied by a detailed paper which was placed in the libraries of both Houses of Parliament and were endorsed by the incoming Labour administration in a written answer dated July 11, 1997 (*Hansard*, HC, Vol.297, July 11, 1997, cols 616–617). See M. Supperstone and J. Coppel, "A New Approach to Public Interest Immunity" [1997] P.L. 211.

68 The doctrine of public interest immunity applies to both criminal and civil proceedings but its application may differ according to the nature of the proceedings and the differing considerations involved (*e.g.* if the liberty of the subject is at stake): *R. v Governor of Brixton Prison, Ex p. Osman* [1991] 1 W.L.R. 281, DC at 287 (*per* Mann L.J.). Public interest immunity rulings in civil cases are therefore not necessarily of direct relevance in criminal cases where the public interest in disclosure may be stronger and where the abandonment of the prosecution always remains a fall-back option in circumstances where both disclosure and non-disclosure are deemed unacceptable.

69 In terms of domestic law see: *Duncan v Cammell Laird & Co Ltd* [1942] A.C. 624, HL; *Asiatic Petroleum Co Ltd v Anglo-Persian Oil Co Ltd* [1916] 1 K.B. 822, CA; *Balfour v Foreign Office* [1994] 1 W.L.R. 681, CA. The European Court of Human Rights has endorsed public interest immunity claims upheld on such grounds in criminal proceedings provided the domestic courts exercise effective control and oversight: *Rowe and Davis v United Kingdom* (2000) 30 E.H.R.R. 1; *Jasper v United Kingdom* (2000) 30 E.H.R.R. 441; *Fitt v United Kingdom* (2000) 30 E.H.R.R. 480; *Edwards and Lewis v United Kingdom*, (2003) 15 B.H.R.C. 189; *The Times*, July 29, 2003. See also: *R. v Smith (Joe)* [2001] 1 W.L.R. 1031, CA; *R v C, R. v H*, [2003] EWCA Crim 2847; [2003] 1 W.L.R. 3006, CA; *R. (DPP) v Acton Youth Court* [2001] 1 W.L.R. 1828, DC at para.34 (*per* Lord Woolf C.J.). See also the Regulation of Investigatory Powers Act 2000, s.17 which prohibits the disclosure in legal proceedings of certain information about interceptions of communications.

70 *Chahal v United Kingdom* (1997) 23 E.H.R.R. 413, ECtHR; *Tinnelly and Sons Ltd v United Kingdom* (1999) 27 E.H.R.R. 249, ECtHR.

71 Provision is made for the appointment and appearance of special advocates in proceedings under: the Special Immigration Appeals Commission Act 1997 and the Special Immigration Appeals Commission (Procedure) Rules 2003 (SI 2003/1034); the Northern Ireland Act 1998 and the Northern Ireland Act Tribunal (Procedure) Rules 1999 (SI 1999/2131); the Terrorism Act 2000 and the Proscribed Organisations Appeal Commission (Procedure) Rules 2001 (SI 2001/443); the Anti-terrorism, Crime and Security Act 2001 and the Pathogens Access Appeal Commission (Procedure) Rules 2002 (SI 2002/1845); the Life Sentences (Northern Ireland) Order 2001 (SI 2001/2564 (NI 2)) and the Life Sentence Review Commissioners' Rules 2001 (SRNI 2001/317); the Employment Tribunals Rules of Procedure at Employment Tribunals (Constitution and Rules of

discretionary power to request the appointment by the Attorney General of, and to hear, special advocates on an extra-statutory basis in other proceedings.[72] Sensitive identities and information can also be protected in legal proceedings through mechanisms which do not involve complete non-disclosure such as: private hearings[73]; orders and directions prohibiting the collateral and onward use of disclosed materials[74]; orders or directions requiring witnesses to give evidence anonymously or screened from public view[75]; and reporting restrictions.[76]

The security bodies: need for an absolutist approach to secrecy?

So far as concerns the treatment of the security bodies in the Freedom of Information Act 2000, the key issue is whether and why the legitimate preservation of their secrecy should be pursued by absolute rather than qualified means: that is to say, does the need for secrecy require or justify the institutional exclusion of the security bodies from the regime of the Act and the absolute exemption of all information supplied by, or relating to, them irrespective of whether its disclosure might harm those bodies or national security? Many of the judicial pronouncements regarding the intelligence services and the importance of, and relationship between, their effectiveness and secrecy have been made in connection with decisions reviewing and affirming the need for a "brightline rule" prohibiting all unauthorised disclosures by their members and former members.[77] 17–023

Procedure) Regulations 2001 (SI 2000/1171, Schs 1–2); the Employment Appeal Tribunal Rules 1993 (SI 1993/2854) as amended by Employment Appeal Tribunal (Amendment) Rules 2001 (SI 2001/1128).

[72] *R. v Shayler* [2002] UKHL 11; [2003] 1 A.C. 247, HL at para.[34] (*per* Lord Bingham) and para.[113] (*per* Lord Hutton); *Secretary of State for the Home Department v Rehman* [2000] 3 W.L.R. 1240, CA at paras 31–32 (*per* Lord Woolf M.R.); *R v C, R v H*, [2003] EWCA Crim 2847; [2003] 1 W.L.R. 3006, CA; *R (Harry Roberts) v Parole Board* [2003] EWHC 3120 (Admin).

[73] *e.g.* Official Secrets Act 1920, s.8(4); Official Secrets Act 1989, s.11(4); Criminal Justice Act 1988, s.159(1); Crown Court Rules 1982 (SI 1982/1109), r.24A; *R. v Shayler* [2003] EWCA Crim 2218, CA at [18]–[22] (*per* Kennedy L.J.); Administration of Justice Act 1960, s.12(1)(c); Civil Procedure Rules 1998, (SI 1998/3132), Pt 39.2(3), 39PD.1 see esp. Pt 39.2(3)(b) "a hearing, or any part of it, may be in private if it involves matters relating to national security."

[74] Criminal Procedure and Investigations Act 1996, ss.17–18; Crown Court (Criminal Procedure and Investigations Act 1996) (Confidentiality) Rules 1997 (SI 1997/699); Civil Procedure Rules 1998 (SI 1998/3132) Pt 31.22; *Davies (Joy Rosalie) v Eli Lilly & Co (No. 1)* [1987] 1 W.L.R. 428, CA at 431–432 (*per* Lord Donaldson M.R.).

[75] *e.g.* Civil Procedure Rules 1998 (SI 1998/3132) Pt 39.2(4), 39PD.1; *Re Ministry of Defence's Application* [1994] N.I. 279, CA (NI); *R. v Lord Saville of Newdigate, Ex p. A* [2000] 1 W.L.R. 1855, CA; *R. v Shayler* [2003] EWCA Crim 2218, CA at paras [10]–[17] (*per* Kennedy L.J.); *Doorson v The Netherlands* (1996) 22 E.H.R.R. 330, ECtHR; *X v United Kingdom* (1993) 15 E.H.R.R. CD 113, ECommHR.

[76] *e.g.* Contempt of Court Act 1981, ss.4 and 11.

[77] *Attorney-General v Guardian Newspapers Ltd* [1990] 1 A.C. 109, HL at 269 (*per* Lord Griffiths). Cited with approval in *Lord Advocate v The Scotsman Publications Ltd* [1990] 1 A.C. 812, HL at 828 (*per* Lord Jauncey) and in *R. v Shayler* [2002] UKHL 11; [2003] 1 A.C. 247, HL at paras [25] and [36] (*per* Lord Bingham). Also approved in *Attorney-General v Blake* [2001] 1 A.C. 268, HL at 287 (*per* Lord Nicholls). A brightline rule against unauthorised disclosures is imposed by

Certain aspects of the rationale for this rule are not relevant in the freedom of information context, however, as disclosures under access to information legislation are not unauthorised and, provided they are controlled by reference to an adequate harm or prejudice test, they should not run the risk of damaging the trust of others in, or the morale of, the intelligence services.[78] Moreover, it is well established that there are occasions when government can and should consider and authorise the disclosure of information supplied by, or relating to, security bodies. Such occasions may arise in relation to: the disclosure and inspection of documents in legal proceedings and the application of the doctrine of public interest immunity[79]; requests for authorisation to publish memoirs and books relating to service with the principal security bodies[80]; and the disclosure of information to, and the inclusion of material in the published versions of reports produced by, oversight bodies.[81] There would appear to be two main justifications for taking an absolutist approach to secrecy in the freedom of information context:

(1) *Mosaic prejudice*. First is the contention that any disclosure of information supplied by, or relating to, security bodies is necessarily harmful because it will contribute pieces to a public domain "mosaic" or "jigsaw" of information about those bodies. This argument gives rise to the theory that such disclosures cause "mosaic prejudice" because apparently innocuous information connected with security and intelligence matters can prove to be acutely revealing when read in conjunction with other pieces of the mosaic or when used as the basis for deductions and inferences about gaps in the picture.[82] Most of the

the Official Secrets Act 1989, s.1 (on members of the intelligence services) and the general law of confidence (on members of the intelligence services and, arguably, others in a similar position). Membership of "the intelligence services" is not necessarily an essential or exclusive pre-condition in this regard: note the reference to "members or former members of those services who have had access to information relating to national security" in *R. v Shayler* [2002] UKHL 11; [2003] 1 A.C. 247, HL at para.[68] (*per* Lord Hope).

[78] *Attorney-General v Blake* [2001] 1 A.C. 268 at 287 (*per* Lord Nicholls); *R. v Shayler* [2002] UKHL 11; [2003] 1 A.C. 247, HL at para.[100] (*per* Lord Hutton).

[79] See para.17–022(5).

[80] *e.g.* S. Rimington, *Open Secret: The Autobiography of the Former Director-General of MI5* (Hutchinson, London, 2001). Refusals of authorisation to publish are judicially reviewable see: *Attorney-General v Guardian Newspapers Ltd (No.2)* [1990] 1 A.C. 109, Ch at 163 (*per* Scott J.); *R. v Shayler* [2002] UKHL 11; [2003] 1 A.C. 247, HL at paras [31]–[35] (*per* Lord Bingham), at paras [72]–[85] (*per* Lord Hope) and at paras [107]–[116] (*per* Lord Hutton); *"R" v Attorney-General for England and Wales* [2003] UKPC 22; [2003] E.M.L.R. 499, PC at para.36 (*per* Lord Hoffmann).

[81] See para.17–024(2), (3) and (6).

[82] See paras 15–015 to 15–016 for a general discussion of "mosaic prejudice." The government certainly regarded mosaic prejudice as a live issue when it published the consultation paper *Freedom of Information: Consultation on Draft Legislation* (Cm.4355) 1999. As mentioned above, cl.19(3) of the draft Bill annexed to this paper contained an express "jigsaw puzzle" exemption which would have ensured the non-disclosure of apparently harmless information which might be harmful when looked at in conjunction with other pieces of the wider puzzle: "Where, in relation to any information ("the information requested"), exemption from section 8(1)(b)–(a) is not

domestic judicial dicta dealing with the dangers of mosaic prejudice have arisen in relation to the need for the brightline rule mentioned above and have stressed the particular risks run by individuals who attempt to assess for themselves how an intended disclosure will add to the public mosaic.[83] It could therefore be argued that the force of these dicta diminishes in the freedom of information context, where decisions to disclose can be taken by or in consultation with the security bodies.[84] Against this, a pre-disclosure assessment and authorisation process might not entail a particularly effective use of time and resources within the security bodies and it would not provide total immunity from mosaic prejudice in any event. While the security bodies

---

required for the purpose of safeguarding national security, but (b) would be required for that purpose if any other information (whether or not held by the public authority and whether or not accessible, or likely to become accessible, to members of the public) became available at the same time or subsequently, the exemption shall be taken for the purposes of this section to be required for that purpose in relation to the information requested." This draft provision was criticised for being too broad (*e.g.* House of Lords Draft Freedom of Information Bill Select Committee First Report Session 1998–1999, *Report from the Select Committee Appointed to Consider the Draft Freedom of Information Bill* (HL 97) 1999, paras 36–37) and was not repeated in the Freedom of Information Bill introduced in the House of Commons on November 18, 1999.

[83] In relation to unauthorised disclosures see: *Attorney-General v Guardian Newspapers Ltd (No.2)* [1990] 1 A.C. 109, HL at 269 "What may appear to the writer to be trivial may in fact be the one missing piece in the jigsaw sought by some hostile intelligence agency" (*per* Lord Griffiths); *R. v Shayler* [2002] UKHL 11; [2003] 1 A.C. 247, HL at para.[101] "such a decision [*i.e.* whether a disclosure would or would not be damaging] could not safely be left to that individual because he may not have a full appreciation of how that piece of information fits into a wider picture and of what effect the disclosure might have on other aspects of the work of the service of which he is unaware or of which he lacks a full appreciation" (*per* Lord Hutton).

[84] The courts in the USA and Australia have usually endorsed the mosaic approach to prejudice in relation to national security exemption claims in the freedom of information context. In relation to the USA see: *Halperin v CIA*, 629 F.(2d) 144, 150 (D.C. Cir. 1980) ("each individual piece of intelligence information, much like a piece of a jigsaw puzzle, may aid in piecing together other bits of information even when the individual piece is not of obvious importance in itself"); *Salisbury v United States*, 690 F.(2d) 966, 971 (D.C. Cir. 1982) (referring to the "mosaic-like nature of intelligence gathering"); *American Friends Serv. Comm. v Department of Defense*, 831 F.(2d) 441, 444–45 (3d Cir. 1987) ("compilation" theory); *Taylor v Department of the Army*, 684 F.(2d) 99, 105 (D.C. Cir. 1982); *National Security Archive v FBI*, 759 F. Supp. 872, 877 (D.D.C. 1991) (held that disclosure of code names and designator phrases could provide a hostile intelligence analyst with a "common denominator" permitting the analyst to piece together seemingly unrelated data into a snapshot of specific FBI counter-intelligence activity); *Jan-Xin Zang v FBI*, 756 F. Supp. 705, 709–10 (W.D.N.Y. 1991) (upholding classification of any source-identifying word or phrase, which could by itself or in aggregate lead to disclosure of intelligence source). Indeed, mosaic prejudice is also now recognised in the USA by Executive Order 12,958, para.1.8(e). In relation to Australia see: *Re Low and Department of Defence* (1984) 2 A.A.R. 142 at 149; *Re Actors' Equity Association of Australia and Australian Broadcasting Tribunal (No.2)* (1985) 7 A.L.D. 584; *Re Robinson and Department of Foreign Affairs* (1986) 11 A.L.N. N48; *Re Throssell and Australian Archives* (1986) 10 A.L.D. 403 at 406 and 407; *Re Throssell and Department of Foreign Affairs* (1987) 14 A.L.D. 296; *Re Slater and Cox (Director-General, Australian Archives)* (1988) 15 A.L.D. 20 at 27; *Re McKnight v Australian Archives* (1992) 28 A.L.D. 95 at 112; *Re Ewer and Australian Archives* (1995) 38 A.L.D. 789. A mechanical application or an unquestioning acceptance of all claims of mosaic prejudice will, of course, emasculate the rights given by the Freedom of Information Act 2000.

can evaluate the pieces of the mosaic they know to be in the public domain and the extent to which a particular disclosure would add to the overall publicly accessible picture, they cannot know every piece of information held by hostile forces and individuals (which may not be in the public domain but may make the proposed disclosure more damaging) and they cannot predict the subsequent emergence of further pieces of information which will elucidate the picture even further.

(2) *Countervailing human rights*. A more defensive argument in support of the absolutist approach takes the need for secrecy and the risk of mosaic prejudice as its starting point before asserting that there is no human rights based reason for taking a more qualified approach. The need to act compatibly with "Convention rights" within the meaning of the Human Rights Act 1998[85] or rights under European Community law that can be relied upon before the domestic courts,[86] may require that disclosures of information are considered by reference to a harm or prejudice test where such rights are in play. In this way, those seeking the disclosure of information in legal proceedings can rely on the right to a fair trial under Art.6 of the ECHR,[87] those requesting authority to publish a memoir can rely on the right to freedom of expression under Art.10 of the ECHR and those seeking access to personal data can rely on the right to respect for private and family life under Art.8 of the ECHR[88] and Community rights under the European Community Data

---

[85] Human Rights Act 1998, s.1(1)–(3), Sch.1 define "the Convention rights" for the purposes of that Act as the rights and fundamental freedoms set out in Arts 2–12 and 14 of the Convention for the Protection of Human Rights and Fundamental Freedoms (Cmd.8969) 1953 ("ECHR"), Arts 1–3 of the First Protocol and Arts 1–2 of the Sixth Protocol. The ECHR, Arts 1 and 13 are notable omissions from "the Convention rights." Primary and subordinate legislation must, so far as possible, be read and given effect in a way which is compatible with the Convention rights (s.3) and it is unlawful for public authorities (including courts) to act in a way which is incompatible with them unless left with no alternative by primary legislation (s.6).

[86] In this regard, reliance can be placed on Community law in accordance with the doctrine of direct effect including the subsidiary or related doctrines of vertical, indirect and incidental direct effect: P. Craig and G. De Búrca, *EU Law: Text, Cases and Materials* (3rd ed., Oxford University Press, Oxford, 2003), Chs 5–6. In particular, the doctrine of indirect direct effect requires that national law implementing Directives is interpreted and applied in accordance with Community law and norms and is therefore relevant to the Data Protection Act 1998 which implements the European Community Data Protection Directive 95/46; ([1995] O.J. L281/31): Case 14/83 *Von Colson v Land Nordrhein-Westfalen* [1984] E.C.R. 1891; Case C-106/89 *Marleasing SA v La Comercial Internacionale de Alimentacion SA* [1990] E.C.R. I-4135; Cases C-240–244/98 *Océano Grupo Editorial v Rocio Murciano Quintero* [2000] E.C.R. I-4491; Craig, "Directives: Direct Effect, Indirect Effect and the Construction of National Legislation", (1997) 22 E.L.Rev. 519. In relation to the interpretation of the Data Protection Act 1998 see in particular: *Campbell v MGN Ltd* [2002] EWCA Civ 1373; [2003] QB 633, CA, para.[96] (*per* Lord Phillips M.R.); *Durant v Financial Services Authority* [2003] EWCA Civ 1746, paras [3]–[4] (*per* Auld L.J.); *R. (Alan Lord) v Secretary of State for the Home Department* [2003] EWHC 2073 (Admin), para.[83] (*per* Munby J.).

[87] *McGinley and Egan v United Kingdom* (1998) 27 E.H.R.R. 1, ECtHR.

[88] *Gaskin v United Kingdom* (1989) 12 E.H.R.R. 36, ECtHR; *Guerra v Italy* (1998) 26 E.H.R.R. 357, ECtHR; *McGinley and Egan v United Kingdom* (1998) 27 E.H.R.R. 1, ECtHR at paras [101] and [103].

Protection Directive 95/46.[89] Although none of these rights is absolute and each of them may have to give way to the requirements of national security,[90] their engagement effectively requires that the competing interests involved be weighed against each other before a final decision is taken on disclosure. The engagement of these rights thus precludes the adoption of an absolutist approach to secrecy and requires that non-disclosure be supported by some evidence of the harm that disclosure would cause.[91] When it comes to general requests for information under the Freedom of Information Act 2000, however, there are unlikely to be any countervailing rights in play as neither the ECHR nor Community law confers a general right of access to information; an absolutist approach may therefore be seen as less objectionable.[92] It should also be remembered that in circumstances where countervailing rights operate in other contexts to require the disclosure of information supplied by, or relating to, the security bodies, it may nevertheless be possible to restrict the number of people to whom that information is disclosed, thus minimising the risk of

89 [1995] O.J. L281/31. Indeed, the connection between rights to privacy (including under the ECHR, Art.8) and data protection is strongly emphasised throughout the recitals to the European Community Data Protection Directive 95/46 (see esp. recitals (1)–(3), (7) and (9)–(11)) and in Art.1. The importance of countervailing rights favouring disclosure in the Data Protection Act 1998 context has been emphasised by the Information Tribunal in *Baker v Secretary of State for the Home Department* [2001] U.K.H.R.R. 1275, paras 50–64 and *Gosling v Secretary of State for the Home Department*, (unreported, decision of the Information Tribunal dated August 1, 2003), para.48. The engagement of countervailing rights and the limited scope for security and defence exemptions under the Data Protection Directive no doubt explain the absence of any institutional exclusion for the security bodies in the Data Protection Act 1998. See further paras 25–022 to 25–027.

90 In relation to ECHR, Art.6 see: *Fayed v United Kingdom* (1994) 18 E.H.R.R. 393, ECtHR at pp.429–430, paras 65–67; *Tinnelly and Sons Ltd v United Kingdom* (1999) 27 E.H.R.R. 249, ECtHR at p.271, para.74; *Lithgow v United Kingdom* (1986) 8 E.H.R.R. 329, ECtHR at p.393, para.194. In relation to ECHR, Arts 8 and 10 see: ECHR, Arts 8(2) and 10(2). In relation to personal data rights see: European Community Data Protection Directive 95/46 ([1995] O.J. L281/31), recital (16) and Art.13(1)(a)–(c); Data Protection Act 1998, s.28. See further paras 1–029 to 1–037.

91 Establishing a real risk of mosaic prejudice may or may not suffice in this regard, but there is no automatic presumption that it will and each case must be dealt with on its merits.

92 Although the right to freedom of expression under ECHR, Art.10 includes "the right to receive and impart information and ideas without interference," it has been consistently held not to confer or entail a general right of access to information: *R. (Persey) v Secretary of State for the Environment, Food and Rural Affairs* [2002] EWHC 371 (Admin); [2003] Q.B. 794, DC at paras [52]–[53] (*per* Simon Brown L.J.); *R. (Howard) v Secretary of State for Health (Note)* [2002] EWHC 396 (Admin) at para.[103] (*per* Scott Baker J.); *Leander v Sweden* (1987) 9 E.H.R.R. 433: ECtHR; *Gaskin v United Kingdom* (1989) 12 E.H.R.R. 36, ECtHR; *Guerra v Italy* (1998) 26 E.H.R.R. 357, ECtHR; *BBC, Petitioners (No.2)* (2000) J.C. 521; *cf. R. (Wagstaff) v Secretary of State for Health* [2001] 1 W.L.R. 292, DC. *cf.* Sir Stephen Sedley, "Information as a Human Right" in J. Beatson and Y. Cripps (eds), *Freedom of Expression and Freedom of Information: Essays in Honour of Sir David Williams* (Oxford University Press, Oxford, 2000). See paras 1–030 to 1–032.

mosaic prejudice[93]; such measures cannot be taken under the Freedom of Information Act 2000.[94]

The security bodies: accountability and oversight

17–024 Having set out the consistently high level of secrecy surrounding the security bodies it is important to understand the wider institutional and constitutional context in which they operate. This context will help determine the practical consequences of the security bodies' exclusion from the Freedom of Information Act 2000 regime in terms of the effect it has on other public authorities and the accessibility of information more generally. The extent to which the security bodies are subject to authorities and mechanisms allowing for the oversight and regulation of their work is also critical to an evaluation of two inter-dependent issues, first, the effectiveness and transparency of their public accountability and, secondly, the justifiability of their institutional exclusion from the Freedom of Information Act 2000 regime. In terms of the ancillary security bodies, the RIPA, IOCA, SSA and ISA Tribunals, the Security Vetting Appeals Panel and the Security Commission are themselves oversight bodies, whilst the Police Complaints Authority handles complaints about the conduct of members of NCIS under s.39 of the Police Act 1997 and Regulations thereunder.[95] In terms of the principal security bodies, which are obviously of most importance here, accountability and oversight is provided by some of the ancillary security bodies, as has already been mentioned, together with (1) the Comptroller and Auditor General and National Audit Office, (2) the Intelligence Services Commissioner, (3) the Interception of Communications Commissioner, (4) the Parliamentary Commissioner for Administration and, in more limited circumstances, (5) the Privy Council. In addition to this, (6) the Intelligence and Security Committee and (7) the Ministerial and Permanent Secretaries' Committees on the Intelligence Services have an oversight role in relation to the intelligence

---

[93] Even where the disclosure of confidential information is required on public interest grounds, the courts recognise that this does not necessarily extend to publication to the world at large and may be limited to the police or appropriate regulators: *Attorney-General v Guardian Newspapers Ltd (No.2)* [1990] 1 A.C. 109, HL at 269 (*per* Lord Griffiths) and 283 (*per* Lord Goff); *Francome v MGN Ltd* [1984] 1 W.L.R. 892; *In re A Company's Application* [1989] Ch.477. *cf. Initial Services Ltd v Putterill* [1968] 1 Q.B. 396, pp.405–406; *Lion Laboratories Ltd v Evans* [1985] Q.B. 526; *Barrymore v News Group Newspapers Ltd* [1997] F.S.R. 600 at 603; *London Regional Transport v Mayor for London* [2001] EWCA Civ 1491. See also para.17–022(5) on the restrictions that may be placed on the collateral and onward use of materials disclosed in legal proceedings.

[94] See paras 15–019 to 15–020.

[95] Police Act 1997, s.39 as amended by the Police Reform Act 2002, s.25; NCIS (Complaints) Regulations 1998 (SI 1998/641) as amended by NCIS (Complaints) (Amendment) Regulations 1999 (SI 1999/1273); *Halsbury's Laws of England* (4th ed.), Vol. 36(1), title "Police", paras 245–260. Under the Police Reform Act 2002 the Police Complaints Authority will be replaced by the Independent Police Complaints Commission with effect from April 1, 2004.

services.[96] A brief outline of the functions of the seven additional oversight bodies follows:

(1) *The Comptroller and Auditor General.* The National Audit Office is listed as a "public authority" in Pt VI of Sch.1 to the Freedom of Information Act 2000 and it supervises, and therefore holds information about, the security bodies and their sponsoring departments.[97] Since 1994 the government has brought forward in a single published vote, known as the Single Intelligence Account, the aggregate expenditure and budget provision for the intelligence services in a form that is "fully open to scrutiny by the Comptroller and Auditor General, apart from limited restrictions to protect the identities of certain sources of information and the details of particularly sensitive operations."[98] The Single Intelligence Account is decided by ministers through the biennial Spending Review mechanism and has the Cabinet Office Security and Intelligence Co-ordinator as its Accounting Officer.[99] The total allocation for the intelligence services is made known to Parliament and the public, but the details (including the apportionment to each service) are only revealed to the Comptroller and Auditor General, the Intelligence and Security Committee and the Chairman of the House of Commons Public Accounts Committee.[1]

---

[96] The special forces are not subject to any equivalent Committees or Commissions, although the House of Commons Defence Select Committee examines the expenditure, administration and policy of the Ministry of Defence: HC Standing Order, No.152; *Departmental Evidence and Response to Select Committees* (1999); A. Bradley and K. Ewing, *Constitutional and Administrative Law* (13th ed., Longman, London, 2003), pp.209–215; P. Jackson, *Hood Phillips and Jackson: Constitutional and Administrative Law* (8th ed., Sweet & Maxwell, London, 2001), paras 12–029 to 12–033.

[97] National Audit Act 1983; *Halsbury's Laws of England* (4th ed.), Vol. 8(2), title "Constitutional Law and Human Rights", paras 716–717, 720 and 724–726; A. Bradley and K. Ewing, *Constitutional and Administrative Law* (13th ed., Longman, London, 2003), pp.358–360; P. Jackson, *Hood Phillips and Jackson: Constitutional and Administrative Law* (8th ed., Sweet & Maxwell, London, 2001), paras 12–018 to 12–019.

[98] *Hansard*, HC, Vol.233, November 24, 1993, col.52 (written answer by the Prime Minister, Mr Major, to a Parliamentary Question tabled by Mr Robinson). See: A. Bradley and K. Ewing, *Constitutional and Administrative Law* (13th ed., Longman, London, 2003), pp.358–359 and 577; Cabinet Office, *National Intelligence Machinery* (2nd ed., HMSO, London, 2001), p.5.

[99] The annual Net Resource and Capital Requirements for the Single Intelligence Account and the security and intelligence services recorded at *Intelligence and Security Committee Annual Report 2002–2003* (Cm.5837) 2003, para.16 are: in 2001–2002, £938m resource and £108m capital (out-turns); in 2002–2003, £1,033m resource and £164m capital (estimates); and 2003–2004, £1,118m resource and £184m capital (forecasts). The Cabinet Secretary acted as Accounting Officer until August 1, 2002 when the role was transferred to the new Cabinet Office Permanent Secretary and Security and Intelligence Co-ordinator, Sir David Omand. The post of Security and Intelligence Co-ordinator was newly created at that time.

[1] Intelligence and Security Committee, *Intelligence Oversight* (London, 2002), p.8. Security Service Act 1989, s.2(3A)(b) permits the disclosure of information by the Security Service to the Comptroller and Auditor General. Intelligence Services Act 1994, ss.2(3)(b) and 4(3)(b) permit the disclosure of information by SIS and GCHQ respectively to the Comptroller and Auditor General.

(2) *The Intelligence Services Commissioner*. The Regulation of Investigatory Powers Act 2000 established a new combined Intelligence Services Commissioner in place of the former Security Service Commissioner and Intelligence Services Commissioner created under the Security Service Act 1989 and Intelligence Services Act 1994 respectively.[2] The Intelligence Services Commissioner is not listed as a "public authority" in Sch.1 to the Freedom of Information Act 2000. The Intelligence Services Commissioner is appointed by the Prime Minister to keep under review, so far as they are not required to be kept under review by the Interception of Communications Commissioner, the exercise and performance by the relevant Secretaries of State, the intelligence services, the Ministry of Defence and the armed forces of various functions relating to the issue of warrants authorising directed and intrusive surveillance, interferences with property and the use of covert human intelligence sources.[3] Those involved are obliged to provide the Intelligence Services Commissioner with all the information he needs and the Commissioner is in turn required to assist the RIPA Tribunal and report to the Prime Minister on particular subjects from time to time and provide him with annual reports which are presented to Parliament and published.[4]

(3) *The Interception of Communications Commissioner*. The Regulation of Investigatory Powers Act 2000 established a new Interception of Communications Commissioner in place of the identically named Commissioner established under the Interception of Communications Act 1985.[5] The Interception of Communications Commissioner is not listed as a "public authority" in Sch.1 to the Freedom of Information Act 2000. The Commissioner is appointed by the Prime Minister and his functions are to review the Secretary of State's role in authorising interception warrants, the operation of the regime for acquiring communications data, any notices requiring the decryption of data authorised by the Secretary of State and the adequacy of the arrangements made by the Secretary of State for the protection of intercepted

2 Regulation of Investigatory Powers Act 2000, ss.59–60. Security Service Act 1989, s.4 (establishing the Security Service Commissioner) and Intelligence Services Act 1994, s.8 (establishing the Intelligence Services Commissioner) were repealed by the Regulation of Investigatory Powers Act 2000, ss.59(8) and 82(2), Sch.5.

3 Regulation of Investigatory Powers Act 2000, s.59; Cabinet Office, *National Intelligence Machinery* (2nd ed., HMSO, London, 2001), p.24.

4 Regulation of Investigatory Powers Act 2000, ss.59(3) and 60. The published reports omit any matter whose publication would be contrary to the public interest or prejudicial to national security and other related interests.

5 Regulation of Investigating Powers Act 2000, ss.57–58 (replacing the Interception of Communications Commissioner established under the Interception of Communications Act 1985, s.8; see the Regulation of Investigatory Powers Act 2000, s.57(8)). See also Regulation of Investigatory Powers Act 2000, s.61 in relation to the Investigatory Powers Commissioner for Northern Ireland.

material.[6] All persons involved in requesting, authorising or carrying out interception are required to co-operate with the Interception of Communications Commissioner and provide him with any information he needs.[7] The Commissioner in turn reports to the Prime Minister on particular subjects from time to time and provides him with annual reports which are presented to Parliament and published.[8]

(4) *The Parliamentary Commissioner for Administration.* The Parliamentary Commissioner for Administration[9] has a limited role to play in relation to the oversight of the security bodies: none of the security bodies is directly subject to his investigative remit[10]; and, although their sponsoring departments are subject to such investigation,[11] various security and defence related matters are nevertheless excluded.[12] As a "public authority" listed in Pt VI of Sch.1 to the Freedom of Information Act 2000, the Parliamentary Commissioner for Administration may be asked to disclose information, but his ability to do so will be subject to the exemptions in Pt II of that Act and the provisions on onward disclosure in s.11 of the Parliamentary Commissioner Act 1967.[13] The Parliamentary Commissioner for Administration may also

6 Regulation of Investigatory Powers Act 2000, s.57; Cabinet Office, *National Intelligence Machinery* (2nd ed., HMSO, London, 2001), p.24.

7 Regulation of Investigatory Powers Act 2000, s.58.

8 Regulation of Investigation Powers Act 2000, s.58(4)–(7). The published reports omit any matter whose publication would be contrary to the public interest or prejudicial to national security and other related interests.

9 Parliamentary Commissioner Act 1967; *Halsbury's Laws of England* (4th ed.), Vol.1(1), title "Administrative Law", paras 41–44; A. Bradley and K. Ewing, *Constitutional and Administrative Law* (13th ed., Longman, London, 2003), pp.685–694; P. Jackson, *Hood Phillips and Jackson: Constitutional and Administrative Law* (8th ed., Sweet & Maxwell, London, 2001), paras 34–005 to 34–014.

10 None of the security bodies is listed as a government department, corporation or unincorporated body subject to investigation by the Commissioner in the Parliamentary Commissioner Act 1967, Sch.2 and it follows that action taken by or on behalf of the security bodies in the exercise of their administrative functions cannot be investigated under the Parliamentary Commissioner Act 1967, s.5.

11 Parliamentary Commissioner Act 1967, Sch.2. The list includes the Cabinet Office (not including any of the Secretariats, the Joint Intelligence Organisation or the office of the Secretary of the Cabinet and Head of the Home Civil Service: *ibid.*, n.6), Foreign and Commonwealth Office, Home Office and Ministry of Defence (including the Defence Council, Admiralty Board, Army Board and Air Force Board: *ibid.*, n.1).

12 Parliamentary Commissioner Act 1967, s.5, Sch.4, paras 1–5. The Parliamentary Commissioner Act 1967, s.11(3) does envisage the Commissioner having access to documents or information whose disclosure might be prejudicial to the safety of the State or otherwise contrary to the public interest and if he did investigate or obtain security or defence information he could, in theory, disclose it to others but only for certain specified purposes (including the purposes of the investigation in question and of any report to be made thereon) and subject also to any notices in writing given by a Minister of the Crown specifying documents or information or classes of documents or information whose disclosure would, in the opinion of the Minister, be prejudicial to the safety of the State or otherwise contrary to the public interest (s.11(2)–(3)).

13 These provisions effectively prevent the disclosure under the Freedom of Information Act 2000 of any information obtained by the Parliamentary Commissioner for Administration in the course of or for the purposes of an investigation under the Parliamentary Commissioner Act 1967. See also Freedom of Information Act 2000, s.44. The provisions on ministerial notices in Parliamentary Commissioner Act 1967, s.11(3) do not apply in relation to disclosures made by

exchange certain types of information with the Information Commissioner[14] and provide him with information which relates to certain matters within the Information Commissioner's remit or the commission of certain offences under the Freedom of Information Act 2000 or the Data Protection Act 1998.[15]

(5) *The Privy Council.* Issues of constitutional importance, including issues connected with security and defence matters, are sometimes referred to *ad hoc* committees of the Privy Council for advice. In this way, public service security arrangements,[16] the legal basis for and practice relating to telephone tapping[17] and government policy towards the Falkland Islands prior to Argentina's invasion in 1982 have been reviewed by such committees.[18] One reason for referring such matters to the Privy Council is that Privy Counsellors take an oath on appointment binding them not to disclose anything said or done "in Council"

---

the Parliamentary Commissioner for Administration under the Freedom of Information Act 2000, as they only operate to prevent the Parliamentary Commissioner Act 1967 from being construed as authorising or requiring the disclosure of any document or information specified in a relevant notice. This is unlikely to be significant, however, as Freedom of Information Act 2000, Pt II and Parliamentary Commissioner Act 1967, s.11(2) will almost inevitably prevent the disclosure of any information that might have been covered by a ministerial notice under Parliamentary Commissioner Act 1967, s.11(3).

14 Freedom of Information Act 2000, s.76(1) (disclosure by the Information Commissioner) and Parliamentary Commissioner Act 1967, s.11AA (disclosure by the Parliamentary Commissioner for Administration) (inserted by Freedom of Information Act 2000, Sch.7, para.2). The Information Commissioner may disclose to the Parliamentary Commissioner for Administration information obtained by, or furnished to, him under or for the purposes of the Freedom of Information Act 2000 or the Data Protection Act 1998 if it appears to him to relate to a matter which could be the subject of an investigation by the Parliamentary Commissioner for Administration (Freedom of Information Act 2000, s.76(1)). Information obtained by the Parliamentary Commissioner for Administration by virtue of this provision is nevertheless subject to Parliamentary Commissioner Act 1967, s.11(2)–(3) on onward disclosure and ministerial notices: Parliamentary Commissioner Act 1967, s.11(5), inserted by Freedom of Information Act 2000, Sch.7, para.1.

15 Parliamentary Commissioner Act 1967, s.11AA (inserted by Freedom of Information Act 2000, Sch.7, para.2). The disclosure of information by the Parliamentary Commissioner for Administration under this provision is nevertheless subject to Parliamentary Commissioner Act 1967, s.11(3) on ministerial notices (Parliamentary Commissioner Act 1967, s.11AA(2)). While such disclosure need not be made for a purpose specified in Parliamentary Commissioner Act 1967, s.11(2), a Minister of the Crown may prevent it by giving the Parliamentary Commissioner for Administration notice in writing under Parliamentary Commissioner Act 1967, s.11(3) that disclosure would, in his or her opinion, be prejudicial to the safety of the State or otherwise contrary to the public interest (see also Freedom of Information Act 2000, s.44).

16 This committee, convened in the aftermath of the Burgess and Maclean defections, was in fact referred to as a conference of Privy Counsellors. For the background see *Hansard*, HC, Vol.545, November 7, 1955, col.1609, and *Hansard*, HC, vol.546, November 23, 1955, col.1462. Its report was not published, but a summary was made public (Cmnd.9715) 1956.

17 The Birkett Committee Report (Cmnd.283) 1957.

18 *Falkland Islands Review: Report of a Committee of Privy Counsellors* (Cmnd.8787) 1983. The Prime Minister, Mrs Thatcher, consulted five former Prime Ministers to secure their consent to the committee on Falkland Islands policy having access to the papers of previous governments and secret intelligence assessments. See: A. Bradley and K. Ewing, *Constitutional and Administrative Law* (13th ed., Longman, London, 2003), pp.245 and 266–267; Lord Hunt, "Access to a Previous Government's Papers", [1982] P.L. 514; *Hansard*, HC, Vol.26, July 1, 1982, col.1039; *Hansard*, HC, Vol.27, July 8 1982, col.469.

without the consent of the Sovereign and sensitive information can therefore be disclosed to them on "Privy Counsellor terms."[19] A further reason is that committees of the Privy Council can be political and yet non-partisan and can also examine the work of past or multiple administrations.[20] It would appear that the Privy Council is not a "public authority" for the purposes of the Freedom of Information Act 2000.[21]

(6) *The Intelligence and Security Committee.* The Intelligence and Security Committee was established under the Intelligence Services Act 1994 to examine the expenditure, administration and policy of the intelligence services.[22] The Committee operates within the so-called "ring of secrecy," which means that the members of the Committee and its Secretariat are formally notified that they are subject to the provisions of s.1 of the Official Secrets Act 1989.[23] The Committee makes an annual report on the discharge of the functions of the intelligence services to the Prime Minister and may at any time report to him on any matter relating to the discharge of those functions.[24] The Prime Minister then publishes the annual reports by laying a copy before each House of Parliament,[25] although he may exclude from the published report any

---

[19] *Halsbury's Laws of England* (4th ed.), Vol.8(2), title "Constitutional Law and Human Rights", para.523; A. Bradley and K. Ewing, *Constitutional and Administrative Law* (13th ed., Longman, London, 2003), pp.244–245; P. Jackson, *Hood Phillips and Jackson: Constitutional and Administrative Law* (8th ed., Sweet & Maxwell, London, 2001), para.16–003.

[20] I. Leigh and L. Lustgarten, "The Security Commission: Constitutional Achievement or Curiosity" [1991] P.L. 215 at 216.

[21] The Privy Council is not listed in the Freedom of Information Act 2000, Sch.1 and it cannot easily be described as a "body or authority exercising statutory functions on behalf of the Crown" and thus a "government department" for the purposes of s.84, Sch.1, Pt I, para.1. However, the Privy Council Office which, under the Lord President of the Council, is responsible for preparing business for the Privy Council and its committees has been described as, to a certain extent, "a real administrative department": *Halsbury's Laws of England* (4th ed.), Vol.8(2), title "Constitutional Law and Human Rights", para.526. See also para.17–010, n.65 on the "immunity" of certain Crown bodies from the provisions of the Freedom of Information Act 2000.

[22] Intelligence Services Act 1994, s.10(1), Sch.3. The Intelligence and Security Committee has published a guide to its work: *Intelligence Oversight* (London, 2002), and it has a website *www.cabinet-office.gov.uk/intelligence*. See also: *Halsbury's Laws of England* (4th ed.), Vol. 8(2), title "Constitutional Law and Human Rights", para.475; A. Bradley and K. Ewing, *Constitutional and Administrative Law* (13th ed., Longman, London, 2003), pp.600–601; Cabinet Office, *National Intelligence Machinery* (2nd ed., HMSO, London, 2001), p.23.

[23] Official Secrets Act 1989, s.1(1)(b) and (6)–(8). This was confirmed by the Foreign Secretary, Mr Hurd, at the press conference on publication of the Intelligence Services Bill on November 23, 1993 and the Chancellor of the Duchy of Lancaster, Mr Waldegrave, subsequently told the House of Commons "The Committee will be fully trusted, and fully inside the secret wall" (*Hansard*, HC, Vol.238, February 22, 1994, col.240). See: Wadham, "The Intelligence Services Act 1994" (1994) 57 M.L.R. 916, pp.926–927; *Intelligence and Security Committee Interim Report 1994–1995* (Cm.2873) 1995; A. Bradley and K. Ewing, *Constitutional and Administrative Law* (13th ed., Longman, London, 2003), p.600; Cabinet Office, *National Intelligence Machinery* (2nd ed., HMSO, London, 2001), p.23; *Intelligence and Security Committee Annual Report 2002–2003* (Cm.5837) 2003, para.2.

[24] Intelligence Services Act 1994, s.10(5).

[25] Intelligence Services Act 1994, s.10(6). In practice, at least some of the non-annual reports on specific subjects are also published in the same way.

matter whose publication would be prejudicial to the continued discharge of the functions of the intelligence services.[26] The Committee is given access to information unless it is "sensitive" or the Secretary of State has determined that it appears to him to be of such a nature that it would not be disclosed to a Departmental Select Committee.[27] The Committee is not a Parliamentary Select Committee as such, but it consists of nine members of Parliament drawn from both Houses of Parliament who are not Ministers of the Crown and who are appointed by the Prime Minister, after consultation with the Leader of the Opposition, on a cross-party basis.[28] Since June 1999, the Committee have also had their own Investigator who they can deploy to pursue specific matters in greater detail.[29] The Foreign and Home Secretaries have both signed a certificate under s.28 of the Data Protection Act 1998 in relation to personal data processed by the Intelligence and Security Committee and its Secretariat.[30] The Committee is not listed as a "public authority" in Sch.1 to the Freedom of Information Act 2000.

(7) *The Ministerial and Permanent Secretaries' Committees on the Intelligence Services*. The Ministerial Committee on the Intelligence Services is chaired by the Prime Minister, further comprises the Deputy Prime Minister, the Defence, Foreign and Home Secretaries and the Chancellor of the Exchequer and has the following terms of reference: "to keep under review policy on the security and intelligence services."[31] The

---

[26] Intelligence Services Act 1994, s.10(6)–(7).

[27] Intelligence Services Act 1994, Sch.3, para.3. "Sensitive information" is defined by Sch.3, para.4 as (a) information which might lead to the identification of, or provide details of, sources of information, other assistance or operational methods available to the intelligence services, (b) information about particular operations which have been, are being or are being proposed to be undertaken in pursuance of any of the functions of those bodies and (c) information provided by, or by an agency of, the Government of a territory outside the United Kingdom where that Government does not consent to the disclosure of the information. Such information may still be disclosed to the Committee if the head of the relevant intelligence service considers it safe to do so or the Secretary of State considers it desirable in the public interest (Sch.3, para.3(2)–(3)). The bases on which information may be withheld from Select Committees are set out in the Cabinet Office Memorandum expressing the "Osmotherly Rules" *Departmental Evidence and Response to Select Committees* (1999); see esp. paras 80–87 which allow for the provision to Select Committees of "sensitive information, including that carrying a protective security marking," on the basis that it will not be published and will be treated in confidence.

[28] Intelligence Services Act 1994, s.10(2)–(3). The Committee has been described as "A committee of Parliamentarians, but emphatically not a committee of Parliament" (HC 300) 1999–2000, para.90.

[29] The introduction of an Investigator was proposed by the Intelligence and Security Committee (see *Intelligence and Security Committee Annual Report 1997–1998* (Cm.4073) 1998, para.69 and *Intelligence and Security Committee Annual Report 1998–1999* (Cm.4532) 1999, paras 84–86) and accepted by the government subject to arrangements set out by the Prime Minister in *Government Response to the Intelligence and Security Committee's Annual Report 1998–1999* (Cm.4569) 2000, para.34. See also Intelligence and Security Committee, *Intelligence Oversight* (London, 2002), p.9.

[30] *Intelligence and Security Committee Annual Report 2001–2002* (Cm.5542) 2002, paras 49–50 and Appendix 2.

[31] Cabinet Office, *National Intelligence Machinery* (2nd ed., HMSO, London, 2001), p.12.

Ministerial Committee is itself assisted by the Permanent Secretaries' Committee on the Intelligence Services, which is chaired by the Cabinet Office Security and Intelligence Co-ordinator and which provides advice periodically on intelligence collection requirements, the intelligence services' programmes and expenditure and other issues related to intelligence.[32] The Intelligence and Security Committee has, however, reported that the Ministerial Committee very rarely meets, that ministers prefer to meet on an *ad hoc* basis to discuss particular crises and that they are not sufficiently engaged in the setting of requirements and priorities for secret intelligence.[33] Neither of these Committees is formally excluded from the Freedom of Information Act 2000 regime: they would appear to be parts of the Cabinet Office, which is a public authority for the purposes of Sch.1 to that Act.[34]

Other parts of the national intelligence machinery

One notable feature of the approach taken to the security bodies is the omission from the list specified in s.23(3) of the Freedom of Information Act 2000 of two other bodies which undoubtedly deal with security matters and which complete the government's "national intelligence machinery",[35] namely, the Defence Intelligence Staff ("DIS") and the Joint Intelligence Committee ("JIC"):[36] 17–025

(1) *The Defence Intelligence Staff*. In the official government publication *National Intelligence Machinery* the DIS is dealt with under the heading, "the intelligence and security agencies", but treated not as a fourth

[32] *ibid*. The Cabinet Secretary acted as Chairman of the Committee until August 1, 2002, when the duty was transferred to the new Cabinet Office Permanent Secretary and Security and Intelligence Co-ordinator, Sir David Omand. The post of Security and Intelligence Co-ordinator was newly created at that time.

[33] *Intelligence and Security Committee Annual Report 1999–2000* (Cm.4897) 2000, para.19; *Intelligence and Security Committee Interim Report 2000–2001* (Cm.5126) 2001, para.15; *Intelligence and Security Committee Annual Report 2001–2002* (Cm.5542) 2002, paras 10–11; *Intelligence and Security Committee Annual Report 2002–2003* (Cm.5837) 2003, paras 54–57. See also: *Government Response to the Intelligence and Security Committee's Annual Report 1999–2000* (Cm.5013) 2000, paras 5–6; *Government Response to the Intelligence and Security Committee's Annual Report 2001–2002* (Cm.5543) 2002, para.20; *Government Response to the Intelligence and Security Committee's Annual Report 2002–2003* (Cm.5838) 2003, para.10.

[34] Freedom of Information Act 2000, s.84 and Sch.1, Pt I, para.1. The Ministerial Committee on the Intelligence Services may also be a "committee of the Cabinet" for the purposes of the Freedom of Information Act 2000, s.35(4).

[35] *Intelligence and Security Committee Annual Report 1999–2000* (Cm.4897) 2000, paras 17–23; *Government Response to the Intelligence and Security Committee's Annual Report 1999–2000* (Cm.5013) 2000, paras 5–9; Cabinet Office, *National Intelligence Machinery* (2nd ed., HMSO, London, 2001); *Intelligence and Security Committee Annual Report 2001–2002* (Cm.5542) 2002, paras 8–12.

[36] For these purposes, references to the JIC should be read as a compendious short-hand for the entirety of the central intelligence machinery within the Cabinet Office which comprises the JIC itself, the Chairman of the JIC and Intelligence Co-ordinator, the Security and Intelligence Co-ordinator and the Joint Intelligence Organisation.

intelligence service as such, but as an "important contributor to" and "an essential element" of the national intelligence machinery.[37] The DIS is a part of the Ministry of Defence funded out of the Defence Votes that was created in 1964 by the amalgamation of the Navy, Army and Air Force intelligence staffs and the civilian Joint Intelligence Bureau.[38] The DIS does not have any statutory basis or identity but its tasks are to analyse information, from both overt and covert sources, and to provide intelligence assessments, advice and strategic warning to the JIC, the Ministry of Defence, military commands and deployed forces.[39] The DIS also has responsibility for two Defence Agencies, the Defence Geographic and Imagery Intelligence Agency and the Defence Intelligence and Security Centre, which are responsible for providing imagery, geographic products and intelligence training.[40] The Defence Secretary is responsible for the DIS and its operations are controlled by the Chief of Defence Intelligence who reports to the Chief of the Defence Staff and the Permanent Secretary of the Ministry of Defence and who is also Deputy Chairman of the JIC.[41]

(2) *The Joint Intelligence Committee*. The JIC is a part of the Cabinet Office under the authority of the Cabinet Secretary which also has no statutory basis or identity.[42] The JIC comprises senior officials in the Foreign and Commonwealth Office, Home Office, Ministry of Defence, Department of Trade and Industry and HM Treasury, the heads of the intelligence services and its Deputy Chairman, the Chief of Defence Intelligence. The JIC is designed to bring an overall coherence to the tasking of the intelligence services, the assessment of their product and the determination of their resource needs and performance.[43] To this end, the JIC has two main functions, first, it produces assessments using secret intelligence and open source material for ministers and officials and, secondly, it establishes the government's requirements and priorities for secret intelligence. The JIC thus advises

[37] Cabinet Office, *National Intelligence Machinery* (2nd ed., HMSO, London, 2001), pp.5 and 11. See: *Inquiry into the Export of Defence Equipment and Dual Use Goods to Iraq and Related Prosecutions* (HC 115) 1995–1996, para.C2.26 (Scott Report); A. Bradley and K. Ewing, Constitutional and Administrative Law (13th ed., Longman, London, 2003), pp.579–580. See also the information on the Ministry of Defence website *www.mod.uk/aboutus/factfiles/dis.htm*.

[38] Cabinet Office, *National Intelligence Machinery* (2nd ed., HMSO, London, 2001), p.11. This followed the enactment of the Defence (Transfer of Functions) Act 1964 and the creation of a unified Secretary of State for Defence and Ministry of Defence: *Halsbury's Laws of England* (4th ed.), Vol.8(2), title "Constitutional Law and Human Rights", paras 439–447.

[39] Cabinet Office, *National Intelligence Machinery* (2nd ed., HMSO, London, 2001), p.11.

[40] *ibid.*

[41] Cabinet Office, *National Intelligence Machinery* (2nd ed., HMSO, London, 2001), pp.11–12.

[42] Parliamentary Commissioner Act 1967, Sch.2, n.6 formally acknowledges the existence of the Joint Intelligence Organisation in providing that the Cabinet Office does not include, for the purposes of its being a department subject to investigation by the Parliamentary Commissioner for Administration, "any of the Secretariats, the Joint Intelligence Organisation or the office of the Secretary of the Cabinet and Head of the Home Civil Service."

[43] Cabinet Office, *National Intelligence Machinery* (2nd ed., HMSO, London, 2001), p.15.

on priorities for intelligence gathering and provides ministers and senior officials with assessments of the resulting intelligence in the fields of security, defence and foreign affairs and is supported by the Joint Intelligence Organisation.[44] The Chairman of the JIC and Intelligence Co-ordinator is responsible for ensuring the proper and effective functioning of the JIC and to this end he has direct access to the Prime Minister and works closely with the Cabinet Office Security and Intelligence Co-ordinator.[45]

Neither the DIS nor the JIC is listed as a "public authority" in Sch.1 to the Freedom of Information Act 2000 but, as already mentioned, they are parts of the Ministry of Defence and Cabinet Office respectively which are both "public authorities" for these purposes.[46] It follows that neither the DIS nor the JIC is institutionally excluded from the Freedom of Information Act 2000 regime.

3. INFORMATION SUPPLIED BY, OR RELATING TO, THE SECURITY BODIES

Terms of the exemption in section 23 of the Freedom of Information Act 2000

As already indicated, information held by a public authority which was directly or indirectly supplied to it by, or which relates to, a security body is subject to an absolute exemption under s.23 of the Freedom of Information Act 2000.[47] 17–026

[44] Cabinet Office, *National Intelligence Machinery* (2nd ed., HMSO, London, 2001), pp.15–17. The JIC's full terms of reference are as follows: "The Committee is charged with the following responsibilities: under the broad supervisory responsibility of the Permanent Secretaries' Committee on the Intelligence Services, to give direction to, and to keep under review, the organisation and working of British intelligence activity as a whole at home and overseas in order to ensure efficiency, economy and prompt adaptation to changing requirements; to submit, at agreed intervals, for approval by Ministers, statements of the requirements and priorities for intelligence gathering and other tasks to be conducted by the Intelligence Agencies; to co-ordinate, as necessary, interdepartmental plans for activity; to monitor and give early warning of the development of direct or indirect foreign threats to British interests, whether political, military or economic; on the basis of available information, to assess events and situations relating to external affairs, defence, terrorism, major international criminal activity, scientific, technical and international economic matters; to keep under review threats to security at home and overseas and to deal with such security problems as may be referred to it; to maintain and supervise liaison with Commonwealth and foreign intelligence organisations as appropriate, and to consider the extent to which its product can be made available to them" (*ibid*., p.19).

[45] Cabinet Office, *National Intelligence Machinery* (2nd ed., HMSO, London, 2001), p.16.

[46] They are both "government departments" within the Freedom of Information Act 2000, s.84 and Sch.1, Pt I, para.1.

[47] Once a record containing particular information directly or indirectly supplied by, or relating to, a security body has been transferred to the Public Record Office ("PRO") or the PRO of Northern Ireland in accordance with the Public Records Act 1958 or the Public Records Act (Northern Ireland) 1923, the exemption conferred on that information by the Freedom of Information Act

Section 1 of the Freedom of Information Act 2000 does not apply in respect of such information and the duty to confirm or deny and the duty to communicate do not arise.[48] So far as concerns the duty to confirm or deny, public authorities need not inform applicants whether they hold information covered by the s.23 exemption if, or to the extent that, this would itself involve the disclosure of information which was directly or indirectly supplied by, or which relates to, a security body, whether or not that information is already recorded.[49] In this regard, the significance of the words "whether or not already recorded" comes about because the term "information" would otherwise be confined to information recorded in any form.[50] Having said this, public authorities cannot avoid specifying the exemption relied upon when refusing to divulge or communicate information in reliance on s.23 and this could itself prove revealing.[51] The exemption in s.23 of the Freedom of Information Act 2000 applies irrespective of whether the information in question is confidential, known to the applicant or wholly non-confidential.[52]

The direct or indirect supply of information by the security bodies

17–027 For information supplied to a public authority by a security body to be caught by the exemption in s.23 of the Freedom of Information Act 2000 it need not have been obtained by the security body in the exercise of any particular function or supplied by it in writing or in confidence. It is clear that the public authority holding the information need not have had it supplied directly by the security body: it may have passed through a number of hands before indirectly reaching that authority. There is no requirement that the information should have originated with the security body: it must simply have been supplied by that body to a third party on its way to the recipient public authority. One result

2000, s.23 ceases to be absolute. As a result, the Freedom of Information Act 2000, s.1 will not apply in respect of such information, and the duty to confirm or deny and the duty to communicate will not arise, only if the public interest in maintaining the exclusion of the relevant duty outweighs the public interest in divulging whether the public authority holds the information or in disclosing the information itself: s.64(2). The latter provision achieves this outcome by providing that, in relation to any information falling within s.23(1) which is contained in a historical record in the PRO or the PRO of Northern Ireland, s.2(3) shall have effect with the omission of the reference to s.23. It is also important to bear in mind here that information contained in a historical record in the PRO or the PRO of Northern Ireland cannot be exempt information by virtue of ss.21–22: s.64(1). In relation to historical records, see paras 6–028 to 6–038.

[48] Freedom of Information Act 2000, s.23(1) engages s.2(2)(a) and (3)(b) so as to prevent the duty to communicate from arising in respect of the exempt information. Freedom of Information Act 2000, s.23(5) engages s.2(1)(a) and (3)(b) so as to prevent the duty to confirm or deny from arising in relation to the exempt information.

[49] Freedom of Information Act 2000, s.23(5).

[50] *ibid.*, s.84.

[51] *ibid.*, s.17(1)(b) and (5). See further paras 17–041 to 17–045.

[52] See para.17–038 in relation to the relevance of confidentiality to the application of Freedom of Information Act 2000, s.24.

of this is that where the same piece of information reaches authority "A" via a security body and authority "B" by some other non-security body route, it will be exempt from disclosure by authority "A" under s.23 but available from authority "B" as of right unless it relates to a security body or is subject to some other exemption in Pt II of the Act. Another result is that a public authority which has received the same piece of information quite independently from both a security body and a non-security body, such as a member of the public, may nevertheless have to conclude that it is exempt under s.23. Lastly, there may be circumstances where a security body forwards information without assessing its contents or considering its dissemination in an active way or where the security body has no intention or desire that it should end up in the hands of the public authority in question: questions could then arise as to whether this has involved a meaningful act of "supply to" that public authority "by" the security body for the purposes of s.23.

Meaning of "relates to"

Whether information "relates to" a security body will be a mixed question of fact and law. The expression is not defined further in the Freedom of Information Act 2000 and will therefore be given its ordinary natural meaning.[53] In this regard, information which relates to a security body's sources, methods, activities, plans or members, will presumably be treated as relating to that body. Some assistance in relation to these questions may be derived from existing authorities on issues of "respection" which have arisen in relation to the legislative competence of devolved or colonial legislatures. In this regard s.4(1) of the Government of Ireland Act 1920 (now repealed) prevented the old Parliament of Northern Ireland from making laws "in respect of" certain excepted matters and formulations of this kind in turn gave rise to the use of the term "respection." In this way, words of respection such as "in respect of", "in relation to" and "dealing with" describe the nature and extent of the connection between a law and particular permitted or, more usually, prohibited subject matters. As a matter of ordinary construction, the "doctrine of dual respection" applies in relation to such expressions, that is to say, it is generally accepted that laws can "relate to" more than one matter.[54] Applying these principles, one would say that information "relates to" a security body if it is respected towards or deals 17–028

[53] See further the discussion and authorities at para.22–007.

[54] See *R. (Hume) v Londonderry Justices* [1972] N.I. 91, DC at 110–113 (*per* Lowry C.J.) (in relation to the Government of Ireland Act 1920, s.4) approving the analysis put forward in H. Calvert *Constitutional Law in Northern Ireland: a study in regional government* (Stevens, London, 1968), pp.187–196 and rejecting the approach taken in *Gallagher v Lynn* [1937] A.C. 863, HL where the "doctrine of pith and substance" (applied in *Russell v The Queen* (1882) 7 App. Cas. 829, PC in relation to the Constitution Act 1867 formerly the British North America Act 1867) was applied at 870 (*per* Lord Atkin). The doctrine of pith and substance evolved in relation to the Constitution Act 1867 because that Act required that a law had to "relate to" a particular matter within the exclusive area of either dominion or provincial legislative competence.

with that body (together with other matters) in a reasonably directed or targeted and non-incidental way. It must do more than merely "touch on" the body in question, but it need not be "solely or mainly" concerned with or focused on that body or have that body as its "pith and substance."

Where the absence of information relating to the security bodies is itself information which relates to those bodies

17–029 In certain circumstances, the fact that a public authority does not hold information which was supplied to it by, or which relates to, a security body could itself reveal the lack of any security body involvement in the subject matter of the relevant information request. The question may therefore arise as to whether the disclosure of the requested information (without reference to or reliance on s.23) will thus involve the disclosure of exempt information falling within s.23 of the Freedom of Information Act 2000. The answer to this may lie in the approach taken to the meaning of "information"[55] in s.23(1)–(2) and the effect of the reference to "information (whether or not already recorded)" in s.23(5). This can be demonstrated by reference to two hypothetical requests for information made to a government department or police authority regarding the involvement of the security bodies in a particular operation: request A asks for a list of every agency that was involved and request B asks for a list of every security body that was involved. If a security body was involved in the operation, the department or authority can respond to both requests with a partial list and a partial refusal notice which states that the authority is not obliged to confirm or deny whether it holds information relating to the involvement of the security bodies or to disclose any such information by virtue of s.23. If no security bodies were involved in the operation, however, the department or authority could only respond in the same fashion if it holds information "recorded in any form" which confirms the non-involvement of the security bodies[56] or if the fact that the security bodies were not involved is "information (whether or not already recorded)" which relates to them for the purposes of s.23(5).

A strained construction and search for each law's single pith and substance was thus required but in the absence of exceptional circumstances requiring such an approach, the doctrine of dual respection will ordinarily apply. Note the gloss on "relates to" in the Scotland Act 1998, s.29(3), the general clarification of "deals with" in the Northern Ireland Act 1998, s.98(2) and the specific qualification of "deals with" in the Northern Ireland Act 1998, Sch.2, para.22 and Sch.3, para.42.

[55] In the default sense of "information recorded in any form": Freedom of Information Act 2000, s.84. As to the meaning of "information" as it is otherwise used in the Act, see paras 7–002 to 7–007.

[56] Freedom of Information Act 2000, s.1(4) would prevent the department or authority from generating a record of security body non-involvement (following receipt of the information request) simply to enable it to say that it therefore holds recorded information relating to the security bodies.

Information which relates to GCHQ and the special forces: identities over time

The terms of the Freedom of Information Act 2000 allow scope for the composition of both GCHQ and the special forces to change over time as different units of the armed forces are transferred to or from duties assisting GCHQ or the remit of the Director of Special Forces.[57] Whether or not such transfers take place at all often in practice, questions could arise as to whether a unit of the armed forces was a part of GCHQ or the special forces at the time it supplied certain information or as to whether information relating to that unit relates to, or has ceased to relate to, GCHQ or the special forces for the purposes of s.23 of the Freedom of Information Act 2000. The relevant references to units of the armed forces being part of GCHQ or the special forces "for the time being" tend to suggest that what matters is their status as such when the information request is made. So far as concerns the supply of information, what matters for the purposes of s.23 is that the unit of the armed forces which directly or indirectly supplied the information to the public authority was a part of GCHQ or the special forces at the time it did so. The question which s.23 appears to pose, namely whether information currently relates to any of the security bodies, is capable of raising more complicated issues. On a straightforward reading, information relating to sensitive work done by a unit of the armed forces at a time when it was a part of GCHQ or the special forces will cease to be exempt under s.23 once that unit ceases to be a part of GCHQ or the special forces. By the same token, information relating to non-sensitive work done by a unit of the armed forces at a time when it was not a part of GCHQ or the special forces will be exempt under s.23 once it becomes a part of GCHQ or the special forces. These outcomes may seem counter-intuitive at first blush because the 17–030

[57] In relation to GCHQ, see Freedom of Information Act 2000, ss.23(4) and 84 (definition of "government department") and Sch.1, Pt I, para.6(b) and note that by virtue of s.23(4) GCHQ in s.23(3)(c) includes units or parts of units of the armed forces which are "for the time being" required to assist GCHQ. Although there is no obvious reason why the Freedom of Information Act 2000, s.23(4) (and the Intelligence Services Act 1994, s.3(3)) refer to units of the armed forces assisting GCHQ "in carrying out its functions" while the Freedom of Information Act 2000, Sch.1, Pt I, para.6(b) refers to them assisting GCHQ "in the exercise of its functions", it is submitted that the different formulations are intended to have the same meaning and effect. In relation to the special forces, see Freedom of Information Act 2000, s.84 (definition of "the special forces") and Sch.1, Pt I, para.6(a) and note that the special forces are those units of the armed forces (no allowance is made for parts of units) the maintenance of whose capabilities is the responsibility of the Director of Special Forces (the words "for the time being" are not included) or which are "for the time being" subject to the operational command of that Director. So far as concerns the words "for the time being" being applied in relation to those units subject to the operational command of the Director of Special Forces but not in relation to those units the maintenance of whose capabilities is the responsibility of that Director, for the latter type of unit to be a part of the special forces it must nevertheless be true to say that the maintenance of its capabilities "*is* the responsibility of the Director of Special Forces." It would therefore appear that the use or non-use of "for the time being" is not of great significance and may simply reflect the fact that periods of "operational command" can be of varying length whilst the maintenance of a unit's capabilities will tend to be a more long-term responsibility.

sensitive information is left unprotected and the non-sensitive information is exempt. However, past membership of GCHQ or the special forces, possibly for a very short period, cannot confer permanent "security body" status under s.23 and the past *modus operandi* of a unit which has since assumed more sensitive duties may well require protection. In practice, of course, the type of information likely to be affected by such questions will very often "relate to" the unchanging core of GCHQ or the special forces in any event and, if not exempted by s.23, there may yet be a role for ss.24 and 26 of the Freedom of Information Act 2000.

Public authorities likely to hold information supplied by, or relating to, the security bodies

17–031 It should be clear from the functions of the security bodies set out above that numerous public authorities listed in Sch.1 to the Freedom of Information Act 2000 will hold information which was supplied to them by, or which relates to, those bodies. Candidates include: major ministerial departments of state such as the Cabinet Office, Department for International Development, Department of Trade and Industry, Foreign and Commonwealth Office, Home Office, Legal Secretariat to the Law Officers, Ministry of Defence, Northern Ireland Office and HM Treasury; the armed forces of the Crown; non-ministerial departments and agencies such as HM Customs and Excise, the Treasury Solicitor's Department and the Defence Vetting Agency; law enforcement agencies and prosecuting authorities such as the police, National Crime Squad, Crown Prosecution Service and Serious Fraud Office; regulatory and financial bodies such as the Bank of England and the Financial Services Authority; oversight bodies such as the National Audit Office and the Parliamentary Commissioner for Administration; and a number of other public authorities such as the Armed Forces Pay Review Body, the Civil Service Appeal Board, the Defence Nuclear Safety Committee, the Diplomatic Service Appeal Board, the Imperial War Museum, the National Army Museum, the National Maritime Museum, the Royal Air Force Museum and the United Kingdom Atomic Energy Authority.

Selection of the security bodies and treatment of other associated bodies

17–032 The selection of the security bodies specified in s.23(3) of the Freedom of Information Act 2000 and the omission of other similar bodies raises some questions about the purpose and effect of s.23. In relation to the principal security bodies, the question arises as to why the DIS and JIC are not also institutionally excluded from the Freedom of Information Act 2000 regime. In relation to the RIPA, IOCA, SSA and ISA Tribunals, the Security Vetting Appeals Panel and the Security Commission, the question arises as to why information supplied by, or relating to, the Interception of Communications Commissioner, the Intelligence and Security Committee and the Intelligence Services Commissioner, (which have similar oversight functions and are also not "public authorities" for the purposes of the Freedom of Information Act 2000), is not also subject to the s.23 exemption. In relation to NCIS and its Service Authority, the question arises as to why the National Crime Squad and its Service Authority and the various police Special Branches are not also excluded from the Freedom of Information Act 2000 regime. In constitutional terms, the answer must be that the selection of the security bodies and the treatment of other associated bodies in the Freedom of Information Act 2000 reflects an overall policy judgement as to the competing public interests involved. For example, NCIS and the National Crime Squad are closely related and similar in many ways, but it is apparent from the Security Service Act 1989 and the Police Act 1997 that NCIS is more closely allied to the Security Service than the National Crime Squad[58] and this presumably tipped the balance in favour of its designation as a security body. The difference of approach between, on the one hand, the other ancillary security bodies, and, on the other hand, the DIS, JIC, Interception of Communications Commissioner, Intelligence and Security Committee and Intelligence Services Commissioner, is more difficult to explain: although it is easy to imagine in relation to the latter group that their designation as security bodies for the purposes of s.23 of the Freedom of Information Act 2000 would not have added much to its impact, it is more difficult to imagine that the non-designation of the former group would have diluted that impact to a significant degree.

4. INFORMATION WHOSE EXEMPTION IS REQUIRED FOR NATIONAL SECURITY PURPOSES

Terms of the exemption in section 24 of the Freedom of Information Act 2000

As already indicated, information held by a public authority which was not directly or indirectly supplied to it by, and which does not relate to, any of the security bodies is subject to a qualified exemption under s.24 of the Freedom of Information Act 2000 if this is required for the purpose of safeguarding 17–033

[58] While the Security Service acts in support of police forces, NCIS, the National Crime Squad and other law enforcement agencies (Security Service Act 1989, s.1(4)) the Director-General of the Security Service only needs to agree formal arrangements for providing this support with the Director General of NCIS (Security Service Act 1989, s.2(2)(c)). Moreover, while the NCIS Service Authority and the National Crime Squad Service Authority have a common core membership as outlined above (Police Act 1997, ss.1, 46–47, 90 and Sch.1, Pt I) only the NCIS Service Authority is statutorily required to include a member of the Security Service (Police Act 1997, s.1(7) and Sch.1, Pt II, para.7(c)).

national security. However, the detailed terms of the exemption require closer examination:

(1) Section 24(1) renders information that does not fall within s.23(1) (*i.e.* information which was not directly or indirectly supplied by, and does not relate to, any of the security bodies) exempt information if or to the extent that exemption from the duty to communicate is required for the purpose of safeguarding national security. The exemption is a qualified exemption, so that even if information falls within the description of the exemption (and is thus exempt information) it is then necessary to consider whether in all the circumstances the public interest favours disclosure of the information or maintenance of the exemption.[59] The fact that the exemption is qualified implies that there may be instances in which it will be in the public interest to disclose information, notwithstanding that exemption is required for the purpose of safeguarding national security.[60]

(2) Section 24(2) provides that "the duty to confirm or deny does not arise if, or to the extent that, exemption from s.1(1)(a) is required for the purpose of safeguarding national security." Unlike s.24(1), this limb of the national security exemption is not expressed to apply only to "information which does not fall within s.23(1)." Indeed s.24(2) is not expressed to relate to any particular category of information and it does not itself stand as a "provision" which "states that the duty to confirm or deny does not arise in relation to any information" for the purposes of s.2(1). As it was plainly not the intention that s.24(2) should operate independently of s.2(1),[61] s.24(2) must nevertheless be made to interact with s.2(1). This can be achieved by reading s.24 as a whole for the purposes of s.2(1), so that s.24 is itself a "provision" which "states that the duty to confirm or deny does not arise in relation to any information."[62] On this basis, s.24 provides that the duty to confirm or deny

[59] Freedom of Information Act 2000, s.2(2)(b).

[60] Otherwise the exemption will be effectively metamorphosed into an absolute exemption.

[61] The same can be said of all the other provisions in Pt II which state that the duty to confirm or deny does not arise without stating that this is the case "in relation to any information", *i.e.* Freedom of Information Act 2000, ss.22(2), 26(3), 27(4)(a), 28(3), 29(3), 31(3), 33(3), 34(2), 38(2), 41(2), 43(3) and 44(2); *cf.* ss.23(5), 27(4)(b), 30(3), 32(3), 35(3), 36(3), 37(2), 39(2) and 42(2).

[62] Reading the Freedom of Information Act 2000, ss.2(1) and 24(1)–(2) together in this way is consistent with s.2(3) in two respects: first, s.2(3) treats whole sections as "provisions in Part II" for the purposes of s.2(1)–(2); and, secondly, s.2(3) does not designate s.24 as conferring absolute exemption and it is therefore clear that s.24 was intended to confer a qualified exemption subject to a public interest balancing test, which in turn requires that s.24(2) should engage s.2(1). It is further clear from Freedom of Information Act 2000, s.24(3) that s.24(2) was not meant to operate independently of s.24(1): national security certificates under s.24(3) may certify that exemption from s.1(1)(b) is or was required for national security reasons (*i.e.* a duty to communicate certificate under s.24(1)) or that exemption from both s.1(1)(a) and (b) is or was required for national security reasons (*i.e.* a duty to confirm or deny and duty to communicate certificate under s.24(1) and (2)). The equivalent provision in the draft Freedom of Information Bill at *Freedom of Information: Consultation on Draft Legislation* (Cm.4355) 1999, Pt II (*i.e.* cl.19(2)) was

does not arise in relation to information which does not fall within s.23(1) (*i.e.* information which was not directly or indirectly supplied by, and does not relate to, any of the security bodies) if, or to the extent that, exemption from s.1(1)(a) is required for the purpose of safeguarding national security. Again, the exclusion is a qualified one, so that even if the terms of s.24(2) are satisfied (and thus the duty to confirm or deny does not arise) it is then necessary to consider whether in all the circumstances the public interest favours confirmation or denial or maintenance of the exclusion.[63] The fact that the exclusion is qualified implies that there may be instances in which it will be in the public interest to divulge the existence of information, notwithstanding that exclusion of that duty is required for the purpose of safeguarding national security.

Terms of the exemption in section 28 of the Data Protection Act 1998

As also indicated above, s.28 of the Data Protection Act 1998 exempts personal data from the provisions of the data protection principles and Pts II–III and V and s.55 of the Data Protection Act 1998 (which include the subject-access right) if exemption from the relevant provision is required for the purpose of safeguarding national security. Personal data may therefore be exempt from the right of access under s.7 of the Data Protection Act 1998, other related rights and the regulatory requirements of the regime of that Act if this is required for the purpose of safeguarding national security. The national security exemption in s.28 of the Data Protection Act 1998 does not operate, and cannot be overridden, by reference to any public interest balancing test. 17–034

Meaning of "national security"

The expression "national security" is not defined in the Freedom of Information Act 2000 or the Data Protection Act 1998 and it has not been the subject of exhaustive definition in any other statutes or judicial decisions.[64] A number of general themes can, however, be extracted from a variety of sources: 17–035

more explicit in this regard: "In relation to information which is exempt information by virtue of subsection (1), the duty to confirm or deny does not arise if, or to the extent that, exemption from section 8(1)(a) is required for the purpose of safeguarding national security." The opening words "[I]n relation to information which is exempt information by virtue of subsection (1)" were not included in the equivalent provision in the Freedom of Information Bill introduced in the House of Commons on November 18, 1999 (*i.e.* cl.22(2)), but this change appears to have been a stylistic one made to all the exemptions based on the same template rather than a deliberate attempt to disengage s.2(1).

63 Freedom of Information Act 2000, s.2(2)(b).

64 *Esbester v United Kingdom* (1993) 18 E.H.R.R. CD 72, ECommHR; *Hitchens v Secretary of State for the Home Department* (unreported, decision of the Information Tribunal dated

(1) In 1985 the Home Office White Paper, *Interception of Communications in the United Kingdom*, stated that the interests of national security encompass "terrorist, espionage or major subversive activity, or [the] support of the Government's defence and foreign policies."[65]

(2) In 1988 the Prime Minister, Mrs Thatcher, stated in answer to a Parliamentary Question,

> "National security is generally understood to refer to the safeguarding of the State and the community against threats to their survival or well-being. I am not aware that any previous administration has thought it appropriate to adopt a specific definition of the term."[66]

(3) The Security Service Act 1989 envisages that the protection of national security requires that it be protected against threats from espionage, terrorism and sabotage, from the activities of agents of foreign powers and from actions intended to overthrow or undermine Parliamentary democracy by political, industrial or violent means,[67] but that it does not itself extend to safeguarding the economic well-being of the United Kingdom against threats posed by the actions or intentions of persons outside the British Islands or preventing or detecting serious crime.[68]

(4) In 1991 the *Report of the Security Service Commissioner for 1990* stated

> "The concept of national security however is wider than this and is not easily defined; indeed it is probably undesirable that I attempt an all-embracing definition. In my opinion it includes the defence of the realm and the government's defence and foreign policies involving the protection of vital national interests in this country and abroad. In this regard I would draw a distinction between national interest and the interests, which are not necessarily the same, of the government of the day. What is a vital national interest is a question of fact and degree, more easily recognised when being considered than defined in advance."[69]

August 4, 2003) para.47. See generally: L. Lustgarten and I. Leigh, *In From the Cold: National Security and Parliamentary Democracy* (Oxford University Press, Oxford, 1994), pp.3–35; I. Cameron, *National Security and the European Convention on Human Rights* (Kluwer Law International, The Hague, 2000), pp.39–58.

65 (Cmnd.9438) 1985, para.21.

66 *Hansard*, HC, Vol.126, January 25, 1988, col.7.

67 Security Service Act 1989, s.1(2).

68 Security Service Act 1989, s.1(3)–(4). The same distinction between the interests of national security, on the one hand, and the interests of the economic well-being of the United Kingdom and the prevention or detection of serious crime, on the other, is drawn in the Security Service Act 1989, s.2(2)(a) and the Intelligence Services Act 1994, ss.1(2), 2(2)(a), 3(2) and throughout the Regulation of Investigatory Powers Act 2000 (see *e.g.* s.5(3)). This is also reflected in the separate provision made for the economic interests of the United Kingdom and law enforcement in Freedom of Information Act 2000, ss.29–31. See further Chs 19 and 20.

69 (Cm.1480) 1991, para.10.

(5) The European Commission of Human Rights and the European Court of Human Rights[70] have held that the following may pose a threat to national security and may therefore be countered in the interests of national security: disloyalty in the public services (in relation to security vetting procedures)[71]; espionage[72]; inciting disaffection of military personnel[73]; indiscipline in the armed forces and the police[74]; separatist organisations[75]; subversion[76]; and terrorism.[77]

(6) *National Security and the European Convention on Human Rights* by Iain Cameron states,

> "It would also seem clear that, in an era of global interdependence, the ordinary meaning of 'national security' cannot be limited to the simple preservation of territorial integrity and political independence from external armed attack, or dictatorial interference by foreign powers. National security must also logically encompass espionage, economic or political, and covert (destabilising) action by foreign powers. Moreover, notwithstanding a lack of foreign involvement, purely internal threats to change the existing political order of the state by force (*i.e.* revolutionary subversion and terrorism) must also be covered. Certainly these are regarded by most if not all governments as legitimate national security concerns."[78]

(7) The following points were made in the most recent and authoritative House of Lords decision on the topic *Secretary of State for the Home Department v Rehman*[79]: "national security" means "the security of the

---

70 In *Hewitt and Harman v United Kingdom* (September 1, 1993) No.20317/92, ECommHR an application based on the ECHR, Art.8 brought following the implementation of the Security Service Act 1989 was ruled inadmissible by the European Commission of Human Rights. In relation to the Security Service Act 1989 the Commission said "the principles referred to above do not necessarily require a comprehensive definition of 'the interests of national security'" and "the Commission considers that in the present case the law is formulated with sufficient precision to enable the applicants to anticipate the role of the Security Service" (at p.13).

71 *Glasenapp v Federal Republic of Germany* (1987) 9 E.H.R.R. 25, ECtHR at paras 86–87; *Kosiek v Federal Republic of Germany* (1987) 9 E.H.R.R. 328, ECtHR at paras 79–80; *Vogt v Federal Republic of Germany* (1996) 21 E.H.R.R. 205, ECtHR at paras 49–51.

72 *Klass v Federal Republic of Germany* (1978) 2 E.H.R.R. 214, ECtHR at para.48; *Hadjianastassiou v Greece* (1992) 16 E.H.R.R. 219, ECtHR at para.43.

73 *Arrowsmith v United Kingdom* (1979) 19 D.R. 5, ECommHR at para.24.

74 *VDSÖ and Gubi v Austria* (1995) 20 E.H.R.R. 56, ECtHR; *Grigoriades v Greece* (1999) 27 E.H.R.R. 464, ECtHR at para.41; *Rekvényi v Hungary* (2000) 30 E.H.R.R. 519, ECtHR at para.39; *Smith and Grady v United Kingdom* (1999) 29 E.H.R.R. 493, ECtHR; *Lustig-Prean and Beckett v United Kingdom* (2000) 29 E.H.R.R. 548, ECtHR.

75 *United Communist Party of Turkey v Turkey* (1998) 26 E.H.R.R. 121, ECtHR at paras 39–41; *Socialist Party v Turkey* (1999) 27 E.H.R.R. 51, ECtHR at paras 33–36.

76 *Leander v Sweden* (1987) 9 E.H.R.R. 433, ECtHR at para.59.

77 *Klass v Federal Republic of Germany* (1978) 2 E.H.R.R. 214, ECtHR at para.48; *Zana v Turkey* (1999) 27 E.H.R.R. 667, ECtHR at paras 48–50.

78 I. Cameron, *National Security and the European Convention on Human Rights* (Kluwer Law International, The Hague, 2000), p.43.

79 [2001] UKHL 47; [2003] 1 A.C. 153, HL. The House of Lords approved the Court of Appeal's rejection of the narrower definition of "national security" adopted by the Special Immigration

United Kingdom and its people;"[80] the interests of national security are not limited to action by an individual which can be said to be "targeted at" the United Kingdom, its system of government or its people[81]; the protection of democracy and the legal and constitutional systems of the state is a part of national security as well as military defence[82]; "action against a foreign state may be capable indirectly of affecting the security of the United Kingdom;"[83] and "reciprocal co-operation between the United Kingdom and other states in combating international terrorism is capable of promoting the United Kingdom's national security."[84]

(8) By way of contrast with the foregoing, the second of the "Johannesburg Principles on National Security, Freedom of Expression and Access to Information" proposes a much narrower formulation,

> "A restriction [on expression or information] sought to be justified on the ground of national security is not legitimate unless its genuine purpose and demonstrable effect is to protect a country's existence or its territorial integrity against the use or threat of force, or its capacity to respond to the use or threat of force, whether from an external source, such as a military threat, or an internal source, such as incitement to violent overthrow of the government."[85]

Appeals Commission, namely, "a person may be said to offend against national security if he engages in, promotes, or encourages violent activity which is targeted at the United Kingdom, its system of government or its people. This includes activities directed against the overthrow or destabilisation of a foreign government if that foreign government is likely to take reprisals against the United Kingdom which affect the security of the United Kingdom or of its nationals. National security extends also to situations where United Kingdom citizens are targeted, wherever they may be" (see the speeches of Lord Slynn at para.[2] and Lord Hoffmann at para.[43]). See also Tomkins, "Defining and delimiting national security" (2002) 118 L.Q.R. 200.

80 [2001] UKHL 47 [2003] 1 A.C. 153, HL at para.[50] (*per* Lord Hoffmann) and para.[64] (*per* Lord Hutton).

81 *ibid.*, at para.[15] (*per* Lord Slynn).

82 *ibid.*, at para.[16] (*per* Lord Slynn).

83 *ibid.*, at paras [16]–[17] (*per* Lord Slynn). See also at paras [53] and [62] (*per* Lord Hoffmann) and para.[64] (*per* Lord Hutton).

84 *ibid.*, at para.[17] (*per* Lord Slynn).

85 Adopted on October 1, 1995 by a group of experts on international law, national security and human rights convened by Art.19, the International Centre Against Censorship, in collaboration with the Centre for Applied Legal Studies of the University of the Witwatersrand, Johannesburg: Art.19 and Liberty, *Secrets, Spies and Whistleblowers: Freedom of Expression and National Security in the United Kingdom* (Liberty, London, 2000), Appendix 1 and recommendation 4; S. Coliver, "Commentary on the Johannesburg Principles" in S. Coliver (ed.), *Secrecy and Liberty: National Security, Freedom of Expression and Access to Information* (Martinus Nijdhoff, Cambridge Mass., 1999). See also *Secretary of State for the Home Department v Rehman* [2001] UKHL 47; [2003] 1 A.C. 153, HL at para.[14] (*per* Lord Slynn).

Judicial approach to national security

Throughout the twentieth century the domestic courts consistently held that national security is the primary responsibility of the executive, that the executive has the particular experience and expertise necessary to make assessments and decisions relating to national security, together with democratic responsibility for doing so, and that the courts are not in a position to question the executive in this regard once it has been shown, on credible evidence, that national security considerations are in play.[86] The degree to which these authorities suggested that national security was non-justiciable or that evidence of national security concerns could be demanded and reviewed to establish their *bona fides* and credibility varied a little from case to case, but the basic message remained the same: the courts would not interfere in the executive's assessment of national security matters. The judicial organs of the ECHR[87] and the European Community[88] have taken a broadly similar approach, but, whilst they have expressly recognised and emphasised the wide margin of appreciation enjoyed by the executive in this area, they have also stressed the need for effective judicial control by means of judicial review on proportionality-based grounds. In the light of this jurisprudence, the domestic courts have recently restated and recast their approach somewhat, whilst retaining the same basic respect and 17–036

[86] *The Zamora* [1916] 2 A.C. 77, PC at 107 "Those who are responsible for national security must be the sole judge of what the national security requires. It would obviously be undesirable that such matters should be made the subject of evidence in a court of law or otherwise discussed in public" (*per* Lord Parker); *Chandler v DPP* [1964] A.C. 763, HL at 798 (*per* Viscount Radcliffe) and 811 (*per* Lord Devlin) (in relation to the defence of the realm); *R. v Secretary of State for the Home Department, Ex p. Hosenball* [1977] 1 W.L.R. 766, CA at 778 and 783 (*per* Lord Denning M.R.) and 783–784 (*per* Lane L.J.); *Council of Civil Service Unions v Minister for the Civil Service* [1985] A.C. 374, HL at 402–403 (*per* Lord Fraser), 404 and 406–407 (*per* Lord Scarman), 410 and 412 (*per* Lord Diplock), 420–421 (*per* Lord Roskill) and 423 (*per* Lord Brightman); *R. v Secretary of State for the Home Department, Ex p. Ruddock* [1987] 1 W.L.R. 1482, at 1490–1492 (*per* Taylor J.); *NHS v Secretary of State for the Home Department* [1988] Imm.A.R. 389, CA at 395 (*per* Dillon L.J.); *R. v Director of GCHQ, Ex p. Hodges* [1988] C.O.D. 123; *R. v Secretary of State for Foreign and Commonwealth Affairs, Ex p. Everett* [1989] Q.B. 811, CA; *R. v Secretary of State for the Home Department, Ex p. B, The Times*, January 29, 1991; *R. v Secretary of State for the Home Department, Ex p. Cheblak* [1991] 1 W.L.R. 890, CA at 902 and 906–907 (*per* Lord Donaldson M.R.), 912 (*per* Beldam L.J.) and 916 (*per* Nolan L.J.); *R. v Secretary of State for the Home Department, Ex p. Chahal* [1995] 1 W.L.R. 526, CA at 531 and 535 (*per* Staughton L.J.); *R. v Secretary of State for the Home Department, Ex p. McQuillan* [1995] 4 All E.R. 400 at 424 (*per* Sedley J.); *Jahromi v Secretary of State for the Home Department* [1996] Imm.A.R. 20, CA at 26 (*per* Roch L.J.). See also: Lee, "GCHQ: Prerogative and Public Law Principles" [1985] P.L. 186; Morris, "The Ban on Trade Unions at Government Communications Headquarters" [1985] P.L. 177; Sir Simon Brown, "Public Interest Immunity" [1994] P.L. 579, pp.589–590; Dickson, "Judicial Review and National Security" in B. Hadfield (ed.), *Judicial Review: A Thematic Approach* (Gill & Macmillan, Dublin, 1995).

[87] *Ireland v United Kingdom* [1979–80] 2 E.H.R.R. 25, ECtHR, para.206; *Chahal v United Kingdom* (1997) 23 E.H.R.R. 413, ECtHR at paras 131 and 138; *Tinnelly and Sons Ltd v United Kingdom* (1999) 27 E.H.R.R. 249, ECtHR at para.78; *R. v Ministry of Defence, Ex p. Smith* [1996] Q.B. 517, CA and *Smith and Grady v United Kingdom* (1999) 29 E.H.R.R. 493, ECtHR.

[88] Case 222/84 *Johnston v Chief Constable of the Royal Ulster Constabulary* [1987] Q.B. 129, ECJ; Case 175/94 *R. v Secretary of State for the Home Department, Ex p. Gallagher* [1995] E.C.R. I-4253, ECJ; Case 273/97 *Sirdar v Secretary of State for Defence*, [1999] E.C.R. I-7403, ECJ.

deference for the conclusions of the executive when it comes to national security matters.[89]

Information whose exemption is required for the purpose of safeguarding national security

17–037 In the light of the authorities mentioned in the foregoing paragraph, it is clear that the executive's assessment of whether exemption from the relevant provisions of the Freedom of Information Act 2000 and Data Protection Act 1998 is required for the purpose of safeguarding national security will not be readily gainsaid. In this regard, the executive may legitimately adopt a preventative or precautionary approach to the protection of national security and may consider not only direct or immediate threats but also the "real possibility" of adverse affects on, and subsequent risks to, national security whether direct or indirect.[90] So far as concerns the communication of information or personal data under s.1(1)(b) of the Freedom of Information Act 2000 or s.7(1)(b)–(d) of the Data Protection Act 1998, the assessment to be made is simply whether non-disclosure is required for the purpose of safeguarding national security on the

[89] *Secretary of State for the Home Department v Rehman* [2001] UKHL 47; [2003] 1 A.C. 153, HL at paras [16] and [26] (per Lord Slynn) and paras [49]–[50], [53]–[54] and [62] (*per* Lord Hoffman). See esp. at para.[31], while "issues of national security do not fall beyond the competence of the courts" it is "self-evidently right that national courts must give great weight to the views of the executive on matters of national security" (*per* Lord Steyn); at para.[50] "the question of whether something is 'in the interests' of national security is not a question of law. It is a matter of judgment and policy. Under the constitution of the United Kingdom and most other countries, decisions as to whether something is or is not in the interests of national security are not a matter for judicial decision. They are entrusted to the executive" (*per* Lord Hoffmann); and at para.[62] "It is not only that the executive has access to special information and expertise in these matters. It is also that such decisions, with serious potential results for the community, require a legitimacy which can be conferred only by entrusting them to persons responsible to the community through the democratic process. If the people are to accept the consequences of such decisions, they must be made by persons whom the people have elected and whom they can remove" (*per* Lord Hoffmann). See also: *Brown v Stott* [2001] 2 W.L.R. 817, PC at 834–835 (*per* Lord Bingham); *R. v DPP, Ex p. Kebilene* [2000] 2 A.C. 326, HL at 380–381 (*per* Lord Hope); *International Transport Roth GmbH v Secretary of State for the Home Department* [2002] EWCA Civ 158; [2003] Q.B. 728, CA at paras [77] and [80]–[87] (*per* Laws L.J.); *R. v Secretary of State for the Home Department, Ex p. Farrakhan* [2002] EWCA Civ 606; [2002] Q.B. 1391, CA; *A v Secretary of State for the Home Department* [2002] EWCA Civ 1502; [2003] 2 W.L.R. 564, CA at para.[40] (*per* Lord Woolf C.J.) and at paras [66] and [81] (*per* Brooke L.J.); *Re Freddie Scappaticci's Application* [2003] NIQB 56 at paras [17]–[19] (*per* Carswell C.J.) (NI); *Baker v Secretary of State for the Home Department* [2001] U.K.H.R.R. 1275, para.76; *Gosling v Secretary of State for the Home Department*, (unreported, decision of the Information Tribunal dated August 1, 2003), paras 44 and 48. In relation to the language of "deference" see now *R. (Pro-Life Alliance) v BBC* [2003] UKHL 23; [2003] 2 W.L.R. 1403, HL at paras [74]–[77] (*per* Lord Hoffmann) and para.[144] (*per* Lord Walker).

[90] *Secretary of State for the Home Department v Rehman* [2001] UKHL 47; [2003] 1 A.C. 153, HL at paras [16]–[17] and [22] (*per* Lord Slynn) and para.[29] (*per* Lord Steyn) (both approving *Secretary of State for the Home Department v Rehman* [2000] 3 W.L.R. 1240, CA at para.[44] (*per* Lord Woolf M.R.)); *Secretary of State for Defence v Guardian Newspapers Ltd* [1985] A.C. 339, HL at 355 (*per* Lord Diplock), 371 (*per* Lord Roskill) and 373 (*per* Lord Bridge).

basis that disclosure would give rise to the real possibility of direct or indirect damage being done to national security. A wider variety of factors may have to be taken into account in relation to confirmation or denial under s.1(1)(a) of the Freedom of Information Act 2000 or s.7(1)(a) of the Data Protection Act 1998, as confirmation that a public authority holds or does not hold information or personal data of a particular description might be harmless in one case and yet give rise to damaging deductions and inferences if similar confirmation has to be withheld in another case. This may be accommodated on the basis that the public interest in disclosing whether the public authority holds information is, by itself, less compelling than the public interest in disclosing information.[91] Reference has already been made to the risk of mosaic prejudice being caused by the disclosure of information in the security and intelligence context and this will undoubtedly be a factor in relation to national security assessments under both s.24 of the Freedom of Information Act 2000 and s.28 of the Data Protection Act 1998.[92]

Non-confidential information

Section 24 of the Freedom of Information Act 2000 and s.28 of the Data Protection Act 1998 are both capable of conferring exemption on information or personal data that is known to the applicant or wholly non-confidential, just as much as on confidential information.[93] The question nevertheless arises whether the exemption of information which is already known to the applicant or in the public domain can realistically be required for the purpose of safeguarding national security.[94] The first point to note here is that where information enters the public domain[95] without there being any official confirmation of its accuracy, it may nevertheless remain inherently unreliable.[96] Formal disclosure by a 17–038

91 See generally para.15–011.
92 See para.17–023(1) and references therein.
93 Neither provision is expressly or impliedly confined to confidential information. See generally para.15–018.
94 Data Protection Act 1998, s.28 could require the exemption of such information, but it may be more difficult to justify this, particularly in relation to a data subject who, for example, is a former servant or agent of the intelligence services or has been subject to a prosecution involving evidence supplied by the intelligence services and who therefore knows that they hold personal data about him. The Information Tribunal has recognised that establishing the need for a neither confirm nor deny response in such cases is not a foregone conclusion: *Baker v Secretary of State for the Home Department* [2001] U.K.H.R.R. 1275, paras 4 and 9; *Gosling v Secretary of State for the Home Department*, (unreported, decision of the Information Tribunal dated August 1, 2003); *Hitchens v Secretary of State for the Home Department*, (unreported, decision of the Information Tribunal dated August 4, 2003).
95 In this regard, it has been said that for information to enter the public domain means "no more than that the information in question is so generally accessible that, in all the circumstances, it cannot be regarded as confidential": *Attorney-General v Guardian Newspapers Ltd (No.2)* [1990] 1 A.C. 109, HL at 282 (*per* Lord Goff).
96 At least while some doubt remains as to whether or not it is true, false or the product of speculation and that doubt is greater than that which ordinarily attaches to official information of the same kind.

public authority will authenticate the information and thus entail the disclosure of an extra piece of information, namely, the fact that the information is true. It is therefore entirely possible for non-confidential information to attract the protection of s.24 of the Freedom of Information Act 2000 or s.28 of the Data Protection Act 1998. This is largely borne out by reference to the experience in the USA under the federal Freedom of Information Act 1966 (USA)[97] where the approach taken is that national security exemption claims are not undermined by a generalised allegation that classified information has been leaked to the press or otherwise made available to members of the public. Information is not considered to be in the public domain unless it has been the subject of an official disclosure.[98] Where a person seeks to defeat a national security claim for exemption on the ground that the information is in the public domain, the burden rests upon that applicant to point to specific information officially placed in the public domain that appears to duplicate[99] the withheld information.[1] Reports in the media, even if widespread, about the general subject matter of the information requested will not defeat a claim for national security exemption for that type of information.[2] Public statements by former government officials do not constitute such an official disclosure[3] and it would appear that even

---

[97] Freedom of Information Act 1966 5 USC 552(b)(1) (1994 & Supp. IV 1998) (USA).

[98] *e.g. Simmons v United States Department of Justice*, 796 F.(2d) 709, 712 (4th Cir. 1986); *Abbotts v NRC*, 766 F.(2d) 604, 607–08 (D.C. Cir. 1985); *Afshar v Department of State*, 702 F.(2d) 1125 (D.C. Cir. 1983) (foreign government can ignore "unofficial leaks and public surmise . . . but official acknowledgement may force a government to retaliate"); *Steinberg v United States Department of Justice*, 801 F. Supp. 800, 802 (D.D.C. 1992) ("passage of time, media reports and informed or uninformed speculation based on statements by participants cannot be used . . . to undermine [government's] legitimate interest in protecting international security [information]"), aff'd at 23 F.(3d) 548, 553 (D.C. Cir. 1994). *Cf. Lawyers Comm. for Human Rights v INS*, 721 F. Supp. 552, 569 (S.D.N.Y. 1989) (national security exemption is not available when the same documents were disclosed by foreign government or when the same information was disclosed to press in "off-the-record exchanges").

[99] It would appear that any material difference between that being requested and that which is in the public domain will allow the national security exemption to be maintained: *Public Citizen v Department of State* 11 F.(3d) at 199 (D.C. Cir. 1993); *Public Citizen v Department of State*, 787 F. Supp. 12, 13, 15 (D.D.C. 1992) (public Congressional testimony of the US Ambassador to Iraq did not constitute such a waiver so as to prevent the agency from invoking the national security exemption to withhold related records; his public testimony had not "waived" Exemption 1 protection because the context of the information in the documents was sufficiently different so as to not negate their confidentiality).

[1] *Fitzgibbon v CIA*, 911 F.(2d) 755, 765 (D.C. Cir. 1990); *Afshar v Department of State*, 702 F.(2d) 1125, 1130 (D.C. Cir. 1983); *Billington v Department of Justice*, 11 F. Supp. 2d 45, 54–56 (D.D.C. 1998); *Steinberg v United States Department of Justice*, 179 F.R.D. 357, 361 (D.D.C. 1998); *Pfeiffer v CIA*, 721 F. Supp. 337, 342 (D.D.C. 1989).

[2] *Schlesinger v CIA*, 591 F. Supp. 60, 66 (D.D.C. 1984) (CIA records relating to Guatemala were properly classified despite the fact that the public domain contained significant information and speculation about CIA involvement in the 1954 coup in Guatemala: "CIA clearance of books and articles, books written by former CIA officials, and general discussions in Congressional publications do not constitute official disclosures").

[3] *Hudson River Sloop Clearwater, Inc v Department of the Navy*, 891 F.(2d) 414, 421–22 (2d Cir. 1989).

Congressional publications may not constitute an official disclosure.[4] Much the same conclusion has been arrived at in Australia in relation to information known to the applicant.[5]

Outweighing the public interest in safeguarding national security

Even if information is rendered exempt information (or if the duty to confirm or deny does not arise) for the purpose of safeguarding national security under s.24 of the Freedom of Information Act 2000, disclosure or divulgence will still have to take place under s.1 of the Act if, in all the circumstances of the case, the public interest in maintaining the exemption or exclusion is outweighed by the public interest in disclosure or divulgence (respectively).[6] The decision of Parliament not to make exemption under s.24 absolute cannot properly be undone by giving the public interest in maintaining the exemption such weight as to make the public interest in disclosure unable to outweigh it. The exercise must be carried out in such a manner as to recognise that in some circumstances the public interest in disclosure will be sufficiently powerful to displace an inherently compelling public interest in maintaining the exemption.[7] The scales could also be made to tip in favour of disclosure or divulgence, for example, in relation to widely known non-confidential information whose exemption is nevertheless necessary for the purpose of safeguarding national security[8]: in such a case, the public interest in maintaining the exemption may have to be ascribed a more limited weight in accordance with the more limited effect it will have. 17–039

4 *e.g. Salisbury v United States*, 690 F.(2d) 966, 971 (D.C. Cir. 1982) (holding that inclusion of information in Senate report "cannot be equated with disclosure by the agency itself"); *Military Audit Project v Casey*, 656 F.(2d) 724, 744 (D.C. Cir. 1981) (publication of Senate report does not constitute official release of agency information).

5 *Re Reithmuller and Australian Federal Police* (1985) 8 A.L.N. N92; *Re Robinson and Department of Foreign Affairs* (1986) 11 A.L.N. N48 (inadvertent earlier disclosure by the agency); *Commonwealth of Australia v Hittich* (1994) 53 F.C.R. 152.

6 Freedom of Information Act 2000, s.2(1)(b) and (2)(b). Data Protection Act 1998, s.28 is not subject to an express public interest override provision but an assessment of the proportionality of any claim that its application is required for the purpose of safeguarding national security will nevertheless involve a similar balancing of national security interests, on the one hand, against the data subject's rights under the Data Protection Act 1998 and the European Community Data Protection Directive 95/46, on the other hand: *Baker v Secretary of State for the Home Department* [2001] U.K.H.R.R. 1275 at paras [63] and [83]; *Gosling v Secretary of State for the Home Department*, (unreported, decision of the Information Tribunal dated August 1, 2003; and *Hitchens v Secretary of State for the Home Department*, (unreported, decision of the Information Tribunal dated August 4, 2003).

7 A crucial factor here will be the engagement of legally recognised countervailing human rights (as against a more generalised public interest) favouring disclosure over non-disclosure. Such rights will not be absolute, and they are unlikely to be determinative in any event, but they will at least provide something extra of substance to go into the balance: see para.(2).

8 See para.17–038.

Approach to national security issues in the United States of America

17–040 In the USA, once a document has engaged the national security exemption by being classified under the federal Freedom of Information Act 1966 (USA)[9] and the relevant Presidential Order thereunder,[10] the focus of challenge becomes the propriety of this classification.[11] While the courts have over the years increased their preparedness to scrutinise claims for exemption on this ground, it remains an exemption in respect of which the courts are loath to substitute their judgment for that of the executive. In 1973 the Supreme Court[12] held that records classified under proper procedures were necessarily exempt from disclosure, without any possibility of judicial scrutiny.[13] Following this decision, Congress amended the Freedom of Information Act in 1974 to provide expressly for *de novo* review by the courts and for the *in camera* review of classified documents.[14] Despite these amendments, the courts, in the absence of evidence of bad faith on the part of an agency, routinely upheld agency classification decisions.[15] Although the courts subsequently increased their use of the *in camera* review procedures in order to facilitate full *de novo* reviews of national security claims even where bad faith was not an issue,[16] it was recognised that they should first "accord substantial weight to an agency's affidavit concerning the details of the classified status of the disputed record."[17] Provided an agency's affidavit evidence discloses no bad faith and the requisite degree of particularity, examination of the documents by the court will either not be required or be limited to sample documents.[18] Claims for exemption can be supported by *in camera* affidavits[19]

---

9 5 USC § 552(b)(1), s.6F(b) (USA).

10 Executive Order 12,356. See further para.2–008(1) and the footnotes therein.

11 Thus the issue on review is whether the classification was justified at the time that it was made: *King v Department of Justice*, 830 F.(2d) 210 at 217 (D.C. Cir. 1987). An agency may, as a matter of discretion, re-examine its classification decisions under a newly issued Executive Order in order to take into account changed international and domestic circumstances: *ibid.*

12 *EPA v Mink* 410 US 73 (1973).

13 *ibid.*, at 84.

14 USC § 552(a)(4)(B).

15 *e.g. Weissman v CIA*, 565 F.2d 692, 698 (D.C. Cir. 1977).

16 Starting with *Ray v Turner*, 587 F.(2d) 1187, 1194–95 (D.C. Cir. 1978).

17 *ibid.* at 1194 (D.C. Cir. 1978).

18 *e.g. Doherty v United States Department of Justice*, 775 F.(2d) 49, 53 (2d Cir. 1985) ("the court should restrain its discretion to order *in camera* review"); *Hayden v NSA*, 608 F.(2d) 1381, 1387 (D.C. Cir. 1979) ("[w]hen the agency meets its burden by means of affidavits, *in camera* review is neither necessary nor appropriate"); *Public Education Center Inc. v Department of Defense*, 905 F. Supp. 19, 22 (D.D.C. 1995) (declining *in camera* review of withheld videotapes after according substantial weight to agency's affidavit that public disclosure would harm national security); *King v United States Department of Justice*, 586 F. Supp. 286, 290 (D.D.C. 1983) (characterising *in camera* review as a last resort).

19 *e.g. Patterson v FBI*, 893 F.(2d) 595, 599–600 (3d Cir. 1990); *Simmons v United States Department. of Justice*, 796 F.(2d) 709, 711 (4th Cir. 1986); *Ingle v Department of Justice*, 698 F.(2d) 259, 264 (6th Cir. 1983) (ruling that *in camera* review should be secondary to testimony or affidavits). The approach taken is that in such cases the agency is under a duty to "create as complete a public record as is possible" before resorting to an *in camera* affidavit: *Phillippi v CIA*, 546 F.(2d) 1009, 1013 (D.C. Cir. 1976). See also *Armstrong*, 97 F.(3d) at 580 (holding that when district court uses

which the legal representatives of the person seeking access will not be allowed to see.[20] The courts will give substantial deference to agency expertise in national security matters[21] and have expressed a reluctance to substitute their judgment for that of the agency's "unique insights" in the areas of national defence and foreign relations.[22] Even where the person requesting access has adduced expert evidence as to the security implications, this has not usually caused the courts to upset the agency's assessment of the national security implications of disclosure.[23] Thus, claims for exemption are generally upheld if the agency's affidavits are reasonably specific and there is no evidence of bad

an *in camera* affidavit, even in national security cases, "it must both make its reasons for doing so clear and make as much as possible of the *in camera* submission available to the opposing party" (citing *Lykins v United States Department of Justice*, 725 F.(2d) 1455, 1465 (D.C. Cir. 1984)); *Patterson v FBI*, 893 F.(2d) 595 at 600 (3d Cir. 1990); *Simmons v United States Department of Justice*, 796 F.(2d) at 710 (4th Cir. 1986); *Scott v CIA*, 916 F. Supp. 42, 48–49 (D.D.C. 1996) (denying request for *in camera* review until agency "creates as full a public rec.ord as possible"); *Public Education Centre, Inc. v Department of Defense*, 905 F. Supp. 19, 22 (D.D.C. 1995) (ordering *in camera* review only after agency created "as full a public record as possible").

20 *Phillippi v CIA*, 546 F.(2d) 1009, 1013 (D.C. Cir. 1976).

21 *e.g. Young v CIA*, 972 F.(2d) 536, 538–39 (4th Cir. 1993) (finding district court properly deferred to agency because no evidence of bad faith); *Bowers v United States Department of Justice*, 930 F.(2d) 350, 357 (4th Cir. 1991) (observing that "[w]hat fact . . . may compromise national security is best left to the intelligence experts"); *Doherty v United States Department of Justice*, 775 F.(2d) 49, 52 (2d Cir. 1985) (according "substantial weight" to agency declaration); *Miller v Casey*, 730 F.(2d) 773, 776 (D.C. Cir. 1984) (same); *Taylor v Department of the Army*, 684 F.(2d) 99, 109 (D.C. Cir. 1982) (holding that classification affidavits are entitled to "the utmost deference") (reversing district court disclosure order); *Badalementi v Department of State*, 899 F. Supp. 542, 546 (D. Kan. 1995) (according substantial weight to agency's affidavit and granting motion for summary judgment in light of agency's expertise in national security matters); *Canning v United States Department of Justice*, 848 F. Supp. 1037, 1042 (D.D.C. 1994) (describing how in according such deference, courts "credit agency expertise in evaluating matters of national security by focusing attention primarily on whether affidavits are sufficiently specific and by ensuring that they are not controverted by contradictory evidence or evidence of bad faith"); *Abbotts v NRC*, 766 F.(2d) 604 (D.C. Cir. 1985) overturning the district court's disclosure because it "did not give the required 'substantial weight' to the [agency's] uncontradicted affidavits."

22 *e.g. Miller v United States Dept of State*, 779 F.(2d) 1378, 1387 (8th Cir. 1985); *Maynard v CIA*, 986 F.2d 547, 556 n.9 (1st Cir. 1993) (a court is "not in a position to 'second-guess'" agency's determination regarding need for continued classification of material); *Krikorian v Department of State*, 984 F.(2d) 461, 464–65 (D.C. Cir. 1993) (where it was held that an agency has "unique insights" in areas of national defence and foreign relations); *Willens v NSC*, 726 F. Supp. 325, 326–27 (D.D.C. 1989) (where it was held that a court cannot second-guess agency's national security determinations when they are "credible and have a rational basis"). But see *King v United States Department of Justice*, 830 F.(2d) 210, 226 (D.C. Cir. 1987) (holding that trial court erred in deferring to agency's judgment that information more than 35 years old remained classified when Executive Order presumed declassification of information over 20 years old and agency merely indicated procedural compliance with Order); *Lawyers Comm. for Human Rights v INS*, 721 F. Supp. 552, 561 (S.D.N.Y. 1989) (reminding that such deference does not give agency *carte blanche* to withhold responsive documents without "valid and thorough affidavit").

23 *e.g. Hudson River Sloop Clearwater, Inc v Department of the Navy*, 891 F.(2d) 414, 421–22 (2d Cir. 1989)(retired admiral's opinion); *Gardels v CIA*, 689 F.(2d) 1100, 1106 n.5 (D.C. Cir. 1982) (former agent of the CIA); *Pfeiffer v CIA*, 721 F. Supp. 337, 340–41 (D.D.C. 1989)(retired CIA historian). Prior to 1986, no appellate court had ever upheld, on the substantive merits of the case, a decision to reject an agency's classification claim.

faith.[24] A similar degree of judicial deference to the assessments of the executive has also been shown by the Australian courts in the freedom of information context.[25]

5. NATIONAL SECURITY CERTIFICATES AND THE OPERATION OF THE RELATED EXEMPTIONS

National security certificates under sections 23 and 24 of the Freedom of Information Act 2000: introduction

National security certificates may be issued under ss.23 and 24 of the Freedom of Information Act 2000 as follows:

17–041 (1) Under s.23(2) of the Freedom of Information Act 2000 a Minister of the Crown may sign a certificate certifying that the information to which it applies was directly or indirectly supplied by, or relates to, any of the security bodies specified in s.23(3). Such a certificate will then stand as conclusive evidence of that fact, thus confirming the engagement of the s.23 exemption, unless and until withdrawn or revoked[26] or quashed on an appeal under s.60 of the Freedom of Information Act 2000. There is no provision allowing such a certificate to identify the information to

[24] *Halperin v CIA*, 629 F.(2d) 144, 148 (D.C. Cir. 1980); *Goldberg v Department of State*, 818 F.(2d) 71 (D.C. Cir. 1987); *Schrecker v United States Dept of Justice*, 74 F. Supp. (2d) 26, 30 (D.D.C. 1999); *Voinche v FBI*, 46 F. Supp. (2d) 26, 29 (D.D.C. 1999); *Billington v Department of Justice*, 11 F. Supp. (2d) 45, 54, 58 (D.D.C. 1998); *Canning v United States Dept of Justice*, 848 F. Supp. 1037, 1042–43 (D.D.C. 1994); *Students Against Genocide v Department of State*, 257 F.3d 828 (D.C. Cir. 2001). Thus, in *Rosenfeld v United States Dept of Justice*, 57 F.(3d) 803, 807 (9th Cir. 1995) the Court affirmed a district court disclosure order, finding the government had failed to show with "any particularity" why classified portions of several documents should be withheld. Similarly, *Wiener v FBI*, 943 F.(2d) 972, 978–79 (9th Cir. 1991); *Oglesby v United States Dept of the Army*, 920 F.(2d) 57, 66 n.12 (D.C. Cir. 1990); *Scott v CIA*, 916 F. Supp. 42, 44–49 (D.D.C. 1996).

[25] *Re Maher and Attorney-General's Department* (1985) 3 A.A.R. 396; *Re Stolpe and Department of Foreign Affairs* (1985) 9 A.L.D. 104; *Re Fewster and Department of Prime Minister and Cabinet (No.2)* (1987) 13 A.L.D. 139; *Re Wang and Department of Employment, Education and Training* (1988) 15 A.L.D. 497; *Re Bayliss and Department of Health and Family Services* (1997) 48 A.L.D. 443; *Gersten v Minister for Immigration & Multicultural Affairs* [2000] F.C.A. 1221; [2001] F.C.A. 159. See further para.2–015(9).

[26] There is no obvious reason for construing the Freedom of Information Act 2000, ss.23(2), 24(3), 34(3) and 36(7), Freedom of Information (Scotland) Act 2002, s.31(2) or Data Protection Act 1998, s.28(2) as preventing the withdrawal or revocation of certificates or rendering the signatories *functus officio*. Changes in circumstances may very well make the withdrawal or revocation of a certificate appropriate without the need (where this route is open) for an appeal to the Information Tribunal. See: *Al Fayed v Secretary of State for the Home Department & Secretary of State for Foreign and Commonwealth Affairs*, (unreported, decision of the Information Tribunal dated February 28, 2002), paras 9 and 15–16; Wade and Forsyth, *Administrative Law* (8th ed., Oxford University Press, Oxford, 2000), pp.235–238; Interpretation Act 1978, s.12.

which it applies by means of a general description or to be expressed to have prospective effect.[27] Such a certificate may only be signed by a Minister of the Crown who is a member of the Cabinet or by the Attorney General, the Advocate General for Scotland or the Attorney General for Northern Ireland.[28]

(2) Under s.24(3) of the Freedom of Information Act 2000 a Minister of the Crown may sign a certificate certifying that exemption from the disclosure duty in s.1(1)(b) or from the divulgence and disclosure duties in s.1(1)(a) and (b) is, or at any time was, required for the purpose of safeguarding national security.[29] Such a certificate will then stand as conclusive evidence of that fact, thus confirming the engagement of the s.24 exemption subject to the application of the public interest balancing tests,[30] unless and until withdrawn or revoked or quashed on an appeal under s.60 of the Freedom of Information Act 2000.[31] It is important to note here that such a certificate cannot certify for the purposes of s.2(1)(a) and (2)(a) of the Freedom of Information Act 2000 that, in all the circumstances of the case, the public interest in maintaining the exemption outweighs the public interest in divulging whether the public authority holds the information or in disclosing the information itself. The assessment and balancing of these competing facets of the public interest will therefore be subject to review by the Information Commissioner in the normal way. A national security certificate under s.24(3) may identify the information to which it applies by means of a general description and may be expressed to have prospective effect.[32] Such a certificate may only be signed by a Minister of the Crown who is a member of the Cabinet or by the Attorney General, the Advocate General for Scotland or the Attorney General for Northern Ireland.[33]

---

[27] *cf.* Freedom of Information Act 2000, s.24(4) and Data Protection Act 1998, s.28(3).

[28] Freedom of Information Act 2000, s.25(3).

[29] Freedom of Information (Scotland) Act 2002, s.31(2)–(3). Under the Freedom of Information (Scotland) Act 2002, s.31(2) a certificate may be signed by a member of the Scottish Executive and will stand as being conclusive of the fact certified (*i.e.* exemption from s.1(1) is required for the purpose of safeguarding national security): the Freedom of Information (Scotland) Act 2002 does not expressly provide or allow for any appeal or review. Under the Freedom of Information (Scotland) Act 2002, s.31(3), such a certificate may identify the information to which it applies by means of a general description and may be expressed to have prospective effect.

[30] Freedom of Information Act 2000, s.2(1)(b) and (2)(b).

[31] As to appeals, see para.28–018.

[32] Freedom of Information Act 2000, s.24(4). Pursuant to the Freedom of Information Act 2000, s.60(4) a public authority may claim in proceedings under or by virtue of that Act that a certificate issued under s.24(3) which identifies the information to which it applies by means of a general description applies to particular information and, subject to any contrary determination by the Information Tribunal on appeal, the certificate will be conclusively presumed so to apply.

[33] Freedom of Information Act 2000, s.25(3).

National security certificates under section 28 of the Data Protection Act 1998: introduction

17–042 Under s.28(2) of the Data Protection Act 1998 a Minister of the Crown may sign a national security certificate certifying that exemption from all or any of the provisions of the data protection principles or Pts II, III or V or s.55 of the Data Protection Act 1998 (which includes the subject access rights given by s.7) is, or at any time was, required for the purpose of safeguarding national security in respect of any personal data. Such a certificate will then stand as conclusive evidence of that fact, thus confirming the engagement of the s.28 exemption, unless and until withdrawn or revoked or quashed on an appeal under s.28(4) of and Sch.6 to the Data Protection Act 1998.[34] Such a certificate may identify the personal data to which it applies by means of a general description and may be expressed to have prospective effect.[35] Such a certificate may only be signed by a Minister of the Crown who is a member of the Cabinet or by the Attorney General, the Advocate General for Scotland or the Attorney General for Northern Ireland.[36]

National security certificates: appeals

17–043 The circumstances in, grounds on and procedures by which national security certificates issued under ss.23(2) and 24(3) of the Freedom of Information Act 2000 and s.28(2) of the Data Protection Act 1998 may be appealed to the Information Tribunal under s.60(1) of the Freedom of Information Act 2000 or s.28(4) of the Data Protection Act 1998 are dealt with elsewhere in this work.[37] For present purposes, however, it should be noted that the Tribunal may allow such appeals and quash the relevant certificate if it finds: in relation to a certificate under s.23(2) of the Freedom of Information Act 2000, that the information referred to in the certificate was not exempt information by virtue of s.23(1)[38]; or, in relation to a certificate under s.24(3) of the Freedom of Information Act 2000 or s.28(2) of the Data Protection Act 1998, that, applying the principles applied by the court on an application for judicial review, the

---

34 As to which, see paras 28–036 to 28–037.

35 Data Protection Act 1998, s.28(3). Pursuant to the Data Protection Act 1998, s.28(6) a data controller may claim in proceedings under or by virtue of that Act that a certificate issued under s.28(2) which identifies the personal data to which it applies by means of a general description applies to any personal data and, subject to any contrary determination by the Information Tribunal on appeal, the certificate will be conclusively presumed so to apply.

36 Data Protection Act 1998, s.28(10).

37 See paras 14–030 to 14–043, 28–028 and 28–036 to 28–037.

38 Freedom of Information Act 2000, s.60(2). The Tribunal is thus given full appellate jurisdiction to review the matter, unconstrained by any caveat that it "apply the principles applied by the court on an application for judicial review" and assess only whether the minister had "reasonable grounds for issuing the certificate" (*cf.* Freedom of Information Act 2000, s.60(3) and Data Protection Act 1998, s.28(5)).

minister did not have reasonable grounds for issuing the certificate.[39] A second type of appeal may be brought under s.60(4) of the Freedom of Information Act 2000 or s.28(6) of the Data Protection Act 1998 by a party to any proceedings under or by virtue of the relevant Act if it is claimed by a public authority or a data controller that a certificate issued under s.24(3) of the Freedom of Information Act 2000 or s.28(2) of the Data Protection Act 1998 which identifies the information or the personal data to which it applies by means of a general description applies to particular information or personal data. Appeals of this type are also dealt with elsewhere in this work,[40] but it should be noted here that the Tribunal has power to determine that the certificate in question does not apply to the information or personal data referred to by the public authority or data controller.[41]

The principle of neither confirming nor denying

Whether described as keeping a secret or concealing the truth, the exercise of withholding information is in substance the same. So long as questions are not asked about the information or its existence, the secret can be kept and the truth concealed, normally without misinformation or evasion.[42] Once such questions are asked, however, the picture changes because truthful answers may betray the underlying secret. The only way to continue withholding the information is then by way of a misleading or evasive response. Where the reply must come from a public authority, a misleading response is unacceptable and an evasive response is therefore the only option consistent with continuing to keep the secret; this will inevitably take the form of a non-committal "neither confirm nor deny" or "no comment" response.[43] The picture becomes even more complicated once 17–044

[39] Freedom of Information Act 2000, s.60(3); Data Protection Act 1998, s.28(5). See further at para.14–038.

[40] See para.14–038.

[41] The Tribunal is thus given full appellate jurisdiction to review such matters unconstrained by any caveat that it "apply the principles applied by the court on an application for judicial review" and assess only whether the minister had "reasonable grounds for issuing the certificate" (*cf.* Freedom of Information Act 2000, s.60(3) and Data Protection Act 1998, s.28(5)). The explanation for this is no doubt that the minister can issue a new certificate with a much clearer application if dissatisfied with a determination made by the Tribunal under Freedom of Information Act 2000, s.60(5) and Data Protection Act 1998, s.28(7). Freedom of Information Act 2000, s.60(4) or Data Protection Act 1998, s.28(6) only provide for the resolution by way of appeal of a dispute over a certificate's applicability where it arises, in relation to the Freedom of Information Act 2000, "in any proceedings under this Act" and, in relation to the Data Protection Act 1998, "in any proceeding under or by virtue of this Act." The reason for the different formulations is unclear and their effect depends on whether the need for "proceedings" is given a strict or generous construction; the latter would expand the scope for having disputes over a certificate's applicability resolved by the Tribunal without the procedural need for separate "proceedings."

[42] The position may be different where there has been official disclosure of other information relating to the same subject and what is not released impinges upon the former's worth or reliability.

[43] The alternative is to not answer at all, but it would then be uncertain whether the question or the answer has reached its intended recipient.

multiple questions may be asked, because it will then be possible to compare evasive and non-evasive responses and the questions which elicited them in order to deduce or infer the underlying existence or nature of withheld information. These complications in part stem from, and are intimately bound up with, the nature of mosaic prejudice.[44] Accommodating these considerations will tend to require that the neither confirm nor deny blanket be extended to cover all requests on a particular topic having such a high degree of specificity that any variation in the use of evasive or non-evasive responses to them could give something away. Courts in the comparative jurisdictions have, in general terms, approved the adoption of a neither confirm nor deny response to statutory information requests where this is necessary to preserve the secrecy of information whose sensitivity is recognised and protected by the legislation in question.[45] The application of these principles to ss.23 and 24 of the Freedom of Information Act 2000 and s.28 of the Data Protection Act 1998 is dealt with below.[46]

The relationship between sections 23 and 24 of the Freedom of Information Act 2000

17–045 Before turning to this, it is first important to note two points regarding ss.23 and 24 of the Freedom of Information Act 2000:

(1) Sections 23 and 24 confer very different types of exemption. Section 23 is absolute and applies in a mechanical way according to the satisfaction of factual criteria regarding the historical supply and current content of the requested information. Section 23 thus leaves little scope for considering the desirability of a neither confirm nor deny approach in the particular circumstances of each case or as a matter of general policy for cases of the same type. By contrast, s.24 is qualified and applies in a purposive way where exemption is required for live and ongoing national security reasons. Section 24 can therefore consider not only the content and sensitivity of the requested information, but also the particular and general consequences of disclosure and, following on from this, the desirability of a neither confirm nor deny approach.

[44] See paras 15–016 to 15–017, and 17–023(1). For a recent exposition and consideration of the reasons for adapting and adhering to a "neither confirm nor deny" policy in the security and intelligence context see: *Re Freddie Scappaticci's Application* [2003] NIQB 56 at paras [6] and [15] (*per* Carswell C.J.) (NI).

[45] In the USA such a response is known as a "Glomar" response after the "Glomar Explorer," a vessel involved in the leading case *Phillippi v CIA* 546 F.(2d). 1009 (D.C. Cir. 1976). See also: Presidential Executive Order No. 12,958, para.3.7(a) "An agency may refuse to confirm or deny the existence or non-existence of requested information whenever... its existence or non-existence is itself classified under this order"; *Gardels v CIA* (1982) 689 Fed. Rep. (2d).Ser. 1100. See further para.2–013 (Australia); para.2–020 (New Zealand); para.2–028 (Canada); and para.2–037 (Ireland).

[46] See paras to 17–046 to 17–049.

(2) Sections 23 and 24 are also mutually exclusive and do not overlap: s.24(1) only applies to information which does not fall within s.23(1); s.24(2) must be read as being subject to the same limitation in order to engage s.2(1)[47]; and s.24(3)–(4) must necessarily share the same limitation as well. Moreover, s.23 takes precedence over s.24: it is not possible to rely on ss.23 and 24 in relation to the same information; and s.24 may only be relied upon if and to the extent that s.23 is not in play.[48] One consequence of this is that reliance on s.23, which must be revealed under s.17(1)(b) of the Freedom of Information Act 2000, will inevitably inform the applicant that his request has engaged information of the kind described in s.23 while reliance on s.24 instead, which must also be revealed under s.17(1)(b), will inevitably inform the applicant that his request has not had this effect. A further consequence is that the effectiveness of s.24 and its ability to have regard to the desirability of the neither confirm nor deny approach are hampered by its confinement to information which does not fall within s.23(1).

National security certificates under sections 23 and 24 of the Freedom of Information Act 2000: the scope for neither confirming nor denying

Under the Freedom of Information Act 2000 a neither confirm nor deny response may be given where the duty to confirm or deny does not arise by virtue of a Pt II exclusion which prevents the application of s.(1)(a).[49] As indicated above, the mutually exclusive operation of ss.23 and 24 of the Freedom of Information Act 2000 means that reliance on one exemption and not the other 17–046

[47] See para.17–033(1).

[48] It will nevertheless be possible to rely on Freedom of Information Act 2000, ss.23 and 24 in relation to a single information request where different pieces of the information requested are subject to ss.23 and 24, and it may also be possible to rely on different exemptions in the alternative. In this latter regard, Freedom of Information Act 2000, ss.23 and 24 may be exclusive but each is capable of overlapping with, *e.g.* ss.26 and 27. So, while there is no room for choosing between reliance on ss.23 or 24 (if s.23 is in play, s.24 is not), it is perfectly possible to rely on ss.26 or 27 in addition or in preference to either ss.23 or 24.

[49] During the passage of the Freedom of Information Bill, the Cabinet Officer Minister, Lord Falconer of Thoroton, gave the following example of a situation in which it might be necessary to give a neither confirm nor deny response to an information request: "The clearest and easiest example is endangering the defence of the realm. You do not have to communicate information which endangers the defence of the realm. Nor do you have to confirm or deny whether such information exists when, if you did confirm or deny its existence, that in itself would endanger the defence of the realm. I give the obvious example. 'Do you have detailed information concerning the chemical warfare capacities of the following countries?'; and then a list of countries is given. It could well damage the defence of the realm if one indicated the extent to which one had that information" (*Hansard*, HL, Vol.617, October 19, 2000, col.1252) (House of Lords Committee Stage). The example illustrates the importance of the specificity of the request. *Quaere* whether confirmation or denial could be refused if the above request did not include any reference to particular countries.

may itself reveal a certain amount. The extent to which this is the case will depend on the practical operation of s.23 in general and s.23(5) in particular[50] and the scope allowed thereunder for the use of neither confirm nor deny responses.[51] In this regard, further reference can be made to the two hypothetical requests for information made to a government department or police authority regarding the involvement of the security bodies in a particular operation, namely, request A asking for a list of every agency that was involved and request B asking for a list of every security body that was involved.[52] As set out above, if a security body was involved in the operation the department can refuse to comment on this in reliance on s.23 and if no security bodies were involved it can adopt the same approach, provided the fact of this non-involvement is information held by it in recorded form or amounts to unrecorded information which relates to the security bodies for the purposes of s.23(5).[53] The use or non-use of s.23 will only prove revealing if it cannot be relied upon in cases of security body non-involvement. However, if it can be used in such circumstances, so as to obscure the significance of the application of s.23, it might in practice need to be relied upon in a very wide range of situations.[54]

---

50 Freedom of Information Act 2000, s.23(5) prevents the duty to confirm or deny the existence or non-existence of recorded information from arising if, or to the extent that, compliance would involve the disclosure of any information, whether or not already recorded, which was supplied by, or relates to, a security body; see also s.17(4). Because s.23(1)–(2) does not include the formulation "whether or not already recorded", national security certificates issued thereunder may apply only to recorded information unless it can be argued (by reference to the default definition of "information" in s.84) that "the context otherwise requires" a different construction of "information" in s.23(2) (*i.e.* one that imports "whether or not already recorded" because these words appear in s.23(5)). Not adopting such a construction would lead to the result that a national security certificate under s.23(1)–(2) could not be issued to support a refusal to confirm or deny the existence of recorded information to the extent that this refusal is based on a need to prevent the disclosure of unrecorded information which was supplied by, or relates to, a security body: the absence of a national security certificate in a s.23 case would then point to reliance on s.23(5) unrecorded information and this could itself be revealing. Nor does the additional category of unrecorded information which falls within s.23(5) present an area of possible overlap with s.24 even though it is not information falling within s.23(1): this is because s.24 itself only applies to "information which does not fall within s.23(1)" in the default sense of "information recorded in any form which does not fall within s.23(1)."

51 The extent to which reliance on Freedom of Information Act 2000, s.23 and not s.24 (or vice versa) will in practice be capable of revealing significant information will, in any event, be somewhat limited for the following reasons: requests for information cannot be made to the security bodies, so it will not be easy to pose strategic questions liable to yield variable responses which are themselves revealing; bare reference to s.23 under s.17(1)(b) will not itself reveal the identity of the security body or bodies in question or anything specific about the nature of their involvement; and information requests may in practice specify information which falls partly within s.23(1), partly within s.24 and wholly within any number of other Pt II exemptions.

52 See para.17–029.

53 See paras 17–026 and 17–029.

54 This is because the fact of security body non-involvement will arise as an implicit issue or piece of information in many situations. Returning to hypothetical requests A and B, the possibility that the only agencies involved in the operation might have been security bodies complicates the picture even further: if the fact of the operation is a matter of public record and no agencies are referred to in response to either request A or request B it could be readily inferred that they must all have been security bodies. Avoiding this through adherence to the principle of neither confirming nor denying would, however, require a blanket refusal to comment on the involvement of state agencies in almost any security or defence type operation.

National security certificates under section 24 of the Freedom of Information Act 2000 and section 28 of the Data Protection Act 1998: the scope for neither confirming nor denying

Leaving to one side the effect which the exclusive precedence of s.23 of the Freedom of Information Act 2000 has on the application of the exemption in s.24 of that Act, the basic purposive formulation of that exemption, and the equivalent exemption in s.28 of the Data Protection Act 1998, leaves scope for both provisions to be applied in a way that has regard to the desirability of a neither confirm nor deny approach in comparable situations and the general risks of mosaic prejudice.[55] This is probably of more immediate significance in relation to s.28 of the Data Protection Act 1998, because s.7 of that Act allows individuals to request that the security bodies themselves confirm whether they are processing personal data of which they are the data subject and disclose the source of any such data and information. The intelligence services in particular have sought to pursue a neither confirm nor deny policy when responding to such requests and various national security certificates have been issued and relied upon under s.28 of the Data Protection Act 1998 in order to allow them to do so. The history and success of this policy to date is outlined in the following two paragraphs. 17–047

National security certificates under the Data Protection Act 1998: original intelligence service certificates

Three national security certificates under s.28(2) of the Data Protection Act 1998 were originally issued by the Home Secretary (in relation to the Security Service) and the Foreign Secretary (in relation to SIS and GCHQ) in July 2000.[56] These certificates purported to confer a blanket exemption, allowing each intelligence service to respond with a vague and non-committal neither confirm nor deny reply to every request made to it under s.7(1)(a) of the Data Protection Act 1998 without considering whether a different response might be acceptable in the particular circumstances of the case in question. On an appeal brought under s.28(4) of the Data Protection Act 1998 the Information Tribunal quashed the Home Secretary's original certificate on the basis that its effect was "unnecessarily wide"[57] 17–048

[55] See para.17–023(1).

[56] The Home Secretary's certificate was dated July 22, 2000 and the Foreign Secretary's certificates were dated July 30, 2000.

[57] *Baker v Secretary of State for the Home Department* [2001] U.K.H.R.R. 1275, an appeal under the Data Protection Act 1998, s.28(4). Having referred in general terms to the Council of Europe Convention for the Protection of Individuals with Regard to Automatic Processing of Personal Data dated January 28, 1981, the European Community Data Protection Directive 95/46 dated October 24, 1995 and the Human Rights Act 1998, ss.1, 3 and 6, the Tribunal asked itself whether the issue of the certificate was "reasonable in the extended sense of proportionate by reference to the precepts of the ECHR" (para.63) and concluded that the certificate had an "unnecessarily wide effect" and should be quashed accordingly (summary, para.14).

and the Foreign Secretary's original certificates were subsequently withdrawn.[58]

National security certificates under the Data Protection Act 1998: replacement intelligence service certificates

17–049 Three replacement certificates under s.28(2) of the Data Protection Act 1998 were therefore issued by the Home Secretary (in relation to the Security Service) and the Foreign Secretary (in relation to SIS and GCHQ) in December 2001, together with documents giving explanatory reasons.[59] The replacement certificates are expressed in broadly similar general and prospective terms and confer exemption from different provisions of the Data Protection Act 1998 on personal data processed by the intelligence services depending on the purposes and types of data involved. Crucially, the replacement certificates provide: first, that no data shall be exempt from s.7(1)(a) of the Data Protection Act 1998 if the intelligence service in question determines that adherence to the principle of neither confirming nor denying whether it holds data about an individual is not required for the purpose of safeguarding national security; and, secondly, that no data shall be exempt from s.7(1)(b)–(d) of the Data Protection Act 1998 if the intelligence service in question determines that the non-communication of such data or any description of such data is not required for the purpose of safeguarding national security. On appeals brought under s.28(4) of the Data Protection Act 1998 the Information Tribunal has effectively upheld the format of all three certificates,[60] although it should be noted that it has only done so in

---

[58] *Al Fayed v Secretary of State for the Home Department & Secretary of State for Foreign and Commonwealth Affairs*, (unreported, decision of the Information Tribunal dated February 28, 2002), paras 9 and 15–16.

[59] The Home Secretary's certificate was dated December 10, 2001 and the Foreign Secretary's certificates were dated December 8, 2001. Copies of the certificate and reasons document relating to the Security Service are annexed to the decisions of the Information Tribunal in *Gosling v Secretary of State for the Home Department*, (unreported, decision dated August 1, 2003) and *Hitchens v Secretary of State for the Home Department*, (unreported, decision dated August 4, 2003). The certificate and reasons document relating to GCHQ were also accompanied by a document headed "GCHQ Arrangements" setting out the Foreign Secretary's policy in relation to requests made under the Data Protection Act 1998, s.7 and the procedure to be followed by GCHQ when responding to them (*Hitchens v Secretary of State for the Home Department*, (unreported, decision of the Information Tribunal dated August 4, 2003), para.48). Copies of the certificates and reasons documents for all three intelligence services were also placed in the Libraries of both Houses of Parliament (*Intelligence and Security Committee Annual Report 2001–2002* (Cm.5542) 2002, para.50). The Foreign and Home Secretaries have both signed a similar certificate under s.28(2) of the Data Protection Act 1998 in relation to personal data processed by the Intelligence and Security Committee established under s.10 of the Intelligence Services Act 1994 or its Secretariat, and the Committee has in turn issued its own explanatory reasons document (*Intelligence and Security Committee Annual Report 2001–2002* (Cm.5542) 2002, paras 49–50 and Appendix 2).

[60] *Gosling v Secretary of State for the Home Department*, (unreported, decision of the Information Tribunal dated August 1, 2003) followed in *Hitchens v Secretary of State for the Home Department*, (unreported, decision of the Information Tribunal dated August 4, 2003).

response to appeals founded on somewhat limited grounds.[61] In this regard, the Information Tribunal held that there were reasonable grounds for, in effect, delegating to the Security Service the power to determine the requirements of national security in relation to each request, bearing in mind the scope for challenging such determinations before the RIPA Tribunal under s.65 of the Regulation of Investigatory Powers Act 2000 or, possibly, by way of judicial review.[62]

The date to which a certificate relates

National security certificates under s.23(2) of the Freedom of Information Act 2000 may certify that information was directly or indirectly supplied by any of the security bodies as a matter of historical fact or that it relates to any of those bodies as a matter of current fact.[63] National security certificates under s.24(3) of the Freedom of Information Act 2000 and s.28(2) of the Data Protection Act 1998 may certify that the exemption of the information or personal data to which it applies "is or at any time was required" for the purpose of safeguarding national security. The past tense formulation "or at any time was" is included to allow for national security certificates which are issued after the relevant exemption has been relied upon by the public authority in question.[64] It does not enable a Minister to claim exemption where this is no longer required for the purpose of safeguarding national security, because the operative exemption provisions only apply in circumstances where exemption "is required" for that purpose.[65] 17–050

6. INFORMATION PREJUDICIAL TO DEFENCE OR THE ARMED FORCES

Introduction

As already indicated, information whose disclosure under the Freedom of Information Act 2000 would, or would be likely to, prejudice the defence of the British Islands or of any colony or the capability, effectiveness or security of the 17–051

[61] *Gosling v Secretary of State for the Home Department* (unreported, decision of the Information Tribunal dated August 1, 2003), para.28; *Hitchens v Secretary of State for the Home Department, (*unreported, decision of the Information Tribunal dated August 4, 2003), para.42.

[62] *Gosling v Secretary of State for the Home Department*, (unreported, decision of the Information Tribunal dated August 1, 2003), para.56; *Hitchens v Secretary of State for the Home Department*, (unreported, decision of the Information Tribunal dated August 4, 2003) para.49.

[63] See para.17–041.

[64] In relation to the Freedom of Information Act 2000, s.24, this was confirmed in House of Commons Public Administration Select Committee Third Report Session 1998–1999 *Freedom of Information Draft Bill* (HC 570-I), 1999, paras 74–77 and Annex 6, para.44.

[65] Freedom of Information Act 2000, s.24(1)–(2); Data Protection Act 1998, s.28(1).

armed forces of the Crown or of any forces co-operating with those forces ("the section 26 defence interests") is also subject to a qualified exemption under s.26 of that Act. A similar exemption is to be found in the freedom of information legislation of each of the comparative jurisdictions.[66] The phrase "would or would be likely to prejudice" is common to most of the prejudice-based exemptions in the Act. The nature of prejudice and the degree of likelihood which the phrase requires are considered elsewhere in this work.[67]

Terms of the exemption in section 26 of the Freedom of Information Act 2000

17–052 Section 26(1) of the Freedom of Information Act 2000[68] provides that information is exempt information if its disclosure under the Act would, or would be likely to, prejudice any of the s.26 defence interests. Having reached that threshhold, the duty to communicate will not apply where, in all the circumstances of the case, the public interest in maintaining the exemption outweighs the public

[66] In the United States, the Freedom of Information Act, 1966, 5 USC 552(b)(1) (USA), exempts from disclosure national security information concerning national defence or foreign policy, provided that that information has been classified in accordance with the requirements of an executive Order: see para.2–008(1). The Freedom of Information Act 1982, s.33(1)(a) (Cth of Aust), provides an exemption where the disclosure of the requested document would, or could be reasonably be expected to, cause damage to (i) the security of the Commonwealth of Australia; or (ii) the defence of the Commonwealth of Australia: see para.2–015(9). The Act provides for a conclusive certificate to be issued in relation to this exemption (see para.2–014) and makes provision for neither confirming nor denying the existence of the requested documents where to do so would or could reasonably be expected to cause damage to these interests (see para.2–013). The Official Information Act 1982, ss.6(a), 7 and 27(1)(a) (NZ) and the Privacy Act 1993, ss.27(1)(a) and 27(2)(a)–(c) provide absolute exemptions where the disclosure of the information would be likely to prejudice the security or defence of New Zealand or certain external dependencies: see para.2–022(1). The Official Information Act 1982 (NZ) provides for a conclusive certificate to be issued in relation to this exemption (see para.2–021) and makes provision for neither confirming nor denying the existence of the requested documents where to do so would or could reasonably be expected to cause damage to these interests (see para.2–020). The Access to Information Act (1982), s.15 Canada, provides a discretionary exemption for records the disclosure of which could reasonably be expected to cause injury to the defence of Canada or allied states: see para.2–032(11). "Defence of Canada", etc., is defined to include the efforts of Canada and of foreign states toward the detection, prevention and suppression of activities of any foreign state directed toward actual or potential attack or other acts of aggression against Canada or any state allied or associated with Canada: s.15(2). The Act provides for a conclusive certificate to be issued in relation to this exemption (see para.2–030). The Freedom of Information Act 1997 s.24(1) (Ireland), provides a discretionary exemption for records the disclosure of which could reasonably be expected to adversely affect the security or defence of the Republic of Ireland: see para.2–039(13). The public body can refuse to confirm or deny the existence of any record falling within the terms of the exemption if it thinks that to do either would be contrary to the public interest: Freedom of Information Act 1997, s.24(3) (Ireland): see para.2–037. A conclusive certificate may be issued in respect of this head of exemption: Freedom of Information Act 1997, s.25 (Ireland): see para.2–037.

[67] See paras 15–012 to 15–020.

[68] Freedom of Information (Scotland) Act 2002, s.31(4).

interest in disclosing the information.[69] Section 26(3) provides a corresponding exclusion of the duty to confirm or deny where, or to the extent that, compliance with the duty to divulge the existence of information would, or would be likely to, prejudice any of the s.26 defence interests. Section 26(3) is not expressed to relate to any particular category of information and does not itself stand as a "provision" which "states that the duty to confirm or deny does not arise in relation to any information" for the purposes of s.2(1). However, for the reasons set out above in relation to s.24(2),[70] the whole of s.26 needs to be read as the "provision" which "states that the duty to confirm or deny does not arise in relation to any information" and which therefore engages s.2(1). On this basis, if the s.26(3) description is met, the duty to confirm or deny does not apply only where, in all the circumstances of the case, the public interest in maintaining the exclusion of the divulgence duty outweighs the public interest in disclosing whether the public authority holds the information requested.[71]

Terms of the exemption in Schedule 7 to the Data Protection Act 1998

As already indicated, Sch.7 to the Data Protection Act 1998 further exempts personal data from the subject access provisions in that Act[72] in any case to the extent to which the application of those provisions would be likely to prejudice the combat effectiveness of any of the armed forces of the Crown.[73] This is a much narrower exemption than s.26 of the Freedom of Information Act 2000 for the following reasons: it does not wholly exempt the type of information in question from the entirety of the Data Protection Act 1998 regime; it is confined to the combat effectiveness of the armed forces of the Crown and does not extend to their general effectiveness; it does not protect the defence of the British Islands or of any colony or the capability or security of the armed forces of the Crown; and it does not protect forces co-operating with them. The adoption of this narrower formulation was not expressly required by the European Community Data Protection Directive 95/46, which allowed for restrictions and exemptions where necessary to safeguard defence.[74] The armed forces exemption in Sch.7 to the Data Protection Act 1998 does not operate, and cannot be overridden, by reference to any public interest balancing test, but its application is subject to the full range of enforcement mechanisms in Pt V of that Act. The 17–053

[69] Freedom of Information Act 2000, s.2(2)(b).

[70] See para.17–033(1).

[71] Freedom of Information Act 2000, s.26(3) (read with s.26(1)) thus engages s.2(1)(b) so as to prevent s.1(1)(a) from applying and the duty to confirm or deny from arising in relation to the exempt information if the public interest balance favours non-divulgence.

[72] The subject information provisions include the subject access rights under s.7: Data Protection Act 1998, ss.27(2) and 71.

[73] Data Protection Act 1998, s.37, Sch.7, para.2. *cf.* Freedom of Information Act 2000, s.26(1) which uses the more exhaustive formulation "would, or would be likely to, prejudice."

[74] [1995] O.J. L281/31. Art.13(1)(b).

remainder of this section concentrates on the exemption in s.26 of the Freedom of Information Act 2000, but the same definition of the armed forces of the Crown and the same considerations as to the executive's assessment of likely prejudice to their combat effectiveness are nevertheless relevant to the armed forces exemption in Sch.7 to the Data Protection Act 1998.

The British Islands and the colonies

17–054 While s.24 of the Freedom of Information Act 2000 is concerned with safeguarding national security, meaning "the security of the United Kingdom and its people,"[75] s.26 of the Act might be thought to have a geographically wider purview in that it is overtly concerned with the defence of the British Islands and of any colony.[76] The significance of this should not be overstated, however, as it has been recognised that action overseas may be capable of indirectly affecting the security of the United Kingdom even if directed towards a foreign State.[77] For the purposes of s.26 of the Freedom of Information Act 2000, the British Islands means the United Kingdom, the Channel Islands and the Isle of Man (but not the Republic of Ireland which could be said to fall within the British Isles).[78] The United Kingdom in turn means Great Britain (*i.e.* England, Scotland and Wales)[79] and Northern Ireland, while the Channel Islands means the Bailiwick of Jersey and the Bailiwick of Guernsey, Alderney and Sark and their respective dependencies.[80] Colony means any part of Her Majesty's dominions outside the British Islands,[81] except countries having fully responsible status within the Commonwealth[82] and their respective dependencies.[83]

[75] *Secretary of State for the Home Department v Rehman* [2001] UKHL 47; [2003] 1 A.C. 153, HL at para.[50] (*per* Lord Hoffmann) and para.[64] (*per* Lord Hutton).

[76] Freedom of Information Act 2000, s.26(1); Freedom of Information (Scotland) Act 2002, s.31(4).

[77] *Secretary of State for the Home Department v Rehman* [2001] UKHL 47; [2003] 1 A.C. 153, HL, at paras [16]–[17] (*per* Lord Slynn). See also at paras [53] and [62] (per Lord Hoffmann) and para.[64] (*per* Lord Hutton). It is at least conceivable that some colonies may be of little or no significance to the national security of the United Kingdom so that considerations relating to their defence could engage Freedom of Information Act 2000, s.26 but not s.24.

[78] Interpretation Act 1978, ss.5, 22(1), Sch.1, Sch.2, para.4(2); F. Bennion, *Statutory Interpretation*, 4th ed. (Butterworths, London, 2002), p.289.

[79] Interpretation Act 1978, ss.5, 22(1), Sch.1, Sch.2, para.5(a); Union with Scotland Act 1706, preamble, Art.1.

[80] F. Bennion, *Statutory Interpretation* (4th ed., Butterworths, London, 2002), pp.289–291.

[81] Interpretation Act 1978, s.5, Sch.1; F. Bennion, *Statutory Interpretation* (4th ed., Butterworths, London, 2002), pp. 291–292. An example would be the Falkland Islands.

[82] *i.e.* countries other than the United Kingdom which are part of Her Majesty's independent dominions.

[83] The statutory expression is territories for whose external relations a country other than the United Kingdom is responsible. Associated states are also excluded from the definition of a colony, but this is now a defunct category as there are no longer any territories maintaining a status of association with the United Kingdom in accordance with the West Indies Act 1967.

The armed forces of the Crown

The expression "the armed forces of the Crown" is not defined in the Freedom of Information Act 2000 or the Data Protection Act 1998 but must include the regular, reserve and auxiliary naval, military and air forces of the Crown and the women's services of those forces.[84] Authority for the existence and maintenance of the naval forces derives from the royal prerogative, while authority for the existence and maintenance of the military and air forces derives from statute.[85] In terms of the principal and most important statutes, the keeping of discipline in the naval forces is authorised by the Naval Discipline Act 1957, the raising and maintenance of, and the keeping of discipline within, the military forces are authorised by the Army Act 1955 and the raising and maintenance of, and the keeping of discipline within, the air forces are authorised by the Air Force (Constitution) Act 1917 and the Air Force Act 1955.[86] Similarly, the territorial forces, the naval, military and air force reserves and the women's services are raised and maintained primarily under the Reserve Forces Act 1996, the 17–055

[84] This is supported by the definition of "the armed forces of the Crown raised in the United Kingdom at the present day" at *Halsbury's Laws of England* (4th ed.), Vol.41, title "Royal Forces", para.1. The Armed Forces Act 1981, s.20(1), Sch.3, Pts I–II further provide that "the armed forces of the Crown" (raised in the United Kingdom and excluding the Royal Navy) includes the women's services of those forces administered by the Defence Council: see also *Halsbury's Laws of England* (4th ed.), Vol.41, title "Royal Forces", para.17. On this basis, the armed forces of the Crown comprise: the regular forces (*i.e.* the Royal Navy, Army, Royal Air Force and Royal Marines); the reserve and auxiliary forces (including the Territorial Army); and the women's services and their reserves. The alternative expression "Her Majesty's forces" is also used in some legislation, *e.g.* Army Act 1955, s.225(1), Air Force Act 1955, s.223(1), Naval Discipline Act 1957, s.135(1) and Regulation of Investigatory Powers Act 2000, s.81(1). As to the armed forces more generally see: A. Bradley and K. Ewing, *Constitutional and Administrative Law* (13th ed., Longman, London, 2003), pp.328–342; P. Jackson, *Hood Phillips and Jackson: Constitutional and Administrative Law* (8th ed., Sweet & Maxwell, London, 2001), paras 19–002 to 19–018; F.W. Maitland, *The Constitutional History of England* (Cambridge University Press, Cambridge, 1919), pp.275–280, 324–329 and 447–462; W. Anson, *Law and Custom of the Constitution* (4th ed.), Oxford University Press, Oxford, 1907), Vol.II(ii), pp.199–222; Ministry of Defence, *Manual of Military Law* (12th ed., HMSO, London, 1972), Pt I, Vols A-B and (10th ed., London, 1989), Pt II, Sec. 1; Rowe "The Crown and Accountability for the Armed Forces" in M. Sunkin and S. Payne (eds), *The Nature of the Crown: a Legal and Political Analysis* (Oxford University Press, Oxford, 1999). The special forces and any unit or part of a unit which is for the time being required by the Secretary of State to assist GCHQ in the exercise of its functions are not excluded from the definition of the armed forces of the Crown for the purposes of the Freedom of Information Act 2000, s.26, *cf.* Sch.1, Pt I, para.6.

[85] Bill of Rights Act (1688 or 1689), s.1 prevents the Crown from raising or keeping a standing army within the United Kingdom in times of peace without the consent of Parliament; *Halsbury's Laws of England* (4th ed.), Vol.8(2), title "Constitutional Law and Human Rights", paras 883 and 886–887; *Halsbury's Laws of England* (4th ed.), Vol.41, title "Royal Forces", paras 1, 3 and 5–8.

[86] The Army Act 1955, Air Force Act 1955 and Naval Discipline Act 1957 are each continued in force for one year at a time by Army, Air Force and Naval Discipline (Continuation) Orders made annually during the course of five year periods, which are in turn instituted by quinquennial Armed Forces Acts: see the Armed Forces Act 2001, s.1 and the Army, Air Force and Naval Discipline Acts (Continuation) Order 2003 (SI 2003/1869) continuing the Service Discipline Acts in force until August 31, 2004; *Halsbury's Laws of England* (4th ed.), Vol.8(2), title "Constitutional Law and Human Rights", para.887; *Halsbury's Laws of England* (4th ed.), Vol.41, title "Royal Forces", para.3.

Army and Air Force (Women's Service) Act 1948 and the prerogative.[87] The supreme government, command and disposition of all the armed forces by sea, land and air, and of all defence establishments, is ultimately vested in the Crown by prerogative right at common law and by statute.[88] However, these powers are now exercised on the advice of ministers and most matters relating to the armed forces are regulated by statute and administered by and through ministers, the Ministry of Defence, the Defence Council and the Admiralty, Army and Air Force Boards.[89]

Other relevant forces

17–056 Although certain forces raised under the law of a colony, protectorate or trust territory and certain visiting forces can become subject to United Kingdom service law and discipline,[90] they are not "armed forces of the Crown" for the purposes of the Freedom of Information Act 2000.[91] Any forces co-operating with the armed forces of the Crown or any part of those forces are, however, relevant forces for the purposes of s.26 of the Freedom of Information Act 2000.[92] Colonial, Commonwealth and other allied armed forces could fall into this category when co-operating with the armed forces of the Crown on operations or exercises on any kind of bilateral or multilateral basis or under the auspices of, for example, the North Atlantic Treaty Organisation or the United Nations.[93] There is also no express requirement that these co-operating forces be either armed or foreign and so it might be argued that domestic or foreign police or security forces are included. One question arising in relation to other relevant

87 Note that some of the Reserve Forces Act 1980 remains unrepealed by the Reserve Forces Act 1996, ss.3(1), 132(4) and Sch.11 (Reserve Forces Act 1996 (Commencement No. 1) Order 1997 (SI 1997/305) and Reserve Forces Act 1996 (Transitional, Consequential and Saving Provisions) Regulations 1997 (SI 1997/306)). See generally: *Halsbury's Laws of England*, Vol.8(2), title "Constitutional Law and Human Rights", paras 888–889.

88 *Halsbury's Laws of England* (4th ed.), Vol 8(2), title "Constitutional Law and Human Rights", para.884.

89 Defence (Transfer of Functions) Act 1964; *Halsbury's Laws of England* (4th ed.), Vol.8(2), title "Constitutional Law and Human Rights", paras 439–447 and 885–886; *Halsbury's Laws of England* (4th ed.),Vol.41, title "Royal Forces", paras 1–2.

90 Army Act 1955, ss.206–207 and 217; Air Force Act 1955, ss.206–207 and 215; Naval Discipline Act 1957, ss.114–115 and 127; Visiting Forces (British Commonwealth) Act 1933, ss.4–6; Visiting Forces Act 1952; International Headquarters and Defence Organisations Act 1964; *Halsbury's Laws of England* (4th ed.), Vol.41, title "Royal Forces", paras 9–10, 19, 21 and 127–134.

91 Note the exclusion of Commonwealth forces from the definitions of "Her Majesty's air forces", "Her Majesty's military forces", "Her Majesty's naval forces" and "Her Majesty's forces" in Army Act 1955, s.225(1) and Air Force Act 1955, s.223(1). Note the inclusion of colonial forces in, but the exclusion of Commonwealth forces, from the definition of "Her Majesty's forces" in Naval Discipline Act 1957, s.135(1).

92 Freedom of Information Act 2000, s.26(2)(b); Freedom of Information (Scotland) Act 2002, s.31(5)(b)(ii).

93 The involvement of foreign States or international organisations might also engage the international relations exemption in the Freedom of Information Act 2000, s.27, Freedom of Information (Scotland) Act 2002, s.32(1).

forces is whether general prejudice to their capability, effectiveness or security is enough to engage s.26 or whether what matters is their capability, effectiveness or security whilst they are "co-operating with" the armed forces of the Crown: the latter interpretation seems preferable, since otherwise account could be taken of prejudice to the capability, effectiveness or security of forces which co-operate only occasionally with the armed forces of the Crown.

Prejudice to the defence of the British Islands or of any colony

Whether disclosure of particular information under the Freedom of Information Act 2000 would prejudice, or would be likely to prejudice, the defence of the British Islands or of any colony cannot properly be determined without some consideration of what the defence of the nation may reasonably require in the prevailing circumstances. Distinctions may be drawn between what is legitimately required for the defence of a nation in peacetime, during a time of preparation for war, during actual hostilities, upon the cessation of hostilities and in the transition to peace.[94] Prejudice to the defence of the nation will reflect those distinctions. The defence of the nation is not confined to the resistance of external threats to the nation, but extends to matters whose purpose is the protection of the nation. Accordingly, there is bound to be some overlap between information whose disclosure would, or would be likely to, prejudice, on the one hand, the defence of the British Islands or of any colony and, on the other hand, the capability, effectiveness or security of any relevant forces, as well as a substantial overlap with information whose non-disclosure is required for the purpose of safeguarding national security. The s.26 defence interests are akin to the national security interests covered by s.24 of the Freedom of Information Act 2000. The courts may therefore be expected to adopt an analogous approach to the executive's assessment of their protection and the type of disclosure which would be likely to cause them prejudice: the executive will thus be entitled to take a preventative or precautionary approach to the protection of the s.26 defence interests, taking into account the risks of mosaic prejudice,[95] 17–057

[94] For a discussion of the fluctuating nature of what may legitimately be done under the aegis of the defence of the nation, see: *Stenhouse v Coleman* (1944) 69 C.L.R. 457 at 471–2. The Constitution of Australia gives the Federal Legislature the power to make laws with respect to the "defence of the Commonwealth." In general terms, the view taken is that in a period of stable and amicable international relations the extent of what may be done in the name of the defence of the Commonwealth is small: there can be no reasonable justification for interference with most ordinary civil activities. But at a period of international discord, the danger to the nation of becoming involved in war may be great and what may legitimately be done in the name of the defence of the nation is broader: *Farey v Burvett* (1916) 21 C.L.R. 433 at 453; *Victorian Chamber of Manufacturers v The Commonwealth of Australia* (1943) 67 C.L.R. 335 at 339; *Adelaide Company of Jehovah's Witnesses Incorporated v Commonwealth of Australia* (1943) 67 C.L.R. 116.

[95] See para.17–023(1). This has been the approach taken by the High Court of Australia in determining whether a law is one with respect to the defence of the Commonwealth: "It is not the duty or the function of the court to consider whether in its opinion such regulations are 'necessary' for

and the courts can be expected to show a certain deference to its conclusions.[96] Section 2 of the Official Secrets Act 1989[97] provides some guidance as to the type of matters that may be relevant to "defence"[98] and the type of effects which are "damaging" to defence interests.[99]

Prejudice to the capability, effectiveness or security of the armed forces

17–058 So far as concerns the capability, effectiveness and security of any relevant forces, the Ministry of Defence publication *The Green Book: Defence and the Media in Times of Emergency* contains "regulations for correspondents accompanying an operational force" which list categories of "operational information" which

defence purposes. Questions of legislative policy are determined by the Legislature, not by the courts. If it can reasonably be considered that there is a real connection between the subject matter of the legislation and defence, the court should hold that the legislation is authorised by the power to make laws with respect to defence." (*Dawson v The Commonwealth* (1946) 73 C.L.R. 157 at 173). However, the High Court has rejected the notion that the Parliament's or the executive's determination of the needs of defence can be conclusive: *The Communist Party v The Commonwealth of Australia* (1951) 83 C.L.R. 1, where the Court held that a law *inter alia* dissolving the Australian Communist Party which, in its recital, was declared to be detrimental to the defence of the nation could not, in fact, be said to be related to the defence of the nation.

[96] See paras 17–036 to 17–040. This was the approach that was taken in relation to regulations made under the Defence of the Realm Act 1914, which permitted regulations to be made for *inter alia* the public safety and the defence of the realm. Provided that the regulations were "conceivably capable" or "reasonably capable" of assisting in the defence of the realm, they were permissible under the Act: *Lipton Ltd v Ford* [1917] 2 K.B. 647; *Hudson's Bay Co v Maclay* (1920) 36 T.L.R. 469; *John Robinson & Co Ltd v The King* [1921] 3 K.B. 183 at 197; and similarly *Fort Frances Pulp and Paper Co v Manitoba Free Press Co* [1923] A.C. 695 at 705–705. This is also the approach that has been taken by the courts of the comparative jurisdictions when determining whether a law is required for the purpose of defence. Thus: ". . .when a nation is in peril, applying the maxim *salus populi suprema lex*, the courts must concede to the Parliament and to the Executive which it contols a wide latitude to determine what legislation is required to protect the safety of the realm" (*Victorian Chamber of Manufactures v Commonwealth of Australia* (1943) 67 C.L.R. 347 at 400); "to the Congress, in the exercise of its powers, not least the war upon which the very life of the nation depends, a wide latitude of discretion must be accorded" (*Hamilton v Kentucky Distilleries & Warehouse Co* (1919) 251 U.S. 146 at 163). It should, however, be noted that in each of the above cases the considerable latitude allowed was in no small part due to the existence of a formal state of war in which the nation found itself.

[97] See para.17–022(1).

[98] Official Secrets Act 1989, s.2(4) defines "defence" to mean (a) the size, shape, organisation, logistics, order of battle, deployment, operations, state of readiness and training of the armed forces of the Crown, (b) the weapons, stores or other equipment of those forces and the invention, development, production and operation of such equipment and research relating to it, (c) defence policy and strategy and military planning and intelligence and (d) plans and measures for the maintenance of essential supplies and services that are or would be needed in time of war.

[99] For the purposes of Official Secrets Act 1989, s.2(1) a disclosure is damaging if it (a) damages the capability of, or any part of, the armed forces of the Crown to carry out their tasks or leads to loss of life or injury to members of those forces or serious damage to the equipment or installations of those forces, (b) endangers the interests of the United Kingdom abroad, seriously obstructs the promotion or protection by the United Kingdom of those interests or endangers the safety of British citizens abroad or (c) would be likely to have any of those effects (s. 2(2)).

"correspondents may not be allowed to include in copy, or in radio or television reports, without specific approval."[1] These categories give some idea of the types of information whose disclosure is capable of prejudicing combat effectiveness.[2] The s.26 defence interests, of course, go much wider than this and are not confined to periods of operational activity.

Outweighing the public interest in preventing prejudice to the section 26 defence interests

Even if non-compliance with the duty to confirm or deny or the duty to communicate is required because divulgence or disclosure would, or would be likely to, prejudice any of the s.26 defence interests, divulgence or disclosure will still have to take place under s.1 of the Freedom of Information Act 2000 if, in all the circumstances of the case, the public interest in divulgence or disclosure is not outweighed by the public interest in preventing, or avoiding the risk of, such prejudice.[3] As with the safeguarding of national security interests under s.24 of the Freedom of Information Act 2000, the decision of Parliament not to make exemption under s.26 absolute cannot properly be undone by giving the public interest in maintaining the exemption such weight as to make the public interest in disclosure unable to outweigh it. The exercise must be carried out in such a manner as to recognise that in some circumstances the public interest in disclosure will be sufficiently powerful to displace an inherently compelling public interest in maintaining the exemption.[4] The following considerations, which will be relevant in this regard, show that the public interest in complying with s.1 of the Freedom of Information Act 2000 is capable of prevailing: where the degree of likelihood attaching to the apprehended prejudice is low, the weight assigned to the public interest in non-disclosure may have to be moderated accordingly; the United Kingdom public interest in defending a colony or protecting the capability, effectiveness or security of foreign forces may also deserve a lower weighting, particularly if the national security and international relations exemptions in ss.24 and 27 of the Freedom of Information Act 2000 are not engaged[5]; it is generally recognised that the public interest in information 17–059

1 Annex A. *The Green Book* can be found at *www.mod.uk/news/green_book/index.htm*.

2 The categories are: (a) composition of the force and the locations of ships, units and aircraft; (b) details of military movements; (c) operational orders; (d) plans or intentions; (e) casualties; (f) organisations; (g) place names; (h) tactics, details of defensive positions, camouflage methods, weapon capabilities or deployments; (i) names or numbers of ships, units or aircraft; (j) names of individual servicemen.

3 Freedom of Information Act 2000, s.2(1)(b) and (2)(b).

4 See para.17–039.

5 By way of a parallel, public interest immunity cannot be claimed by a foreign state or on the ground that disclosure would infringe the public interest of a foreign state: *Buttes Gas & Oil Co v Hammer (No.3)* [1981] Q.B. 223, CA at 247, 251 and 262. However, it has been recognised that because the public interest of the United Kingdom requires continued co-operation, and recognises a convergence of interests, with foreign sovereign states, public interest immunity can nevertheless apply to various communications between British and foreign government departments

about defence matters can be very great and in this regard reference can be made to the *Guidance on Interpretation* accompanying the *Code of Practice on Access to Government Information* which stated in relation to the exemption for "information whose disclosure would harm defence"[6] that the exemption was not intended to prevent the disclosure of "factual information relating to legitimate concerns on such matters as loss of life, or hazards and environmental intrusion arising from military operations or use of land."[7]

or prosecuting authorities on international relations grounds: *Buttes Gas & Oil Co v Hammer (No.3)* [1981] Q.B. 223, CA at 256; *R. v Governor of Brixton Prison, Ex p. Osman* [1991] 1 W.L.R. 281, DC at 285–286; *R. v Horseferry Road Magistrates' Court, Ex p. Bennett (No.2)* (1995) 99 Cr.App.R. 123, DC at 126. Mention has already been made of the fact that action overseas may be capable of indirectly affecting the security of the United Kingdom, even if directed towards a foreign State: *Secretary of State for the Home Department v Rehman* [2001] UKHL 47; [2003] 1 A.C. 153, HL, at paras [16]–[17] (*per* Lord Slynn). See also *ibid.*, at paras [53] and [62] (*per* Lord Hoffmann) and para.[64] (*per* Lord Hutton).

6 *Open Government Code of Practice on Access to Government Information* (2nd ed., 1997), Pt II, para.1(a).

7 *Government Code of Practice on Access to Government Information: Guidance on Interpretation* (2nd ed., 1997), Pt II, para.1.1.

CHAPTER 18

International and Internal Relations

1. INTERNATIONAL RELATIONS

Introduction

Section 27(1) of the Freedom of Information Act 2000[1] provides a four-limbed exemption in respect of information the disclosure of which, broadly speaking, 18–001

[1] The Freedom of Information (Scotland) Act 2002, s.32(1)(a) is in similar terms, save that "substantial prejudice" to the protected matters is required, rather than prejudice simpliciter. The

would be likely to be prejudicial to relations between the government of the United Kingdom and a foreign state or which otherwise would be likely to be prejudicial to the interests of the United Kingdom abroad.[2] Section 27(2) of the Act provides a separate exemption for confidential information obtained from a foreign state or from an international organisation or international court.[3] The latter exemption is purely class-based, with no requirement of harm or likelihood of harm resulting from disclosure. Both exemptions are qualified exemptions, so that whether or not there is a duty to disclose such exempt information will turn upon whether in all the circumstances of the case the public interest in maintaining the exemption outweighs the public interest in disclosing the information.[4] Section 27 also includes a corresponding exclusion of the duty to confirm or deny. Although a particular piece of information may readily fall within both sub-sections, the focus of each of the two provisions is basically different. Section 27(1) is concerned to protect the interests of the United Kingdom in its dealings with and in other States. Section 27(2) is concerned to protect a facet of international comity. Whilst it can be said that any conduct that is potentially harmful to international comity is indirectly harmful to the interests of the United Kingdom, that harm may often be difficult to identify or measure at the time of proposed disclosure and it may have to compete with immediate interests that are clearly served by disclosure. Section 27(2) is thus capable of applying to information not captured by s.27(1). Moreover, determination of the applicability of s.27(2) is more straightforward, looking to the character of the information (*i.e.* whether it is confidential) and to the source of the information (*i.e.* whether it was obtained from a State other than the United Kingdom or from an international organisation or international court), rather than conjecturing about the effect of disclosure upon "the interests of the United Kingdom abroad" and upon international relations. The issue of confidentiality and the scope of the s.27(2) exemption are considered in the main chapter on confidentiality.[5] The s.27(1) exemption, as well as the required sources of information for the s.27(2) exemption to operate, are considered in this chapter. With the

Scottish provision may be open to challenge. Under the Scotland Act 1998, the Scottish Parliament cannot make legislation which relates to or modifies the law on "reserved matters" and corresponding restrictions apply in relation to the exercise of certain functions by the Scottish Ministers: Scotland Act 1998, ss.28–30, Sch.4, Pt I, paras 2, 3, Sch.5 (on "legislative competence"), and Scotland Act 1998, ss.53–54 (on "devolved competence"). The following are in turn defined as "reserved matters" for the purposes of the Scotland Act 1998: (1) international relations, including relations with territories outside the United Kingdom, the European Communities (and their institutions) and other international organisations (under the heading "foreign affairs etc."), Scotland Act 1998, s.30, Sch.5, Pt I, para.7; and (2) public access to information held by public bodies or holders of public offices other than certain Scottish public authorities: Scotland Act 1998, s.30, Sch.5, Pt II, s.B13.

2 The provision echoes the language used in ss.3 and 6 of the Official Secrets Act 1989.
3 The Freedom of Information (Scotland) Act 2002, s.32(1)(b) is identical.
4 Freedom of Information Act 2000, s.2(2); Freedom of Information (Scotland) Act 2002, s.2(1).
5 See in particular paras 25–039 to 25–042.

exception of the USA, similar exemptions of varying width exist in each of the comparative jurisdictions.[6]

Scope of the section 27(1) exemption

Section 27(1) of the Freedom of Information Act 2000[7] provides that where the disclosure of information under the Act would or would be likely to prejudice: 18–002

[6] In the United States, the Freedom of Information Act, 1966, contains no specific exemption for information that might damage international relations or for information that was obtained from a foreign government in confidence. In practice, such information may be found to be exempt under Exemption 1 (national security information) provided that it has been earlier classified: see para.2–008(1) and Executive Order No. 12,958, s.1.1(d). In order to be exempted, "foreign government information" must be shown to have been provided to the US Government with an expectation of confidentiality and classified at the time as such: see *Weatherhead v United States*, 157 F.(3d) 735 (9th Cir. 1998) and, on appeal, *Weatherhead v United States*, 527 US 1063 (1999), where a letter sent by the British Home Office to the Department of Justice was ordered to be disclosed because it had not been so classified. In *Weatherhead*, the British Government, upon being asked by the State Department whether it consented to release, stated that it was unable to agree because "the normal line in cases like this is that all correspondance between Governments is confidential unless papers have been formally requisitioned". If it has been classified, then exemption will generally be upheld. Thus, in *Krikorian v Department of State*, 984 F.(2d) 461 (D.C. Cir. 1993) the court found that a telegram reporting discussion between an agency official and a high-ranking foreign diplomat regarding terrorism was properly withheld as foreign government information; release would jeopardise reciprocal confidentiality between governments. Differing views have been taken on whether the agency must demonstrate that the foreign state provided the information in confidence or whether that is to be presumed: *Steinberg v United States Department of Justice*, 179 F.R.D. 357 (D.D.C. 1998) and *Billington v Department of Justice*, 11 F. Supp. (2d) 45 (D.D.C. 1998) and 69 F. Supp. (2d) 128 (D.D.C. 1999). Exemption can also be secured under Exemption 7: para.2–008(7). The Freedom of Information Act 1982 (Cth of Australia), s.33, provides two exemptions that broadly correlate to the two provisions in Freedom of Information Act 2000, s.27(1) and (2). Under Freedom of Information Act 1982, s.33(1)(a)(iii), a document is exempt where its disclosure would, or could be reasonably be expected to, cause damage to the international relations of Australia; under s.33(1)(b) a document is exempt if its disclosure would divulge any information communicated in confidence by or on behalf of a foreign government, etc.: see para.2–015(9). A conclusive certificate to this effect may be issued. The provision does not involve a consideration of the public interest. The Official Information Act 1982 (New Zealand), provides two separate absolute exemptions to cover analogous information. First, information may be withheld without a consideration of the public interest where disclosure would be likely to prejudice the international relations of the New Zealand government: Official Information Act 1982, ss.6(b) and 27(1)(a); Privacy Act 1993, s.27(1)(b); and see para.2–022(1). Secondly, information may also be withheld without a consideration of the public interest where disclosure would be likely to prejudice the entrusting of information to the government of New Zealand on a basis of confidence by the government of any other country or any agency of such a government, or by any international organisation: Official Information Act 1982, ss.6(b) and 27(1)(a); Privacy Act 1993, s.27(1)(b); and see para.2–022(1). The Act provides for the Prime Minister to issue a conclusive certificate in support of the first: s.31. The Access to Information Act (Canada), s.15 provides a discretionary exemption for records the disclosure of which could "reasonably be expected" to cause injury to the conduct of international affairs: see para.2–032(11). The Canada Evidence Act allows the Attorney-General to issue a certificate prohibiting the disclosure of information in connection with a legal proceeding for the purpose of *inter alia* protecting information obtained in confidence from foreign entities. The Freedom of Information Act 1997 (Ireland), ss.24(1)(c) provides a discretionary exemption for records the disclosure of which could reasonably be expected to affect adversely the international relations of the State of Ireland: see para.2–039(13). The Act provides for a conclusive certificate in support of the exemption: s.25.

(a) relations between the United Kingdom[8] and any other State,
(b) relations between the United Kingdom and any international organisation or international court,
(c) the interests of the United Kingdom abroad, or
(d) the promotion or protection by the United Kingdom of its interests abroad,

then the information is exempt information. The phrase "would or would be likely to prejudice" is common to most of the prejudice-based exemptions in the Act. The nature of prejudice and the degree of likelihood which the phrase requires are considered elsewhere in this work.[9]

The State and its organs

18–003 The Freedom of Information Act 2000 defines the word "State" to include the "government of any State and any organ of its government,"[10] thereby alluding to its meaning in international law. There is no means of determining objectively the existence of a State: it is a matter of recognition by one State of another State, with recognition being largely presumed.[11] The stated view of the United Kingdom is:

> "The normal criteria which the government apply for recognition as a state are that it should have, and seem likely to continue to have, a clearly defined territory with a population, a government who are able of themselves to exercise effective control of that territory, and independence in their external relations. Other factors, including some United Nations resolutions, may also be relevant."[12]

---

7 And similarly the Freedom of Information (Scotland) Act 2002, s.32(1)(a), but with a requirement of substantial prejudice.

8 "United Kingdom" bears its ordinary meaning under the Interpretation Act 1978: in other words, Great Britain and Northern Ireland: s.5 and Sch.1. Great Britain consists of England, Scotland and Wales.

9 See paras 15–012 to 15–020.

10 Freedom of Information Act 2000, s.27(5); Freedom of Information (Scotland) Act 2002, s.32(3).

11 See generally R.Y. Jennings and A.D. Watts (eds), *Oppenheim's International Law* (9th ed.) (Longman, London, 1992), pp.120–123.

12 *Hansard*, HC, Vol.102, October 23, 1986, col.977 (written answer). See also *Hansard*, HC, Vol.169, March 19, 1990, cols 449–450 (written answer). This accords with the view taken in R.Y. Jennings and A.D. Watts (eds), *Oppenheim's International Law* (9th ed.) (Longman, London, 1992), pp.120–123, where four conditions are identified as being necessary for the existence of a state: (1) a people, being an aggregate of individuals who live together as a community; (2) a territory in which the people are settled, even if its frontiers be disputed; (3) a government, meaning that there must be one or more persons who act for the people and govern according to the law of the land; and (4) a sovereign government, meaning that its domestic authority must not be dependent upon any other earthly authority.

An entity unrecognised by the Foreign Office as a state will generally be treated by the courts as if it did not exist.[13] The constituent parts of a federated State, although often termed "states" in their domestic law, are not States in the international law sense.[14] Whilst identification of a State itself will generally be straightforward, identification of the "organs of its government" involves a consideration of the degree to which an entity is distinct from the executive elements of the government of the State.[15] The above starting point has, in part, been displaced by the definition of "State" given in s.27(5). Certainly so far as s.27(2) is concerned and seemingly so far as section 27(1) is concerned, the phrase "State other than the United Kingdom" is defined to include references to any territory outside the United Kingdom. This is considerably wider than a State in its international law sense, and is sufficiently broad to include British territories.[16]

International organisations

Section 27(5) of the Freedom of Information Act 2000 defines "international organisation" to mean "any international organisation whose members include any two or more States, or any organ of such an organisation,"[17] thereby alluding to its meaning in international law. There is no fixed meaning in international law of the phrase "international organisation." However, the universal core attributes of an international organisation are: 18–004

- — that it is created by a treaty between two or more states[18];
- — possession of what might be called a constitution;
- — that it is a legal entity in international law, in the sense of being a juridical person or having legal personality; and
- — generally, but not always, having an exclusive membership of States or governments, or at any rate membership that is predominantly comprised of States or governments.[19]

[13] *The Annette* [1919] P. 105; *Luther v Sagor* [1921] 1 K.B. 456, [1921] 3 K.B. 532.

[14] Such as the 50 states of the United States or the six states of Australia.

[15] *Coreck Maritime v Sevrybokholodflot* 1994 S.L.T. 893 (a state-owned shipping company held not to be an organ of the state on the basis that it was a commercial company, it had its own legal personality, it was substantially free of government control and it exercised no governmental functions).

[16] That is: Anguilla, Ascension Island, Bermuda, British Antarctic Territory, British Indian Ocean Territory, British Virgin Islands, Cayman Islands, Falkland Islands, Gibraltar, Monserrat, Pitcairn Islands, St Helena, South Georgia and South Sandwich Islands, Tristan da Cunha, and Turks & Caicos Islands.

[17] Similarly Freedom of Information (Scotland) Act 2002, s.32(3).

[18] *JH Rayner (Mincing Lane) Ltd v Department of Trade and Industry* [1989] 1 Ch.72 at 143 *per* Kerr L.J. where he also observed that most such treaties will be called a "convention" or "agreement."

[19] See C.F. Amerasinghe, *Principles of the Institutional Law of International Organizations* (Cambridge University Press, Cambridge, 1996), p.9; G. Schwarzenberger, *International Law as applied by International Courts and Tribunals* (Stevens & Sons, London, 1976), vol.III, pp.5–8.

International organisations of which the United Kingdom is a member are readily identifiable as they are declared to be such by Order in Council[20] or, in a limited number of cases, by statute.[21] Some international organisations of which the United Kingdom is not a member are also readily identifiable by virtue of their having certain privileges and immunities conferred on them by Order in Council.[22] The list of international organisations that the United Kingdom has either recognised or upon which it has conferred privileges and immunities is extensive,[23] but more notable inclusions are: the Asian Development Bank[24]; the Council of Europe[25]; the European Court of Human Rights[26]; the European Bank for Reconstruction and Development[27]; the European Space Agency[28]; the European Union and its organs[29]; the International Atomic Energy Agency; the International Bank for Reconstruction and Development[30]; the International Court of Justice[31]; the International Monetary Fund[32]; the International

20 See the International Organisations Act 1968, s.1, replacing the International Organisations (Immunities and Privileges) Act 1950. Any such Order in Council must be laid in draft before Parliament and approved by a resolution of each House: s.10(1).

21 Such as the Bretton Woods Agreements Act 1945 and the International Sugar Organisation Act 1973.

22 For example, because the United Kingdom has entered into "headquarters agreement" with an international organisation which has its headquarters in the United Kingdom. This includes: the International Cocoa Organisation; the International Coffee Organisation; the International Whaling Commission; the International Maritime Organisation; INTELSAT. A full list appears in *Halsbury's Laws of England* (4th ed., 2000 re-issue), vol.18(2), para.914.

23 See the list in Halsbury's Laws of England (4th ed, 2000 re-issue), vol.18(2), paras 916–919.

24 Asian Development Bank (Immunities and Privileges) Order 1974, (SI 1974/1251).

25 General Agreement on Privileges and Immunities of the Council of Europe, Paris, September 2, 1949, Cmd 8852.

26 Second Protocol to the General Agreement on Privileges and Immunities of the Council of Europe, Paris, December 15, 1956, Cmnd 579 (Commission of Human Rights); Fourth Protocol to the General Agreement on Privileges and Immunities of the Council of Europe, Paris, December 16, 1961, Cmnd 4739.

27 European Bank for Reconstruction and Development (Immunities and Privileges) Order 1991, (SI 1991/757).

28 European Space Agency (Immunities and Privileges) Order 1978, (SI 1978/1105).

29 Protocol on the Privileges and Immunities of the European Communities, Brussels, April 8, 1965, Cmnd 5179 (as amended).

30 Articles of Agreement of the International Bank for Reconstruction and Development (Washington, December 27, 1945; TS 21 (1946); Cmd 6885), Art.I. The International Bank for Reconstruction and Development was established by an agreement drawn up at the United Nations Monetary and Financial Conference held at Bretton Woods, New Hampshire, USA in July 1944: see the Bretton Woods Agreement Act 1945 preamble (repealed). See also International Bank for Reconstruction and Development (1988 General Capital Increase) Order 1988, (SI 1988/1486).

31 United Nations and International Court of Justice (Immunities and Privileges) Order 1974, (SI 1974/1261).

32 The International Monetary Fund was created at the Bretton Woods Conference in 1944. The constitution of the International Monetary Fund can be found in the Articles of Agreement of the International Monetary Fund (Washington, December 27, 1945; TS 21 (1946); Cmd 6885) (amended by TS 44 (1978); Cmnd 7205; TS 83 (1978); Cmnd 7331). See aslo International Monetary Fund Act 1979, s.5.

Finance Corporation[33]; the North Atlantic Treaty Organisation[34]; the Organisation for Economic Co-operation and Development[35]; the United Nations (including various specialised agencies of the United Nations, such as the Food and Agriculture Organisation, the International Labour Organisation, the International Telecommunications Union, the United Nations Educational, Scientific and Cultural Organisation, the Universal Postal Union, the World Health Organisation, the World Meteorological Organisation, and the World Intellectual Property Organisation)[36]; and the World Trade Organisation.[37] In addition to these readily recognisable international organisations, there exist many other international organisations (in the international law sense) including the Arab League, The Organisation of American States, The Organisation of African Unity, and The Association of South-East Asian Nations. These, too, will fall within the definition given by s.27(5), notwithstanding that these organisations do not enjoy any privileges and immunities in the United Kingdom.[38]

International courts

Section 27(5) of the Freedom of Information Act 2000 defines "international court" to mean 18–005

> "any international court which is not an international organisation and which is established: (a) by a resolution of an international organisation of which the United Kingdom is a member, or (b) by an international agreement to which the United Kingdom is a party."

A number of notable international courts are international organisations,[39] but the operation of s.27 is the same whether the body falls within the definition of "international organisation" or within the definition of "international court."

[33] The International Finance Corporation is an affiliate of the International Bank for Reconstruction and Development: Articles of Agreement of the International Finance Corporation (Washington, May 25, 1955; TS 37 (1961); Cmnd 1377), Art.I. See also International Finance Corporation (1991 General Capital Increase) Order 1993, (SI 1993/1059).

[34] Agreement on the Status of the North Atlantic Treaty Organisation, National Representatives and International Staff, Ottawa, September 20, 1951, Cmnd 9383.

[35] Organisation for Economic Co-operation and Development (Immunities and Privileges) Order 1974, (SI 1974/1258).

[36] Specialised Agencies of the United Nations (Immunities and Privileges) Order 1974, (SI 1974/1260).

[37] World Trade Organisation (Immunities and Privileges) Order 1995, (SI 1995/266).

[38] See *Arab Monetary Fund v Hashim (No. 3)* [1991] 1 A.C. 114 at 167, which suggests that in such cases, in order to be recognised as an international organisation, the entity must be created not by treaty but by one or more of the member states.

[39] The European Court of Human Rights, see n.26; the International Court of Justice, see n.31; and the International Criminal Court.

The phrase "international court" has no fixed meaning in international law, but the essential attributes would appear to be that:

— it is created by a treaty between two or more states;
— it has a legal personality derived from international law;
— it enjoys the usual immunities enjoyed by an international organisation; and
— it is bestowed with powers and duties that are essentially judicial, even if it also performs administrative acts.[40]

International courts vary in nature, but may be divided into:

(1) Courts of universal scope, which includes the International Court of Justice, the International Tribunal for the Law of the Sea, the Dispute Settlement System of the World Trade Organisation, and the International Criminal Court.
(2) Ad hoc criminal tribunals, which includes the International Criminal Tribunal for the former Yugoslavia and the International Tribunal for Rwanda.
(3) Regional Human Rights Courts, which includes the European Court of Human Rights, the Inter-American Court of Human Rights, and the African Court of Human and Peoples Rights.
(4) Judicial bodies of regional economic integration and the like, including the Court of Justice of the European Communities (comprising the European Court of Justice and the European Court of First Instance), the Court of Justice of the European Free Trade Agreement, the Court of Justice of the Benelux Economic Union, the Central American Court of Justice, the Court of Justice of the Andean Community, the Court of Justice of the Common Market for Eastern and Southern Africa, the Common Court of Justice and Arbitration of the Organisation for the Harmonisation of Corporate Law in Africa, the Judicial Tribunal of the Organisation of Arab Petroleum Exporting Countries, and the Court of Justice of the Arab Maghrev Union.

Prejudice to international relations

18–006 There are basically two broad classes of information the disclosure of which may cause any of the types of prejudice identified in s.27(1)(a)–(b). The first class is information that has been supplied by a foreign State on the under-

40 See P. Sands *et al.*, *Manual on International Courts and Tribunals* (Butterworths, London, 1999); C.F. Amersainghe, *Jurisdiction of International Tribunals* (Kluwer Law International, The Hague, 2003) pp.42–43.

standing or in the expectation that it will not be further disseminated without the approval of the foreign State. Whilst information in this class may, of course, be rendered exempt information by s.27(2), it is also potentially exempt under s.27(1). The second class embraces information the disclosure of which, on the basis of what would actually be disclosed, could be expected to cause prejudice to relations between the United Kingdom and another State or an international organisation or court. Here, the potential prejudice does not arise from the mere fact of disclosure of information that has been provided by a foreign State upon a particular understanding: it arises from a likely effect of the disclosure of particular information upon the international relations of the United Kingdom having regard to the information itself.

Prejudice by breaking an understanding

The jurisprudence of the comparative jurisdictions reveals that public authorities often maintain that disclosure of information in the first class would damage international relations. These claims have enjoyed a measure of success, although such claims have been approached with a degree of circumspection in order not to convert what is a prejudice-based exemption into a purely class-based exemption. In Australia, the Administrative Appeals Tribunal has been generally receptive to such claims. In *Re Maher and Attorney-General's Department*[41] the President of the Tribunal upheld exemption on this basis for documents revealing negotiations that led to a treaty between Australia and United States on limiting the extra-territorial effect of anti-trust litigation in the United States: 18–007

> "The phrase 'damage to international relations of the Commonwealth' [of Australia] comprehends intangible damage to Australia's reputation though such damage may be difficult to assess. International relations have never been matters easy to define or to quantify. Regard must be had, *inter alia*, to the relationships between particular persons in one government and persons in another. Damage to personal relationships may cause considerable harm for a time at least.
>
> I accept that it must be shown that the publication of a document claimed to be exempt could reasonably be expected to cause damage to the international relations of the Commonwealth. A mere allegation to that effect is not enough. There must be cause and effect which can reasonably be anticipated. But if it can reasonably be anticipated that disclosure of the document would lessen the confidence which another country would place on the Government of Australia, that is a sufficient ground for a finding

[41] (1985) 7 A.L.D. 731; 3 A.A.R. 396 at paras 40–41.

> that the disclosure of the document could reasonably be expected to damage international relations. Trust and confidence are intangible aspects of international relations."

In *Re Slater and Cox (Director-General of Australian Archives)*[42] the Tribunal was concerned with documents relating to the establishment of the Australian Secret Service and the Australian Secret Intelligence Service some 30 or so years before the making of the request. In its necessarily sparse reasons[43] the Tribunal said:

> "It is necessary to have some regard to differences in attitude, and to reflect the views, of foreign governments which provide information, etc. to the Australian Government or its agencies. Failure to respect such views could lead to a diminution in co-operation and consequently damage relations. Considerable weight should be given by the Tribunal to the views of objecting foreign governments since they are usually in the best position to assess the local, regional or international consequences of disclosure . . . .
>
> If it can be anticipated that disclosure of the document would lessen the confidence which another country would place in the Government of Australia, that is sufficient ground for a finding that the disclosure of the document could reasonably be expected to damage international relations (though a mere allegation of damage or an expression of concern may not be sufficient)."[44]

It is, of course, important to distinguish contrived prejudice (which may or may not be supported by the foreign government that supplied the information) or mere diplomatic irritation from true prejudice to relations between the United Kingdom and another State. In this regard, it is worth remembering that information supplied by the United Kingdom to the United States was from time to time disclosed under the Freedom of Information Act (USA) without any

42 (1988) 15 A.L.D. 20.

43 As the Tribunal explained: "The Scylla of disclosure of confidential material (or worse, of the contents of a document in issue), and the Charybdis of inadequate explanation must each be avoided."

44 At paras 35–36 and 50. The Tribunal quoted with approval from the decision of Neaves J. in *Re Throssell and Department of Foreign Affairs (No. 2)* (1987) 14 A.L.D. 296 at para.16: "The material before the Tribunal tends to support the conclusion that the disclosure to the public of the records identified in the certificate could have the result of impairing the degree of trust and confidence which foreign governments place in the Government of the Commonwealth and, in consequence, of inhibiting the flow of information relating to security which might otherwise come to Australia from the overseas governmental agencies concerned and, possibly, similar agencies in other overseas countries. If such a result ensued, damage would be caused to the security and international relations of the Commonwealth. Whether such action on the part of the foreign governments and agencies would be a rational or otherwise proper reaction to the disclosure of these particular records is not to the point. The question is whether such action could reasonably be expected in the event of access being granted."

apparent prejudice to the publicly-declared special relationship between the two countries.

Inherent prejudice

Quite apart from breaking any understanding with a foreign State, disclosure of certain information may risk souring relations between the United Kingdom and another State because of the very contents of that information. In *Kuijer v EU Council (No.2)*[45] the applicant had made a request to the Secretary General of the European Council for access to certain reports that had been prepared by or with the Centre for Information, Discussion and Exchange on Asylum. The request was refused on the ground that: 18–008

> "This report contains very sensitive information about the political, economical and social situation in [the country concerned], which was provided by the heads of the European Union member state missions in that country. The Council is of the opinion that disclosure of this information might damage the relations between the European Union and [country]. The Council has therefore decided that access to this document has to be denied on the basis of article 4(1) of [Decision 93/731] (international relations)."

The Council explained that the Report contained very detailed information on the general political situation and the protection of human rights in third countries, which could be construed as criticism of those countries. The Court upheld the applicant's application for annulment of the decision to refuse access to the reports. While the Court accepted the principle that the contents of a document could be of such a nature as to make its disclosure harmful to international relations,[46] it did not accept that that could be said of the documents in question:

> "Although it is the case that some documents, such as reports containing sensitive military information, may have sufficient features in common for their disclosure to be refused, that is not the case of the documents at issue. In such circumstances, the mere fact that certain documents contain information or negative statements about the political situation, or the protection of human rights, in a third country does not necessarily mean that access to them may be denied on the basis that there is a risk that the public interest may be undermined. That fact, in itself and in the abstract, is not a sufficient basis for refusing a request for access. Rather, refusal of

---

[45] [2002] 1 W.L.R. 1941, Court of First Instance of the European Communities.

[46] Although the various examples given by the Court would, in fact, have engaged other exemptions.

> access to the reports in question must be founded on an analysis of factors specific to the contents or the context of each report, from which it can be concluded that, because of certain specific circumstances, disclosure of such a document would pose a danger to a particular public interest. As regards their contents, the reports at issue do not concern directly or primarily the relations of the European Union with the countries concerned. They contain an analysis of the political situation and of the position as regards the protection of human rights in general in each of those countries and also refer to the ratification of international treaties concerning human rights. They also contain more specific information on the protection of human rights, the possibility of internal migration to escape persecution, the return of nationals to their country of origin and the economic and social situation."[47]

It was relevant that much of the information related to facts that had already been made public or that were common knowledge.[48] The risk of the claimed harm was reduced:

- by the significant political changes that had occurred since the analysis recorded in the report;
- by the fact that the situation in the country concerned had already been criticised by institutions of the European Union;
- by the fact that relations with the country concerned might be such that they could not be damaged by disclosure of criticism; and
- by the fact that some of the observations in the report were positive.[49]

The only parts of the requested documents that the court was prepared to withhold from disclosure were those that would reveal the names of persons who had provided the information in question. Whilst the above authority exemplifies an attempt to employ the spectre of harm to international relations so as to secure exemption for commonplace material, it is suggested that prejudice to international relations can properly be said to be likely where, for example, the requested information comprises current appraisals of foreign political leaders or assessments of the relations between two foreign nations and so forth (at least to the extent that these views have not been previously made officially known).

47 At paras 60–62.
48 At para.63.
49 At para.66.

Prejudice to the interests of the United Kingdom

Paragraphs (c)–(d) of s.27(1) protect from disclosure information that would or would be likely to prejudice "the interests of the United Kingdom abroad." The phrase is sufficiently elastic to potentially embrace any financial, economic or proprietary interest abroad with which the United Kingdom (as a State) has some interest. On the other hand, it is also susceptible to a narrower interpretation that confines it to matters of sovereign interest abroad. 18–009

The public interest

As noted above, the exemption is qualified: it only applies if the public interest in maintaining the exemption outweighs the public interest in disclosing the information.[50] There is a recognised public interest in maintaining the confidentiality of diplomatic communications: it allows states to negotiate delicate situations frankly and quickly. If one State were to begin to reveal such communications with a resultant prospect of damage to the ability to negotiate, that is contrary to one facet of the public interest, bearing in mind the often fragile nature of such matters.[51] The public interest in avoiding other forms of prejudice to relations between the United Kingdom and other States or international organisations or courts, such as might result from revealing previously-undisclosed critical appraisals of foreign States or their institutions, is generally self-evident. The *Code of Practice on Access to Government Information* contained exemptions for "information whose disclosure would harm the conduct of international relations or affairs" and "information received in confidence from foreign governments, foreign courts or international organisations."[52] The accompanying *Guidance on Interpretation* stated that harm or risk of harm to the effective conduct of international relations included disclosures which 18–010

[50] See: Freedom of Information Act 2000, ss.2(1)(b) and 2(2)(b) and Freedom of Information (Scotland) Act 2002, s.2(1)(b). For a general discussion of this topic, see paras 15–001 to 15–011.

[51] This is the line that was taken by the Federal Court of Canada in *Do-Ky v Canada (Minister of Foreign Affairs & International Trade)* [1997] 2 F.C. 907. The difference with the "candour" argument in relation to the development of government policy by officials (see para.22–009) is that the relationship is not one of master and servant, with the foreign State being under no obligation to convey information to the United Kingdom and potentially having an agenda of its own that may be compromised by the disclosure.

[52] *Open Government Code of Practice on Access to Government Information* (2nd ed., 1997), Pt II, para.1(b)–(c). The first of these exemptions (for international relations or affairs) referred to "harm" and there was thus a presumption that such information should be disclosed unless the harm likely to arise from disclosure would outweigh the public interest in making the information available whilst the second of these exemptions (for confidential international information) did not refer to harm or prejudice was not therefore subject to any such balancing exercise weighing the public interest in disclosure against the public interest in non-disclosure: *ibid.*, Pt II. See also: the *White Paper on Open Government* (Cm.2290, 1993), paras 3.8–3.9 and Annex A, Pt II, para.i; the Scottish Executive's *Code of Practice on Access to Scottish Executive Information* (2nd ed., 2003), Pt II; and the National Assembly for Wales's *Code of Practice on Public Access to Information* (2nd ed., 2001), Annex B.

would "impede negotiations, for example, by revealing a negotiating or fall-back position, or weakening the Government's bargaining position", "undermine frankness and candour in diplomatic communications, for example the appraisal of personalities or political situations" or "impair confidential communications and candour between governments or international bodies."[53] In weighing the public interest in maintaining the exemption, it may be relevant to take into account the general attitude taken by the foreign State to the disclosure of official information. For example, the public interest in maintaining exemption under s.27(1) in relation to a communication from the European Commission (which is an international organisation) where that exemption is founded upon likely prejudice to relations arising from the mere fact of disclosure is arguably diminished by the encouragement which various European Union instruments give to disclosure of official documents.[54] Although what is in the public interest of a foreign State is not directly relevant to an assessment of the public interest under the Freedom of Information Act 2000, it may indirectly impinge upon that assessment.[55]

The duty to confirm or deny

18–011 Where, if a public authority were to inform an applicant that it holds or does not hold information of the description specified in the applicant's request, that revelation:

(a) would or would be likely to prejudice any of the matters set out in s.27(1); or
(b) would involve the disclosure of information (whether or not already recorded) which is confidential information obtained from a State other than the United Kingdom or from an international organisation or an international court,

[53] *Open Government Code of Practice on Access to Government Information: Guidance on Interpretation* (2nd ed., 1997), Pt II, para.1.5.

[54] Most notably, Art.255 of the Treaty of Amsterdam and Art.42 of the Charter of Fundamental Rights of the European Union: see paras 3–003 to 3–004. It will, in each case, be necessary to consider the general thrust of the legislative regime.

[55] By way of a parallel, public interest immunity cannot be claimed by a foreign state or on the ground that disclosure would infringe the public interest of a foreign state: *Buttes Gas & Oil Co. v Hammer (No. 3)* [1981] Q.B. 223, CA at 247, 251 and 262. However, it has been recognised that because the public interest of the United Kingdom requires continued co-operation, and recognises a convergence of interests, with foreign sovereign states, public interest immunity can nevertheless apply to various communications between British and foreign government departments or prosecuting authorities on international relations grounds: *Buttes Gas & Oil Co. v Hammer (No. 3)* [1981] Q.B. 223, CA at 256; *R v Governor of Brixton Prison, Ex p. Osman* [1991] 1 W.L.R. 281, DC at 285–286; *R v Horseferry Road Magistrates' Court, Ex p. Bennett (No. 2)* (1994) 99 Cr.App.R. 123, DC at 126.

then, to that extent, the duty to confirm or deny does not arise.[56] The precise terms of the request are critical to determining what would be revealed by confirming or denying that such information is held. A request that more specifically identifies the information sought will be more likely to fall within the exclusion than a request in general terms. The exclusion of the duty to confirm or deny is qualified. Accordingly, even if the request satisfies the terms of s.27(4) it will be necessary to consider whether, in all the circumstances, the maintenance of the exclusion of this duty outweighs by the public interest in disclosing whether the public authority holds the information. This public interest balancing exercise is materially different from that employed for the purpose of determining whether the duty to communicate does not apply.[57]

Scope of the confidential information exemption

Section 27(2) of the Freedom of Information Act 2000[58] provides that "confidential information" obtained by a State other than the United Kingdom[59] or from an international organisation[60] or international court[61] is exempt information. Section 27(3) defines what is meant by confidential information: 18–012

> "For the purposes of this section, any information obtained from a State, organisation or court is confidential at any time while the terms on which it was obtained require it to be held in confidence or while the circumstances in which it was obtained make it reasonable for the State, organisation or court to expect that it will be so held."

The special provision of an exemption for confidential information emanating from foreign state bodies and the like (in addition to the general exemption for confidential information provided by s.41), reflects the particular sensitivities arising from the disclosure of such material.[62] The scope of the exemption is considered in the chapter dealing with confidential information.[63]

The Data Protection Act 1998

There is no analogous exemption under the Data Protection Act 1998 or any statutory instrument made under it. 18–013

[56] Freedom of Information Act 2000, s.27(4). There is no equivalent provision under the Freedom of Information (Scotland) Act 2002.
[57] See paras 15–010 to 15–011 as to what it involves.
[58] And Freedom of Information (Scotland) Act 2002, s.32(1)(b).
[59] As to the meaning of "a State other than the United Kingdom," see para.18–003.
[60] As to the meaning of "international organisation," see para.18–004.
[61] As to the meaning of "international court," see para.18–005.
[62] See para.18–006.
[63] See paras 25–039 to 25–042.

2. INTERNAL RELATIONS

Scope of the section 28(1) exemption

18–014 Section 28(1) of the Freedom of Information Act 2000 provides that information is exempt information if its disclosure under the Act would, or would be likely to, prejudice relations between any administration in the United Kingdom[64] and any other such administration ("internal relations").[65] The phrase "would or would be likely to prejudice" is common to most of the prejudice-based exemptions in the Act. The nature of prejudice and the degree of likelihood which the phrase requires are considered elsewhere in this work.[66] Section 28(2) defines "administration in the United Kingdom" for the purposes of the section to mean:

(a) the government of the United Kingdom ("the Westminster government");
(b) the Scottish Administration;
(c) the Executive Committee of the Northern Ireland Assembly; or
(d) the National Assembly for Wales.

Section 28(3) provides that the duty to confirm or deny does not arise if, or to the extent that, compliance with s.1(1)(a) of the Freedom of Information Act 2000 would, or would be likely to, prejudice internal relations. The exclusion and the exemption in s.28 of the Freedom of Information Act 2000 are non-absolute: the duty to confirm or deny does not arise in relation to information prejudicial to internal relations only if, in all the circumstances of the case, the public interest in maintaining the exclusion of that duty outweighs the public interest in divulging whether the public authority holds the information[67]; and the duty to communicate in relation to such information does not arise only if, or to the extent that, in all the circumstances of the case, the public interest in maintaining the exemption outweighs the public interest in disclosing the information.[68]

---

64 United Kingdom means Great Britain (*i.e.* England, Scotland and Wales) and Northern Ireland: Interpretation Act 1978, ss.5, 22(1), Sch.1, Sch.2, para.5(a); Union with Scotland Act 1706, preamble, art. 1.

65 Freedom of Information (Scotland) Act 2002, s.28 is identically worded save that it follows the slightly different drafting format and "substantial prejudice" test adopted elsewhere in that Act. Information contained in a "historical record" (as to the meaning of which, see para.6–033) for the purposes of the Freedom of Information Act 2000, s.62 cannot be exempt information by virtue of s.28 and compliance with the duty to confirm or deny under s.1(1)(a) in relation to such a record is not to be taken to be capable of having any of the effects referred to in s.28(3): Freedom of Information Act 2000, s.63(1)–(2).

66 See paras 15–012 to 15–020.

67 Freedom of Information Act 2000, s.28(3) (read with s.28(1)) engages s.2(1)(b) so as to prevent s.1(1)(a) from applying and the duty to confirm or deny from arising in relation to the exempt information if the public interest balance favours non-divulgence.

68 Freedom of Information Act 2000, s.28(1) thus engages s.2(2)(b) so as to prevent s.1(1)(b) from applying and the duty to communicate from arising in relation to the exempt information if the public interest balance favours non-disclosure.

The administrations in the United Kingdom

As already indicated, the administrations covered by s.28 of the Freedom of Information Act 2000 are the Westminster government, together with the "devolved administrations": namely, the Scottish Administration, Executive Committee of the Northern Ireland Assembly and National Assembly for Wales. A brief outline of each devolved administration follows[69]: 18–015

(1) The Scottish Administration. The Scottish Administration was established under Pt II of the Scotland Act 1998[70] and the reference in s.28(2)(b) of the Freedom of Information Act 2000 to the Scottish Administration must be construed as a reference to both its office-holders and their staff.[71]

(2) The Executive Committee of the Northern Ireland Assembly. The Executive Committee of the Northern Ireland Assembly was established under Pt III of the Northern Ireland Act 1998.[72] The Committee consists of the First Minister and deputy First Minister and the Northern Ireland Ministers appointed under that Act.[73] However, devolution in Northern Ireland was suspended for the time being on October 15, 2002 and the Executive Committee is therefore in abeyance; the functions of its members are instead exercised by the Secretary of State for Northern Ireland.[74]

---

[69] As to devolution generally see: P. Jackson, *Hood Phillips and Jackson: Constitutional and Administrative Law* (8th ed., Sweet & Maxwell, London, 2001), Ch.5; Mitchell, "The Creation of the Scottish Parliament: Journey without End" (1999) 52 Parl. Affairs 651; McAllister, The "Road to Cardiff Bay: The Process of Establishing the National Assembly for Wales", (1999) 52 Parl. Affairs 635.

[70] The Scotland Act 1998 was passed to implement policy proposals set out in the government White Paper *Scotland's Parliament* (Cm.3658), 1997 and followed a referendum held in Scotland in September 1997 under the Referendums (Scotland and Wales) Act 1997.

[71] Scotland Act 1998, s.126(6)–(7). The office-holders are the members of the Scottish Executive (*i.e.* the Scottish Ministers including the First Minister and the Lord Advocate and Solicitor General for Scotland), junior Scottish Ministers and the holders of offices in the Scottish Administration which are not ministerial offices (*i.e.* the Registrar General of Births, Deaths and Marriages for Scotland, the Keeper of the Registers of Scotland, the Keeper of the Records of Scotland and certain other specified officers): Scotland Act 1998, ss.44–49, 126(7)(a) and (8); Scottish Administration (Offices) Order 1999 (SI 1999/1127).

[72] The Northern Ireland Act 1998 was passed (together with the Northern Ireland (Sentences) Act 1998) to implement the Belfast Agreement (also known as the Good Friday Agreement) set out in the *Agreement Reached at Multi-Party Talks on Northern Ireland* (Cm.3883), 1998 and followed referendums held in Northern Ireland and the Republic of Ireland in May 1998. See also the related agreements between the United Kingdom and Republic of Ireland Governments: *Agreement Establishing Implementing Bodies* (Cm.4293), 1998; *Agreement Establishing a North-South Ministerial Council* (Cm.4294), 1998; *Agreement Establishing a British-Irish Council* (Cm. 4296), 1998.

[73] Northern Ireland Act 1998, s.20.

[74] Northern Ireland Act 2000, ss.1, 4, Sch.1; Northern Ireland Act 2000 (Suspension of Devolved Government) Order 2002, (SI 2002/2574), art.2.

(3) The National Assembly for Wales. The National Assembly for Wales was established under Pt I of the Government of Wales Act 1998[75] as a body corporate consisting of elected members.[76]

It can therefore be noted that, for the purposes of s.28 of the Freedom of Information Act 2000, the Scottish Administration includes staff as well as office-holders, whilst the Northern Ireland and Wales devolved administrations include only their elected ministers and members respectively and not their staff.

Background

18–016 No exemption equivalent to s.28 of the Freedom of Information Act 2000 was included in the *Code of Practice on Access to Government Information*[77] or proposed in the White Paper *Your Right to Know: The Government's Proposals for a Freedom of Information Act*.[78] This is not surprising as both documents preceded the establishment of the devolved administrations.[79] The draft Freedom of Information Bill published on May 24, 1999[80] and the Freedom of Information Bill introduced in the House of Commons on November 18, 1999 post-dated the 1998 devolution statutes and both contained clauses equivalent to s.28 of the Freedom of Information Act 2000.[81] During the passage of the Freedom of Information Bill two examples were given by the government of information held by a Westminster government department which might be covered by the exemption, namely, "a thumbnail sketch of the strengths and weaknesses of the individual members of an executive" and "comments . . . on a devolved administration's policy proposals or Acts."[82]

The comparative jurisdictions

18–017 Exemptions similar to s.28 of the Freedom of Information Act 2000 are provided for in the comparable legislation of Australia, New Zealand and Canada. Sections 26A and 33A of the Freedom of Information Act 1982 (Cth of Aust)

[75] The Government of Wales Act 1998 was passed to implement policy proposals set out in the government White Paper *A Voice for Wales* (Cm.3718), 1997 and followed a referendum held in Wales in September 1997 under the Referendums (Scotland and Wales) Act 1997. See also: National Assembly for Wales (Transfer of Functions) Order 1999, (SI 1999/672); National Assembly for Wales (Transfer of Functions) Order 2000, (SI 2000/253); National Assembly for Wales (Transfer of Functions) (No. 2) Order 2000, (SI 2000/1830).

[76] Government of Wales Act 1998, ss.1(2), 2.

[77] *Open Government Code of Practice on Access to Government Information* (2nd ed.), 1997.

[78] (Cm.3818), 1997.

[79] Note, however, the reference to devolution in the White Paper (Cm.3818), 1997, para.2.1.

[80] *Freedom of Information: Consultation on Draft Legislation* (Cm.4355), 1999, Pt II.

[81] Draft Bill, cl.23; Introduction Print of Bill, cl.26.

[82] Cabinet Office Minister, Lord Falconer of Thoroton, *Hansard*, HL, Vol.617, col.1280, October 19, 2000 (House of Lords Committee Stage).

contain a discretionary exemption for information whose disclosure would, or could reasonably be expected to, cause damage to relations between the Commonwealth and a State or divulge certain confidential Commonwealth-State communications.[83] As with s.28 of the Freedom of Information Act 2000, the Australian equivalent is subject to a public interest override for information whose disclosure would, on balance, be in the public interest.[84] Section 7(a) of the Official Information Act 1982 (NZ) provides that information may be withheld if its disclosure would be likely to prejudice relations between any of the Governments of New Zealand, the self-governing state of the Cook Islands or the self-governing state of Niue. Section 14 of the federal Access to Information Act (1982) (Canada) contains a discretionary exemption for information which could reasonably be expected to be injurious to the conduct by the Government of Canada of federal-provincial affairs including information on federal-provincial consultations or deliberations and the strategy or tactics adopted or to be adopted by the Government of Canada relating to the conduct of federal-provincial affairs.

Prejudice to internal relations

All the administrations have agreed a Memorandum of Understanding and a series of Supplementary Agreements "setting out the principles which underlie the relations between them" and a series of bilateral agreements have also been agreed between various Westminister government departments and their devolved counterparts.[85] Although these agreements are expressed to be non-binding statements of political intent, they reflect the way in which the administrations intend and would wish to relate to each other and may therefore provide a useful guide for what would and would not be liable to prejudice internal relations.[86] Although in legal terms each of the devolved 18–018

[83] Ministers can issue conclusive certificates specifying the relevant ground of exemption, the part or parts of the document covered and the particular kind of document in respect of which the exemption has been claimed: Freedom of Information Act 1982, s.33A(2) and (4) (Cth of Aust). Such certificates are conclusive in their effect subject to the relevant review procedures in Freedom of Information Act 1982, Pt VI (Cth of Aust). See para.14–036(1). The words "relations between the Commonwealth and a State" refer to the totality of their relationships at every level: *Arnold v Queensland* (1987) 6 A.A.R. 463 at 472 (*per* Wilcox J.).

[84] Freedom of Information Act 1982, s.33A(5) (Cth of Aust).

[85] See the *Memorandum of Understanding and Supplementary Agreements Between the United Kingdom Government, Scottish Ministers, the Cabinet of the National Assembly for Wales and the Northern Ireland Executive Committee* (Cm.5240), 2001. The principal agreement is the Memorandum of Understanding and there are five supplementary agreements: an Agreement on the Joint Ministerial Committee; and four Concordats on Co-ordination of European Union Policy Issues, Financial Assistance to Industry, International Relations and Statistics. In very general terms, the importance of communicating and exchanging information between the administrations is stressed throughout (Cm.5240), 2001, but there is also a recognition that some of this may need to take place on a confidential basis: see the Memorandum, paras 5, 9–11 and 16.

[86] The Westminster government department with overall responsibility for devolution (currently the Office of the Deputy Prime Minister, formerly the Cabinet Office) also publishes Devolution

administrations exercises its functions on behalf of the same Crown, their members may have very different political views and there is a constitutional distinction between the Crown in right of Her Majesty's Government in the United Kingdom, the Crown in right of the Scottish Administration and the Crown in right of Her Majesty's Government in Northern Ireland.[87] The logic of s.28 of the Freedom of Information Act 2000 is as follows: given that the Westminster government and the devolved administrations do need to co-operate closely in a variety of areas, particularly in relation to the implementation of and compliance with the United Kingdom's obligations under European Community law, good internal relations are plainly a matter of great practical importance and they should not therefore be needlessly prejudiced or put at risk unless this is necessary on overriding public interest grounds. Whether the remaining exemptions in Pt II of the Freedom of Information Act 2000 ought to suffice for these purposes is another matter, but the comparative jurisdictions at least show some consistency of approach to such issues and provide a precedent for s.28.

The Data Protection Act 1998

18–019 There is no analogous exemption under the Data Protection Act 1998 or any statutory instrument made under it.

Guidance Notes on various topics and these may be capable of providing some illumination in relation to the same issues: *e.g. Devolution Guidance Note No.6: Circulation of Inter-Ministerial And Inter-Departmental Correspondence*, 2002.

87 See: Scotland Act 1998, s.99; Northern Ireland Act 1998, Sch.13, para.9(3); Government of Wales Act 1998, s.1(3).

CHAPTER 19

Economic and Financial Interests

Introduction

By s.29(1) of the Freedom of Information Act 2000 information is rendered exempt information where its disclosure would prejudice, or would be likely to prejudice: 19–001

(a) the economic interests of the United Kingdom[1] or of any part of the United Kingdom; or

(b) the financial interests of any administration in the United Kingdom.[2]

An "administration in the United Kingdom" is defined to mean the government of the United Kingdom, the Scottish Administration, the Executive Committee of the Northern Ireland Assembly and the National Assembly for Wales.[3] The phrase "would or would be likely to prejudice" is common to most of the prejudice-based exemptions in the Act. The nature of prejudice and the degree of

---

[1] The United Kingdom means Great Britain (*i.e.* England, Scotland and Wales) and Northern Ireland: Interpretation Act 1978, ss.5 and 22(1), Sch.1, Sch.2, para.5(a); Union with Scotland Act 1706, preamble, art.1.

[2] Freedom of Information (Scotland) Act 2002, s.33(2) is in similar terms, save that the prejudice must be substantial.

[3] Freedom of Information Act 2000, s.28(2); Freedom of Information (Scotland) Act 2002, s.28(2).

likelihood which the phrase generally requires are considered elsewhere in this work.[4] Section 29(2) provides that the duty to confirm or deny does not arise if, or to the extent that, compliance with that duty would prejudice, or would be likely to prejudice, the interests protected by s.29(1). Both exemption from the disclosure duty and exclusion from the duty to divulge are non-absolute. Thus, the duty to communicate information whose disclosure would be prejudicial (or would be likely to be prejudicial) to the interests protected by s.29 does not arise only if, or to the extent that, in all the circumstances of the case, the public interest in maintaining the exemption outweighs the public interest in disclosing the information.[5] Similarly, the duty to confirm or deny that such information is held remains excluded only if, in all the circumstances of the case, the public interest in maintaining the exclusion of that duty outweighs the public interest in divulging whether the public authority holds the information.[6] A broadly equivalent exemption is to be found in the freedom of information legislation of most of the comparative jurisdictions.[7]

---

4 See paras 15–012 to 15–020.

5 Freedom of Information Act 2000, s.2(2)(b).

6 *ibid*, s.2(1)(b).

7 There is no directly comparable exemption in the Freedom of Information Act, 1966 (USA). The Freedom of Information Act 1982 (Cth of Australia), s.44, provides an exemption where the disclosure of the requested document would, or could be reasonably be expected to, have a substantial adverse effect on the ability of the Commonwealth to manage the economy: see para.2–015(19). The exemption does not involve a consideration of the public interest. The AAT in *Re Waterford and Treasurer of Commonwealth of Australia (No 2)* (1985) 8 A.L.N. N37 stated that if the document entitled Forward Estimates of Budget Receipts had the potential to have a significant impact on the government's ability to control the economy, then its disclosure would be contrary to the public interest and it would be exempt. The Administrative Review Council in its review of the Australian Act considered the exemption superfluous (because information could be exempted under other provisions) and recommended that it be repealed: Australian Law Reform Commission and the Administrative Review Council, "Open Government: a review of the federal Freedom of Information Act 1982", A.L.R.C. 77; A.R.C. 40, Canberra, 1995, para.9.28. The Official Information Act 1982 (New Zealand), ss.6(e) and 27(1)(a) provide absolute exemptions where the disclosure of the information would be likely to damage seriously the New Zealand economy by disclosing prematurely decisions to change or continue government economic or financial policies relating to: exchange rates or the control of overseas exchange transactions; the regulation of banking or credit; taxation; the stability, control, and adjustment of prices of goods and services, rents, and other costs, and rates of wages, salaries, and other incomes; the borrowing of money by the New Zealand government; and the entering into of overseas trade agreements: see para.2–022(5). The Official Information Act 1982 makes provision for neither confirming nor denying the existence of the requested documents where to do so would or could reasonably be expected to cause damage to the economy (see para.2–020). The Access to Information Act (Canada), s.18, provides a discretionary exemption for records the disclosure of which could reasonably be expected to cause injury to the financial or economic interests of Canada: see para.2–032(17). The Canadian Courts have required clear proof of a reasonable belief on the part of the Minster that there was a reasonable expectation of probable harm of the prescribed kinds: see *Canadian Council of Christian Charities v Canada (Minister of Finance)* [1999] 4 F.C. 245. In that case, the Federal Court held that the phrase "injurious to the financial interests of the Government of Canada" in s.18(d) should not be interpreted as including revenue loss resulting from an increase in legitimate claims to deduction under the Income Tax Act. The Freedom of Information Act 1997 (Ireland), s.24(1), provides a discretionary exemption for records the disclosure of which could reasonably be expected to have a serious adverse effect upon the financial interests of the state or on the ability to manage the economy: see para.2–039(16).

Provenance of the exemption

Although the terms of the exemption are imprecise, the provenance of the exemption gives some clue as to its intended breadth. The exclusion of information whose disclosure could be harmful to the economy has always been in the Code of Practice.[8] The amended version of the Code includes an exemption for: 19–002

> "information whose disclosure would harm the ability of the Government to manage the economy, prejudice the conduct of official market operations, or could lead to improper gain or advantage."[9]

The Explanatory Guidance on the Code gives a non-exhaustive list of examples of information that is considered to fall within the exemption, as well as the underlying rationale for the exemption:

> "Information about some types of proposals, or even the admission that certain possibilities are being considered, can lead to speculation, disturbance of the markets and even improper gain. It will therefore be necessary to consider the harm test set out in the exemption before releasing information regarding such matters as:
>
> — the currency, coinage or legal tender of the United Kingdom;
> — proposals for expenditure;
> — a contemplated change in the rate of bank interest or in Government borrowing;
> — a contemplated change in tariff rates, taxes, duties or any other revenue services;
> — a contemplated change in the conditions of operation of financial institutions;
> — a contemplated sale or acquisition of land or property; or
> — a contemplated sale or purchase of securities or of foreign or United Kingdom currency."[10]

The fact that information relates to one of these matters is, of course, not enough in itself: the exemption in the Code, as in the Freedom of Information Act 2000, is harm-based. The Explanatory Guidance simply sets out those classes of information that might, if disclosed, result in harm to the economy.

---

[8] See further para.5–001 to 5–010.

[9] *Open Government Code of Practice on Access to Government Information* (2nd ed., 1997), Pt II, para.6(a).

[10] Cabinet Office, *Open Government: Code of Practice on Access to Government Information Guidance on Interpretation* (2nd ed., 1997), para.6.1.

Legislative history

19–003 The Bill leading to the Freedom of Information Act 2000 included an exemption[11] in substantially the same terms as s.29. An attempt was made to amend the Bill so that its terms would more closely resemble the exemption in the Code:

> "I can be brief on this, because it is a straightforward argument between the terms of the Bill and the code of practice. The Government thought the code of practice inadequate, but it is stronger than the Bill. The amendment would replace the provisions for a contents exemption in the Bill with the wording used in the code of practice. It would tighten up the Bill, ensuring that only information that would genuinely harm a specific economic interest would be exempt. At the moment, the clause would catch all information relating to the economy. The Government must not be allowed to include such catch-all exemptions, especially as they have drawn up the Bill in such a way that, if information is covered by an exemption, the public authority, rather than the information commissioner, decides whether it should be released. For those reasons, the exemptions should be worded as tightly as possible. The wording in the code is far superior in this regard to that in the Bill. The Government's supporters, who have just come so willingly to their aid in the Division, should ask themselves whether they believed that they fought the election for a Bill that is weaker than the code introduced by the previous Government."[12]

The answer given by Lord Bach was:

> "I do not dispute that the interests identified in the amendment are important, but the Government do not believe that they are the only important economic or financial considerations in relation to which the inappropriate disclosure of information could lead to real harm being done to the economy."[13]

Lord Bach gave an example of information that would be captured by the proposed exemption but which would not be captured by the exemption in the code:

> "Public authorities such as the DTI may hold documents which set out the advantages and disadvantages of investing in different regions. If that type of information were disclosed to an overseas business organisation which was contemplating setting up a factory in the UK, the organisation may be

[11] Cl.24.
[12] *Hansard*, HL, Vol.617, October 19, 2000, col.1286, Lord Mackay of Ardbrecknish.
[13] *Hansard*, HL, Vol.617, October 19, 2000, col.1288.

put off its proposed investment. However, if this amendment were carried, that would not exempt such information from disclosure."[14]

Other examples of information thought to be captured by s.29 but not by the Code were given by Lord Bassam of Brighton:

"I should like to assist Members of the Committee by providing some examples. First, the Treasury holds information about the performance of different sectors of the economy and information about whether it intends to raise or lower taxes—important information. Such information has an effect on the United Kingdom economy and its release needs to be carefully managed. Secondly, there exist research projects, the findings of which it would be unreasonable, impractical and inappropriate to publish before the project has been completed. Some research projects could easily run for longer than three months, but under this exemption they would have to supply information on request before the project was completed, with the possible effect of nullifying the results of that project."[15]

As will be seen, the difference between the exemption in the Code and the exemption created by s.29 presents its own difficulties. Information captured by an exemption in the Freedom of Information Act 2000 is not, of course, precluded from disclosure: it merely means that the entitlement given by s.1 is disapplied. Although the Code does not bestow a right of access insofar as it encourages disclosure of information not rendered exempt by its own provisions, that encouragement applies whether or not information is exempt information under the terms of the Freedom of Information Act 2000.

Scope of the exemption

The terms "economic interests" and "financial interests" are capable of a considerable degree of overlap. However, the scope for overlap, as well as the ambit of the exemption itself, is reduced by these two interests being tied to different entities. In each case it is that entity whose interests are required to be prejudiced by disclosure. In order to be captured by s.29(1)(a), the economic interests required to be prejudiced by the disclosure are those of the United Kingdom or any part of the United Kingdom. In order to be captured by s.29(1)(b), the financial interests required to be prejudiced by the disclosure are those of any administration in the United Kingdom.[16] A further insight into the scope of the exemption comes from Pt VI of the Act dealing with historical records.[17] It is 19–004

14 *Hansard*, HL, Vol.617, October 19, 2000, col.1288.
15 *Hansard*, HL, Vol.617, October 19, 2000, col.1244.
16 As to the meaning of "any administration in the United Kingdom" see para.19–001.
17 See, more generally, Ch.6.

not easy to conceive of information 30, 60 or 100 years old the disclosure of which would prejudice, or would be likely to prejudice, the economic interests of the United Kingdom or the financial interests of any administration of the United Kingdom. Nevertheless, the s.29 exemption is not removed where the information is contained in a historical record,[18] nor where it is contained in a record created 60 or 100 years earlier.[19] The decision to exclude s.29 from the exemptions that fall away with time can best be explained by the importance of the interest that is protected by the exemption, rather than by the nature of the information itself. While the quantity and type of information the disclosure of which would prejudice the economic interests of the United Kingdom, etc. may be very greatly diminished when the information is, say, 60 years old, if that in fact is what the effect of its disclosure would be, then the desirability of avoiding the adverse effect is not lessened by the age of the information.

Economic interests

19–005 Not all information relating to the economy of the United Kingdom (or a part of the United Kingdom) will be exempted from disclosure by s.29. It is information prejudicing economic interests, rather than economic affairs, which is exempted by the section. Beyond the obvious instances of economic interests affecting the United Kingdom generally at a national level, such as forthcoming budgetary or fiscal policy decisions, the exemption would appear to cover information relating to a whole sector of the national economy.[20] As well as making strategic decisions, the State also acts as economic participant (buyer, seller, investor and lender) and as regulator and enforcer. It is arguable that, bearing in mind the scope of its activities in the economy and its corresponding interests, disclosure of information prejudicing or likely to prejudice these interests is also captured by the exemption.

Financial interests

19–006 So far as financial interests are concerned, the exemption would appear to have a narrower application than in relation to economic interests. As noted above, the financial interests exemption may only be invoked if it relates to the financial interests of an administration as defined. A substantial part of the finances of such administrations are a matter of public record, as in the case of the public sector pay review, for example.

[18] Freedom of Information Act 2000, s.63(1).
[19] Freedom of Information Act 2000, s.63(3) and (4).
[20] See *Norway v EFTA Surveillance Authority* [1999] 1 C.M.L.R. 851.

The Bank of England

It is to be noted that, while "any government department" is deemed to be a public authority[21] (and therefore the Treasury is a potential recipient of a request), the Bank of England is only a public authority for the purposes of the Act in respect of information held for purposes other than those of its functions with respect to: 19–007

— monetary policy
— financial operations intended to support financial institutions for the purposes of maintaining stability, and
— the provision of private banking services and related services.[22]

Thus information relating to future or past interest rate changes or interventions to support a market sector is inaccessible as the Bank of England is not a public authority for the purposes of a request for such information.

Actual or likely prejudice

Demonstrating the likely prejudice from a disclosure of information under the Act presents particular problems so far as this exemption is concerned: 19–008

(1) In terms of the type of prejudice which must be shown, it is reasonably clear that one of the aims of s.29 is to preclude the obtaining of an unfair pecuniary advantage by those seeking information in such a way that it will have an adverse impact on the management of the economy and the conduct of business in general. It is easy to assert such prejudice: proof, even to a level sufficient for an administrative decision, will often be rather more difficult. Expert evidence may be required to demonstrate the likelihood of such prejudice. The currency of the information will often be critical to the application of the exemption, as it is difficult to see how the disclosure of past information could be deemed to be prejudicial. It is also difficult to see how the public authority concerned would be prejudiced by the disclosure of current information where such information comprised no more than a compilation of information obtainable from other publicly-available sources.

(2) Since 1997, the Government have continued to publish the minutes of monthly meetings between the Chancellor of the Exchequer and the Bank of England. These minutes disclose sensitive economic and financial information. That this information is regularly dispersed to the public without apparent damage makes it more difficult to contend that

[21] Freedom of Information Act 2000, s.3(1)(a)(i) and Sch.1, para.1.
[22] Freedom of Information Act 2000, Sch.1, Pt VI.

disclosure of other economic information has, or would be likely to have, the prejudicial effect required by s.29.

(3) Some consideration must also be given to official information relating to the economy that is otherwise liable to be disclosed. Section 27 of the Industry Act 1975 provides that Ministers of the Crown and the Treasury must publish , make available and provide access to information and analysis as set out in Sch.5 to that Act. That Schedule provides:

"1. For the purposes of this Schedule the Treasury shall keep a macro-economic model suitable for demonstrating the likely effects on economic events in the United Kingdom of different assumptions about the following matters, namely—
   (a) government economic policies;
   (b) economic events outside the United Kingdom; and
   (c) such (if any) other matters as appear to the Treasury from time to time likely to have a substantial effect on economic events in the United Kingdom.
2. The model shall enable forecasts to be made—
   (a) of any of the following, namely—
      (i) the level of growth domestic product;
      (ii) unemployment;
      (iii) the balance of payments on current account;
      (iv) the general index of retail prices; and
      (v) average earnings; and
   (b) of such (if any) other economic variables as are appropriate in the opinion of the Treasury from time to time.

....

6. Not less than twice in each year commencing with a date not later than one year from the coming into force of this Act, the Treasury shall publish forecasts produced with the aid of the model as to such matters and based on such alternative assumptions as appear to them to be appropriate.
7. Any forecast under this Schedule shall indicate, where possible, the margin of error attaching to it.
8. The Treasury shall from time to time publish an analysis of errors in such forecasts that would have remained even if the assumptions set out in the forecasts and on which they were based had been correct."

It is difficult to contend that disclosure of analogous information (for example, a micro-economic model) under the Freedom of Information Act 2000 would or would be likely to prejudice the economic interests of the United Kingdom if that class of information is liable to be disclosed under another Act of Parliament. The existence of this free-standing right to certain information that may impinge upon the economic interests of the United Kingdom is also relevant to the weighing exercise required by s.2 of the Act: it is difficult to see that the public interest in maintaining the exemption has particular force if another Act of Parliament gives a statutory entitlement to the disclosure of information of the same class.

The public interest

Even if information is exempt because it answers the terms of s.29(1), an applicant will still be entitled to have the information communicated to him unless, in all the circumstances of the case, the public interest in maintaining the exemption outweighs the public interest in disclosing the information.[23] Similarly, even if the duty to confirm or deny does not arise as a result of the operation of s.29(2), an applicant will still be entitled to be informed that the public authority holds the information requested unless, in all the circumstances of the case, the public interest in maintaining the exclusion outweighs the public interest in divulging its existence.[24] The decision of the Legislature not to make exemption under s.29 absolute cannot properly be undone by giving the public interest in maintaining the exemption such weight as to make the public interest in disclosure unable to outweigh it. The exercise must be carried out in such a manner as to recognise that in some circumstances the public interest in disclosure will be sufficiently powerful to displace an inherently compelling public interest in maintaining the exemption. In practice, the balancing exercise will comprise mainly weighing up the public interest in disclosure against the public interest in protecting the economic and financial welfare of the nation, the constituent parts of the nation, and the various national administrations. For information relating to past and current decisions involving the matters protected by s.29, it may be more difficult to find that the public interest in maintaining the exemption outweighs the public interest in disclosure. So far as information relating to future decisions involving the protected matters, for example the imposition of exchange rate controls, the public interest in maintaining the exemption will, as a general rule, more readily outweigh the public interest in disclosure. The years since Black Wednesday have provided ample illustration of how entire markets and economic sectors can be destabilised by the acts of a very few speculators. Access to information which enables or informs such speculation cannot readily be characterised as being in the public interest. On the other hand, an inward investor seeking information about the future of the regional development will not necessarily be acting contrary to the public interest. Such an investor may well argue that a whole region will benefit from enhanced infrastructure and the creation of jobs by inward investment and that it is in the public interest that access to such information is provided. 19–009

[23] Freedom of Information Act 2000, s.2(2)(b).
[24] *ibid.*, s.2(1)(b).

The Data Protection Act 1998

19–010 There is no directly comparable exemption in the Data Protection Act 1998. However, para.6(1) of Sch.7[25] provides that where personal data are processed for the purposes of, or in connection with, a "corporate finance service"[26] provided by a "relevant person"[27] they may be exempt from the "subject information provisions" (which includes the s.7 access rights) if the "exemption is required for the purpose of safeguarding an important economic or financial interest of the United Kingdom." Paragraph 6(2) of Sch.7 enables the Secretary of State to specify by order"matters to be taken into account in determining whether exemption from the subject information provisions is required for the purposes of safeguarding an important economic or financial interest of the United Kingdom." The Secretary of State has exercised this power,[28] with the matters to be taken into account spelled out as:

> ". . . the inevitable prejudicial effect on—
> (a) the orderly functioning of financial markets, or
> (b) the efficient allocation of capital within the economy,
> which will result from the application (whether on an occasional or regular basis) of the subject information provisions to data to which paragraph (3) applies."

The data referred to is personal data to which application of the relevant provisions of the Data Protection Act 1998 could reasonably be believed to affect: (a) any decision of any person whether or not to deal in, subscribe or issue any instrument which is already in existence or is to be or may be created; or (b) any decision of any person to act or not to act in a way that is likely to have an effect on any business activity.

---

[25] Sch.7 provides miscellaneous exemptions for the purposes of the "subject information provisions," which are defined in s.27(2) to include the access right provided by s.7 of the Data Protection Act 1998.

[26] Defined in para.6(3) of Sch.7.

[27] Also defined in para.6(3) of Sch.7: in very general terms, a person who is authorised under C.III of Pt I of the Financial Services Act 1986 or who is an exempted person under C.IV of Pt I of that Act.

[28] Data Protection (Corporate Finance Exemption) Order 2000, (SI 2000/184).

CHAPTER 20

Investigation, audit, law enforcement and the courts

1. INTRODUCTION

Nature of exemptions covered

20–001 This chapter is principally concerned with a group of provisions which exempt numerous categories of information from the disclosure obligations so as not to undermine the enforcement of the law (principally, but not exclusively, the criminal law) and the administration of justice. The exemptions take many different forms and often overlap in a haphazard way. Some depend on the purposes for which the information is held, some on whether disclosure will cause prejudice (and some on a combination of the two)[1]; some require the information still to be held for the relevant purpose, some that it was once so held; in some cases the current holder of the information must have had the relevant purpose, in others this is not required; in some the original source of the information or the

[1] See in particular Data Protection Act 1998, s.29(1). In relation to the Freedom of Information Act 2000, see paras 14–021 to 14–022.

purposes for which it was communicated to the public authority is relevant, in others not. In this chapter, this group of exemptions has been divided into seven loose sections. For each section, separate consideration is given: to the scope of the exemption from the duty to communicate under the Freedom of Information Acts; to the role of the public interest; to the duty to confirm or deny; and to the equivalent exemption under the Data Protection Act 1998.

The public interest generally

With the exception of provisions relating to court records,[2] none of the Freedom of Information Act exemptions in this group is absolute: they only apply if the public interest in maintaining the exemption outweighs the public interest in disclosing the information.[3] This public interest requirement must be satisfied even in cases where the test for exemption is whether prejudice will or is likely to be caused. Thus it is possible that although a particular disclosure would cause prejudice to the enforcement of the law or the administration of justice, nevertheless the information must be disclosed because the public interest in disclosure outweighs the prejudice. As with the other qualified exemptions, in weighing the competing public interests, the relevant decision maker[4] will have to take into account all the circumstances of the case[5] and any relevant provisions of the European Convention for the Protection of Human Rights and Fundamental Freedoms.[6] There is no express public interest requirement to be satisfied in relation to this group of exemptions as they appear in the Data Protection Act 1998. 20–002

Limits on exemptions

As with all exemptions under Pt II of the Freedom of Information Act 2000 and Pt IV of the Data Protection Act 1998, they only operate in relation to the obligations of disclosure provided by the relevant Act: they do not exempt a public authority from making disclosures required by other legislation or rules of law. Thus, they do not exempt a public authority from its obligations to disclose 20–003

[2] Namely, Freedom of Information Act 2000, s.32; Freedom of Information (Scotland) Act 2002, s.37.

[3] See Freedom of Information Act 2000, ss.2(1)(b) and 2(2)(b) and Freedom of Information (Scotland) Act 2002, s.2(1)(b). For a general discussion of this topic, see paras 15–001 to 15–011.

[4] *i.e.* the public authority from which information is sought, the Information Commissioner, the Information Tribunal or the courts.

[5] Freedom of Information Act 2000, ss.2(1)(b) and 2(2)(b); Freedom of Information (Scotland) Act 2002, s.2(1)(b).

[6] As to which, see paras 1–029 to 1–037.

material to the accused in criminal proceedings[7] or to the other party in civil proceedings[8] and they do not affect its power to do so.[9]

2. INFORMATION HELD FOR CRIMINAL INVESTIGATION, ETC., PURPOSES

Introduction

20–004 This and the following two sections involve three separate, but in practice largely overlapping, heads of exemption:

(1) information held for the purposes of a criminal investigation or proceedings;
(2) information relating to the obtaining of information from confidential sources; and
(3) information whose disclosure might prejudice the enforcement of criminal law.

It will be noted that only the third involves a consideration of resultant prejudice. Similar exemptions are to be found in each of the comparative jurisdictions.[10]

The exemption

20–005 Section 30(1) of the Freedom of Information Act 2000 exempts information held by a public authority if it has been held by it at any time for the purposes

7 See Criminal Procedure and Investigations Act 1996, Pt I.

8 See CPR Pt 31.

9 See, *e.g.* Freedom of Information Act 2000, s.78; Freedom of Information (Scotland) Act 2002, s.66; Data Protection Act 1998, s.35.

10 In the United States, the Freedom of Information Act, 1966, 5 USC § 552(b)(7), exempts from disclosure records or information compiled for law enforcement purposes: see para.2–008(7). The Freedom of Information Act 1982 (Cth of Australia), s.37, provides an exemption where the disclosure of the requested document would, or could be reasonably be expected to, cause damage to law enforcement, confidential sources of information relating to law enforcement, fair trials, or methods of criminal investigation: see para.2–015(12). The Official Information Act 1982 (New Zealand), ss.6(c) and 27(1)(a), provides an exemption where the disclosure of the information would be likely to prejudice the maintenance of the law, including the prevention, investigation, and detection of offences, and the right to a fair trial: see para.2–022(3). The Access to Information Act (Canada), s.16(1)(c), provides a discretionary exemption for records the disclosure of which could reasonably be expected to cause injury to law enforcement or conduct of lawful investigations: see para.2–032(12). The Freedom of Information Act 1997 (Ireland), provides a discretionary exemption for records the disclosure of which could reasonably be expected to prejudice law enforcement and investigations or matters of internal security, or to reveal the name of a police informer: see para.2–039(12).

of any investigation which it has a duty to carry out with a view to it being ascertained whether to charge someone with an offence or whether a person charged is guilty,[11] or, if the authority itself has power to conduct criminal proceedings, for the purposes of an investigation carried out by it which may lead to criminal proceedings[12] or for the purposes of such criminal proceedings.[13] This is a class-based exemption: in spite of considerable Parliamentary pressure,[14] and in contrast to the position in much of the comparative legislation,[15] there is no requirement for any prejudice to any investigation or proceedings to be shown for the exemption to apply. The exemption appears to be designed to relate to information held for the purposes of specific investigations or criminal proceedings, rather than to investigations or proceedings generally,[16] although the wording of the provision is possibly ambiguous.[17] It applies most obviously to information coming to the police, the Serious Fraud Office, the Crown Prosecution Service or the Director of Public Prosecutions in the course of specific investigations; but it may also apply to information held by many other bodies which have the power to conduct criminal proceedings of all sorts, including proceedings relating to quite minor offences.[18] For the exemption to apply the authority holding the information must be the same as the one which held it for the relevant purpose,[19] but it can have held it for that purpose at any time in the past, it need not have obtained it for that purpose originally and the information does not have to be required any longer for that purpose. Thus, information once coming within the exemption is always potentially exempt and the potential exemption applies even if a decision was made not to prosecute or if a prosecution has been completed, however long ago the investigation or prosecution was completed.[20]

---

11 See Freedom of Information Act 2000, s.30(1)(a).

12 *ibid.* s.30(1)(b).

13 *ibid.* s.30(1)(c).

14 *e.g. Hansard*, HL, Vol.617, October 19, 2000, col.1291.

15 See, *e.g.* Freedom of Information Act 1982 (Cth of Aust), s.37(1)(a); Freedom of Information Act 1997, (Ireland) s.23(1)(a).

16 As, for example, internal documents of the police showing investigation methods or procedures which are likely to be covered by Freedom of Information Act 2000, s.31(1)(a) and (b).

17 See the view of the Minister, Lord Falconer of Thoroton, in *Hansard*, HL, Vol.612, April 20, 2000, col.827.

18 *e.g.* local authorities which have numerous prosecutorial functions, the Health and Safety Executive, the Environment Agency. Note that Freedom of Information Act 2000, s.30(5) expressly includes proceedings before courts-martial and other military courts within the concept of criminal proceedings.

19 The exemption is designed for prosecuting authorities as such.

20 This appears to go further than was necessary to carry out the Government's expressed purpose for the provision, Lord Falconer of Thoroton stating that it was necessary "to ensure that criminal proceedings are not jeopardised by the premature disclosure of information and to preserve the criminal courts as the sole forum for determining guilt": *Hansard*, HL, Vol.612, April 20, 2000, col.827. But these issues may be relevant in assessing where the "public interest" lies: see para.20–006.

The public interest

20–006 If the information in question comes within the section, the duty to disclose does not apply only if or to the extent that if the public interest in maintaining the exemption outweighs the public interest in disclosing the information.[21] The weighing exercise necessitates an identification of the public interest in the maintenance of the exemption, always recognising that that public interest must be delineated in such a fashion that it is capable in practice of being outweighed.[22] Although the public interest in maintaining the exemption is, to a certain extent, self-evident to those concerned to abide by or maintain the law, a useful statement of purpose was set out in the White Paper leading to the introduction of the Act:

> "[freedom of information] should not undermine the investigation, prosecution or prevention of crime, or the bringing of civil or criminal proceedings by public bodies. The investigation and prosecution of crime involve a number of essential requirements. These include the need to avoid prejudicing effective law enforcement, the need to protect witnesses and informers, the need to maintain the independence of the judicial and prosecution processes, and the need to preserve the criminal court as the sole forum for determining guilt. Because of this, the Act will exclude information relating to the investigation and prosecution functions of the police, prosecutors, and other bodies carrying out law enforcement work such as the Department of Social Security or the Immigration Service. The Act will also exclude information relating to the commencement or conduct of civil proceedings."[23]

The force of the public interest in maintaining this exemption will in material part depend on the importance of the information to the investigation or proceedings, the currency of the investigation or proceedings, whether the information, or like information, has been earlier released and, if so, to whom, on what basis and for what purpose. On the other hand, there is likely to be a public interest in the disclosure of information about the commission of a criminal offence and the passage of time, the completion of a prosecution, the release of similar information into a public forum and the inconsequentiality of the infor-

[21] Freedom of Information Act 2000, ss.30(1) and 2(2)(b). That there is a particular public interest in the disclosure of information relating to the commission of a criminal offence is reflected in Pt IVA of the Employment Rights Act 1996 as inserted by the Public Interest Disclosure Act 1998, which sanctions as being in the public interest a disclosure by an employee tending to show "that a criminal offence has been committed, is being committed or is likely to be commited"—s.43B(1)(a).

[22] To avoid metamorphosing it into an absolute exemption.

[23] *Your Right to Know. The Government's Proposals for a FOI Act*, Cm.3818, December 11, 1997, para.2.21. Although the form of the Act as enacted was quite different from that intended in 1997, the basic intention behind the provisions dealt with in this chapter is that revealed in the quotation.

mation can all be expected to weaken the public interest in the maintenance of the exemption.[24] On the other hand, the public interest in disclosure may, for example, be heightened:

— where disclosure would allay legitimate public concerns about an investigation or prosecution;
— where the information already officially released relating to an investigation or prosecution is unrepresentative of all such information held by the public authority[25]; or
— where some decision affecting the applicant has been made that is based, whether in whole or in part, on the information.[26]

Duty to confirm or deny

Where the requested information is, or if it were held would be, exempt information under s.30(1), then the discrete duty to confirm or deny that that information is held by the public authority does not arise. Again, this is a qualified exclusion of duty. It will be necessary to consider whether, in all the circumstances, the maintenance of the exclusion of this duty outweighs by the public interest in disclosing whether the public authority holds the information. Despite its superficial similarity, this public interest balancing exercise is materially different from that employed for the purpose of determining whether the duty to communicate does not apply.[27] As a general rule, the broader the terms of the request, the more difficult it will become for the public authority to contend that the public interest in excluding the duty to confirm or deny that such information is held by it outweighs the public interest in compliance with that duty; if only because it will be self-evident that the public authority does hold information of that description. 20–007

Scottish Act

The Scottish counterpart to s.30(1) is s.34(1) of the Freedom of Information (Scotland) Act 2002. The Scottish provision does not in terms require the information to be held by the Scottish public authority which previously held it for the purposes of the investigation. Also, it does not cover the possibility of the 20–008

[24] See *Hansard*, HL, Vol.618, October 24, 2000, col.274 and Vol.619, November 14, 2000, col.223/4. Note also the Access to Information Act 1982 (Canada) which provides at s.16(1)(a) that the corresponding exemption only applies to information less than 20 years old.

[25] See para.15–008.

[26] The public interest is capable of recognising the peculiar interest of an applicant in having access to information that touches upon or relates to that individual's rights or to matters of particular and legitimate concern to that individual: see para.15–009.

[27] See paras 15–010 to 15–011 as to what it involves.

authority which held the information itself having power to institute criminal proceedings; rather, it refers to an investigation which may lead to a report to the Procurator Fiscal.[28] There is also a special provision in s.34(2) of the Scottish Act making information exempt if it is held by a Scottish public authority for the purposes of an inquiry under the Fatal Accidents and Sudden Deaths Inquiry (Scotland) Act 1976[29] or if it has been held by such an authority for the purposes of any other investigation into the cause of death of any person. Apart from these differences, as well as the different manner in which the Scottish Act generally deals with the duty to confirm or deny,[30] the Scottish provision is materially the same as s.30(1) of the Freedom of Information 2000.

3. INFORMATION RELATING TO THE OBTAINING OF INFORMATION FROM CONFIDENTIAL SOURCES

First requirement of the exemption

20–009 Section 30(2) of the Freedom of Information Act 2000 contains specific provisions exempting information held by a public authority which was obtained or recorded for the purposes of the public authority's functions relating to criminal investigations or proceedings, as well as certain civil investigations or proceedings. In each such case, however, there is an additional requirement that the information "relates to the obtaining of information from confidential sources."[31] Insofar as this exemption relates to information obtained or recorded for the purpose of criminal investigation or proceedings, such information will very likely also be rendered exempt information by s.30(1). However, s.30(2), unlike s.30(1), would seem not to require that the information have been held for the purpose of any particular investigation: it would seem to be enough that the information was obtained for the purposes of the public authority's functions relating to criminal investigations and proceedings generally. Insofar as this exemption relates to particular civil investigations and proceedings, it does not overlap with s.30(1).

Second requirement of the exemption

20–010 The second requirement in s.30(2) is that the information "relates to the obtaining of information from confidential sources." This was said to be intended to protect the identity of particular sources of information,[32] but it is arguable that

[28] There are similar provisions in the Freedom of Information Act 2000 in the application of s.30 to Scotland: see s.30(6).
[29] But if the inquiry is still continuing, see Freedom of Information (Scotland) Act 2002, s.34(2)(a).
[30] See para.1–025.
[31] Freedom of Information Act 2000, s.30(2)(a)(i) and (ii) and (b).
[32] See Lord Falconer of Thoroton in *Hansard*, HL, Vol.619, November 14, 2000, col.220.

it is more limited. A neutral reading of the exemption results in it only comprehending general information relating to the obtaining of information from confidential sources, and not a particular piece of information obtained from such a source in the course of a specific investigation or the identity of the particular source.[33] Whatever is precisely covered by the section, it is clear that the information itself need not be "confidential:" it is dealing with information "from confidential sources," a phrase which is likely to be construed as referring to information from someone who has supplied it "on the understanding, whether express or implied, that his or her identity will remain confidential."[34] The information itself could be "old, out-of-date, or simply wrong."[35]

The public interest

Exemption under s.30(2) is qualified.[36] An assessment of the public interest in maintaining this exemption should involve a consideration of both paragraphs of the exemption. So far as para.(a) is concerned, where the information relates to a criminal investigation or proceedings, the relevant factors will be similar to those which arise upon an assessment of the public interest under s.30(1).[37] So far as para.(b) is concerned, the public interest in the maintenance of confidential sources of information will be of particular significance,[38] as will the ability of a person adversely affected by a decision based on the information to controvert it. 20–011

Duty to confirm or deny

Where the requested information is, or if it were held would be, exempt information under s.30(2), then the discrete duty to confirm or deny that that information is held by the public authority does not arise. The exclusion of this duty is a qualified one. It will be necessary to consider whether, in all the circumstances, the 20–012

[33] Compare the clearer and more explicit foreign legislation: Freedom of Information Act 1982 (Cth of Aust) s.37(1)(b); Official Information Act 1982 (New Zealand), s.9(2)(ba)(i); Access to Information Act,1982 (Canada), s.16(1)(c)(ii); Freedom of Information Act 1997 (Ireland), s.23(1)(a)(i) and (b); exemption 7(D) in the Freedom of Information Act 1966 (USA) referred to in *Pope v USA* (1979) 599 F.(2d) 1383 and note not only the wording of Freedom of Information Act 2000, s.30(2)(b) but also the use of the phrase "for the purposes of its functions relating to... investigations [and]...proceedings" in s.30(2)(a). It is likely that the identity of confidential sources would be protected in any event by the very general prejudice based exemption in s.31(1)(a) and (b) or by s.30(1).

[34] See *Dept of Health v Jephcott* (1985) 62 A.L.R. 421 at 426. See also *Luzaich v United States* (1977) 435 F. Supp 31 at 35, which talks of a "pledge of confidentiality."

[35] See: *Dale v Australian Federal Police* (1997) 47 A.L.D. 417.

[36] Freedom of Information Act 2000, s.2(3).

[37] As to which, see para.20–006.

[38] See for a discussion of the public interest in preserving confidential sources in this and analogous contexts: *D v NSPCC* [1978] A.C. 171 (in particular 218C–F, 230A–B, 232F–G, 241C–D). See also *Pope v USA* (1979) 599 F.(2d) 1383 and *Jarvie v Magistrates' Court of Victoria at Brunswick* [1995] 1 V.R. 84 *per* Brooking J. at 88:

maintenance of the exclusion of this duty is outweighed by the public interest in disclosing whether the public authority holds the information. As noted above,[39] this public interest balancing exercise is materially different from that employed for the purpose of determining whether the duty to communicate does not apply.[40]

Scottish provisions

20–013 Analogous provisions exist in the Freedom of Information (Scotland) Act 2002,[41] albeit slightly narrower in scope than under the Westminster Act.[42]

4. INFORMATION WHOSE DISCLOSURE MIGHT PREJUDICE THE ENFORCEMENT OF CRIMINAL LAW

The exemption

20–014 By s.31(1)(a) and (b) of the Freedom of Information Act 2000 information which is not exempt under s.30[43] is nevertheless exempt if its disclosure under the Act would, or would be likely to, prejudice the prevention or detection of crime or the apprehension or prosecution of offenders.[44] The basic distinction between ss.30 and 31 is that:

— the former is concerned with information held by the public authority for the purpose of a specific investigation or criminal proceedings conducted by it, and with investigative material that relates to the obtaining of information from confidential sources;
— the latter is concerned with information, which although not held by the public authority for the purpose of a specific investigation or criminal proceedings conducted by it (nor relating to the obtaining of

"There is a public interest in preserving the anonymity of informers, since otherwise these wells of information will dry up and the police will be hindered in preventing and detecting crime; moreover, the public interest on which the need to protect informers rests is based in part on a regard for their personal safety, considered, not as a matter of expediency, but as an object in itself."

[39] See para.20–007, where this duty is considered further.
[40] See paras 15–010 to 15–011 as to what it involves.
[41] Note Freedom of Information (Scotland) Act 2002, s.34(3).
[42] The Freedom of Information (Scotland) Act 2002 does not include an equivalent of the Freedom of Information Act 2000, s.30(2)(a)(i) or (ii). The Freedom of Information Act 2000, s.30(2)(a)(iii) is equivalent to the Freedom of Information (Scotland) Act 2002, s.34(3); s.30(2)(a)(iv) is equivalent to 34(4), save that the second requirement is absent in Scotland. In relation to the duty to confirm or deny that the requested information is held, see para.20–008.
[43] See paras 20–004 to 20–008.
[44] Freedom of Information Act 2000, s.31(1)(a) and (b).

information from confidential sources), nevertheless would, if disclosed, prejudice or be likely to prejudice the enforcement of the law.

The latter is, therefore, more concerned with adverse revelations of methodology.[45] Similar exemptions as to law enforcement procedures are to be found in the comparative jurisdictions.[46] It is thought that the phrase "would be likely to prejudice" in the context of this provision will be taken to mean that the prejudice must be a real possibility, or something which "may well" result, as opposed to being "more probable than not."[47] Thus, not only insignificant harm but also fanciful or improbable risks of harm to the relevant interest are to be disregarded. Provided the relevant likelihood of prejudice is established, it does not matter which public authority holds the information and it need not relate to a specific investigation or prosecution. Thus, the exemption might apply not only to information held for the purposes of a current investigation (assuming for some reason it was not in any event covered by s.30(1) of the Freedom of Information Act 2000) but also to information disclosing methods and procedures for investigating crime.[48] For example:

[45] It is questionable whether s.31 can be used to prevent the disclosure of confidential source information to any useful extent. First, the information will be exempt information by virtue of s.30 and therefore outside s.31. Secondly, a general assertion that the disclosure of such material will, or would be likely to, prejudice enforcement of the law is apt to metamporphose s.31 into a pure class-based exemption. This approach has been rejected elsewhere. In Canada, the Courts have required the public authority to identify a particular investigation that would be prejudiced, and have declined to uphold a refusal to disclose upon a assertion that investigative processess would generally be prejudiced: *Rubin v Canada (Clerk of the Privy Council)* [1993] 2 F.C. 391, TD; [1994] 2 F.C. 707, CA; (1996), 179 N.R. 320, SCC; *Lavigne v Canada (Commissioner of Official Languages)* [2000] F.C.J. 1412, QL FCA; *Information Commissioner v Minister of Citizenship and Immigration* [2002] F.C.A. 270 ("chilling effect" argument rejected).

[46] In the United States, the Freedom of Information Act, 1966, 5 USC § 552(b)(7)(E), exempts from disclosure records or information that would reveal techniques and procedures for law enforcement investigations or prosecutions or that would disclose guidelines for law enforcement investigations or prosecutions, provided that disclosure of the information could reasonably be expected to risk circumvention of the law: see para.2–008(7)(E). The Freedom of Information Act 1982 (Cth of Australia), s.37, provides an exemption where the disclosure of the requested document would, or could be reasonably be expected to, prejudice an investigation or enforcement of the law or to disclose confidential sources of information in relation to the enforcement or administration of the law: see para.2–015(12). The Official Information Act 1982 (New Zealand), ss.6(c) and 27(1)(a), provides an exemption where the disclosure of the information would be likely to prejudice the maintenance of the law, including the prevention, investigation, and detection of offences, and the right to a fair trial: see para.2–022(3). The Access to Information Act (Canada), s.16(1)(c), provides a discretionary exemption for records the disclosure of which could reasonably be expected to cause injury to law enforcement or conduct of lawful investigations: see para.2–032(12). The Freedom of Information Act 1997 (Ireland), provides a discretionary exemption for records the disclosure of which could reasonably be expected to prejudice law enforcement and investigations or matters of internal security, or to reveal the name of a police informer: see para.2–039(12).

[47] See, in relation to analogous provisions in Australia and New Zealand, *Ward v Victoria Police* [1986] 1 V.A.R. 334 at 335–6; *Commissioner of Police v Ombudsman* [1988] 1 N.Z.L.R. 385 and, in different statutory contexts in England, *Three Rivers District Council v Bank of England (Disclosure No. 1)* [2002] EWCA Civ 1182; [2003] 1 W.L.R. 210; [2002] 4 All E.R. 881 and *Re Harris Simons Construction Ltd* [1989] 1 W.L.R. 368. Generally, see paras 15–012 to 15–020.

[48] See the corresponding provision in the Freedom of Information Act 1982 (Cth of Aust), s.37(2)(b).

— policy documents setting out in what circumstances a public authority would prosecute for a breach of statute[49];
— investigation manuals[50];
— information about the criteria the police apply when considering the possible installation of secret surveillance equipment;
— information as to the registration numbers of unmarked police cars;
— information as to numbers of police officers deployed in a particular area.

It should also be noted that the particular information in itself may appear innocuous but nevertheless come within the exemption because, when combined with other information which may be in the public domain or be otherwise accessible, its disclosure will or may result in the relevant prejudice.[51]

The public interest

20–015 If the information in question comes within the section, the duty to disclose the information does not apply if the public interest in maintaining the exemption outweighs the public interest in disclosing the information.[52] The principles relating to the public interest weighing exercise are the same as those in relation to s.30(1).[53]

The duty to confirm or deny

20–016 Where the requested information is, or if it were held would be, exempt information under s.31(1)(a) or (b), then the discrete duty to confirm or deny that that information is held by the public authority does not arise. The exclusion of this duty is a qualified one, and the principles relating to the public interest weighing exercise are the same as those in relation to s.30(2).[54]

---

[49] For a similar example in Australia, see: *Re Murphy and Australian Electoral Commission* (1994) 33 A.L.D. 718.

[50] For a similar example in Australia, see: *Re Arnold Bloch Leibler & Co and Australian Taxation Office (No. 2)* (1985) 4 A.A.R. 178, 9 A.L.D. 7.

[51] The so-called "mosaic" or "jigsaw" principle. See paras 15–016 to 15–017.

[52] Freedom of Information Act 2000, ss.30(1) and 2(2)(b). If disclosure would reveal a miscarriage of justice, then this will almost certainly trump the harm that might be caused to enforcement of the criminal law. That there is a particular public interest in the disclosure of information relating to the miscarriage of justice is reflected in Pt IVA of the Employment Rights Act 1996, as inserted by the Public Interest Disclosure Act 1998, which sanctions as being in the public interest a disclosure by an employee tending to show "that a miscarriage of justice has occured, is occuring or is likely to occur"—s.43B(1)(c).

[53] See para.20–006.

[54] See para.20–012.

Scottish provisions

The Freedom of Information (Scotland) Act 2002 contains provisions that are identical to those in the Freedom of Information Act 2000, save that the relevant prejudice must be "substantial."[55] 20–017

Data Protection Act 1998

Section 29(1) of the Data Protection Act 1998 provides an analogous exemption in relation to a request for personal data. Under that section, personal data processed (which includes information "held") for the purposes of the prevention or detection of crime or the apprehension or prosecution of offenders is exempt from the subject access rights in any case where disclosure would be likely to prejudice those purposes.[56] Section 29(2) of the Act also provides an exemption for information being processed for the purpose of discharging statutory functions which has been obtained for that purpose from a person who had it in his possession for the purpose of preventing or detecting crime or apprehending or prosecuting offenders, provided that disclosure would be likely to prejudice the latter purposes. 20–018

5. OTHER LAW ENFORCEMENT

Introduction

All three Acts exempt information from disclosure if its disclosure is likely to prejudice[57] any of a large number of other law enforcement and regulatory activities outside the criminal context.[58] All three Acts are cast in slightly different terms, but their scope is broadly the same. The most obvious difference of substance, apart from the different structure and terminology used in the Data Protection Act 1998, is that the Freedom of Information (Scotland) Act 2002 requires substantial prejudice to be shown, as opposed to prejudice simpliciter.[59] 20–019

---

[55] Freedom of Information (Scotland) Act 2002, s.35(1)(a) and (b).

[56] Data Protection Act 1998, s.29(1)(a) and (b). In relation to the meaning of this provision see *R. (on the application of Lord) v Secretary of State for the Home Department* [2003] EWHC 2073 (Admin) at [102]; *R. (on the application of Ellis) v Chief Constable of the Essex Police* [2003] EWHC 1321 (Admin) at [29].

[57] For the meaning of "prejudice" and the degree of likelihood required, see paras 15–012 to 15–020.

[58] Freedom of Information Act 2000, s.31; Freedom of Information (Scotland) Act 2002, s.35; Data Protection Act 1998, s.31.

[59] As to the practical difference that the adjective "substantial" makes, see para.15–013.

Tax and similar impositions

20–020 The two Freedom of Information Acts exempt information if its disclosure will or is likely to prejudice "the assessment or collection of any tax or duty or of any imposition of a similar nature".[60] This would cover not only information which might prejudice a particular investigation of a taxpayer's affairs but also internal Inland Revenue information which showed, say, minimum financial limits below which the Revenue do not, as a matter of policy, investigate a self-assessment. The Data Protection Act 1998 contains more elaborate provisions relating to tax assessment and collection. Under it, personal data processed for the purposes of tax assessment or collection are exempt if disclosure would be likely to prejudice such assessment or collection.[61] And personal data held by government departments, local authorities and authorities administering council tax and housing benefit are exempt from the subject access rights to the extent that the exemption is necessary for the operation of a system of risk assessment for the purpose of collecting and assessing tax or similar impositions or of preventing, detecting or prosecuting offenders for making unlawful claims to, or applications of, public funds.[62]

Immigration

20–021 The two Freedom of Information Acts exempt information if its disclosure will or is likely to prejudice the operation of immigration controls.[63] This might cover, for example, instructions to immigration officers as to how to conduct inquiries of those seeking entry to the country.

Prisons

20–022 The two Freedom of Information Acts exempt information if its disclosure will or is likely to prejudice the maintenance of security and good order in prisons and other lawful detention centres.[64] This would cover, for example, plans of the layout of prisons.

---

60 See Freedom of Information Act 2000, s.31(1)(d); Freedom of Information (Scotland) Act 2002, s.35(1)(d).

61 Data Protection Act 1998, s.29(1)(c); see also Data Protection Act 1998, s.29(2) referred to in para.20–018.

62 *ibid*. ss.29(4) and (5).

63 Freedom of Information Act 2000, s.31(1)(e); Freedom of Information (Scotland) Act 2002, s.35(1)(e).

64 Freedom of Information Act 2000, s.31(1)(f); Freedom of Information (Scotland) Act 2002, s.35(1)(f).

The public interest

If the information in question comes within the section, the duty to disclose the information does not apply if the public interest in maintaining the exemption outweighs the public interest in disclosing the information.[65] The principles relating to the public interest weighing exercise are the same as those in relation to s.30(1).[66] The particular public interest in maintaining these exemptions is, in large part, self-evident. 20–023

The duty to confirm or deny

Where the requested information is, or if it were held would be, exempt information under s.31(1), then the discrete duty to confirm or deny that that information is held by the public authority does not arise. The exclusion of this duty is a qualified one, and the principles relating to the public interest weighing exercise are the same as those in relation to s.30(2).[67] 20–024

6. OTHER INVESTIGATORY AND REGULATORY FUNCTIONS

Regulatory functions

All three Acts exempt the disclosure of information if that is likely to prejudice the discharge of a wide range of investigatory and regulatory functions of public authorities.[68] The relevant functions are defined in the Data Protection Act 1998 as meaning functions conferred on any person by or under an enactment, any function of the Crown or a Minister or government department and any other function of a public nature exercised in the public interest.[69] The exemption in each of the Acts applies to the exercise of the relevant functions for specified purposes. These purposes include: 20–025

— ascertaining whether any person has failed to comply with the law[70];
— ascertaining whether any person is responsible for improper conduct[71];

---

[65] Freedom of Information Act 2000, ss.31(1) and 2(2)(b).
[66] See para.20–006.
[67] See para.20–012.
[68] Data Protection Act 1998, s.31(1)–(3); Freedom of Information Act 2000, s.31(1)(g) and (2); Freedom of Information (Scotland) Act 2002, s.35(1)(g) and (2).
[69] Data Protection Act 1998, s.31(3).
[70] Freedom of Information Act 2000, s.31(1)(g) and (2)(a); Freedom of Information (Scotland) Act 2002, s.35(1)(g) and (2)(a).
[71] Freedom of Information Act 2000, s.31(1)(g) and (2)(b); Freedom of Information (Scotland) Act 2002, s.35(1)(g) and (2)(b). See also Data Protection Act 1998, s.31(1) and (2)(a)(i)–(iii): the Data

- ascertaining whether circumstances exist which would justify regulatory action under an enactment[72];
- ascertaining a person's fitness or competence in relation to management of companies or in any professional activity[73];
- ascertaining the cause of an accident[74];
- protecting charities against misconduct and mismanagement and the loss of their property and recovering property which has been lost[75]; and
- securing the health safety and welfare of people at work[76] and protecting the public against risks to their health and safety from those at work.[77]

Information covered by regulatory functions exemption

20–026 It is clear that this group of exemptions will cover information whose disclosure might prejudice inquiries into the causes of all kinds of matters which come within the purview of particular public authorities (*e.g.* local authorities, the Civil Aviation Authority, the Health and Safety Executive, the Official Receiver). What is not so clear is whether, and if so the extent to which, the prejudice need not relate to the specific inquiry for which the information has been obtained. The Canadian case *Rubin v Canada (Minister of Transport)*[78] neatly illustrates the issue. The applicant sought from Transport Canada a post-accident safety review report undertaken as a result of a Nationair aircraft crash in Jeddah, Saudi Arabia on July 11, 1991, in which 249 Nigerian passengers and 14 Canadian crew members were killed. It had been the worst airline disaster in Canadian history. Transport Canada refused the request. The trial judge ordered that Transport Canada should disclose only those parts of the report

Protection Act 1998 refers to functions designed to protect the public against financial loss caused by improper conduct of those carrying on financial services or managing companies or those who are bankrupts or improper conduct of persons authorised to carry on professions or other activities, but it is thought that the same type of information is likely to be exempted under these differently worded provisions.

72 Freedom of Information Act 2000, s.31(2)(c); Freedom of Information (Scotland) Act 2002, s.35(2)(c). See again note above in relation to Data Protection Act 1998, s.31(2)(a).

73 Freedom of Information Act 2000, s.31(2)(d); Freedom of Information (Scotland) Act 2002, s.35(2)(d). See again note above in relation to Data Protection Act 1998, s.31(2)(a).

74 Freedom of Information Act 2000, s.31(2)(e); Freedom of Information (Scotland) Act 2002, s.35(2)(e).

75 Freedom of Information Act 2000, s.31(2)(f)–(h); Freedom of Information (Scotland) Act 2002, s.35(2)(f)–(h); Data Protection Act 1998, s.31(2)(b)–(d).

76 Freedom of Information Act 2000, s.31(2)(i); Freedom of Information (Scotland) Act 2002, s.35(2)(i); Data Protection Act 1998, s.31(2)(e).

77 Freedom of Information Act 2000, s.31(2)(j); Freedom of Information (Scotland) Act 2002, s.35(2)(j); Data Protection Act 1998, s.31(2)(f).

78 [1998] 2 F.C. 430, (1997) 154 DLR (4th) 414, Court of Appeal. The analogous provision is the Access to Information Act, s.16(1)(c).

which could have been obtained through regulatory means or otherwise, without relying on confidential sources, but refused access to the remainder. He found a reasonable expectation of probable harm to the conduct of *future* accident safety reviews were the report to be disclosed, and that the public interest in maintaining confidential reviews outweighed the public right to access contemplated in the Canadian Act. Mr Rubin appealed and the Court of Appeal allowed his appeal, rejecting the trial judge's reasoning:

> "to allow his judgment to stand, would protect from public review most non-regulatory investigations 'past, present and future' on the nebulous ground that to disclose this information might have a chilling effect on future investigations. Given that the purpose of the Act is to broaden the public's access to government information, this cannot have been Parliament's intent."

The Court of Appeal was also influenced by the fact that such a broad interpretation of the exemption would render other exemptions in the Act practically superfluous. The Court of Appeal concluded that the exemption only referred to a specific, ongoing investigation or one that was about to be undertaken: it did not apply to the general investigative process.

The public interest

If the information in question comes within the section, the duty to disclose the information does not apply if the public interest in maintaining the exemption outweighs the public interest in disclosing the information.[79] The broad principles relating to the public interest weighing exercise have been considered above.[80] However, the nature of the investigations and regulatory activities with which the exemptions at hand are concerned will often be of wider public concern than the run-of-the-mill prosecution: accidents, particularly those involving trains or aircraft, invariably provoke public concern; so, too, maladministration that has been the subject of an official investigation of any sort. This particular public interest must be reflected in the balancing exercises that must be carried out under s.2 of the Freedom of Information Act 2000. The particular public interest was recognised by the Canadian Court of Appeal in *Rubin v Canada (Minister of Transport)*[81]: 20–027

> "Having stated the important role that post-accident safety reviews play in the overall safety of the aeronautics industry, I think it is also important

[79] Freedom of Information Act 2000, ss.30(1) and 2(2)(b).
[80] See para.20–006.
[81] [1998] 2 F.C. 430, (1997) 154 DLR (4th) 414, CA. The analogous provision is the Access to Information Act, s.16(1)(c).

> not to underestimate the public's interest in disclosure and the positive impact disclosure may have on the regulation of the aeronautics industry. It should not be forgotten that in passing this Act, Parliament has specified the important role public scrutiny of government information plays in a democratic system. Indeed, as Justice La Forest recently affirmed in *Dagg*,[82] 'The overarching purpose of access to information legislation . . . is to facilitate democracy. It does so in two related ways. It helps to ensure first, that citizens have the information required to participate meaningfully in the democratic process, and secondly, that politicians and bureaucrats remain accountable to the citizenry.'"

The duty to confirm or deny

20–028 Where the requested information is, or if it were held would be, exempt information under s.31(1), then the discrete duty to confirm or deny that that information is held by the public authority does not arise. The exclusion of this duty is a qualified one, and the principles relating to the public interest weighing exercise are the same as those in relation to s.30(2).[83]

Data Protection Act 1998

20–029 Given that the Data Protection Act 1998 is concerned with "personal data," the significance of this head of exemption is less immediate than it is under the Freedom of Information Act 2000. Nevertheless, the Data Protection Act 1998 provides a broadly analogous ground of exemption for information the disclosure of which would prejudice regulatory bodies.[84] Specific exemption is provided for personal data processed for the purpose of discharging any function conferred on various commissioners and ombudsmen, as well the Director General of Fair Trading, provided that those functions are designed to protect members of the public against maladministration, failures and other forms of sub-standard conduct.[85]

---

82 *Dagg v Canada (Minister of Finance)* [1997] 2 S.C.R. 403 at 432–433.
83 See para.20–012.
84 Data Protection Act 1998, s.31(1)–(2).
85 *ibid*. s.31(4)–(5).

7. CIVIL PROCEEDINGS

Investigations

There are specific provisions in the two Freedom of Information Acts relating to information obtained by public authorities for the purposes of civil proceedings arising out of investigations of various sorts, although the details of the provisions in the two Acts differ. Section 30(2)(a)(iv) of the Freedom of Information Act 2000 exempts information obtained for the purposes of civil proceedings brought by or on behalf of the authority arising out of investigations conducted by it for any of the purposes set out in s.31(2),[86] provided the information relates to the obtaining of information from confidential sources.[87] Section 34(4) of the Freedom of Information (Scotland) Act 2002 exempts information held by a Scottish public authority if it was obtained for the purposes of civil proceedings arising out of such investigations or out of criminal investigations, but there is no requirement about confidential sources. In neither case is it necessary for there to be any prejudice shown. 20–030

Prejudice to administration of justice

Both Freedom of Information Acts specifically exempt information held by a public authority the disclosure of which would or would be likely to prejudice "the administration of justice"[88]: this provision might include information held by the public authority in connection with civil proceedings being brought by or against it. Both Freedom of Information Acts also exempt information if its disclosure would or would be likely to prejudice any civil proceedings brought by any public authority and arising out of an investigation conducted for any of the purposes set out in s.31(2) of the Freedom of Information Act 2000[89] by virtue of the royal prerogative or under statutory powers.[90] 20–031

86 See para.20–025.
87 Freedom of Information Act 2000, s.30(2)(b).
88 Freedom of Information Act 2000, s.31(1)(c); Freedom of Information (Scotland) Act 2002, s.35(1)(c). As to the phrase "likely to prejudice," see para.20–014.
89 Or the Freedom of Information (Scotland) Act 2002, s.35(2).
90 See: Freedom of Information Act 2000, s.31(1)(h); Freedom of Information (Scotland) Act 2002, s.35(1)(h). The Freedom of Information Act 2000, s.31(1)(i) contains a similar exemption if disclosure may prejudice an inquiry held under the Fatal Accidents and Sudden Deaths Inquiries (Scotland) Act 1976.

Court documents

20–032 Information is exempt under the Freedom of Information Act 2000 if it is held by a public authority only by virtue of being contained in a document filed or lodged with a court[91] or served on or by the authority or created by the court or its officials for the purposes of court proceedings in a particular cause or matter.[92] This exemption would cover information contained in statements of case, application notices, witness statements, affidavits, skeleton arguments, and disclosed documents served in the course of proceedings, provided always that the information is held by the public authority only by virtue of being contained in such a document. The thinking behind the exemption is that the disclosure of information contained in court documents should be regulated by the procedure applying in the court or tribunal in question, which are not themselves "public authorities" for the purposes of the Acts, and not by a separate regime.[93] Information is also exempt if it is held only by virtue of being contained in a document lodged with a person conducting an inquiry or arbitration or created by such a person for the purposes thereof.[94] The corresponding provisions in the Freedom of Information (Scotland) Act 2002 are slightly differently worded but the effect is the same in relation to information held by Scottish public authorities.[95] Information held by a Scottish public authority for the purposes of an inquiry under the Fatal Accidents and Sudden Deaths Inquiry (Scotland) Act 1976 is not covered by this exemption, however.[96] These exemptions are absolute. They may also apply in the context of criminal proceedings.[97]

91 "Court" is defined as including any tribunal or body exercising the judicial power of the State for the purposes of this exemption: see Freedom of Information Act 2000, s.32(4)(a); Freedom of Information (Scotland) Act 2002, s.37(2). This would include, *e.g.* employment tribunals, the Employment Appeal Tribunal, mental health tribunals, Special Educational Needs Tribunals etc. It probably also encompasses the European Court of Justice and the European Court of Human Rights, which, though they do not exercise the judicial power of any State, are undoubtedly courts.

92 Freedom of Information Act 2000, s.32(1).

93 Thus, for example, in the High Court and county courts, CPR 5.4(2) governs access by non-parties to documents coming into existence in the course of proceedings (broadly speaking there is a right to inspect served claim forms and judgments of the court and other documents lodged with the court may be inspected with permission), while witness statements which have formed evidence in chief are open to inspection unless the court otherwise directs and the circumstances set out in CPR 32.13(3) apply (see CPR 32.13).

94 Freedom of Information Act 2000, s.32(2).

95 Freedom of Information (Scotland) Act 2002, s.37(1).

96 *ibid.* s.37(3).

97 "Cause or matter" is not defined in the Freedom of Information Act 2000 but the Supreme Court Act 1981, s.151(1) defines cause to mean "any action or any criminal proceedings."

The duty to confirm or deny

Where the requested information is, or if it were held would be, exempt information under s.32(1) or (2), then the discrete duty to confirm or deny that that information is held by the public authority does not arise.[98] The exclusion of this duty is an absolute one.[99] 20–033

Data Protection Act 1998

Analogous grounds of exemption are provided by s.35(2) of the Data Protection Act 1998. 20–034

8. AUDIT

Introduction

There are provisions in both Freedom of Information Acts exempting information held by public authorities in relation to auditing the accounts of other public authorities or examining the economy, efficiency and effectiveness with which they use their resources if its disclosure would or would be likely to prejudice (or, in the case of Scottish public authorities, prejudice substantially) the exercise of such audit functions.[1] This will most obviously cover information held by the National Audit Office or the Audit Commission for Local Authorities and the National Health Service in England and Wales. It does not relate to internal audits by public authorities. Although private firms of accountants employed by public audit bodies are not themselves subject to the Freedom of Information Acts, the information generated by them in the course of carrying out work for a public authority may be information "held" by the public authority even if it is in the physical possession of the private firm.[2] 20–035

---

[98] Freedom of Information Act 2000, s.32(3).

[99] *ibid.* s.2(3).

[1] Freedom of Information Act 2000, s.33; Freedom of Information (Scotland) Act 2002, s.40. There are similar exemptions in three of the comparative regimes. The Freedom of Information Act 1982 (Cth of Australia), s.40, provides an exemption where the disclosure of the requested document would, or could be reasonably be expected to, prejudice the effectiveness of audits or tests or to have a substantial adverse effect upon the running of an agency: see para.2–015(14). The Access to Information Act (Canada), s.22, provides a discretionary exemption for records the disclosure of which could reasonably be expected to prejudice the use of audits or tests: see para.2–032(18). The Freedom of Information Act 1997 (Ireland), s.46(1), treats records relating to audits as "exempt records," thereby taking them outside the scope of the Act: see para.2–035.

[2] See *Chantrey Martin v Martin* [1953] 2 Q.B. 286 at 293; *Gibbon v Pease* [1905] 1 K.B. 810; *Leicestershire County Council v Michael Faraday & Partners* [1941] 2 All E.R. 483; *Formica Ltd v ECGD* [1995] 1 Lloyd's Rep. 692 at 703.

The public interest

20–036 If the information in question comes within the section, the duty to disclose the information does not apply if the public interest in maintaining the exemption outweighs the public interest in disclosing the information.[3] The principles relating to the public interest weighing exercise are the same as those in relation to s.30(1).[4] Given that the exemption is prejudice-based, the particular public interest in maintaining these exemptions is self-evident.

The duty to confirm or deny

20–037 Where the requested information is, or if it were held would be, exempt information under s.32(1) or (2), then the discrete duty to confirm or deny that that information is held by the public authority does not arise.[5] The exclusion of this duty is an absolute one.[6]

Data Protection Act 1998

20–038 Analogous grounds of exemption are provided by s.35(2) of the Data Protection Act 1998.

[3] Freedom of Information Act 2000, ss.33(2) and 2(2)(b).
[4] See para.20–006.
[5] Freedom of Information Act 2000, s.32(3).
[6] *ibid*. s.2(3).

CHAPTER 21

Privilege

1. PARLIAMENTARY PRIVILEGE

Introduction

Where the communication of particular information pursuant to a request under the Freedom of Information Act 2000 would constitute an infringement of the privileges of either House of Parliament, that information is exempt 21–001 information for the purposes of the Act.[1] The exemption is an absolute one, so that there is no need to consider whether the public interest in disclosing the information outweighs the public interest in maintaining the exemption.[2] Similarly, where the mere confirmation or denial by a public authority that it holds the information requested would constitute an infringement of the privileges of either House of Parliament, the duty to confirm or deny will not arise.[3] Similar exemptions are to be found in each of the comparative jurisdictions except the United States and Canada.[4]

Scope and meaning

21–002 The Freedom of Information Act 2000 protects the privileges of "either House of Parliament." There is no statutory definition of a "privilege" of House of Parliament.[5] By convention, the Parliament at Westminster and its members and officers carrying out its functions enjoy a number of benefits, or "privileges," not available to other citizens or institutions, such as exemption from jury service and the right to discipline its own members for misconduct. The scope for an answer to a request for information (still less a confirmation or denial that that information is held) to infringe any of these privileges is limited.

---

1 Freedom of Information Act 2000, s.34(1). With the result that the duty to communicate the information, under Freedom of Information Act 2000, s.1(1)(b), does not apply. No such exemption operates under the Freedom of Information (Scotland) Act 2002.

2 Freedom of Information Act 2000, s.2(3). This does not, of itself, mean that there cannot be discretionary disclosure of the information: see paras 14–006 to 14–013.

3 *ibid.* s.34(2). The disapplication of this duty is also absolute, so that it is not necessary to consider the public interest. Disapplication of the duty to confirm or deny is more likely to arise where the request is very specific, such that mere confirmation or denial is revelatory of the information sought.

4 The Freedom of Information Act 1982 (Cth of Australia), s.46(b), provides an exemption where the disclosure of the requested document would infringe the privileges of the Commonwealth Parliament, State Parliaments and Territorial Assemblies: see para.2–015(6). The Official Information Act 1982 (New Zealand), ss.18(c)(ii) and 52(1), provides an absolute exemption where the disclosure of the information would constitute a contempt of the House: see para.2–022(7). This is a wider concept than Parliamentary privilege, and includes anything which has a tendency to obstruct or impede the House in its business, even something for which there is no precedent. The Freedom of Information Act 1997 (Ireland), s.22(1)(c), provides a mandatory exemption where the record consists of the private papers of a member of the European Parliament, a member of a local authority or of a health board, or it consists of the opinions, advice, recommendations or the results of consultations considered by either House of the Oireachtas or its committees: see para.2–039(3).

5 This was intentional—see House of Commons, *Research Paper 99/98, The Freedom of Information Bill*, December 3, 1999, p.38.

Debates and speeches

Parliamentary privilege protects the primary right not to have called into question any "proceedings in Parliament" outside of the Houses nor to be required to produce documents which are in the custody of the House.[6] It is protected by Art.9 of the Bill of Rights 1689[7] and by common law authorities refusing to allow any challenge to what is said or done within the walls of Parliament in performance of its legislative function and established privileges.[8] This aspect of the privilege covers proceedings in the chambers of both the House of Commons and the House of Lords while in session. Most debates are conducted in public, and most Parliamentary reports are available to the public. However Parliament retains the right to prohibit publication of its proceedings as it considers appropriate. Since 1971 this has been restricted to proceedings conducted in private or when publication has been expressly prohibited by the House.[9] These are rare events. 21–003

Committees and Commissioners

The term "proceedings in Parliament"[10] covers emanations of either House, such as committees and the workings of the Parliamentary Commissioner for Standards.[11] Parliament has the right to prevent publication of the evidence taken by a select committee before it has been reported to the House.[12] So, for example, an application for disclosure of a Parliamentary Select Committee report, or of workings of that Committee, could not be sustained if such documents have not been released by Parliament itself. The same would apply to an unpublished draft report. If reports of departmental officials advising 21–004

[6] This would include documents in the possession of officers of Parliament and officers of its Committees, and Members of Parliament, held for some function of the work of Parliament and its committees.

[7] "That the freedom of speech and debates or proceedings in Parlyament ought not to be impeached or questioned in any court or place out of Parlyament."

[8] *Prebble v Television New Zealand* [1995] 1 A.C. 321 at 332. In a defence to a defamation action, Television New Zealand asserted justification and relied *inter alia* on statements by ministers in the House which Television New Zealand alleged were calculated to mislead the House or were otherwise improperly motivated. Mr Prebble, a government minister and plaintiff in the defamation action, applied to strike out that part of the defence said to rely on privileged material. The Privy Council upheld the striking out of pleadings, ruling that the privilege applied to the material in question. It was an infringement of the privilege for any party to question in legal proceedings words spoken or actions done in Parliament by suggesting they were untrue, misleading or done for improper motives, even when done in defence of proceedings brought by a member of the legislature.

[9] See 226 *Commons Journal*, 548–549.

[10] In art.9 of the Bill of Rights 1689.

[11] *Hamilton v Al-Fayed (No.1)* [2001] 1 A.C. 395.

[12] This would certainly be the case where Parliament has actively proscribed publication. It could arguably be otherwise where Parliament has merely taken no steps to publish committee evidence. However it is likely that the privilege applies in this latter situation as well, unless and until Parliament has taken a positive step to waive the privilege that would otherwise attach.

Parliamentary committees are treated as confidential and not published, then it is arguable whether they would be susceptible to an FOI application.[13]

Internal documents and correspondence

21–005 Parliamentary privilege probably extends to letters and other documentation directly connected with proceedings in Parliament and internal documents of a House directly relating to its own proceedings.[14] The privilege does not extend to information volunteered to members of either House in their personal capacity.[15] It also probably does not cover letters sent by Members to Ministers.[16] Papers held by MPs, parties and their Committees which do not relate to Parliament's public functions are not caught by the Freedom of Information Act 2000 in any event.[17]

Parliamentary papers

21–006 In theory it may infringe the privilege to disclose parliamentary papers before they have been tabled in the House, where they are required to be so tabled.[18]

---

13 Two competing views are presented in Eagles, Taggart and Liddell, *Freedom of Information in New Zealand* (Oxford University Press, Auckland, 1992), pp.474–475. The argument in favour of access to such material rests on the aim of increased public participation in the legislative process, and the fact that while such departmental officials are Ministerial advisers, it is usual practice for them to be present during select committee proceedings. Against these considerations is the classic constitutional role of such officials as Ministerial advisers, and the practice that when acting in such an advisory capacity their reports continue to be confidential even after the committee has reported. It is for the committee to determine whether to treat such officials as witnesses or advisers.

14 Joint Committee on Parliamentary Privilege, *Report*, April 1999, HL Paper 43, HC 214, para.12.

15 See *Halsbury's Laws of England*, (4th ed., Butterworths, 1997 re-issue) Vol.34, para.1015.

16 In 1958 the House ruled that a letter sent by a Member of Parliament to a Minister was not covered by privilege as a proceeding of the House. An MP, Mr Strauss, wrote a letter to the Minister for Power complaining about various actions of the London Electricity Board. The Minister referred the letter to the Board, who took issue with the allegations in the letter and threatened to sue Mr Strauss unless he retracted the comments. The House Committee on Privileges determined that the letter was subject to privilege and the Board and its solicitors had acted in breach of the privilege. Following a lengthy debate the Commons voted 218 to 213 to hold that the letter was not a "proceeding in Parliament" and therefore the Board and its solicitors had not breached the privileges of the Parliament. See *Hansard*, HC, Deb. vol.591, July 8, 1958, cols 208–346.

17 House of Commons, *Public Administration Committee, Third Report, Session 1997–98*, May 19, 1998, para.37. Such papers are outside the scope of the regime in Australia (see para.2–011), New Zealand (see para.2–018), Canada (see para.2–026) and Ireland (see para.2–035).

18 The author is not aware of any authority directly on the issue. In practice the remedy would perhaps be the tabling of the report in the House and/or reprimand of the offender, rather than the withholding of the document.

Exclusive cognisance

The privilege extends to the "exclusive cognisance" or exclusive jurisdiction of Parliament. This covers determination of Parliamentary procedures, whether a procedure has been breached, and how breaches are to be dealt with.[19] It would probably also cover arrangements made by the Black Rod and Sarjeant-at-Arms for the security and proper functioning of the Houses and action taken on decisions relating to the use of committee rooms or the rules governing parliamentary groups.[20] There is uncertainty as to whether registration of members' interests is a proceeding in Parliament. [21] Where a matter is within the exclusive cognisance of Parliament, disclosure of confidential information held by Parliament dealing with that matter would infringe the privilege. 21–007

Administrative functions

Many administrative functions of Parliament would not be considered within the privilege, such as personnel matters, catering and other household activities.[22] 21–008

Conclusive certificates

The Speaker of the House of Commons or, in relation to the House of Lords, the Clerk of the Parliaments may issue a conclusive certificate for the purpose of exempting a public authority from its disclosure duty or both its disclosure duty and its duty to confirm or deny that it holds any of the information requested. Such a certificate is conclusive evidence of the "fact" that exemption from the duty or duties is, or at any time was, required for the purpose of avoiding an infringement of the privileges of either House of Parliament.[23] The effect of such a certificate in relation to information to which it applies is to remove practically all, if not all, an applicant's rights to challenge a decision not to 21–009

[19] Joint Committee on Parliamentary Privilege, *Report*, April 1999, HL Paper 43, HC 214, para.13.
[20] Joint Committee on Parliamentary Privilege, *Report*, April 1999, HL Paper 43, HC 214, para.117; House of Commons, *Research Paper 99/98, The Freedom of Information Bill*, December 3, 1999, p.40.
[21] Joint Committee on Parliamentary Privilege, *Report*, April 1999, HL Paper 43, HC 214, para.122.
[22] House of Commons, *Research Paper 99/98, The Freedom of Information Bill*, December 3, 1999, p.40. For the background on whether administrative functions were to be covered by the Freedom of Information Act 2000 see *ibid*. pp.39–40. The House of Commons Select Committee on Pub lic Administration stated that such information should not be protected from disclosure: see their Third Report, Session 1997–98, May 19, 1998, para.37.
[23] Freedom of Information Act 2000, s.34(3–(4).

communicate the information sought and a decision neither confirming nor denying that the information requested is held by the public authority.[24]

The Data Protection Act 1998

21–010 Section 35A of the Data Protection Act 1998 provides an exemption from the subject access rights that is in materially identical terms to s.34(1) of the Freedom of Information Act 2000.[25] As with all exemptions under the *Data Protection Act 1998*, there is no public interest "override." Nor is there provision for a conclusive certificate under s.35A of the Data Protection Act 1998.

2. LEGAL PROFESSIONAL PRIVILEGE

Introduction

21–011 Information in respect of which a claim to legal professional privilege could be maintained in legal proceedings is rendered exempt information under the Freedom of Information Act 2000.[26] The exemption under the Freedom of Information Act 2000 is not absolute, so that disapplication of the disclosure duty requires consideration of whether maintenance of the exemption outweighs the public interest in disclosure.[27] There is a correlative exemption from the duty to confirm or deny that information answering the terms of the request is held by the public authority.[28] Similar exemptions are to be found in each of the comparative jurisdictions.[29]

24 Appeals are considered generally in Ch.28. A potential avenue of challenge in relation to a s.34(2) certificate is considered at para.28–027.

25 See Data Protection Act 1998, s.35A, with effect from November 30, 2005, unless the Secretary of State appoints an earlier date.

26 Freedom of Information Act 2000, s.42(1); Freedom of Information (Scotland) Act 2002, s.36(1).

27 Freedom of Information Act 2000, s.2(3).

28 *ibid*. s.42(2). See para.21–017.

29 In the United States, the Freedom of Information Act, 1966, 5 USC 552(b)(5), exempts from disclosure inter-agency or intra-agency memoranda or letters "which would not be available by law to a party other than an agency in litigation with the agency," which has been interpreted to include records or information covered by attorney work-product privilege and attorney-client privilege: see para.2–008(5). The Freedom of Information Act 1982 (Cth of Australia), s.42, provides an exemption where the requested documents are subject to legal professional privilege: see para.2–015(4). In New Zealand, the Official Information Act 1982, ss.9(2)(h) and 27(1)(h), the Local Government Official Information and Meetings Act 1987, ss.7(2)(g) and 26(1)(h), and the Privacy Act 1993, s.29(1)(f), each provides a qualified exemption where non-disclosure is required to maintain legal professional privilege: see para.2–023(9). In Canada, the Access to Information Act, 1982, s.23, provides a discretionary exemption for solicitor-client privileged information: see para.2–032(8). The Freedom of Information Act 1997 (Ireland), s.22(1), provides a mandatory

Scope and meaning

Legal professional privilege is a rule or a collection of rules which seek to protect the confidentiality of legal communications, specifically: 21–012

(1) information imparted by a client to a lawyer for the purpose of seeking advice;
(2) communications in which advice is given; and
(3) certain communications between a lawyer and third parties for the purpose of preparing for litigation.[30]

The privilege is a bar to the compulsion of evidence: it is not a rule of inadmissibility. The confidentiality of legal communications is recognised as a human right under both Arts 6 and 8 of the European Convention on Human Rights.[31]

Legal advice privilege and litigation privilege

There are two distinct branches of legal professional privilege: legal advice privilege and litigation privilege. Legal advice privilege covers confidential[32] communications between a lawyer[33] and client for the purpose of giving or obtaining legal advice. Litigation privilege covers confidential communication after litigation has commenced or once litigation is contemplated, between a lawyer and his client, a lawyer and his non-professional agent or a lawyer 21–013

exemption where the record would be exempt from production in a court on the grounds of legal professional privilege: see para.2–039(3).

30 See generally: P. Matthews and H. Malek, *Disclosure* (2nd ed., Sweet & Maxwell, 2001) Chs 9 and 10; J. Auburn, *Legal Professional Privilege: Law and Theory* (Hart Publishing, 2000); C. Passmore, *Privilege* (CLT Publishing, 1998).

31 *e.g. Golder v United Kingdom* (1979–80) 1 E.H.R.R. 524 (Art.6); *Niemietz v Germany* (1993) 16 E.H.R.R. 97 (Art.8). See the pre-incorporation House of Lords decision in *R. v Secretary of State for the Home Department Ex p. Simms* [2000] 2 A.C. 115. Also see *Tamosius v United Kingdom* (2002) 35 E.H.R.R. CD323; *Foxley v United Kingdom* (2001) 31 E.H.R.R. 25.

32 Communications between a lawyer and client in circumstances where they could not reasonably have expected confidentiality to be maintained are not covered, for example where the lawyer and client speak in a room with a police officer present.

33 This will include: solicitors in private practice, as well as their employees and trainees acting on their behalf (*Wheeler v Le Marchant* (1881) 17 Ch.D. 675 at 682); barristers in private practice; in-house solicitors and barristers (*Geraaghty v Minister for Local Government* [1975] I.R. 300; *Attorney-General for the Northern Territory v Kearney* (1985) 158 C.L.R. 500; *Waterford v Commonwealth of Australia* (1987) 163 C.L.R. 54; ; *Commonwealth of Australia v Dutton* (2000) 102 F.C.R. 168; *Three Rivers District Council v Bank of England (No.3)* EWCA Civ 474; [2003] 3 W.L.R. 667. See further: Matthews and Malek, *Disclosure* (2nd ed., Sweet & Maxwell, 2001), pp.215–218, 226–228.

and third party for the sole or dominant[34] purpose of the litigation.[35] Communications between parties with a common interest in litigation for the dominant purpose of informing each other of the advice received or of obtaining legal advice are also protected.[36]

Exceptions to the privilege

21–014 Certain communications that would otherwise fall within the general scope of the rule[37] are excepted from the privilege:

(1) Communications in furtherance of a crime or fraud are not communications within the ordinary scope of the professional lawyer-client relationship and so not privileged.[38]
(2) The privilege in the totality of a document may be waived or lost where part of that document has been disclosed such that it would be unfair for the disclosing party to continue to assert privilege over the remainder.[39]
(3) Privilege will be waived where reference to a document is made in court documents, such as statements of case and witness statements.[40]
(4) Privilege in a document will be waived where reference is made to it during the course of a trial, including in the course of advocate's speeches to the court, or by calling evidence of a privileged conversation[41] or having taken counsel's advice.
(5) Privilege does not extend to a copy of a privileged document in the hands of another party.[42]

---

[34] This test has been thought to be too broad as the foundation for an FOI exemption: see Australian Law Reform Commission, *Open Government, report No.77*, 1995, para.10.26. Its breadth under the Freedom of Information Act 2000 is tempered by the public interest override: see below.
[35] *Anderson v Bank of British Columbia* (1876) 2 Ch. D. 644; *Wheeler v Le Marchant* (1881) 17 Ch.D. 675.
[36] *Buttes Gas and Oil Co v Hammer (No 3)* [1981] Q.B. 223.
[37] See para.21–012.
[38] *R. v Cox and Railton* (1884) 14 Q.B.D. 153; *Derby & Co v Weldon (No. 7)* [1990] 1 W.L.R. 1156; *R. v Central Criminal Court, Ex p. Francis & Francis* [1989] 1 A.C. 346.
[39] *Great Atlantic Insurance Co v Home Insurance Co* [1981] 2 All E.R. 485; *Nea Karteria Maritime Co Ltd v Atlantic and Great Lakes Steamship Corp* [1981] Comm. L.R. 138; *General Accident Corp v Tanter* [1984] 1 W.L.R. 100; *Re Konigsberg (a bankrupt)* [1989] 3 All E.R. 289; *R. v Secretary of State for Transport and Factortame Ltd* [1998] 1 All E.R. 736 (Note); *Somatra Ltd v Sinclair, Roche & Temperley* [2000] 1 W.L.R. 2453.
[40] *Great Atlantic Insurance Co v Home Insurance Co* [1981] 1 W.L.R. 529 at 538; *Derby v Weldon (No.10)* [1991] 2 All E.R. 908. The rule is based on the need to ensure the disclosing party has not misled the court by disclosing a selection of the document out of context or in a manner that is not properly representative of the whole. The material must be "deployed" in court. Mere reference is usually insufficient.
[41] *George Doland Ltd v Blackburn Robson Coates & Co* [1972] 1 W.L.R. 1338.
[42] *Calcraft v Guest* [1898] 1 Q.B. 759; though the privilege-holder may seek an injunction under the principles in *Ashburton v Pape* [1913] 2 Ch.469.

(6) In some jurisdictions (though not in England[43] or Australia[44]) the privilege may be taken to be overridden where the evidence may prove an accused innocent of a serious criminal charge.[45]

(7) There are various statutory exceptions to the privilege, such as s.39 of the Banking Act 1987, which allows the Bank of England to require a person to produce material, including privileged material in certain circumstances; and s.291 of the Insolvency Act 1986, by which a bankrupt cannot withhold privileged documents from the Official Receiver. To the opposite effect it has been held that there was no express reference in s.20(1) of the Taxes Management Act 1970 to legal professional privilege and that section could not be construed as necessarily implying that a tax inspector could, by the issue of a notice, require the disclosure of documents which were subject to legal professional privilege.[46]

The public interest—the conceptual issue

It may be thought odd that the exemption for legal professional privilege is a qualified one.[47] It has been a defining feature of legal professional privilege that it involves no such balancing exercise. Courts in the United Kingdom and in the rest of the Commonwealth have frequently stated that the concept of legal professional privilege is itself the result of a balancing process,[48] which was performed once and for all in the sixteenth century,[49] and that such arguments were either presumed[50] or considered and rejected[51] in the course of the development of the common law, and therefore once the rule applies no further balancing process should be carried out[52]: 21–015

43 *R. v Derby Magistrates' Court, Ex p. B* [1996] 1 A.C. 487. It may be doubted whether this decision will survive the incorporation into domestic English law of Art.6 of the European Convention on Human Rights.

44 *Carter v The Managing Partner, Northmore Hale Davy & Leake* (1995) 183 C.L.R. 121.

45 *R. v Gray* (1992) 74 C.C.C. (3d) 267) (British Columbia Supreme Court); *S v Safatsa* 1988 (1) S.A. 868 (Appellate Division, South Africa). Also see *R. v Craig* [1975] 1 N.Z.L.R. 597 (NZ) and *R. v Dunbar and Logan* (1982) 138 D.L.R. (3d) 221. *R. v McClure* (2001) 195 D.L.R. (4th) 513; *R. v Brown* (2000) 210 D.L.R. (4th) 341 (Canada).

46 *R. (on the application of Morgan Grenfell & Co Ltd) v Special Commissioner of Income Tax* [2002] UKHL 21; [2003] 1 A.C. 563. See also: *B v Auckland District Law Society* [2003] UKPC 8; *Woolworths v FELS* [2002] HCA 50, (2002) 193 A.L.R. 1; *Daniels Corp v Accc* [2002] HCA 49, (2002) 194 A.L.R. 561.

47 As is the case in New Zealand: see para.2–023(9).

48 e.g. *Waterford v The Commonwealth* (1987) 163 C.L.R. 54 at 64–65; *Australian Federal Police v Propend Finance* (1997) 141 A.L.R. 545 at 592, 609.

49 *R. v Derby Magistrates' Court; Ex p. B* [1996] 1 A.C. 487 at 508.

50 *R. v Uljee* [1982] 1 N.Z.L.R. 561 at 576–577.

51 *Carter v The Managing Partner, Northmore Hale Davy & Leake* (1995) 183 C.L.R. 121 at 138.

52 *Waterford v The Commonwealth* (1987) 163 C.L.R. at 64, 74, 98–99; *Attorney-General (N.T.) v Kearney* (1985) 158 C.L.R. 500 at 532; *Carter v The Managing Partner, Northmore Hale Davy & Leake* (1995) 183 C.L.R. 121 at 128, 134 and 137; *Australian Federal Police v Propend Finance* (1997) 141 A.L.R. at 592, 609.

> "courts have for very many years regarded legal professional privilege as the predominant public interest. A balancing exercise is not required in individual cases, because the balance must always come down in favour of upholding the privilege."[53]

The use of a balancing test within the privilege would, it has been repeatedly said, fundamentally undermine the *raison d'être* of the privilege: a client's confidence in the sanctity of his legal communications:

> "once any exception to the rule is allowed, the client's confidence is necessarily lost."[54]

Section 34 of the Freedom of Information Act 2000 cuts across these notions, but in a more measured fashion than a general consideration of the public interest would entail.

The public interest balancing exercise

21–016 The weighing exercise imposed by s.2 of the Freedom of Information Act 2000 necessitates an identification of the public interest in the maintenance of the exemption, always recognising that that public interest must be delineated in such a fashion that it is capable in practice of being outweighed.[55] A proper weighing of the public interest in maintaining the exemption will involve both general and specific considerations.

(1) In relation to the former, the general maintenance of the confidentiality of communications between any lawyer and his client is a matter which is in the public interest. Here, the issue is not the effect that dis-

---

[53] Lord Lloyd in *R. v Derby Magistrates' Court; Ex p. B* [1996] 1 A.C. 487 at 509. Also see *Carter v The Managing Partner, Northmore Hale Davy & Leake* (1995) 183 C.L.R. at 128–9, where Brennan J. held that "there is no occasion for the courts to undertake a balancing of public interests: the balance is already struck by the allowing of the privilege . . . if there can be no public interest which defeats the privilege, there can be no individual interest which does so."

[54] *R. v Derby Magistrates' Court; Ex p. B* [1996] 1 A.C. 487 at 508. In *Carter v The Managing Partner, Northmore Hale Davy & Leake* (1995) 183 C.L.R. 121 at 139 the view expressed was that departure from this principle would mean that lawyers would become duty-bound to recite the court's powers as to disclosure and this would intensify the chilling effect.

[55] To avoid metamorphosing it into an absolute exemption. The exercise is antithetical to orthodox privilege theory that "once privileged, always privileged." Thus, in *Calcraft v Guest* [1898] 1 Q.B. 759 the privilege was asserted 110 years after the relevant communication. The House of Commons Select Committee favoured widespread disclosure of old opinions. Thus the House of Commons Public Administration Committee in its *Third Report, Session 1997–98*, May 19, 1998, stated at para.31: "In the spirit of openness, the Government's vast storehouse of legal opinions on every conceivable subject should be made available to interested members of the public."

closure might have on particular information or in a particular solicitor-client relationship: it is the effect that disclosure might have on future legal communications in general.[56] This is a highly speculative exercise at best, and there are widely differing views on the effect of individual disclosures on the continued confidence of clients in the sanctity of their legal communications. On the one hand it is often claimed that it is essential to the maintenance of continued candid lawyer-client relations that there are no new exceptions to the privilege.[57] The preferable view is that these concerns have been overplayed, and that the privilege could survive the recognition of exceptions without the collapse of lawyer-client relations.[58]

(2) In relation to the latter, this will involve a consideration of the particular information that stands to be disclosed. One set of relevant factors may relate to the age of the relevant information: when it was created; whether the purpose for which it was created is "spent;" whether all limitation periods for an action based on the information have expired. Another relevant factor may be the official release by the requested or another public authority of other information on the same subject matter as the information which enjoys legal professional privilege: if the information officially released, particularly if released as a discretionary disclosure, is unrepresentative of the entirety of the information held, the public interest in maintaining the exemption may be weakened where disclosure would redress the situation.

The public interest in disclosure[59] will vary according to the information sought. A number of Commonwealth courts have developed a principle that the privilege may give way to a far weightier public interest where the privilege-holders no longer have a recognised interest to protect.[60] It may be that this principle, previously disfavoured in England (as well as Australia)[61] will now be relevant in weakening the case for continued confidentiality.

[56] See para.21–015.

[57] *e.g.* Lord Taylor C.J. in *R. v Derby Magistrates' Court, Ex p. B* [1996] 1 A.C. 487 at 508 "once any exception to the rule is allowed, the client's confidence is necessarily lost."

[58] *e.g. Saunders v Punch* [1998] 1 W.L.R. 986 at 996.

[59] See para.15–006.

[60] *R. v Craig* [1975] 1 N.Z.L.R. 597 (NZ); *R. v Dunbar and Logan* (1982) 138 D.L.R. (3d) 221 at 252; *R. v McClure* (2001) 195 D.L.R. (4th) 513, [2001] 1 SCR 45; *R. v Brown* [2002] 210 D.L.R. (4th) 341 (Canada); *R v Ataou* [1988] Q.B. 798, but over-ruled in *R. v Derby Magistrates' Court*, Ex p. B [1996] 1 A.C. 487; *Carter v The Managing Partner, Northmore Hale Davy & Leake*, (unreported) July 15, 1993, Supreme Court of Western Australia (Full Court) *per* Rowland J. at 30–31.

[61] *Carter v The Managing Partner, Northmore Hale Davy & Leake* (1995) 183 C.L.R. 121.

Duty to confirm or deny

21–017 Where or to the extent that a public authority, by confirming or denying that it holds the requested information, would thereby disclose exempt information under s.42(1), then the discrete duty to confirm or deny that that information is held by the public authority does not arise.[62] Confirmation or denial that information answering the terms of a request is held will only be likely to involve the disclosure of information in respect of which a claim to legal professional privilege could be maintained where the request is couched in very specific terms: for example, a request for advice to a particular effect. Again, this is a qualified exclusion of duty. It will be necessary to consider whether, in all the circumstances, the maintenance of the exclusion of this duty is outweighed by the public interest in disclosing whether the public authority holds the information. Despite its superficial similarity, this public interest balancing exercise is materially different from that employed for the purpose of determining whether the duty to communicate does not apply.[63] As a general rule, the broader the terms of the request, the more difficult it will become for the public authority to contend that the public interest in excluding the duty to confirm or deny that such information is held by it outweighs the public interest in compliance with that duty; if only because it will be self-evident that the public authority does hold information of that description.

Scotland

21–018 The Scottish exemption is much wider, covering any information for which a claim to "confidentiality of communications" could be maintained in legal proceedings.[64] In Scotland priests may have a form of privilege not recognised in England and Wales.[65] There already existed in Scottish law a general judicial discretion not to require answers that may betray confidences, even though the evidence is otherwise relevant and admissible.[66]

[62] Freedom of Information Act 2000, s.42(2).

[63] See paras 15–010 to 15–011 as to what it involves.

[64] Freedom of Information Act 2000, s.42(2); Freedom of Information (Scotland) Act 2002, s.36(1).

[65] I.D. Macphail, *Research paper on the Law of Evidence of Scotland* (Scottish Law Commission, Edinburgh, 1979), paras 18.38–18.40; D. Field, *The Law of Evidence in Scotland* (W. Green, Edinburgh, 1988), p.265. Compare the position in England: *R. v Hay* (1860) 2 F. & F. 4; *Pais v Pais* [1971] P. 119, though the waiver analysis in this case is questionable if there is no privilege recognised.

[66] *HM Advocate v Airs* [1975] J.C. 64 at 70; S.L.T. 177 at 180. However this is unlikely to be a sufficient explanation for the very different Scottish FOI exemption, as a similar discretion operated in England: *Attorney-General v Clough* [1963] 1 Q.B. 773 at 792; *Attorney-General v Mulholland* [1963] 2 Q.B. 477 at 489–490, 492.

Related FOI exemptions

There is a separate exemption for communications relating to advice given by Law Officers.[67] Law Officers include the Attorney-General, Solicitor General, Advocate-General for Scotland, Lord Advocate, Solicitor-General for Scotland and the Attorney-General for Northern Ireland.[68] 21–019

The Data Protection Act 1998

The Data Protection Act 1998 exempts privileged documents from the non-disclosure provisions.[69] As with all exemptions under the Data Protection Act 1998, there is no public interest "override," but otherwise the principles are the same as under s.34 of the Freedom of Information Act 2000. 20–020

[67] Freedom of Information Act 2000, s.35(1)(c).
[68] *ibid*. s.35(5).
[69] Data Protection Act 1998, s.35; also see Sch.7, para.10.

CHAPTER 22

Policy Formulation and Public Affairs

1. INTRODUCTION

Nature of the exemptions covered

This chapter is concerned with two connected provisions of the Freedom of Information Act 2000 which exempt: 22–001

— information relating to government policy and Ministerial communications[1] and
— information the disclosure of which would be prejudicial to the conduct of public affairs.[2]

The first of these exemptions applies only to information held by government departments or by the National Assembly for Wales: it does not apply to information held by any other public authority.[3] The exemption is a purely class-based exemption, such that it does not matter that harm will not result from disclosure of the information concerned.[4] The exemption is a qualified exemption, so that even if information falls within the description of the exemption, it is then necessary to consider whether the public interest favours disclosure or the maintenance of the exemption. The second exemption can apply to information held by any type of public authority, but so far as information held by a government department or the National Assembly of Wales is concerned, those bodies may only rely on it if the first exemption is inapplicable. The second exemption is a prejudice-based exemption. It is only applicable if disclosure would, or would be likely to, prejudice the effective conduct of public affairs in any one or more of the ways specified in s.36(2). This exemption is an absolute

[1] Freedom of Information Act 2000, s.35; Freedom of Information (Scotland) Act 2002, s.29.
[2] Freedom of Information Act 2000, s.36. The comparable provision in the Freedom of Information (Scotland) Act 2002, s.30, is in materially different terms: see para.22–019.
[3] In Scotland, the comparable exemption is only applicable to information held by the Scottish Administration.
[4] Though it may be relevant to a consideration of the public interest.

exemption in the case where the information is held by the House of Commons or the House of Lords; but otherwise it is a qualified exemption.[5]

Application of the "public interest" test

22–002 Apart from information held by the House of Commons or the House of Lords,[6] the exemptions and the exclusions considered in this chapter are all qualified. Accordingly, even if information falls within any of the descriptions in s.35 or s.36, the duty to disclose (and the duty to confirm or deny) will still apply unless the public interest in maintaining the exemption outweighs the public interest in disclosure (or the public interest in maintaining the exclusion of the duty to confirm or deny outweighs the public interest in disclosing whether the public authority holds the information). Thus, s.36 of the Freedom of Information Act 2000 allows for the possibility that the disclosure of information relating to public affairs may be prejudicial in the relevant sense, but nonetheless be in the public interest. By contrast, policy information falling under s.35 of the Act is exempt from the duty of disclosure irrespective of whether or not its disclosure would be "prejudicial." However, the fact that no prejudice is caused to anyone by the disclosure of such information in any given case may well count as a significant consideration in favour of it being in the public interest that the exemption should not be maintained and that the information should be disclosed. As with the other qualified exemptions, the relevant decision-maker will have to take into account all of the circumstances of the case and any relevant provisions of the European Convention for the Protection of Human Rights and Fundamental Freedoms.[7] The weighing of the competing public interests poses particular problems in relation to information that falls within s.35(1). As noted previously,[8] on one side of the "balance" introduced by s.2 is the public interest in *maintaining the exemption*: it is not the public interest in non-disclosure. A public authority must therefore identify the public interest that is expressed in the particular exemption and adjudge the extent to which disclosure of each item of information falling within the terms of the request would offend that public interest. The exercise requires the public authority to stand back and abnegate its own interests except and insofar as those interests are properly viewed as part of the public interest. Where what is at stake is national security, the defence of the realm, international relations, criminal investigations and so forth, that task is difficult, but may be achieved through intellectual rigour and discipline. The public interest in maintaining an exemption for information held by a government department relating to "the formulation or development of public policy" (to use the first of the limbs of

[5] Freedom of Information Act 2000, s.2(3)(e); Freedom of Information (Scotland) Act 2002, s.2(2).
[6] But only insofar as the exemption and exclusion provided by s.36 is concerned.
[7] See paras 1–029 to 1–037.
[8] Para.15–005.

exemption in s.35(1))[9] presents two additional challenges. First, there is nothing in the description itself that urges non-disclosure, or at least, not without some rejection of the underlying premise of all freedom of information legislation. This is further evidenced by the limited range of public authorities to which the exemption applies: if there is a public interest served by exempting information relating to the formulation or development of policy, it is not immediately obvious why that public interest stops with government departments and does not include the formulation or development of policy of, say, a local authority. Secondly and largely because of the first, a public authority's self-interest in non-disclosure of this class of information is apt to be presented or even perceived as the public interest in maintaining the exemption, with the public authority effectively determining its own cause. The exemptions therefore require government departments to steel themselves, and where required find that the public interest in maintaining these exemptions is outweighed by the public interest in disclosure.[10]

Inter-relationship between the two provisions

Apart from the restriction of s.35 to "information held by a government department or by the National Assembly for Wales," the two provisions have a fair measure of overlap. In particular, the proceedings of the Cabinet, of the Executive Committee of the Northern Ireland Assembly and of the executive committee of the National Assembly for Wales are apt to be caught by both provisions. Similarly, it is to be anticipated that it will often be claimed that the disclosure of information relating to the formulation or development of government policy would, or would be likely to, inhibit the free and frank exchange of views for the purpose of deliberation. The inapplicability of s.36 to information held by a government department or by the National Assembly for Wales that is not exempt information by virtue of s.35[11] has wide-reaching consequences. Because s.35 is purely class-based and because it is cast in such wide terms, there will be much that will be "exempt information by virtue of s.35." As noted above, the bland attributes required to render information exempt under s.35 may often result in a public authority struggling to conclude that the public interest in maintaining that exemption outweighs the public interest in disclosure, with the result that that provision may well not operate to disapply the disclosure or existence duty. However, the result of the public interest weighing exercise does not affect the inapplicability of s.36 to such information. The criterion in s.36(1)(a) is that it not be "exempt information by virtue of section 35." 22–003

[9] The point applies equally to the other three limbs of exemption in s.35(1).
[10] To do otherwise will effectively promote the exemptions into absolute exemptions.
[11] See Freedom of Information Act 2000, s.36(1)(a). This does not apply under the Freedom of Information (Scotland) Act 2002: information can be rendered exempt information upon both ss.29 and 30 of the Act.

Where the public interest in maintaining the exemption does not outweigh the public interest in disclosing the information, s.2(2) does not metamorphose that exempt information into non-exempt information: it merely disapplies the rights bestowed by s.1(1) of the Act in relation to that exempt information. Thus, it is to be anticipated that there will be circumstances where a government department holding information relating to, say, the formulation of government policy finds that the public interest in maintaining the s.35 exemption does not outweigh the public interest in disclosure, but is unable to look to s.36 as an alternative means of refusing disclosure of the information. Because the public interest exercise is concerned with the *maintenance* of the exemption conferred by the particular provision it will not be permissible to sweep in under the rubric of "the public interest" the attributes which, in s.36(2), are used to render information exempt information. To do that, would, of course, make s.36(1)(a) pointless.

Legislative history

22–004 The two kinds of information that are now dealt with separately in ss.35 and 36 of the Freedom of Information Act 2000 were not distinguished in the 1997 White Paper. Instead, they were both considered under the single heading of information relating to government decision-making and policy-advice.[12] In the White Paper, the Government proposed that the question of whether or not such information would be disclosed should be determined by a test of "harm," whereas the test to be applied in the great majority of cases would be one of "substantial harm."[13] The draft Bill published in May 1999 substituted the term "prejudice" for that of "harm" as the key term in the applicable test,[14] and made information now falling within the scope of s.35 of the Freedom of Information Act 2000 subject to a purely class-based exemption.[15] The "prejudice" test and the introduction of a class-based exemption in respect of policy information held by government departments were also retained in the Bill published in November 1999,[16] which later became the Freedom of Information Act 2000.

[12] Cabinet Officer, *Your Right to Know: The Government's Proposals for a Freedom of Information Act*, Cm.3818, December 11, 1997, para.3.12.

[13] *ibid.*, paras 3.7, 3.12. The decision to impose a simple "harm" test on such information rather than a test of "substantial harm" was explained on the basis that "now, more than ever, government needs space and time in which to assess arguments and conduct its own debates with a degree of privacy. Experience from overseas suggests that the essential governmental functions of planning ahead, delivering solutions to issues of national importance and determining options on which to base policy decisions while still maintaining collective responsibility, can be damaged by random and premature disclosure of its deliberations under Freedom of Information legislation . . .": *ibid.*, para.3.12.

[14] This was done in order to make the Bill consistent in its terminology with other legislation including, notably, the Data Protection Act 1998 and the Local Government Act 1972: see House of Commons Select Committee on public administration, *Third Report* (Cm.4355), July 19, 1999, para.65.

[15] cl.28.

[16] cl.33 and 34.

Controversies surrounding the form of the exemptions

The provisions of the Freedom of Information Bills concerning government information were recognised to be "one of the especially difficult areas for freedom of information legislation."[17] Both the introduction of a class-based exemption in relation to policy information held by government departments and the imposition of a test of "prejudice" rather than "substantial prejudice" in respect of information relating to public affairs were controversial. They were stringently criticised both at the Committee stage and in Parliament.[18] In particular, the introduction of a class-based exemption in respect of policy information held by government departments was objected to on the basis that the exemption was more restrictive than the provisions of the Code that applied in respect of this kind of information, according to which such information should only be withheld if its disclosure would harm the frankness and candour of internal discussion, and if that harm outweighed the public interest in openness.[19] 22–005

Justification for the current form of the exemptions

The Government nevertheless insisted that the exemptions in respect of policy information and of information relating to public affairs were both justified. The imposition of a class-based exemption in respect of policy information was said to be necessary on the basis that, while the purpose of the Freedom of Information Bill was to increase openness in government, it was "appropriate that policy-making should not take place in a goldfish bowl" and that there should be a process which allowed Ministers, public authorities and civil 22–006

17 House of Commons Select Committee on public administration, *Third Report* (Cm.4355), July 19, 1999, para.83.

18 For criticism of the former class-based exemption, see, for example, House of Commons Select Committee on public administration, *Third Report* (Cm.4355), July 19, 1999, para.89; Mr Robert McLennan M.P., *Hansard*, HC, Vol.340, December 7, 1999, col.748; Lord Mackay of Ardbrecht, *Hansard*, HL, Vol.618, October 24, 2000, col.275–276. For criticisms of the imposition of a test of "prejudice" as opposed to "substantial prejudice," see, for example, House of Lords, *Draft Freedom of Information Bill: First Report*, July 27, 1999, paras 32, 34–35.

19 See for example Lord Mackay of Ardbrecht, *Hansard*, HL, Vol.618, October 24, 2000, col.275–276. It is to be noted that in the 1997 White Paper, the Government itself criticised the Code of Practice on the basis that the tests for harm contained therein were "insufficient." In particular, the exemptions contained in the Code of Practice, for the most part, gave "no indication of the extent of harm against which the disclosure or withholding of the information should be judged." In the Government's view, as expressed in the White Paper, "the test to determine whether disclosure is to be refused should normally be set in specific and demanding terms. We therefore propose to move in most areas from a simple harm test to a substantial harm test, namely will the disclosure of this information cause substantial harm?": *Your Right to Know: The Government's Proposals for a Freedom of Information Act*, paras 3.6–3.7. Note also that, whereas the White Paper proposed (in para.3.12) that a simple harm test should nevertheless be retained in respect of information relating to government decision-making and policy advice, the Government's final position, as explained by Lord Falconer of Thoroton, appears to be that the test of "prejudice" applicable in respect of information relating to public affairs in fact requires a demonstration of "substantial prejudice" before the exemption can be said to apply.

servants "to exchange views in a way that they feel will be private to give them space to think and make decisions."[20] The preference for a test of "prejudice" as opposed to "substantial prejudice" was explained on the basis that a public authority who sought to justify a decision to apply the exemption from the duty of disclosure to information relating to public policy on the basis that its disclosure would cause "prejudice" of the relevant kind would in any event be required to show that the prejudice in question, or the risk of prejudice, was "real, actual or of substance." Consequently, there was nothing to be gained by including an additional requirement in the Bill that any "prejudice" should also be "substantial."[21] The fact that "prejudice," when viewed properly, entails real, actual or substantial prejudice provides a further indication of the Government's rationale in subjecting policy-information to a class-based exemption, rather than a "simple prejudice" exemption.[22]

2. INFORMATION RELATING TO THE FORMULATION OF GOVERNMENT POLICY, ETC.

Introduction

22–007 Information held by a government department or by the National Assembly for Wales is exempt information if it relates to:

(a) the formulation or development of government policy[23];
(b) Ministerial communications[24];
(c) the provision of advice by any of the Law Officers or any request for the provision of such advice[25]; or
(d) the operation of any Ministerial private office.[26]

---

[20] *Hansard*, HL, Vol.612, April 20, 2000, col.827 *per* Lord Falconer. The explanation of the rationale for the exemption illuminates the public interest weighing exercise: if the policy decision has been made by the time that the request is received there will be little public interest in maintaining the exemption; they will have had their space to think and make decisions. Moreover, so far as the existence duty is concerned, it is difficult to see how confirming or denying that information is held should stop anyone of normal sensitivity from having "space to think and make decisions."

[21] Lord Falconer of Thoroton, *Hansard*, HL, Vol.612, April 20, 2000, col.827.

[22] That is, in accordance with the approach taken in the White Paper (*Your Right to Know: The Government's Proposals for a Freedom of Information Act*, paras 3.6–3.7 and 3.12).

[23] Freedom of Information Act 2000, s.35(1)(a); Freedom of Information (Scotland) Act 2002, s.29(1)(a). "Government policy" is defined in s.35(5) of the former Act and s.29(4) of the Scottish Act.

[24] Freedom of Information Act 2000, s.35(1)(b); Freedom of Information (Scotland) Act 2002, s.29(1)(b). "Ministerial communications" is defined in s.35(5) of the former Act and s.29(4) of the Scottish Act.

[25] Freedom of Information Act 2000, s.35(1)(c); Freedom of Information (Scotland) Act 2002, s.29(1)(c). "The Law officers" are defined in s.35(5) of the former Act and s.29(4) of the Scottish Act.

[26] Freedom of Information Act 2000, s.35(1)(d); Freedom of Information (Scotland) Act 2002, s.29(1)(d). "Ministerial private office" is defined in s.35(5) of the former Act and s.29(4) of the Scottish Act.

As noted at the outset of this Chapter, the exemption applies only to information held by government departments or by the National Assembly for Wales: it does not apply to information held by any other public authority.[27] The exemption has four discrete limbs, which need to be considered separately. So far as the first and second limbs of the exemption are concerned, special provision is made in relation to background statistical information.[28] So far as the first limb is concerned, special provision is also made in relation to background factual information.[29] The exemption is a qualified exemption,[30] and there is a corresponding exclusion of the duty to confirm or deny.[31] In relation to each of the limbs, the required connection is that the information "relate to" what is described by the limb. The phrase "relate to" and cognate expressions are notoriously vague.[32]

---

[27] In Scotland, the comparable exemption is only applicable to information held by the Scottish Administration.

[28] Freedom of Information Act 2000, s.35(2); Freedom of Information (Scotland) Act 2002, s.29(2). See para.22–014.

[29] Freedom of Information Act 2000, s.35(4); Freedom of Information (Scotland) Act 2002, s.29(3). See para.22–015.

[30] See paras 22–001 to 22–002.

[31] Freedom of Information Act 2000, s.35(3). There is no separate duty to confirm or deny under the Freedom of Information (Scotland) Act 2002. See para.22–017.

[32] See, for example: *R. v Smith* [1975] Q.B. 531 at 542B ("the words 'relating to' are very wide. They are equivalent to 'connected with' or 'arising out of.'") *per* Lord Denning; *R. v Sheffield Crown Court, Ex p. Brownlow* [1980] 2 W.L.R. 892 at 896–898 ("So once again we have the problem of statutory interpretation. It vexes us daily. Not only us. But also the House of Lords. Even the simplest words give rise to acute differences between us. Half of the judges think the interpretation is clear one way. The other half think it is clear the other way . . . So I approach the two words 'relating to' fully appreciating that others may interpret them differently from me. They are two words in common use but they are not clear or specific. Like many English words or phrases they are flexible enough to be capable of two or more interpretations . . . just as one person may be closely related to, or distantly related to, another: so may one matter be closely related to, or distantly related to, another. There is a choice before the judges: either to give the words "relating to" a wide interpretation or a narrow interpretation.") *per* Lord Denning. *In re Smalley* [1985] A.C. 622 Lord Bridge, in considering the phrase "relating to trial on indictment" said (at 643H) "If the statutory language is, as here, imprecise, it may well be impossible to prescribe in the abstract a precise test to determine on which side of the line any case should fall and, therefore, necessary to proceed . . . on a case by case basis." Of the same provision, the Divisional Court in *R. v Central Criminal Court, Ex p. Randle* [1991] 1 W.L.R. 1087 said (at 1093B) "One perfectly sensible construction involves interpreting the words 'relating to' as meaning 'having to do with.' On the other hand, the words could be understood as meaning 'arising in the course of.' It is the very simplicity of the phrase that admits of such differing constructions." In *Pickering v Liverpool Daily and Echo Newspapers plc* [1991] 2 A.C. 370 the House of Lords considered whether certain information disclosed by a newspaper constituted "the publication of information relating to proceedings before any court" within the meaning of s.12(1) of the Administration of Justice Act, which provides that certain matters are not capable of constituting a contempt of court. On the basis that they were not "information relating to the proceedings" (as well as not being "information about proceedings" for the purposes of r.21(5) of the Mental Health Tribunal Rules 1983), it concluded that it was not a contempt to publish the fact that a named patient had made an application to a tribunal for his discharge, nor was it a contempt to publish information as to the date, time or place at which the proceedings had been or were to be heard, nor the fact that a patient had been released from detention: at 384, CA and 423, HL.

Formulation or development of government policy: scope

22–008 The first limb of s.35(1) renders material exempt information if it relates to the formulation or development of government policy. A broadly similar class of exemption is found in most of the comparable jurisdictions, with differences partly reflecting the differences in the systems of governance.[33] "Government policy" is defined to include the policy of the Executive Committee of the Northern Ireland Assembly and the policy of the National Assembly for Wales.[34] The 1997 White Paper considered that there was a readily-identifiable core class of documents and materials that contain information falling within the exemption, including "high-level" government records such as Cabinet and Committee papers,[35] as well as draft consultation papers and advice on policy prepared by civil servants for the benefit of Ministers. The House of Commons Select Committee on public administration, on the other hand, doubted that "information relating to the formulation or development of policy" was a sufficiently well-defined class of information. It also took the view that such information should be included within the scope of the prejudice-based exemption contained in what is now s.36 of the Freedom of Information Act 2000.[36] There are two grey areas in relation to the limb, at least at its extremities:

(1) in determining what is and what is not "policy"; and
(2) in determining when the "formulation or development" of policy starts and ends.

In relation to the first area, the wording of the limb appears to contemplate a dichotomy between "policy" decisions and operational decisions made by government departments, with information relating to the latter falling outside of the scope of the exemption. As was recognised at the time of the Bill, however,

---

[33] In the United States, the Freedom of Information Act, 1966, 5 USC 552(b)(5), exempts from disclosure records that enjoy "deliberative process privilege:" see para.2–008(5). The Freedom of Information Act 1982 (Cth of Australia), s.33, provides an exemption in relation to "matter in the nature of, or relating to, opinion, advice or recommendation . . . in the course of the deliberative processes involved in the functions of an agency or Minister . . . and [the disclosure of which] would be contrary to the public interest:" see para.2–015(11). The Official Information Act 1982 (New Zealand), ss.6(e) and 27(1)(a), provides a comparatively narrow, but absolute, exemption in relation to information relating to decisions to change or continue government economic or financial policies: see para.2–022(5). The Access to Information Act (Canada), s.21(1), provides a discretionary exemption for records that contain advice or recommendations developed by or for a government institution or a minister of the Crown and for any account of governmental consultations or deliberations: see para.2–032(4) and (5). The Freedom of Information Act 1997 (Ireland), s.20(1), provides a discretionary exemption where the record contains matter relating to the deliberative process of the public body: see para.2–039(9).

[34] Freedom of Information Act 2000, s.35(5).

[35] Cabinet Office, *Your Right to Know: The Government's Proposals for a Freedom of Information Act* 1997, Cm.3813, December 11, para.3.12.

[36] *House of Commons Select Committee on public administration—Third Report* (Cm.4355), July 19, 1999, para.89.

the distinction will not always be clear,[37] and this is borne out by those occasions on which the word has been subject to judicial consideration.[38] In relation to the second area, s.35(2) recognises that at some identifiable point a decision will be taken as to government policy such that it can no longer be said to be being formulated or developed. Equally, it is not clear whether information relating to a review of the practical efficacy of a policy already in place is properly to be characterised as representing information relating to the development of that policy. Finally, the information in question must "relate to" the development or formulation of government policy.[39] It is unclear whether the relationship must be apparent from the face of the information or whether it is permissible to demonstrate the link by reference to other material.

Formulation or development of government policy: the public interest

The public interest generally thought to be embraced by this head of exemption is that disclosure of the deliberative process whilst it is being undertaken will cramp the ability of those engaging in it to freely explore the full range of options, including toying with the presently-unthinkable.[40] Although this 22–009

[37] The breadth of the exemption under s.35(1)(a) was objected to in Parliament: see, *e.g. Hansard*, HL, Vol.618, October 24, 2000, col.276. The Campaign for Freedom of Information described the exemption under s.35(1)(a) of the FOI Act as a "gigantic" class exemption: see *ibid.*, col.278.

[38] In *Bushell v Secretary of State for the Environment* [1981] A.C. 75, which involved consideration of the refusal by an Inspector at a public inquiry into the construction of certain motorways to permit certain questions by way of cross-examination, Lord Diplock (at 98B) said: "'Policy' as descriptive of departmental decisions to pursue a particular course of conduct is a protean word and much confusion in the instant case has, in my view, been caused by the failure to define the sense in which it can properly be used to describe a topic which is unsuitable to be the subject of an investigation as to the merits at an inquiry at which only persons with local interestes affected by the scheme are entitled to be represented. A decision to construct a nationwide network of motorways is clearly one of government policy in the widest sense of the word." Lord Edmund Davies said (at 115D) ". . . matters of policy are matters which involve the exercise of political judgment, and matters of fact and expertise do not become 'policy' merely because a department of government relies on them." In *Auckland Regional Council v North Shore City Council* [1995] 3 N.Z.L.R. 18 at 23 the New Zealand Court of Appeal expressed similar sentiments in attempting to ascertain the meaning of the word "policy" in the *Resources Management Act 1991*: "It is obvious that in ordinary present-day speech a policy may be either flexible or inflexible, either broad or narrow. Honesty is said to be the best policy. Most people would prefer to take some discretion in implementing it, but if applied remorselessly it would not cease to be a policy. Counsel for the defendants are on unsound ground in suggesting that in everyday speech or in parliamentary drafting or in etymology, policy cannot include something highly specific."

[39] See n.32.

[40] See the quotations at para.22–006. The fact that the "thinking" has been thought worthy of articulation and then of being recorded in some form immediately distinguishes it from the cogitation and general discussion which generally precede the preparation of drafts, option statements and the like. It may be thought that the fact of something having been thought worthy of recording and official retention indicates that it has taken more definite form than the mere thoughts and dialectic leading to it.

apprehension is predicated upon a certain sensitivity[41] on the part of high-level individuals who might be expected to be both capable and experienced in shrugging off ill-considered criticism and in appreciating well-founded criticism, the notion has at times found favour in the United Kingdom as well as in the comparative jurisdictions.

(1) In the United Kingdom, the exemption resembles one of the grounds of public interest immunity that the Crown used to rely upon to avoid what would otherwise have been its disclosure obligations in litigation.[42] That exemption enjoyed diminishing success in the Courts over the last half of the twentieth century, partly on the basis of the countervailing public interest in disclosure but also because the very notion that potential disclosure would inhibit candour was received with increasing scepticism.[43] It is fair to say that some judges were more receptive to the sentiment than others, but the preponderance of judicial view leaned increasingly against the notion that the potential of disclosure would adversely affect the candour of civil servants:

> "The notion that any competent and conscientious public servant would be inhibited at all in the candour of his writings by consideration of the off-chance that they might have to be produced in a litigation is in my opinion grotesque. To represent that the possibility of it might significantly impair the public service is even more so. Nowadays the state in multifarious manifestations impinges closely upon the lives and activities of individual citizens. Where this has involved a citizen in litigation with the state or one of its agencies, the can-

---

[41] Lord Radcliffe in the *Glasgow Corporation v Central Land Board* [1956] S.C. (HL) 1 at 20 that he would have supposed Crown servants to be "made of sterner stuff," a view shared by Harman L.J. in *Re Grosvenor Hotel, London (No.2)* [1965] Ch. 1210 at 1255E.

[42] This class of exemption was referred to in *Smith v East India Co* (1841) 1 Ph. 50 at 55 *per* Lord Lyndhurst: "it is quite obvious that public policy requires . . . that the most unreserved communication should take place . . . that it should be subject to no restraints or limitations; but it is also quite obvious, that if, at the suit of a particular individual, those communications should be subject to be produced in a court of justice, the effect of that would be to restrain the freedom of the communications, and to render them more cautious, guarded and reserved."

[43] Starting with *Duncan v Cammell, Laird & Co* [1942] A.C. 642. In *Conway v Rimmer* [1968] A.C. 910 the House of Lords, whilst recognising that candour could be impaired by disclosure, rejected this as a class-claim. Lord Upjohn was more sceptical of the claim: ". . . the executive have relied upon the *Cammell, Laird* case to claim privilege in class cases on the ground that the public interest requires that the writings of every member of the executive from the highest to the lowest . . . must be protected from production for the reason that the writer of the document must have a full, free and uninhibited right to pen his views without fear that they will ever be subject to the public gaze; in other words, secure in such knowledge he can then, and apparently only then, write with the complete candour necessary for the discharge of his functions as a member of the public service" (at 992). And later: "I cannot believe that any Minister or any high level military official or civil servant would feel in the least degree inhibited in expressing his honest views in the course of his duty on some subject, such as even the personal qualifications and delinquencies of some colleague, by the thought that his observations might one day see the light of day" (at 994).

dour argument is an utterly insubstantial ground for denying him access to relevant documents."[44]

The concept is no longer employed by government departments in support of public interest immunity claims.[45]

(2) In the USA, the Supreme Court has held that the comparable "deliberative process privilege" exists to "prevent injury to the quality of agency decisions."[46] The injuries are thought to be occasioned by:

(1) an impairment of open, frank discussions on matters of policy between subordinates and superiors;
(2) premature disclosure of proposed policies before they are finally adopted; and
(3) public confusion that might result from disclosure of reasons and rationales that were not in fact ultimately the grounds for an agency's action.[47]

(3) In Canada, the Federal Court has held that "despite the importance of governmental openness as a safeguard against the abuse of power, and

[44] *Burmah Oil Company Limited v Bank of England* [1980] A.C. 1090 at 1133 *per* Lord Keith. See also: *Sankey v Whitlam* (1978) 148 C.L.R. 1 at 40 *per* Gibbs A.C.J., 63 *per* Stephen J. and 96 *per* Mason J.; *Williams v Home Office* [1981] 1 All E.R. 1151. Contrast with Lord Wilberforce in *Burmah Oil Company Limited v Bank of England* [1980] A.C. 1090 at 1112; *Air Canada v Secretary of State for Trade* [1983] 2 A.C. 394 at 437.

[45] In a statement to the House of Commons on the future of public interest immunity in relation to Government documents, the Attorney-General (Sir Nicholas Lyell) spelled out that the new approach was to focus directly on the damage that disclosure would cuase, with the former division between class exemptions and contents exemptions no longer being maintained: *Hansard*, HC, Vol.287, December 18, 1996, cols 949–950; see also *Hansard*, HC, Vol.297, July 11, 1997, cols 616–617. The Government's new approach was set out in a document that was placed in the libraries of both Houses of Parliament. Entitled *Annex C: Paper which Accompanied 1996 HMG Hansard Statement on PII*, it reiterates the abandonment of purely class-based claims (para.2.3), describing the distinction between class claims and contents claims as "unhelpful and obscure" (para.3.3) and noting the particular difficulty with "the advice to ministers class" (para.3.4). The new approach heralded is "therefore based on the principle that PII can only ever apply where disclosure of material could cause real damage to the public interest" (para.4.1). In the section on "Examples of the Government's approach," under the heading "Internal discussion and advice" the paper states: "The class is widely represented as reinforcing the executive's tendency to secrecy and unaccountability. In practice this type of PII claim is only considered, let alone made, on comparatively rare occasions, since it is only rarely this kind of document is relevant to litigation. Government documents should not attract PII on the basis of any special privilege but merely on the basis, as for any other document, that in certain circumstances their disclosure would cause real harm. The Government accepts that an approach to PII which claimed a kind of blanket protection for pre-defined categories of documents would be wrong in principle. . .A claim will not be made simply because the document constitutes high level advice to ministers" (paras 5.5–5.6, 5.12). Wholly absent from the document was any suggestion that a claim might be made out on the basis that disclosure would inhibit the candour of civil servants or somehow prevent the free and frank exchange of ideas.

[46] *National Labor Relations Board v Sears, Roebuck & Co.* (1975) 421 U.S. 132 at 151.

[47] *Russell v Department of the Air Force*, 682 F.(2d) 1045 (D.C. Cir. 1982); *Coastal States Gas Corp. v Department of Energy*, 617 F.(2d) 854 (D.C. Cir. 1980); *Jordan v United States Department of Justice*, 591 F.(2d) 753 (D.C. Cir. 1978).

as a necessary condition for democratic accountability, it is equally clear that governments must be allowed a measure of confidentiality in the policy-making process. To permit or to require the disclosure of advice given by officials, either to other officials or to ministers, and the disclosure of confidential deliberations within the public service on policy options, would erode government's ability to formulate and to justify its policies. It would be an intolerable burden to force ministers and their advisors to disclose to public scrutiny the internal evolution of the policies ultimately adopted. Disclosure of such material would often reveal that the policy-making process included false starts, blind alleys, wrong turns, changes of mind, the solicitation and rejection of advice, and the re-evaluation of priorities and the re-weighing of the relative importance of the relevant factors as a problem is studied more closely. In the hands of journalists or political opponents this is combustible material liable to fuel a fire that could quickly destroy governmental credibility and effectiveness. On the other hand, of course, democratic principles require that the public, and this often means the representatives of sectional interests, are enabled to participate as widely as possible in influencing policy development. Without a degree of openness on the part of government about its thinking on public policy issues, and without access to relevant information in the possession of government, the effectiveness of public participation will inevitably be curbed."[48]

(4) In Australia, the Federal Court had, for the purposes of the Freedom of Information Act 1982, held that disclosure of communications made in the course of the development and subsequent promulgation of policy tended not to be in the public interest; and that such disclosure could inhibit frankness and candour in future pre-decisional communications, could lead to confusion and "unnecessary debate." In particular, disclosure of documents that did not fairly disclose the reasons for a decision subsequently taken might be unfair to a decision-maker and may prejudice the integrity of the decision-making process.[49] This view, briefly held and sitting uncomfortably with the approach taken in

[48] *Canadian Council of Christian Charities v Canada (Minister of Finance)* [1999] 4 F.C. 245 at paras 30–32.

[49] *Re Howard and the Treasurer* (1985) 7 A.L.D. 626; 3 A.A.R. 169, in which the then-Deputy Leader of the Opposition sought access to the documents provided by the Treasurer or his department to the Australian Council of Trade Unions during the government's bargaining session over the content and shape of the 1984/85 Budget. See also *Harris v Australian Broadcasting Corporation* (1983) 50 A.L.R. 551; 78 F.L.R. 236. Other decisions have been more circumspect in their acceptance of the candour argument: *Re Rae and Department of Prime Minister and Cabinet* (1986) 12 A.L.D. 589; *Re Fewster and Department of Prime Minister and Cabinet (No.2)* (1987) 13 A.L.D. 139; *Re Kamenka and the Australian National University* (1992) 26 A.L.D. 585; *Re Cleary and Department of the Treasury* (1993) 31 A.L.D. 214; *Re Eccleston and Department of Family Services and Aboriginal and Islander Affairs* (1993) 1 Q.A.R. 60.

public interest immunity claims,[50] has lost favour, although the argument continues to be run from time to time.[51]

The position reached would appear to be that in the United Kingdom, in the absence of freedom of information legislation, there has been a rejection of the notion that those involved in the formulation or development of government policy would be legitimately inhibited in expressing their views or giving advice were it apprehended that those views or that advice might be disclosed.[52]

Information relating to ministerial communications: scope

The second limb of s.35(1) renders material exempt information if it relates to "Ministerial communications." That phrase is defined to mean any communications between Ministers of the Crown; or between Northern Ireland Ministers, including Northern Ireland junior Ministers; or between Assembly Secretaries, including the Assembly Secretary.[53] The terms also includes, in particular, proceedings of the Cabinet or of any committee of the Cabinet, proceedings of the Executive Committee of the Northern Ireland Assembly, and proceedings of the Executive Committee of the National Assembly for Wales. "Northern Ireland junior Minister" is itself defined to mean a member of the Northern Ireland Assembly appointed as a junior Minister under s.19 of the Northern Ireland Act 1998.[54] It is to be noted that the exemption is for information that "relates to" Ministerial communications, rather than being for Ministerial communications themselves. Thus, information that recounts or relays a Ministerial communication will be captured by the exemption, but, possibly, not the communication itself. As the number of degrees of remove between the information in question and the original Ministerial communication increases, it will become harder to maintain that the information "relates to" the Ministerial communication.[55] 22–010

50 See *Sankey v Whitlam* (1978) 148 C.L.R. 1 at 40 *per* Gibbs A.C.J., 63 *per* Stephen J. and 96 *per* Mason J. and para.22–023 n.4 and para.22–024 n.8.

51 See most recently *Accredited (Wholesale Tobacco) Distributors Pty Ltd v Griffiths* [2003] V.S.C. 20.

52 In *Rogers v Home Secretary* [1973] A.C. 388 at 413E-F Lord Salmon spoke of a "candour argument" run by the Attorney-General as "smack[ing] of the old fallacy that any official in the government service would be inhibited from writing frankly and possibly at all unless he could be sure that nothing he wrote could ever be exposed to the light of day". See also *R. v Secretary of State for the Home Department*, Ex p. Duggan [1994] 3 All E.R. 277 at 285e.

53 Freedom of Information Act 2000, s.35(5).

54 Freedom of Information Act 2000, s.35(5).

55 See n.38.

Information relating to ministerial communications: public interest

22–011 This exemption has no analogous exemption in any of the comparative jurisdictions. The exemption presents peculiar difficulties so far as the public interest is concerned. Save for the effect of s.2, the exemption effectively takes out of the access regime all information relating to ministerial communications, irrespective of their content, irrespective of the harmlessness of their disclosure and irrespective of the origins of the information itself. This removal of a class of information that, on its face, has no characteristic requiring it to be cloaked in secrecy may be thought to be antithetical to the purpose of the Act.[56] The Secretary of State for the Home Department began the second reading speech for the Bill thus:

> "Unnecessary secrecy in Government and our public services has long been held to undermine good governance and public administration, and my party has long been committed to change. At the last election, our manifesto stated: 'We are pledged to a Freedom of Information Act, leading to more open government.' The Bill will make that promise a reality. The Bill, by its first clause, lays down for the first time in our constitutional history that the public have a right to know about the work of Government and all other public authorities. Again for the first time, that right of access to information will be enforced by an independent Information Commissioner and an Information Tribunal with clear powers to override the decisions of Ministers or any other public authority as to whether information should be released. Moreover, the Bill will not only provide legal rights for the public and place legal duties on Ministers and public authorities, but will help to transform the culture of Government from one of secrecy to one of openness. It will transform the default setting from 'this should be kept quiet unless' to 'this should be published unless.' By doing so, it should raise public confidence in the processes of government, and enhance the quality of decision making by the Government."[57]

A full reconciliation of this sentiment with the terms of s.35(1)(b) is only possible through the public interest balancing exercise prescribed in s.2 of the Act.[58] Against the backdrop of the Freedom of Information Act 2000 having set its face against non-disclosure of official information without objectively good reason and of s.35(1)(b) not having been made an absolute exemption, the decision-maker must identify the public interest which is served by maintaining an exemption for information whose only required attribute is that it relates to Ministerial communications. It will not be permissible to elevate the limb into

56 See paras 1–010 to 1–014 and para.22–009.
57 *Hansard*, HC, Vol.340, col.714, December 7, 1999.
58 See the introductory remarks at para.22–002.

a *de facto* absolute exemption by alighting on characteristics that invariably attend a Ministerial communication. To the extent that such information would reveal the proceedings of the Cabinet, etc. the public interest question may be fairly readily answered: the purpose served by the secrecy attaching to the records of Cabinet proceedings is well-recognised.[59] Otherwise, however, the public interest in maintaining the exemption is not readily divined.

Information relating to advice from a Law Officer

The third limb of s.35(1) renders material exempt information if it relates to the provision of advice by any of the "Law Officers" or any request for the provision of such advice. The phrase the "Law Officers" is defined to mean the Attorney General, the Solicitor General, the Advocate General for Scotland, the Lord Advocate, the Solicitor General for Scotland and the Attorney General for Northern Ireland.[60] This exemption will inevitably overlap with the exemption for information in respect of which a claim to legal professional privilege could be maintained.[61] It extends the scope of protection by picking up information that might not be privileged itself: for example, because it merely recounts or relays legal advice received. The public interest in the maintenance of this exemption is akin to the public interest in maintaining the exemption for information in respect of which a claim to legal professional privilege could be maintained.[62] 22–012

Information relating to the operation of any Ministerial private office

The final limb of s.35(1) renders material exempt information if it relates to the operation of any "Ministerial private office." This phrase is defined to mean any part of a government department which provides personal administrative support to a Minister of the Crown, to a Northern Ireland Minister or a Northern Ireland junior Minister, or any part of the administration of the National Assembly for Wales providing personal administrative support to the 22–013

[59] See *Conway v Rimmer* [1968] A.C. 910 at 952 and *Attorney-General v Jonathan Cape Ltd* [1976] Q.B. 752. Similar statements are made in the comparative jurisdictions, apart from the USA: *Attorney-General v Hamilton* [1993] 2 I.R. 250 at 266; *Egan v Chadwick* [1999] N.S.W.C.A. 176; (1999) 46 N.S.W.L.R. 563 esp. at 573–576 and at 589–592, which sets out a very useful history of the convention and its rationale. However, some chinks in the armour have started to appear: see *Commonwealth v Northern Land Council* (1993) 176 C.L.R. 604; *Commonwealth v Construction, Forestry, Mining and Energy Union* (2000) 98 F.C.R. 31.

[60] Freedom of Information Act 2000, s.35(5).

[61] Freedom of Information Act 2000, s.42; Freedom of Information (Scotland) Act 2002, s.36(1). See Ch.21.

[62] See para.21–001 to 21–016.

Assembly First Secretary or an Assembly Secretary.[63] Most of the comparative jurisdictions remove such material from the operation of the legislation.[64] The policy underpinning this exemption is that information relating to the operation of a Minister's private office does not serve any of the purposes of the Act. On that basis, the public interest in disclosure of such information may be expected to be readily displaced by the public interest in maintaining the exemption.

Statistical information

22–014 Section 35(2) of the Freedom of Information Act 2000 provides that once a decision as to government policy has been taken, then any statistical information that has been used to provide "an informed background" to that decision is to be taken out of the scope of the first two limbs of s.35(1). The fact that statistical information is at a certain point taken out of the scope of s.35 does not mean that that information must be disclosed. Indeed, once exemption under s.35 drops away, the limitation imposed by the concluding words in s.36(1)(a) is disengaged, enabling the public authority to rely on this section to protect it from having to disclose to a member of the public any statistical information that it used to inform its policy decisions.[65] The subsection implies that statistical information can represent information relating to the formulation or development of government policy.

Factual information: background

22–015 It is conventional for freedom of information legislation, when exempting policy deliberations from disclosure, to make some sort of exception for the factual

---

[63] Freedom of Information Act 2000, s.5. The House of Commons Select Committee on public administration stated, in their *Third Report* (Cm.4355), July 19, 1999, (para.89) that they did not believe that a class-based exemption for the operation of a private Ministerial office was appropriate. In their view, such information should be included within the scope of the prejudice-based exemption that is now to be found in s.36 of the Freedom of Information Act 2000.

[64] In Australia, such material is excluded as a result of the definition of "official document" in s.4 of the Freedom of Information Act 1982: see para.2–011. The definition of "official information" in s.2 of the Official Information Act 1982 (New Zealand) excludes some, but not all, such information. The Freedom of Information Act 1997 (Ireland), s.46(1), treats such material as "exempt records" and therefore outside the main operation of the Act: see para.2–035.

[65] See para.22–003. In relation to statistical information falling within the scope of s.36, the Commissioner has the power to review the decision not to disclose that information without being subject to the restriction that is applicable in respect of other kinds of information falling under s.36: namely, that that review must be limited to a consideration of whether the view of the relevant "qualified person" that such information should not be disclosed was "reasonable." The Government conferred this broader power of review upon the Commissioner in respect of statistical information in order to underline its stated commitment to openness: Lord Falconer of Thoroton, *Hansard*, HL, Vol.618, October 24, 2000, col.287.

material used in the course of those deliberations.[66] In introducing freedom of information legislation into Westminster, the Government indicated that it intended that as much as possible factual and background information gathered by public authorities in the process of devising policy and making decisions should be made publicly available.[67] Thus, the 1997 White Paper recorded that the protection which the Government envisaged would be imposed with respect to the disclosure of information relating to policy and public affairs was intended "primarily to protect opinion and analytical information, not the raw data and factual background material which have contributed to the policy-making process."[68] The White Paper promised that public authorities would be encouraged to make such information available, even where opinion and advice based upon it needed to remain confidential. Nonetheless, neither the draft Bill published in May 1999 nor the second draft introduced into Parliament on November 18, 1999 distinguished between policy information and advice, on the one hand, and factual or statistical background material on the other. Both versions of the Bill were heavily criticised for this. In its first Report on the May 1999 draft Bill, the House of Commons Select Committee on Public Administration recommended that the exemption for decision-making and policy formulation should "specifically not be taken to apply to purely factual information held by public authorities, not to analysis, if that information has been created in order to inform policy decisions, and this distinction should be drawn clearly in the Bill."[69] This position was also endorsed by the House of Lords Select Committee that commented on the Bill. Parliament, likewise, pressed strongly for a distinction between factual and statistical information, on the one hand, and policy information, on the other, to be made in the Bill, and for factual and

[66] In the United States, under the Freedom of Information Act, 1966, 5 USC 552(b)(5), the "deliberative process privilege" does not include the underlying factual material: see para.2–008(5). The Freedom of Information Act 1982 (Cth of Australia), s.36(5) takes out of the "deliberative process" exemption "purely factual material:" see para.2–015(11). However, purely factual material within Cabinet records or records of the Executive Council remain within these exemptions: see para.2–015(1)–(2). The Official Information Act 1982 (New Zealand), bucks convention so as to retain an exemption for factual and statistical information. The New Zealand Law Commission, in its Review of the Official Information Act 1982, October 1997, saw no reason to change this. In Canada, factual material falls outside of the exemption provided by the Access to Information Act, s.21(1): see para.2–032(4)–(5). The exemption provided by the Freedom of Information Act 1997 (Ireland), s.19(1), does not extend to factual material and the exemption provided by s.20 extends neither to factual information nor to statistical information: see para.2–039(1) and 2–039(9).

[67] Cabinet Office, *Your Right to Know: The Government's Proposals for a Freedom of Information Act* 1997, Cm.3813, December 11, para.3.13.

[68] *ibid.*, para.3.13.

[69] House of Commons Select Committee on Public Administration, *Third Report* (Cm.4355), July 19, 1999, para.93. The House of Lords Select Committee, in its *First Report on the Draft Freedom of Information Bill* (July 27, 1999) accepted the arguments justifying a class-based exemption for policy advice, but agreed with the House of Commons Select Committee that policy advice should be distinguished from "separable factual background" to that advice; and that "such factual background should be exempt only if its disclosure 'would substantially or would be likely substantially to prejudice the interests set forth in clause 28(3)'": House of Lords, *Draft Freedom of Information Bill: First Report* (July 27, 1999), para.34.

statistical information to be excluded from the scope of the policy exemption.[70] The Government resisted these criticisms on the basis that, while factual material used to provide an informed background to decision-taking should be made available wherever possible, it could not be made available as of right, because "the dividing line between facts and opinions, or advice, is simply not that clear . . . There will be occasions where 'facts' are part of the discussion or argumentation about options under consideration and where it will not be possible to disentangle facts from opinions or advice. On these occasions the disclosure of such information would, of itself, affect the decision-taking process. Thus there will be a need to withhold such information on a few occasions."[71] The Government agreed, however, that greater openness could be achieved than the Bill allowed for[72] and amendments containing the provisions now to be found in ss.35(2)[73] and 35(4)[74] were introduced as a result.[75]

Factual information: approach

22–016 The approach taken by s.35(4) of the Freedom of Information Act 2000 is to exhort the decision-maker, when weighing the competing public interests in s.2, to have regard "to the particular public interest in the disclosure of factual information which has been used, or is intended to be used, to provide an informed background to decision-making."[76] This, of course, requires an

[70] Dr Tony Wright M.P. (Cannock Chase), for example, said in the course of the second reading of the second draft Bill "We had discussions on the [first draft Bill] and the Home Secretary told the Select Committee on public administration that the 'issue of factual or background information is important . . . and I think on the whole ought to be disclosed'. Unfortunately, the Bill does not convert that desire into legislative provision, but I am heartened by the fact that it might still do that. . . . We have a cumulative body of evidence which says that it is both desirable and practical to have such distinctions. However, the distinction is not made in the Bill, contrary to the developing practice to which I have pointed, and contrary to freedom of information regimes elsewhere, notably in New Zealand and Ireland. Hon members should be clear about what that means. It means that all information relating in any way to the development of policy—including purely factual background information—stands exempt. I simply do not believe that the House will allow that to be sustained. Clauses 33 and 34 [the precursors to ss.35 and 36] represent the hole in the centre of the Bill. At the very least, we need the facts, and an analysis of them . . .." *Hansard*, HC, Vol.340, December 7, 1999, col.753.

[71] Lord Falconer of Thoroton, *Hansard*, HL, Vol.612, April 20, 2000, col.827; *Hansard*, HL, Vol.619, November 22, 2000, col.832. See also Jack Straw, *Hansard*, HC, Vol.347, April 5, 2000, col.1027.

[72] Lord Falconer of Thoroton, *Hansard*, HL, Vol.618, October 24, 2000, col.287.

[73] *ibid.*

[74] *Hansard*, HL, Vol.619, November 14, 2000, col.147. The formulation contained in s.35(4) was preferred to various alternatives that were proposed which would have had the effect of excluding factual information from the scope of the exemption now contained in s.35(1) altogether: see for example *Hansard*, HC, Vol.347, April 5, 2000, col.997.

[75] The amendment with respect to statistical information was welcomed in Parliament, but the majority of members of the House of Commons and House of Lords who spoke on the Bill continued to press for an exception from the exemption in respect of factual information, as well as statistical information: see, *e.g. Hansard*, HL, Vol.618, cols 288–302.

[76] In Scotland, Freedom of Information (Scotland) Act 2002, s.29(3).

identification of what is and what is not "factual information." As Wigmore observed at the outset of his treatise on evidence "everything in the cosmos is a fact or a phenomenon."[77] The phrase "factual information" is innately vague: whether an opinion is held is a matter of fact even if the opinion itself is not.[78] On the other hand, the choice of factual material and its presentation may consitute a matter of opinion,[79] just as the reaching of a conclusion or a view upon factual material may itself be a fact.[80] These complexities and distinctions are borne out by the comparative jurisprudence. In the United States, the Courts will normally allow agencies to withhold factual material in an otherwise "deliberative" document in two situations. First, if a document comprises or includes a conscious selection of factual information out of a larger group of factual information, the act of selection of those facts is treated as deliberative in nature, entitling the selected facts to enjoy the deliberative process privilege exemption.[81] Secondly, factual information may be withheld in circumstances where it is so inextricably connected to the deliberative material that its disclosure would expose or cause harm to the agency's deliberations.[82]

The duty to confirm or deny

Section 35 also provides a corresponding qualified exclusion from the duty to confirm or deny.[83] The way in which the exclusion is worded is such that, if a given piece of information relating to the formulation of policy, etc. is exempt information under s.35(1), then the corresponding duty to confirm or deny that the information is held does not arise. It should be noted that the public interest exercise differs for the two duties, so that even though the public interest 22–017

[77] J.H. Wigmore, *Treatise on the Anglo-American System of Evidence in Trials at Common Law*, (3rd ed., Little Brown, Boston, 1940), Vol.1, p.1, para.1.

[78] That there is no logical dichotomy between fact and opinion is recognised in the Freedom of Information Act 2000 itself: s.36(2) and (7) involve a statutory transposition of fact and opinion.

[79] The Federal Court of Australia in *Harris v Australian Broadcasting Corporation* (1984) 51 A.L.R. 571 held that summaries of factual material could not be classified as "purely factual material" for the purposes of s.36 of the Freedom of Information Act 1982 if they were "of such a character as to disclose a process of selection involving opinion, advice or recommendation for the purpose of the deliberative process."

[80] In *Harris v Australian Broadcasting Corporation* (1984) 51 A.L.R. 571 the Federal Court held that "conclusions expressed as findings" could be a statement of "purely factual material notwithstanding it involves a conclusion based upon primary facts."

[81] *Montrose Chemical Corp. v Train*, 491 F.(2d) 63, 66 (D.C. Cir. 1974); *Mapother v Department of Justice*, 3 F.(3d) 1533 (D.C. Cir. 1993), where the Court held, in relation to a report which consisted of factual materials prepared for the Attorney-General's decision whether to allow former UN Secretary General Kurt Waldheim to enter the United States, that "the majority of [the report's] factual material was assembled through an exercise of judgment in extracting pertinent material from a vast number of documents for the benefit of an official called upon to take discretionary action," and that it therefore fell within the deliberative process privilege. On the other hand, the Court held that a chronology of his military career was not deliberative, as it was "neither more nor less than a comprehensive collection of the essential facts" and "reflect[ed] no point of view."

[82] *Wolfe v United States Department of Health and Human Services*, 839 F.(2d) 768 (D.C. Cir. 1988).

[83] Freedom of Information Act 2000, s.35(3).

may weigh in favour of maintaining the exemption from disclosure, it may nevertheless not weigh in favour of maintaining the exclusion of the duty to confirm or deny.

3. INFORMATION THE DISCLOSURE OF WHICH WOULD BE PREJUDICIAL TO PUBLIC AFFAIRS

Introduction

22–018 Section 36 of the Freedom of Information Act 2000 provides a further array of exemptions for what might loosely be described as information recording the deliberations of a public authority.[84] The scope and operation of the provision varies according to the identity of the public authority holding the information:

— If the information is held by a government department or by the National Assembly for Wales and the information is exempt information by virtue of s.35, then s.36 is inapplicable.[85]
— If the information is held by the House of Commons or the House of Lords, then the exemption is an absolute exemption for the purposes of s.2[86] and provision is made for a conclusive certificate.[87]
— If the information is held by any other public authority, then the exemption is a qualified exemption and there is no provision for a conclusive certificate.

The section provides three overlapping heads of exemption, each of which requires a reasonable expectation of prejudice, or the likelihood of prejudice, to the interest protected by the head. A similar exemption exists in each of the comparative jurisdictions except, for obvious reasons, the United States of America.[88] In that the exemption in the Freedom of Information Act 2000 is

[84] Similarly, Freedom of Information (Scotland) Act 2002, s.30.
[85] Freedom of Information Act 2000, s.36(1)(a). As to the inter-relationship of the two provisions, see para.22–003. There is no equivalent restriction under the Freedom of Information (Scotland) Act 2002.
[86] Freedom of Information Act 2000, s.2(3)(e). No analogous distinction is drawn in the Freedom of Information (Scotland) Act 2002. The House of Commons Select Committee on Public Administration did not accept that the justification for the exclusion of Parliament from the right to official information had been made out. In their view, "the exclusion of Parliament may well convey the wrong impression to the general public, given the purpose of this legislation" (*Third Report* (Cm.4355) July 29, 1999, para.37).
[87] Freedom of Information Act 2000, s.36(7). No provision is made for a conclusive certificate under s.30 of the Freedom of Information (Scotland) Act 2002.
[88] The Freedom of Information Act 1982 (Cth of Australia), s.34(1) provides a very broad exemption that embraces any record of Cabinet, a document brought into existence for the purpose of submission to Cabinet and so submitted, extracts from such documents, and any document that would disclose the deliberations or decisions of Cabinet other than an official document. An exception is made for purely factual material: s.34(1A). Provision is also made for conclusive

prejudice-based as well as subject to a public interest override, it is the narrowest exemption of its type amongst the comparative juridictions.[89] The meaning of "prejudice" and the required probability of prejudice are generally considered earlier in this work.[90] It is worth bearing in mind that the Government's preference for a test of "prejudice," rather than substantial prejudice, was the source of some controversy during the passage of the Bill through Parliament. The decision to retain a test of "prejudice" was, however, justified on the ground that, according to the Government, the test of prejudice was not a weak test; and the commissioner, who would have the power to overrule an authority if it was thought that any prejudice caused by a disclosure would be trivial or insignificant, would ensure that the authority was able to point to prejudice that was "real, actual, or of substance."[91] Finally, it should be noted that the

certificates, conclusively certifying that a particular document falls within s.34(1). There is no public interest requirement or override and there is no requirement that prejudice result from the disclosure. The Official Information Act 1982 (New Zealand), s.9(2)(f)(ii) is in substantially identical terms to s.36(2)(a) of the Freedom of Information Act 2000. The provision has the effect of affording a good reason for non-disclosure for the purposes of s.5 of the Act unless "the withholding of that information is outweighed by other considerations which render it desirable, in the public interest, to make that information available." The New Zealand Law Commission, in its Review of the Official Information Act 1982, October 1997, para.217, noted that this had been interpreted to mean that "the protection afforded is not a categorical one. It is not enough, for instance, to show that the relevant information is set out in a Cabinet document. Rather a judgment, involving an element of damage, is required: the person wishing to withhold must show that the withholding is necessary to maintain the particular interest. That phrase has been interpreted by the Ombudsmen as requiring that release would go 'to the heart' of the relevant interest. Factors such as the age of the information, or the timing of the request, may be relevant." In Canada, s.69 of the Access to Information Act provides that the Act does not apply to confidences of the Queen's Privy Council for Canada (which includes the Cabinet and committees of Cabinet), including memoranda the purpose of which is to present proposals or recommendations to Council; discussion papers the purpose of which is to present background explanations, analyses of problems or policy options to Council for consideration by Council in making decisions; agenda of Council or records recording deliberations or decisions of Council; records used for or reflecting communications or discussions between ministers of the Crown on matters relating to the making of government decisions or the formulation of government policy; records the purpose of which is to brief ministers of the Crown in relation to matters that are before, or are proposed to be brought before, Council; and records that contain information about the contents of any record within any of the preceding classes of records. S.19(1) of the Freedom of Information Act 1997 (Ireland), provides a mandatory exemption (it was, until the amendments made in 2003, a discretionary exemption) for any record: submitted, or proposed to be submitted, to the Government for their consideration by a Minister; containing information (including advice) for a member of the Government, the Attorney General, a Minister of State, the Secretary to the Government or the Assistant Secretary to the Government for use by him solely for the purpose of the transaction of any business of the Government at a meeting of the Government; that consists of a communication between two or more members of the Government relating to a matter that is under consideration by the Government or is proposed to be submitted to the Government. "Government" is defined in s.19(6) to be broadly akin to the Cabinet.

89 Although the information may independently be rendered exempt by s.35.

90 See paras 15–012 to 15–020.

91 Lord Falconer of Thoroton, *Hansard*, HL, Vol.612, April 20, 2000, col.827. Lord Falconer said "I want to emphasise the strength of the prejudice test . . . . It is not a weak test. The commissioner will have the power to overrule an authority if she feels that any prejudice caused by a disclosure would be trivial or insignificant. She will ensure that an authority must point to prejudice

Freedom of Information (Scotland) Act 2002 requires "substantial prejudice" for the purposes of this and other prejudice-based exemptions.

The reasonable opinion of a qualified person

22–019 Section 36 is unique amongst the 23 sections of the Act conferring exemptions in its making the "reasonable opinion" of a particular person determinative of its operation.[92] The reaching of a reasonable opinion is, in relation to each public authority, entrusted to a particular "qualified person," who is invariably at the highest level of accountability so far as that public authority is concerned.[93] This unique aspect of the exemption was controversial and was criticised, both at the Committee stage and as the Bill went through Parliament, on the basis that the question of whether or not such information should be disclosed was one that the Commissioner should be free to determine on the merits, without being limited to a review of the qualified person's opinion.[94] The role of the qualified person's opinion in determining whether a public authority is under a duty to disclose has two related limitations. First, the "reasonable opinion" determinant is confined to deciding whether the disclosure of the information would have, or would be likely to have, any of the effects set out in paras (a)–(c) of s.36(2). As noted above, except in relation to information held by the House of Commons or the House of Lords the exemption is a qualified exemption. Accordingly, the exercise prescribed by s.2(1) and (2) must then be carried out, not necessarily by the "qualified person" who held the "reasonable opinion," to determine whether the public interest in maintaining the exemption outweighs the public interest in disclosing the information. The public interest in maintaining the exemption will, in part, be informed by the fact that the

---

which is 'real, actual or of substance.' We do not think that reliance on undefined words such as 'substantial' or 'significant' is a sensible way forward. We do not know how they will be interpreted by the commissioner or the courts. We can never deliver absolute certainty, but we can avoid making uncertainty worse by adding ill-defined terminology into the Bill."

[92] Although, of course, there are provisions for conclusive certificates under ss.23, 24 and 34. There is no such system under the Freedom of Information (Scotland) Act 2002, which adopts the straightforward approach adopted by each of the other exemptions.

[93] The qualified person for each type of public authority is set out in Freedom of Information Act 2000, s.36(5).

[94] See the House of Commons Select Committee on Public Administration, *Third Report* (Cm.4355), July 19, 1999, para.90; the House of Lords, *Draft Freedom of Information Bill: First Report*, July 27, 1999, para.35; *Hansard*, HC, Vol.340, December 7, 1999, col.782; *Hansard*, HC, Vol.347, April 5, 2000, col.1079–1088; *Hansard*, HL, Vol.618, October 24, 2000, cols 303–313; and *Hansard*, HL, Vol.619, November 22, 2000, cols 833–842. The Government justified the retention of the clause on the basis that "the issues involved in the decision-taking process of public authorities are so near the heart of government that . . . only a qualified person, as defined by the Bill, can have a full understanding of them. Although the issues in [s.36] are less sensitive than those in [s.35] and a class exemption is not justified, the Government do not believe that it would be right for the commissioner to substitute her view for that of the authority on the question of prejudice; hence the test of the reasonable opinion of a qualified person": *Hansard*, HC, Vol.347, April 5, 2000, col.1085.

exemption is engaged by an opinion rather than an actuality. In this way, it may be that the extent to which the qualified person's opinion is borne out by the actuality will fall to be considered at this stage. Secondly, on its face, s.36 restricts the Commissioner's role in an appeal to assessing whether the qualified person's opinion was reasonable: in other words, a review of the qualified person's decision akin to the *Wednesbury* irrationality test.[95] Again, however, even if the Commissioner does find that the qualified person's opinion is reasonable, he must then decide whether or not the information should be disclosed in accordance with the provisions of s.2 of the Freedom of Information Act 2000. In so doing, the Commissioner will have to determine how much weight should be given to the opinion of the qualified person that disclosing the information will have a prejudicial effect. That task cannot properly be carried out without the Commissioner reaching his own view of whether the protected interests set out in paras (a)–(c) of s.36(2) would be, or would be likely to be, prejudiced by the disclosure of the information.[96]

Statistical information

Section 36(4) of the Freedom of Information Act 2000 makes special provision in relation to the rendering of "statistical information" into exempt information. In relation to statistical information, the exemption created by s.36(2) operates like any of the other 22 provisions in the Act creating exemptions. In other words, the statistical information is exempt information if its disclosure would have, or would be likely to have, any of the consequences set out in paras (a)–(c): it is not exempt information merely because, in the reasonable opinion of the qualified person, its disclosure would have, or would be likely to have, any of the consequences set out in paras (a)–(c). On any review by the Information Commissioner, the question for the Commissioner will be similarly modified where the information in question is statistical information. 22–020

The convention of the collective responsibility of Ministers of the Crown: scope

The first of the three limbs in s.36(2) describes information the disclosure of which would, or would be likely to, prejudice "the maintenance of the convention of the collective responsibility of Ministers of the Crown." In order to appreciate whether something would prejudice or would be likely to prejudice 22–021

[95] Thus Lord Falconer of Thoroton indicated that the Commissioner might overturn the qualified person's decision if she took the view that it was "irrational" or "perverse", or a view that "no reasonable Minister or qualified person" would take; and he added that the Commissioner's review of the qualified person's decision would be conducted "on a judicial review basis": see *Hansard*, HL, Vol.618, cols 305 and 306. See also *Hansard*, HC, Vol.347, April 5, 2000, col.1085.

[96] See *Hansard*, HL, Vol.619, November 22, 2000, col.836 (Lord Falconer).

the convention, it is necessary to understand the exact nature of the convention and what end it is designed to serve. The matter was considered in *Attorney-General v Jonathan Cape Ltd*,[97] where the Attorney-General sought in 1975 to prevent the publication of a book, entitled *Diaries of a Cabinet Minister*, written by Richard Crossman, who had been a Cabinet Minister from 1964 to 1970, based upon a diary he had kept recording Cabinet discussions. The Attorney-General contended that publication of the book would undermine the doctrine of joint Cabinet responsibility, that it would represent a breach of the confidentiality and a breach of oath that every Cabinet Minister, as a Privy Councillor, is required to take, and that publication was therefore contrary to the public interest. Lord Widgery disagreed and the action was dismissed. The Court heard extensive evidence as to the nature of the convention, not all of it consistent, and concluded:

> "It has always been assumed by lawyers and, I suspect, by politicians, and the Civil Service, that Cabinet proceedings and Cabinet papers are secret, and cannot be publicly disclosed until they have passed into history. It is quite clear that no court will compel the production of Cabinet papers in the course of discovery in an action, and the Attorney-General contends that not only will the court refuse to compel the production of such matters, but it will go further and positively forbid the disclosure of such papers and proceedings if publication will be contrary to the public interest.
>
> The basis of this contention is the confidential character of these papers and proceedings, derived from the convention of joint Cabinet responsibility whereby any policy decision reached by the Cabinet has to be supported by all members of the Cabinet whether they approve of it or not, unless they feel compelled to resign. It is contended that Cabinet decisions and papers are confidential for a period to the extent at least that they must not be referred to outside the Cabinet in such a way as to disclose the attitude of individual Ministers in the argument which preceded the decision. Thus, there may be no objection to a Minister disclosing (or leaking, as it was called) the fact that a Cabinet meeting has taken place, or, indeed, the decision taken, so long as the individual views of Ministers are not identified."[98]

The Attorney-General had argued that all Cabinet papers and discussions were *prima facie* confidential and that publication of them ought to be restrained if the public interest in concealment outweighed the public interest in a right to free publication: the court could, it was argued, restrain disclosure of Cabinet documents or proceedings that would reveal the individual views or attitudes of

97 [1976] Q.B. 752.
98 At 764.

a Minister and confidential advice from civil servants (whether contained in Cabinet papers or not).[99] Lord Widgery C.J. concluded:

> "... it seems to me that the degree of protection afforded to Cabinet papers and discussion cannot be determined by a single rule of thumb. Some secrets require a high standard of protection for a short time. Others require protection until a new political generation has taken over.
>
> ... I find overwhelming evidence that the doctrine of joint responsibility is generally understood and practised and equally strong evidence that it is on occasion ignored ... To leak a Cabinet decision a day or so before it is officially announced is an accepted exercise in public relations, but to identify the Ministers who voted one way or another is objectionable because it undermines the doctrine of joint responsibility."[1]

Lord Widgery C.J. concluded that publication of the Crossman diaries would, as a matter of fact, not prejudice the maintenance of the convention of the collective responsibility of Ministers of the Crown:

> "... I cannot believe that the publication at this interval [*i.e.* 1975 in a volume relating to 1964–1966] of anything in volume one would inhibit free discussion in the Cabinet of today, even though the individuals involved are the same, and the national problems have a distressing similarity with those of a decade ago. It is unnecessary to elaborate the evils which might flow if at the close of a Cabinet meeting a Minister proceeded to give the press an analysis of the voting, but we are dealing in this case with a disclosure of information nearly 10 years later. It may, of course, be intensely difficult in a particular case, to say at what point the material loses its confidential character, on the ground that publication will no longer undermine the doctrine of joint Cabinet responsibility. It is this difficulty which prompts some to argue that Cabinet discussions should retain their confidential character for a longer and arbitrary period such as 30 years, or even for all time, but this seems to me to be excessively restrictive. The court should intervene only in the clearest of cases where the continuing confidentiality of the material can be demonstrated. In less clear cases—and this, in my view, is certainly one—reliance must be placed on the good sense and good taste of the Minister or ex-Minister concerned.
>
> ... The Attorney-General ... has not satisfied me that publication would in any way inhibit free and open discussion in Cabinet hereafter."[2]

It is suggested that unless there is some measure of contemporaneity about the information or the subject-matter of the information that falls to be released, it

[99] At 765.
[1] At 767, 770.
[2] At 771.

will be difficult to reasonably conclude that its disclosure would be likely to prejudice the maintenance of the convention of the collective responsibility of Minsters of the Crown.[3]

The convention of the collective responsibility of the Cabinet: the public interest

22–022 Lord Widgery's judgment in *Attorney-General v Jonathan Cape Ltd* also provides a useful insight into the public interest embodied in the exemption:

> "I have already indicated some of the difficulties which face the Attorney-General when relied simply on the public interest as a ground for his actions. That such ground is enough in extreme cases is shown by the universal agreement that publication affecting national security can be restrained in this way. It may be that in the short run (for example, over a period of weeks or months) the public interest is equally compelling to maintain joint Cabinet responsibility and the protection of advice given by civil servants, but I would not accept without close investigation that such matters must, as a matter of course, retain protection after a period of years."[4]

Quite apart from its diminution in the likelihood of prejudice to the maintenance of the convention of the collective responsibility of Minsters of the Crown, the passage of time is likely also to diminish the public interest in the maintenance of the exemption.

Inhibiting the free and frank provision of advice, etc.

22–023 The second limb in s.36(2) describes information the disclosure of which would, or would be likely to, inhibit "the free and frank provision of advice or the free and frank exchange of views for the purposes of deliberation." The shortcomings in the "candour argument" and its fate as a head of public interest immunity in this country have already been noted in relation to the parallel exemption

[3] Some further support for this proposition comes from the fact that such information in a "historical record" cannot be exempt information: see Freedom of Information Act 2000, s.63(1) and paras 6–032 to 6–033.

[4] [1976] Q.B. 752 at 768. In *Sankey v Whitlam* (1978) 148 C.L.R. 1, Mason J., in referring to Lord Widgery's judgment, said: "I also agree with his Lordship that the efficiency of government would be seriously compromised if Cabinet decisions and papers were disclosed whilst they or the topics to which they relate are still current or controversial. But I base this view, not so much on the probability of ill-formed criticism with its inconvenient consequences, as upon the inherent difficulty of decision making if the decision-making processes of Cabinet and the materials on which they are based are at risk of premature publication. Cabinet proceedings have always been regarded as secret and confidential" (at 98).

in s.35.[5] On the basis of these, it is suggested that, whatever might have been the position in past decades, it can no longer seriously be maintained that officials, either by dint of advising on matters of policy or of their seniority, would be likely to neglect their duty to give frank advice if that advice were to be released pursuant to a legislative obligation to do so.[6] Moreover, even if an official were to attest that he would compromise his professionalism should that professionalism see the light of day, it is difficult to see that very much weight could be attached to the public interest in maintaining such a stance.[7] As noted above, it is to be expected that the individuals who prepare such advice are both capable and experienced in shrugging off ill-considered criticism and in appreciating well-founded criticism. Moreover, they operate in a regime in which executive decisions are regularly subject to judicial scrutiny and in which, now, most information held by a public authority starts with a presumption that it is to be disclosed to anyone who makes a request.

Otherwise prejudicing the effective conduct of public affairs

The last of the three limbs in s.36(2) describes information the disclosure of which would, or would be likely to, "otherwise prejudice the effective conduct of public affairs." It is difficult to imagine what prejudice, apart from undermining Cabinet secrecy and the questionable impact upon public officials' ability to advise candidly, would be likely to be caused to the effective conduct of public affairs from the "disclosure of . . . information under [the Freedom of Information Act]."[8] If the information has a further attribute (*e.g.* it is confidential information or it comprises sensitive national security material) then it 22–024

[5] See para.22–009.

[6] In *R. (on the Application of Wagstaff) v Secretary of State for Health* [2001] 1 W.L.R. 292 the Divisional Court described the candour argument, which was there being used in support of the decision to hold in private an inquiry into a series of deaths caused by a NHS medical practitioner, as "plainly now what might be described as a diminishing minority point of view, incapable in the circumstances of this case, where no vulnerable witnesses are apparently involved, of standing up to the weight of the arguments in favour of an open inquiry." See also *R. (on the Application of Persey) v Environment Secretary* [2002] EWHC 371 (Admin); [2002] 3 W.L.R. 704.

[7] See para.22–009 n.45.

[8] In *Sankey v Whitlam* (1978) 148 C.L.R. 1 a similar "sweep-up" claim was made in support of a public interest immunity claim: "They [the Executive] have sought refuge in the amorphous statement that non-disclosure is necessary for the proper functioning of the Executive Government and of the public service, without saying why disclosure would be detrimental to their functions, except for the reference to want of 'candour.' Perhaps affidavits in this form were acceptable in the days when it was thought that the court should uphold an objection once made by the Crown through its appropriate representative. But they are plainly unacceptable now that the court is to resolve the issue for itself, after an inspection of the documents when that is thought to be appropriate. An affidavit claiming Crown privilege should state with precision the grounds on which it is contended that documents or information should not be disclosed so as to enable the court to evaluate the competing interests" (at 97, per Mason J.).

may be that disclosure will result in prejudice to the effective conduct of public affairs: however, that additional attribute will invariably render the information exempt information under another provision of the Act. It is suggested that resultant criticism cannot properly be characterised as representing prejudice to the effective conduct of public affairs.[9]

The duty to confirm or deny

22–025 Section 36 also provides a corresponding exclusion from the duty to confirm or deny.[10] There is a subtle but important distinction in the operation of this exclusion from the exclusion given by s.35(3). Under s.35(3), if a given piece of information relating to the formulation of policy, etc. is exempt information under s.35(1), then the corresponding duty to confirm or deny that the information is held does not arise. Under s.36(3), where information is exempt from the duty of disclosure under s.36(2), that is not determinative of whether the duty to confirm or deny arises under s.36(3).[11] Instead, the duty to confirm or deny does not arise where, in the reasonable opinion of a "qualified person," informing the applicant that the public authority holds or does not hold the

[9] In *Commonwealth of Australia v John Fairfax & Sons Ltd* (1980) 147 C.L.R. 39 at 50–51 Mason J. in granting an interlocutory injunction restraining the defendant on breach of copyright grounds from publishing but declining to grant an injunction on breach of duty-of-confidence grounds on the basis that disclosure was unlikely to injure the public interest said: "The question then, when the executive government seeks the protection given by equity, is: What detriment does it need to show? The equitable principle has been fashioned to protect the personal, private and proprietary interests of the citizen, not to protect the very different interests of the executive government. It acts, or is supposed to act, not according to standards of private interest, but in the public interest. This is not to say that equity will not protect information in the hands of the government, but it is to say that when equity protects government information it will look at the matter through different spectacles. It may be a sufficient detriment to the citizen that disclosure of information relating to his affairs will expose his actions to public discussion and criticism. But it can scarcely be a relevant detriment to the government that publication of material concerning its actions will merely expose it to public discussion and criticism. It is unacceptable in our democratic society that there should be a restraint on the publication of information relating to government when the only vi ce of that information is that it enables the public to discuss, review and criticise government action. . . . The court will not prevent the publication of information which merely throws light on the past workings of government, even if it be not public property, so long as it does not prejudice the community in other respects. Then disclosure will itself serve the public interest in keeping the community informed and in promoting discussion of public affairs. If, however, it appears that disclosure will be inimical to the public interest because national security, relations with foreign countries or the ordinary business of government will be prejudiced, disclosure will be restrained." This authority was cited with approval in *Attorney-General v Observer Ltd* [1990] 1 A.C. 109 *per* Scott J. at 151–152; *per* Dillon L.J. at 203; *per* Bingham L.J. at 218, 221; *per* Lord Keith at 258; *per* Lord Griffiths at 270; *per* Lord Goff at 283 ("in a free society there is a continuing public interest that the workings of government should be open to scrutiny and criticism").

[10] Freedom of Information Act 2000, s.36(3).

[11] Freedom of Information Act 2000, s.2(1).

information requested would, or would be likely to, be prejudicial to public affairs in one of the ways set out in s.36(2).[12] The exemption is qualified: the matters to be weighed, which are different from those weighed for the purposes of determining whether the duty to disclose applies, is treated elsewhere in this work.[13]

[12] The different ways in which the duty to confirm or deny has been made not to arise under the Freedom of Information Act 2000 is considered in para.14–004.

[13] See paras 15–010 to 15–011.

CHAPTER 23

Health and Safety

Introduction

23–001 Where the disclosure of information under the Freedom of Information Act 2000 would or would be likely: (a) to endanger the physical or mental health of any individual; or (b) to endanger the safety of any individual, then that information is exempt information by virtue of s.38(1).[1] The exemption is a qualified exemption, so that whether or not there is a duty to disclose such exempt information will turn upon whether in all the circumstances of the case the public interest in maintaining the exemption outweighs the public interest in disclosing the information. Similarly, to the extent that, if a public authority were to inform an applicant that it held information of the description specified in the applicant's request, that informing would or would be likely: (a) to endanger the physical or mental health of any individual; or (b) to endanger the safety of any individual, then the duty to confirm or deny does not arise.[2] The exclusion of this duty is also qualified, so that in such circumstances the public authority will be excused from informing the applicant that it holds the requested information only if the public interest in maintaining the exclusion outweighs the public interest in disclosing whether the public authority holds

[1] s.39(1) of the Freedom of Information (Scotland) Act 2002 is effectively identical.

[2] Freedom of Information Act 2000, s.38(2). There is no separate duty to confirm or deny under the Freedom of Information (Scotland) Act 2002.

the information. Similar exemptions of varying width exist in each of the comparative jurisdictions.[3]

Scope of the exemption

The scope for the disclosure of information to directly endanger health or safety is limited. If the applicant, or a person to whom the information can reasonably be expected to be conveyed, has a vulnerability or sensitivity, then it is conceivable that receipt of the information, if touching upon that vulnerability or sensitivity, may directly endanger that individual's health. In those circumstances, the information will be exempt information. Such a determination by a public authority presupposes some knowledge on its part of the individual's vulnerabilities or sensitivities. Apart from such direct endangering, information that is disclosed under the Freedom of Information Act 2000 may be *used* in such a way 23–002

[3] In the United States, the Freedom of Information Act, 1966, 5 USC 552(b)(7), exempts from disclosure records or information the production of which could reasonably be expected to endanger the life or physical safety of any individual: see para.2–008(7)(F). The Freedom of Information Act 1982 (Cth of Australia), s.37(1)(c), provides an exemption where the disclosure of the requested document would, or could be reasonably be expected to, endanger the life or physical safety of any person. S.37(2)(c) provides a separate exemption for a document the disclosure of which would, or could reasonably be expected to, prejudice the maintenance or enforcement of lawful methods for the protection of public safety. S.41(3) provides a special method of disclosure where it appears to the agency that the disclosure of the information to the applicant might be detrimental to the applicant's physical or mental health, or well-being. The Official Information Act 1982 (New Zealand), s.9(2)(c) provides a qualified exemption where disclosure would cause prejudice to measures protecting the health or safety of members of the public: see para.2–023(4). Ss.6(d) and 27(1)(a) provide an absolute exemption where disclosure would be likely to endanger the safety of any person: see para.2–022(4). The Access to Information Act (Canada), s.17 provides a discretionary exemption for records the disclosure of which could "reasonably be expected" to cause a threat to an individual's safety: see para.2–032(14). There is no analogous exemption in respect of information the disclosure of which could reasonably be expected to threaten an individual's physical or mental health. The *Report of the Access to Information Task Force* (June 2002, Ottawa), p.56, recommended that one be included. The Privacy Act (Canada), s.28, provides discretionary exemption for any personal information that relates to the physical or mental health of the individual who requested it where the examination of the information by the individual would be contrary to the best interests of the individual. S.25 of that Act provides a discretionary exemption where disclosure could reasonably be expected to threaten the safety of individuals. S.20(6) of the Access to Information Act also specifically provides that the head of a government institution (being the primary decision-maker for the purposes of the Act) may disclose third party confidential information (which would otherwise be exempt) where disclosure under the Act "would be in the public interest as it relates to public health, public safety or protection of the environment and, if the public interest in disclosure clearly outweighs in importance any financial loss or gain to, prejudice to the competitive position of or interference with contractual or other negotiations of a third party." The Freedom of Information Act 1997 (Ireland), ss.23(1)(aa) and 28(3), respectively provide a discretionary exemption for records the disclosure of which might endanger the life or safety of any person or that might be prejudicial to the health of the applicant: see para.2–039(14). A separate exemption is provided for disclosures that could reasonably be expected to prejudice or impair lawful methods, etc., for ensuring the safety of the public and of persons. Ss.27(2)(e) and 28(2)(e) provide a similar override to the Canadian Act in relation to confidential third party information the disclosure of which is "necessary in order to avoid a serious and imminent danger to the life or health of an individual."

as to endanger an individual's health or safety. Whether in these circumstances it is apposite to describe *the disclosure* of the information as endangering health or safety, as opposed to *the likely use* that will be made of disclosed information endangering health or safety, is essentially a question of causation. On the usual principles of causation, if it is readily predictable that particular information, once disclosed, will be used so as to harm the health or safety of an individual, then it may be said that the disclosure of the information will endanger the health or safety of that individual.[4] On the other hand, where there is a mere possibility that certain information may be misused in such a way as to endanger health or safety it becomes more difficult to say the disclosure of that information "would or would be likely to endanger" health or safety. This is particularly so if there is an obvious use that may be made of the information that would not be likely to endanger health or safety. The level of probability required by the exemption is the same as that used in other exemptions ("would or would be likely to"): this is considered elsewhere in this work.[5] The exemption is unique in its use of the word "endanger" rather than the word "prejudice." Arguably, it is easier for a disclosure to "endanger" an interest than it is for a disclosure to prejudice that interest, as the word "endanger" connotes a risk of harm rather than harm itself.[6]

The distinction between health and safety

23–003 Although there is a considerable degree of potential overlap between the information caught by s.38(1)(a) (physical or mental health) and the information caught by s.38(1)(b) (safety), the comparative jurisprudence illustrates that their coverage is by no means identical. In particular, whereas the former exemption has greater potential direct application, the latter is only readily engaged by some predicted use of the information.

---

4 In other areas of the law it is conventional to seek to identify the "effective" or "dominant" cause of an outcome: *Galoo v Bright Grahame Murray* [1994] 1 W.L.R. 1360 at 1374–1375. Ultimately it will depend upon a commensense interpretation of the facts. Intervening acts by third persons have always presented particular problems in relation to causation, and the following authorities provide useful illustrations, albeit in different contexts: *Weld-Blundell v Stephens* [1920] A.C. 956 (where the defendant, in breach of his contract, negligently left a libellous letter written by the plaintiff, where it was read by a third party, who was likely to, and did, communicate its contents to the persons libelled: the latter recovered damages for libel from the plaintiff, who then turned around and sued the defendant. The House of Lords, by a majority, held that the act of the third party, although foreseeable, was a "new and independent" cause).

5 See paras 15–014 to 15–018.

6 See in a very different context *R. v Whitehouse* [2000] Crim. L.R. 172 which concerned the issue of whether the use of a mobile phone on an aircraft was doing an act "likely to endanger an aircraft" contrary to Art.5 Air Navigation (No.2) Order 1995. The Court of Appeal concluded that "likely to endanger" in this context would be satisfied if there was a real risk of endangerment. This case turned more on the meaning of "likely" than of "endanger." In *R. v Pearce* [1966] 3 W.L.R. 823 at 827 the Court of Appeal, again in a different context, spoke of endangering as being concerned with "causing a source of danger".

— In the USA, under the safety exemption, where the applicant had previously threatened federal employees and third persons connected with law enforcement matters, the courts have upheld non-disclosure of the names and identifying information of persons in that class, provided that withholding that information is necessary in order to protect them from possible harm.[7]

— In Australia, exemption on the analogous safety ground has been upheld for documents relating to a surveillance operation carried out by the police into members of a sect, the Tribunal considering that release would give rise to a reasonable expectation that the life or physical safety of a person might be in danger.[8] Similarly, exemption has been upheld where disclosure of information such as a person's identity, views or whereabouts would make that person a potential target of violence by another person or group of persons. However, the Tribunal and Courts have required objective evidence to support a reasonable apprehension of danger.[9] Thus, where an applicant, who had four convictions for assault and who had been a recipient of a disability support pension that had been cancelled and then reinstated, sought access to the underlying documents for the cancellation decision, it was held not to be enough to engage the safety exemption that (a) the psychologist who had examined the applicant had requested that his report not be provided to the applicant because of his potential to react violently; (b) the applicant had made statements suggesting that he would act violently; and (c) when interviewed, the applicant had had a threatening demeanour, and the officer concerned had felt threatened by him.[10]

— Also in Australia, disclosure has been refused on safety grounds in relation to a portion of an army manual relating to the tactical response to terrorism and to Army procedures to meet requests for assistance in

7 *Blanton v United States Department of Justice*, 182 F. Supp.(2d) 81 (D.D.C. 2002), where, on the grounds of safety, the Court refused to order disclosure so as to protect the identities of FBI Special Agents and non-law enforcement personnel assisting in an investigation, even though the requester was incarcerated, on the basis that his threats against persons responsible for his arrest and conviction made it possible that those individuals could be targets of physical harm.

8 *Re Anderson and Australian Federal Police* (1987) 11 A.L.D. 356.

9 *Re Boehm and Department of Industry Technology and Commerce* (1985) 7 A.L.N. N186. On the other hand, the exemption has been held not to be satisfied where evidence was produced that one of several institutions where animal experiments were conducted had received a bomb threat. It was held that danger to lives or physical safety was only considered to be a possibility, not a real chance: *Re Binnie and Department of Agriculture and Rural Affairs* (1987) 1 V.A.R. 361.

10 *Centerlink v Dykstra* [2002] F.C.A. 1442. The Tribunal had taken into account that the medical evidence was 2 years old and that the applicant had never actually attempted to harm any official. Although the Federal Court allowed an appeal, that was on the basis that the Tribunal had failed to take into account relevant material, and it otherwise upheld the decision-making methodology of the Tribunal: in particular, that the fear of the officers could not be determinative of the issue.

dealing with terrorism on the basis that if the relevant section of the manual were made public, there would be a significant risk to security.[11]
— In New Zealand, the disclosure of possible examination questions for pilots has been refused on safety grounds.[12]

Other safety examples can be expected to include: the disclosure of plans of a prison,[13] and the disclosure of the new identity, or the location of, a recently released convicted child killer.[14] In each of these two cases it is difficult to see a legitimate need for the information sought by any applicant under the Act.

The public interest

23–004 As noted above, the health and safety exemption is qualified or non-absolute: it only applies if the public interest in maintaining the exemption outweighs the public interest in disclosing the information.[15] This public interest must be satisfied even in cases where the endangerment of physical or mental health or safety is likely to occur. As with the other qualified exemptions, in weighing the competing public interests, the relevant decision maker[16] will have to take into account all the circumstances of the case[17] and any relevant provisions of the European Convention for the Protection of Human Rights and Fundamental Freedoms. Arts 2, 3 and 8 ECHR are all potentially engaged in relation to this exemption.[18] Relevant factors that will need to be considered no doubt include the risk and severity of any adverse effects on someone's health and the strength of the public interest in disclosure. It is suggested that the public interest in maintaining an exemption where it is the anticipated *use* of information that

[11] *Re Hocking and Department of Defence* (1987) 12 A.L.D. 554.

[12] 8 CCNO 78 and 9 CCNO 143.

[13] In Australia, the Administrative Appeals Tribunal upheld an exemption in relation to a request by an applicant who had been interned during the Second World War on the grounds that the information referred to methods for protecting public safety during wartime: *Re Parisi and Australian Federal Police* (1987) 14 A.L.D. 11 at 17. It is not clear how the Tribunal considered this continued to remain a threat to safety some 40 years later.

[14] See *Venables v News Group Newspapers* [2001] Fam. 430. In such circumstances Art.2 ECHR protecting the right to life is likely to be relevant when carrying out the balancing test relating to the public interest.

[15] See: Freedom of Information Act 2000, ss.2(1)(b) and 2(2)(b) and Freedom of Information (Scotland) Act 2002, s.2(1)(b). For a general discussion of this topic, see paras 15–001 to 15–011. That there is particular public interest in the disclosure of information relating to health and safety of an individual is reflected in Pt IVA of the Employment Rights Act 1996, as inserted by the Public Interest Disclosure Act 1998, which sanctions on the basis of it being in the public interest of a disclosure by an employee tending to show "that the health and safety of any individual has been, is being or is likely to be endangered"—s.43B(1)(d).

[16] That is: the public authority from which information is sought; the Information Commissioner; the Information Tribunal; or the courts.

[17] Freedom of Information Act 2000, ss.2(1)(b) and 2(2)(b); Freedom of Information (Scotland) Act 2002, s.66; Data Protection Act 1998, s.35.

[18] See paras 1–029 to 1–037.

renders it exempt information will be liable to be displaced by the public interest in disclosure if there are legitimate uses for the information. Thus, the public interest in maintaining an exemption for information revealing the risks, however slight, in treatments or medicines on the basis that a proportion of the population will turn away from them (despite their beneficial effects), can only readily predominate over the public interest in disclosure of such information by rejecting the fundamental precepts of freedom of information legislation. In the parliamentary debates there was considerable discussion about withholding information about the risks of eating beef during the BSE controversy. Mr O'Brien, the Parliamentary Under-Secretary of State for the Home Department stated:

> "Where public health is seriously at risk and information is held by the Government, it is difficult to see, on any reading of the Bill, how it could be justified for a Minister to take the view that the public interest was in favour of secrecy, unless a criminal investigation were about to be undertaken, in which case the public interest would have to be weighed very carefully. In circumstances where there is a clear view that public health would be at risk—particularly in the sort of situation in which BSE arose—under the Bill, it would always be in the public interest for that information to be in the public domain . . . ."[19]

The duty to confirm or deny

Where the requested information is, or if it were held would be, exempt information under s.38 (1), then the discrete duty to confirm or deny that the information is held by the public authority does not arise. The exclusion of this duty is a qualified one. It will be necessary to consider whether, in all the circumstances, the maintenance of the exclusion of this duty is outweighed by the public interest in disclosing whether the public authority holds the information. As noted above,[20] this public interest balancing exercise is materially different from that employed for the purpose of determining whether the duty to communicate does not apply.[21] It will only be in limited circumstances where the decision maker will be exempted from confirming or denying that it holds such information. The need for a exemption to the duty to confirm or deny was debated by Parliament. Lord Goodhart, the Liberal Democrat peer, commented: 23–005

> "There are certain possible circumstances in which the mere disclosure that information was held would be a potential danger, either to someone who

[19] *Hansard*, HC, Vol.357, November 27, 2000, col.723.

[20] See para.20–007, where this duty is considered further.

[21] See paras 15–010 to 15–011 as to what it involves.

> would be seriously upset—mentally perhaps—by the realisation that such information was in the possession of a public authority, or to someone who had supplied the information. The fact that that was known might induce someone to take steps against him."[22]

Whilst, it is suggested, upset—whether mental or otherwise—is not a sufficient reason for refusing to confirm or deny the existence of information, there may be certain circumstances where such disclosure could cause, or exacerbate, mental illness. Further, the disclosure of the existence of information, provided that the request is sufficiently narrowly formulated, might indicate the identity of an informer.

The Data Protection Act 1998

23–006 The Data Protection (Subject Access Modification) (Health) Order 2000[23] provides an analogous exemption in relation to a request for personal data. Under this Order, data is exempted from subject access requirements of s.7 of the Data Protection Act 1998 to the extent to which disclosure under the section would be likely to cause serious harm to the physical or mental health or condition of the data subject or any other person.[24] The qualification of harm as limited to "serious" harm is likely to compensate for the absence of an express public interest requirement in the Data Protection Act 1998 and as such exemption from disclosure under both Acts is likely to be similar. It is suggested that the addition of the word "condition" adds little. The phrase "mental health" is sufficiently broad to include mental conditions.

[22] *Hansard*, HL, Vol.617, October 19, 2000, col.1250.
[23] SI 2000/413.
[24] See para.4–055.

CHAPTER 24

Personal Information

1. BACKGROUND

Introduction

24–001 Section 40 of the Freedom of Information Act 2000[1] is a complex provision which seeks to achieve two aims:

(1) To channel any request by an applicant for personal data[2] relating to himself through those access provisions of the Data Protection Act 1998 by rendering that data exempt information for the purposes of the Freedom of Information Act 2000.[3] As noted earlier,[4] under the Data Protection Act 1998 an individual has a right of access to information held by a public authority relating to himself.[5]

(2) To limit the s.1 rights of an applicant in relation to personal information concerning other persons.[6] The right of an individual to obtain access to third-party personal information is exclusively that given by s.1(1) of the Freedom of Information Act 2000. Similarly, where a corporate entity seeks any personal information held by a public authority, including information relating to itself, the right of access to that information is that given by the Freedom of Information Act 2000. By rendering certain third-party personal information "exempt information," the right of access given by s.1(1) is shaped so as not to extend to that information.

This chapter is concerned with the scope and operation of the two exemptions in s.40 which give effect to these aims. As both exemptions are expressly inter-related with the Data Protection Act 1998, reference to that Act must necessarily be made. With one exception,[7] the two exemptions are absolute exemptions, so that a consideration of the public interest is not involved in determining their applicability.[8] These two exemptions do not, of course, preclude a request for information being made under the Data Protection Act 1998. Indeed, so far as a request by an applicant for personal data relating exclusively

1 And the Freedom of Information (Scotland) Act 2002, s.38.

2 As to the meaning of "personal data" see paras 4–010 and 4–017 to 4–020. Broadly speaking, "personal data" are data relating to living and identified or identifiable individuals.

3 Freedom of Information Act 2000, s.40(1); Freedom of Information (Scotland) Act 2002, s.38(1)(a).

4 See para.4–002.

5 If a request is made for this sort of information under the Freedom of Information Act 2000, the public authority is entitled to refuse the request without any consideration of the public interest: see s.2 of that Act; Freedom of Information (Scotland) Act 2002, s.2.

6 Freedom of Information Act 2000, s.40(2)–(4); Freedom of Information (Scotland) Act 2002, s.38(1)(b).

7 Freedom of Information Act 2000, s.40(3)(a)(ii); Freedom of Information (Scotland) Act 2002, s.38(2)(a)(ii).

8 Freedom of Information Act 2000, s.2; Freedom of Information (Scotland) Act 2002, s.2.

to himself is concerned, a request under the Data Protection Act 1998 is the appropriate statutory route and is expressly catered for in that Act.[9] Under that Act, however, the correlation between the identity of the applicant and the data subject of the information sought is critical to the success of the request for information. The scope of the access right bestowed by that Act is thus narrower than the general right of access given by s.1(1) of the Freedom of Information Act 2000. Section 40 also contains two correlative exclusions of the duty to confirm or deny.[10]

The rationale for the first exemption

Access to personal information is a key element of any freedom of information regime. It is to be anticipated that requests for personal information will form the majority of requests for information under the Freedom of Information Act 2000. This would reflect the experience of other jurisdictions.[11] Individuals in the United Kingdom have for a number of years enjoyed rights of access to certain types of personal information about themselves. Since 1998 those rights have been provided principally by the Data Protection Act 1998 (which implements the Data Protection Directive).[12] That Act, like the earlier Data Protection Act 1984, also provides safeguards in respect of the processing of personal data, perhaps most importantly by requiring data controllers to comply with eight data protection principles.[13] The advent of the Freedom of Information Act 2000, having at its core a general right of access to information held by a public authority, gave rise to a potential overlap between the two Acts in respect of access to personal information held by public authorities. In fact, the intention was that the Freedom of Information Act 2000 should go further than the Data Protection Act 1998, in affording access to any information held by a public authority, not just the specific categories to which access was permitted under the Data Protection Act 1998. For these reasons, it was necessary to consider how requests for personal information should be dealt with on the coming into force of the Freedom of Information Act 2000. The solution arrived at, which is discussed in greater depth below, is essentially that all requests for personal 24–002

[9] The rights of access under the Data Protection Act 1998 are considered in Ch.4 of this work.

[10] Freedom of Information Act 2000, s.40(5). There is no separate duty to confirm or deny under the Freedom of Information (Scotland) Act 2002.

[11] See: Australian Law Reform Commission and Administrative Review Council, "Open Government: a Review of the Federal Freedom of Information Act 1982", A.L.R.C. 77, A.R.C. 40, Canberra, 1995, para.2.10. In Canada, access to personal information is dealt with through the Privacy Act. The analogous exemption, s.19 of the Access to Information Act, is the most frequently claimed exemption in the Canadian Act, accounting for just under a third of all claimed exemptions: Government of Canada, *Report of the Access to Information Review Task Force* (Ottawa, 2002), p.58.

[12] See Ch.4.

[13] As to which, see para.24–011.

information about oneself from public authorities, the first main category of requests for personal information, are channelled through the Data Protection Act 1998. Accordingly, such requests are taken out of the scope of the Freedom of Information Act 2000.[14] Because the Data Protection Act 1998, as originally passed, applied only to specific categories of information,[15] amendments were made to it to bring within its ambit any information held by a public authority, thereby reflecting the broader coverage of the Freedom of Information Act 2000.[16] This expansion was accompanied by certain modifications of the subject access provisions for certain requests, reflecting the potential difficulties of complying with requests relating to unstructured paper files. So, where a request relates to unstructured manual data, the data subject has to provide a description of the data, and the data controller need not comply with the request if the cost of doing so would be excessive.[17]

The rationale for the second exemption

24–003 The second main category of requests for personal information—requests for personal information about third parties—was placed within the province of the Freedom of Information Act 2000. However, because of the interplay between it and the Data Protection Act 1998 with its protection against unwarranted disclosure of personal information, there is complex exemption in the Freedom of Information Act 2000 from the obligation to comply with such requests reflecting (and cross-referring to) various protections given by the Data Protection Act 1998.[18] There is, of course, an inherent tension between the objective of freedom of information and the objective of protecting personal privacy. These conflicting objectives inevitably conflict when an individual seeks access to personal information about a third party. The conflict poses two related challenges for governments: first, to determine where the balance should be struck between those aims; and, secondly, to determine the mechanisms for dealing with requests for such information. This will frequently involve an interplay between privacy legislation and freedom of information legislation.[19] The conflict between the right to personal privacy and the public interest in the disclosure of personal information was recognised by the Government when it first proposed a freedom of information Act[20] and there was continued

[14] Freedom of Information Act 2000, s.40; Freedom of Information (Scotland) Act 2002, s.38.
[15] See para.4–011(1)–(4).
[16] Data Protection Act 1998, s.1(1)(e), inserted by Freedom of Information Act 2000, s.68(2)(a).
[17] See para.4–037.
[18] Freedom of Information Act 2000, s.40; Freedom of Information (Scotland) Act 2002, s.38.
[19] This is reflected in the approach taken by the majority of the comparative jurisdictions, where the right of access to personal information is found exclusively in a Privacy Act and not in the freedom of information legislation: see para.4–002.
[20] Cabinet Office, *Your Right to Know: The Government's Proposals for a Freedom of Information Act*, (White Paper) (Cm.3818), December 11, 1997, para.3.11(3).

recognition of that difficulty throughout the passage of the Bill.[21] Overall, the balance appears to have been struck in favour of administrative convenience, whilst adhering to the structure of the Data Protection Directive.[22] Thus, while aspects of the scheme appear to favour a third party's privacy,[23] the Freedom of Information Act 2000 is alone amongst its comparators in not making provision for consulting a third party where information relating to that third party is sought by an applicant.[24]

The approach adopted

As regards the mechanism for dealing with requests for access to personal information, as in many jurisdictions the government was faced with different legislation dealing with freedom of information, privacy and human rights.[25] When the Freedom of Information Act was first proposed, it was intended that the two access schemes (*i.e.* under the Data Protection Act 1998 and the Freedom of Information Act) would run in parallel as a dual access regime, with their systems aligned as far as possible.[26] However, that proposal was abandoned when the Bill was drafted. As already indicated, the replacement provisions direct requests for personal information either to the Data Protection Act 1998 (subject access) or to the Freedom of Information Act 2000 (third party information), but in consequence suffer from considerable complexity.[27] One alternative approach debated when the Bill received its third reading was to make the third party disclosure exemption under the Freedom of Information Act **24–004**

21 See *e.g.* House of Commons, *Select Committee on Public Administration Third Report, Session 1997–1998*, May 19, 1998, paras 10–18.

22 As to which, see paras 4–004 to 4–005. As noted at para.4–002, the separate legislative treatment of an applicant's right of access to information relating to himself is common.

23 For example, in relation to personal information about public officials, where the Freedom of Information Act 2000 draws no distinction between personal information that might be termed "public" and that which is "private." The Data Protection Registrar had suggested that public officials should be afforded the same level of protection for information relating to their private lives as that enjoyed by others, but that there should be provision for greater disclosure of information relating to their public activities: *Third Report of 1998–1999, Freedom of Information Draft Bill*, Vol. II: HC 570-II of 1998–99, August 16, 1999, memorandum 2, p.19 paras 4.4–4.5. The Access to Information Act (Canada), s.3, definition of "personal information," draws this distinction.

24 See further paras 11–042 to 11–049.

25 The Data Protection Act 1998 was brought forward before the Freedom of Information Act 2000 because of the obligation to comply with the Data Protection Directive by October 24, 1998: see paras 4–004 to 4–005.

26 Cabinet Office, *Your Right to Know. The Government's Proposals for a Freedom of Information Act*, (White Paper) (Cm. 3818), December 11, 1997, paras 4.6–4.11; House of Commons Library, *The Freedom of Information Bill: Data Protection Issues*, Research Paper 99/99, December 3, 1999, p.7.

27 For example, from the Data Protection Registrar in her evidence to the Public Administration Committee: *Third Report of 1998–1999, Freedom of Information Draft Bill*, Vol II: HC 570-II of 1998–99, August 16, 1999, memorandum 2, p.18 para.4; *Third Report of 1998–1999, Freedom of Information Draft Bill*, Vol II: HC 570-I of 1998–99, 29 July 1999, para. 98.

2000 applicable simply when disclosure would be likely to result in a public authority breaching its obligation to respect the private life of individuals pursuant to Art.8 of the European Convention on Human Rights; but this did not find favour.[28]

2. PERSONAL DATA OF WHICH THE APPLICANT IS THE DATA SUBJECT

Introduction

24–005 Under s.40(1) of the Freedom of Information Act 2000,[29] where information constitutes "personal data"[30] of which the applicant is the "data subject,"[31] it is thereby rendered exempt information. The exemption is an absolute exemption.[32] The result is that an applicant seeking information about himself has no rights under s.1 of the Freedom of Information Act 2000 but, instead, must look to the Data Protection Act 1998 to secure that information. Under the 1998 Act, such a request is termed a "subject access request." The data answering the terms of a subject access request may also reveal personal information relating to a third party. Such requests are also dealt with under the Data Protection Act 1998. Under that Act, where a data controller cannot comply with a subject access request without disclosing information relating to another identifiable individual he is not obliged to do so unless that individual has consented to the disclosure or it is reasonable in all the circumstances to comply with the request without such consent.[33]

The duty to confirm or deny

24–006 Section 40(5)(a) grants a correlative exclusion of the duty to confirm or deny in relation to information which constitutes personal data of which the applicant is the data subject. It is to be noted that the exclusion of the duty does not require that confirmation or denial would or might itself disclose the existence of the information or cause any particular prejudice.[34] The exclusion of the

[28] *Hansard*, HC, Vol.347, April 5, 2000, col.982; *Hansard*, HL, Vol.618, October 25, 2000, cols 409–412.

[29] And Freedom of Information (Scotland) Act 2002, s.38(1)(a).

[30] Defined in Freedom of Information Act 2000, s.40(7) and Freedom of Information (Scotland) Act 2002, s.38(5). See paras 4–010 and 4–017 to 4–020. Broadly speaking, "personal data" are data relating to living and identified or identifiable individuals.

[31] Defined in Freedom of Information Act 2000, s.40(7) and Freedom of Information (Scotland) Act 2002, s.38(5). A data subject is an individual who is the subject of personal data: see para.4–022.

[32] Freedom of Information Act 2000, s.2(3)(f); Freedom of Information (Scotland) Act 2002, s.2(2)(e).

[33] Data Protection Act 1998, s.7(4). This provision is considered at para.4–041.

[34] See the distinctions drawn in para.14–004.

duty to confirm or deny is absolute.[35] Thus, where or to the extent that a public authority receives a request under the Freedom of Information Act 2000 for information that constitutes personal data of which the applicant is the data subject, the public authority need neither provide the information nor advise the applicant whether or not it holds the information.

3. PERSONAL DATA OF WHICH THE APPLICANT IS NOT THE DATA SUBJECT

Introduction

The second exemption in s.40 deals with personal information about third parties.[36] In order for the exemption to apply, two requirements must be satisfied. The first requirement is universal. The second requirement can be met in a number of different ways, the availability of which partly depends upon whether the information in question falls within paras (a) to (d) of the definition of "data" in s.1(1) of the Data Protection Act 1998[37] or whether, instead, it falls within para.(e) of that definition; the latter being termed "manual data."[38] There is a correlative exclusion of the duty to confirm or deny. This is also dependant upon two requirements being satisfied, although there are differences between these and those required to render information "exempt information." 24–007

Overview of the exemption

Ignoring for the moment the different treatment of of "manual data," this part of s.40 of the Freedom of Information Act 2000 can be crudely summarised as follows: personal data of which the applicant is not the data subject is rendered exempt information for the purposes of the Freedom of Information Act 2000 if its disclosure would: 24–008

— contravene any of the data protection principles[39];
— contravene s.10 of the Data Protection Act 1998 by causing substantial damage or distress to the data subject[40]; or

[35] Freedom of Information Act 2000, s.2(3)(f); Freedom of Information (Scotland) Act 2002, s.2(2)(e).
[36] Freedom of Information Act 2000, s.40(2)–(7); Freedom of Information (Scotland) Act 2002, s.38(1)(b) and (2)–(5).
[37] See paras 4–011 to 4–016.
[38] See para.4–013.
[39] Considered at greater length at paras 24–009 to 24–013.
[40] Considered at greater length at para.24–014.

— not be required under the Data Protection Act 1998 by virtue of one of the exemptions in Pt IV of that Act.[41]

It is helpful to use this overview as a lodestar to guide one's travels through subss.40(2)–(7).

First requirement: personal information not relating to the applicant

24–009 In order for information to be exempt under this exemption, the first requirement is that the information must constitute personal data of which the applicant is not the data subject.[42] That is to say, the data must relate to a living individual whom it is possible to identify either from those data alone or from those data and any other information that is in the possession of the data controller or is likely to come into his possession,[43] and the request for information must be made by an individual who is not the subject of those personal data.

Second requirement, first alternative: disclosure would contravene the data protection principles

24–010 As noted above, what is required in order to meet the second requirement is partly dependant upon whether the information falls within any of paras (a) to (d) of the definition of "data" in s.1(1) of the Data Protection Act 1998.[44] Where information does fall within any of those paragraphs, then, if disclosure of the information to a member of the public would breach any of the data protection principles, the second requirement will be met and the information will be exempt information.[45] This is an absolute exemption.[46] The application of this requirement is complicated by the potential applicability of the exemptions in Pt IV of the Data Protection Act 1998. Section 27(1) of that Act provides that references in any of the data protection principles to "personal data" or to the "processing of personal data" do not include references to data or processing which, by virtue of Pt IV of the Data Protection Act 1998, are exempt from that

41 Considered at greater length at para.24–016.

42 Freedom of Information Act 2000, s.40(1), (2)(a) and (7). This is not a requirement under the Freedom of Information (Scotland) Act 2002.

43 Data Protection Act 1998, s.1(1). See paras 4–017 to 4–022.

44 As to which, see paras 4–011 to 4–015.

45 Freedom of Information Act 2000, s.40(2), (3)(a)(i), (3)(b); Freedom of Information (Scotland) Act 2002, s.38(1)(b), (2)(a)(i), (2)(b). The data protection principles, so far as potentially applicable, are considered at para.24–011.

46 Freedom of Information Act 2000, s.2(3)(f)(ii), s.40(2), (3)(a)(i), (3)(b); Freedom of Information (Scotland) Act 2002. s.2(2)(e)(ii).

principle.[47] The exemptions in Pt IV of the Data Protection Act 1998 are considered elsewhere in this work.[48] The upshot of this feeding in of the exemptions in Pt IV is that once it is established that disclosure would contravene one of the data protection principles as set out in Pt I of Sch.I, it will then be necessary to consider whether that or those applicable principle or principles or the data itself is nevertheless exempt by virtue of one of the exemptions in Pt IV of the Data Protection Act 1998. If one of those exemptions is applicable, then:

— disclosure will be exempt from the data protection principle;
— disclosure under the Freedom of Information Act 2000 will accordingly not breach a data protection principle, and
— the exemption under the 2000 Act will not apply.

The odd consequence is, therefore, that the applicability of one of the exemptions in Pt IV of the Data Protection Act 1998 has the effect of increasing the likelihood of disclosure under the Freedom of Information Act 2000.[49] In relation to the duty to confirm or deny, the position is similar to the disclosure duty: if the mere confirmation or denial of the holding of information answering the terms of the request would contravene any of the data protection principles, then the duty to confirm or deny will be excluded. Exclusion of the duty is qualified, so that it is necessary for a public authority to consider whether the public interest in maintaining the exclusion of the duty to confirm or deny outweighs the public interest in disclosing the information.[50]

Contravention of data protection principles

The eight data protection principles are contained in Pt I of Sch.1 to the Data Protection Act 1998.[51] Pt II of Sch.1 sets out a binding[52] statement of the manner in which those principles in Part I are to be interpreted. It must always be borne in mind that s.1(1) of the Data Protection Act 1998 defines "processing" very widely, and that it expressly includes holding, disclosure or otherwise making available of information. In very general terms, the eight data protection principles are principles that must be followed by every data controller in his 24–011

47 It is clear from the definition of "the data protection principles" in Freedom of Information Act 2000, s.40(7), that the data protection principles are not simply to be read in their "raw" form, as they appear in Sch.1, but must be read in the light of the exemption in Pt IV of the Data Protection Act 1998. Similarly, the definition in Freedom of Information Act 2000, s.38(5).
48 paras 4–051 to 4–076.
49 But see para.24–016.
50 Freedom of Information Act 2000, ss.2(1), 2(3) and 40(5)(b)(i). Scottish public authorities are deprived of this pleasure and must content themselves with Freedom of Information (Scotland) Act 2002, s.16(3).
51 Data Protection Act 1998, s.4, Sch.1; see also Sch.2. These replaced the eight data protection principles that were in the Data Protection Act 1984.
52 Data Protection Act 1998, s.4(2).

processing of personal data. Because the Data Protection Act 1998 relates to all aspects of the "processing"[53] of data, the data protection principles reflect the breadth of that term and do not always have an immediate application to the disclosure of data. Nevertheless, as disclosure is one of the defined facets of "processing," if disclosure of personal data of which the applicant is not the data subject that contravenes any of the data protection principles this will render those data "exempt information" for the purposes of the Freedom of Information Act 2000. It is therefore necessary to consider each of the data protection principles, recognising that some are inapposite to the operation of the exemption. For the reasons set out below, it is suggested that only contravention of the first and sixth principles will have any potential application to a disclosure under the Freedom of Information Act 2000.

(1) *First Principle*: Personal data must be processed fairly and lawfully and must, in particular, not be processed unless: (a) at least one of the conditions in Sch.2 of the Data Protection Act 1998 is met;[54] and (b) in the case of sensitive personal data, at least one of the conditions in Sch.3 of the Data Protection Act 1998 is met.[55] Paras 1 to 4 of Pt II of Sch.I provide binding interpretive guidance upon the first principle and impose further obligations upon data controllers in respect of the requirement to process fairly and lawfully. Because of the intricacies of the first principle and given its potential to apply to a disclosure under the Freedom of Information Act 2000, it has been considered separately below.

(2) *Second Principle*: Personal data must be obtained only for one or more specified and lawful purpose(s), and must not be further processed in any manner that is incompatible with that purpose or those purposes. The first part of the second principle relates to the obtaining of personal data: disclosure under the Freedom of Information Act 2000 is not going to result in a contravention of this part of the principle. The second part of the second principle is directed to all forms of processing, which will include disclosure. Paragraph 6 of Pt II of Sch.1 explains that in determining whether any disclosure of personal data is compatible with the purpose or purposes for which the data were obtained, regard is to be had to the purpose or purposes for which the personal data are intended to be processed by any person to whom they are disclosed. It is questionable whether this has any application to a disclosure under the Freedom of Information Act 2000. It will almost always be possible to contend that a public authority will not have obtained data for the purpose of being able to release it under the Freedom of

[53] Defined in the Data Protection Act 1998, s.1(1) to include obtaining, recording, holding, organising, retrieving, consulting, use, transmitting, etc., of data.

[54] See para.24–012.

[55] See para.24–013.

Information Act 2000. It is suggested that the second element of the second principle is directed to a voluntary disclosure; that is, to a disclosure that is not given in obedience to a statutory or other legal requirement. On this view, the second element of the second principle will have no real application to a disclosure under the Freedom of Information Act 2000.

(3) *Third Principle*: Personal data must be adequate, relevant and not excessive in relation to the purposes for which they are processed. Part II of Sch.1 does not include interpretive provisions for this principle and there is no definition of or guidance as to what is "adequate," "relevant" or "excessive." As this principle is principally directed to the obtaining of data, it is difficult to see how disclosure under the Freedom of Information Act 2000 could by itself involve a contravention of the principle.

(4) *Fourth Principle*: Personal data should be accurate and, where necessary, kept up-to-date. Paragraph 7 of Pt II of Sch.1 explains that the fourth principle is not to be regarded as being contravened by reason of any inaccuracy in personal data which accurately record information obtained by the data controller from the data subject or a third party in a case where: (a) having regard to the purpose or purposes for which the data were obtained and further processed, the data controller has taken reasonable steps to ensure the accuracy of the data; and (b) if the data subject has notified the data controller of the data subject's view that the data are inaccurate, the data indicate that fact. As this principle is directed to the holding or keeping of data, it is difficult to see how disclosure under the Freedom of Information Act 2000 could by itself involve a contravention of the principle.

(5) *Fifth Principle*: Personal data processed for any purpose or purposes must not be kept longer than is necessary for that purpose or those purposes. The Act gives no guidance as to what is meant by "not . . . longer than necessary" or the factors that are to be taken into account. However, as this principle is directed to the keeping of data, it is difficult to see how disclosure under the Freedom of Information Act 2000 could by itself involve a contravention of the principle.

(6) *Sixth Principle*: Personal data must be processed in accordance with a data subject's rights under the Data Protection Act 1998. Paragraph 8 of Pt II of Sch.1 explains that this principle is only to be regarded as having been contravened by failing to supply information in accordance with s.7 or by failing to comply with a notice under s.10(1), 11(1) or 12(1). The only potential contravention of this principle by a disclosure under the Freedom of Information Act 2000 would be where a data subject has previously written to the public authority as data controller requiring it to cease, or not begin, processing personal information in respect of which he is the data subject on the ground that that processing would cause or would be likely to cause substantial damage or distress to him or another which is unwarranted.

(7) *Seventh Principle*: Appropriate technical and organisational measures must be taken against unauthorised or unlawful processing of personal data and against accidental loss or destruction of, or damage to, personal data. This is further explained in paras 9 to 12 of Pt II of Sch.1. This underscores the focus of the seventh principle, which is the taking of technical and organisational measures to safeguard personal data. Again, it is difficult to see how disclosure under the Freedom of Information Act 2000 could by itself involve a contravention of the principle.

(8) *Eighth Principle*: Personal data must not be transferred to a country or territory outside the European Economic Area[56] unless that country or territory ensures an adequate level of protection of the rights and freedoms of data subjects in relation to the processing of personal data. This principle is further explained in paras 13 to 15 of Pt II of Sch.1. This, too, is unlikely to have any particular relevance to a disclosure under the Freedom of Information Act 2000.

The conditions in Schedule 2 of the Data Protection Act 1998

24–012 As noted above, the first principle requires personal data to be processed fairly and lawfully, and prohibits their processing (which would include disclosure to a third party) unless one of a number of specific conditions is met.[57] So far as potentially relevant to a disclosure under the Freedom of Information Act 2000, the conditions are:

1. That the data subject has given his consent to the processing;
2. .....
3. That the processing is necessary for compliance with any legal obligation to which the data controller is subject, other than an obligation imposed by contract.
4. .....
5. That the processing is necessary-
   - (a) for the administration of justice;
   - (b) for the exercise of any functions conferred on any person by or under any enactment;
   - (c) for the exercise of any functions of the Crown, a Minister of the Crown or a government department; or
   - (d) for the exercise of any other functions of a public nature exercised in the public interest by any person.

[56] Comprising the 15 Member States, Norway, Iceland and Liechtenstein. Art.25(1) of the Directive imposes a stricter prohibition on any transfer outside the European Union.

[57] Data Protection Act 1998, s.4, Sch.1.

6. (1) That the processing is necessary for the purposes of legitimate interests pursued by the data controller or by the third party or parties to whom the data are disclosed, except where the processing is unwarranted in any particular case by reason of prejudice to the rights and freedoms or legitimate interests of the data subject.

(2) ....

The first condition is straightforward enough. The third condition raises a conundrum. It will be seen, then, that whilst s.40 of the Freedom of Information Act 2000 potentially renders information exempt information (thereby removing that information from the legal obligation to which the public authority/data controller would otherwise be subject by s.1(1)) on the basis of contravention of a data protection principle, contravention of the first such principle itself potentially turns upon whether disclosure is necessary for compliance with a statutory obligation (which of course may include a disclosure required by the Freedom of Information Act 2000). A similar conundrum may be thought to arise in relation to the fifth condition.[58]

The conditions in Schedule 3 of the Data Protection Act 1998

Under the first data protection principle, where the data being processed are "sensitive personal data,"[59] they must not be processed unless at least one of the conditions in Sch.3 of the Data Protection Act 1998 is also met. So far as potentially relevant to a disclosure under the Freedom of Information Act 2000, the conditions are: 24–013

1. That the data subject has given his explicit consent to the processing of the personal data.
2. .....
3. The processing is necessary—

   (a) in order to protect the vital interests of the data subject or another person, in a case where—

[58] In order to be "necessary" the disclosure must be proportionate in the sense applicable to Art.8 of the ECHR: see *R. (on the application of Ellis) v Chief Constable of the Essex Police* [2003] EWHC 1321 (Admin) Div Ct at [29].

[59] Which, under s.2 of the Data Protection Act 1998, means personal data consisting of information as to: (a) the racial or ethnic origin of the data subject; (b) his political opinions; (c) his religious beliefs or other beliefs of a similar nature; (d) whether he is a member of a trade union (within the meaning of the Trade Union and Labour Relations (Consolidation) Act 1992); (e) his physical or mental health or condition; (f) his sexual life; (g) the commission or alleged commission by him of any offence; or (h) any proceedings for any offence committed or alleged to have been committed by him, the disposal of such proceedings or the sentence of any court in such proceedings.

(i) consent cannot be given by or on behalf of the data subject; or

(ii) the data controller cannot reasonably be expected to obtain the consent of the data subject;

or

(b) in order to protect the vital interests of another person, in a case where consent by or on behalf of the data subject has been unreasonably withheld.

4. ....

5. The information contained in the personal data has been made public as a result of steps deliberately taken by the data subject.

6. The processing—

(a) is necessary for the purpose of, or in connection with, any legal proceedings (including prospective legal proceedings);

(b) is necessary for the purpose of obtaining legal advice; or

(c) is otherwise necessary for the purposes of establishing, exercising or defending legal rights.

7(1). The processing is necessary-

(a) ...

(b) for the exercise of any functions conferred on any person by or under an enactment; or

(c) for the exercise of any functions of the Crown, a Minister of the Crown or a government department.

8–9. ....

10. The personal data are processed in circumstances specified in an order made by the Secretary of State for the purposes of this paragraph.

The condition in para.7(1) raises the same conundrum as is raised by conditions 3 and 5 in the second Schedule.[60] A further tier of complexity is introduced by para.10. Pursuant to this paragraph an Order has been passed[61] setting out ten circumstances in which sensitive personal data may be processed. These broadly relate to processing that is necessary for:

— preventing or detecting any unlawful act;
— protecting the public against certain improper conduct or maladministration;
— providing confidential counselling, advice or support;

[60] See para.24–012.

[61] The Data Protection (Processing of Sensitive Personal Data) Order 2000 (SI 2000/417). The exemptions introduce a requirement of "the substantial public interest."

— carrying on insurance business or administering occupational pension schemes;
— monitoring equality of opportunity;
— carrying on political activities by registered political parties;
— research;
— exercising functions conferred on constables by law.

Working it through, if one of the exemptions in the Order is applicable, then para.10 of Sch.3 will apply (so that one of the conditions in Sch.3 will have been met for the purposes of the first data protection principle), disclosure will accordingly be exempt from the data protection principle, disclosure under the Freedom of Information Act 2000 will accordingly not breach a data protection principle, and the exemption under the 2000 Act will not apply. Again, therefore, the odd consequence is that the applicability of one of the exemptions in the Order has the effect of increasing the likelihood of disclosure under the Freedom of Information Act 2000.[62]

Second requirement, second alternative: disclosure would contravene section 10 of the Data Protection Act 1998

The second alternative also only applies where the information falls within any of paras (a) to (d) of the definition of "data" in s.1(1) of the Data Protection Act 1998.[63] Provided that the first requirement is also met, where disclosure of the information to a member of the public would contravene the right to prevent processing likely to cause damage or distress under s.10 of the Data Protection Act,[64] that information will be rendered exempt information under the Freedom of Information Act 2000.[65] The right to prevent such disclosure is inchoate until such time as the individual has served a written notice on the data controller and a reasonable time has elapsed.[66] However, in the case of the duty to confirm or deny, the exclusion applies to all categories of data: the s.33A exemption is to be disregarded for that purpose.[67] Both the exemption and the exclusion are qualified,[68] so that the public authority is required to weigh the public interests in order to determine what the applicant's rights are. 24–014

[62] But see para.24–016.
[63] The limiting of this alternative to the first four categories of data reflects the position under s.33A of the Data Protection Act 1998, by virtue of which s.10 does not apply to manual data held by public authorities.
[64] This right is disapplied where any of the conditions in paras 1 to 4 of Sch.2 to the Data Protection Act 1998 is met: see s.10(2)(a) of that Act.
[65] Freedom of Information Act 2000, s.40(3)(a)(ii); Freedom of Information (Scotland) Act 2002, s.38(2)(a)(ii).
[66] Data Protection Act 1998, s.10(1).
[67] Freedom of Information Act 2000, s.40(5)(b)(i). This does not apply to Scotland.
[68] Freedom of Information Act 2000, s.2; Freedom of Information (Scotland) Act 2002, s.2(2)(e).

Second requirement, third alternative: manual data held by public authorities

24–015 Information that does not fall within any of paras (a)–(d) of the definition of "data" in s.1(1) of the Data Protection Act 1998, but does fall within para.(e) of that definition, is termed "manual data."[69] The second exemption in s.40 of the Freedom of Information Act 2000 deals separately with the second requirement so far as manual data held by public authorities are concerned.[70] This difference in treatment arises out of the fact that manual data held by public authorities are exempted as a class from a number of the data protection principles by s.33A of the Data Protection Act 1998. So far as manual data are concerned, the position is the same as the first alternative[71] save that the exemptions in s.33A(1) of the Data Protection Act 1998 (which are peculiar to manual data)[72] are disregarded.

Second requirement, fourth alternative: other Data Protection Act 1998 exemptions

20–016 Information falling within any of the paragraphs of the definition of "data" is exempt information (and the duty to confirm or deny is excluded) if it would be exempt from the corresponding provision of the Data Protection Act 1998.[73] In other words, if, under the Data Protection Act 1998, data are by virtue of any provision in Pt IV of that Act exempt from the data subject's right to have the personal data communicated to him,[74] then the second requirement of the second exemption in s.40 of the Freedom of Information Act 2000 will be satisfied. And if, under the Data Protection Act 1998, data are by virtue of any provision in Pt IV of that Act exempt from the data subject's right to be informed whether personal data are being processed by the data controller, then the duty to confirm or deny does not arise in relation to the information that constitutes those data. Both the exemption and the exclusion are qualified.[75]

---

69 See para.4–013.

70 Freedom of Information Act 2000, s.40 (3)(a)(i) and (3)(b) respectively; Freedom of Information (Scotland) Act 2002, s.38(2)(a)(i) and (2)(b) respectively.

71 Set out at paras 24–009 to 24–013.

72 See para.4–062.

73 Freedom of Information Act 2000, s.40(4) and 40(5)(b)(ii) respectively; Freedom of Information (Scotland) Act 2002, s.38(3). It is thought that the reference to "*either* the first condition *or* the second condition" in s.40(2)(b) is for the purpose of emphasis, rather than to require that one, but not both, conditions be satisfied. The corresponding rights are, respectively, the subject's right to have the data communicated to him under s.(1)(c) and his right to be informed whether data of which he is the subject are being processed under s.7(1)(a).

74 As to which, see paras 4–051 to 4–076.

75 Freedom of Information Act 2000, ss.2, 40(4), (5)(b)(ii); Freedom of Information (Scotland) Act 2002, ss.2 and 38(3).

CHAPTER 25

Confidential Information

1. INFORMATION PROVIDED IN CONFIDENCE

Introduction

25–001 By s.41(1) of the Freedom of Information Act 2000 information is rendered exempt information where it was obtained by a public authority from any other person (including another public authority)[1] and the disclosure of the information to the public (otherwise than under the Act) by the public authority holding it would constitute a breach of confidence actionable by that or any other person.[2]

[1] But see para.25–003.

[2] Freedom of Information Act 2000, s.41(1); Freedom of Information (Scotland) Act 2002, s.36(2). Under the Data Protection Act 1998, there is an exemption for confidential references, but otherwise no exemption for confidential information: Data Protection Act 1998, s.37, Sch. 7, para. 1, and see para.4–067.

Similarly, the duty to confirm or deny does not arise if, or to the extent that, a confirmation or denial that the public authority holds the information specified in the request would (apart from the Act) constitute an actionable breach of confidence.[3] The exemption and the exclusion of the duty to confirm or deny are absolute.[4] Accordingly, disapplication of the duty to disclose and of the duty to confirm or deny does not expressly depend upon a balancing of the public interest in maintaining the exemption (or in excluding the duty to confirm or deny) against the public interest in disclosure (or in disclosing whether the public authority holds the requested information).[5] However, a consideration of the public interest is required to determine whether disclosure would constitute an actionable breach of confidence, as there is a public interest defence to any common law claim for breach of confidence. In addition, where government secrets are concerned, the Crown is not entitled to restrain disclosure or to obtain redress on confidentiality grounds unless it can establish that disclosure has damaged or would be likely to damage the public interest.[6] For these reasons, although the wording of the Act itself does not require any such evaluation to be made, the applicability of s.41 will involve in each instance some consideration of the public interest in disclosure and the public interest in maintaining the confidence. A similar exemption for confidential information is to be found in each of the comparative jurisdictions.[7]

Information obtained from another

Because the exemption only applies to information obtained by the public authority from another person it has no application to the public authority's 25–002

[3] Freedom of Information Act 2000, s.41(2): see further paras 25–021, 25–034 and 25–038. In relation to Scotland, see para.1–025(1).

[4] Freedom of Information Act 2000, s.2(3)(g); Freedom of Information (Scotland) Act 2002, s.2(2)(c). Presumably because consideration of the public interest is inherent in determining whether there is an actionable breach of confidence.

[5] Freedom of Information Act 2000, s.2(1)–(2).

[6] *Attorney-General v Guardian Newspapers Ltd (No.2)* [1990] 1 A.C. 109, 256, 265, 270, 282 and 293. See further para.25–018.

[7] In the United States, the Freedom of Information Act, 1966, 5 USC § 552(b)(4), exempts from disclosure records or information obtained from a person that is confidential: see para.2–008(4). The Freedom of Information Act 1982 (Cth of Australia), s.45, provides an exemption where the disclosure of the requested document would represent a breach of confidence other than that of the Commonwealth: see para.2–015(20). In New Zealand, the Official Information Act 1982, ss. 9(2)(b)(ii) and 27(1)(c), the Local Government Official Information and Meetings Act 1987, ss. 7(2)(b)(ii) and 26(1)(c) and the Privacy Act 1993, s.29(1)(b) provide a qualified exemption where the non-disclosure is required to protect information which is subject to an obligation of confidence: see para.2–023(2). The Access to Information Act (Canada), s.16(1)(c), provides a mandatory exemption for financial, commercial, scientific or technical information received in confidence from a third party: see para.2–031(5). The Freedom of Information Act 1997 (Ireland), provides a mandatory exemption where the requested record contains information given to the public body in confidence or the disclosure of which would constitute a breach of confidence: see para.2–039(5).

own information. The public authority therefore cannot rely upon the exemption as a basis for refusing to disclose information that it has itself created.

Claims between government departments

25–003 The effect of s.81 of the Freedom of Information Act 2000[8] is that, in general, the disclosure by one government department of information originating from another government department is not to be regarded as giving rise to an actionable breach of confidence, and so will fall outside the scope of the exemption. The reason for this is that, although s.81(1) provides that for the purposes of the Act each government department is to be treated as a person separate from any other government department, s.81(2) goes on to provide that s.81(1) does not enable:

(a) a government department which is not a Northern Ireland department to claim for the purposes of s.41(1)(b) that the disclosure of any information by it would constitute a breach of confidence actionable by any other government department (not being a Northern Ireland department); or

(b) a Northern Ireland department to claim for those purposes that the disclosure of information by it would constitute a breach of confidence actionable by any other Northern Ireland department.

As s.81(2) does not apply to information provided by a Northern Ireland department to a government department, and vice versa, the disclosure of such information may constitute an actionable breach of confidence, and it may fall within the scope of the exemption. This appears to have been the intention of the legislature. If the information supplied by a government department originates from a third party (in other words, not another government department), then, subject to any loss of confidentiality resulting from the transmission between departments, it will retain the confidentiality it had when held by the transmitting department.

The meaning of "actionable"

25–004 The exemption applies only to any disclosure by the public authority holding the information which would constitute a breach of confidence "actionable" by the person who provided the information to that authority or by any other person.[9]

[8] There is no equivalent under the Freedom of Information (Scotland) Act 2002.

[9] One possible reason for the inclusion of the word "actionable" was to avoid the uncertainties which the equivalent provision in the Freedom of Information Act 1982 (Cth of Aust) encountered before its amendment: see para.2–015(20).

One possible meaning of the word "actionable" is that it will be satisfied whenever the circumstances afford "grounds for an action at law."[10] If that meaning were applied in the present context, the exemption would appear to be available wherever there is in existence a claim for breach of confidence which satisfies the test of "real prospect of success" or that affords grounds for resisting the striking out of a statement of case.[11] Another possible interpretation is that "actionable" means a breach of confidence that satisfies the essential elements for a successful breach of confidence claim,[12] but without a consideration of whether any of the public interest defences to the claim would defeat it.[13] However, during the introduction of the Act into Parliament, Lord Falconer of Thoroton, Minister of State at the Cabinet Office, advised Parliament that an "actionable breach" meant one that affords grounds for a claim for breach of confidence that will succeed: in other words, one that "would be upheld by the courts."[14] This is in line with the suggestion of the Queensland Information Commissioner[15] who, in considering a like-worded provision, said that the test of exemption is to be evaluated:

> "by reference to a hypothetical legal action in which there is a clearly identified [claimant], possessed of appropriate standing to bring a suit to enforce an obligation of confidence said to be owed to that [claimant], in possession or control of the agency or the Minister faced with an application for access."

Under each approach, the wording of the section points to a consideration of the elements of the common law claim for breach of confidence. It also requires consideration of the grounds on which such a claim may be defeated.

[10] *Oxford English Dictionary*. That is, for example, the sense in which the word is used in the head note to *Stephens v Avery* [1988] Ch.449; [1988] 2 All E.R. 477, [1988] F.S.R. 510, in which Browne-Wilkinson V.C. refused to strike out a statement of case complaining of the misuse of information relating to a lesbian sexual relationship between the claimant and another woman, on the basis that it was arguable that the claimant's confidant and the editor and publisher of a newspaper to whom the confidant had imparted the information were bound by a duty of confidence with regard to the information.

[11] Under CPR r.3.4; or for resisting a claim for summary judgment under CPR r.24. A claim satisfies that test if it is not merely fanciful: *Swain v Hillman* [2001] 1 All E.R. 91; *Kraft v London Borough of Camden* (2001) 3 L.G.R. 37. In *Three Rivers District Council v Bank of England (No.3)* [2001] UKHL 16; [2001] 2 All E.R. 513 Lord Hope of Craighead observed that: "The difference between a test which asks the question 'is the claim bound to fail?' and one which asks the question 'does the claim have a real prospect of success?' is not easy to determine."

[12] See para.25–006.

[13] See para.25–014.

[14] House of Lords, *Hansard*, Vol.617, October 17, 2000, col.92; Vol.618, October 25, 2000, col.416; Vol.619, November 14, 2000, col.175 .

[15] *Re B and Brisbane North Regional Health Authority* [1994] 1 Q.A.R. 279, 296.

The sources of obligations of confidentiality

25–005 Obligations of confidence at common law may be express or implied.[16] It is arguable that an express contractual duty of confidence carries more weight, at least when balanced against the restriction of the right of freedom of expression, than an implied duty of confidentiality.[17] In addition, the scope of express and implied obligations may, of course, be different. In *Balston Ltd v Headline Filters Ltd*,[18] for example, Scott J. observed in the context of contracts of employment:

> "... the criteria that determine whether or not an express covenant in a contract of employment restricting the use or disclosure of particular information after the determination of the employment is enforceable are very different from the criteria that determine whether or not an obligation restricting the use or disclosure of that information can be implied into the contract. The implied obligation will always, I think be unlimited in time and probably in area as well .... If the information sought to be protected is not fit for protection, unlimited by time or area, it is very difficult to see how protection can be supplied by an implied term. On the other hand, an express covenant against use or disclosure is very likely to be limited both as to time and as to area."

The essential elements of an actionable breach of confidence

25–006 The conventional starting point for considering the nature and scope of the duty of confidentiality remains[19] the three-fold test identified in the judgment of Megarry J. in *Coco v A N Clark (Engineers) Ltd*[20]:

> "In my judgment, three elements are normally required if, apart from contract, a case of breach of confidence is to succeed. First, the information itself, in the words of Lord Greene M.R. in *Saltman Engineering Co Ltd v*

[16] For a more general treatment of the law of confidentiality, see: R.G. Toulson and C.M. Phipps, *Confidentiality* (Sweet & Maxwell, London, 1996); F. Gurry, *Breach of Confidence* (Oxford University Press, Oxford, 1984); B.C. Reid, *Confidentiality and the Law* (Waterlow, London, 1986); L. Clarke (ed.), *Confidentiality and the Law* (Lloyd's of London, London, 1990); S. Ricketson, *The Law of Intellectual Property: Copyright, Designs & Confidential Information* (2nd ed., Law Book Company, Sydney, 1999); P. Lavery, *Commercial Secrets: the action for Breach of Confidence in Ireland* (Round Hall, Dublin, 1996).

[17] *Campbell v Frisbee* [2002] EWCA Civ 1374; [2003] E.M.L.R. 3, para.22, contrasting *London Regional Transport v Mayor of London* [2001] EWCA Civ 1491; [2003] E.M.L.R. 4, para.46 and *Attorney-General v Barker* [1990] 3 All E.R. 257 at 260.

[18] [1987] F.S.R. 330 at 348.

[19] See *R. v Department of Health, Ex p. Source Informatics Ltd* [2001] Q.B. 424; [2001] 1 All E.R. 786, para.14.

[20] [1969] R.P.C. 41 at 47. See more recently: *Murray v Yorkshire Fund Managers Ltd* [1998] 1 W.L.R. 96, CA; *A v B plc* [2001] 1 W.L.R. 2341; [2002] 1 All E.R. 449.

Campbell Engineering Co Ltd,[21] must 'have the necessary quality of confidence about it'. Secondly, that information must have been imparted in circumstances importing an obligation of confidence. Thirdly, there must be an unauthorised use of that information to the detriment of the party communicating it."

In *Attorney-General v Guardian Newspapers Ltd (No.2)*[22] Lord Goff of Chieveley stated the broad, general principle (non-definitively) as being:

> "that a duty of confidence arises when confidential information comes to the knowledge of a person (the confidant) in circumstances where he has notice, or is held to have agreed, that the information is confidential, with the effect that it would be just in all the circumstances that he should be precluded from disclosing the information to others . . . in the vast majority of cases . . . the duty of confidence will arise from a transaction or relationship between the parties . . . But it is well settled that a duty of confidence may arise in equity independently of such cases . . ."

Underlying public policy considerations

The jurisdiction is founded on obligations of conscience, and its essential basis is the duty to act in good faith.[23] It also rests on the notion that there is a public interest in the maintenance of confidences, and to this extent it is governed by public policy considerations. These public policy considerations mean that regard must be had to countervailing public interests. One such countervailing public interest is that of freedom of trade. Concern for this interest, coupled with the difficulties for employees of identifying what information of their employers is truly confidential, as opposed to forming part of the general stock of knowledge of those engaged in any particular line of business, has led the courts to observe that the proper way for employers to protect themselves: 25–007

> "would be by exacting covenants from their employees restricting their field of activity after they have left their employment, not by asking the court to extend the general equitable doctrine to prevent breaking confidence beyond all reasonable bounds."[24]

Another countervailing public interest is that of freedom of expression. As Lord Keith of Kinkel said in *Attorney-General v Guardian Newspapers Ltd (No.2)*[25]:

[21] [1948] 65 R.P.C. 203 at 215; [1963] 3 All E.R. 413 (Note).
[22] [1990] 1 A.C. 109 at 281.
[23] See the discussion of the relevant principles of law by Bingham L.J. in *Attorney-General v Guardian Newspapers Ltd (No.2)* [1990] 1 A.C. 109 at 214–216.
[24] *Printers & Finishers Ltd v Holloway* [1965] 1 W.L.R. 1 at 6; [1963] 3 All E.R. 731.
[25] [1990] 1 A.C. 109 at 256.

> "The general rule is that anyone is entitled to communicate anything he pleases to anyone else, by speech or in writing or in any other way. That rule is limited by the law of defamation and other restrictions similar to those mentioned in Article 10 of [the Convention]. All those restrictions are imposed in the light of considerations of public interest such as to countervail the public interest in freedom of expression."

There is also a public interest in promoting the accountability of government. It is this consideration that underpins the distinction made by Lord Scott of Foscote between the principles that ought to represent the foundation of the law of confidence.[26] Lord Scott expressed the view that, on the one hand, there is a principle that private persons are entitled to protection against disclosure without their consent of confidential information about themselves and their activities in the absence of a sufficient public interest reason for disclosure of such information; but, on the other hand, there is a principle that the various manifestations of government are not entitled to protection against disclosure of information about themselves and their activities unless there is a sufficient public interest requiring such information to be protected from disclosure.[27]

The first element: the necessary quality of confidence

25–008 The necessary quality of confidence is that "the information must not be something which is public property and public knowledge."[28] In other words, in order to be confidential the information must have about it "the basic attribute of inaccessibility."[29] Information ceases to have this quality once it has entered the public domain, which means "no more than that the information in question is so generally accessible that, in all the circumstances, it cannot be regarded as confidential."[30] Whether information is so generally accessible that it is not confidential is a matter of fact and degree. Relevant considerations include the realities of accessibility, the nature of the information, and the lapse of time since dissemination took place. For example, information in a library book filed under a specialised heading or on the website of a government department which would not be accessed without some degree of background knowledge may not be "realistically accessible" or properly regarded as "public knowledge."[31] In addition, where personal information is concerned "the fact

[26] See Lord Scott's essay "Confidentiality" in *Freedom of Information—Essays in Honour of Sir David Williams*, (OUP, Oxford, 2000) pp.267–274.

[27] See paras 15–006 to 15–007 for a treatment of the public interest considerations weighing in favour of disclosure.

[28] *Saltman Engineering Co Ltd v Campbell Engineering Co Ltd* [1948] 65 R.P.C. 203 at 215.

[29] *Attorney-General v Guardian Newspapers Ltd (No.2)* [1990] 1 A.C. 109 at 215.

[30] See *Attorney-General v Guardian Newspapers (No.2) Ltd* [1990] 1 A.C. 109 at 282.

[31] *Attorney-General v Greater Manchester Newspapers Ltd* [2001] T.L.R. 668; (2001) 145 S.J.L.B. 279, paras 33–34.

that a matter has once been in the public domain cannot prevent its resurrection, possibly many years later, from being an invasion of privacy. Whether in such a case there is an unwarranted invasion of privacy is a matter of fact and degree."[32] As discussed below,[33] this type of invasion of privacy forms part of the developing law of confidence. As this consideration is unlikely to be held to be applicable to commercial information, to this extent the courts may be inclined to afford greater protection to personal information than to commercial information. As against that, however, the decided cases concerning personal information contain statements to the effect that a person who has placed or allowed to be placed in the public domain information concerning a certain aspect of his private life may not be entitled to complain about the publication of other information concerning the same area—or, possibly, in an extreme case, any area—of his private life.[34] There is faint echo of this approach in the decided cases concerning commercial confidences,[35] where "within the law of confidentiality in its normal reach" the exceptions to protection of (among other things) public domain are specific to the material in question.[36] To that extent, therefore, it appears that the courts may be prepared to afford less protection to personal information than to commercial information. But in *Campbell v MGN Ltd*[37] the Court of Appeal sounded a note of caution about the extent to which the courts will be prepared to adopt this approach to the ambit of the public domain exception in cases involving personal information:

> "When Lord Woolf CJ spoke of the public having 'an understandable and so a legitimate interest in being told' information, even including trivial facts, about a public figure, he was not speaking of private facts which a fair-minded person would consider it offensive to disclose. That is clear from his subsequent commendation of the guidance on striking a balance between Article 8 and Article 10 rights provided by the Council of Europe Resolution 1165 of 1998.
>
> For our part we would observe that the fact that an individual has achieved prominence on the public stage does not mean that his private life can be laid bare by the media. We do not see why it should necessarily be in the public interest that an individual who has been adopted as a role model, without seeking this distinction, should be demonstrated to have feet of clay."[38]

[32] *R. v BCC Ex p. Granada Television Ltd* [1995] E.M.L.R. 163 at 168.

[33] At paras 25–022 to 25–027.

[34] *Theakston v MGN Ltd* [2002] EWHC 137; [2002] E.M.L.R. 398, para.68; *A v B plc* [2002] EWCA Civ 337; [2003] Q.B. 195; [2002] 2 All E.R. 545, para.11(xii); *Lennon v News Group Newspapers Ltd* [1978] F.S.R. 573, 574–575.

[35] But see *Jockey Club v Buffham* [2002] EWHC 1866; [2003] Q.B. 462 at 479 where Gray J. said at para.57(v) with regard to certain press releases issued by the claimant that "The effect of placing such material in the public domain does in my view result in some loosening of the ties of confidence."

[36] *Theakston v MGN Ltd* [2002] EWHC 137; [2002] E.M.L.R. 398, paras 65–66.

[37] [2002] EWCA Civ 1373; [2003] Q.B. 633; [2003] 1 All E.R. 224.

[38] At paras 40–41.

The effect of a disclosure upon the duty of confidence

25–009 The basic principle is that the duty of confidence is imposed not only on the person to whom information is confided but also on any third party who acquires the information and who knows that it is subject to an obligation of confidence. In this context, the question arises whether a recipient who is bound by an obligation of confidence can rely upon disclosure to the world at large, including his own disclosure, to say that he is no longer bound by that obligation. On one view, he can, because the consequence of any disclosure to the world at large, including his own disclosure, is that "the secret, as a secret, has ceased to exist."[39] The contrary view is that of the majority in *Schering Chemicals Ltd v Falkman Ltd*.[40] In that case Shaw L.J. said:

> "It is not the law that where confidentiality exists it is terminated or eroded by adventitious publicity. Nor is the correlative duty to preserve that confidentiality. The public interest may demand that the duty be gainsaid; but it cannot be arbitrarily cast aside. An order of a court of law may relieve the confidant of the burden of secrecy and may, after due inquiry, require him to reveal the subject matter of the confidence; but it is not to be sloughed at will for self-interest."[41]

The significance of this approach to the exemption contained in s.41 of the Freedom of Information Act 2000 is that it cannot be assumed that the fact that information in the possession of the public authority that is subject to an obligation of confidence has been placed in the public domain releases the public authority from that obligation—particularly in the event that the information has been placed in the public domain in breach of the public authority's own obligation. The disclosure or further disclosure by the public authority of the information that it holds may still be actionable against it, in spite of the fact that the information is already in the public domain.

The second element: the circumstances of acquisition

25–010 Plainly, where the person providing the information to the public authority expressly states that it is being provided in confidence, that will usually suffice to satisfy the second element.[42] However, Lord Goff's non-definitive formulation of the broad general principle makes clear that it is not essential that there should be a pre-existing relationship between the person seeking to enforce the

---

[39] *O. Mustad & Son v Dosen (Note)* [1964] 1 W.L.R. 109, 111.
[40] [1982] Q.B. 1; [1981] 2 All E.R. 321.
[41] At 26–27, and see Templeman L.J. at 37–38. See also *Exchange Telegraph Co Ltd v Central News Ltd* [1897] 2 Ch.48.
[42] As in *Dunford & Elliott v Johnson & Firth Brown* [1978] F.S.R. 143.

duty and the person to whom the information was disclosed. In this regard, the statements of Laws J. in *Hellewell v Chief Constable of Derbyshire*[43] and of Butler Sloss P. in *Venables v News Group Newspapers Ltd*[44] were echoed in the arguments of the UK Government in *Earl Spencer v United Kingdom*[44A] and in the judgments of the Court of Appeal in *Douglas v Hello! Ltd*[44B], and, at least so far as personal information in concerned, appear to have been provisionally endorsed by Lord Hoffmann in *Wainwright v Home Office*[45], who summed the matter up as follows:

> "The claimants placed particular reliance upon the judgment of Sedley L.J. in *Douglas v Hello! Ltd*[45A]. Sedley L.J. drew attention to the way in which the development of the law of confidence had attenuated the need for a relationship of confidence between the recipient of the confidential information and the person from whom it was obtained—a development which enabled the UK Government to persuade the European Human Rights Commission in *Earl Spencer v United Kingdom*[45B] that English law of confidence provided an adequate remedy to restrain the publication of private information about the applicants' marriage and medical condition and photographs taken with a telephoto lens. These developments showed that the basic value protected by the law in such cases was privacy. Sedley L.J. said, at p.1001, para.126:
>
> > 'What a concept of privacy does, however, is accord recognition to the fact that the law has to protect not only those people whose trust has been abused but those who simply find themselves subjected to an unwanted intrusion into their personal lives. The law no longer needs to construct an artificial relationship of confidentiality between intruder

43 [1995] 1 W.L.R. 804; [1994] 4 All E.R. 473, where it was said:
"If someone with a telephoto lens were to take from a distance and with no authority a picture of another engaged in some private act, his subsequent disclosure of the photograph would, in my judgment, as surely amount to a breach of confidence as if he had found or stolen a letter or diary in which the act was recounted and proceeded to publish it. In such a case, the law would protect what might reasonably be called a right of privacy, although the name accorded to the cause of action would be breach of confidence."

44 [2001] Fam. 430, [2001] 1 All E.R. 908, where it was held that the law of confidence could, exceptionally, extend to cover information as to the identity or whereabouts of individuals where its disclosure would put them at risk of serious injury or death. Butler Slass P. said at para.81:
"The duty of confidence may arise in equity independently of a transaction or relationship between parties. In this case it would be a duty placed upon the media. A duty of confidence does already arise when confidential information comes to the knowledge of the media, in circumstances in which the media have notice of its confidentiality. An example is the medical reports of a private individual which are recognised as being confidential."

44A [1998] 25 E.H.R.R. CD 105.

44B [2001] Q.B. 967.

45 [2003] 3 W.L.R. 1137, at 1145 paras 28–29, giving the leading speech with which the other members of the House of Lords agreed.

45A [2001] Q.B. 967.

45B [1998] 25 E.H.R.R. CD 105.

> and victim: it can recognise privacy itself as a legal principle drawn from the fundamental value of personal autonomy.'
>
> I read these remarks as suggesting that, in relation to the publication of personal information obtained by intrusion, the common law of breach of confidence has reached the point at which a confidence relationship has beome unnecessary. As the underlying value protected is privacy, the action might as well be renamed invasion of privacy. 'To say this' said Sedley L.J., at p.1001, para.125, 'is in my belief to say little, save by way of a label, that our courts have not said already over the years.'"

It is thus also possible for information acquired by a public authority without anyone's consent (*e.g.* by telephone tapping) to be subject to an obligation of confidence.[46]

The third element: detriment

25–011 The better view is that it is an open question whether detriment to the claimant is an essential ingredient of an action for breach of confidence.[47] If detriment does need to be established, however, it may well constitute sufficient detriment to the confider that information is to be disclosed to persons whom he would prefer not to know of it.[48]

Limiting principles

25–012 In *Attorney-General v Guardian Newspapers (No.2) Ltd*[49] Lord Goff identified three limiting concepts to the broad general principle that he had stated. The first, that the principle of confidentiality does not apply to information which is generally accessible, has already been considered above.[50] The second is that the duty of confidence does not apply to information that is useless or trivial.[51] Although Lord Goff said that he did not need to develop this point, it has since assumed particular importance as a result of recent developments which have extended the law of confidence beyond its traditional boundaries and into the realms of intrusion into personal autonomy.[52] The third limiting concept

[46] *Francome v Mirror Group Newspapers Ltd* [1984] 1 W.L.R. 892; [1984] 2 All E.R. 408; *English and American Insurance Co Ltd v Herbert Smith* [1988] F.S.R. 232, but see also *Malone v Commissioner of Police of the Metropolis* [1979] Ch.344 at 375–376, [1979] 2 W.L.R. 700, [1979] 2 All E.R. 620.

[47] *Attorney-General v Guardian Newspapers Ltd (No.2)* [1990] 1 A.C. 109 at 281–282.

[48] *ibid.* at 255–256.

[49] [1990] 1 A.C. 109 at 282.

[50] See paras 25–008 to 25–009.

[51] This is dealt with at para.25–013.

[52] See further paras 25–022 to 25–027.

identified by Lord Goff is that in certain circumstances the public interest in maintaining confidence may be outweighed by the public interest in disclosure.[53]

Useless or trivial information

Where the information for which a claim for confidence is made is of a commercial nature, if the information is, from an objective standpoint, trivial or useless, that will defeat the claim. On the other hand, in cases involving the misuse or disclosure of personal or private information, the fact that the information in question is "trivial or useless" may not preclude the existence of an actionable breach of confidence. For example, information contained in a photograph taken with a long lens of someone carrying out an entirely mundane activity inside his own home may give rise to an actionable breach of confidence having regard to some or all of the following factors: the home is specifically mentioned in Art.8 of the Convention and has a particular status in the sphere of an individual's private life; the means by which the information was obtained; and the consideration that the information is recorded in permanent form and as an image.[53A] There seems no reason in principle why the fact that the information thus recorded is, objectively speaking, trivial and of no practical or commercial use should be fatal to an action for breach of confidence which embraces a reasonable expectation of privacy. It may be, however, that the correct analysis is that such information is not to be regarded as "trivial" because it is not trivial to the person whose privacy has been infringed. The decision of the European Court of Human Rights in *Peck v United Kingdom (Application No.44647/98)*[54] seems consistent with the approach suggested above, while at the same time providing some indication of how far-reaching the potential implications of Art.8 considerations for the law of confidence may be. In that case, the court held, among other things, as follows. First, 25–013

[53] This is dealt with at para.25–014.

[53A] For the particular significance which may be attached to photographs taken without consent see *R. v Broadcasting Standards Commission, Ex p. BBC (Liberty intervening)* [2001] Q.B. 885, [2000] 3 W.L.R. 1327, [2000] 3 All E.R. 989; *R. v Loveridge* [2001] EWCA Crim 973; *Theakston v MGN Ltd* [2002] EWHC 137, [2002] E.M.L.R. 398, paras 40–41.

[54] [2003] E.M.L.R. 15; (2003) 36 E.H.R.R. 41; 13 B.H.R.C. 669. Peck had been captured on closed circuit television when he had attempted suicide by cutting his wrists on a high street. Although the images used did not show the attempted suicide, they clearly identified Peck brandishing a kitchen knife in a public place. Although the police had attended the scene, Peck was not charged with any criminal offence. The images were used in a campaign to reflect the effectiveness of closed circuit television in combatting crime. No attempt was made to mask Peck's identity. He subsequently appeared on a number of television broadcasts to discuss the publications of the footage and photographs, but nevertheless complained to the relevant media commissions about the disclosures. Peck tried unsuccessfully to obtain judicial review of the local authority's disclosure. Before the European Court, Peck complained: (1) that the disclosure by a local authority of closed circuit television footage and photographs which had resulted in images of himself being published and broadcast on a local and national level was a breach of his right to respect for family and private life under Art.8; and (2) that it had been a breach of Art.13 in that no effective domestic remedy existed in relation to the violation of his Art.8 right.

private life is a broad term not susceptible to exhaustive definition but includes the right to establish and develop relationships with other human beings, such that there is a zone of interaction of a person with others, even in a public context, which may fall within the scope of "private life."[55] Secondly, disclosure of material to the public in a manner which could never have been foreseen may give rise to such an interference.[56] Thirdly, where photographs are concerned, it is relevant to consider whether they relate to private or public matters and whether they were envisaged for limited use or likely to be made available to the general public.[57] Fourthly, disclosure to an extent which far exceeds the exposure to the public at the time may also constitute a serious interference with the right to respect for private life.[58] Fifthly, Art.8, in conjunction with Art.13, requires effective protection to be granted against unwarranted interference with a person's private life.[59]

In *Wainwright v Home Office*[59A], however, when rejecting the argument that the decision in Peck's case demonstrated the need for a general tort of invasion of privacy, Lord Hoffmann said that in his opinion, "it shows no more that the need, in English law, for a system of control of the use of film from CCTV cameras which shows greater sensitivity to the feelings of people who happen to have been caught by the lens".

Public interest defence: the principle

25–014 Public interest is available as a defence[60] to claims for breach of confidence, and it is a general defence[61] not limited to the refusal of equitable relief.[62] The basic principles are that:

---

[55] para.57.
[56] para.60.
[57] para.61.
[58] para.62.
[59] para.78.
[59A] [2003] 3 W.L.R. 1137, at 1146 para.33.
[60] This is how the point is characterised in, for example, *London Regional Transport v Mayor of London* [2003] EWCA Civ 1491; [2003] E.M.L.R. 4, by Robert Walker L.J. at para.35. There is a school of thought that the true analysis is not so much that the public interest affords a defence but rather that the public interest principle is of relatively narrow application and that, where it does apply, it has the effect that no obligation of confidence arises at all. See, for example, R.G. Toulson and C.M. Phipps, *Confidentiality* (Sweet & Maxwell, London, 1996), para.6–11: "the true principle is not . . . that the court will permit a breach of confidence wherever it considers that disclosure would serve the public interest more than non-disclosure, but rather that no obligation of confidence exists in contract or in equity, in so far as the subject matter concerns a serious risk of public harm . . . and the alleged obligation would prevent disclosure appropriate to prevent such harm." This characterisation has usually been preferred by the Australian courts: *Corrs Pavey Whiting & Byrne v Collector of Customs (Vic)* (1987) 14 F.C.R. 434 at 451; 74 A.L.R. 428 at 445 *et seq.*; *Smith Kline & French Laboratories (Aust) Ltd v Secretary, Department of Community Services and Health* (1990) 22 F.C.R. 87 at 110, 95 A.L.R. 87 at 124.
[61] Although most of the reported cases have been concerned with the grant or refusal of an interlocutory injunction, it is submitted that the policy reasons given in the judgments apply with equal force to final injunctions and to pecuniary remedies.

(1) the public interest in disclosure may outweigh the public interest that confidences should be protected and the right of the claimant to protect his confidences;
(2) where the balancing exercise comes down in favour of disclosure, it may favour only limited disclosure—either in the form of disclosure to less than the world at large or in the form of partial disclosure; and
(3) in the era of the Human Rights Act 1998, the Court, as a public authority, must take into account the right to freedom of expression conferred by Art.10 of the Convention, which has the practical effect that any relief which interferes with that right must be justified as being no more than is necessary in a democratic society for the legitimate aim or aims pursued.[63]

In *Attorney-General v Guardian Newspapers (No.2)*[64] Lord Goff of Chieveley summed the matter up as follows:

> "The third limiting principle is of far greater importance. It is that, although the basis of the law's protection of confidence is that there is a public interest that confidences should be preserved and protected by the law, nevertheless that public interest may be outweighed by some other countervailing public interest which favours disclosure. This limitation may apply, as the learned judge pointed out, to all types of confidential information. It is this limiting principle which may require a court to carry out a balancing operation, weighing the public interest in maintaining confidence against a countervailing public interest favouring disclosure. Embraced within this limiting principle is, of course, the so called defence of iniquity. In origin, this principle was narrowly stated, on the basis that a man cannot be made 'the confidant of a crime or a fraud': see *Gartside v Outram*[65] per Sir William Page Wood V.C. But it is now clear that the principle extends to matters of which disclosure is required in the public interest: see *Beloff v Pressdram Ltd*,[66] per Ungoed-Thomas J, and *Lion Laboratories Ltd v Evans*[67] per Griffiths L.J. It does not however follow

[62] Indeed, it now seems clear that essentially the same defence is also available to a claim for infringement of copyright (which, unlike a claim for breach of confidence, is clearly a claim that is based on a property right), and that the existence and scope of the defence is informed and bolstered by free-speech considerations in view of the effective incorporation into English law of Art.10 by the Human Rights Act 1998: see *Hyde Park Residence Ltd v Yelland* [2001] Ch.143; *Ashdown v Telegraph Ltd* [2002] Ch.149.

[63] See *Imutran v Uncaged Campaigns Ltd* [2001] 2 All E.R. 385; [2001] E.M.L.R. 21, Sir Andrew Morritt V.C., paras 20–21.

[64] [1990] 1 A.C. 109 at 282.

[65] (1857) 26 L.J. Ch 113 at 114.

[66] [1973] 1 All E.R. 241 at 260.

[67] [1985] Q.B. 526 at 550. In that case, claims for breach of confidence and infringement of copyright were made in respect of documents taken by former employees which cast doubt on the accuracy of electronic breath testing equipment supplied by the claimant company to the police for the purpose of measuring the level of intoxication of motorists. Public interest was the only

> that the public interest will in such cases require disclosure to the media, or to the public by the media. There are cases in which a more limited disclosure is all that is required: see *Francome v Mirror Group Newspapers Ltd.*[68] A classic example of a case where limited disclosure is required is a case of alleged iniquity in the Security Service."

The circumstances in which a public interest defence to a breach of confidence may enjoy success can conveniently be considered under three headings, which may, of course, overlap: first, the public interest in the disclosure of iniquity; secondly, the public interest in the public not being misled; and, thirdly, the public interest in the disclosure of matters of public concern.

Public interest in the disclosure of iniquity

25–015 Although the defence of public interest is not confined to cases involving wrongdoing, that is the paradigm instance in which it operates. The courts have always refused to uphold the right to confidence when to do so would cover up wrongdoing: in the words of Wood V.C. in *Gartside v Outram*[69] there is "no confidence as to the disclosure of iniquity." In addition, in the era of the Human Rights Act 1998, such a public interest consideration may be an exception under Art.8(2) to the Art.8(1) right to respect for private and family life. The reason that exposure of wrongdoing should not be prevented, even if it is in breach of confidence, is that "no private obligations can dispense with that universal one which lies on every member of society to discover every design which may be formed contrary to the laws of the society to destroy the public welfare."[70] An allegation of wrongdoing will justify exposure in the public interest if it is a credible allegation from an apparently reliable source.[71]

Public interest in the public not being misled

25–016 There is also a public interest in the public not being misled. Typically, this principle comes into play if a public figure misleads the public, in which

defence argued in the Court of Appeal, which held that the public interest may afford just cause or excuse for breaking confidence or infringing copyright, and that there was on the facts sufficient just cause and excuse so that no interim injunction should be granted restraining use or disclosure. All three judges held that the defence was not limited to cases of wrongdoing on the part of the claimant, that the disclosure of iniquity was merely an instance of the essential just cause or excuse, and that the test is whether there is legitimate ground for supposing that it is in the public interest for disclosure to be made. See, in particular, Stephenson L.J. at 538.

[68] [1984] 1 W.L.R. 892.

[69] (1857) 26 L.J. Ch (N.S.) 113 at 114. The case is reported in differing terms in three other sets of reports: (1856) 3 Jur. (N.S.) 39, 5 W.R. 35 and 28 L.T. (O.S.) 120.

[70] *Annersley v Anglesea (Earl)* (1743) L.R. 5 Q.B. 317n; 17 State Tr. 1139, cited by Lord Denning M.R. in *Initial Services v Putterill* [1968] 1 Q.B. 396 at 405.

[71] *Attorney-General v Guardian Newspapers Ltd (No.2)* [1990] 1 A.C. 109 at 283.

circumstances the media may well be entitled to put the record straight.[72] The application of this principle on the facts of any particular case, and especially one involving the media, is, also, informed by free speech considerations. In *Campbell v MGN Ltd*,[73] for example, the Court of Appeal applied the reasoning of the European Court of Human Rights in *Fressoz and Roire v France*[74] in holding that:

> "the information published by [the newspaper] was justified in order to provide a factual account of [the claimant's] drug addiction that had the detail necessary to carry credibility. Provided that publication of particular confidential information is justifiable in the public interest, the journalist must be given reasonable latitude as to the manner in which that information is conveyed to the public or his Article 10 right to freedom of expression will be unnecessarily inhibited."

In the context of giving guidance as to grant of interim injunctions, the Court of Appeal has said that in many situations the public have an understandable and so legitimate interest in being told the information which can be taken into account by the Court in deciding on what side of the line a case falls; and that the Court must not ignore the fact that if newspapers do not publish information in which the public are interested, there will be fewer newspapers published which will not be in the public interest.[75] This is not to equate the public interest with what is of interest to the public (or the media), which would be wrong.[76] However, it does underline that there is a public interest in freedom of expression itself; and, although there is also a public as well as a private interest in the maintenance of confidences, this may mean that, at least in some cases, the public interest defence to the cause of action for breach of confidence should be interpreted more liberally and treated as having more strength and breadth in the post-Human Rights Act 1998 era than it did in the past.

---

[72] See, for example, *Woodward v Hutchins* [1977] 1 W.L.R. 760. See also *Theakston v MGN Ltd* [2002] EWHC 137; [2002] E.M.L.R. 22.

[73] [2003] Q.B. 633.

[74] (2001) 31 E.H.R.R. 2; 5 B.H.R.C. 654 at paras 63–64.

[75] See *A v B plc* [2003] Q.B. 195, para.11(xii). The Court of Appeal in *Campbell v MGN Ltd* [2003] Q.B. 633 later explained (at para.40) that this was not intended to refer to private facts which a fair-minded person would consider it offensive to disclose and (at para.41) that the fact that an individual has achieved prominence on the public stage does not mean that his private life can be laid bare by the media.

[76] See, *e.g.*, *Francome v Mirror Group Newspapers Ltd* [1984] 1 W.L.R. 892, Sir John Donaldson M.R. at 898: "The 'media', to use a term which comprises not only the newspapers, but also television and radio, are an essential foundation of any democracy. In exposing crime, anti-social behaviour and hypocrisy and in campaigning for reform and propagating the view of minorities, they perform an invaluable function. However, they are peculiarly vulnerable to the error of confusing the public interest with their own interest. Usually these interests march hand in hand, but not always. In the instant case, pending a trial, it is impossible to see what public interest would be served by publishing the contents of the tapes which would not equally be served by giving them to the police or to the Jockey Club. Any wider publication could only serve the interests of the 'Daily Mirror'."

Public interest in the disclosure of matters of public concern

25–017 In *Initial Services Ltd v Putterill*,[77] the Court of Appeal held, first, that the exception allowing disclosure of information and documents obtained by an employee in the course of his employment extended to any disclosure that was justified in the public interest and operated with regard to a claim in damages; and, second, that disclosure to the press can fall within the principle. In *Fraser v Evans*[78] Lord Denning M.R. said:

> "There are some things which are of such public concern that the newspapers, the Press, and, indeed, everyone is entitled to make known the truth and to make fair comment on it. This is an integral part of the right of free speech and expression. It must not be whittled away".

In *London Regional Transport v Mayor of London*[79] the Court of Appeal held that there was a public interest in enabling the general public (and especially the travelling public in London) to be informed of serious criticism from a responsible source of the value for money evaluation of the proposed public-private partnership involvement in the London Underground; and that this outweighed the preservation of commercial confidentiality in an interim report prepared by a firm of accountants which was based on commercially sensitive and confidential information that had been disclosed by private-sector bidders subject to express confidentiality agreements. An injunction to restrain the publication of a redacted version of that report—which, although interim in form, would in practice have irreversible consequences—was, accordingly, refused. The Court accepted the concession that there is a need for proportionality in any restraint of freedom of expression if the restraint is to be justifiable under Art.10(2) of the Convention.[80] Sedley L.J. suggested that the concept of proportionality that formed the basis for deciding a variety of Convention issues in accordance with the jurisprudence of the European Court of Human Rights enabled the elastic concept of whether a reasonable recipient's conscience would be troubled to be replaced by a structured inquiry:

> "Does the measure meet a recognised and pressing social need? Does it negate the primary right or restrict it more than is necessary? Are the reasons given for it logical? . . . for my part, I find it more helpful today to postulate a recipient who, being reasonable, runs through the proportionality checklist in order to anticipate what a court is likely to decide, and who adjusts his or her conscience and conduct accordingly".[81]

---

[77] [1968] 1 Q.B. 396.
[78] [1969] 1 Q.B. 349 at 363.
[79] [2003] EWCA Civ 1491; [2003] E.M.L.R. 4.
[80] Robert Walker L.J. at para.49.
[81] Sedley L.J. at paras 57–58.

In *Jockey Club v Buffham*,[82] Gray J. held that questions of the integrity and fairness of bookmaking to the betting public; the relationship of bookmakers to trainers and racing stables; and the effectiveness of the Jockey Club's regulatory role over the sport and industry of horseracing, are questions of proper and serious interest and concern to the public and, in particular, to the very many hundreds of thousands of people interested in horseracing, very many of whom will place bets from time to time. Accordingly, he ruled that the BBC should be allowed to broadcast information relating to such matters notwithstanding that it had been obtained from a "whistleblower" who divulged it to the BBC in breach of express contractual obligations.[83] Gray J. also had to consider and apply s.12(4) of the Human Rights Act 1988. In this regard, although they were not directly in point in that particular case, it is relevant to note the following matters. First, one of the matters that the Court is required by s.12(4)(b) of the Human Rights Act 1998 to take into account is the Press Complaints Commission Code of Conduct. Secondly, cl.3 of that Code is one of the clauses that is marked with an asterisk to indicate that it is subject to the public interest exception contained in that Code. Thirdly, the wording of cl.3(i) closely follows the wording of Art.8 of the Convention—such that the effect of cl.3 and the public interest exemption taken together is substantially the same as Art.8 of the Convention. Fourth, in accordance with that Code:

> "The public interest includes:
> (i) Detecting or exposing crime or serious misdemeanour.
> (ii) Protecting public health and safety.
> (iii) Preventing the public from being misled by some statement or action of an individual or organization".

Examples of cases where, at least at the interim stage, only limited disclosure was held to be justified in the public interest include *Francome v Mirror Group Newspapers Ltd*[84] and *Re a Company's Application*.[85] In *W v Edgell*[86] a consultant psychiatrist retained by the claimant to report on his state of mental health for the purposes of an application to a mental health review tribunal for

[82] [2003] Q.B. 462.

[83] In reaching this decision, Gray J. had regard to what the Court of Appeal had said in *Grobbelaar v News Group Newspapers Ltd* [2001] 2 All E.R. 437 at paras 47, 201 about the public interest in whether there was corruption in football, to what Morland J. had said in *Chandler v Buffham* [2002] EWHC 1426 on an earlier application for injunctive relief in relation to two of the documents with which the application before Gray J. was concerned, and to what had been said by Sir Thomas Bingham M.R. in *R. v Disciplinary Committee of the Jockey Club, Ex p. Aga Khan* [1993] 1 W.L.R. 909 at 912, 914.

[84] [1984] 1 W.L.R. 892 (injunction restraining until trial the publication in the media of allegations of breaches of the rules of racing varied to allow the defendants to seek permission to make disclosure to the Jockey Club and to the police).

[85] [1989] Ch.477 (no injunction granted until trial to prevent an employee who alleged that his employer was guilty of breaches of a regulatory scheme and improprieties in relation to tax from disclosing his employer's confidential information to the regulatory body or the Inland Revenue).

[86] [1990] 1 Ch. 359; [1990] 1 All E.R. 835.

his release from a secure hospital was so concerned about the difference between his views and those of the medical officer responsible for the claimant's treatment that, after the proposed application had been withdrawn due to the adverse views expressed in his report, and without the consent of the claimant, he forwarded a copy of his report to the medical director of the hospital. The claimant was a paranoid schizophrenic who had shot and killed a number of people and wounded others, and who had been ordered to be detained in the secure hospital after he had pleaded guilty to manslaughter on the grounds of diminished responsibility. The central concern of the psychiatrist was of the danger that would be presented to the public if the claimant was released prematurely. Scott J. dismissed the claimant's claim for breach of confidence, reasoning that it would plainly have been a breach of his duty of confidence for the psychiatrist to have sold the information to a newspaper, but that, applying the limiting principle identified by Lord Goff in *Attorney-General v Guardian Newspapers (No.2)*[87] it was not a breach of duty for him to disclose it to the medical director of the hospital. On appeal, that decision was upheld by the Court of Appeal.

Government secrets

25–018 Where confidential information is produced by the workings of government,[88] the question arises as to the extent to which it is open to the government to rely upon the law of confidence to restrain use and disclosure of such information (whether by its own servants or agents, or by third parties to whom such information has been communicated). The reasons why a different approach is appropriate in the case of government secrets[89] than that which applies to

[87] [1990] 1 A.C. 109 at 282.

[88] Where government is not the source, but the recipient, of confidential information different considerations apply, for here the essential confidence is, or is likely to be, that of others, typically citizens. Broadly speaking, two different sets of circumstance are likely to arise. First, the information may have been imparted consensually, in which case it will be subject to ordinary principles, and confidence will not be lost unless, for example, the public interest in disclosure outweighs the public interest in maintaining the confidence: *London Regional Transport v Mayor of London* [2003] EWCA Civ 1491; [2003] E.M.L.R. 4 provides an illustration of how this might work in practice. Secondly, the information may have been imparted pursuant to an obligation imposed on the citizen (typically by statute), in which case the material legislation may impress the information with confidentiality, and, in some instances, may expressly prohibit disclosure or restrict the uses to which the information may be put: the census and fiscal legislation provide examples.

[89] In *British Steel Corp v Granada Television Ltd* [1981] A.C. 1096, the majority of the House of Lords held or assumed that the need for a different approach did not extend to statutory corporations, treated the claimant public authority as entitled to the same rights as a private organization, and regarded accountability to Parliament as a sufficient check. Contrast the approach taken by the High Court of Australia in *Esso Australia Resources Ltd v Plowman* (1985) 183 C.L.R. 10; 128 A.L.R. 391.

private or commercial confidences were explained in *A-G (UK) v Heinemann Publishers Pty Ltd*[90] by McHugh J.A. in the following terms:

> ". . . the relationship between the modern State and its citizens is so different in kind from that which exists between private citizens that rules worked out to govern the contractual, property, commercial and private confidences of citizens are not fully applicable where the plaintiff is a government or one of its agencies. Private citizens are entitled to protect or further their own interests, no matter how selfish they are in doing so. Consequently, the publication of confidential information which is detrimental to the private interest of a citizen is a legitimate concern of a court of equity. But governments act, or at all events are constitutionally required to act, in the public interest. Information is held, received and imparted by governments, their departments and agencies to further the public interest. Public and not private interest, therefore, must be the criterion by which equity determines whether it will protect information which a government or governmental body claims is confidential."

Role of the public interest in relation to government secrets

In *Attorney-General v Jonathan Cape Ltd*[91] the Attorney General sought an injunction to restrain publication of Richard Crossman's book *Diaries of a Cabinet Minister*. Having said that "when a Cabinet Minister receives information in confidence the improper publication of such information can be restrained by the court," Lord Widgery C.J. went on to hold that the claimant had to establish not only (a) that publication would be a breach of confidence but in addition (b) that the public interest required that the publication be restrained, and (c) that there were no other facets of the public interest contradictory of and more compelling than that relied upon (by the claimant). In fact, the events described in the diaries were 10 years old, and there had been three general elections in the intervening period. In the result, Lord Widgery C.J. refused an injunction, because: 25–019

> "I cannot believe that publication at this interval of anything in volume one would inhibit free discussion in the Cabinet of today, even though the individuals involved are the same, and the national problems have a distressing similarity with those of a decade ago."

[90] (1987) 10 N.S.W.L.R. 86 at 191; 75 A.L.R. 353 at 451, and subsequently adopted in *Coulthard v South Australia* (1995) 63 S.A.S.R. 531 and in *Smith, Kline & French Laboratories (Aust) Ltd v Secretary, Department of Community Services and Health* (1991) 99 A.L.R. 679; 23 F.C.R. 291.

[91] [1976] Q.B. 752 at 770–771.

In *Commonwealth v John Fairfax and Sons Ltd*[92] Mason J. proceeded on the basis that detriment was a necessary element of a cause of action for breach of confidence, and continued:

> "The question then, when the executive government seeks the protection given by equity, is: What detriment does it need to show?
>
> The equitable principle has been fashioned to protect the personal, private and proprietary interests of the executive government. It acts, or is supposed to act, not according to standards of private interest, but in the public interest. This is not to say that equity will not protect information in the hands of the government, but it is to say that when equity protects government information it will look at the matter through different spectacles.
>
> It may be a sufficient detriment to the citizen that disclosure of information relating to his affairs will expose his actions to public discussion and criticism. But it can scarcely be a relevant detriment to the government that publication of material concerning its actions will merely expose it to public discussion and criticism. It is unacceptable in our democratic society that there should be a restraint on the publication of information relating to government when the only vice of that information is that it enables the public to discuss, review and criticize government action.
>
> Accordingly, the court will determine the government's claim to confidentiality by reference to the public interest. Unless disclosure is likely to injure the public interest, it will not be protected.
>
> The court will not prevent the publication of information which merely throws light on the past workings of government, even if it be not public property, so long as it does not prejudice the community in other respects. Then disclosure will itself serve the public interest in keeping the community informed and in promoting discussion of public affairs. If, however, it appears that disclosure will be inimical to the public interest because national security, relations with foreign countries or the ordinary business of government will be prejudiced, disclosure will be restrained. There will be cases in which the conflicting considerations will be finely balanced, where it is difficult to decide whether the public's interest in knowing and expressing its opinion outweighs the need to protect confidentiality."

Mason J. and Lord Widgery C.J. accordingly adopted substantially the same approach. The passage from the judgment of Mason J. set out above has been accepted as representing the law in England[93] and in Scotland.[94]

[92] (1980) 147 C.L.R. 39 at 51.

[93] See *Attorney-General v Guardian Newspapers Ltd* [1987] 1 W.L.R. 1248 at 1261–1262; [1987] 3 All E.R. 316 at 325–6; *Attorney-General v Guardian Newspapers Ltd (No.2)* [1990] 1 A.C. 109 at 150–2, 203, 218, 221–2, 257–8, 270, 283; *Attorney-General v Punch Ltd* [2001] Q.B. 1028 at para.40; *R. v Department of Health, Ex p. Source Informatics Ltd* [2001] Q.B. 424 at para.25; *R. v Shayler* [2001] 1 W.L.R. 2206 at paras 71–72. See also (in related litigation) the position in New Zealand (*A-G for UK v Wellington Newspapers Ltd* [1988] 1 N.Z.L.R. 129 at 176.

[94] *Lord Advocate v Scotsman Publications Ltd* [1990] 1 A.C. 812 at 828; [1989] 2 All E.R. 852 at 862.

Consultation with other persons

There is no statutory obligation on the public authority to consult with persons to whom the information requested relates or whose interests are likely to be affected by the disclosure of information to the public pursuant to s.41 of the Freedom of Information Act 2000. In accordance with s.45(2)(c) of the Act, however, consultation with such persons is one of the matters that is required to be covered by the code of practice issued by the Lord Chancellor pursuant to s.45(1) "providing guidance to public authorities as to the practice which he considers it desirable for them to follow in connection with the discharge of their functions under Part I of the Act". In practice, therefore, such persons are very likely to be consulted by the public authority before any disclosure is made. If the persons consulted consent to disclosure, and no other person is entitled to maintain any claim to confidentiality with regard to the information in question, then the public authority will be released from any obligation of confidence that it would otherwise have had, and it will not be able to rely on the exemption to resist disclosure. If the persons consulted do not consent to disclosure, and the public authority considers that disclosure would constitute a breach of confidence actionable by them, it is likely that the terms of their objection will bolster the public authority's stance. If the persons consulted do not consent to disclosure and claim it would constitute a breach of confidence actionable by them and the public authority disagrees with that view, the matter may well end up being resolved by the court either in proceedings brought by such persons for injunctive relief, or, conceivably, in proceedings brought against them by the public authority for declaratory relief.[95] If any dispute is not resolved by those means, and the public authority decides to make disclosure in spite of such claims, any person whose rights of confidentiality are breached by the disclosure will be entitled to claim pecuniary relief in respect of such disclosure, subject to any common law defences that may be available to the public authority: these rights are not conferred by the Act, but arise at common law. 25–020

The duty to confirm or deny

The duty to confirm or deny does not arise if, or to the extent that, a confirmation or denial that the public authority holds the information specified in the request would (apart from the Act) constitute an actionable breach of confidence.[96] This is an absolute exclusion of duty.[97] As a matter of practice, other than where the request is so specific that the mere confirmation that the information is held (without a disclosure of that information) would be to disclose 25–021

[95] See paras 28–028 to 28–030.
[96] Freedom of Information Act 2000, s.41(2). In relation to Scotland, see para.1–025(1).
[97] *ibid.*, s.2(3).

the gist of the information, it is difficult to contemplate circumstances in which a public authority could properly refuse to confirm or deny that it held information under s.41(2).

2. PRIVACY AND ACTIONABLE BREACH OF CONFIDENCE

Introduction

25–022 By tying the exemption in s.41 to an actionable breach of confidence, the Freedom of Information Act 2000 imports the conceptual difficulties which surround the basis upon which the common law is prepared to offer protection against certain invasions of privacy. Because of these difficulties and the resultant uncertainties, it is convenient to give separate consideration to the interrelationship between an actionable breach of confidence and a breach of privacy. Whatever the nomenclature used, information will only be exempt from the disclosure duty if that disclosure may properly be characterised as an actionable breach of confidence.[98]

English law of privacy before the Human Rights Act 1998

25–023 The view that English law does not recognise invasion of privacy as an independent cause of action was clearly articulated by the Court of Appeal in *Kaye v Robertson*.[99] Even at that time, however, that starting point was subject to two significant qualifications. First, the facts of cases in which privacy issues arise often constitute another cause of action that is recognised by English law, most notably for a breach of confidence. Lord Hoffmann in his 1996 Goodman Lecture[1] expressed the view that breach of confidence—which was not even argued—would have afforded a basis for relief in *Kaye v Robertson*.[2] In *Attorney-General v Guardian Newspapers Ltd (No.2)*,[3] Lord Keith referred to cases "where the breach of confidence involves no more than an invasion of

[98] *ibid.*, s.41(1); Freedom of Information (Scotland) Act 2002, s.36(2).

[99] [1991] F.S.R. 62: "It is well-known that in English law there is no right to privacy, and accordingly there is no right of action for breach of a person's privacy. The facts of the present case are a graphic illustration of the desirability of Parliament considering whether and in what circumstances statutory provision can be made to protect the privacy of individuals", *per* Glidewell L.J. at 66; "This case nonetheless highlights, yet again, the failure of both the common law of England and statute to protect in an effective way the personal privacy of individual citizens", *per* Bingham L.J. at 70; "This right has so long been disregarded here that it can be recognised now only by the legislature", *per* Leggatt L.J. at 71.

[1] Lord Bingham, on the other hand, saw a need for development: see "Should There be a Law to Protect Rights of Personal Privacy?" [1996] E.H.L.R. 45.

[2] [1991] F.S.R. 62.

[3] [1990] 1 A.C. 109 at 255.

personal privacy," specifically mentioned *Argyll v Argyll*[4] and marital confidences, and concluded that "the right to personal privacy is clearly one which the law should in this field seek to protect." Second, even before the Human Rights Act 1988 came into force on October 2, 2000 the law appeared to be moving toward recognition of a discrete right of privacy of some description. In *Morris v Beardmore*[5] the question was whether a motorist who refused to take a breath test at the request of a policeman who was trespassing at the time was acting unlawfully. The House of Lords held that he was not. The common law rights in question were trespass to land and physical compulsion to blow into a breathalyser. Lord Edmund Davies, Lord Keith, Lord Scarman and Lord Roskill nevertheless alluded to the exercise of the relevant police powers in terms of invasion of privacy. Lord Scarman referred to the "invasion of fundamental private rights and liberties" and said that "the adjective . . . 'fundamental'. . . is apt to describe the importance attached by the common law to the privacy of the home." Lord Roskill referred to "the right of the ordinary citizen not to have his property, and thus his privacy, invaded against his will, save where such invasion is directly authorised by law." In *R. v Khan*,[6] Lord Nolan said that there was no right of privacy in English law in terms similar to Art.8 of the Convention, and Lord Keith agreed with him. As against that, Lord Browne-Wilkinson, Lord Slynn and Lord Nicholls expressly left open the question whether English law recognised a right of privacy, and, if so, what were the limitations of that right. Lord Nicholls referred to "the important question whether the present, piecemeal protection of privacy has now developed to the extent that a more comprehensive principle can be seen to exist."

The Human Rights Act 1998 and relevant Convention rights

In accordance with s.1 of the Human Rights Act 1998, the Convention rights to which the Act applies include the rights and fundamental freedoms set out in Arts 8 and 10 of the Convention.[7] The rights set out in both Articles are qualified. In the case of Art.8, the qualifications include the Art.10 right to freedom of expression. In the case of Art.10, the qualifications include both the Art.8 right to respect for private and family life and the protection of information received in confidence (although the latter is not, itself, a Convention right; any more than the right to protection of reputation is a Convention right). In the case of both Articles, the restrictions can only apply where three conditions are satisfied. First, the restrictions must pursue a legitimate aim or aims. Secondly, the restrictions must be "prescribed by law:" in other words, they must be easily accessible and formulated with sufficient precision for the ordinary citizen to 25–024

4 [1967] Ch. 302.
5 [1981] A.C. 446; [1980] 2 All E.R. 753.
6 [1997] A.C. 558; [1996] 3 All E.R. 289.
7 These are set out at para.1–029 and para.1–033.

rely upon them to regulate his conduct.[8] Thirdly, they must be necessary in a democratic society for the protection of the legitimate aim or aims of the countervailing rights or qualifications: in other words, they must be proportionate to the end pursued, securing what is necessary for the protection of those countervailing rights or qualifications and no more. It has been said of the right to freedom of expression that it is a constitutional right and that "by categorising this basic and fundamental right as a constitutional right its higher normative force is emphasised."[9] In addition, as a matter of Convention law, the position is that, in deciding whether a given interference with free expression is necessary in a democratic society, the court "is faced not with a choice between two conflicting principles, but with a principle of freedom of expression that is subject to a number of exceptions which must be narrowly interpreted."[10] However, there is no hierarchy of rights as between Art.8 and Art.10. This appears, for example, from Council of Europe Resolution 1165 of 1998:

> "11. The Assembly reaffirms the importance of every person's right to privacy, and of the right to freedom of expression, as fundamental to a democratic society. These rights are neither absolute nor in any hierarchical order, since they are of equal value."

The effect of the Human Rights Act 1998

25–025 Section 2 of the Human Rights Act 1998 requires any court or tribunal determining a question which has arisen in connection with a Convention right to take into account any relevant Strasbourg jurisprudence. Section 6(1) provides that it is unlawful for a public authority to act in a way which is incompatible with a Convention right. By virtue of s.6(3), a "public authority" includes a court or tribunal. The effect of these provisions is to make it the duty of the court to exercise its judicial powers in a way that is compatible with Convention rights, as interpreted by the Strasbourg institutions and the English courts, even if it means not following previous case law which would otherwise have been binding on the court at common law: thus a court is not bound by previous decisions of English courts which are incompatible with Convention rights, unless those previous decisions have had regard to and given effect to any relevant Convention right and relevant case law. At the same time, the Convention rights in accordance with the Human Rights Act 1998 do not include Art.1,

---

[8] *Sunday Times v United Kingdom (No.1)* (1979–80) 2 E.H.R.R. 245; *Rantzen v Mirror Group Newspapers Ltd* [1994] Q.B. 670 at 693; [1993] 4 All E.R. 975.

[9] *R v Secretary of State for the Home Department, Ex p. Simms* [2000] 2 A.C. 115 at 126 *per* Lord Steyn. See also: *Reynolds v Times Newspapers Ltd* [2001] 2 A.C. 127; [1999] 4 All E.R. 609; *McCartan Turkington Breen v Times Newspapers Ltd* [2001] 2 A.C. 277; [2000] 4 All E.R. 913.

[10] *Sunday Times v United Kingdom (No.1)* (1979–80) 2 E.H.R.R. 245 at 281. See also: *Bergens Tidende v Norway* (2001) 31 E.H.R.R. 16; *Bladet Tromso v Norway* (2000) 29 E.H.R.R. 125; 6 B.H.R.C. 599.

which forms the foundation of the positive duty of a State when it is brought before the international court which has the duty of enforcing the duties of Member States under the Convention. This raises a potential difficulty for a court called upon to determine a question which has arisen in connection with a Convention right within the meaning of the Act and which is required to take into account a relevant Strasbourg judgment which has made it clear that the law-making body of the Member States has a positive duty. Guidance as to the correct approach appears from *Venables v News Group Newspapers Ltd*,[11] where Dame Elizabeth Butler-Sloss P. stated:

> "The decisions of the European Court of Human Rights in Glaser's case[12] and X *and Y v The Netherlands*,[13] seem to dispose of any argument that a court is not to have regard to the Convention in private law cases . . . .
> . . . That obligation on the court does not seem to me to encompass the creation of a free-standing cause of action based directly upon the articles of the Convention . . . . The duty on the court, in my view, is to act compatibly with Convention rights in adjudicating upon existing common law causes of action, and that includes a positive as well as a negative obligation."

Privacy and confidence since the Human Rights Act 1998

In *A v B plc*[14] the Court of Appeal set out guidelines to be followed by judges of first instance on applications for interim injunctions in cases involving personal information. The Court explained that: 25–026

> "The applications for interim injunctions have now to be considered in the context of Articles 8 and 10 of the European Convention for the Protection of Human Rights and Fundamental Freedoms. These articles have provided new parameters within which the court will decide, in an action for breach of confidence, whether a person is entitled to have his privacy protected by the court or whether the restriction of freedom of expression which such protection involves cannot be justified. The court's approach to

[11] [2001] Fam. 430; [2001] 1 All E.R. 908 at paras 25–27. And in *Douglas v Hello! Ltd* [2001] 1 Q.B. 967; [2001] 2 All E.R. 289 Brooke L.J. observed at para.91: "Where Parliament in this country has been so obviously content to leave the development of the law to the judges, it might seem strange if the absence of Art.1 from our national statute relieved the judges from taking into account the positive duties identified by the court at Strasbourg when they develop the common law."

[12] *Glaser v United Kingdom* [2000] 3 F.C.R. 193 at 208–209; [2001] 1 FLR 153; (2001) 33 E.H.R.R. 1, where the European Court of Human Rights, sitting as a Chamber, declared admissible an application by a father seeking the enforcement of contact orders made in private law proceedings between him and the mother of his children.

[13] (1985) 8 E.H.R.R. 235.

[14] [2002] EWCA Civ 337; [2003] Q.B. 195; [2002] 2 All E.R. 545.

> the issues which the applications raise has been modified because, under section 6 of the 1998 Act, the court, as a public authority, is required not to act 'in a way which is incompatible with a Convention right'. The court is able to achieve this by absorbing the rights which Articles 8 and 10 protect into the long-established action for breach of confidence. This involves giving a new strength and breadth to the action so that it accommodates the requirements of those articles."[15]

The guidelines laid down by the Court of Appeal included the following:

> "(vi) It is most unlikely that any purpose will be served by a judge seeking to decide whether there exists a new cause of action in tort which protects privacy. In the great majority of situations, if not all situations, where the protection of privacy is justified, relating to events after the Human Rights Act 1998 came into force, an action for breach of confidence now will, where this is appropriate, provide the necessary protection. This means that at first instance it can be readily accepted that it is not necessary to tackle the vexed question of whether there is a separate cause of action based upon a new tort involving the infringement of privacy.
>
> (ix) . . . A duty of confidence will arise whenever the party subject to the duty is in a situation where he either knows or ought to know that the other person can reasonably expect his privacy to be protected: see Lord Goff of Chieveley in *Attorney-General v Guardian Newspapers Ltd (No.2)*.[16] The range of situations in which protection can be provided is therefore extensive. Obviously, the necessary relationship can be expressly created. More often its existence will have to be inferred from the facts. Whether a duty of confidence does exist which courts can protect, if it is right to do so, will depend on all the circumstances of the relationship between the parties at the time of the threatened or actual breach of the alleged duty of confidence.
>
> (x) If there is an intrusion in a situation where a person can reasonably expect his privacy to be respected then that intrusion will be capable of giving rise to liability in an action for breach of confidence unless the intrusion can be justified . . .".[17]

It seems tolerably clear from this general statement of principle and these particular guidelines that where a person has a reasonable expectation of privacy he has a right to be protected against intrusion into that privacy, and that the law of confidence will provide protection for that right unless the intrusion in question can be justified. That the Court of Appeal intended to make clear that the right of protection against intrusion on personal privacy falls within, and,

[15] At para.4.

[16] [1990] 1 A.C. 109 at 281.

[17] [2002] EWCA Civ 337; [2003] Q.B. 195; [2002] 2 All E.R. 545 at para.11.

in the era following the coming into force of the Human Rights Act 1988, can properly be assimilated into, the law of confidence seems apparent from the reformulation of Lord Goff's words in *Attorney-General v Guardian Newspapers Ltd (No.2)*[18] that appear in guideline (ix).[19]

Infringement of privacy as a free-standing tort

In *Campbell v MGN Ltd*[20] the Court of Appeal recognised a distinction between infringement of privacy as a free-standing tort (which occurs where there is intrusion into privacy which does not involve disclosure of private facts) and infringement of privacy as a species of breach of confidence (which involves the misuse or disclosure of personal or private information). The Court of Appeal stated that the courts were in the process of identifying, on a case-by-case basis, the principles by which the law of confidentiality must accommodate the rights under Art.8 and Art.10 of the Convention. The Court observed that the development of the law of confidentiality since the Human Rights Act 1998 came into force had seen information described as "confidential" not only where it has been confided by one person to another, but also where it related to an aspect of an individual's private life which he chose not to make public, and that it considered that the unjustifiable publication of such information would better be characterised as a breach of privacy rather than as a breach of confidence. On the basis that this was the test for which the defendant newspaper contended and that the claimant accepted this test subject to "two small cavils," the Court adopted as a test of what is private whether disclosure would be offensive—or, possibly, highly offensive—to a reasonable person of ordinary sensibilities. The source of this test was a passage in the judgment of Gleeson C.J. in *Australian Broadcasting Corporation v Lenah Game Meats Pty Ltd*[21]: 25–027

> "The requirement that disclosure or observation of information or conduct would be highly offensive to a reasonable person of ordinary sensibilities is in many circumstances a useful practical test of what is private."

Although neither side had cited that decision in argument in *A v B plc*,[22] that passage had been quoted by the Court of Appeal in *A v B plc* for the purpose of demonstrating, in the context of applications for interim injunctions which formed the subject of the guidelines laid down in that case, "the advantage of not having to distinguish between acts which are public and those which are private in a difficult case." The judge at first instance in *Campbell v MGN Ltd*,[23]

18 [1990] 1 A.C. 109 at 281.

19 See, further, *Douglas v Hello! Ltd* [2003] EWHC 786, Ch, Lindsay J. paras 186(ix)–(x).

20 [2002] EWCA Civ 1373; [2003] Q.B. 633; [2003] 1 All E.R. 224.

21 [2001] H.C.A. 63; (2001) 208 C.L.R. 199; (2001) 185 A.L.R. 1 at para.41.

22 [2002] EWCA Civ 337; [2003] Q.B. 195; [2002] 2 All E.R. 545 (at para.11(vii)).

23 Morland J. whose decision can be found at [2002] EWHC 449; [2002] E.M.L.R. 30.

having reserved judgment until the decision of the Court of Appeal in *A v B plc*[24] became available, had applied the test suggested by Gleeson C.J. Accordingly, in *Campbell v MGN Ltd*[25] in the Court of Appeal, the defendant newspaper relied on that test, while arguing that Morland J. had applied it wrongly on the facts.[26]

In *Wainwright v Home Office*[26A] the House of Lords held that there is no common law tort of invasion of privacy, that the creation of such a tort would be a matter for legislation, and that the adoption of a right of privacy as a principle of law in itself in not necessary to comply with Art.8 of the Convention. At the same time, Lord Hoffmann[26B], giving the leading speech with which each of the other members of the House of Lords agreed, cited the evolution of the law of confidence in recent years, in particular as appears from the judgment of the Court in *Campbell v MGN Ltd*[26C], as an illustration of the judicious development of an existing principle to cover cases in which the courts have considered that an invasion of privacy deserves a remedy which the existing law does not offer. The decision in that case accordingly seems to be directly in line with the reasoning of the Court of Appeal in *Campbell v MGN Ltd*[26C]. Lord Hoffmann nevertheless left open to doubt the extent to which the law of confidence could properly be developed any further than was contemplated by the decision in *Campbell v MGN Ltd*[26C], concluding his observations that are quoted above[26D] with the following remarks[26E]:

> "I do not understand Sedley L.J. to have been advocating the creation of a high-level principle of invasion of privacy. His observations are in my opinion no more (although certainly no less) than a plea for the extenstion and possibly renaming of the old action for breach of confidence. As Buxton L.J. pointed out in this case in the Court of Appeal[26F], such an extension would go further than any English court has yet gone and would be contrary to some cases (such as *Kaye v Robertson*)[26G] in which it positively declined to do so. The question must wait for another day. But Sedley L.J.'s

[24] [2002] EWCA Civ 337; [2003] Q.B. 195; [2002] 2 All E.R. 545.
[25] [2002] EWCA Civ 1373; [2003] Q.B. 633; [2003] 1 All E.R. 224.
[26] There is no trace in the Strasbourg jurisprudence of the test suggested by Gleeson C.J. in *Australian Broadcasting Corporation v Lenah Game Meats Pty Ltd* [2001] H.C.A. 63; (2001) 208 C.L.R. 199; (2001) 185 A.L.R. 1. Moreover, as was pointed out in *Douglas v Hello! Ltd* [2003] EWHC 786, Ch, Lindsay J. paras 189–191, Gleeson C.J.'s test was articulated (a) in the context of considering the difficulties in constructing a new tort involving broad concepts of unconscionability and privacy; (b) in a case which did not concern personal confidence; and (c) in terms that do purport to constitute an exclusive definition of what is private. The House of Lords is due to hear the appeal of the claimant in *Campbell v MGN Ltd* on February 17–18, 2004, and it is possible that the decision on that appeal will provide guidance as to whether the test suggested by Gleeson C.J. is indeed the appropriate test.
[26A] [2003] 3 W.L.R. 1137.
[26B] At 1142, para.18.
[26C] [2002] EWCA Civ 337; [2003] Q.B. 135; [2002] 2 All E.R. 545.
[26D] At para.25–010.
[26E] At 1145–1146, para.30.
[26F] [2002] Q.B. 1334, 1361–1362, paras 96–99.
[26G] [1991] F.S.R. 62.

dictum does not support a principle of privacy so abstract as to include the circumstances of the present case."

3. TRADE SECRETS

Introduction

Information that constitutes a trade secret[27] is rendered exempt information by s.43(1) of the Freedom of Information Act 2000.[28] The exemption is a class exemption, in that it applies to any information that amounts to a trade secret, irrespective of the consequences of disclosure. The exemption is not absolute, so that disapplication of the duty to disclose requires a weighing of the public interest in maintaining the exemption against the public interest in disclosure of the information.[29] There is no correlative disapplication of the duty to confirm or deny. A similar exemption is to be found in each of the comparative jurisdictions.[30] 25–028

The nature of a trade secret

The ambit of this exemption depends upon the scope of the concept of a trade secret in English law.[31] As there is no statutory definition of what constitutes a 25–029

[27] For a more general treatment of the law of trade secrets, see: S. Mehigan and A. Kamerling, *Restraint of Trade and Business Secrets* (4th ed., Sweet & Maxwell, London, 2004); A.E. Turner, *The Law of Trade Secrets* (Sweet & Maxwell, London, 1962); R. Dean, *The Law of Trade Secrets and Personal Secrets* (Law Book Company, Sydney, 2002); A. Coleman, *The Legal Protection of Trade Secrets* (Sweet & Maxwell, London, 1992); The Institute of Law Research and Reform, *Trade Secrets* (The Institute of Law Research, Edmonton, 1986); P. Lavery, *Commercial Secrets* (Round Hall, Dublin, 1996).

[28] And by Freedom of Information (Scotland) Act 2002, s.33(1)(a). There is a limited exemption for trade secrets under Data Protection Act 1998, s.8(5): see para.4–030.

[29] Freedom of Information Act 2000, s.2(2)(b).

[30] In the United States, the Freedom of Information Act, 1966, 5 USC § 552(b)(4), exempts from disclosure trade secrets: see para.2–008(4). The Freedom of Information Act 1982 (Cth of Australia), s.43(1)(a), provides an exemption for trade secrets: see para.2–015(5). The Official Information Act 1982 (New Zealand), ss.9(2)(b)(i) and 27(1)(a), provide a qualified exemption where the disclosure would disclose a trade secret: see para.2–023(2). The Access to Information Act (Canada), s.20(1)(a), provides a mandatory exemption for trade secrets: see para.2–031(4); s.18(a) provides a discretionary exemption for trade secrets belonging to the Government of Canada: see para.2–032(3). The Federal Court has held that given the existence of other, restricted exemptions for confidential information, the term "trade secrets" had to be given a reasonably narrow interpretation. It considered that a trade secret must be something probably of a technical nature which is guarded very closely and is of such peculiar value to the owner of the trade secret that harm to him would be presumed by its mere disclosure: *Société Gamma Inc. v Canada (Secretary of State)* (1994) 56 C.P.R. (3d) 58; 79 F.T.R. 42. The Freedom of Information Act 1997 (Ireland), s.27(1) provides a mandatory exemption for any record that contains a trade secret: see para.2–039(6).

[31] As to the meaning given to "trade secret" in the context of freedom of information legislation in Australia, see: *Searle Australia Pty Ltd v Public Interest Advocacy Centre* (1992) 108 A.L.R. 163; 36 F.C.R. 111, where it was held by the full court of the Federal Court that the essential attributes

trade secret, guidance on the point needs to be sought in the case law.[32] Although the case law yields no exact definition of a trade secret, it does provide useful indicia. In *Ansell Rubber Co Pty Ltd v Allied Rubber Industries Pty Ltd*,[33] Gowans J. suggested the following guidelines:

> "An exact definition of a trade secret is not possible. Some factors to be considered in determining whether given information is one's trade secret are: the extent to which information is known outside of his business; the extent to which it is known by employees and others involved in his business; the extent of measures taken by him to guard the secrecy of the information; the value of the information to him and his contemporaries; the amount of effort or money expended by him in developing the information; the ease or difficulty with which the information could be properly acquired or duplicated by others."

Similar indicia are found in the judgment of Sir Robert Megarry V.C. in *Thomas Marshall (Exports) Ltd v Guinle*.[34] Although in the following passage he did not attempt to distinguish between trade secrets and other confidential commercial information, his criteria are of assistance in establishing the minimum requirements that must be met before information could properly be said to amount to a trade secret:

> "If one turns from the authorities and looks at the matter as a question of principle, I think (and I say this very tentatively, because the principle has not been argued out) that four elements may be discerned which may be of some assistance in identifying confidential information or trade secrets which the court will protect. I speak of such information or secrets only in an industrial or trade setting. First, I think that the information must be information the release of which the owner believes would be injurious to him or of advantage to his rivals or others. Second, I think the owner must believe that the information is confidential or secret, *i.e.*, that it is not already in the public domain.[35] It may be that some or all of his rivals

of a trade secret were: (a) that it must be used in or usable in trade; in other words, an asset of the trade; (b) it must be used for the benefit of the owner's business; (c) it must not be in the public domain; (d) technicality is not required, but the more technical the information is, the more likely it is to be characterised as a trade secret. The Federal Court accepted that, in "an appropriate case," the names of customers and the goods that they buy would be a trade secret where that would be to the advantage of rivals to obtain.

[32] The term has been used for over a century: in *Allsopp v Wheatcroft* (1872) Law Rep. 15 Eq. 59 at 64–65 Sir John Wickens referred to a "clearly lawful restriction against divulging a trade secret." See also: *Davies v Davies* (1887) 36 Ch.D. 359 at 385.

[33] [1967] V.R. 373.

[34] [1979] Ch.227; [1978] 3 All E.R. 193; [1979] F.S.R. 208.

[35] Thus, under the equivalent provision under the Canadian Access to Information Act 1982, the Federal Court held that dosage information for a drug which was disclosed in a monograph available to health professionals was in the public domain: *Merck Frosst Canada Inc. v Canada (Minister of Health and Welfare)* (1988) 20 F.T.R. 73; 30 C.P.R. (3d) 473; *Canada Post Corp. v Canada*

already have the information: but as long as the owner believes it to be confidential I think he is entitled to try and protect it. Third, I think that the owner's belief under the two previous heads must be reasonable. Fourth, I think that the information must be judged in the light of the usage and practices of the particular industry or trade concerned. It may be that information which does not satisfy all these requirements may be entitled to protection as confidential information or trade secrets: but I think that any information which does satisfy them must be of a type which is entitled to protection."

Distinction between trade secrets and ordinarily-acquired work knowledge

In *Faccenda Chicken Ltd v Fowler*[36] the Court of Appeal distinguished between trade secrets (which at common law may not be disclosed, quite apart from any contractual proscription against disclosure) and the information which an employee will inevitably acquire whilst employed (which is not subject to an implied obligation not to disclose). The correct characterisation of any particular item of information does not depend purely upon the attributes of the information, but will also depend upon the nature of the employment, the degree to which the employer impressed on the employee the confidentiality of the information, and whether the relevant information can be easily isolated from other information which the employee is free to use or disclose. When discussing those matters, the court said: 25–030

"In our judgment the information will only be protected if it can properly be classed as a trade secret or as material which, while not properly to be described as a trade secret, is in all the circumstances of such a highly confidential nature as to require the same protection as a trade secret eo nomine . . . . It is clearly impossible to provide a list of matters which will qualify as trade secrets or their equivalent. Secret processes of manufacture provide obvious examples, but innumerable other pieces of information are *capable* of being trade secrets, though the secrecy of some information may be only short-lived. In addition, the fact that the circulation of certain information is restricted to a limited number of individuals may throw light on the status of the information and its degree of confidentiality . . . though an employer cannot prevent the use or disclosure *merely* by telling the employee that certain information is confidential, the attitude of the employer towards the information provides evidence which may assist in

(Minister of Public Works) [1993] 3 F.C. 320, aff'd (1993) 64 F.T.R. 62 (Fed. Court of Appeal); *Matol Botanical International Inc. v Canada (Minister of National Health & Welfare)* (1994) 84 F.T.R. 168.

[36] [1987] 1 Ch.117; [1986] 1 All E.R. 617; [1986] F.S.R. 291.

> determining whether or not the information can properly be regarded as a trade secret . . . . For our part we would not regard the separability of the information in question as being conclusive, but the fact that the alleged 'confidential' information is part of a package and that the remainder of the package is not confidential is likely to throw light on whether the information in question is really a trade secret."

The distinction made by the Court of Appeal in *Faccenda* was considered by Hoffmann J. in *Lock International Plc v Beswick*[37]:

> "There will be a good deal of . . . information which an employee could not without breach of duty disclose while he was employed but which he is free to use as part of his own skill and knowledge after his employment has ceased . . . . It would not, for example, be sufficient to say in general terms that they were extremely familiar with the way Metalcheck detectors worked—with, as the plaintiff's witnesses repeatedly say, their 'strengths and weaknesses.' There may have been some particular strength or weakness which was indeed a trade secret, but general familiarity is pre-eminently the kind of skill and knowledge which the honest employee cannot help taking away with him . . . . In the Technical Appendix I have considered all the alleged secrets and it seems to me that the only one in respect of which the plaintiff has even an arguable case is that relating to a particular weakness in the tuner diodes used in one circuit. Some of the claims to trade secrets, such as the use of marine ply or a common microprocessor, I regard as frankly absurd . . . . Many [employers] have great difficulty in understanding the distinction between genuine trade secrets and skill and knowledge which the employee may take away with him. In cases in which the plaintiff alleges misuse of trade secrets or confidential information concerning a manufacturing process, a lack of particularity about the precise nature of the trade secrets is usually a symptom of an attempt to prevent the employee from making legitimate use of the knowledge and skills gained in the plaintiff's service . . . . Judges dealing with ex parte applications are usually also at a disadvantage in dealing with alleged confidential knowledge of technical processes described in technical language, such as the electric circuitry in this case. It may look like magic but turn out merely to embody a principle discovered by Faraday or Ampere."[38]

[37] [1989] 1 W.L.R. 1268; 1274–1275, 1281; [1989] 3 All E.R. 373.

[38] See also: *Lansing Linde v Kerr* [1991] 1 W.L.R. 251, where Staughton L.J. referred to *Herbert Morris Ltd v Saxelby* [1916] 1 A.C. 688, *Faccenda Chicken Ltd v Fowler* [1987] Ch 117, *Balston Ltd v Headline Filters Ltd* [1987] F.S.R. 330 and *Lock International Plc v Beswick* [1989] 1 W.L.R. 1268, and went on to say (at 259–260): "It appears to me that the problem is one of definition: what are trade secrets, and how do they differ (if at all) from confidential information?" Staughton L.J. considered a definition suggested by Counsel that "a trade secret is information which, if disclosed to a competitor, would be liable to cause real (or significant) harm to the owner of the secret," and continued: "I would add first, that it must be information used in a trade or business, and secondly that the owner must limit the dissemination of it or at least not

Employee may take away with him; in which case, it will not constitute a trade secret. Conversely, although financial and customer information often may not constitute a trade secret it may do so in an appropriate case: for example, if dissemination of it has been restricted, and if it is of great value and release of it would cause serious harm to the originator.

Trade secrets—examples

The case law needs to be considered with care, as the distinction between confidential information and trade secrets is often unarticulated, if appreciated at all. Nevertheless, the following appear to have been characterised as trade secrets in the properly-understood sense: 25–031

— special methods of design and construction[39];
— technical knowledge and experience connected with the manufacture of particular goods[40];
— trade practices and processes which would be harmful if it fell into the hands of competitors[41]; and
— information relating to sales, prices and customers which would be of advantage to a competing company.[42]

Trade secrets—unifying principles

In summary, therefore, in order for information to amount to a trade secret more is required than that it should be (a) trade information having a commercial value and (b) confidential to the person(s) claiming that it constitutes a 25–032

encourage or permit widespread publication. That is my preferred view of the meaning of trade secret in this context. It can thus include not only secret formulae for the manufacture of products but also, in an appropriate case, the names of customers and the goods which they buy. But some may say that not all such information is a trade secret in ordinary parlance. If that view be adopted, the class of information which can justify a restriction is wider, and extends to some confidential information which would not ordinarily be called a trade secret."

39 *Reid & Sigrist Ltd v Moss and Mechanism Ltd* (1932) 49 R.P.C. 461 (manufacture of aircraft turn indicators); *Standex International Ltd v CB Blades Ltd* [1976] F.S.R. 114 (a unique mould engraving process).

40 *Cranleigh Precision Engineering v Bryant* [1964] 3 All E.R. 289 (a swimming pool); *Balston Ltd v Headline Filters* [1987] F.S.R. 330; *Nordenfelt v Maxim Nordenfelt Guns and Ammunition Company* [1894] A.C. 535 (know-how in relation to machine guns); *Amber Size and Chemical Company, Limited v Menze* [1913] 2 Ch. 239.

41 *Malden Timber v McLeish* [1992] S.L.T. 727; *Littlewoods Organisation v Harris* [1977] 1 W.L.R. 1472.

42 *Sir W.C. Leng & Co Ltd v Andrews* [1909] 1 Ch. 763; *Harben Pumps (Scotland) v Lafferty* [1989] S.L.T. 752; *Lansing Linde Ltd v Kerr* [1991] 1 All E.R. 418; *cf. Faccenda Chicken Ltd v Fowler* [1987] 1 Ch. 117; [1986] 1 All E.R. 617; [1986] F.S.R. 291.

trade secret.[43] What is required is a sufficiently high degree of confidentiality. Whether or not information is of such a high degree of confidentiality as to constitute a trade secret will depend on all the circumstances. Relevant considerations include: the value of the information, the investment made in developing the information, the extent to which it truly is secret, the extent to which access to it has been restricted or its secrecy and importance have been emphasised, and the extent to which it is separate and distinct from other information which cannot properly be regarded as a trade secret. Technicality is not required, although secret processes of manufacture, formulae and designs and so forth may more readily be regarded as trade secrets than information about costs, prices, sales and customers.[44] Technical information may have the appearance of distinctiveness and sophistication, but in truth be trite or inseparable from a general stock of skill and knowledge which an employee may take away with him; in which case, it will not constitute a trade secret. Conversely, although financial and customer information often may not constitute a trade secret it may do so in an appropriate case; for example, if dissemination of it has been restricted, and if it is of great value and release of it would cause serious harm to the originator.

The public interest

25–033 If the information in question constitutes a trade secret, the duty to disclose the information does not apply if the public interest in maintaining the exemption outweighs the public interest in disclosing the information.[45] The weighing exercise necessitates an identification of the public interest in the maintenance of the exemption, always recognising that that public interest must be delineated in such a fashion that it is capable in practice of being outweighed.[46] The public interest in the maintenance of this exemption should, it is suggested, involve an appreciation of:

- — the maintenance of rights of intellectual property; and
- — the potential of a chilling effect upon the provision to public authorities of information constituting trade secrets if such secrets are routinely disclosed upon a request being made under the Freedom of Information Act 2000.

[43] Contrast the suggestion made by the House of Lords Select Committee which considered the draft Freedom of Information Bill that a trade secret is "information of commercial value which is protected by the law of confidence:" *Report of the Select Committee*, July 27, 1998, para.45.

[44] In Canada, in the equivalent provision of the Access to Information Act 1982, the Federal Court held that the term "trade secret" should be reserved for more technical production information: *Merck Frosst Canada Inc. v Canada (Minister of Health and Welfare)* (1988) 20 F.T.R. 73; 30 C.P.R. (3d) 473.

[45] Freedom of Information Act 2000, s.2(2)(b).

[46] To avoid metamorphosing it into an absolute exemption.

The duty to confirm or deny

The discrete duty to confirm or deny upon a public authority that it holds information of the description specified in a request[47] is not displaced on the ground that to comply with that duty would disclose a trade secret. 25–034

4. PREJUDICE TO COMMERCIAL INTERESTS

Introduction

By s.43(2) of the Freedom of Information Act 2000 information is rendered exempt if its disclosure would, or would be likely to, prejudice the commercial interests of any person, including the public authority holding it.[48] The exemption is not absolute, so that disapplication of the duty to disclose requires a weighing of the public interest in maintaining the exemption against the public interest in disclosure of the information.[49] The duty to confirm or deny is similarly excluded where, or to the extent that, informing the applicant that the information specified in the request is or is not held would, or would be likely to, prejudice the commercial interests of any person.[50] The exclusion of the duty to confirm or deny is also not absolute.[51] Of the comparative jurisdictions, a similar exemption is only to be found in the Australian and New Zealand regimes.[52] 25–035

The scope of the exemption

The exemption involves a consideration of: 25–036

— the notion of "prejudice;"
— the requisite degree of likelihood of prejudice; and

[47] Freedom of Information Act 2000, s.1(1)(a).
[48] And by Freedom of Information (Scotland) Act 2002, s.33(1)(b).
[49] Freedom of Information Act 2000, s.2(2)(b).
[50] *ibid.*, s.43(3).
[51] *ibid.*, s.2(1)(b).
[52] The Freedom of Information Act 1982 (Cth of Australia), s.43(1)(c)(i), provides an exemption in respect of information concerning a person in respect of his or her business or professional affairs or concerning the business, commercial or financial affairs of an organization or undertaking, being information the disclosure of which would, or could reasonably be expected to, unreasonably affect that person adversely in respect of his or her lawful business or professional affairs or that organisation or undertaking in respect of its lawful business, commercial or financial affairs see para.2–015(17). The Official Information Act 1982 (New Zealand), ss.9(2)(b)(i) and 27(1)(a), provides a qualified exemption where the making available of that information would be likely to unreasonably prejudice the commercial position of the person who supplied or who is the subject of the information.: see para.2–023(2). In the other jurisdictions, protection from disclosure is provided through the confidentiality and trade secrets exemptions: see nn.2 p.635 and 30, p.663 above.

— the matter that is the proper subject of protection from that prejudice or likely prejudice.

The concept of "prejudice" and the requisite degree of likelihood of prejudice are the same as those which are used for most of the other harm-based exemptions. These have been considered elsewhere in this work.[53] The object of the harm that forms the subject of the provision is the commercial interests of any person (including the public authority holding the information in question). This wording is of wide scope. In particular, there is no limitation on the nature or extent of the commercial interests that are material to the operation of the exemption. For example, there is no requirement that such interests should be serious or substantial[54]; nor is there any requirement that the protection of such interests should have any public interest element or justification. The phrase "commercial interests" is apt to cover:

— the existing business of a person or organisation, including its know-how[55];
— a proposed venture; and
— the assets of a commercial enterprise, including its contracts.

The public interest

25–037 If the information in question comes within the section, the duty to disclose the information does not apply if the public interest in maintaining the exemption outweighs the public interest in disclosing the information.[56] The weighing

[53] In relation to "prejudice" generally, see paras 15–012 to 15–020. In relation to the required degree of likelihood, see specifically para.15–014.

[54] This is, it seems, the deliberate intention of the legislature. The Select Committee had recommended that the phrase "substantial prejudice" be used, but this recommendation was rejected: *Report from the Select Committee Appointed to Consider the Draft Freedom of Information Bill 1998–9*, July 1999, HL, para.32; *Select Committee on Public Administration, Third Report*, Sessions 1998–9, July 1999, HC 570–1, para.71. Contrast, also, the test of "substantial harm" which had been proposed in the White Paper *Your Right to Know. The Government's Proposals for a Freedom of Information Act* (Cm.3818) December 11, 1997, para.3.7.

[55] In Australia, under the equivalent provision in the Freedom of Information Act 1982, this exemption has been successfully invoked to exempt documents with information as to the nature of, techniques used in, and results of tests carried out into a pharmaceutical product (*Re Pfizer Pty Ltd and the Department of Health, Housing and Community Services* (1993) 30 A.L.D. 647). See also: *Re Organon (Australia) Pty Ltd and Department of Community Services and Health* (1987) 13 A.L.D. 588 at 595 (the fact that considerable time and money had been expended upon the compilation of statistical information supplied to the department and that the publication of the statistics would reduce the value of that investment was sufficient to meet the requirements of the exemption); *Gill v Department of Industry, Technology and Resources* [1987] V.R. 681 at 687; *Re The Staff Development and Training Centre and Secretary, Department of Employment, Workplace Relations and Small Business* (2000) 30 A.A.R. 330 at 365–368; *Searle Australia v Public Interest Advocacy Centre* (1992) 36 F.C.R. 111; 108 A.L.R. 163 (the exemption does not apply to the compilation of material otherwise publicly available).

[56] Freedom of Information Act 2000, s.2(2)(b).

exercise necessitates an identification of the public interest in the maintenance of the exemption, always recognising that that public interest must be delineated in such a fashion that it is capable in practice of being outweighed.[57] Given the quintessentially private nature of the interest being protected by the exemption (the commercial interests of a person), it is difficult to see immediately what particular public interest there is in maintaining the exemption without importing interests that already stand to be protected by other provisions in Pt II of the Act. It is suggested that it would be impermissible to use the public interest weighing exercise for the purposes of s.43(2) to effectively reshape and enlarge the discrete exemptions provided elsewhere in the Act: most notably, the exemptions for confidential information and trade secrets.

Duty to confirm or deny

Where compliance with the duty to confirm or deny would, or would be likely to, prejudice the commercial interests of any person (including the public authority holding the information), then the discrete duty to confirm or deny that that information is held by the public authority does not arise.[58] This is a qualified exclusion of duty.[59] It will therefore be necessary to consider whether, in all the circumstances, the maintenance of the exclusion of this duty is outweighed by the public interest in disclosing whether the public authority holds the information. As noted previously, despite its superficial similarity, this public interest balancing exercise is materially different from that employed for the purpose of determining whether the duty to communicate does not apply.[60] Short of a purely confirmatory request that, in its terms, sets out the information or the gist of the information sought, it is difficult to imagine any particular public interest in maintaining an exemption from the duty to confirm or deny that information is held. On the other hand, other than the public interest articulated through the Freedom of Information Act 2000 itself, it is also difficult to identify any particular public interest in confirming or denying the holding. 25–038

5. INTERNATIONAL CONFIDENCES

Introduction

Section 27(2) of the Freedom of Information Act 2000 exempts information if it is confidential information obtained from a State other than the United 25–039

[57] To avoid metamorphosing it into an absolute exemption.
[58] Freedom of Information Act 2000, s.43(3).
[59] *ibid.*, s.2(1).
[60] See paras 15–010 to 15–011 as to what it involves.

Kingdom or from an international organisation or international court.[61] The exemption is a qualified exemption. What is confidential for the purposes of s.27(2) is statutorily defined by the Act as any information obtained from a State, organisation or court while (a) the terms on which it was obtained require it to be held in confidence or (b) the circumstances in which it was obtained make it reasonable for the State, organisation or court to expect that it will be held in confidence.[62] "State," "international organisation" and "international court" are each statutorily defined by the Act.[63] The definitions are cast in wide terms.[63A]

Scope of the exemption

25–040 This is a class exemption, so that it applies to any information that falls within this definition without regard to the consequences of disclosure. It is therefore potentially of wide scope. The exemption is capable of exempting information the disclosure of which would not "constitute a breach of confidence actionable" by the supplier of the information or another person.[64] However, its

[61] Also Freedom of Information (Scotland) Act 2002, s.32(2). There is no comparable exemption under the Data Protection Act 1998. In the United States, exemption for information communicated by foreign governments in confidence is generally secured through Executive Order 12,958 and exemption 1: see para.2–008(1) and *Krikorian v Department of State* 984 F.(2d) 461 (D.C. Cir. 1993). There must be a contemporaneous expectation of confidentiality: *Weatherhead v United States*, 157 F.(3d) 735 (9th Cir. 1998), concerning information from the British Government. The Freedom of Information Act 1982 (Cth of Australia), s.33(1), exempts a document the disclosure of which would divulge any information communicated in confidence by or on behalf of a foreign government, an authority of a foreign government or an international organization to the Australian Government: see para.2–015(9). The Official Information Act 1982 (New Zealand), ss.6(b) and 27(1)(a), provides an absolute exemption where the disclosure of the information would be likely to prejudice the entrusting of information to the government of New Zealand on a basis of confidence by the government of any other country or any agency of such a government, or by any international organisation: see para.2–022(2). The Access to Information Act (Canada), s.13(1), provides a mandatory exemption for records containing information received in confidence from other governments: see para.2–031(1). The Freedom of Information Act 1997 (Ireland), s.24(2) provides a mandatory exemption for records containing information revealing diplomatic communications; or revealing confidential communications from foreign state organisations: see para.2–039(4).

[62] Freedom of Information Act 2000, s.27(2); Freedom of Information (Scotland) Act 2002, s.32(2).

[63] See Freedom of Information Act 2000, s.27(5); Freedom of Information (Scotland) Act 2002, s.32(3).

[63A] See paras.18–003 to 18–007 for a consideration of the exemption under Freedom of Information Act 2000, s.27(1). The exemption may, in some circumstances, be able to be relied upon to exempt foreign confidential information on the basis that to disclose such information would be prejudicial to international relations.

[64] Being the words used in Freedom of Information Act 2000, s.41(1)(b) and Freedom of Information (Scotland) Act 2002, s.36(2)(b). In Australia, where the Freedom of Information Act 1982 s.33(1)(b) provides an exemption where disclosure "would divulge any information or matter communicated in confidence by or on behalf of a foreign government, an authority of a foreign government or an international organization to the Government of the Commonwealth, to an authority of the Commonwealth . . ." it has been held that that exemption is not confined to communications which if disclosed would give rise to an action in breach of confidence. It

practical operation is materially reduced by two considerations. First, although the focus of the definition is on the terms on which or the circumstances in which the information was obtained, and whether those terms or circumstances require it to be held or give rise to a reasonable expectation that it will be held in confidence, the definition also contains a temporal limitation. Information is only confidential within the meaning of the statutory definition for so long as that requirement or that expectation continues in effect.[65] For example, the terms on which the information was obtained may have the effect that if and in so far as it enters the public domain it is no longer required to be held in confidence by the public authority.[66] Similarly, the circumstances in which the information was obtained may mean that if and in so far as it enters the public domain there ceases to be a reasonable expectation that it will be held in confidence. Secondly, the section only applies to information that has itself been obtained from a foreign state or international organisation. Where the information sought originates from a public authority in the United Kingdom, but has been prepared using information from a foreign state or an international organisation, unless and to the extent that the former will reveal the latter, the domestic information will not be exempt information under this provision.[67]

The public interest

As noted above, the exemption is a qualified exemption. In other words, in each instance the exemption is subject to whether the public interest in maintaining 25–041

extends to information which was communicated and received under an express or inferred understanding that it would be kept confidential: *Re Maher and Attorney-General's Department* (1985) 7 A.L.D. 731 (it was enough that the information was supplied pursuant to a general understanding that communications of a particular nature would be treated in confidence); *Re Throssell and Australian Archives (No.2)* (1987) 14 A.L.D. 296. Nor is it necessary that the agency make inquiries as to the motives of the person who supplied the information or whether it is based on false information: *Gersten v Minister for Immigration & Multicultural Affairs* [2000] F.C.A. 1221. Nor, apparently, does it make any difference that the information is in the public domain: *Commonwealth of Australia v Hittich* (1994) 53 F.C.R. 152; 35 A.L.D. 717. The view taken in the comparative jurisdictions is that the evidence of the views of foreign governments should be afforded considerable weight, but is not determinative: *Re Slater and Cox*, (1988) 15 A.L.D. 20, *RC O'Donovan and Attorney-General's Dept* (1985) 8 A.L.D. 528 at 534; *Do-Ky v Minister for Foreign Affairs* [1997] 2 FC 907.

65 Freedom of Information Act 2000, s.27(3); Freedom of Information (Scotland) Act 2002, s.32(2).

66 In the United States, a distinction is drawn between information that has unofficially "leaked" into the public domain and that which has officially come into the public domain. Thus, in *Afshar v Department of State* 702 F.(2d) 1125 (D.C. Cir. 1983) it was observed that a foreign government can ignore "unofficial leaks and public surmise . . . but official acknowledgment may force a government to retaliate."

67 This is the approach which was taken by the Federal Court of Appeal in Canada in *Sherman v Canada (Minster of National Revenue)* [2003] F.C.A. 202, where the applicant sought records containing statistics generated by the Canadian Revenue but derived from information obtained in confidence from the United States pursuant to a bilateral convention with respect to taxes on income and capital.

it outweighs the public interest in disclosure.[68] Where no specific harm would result from the disclosure of the information, the public interest requirement may have the effect that the exemption does not apply. As against that, however, it may be argued that harm generally results from the disclosure of information in circumstances where that contradicts either the terms on which it was obtained or the reasonable expectation of the entity from which it was obtained, and that there is a public interest in upholding compliance with such terms or expectations and avoiding the harm in the shape of lack of trust (and, in all probability, a reduced flow of information) that results from not upholding compliance with the same. Against that and underpinned by the rules of comity and international law, lies the principle that foreign states and organisations dealing with the public authorities in the United Kingdom must take the country as it is, including its laws relating to the disclosure of information. By conveying or transmitting information to a public authority in this country, the foreign entity must accept that that will be attended by certain loss of control over the further dissemination of the information.[69] Accordingly, a consideration of the public interest in maintaining the exemption will, it is suggested, need to take into account:

- whether the particular information or information of that class has been identified by the source as being confidential;
- whether, quite apart from any formal identification, the information is of a sort conventionally considered to be confidential; and
- whether, if the source of the information has designated it as confidential, that was done as a matter of course or perfunctorily; and
- if the information emenates from the European Union, Art.255 of the Amsterdam Treaty.

Duty to confirm or deny

25–042 The duty to confirm or deny does not arise if, or to the extent that, the confirmation or denial that would have to be given to comply with the duty would, or would be likely to, involve the disclosure of any information (whether or not already recorded) which is obtained from a State other than the United Kingdom or from an international organisation or international

[68] Freedom of Information Act 2000, s.2(2)(b); Freedom of Information (Scotland) Act 2002, s.2(1)(b).

[69] Just as the foreign entity would have to accept that if the information it conveyed to the public authority was personal information relating to the applicant, then that information would, notwithstanding that it had been conveyed to the public authority in confidence, have to be conveyed to the applicant if an application were made under s.7 of the Data Protection Act 1998, subject to any applicable exemptions under that Act.

court.[70] This disapplication of the duty to confirm or deny is only operative if, in all the circumstances of the case, the public interest in maintaining the exclusion of the duty outweighs the public interest in disclosing whether the public authority holds the information.[71]

[70] Freedom of Information Act 2000, s.27(4)(b). There is no free-standing duty to confirm or deny in Scotland.

[71] Freedom of Information Act 2000, s.2(1)(b).

CHAPTER 26

Miscellaneous Exemptions

1. COMMUNICATIONS WITH HER MAJESTY, ETC.

Introduction

26–001 By virtue of s.37(1)(a) of the Freedom of Information Act 2000, information that relates to communications with Her Majesty,[1] other members of the Royal Family or the Royal Household is exempt information.[2] Similarly, the duty to confirm or deny does not arise in relation to such information.[3] Both the exemption and the exclusion are qualified.[4] Accordingly, even if information is exempt information under this provision, the public authority holding that information must disclose it unless the public interest in maintaining the exemption outweighs the public interest in disclosing the information.[5]

Background

26–002 The *Code of Practice on Access to Government Information* contained a similar, but narrower, exemption for "information relating to confidential communications between Ministers and Her Majesty the Queen or other Members of the Royal Household, or relating to confidential proceedings of the Privy Council."[6] The accompanying *Guidance on Interpretation* stated that that exemption was designed to protect confidences.[7] More long-standing restrictions have prevented parliamentary questions being asked of ministers regarding certain matters connected with the monarch, the Royal Family and the Royal Household.[8] The relevant exemptions in the draft Freedom of

[1] The reference to Her Majesty is to be construed as a reference to the Sovereign for the time being: Interpretation Act 1978, s.10.

[2] Similarly, the Freedom of Information (Scotland) Act 2002, s.41. See para.26–013.

[3] Freedom of Information Act 2000, s.37(2). There is no discrete duty to confirm or deny under the Freedom of Information (Scotland) Act 2002.

[4] Freedom of Information Act 2000, s.2(3); Freedom of Information (Scotland) Act 2002, s. 2(2).

[5] Similarly, the duty to confirm or deny. Freedom of Information Act 2000, s.37(1) and (2) engage s.2(2)(b) and (1)(b) respectively so as to prevent from arising, first, the duty to confirm or deny and, secondly, the duty to communicate, if the public interest in divulgence or disclosure (as the case may be) is outweighed.

[6] *Open Government Code of Practice on Access to Government Information* (2nd ed., 1997), Pt II, para.3. The exemption did not refer to harm or prejudice and it was not therefore subject to any balancing exercise weighing the public interest in disclosure against the public interest in non-disclosure: *ibid.*, Pt II. See also: the Scottish Executive's *Code of Practice on Access to Scottish Executive Information* (2nd ed., 2003), Pt II, para.3; and the National Assembly for Wales's *Code of Practice on Public Access to Information* (2nd ed., 2001), Annex B.

[7] *Open Government Code of Practice on Access to Government Information: Guidance on Interpretation* (2nd ed., 1997), Pt II, paras 3.1–3.2.

[8] Erskine May, *Parliamentary Practice* (22nd ed., Butterworths, London, 1997), p.298. Although the *White Paper on Open Government* (Cm.2290), 1993 did not offer any additional commentary upon the exemption which eventually found expression in the *Open Government Code of Practice on Access to Government Information* (2nd ed., 1997), Pt II, para.3, it did propose a further exemption which was not taken further for "information which could not be sought in a parliamentary question" (see Annex A, Pt II, para.xv).

Information Bill published on May 24, 1999[9] and the Freedom of Information Bill introduced in the House of Commons on November 18, 1999[10] were identically worded.

The comparative jurisdictions

Section 9(2)(f)(i) of the Official Information Act 1982 (NZ) provides for the withholding of information where necessary to maintain the constitutional conventions that protect the confidentiality of communications by or with the Sovereign or her representative unless it is more desirable in the public interest that the information be made available.[11] Section 46(1)(d) of the Freedom of Information Act 1997 (Ireland) also excludes records relating to the President from the provisions of that Act. Beyond this, none of the comparative jurisdictions has any exemptions in their access to information regimes equivalent to s.37(1) of the Freedom of Information Act 2000. 26–003

The Royal Family

Her Majesty and the other members of the Royal Family are not "public authorities" for the purposes of the Freedom of Information Act 2000[12] and are thus not subject to the regime established by the Act.[13] The expression "the Royal Family" is not defined in the Freedom of Information Act 2000 and does not 26–004

---

[9] *Freedom of Information: Consultation on Draft Legislation* (Cm.4355), 1999, Pt II, cl.29(1).

[10] cl.35(1).

[11] See I. Eagles, M. Taggart & G. Liddell, *Freedom of Information in New Zealand* (Oxford University Press, Auckland, 1992), pp.364–367.

[12] Her Majesty and the other members of the Royal Family are also not "Scottish public authorities" for the purposes of the Freedom of Information (Scotland) Act 2002, s.3, Sch.1: see also the Scotland Act 1998, ss.29–30, Sch.5, Pt II, s.B13.

[13] Furthermore, the Freedom of Information Act 2000 does not expressly bind the Crown and therefore only binds the Crown to the extent required by necessary implication: *Province of Bombay v Municipal Corporation of Bombay* [1947] A.C. 58; *Attorney-General of Ceylon v A D Silva* [1953] A.C. 461; *Madras Electric Supply Corp Ltd v Boarland* [1955] A.C. 667; *Ministry of Agriculture v Jenkins* [1963] 2 Q.B. 317; *Wood v Leeds Area Health Authority* [1974] I.C.R. 535; and *Lord Advocate v Strathclyde Regional Council* [1990] 2 A.C. 580. This "doctrine of Crown immunity" is expressly saved and recognised by the Crown Proceedings Act 1947, ss.31(1) and 40(2)(f). Following *BBC v Johns (Inspector of Taxes)* [1965] Ch. 32 at 81 (*per* Diplock L.J.), the Crown's "immunity" from the Freedom of Information Act 2000 regime will also be enjoyed by the Crown's servants and agents to the extent that they are not brought under that regime by express provision or necessary implication (see also F. Bennion, *Statutory Interpretation* (4th ed., Butterworths, London, 2002), p.164 and Wade and Forsyth, *Administrative Law* (8th ed., Oxford University Press, Oxford, 2000), p.820). In practice, a great number of servants and agents of the Crown and other Crown bodies are brought under the Freedom of Information Act 2000 regime by being expressly listed as "public authorities" in the Freedom of Information Act 2000, Sch 1. The criminal offence provisions in the Freedom of Information Act 2000, s.77 and Sch.3, para.12 are also applied to persons in the public service of the Crown as they apply to any other person: Freedom of Information Act 2000, s.81(3).

have any specific legal definition elsewhere. The monarch, his or her parents and grandparents, his or her spouse and their children, children-in-law and grandchildren are plainly members of the Royal Family. How much further the Royal Family extends to others who are related to the monarch by blood or marriage falls to be answered by reference to convention, their styles, titles, forms of precedence and special privileges, their subjection to the monarch's general authority in relation to the supervision of minors and Royal Marriages, their inclusion in the Civil List and the applicability of special common law and statutory provisions.[14] While it will often be clear in practice whether a particular communication has passed from or to someone who is a member of the Royal Family for the purposes of s.37(1)(a) of the Freedom of Information Act 2000, formal membership for these purposes may depend upon questions of fact in the circumstances of each case. Once membership has been established, however, it is notable that s.37(1)(a) of the Freedom of Information Act 2000 exempts all information regardless of whether the Family member in question was acting in a public or private capacity in relation to the relevant communication.

The Royal Household

26–005 The Royal Household is also not a "public authority" for the purposes of the Freedom of Information Act 2000[15] and is not subject to the Freedom of Information Act 2000 regime.[16] The expression "the Royal Household" is not defined in the Freedom of Information Act 2000 and does not have any specific legal definition elsewhere. The Royal Household assists the monarch in carrying out official duties and it includes the monarch's Household together with the Households of other members of the Royal Family who undertake public engagements. The Royal Household is under the overall authority of the Lord Chamberlain who is the senior member of the monarch's Household and is divided into five departments: the Private Secretary's Office; the Privy Purse and

[14] *Halsbury's Laws of England* (4th ed., 1998 re-issue), Vol.12(1), paras 27, 35–36. The Royal Family would certainly appear to extend beyond those entitled to the style of "Royal Highness:" *ibid.*, para.34. Complications may arise in relation to current monarchs or members of the Royal Family who did not have their current status when a particular communication took place and, conversely, in relation to former monarchs or members of the Royal Family who have lost that status since a particular communication took place. It is notable that a less comprehensive protection from the regime is afforded to information that relates to communications with the Royal Family and Household than is afforded by s.23(1) to information supplied by or relating to the security bodies. Basic precepts of statutory interpretation suggest that some effect must be given to the use of different formulae. It is also significant that information contained in a "historical record" (as to the meaning of which, see para.6–033) cannot be exempt information by virtue of s.37(1)(a), suggesting that the contemporaneity of the information is central to the rationale for the exemption.

[15] The Royal Household is also not a "Scottish public authority" for the purposes of the Freedom of Information (Scotland) Act 2002, s.3, Sch.1: see also the Scotland Act 1998, ss.29–30, Sch.5, Pt II, s.B13.

[16] See also n.13 above.

Treasurer's Office; the Master of the Household's Department; the Lord Chamberlain's Office; and the Royal Collection Department.[17] While it will often be clear in practice whether a particular communication has passed from or to someone who is a member of the Royal Household for the purposes of s.37(1)(a) of the Freedom of Information Act 2000, the precise boundaries of that organisation may depend upon questions of fact in the circumstances of each case.[18] Furthermore, s.37(1)(a) of the Freedom of Information Act 2000 only exempts information relating to communications "with the Royal Household" (and not merely communications with its members) so that the exemption only applies to communications with Household members if and in so far as they were acting in their official capacity in relation to the relevant communication.[19] A possible complication could arise in this regard out of the fact that certain officers of the Household are *ex-officio* government whips who continue to be appointed on a political basis at the nomination of the Prime Minister.[20]

---

[17] The respective heads of these five departments are: the Private Secretary (constitutional, official and political matters and media relations); the Keeper of the Privy Purse (financial, personnel, property and revenue matters and the management of the Civil List); the Master of the Household (domestic, hospitality and staff matters); the Comptroller (ceremonial and formal matters); and the Director of the Royal Collection (co-ordinating the work of the Surveyor of the Queen's Pictures, the Surveyor of the Queen's Works of Art and the Royal Librarian). The five heads of department meet under the chairmanship of the Lord Chamberlain as the Lord Chamberlain's Committee. The Private Secretary is also a Privy Counsellor: Hood, Phillips and Jackson, *Constitutional and Administrative Law* (8th ed., Oxford University Press, Oxford, 2001), para.14–011. The Royal Household also includes the Great Officers of State (*e.g.* the Earl Marshal and the Lord Great Chamberlain), other ancient officers together with numerous other domestic servants and staff who work for or on behalf of the Royal Family (*e.g.* ladies-in-waiting and footmen).

[18] For example, Royal Collection Enterprises Limited is a trading subsidiary of the Royal Collection Trust which in turn funds the activities of the Royal Collection Department within the Royal Household. To this end, Royal Collection Enterprises Limited manages public access to certain castles and palaces, connected shops and certain image and intellectual property rights. The Keeper of the Privy Purse is Chairman of Royal Collection Enterprises Limited. The Director of the Royal Collection is responsible for its day-to-day operation but the company has its own Managing Director. It will be a question of fact in each case whether a particular communication with someone working for or on behalf of Royal Collection Enterprises Limited constitutes a communication with the Royal Household for the purposes of the Freedom of Information Act 2000, s.37(1)(a). Although each Royal Household is formally dissolved upon the death of its monarch (signified by the symbolic breaking of the Lord Chamberlain's staff over the grave of the deceased monarch), information relating to prior communications with that Household may nevertheless benefit from the exemption in the Freedom of Information Act 2000, s.37(1)(a). See also n.14 above.

[19] Any information relating to a letter sent by Her Majesty is exempt under the Freedom of Information Act 2000, s.37(1)(a), but information relating to a private letter sent by someone who happens to be a member of Her Household is not, unless sent on behalf of the Royal Household and in the course of their official duties.

[20] These are the Treasurer, Comptroller and Vice-Chamberlain of Her Majesty's Household in the House of Commons and the Captain of the Honourable Corps of the Gentlemen-at-Arms, the Captain of the Queen's Bodyguard of the Yeomen of the Guard and up to five Lords and/or Baronesses in Waiting in the House of Lords: *Halsbury's Laws of England* (4th ed., 1996 re-issue), Vol.8(2), para.546; Hood Phillips & Jackson, *Constitutional and Administrative Law* (8th ed., Sweet & Maxwell, London, 2001), para.10–024. Strictly speaking these whips are members

Communications with the Royal Family and Household

26–006 The reference in s.37(1)(a) of the Freedom of Information Act 2000 to "communications with" a member of the Royal Family or the Royal Household is broad enough to encompass all manner of written and oral transmissions and exchanges of information whether conducted directly or indirectly and whether passing from or to the Royal side.[21] The exemption in s.37(1)(a) of the Freedom of Information Act 2000 also applies irrespective of whether the public authority which holds the requested information, or indeed any public authority, is or was involved in or party to the communication in question. Information regarding the fact of such communications, details of the "when, where, how, why, by whom, to whom" kind and the content of the information communicated can all "relate to" those communications and so the exemption is of potentially broad application. However, it is also important to recognise its limitations: the exemption does not extend as far as all information directly or indirectly supplied by or relating to the Royal Family or the Royal Household[22]; it does not exempt information about the Royal Family or the Royal Household *per se*; and the precise meaning and limits of the expression "communications with" will need to be established on a case-by-case basis. So far as the last point is concerned, it might be said that communicating "with" someone requires that they be engaged to some degree so that unsuccessful or incomplete transmissions of information (*e.g.* a letter that is sent but recalled or not understood) do not count. Questions may also arise as to whether the copying or side-copying of documents to members of the Royal Family or the Royal Household necessarily entails any "communication with" the relevant copy-recipients.

of the Royal Household and it could therefore be argued that information relating to communications with them is subject to the exemption in the Freedom of Information Act 2000, s.37(1)(a). However, they are paid their salaries out of money provided by Parliament as part of the expenses of the Treasury and the argument that communications with them should be regarded as "communications with the Royal Household" for the purposes of the Freedom of Information Act 2000, s.37(1)(a) is therefore weak: Ministerial and other Salaries Act 1975, s.3(1)(a) and (b), Sch.1, Pts IV and V, para.2(f).

[21] Such information could take the form of answers, assertions, claims, demands, ideas, messages, offers, opinions, propositions, questions, requests, responses or warnings and could be exchanged or transmitted by way of conversation, correspondence or discussion and on any basis ranging from one-off unilateral notification to fully inter-active dialogue. The choice of "communications with" over "communications between" leaves more room for the inclusion of one-sided or passive transmissions and exchanges. In this regard, the use of "communications" in the plural should not be seen as requiring a sequence or series of communications: Interpretation Act 1978, s.6(c) "words in the plural include the singular."

[22] *cf.* Freedom of Information Act 2000, s.23 on information directly or indirectly supplied by or relating to any of the security bodies: see n.14 above and paras 17–026 to 17–032.

Communications with the Royal Family and Household: the public interest

As the exemption conferred by s.37(1)(a) of the Freedom of Information Act 2000 is a qualified exemption, it is implicit that some information relating to communications with Her Majesty or with other members of the Royal Family or with the Royal Household is to be disclosed under the Freedom of Information Act 2000.[23] The task of weighing the public interest in maintaining an exemption that is purely class-based (in other words, that does not have some type of prejudice as one of its composite elements) is always difficult. The task is particularly difficult where, as in s.37(1), the exemption does not reflect a well-understood proscription against disclosure: for example, safeguarding national security, legal professional privilege, trade secrets and so forth. Whereas in the latter cases it is always possible to assess the extent to which exemption is required in order to protect against that well-recognised harm, there is no such familiar protection to be secured by s.37(1), leaving the weighing exercise particularly prone to idiosyncratic views of the underlying public interest perceived to be protected by the exemption. With this caveat, it is suggested that the strength of the public interest in maintaining the exclusion of the duty to confirm or deny the existence of, or the duty to communicate, information relating to communications with members of the Royal Family or with the Royal Household will depend on the nature and public importance of that information. 26–007

The monarch performs a number of important constitutional, legal and political functions and maintains open lines of communication with Parliament and the government at the highest level at all times. The Royal Family more generally fulfil other public and official functions and are the recipients of public funds in return. The nature and content of their interactions with the outside world when they are acting in a public capacity and at public expense may therefore be of very great public interest and the countervailing factors favouring non-disclosure will turn largely on the extent to which exposure to public scrutiny would prejudice the effective working of the Royal Family and the Royal Household given their status and importance. Where communications have taken place with members of the Royal Family acting in their private capacities, however, the public interest in disclosure may be less strong and the legitimate interest in ensuring their privacy and dignity will acquire more force.

2. HONOURS AND DIGNITIES

Introduction

By virtue of s.37(1)(b) of the Freedom of Information Act 2000, information that relates to the conferring by the Crown of any honour or dignity is exempt 26–008

[23] See para.15–005.

information.[24] Similarly, the duty to confirm or deny does not arise in relation to such information.[25] Both the exemption and the exclusion are qualified.[26] Accordingly, even if information is exempt information under this provision, the public authority holding that information must disclose it unless the public interest in maintaining the exemption outweighs the public interest in disclosing the information.[27]

Background

26–009 The *Code of Practice on Access to Government Information* contained a similar, but narrower, exemption for "information, opinions and assessments given in relation to recommendations for honours."[28] The accompanying *Guidance on Interpretation* stated that the exemption was aimed at ensuring frankness, candour and honesty in the honours recommendation and selection process.[29] More long-standing restrictions have prevented parliamentary questions being asked of ministers regarding the grant of honours.[30] The relevant exemptions in the draft Freedom of Information Bill published on May 24, 1999[31] and the Freedom of Information Bill introduced in the House of Commons on November 18, 1999[32]

[24] The Freedom of Information (Scotland) Act 2002, s.41 is identically worded save that reference is made to "the exercise by Her Majesty of Her prerogative of honour" (*ibid.*, s.41(a)) instead of "the conferring by the Crown of any honour or dignity" (Freedom of Information Act 2000, s.37(1)(b)): see para.26–013.

[25] Freedom of Information Act 2000, s.37(2). There is no discrete duty to confirm or deny under the Freedom of Information (Scotland) Act 2002.

[26] Freedom of Information Act 2000, s.2(3); Freedom of Information (Scotland) Act 2002, s. 2(2).

[27] Similarly, the duty to confirm or deny. Freedom of Information Act 2000, s.37(1) and (2) engage s.2(2)(b) and (1)(b) respectively so as to prevent from arising, first, the duty to confirm or deny and, secondly, the duty to communicate, if the public interest in divulgence or disclosure (as the case may be) is outweighed. Information cannot be exempt information by virtue of s.37(1)(b) after the end of the period of 60 years beginning with the year following that in which the record containing the information was created: *ibid.*, s.63(3).

[28] *Open Government Code of Practice on Access to Government Information* (2nd ed., 1997), Pt II, para.8c. The exemption did not refer to harm or prejudice and it was not therefore subject to any balancing exercise weighing the public interest in disclosure against the public interest in non-disclosure: *ibid.*, Pt II. See also: the Scottish Executive's *Code of Practice on Access to Scottish Executive Information* (2nd ed., 2003), Pt II, para.8c; and the National Assembly for Wales's *Code of Practice on Public Access to Information* (2nd ed., 2001), Annex B.

[29] *Open Government Code of Practice on Access to Government Information: Guidance on Interpretation* (2nd ed., 1997), Pt II, paras 8.9–8.12. Para.8.12 states that the exemption for information, opinions and assessments given in relation to recommendations for honours "links in with" the restriction on the matters subject to investigation by the Parliamentary Commissioner for Administration in the Parliamentary Commissioner for Administration Act 1967, s.5, Sch.4, para.11: "the grant of honours, awards or privileges within the gift of the Crown, including the grant of Royal Charters."

[30] Erskine May, *Parliamentary Practice* (22nd ed., Butterworths, London, 1997), p.298. The *White Paper on Open Government* (Cm.2290), 1993 did not offer any additional commentary upon the exemptions which eventually found expression in the *Open Government Code of Practice on Access to Government Information* (2nd ed., 1997), Pt II, para.8c.

[31] *Freedom of Information: Consultation on Draft Legislation* (Cm.4355), 1999, Pt II, cl.29(1).

[32] cl.35(1).

were identically worded. The only difference between these provisions and s.37(1) of the Freedom of Information Act 2000 is the additional inclusion in the latter of a reference to the conferring by the Crown of dignities as well as honours.[33]

Honours and dignities

There is an important distinction between honours and dignities which is maintained in numerous statutes.[34] Reference has already been made to the inclusion in s.37(1)(b) of the Freedom of Information Act 2000 of the reference to dignities (as well as honours) which was specifically achieved by way of amendment to the Freedom of Information Bill.[35] Awards, decorations and medals for bravery, gallantry, heroism and public service in the civilian and military spheres, the civic styles "lord mayor," "deputy lord mayor" and "right honourable" and civic status as a city or royal borough are all conferred under the prerogative of honour.[36] Peerages, baronetcies, knighthoods, arms and precedence are conferred as 26–010

[33] Freedom of Information Act 2000, s.37(1)(b). The words "or dignity" were inserted pursuant to a government amendment moved by Lord Falconer of Thoroton at Committee Stage in the House of Lords: *Hansard*, HL, Vol.618, October 24, 2000, col.315. The amendment was described as "merely clarificatory" and explained as follows: "The term 'dignity' refers to peerages, and the amendment ensures that the exemption applies to the granting of peerages as well as meritorious awards" (*ibid.*). *cf.* Freedom of Information (Scotland) Act 2002, s.41(a).

[34] For example, Honours (Prevention of Abuses) Act 1925, s.1; Legitimation (Scotland) Act 1968, s.8; Adoption Act 1976, s.44; Legitimacy Act 1976, Sch.1 , paras 3–4; Race Relations Act 1976, s.76; Law Reform (Parent And Child) (Scotland) Act 1986, s.9; Family Law Reform Act 1987, ss.19 and 27; Human Fertilisation And Embryology Act 1990, s.29; Private International Law (Miscellaneous Provisions) Act 1995, s.6; Scotland Act 1998, s.30, Sch.5, para.2(3); Northern Ireland Act 1998, s.4, Sch.2, para.6; Adoption and Children Act 2002, s.71. It is notable that the Freedom of Information (Scotland) Act 2002, s.41 refers to "the exercise by Her Majesty of Her prerogative of honour" without mentioning the conferring of dignities.

[35] See para.26–009. The Freedom of Information Act 2000 also amended the Data Protection Act 1998 so as to exempt personal data processed for the purposes of the conferring of any dignity (as well as any honour) from the subject information provisions in that Act: Data Protection Act 1998, Sch.7, para.3 as amended by the Freedom of Information Act 2000, s.73, Sch.6, para.6 (this amendment having come into force on May 14, 2001 under the Freedom of Information Act 2000, s.87(3) and the Freedom of Information Act 2000 (Commencement No. 1) Order 2001, SI 2001/1637, art.2(d)). The Freedom of Information Act 2000, s.73, Sch.6, para.6 was itself inserted into the Freedom of Information Bill by way of amendment at the same time as the words "or dignity" were added to what became s.31(1)(b) in order to ensure "that the corresponding provision in the Data Protection Act is similarly amended": *Hansard*, HL, Vol.618, October 24, 2000, col.315.

[36] *Prince's Case* (1606) 8 Co. Rep. 1a at 18b; 4 Co. Inst. 361, 363, 1 Bl. Com. (14th ed.) 271; *Halsbury's Laws of England*, (4th ed., 1996 re-issue), Vol.8(2), paras 831, 834; *Halsbury's Laws of England* (4th ed., 1994 re-issue), Vol.35, para.969. Examples are the Victoria Cross, the Order of Victoria and Albert, the Albert Medal, the George Cross, the Imperial Order of the Crown of India, the Royal Red Cross, the Distinguished Service Order, the Order of Merit, the Imperial Service Order, the Edward Medal, the Territorial Decoration, the Order of the Companions of Honour and the Order of the British Empire. It is arguable whether the grant of borough status by royal charter under the Local Government Act 1972, ss.245–245A amounts to the conferring by the Crown of an honour for the purposes of the Freedom of Information Act 2000, s.37(1)(b).

dignities.[37] Appointment by the Crown as a Privy Counsellor or Queen's Counsel also carries with it certain consequences in terms of precedence and the right to use (as appropriate) the style "right honourable" or the post-nominal initials "QC".[38] While the office of Queen's Counsel would not appear to constitute an honour or dignity as such, it has been suggested that the office of Privy Counsellor does constitute an honour.[39] That peerages are a type of dignity is probably the most important point to note here because, at least for the time being, the conferral of a life peerage carries with it the right to sit and vote in the House of Lords.[40] In November 2001 the government published plans to promote legislation abolishing the link between peerages and membership of

[37] *Halsbury's Laws of England*, (4th ed., 1994 re-issue), Vol.35, paras 901, 919, 963 and 967. The right to bear arms is a dignity but the Crown's power to grant armorial bearings to individuals is delegated to the Kings of Arms: *Manchester Corporation v Manchester Palace of Varieties Ltd* [1955] P. 133 at 147 (*per* Lord Goddard) (Court of Chivalry); *Halsbury's Laws of England* (4th ed., 1994 re-issue), Vol.35, paras 901, 970–973. Arms are therefore not conferred on individuals "by the Crown" for the purposes of the Freedom of Information Act 2000, s.37(1)(b). The position in relation to the conferring of arms on local authorities is more complicated: the power of grant was historically exercised by the Royal College of Arms (*Halsbury's Laws of England* (4th ed., 2001 re-issue), Vol.29(1) para.100); but Her Majesty may by Order in Council authorise a new local authority to bear and use specified armorial bearings in certain circumstances under the Local Government Act 1972, s.247 and such grants arguably amount to the conferring "by the Crown" of a dignity for the purposes of the Freedom of Information Act 2000, s.37(1)(b) (*e.g.* the Local Authorities (Armorial Bearings) Order 2001 (SI 2001/1454)).

[38] *Halsbury's Laws of England* (4th ed., 1996 re-issue), Vol.8(2), (paras 521–522 and 524; *Halsbury's Laws of England* (4th ed., 1989 re-issue), Vol.3(1), paras 359 and 434.

[39] See, *e.g.* Bradley and Ewing, *Constitutional and Administrative Law* (13th ed., Longman, 2003), p.270 where membership of the Privy Council is described as a "titular honour" and it is recorded that, "[T]he office is a recognised reward for public and political service, and appointments to it figure in the honours lists." As to Queen's Counsel, see the Data Protection Act 1998, s.37, Sch.7, para.3(a) and note the inclusion of honours and dignities in *ibid.*, para.3(b).

[40] *Norfolk Earldom Case* [1907] A.C. 10; *Wensleydale Peerage Case* (1856) 5 H.L.C. 958; L.J. 38; Appellate Jurisdiction Act 1876, s.6; Life Peerages Act 1958, s.1(2)(b); *Halsbury's Laws of England* (4th ed., 1994 re-issue), Vol.35, para.930; House of Lords Act 1999. The House of Lords currently comprises the Lords Spiritual and the Lords Temporal. All of the Lords Temporal are entitled to sit and vote in the House of Lords by virtue of the conferring by the Crown of a dignity (i.e. their peerage) while the Lords Spiritual are not because, while they are Lords of Parliament, they are not peers as such: *Halsbury's Laws of England* (4th ed., 1997 re-issue), Vol.34, para.531; Erskine May, *Parliamentary Practice* (22nd ed., Butterworths, London, 1997), p.12; Hood Phillips & Jackson, *Constitutional and Administrative Law* (8th ed., Sweet & Maxwell, London, 2001), p.176, n.19; and HL Standing Orders (Public Business) (2003), no.6. For these purposes, the Lords Spiritual are the archbishops and certain bishops of the Church of England and the Lords Temporal are life peers created under the Life Peerages Act 1958, Lords of Appeal in Ordinary created peers for life under the Appellate Jurisdiction Act 1876 and 92 hereditary peers given continued membership of the House of Lords under the House of Lords Act 1999 and relevant standing orders: *Halsbury's Laws of England* (4th ed., 1997 re-issue), Vol.34, paras 527 and 533–533A; *Halsbury's Laws of England* (4th ed., 2002 re-issue), Vol.10, para.352. Since the implementation of the House of Lords Act 1999, only the following 92 members of the House of Lords have been hereditary peers: 75 elected under that Act either by their own political party's hereditary peers or cross-bench grouping in proportion to that party or grouping's share of the hereditary peers, 15 elected under that Act by the House as a whole to act as Deputy Speakers or Committee Chairmen plus the hereditary Royal appointments of Earl Marshal and the Lord Great Chamberlain.

the House of Lords but these proposals were subsequently withdrawn in September 2003.[41]

The conferring by the Crown of any honour or dignity

The monarch is the fountain of all honour and dignity and enjoys the sole right of conferring all titles of honour and dignities.[42] By convention the monarch's powers in relation to titles of honour and dignities are exercised on the advice of the Prime Minister.[43] In relation to honours, each incoming Prime Minister appoints three Privy Counsellors to act as a Political Honours Scrutiny Committee for the purpose of considering the character and antecedents of persons on whom it is proposed to confer honours and to report to the Prime Minister.[44] 26–011

[41] Following the Report of the Royal Commission on the Reform of the House of Lords *A House for the Future* (Cm.4534), 2000, the government published a White Paper outlining plans for a second phase of House of Lords Reform *The House of Lords: Completing the Reform* (Cm.5291), 2001: "The Government proposes that membership of the House of Lords should cease to be connected to the peerage. As the Royal Commission emphasised, membership of the Lords should constitute a commitment to active engagement in the life of Parliament rather than the acceptance of an honour. At present the two purposes of a life peerage are muddled, with some members regarding the title as a necessary (but not always welcome) route to a seat in Parliament, while others accept peerages essentially as an honour (with any Parliamentary contribution being ancillary to the title). The Government proposes that in future Members of the House of Lords will not become peers. Equally, new peers will not in future become members of the House of Lords unless appointed or elected to it. This will free the award of a peerage to become wholly a mark of honour. Individuals may become, through separate routes, both peers and Members of the House of Lords, but the two would cease to be intertwined. Members of the second chamber would be designated 'Member of the Lords' (ML)" (*ibid.*, paras 78–79). The consultation paper published by the Department for Constitutional Affairs in September 2003, entitled *Constitutional Reform: Next Steps for the House of Lords* (CP 14/03), September 2003, paras 21 and 24–28 confirmed the plan to remove all hereditary peers from the House of Lords but indicated that the government no longer planned to "break the link" between peerages and membership of the House of Lords. This followed the publication of a report by the House of Commons Public Administration Select Committee, *The Second Chamber: Continuing the Reform*, (Session 2001–2002, Fifth Report, HC 494–I) and two reports by a House of Lords and House of Commons Joint Committee on House of Lords Reform (Session 2002–2003: First Report, HL Paper 17, HC 171 (December 2002); and Second Report, HL Paper 97, HC 668, (April 2003)). The first of the Joint Committee reports was debated by both Houses of Parliament in January-February 2003 and the second was responded to by the government (Session 2002–2003, HL Paper 155, HC 1027 (July 2003)).

[42] *Prince's Case* (1606) 8 Co. Rep. 1a at 18b; 4 Co. Inst. 361, 363; 1 Bl. Com. (14th ed.) 271; *Halsbury's Laws of England* (4th ed., 1996 re-issue), Vol.8(2), para.831; *Halsbury's Laws of England* (4th ed., 2001 re-issue), Vol.29(1), para.95; *Halsbury's Laws of England* (4th ed., 1994 re-issue), Vol.35, paras 901, 910–918; Hood Phillips & Jackson, *Constitutional and Administrative Law* (8th ed., Sweet & Maxwell, London, 2001), para.15–015(f).

[43] Although the monarch reserves absolute discretion in conferring the Order of Merit, the Order of the Garter, the Order of the Thistle and the Royal Victorian Order: *Halsbury's Laws of England* (4th ed., 1996 re-issue), Vol.8(2), paras 831–832. Thus Elizabeth II made the Governor of Southern Rhodesia a KCVO at the time of the Unilateral Declaration of Independence in November 1965: Hood Phillips & Jackson, *Constitutional and Administrative Law* (8th ed., Sweet & Maxwell, London, 2001), p.316, n.4.

[44] Report of the Royal Commission on Honours (Cmd.1789), 1922, paras 24–28; 57 HL Official Report (5th series) June 26, 1924, col.1068; *Halsbury's Laws of England* (4th ed., 1996 re-issue),

In relation to peerages, an independent House of Lords Appointments Commission recommends non-party-political persons for cross-bench life peerages (a role previously undertaken by the Prime Minister) and scrutinises the propriety and suitability of all nominations to life peerages including those put forward by the political parties but excluding those appointed to take on ministerial responsibility (a role previously undertaken by the Political Honours Scrutiny Committee).[45] Both the Political Honours Scrutiny Committee and the House of Lords Appointments Commission are listed as "public authorities" in Sch.1 to the Freedom of Information Act 2000.[46] Titles of honour are conferred by express grant in the form of letters patent and dignities are conferred by writ of summons in the case of peerages, by letters patent in the case of baronetcies and some knighthoods, by direct corporeal investiture in the case of most knighthoods or by warrants of precedence.[47] The expression "the conferring by the Crown" in s.37(1)(b) of the Freedom of Information Act 2000 raises questions as to how far the exemption captures information relating to the earlier selection and recommendation process which precedes formal conferral by the Crown itself as well as information relating to non-conferral where a candidate is rejected, for whatever reasons, by the Crown or by those involved lower down.

The conferring by the Crown of any honour or dignity: the public interest

26–012 The particular difficulties affecting the public interest so far as s.37(1) of the Freedom of Information Act 2000 is concerned have already been considered in relation to s.37(1)(a), and these are equally applicable to s.37(1)(b).[48] While the

Vol.8(2), paras 526, 832; Hood Phillips & Jackson, *Constitutional and Administrative Law* (8th ed., Sweet & Maxwell, London, 2001), para.15–015(f).

45 The House of Lords Appointments Commission is an advisory non-departmental public body established by the Prime Minister on May 4, 2000 on a non-statutory basis pursuant to proposals set out in the government White Paper *Modernising Parliament: Reforming the House of Lords* (Cm.4183), 1999, ch.6, paras 9–14. In relation to cross-bench life peerages, the Prime Minister invites a fixed number of recommendations from the Commission and passes these on to Her Majesty for approval "except in the most exceptional of circumstances." In 2001, the government published a White Paper on House of Lords reform which proposed, *inter alia*, the replacement of the current House of Lords Appointments Commission with a statutory Appointments Commission with greatly expanded functions: *The House of Lords: Completing the Reform* (Cm.5291), 2001, paras 65–68 published following the Report of the Royal Commission on the Reform of the House of Lords *A House for the Future* (Cm.4534), 2000. See also: Hood Phillips & Jackson, *Constitutional and Administrative Law* (8th ed., Sweet & Maxwell, London, 2001), para.9–011; Department for Constitutional Affairs Consultation Paper, *Constitutional Reform: Next Steps for the House of Lords* (CP 14/03, 2003), September 2003, paras 29–43 and 53–60.

46 Freedom of Information Act 2000, s.3, Sch.1, Pt VI.

47 Bl Com (14th ed.) 272; *Halsbury's Laws of England* (4th ed., 1996 re-issue), Vol.8(2), para.831; *Halsbury's Laws of England* (4th ed., 1994 re-issue), Vol.35, paras 901, 963, 967; the Appellate Jurisdiction Act 1876, s.6; the Life Peerages Act 1958, s.1.

48 See para.26–007.

conferring of honours and dignities is undoubtedly a matter of public interest,[49] it does not often carry any great practical consequences in legal, political or constitutional terms and the selection process often involves an evaluative assessment of personal information and the exercise of a very broad discretion. A public interest in maintaining the exclusion of the duty to communicate related information may therefore arise out of the need to protect confidences and to ensure frankness, candour and honesty in the recommendation and selection process[50] and the need to protect the feelings and privacy of those considered and their families particularly where it has been decided not to confer an honour.[51] A public interest in maintaining the exclusion of the duty to confirm or deny may also arise out of the same considerations, although this is less likely to be the case in circumstances where an honour or dignity *has* been conferred. So far as concerns information relating to the conferring of honours and most dignities (other than life peerages) on individuals, the public interest balance may therefore be thought normally to weigh in favour of non-disclosure rather than disclosure. The public interest balance may, however, be more likely to shift in favour of disclosure in relation to the conferring of honours on corporations or groups of people (where questions of privacy and personal distress are less likely to arise)[52] and in relation to the conferring of life peerages (where receipt of the dignity carries with it important consequences in terms of the right to sit and vote in Parliament and eligibility for ministerial office).

---

[49] The public interest in the fairness and transparency of the honours system has long been recognised: *Report of the Royal Commission on Honours* (Cmd.1789), 1922, paras 24–28; 57 HL Official Report (5th series) June 26, 1924, col.1068; the Honours (Prevention of Abuses) Act 1925. The public interest in the conferring of both honours and dignities more generally is also implicitly recognised by the inclusion of the Political Honours Scrutiny Committee and the House of Lords Appointments Commission in the Freedom of Information Act 2000, Sch.1, Pt VI as "public authorities."

[50] See para.26–009 and *Open Government Code of Practice on Access to Government Information: Guidance on Interpretation* (2nd ed., 1997), Pt II, paras 8.9–8.12 on the equivalent exemption in the *Open Government Code of Practice on Access to Government Information* (2nd ed., 1997), Pt II, para.8c. The exemptions for personal and confidential information in the Freedom of Information Act 2000, ss.40–41 would protect a certain amount of personal information in any event.

[51] See the remarks made by Lord Falconer of Thoroton at Committee Stage in the House of Lords in connection with a proposed government amendment to the relevant clause in the Freedom of Information Bill: "The conferring of honours raises questions of personal confidentiality and the government believes that it should receive substantial protection under the Bill. The conferring of honours raises such questions not just in relation to the candidates for honours themselves and members of their families, but also in relation to those who contribute to the process of selection. Questions of confidentiality can arise just as easily in regard to posthumous awards. It will be obviously embarrassing, and potentially distressing, for surviving relatives to discover that the deceased was considered but rejected for an honour" (*Hansard*, HL, Vol.618, October 24, 2000, col.315).

[52] For example, the conferring of city or royal borough status on a local authority, the award of the George Cross to "the Island Fortress of Malta" by George VI on April 15, 1942 and the award of the George Cross to the Royal Ulster Constabulary by Elizabeth II on November 23, 1999. Where a local authority has applied for and been refused city status it may well want to disclose information relating to its application in order to show it put forward the best case possible and in such cases it may make voluntary disclosure regardless of the Freedom of Information Act 2000, s.37(1)(b).

Communications with Her Majesty, etc. and honours: the Freedom of Information (Scotland) Act 2002

26–013 Section 41 of the Freedom of Information (Scotland) Act 2002 is the Scottish equivalent of s.37 of the Freedom of Information Act 2000 and, as mentioned above, it follows the wording of its Westminster counterpart save that reference is made to "the exercise by Her Majesty of Her prerogative of honour" instead of "the conferring by the Crown of any honour or dignity."[53] Information held by Scottish public authorities which relates to the conferring by the Crown of any dignity will not therefore be exempt under the terms of s.41(b) of the Freedom of Information (Scotland) Act 2002. The only way of avoiding this conclusion is to argue that the conferring of dignities is an "exercise by Her Majesty of Her prerogative of honour" but this is not a particularly persuasive proposition given the distinction drawn between honours and dignities elsewhere. The different approach in s.41(b) of the Freedom of Information (Scotland) Act 2002 also raises two other questions which may lead to different results under the two regimes: first, whether there are any honours which may be conferred by the Crown other than in the exercise of Her prerogative of honour; and, secondly, whether there is any difference between the amount and type of honours-related information capable of "relating to" the conferring by the Crown of any honour or dignity, on the one hand, and the exercise by Her Majesty of Her prerogative of honour, on the other.

Communications with Her Majesty, etc. and honours: the Data Protection Act 1998

26–014 The Data Protection Act 1998 binds the Crown and contains special provision for its application to the Royal Household, the Duchy of Lancaster and the Duchy of Cornwall.[54] Personal data processed for the purposes of the

[53] It might be argued that the Freedom of Information (Scotland) Act 2002 is outside the legislative competence of the Scottish Parliament to the extent that it confers a qualified entitlement (subject to a public interest override) to information about honours and a general entitlement to information about dignities because the Scottish Parliament cannot enact provisions which "relate to" "reserved matters" (Scotland Act 1998, ss.28–30; "honours and dignities" are defined as "reserved matters" by the Scotland Act 1998, s.30, Sch.5, paras 1, 2(3)). This is not a strong argument for a number of reasons. First, the Freedom of Information (Scotland) Act 2002 does not obviously contain any provisions which "relate to" the conferring of honours or dignities when the expression "relates to" is read in accordance with the Scotland Act 1998, s.29(3). Secondly, if and in so far as Scottish public authorities hold information about honours and dignities, it would be odd if the Scottish Parliament were unable to regulate public access to it particularly when the Freedom of Information Act 2000 regulates public access to such information when held by other (non-Scottish) public authorities. Thirdly, the proviso to the Scotland Act 1998, Sch.5, Pt II, s.B13 would appear to envisage legislation along the lines of the Freedom of Information (Scotland) Act 2002.

[54] Data Protection Act 1998, s.63 provides that: where the purposes for which and the manner in which any personal data are, or are to be, processed are determined by, *inter alia*, any person

conferring by the Crown of any honour or dignity are also exempt from the subject information provisions in the Data Protection Act 1998.[55]

3. STATUTORY PROHIBITIONS ON DISCLOSURE

Introduction

By s.44(1) of the Freedom of Information Act 2000 information is exempt from the disclosure obligation in s.1(1)(b) "if its disclosure (otherwise than under [the Act itself]) by the public authority holding it (a) is prohibited by or under any enactment, (b) is incompatible with any Community obligation or (c) would constitute or be punishable as a contempt of court." The exemption is an absolute one, so that no question of weighing competing public interests arises.[56] The duty to confirm or deny whether the public authority holds information requested provided by s.1(1)(a) of the Act does not arise if compliance with that duty would fall within any of paras (a), (b) or (c) above.[57] Section 26 of the Freedom of Information (Scotland) Act 2002 contains a provision in almost identical terms to s.44(1) of the 2000 Act.[58] The basic position under the two Freedom of Information Acts is therefore that existing legal prohibitions on disclosure "trump" any rights given by the Acts. This is in contrast to the position under the Data Protection Act 1998, which provides that the "subject information provisions" have effect notwithstanding any enactment or rule of law prohibiting or restricting the disclosure.[59] 26–015

General difficulties

Before considering separately these three categories of prohibition, it should be noted that although s.44 is on its face fairly straightforward there may be 26–016

acting on behalf of the Royal Household, the data controller in respect of those data for the purposes of that Act shall be the Keeper of the Privy Purse (*ibid.*, s.63(3)(a)); the Keeper of the Privy Purse is not liable to prosecution under the Data Protection Act 1998 but the criminal offence and liability provisions in s.55 and Sch.9, para.12 do apply to persons in the service of the Crown as they apply to any other person (*ibid.*, s.63(5)).

[55] Data Protection Act 1998, s.37, Sch.7, para.3(b) as amended by the Freedom of Information Act 2000, s.73, Sch.6, para.6. This amendment having come into force on May 14, 2001 under the Freedom of Information Act 2000, s.87(3) and the Freedom of Information Act 2000 (Commencement No.1) Order 2001(SI 2001/1637), art.2(d).

[56] Freedom of Information Act 2000, s.2(2)(a), 2(3)(h).

[57] *ibid.*

[58] See also Freedom of Information (Scotland) Act 2002, s.2(2)(b); the duty to confirm or deny whether the public authority holds requested information does not arise under the Scottish legislation.

[59] Data Protection Act 1998, s.27(5).

practical difficulties in applying it.[60] In particular, although the section is likely to raise questions of law and issues particularly appropriate for decision by a court, the question whether the requested disclosure would be prohibited by any enactment or incompatible with a Community obligation or would constitute a contempt of court falls to be decided in the first instance by the public authority itself; and subsequently, if the applicant pursues the matter further, by the Information Commissioner.[61] It is only at the stage of the Information Tribunal[62] (or, in Scotland, the Court of Session[63]) that the decision-maker will necessarily be legally-qualified and sitting in a judicial capacity. There is also a potential problem in that the decision whether the section applies involves (particularly in relation to contempt of court) a prediction of whether or not something which has not happened would infringe the law. Moreover, the assumed facts on which the prediction is to be based are not made entirely clear by the section: thus, it is not made clear to whom, for what purpose and in what circumstances the disclosure whose legality is to be judged would be made (other than that it is otherwise than under the Act). This is in contrast to the position in the corresponding provision dealing with contempt of court under the Australian legislation which refers to "public disclosure" of the relevant document.[64]

Prohibition under any "enactment"

26–017 In its ordinary sense, an "enactment" is a legal proposition laid down in an Act or other legislative text with the effect that, when facts fall within an indicated area, specified legal consequences follow.[65] It seems clear that the word "enactment" in the section is intended to include any enactment made by subordinate legislation, although the word is not expressly defined in these terms for the purposes of s.44.[66] The relevant enactment can have been passed at any time as long as it prohibits the disclosure of the information at the time the question falls to

[60] As it appears there were under the original s.38 of the Freedom of Information Act 1982 (Cth of Australia) which contained the corresponding provisions in relation to statutory provisions: *News Corp Ltd v National Companies and Securities Commission* (1984) 52 A.L.R. 277; *Kavvadias v Ombudsman (Cth)* (1984) 1 F.C.R. 80; 52 A.L.R. 728; *Federal Commissioner of Taxation v Swiss Aluminium Ltd* (1986) 10 F.C.R. 321.

[61] See paras 28–001 and 28–006.

[62] See para.28–015.

[63] See para.28–022.

[64] Freedom of Information Act 1982 (Cth of Australia), s.46.

[65] This definition is taken from F. Bennion, *Statutory Interpretation*(4th ed., Butterworths, London, 2002), p.337. As the author notes, the proposition containing the enactment may, as is most usual, be embodied in a single sentence of an Act or other instrument; or it may fall to be collected from two or more sentences, whether consecutive or not. The Interpretation Act 1889, s. 35(1) appeared to take the view that an enactment was to be found within a single section or subsection. The provision is not repeated in the Interpretation Act 1978.

[66] See: Freedom of Information Act 2000, ss.75(2)(b) and 84; Freedom of Information (Scotland) Act 2002, ss.46(2) and 73.

be considered. It is thus possible in principle for rights under the Freedom of Information Acts to be removed by subordinate legislation made under different primary legislation without the Acts themselves being amended. However, the provision clearly does not cover departmental circulars or codes of practice even if issued under statutory authority; nor does it cover any prohibition on disclosure provided by the common law.

Comparative legislation

In contrast to the position in other jurisdictions, the section applies to "any enactment" rather than to enactments that are expressly listed in the Act concerned.[67] There is no provision, as in Ireland, for particular enactments to be listed as not applying.[68] Nor, unlike the position in New Zealand, is there an express requirement that the decision-maker who relies on the section specifies the enactment relied on.[69] On the other hand, in some ways this exemption in the Freedom of Information Acts is narrower in scope than in some of the comparable legislation. Thus, the enactment must "prohibit" the disclosure rather than "restrict" it, as is the case in Canada and New Zealand[70]; and there is no scope for continued reliance on statutory provisions which give the public authority a discretion whether to disclose information or not, as is the case in the United States and Ireland.[71] 26–018

Review and repeal or amendment

Further, the application of the section to "any enactment" without any limitation is mitigated by the Government's avowed intention to review all existing statutory prohibitions to disclosure and to repeal or amend any which on consideration can no longer be justified.[72] This intention has found expression in s.75 of the Freedom of Information Act 2000, which enables the Secretary of 26–019

67 Compare Access to Information Act (Canada) s.24(1) and Sch.II and Freedom of Information Act 1982 (Cth of Australia), s.38(1)(b).

68 See Freedom of Information Act 1997 (Ireland), s.32(1).

69 See Official Information Act 1982 (New Zealand), s.18(c)(i); in practice this is very likely to happen in any event in the United Kingdom by reason of Freedom of Information Act 2000, s.17(1)(c) and Freedom of Information (Scotland) Act 2002, s.16(1)(d).

70 See Access to Information Act (Canada), s.24(1); Official Information Act 1982 (New Zealand), s.52(3)(b)(i).

71 See: Freedom of Information Act, 5 USC 552(b)(3)(B); Freedom of Information Act 1997 (Ireland), s.32(1)(b). The Lord Chancellor's Department's second report to Parliament on its review of legislation governing the disclosure of information (November 2002: *www.dca.gov.uk/foi/foidoirpt2.htm*) states that the Freedom of Information Act 2000 will "overlay . . . existing discretionary powers with an access right . . ." (see para.7).

72 See *Hansard*, Standing Committee B, Freedom of Information Bill, February 1, 2000, col.385 *per* David Lock (Parliamentary Secretary, Lord Chancellor's Dept) and *Hansard*, HL (series 5) Vol.617, October 17, 2000, col.905, *per* Lord Falconer.

State for Consitutional Affairs[73] to repeal or amend any enactment by order[74] if it appears that by virtue of s.44(1) the enactment is capable of preventing the disclosure of information under the Act, and in the ongoing review of legislation governing the disclosure of information being carried out by the Lord Chancellor's Department (now the Department for Constitutional Affairs).

Secretary of State's power to remove statutory prohibitions

26–020 Section 75 of the Freedom of Information Act 2000 empowers the Secretary of State for Consitional Affairs to repeal or amend the enactment "for the purpose of removing or relaxing the prohibition." Section 75(2) expressly defines "enactment" for the purposes of the section as any enactment contained in an Act passed before or in the same Session as the Freedom of Information Act 2000 and any enactment contained in Northern Ireland legislation or subordinate legislation passed or made before the passing of the Act. It is therefore clear that the power does not relate to legislation passed after the Freedom of Information Act 2000; this is presumably on the basis that Parliament and other legislators will be expected to take account of the principles enshrined in the Freedom of Information Act 2000 when passing new legislation. There is an ambiguity in s.75(2)(b) as to whether the subordinate legislation there referred to is only Northern Ireland subordinate legislation; it may be that the draftsman did intend this result on the basis that there would automatically be power to amend or repeal United Kingdom secondary legislation without the need for the express power[75] but this is unlikely to arise as an issue in practice. There is a similar power in the *Freedom of Information (Scotland) Act 2002*,[76] which allows Scottish Ministers to repeal or amend an enactment for the same purposes "in so far as it relates to any Scottish public authority." Subject to that limitation it is clear that the Scottish Ministers have power under the section to amend by order provisions in a United Kingdom Act of Parliament.[77]

Government review

26–021 At the time of writing there have been two reports by the former Lord Chancellor's Department.[78] The second report, dated November 2002, contains

[73] See The Secretary of State for Constitutional Affairs Order 2003 (SI 2003/1887).
[74] Subject to approval by a resolution of each House of Parliament (Freedom of Information Act 2000, s.82(2)(b)) or the Scottish Parliament (Freedom of Information (Scotland) Act 2002, s.72(2)(b)).
[75] See Interpretation Act 1978, s.14.
[76] See Freedom of Information (Scotland) Act 2002, s.64.
[77] See definition of "enactment" in Freedom of Information (Scotland) Act 2002, s.64(2).
[78] In May 2002, reproduced at *www.dca.gov.uk/foi/foidoirpt.htm* and in November 2002, reproduced at *www.dca.gov.uk/foi/foidoirpt2.htm*.

a list (based on contributions by all "the major legislation-making departments") of primary and secondary legislation which prohibits disclosure of information and legislation which provides a discretion to disclose. The report states that the Government is committed to reducing the number of provisions prohibiting disclosure. It has identified primary criteria for retaining such provisions as follows: (a) provisions fulfilling an international obligation; (b) cases where the information being protected may be held by a person or body not covered by Freedom of Information Act 2000; (c) cases where the information being protected has been collected under compulsion; and (d) cases where the information is protected as part of a specific and limited access regime.[79] The report states that 381 items have been identified of which 97 will be repealed or amended, 79 will be retained and the balance remain under review.[80] It also states that where legislation is retained, time limits for non-disclosure obligation will be introduced.[81] It will be for the Scottish Parliament to determine what should be done as regards Scotland.[82]

Form and content of enactments prohibiting disclosure

Legislation which potentially prohibits disclosure of information by public authorities covers the whole range of government activities, including: national security,[83] defence,[84] international relations,[85] crime,[86] human fertilisation and embryology,[87] the census,[88] taxation,[89] company regulation,[90] medicines,[91] betting and gaming,[92] environmental protection,[93] estate agents[94] and air transport.[95] The precise wording of this sort of statutory provision varies substantially from enactment to enactment. In general, the legislation creates offences if certain categories of information are disclosed by members or employees of the relevant body without lawful authority or excuse and/or 26–022

[79] November 2002 report, para.5.
[80] *ibid.*, para.11.
[81] *ibid.*, para.8.
[82] *ibid.*, para.4. The Scottish Ministers' report to the Scottish Parliament on implementation of the Freedom of Information (Scotland) Act 2002 dated May 28, 2003 deals with the review of statutory bars and Freedom of Information (Scotland) Act 2002, s.64. At para.4.1 it states that a review of Scottish legislation and of pre-devolution Westminster legislation is to be carried out.
[83] Official Secrets Act 1911, s.1; Official Secrets Act 1989, s.1.
[84] Army Act 1955, s.60; Official Secrets Act 1989, s.2.
[85] Official Secrets Act 1989, s.3.
[86] *ibid.*, s.4.
[87] Human Fertilisation and Embryology Act 1990, s.33.
[88] Census Act 1920, s.8.
[89] Finance Act 1989, s.182.
[90] Companies Act 1985, s.449.
[91] Medicines Act 1968, s.118.
[92] Betting Gaming and Lotteries Act 1963, s.28(10).
[93] Environment Act 1995, s.113(3).
[94] Estate Agents Act 1979, s.10.
[95] Airports Act 1986, ss.30(7) and 74(1).

otherwise than in the course of his duties and/or otherwise than for specified purposes and/or for prohibited purposes.[96] There are often defences provided which apply if the defendant can show a subjective belief that he had lawful authority or that he did not know that the information came within the relevant category.[97]

Rationale for enactments

26–023 The rationale for the legislative prohibitions on disclosure of information obviously varies from enactment to enactment. In many cases an exemption provided by a specific provision of Pt II of the Freedom of Information Act 2000[98] (relating to defence, security, etc.) would potentially (subject to public interest balance where appropriate) exclude disclosure under the Act even in the absence of the express legislative prohibition.[99] In some cases Ministers are given express powers effectively to prohibit the disclosure of information on the grounds of national security, or commercial confidentiality or simply the "public interest."[1]

Application of section 44(1)(a) to specific requests

26–024 As stated, there may be difficulties in practice in applying s.44(1)(a) in the way it was probably intended in response to specific requests for information. The subsection exempts information whose disclosure by the public authority is prohibited by or under an enactment; but generally the enactments identified prohibit disclosure by individual civil servants otherwise than in the course of their duties and/or without lawful authority and, furthermore, provide a defence based on a subjective belief in such authority. In many cases it might be argued that, if the public authority as a body was able to decide, in response to a specific request, that information should be disclosed notwithstanding the other exemptions in Pt II, there was the appropriate lawful authority for disclosure by the individual civil servant on behalf of the public authority. This would leave

---

[96] For example, "for any purpose prejudicial to the safety or interests of the State:" Official Secrets Act 1911, s.1.

[97] See, for example, Army Act 1955, s.60; Census Act 1920, s.8; Finance Act 1989, s.182.

[98] Or Pt 2 of Freedom of Information (Scotland) Act 2002.

[99] See for example: Official Secrets Act 1911, s.1 and Official Secrets Act 1989, s.1, under Freedom of Information Act 2000, ss.23 and 24; Airports Act 1986, s.30(7), under Freedom of Information Act 2000, s.24; Official Secrets Act 1989, s.2 and Army Act 1955, s.60, under Freedom of Information Act 2000, s.26; Official Secrets Act 1989, s.3, under Freedom of Information Act 2000, s.27; Official Secrets Act 1989, s.4, under Freedom of Information Act 2000, s.31(1)(a) and (b); Environment Act 1995, s.113(3), under Freedom of Information Act 2000, ss.24 and 43; Human Fertilisation and Embryology Act 1990, s.33, Census Act 1920, s.8, Finance Act 1989, s.182, Estate Agents Act 1979, s.10, under Freedom of Information Act 2000, ss.40 and/or 41.

[1] See, for example: Parliamentary Commissioner Act 1967, s.11, Environment Act 1995, s.113(3), Airports Act 1986, s.30(7).

the vital interests identified in ss.21–43 of Freedom of Information Act 2000 protected in so far as necessary.

Repeal or amendment

In the light of these considerations it may be thought that all such provisions should be repealed and that the question of whether disclosure should be made should be left to the regime established by the Freedom of Information Act 2000. However, a straightforward repeal is unlikely to be appropriate in most cases because, whatever the position under the Freedom of Information Acts, it will remain appropriate to have criminal sanctions against civil servants (or indeed ministers) making unauthorised disclosures of particular types of information. There is also a category of rationale for legislative prohibition on disclosure of information by public authorities which is not reflected (save in so far as it comes within s.41) in Pt II of Freedom of Information Act 2000, namely where the information does not relate to an individual but was obtained by compulsion[2]: this is one of the categories where the Lord Chancellor's Department's report indicates that the legislative prohibition might be retained. Overall, the better course would probably be the amendment or repeal of s.44(1)(a) and possibly the insertion of a new exemption to cater for the "compulsion" issue. 26–025

4. COMMUNITY OBLIGATIONS

Introduction

As noted earlier, s.44(1) of the Freedom of Information Act 2000 bestows an absolute exemption on information the disclosure of which (but for any obligation under the Act itself) is incompatible with any Community obligation.[3] "Community obligation" is defined as any obligation created by or arising under the Treaties (as defined in the European Communities Act 1972), whether an enforceable Community obligation or not[4]: such obligations comprise any legal obligation in the Treaties or emanating from any of the European institutions whether or not they are directly enforceable without further enactment in the United Kingdom.[5] An example of such a provision is Art.19 of the European Council Directive of April 23, 1990 on the deliberate release into the 26–026

[2] See, for example: Companies Act 1985, s.449; Airports Act 1986, s.74(1).
[3] See the remarks made at paras 26–015 to 26–016.
[4] See: Interpretation Act 1978, s.5 and Sch.1 and European Communities Act 1972, s.1 and Sch.1 Pt II.
[5] See European Communities Act 1972, s.2(1) for definition of "enforceable Community obligation."

environment of genetically modified organisms.[6] This Article provides that the competent authorities in the member states (which would be "public authorities" under the Freedom of Information Acts) shall not divulge to third parties any confidential information notified to them under the Directive[7] and that, if a notification under the Directive is withdrawn, the competent authorities must respect the confidentiality of information supplied.[8] If the relevant information comes within the terms of the prohibition in the Directive there is no question of applying the public interest test as there would be if the public authority were applying, say, the exemption in s.43 of Freedom of Information Act 2000 ("commercial interests"), though of course it must be recognised that the concept of "confidentiality" itself is somewhat elastic and the decision whether information is confidential may itself involve public interest considerations.[9]

European Regulation 1049/2001

26–027 The House of Commons Public Administration Committee expressed concern about s.44(1)(b): the Committee said that they considered the European rules on disclosure of information to be too restrictive.[10] Since the publication of the Committee's Report, the European Parliament and Council have adopted Regulation 1049/2001 of May 30, 2001 regarding access to European Parliament, Council and Commission documents.[11] This is considered in more detail elsewhere in this work,[12] but in brief the Regulation provides a right of access to documents of the institutions subject to exceptions set out in Art.4. Article 5 of the Regulation provides a special regime for documents held by Member States which originate from a European institution. In view of the supremacy of European law, this special regime would apply in place of the provisions of the Freedom of Information Acts in relation to requests for access to such documents or information contained therein. Unless it is clear under the terms of the Regulation that a particular document or information should or should not be disclosed, the Member State must consult the institution concerned in order to take a decision on the matter or may simply refer the matter to the institution concerned. Article 4(1), (2) and (3) provide that access to a document must be refused in the circumstances there set out. That proscription would therefore engage s.44(1)(b) of the Freedom of Information Act 2000 so as to defeat the domestic rights bestowed by s.1. Although the exceptions in the

6 Council Directive 90/220.

7 Art.19(1).

8 Art.19(5).

9 See paras 25–014 to 25–019.

10 See House of Commons *Public Administration Committee Third Report 1998–9 Session* (Cm.4355), July 29, 1999), para.111.

11 The Regulation entered into force on December 3, 2001 and is binding in its entirety and directly applicable in all Member States.

12 See paras 3–010 to 3–017.

Regulation are broadly similar to the exemptions provided in Pt II of the Freedom of Information Acts, they are not identical.[13] Accordingly, the information that must be disclosed under the Regulation will not be exactly the same as the information that must be disclosed under the Freedom of Information Act 2000. In particular, the question of where the public interest lies in a particular case will be a matter not for the public authority in the United Kingdom but for the Community institution and, ultimately, the European Court of Justice. It should also be noted that if disclosure is required under the Regulation it must be given even if under the Freedom of Information Acts it could have been refused.

5. CONTEMPT OF COURT

Introduction

Information whose disclosure by the public authority holding it would constitute or be punishable as a contempt of court is exempt from disclosure under the Freedom of Information Acts.[14] There are similar provisions in the freedom of information statutes in Australia,[15] New Zealand[16] and Ireland.[17] This exemption appears to give precedence to the policy of preventing interference with the administration of justice (which is the underlying policy of the law of contempt of court) over the policy of free disclosure of information held by public authorities (which is the policy underlying the Freedom of Information Acts).[18] It should be noted that in many cases, the exemption provided by s.44(1)(c) of the Freedom of Information Act 2000 will also be provided by another provision in Pt II, though generally the other provision will be subject to the public interest test in s.2.[19] 26–028

[13] See para.3–012.

[14] Freedom of Information Act 2000, s.44(1)(c); Freedom of Information (Scotland) Act 2002, s.26(c). See the introductory comments made at paras 26–015 to 26–016.

[15] Freedom of Information Act 1982 (Cth of Australia), s.46(a).

[16] Official Information Act 1982 (New Zealand), ss.18(c)(ii) and 52(1).

[17] Freedom of Information Act 1997 (Ireland), s.22(1)(b).

[18] See *Attorney General v Times Newspapers Ltd* [1974] A.C. 273 at 294E *per* Lord Reid for a discussion of the public policy underlying the law of contempt and its interaction with the public interest in freedom of speech.

[19] This applies in particular to the exemptions provided by ss.30(1)(c), 31(1)(c), 32, 40, 41, 42 and 43; the same comment applies *mutatis mutandis* in relation to Freedom of Information (Scotland) Act 2002.

The law of contempt

26–029 The law of contempt can be highly technical and uncertain and is largely governed by common law rules.[20] The European Convention for the Protection of Human Rights and Fundamental Freedoms often plays an important role.[21] A person's guilt or innocence of contempt can depend on subjective knowledge and intent and on the practical effect of the act concerned and may be dependent on such questions as whether the legal proceedings concerned are civil or criminal, what stage they have reached, whether there is a jury, and the extent to which any information is already in the public domain. Proceedings are generally taken at the behest of the Attorney General who has to make a fine judgment in the public interest as to whether they are appropriate.

Classification of contempts of court

26–030 Contempt of court can arise in a myriad of ways. The traditional classification into "civil" and "criminal" contempts is no longer helpful. Of greater assistance is a re-classification into (a) conduct which involves a breach, or which assists in a breach, of a court order and (b) any other conduct which involves an interference with the due administration of justice, either in a particular case or, more generally, as a continuing process, the first category being a special form of the latter, with such interference being a characteristic common to all contempts. In general, breach of a court order is treated as a matter for the parties to raise by way of complaint to the court, whereas other forms of contempt are considered to be a matter for the Attorney General to raise as guardian of the public interest in the administration of justice.[22] The Phillimore Report on the law of contempt[23] divided contempts between:

(a) "contempt in the face of the court," for example, throwing missiles at the judge, insulting persons in court, demonstrating in court; and
(b) "contempt out of court," subdivided into:

---

[20] Notwithstanding the Contempt of Court Act 1981. For a more detailed account of the law of contempt, reference should be made to the authoritative texts: D. Eady and A. Smith, *Aldridge, Eady & Smith on Contempt* (2nd ed., Sweet & Maxwell, London, 2000); Borrie and Lowe, *The Law of Contempt* (3rd ed., Butterworths, London, 1996); C.J. Miller, *Contempt of Court* (3rd ed., Oxford University Press, Oxford, 2000). For a general account see *Halsbury's Laws of England* (4th ed., 1998 re-issue), Vol.9(1), paras 401 *et seq*. and *White Book* (2003 edition), pp.1625 *et seq*.

[21] In particular Arts 6 (fair trial), 8 (private life) and 10 (freedom of expression): see *Sunday Times v UK* (1979–80) 2 E.H.R.R. 245; *Goodwin v United Kingdom* (1996) 22 E.H.R.R. 123; *Omar v France* (2000) 29 E.H.R.R. 210.

[22] See *Attorney General v Newspaper Publishing Ltd* [1988] Ch. 333 *per* Sir John Donaldson M.R. at 362.

[23] *Report of the Committee on Contempt of Court*, Cmnd.5794, December 1974.

(i) reprisals against witnesses after the conclusion of proceedings;
(ii) "scandalising the court," for example, abusing a judge qua judge or attacking his impartiality or integrity;
(iii) disobedience to court orders;
(iv) conduct, whether intentional or not, liable to interfere with the course of justice in particular proceedings.[24]

Disclosure of information by a public authority is only ever likely to constitute a contempt under (b)(iii) or (iv) in this classification, by being contrary to a court order or undertaking or by tending to prejudice proceedings or to undermine the administration of justice.

Decisions on the application of section 44(1)(c)

As has been pointed out,[25] the application of this difficult area of law will have to be carried out in the first instance by the decision-maker in the relevant public authority or the Information Commissioner. This task is not made easier by the fact that the precise circumstances of the assumed disclosure by the public authority are not made clear by the section. What is clear, however, is that it is the act of disclosure by the public authority itself which must constitute the act of contempt (rather than possible acts by the recipient of the information,[26] although knowledge of the intentions of the recipient may be relevant). It is also clear that in order for the exemption to apply there must be almost certainty that a contempt will be committed.[27] 26–031

Practical examples

Cases where the exemption may apply are as follows: 26–032

(1) The most obvious and straightforward example would be a case where there is an order addressed directly to, or an undertaking[28] given expressly by, the public authority in question forbidding it from disclosing the relevant information[29]: in these circumstances there would

[24] See *The Sunday Times v UK* (1979) 2 E.H.R.R. 245 at 257.
[25] See paras 26–014 to 26–015.
[26] See *Altman v Family Court of Australia* (1992) 15 A.A.R. 236 (Administrative Appeals Tribunal) at para.38.
[27] The section requires that disclosure would constitute or be punishable as a contempt: see the discussion in relation to the New Zealand legislation in I. Eagles, M. Taggart & G. Liddell, *Freedom of Information in New Zealand* (Oxford University Press, Auckland, 1992), at p.456.
[28] As to undertakings, see *Halsbury's Laws of England* (4th ed., 1998 re-issue), Vol.9(1), para.482.
[29] Such information is also likely to come within one or more other exemptions: *e.g.* under Freedom of Information Act 2000, s.40 (personal information), 41 (information provided in confidence), or 43 (commercially sensitive information).

clearly be no obligation to disclose it pursuant to a request purportedly made under Freedom of Information Act 2000 as to do so would almost certainly constitute a contempt of court.[30]

(2) If a public authority is a party to litigation it will be subject to the implied undertakings as to the use of disclosed documents which are now codified in CPR r.31.22: to disclose a document or the information contained therein in breach of the terms of that rule would almost certainly constitute a contempt of court.[31]

(3) A public authority with the requisite knowledge and intent could also be in contempt of court if it disclosed information whose disclosure by another party was in breach of an injunction or undertaking on the basis either that it was aiding and abetting the third party's breach of the order or undertaking[32] or, in the case of an interlocutory order or undertaking preventing the disclosure of information which may be confidential, on the basis that the disclosure destroyed the confidentiality which it was the purpose of the order or undertaking to preserve and that there had therefore been an interference with the administration of justice.[33]

(4) It is a contempt of court under the "strict liability rule" to publish information which creates a substantial risk that the course of justice in particular proceedings will be seriously impeded or prejudiced[34] if the proceedings are "active" (regardless of intent)[35]: however, it seems unlikely that a public authority complying with a request for information under the Freedom of Information Acts would be committing such a contempt since the disclosure of any such information would be unlikely to constitute a "publication" for the purposes of the "strict

[30] Assuming, of course, that the public authority was aware of the order and its terms: see *Halsbury's Laws of England* (4th ed., 1998 re-issue), Vol.9(1), para.458, note 3.

[31] See, for example: *Home Office v Harman* [1983] A.C. 280; *Alterskye v Scott* [1948] 1 All E.R. 469. The information may well also be exempt information under Freedom of Information Act 2000, s.41 and such disclosure would probably also be exempt under s.44(1)(a) as being prohibited by CPR r.31.22.

[32] On aiding and abetting, see *Halsbury's Laws of England* (4th ed., 1998 re-issue), Vol.9(1), para.490.

[33] See, on this form of contempt: *Attorney General v Times Newspapers Ltd* [1992] 1 A.C. 191; *Jockey Club v Buffham* [2003] Q.B. 462; *Attorney General v Punch Ltd* [2003] 2 W.L.R. 49. Note that information in this category is likely to be exempt under Freedom of Information Act 2000 s.31(1)(c).

[34] The forms of information which might have this effect are numerous, including: information inducing bias in the court (*e.g.* information on the personal character or antecedents of an accused which would tend to influence a jury, information as to alleged confessions, comments on the merits of litigation or the court by the Government), information prejudicing the court's ability to determine the true facts (*e.g.* comments tending to discourage witnesses or to affect the content of their evidence, information as to without prejudice offers in civil litigation, reports of private investigations or interviews with witnesses), information tending to discourage or deter a litigant from pursuing litigation.

[35] See Contempt of Court Act 1981, ss.1–5.

liability rule."[36] It may be that if the public authority knew that a journalist or news organisation seeking information intended to publish it in breach of the "strict liability rule," disclosure by the public authority would amount to a contempt by aiding and abetting, which would allow the public authority to refuse disclosure under s.44(1)(c).[37]

(5) It is also a contempt of court to create a real risk of prejudice to the administration of justice (regardless of whether the proceedings are active) with the intention of doing so.[38] Since this form of contempt normally takes the form of a publication to the public and since it is hard to see how the public authority, if it had the relevant intent, would seek to rely on it in order to avoid the very disclosure which it intended to make, it seems most unlikely that this form of contempt would ever be relevant for the purposes of the Freedom of Information Acts.

(6) It is a contempt of court to disclose particulars of anything said in the jury room.[39] Thus, if for some reason (which it is hard to imagine in practice) a public authority had such information it would be committing a contempt in disclosing it and it would therefore be exempt information for the purposes of Freedom of Information Acts.

(7) There are numerous specific statutory restrictions on the reporting of criminal and civil proceedings whose breach may also amount to a contempt of court.[40] Again, there will be a question whether disclosure of the information by the public authority itself pursuant to a request under the Freedom of Information Acts would involve publishing it sufficiently widely so as to breach such a restriction, but knowledge of an intention to do so by a journalist or news organization seeking the information is likely to mean that the public authority could rely on s.44(1)(c) on the basis that such disclosure would amount to aiding and abetting such a breach.[41] In this context it should also be noted that the court itself has various powers to make orders binding on the world

36 A publication must be "addressed to the public at large or any section of the public": see Contempt of Court Act 1981, s.2(1).

37 The factual hypothesis is perhaps unlikely; if these circumstances applied the public authority would probably be able to rely on Freedom of Information Act 2000, s.31(1)(b) or (c) and/or s.30(1)(c).

38 See Contempt of Court Act 1981, s.6(c) and *Attorney General v News Group plc* [1989] Q.B. 110; *Attorney General v Hislop* [1991] 1 Q.B. 514; *Attorney General v Sport Newspapers Ltd* [1991] 1 W.L.R. 1194: the precise scope of this form of contempt is not at all clear.

39 Contempt of Court Act 1981, s.8.

40 See *Halsbury's Laws of England* (4th ed., 1998 re-issue), Vol.9(1), paras 430 and 431; Magistrates' Court Act 1980, s.8; Criminal Justice Act 1987, s.11; Sexual Offences (Amendment) Act 1976; Children and Young Persons Act 1933, s.39; Youth Justice and Criminal Evidence Act 1999, ss.44 and 45, Administration of Justice Act 1960, s.12. In theory, these statutory provisions might give rise to a prohibition on disclosure by or under an enactment for the purposes of s.44(1)(a) of Freedom of Information Act 2000, but the act of disclosure itself is unlikely to amount to publication (though if the journalist was known to have the relevant intention it might amount to aiding and abetting the relevant offence).

41 And no doubt it could also rely on Freedom of Information Act 2000, ss.30 and/or 31.

which restrict the publication of information concerning criminal or civil proceedings[42] and that a breach of such orders would also constitute a contempt of court. The same comments apply in relation to such orders as to the statutory provisions mentioned above.

(8) There is a class of contempt referred to as "scandalising the court" which arises when a court or judicial officer is grossly insulted or has its integrity impugned.[43] It is just conceivable that there exist in the Lord Chancellor's Department (or the Department for Constitutional Affairs) comments about individual judges which if disclosed would involve such a contempt.

Disclosure punishable as a contempt

26–033 Section 44(1)(c) of Freedom of Information Act 2000 also exempts information whose disclosure by the public authority would "be punishable as a contempt of court." Various statutes provide that where a person does anything in relation to a particular tribunal which, if it were a court, would amount to a contempt of court, the tribunal can certify that fact to a court and the court can investigate the matter and punish the person as if they had committed a contempt of court.[44] It is thought that the words "punishable as a contempt of court" are designed to deal with actions which would be caught by this kind of provision. Given that the tribunals in question may have limited powers to grant injunctions and given that they are unlikely to be easily influenced by publications in the way that a jury would, it seems unlikely that this provision would arise for consideration very often.

[42] Note in particular Contempt of Court Act 1981, ss.4(2) and 11 (examples of information which the court has power to withhold from the public apart from those provided by statute are secret processes and the name of complainants in blackmail cases (*R. v Socialist Worker* [1975] Q.B. 637)), Children and Young Persons Act 1933, s.39 and the inherent power of the Family Division of the High Court in certain circumstances to make orders which protect children from publicity (see: *Re S* [2003] EWCA Civ 963 (July 10, 2003)).

[43] See *Halsbury's Laws of England* (4th ed., 1998 re-issue), Vol.9(1), para.433 and *Altman v Australian Family Court* (1992) 15 A.A.R. 236 at para.37 (Administrative Appeals Tribunal).

[44] See, for example: Army Act 1955, s.101; Airforce Act 1955, s.101; Naval Discipline Act 1957, s.65; Tribunals of Inquiry (Evidence) Act 1921, s.1(2); Parliamentary Commissioner Act 1967, s.9.

6. MISCELLANEOUS EXEMPTIONS UNDER THE DATA PROTECTION ACT 1998

Information held only for research purposes

Personal data processed only for research purposes are exempt from the subject access rights under the Data Protection Act 1998 provided: 26–034

- that the data are not processed in order to support measures or decisions with respect to particular individuals;
- that they are not processed in such a way that substantial damage or distress is, or is likely to be, caused to any data subject; and
- that the results of the research or any resulting statistics are not made available in a form which identifies any data subject.[45]

Research purposes includes statistical and historical purposes.[46] Personal data are not treated as processed otherwise than for research purposes simply because they are disclosed to a person for research purposes, or are disclosed to the data subject or a person acting on his behalf, or are disclosed at the request or with the consent of the data subject or a person acting on his behalf.[47] Further, they are not treated as being so processed where the person making the disclosure has reasonable grounds for believing that one of those circumstances applies.[48] The Information Commissioner advises that, as a matter of good practice, when processing for research, historical or statistical purposes, data controllers should always consider whether it is necessary to process personal data in order to achieve their purpose, and that wherever possible they should only process data that have been stripped of all identifying features.[49]

Manual data relating to Crown employment

Personal data falling within the final limb of the definition of data, *i.e.* manual data recorded by a public authority, and that relate to personnel matters concerning Crown employment are exempt from the subject access rights (and other provisions) of the Data Protection Act 1998.[50] The types of personnel matters concerned include appointments and removals, pay, discipline and superannuation.[51] The exemption covers service in the armed forces, service in 26–035

[45] Data Protection Act 1998, s.33(1), (4).
[46] *ibid.*, s.33(1).
[47] *ibid.*, s.33(5)(a)–(c).
[48] *ibid.*, s.33(5)(d).
[49] The Information Commissioner, *Data Protection Act 1998: Legal Guidance* para.5.7.
[50] Data Protection Act 1998, s.33A(2).
[51] *ibid.*, s.33A(2).

any office or employment under the Crown or a public authority, and service in any other office or employment or under any contract for services where the power to take action in respect of such personnel matters rests with Her Majesty, a Minister of the Crown, the National Assembly for Wales, a Northern Ireland Minister or any public authority.[52] This exemption is designed to achieve parity between those who work for public authorities and those who work in the private sector. The view is taken that the former should not have additional rights of access in the employment context merely because of the identity of their employer.

Journalistic, literary and artistic material held with a view to publication

26–036 Personal data processed only for journalistic, artistic or literary purposes ("the special purposes") are exempt from the subject access rights (and certain other provisions) of the Data Protection Act 1998 if they are processed with a view to the publication of journalistic, literary or artistic material and the data controller reasonably believes both that publication would be in the public interest and that compliance with the subject access rights would be incompatible with the special purposes.[53] As the Information Commissioner has noted in her published Legal Guidance on the Data Protection Act 1998, the data controller must be satisfied that each of the four conditions (processing solely for the special purposes, processing with a view to publication of journalistic, literary or artistic material, belief that publication would be in the public interest, belief that compliance with the Data Protection Act 1998 would be incompatible with the special purposes) is satisfied in respect of the specific provision of the Data Protection Act 1998 from which exemption is claimed.[54] This exemption, which has its origins in Art.9 of the Data Protection Directive, is concerned with the balance between the protection of individual privacy and the right to freedom of expression. Thus, in considering whether publication would be in the public interest, the data controller is required to have particular regard to the special importance of the public interest in freedom of expression.[55]

Confidential references

26–037 A number of exemptions relate broadly to information provided or processed in relation to the employment, engagement or appointment of individuals to posts, offices and the like. The first relates to confidential references. Personal

---

[52] Data Protection Act 1998, s.33A(2).
[53] *ibid.*, s.32(1), (2).
[54] The Information Commissioner, *Data Protection Act 1998: Legal Guidance* para.5.6.
[55] Data Protection Act 1998, s.32(1)(b).

data are exempt from the subject access rights if they consist of a reference given (or to be given) in confidence by the data controller for the purposes of the education, training or employment of the data subject; his or her appointment to any office; or the provision by him or her of any service.[56] It is notable that this exemption applies only to references given or to be given by the data controller. If the data controller has on file references provided by a previous employer, they do not fall within the scope of the exemption.[57] However, the data controller may, for example, decline to reveal the identity of the author of the reference, pursuant to s.7(4) and (5).

Judicial appointments and honours

The next related exemption concerns judicial appointments and honours. It covers a broader category of information than confidential references: all personal data processed for the purposes of assessing a person's suitability for judicial office or the office of Queen's Counsel, or for the purposes of the conferring by the Crown of any honour or dignity,[58] are exempt from the subject access rights (and other provisions).[59] 26–038

Crown employment and Crown or Ministerial appointments

The final related exemption concerns other Crown and Ministerial appointments or employment. Again, it covers a broader category of information than confidential references. Rather than providing a blanket exemption, the Data Protection Act 1998 confers a power on the Secretary of State to exempt from the subject access rights personal data processed for the purposes of assessing a person's suitability for Crown employment or appointment to any office by Her Majesty, a Minister of the Crown or a Northern Ireland department.[60] This power has been exercised in relation to a variety of Crown appointments, including archbishops, bishops and certain other clergy; Lord-Lieutenants; Masters of certain Cambridge colleges; the Provost of Eton; the Poet Laureate and the Astronomer Royal.[61] 26–039

[56] Data Protection Act 1998, s.37, Sch.7, para.1.
[57] See also: The Information Commissioner, *Data Protection Act 1998: Legal Guidance*, para.5.13.
[58] As to the meaning of which, see paras 26–008 to 26–014.
[59] Data Protection Act 1998, s.37, Sch.7, para.3.
[60] *ibid.*, para.4.
[61] The Data Protection (Crown Appointments) Order 2000 (SI 2000/416).

Armed forces

26–040 Personal data are exempt from the subject access rights (and other provisions) in any case to the extent to which the application of those provisions would be likely to prejudice the combat effectiveness of any of the armed forces of the Crown.[62]

Management forecasts

26–041 Personal data processed for the purposes of management forecasting or management planning to assist the data controller in the conduct of any business or other activity are exempt from the subject access rights (and other provisions) in any case to the extent to which the application of those provisions would be likely to prejudice the conduct of that business or activity.[63]

Corporate finance

26–042 There is an exemption in relation to personal data processed for the purposes of, or in connection with, a corporate finance service.[64] The concept of a 'corporate finance service' is derived from the EC Directive on investment services in the securities field.[65] It covers certain activities relating to issues of specified instruments, as well as the provision of advice to undertakings on matters such as capital structure, industrial strategy and mergers.[66] Where personal data are processed for the purposes of, or in connection with, a corporate finance service provided by a relevant person,[6] the data are exempt from the subject access rights (and other provisions) to the extent to which the application of those provisions could affect the price of any specified instrument (whether it already exists, or is to be or may be created).[68] This limb of exemption also extends to circumstances in which the data controller reasonably believes that the price of such an instrument could be so affected.[69] Such data are also exempt if exemption is required to safeguard an important economic or financial interest of the United Kingdom.[70] The Secretary of State has a power to specify matters to be taken into account in determining whether exemption on the latter ground is required, or circumstances in which exemption is (or is not) to be taken to be

[62] Data Protection Act 1998, s.37, Sch.7, para.2. See generally paras 17–051 to 17–059.
[63] *ibid.*, para.5.
[64] *ibid.*, para.6.
[65] Council Directive 93/22. See Data Protection Act 1998, Sch.7, para.6(3).
[66] Data Protection Act 1998, Sch.7, para.6(3).
[67] Defined in Data Protection Act 1998, Sch.7, para.6(3).
[68] Data Protection Act 1998, Sch.7, para.6(1)(a)(i).
[69] *ibid.*, para.6(1)(a)(ii).
[70] *ibid.*, para.6(1)(b).

required.[71] This power has been exercised in relation to personal data to which the application of the subject information provisions could affect decisions whether to deal in, subscribe for or issue instruments or decisions which are likely to affect any business activity.[72] In such cases, the matter to be taken into account is the inevitable prejudicial effect on the orderly functioning of financial markets or the efficient allocation of capital within the economy resulting from the application of the subject access rights.[73]

Negotiations

Personal data comprising records of the data controller's intentions in relation to any negotiations with the data subject are exempt from the subject access rights (and other provisions) in any case to the extent to which the application of those provisions would be likely to prejudice those negotiations.[74] One example of the application of this exemption is the situation in which an organisation is in dispute with a former employee and records a potential settlement figure for its own budget forecasting. Disclosure of the figure to the ex-employee might prejudice the negotiations between those parties.[75] **26–043**

Examination marks and scripts

A group of exemptions and modifications relates to examination marks and scripts. Examination scripts, that is to say personal data consisting of information recorded by candidates during an academic, professional or other examination,[76] are exempt from the subject access rights.[77] Those rights are modified in relation to examination marks or other information processed for the purpose of determining examination results, or of enabling those results to be determined, or in consequence of their determination.[78] The modifications prevent a data subject from using his or her subject access rights to obtain examination results before they are announced. They achieve this by extending the period for compliance with a subject access request.[79] **26–044**

---

71 Data Protection 1998 Act, Sch.7, para.6(2).
72 Data Protection (Corporate Finance Exemption) Order 2000, SI 2000/184, art.2(3).
73 *ibid.*, art.2.
74 Data Protection Act 1998, s.37, Sch.7, para.7.
75 The Information Commissioner, *Data Protection Act 1998: Legal Guidance*, para.5.18.
76 Data Protection Act 1998, Sch.7, para.9(1).
77 *ibid.*, s.37, Sch.7, para.9.
78 *ibid.*, s.37, Sch.7, para.8(1), (5).
79 *ibid.*, Sch.7, para.8.

Self-incrimination

26–045 The privilege against self-incrimination is preserved by the Data Protection Act 1998. A person is not required to comply with a subject access request (or order under s.7) to the extent that to do so would, by revealing evidence of the commission of any offence (other than an offence under the Data Protection Act 1998) expose him to proceedings for that offence.[80] Furthermore, information disclosed by a person in compliance with such a request or order is not admissible against him in proceedings for an offence under the Data Protection Act 1998.[81]

Disclosure prohibited by other legislation

26–046 In addition to the exemptions conferred by the *Data Protection Act 1998* itself, there are additional exemptions from the subject access rights made pursuant to a further general power of exemption conferred on the Secretary of State by the Act in respect of information the disclosure of which is already prohibited or restricted by other legislation.[82] The Secretary of State may exempt personal data consisting of such information, where he considers it necessary for safeguarding the interests of the data subject or the rights and freedoms of any other individual that the prohibition or restriction should prevail over the subject access rights.[83] Pursuant to this power, there are exemptions in respect of certain information relating to human fertilisation and embryology,[84] adoption records and reports,[85] statements of special educational needs[86] and parental order records and reports.[87]

80 Data Protection Act 1998, s.37, Sch.7, para.11(1).
81 *ibid*., s.37, Sch.7, para.11(2).
82 As to the potential scope of the provision, see paras 26–015 to 26–025.
83 Data Protection Act 1998, s.38(1).
84 The Data Protection (Miscellaneous Subject Access Exemptions) Order 2000 (SI 2000/419), art.2, Sch. Pt I.
85 *ibid*., Sch. Pts II(a), III(a), IV(a) as amended by the Data Protection (Miscellaneous Subject Access Exemptions) (Amendment) Order 2000 (SI 2000/1865). In Scotland information provided by a principal reporter for a children's hearing is also exempted: The Data Protection (Miscellaneous Subject Access Exemptions) Order 2000 (SI 2000/419), art.2, Sch. Pt III(b).
86 The Data Protection (Miscellaneous Subject Access Exemptions) Order 2000 (SI 2000/419), art.2, Sch. Pts II(b), III(c) (record of special educational needs in Scotland), IV(b).
87 *ibid*., Sch. Pts II(c), III(d), IV(c).

CHAPTER 27

The Information Commissioners and the Information Tribunal

1. THE FUNCTIONS AND DUTIES OF THE INFORMATION COMMISSIONERS

The Information Commissioner

27–001 The main responsibility for enforcing the Data Protection Act 1998 and the Freedom of Information Act 2000 lies with the Information Commissioner.[1] The office was originally established as that of the Data Protection Registrar.[2] It was renamed the Data Protection Commissioner by the Data Protection Act 1998[3] and later the Information Commissioner by the Freedom of Information Act 2000.[4] The last name change coincided with the office being given responsibilities under that Act in addition to its responsibilities under the Data Protection Act 1998.[5] The Information Commissioner is also the "supervisory authority" in the United Kingdom for the purposes of the Data Protection Directive and the "designated authority" in the United Kingdom for the purpose of Art.13 of the 1981 Convention.[6] The Information Commissioner is subject to the supervision of the Tribunals and Inquiries Act 1992.[7]

Terms of appointment

27–002 The Information Commissioner is appointed by the Crown by Letters Patent.[8] Part I of Sch.5 to the Data Protection Act 1998 lays down the detailed terms of his appointment and powers. The Commissioner is a corporation sole and neither he nor his officers and staff are servants or agents of the Crown.[9] His tenure is normally for five years (renewable twice) and he can be removed from office only in pursuance of an address by both Houses of Parliament.[10] Provision is made for his salary and pension and for the appointment of one or two

[1] The Commissioner at the time of writing was Elizabeth France. The office of the Commissioner was at Wycliff House, Water Lane, Wilmslow, Cheshire SK9 5AF (tel. 01625 545 700). The website address is *www.dataprotection.gov.uk* or *www.informationcommissioner.gov.uk*.

[2] Under the Data Protection Act 1984, s.3(1)(a).

[3] Data Protection Act 1998, s.5(1).

[4] Freedom of Information Act 2000, s.18(1), with effect from January 30, 2001.

[5] The combination of the two roles into one post was the source of some controversy in Parliament. The Government's justifications for combining the two roles were given in *Hansard*, HC, Vol.347, April 5, 2000, cols 1040–1042 as: (1) the two roles were said by the Commissioner to be complementary and she supported the idea; (2) consistent decisions would be made as to what should be disclosed; (3) the public would have a single point of contact when they sought information; (4) this was said to be the course adopted in Australia, New Zealand and Ireland. See also *Hansard*, HL, Vol.617, October 15, 2000, col.1214 .

[6] Data Protection Act 1998, s.54(1).

[7] Tribunals and Inquiries Act 1992, s.1 and Sch.I, Pt I, para.14(a).

[8] Data Protection Act 1998, s.5(2).

[9] Data Protection Act 1998, Sch.5, Pt I, para.1.

[10] *ibid.*, Sch.5, Pt I, para.2.

deputy commissioners and other officers and staff by him.[11] The funds required by the Commissioner are to be paid to him by the Secretary of State for Constitutional Affairs out of money provided by Parliament.[12] He must keep proper accounts and records.[13] Each year he must lay a general report before Parliament on the exercise of his functions under the Data Protection Act 1998 and the Freedom of Information Act 2000.[14]

Data Protection Act 1998 functions

The main functions of the Information Commissioner under the Data Protection Act 1998 are: 27–003

- maintaining the register of notifications by "data controllers"[15] under Pt III of the Data Protection Act 1998;
- enforcing compliance with the "data protection principles"[16] by data controllers by issuing "enforcement notices"[17] and investigating compliance with the Act and those principles in respect of the processing of "personal data"[18] by data controllers[19];
- promoting good practice and the observance of the requirements of the Act by data controllers[20];
- disseminating information about the Act to the public[21] and preparing and disseminating codes of practice if he considers it appropriate or the Secretary of State for Constitutional Affairs so directs by order[22];
- encouraging trade associations to prepare and disseminate and approve codes of practice[23];
- disseminating information about European decisions and the protection of data subjects' rights in the rest of the world[24];

[11] Data Protection Act 1998, Sch.5, Pt I, paras 5 and 6.

[12] *ibid.*, Sch.5, Pt I, para.8. The Lord Chancellor's functions were transfered by Art.4 of the Secretary of State for Constitutional Affairs Order 2003 (SI 2003/1887).

[13] *ibid.*, Sch.5, Pt I, para.10.

[14] *ibid.*, s.52(1); Freedom of Information Act 2000, s.49(1). The reports are prepared for the year ending March 31 and can be accessed on the Information Commissioner's website. See n.1 above for details.

[15] As to the meaning of "data controller," see para.4–023.

[16] These principles are set out in Data Protection Act 1998, Sch.1, Pt I, and elucidated in Sch.1 Pt II and Schs 2–4 .

[17] Data Protection Act 1998, ss.40 and 41. As to enforcement notices, see para.4–081.

[18] As to the meaning of "personal data," see paras 4–017 to 4–020.

[19] Data Protection Act 1998, ss.42–46: processing is defined by s.1(1) of the Act to mean obtaining, recording, holding or carrying out defined operations on the data.

[20] Data Protection Act 1998, s.51(1).

[21] *ibid*., s.51(2).

[22] *ibid.*, s.51(3). No orders have been made by the Lord Chancellor or the Secretary of State for Constitutional Affairs under s.51(3)(a).

[23] *ibid.*, s.51(4).

[24] *ibid.*, s.51(6).

— providing assistance to individuals who are parties to proceedings under Pt II of the Act[25] which relate to personal data processed for the "special purposes"[26] if he considers the case to involve a matter of substantial public importance[27];
— instituting proceedings for offences under the Act[28]; and
— carrying out various functions under the Data Protection Directive and the Convention and other international obligations of the United Kingdom as provided by the Secretary of State for Constitutional Affairs.[29]

The Information Commissioner has sole authority with the Director of Public Prosecutions for bringing prosecutions under the Act.[30] The Information Commissioner is also responsible for enforcing the Telecommunications (Data Protection and Privacy) Regulations 1999.[31]

Freedom of Information Act 2000 functions

27–004 The main function of the Information Commissioner under the Freedom of Information Act 2000 is investigating and determining whether public authorities have dealt with requests for information in accordance with Pt I of the Act, or are otherwise complying with Pt I of the Act and the codes of practice issued by the Lord Chancellor or the Secretary of State for Constitutional Affairs under it, and enforcing such compliance.[32] His general functions are:

— approving "publication schemes" by public authorities[33];
— preparing and/or approving "model publication schemes"[34];
— promoting good practice by public authorities in following the provisions of the Act and the Lord Chancellor's codes of practice[35];
— disseminating information about the Act and good practice[36];

---

[25] These include proceedings under Data Protection Act 1998, s.7(9) to enforce the right of access to personal data by individuals who are the subject of it.
[26] As to the "special purposes," see para.4–060.
[27] Data Protection Act 1998, s.53; special purposes are defined by s.3 as the purposes of journalism, artistic purposes and literary purposes.
[28] Data Protection Act 1998, s.60. Offences under the Act are considered at paras 4–085 to 4–089 and 29–012.
[29] Data Protection Act 1998, s.54. The following orders have been made under the section: Data Protection (Functions of Designated Authority) Order 2000 (SI 2000/186) and the Data Protection (International Co-operation) Order 2000 (SI 2000/190).
[30] Data Protection Act 1998, s.60(1).
[31] SI 1999/2093, made to implement Directive 97/66 [1996] O.J. L23/26. See: reg.36 which extends the provisions of Pt V of Data Protection Act 1998 for the purposes of the regulations.
[32] Freedom of Information Act 2000, Pt IV (ss.50 – 56).
[33] *ibid.*, s.19(1)(a). As to publication schemes, see Ch.10.
[34] *ibid.*, s.20(1).
[35] *ibid.*, s.47(1). As to codes of practice, see Ch.9.
[36] *ibid.*, s.47(2).

- assessing (with consent) whether public authorities are following good practice[37];
- consulting the Keeper of Public Records about the promotion of the observance by local authorities of codes of practice issued by the Lord Chancellor under s.46[38];
- giving recommendations to public authorities if it appears that their practice does not comply with such codes of practice[39];
- reporting to Parliament at least annually on the exercise of his functions[40];
- disclosing information to the appropriate ombudsman if it appears to him that it could be relevant to an investigation by such ombudsman.[41]

The Secretary of State for Constitutional Affairs must consult the Information Commissioner before issuing or revising a code of practice under s.45(1) of the Act providing guidance to public authorities in connection with the discharge of their functions under Pt I and a code of practice under s.46(1) in connection with the keeping, management and destruction of public records.[42] The Information Commissioner also has responsibility for bringing criminal proceedings against a public authority or its officers and employees who alters records to prevent disclosure pursuant to the Act or the Data Protection Act 1998.[43]

The Scottish Information Commissioner

The Freedom of Information (Scotland) Act 2002 is enforced by the Scottish Information Commissioner. He is appointed by Her Majesty on the nomination of the Scottish Parliament.[44] He holds office for an initial term not exceeding five years on the terms and conditions determined by the Scottish Parliamentary corporation.[45] Schedule 2 to the Freedom of Information (Scotland) Act 2002 lays down similar terms in relation to the Scottish Information Commissioner as Sch.5 to the Data Protection Act 1998. The Scottish Information Commissioner must also lay a report each year before the Scottish Parliament on the exercise of his functions under the Act, which must include a record of the number of occasions on which he failed to reach a decision on a s.47(1) application within the four months specified by s.47(3)(b).[46] 27–005

[37] Freedom of Information Act 2000, s.47(3).
[38] *ibid.*, s.47(5). As to codes of practice under s.46, see para.9–006.
[39] *ibid.*, s.48.
[40] *ibid.*, s.49.
[41] *ibid.*, s.76.
[42] *ibid.*, s.45(4) and 46(5)(b). See further para.9–006.
[43] *ibid.*, s.77(4). See also para.29–007.
[44] Freedom of Information (Scotland) Act 2002, s.42(1).
[45] *ibid.*, s.42(2)–(5).
[46] *ibid.*, s.46(1) and (2).

Functions of Scottish Information Commissioner

27–006 The main function of the Scottish Information Commissioner is enforcing the Freedom of Information (Scotland) Act 2002 by investigating and deciding whether Scottish public authorities have dealt with requests for information in accordance with Pt 1 of the Act or are otherwise complying with Pt 1.[47] He also has the general functions of:

— promoting the following of good practice by Scottish public authorities in relation to the Act and the codes of practice issued under it and assessing whether they are following such good practice[48];
— disseminating information to and advising the public about the operation of the Act[49];
— making proposals to the Scottish Ministers about their power under ss.4 and 5 of the Act to designate Scottish public authorities for the purpose thereof[50]; and
— issuing practice recommendations to Scottish public authorities if he considers they are not following the codes of practice issued by the Scottish Ministers as to their functions under the Act and as to keeping, management and destruction of records issued under ss 60 and 61 thereof.[51]

Information Commissioners' duties of confidentiality

27–007 The Information Commissioners have extensive powers and opportunities to obtain information in the course of enforcing compliance with the Data Protection Act 1998 and Freedom of Information Act 2000 and the Freedom of Information (Scotland) Act 2002, respectively, including information held by public authorities.[52] Further, no enactment or rule of law prohibiting or restricting the disclosure of information precludes any person from furnishing the Commissioner with any information necessary for the discharge of his functions under the Data Protection Act 1998 or the Freedom of Information Act 2000.[53] The Commissioners and their staff are therefore potentially privy to much sensitive information, which may not in the event be made public. They commit an offence if they disclose, without lawful authority, any information

[47] Freedom of Information (Scotland) Act 2002, Pt 4 (ss.50–56), which is in similar terms to Freedom of Information Act 2000, Pt IV (ss.47–56).
[48] *ibid.*, s.43(1) and (3). As to codes of practice, see Ch.9.
[49] *ibid.*, s.43(2).
[50] *ibid.*, s.43(4).
[51] *ibid.*, s.44. As to public records, see Ch.4.
[52] In particular by virtue of: Freedom of Information Act 2000, s.51; Freedom of Information (Scotland) Act 2002, s.50; and Data Protection Act 1998, s.43.
[53] Data Protection Act 1998, s.58 (which applies to the discharge of functions under the Freedom of Information Act 2000 as well); Freedom of Information (Scotland) Act 2002, s.50(7).

which has been furnished to the Commissioner under the Data Protection Act 1998 or the Freedom of Information Act 2000 which relates to an identified or identifiable individual or business and which is not available to the public from other sources.[54] There appears to be a hiatus in the English legislation, however, in that there is no provision making it an offence for the Commissioner or his staff to disclose information which comes to them under the Freedom of Information Act 2000 unless it relates to an identified or identifiable individual or business; there is no such hiatus in the Freedom of Information (Scotland) Act 2002, which provides that the Scottish Commissioner or his staff or agents commit an offence (punishable on summary conviction by the maximun fine and on indictment by an unlimited fine) if they disclose without lawful authority any information which is received by them under the Act and which is not in the public domain.[55]

Disclosure with lawful authority

Disclosure with lawful authority is defined for the purposes of the Data Protection Act 1998 and the Freedom of Information Act 2000 as being where: 27–008

(1) the disclosure is with consent of the individual or person carrying on the business concerned;
(2) the information was provided for the purpose of being made available to the public under any provision of the Acts;
(3) the disclosure is made for the purposes of and is necessary for the discharge of functions under the Acts or any Community obligation;
(4) the disclosure is made for the purposes of any proceedings, whether criminal or civil; or
(5) the disclosure is necessary in the public interest having regard to the rights and freedoms or legitimate interests of any person.

Under the Freedom of Information (Scotland) Act 2002 the definition of disclosure with lawful authority is similar save that:

(1) provides that the disclosure is made with the consent of the person from whom the information was obtained; and
(2) provides that the disclosure would have been required under the Act itself if the public authority from whom it was obtained or the Commissioner himself had received a request under s.1(1) thereof.[56]

[54] Data Protection Act 1998, s.59.
[55] Freedom of Information (Scotland) Act 2002, s.45(1), (3), (4).
[56] Data Protection Act 1998, s.59(2), Freedom of Information (Scotland) Act 2002, s.45(2), in particular paras (c) and (b).

Both the Freedom of Information Act 2000 and the Freedom of Information (Scotland) Act 2002 contain specific provisions authorising the Commissioners to disclose information coming to them under the Freedom of Information Act 2000 and Data Protection Act 1998 or the Freedom of Information (Scotland) Act 2002 respectively to various ombudsmen where the Commissioner believes the information would be relevant to such ombudsmen's investigations.[57]

Human Rights Act 1998

27–009 The Information Commissioners are themselves subject to the Human Rights Act 1998.[58] Articles 6, 8 and 10 of the European Convention on Human Rights are potentially relevant to the exercise of their functions, but it seems unlikely that they will impinge greatly on their work, although at this stage it is not possible to say so definitively.[59] Article 6 of the Convention probably does not apply to the work of the Commissioners in deciding whether applicants are entitled to information under the Acts on the basis that the rights granted are not "civil rights"[60] within the meaning of the Convention, and, in any event, the various rights of appeal against their decisions probably mean that Art.6 will be satisfied. The European Court has decided that Art.10 (which includes the right "to receive information") only prohibits a government from restricting a person from receiving information from others who want to provide it and does not cast any obligation to provide information to an applicant against its will but in the same case decided that the failure by a public authority to disclose certain personal data might involve a breach of the right to respect for private and family life provided by Art.8.[61] It seems likely that this decision would only impinge on applications for information under the Data Protection Act 1998. The Commissioners are also themselves public authorities for the purposes of the Freedom of Information Acts[62] and potentially "data controllers" subject to the Data Protection Act 1998, and they must accordingly comply with the provisions of these Acts.

---

57 Freedom of Information Act 2000, s.76 and Freedom of Information (Scotland) Act 2002, s.63.

58 See, in relation to England and Wales, Human Rights Act 1998, s.6(1) and (3).

59 See paras 1–029 to 1–037.

60 See the admissibility decision of the European Human Rights Commission in *Barry v France* (App. No.14497/89, October 14, 1991) and *McGinley v United Kingdom* (1998) 27 E.H.H.R. 1 at paras 85–6.

61 *Gaskin v United Kingdom* (1990) 12 E.H.R.R. 36. The actual decision in *Gaskin* was that the failure to provide medical records relating to the applicant at his request was an interference with his Article 8 right to respect for his private and family life; this decision led to the enactment of Data Protection Act 1998, ss.68 and 69 which *inter alia* make health records, in whatever form they are kept, subject to the Data Protection Act 1998 and in pticular the access rights provided by s.7, thereby potentially allowing individuals a right to obtain access to their own health records. See, further, paras 1–033 to 1–035.

62 Freedom of Information Act 2000, Sch.1, Pt VI; Freedom of Information (Scotland) Act 2002, Sch.1, Pt 7.

2. MONITORING COMPLIANCE WITH THE ACTS

Monitoring the right of access to personal data

The right of access to "personal data"[63] held by a "data controller" provided by Pt II of the Data Protection Act 1998 is mainly enforced by means of an application to court by the individual who is the subject of such personal data.[64] The Information Commissioner's monitoring and enforcement functions relate to data controllers' "processing" of personal data and their compliance with "the data protection principles,"[65] rather than directly to their compliance with their obligations to give access to personal data. 27–010

Monitoring the right of access to information held by public authorities

There is no express provision of the Freedom of Information Act 2000 requiring the Information Commissioner to monitor compliance by public authorities with their duty to give access to information pursuant to Pt I of the Act, and the normal mechanism for enforcement of that duty is for a complainant to apply to the Commissioner seeking from him a decision notice requiring steps to be taken by a public authority pursuant to s.50 of the Act.[66] However, there are a number of provisions of the Act from which such a free-standing obligation on the part of the Commissioner can be implied: 27–011

(1) The Commissioner has power, with the consent of the public authority, to assess whether it is following "good practice" in the discharge of its functions under Pt I of the Act[67];
(2) The Commissioner can make recommendations as to good practice in any case where it appears to him that the practice of a public authority does not comply with a code of practice issued under s.45 of the Act in connection with the discharge of public authorities' functions under Pt I thereof[68];
(3) The Commissioner has power to require a public authority to furnish him with information for the purpose of determining whether it has complied with Pt I of the Act or a code of practice issued under s.45[69] and power to seek a warrant allowing entry, search and seizure of

[63] As to the meaning of "personal data," see paras 4–017 to 4–020.
[64] Data Protection Act 1998, s.7(9). See para.4–077.
[65] See in particular Data Protection Act 1998, ss.40(1), 42(1) and 43(1).
[66] See para.28–009.
[67] See Freedom of Information Act 2000, ss.47(3) and (6).
[68] Freedom of Information Act 2000, s.48.
[69] *ibid.*, s.51(1)(b).

documents and other evidence if there is reason for suspecting a breach of Pt I of the Act,[70] whether or not there has been a complaint and, if he is satisfied that the public authority has failed to comply with any requirement of Pt I of the Act, he has power to serve an "enforcement notice" on the public authority under s.52(1) of the Act, again whether or not there has been a complaint.

Monitoring the right of access to information held by Scottish public authorities

27–012 The position under the Freedom of Information (Scotland) Act in relation to the Scottish Information Commissioner is very similar,[71] save that the Scottish Information Commissioner does not require the consent of the public authority before undertaking an assessment as to whether the authority is following good practice and in particular complying with the requirements of the Act.[72]

3. THE INFORMATION TRIBUNAL

The Information Tribunal

27–013 Judicial supervision of the Freedom of Information Act 2000 is primarily provided by the Information Tribunal.[73] There is no equivalent in relation to the Freedom of Information (Scotland) Act 2002.[74] The Information Tribunal was originally constituted as a statutory tribunal under the Data Protection Act 1984[75] as the Data Protection Tribunal. It was continued in existence by the Data Protection Act 1998[76] and its name was changed to the Information Tribunal by s.18(2) of the Freedom of Information Act 2000,[77] which Act also extended its functions substantially. The jurisdiction of the Tribunal is purely statutory.[78] It is subject to supervision under the Tribunals and Inquiries Act

[70] Freedom of Information Act 2000, s.55, Sch.3 paras 1 and 2.

[71] See Freedom of Information (Scotland) Act 2002, ss.43(3), 44(1), 50(1)(b) and 51, and Sch.3.

[72] *ibid.*, s.43(1), (3) and (8).

[73] Freedom of Information Act 2000, ss.57 and 60. In relation to the Data Protection Act 1998, where no national security certificate has been issued under the Data Protection Act 1998, judicial supervision is provided by the County Courts and the High Court (see paras 4–077 and 28–032); where a national security certificate has been issued, judicial supervision is provided by the Information Tribunal (see paras 4–078 and 28–036).

[74] Appeals are heard by the Court of Session: Freedom of Information (Scotland) 2002.

[75] Data Protection Act 1984, s.3(1)(b).

[76] Data Protection Act 1998, s.6(3).

[77] With effect from January 30, 2001.

[78] The Information Tribunal is a "court" and appeals before it are "civil proceedings" for the purposes of the Supreme Court Act 1981, s.42 (restriction of vexatious legal proceedings in any civil proceedings, whether in the High Court or any inferior court): *Re Ewing* [2002] All E.R. (D) 350 (Dec).

1992.[79] At the moment it is administered by an official in the Lord Chancellor's Department.[80]

Membership of the Tribunal

The members of the Tribunal, including a chairman[81] and such number of deputy chairmen as he may determine, are appointed by the Lord Chancellor, after consultation with the Secretary of State in relation to the chairman.[82] The chairman and deputy chairmen must be lawyers of seven years' standing[83] and the remaining members must be persons who represent the interests of "data subjects", "data controllers,"[84] those making requests for information under the Freedom of Information Act 2000 or public authorities.[85] The chairman and deputy chairman must retire at 70 unless authorised to continue to 75; otherwise, members of the tribunal hold and vacate office in accordance with the terms of their appointment.[86] Remuneration of the Tribunal members, officers and staff and the expenses of the Tribunal are all determined by the Lord Chancellor.[87] 27–014

Constitution of Tribunal in particular cases

The Lord Chancellor must designate, from among the chairman and deputy chairmen of the Information Tribunal, those capable of hearing national security cases.[88] Save when the Tribunal sits ex parte,[89] it is duly constituted in national security cases if it consists of three such designated persons. In other cases, the Tribunal is duly constituted if it consists of a chairman or deputy chairman sitting with an equal number of representatives of data subjects and data controllers in an appeal under the Data Protection Act 1998[90] and an equal number of representatives of those making requests for information and public 27–015

[79] See Tribunals and Inquiries Act 1992, s.1 and Sch.I, Pt I, para.14(b).

[80] The contact details are: Charlotte Mercer, Secretary to the Information Tribunal, Department for Constitutional Affairs, Selborne House, 54 Victoria Street London SW1E 6QW.

[81] Currently David Marks.

[82] Data Protection Act 1998, s.6(4). Note the functions of the Secretary of State under s.6(4)(c) were transferred to the Lord Chancellor with effect from November 26, 2001 by the Transfer of Functions (Miscellaneous) Order 2001 (SI 2001/3500) and from the Lord Chancellor to the Secretary of State for Constitutional Affairs by SI 2003/1887.

[83] Data Protection Act 1998, s.6(5).

[84] As defined in the Data Protection Act 1998.

[85] Data Protection Act 1998, s.6(6), as amended by Freedom of Information Act 2000, Sch.2, Pt II, para.16.

[86] *ibid.*, Sch.5, Pt II, para.12.

[87] *ibid.*, Sch.5, Pt II, paras 13–15. The Secretary to the Tribunal is based at the Lord Chancellor's Deptment at Selbourne House, 54 Victoria St, London SW1E 6QW.

[88] Namely appeals under the Data Protection Act 1998, s.28(4) and (6) and the Freedom of Information Act 2000, s.60(1) and (4). See paras 28–018 to 28–019 and 28–036.

[89] Pursuant to Data Protection Act 1998, Sch.6, para.6.

[90] Save for an appeal under the Data Protection Act 1998, s.48(3).

authorities in an appeal under the Freedom of Information Act 2000.[91] The members of the Tribunal who sit in any case are to be nominated by the chairman or a deputy chairman if he cannot act.[92] The determination of the Tribunal is by a majority of those sitting.[93] Subject to any rules made by the Secretary of State for Constitutional Affairs, the Tribunal can sit ex parte in appeals under ss.28(4) or (6) of the Data Protection Act 1998 (which concern national security and in which case the jurisdiction can be exercised by one or more of the persons designated to hear national security cases) or appeals under s.48(3) of that Act (which relate to urgent cases and in which case the jurisdiction shall be exercised by the chairman or a deputy chairman sitting alone).[94]

Data Protection Act 1998 appeals

27–016 The Information Tribunal has jurisdiction to determine the following appeals under the Data Protection Act 1998:

- an appeal under s.28(4) of the Act to quash a certificate relating to national security issued under s.28(2) of the Act;[95]
- an appeal under s.28(6) of the Act for a determination under s.28(7) that such a certificate does not relate to particular personal data;
- an appeal under s.48(1) of the Act against an "enforcement notice,"[96] an "information notice"[97] or a "special information notice"[98] served by the Information Commissioner;
- an appeal under s.48(2) of the Act against the refusal of the Information Commissioner to cancel or vary an enforcement notice after an application under s.41(2);
- an appeal under s.48(3) against a statement of urgency in relation to an enforcement notice, information notice or special information notice included by the Information Commissioner under ss.40(8), 43(5) or 44(6) of the Act respectively; and

91 Data Protection Act 1998, Sch.6, para.4(1) and (1A).
92 *ibid.*, Sch.6, para.4(2).
93 *ibid.*, Sch.6, para.5.
94 *ibid.*, Sch.6 para.6.
95 A certificate signed by a Minister of the Crown is, by virtue of the Data Protection Act 1998, s.28(2), conclusive evidence that exemption from the provisions of all or any of the provisions mentioned in s.28(1) (which include Pt II, which itself includes s.7: the right of access to personal data) is required for the purposes of safeguarding national security.
96 Data Protection Act 1998, s.40. Enforcement notices under the Data Protection Act 1998 are considered at para.4–081.
97 Data Protection Act 1998, s.43. Information notices under the Data Protection Act 1998 are considered at para.4–082.
98 Data Protection Act 1998, s.44. As to the meaning of "special purposes," see para.4–060.

— an appeal under s.48(4) of the Act by a data controller against a determination by the Information Commissioner under s.45(1) that particular data is not being processed only for "special purposes."[99]

Freedom of Information Act 2000 appeals

The Information Tribunal has jurisdiction to determine the following appeals under the Freedom of Information Act 2000: 27–017

— an appeal under s.57(1) by a complainant or a public authority[1] against a decision notice served by the Information Commissioner under s.50(3)(b) following a complaint under s.50(1) that the public authority had failed to deal with a request for information in accordance with Pt I of the Act;

— an appeal under s.57(2) by a public authority against an "information notice"[2] or an "enforcement notice"[3] served on it[4];

— an appeal under s.60(1) by the Information Commissioner or any applicant whose request for information has been affected by the issue of a national security certificate under s.23(2)[5] or s.24(3)[6]; and

— an appeal under s.60(4) by a party to proceedings under the Act on the grounds that a certificate issued under s.24(3) identifying the information to which it applies by means of a general description does not apply to the particular information in question as claimed by the public authority holding it.

[99] See Data Protection Act 1998, ss.3 and 45(1)(b).

[1] Or, in the case of "transferred public records" (Freedom of Information Act 2000, s.15(4)) within s.66 of the Act, the "responsible authority" as defined in s.15(5) thereof: s.57(3).

[2] Freedom of Information Act 2000, s.51(1). Information notices under the Freedom of Information Act 2000 are dealt with at para.28–010.

[3] Freedom of Information Act 2000, s.52(1). Enforcement notices under the Freedom of Information Act 2000 are dealt with at para.28–011.

[4] Or, in the case of "transferred public records" (Freedom of Information Act 2000, s.15(4)) within s.66 of the Act, the "responsible authority" as defined in s.15(5) thereof: s.57(3).

[5] Freedom of Information Act 2000, s.23(2) provides that a certificate signed by a Minister of the Crown certifying that information was supplied by or relates to any of the security bodies listed in s.23(3) is conclusive evidence of that "fact" so as to make it "exempt information" by virtue of s.23(1). Conclusive certificates on the grounds of national security are dealt with at paras 17–041 to 17–050. Appeals where there has been such a certificate are dealt with at paras 28–015, 28–018 to 28–019.

[6] Freedom of Information Act 2000, s.24(3) provides that a certificate signed by a Minister of the Crown certifying that exemption from s.1(1)(b) or ss.1(1)(a) and (b) is required shall be conclusive evidence of that "fact" for the purposes of s.24(1) and (2) which provide exemption in those circumstances from the duties to state whether information is held and to communicate it pursuant to s.1(1)(a) and (b) of the Act respectively. Conclusive certificates under s.24 are dealt with at paras 17–041 to 17–050. Appeals where there has been such a certificate are dealt with at paras 28–015, 28–018 to 28–019.

Practice and procedure

27–018 The Secretary of State for Constitutional Affairs (formerly the Lord Chancellor) can make rules regulating the exercise of rights of appeal under the Data Protection Act 1998 and the Freedom of Information Act 2000 and the practice and procedure of the Information Tribunal.[7] There is express provision in the Data Protection Act 1998 dealing with the equivalent of contempt of court in relation to the Tribunal: if an act or omission which would amount to a contempt of court is done in relation to proceedings before the Tribunal, the Tribunal can certify the fact to the High Court which can inquire into the matter and deal with it as a contempt of court.[8] Since under its current jurisdiction in relation to Freedom of Information Act 2000 and Data Protection Act 1998 (at least relating to access to information) the Tribunal will rarely issue orders (save of a procedural nature) it seems likely that this provision is mainly designed to deal with the equivalent of contempt in the face of the court or other interference with the course of justice, such as interfering with witnesses. The normal way in which such a contempt would be treated would be committal for up to two years or a fine.[9] As discussed later,[10] in relation to the enforcement of notices of the Information Commissioner there are difficulties with this provision although in practice they are perhaps unlikely to arise. It is sufficient to note that the power to punish for contempt given by the Data Protection Act 1998 can be exercised by a single judge of the Queen's Bench Division[11] and that it seems likely that if the Tribunal made a certificate under the Act, the proceedings would be conducted before the court by the Attorney-General.[12]

---

[7] Data Protection Act 1998, Sch.6, para.7. At time of writing there were three sets of rules made under para.7: Data Protection Tribunal (Enforcement Appeals) Rules (SI 2000/189); Data Protection Tribunal (National Security Appeals) Rules 2000 (SI 2000/206); and Information Tribunal (National Security Appeals)(Telecommunications) Rules (SI 2000/731). The intention of the Lord Chancellor was to produce a new consolidated set of rules replacing these and covering appeals under the Freedom of Information Act 2000 (see Lord Chancellor's Annual Report on implementation of the Act presented to Parliament under Freedom of Information Act 2000, s.87(5) in November 2001, HC 367, p.12 and the consultation document dated March 2002 at *www.dca.gov.uk/foi/inftribprop.htm*). The rules of procedure are dealt with at para.28–017.

[8] Data Protection Act 1998, Sch.6, para.8.

[9] See generally *Halsbury's Laws of England* (4th ed., Butterworths, 1998 re-issue) Vol.9(1), paras 506–509.

[10] para.29–003.

[11] RSC Ord.52, r.1(4).

[12] As in the analogous case of *Attorney-General v Clough* [1963] 1 Q.B. 773.

Human Rights Act 1998

The Information Tribunal is itself subject to the Human Rights Act 1998.[13] It seems unlikely that the ECHR will have much impact on its work in practice.[14] The Information Tribunal is not a public authority for the purposes of the Freedom of Information Act 2000 itself, though it may be a "data controller" for the purposes of the Data Protection Act 1998. 27–019

13 Human Rights Act 1998, s.6(1) and (3).
14 See the discussion at paras 1–029 to 1–037, and 27–009.

CHAPTER 28

Appeals

A. Appeals under the Freedom of Information Acts

B. APPEALS UNDER THE DATA PROTECTION ACT 1998

A. APPEALS UNDER THE FREEDOM OF INFORMATION ACTS

1. FIRST STAGE: INTERNAL RECONSIDERATION

First stage

28–001 A person who is dissatisfied with the response of a public authority to his request for information under the Freedom of Information Act 2000 will normally first seek internal reconsideration by the public authority before resorting to the Information Commissioner, the Information Tribunal or the courts.

Complaints under the s.45 Code of Practice

28–002 The code of practice issued under s.45 of the Freedom of Information Act 2000 requires public authorities to provide internal procedures for dealing with complaints about the handling by them of requests for information.[1] Such complaints will include complaints by persons who have made requests for information about a failure to comply with s.1(1)(a) or (b) of the Act promptly[2] or objecting to the contents of a notice of refusal by the public authority made under s.17(1), (3) or (5) relying on an exemption in Pt II of the Act or stating that s.12 or s.14 apply to relieve it of the duty to comply with the request.[3] A notice under s.17 must, if appropriate, contain reasons for reliance on an exemption in Pt II of the Act and reasons for claiming that the public interest in disclosure is outweighed by the public interest in maintaining the exemption[4] and must contain details of any complaints procedure and of the right to complain' to the Information Commissioner under s.50.[5] The code provides that any

---

1 See Freedom of Information Act 2000, s. 45(2)(e) and Pt XII of the Code. The Code was issued by the Lord Chancellor in November 2002 and is available at *www.dca.gov.uk/foi/codepafunc.htm*. The Code is dealt with more specifically in Ch.9.

2 Sections 1(1)(a) and (b) give the basic rights to be informed whether the public authority holds the information and to have it communicated; s.10(1) generally requires compliance within 20 working days of a request, but permits extensions in certain circumstances: see paras 11–022 to 11–030.

3 Section 12 provides exemption where the cost of compliance would exceed an appropriate limit and s.14 provides exemption where the request is vexatious. See Ch.12.

4 See Freedom of Information Act 2000, s.17(1)(c) and 17(3) and paras 13–009 to 13–010.

5 Freedom of Information Act 2000, s.17(7).

written reply from an applicant expressing dissatisfaction with a public authority's response to a valid request for information should be treated as a complaint.[6] The complaints procedure should be a fair and impartial means of dealing with problems and reviewing decisions under the Act; it should be possible to reverse or amend decisions already taken; procedures should be clear and not unnecessarily bureaucratic and capable of producing a prompt determination of the complaint[7]; if possible, complaints should be handled by someone who was not a party to the original decision[8]; complainants should be informed of the outcome of their complaint and complaints should be dealt with within target time periods[9]; the information requested should be provided as soon as practicable if that is the outcome of the procedure[10]; and a complainant should be informed of his right to apply to the Information Commissioner if still dissatisfied.[11]

Statutory encouragement for internal procedure

The policy of the Act is to encourage attempts at resolving disputes by means of the internal complaints procedure. Thus, any notice of refusal of a request under s.17 of the Act must include particulars of any complaints procedure maintained by the public authority or state that it does not have one[12] and the Information Commissioner should not deal with an application to him under s.50 of the Act if it appears to him that the complainant has not exhausted any complaints procedure which complies with the Code of Practice.[13] 28–003

Scottish provisions

The Freedom of Information (Scotland) Act 2002 adopts a somewhat different approach. It provides that the Scottish Ministers are to issue codes of practice which must require the provision by public authorities of complaints procedures in respect of their handling of requests for information under the Act[14] and that notices issued by public authorities refusing to supply information pursuant to a request must contain particulars of their complaints procedure.[15] However, there is no sanction for failure to make use of a complaints procedure; rather there is a statutory procedure for an internal review by the public authority 28–004

[6] Freedom of Information Act 2000, s.45; Code of Practice, para.55.
[7] *ibid.*, para.56.
[8] *ibid.*, para.57.
[9] *ibid.*, para.58.
[10] *ibid.*, para.61.
[11] *ibid.*, para.63.
[12] Freedom of Information Act 2000, s.17(7)(a).
[13] *ibid.*, s.50(2)(a).
[14] Freedom of Information (Scotland) Act 2002, s.60(2)(e).
[15] *ibid.*, s.19(a).

which is a precondition of any application to the Scottish Information Commissioner.[16]

Internal review by Scottish public authorities

28–005 The statutory procedure allows an applicant who is dissatisfied with the way that a Scottish public authority has dealt with a request for information under the Act to require the authority to review its actions and decisions in relation to the request.[17] The requirement for a review must be made not later than the fortieth working day after the time limit for dealing with a request or a purported compliance with a request or service of a notice refusing to supply the information if later,[18] but the public authority can, in effect, extend time.[19] Unless the requirement for a review or the original request for information was vexatious,[20] the public authority must comply with a requirement for a review promptly and in any event not later than the twentieth working day after receipt thereof.[21] On the review, the public authority can confirm, vary or substitute any decision or reach an original decision if the complaint is that no decision has been reached.[22] The public authority must give the applicant a notice in writing as to what it has done on the review or that it considers the requirement or request to have been vexatious.[23] Special provisions apply in relation to certain reviews when the relevant public authority is the Keeper of the Records of Scotland.[24]

2. SECOND STAGE: APPLICATION TO THE INFORMATION COMMISSIONER

Application to Information Commissioner

28–006 The second stage for a person who is dissatisfied with the response by a public authority to a request for information is an application to the Information Commissioner under s.50(1) of the Freedom of Information Act 2000. The

[16] Freedom of Information (Scotland) Act 2002, s.47(1) which provides for applications to the Commissioner only by a person dissatisfied with a decision given by the public authority on such review under ss.21(5) or (9) or with the failure of the public authority to deal with a requirement for a review.
[17] *ibid.*, s.20(1).
[18] *ibid.*, s.20(5).
[19] *ibid.*, s.20(6).
[20] *ibid.*, s.21(8).
[21] *ibid.*, s.21(1).
[22] *ibid.*, s.21(4).
[23] Freedom of Information (Scotland) Act 2002, ss.21(5) and (9). It is against notices under these subsections or a failure to carry out a review that application is made to the Scottish Commissioner under s.47(1).
[24] Freedom of Information (Scotland) Act 2002, ss.21(2) and 22.

section is framed in such a way that it is only the person who made the original request for information who can apply. The application is for a decision whether, in any specified respect, the request for information has (or, by implication, has not) "been dealt with in accordance with the requirements of Part I [of the Act]."[25]

Commissioner's jurisdiction on a complaint—procedural matters

The reference in s.50(1) to a request not having been dealt with in accordance with the requirements of Pt I of the Act comprehends a wide range of potential complaints. A complainant may apply to the Commissioner for a decision whether any of the following matters are in accordance with the Act: 28–007

(1) The level of fee sought by the public authority for complying with its duty to inform the applicant whether it holds information of the description specified in the request and for communicating that information to him[26];
(2) The time taken by the public authority for complying with the request[27];
(3) The means by which the public authority communicated the information to the applicant[28];
(4) The refusal of a public authority to comply with a request on the basis of the cost of compliance being estimated to exceed the appropriate limit[29];
(5) The refusal of a public authority to deal with a request on the basis that it is vexatious or is identical or substantially identical to an earlier request from the applicant[30];
(6) The failure by an appropriate records authority upon receipt of a request to comply with its obligations under s.15 of the Act;
(7) The failure by a public authority to provide advice and assistance[31]; and
(8) The failure of a refusal notice to contain the information required under s.17 of the Act.

[25] Freedom of Information Act 2000, s.50(1).
[26] *ibid.*, s.9.
[27] *ibid.*, s.10.
[28] *ibid.*, s.11.
[29] *ibid.*, ss.12 and 13.
[30] *ibid.*, s.14.
[31] *ibid.*, s.16.

Commissioner's jurisdiction on a complaint—refusals

28–008 Where a public authority either:

— does not inform an applicant whether or not it holds information of the description specified in his request; or
— does not communicate to that applicant some or all of the requested information held by it,

the applicant's request will not have been dealt with in accordance with the requirements of Pt I of the Act unless one or more of the qualifications introduced by s.1(2) are engaged.[32] A person who has either not been informed by a public authority that it holds information of the description specified in his request or who has not had that information communicated to him may therefore apply to the Commissioner for a decision whether his request has been dealt with in accordance with the requirements of Pt I on the basis that none of the qualifications in s.1(2) applies so as to deprive him of his rights in s.1(1).[33] In order to determine whether any of the qualifications in s.1(2) apply, the Commissioner necessarily must consider:

(1) whether the information held by the public authority answering the terms of the request is exempt information by virtue of any provision in Pt II (ss.21–44);
(2) if a provision by which the information is rendered exempt information does not confer absolute exemption, whether the public interest in maintaining the exemption outweighs the public interest in disclosing that information;
(3) whether the duty to confirm or deny that the public authority holds information of the description specified in the request has been disapplied by any provision in Pt II; and
(4) if the duty to confirm or deny has been disapplied by any provision in Pt II, whether the public interest in maintaining the exclusion of that duty outweighs the public interest in disclosing whether the public authority holds that information.

Depending upon the exemption, (1) and (3) involve considering, in relation to each piece of information, whether the particular attributes identified in the exemption are present or the likely effects of its disclosure upon an identified interest. Where a conclusive certificate has been issued, (1) and (3) above will be answered to the extent that the information sought is covered by the certificate. It is for the Information Commissioner himself to decide in any particular case

---

32 All of the qualifications enumerated in s.1(2) are within Pt I of the Act.
33 As is clear from Freedom of Information Act 2000, s.50(4)(a).

whether any provision of Pt II applies[34] and, in particular, where the "public interest" lies in the case of a non-absolute exemption[35] (as opposed to it being for him to review the decision of the public authority on the question). Further, it seems clear that it is open to the Commissioner to decide that, although the grounds relied on by the public authority are not valid, there are other grounds which justify withholding the information in question.[36] Indeed, if the Commissioner concludes that the information sought has all the attributes identified in one or more of the provisions of Pt II of the Act, then, subject to a consideration of the public interest, the preconditions for a decision notice under s.50(4) will not be satisfied.[37] There is no provision dealing with who bears the burden of persuading the Information Commissioner whether the public authority has not acted in accordance with the Act.[38]

Formalities of Commissioner's decision

Unless the Information Commissioner forms the view that the complainant has not exhausted an internal complaints procedure, that there has been "undue delay" in making the application, that it is frivolous or vexatious or that it has been withdrawn or abandoned,[39] he must make a decision on the application and serve a "decision notice" on the complainant and the public authority in question.[40] If the decision is that the public authority has failed to communicate information or confirm or deny whether it holds the information as required by s.1(1) of the Act or that it has failed to comply with any of the requirements of s.11[41] or s.17,[42] the decision notice must specify the steps to be taken by the authority to comply with its obligations and the period within which they must be taken.[43] The decision notice must also contain details of the right of appeal 28–009

[34] Subject to the certification procedure under Freedom of Information Act 2000, ss.23(2), 24(3) 34(3) or 36(7).

[35] See Freedom of Information Act 2000, s.2(1)(b) and 2(2)(b); note the debate in House of Lords, *Hansard*, Vol.619, November 14, 2000, col.218 Lord Goodhart. This decision would also be subject to an appropriate certificate under Freedom of Information Act 2000, s.53: see below at para.28–012.

[36] See in particular in this context the wording of Freedom of Information Act 2000, s.50(4)(a) which specifies the position where the public authority ". . . has failed to communicate information . . . *in a case where it is required to do so . . .*".

[37] *Spurlock v FBI*, 69 F.(3d) 1010, 1016–18 (9th Cir. 1995), dealing with the position in the USA; *Re Waterford and Department of Health* (1983) 5 A.L.N. N139; *Re Waterford and Department of Treasury* (1983) 5 A.L.D. 193 (dealing with the position in Australia).

[38] Compare the Australian Freedom of Information Act 1982, s.61 referred to para.28–016. In relation to the burden of proof, see paras 14–023 to 14–029.

[39] In any of which cases he must notify the complainant accordingly and let him know the grounds for not making a decision: Freedom of Information Act 2000, ss.50(2) and 50(3)(a).

[40] *ibid.*, s.50(3)(b).

[41] Obligations of public authority as to means by which information is communicated.

[42] Obligations of public authority in relation to notices of refusal of requests for information.

[43] Freedom of Information Act 2000, s.50(4).

to the Information Tribunal provided by s.57 if the Act.[44] It is not clear whether there would be a duty on the Commissioner to provide reasons for the decision in the decision notice[45]: there is no express provision requiring that reasons be given, but there are arguments both for and against[46]; the better view is probably that the Commissioner is under a duty to provide such reasons as he can.

Information notices

28–010 The Information Commissioner has power, in connection with an application by a complainant under s.50(1) (or if he reasonably requires information to determine whether a public authority is complying with Pt I of the Act or any code of practice issued under s.45 or 46), to serve on the public authority "an information notice" requiring it to furnish him with relevant information (including unrecorded information) within such time as may be specified.[47] The notice must contain details of the right of appeal to the Information Tribunal provided by s.57 of the Act and if an appeal is brought it need not be complied with pending appeal[48]; and the public authority is not required to provide legally privileged information,[49] but otherwise the public authority must comply with the notice.[50] Thus, the Information Commissioner is able to see the information which is being sought by the applicant in order to form a judgment as to whether it or its existence ought to be disclosed under the Freedom of Information Act 2000.[51]

44 Freedom of Information Act 2000, s.50(5).
45 See generally in relation to the duty to give reasons: *Halsbury's Laws of England* (4th ed., Butterworths 2001), Vol.1(1), 2001 re-issue, paras 112 and 113.
46 For example: against: (1) the fact that there is an express requirement to give "grounds" when refusing to make a decision in Freedom of Information Act 2000, s.50(3)(a); (2) the fact that in many cases there may be difficulties in giving reasons which do not themselves reveal the information which is the subject-matter of a request and the lack of any statutory guidance as to how this problem should be dealt with (compare in relation to the Information Tribunal: the Information Tribunal (Enforcement Appeals) Rules 2000 (SI 2000/189) r.24 and the Information Tribunal (National Security Appeals) Rules 2000 (SI 2000/206) r.27 and the Lord Chancellor's Consultation Paper on new procedural rules following the introduction of the Freedom of Information Act 2000 at para.37); for: (1) the need for a party considering an appeal under Freedom of Information Act 2000 s.57 to have some basis for deciding whether or not to appeal (2) in particular the provision at s.58(2) that the Tribunal can review "any finding of fact on which the notice in question was based" and (3) the fact that the public authority in question must give reasons for deciding that an exemption under Pt II of Freedom of Information Act 2000 applies and for claiming that the public interest in disclosing the information in question is outweighed by maintaining the exemption (see Freedom of Information Act 2000 ss.17(1)(c) and 17(3)).
47 Freedom of Information Act 2000, ss.51(1), (7).
48 *ibid.*, ss.51(3), (4).
49 *ibid.*, ss.51(5), (6).
50 Note there is no provision against self incrimination similar to that in Data Protection Act 1998, s.43(8).
51 See, in relation to the Commissioner's duties of confidentiality, see para.27–007.

Enforcement notices

If the Information Commissioner is satisfied that a public authority has failed to comply with any of the requirements of Pt I of the Act,[52] he may serve on it an "enforcement notice" requiring it to take within a specified time such steps as may be specified to comply.[53] In general such a notice would be served following an independent investigation by the Information Commissioner rather than following a complaint under s.50(1), although there is nothing in Pt IV of the Act to prevent an enforcement notice being served in respect of the same matter which is the subject of a decision notice. An enforcement notice must give details of the failure to comply with Pt I and of the right of appeal under s.57 of the Act.[54] The obligation to comply with the notice is suspended pending an appeal.[55] 28–011

Certificated exemption from compliance with certain decision or enforcement notices

There is a provision allowing a government department or the National Assembly for Wales (or any other public authority specified in an order made by the Secretary of State for Constitutional Affairs) to avoid the effect of a decision or enforcement notice served on it relating to a failure to comply with s.1(1) in respect of exempt information[56] where within 20 days of the notice there is a certificate signed by an "accountable person" given to the Information Commissioner stating that he has on reasonable grounds formed the opinion that there was no failure.[57] The "accountable person" must give reasons to the complainant for the opinion he has formed unless that would involve the disclosure of exempt information.[58] An "accountable person" (apart from special provisions about the National Assembly of Wales and the Northern Ireland Assembly) is a member of the cabinet or the Attorney General and a copy of the certificate must be laid before Parliament.[59] This provision in effect removes the supervision of the Information Tribunal as to where the public interest lies in relation to the disclosure of exempt information and represents a kind of 28–012

[52] This would include in particular Freedom of Information Act 2000, ss.1, 10, 11, 15, 16, 17 and 19.
[53] *ibid.*, s.52(1).
[54] *ibid.*, s.52(2).
[55] *ibid.*, s.52(3).
[56] In other words, information falling within one or more of the provisions in Pt II of the Act, irrespective of whether the public interest weighs in favour of disclosure: Freedom of Information Act 2000, s.84.
[57] *ibid.*, ss.53(1), (2).
[58] *ibid.*, ss.53(6) and (7).
[59] *ibid.*, s.53(8) and (3).

"trump card" in the hand of the higher executive.[60] The only way of challenging such a certificate would be by an application for judicial review.[61]

Scottish provisions

28–013 Under the Freedom of Information (Scotland) Act 2002 a person dissatisfied with the decision (or failure to take a decision) of a Scottish public authority on a review under the statutory review procedure set out in ss.20–22 of that Act, can apply to the Scottish Information Commissioner for a decision whether the request for information was dealt with in accordance with Pt 1 of the Act.[62] Unlike the Freedom of Information Act 2000, the Scottish Act lays down detailed provisions as to the form and contents of the application and the time within which it is to be brought (basically, six months from the date of the review).[63] Once he has received an application the Scottish Information Commissioner must make a decision unless it is excluded[64] or he thinks it is frivolous or vexatious or has been withdrawn or abandoned.[65] Again, unlike the Freedom of Information Act 2000, the Scottish Act provides a four-month time limit for the Scottish Information Commissioner to make a decision and expressly provides that the Scottish Information Commissioner must invite the public authority's comments on the application and that he may endeavour to effect a settlement of the case.[66] Once he has made a decision the Scottish Information Commissioner must serve a "decision notice" on the parties and must specify the steps which the Scottish public authority must take and time within which it must do so in order to comply with Pt 1 of the Scottish Act.[67] The decision notice must also contain particulars of the right of appeal against

[60] See para.28–027 for a discussion of the effect of s.53: it seems clear that a certificate can only relate to the public interest question and not to the anterior question of whether information is exempt. The trumping effect of such certificates is a feature of freedom of information legislation in each of the Westminster-style comparative jurisdictions. See: 2–016 (Australia); 2–021 (New Zealand); 2–030 (Canada); and 2–038 (Ireland). In the USA, an equivalent is achieved with exclusions: see para.2–003.

[61] See para.28–023. There is a question whether s.53, by effectively removing the jurisdiction of the Tribunal, might involve a breach of Art.6.1 of the European Convention on Human Rights. It is thought that this is unlikely for at least two reasons: (1) it seems unlikely that in many cases the right of access to information could properly be categorised as a "civil right" within the meaning of Art.6.1, since there is unlikely to be any direct financial or property right at stake (see: decision of the European Human Rights Commission on admissibility in *Barry v France*, App. No.14497/89, October 14, 1991) and (2) the question of entitlement involves a weighing of the public interest and the decision of the minister on the matter will be open to judicial review, which is an appropriate way of testing such a decision in any event.

[62] Freedom of Information (Scotland) Act 2002, s.47(1). The language is materially the same as the Freedom of Information Act 2000, s.50(1): see para.28–010.

[63] Freedom of Information (Scotland) Act 2002, s.47(2)–(7).

[64] By s.48, which excludes such applications in relation to the Commissioner himself, the Procurator Fiscal and the Lord Advocate in his prosecutorial role.

[65] Freedom of Information (Scotland) Act 2002, s.49(1), (2).

[66] *ibid.*, s.49(3), (4).

[67] *ibid.*, s.49(5)–(7).

the notice provided by s.56 of the Scottish Act, which, unlike the position under the Freedom of Information Act 2000, is an appeal to the Court of Session on a point of law. As with decisions of the Information Commissioner,[68] there is no express requirement on the Scottish Information Commissioner to give reasons in a decision but it is thought that the arguments in favour of an implied requirement to do so must be stronger given the nature of the right of appeal against such a notice.

Scottish provisions as to information notices and enforcement notices

There are very similar provisions in the Freedom of Information (Scotland) Act 2002 in relation to information and enforcement notices as there are in the Freedom of Information Act 2000.[69] The Scottish Act expressly provides that neither an obligation to maintain secrecy nor any other restriction on disclosure affects the public authority's duty to comply with an information notice[70] and the particulars of a right of appeal which are to be given are of an appeal under s.56 of the Scottish Act, namely to the Court of Session on a point of law. The exception from compliance with a decision or enforcement notice provided by s.53 of the Freedom of Information Act 2000[71] is mirrored in s.52 of the Scottish Act, but in more limited terms: the decision or enforcement notice must have been given to the Scottish Administration,[72] the categories of exempt information on which a certificate can rely are expressly set out,[73] and the certificate can only be given by the First Minister and he must also certify his opinion that the information requested is "of exceptional sensitivity."[74] 28–014

3. THIRD STAGE: APPEAL TO THE INFORMATION TRIBUNAL

Appeal to the Information Tribunal

The third stage for someone dissatisfied with the outcome of a request for information under the Freedom of Information Act 2000 is an appeal against the Information Commissioner's decision notice to the Information Tribunal.[75] The Freedom of Information Act 2000 also provides for a right of appeal by a 28–015

[68] See para.28–025.
[69] Freedom of Information (Scotland) Act 2002, ss.50, 51: see paras 28–010 to 28–011.
[70] *ibid.*, s.50(7).
[71] See para.28–012.
[72] Freedom of Information (Scotland) Act 2002, s.52(1)(a).
[73] *ibid.*, s.52(1)(b).
[74] *ibid.*, s.52(2).
[75] Freedom of Information Act 2000, s.57(1).

public authority to the Information Tribunal against a decision notice of the Commissioner and provides for such an appeal by a public authority against an information or enforcement notice.[76] The Act further provides the Information Commissioner or the applicant for information with the right to appeal to the Information Tribunal against a national security certificate issued under s.23(2) or 24(3) of the Act,[77] although there is no equivalent provision for an appeal against conclusive evidence certificates issued under s.34(3) ("parliamentary privilege") and s.36(7) ("prejudice to effective conduct of public affairs") or a certificate issued under s.53(2).[78] There is no equivalent of an appeal to the Information Tribunal in the Freedom of Information Act (Scotland) Act 2002.

Nature of appeals to Information Tribunal against decisions of Information Commissioner under section 57 of the Freedom of Information Act 2000

28–016 On an appeal against a decision, enforcement or information notice, the Information Tribunal must allow the appeal or substitute an alternative notice if the notice is "not in accordance with the law" or, to the extent that the notice involved the exercise of discretion by the Commissioner, that he ought to have exercised such discretion differently; but otherwise it must dismiss the appeal.[79] On such an appeal the Tribunal can review any finding of fact on which the notice was based.[80] There is nothing in s.57 of the Act to suggest that the onus of persuading the Tribunal to allow the appeal would not lie on the appellant in the normal way; this is in contrast to the position in Australia, where it is expressly provided that in an appeal to the Australian Administrative Appeals Tribunal the burden of establishing that a decision to withhold information was justified lies on the public authority.[81]

---

[76] Freedom of Information Act 2000, s.57(1)–(3).

[77] *ibid.*, s.69(1).

[78] For s.53(2) certificate see para.28–012. It may be possible to seek a judicial review of these three types of certificates: see paras 28–023 to 28–027.

[79] Freedom of Information Act 2000, s.58(1): such a discretion would include the "balancing exercise" required of the Information Commissioner by ss.2(1)(b) and 2(2)(b).

[80] Freedom of Information Act 2000, s.58(2). The Act does not specify whether the review is a "*de novo*" review or a consideration of the reasonableness of the earlier fact-finding exercise. Given the marked change in language in s.59, the existence of a subsequent right of review on a point of law and the nature of the Tribunal, any such review would seem to be "*de novo*." This would not include facts based on the conclusive evidence provided by national security certificates issued under s.23(2) or 24(3) or the presumption set out in s.60(4) or certificates under s.34(3) or 36(7) relating to Parliament until, in the case of national security certificates, they were quashed under s.60(1) or (2) or a relevant determination made under s.60(5).

[81] See Australian Freedom of Information Act 1982, s.61.

Practice and procedure

At the time of writing there are no rules of procedure relating to an appeal under s.57(1) of the Freedom of Information Act 2000 by a complainant or public authority against a decision notice.[82] Subject to any such rules, the Information Tribunal shall be duly constituted for the purposes of hearing such an appeal if it consists of a presiding chairman or deputy chairman and an equal number of the members of the Tribunal appointed to represent the interests of those who make request for information under the Act and the interests of public authorities.[83] Rules in relation to appeals under s.57(2) of the Freedom of Information Act 2000 by a public authority against an information or enforcement notice are the same as those in relation to appeals under s.48 of the Data Protection Act 1998, which are discussed below.[84] 28–017

Nature of appeals against national security certificates under section 60 of the Freedom of Information Act 2000

The certificate of a Minister of the Crown[85] under s.23(2) (to the effect that cer- 28–018
tain information was supplied by or relates to certain security bodies[86]) or s.24(3) (to the effect that exemption from the right of access to information is required for the purpose of safeguarding national security[87]) is conclusive

[82] The Secretary of State for Constitutional Affairs has power to make such rules under Data Protection Act 1998, Sch.6, para.7. The current intention is to institute a single set of rules for appeals under both Data Protection Act 1998, s.48 (including in its application to the Telecommunications (Data Protection and Privacy) Regulations 1999 (SI 1999/2093): see reg.36(1) and Sch.4 of the regulations) and Freedom of Information Act 2000, s.57 but rules in relation to s.57(1) are unlikely to be made until close to January 2005 when the substantive rights in Freedom of Information Act 2000 come into effect. The proposals set out in the Lord Chancellor's Department's Consultation Paper dated March 2002 (see: *www.lcd.gov.uk/foi/inftribprop.htm*) differ very little from the existing rules (SI 2000/189): see below para.28–035) save that it is proposed that the default position for appeals under the Freedom of Information Act 2000 should be for appeals to be considered on the papers only and that the Tribunal would have power to refuse an oral hearing as " . . .this will enable the Tribunal to function more efficiently . . ."! (see consultation paper paras 26 and 27 and compare the position under the Information Tribunal (Enforcement Appeals) Rules 2000 (SI 2000/189) r.13 which by implication requires a hearing unless the parties agree otherwise in cases where a public authority is appealing under s.57(2)). Note also that the Consultation Paper does not appear to address the important question of the circumstances in which the Information Tribunal should have power to inspect documents without them being shown to the complainant if the circumstances require. Note this matter is expressly dealt with by the Australian legislation at Freedom of Information Act 1982, s.63.

[83] Data Protection Act 1998, Sch.6, para.4(1A) and s.6(6).

[84] These are the Information Tribunal (Enforcement Appeals) Rules 2000 (SI 2000/189) applied to s.57(2) Freedom of Information Act 2000 appeals by the Information Tribunal (Enforcement Appeals) (Amendment) Rules 2002 (SI 2002/2722): see further para.28–035 below.

[85] Who is a member of the Cabinet or the Attorney-General or in Scotland the Advocate-General: Freedom of Information Act 2000, s.25(3).

[86] Listed in the Freedom of Information Act 2000, s.23(3).

[87] The relevant information for the purposes of such a certificate can be identified by means of a general description: *ibid.*, s.24(4).

evidence of the "fact" certified and, accordingly, if the certificate applies to the information in question, provides exemption to the public authority under the Act. Further, if in any proceedings under the Act the public authority claims that a certificate under s.24(3) which identifies information in general terms covers the information in question, it shall be conclusively presumed that the certificate does cover that information.[88] Section 60 provides an appeal against a certificate under ss.23(2) or 24(3) to the applicant for information or the Information Commissioner[89] and an appeal against the presumption that a s.24(3) certificate covers the information in question to any other party to the proceedings.[90] An appeal relating to a certificate under s.23(2) or relating to the presumption as to the applicability of a s.24(3) certificate is in the nature of a determination whether, as a matter of fact, the certificate is true or does apply to the information in question.[91] The appeal relating to a certificate under s.24(3) is quite different: the appeal can be allowed and the certificate quashed if the Tribunal, applying judicial review principles, finds that the Minister did not have reasonable grounds for issuing the certificate.[92]

---

88 Freedom of Information Act 2000, s.60(4).

89 *ibid.*, s.60(1).

90 *ibid.*, s.60(4).

91 *ibid.*, ss.60(2) and 60(5).

92 *ibid.*, s.60(3); Data Protection Act 1998, s.28(5). In determining whether the minister did or did not have reasonable grounds for issuing the certificate, the Tribunal will inevitably have to assess whether the minister did or did not have reasonable grounds for concluding that exemption from the relevant provision is, or at any time was, required for the purpose of safeguarding national security. It would appear that the Tribunal is thus confined to applying only one of the three heads of judicial review identified in *Council of Civil Service Unions v Minister for the Civil Service* [1985] A.C. 374 at 410 (*per* Lord Diplock) (*i.e.* irrationality but not illegality or procedural impropriety): if the minister took into account an irrelevant consideration or failed to take into account a relevant consideration, made an error of law or failed to act fairly in a procedural sense this will only be relevant if and in so far as it led or contributed to him not having reasonable grounds for issuing the certificate. So far as concerns "the principles applied by the court on an application for judicial review" in relation to "reasonable grounds", the Tribunal will review whether the minister's decision was reasonable or so unreasonable that no reasonable minister could have taken it (*Associated Provincial Picture Houses Ltd v Wednesbury Corpn* [1948] 1 K.B. 223) and the intensity of its scrutiny will increase if it can be shown that "fundamental rights" are engaged (*R. v Ministry of Defence, Ex p. Smith* [1996] Q.B. 517 at 554 (*per* Sir Thomas Bingham M.R.). If satisfied that a "Convention right" as defined by the Human Rights Act 1998 has also been affected by the minister's decision and the appellant may have been the "victim" of this for the purposes of that Act, the Tribunal will also need to go further and determine whether the decision to issue a certificate was compatible with that Convention right and would thus have to apply a more intensive proportionality-based standard of review: *R. (Daly) v Secretary of State for the Home Department* [2001] UKHL 26; [2001] 2 A.C. 532 at [26]–[27] (*per* Lord Steyn); *Baker v Secretary of State for the Home Department* [2001] U.K.H.R.R. 1275 para.63. On the question whether Convention rights will be engaged: see paras 14 to 14 . The language used in the Freedom of Information Act 2000, s.60(3) and Data Protection Act 1998, s.28(5) might also be thought to suggest that the Tribunal must focus solely on the grounds which the minister had in his mind at the time he issued the certificate (to the exclusion of other grounds which he might now wish to rely upon). However, this will not affect the eventual outcome because there is nothing to prevent a minister from issuing a fresh certificate on new grounds to replace one that has been quashed.

Practice and procedure

The Tribunal hearing an appeal under s.60 of the Act is duly constituted if it consists of three of the persons designated by the Lord Chancellor as capable of hearing such appeals.[93] At the time of writing, no rules expressly relating to such appeals have been made[94] but appeals under the section[95] are closely analogous to national security appeals under s.28 of the Data Protection Act 1998, for which rules have been made[96] and similar rules are likely to apply.[97] The significant features of those rules are set out below.[98] There is no provision for an appeal from a decision of the Tribunal itself under s.60 of the Freedom of Information Act 2000; there may be circumstances where it would be appropriate for there to be a judicial review of such a decision.[99] 28–019

4. FOURTH STAGE: APPEAL TO THE HIGH COURT

Appeal to High Court

Any party[1] to an appeal under s.57 of the Freedom of Information Act 2000 against a decision notice, an enforcement notice or an information notice, may appeal from the decision of the Information Tribunal on a "point of law" to the High Court if the address of the public authority is in England or Wales, to the Court of Session if it is in Scotland and to the High Court in Northern Ireland if it is in Northern Ireland.[2] An appeal on a "point of law" would be on the grounds (a) that the Tribunal misdirected itself in law or misunderstood or misapplied the law; (b) that there was no evidence to support a particular conclusion or finding of fact made by the Tribunal; or (c) that the decision was perverse in that it was one which the Tribunal, directing itself properly on the law, could not have reached or one which was obviously wrong.[3] 28–020

---

93 Data Protection Act 1998, Sch.6, paras 2 and 3(b).

94 The Secretary of State for Constitutional Affairs has power to make them under Data Protection Act 1998, Sch.6, para.7.

95 At least those referred to in Freedom of Information Act 2000, s.60(3) and (4).

96 The Information Tribunal (National Security Appeals) Rules 2000 (SI 2000/206): see r.2(1).

97 The Lord Chancellor's Department has indicated an intention to consult on proposals for a new set of rules governing national security appeals under both Acts and under the Telecommunications (Data Protection and Privacy) Regulations 1999 (SI 1999/2093): see para.6 of March 2002 Consultation Paper on Procedural Rules for Appeals and Hearings before the Information Tribunal at *www.dca.gov.uk/foi/inftribprop.htm*.

98 See para.28–036 which deals with national security appeals under the Data Protection Act 1998.

99 See paras 28–023 to 28–027.

1 Namely, the complainant, the public authority or the responsible authority as relevant.

2 Freedom of Information Act 2000, s.59.

3 See, in relation to the analogous provisions in relation to appeals from employment tribunals to the Employment Appeal Tribunal: *British Telecommunications plc v Sheridan* [1990] I.R.L.R. 27 at 30; *Melon v Hector Powe Ltd* [1981] I.C.R. 43; [1980] I.R.L.R. 477; *Neale* v *Hereford and Worcester County Council* [1986] I.C.R. 471; [1986] I.R.L.R. 168; *Watling v William Bird & Son (Contractors) Ltd* 1976 I.T.R. 70.

Practice and procedure

28–021 The procedure on an appeal to the High Court under s.59 of the Freedom of Information Act 2000 will be in accordance with Pt 52 of the Civil Procedure Rules 1998[4] and the Pt 52 Practice Direction, and in particular s.II thereof. Permission is not required for the appeal, the appellant's notice must be filed within 28 days after the decision of the Information Tribunal and it must be served on the chairman of the Tribunal as well as the respondent to the appeal.[5] A further appeal to the Court of Appeal from the decision of the High Court on an appeal under s.59 would require the permission of the Court of Appeal which will only be granted if the appeal would raise an important point of principle or practice or that there is some other compelling reason for it to be heard.[6]

Appeals under section 56 of the Freedom of Information (Scotland) Act 2002

28–022 Section 56 of the Freedom of Information (Scotland) Act 2002 gives a direct right of appeal on a point of law to the Court of Session against decisions of the Scottish Commissioner under ss.49, 50 and 51 of the Scottish Act in relation to decision notices, enforcement notices and information notices.[7] Such an appeal may be expected to be analogous to that to the High Court under s.59 of the Freedom of Information Act 2000.[8]

5. JUDICIAL REVIEW

Limits to judicial review

28–023 The Freedom of Information Act 2000 provides for numerous decisions and actions to be taken by "public authorities," and by the Information Commissioner, the Information Tribunal, the Secretary of State for Constitutional Affairs, and Ministers and others who are given power to sign certificates (in particular, the Speaker of the House of Commons and the Clerk of the Parliaments).[9] There is no provision in the Act expressly excluding the supervisory jurisdiction of the Administrative Court to grant judicial review under

4 See: r.52.1(1).
5 Practice Direction supplementing CPR Pt 52, paras 17.3–17.5.
6 CPR r.52.13.
7 See para.28–014.
8 See para.28–020.
9 See, for example: Freedom of Information Act 2000, ss.23(2), 24(3), 34(3), 36(7) and 53(2).

Pt 54 of the Civil Procedure Rules 1998 in relation to such decisions and actions,[10] so that in principle they would be susceptible to judicial review. In most cases, however, the Act itself provides an appeal or other means of challenge[11] and the court would be unlikely to give permission for, or grant, judicial review in such cases unless there were exceptional circumstances.[12] There are, however, a few cases where judicial review by an applicant may be appropriate because of a gap in the appeal rights provided by the Act.

Public authorities

It is thought unlikely that any judicial review would lie against the handling by a public authority of a request for information given the wide powers of the Information Commissioner under s.50 of the Act. 28–024

Information Commissioner

As for the Commissioner, the exercise of more general powers such as issuing codes of practice might in principle be open to judicial review, but his decision notices, enforcement notices and information notices, which are subject to the extensive rights of appeal given by s.57, are unlikely to be open to such review. There is one decision of the Commissioner, namely a decision not to pursue a complaint under s.50(2), however, which appears not to be subject to any right of appeal under the Act and which would therefore be susceptible to judicial review. A failure by the Commissioner to take a decision within a reasonable time might also be the subject of a judicial review even though, in contrast to the position in Scotland,[13] there is no express time limit on the taking of a decision. 28–025

[10] Section 56(1) states that the Act "does not confer any right of action in civil proceedings in respect of any failure to comply with any duty imposed by or under [it]" but is unlikely to be construed as excluding judicial review: compare similar (but stronger) exclusionary wording considered in *Ex p. Waldron* [1986] Q.B. 824; [1985] 3 All E.R. 775, CA.

[11] *e.g.* the right to complain to the Information Commissioner under s.50(1) that a public authority has not complied with Pt I of the Act, the right to appeal against a decision of the Information Commissioner under s.57(1), the right to appeal against national security certificates under s.60, the right to appeal against the decisions of the Information Tribunal under s.59.

[12] See: *Halsbury's Laws of England*, (4th ed., Butterworths 2001 re-issue), Vol.1(1), para.67.

[13] See Freedom of Information (Scotland) Act 2002, s.49(3)(b).

Information Tribunal

28–026 As for decisions of the Information Tribunal, those under s.57 are subject to an appeal to the High Court under s.59, but those relating to national security certificates are not the subject of any appeal procedure under the Act. It is therefore likely that the Tribunal would be susceptible in principle to judicial review in respect of its decisions on appeals relating to national security certificates. In practice, foreign experience suggests it will be difficult to challenge successfully any such certificate.[14]

Certificates

28–027 National security certificates are open to challenge under s.60 so there is unlikely to be any basis for a judicial review of the act of the relevant Minister in signing the certificate.[15] However, certificates signed under ss.34(3), 36(7) and 53(2) are not open to such challenge. Certificates signed by a Cabinet minister or the Attorney-General will be open to judicial review.[16] Those signed by the Speaker of the House of Commons or the Clerk of the Parliaments under ss.34(3) and 36(7) are probably not amenable to judicial review, on the basis of parliamentary privilege.[17] However the scope of Parliamentary privilege is ultimately for the courts and not Parliament itself to define. Parliament cannot create new forms of privilege. Therefore a certificate may only be conclusive as to whether disclosure would infringe an established privilege. It would still appear to be open to an individual or the Information Commissioner to challenge non-disclosure on the basis that disclosure would not infringe any

---

14 See paras 2–008(1), 2–015(9) and 2–032(11).

15 There is a suggestion in para.48 of the decision of the Information Tribunal in *Norman Baker MP* [2001] U.K.H.R.R. 1275 (see n.63, p.750) that there may be a distinction between the Minister not having reasonable grounds for issuing a national security certificate and it being unlawful for him to have done so; in the latter case there is no express provision for an appeal to the Information Tribunal in s.60(3) so that, the Tribunal thought, in such a case it would be necessary (and presumably possible) to apply to the Administrative Court for judicial review. It is thought unlikely that this would arise in practice.

16 As the Minister, Lord Falconer of Thoroton, assured Parliament at the second reading of the Bill in dealing with what became s.53. He also stated that the Commissioner would have locus to apply for such a judicial review. (see: *Hansard*, HL, Vol.612, April 20, 2000, col.828). See also the Australian case *Shergold v Tanner* [2002] H.C.A. 19; (2002) 188 A.L.R. 302, HCA.

17 See on parliamentary privilege *Halsbury's Laws of England* (4th ed., Butterworths 1997 re-issue), Vol.34, para.1008 and *R. v Parliamentary Commissioner for Standards Ex p. Al Fayed* [1998] 1 W.L.R. 669; [1998] 1 All E.R. 93, CA. There may be a legitimate distinction to be drawn between s.34(3) certificates and s.36(7) certificates: s.34(3) certificates are to the effect that the relevant parliamentary officer certifies that exemption is necessary to avoid an infringement of parliamentary privilege (more likely to be privileged) whereas s.36(7) certificates relate to the opinion of such officer that disclosure of information by Parliament would prejudice the effective conduct of public affairs (an opinion which may be open to review without considering whether parliamentary privilege is properly claimed).

established form of privilege, and that the Speaker of the House of Commons or the Clerk of the Parliaments has misconstrued the ambit of Parliamentary privilege.[18]

6. THIRD PARTIES: INSTITUTION OF APPEALS AND PARTICIPATION IN APPEALS

Introduction

As noted earlier,[19] a person or body other than the public authority to which a request for information is made may have a legitimate interest in seeing that some or all of the information answering the terms of a request is not communicated, either to that applicant or to anyone else.[20] That third party may be similarly concerned to see that any appeal against a refusal to communicate is adequately resisted and that the third party's interests in having the information not disclosed are properly articulated before the appellate body. As well as participating in any appeal, a third party may himself wish to initiate proceedings or an appeal where a decision has been or is proposed to be made by the public authority or by the appellate body to disclose information. 28–028

Participation in appeals

Although a public authority, when making its original decision in relation to disclosure, may have informed the third party of the request and invited the third party's views on disclosure, there is nothing in either the Act or the Code requiring the public authority to inform the third party either of the outcome of the request or of whether an appeal has been instituted.[21] Similarly, there is nothing obliging the Information Commissioner, when an application has been made to him, to inform a third party of that application, to invite representations from the third party or to advise the third party of the outcome of it. Where information is rendered exempt information by more than one provision in Pt II of the Freedom of Information Act 2000, a public authority is not required under the Code to consult with any third party even if the information 28–029

---

[18] However for a more restrictive interpretation of the court's powers in determining the ambit of Parliamentary privilege see Eagles, Taggart and Liddell, *Freedom of Information in New Zealand*, (OUP, Auckland 1992), pp.469–470. Also see Lock [1985] *Public Law* 64.

[19] See paras 11–044 to 11–047.

[20] Disclosure under the Act is disclosure to the world: the public authority cannot itself restrict what the applicant does with the information once disclosed to him.

[21] The Code appears to exclude a third party from the ambit of a complaints procedure or to be advised that it has been engaged or its outcome: see Code paras 52–63.

relates to that third party.[22] If, on any form of reconsideration,[23] the reconsidering body does not find made out any of the grounds of exemption other than that relating to the third party, the spirit of the Code might seem to require consultation with that third party before a final determination of the applicability of that ground is made.[24]

Institution of appeals and other proceedings

28–030 A third party is given no entitlement to seek internal reconsideration under the Code,[25] no entitlement to apply to the Commissioner for a decision whether a request has been dealt with in accordance with Pt I of the Act,[26] and no entitlement to appeal to the Information Tribunal.[27] On ordinary principles, a third party who has a recognised interest in seeing that information is not disclosed may apply for judicial review of a decision of a public authority, of the Information Commissioner or of the Information Tribunal that will result in the disclosure of that information.[28] Also, in certain circumstances a third party will be able to institute proceedings to restrain disclosure.[29]

B. Appeals under the Data Protection Act 1998

7. ORDINARY APPEALS

Subject access rights

28–031 The means by which the subject access rights under s.7 of the Data Protection Act 1998 are pursued are quite different from those by which the equivalent rights under the Freedom of Information Act 2000 are pursued. First, in contrast to the position under the Freedom of Information Act 2000, there is no specific requirement for codes of practice issued or approved by the

[22] Code, para.37.

[23] In other words, internal reconsideration under the Code, an application to the Information Commissioner under s.50 or an appeal to the Information Tribunal under s.57.

[24] As to the role that, in the comparative jurisdictions, it has been held third parties in appeals can play, see: paras 2–013 and 2–014 (Australia); paras 2–031 and 2–033 (Canada); para.2–038 (Ireland).

[25] In Scotland, only an applicant is entitled to seek internal review: Freedom of Information (Scotland) Act 2002, s.20(1).

[26] Similarly, in Scotland: Freedom of Information (Scotland) Act 2002, s.47(1).

[27] In Scotland, to the Court of Session: Freedom of Information (Scotland) Act 2002, s.56.

[28] This is the route adopted in the USA: see para.2–009.

[29] See para.25–014.

Commissioner under s.51(3) of the Data Protection Act 1998 to require authorities to institute internal complaints procedures and at the time of writing the Information Commissioner had not issued a code laying down such a requirement in relation to s.7 requests.[30]

Application to court under section 7(9) of the Data Protection Act 1998

The main remedy for an individual dissatisfied with the response to a request under s.7(1) of the Data Protection Act 1998 in relation to data of which he is the "data subject" is by way of an application to a court under s.7(9), rather than an application to the Information Commissioner. If the court on such an application is satisfied that the data controller in question has failed to comply with the request in contravention of any provision of s.7 it can order him to comply with the request.[31] 28–032

Practice and procedure on an application under section 7(9)

Both the High Court and a county court (or in Scotland the Court of Session or the sheriff) have jurisdiction to hear such an application.[32] The question for the court on such an appeal is whether the data controller has failed to comply with the request in contravention of the provisions of s.7 of the Data Protection Act 1998.[33] In other words, the right of appeal involves the court considering afresh the applicability of any exemption, unfettered by the decision of the data controller: it is not a review of the reasonableness of the data controller's decision or of the methodology applied by the data controller in reaching the appealed decision. In determining whether an applicant is entitled to the information which he seeks (including any question whether it is exempt from s.7 by virtue of Pt IV of the Act) the court has power to require the information in question[34] to be made available for its own inspection but must not, pending a decision in the applicant's favour, require it to be disclosed to him whether by way of discovery or otherwise.[35] Subject to the rights of appeal to the Information 28–033

---

[30] The Lord Chancellor issued non-statutory guidance dated April 2002 to government departments which makes no such requirement: see *www.dca.gov.uk/foi/dpasaguide.htm*.

[31] Data Protection Act 1998, s.7(9).

[32] *ibid.*, s.15(1).

[33] *ibid.*, s.7(9). As the applicant's entitlement under s.7(1) is "subject to the following provisions of [ss.7,] 8, 9 and 9A" of the Act, the court will have jurisdiction to consider whether the procedural requirements set out in those sections have been met in order to determine whether the failure to comply with the applicant's request is, in fact, in contravention of the applicant's entitlement.

[34] And information as to the logic involved in any decision-taking as mentioned in s.7(1)(d).

[35] Data Protection Act 1998, s.15(2).

Tribunal mentioned below,[36] if a national security certificate has been issued under s.28(1) of the Act in relation to any data which is relied on by the data controller in the proceedings, this will constitute conclusive evidence that the exemption of that data from the provisions of s.7 of the Act is required for the purpose of safeguarding national security.[37] If the data controller claims in the course of the proceedings that a national security certificate in general terms applies to the personal data in question, the certificate will be conclusively presumed so to apply.[38] Presumably, if an applicant faced with such a certificate indicated that he wished to appeal to the Information Tribunal on either of those points, the court would grant an adjournment of the proceedings pending a decision of the Information Tribunal. There are no specific rules of procedure relating to an application to the court under the Data Protection Act 1998 and the Civil Procedure Rules 1998 will therefore apply[39]; it is likely that most claims will be brought under Pt 8 of the Civil Procedure Rules 1998. An appeal from the decision of the court dealing with the application may with leave be made to either the High Court or the Court of Appeal under Pt 52 of the Civil Procedure Rules 1998.[40]

The roles of the Information Commissioner and Information Tribunal

28–034 In relation to the access rights as against public authorities granted by s.7 of the Data Protection Act 1998, the roles of the Information Commissioner and the Information Tribunal are likely to be limited. Contravention of s.7 by a public authority by failing to supply information in accordance with that section would constitute a breach of the "sixth data protection principle."[41] Such contravention could be the subject of an "enforcement notice" by the Information Commissioner pursuant to s.40 of the Act requiring the public authority to take steps to comply with its obligations, and could also in principle be the subject of a request for an assessment by the Information Commissioner under s.42 of the Act[42] and of an "information notice" served by the Information Commissioner

[36] See para.28–036 for rights of appeal which are provided by Data Protection Act 1998, ss.28(4) and (6).

[37] Data Protection Act 1998, s.28(2).

[38] *ibid.*, s.28(6).

[39] CPR r.2.1.

[40] CPR r.52.3; an appeal from the High Court is to the Court of Appeal; an appeal from the county court is normally to the High Court but is likely to be assigned to the Court of Appeal either on the basis that it is not a Pt 8 claim and it has been allocated to the multi-track under rr.26.5 and 26.7(2) or if the court exercises its power under r.52.14 (see: Pt 52 Practice Direction, paras 2A.1, 2A.2 and 2A.6) .

[41] Data Protection Act 1998, s.4(4), Sch.1, Pt I, para.6; Sch.1, Pt II, para.8(a).

[42] Such a request must be complied with by the Information Commissioner unless he has not been supplied with sufficient information to identify the person requesting the assessment and the "processing" in question: Data Protection Act 1998, s.42(2).

on the public authority under s.43[43] of the Act in connection with such an assessment or for determining whether the data protection principles had been complied with.[44] An information notice under s.43 is very similar to one under s.51 Freedom of Information Act 2000 save that s.43 includes an express provision, not found in s.51, that a person does not have to comply with an information notice if to do so would expose him to proceedings for an offence save for an offence under the Data Protection Act 1998 itself.[45]

Appeal against enforcement or information notice

An appeal lies under s.48 of the Data Protection Act 1998 to the Information Tribunal by the data controller against any such enforcement or information notice issued by the Information Commissioner. The Tribunal must allow such an appeal if it considers that the notice was not in accordance with the law or if any discretion of the Information Commissioner ought to have been exercised differently and it may review any determination of fact on which the notice was based.[46] These appeals are currently governed by the Data Protection Tribunal (Enforcement Appeals) Rules 2000.[47] The rules provide *inter alia* that in general the notice of appeal must be served within 28 days of the service of the notice to which it relates[48]; the Commissioner is in effect the respondent to the appeal[49]; it is a condition of any disclosure order that material is used only for the purposes of the appeal[50]; the Tribunal has powers of entry and inspection[51]; the hearing is normally by the chairman alone[52]; the hearing is in public unless the Tribunal orders otherwise where that is desirable for protecting the privacy of data subjects or commercially sensitive information[53]; it is for the Commissioner to satisfy the Tribunal that the disputed decision should be upheld[54]; the Tribunal must arrange for its decision to be published save to the extent that 28–035

[43] Or, in theory, a "special information notice" under s.44, though it is probably unlikely that a public authority will claim that "personal data" was being processed by it for journalistic, artistic or literary purposes.

[44] But note in this context Data Protection Act 1998, s.42(3)(c), which would suggest that the Commissioner would generally expect a data subject to seek to exercise his rights to apply to court under s.7(9) before proceeding with any assessment or serving an enforcement notice; presumably the failure of the Commissioner to carry out an assessment or serve an enforcement notice could in principle be the subject of an application for judicial review, but since a direct application under s.7(9) could be made against the real wrong-doer this is unlikely to be granted in practice.

[45] Data Protection Act 1998, s.43(8).

[46] *ibid.*, s.49(1), (2).

[47] SI 2000/189.

[48] Data Protection (Enforcement Appeals) Rules 2000, r.4(1).

[49] *ibid.*, r.6.

[50] *ibid.*, r.11(5).

[51] *ibid.*, r.12.

[52] *ibid.*, r.18.

[53] *ibid.*, r.19.

[54] *ibid.*, r.22.

publication is undesirable in the interests of safeguarding the privacy of data subjects or commercially sensitive information.[55] There appears to be a hiatus in the rules in that there is no provision dealing with the case where the data controller is a public authority which is unwilling to comply with a request for information under s.7 Data Protection Act 1998 on the grounds that to comply would prejudice, for example, the prevention of crime or the enforcement of regulatory functions and the Information Commissioner issues an enforcement notice in relation to the public authority's failure to comply; in a case like this, it may well be undesirable to have a public hearing or a published decision since the very information in question may be revealed even if the public authority was right. As far as the writer is aware, this problem has not arisen in practice and it may be that the Information Commissioner will decline to get involved where the data subject is able to pursue his rights through the courts.[56] There is a statutory right of appeal on a point of law to the High Court or Court of Session against the decision of the Tribunal on an appeal under s.48.[57]

8. NATIONAL SECURITY CERTIFICATE APPEALS

National security certificate appeals

28–036 Where a national security certificate has been issued certifying in respect of some or all of the data sought that exemption from the subject access rights[58] is, or at any time was, required for the purpose of safeguarding national security, then the certificate will be conclusive evidence of that "fact."[59] Although an applicant is not disentitled from appealing to a court where a conclusive certificate has been issued, the certificate will render the proceedings a foregone conclusion provided that it relates to the information sought.[60] Instead, two discrete rights of appeal to the Information Tribunal are given:

55 Data Protection Tribunal (Enforcement Appeals) Rules 2000, r.24.

56 See Data Protection Act 1998, ss.7(9) and 15(2) which appears to cover the point. Compare the provisions of the Canadian Access to Information Act, s.47.

57 Data Protection Act 1998, s.49(6): see paras 28–020 to 28–022 in relation to the Freedom of Information Act, s.59, which provides for an analogous appeal to the High Court under that Act.

58 Whether specifically or as part of any of the provisions mentioned in s.28(1) of the Data Protection Act *1998*.

59 Data Protection Act 1998, s.28(2). A certificate may identify the personal data to which it applies by means of a general description; and it may be expressed to have prospective effect: Data Protection Act 1998, s.28(3). Conclusive certificates are considered further in para.14–030.

60 If there is an issue whether or not the certificate applies to some or all the information sought, the correct procedure is: (1) for the dissatisfied applicant to make an application to the relevant court under the Data Protection Act 1998, s.7(9); (2) for the data controller to claim in those proceedings that a certificate under the Data Protection Act 1998, s.28(2) identifies the information sought by means of a general description; and (3) for any other party to the proceedings to appeal to the Information Tribunal on the ground that the certificate does not apply to the personal data in question: Data Protection Act 1998, s.28(6).

(1) A person directly affected by the issuing of a conclusive certificate may appeal against the decision to issue the conclusive certificate. The task for the Information Tribunal is to consider whether, applying the principles applied by a court on an application for judicial review, the Minister did not have reasonable grounds for issuing the certificate: the Tribunal does not consider afresh whether exemption is in fact required for the purpose of safeguarding national security.[61] Unless the Information Tribunal finds that the Minister did not have reasonable grounds for issuing the certificate, the Tribunal must dismiss the appeal; if it finds that the Minister did not have reasonable grounds for issuing the certificate, it may allow the appeal and quash the certificate.[62]

(2) Where a dissatisfied applicant has made a "merit review" application to the relevant court against a failure to comply with a subject access request [63] and the data controller has claimed in those proceedings that a national security certificate that identifies information by means of a general description[64] applies to the information sought, then any other party to those proceedings may appeal to the Information Tribunal on the ground that the certificate does not apply to the personal data in question.[65] The task for the Information Tribunal is to consider whether the generally-worded certificate is apt to apply to all the information sought.

Practice and procedure

Save in cases of summary dismissal, where the jurisdiction of the Tribunal may be exercised by one designated member ex parte, national security appeals are heard by three from among the chairman and deputy chairmen of the Tribunal 28–037

[61] Data Protection Act 1998, s.28(4)–(5). The Information Tribunal is a "court" and appeals before it are "civil proceedings" for the purposes of the Supreme Court Act 1981, s.42 (restriction of vexatious legal proceedings in any civil proceedings, whether in the High Court or any inferior court): *Re Ewing* [2002] All E.R. (D) 350 (Dec).

[62] Data Protection Act 1998, s.28(5). In *Norman Baker MP v Secretary of State for the Home Department* [2001] U.K.H.R.R. 1275 the Data Protection Tribunal (as the Information Tribunal was then known) held that a national security exemption certificate applying effectively a blanket exemption to files held by MI5 was unreasonably wide. The difficulty with the exemption was that the security service did not have to consider in any individual case whether responding to the request (even with a "neither confirm nor deny" response) would harm national security. A revised form of the certificate was considered by the High Court in *Re Ewing* [2002] All E.R. (D) 350 (Dec), where it was held that the criticisms of the Information Tribunal had been addressed.: ". . . a general [neither confirm nor deny] policy, in response to requests for personal data, including as to the existence (or non-existence) of personal data, is in principle justifiable and cannot be criticised as unreasonable or unnecessary" (at [60]).

[63] *i.e.* under the Data Protection Act 1998, s.7(9).

[64] Relying on Data Protection Act 1998, s.28(3).

[65] Data Protection Act 1998, s.28(6).

designated by the Lord Chancellor as capable of hearing such appeals.[66] The appeals are governed by the Information Tribunal (National Security Appeals) Rules 2000. The significant features of these rules are:

— the Tribunal has a general duty in exercising its functions to secure that information is not disclosed contrary to the interests of national security[67];
— the time limit for an appeal against a certificate is any time during the currency of the disputed certificate and, in respect of an appeal under s.28(6), within 28 days of the claim being made that the certificate covers the information in question[68];
— there is provision for the relevant Minister to be notified of an appeal under s.28(6) and for him to make representations and to put in evidence, even though he will not be a party to the underlying proceedings[69];
— the Minister can object (unless overruled by the Tribunal) to the disclosure of his or the data controller's reply, to any proposed direction of the Tribunal, to the issue of a witness summons or to the publication of the Tribunal's decision if he considers that information will be disclosed thereby contrary to the interests of national security[70];
— all hearings are in private unless the Tribunal, with the consent of the parties and the Minister, directs otherwise and the Tribunal can exclude any party other than the Minister from the proceedings in order to secure that information is not disclosed contrary to the interests of national security[71];
— the Tribunal's decision should only include findings of fact and reasons if and to the extent possible without disclosing information contrary to the interests of national security[72];
— there are special costs rules such that, in an appeal under s.28(4), costs will only be awarded to the Minister if the appeal was "manifestly unreasonable"[73] but will be awarded against the Minister where it "allows the appeal and quashes the disputed certification, or does so to any extent."[74]

66 See: Data Protection Act 1998, Sch.6, paras 2, 3 and 6(1) and Information Tribunal (National Security) Rules 2000 (SI 2000/206), r.3(2) and 11.
67 Information Tribunal (National Security Appeals) Rules 2000 (SI 2000/206), r.3(1).
68 r.5(1)–(2). There is provision for extending time in r.5(3).
69 rr.6 and 7(2)(b).
70 See rr.12, 16 and 17.
71 r.23(1) and (3).
72 r.27(2).
73 r.28(1)(a)(I).
74 r.28(1)(a)(ii). This provision was the subject of the decision of the Tribunal in the reported decision in the case of *Mohammed al Fayed v The Secretary of State for the Home Department and the Secretary of State for Foreign and Commonwealth Affairs* (February 28, 2002, Sir Anthony Evans, James Goudie Q.C. and Kenneth Parker Q.C.: for decision see link on the Department of Constitutional Affairs website): the Tribunal found that it still had power to allow the appeal of

There is no express provision for an appeal from a determination of the Information Tribunal on an appeal relating to a national security certificate, so that judicial review of the Tribunal's decision should, in principle, be possible.

9. JUDICIAL REVIEW

Judicial review

The position in relation to judicial review of acts and decisions under the Data Protection Act 1998 is similar to that under the Freedom of Information Act 2000.[75] Again, there is no provision expressly excluding judicial review but, so far as an applicant is concerned, it will ordinarily be excluded by the principle that the court will not generally grant judicial review where there is some other remedy available. This exclusion does not apply to decisions of the Information Tribunal on national security appeals under s.28 of the Data Protection Act 1998 or to a failure to act on the part of the Information Commissioner on a request for an assessment under s.42(2) of the Act, both of which are likely to be amenable to judicial review by a dissatisfied applicant.[76] 28–038

10. THIRD PARTIES: INSTITUTION OF AND PARTICIPATION IN APPEALS

Introduction

The issues which arise under the Data Protection Act 1998 in respect of third party participation in appeals are very similar to those which arise under the Freedom of Information Act 2000.[77] However, the manner in which these issues have been addressed under the Data Protection Act 1998 is slightly different. 28–039

Mr Al-Fayed under the Data Protection Act 1998, s.28(4) so as to give it jurisdiction to award costs notwithstanding that the certificates in question had already been quashed in other proceedings (brought by Norman Baker MP against the Home Secretary [2001] U.K.H.R.R. 1275) or revoked (in the case of the Foreign Secretary).

[75] See paras 28–023 to 28–027.

[76] See para.28–026.

[77] See paras 28–028 to 28–030.

Participation in and institution of appeals

28–040 A third party is not entitled to initiate an appeal under s.7 of the Act.[78] However, the Data Protection Act 1998 provides a free-standing right by any person who is, or believes himself to be, directly affected by any processing of personal data for an assessment by the Information Commissioner as to whether it is likely or unlikely that the processing has been or is being carried out in compliance with the provisions of the Act.[79] As "processing" is defined to include the disclosure of information, this would appear to permit a third party who is, or would stand to be, directly affected by the disclosure of information to make application to the Information Commissioner for an assessment. The Commissioner is only required to provide the person making the request with details of any view formed or action taken to the extent that the Information Commissioner considers appropriate.[80] Upon such an application being made, the Information Commissioner can issue an information notice,[81] a special information notice[82] or an enforcement notice.[83] The statutory right of appeal to the Information Tribunal only extends to a public authority against whom one or more of the above three notices has been served.[84] Outside these statutory rights of appeal, the position of a dissatisfied third party is akin to that of a like person under the Freedom of Information Act 2000.[85]

---

78 An appeal can only be made by the person who has made the request under s.7: Data Protection Act 1998, s.7(9).
79 *ibid.*, s.42(1).
80 *ibid.*, s.42(2).
81 *ibid.*, s.43.
82 *ibid.*, s.44.
83 *ibid.*, s.40.
84 *ibid.*, s.48. These appeals are considered above at para.28–035.
85 See paras 28–028 to 28–030.

CHAPTER 29

Enforcement

1. FREEDOM OF INFORMATION ACTS

Immunities from private suit

Both the Freedom of Information Act 2000 and the Freedom of Information (Scotland) Act 2002 provide that they do not confer any right of action in civil proceedings in respect of a failure to comply with a duty imposed by or under the Act.[1] There is also specific provision giving protection against proceedings for defamation brought in respect of information supplied to a public authority by a third party which is published to applicants under the Acts unless the publication is made with malice.[2] 29–001

[1] Freedom of Information Act 2000, s.56(1), Freedom of Information (Scotland) Act 2002, s.55(1). Note that these provisions are unlikely to exclude judicial review proceedings: *Re Waldron (No.1)* [1986] Q.B. 824, [1985] 3 All E.R. 775, CA.

[2] See Freedom of Information Act 2000, s.79 and Freedom of Information (Scotland) Act 2002, s.67.

Enforcement by Information Commissioners

29–002 Enforcement of the duties of public authorities under the Acts is primarily in the hands of the two Information Commissioners. If a public authority fails to comply with a decision notice,[3] an enforcement notice,[4] or an information notice[5] issued by the Information Commissioner (and not successfully appealed against[6]), the Information Commissioner may certify that that is the case to the High Court or the Court of Session.[7] The court may then inquire into the matter and, after hearing evidence and any statement which may be offered in defence, it may deal with the public authority "as if it had committed a contempt of court."[8]

Means of dealing with a contempt of court

29–003 If it was ever required in practice,[9] there may be difficulties in applying this provision. The normal ways of dealing with a person who has committed a contempt of court are by way of an order of committal to prison, a sequestration order, a fine, an injunction, an order that the contemnor pay the costs of the hearing (often on an indemnity basis) and (possibly) a declaration.[10] It seems unlikely that committal, sequestration or a fine would ever be appropriate in relation to a public authority (even assuming the public authority in question was an individual and therefore amenable to an order of committal) and, at least in relation to government departments, the House of Lords has expressed the view that a *finding* of contempt should suffice in any case.[11] Because the provision refers to dealing with the authority it does not seem that the court could make an order of committal or sequestration against individual officers who were personally responsible (even in a contumacious way) for the failure of the

3 See Freedom of Information Act 2000, s.50 and Freedom of Information (Scotland) Act 2002, s.49, discussed in paras 28–009 and 28–013.

4 See Freedom of Information Act 2000, s.52 and Freedom of Information (Scotland) Act 2002, s.52 discussed in paras 28–011 and 28–014.

5 See Freedom of Information Act 2000, s.51 and Freedom of Information (Scotland) Act 2002, s.50 discussed in paras 28–010 and 28–014. Note that failure to comply with an information notice includes making a false statement in purported compliance with the information notice: Freedom of Information Act 2000, s.54(2) and Freedom of Information (Scotland) Act 2002, s.53(2).

6 See Freedom of Information Act 2000, s.57 and Freedom of Information (Scotland) Act 2002, s.56.

7 Freedom of Information Act 2000, s.54(1) and Freedom of Information (Scotland) Act 2002, s.53(1).

8 Freedom of Information Act 2000, s.54(3) and Freedom of Information (Scotland) Act 2002, s.53(3).

9 The Home Office's Freedom of Information Unit expressed the view that the provision was only there "to give the Commissioner's notices the appropriate status:" see Public Administration Committee, *Third Report*, 1998–99 Session, Annex 6, para.90.

10 *Halsbury's Laws of England* (4th ed., Butterworths 1998 re-issue) Vol.9(1), paras 506–509.

11 See *M v Home Office* [1994] 1 A.C. 377; [1993] 3 All E.R. 537, *per* Lord Woolf.

authority to comply with a notice by the Commissioner, as the court can normally do in the case of a breach of one of its own orders,[12] although it would presumably be open to the court to grant an injunction which could itself thereafter be enforced if still not complied with in this way.

Procedure

The power of the High Court to punish for contempt under the Freedom of Information Act 2000 can be exercised by a single judge of the Queen's Bench Division.[13] There is no procedure expressly laid down but it is thought that the matter would be brought before the court by the Attorney-General issuing a claim form[14] and that it would be dealt with in accordance with RSC Ord.52 and the Practice Direction thereto. There is an automatic right of appeal to the Court of Appeal against the making of a committal order by a High Court judge if that were the outcome.[15] 29–004

Search and seizure

As well as the power to serve information notices against public authorities in order to collect evidence in relation to compliance with the Freedom of Information Acts, both Commissioners have power to seek a warrant from a circuit judge or a sheriff authorising them or their officers to enter and search premises, inspect and seize documents or other material which might be evidence of non-compliance with the Act, and to inspect, examine, operate and test equipment found there in which information may be recorded if there are reasonable grounds for suspecting such non-compliance and that evidence thereof is to be found on any premises.[16] Save in cases of urgency or where this would defeat the object of the exercise, the occupier of the premises must have been given seven days notice that access was required and have refused it and been warned of the application for a warrant and been heard on the matter.[17] This reflects a clear policy that agreement should be reached if possible which no doubt 29–005

---

12 See RSC Ord.45 r5(1)(b)(ii) and (iii).

13 See RSC Ord.52 r1(4).

14 See, *e.g. Attorney-General v Clough* [1963] 1 Q.B. 773 (showing practice under Tribunals of Enquiry (Evidence) Act 1921) and RSC Ord.52 r.4.

15 CPR 52.3(1)(a)(i).

16 Freedom of Information Act 2000, s.55 and Sch.3, para.1; Freedom of Information (Scotland) Act 2002, s.54 and Sch.3, para.1. These powers are comparable to those given to the Inland Revenue Commissioners in relation to serious fraud by the Taxes Management Act 1970, s.20C and to constables by the Companies Act 1985, s.448, with the interesting result that, under the Freedom of Information Acts, it would be public authorities which are on the receiving end of the search and seizure order.

17 Freedom of Information Act 2000, Sch.3, para.2; Freedom of Information (Scotland) Act 2002, Sch.3, para.2.

also reflects the fact that public authorities are not generally expected to disguise evidence.

Procedure on warrant

29–006 The warrant must be executed within seven days[18] and the person executing it can use reasonable force and must execute it at a reasonable time unless this would mean the evidence would not be found.[19] The powers of inspection and seizure are not exercisable in respect of information which is exempt on national security grounds or communications subject to legal professional privilege in relation to advice or proceedings about obligations, rights or liabilities arising under the Freedom of Information Acts themselves.[20]

Criminal offences

29–007 There are various criminal offences underpinning this system of enforcement. The Freedom of Information Acts both make it an offence to interfere with any records held by a public authority with the intention of preventing disclosure by the authority of information to which the applicant would have been entitled after a request has been made for information.[21] The offence can be committed by a public authority or any of its officers or employees or anyone subject to its direction[22] but a government department[23] (or, in Scotland, the Parliament or the Parliamentary corporation or the Scottish Administration) is not liable to prosecution under the Acts, though servants of the Crown (and members of staff of the Scottish bodies mentioned) are.[24] It is a summary offence, punishable with a fine on level 5.[25] Under the Freedom of Information Act 2000 a prosecution can only be brought in England and Wales by the Information Commissioner or by or with the consent of the Director of Public Prosecutions.[26] It is also an offence to obstruct or to fail, without reasonable excuse, to give reasonably required assistance to a person executing a warrant under the

[18] Freedom of Information Act 2000, Sch.3, para.1(2); Freedom of Information (Scotland) Act 2002, Sch.3, para.1(2).
[19] Freedom of Information Act 2000, Sch.3, paras 4 and 5; Freedom of Information (Scotland) Act 2002, Sch.3, paras 3 and 4.
[20] Freedom of Information Act 2000, Sch.3, paras 8 and 9; Freedom of Information (Scotland) Act 2002, Sch.3, paras 7 and 8.
[21] Freedom of Information Act 2000, s.77(1); Freedom of Information (Scotland) Act 2002, s.65(1).
[22] Freedom of Information Act 2000, s.77(2); Freedom of Information (Scotland) Act 2002, s.65(2).
[23] As defined in Freedom of Information Act 2000, s.84 (with certain exceptions, "any body or authority exercising statutory functions on behalf of the Crown").
[24] *ibid.*, s.81(3); Freedom of Information (Scotland) Act 2002, s.68.
[25] Freedom of Information Act 2000, s.77(3); Freedom of Information (Scotland) Act 2002, s.65(3).
[26] Freedom of Information Act 2000, s.77(4).

procedure set out above.[27] The Scottish Act specifies that this is a summary offence punishable with a fine at level 5.[28]

2. DATA PROTECTION ACT 1998

Private action to enforce access rights

As discussed in Chapter 28,[29] the primary means by which the access rights under the Data Protection Act 1998 are pursued are by an application to the court under s.7(9), which provides that the court can, if satisfied that the data controller has failed to comply with a request in contravention of the Act, order it to do so. The jurisdiction is exercisable by both the High Court or the county court, or, in Scotland, by the Court of Session or the sheriff. If a public authority was ordered to comply with a request and failed to do so, it would be open to the applicant to seek enforcement of the order in the normal way pursuant to the relevant rules of court.[30] As discussed above, it is most unlikely that a public authority would ever be committed to prison (assuming, of course, that the authority in question was a natural person) or that an order for sequestration or a fine would be made, but it would be open, in principle, for the court to make an order for committal against an individual officer of the authority[31] in appropriate circumstances, no doubt involving actual fault on the part of the officer. 29–008

Compensation

Under the Data Protection Act 1998 it is also open to an individual who suffers damage by reason of a contravention of the Act by a data controller to obtain compensation for the damage, and such compensation can include compensation for distress provided there is other damage.[32] The jurisdiction is again in the High Court or a county court (or as appropriate in Scotland) and there is a defence that the data controller took reasonable care to comply with the requirements of the Act.[33] 29–009

[27] *ibid.*, Sch.3, para.12; Freedom of Information (Scotland) Act 2002, Sch.3, para.10. See para.29–006.
[28] Freedom of Information (Scotland) Act 2002, Sch.3, para.10(2).
[29] See paras 28–031 to 28–033.
[30] In the High Court RSC Ord.45 r.5 and Ord.52 and in a county court CCR Ord.29.
[31] See RSC Ord.45 r.5(1)(b)(iii) and CCR Ord.29 r.1(1).
[32] Data Protection Act 1998, s.13.
[33] *ibid.*, s.13(3).

Information Commissioner's role

29–010 As discussed earlier,[34] there is also a possible, though limited, role for the Information Commissioner in enforcing the right of access to personal data provided by the Data Protection Act 1998. The Commissioner can serve enforcement notices on the data controller if satisfied that it has contravened any of the data protection principles[35] (including the sixth principle, which can be contravened by a contravention of s.7 of the Act[36]) and can serve information notices in connection with inquiries into such a contravention.[37] A failure to comply with any such notice (including, in the case of an information notice, deliberately or recklessly making a false statement in response thereto) is an offence.[38] It is a defence to the charge to show that all due diligence was exercised.[39] The offence is triable either summarily or on indictment and punishable with the maximum or an unlimited fine. Proceedings must be brought by the Information Commissioner or by or with the consent of the DPP.[40] No government department[41] is liable to prosecution under the Data Protection Act 1998[42] but individual servants of the Crown may be.[43]

Search and seizure

29–011 As with the Freedom of Information Acts, the Information Commissioner has power to seek a warrant authorising entry search and seizure if there are reasonable grounds for suspecting a contravention of the data protection principles or that an offence under the Data Protection Act 1998 is being or has been committed and that evidence of the contravention or the offence is to be found on any premises.[44] The detailed provisions in Data Protection Act 1998 in relation to these powers are very similar to those in the Freedom of Information Acts.[45]

34 para.28–034.
35 Data Protection Act 1998, s.40(1).
36 *ibid.*, Sch.1, Pt II, para.8(a).
37 *ibid.*, s.43(1).
38 *ibid.*, s.47(1) and (2).
39 *ibid.*, s.47(3).
40 *ibid.*, s.60(1) and (2).
41 Defined by the Data Protection Act, s.70(1) as including any "body or authority exercising statutory functions on behalf of the Crown."
42 *ibid.*, s.63(5).
43 The position is unclear: the Data Protection Act, s.63(5) does not refer expressly to offences under s.47 of failing to comply with a notice and the effect of *ibid.*, s.61(1) is not clear where the body corporate (in this case the government department) is itself not "liable to prosecution."
44 *ibid.*, s.50 and Sch.9, para.1.
45 See para.29–005.

Criminal offences

As in relation to the Freedom of Information Acts, it is a criminal offence to interfere with records held by a public authority with the intention of preventing the disclosure of information to which a person who had made a request would have been entitled in accordance with s.7 of the Data Protection Act 1998.[46] It is also an offence under the Data Protection Act 1998 to obstruct a person in the execution of a warrant under the Act or to fail to give reasonable assistance in the same way as in relation to a warrant under the Freedom of Information Acts.[47] Proceedings for this offence must be brought by the Information Commissioner or by or with the consent of the DPP, it is triable summarily and the maximum penalty is a fine on level 5[48]; although a government department cannot be liable to prosecution for this offence Crown servants can be guilty of the offence.[49] 29–012

[46] Freedom of Information Act 2000, ss.77 and 81(3).
[47] Data Protection Act 1998, Sch.9, para.12; see para.29–006.
[48] *ibid.*, s.60(1) and (3).
[49] *ibid.*, s.63(5).

APPENDICES

Contents

APPENDIX A

Legislation

*These can be viewed at *www.sweetandmaxwell.co.uk/informationrights*.

APPENDIX 1

Principal UK Statutes

Freedom of Information Act 2000

(2000, c.36)

ARRANGEMENT OF SECTIONS

PART I

ACCESS TO INFORMATION HELD BY PUBLIC AUTHORITIES

Right to information

Refusal of request

17. Refusal of request.

The Information Commissioner and the Information Tribunal

18. The Information Commissioner and the Information Tribunal.

Publication schemes

19. Publication schemes.
20. Model publication schemes.

PART II

EXEMPT INFORMATION

21. Information accessible to applicant by other means.
22. Information intended for future publication.
23. Information supplied by, or relating to, bodies dealing with security matters.
24. National security.
25. Certificates under ss. 23 and 24: supplementary provisions.
26. Defence.
27. International relations.
28. Relations within the United Kingdom.
29. The economy.
30. Investigations and proceedings conducted by public authorities.
31. Law enforcement.
32. Court records, etc.
33. Audit functions.
34. Parliamentary privilege.
35. Formulation of government policy, etc.
36. Prejudice to effective conduct of public affairs.
37. Communications with Her Majesty, etc. and honours.
38. Health and safety.
39. Environmental information.
40. Personal information.
41. Information provided in confidence.
42. Legal professional privilege.
43. Commercial interests.
44. Prohibitions on disclosure.

PART III

GENERAL FUNCTIONS OF SECRETARY OF STATE, LORD CHANCELLOR AND INFORMATION COMMISSIONER

45. Issue of code of practice by Secretary of State.
46. Issue of code of practice by Lord Chancellor.
47. General functions of Commissioner.
48. Recommendations as to good practice.
49. Reports to be laid before Parliament.

PART IV

ENFORCEMENT

50. Application for decision by Commissioner.
51. Information notices.
52. Enforcement notices.
53. Exception from duty to comply with decision notice or enforcement notice.
54. Failure to comply with notice.
55. Powers of entry and inspection.
56. No action against public authority.

PART V

APPEALS

57. Appeal against notices served under Part IV.
58. Determination of appeals.
59. Appeals from decision of Tribunal.
60. Appeals against national security certificate.
61. Appeal proceedings.

PART VI

HISTORICAL RECORDS AND RECORDS IN PUBLIC RECORD OFFICE OR PUBLIC RECORD OFFICE OF NORTHERN IRELAND

62. Interpretation of Part VI.
63. Removal of exemptions: historical records generally.
64. Removal of exemptions: historical records in public record offices.
65. Decisions as to refusal of discretionary disclosure of historical records.

66. Decisions relating to certain transferred public records.
67. Amendments of public records legislation.

Part VII

Amendments of Data Protection Act 1998

Amendments relating to personal information held by public authorities

68. Extension of meaning of "data".
69. Right of access to unstructured personal data held by public authorities.
70. Exemptions applicable to certain manual data held by public authorities.
71. Particulars registrable under Part III of Data Protection Act 1998.
72. Availability under Act disregarded for purpose of exemption.

Other amendments

73. Further amendments of Data Protection Act 1998.

Part VIII

Miscellaneous and Supplemental

74. Power to make provision relating to environmental information.
75. Power to amend or repeal enactments prohibiting disclosure of information.
76. Disclosure of information between Commissioner and ombudsmen.
77. Offence of altering etc. records with intent to prevent disclosure.
78. Saving for existing powers.
79. Defamation.
80. Scotland.
81. Application to government departments, etc.
82. Orders and regulations.
83. Meaning of "Welsh public authority".
84. Interpretation.
85. Expenses.
86. Repeals.
87. Commencement.
88. Short title and extent.

SCHEDULES

An Act to make provision for the disclosure of information held by public authorities or by persons providing services for them and to amend the Data Protection Act 1998 and the Public Records Act 1958; and for connected purposes. App 1–01

[NOVEMBER 30, 2000]

BE IT ENACTED by the Queen's most Excellent Majesty, by and with the advice and consent of the Lords Spiritual and Temporal, and Commons, in this present Parliament assembled, and by the authority of the same, as follows:

Part I

Access to Information Held by Public Authorities

Right to information

General right of access to information held by public authorities

1.—(1) Any person making a request for information to a public authority is entitled—

(a) to be informed in writing by the public authority whether it holds information of the description specified in the request, and
(b) if that is the case, to have that information communicated to him.

(2) Subsection (1) has effect subject to the following provisions of this section and to the provisions of sections 2, 9, 12 and 14.

(3) Where a public authority—

(a) reasonably requires further information in order to identify and locate the information requested, and
(b) has informed the applicant of that requirement,

the authority is not obliged to comply with subsection (1) unless it is supplied with that further information.

(4) The information—

(a) in respect of which the applicant is to be informed under subsection (1)(a), or
(b) which is to be communicated under subsection (1)(b),

is the information in question held at the time when the request is received, except that account may be taken of any amendment or deletion made between that time and the time when the information is to be communicated under subsection (1)(b), being an amendment or deletion that would have been made regardless of the receipt of the request.

(5) A public authority is to be taken to have complied with subsection (1)(a) in relation to any information if it has communicated the information to the applicant in accordance with subsection (1)(b).

(6) In this Act, the duty of a public authority to comply with subsection (1)(a) is referred to as "the duty to confirm or deny".

Effect of the exemptions in Part II

2.—(1) Where any provision of Part II states that the duty to confirm or deny does not arise in relation to any information, the effect of the provision is that where either—

(a) the provision confers absolute exemption, or
(b) in all the circumstances of the case, the public interest in maintaining the exclusion of the duty to confirm or deny outweighs the public interest in disclosing whether the public authority holds the information,

section 1(1)(a) does not apply.

(2) In respect of any information which is exempt information by virtue of any provision of Part II, section 1(1)(b) does not apply if or to the extent that—

(a) the information is exempt information by virtue of a provision conferring absolute exemption, or

(b) in all the circumstances of the case, the public interest in maintaining the exemption outweighs the public interest in disclosing the information.

(3) For the purposes of this section, the following provisions of Part II (and no others) are to be regarded as conferring absolute exemption—

(a) section 21,
(b) section 23,
(c) section 32,
(d) section 34,
(e) section 36 so far as relating to information held by the House of Commons or the House of Lords,
(f) in section 40—

(i) subsection (1), and
(ii) subsection (2) so far as relating to cases where the first condition referred to in that subsection is satisfied by virtue of subsection (3)(a)(i) or (b) of that section,

(g) section 41, and
(h) section 44.

Public authorities

3.—(1) In this Act "public authority" means—

(a) subject to section 4(4), any body which, any other person who, or the holder of any office which—
(i) is listed in Schedule 1, or
(ii) is designated by order under section 5, or

(b) a publicly-owned company as defined by section 6.

(2) For the purposes of this Act, information is held by a public authority if—

(a) it is held by the authority, otherwise than on behalf of another person, or
(b) it is held by another person on behalf of the authority.

Amendment of Schedule 1

4.—(1) The [Secretary of State][1] may by order amend Schedule 1 by adding to that Schedule a reference to any body or the holder of any office which (in either case) is not for the time being listed in that Schedule but as respects which both the first and the second conditions below are satisfied.

(2) The first condition is that the body or office—

(a) is established by virtue of Her Majesty's prerogative or by an enactment or by subordinate legislation, or
(b) is established in any other way by a Minister of the Crown in his capacity as Minister, by a government department or by the National Assembly for Wales.

(3) The second condition is—

(a) in the case of a body, that the body is wholly or partly constituted by appointment made by the Crown, by a Minister of the Crown, by a government department or by the National Assembly for Wales, or

1 Words substituted by SI 2003/1887 (Secretary of State for Constitutional Affairs Order), Sch.2, para.12(1)(a).

(b) in the case of an office, that appointments to the office are made by the Crown, by a Minister of the Crown, by a government department or by the National Assembly for Wales.

(4) If either the first or the second condition above ceases to be satisfied as respects any body or office which is listed in Part VI or VII of Schedule 1, that body or the holder of that office shall cease to be a public authority by virtue of the entry in question.

(5) The [Secretary of State][2] may by order amend Schedule 1 by removing from Part VI or VII of that Schedule an entry relating to any body or office—

(a) which has ceased to exist, or
(b) as respects which either the first or the second condition above has ceased to be satisfied.

(6) An order under subsection (1) may relate to a specified person or office or to persons or offices falling within a specified description.

(7) Before making an order under subsection (1), the [Secretary of State][3] shall—

(a) if the order adds to Part II, III, IV or VI of Schedule 1 a reference to—
  (i) a body whose functions are exercisable only or mainly in or as regards Wales, or
  (ii) the holder of an office whose functions are exercisable only or mainly in or as regards Wales,

consult the National Assembly for Wales, and

(b) if the order relates to a body which, or the holder of any office who, if the order were made, would be a Northern Ireland public authority, consult the First Minister and deputy First Minister in Northern Ireland.

(8) This section has effect subject to section 80.

(9) In this section "Minister of the Crown" includes a Northern Ireland Minister.

Further power to designate public authorities

5.—(1) The [Secretary of State][4] may by order designate as a public authority for the purposes of this Act any person who is neither listed in Schedule 1 nor capable of being added to that Schedule by an order under section 4(1), but who—

(a) appears to the [Secretary of State][5] to exercise functions of a public nature, or
(b) is providing under a contract made with a public authority any service whose provision is a function of that authority.

(2) An order under this section may designate a specified person or office or persons or offices falling within a specified description.

(3) Before making an order under this section, the [Secretary of State][6] shall consult every person to whom the order relates, or persons appearing to him to represent such persons.

(4) This section has effect subject to section 80.

---

2 Words substituted by SI 2003/1887 (Secretary of State for Constitutional Affairs Order), Sch.2, para.12(1)(a).
3 *ibid*.
4 *ibid*.
5 *ibid*.
6 *ibid*.

Publicly-owned companies

6.—(1) A company is a "publicly-owned company" for the purposes of section 3(1)(b) if—

(a) it is wholly owned by the Crown, or
(b) it is wholly owned by any public authority listed in Schedule 1 other than—

(i) a government department, or
(ii) any authority which is listed only in relation to particular information.

(2) For the purposes of this section—

(a) a company is wholly owned by the Crown if it has no members except—

(i) Ministers of the Crown, government departments or companies wholly owned by the Crown, or
(ii) persons acting on behalf of Ministers of the Crown, government departments or companies wholly owned by the Crown, and

(b) a company is wholly owned by a public authority other than a government department if it has no members except—

(i) that public authority or companies wholly owned by that public authority, or
(ii) persons acting on behalf of that public authority or of companies wholly owned by that public authority.

(3) In this section—

"company" includes any body corporate;

"Minister of the Crown" includes a Northern Ireland Minister.

Public authorities to which Act has limited application

7.—(1) Where a public authority is listed in Schedule 1 only in relation to information of a specified description, nothing in Parts I to V of this Act applies to any other information held by the authority.

(2) An order under section 4(1) may, in adding an entry to Schedule 1, list the public authority only in relation to information of a specified description.

(3) The [Secretary of State][7] may by order amend Schedule 1—

(a) by limiting to information of a specified description the entry relating to any public authority, or
(b) by removing or amending any limitation to information of a specified description which is for the time being contained in any entry.

(4) Before making an order under subsection (3), the [Secretary of State][8] shall—

(a) if the order relates to the National Assembly for Wales or a Welsh public authority, consult the National Assembly for Wales,
(b) if the order relates to the Northern Ireland Assembly, consult the Presiding Officer of that Assembly, and
(c) if the order relates to a Northern Ireland department or a Northern Ireland public authority, consult the First Minister and deputy First Minister in Northern Ireland.

---

7 *ibid.*
8 *ibid.*

(5) An order under section 5(1)(a) must specify the functions of the public authority designated by the order with respect to which the designation is to have effect; and nothing in Parts I to V of this Act applies to information which is held by the authority but does not relate to the exercise of those functions.

(6) An order under section 5(1)(b) must specify the services provided under contract with respect to which the designation is to have effect; and nothing in Parts I to V of this Act applies to information which is held by the public authority designated by the order but does not relate to the provision of those services.

(7) Nothing in Parts I to V of this Act applies in relation to any information held by a publicly-owned company which is excluded information in relation to that company.

(8) In subsection (7) "excluded information", in relation to a publicly-owned company, means information which is of a description specified in relation to that company in an order made by the [Secretary of State][9] for the purposes of this subsection.

(9) In this section "publicly-owned company" has the meaning given by section 6.

Request for information

8.—(1) In this Act any reference to a "request for information" is a reference to such a request which—

(a) is in writing,
(b) states the name of the applicant and an address for correspondence, and
(c) describes the information requested.

(2) For the purposes of subsection (1)(a), a request is to be treated as made in writing where the text of the request—

(a) is transmitted by electronic means,
(b) is received in legible form, and
(c) is capable of being used for subsequent reference.

Fees

9.—(1) A public authority to whom a request for information is made may, within the period for complying with section 1(1), give the applicant a notice in writing (in this Act referred to as a "fees notice") stating that a fee of an amount specified in the notice is to be charged by the authority for complying with section 1(1).

(2) Where a fees notice has been given to the applicant, the public authority is not obliged to comply with section 1(1) unless the fee is paid within the period of three months beginning with the day on which the fees notice is given to the applicant.

(3) Subject to subsection (5), any fee under this section must be determined by the public authority in accordance with regulations made by the [Secretary of State].[10]

(4) Regulations under subsection (3) may, in particular, provide—

(a) that no fee is to be payable in prescribed cases,
(b) that any fee is not to exceed such maximum as may be specified in, or determined in accordance with, the regulations, and
(c) that any fee is to be calculated in such manner as may be prescribed by the regulations.

(5) Subsection (3) does not apply where provision is made by or under any enactment as to the fee that may be charged by the public authority for the disclosure of the information.

---

[9] Words substituted by SI 2003/1887 (Secretary of State for Constitutional Affairs Order), Sch.2, para.12(1)(a).

[10] *ibid.*

Time for compliance with request

10.—(1) Subject to subsections (2) and (3), a public authority must comply with section 1(1) promptly and in any event not later than the twentieth working day following the date of receipt.

(2) Where the authority has given a fees notice to the applicant and the fee is paid in accordance with section 9(2), the working days in the period beginning with the day on which the fees notice is given to the applicant and ending with the day on which the fee is received by the authority are to be disregarded in calculating for the purposes of subsection (1) the twentieth working day following the date of receipt.

(3) If, and to the extent that—

(a) section 1(1)(a) would not apply if the condition in section 2(1)(b) were satisfied, or

(b) section 1(1)(b) would not apply if the condition in section 2(2)(b) were satisfied,

the public authority need not comply with section 1(1)(a) or (b) until such time as is reasonable in the circumstances; but this subsection does not affect the time by which any notice under section 17(1) must be given.

(4) The [Secretary of State][11] may by regulations provide that subsections (1) and (2) are to have effect as if any reference to the twentieth working day following the date of receipt were a reference to such other day, not later than the sixtieth working day following the date of receipt, as may be specified in, or determined in accordance with, the regulations.

(5) Regulations under subsection (4) may—

(a) prescribe different days in relation to different cases, and
(b) confer a discretion on the Commissioner.

(6) In this section—

"the date of receipt" means—

(a) the day on which the public authority receives the request for information, or
(b) if later, the day on which it receives the information referred to in section 1(3);

"working day" means any day other than a Saturday, a Sunday, Christmas Day, Good Friday or a day which is a bank holiday under the Banking and Financial Dealings Act 1971 in any part of the United Kingdom.

Means by which communication to be made

11.—(1) Where, on making his request for information, the applicant expresses a preference for communication by any one or more of the following means, namely—

(a) the provision to the applicant of a copy of the information in permanent form or in another form acceptable to the applicant,
(b) the provision to the applicant of a reasonable opportunity to inspect a record containing the information, and
(c) the provision to the applicant of a digest or summary of the information in permanent form or in another form acceptable to the applicant,

the public authority shall so far as reasonably practicable give effect to that preference.

[11] Words substituted by SI 2003/1887 (Secretary of State for Constitutional Affairs Order), Sch.2, para.12(1)(a).

(2) In determining for the purposes of this section whether it is reasonably practicable to communicate information by particular means, the public authority may have regard to all the circumstances, including the cost of doing so.

(3) Where the public authority determines that it is not reasonably practicable to comply with any preference expressed by the applicant in making his request, the authority shall notify the applicant of the reasons for its determination.

(4) Subject to subsection (1), a public authority may comply with a request by communicating information by any means which are reasonable in the circumstances.

Exemption where cost of compliance exceeds appropriate limit

12.—(1) Section 1(1) does not oblige a public authority to comply with a request for information if the authority estimates that the cost of complying with the request would exceed the appropriate limit.

(2) Subsection (1) does not exempt the public authority from its obligation to comply with paragraph (a) of section 1(1) unless the estimated cost of complying with that paragraph alone would exceed the appropriate limit.

(3) In subsections (1) and (2) "the appropriate limit" means such amount as may be prescribed, and different amounts may be prescribed in relation to different cases.

(4) The [Secretary of State][12] may by regulations provide that, in such circumstances as may be prescribed, where two or more requests for information are made to a public authority—

(a) by one person, or
(b) by different persons who appear to the public authority to be acting in concert or in pursuance of a campaign,

the estimated cost of complying with any of the requests is to be taken to be the estimated total cost of complying with all of them.

(5) The [Secretary of State][13] may by regulations make provision for the purposes of this section as to the costs to be estimated and as to the manner in which they are to be estimated.

Fees for disclosure where cost of compliance exceeds appropriate limit

13.—(1) A public authority may charge for the communication of any information whose communication—

(a) is not required by section 1(1) because the cost of complying with the request for information exceeds the amount which is the appropriate limit for the purposes of section 12(1) and (2), and
(b) is not otherwise required by law,

such fee as may be determined by the public authority in accordance with regulations made by the [Secretary of State].[14]

(2) Regulations under this section may, in particular, provide—

(a) that any fee is not to exceed such maximum as may be specified in, or determined in accordance with, the regulations, and
(b) that any fee is to be calculated in such manner as may be prescribed by the regulations.

---

[12] Words substituted by SI 2003/1887 (Secretary of State for Constitutional Affairs Order), Sch.2, para.12(1)(a).

[13] *ibid.*

[14] *ibid.*

(3) Subsection (1) does not apply where provision is made by or under any enactment as to the fee that may be charged by the public authority for the disclosure of the information.

Vexatious or repeated requests

14.—(1) Section 1(1) does not oblige a public authority to comply with a request for information if the request is vexatious.

(2) Where a public authority has previously complied with a request for information which was made by any person, it is not obliged to comply with a subsequent identical or substantially similar request from that person unless a reasonable interval has elapsed between compliance with the previous request and the making of the current request.

Special provisions relating to public records transferred to Public Record Office, etc.

15.—(1) Where—

(a) the appropriate records authority receives a request for information which relates to information which is, or if it existed would be, contained in a transferred public record, and
(b) either of the conditions in subsection (2) is satisfied in relation to any of that information,

that authority shall, within the period for complying with section 1(1), send a copy of the request to the responsible authority.

(2) The conditions referred to in subsection (1)(b) are—

(a) that the duty to confirm or deny is expressed to be excluded only by a provision of Part II not specified in subsection (3) of section 2, and
(b) that the information is exempt information only by virtue of a provision of Part II not specified in that subsection.

(3) On receiving the copy, the responsible authority shall, within such time as is reasonable in all the circumstances, inform the appropriate records authority of the determination required by virtue of subsection (3) or (4) of section 66.

(4) In this Act "transferred public record" means a public record which has been transferred—

(a) to the Public Record Office,
(b) to another place of deposit appointed by the Lord Chancellor under the Public Records Act 1958, or
(c) to the Public Record Office of Northern Ireland.

(5) In this Act—

"appropriate records authority", in relation to a transferred public record, means—

(a) in a case falling within subsection (4)(a), the Public Record Office,
(b) in a case falling within subsection (4)(b), the Lord Chancellor, and
(c) in a case falling within subsection (4)(c), the Public Record Office of Northern Ireland;

"responsible authority", in relation to a transferred public record, means—

(a) in the case of a record transferred as mentioned in subsection (4)(a) or (b) from a government department in the charge of a Minister of the Crown, the Minister of the Crown who appears to the Lord Chancellor to be primarily concerned,
(b) in the case of a record transferred as mentioned in subsection (4)(a) or (b) from any other person, the person who appears to the Lord Chancellor to be primarily concerned,

(c) in the case of a record transferred to the Public Record Office of Northern Ireland from a government department in the charge of a Minister of the Crown, the Minister of the Crown who appears to the appropriate Northern Ireland Minister to be primarily concerned,

(d) in the case of a record transferred to the Public Record Office of Northern Ireland from a Northern Ireland department, the Northern Ireland Minister who appears to the appropriate Northern Ireland Minister to be primarily concerned, or

(e) in the case of a record transferred to the Public Record Office of Northern Ireland from any other person, the person who appears to the appropriate Northern Ireland Minister to be primarily concerned.

Duty to provide advice and assistance

16.—(1) It shall be the duty of a public authority to provide advice and assistance, so far as it would be reasonable to expect the authority to do so, to persons who propose to make, or have made, requests for information to it.

(2) Any public authority which, in relation to the provision of advice or assistance in any case, conforms with the code of practice under section 45 is to be taken to comply with the duty imposed by subsection (1) in relation to that case.

Refusal of request

Refusal of request

17.—(1) A public authority which, in relation to any request for information, is to any extent relying on a claim that any provision of Part II relating to the duty to confirm or deny is relevant to the request or on a claim that information is exempt information must, within the time for complying with section 1(1), give the applicant a notice which—

(a) states that fact,

(b) specifies the exemption in question, and

(c) states (if that would not otherwise be apparent) why the exemption applies.

(2) Where—

(a) in relation to any request for information, a public authority is, as respects any information, relying on a claim—

(i) that any provision of Part II which relates to the duty to confirm or deny and is not specified in section 2(3) is relevant to the request, or

(ii) that the information is exempt information only by virtue of a provision not specified in section 2(3), and

(b) at the time when the notice under subsection (1) is given to the applicant, the public authority (or, in a case falling within section 66(3) or (4), the responsible authority) has not yet reached a decision as to the application of subsection (1)(b) or (2)(b) of section 2,

the notice under subsection (1) must indicate that no decision as to the application of that provision has yet been reached and must contain an estimate of the date by which the authority expects that such a decision will have been reached.

(3) A public authority which, in relation to any request for information, is to any extent relying on a claim that subsection (1)(b) or (2)(b) of section 2 applies must, either in the notice under subsection (1) or in a separate notice given within such time as is reasonable in the circumstances, state the reasons for claiming—

(a) that, in all the circumstances of the case, the public interest in maintaining the exclusion of the duty to confirm or deny outweighs the public interest in disclosing whether the authority holds the information, or

(b) that, in all the circumstances of the case, the public interest in maintaining the exemption outweighs the public interest in disclosing the information.

(4) A public authority is not obliged to make a statement under subsection (1)(c) or (3) if, or to the extent that, the statement would involve the disclosure of information which would itself be exempt information.

(5) A public authority which, in relation to any request for information, is relying on a claim that section 12 or 14 applies must, within the time for complying with section 1(1), give the applicant a notice stating that fact.

(6) Subsection (5) does not apply where—

(a) the public authority is relying on a claim that section 14 applies,
(b) the authority has given the applicant a notice, in relation to a previous request for information, stating that it is relying on such a claim, and
(c) it would in all the circumstances be unreasonable to expect the authority to serve a further notice under subsection (5) in relation to the current request.

(7) A notice under subsection (1), (3) or (5) must—

(a) contain particulars of any procedure provided by the public authority for dealing with complaints about the handling of requests for information or state that the authority does not provide such a procedure, and
(b) contain particulars of the right conferred by section 50.

The Information Commissioner and the Information Tribunal

The Information Commissioner and the Information Tribunal

18.—(1) The Data Protection Commissioner shall be known instead as the Information Commissioner.

(2) The Data Protection Tribunal shall be known instead as the Information Tribunal.

(3) In this Act—

(a) the Information Commissioner is referred to as "the Commissioner", and
(b) the Information Tribunal is referred to as "the Tribunal".

(4) Schedule 2 (which makes provision consequential on subsections (1) and (2) and amendments of the Data Protection Act 1998 relating to the extension by this Act of the functions of the Commissioner and the Tribunal) has effect.

(5) If the person who held office as Data Protection Commissioner immediately before the day on which this Act is passed remains in office as Information Commissioner at the end of the period of two years beginning with that day, he shall vacate his office at the end of that period.

(6) Subsection (5) does not prevent the re-appointment of a person whose appointment is terminated by that subsection.

(7) In the application of paragraph 2(4)(b) and (5) of Schedule 5 to the Data Protection Act 1998 (Commissioner not to serve for more than fifteen years and not to be appointed, except in special circumstances, for a third or subsequent term) to anything done after the passing of this Act, there shall be left out of account any term of office served by virtue of an appointment made before the passing of this Act.

Publication schemes

Publication schemes

19.—(1) It shall be the duty of every public authority—

(a) to adopt and maintain a scheme which relates to the publication of information by the authority and is approved by the Commissioner (in this Act referred to as a "publication scheme"),
(b) to publish information in accordance with its publication scheme, and
(c) from time to time to review its publication scheme.

(2) A publication scheme must—

(a) specify classes of information which the public authority publishes or intends to publish,
(b) specify the manner in which information of each class is, or is intended to be, published, and
(c) specify whether the material is, or is intended to be, available to the public free of charge or on payment.

(3) In adopting or reviewing a publication scheme, a public authority shall have regard to the public interest—

(a) in allowing public access to information held by the authority, and
(b) in the publication of reasons for decisions made by the authority.

(4) A public authority shall publish its publication scheme in such manner as it thinks fit.

(5) The Commissioner may, when approving a scheme, provide that his approval is to expire at the end of a specified period.

(6) Where the Commissioner has approved the publication scheme of any public authority, he may at any time give notice to the public authority revoking his approval of the scheme as from the end of the period of six months beginning with the day on which the notice is given.

(7) Where the Commissioner—

(a) refuses to approve a proposed publication scheme, or
(b) revokes his approval of a publication scheme,

he must give the public authority a statement of his reasons for doing so.

Model publication schemes

20.—(1) The Commissioner may from time to time approve, in relation to public authorities falling within particular classes, model publication schemes prepared by him or by other persons.

(2) Where a public authority falling within the class to which an approved model scheme relates adopts such a scheme without modification, no further approval of the Commissioner is required so long as the model scheme remains approved; and where such an authority adopts such a scheme with modifications, the approval of the Commissioner is required only in relation to the modifications.

(3) The Commissioner may, when approving a model publication scheme, provide that his approval is to expire at the end of a specified period.

(4) Where the Commissioner has approved a model publication scheme, he may at any time publish, in such manner as he thinks fit, a notice revoking his approval of the scheme as from the end of the period of six months beginning with the day on which the notice is published.

(5) Where the Commissioner refuses to approve a proposed model publication scheme on the application of any person, he must give the person who applied for approval of the scheme a statement of the reasons for his refusal.

(6) Where the Commissioner refuses to approve any modifications under subsection (2), he must give the public authority a statement of the reasons for his refusal.

(7) Where the Commissioner revokes his approval of a model publication scheme, he must include in the notice under subsection (4) a statement of his reasons for doing so.

PART II

EXEMPT INFORMATION

Information accessible to applicant by other means

21.—(1) Information which is reasonably accessible to the applicant otherwise than under section 1 is exempt information.

(2) For the purposes of subsection (1)—

(a) information may be reasonably accessible to the applicant even though it is accessible only on payment, and

(b) information is to be taken to be reasonably accessible to the applicant if it is information which the public authority or any other person is obliged by or under any enactment to communicate (otherwise than by making the information available for inspection) to members of the public on request, whether free of charge or on payment.

(3) For the purposes of subsection (1), information which is held by a public authority and does not fall within subsection (2)(b) is not to be regarded as reasonably accessible to the applicant merely because the information is available from the public authority itself on request, unless the information is made available in accordance with the authority's publication scheme and any payment required is specified in, or determined in accordance with, the scheme.

Information intended for future publication

22.—(1) Information is exempt information if—

(a) the information is held by the public authority with a view to its publication, by the authority or any other person, at some future date (whether determined or not),

(b) the information was already held with a view to such publication at the time when the request for information was made, and

(c) it is reasonable in all the circumstances that the information should be withheld from disclosure until the date referred to in paragraph (a).

(2) The duty to confirm or deny does not arise if, or to the extent that, compliance with section 1(1)(a) would involve the disclosure of any information (whether or not already recorded) which falls within subsection (1).

Information supplied by, or relating to, bodies dealing with security matters

23.—(1) Information held by a public authority is exempt information if it was directly or indirectly supplied to the public authority by, or relates to, any of the bodies specified in subsection (3).

(2) A certificate signed by a Minister of the Crown certifying that the information to which it applies was directly or indirectly supplied by, or relates to, any of the bodies specified in subsection (3) shall, subject to section 60, be conclusive evidence of that fact.

(3) The bodies referred to in subsections (1) and (2) are—

(a) the Security Service,
(b) the Secret Intelligence Service,
(c) the Government Communications Headquarters,
(d) the special forces,
(e) the Tribunal established under section 65 of the Regulation of Investigatory Powers Act 2000,
(f) the Tribunal established under section 7 of the Interception of Communications Act 1985,
(g) the Tribunal established under section 5 of the Security Service Act 1989,
(h) the Tribunal established under section 9 of the Intelligence Services Act 1994,
(i) the Security Vetting Appeals Panel,
(j) the Security Commission,
(k) the National Criminal Intelligence Service, and
(l) the Service Authority for the National Criminal Intelligence Service.

(4) In subsection (3)(c) "the Government Communications Headquarters" includes any unit or part of a unit of the armed forces of the Crown which is for the time being required by the Secretary of State to assist the Government Communications Headquarters in carrying out its functions.

(5) The duty to confirm or deny does not arise if, or to the extent that, compliance with section 1(1)(a) would involve the disclosure of any information (whether or not already recorded) which was directly or indirectly supplied to the public authority by, or relates to, any of the bodies specified in subsection (3).

National security

24.—(1) Information which does not fall within section 23(1) is exempt information if exemption from section 1(1)(b) is required for the purpose of safeguarding national security.

(2) The duty to confirm or deny does not arise if, or to the extent that, exemption from section 1(1)(a) is required for the purpose of safeguarding national security.

(3) A certificate signed by a Minister of the Crown certifying that exemption from section 1(1)(b), or from section 1(1)(a) and (b), is, or at any time was, required for the purpose of safeguarding national security shall, subject to section 60, be conclusive evidence of that fact.

(4) A certificate under subsection (3) may identify the information to which it applies by means of a general description and may be expressed to have prospective effect.

Certificates under ss. 23 and 24: supplementary provisions

25.—(1) A document purporting to be a certificate under section 23(2) or 24(3) shall be received in evidence and deemed to be such a certificate unless the contrary is proved.

(2) A document which purports to be certified by or on behalf of a Minister of the Crown as a true copy of a certificate issued by that Minister under section 23(2) or 24(3) shall in any legal proceedings be evidence (or, in Scotland, sufficient evidence) of that certificate.

(3) The power conferred by section 23(2) or 24(3) on a Minister of the Crown shall not be exercisable except by a Minister who is a member of the Cabinet or by the Attorney General, the Advocate General for Scotland or the Attorney General for Northern Ireland.

Defence

26.—(1) Information is exempt information if its disclosure under this Act would, or would be likely to, prejudice—

(a) the defence of the British Islands or of any colony, or
(b) the capability, effectiveness or security of any relevant forces.

(2) In subsection (1)(b) "relevant forces" means—

(a) the armed forces of the Crown, and
(b) any forces co-operating with those forces,

or any part of any of those forces.

(3) The duty to confirm or deny does not arise if, or to the extent that, compliance with section 1(1)(a) would, or would be likely to, prejudice any of the matters mentioned in subsection (1).

International relations

27.—(1) Information is exempt information if its disclosure under this Act would, or would be likely to, prejudice—

(a) relations between the United Kingdom and any other State,
(b) relations between the United Kingdom and any international organisation or international court,
(c) the interests of the United Kingdom abroad, or
(d) the promotion or protection by the United Kingdom of its interests abroad.

(2) Information is also exempt information if it is confidential information obtained from a State other than the United Kingdom or from an international organisation or international court.

(3) For the purposes of this section, any information obtained from a State, organisation or court is confidential at any time while the terms on which it was obtained require it to be held in confidence or while the circumstances in which it was obtained make it reasonable for the State, organisation or court to expect that it will be so held.

(4) The duty to confirm or deny does not arise if, or to the extent that, compliance with section 1(1)(a)—

(a) would, or would be likely to, prejudice any of the matters mentioned in subsection (1), or
(b) would involve the disclosure of any information (whether or not already recorded) which is confidential information obtained from a State other than the United Kingdom or from an international organisation or international court.

(5) In this section—

"international court" means any international court which is not an international organisation and which is established—

(a) by a resolution of an international organisation of which the United Kingdom is a member, or
(b) by an international agreement to which the United Kingdom is a party;

"international organisation" means any international organisation whose members include any two or more States, or any organ of such an organisation;

"State" includes the government of any State and any organ of its government, and references to a State other than the United Kingdom include references to any territory outside the United Kingdom.

Relations within the United Kingdom

28.—(1) Information is exempt information if its disclosure under this Act would, or would be likely to, prejudice relations between any administration in the United Kingdom and any other such administration.

(2) In subsection (1) "administration in the United Kingdom" means—

(a) the government of the United Kingdom,
(b) the Scottish Administration,
(c) the Executive Committee of the Northern Ireland Assembly, or
(d) the National Assembly for Wales.

(3) The duty to confirm or deny does not arise if, or to the extent that, compliance with section 1(1)(a) would, or would be likely to, prejudice any of the matters mentioned in subsection (1).

The economy

29.—(1) Information is exempt information if its disclosure under this Act would, or would be likely to, prejudice—

(a) the economic interests of the United Kingdom or of any part of the United Kingdom, or
(b) the financial interests of any administration in the United Kingdom, as defined by section 28(2).

(2) The duty to confirm or deny does not arise if, or to the extent that, compliance with section 1(1)(a) would, or would be likely to, prejudice any of the matters mentioned in subsection (1).

Investigations and proceedings conducted by public authorities

30.—(1) Information held by a public authority is exempt information if it has at any time been held by the authority for the purposes of—

(a) any investigation which the public authority has a duty to conduct with a view to it being ascertained—

(i) whether a person should be charged with an offence, or
(ii) whether a person charged with an offence is guilty of it,

(b) any investigation which is conducted by the authority and in the circumstances may lead to a decision by the authority to institute criminal proceedings which the authority has power to conduct, or
(c) any criminal proceedings which the authority has power to conduct.

(2) Information held by a public authority is exempt information if—

(a) it was obtained or recorded by the authority for the purposes of its functions relating to—

(i) investigations falling within subsection (1)(a) or (b),
(ii) criminal proceedings which the authority has power to conduct,
(iii) investigations (other than investigations falling within subsection (1)(a) or (b)) which are conducted by the authority for any of the purposes specified in section 31(2) and either by virtue of Her Majesty's prerogative or by virtue of powers conferred by or under any enactment, or
(iv) civil proceedings which are brought by or on behalf of the authority and arise out of such investigations, and

(b) it relates to the obtaining of information from confidential sources.

(3) The duty to confirm or deny does not arise in relation to information which is (or if it were held by the public authority would be) exempt information by virtue of subsection (1) or (2).

(4) In relation to the institution or conduct of criminal proceedings or the power to conduct them, references in subsection (1)(b) or (c) and subsection (2)(a) to the public authority include references—

(a) to any officer of the authority,
(b) in the case of a government department other than a Northern Ireland department, to the Minister of the Crown in charge of the department, and
(c) in the case of a Northern Ireland department, to the Northern Ireland Minister in charge of the department.

(5) In this section—

"criminal proceedings" includes—

(a) proceedings before a court-martial constituted under the Army Act 1955, the Air Force Act 1955 or the Naval Discipline Act 1957 [. . .],[15]
(b) proceedings on dealing summarily with a charge under the Army Act 1955 or the Air Force Act 1955 or on summary trial under the Naval Discipline Act 1957,
(c) proceedings before a court established by section 83ZA of the Army Act 1955, section 83ZA of the Air Force Act 1955 or section 52FF of the Naval Discipline Act 1957 (summary appeal courts),
(d) proceedings before the Courts-Martial Appeal Court, and
(e) proceedings before a Standing Civilian Court;

"offence" includes any offence under the Army Act 1955, the Air Force Act 1955 or the Naval Discipline Act 1957.

(6) In the application of this section to Scotland—

(a) in subsection (1)(b), for the words from "a decision" to the end there is substituted "a decision by the authority to make a report to the procurator fiscal for the purpose of enabling him to determine whether criminal proceedings should be instituted",
(b) in subsections (1)(c) and (2)(a)(ii) for "which the authority has power to conduct" there is substituted "which have been instituted in consequence of a report made by the authority to the procurator fiscal", and
(c) for any reference to a person being charged with an offence there is substituted a reference to the person being prosecuted for the offence.

Law enforcement

31.—(1) Information which is not exempt information by virtue of section 30 is exempt information if its disclosure under this Act would, or would be likely to, prejudice—

(a) the prevention or detection of crime,
(b) the apprehension or prosecution of offenders,
(c) the administration of justice,
(d) the assessment or collection of any tax or duty or of any imposition of a similar nature,
(e) the operation of the immigration controls,
(f) the maintenance of security and good order in prisons or in other institutions where persons are lawfully detained,

[15] Words repealed by Armed Forces Act (2001, c.19), Sch.7(1), para.1.

(g) the exercise by any public authority of its functions for any of the purposes specified in subsection (2),
(h) any civil proceedings which are brought by or on behalf of a public authority and arise out of an investigation conducted, for any of the purposes specified in subsection (2), by or on behalf of the authority by virtue of Her Majesty's prerogative or by virtue of powers conferred by or under an enactment, or
(i) any inquiry held under the Fatal Accidents and Sudden Deaths Inquiries (Scotland) Act 1976 to the extent that the inquiry arises out of an investigation conducted, for any of the purposes specified in subsection (2), by or on behalf of the authority by virtue of Her Majesty's prerogative or by virtue of powers conferred by or under an enactment.

(2) The purposes referred to in subsection (1)(g) to (i) are—

(a) the purpose of ascertaining whether any person has failed to comply with the law,
(b) the purpose of ascertaining whether any person is responsible for any conduct which is improper,
(c) the purpose of ascertaining whether circumstances which would justify regulatory action in pursuance of any enactment exist or may arise,
(d) the purpose of ascertaining a person's fitness or competence in relation to the management of bodies corporate or in relation to any profession or other activity which he is, or seeks to become, authorised to carry on,
(e) the purpose of ascertaining the cause of an accident,
(f) the purpose of protecting charities against misconduct or mismanagement (whether by trustees or other persons) in their administration,
(g) the purpose of protecting the property of charities from loss or misapplication,
(h) the purpose of recovering the property of charities,
(i) the purpose of securing the health, safety and welfare of persons at work, and
(j) the purpose of protecting persons other than persons at work against risk to health or safety arising out of or in connection with the actions of persons at work.

(3) The duty to confirm or deny does not arise if, or to the extent that, compliance with section 1(1)(a) would, or would be likely to, prejudice any of the matters mentioned in subsection (1).

Court records, etc.

32.—(1) Information held by a public authority is exempt information if it is held only by virtue of being contained in—

(a) any document filed with, or otherwise placed in the custody of, a court for the purposes of proceedings in a particular cause or matter,
(b) any document served upon, or by, a public authority for the purposes of proceedings in a particular cause or matter, or
(c) any document created by—

(i) a court, or
(ii) a member of the administrative staff of a court,

for the purposes of proceedings in a particular cause or matter.

(2) Information held by a public authority is exempt information if it is held only by virtue of being contained in—

(a) any document placed in the custody of a person conducting an inquiry or arbitration, for the purposes of the inquiry or arbitration, or

(b) any document created by a person conducting an inquiry or arbitration, for the purposes of the inquiry or arbitration.

(3) The duty to confirm or deny does not arise in relation to information which is (or if it were held by the public authority would be) exempt information by virtue of this section.

(4) In this section—

(a) "court" includes any tribunal or body exercising the judicial power of the State,
(b) "proceedings in a particular cause or matter" includes any inquest or post-mortem examination,
(c) "inquiry" means any inquiry or hearing held under any provision contained in, or made under, an enactment, and
(d) except in relation to Scotland, "arbitration" means any arbitration to which Part I of the Arbitration Act 1996 applies.

Audit functions

33.—(1) This section applies to any public authority which has functions in relation to—

(a) the audit of the accounts of other public authorities, or
(b) the examination of the economy, efficiency and effectiveness with which other public authorities use their resources in discharging their functions.

(2) Information held by a public authority to which this section applies is exempt information if its disclosure would, or would be likely to, prejudice the exercise of any of the authority's functions in relation to any of the matters referred to in subsection (1).

(3) The duty to confirm or deny does not arise in relation to a public authority to which this section applies if, or to the extent that, compliance with section 1(1)(a) would, or would be likely to, prejudice the exercise of any of the authority's functions in relation to any of the matters referred to in subsection (1).

Parliamentary privilege

34.—(1) Information is exempt information if exemption from section 1(1)(b) is required for the purpose of avoiding an infringement of the privileges of either House of Parliament.

(2) The duty to confirm or deny does not apply if, or to the extent that, exemption from section 1(1)(a) is required for the purpose of avoiding an infringement of the privileges of either House of Parliament.

(3) A certificate signed by the appropriate authority certifying that exemption from section 1(1)(b), or from section 1(1)(a) and (b), is, or at any time was, required for the purpose of avoiding an infringement of the privileges of either House of Parliament shall be conclusive evidence of that fact.

(4) In subsection (3) "the appropriate authority" means—

(a) in relation to the House of Commons, the Speaker of that House, and
(b) in relation to the House of Lords, the Clerk of the Parliaments.

Formulation of government policy, etc.

35.—(1) Information held by a government department or by the National Assembly for Wales is exempt information if it relates to—

(a) the formulation or development of government policy,
(b) Ministerial communications,
(c) the provision of advice by any of the Law Officers or any request for the provision of such advice, or
(d) the operation of any Ministerial private office.

(2) Once a decision as to government policy has been taken, any statistical information used to provide an informed background to the taking of the decision is not to be regarded—

(a) for the purposes of subsection (1)(a), as relating to the formulation or development of government policy, or
(b) for the purposes of subsection (1)(b), as relating to Ministerial communications.

(3) The duty to confirm or deny does not arise in relation to information which is (or if it were held by the public authority would be) exempt information by virtue of subsection (1).

(4) In making any determination required by section 2(1)(b) or (2)(b) in relation to information which is exempt information by virtue of subsection (1)(a), regard shall be had to the particular public interest in the disclosure of factual information which has been used, or is intended to be used, to provide an informed background to decision-taking.

(5) In this section—

"government policy" includes the policy of the Executive Committee of the Northern Ireland Assembly and the policy of the National Assembly for Wales;

"the Law Officers" means the Attorney General, the Solicitor General, the Advocate General for Scotland, the Lord Advocate, the Solicitor General for Scotland and the Attorney General for Northern Ireland;

"Ministerial communications" means any communications—

(a) between Ministers of the Crown,
(b) between Northern Ireland Ministers, including Northern Ireland junior Ministers, or
(c) between Assembly Secretaries, including the Assembly First Secretary,

and includes, in particular, proceedings of the Cabinet or of any committee of the Cabinet, proceedings of the Executive Committee of the Northern Ireland Assembly, and proceedings of the executive committee of the National Assembly for Wales;

"Ministerial private office" means any part of a government department which provides personal administrative support to a Minister of the Crown, to a Northern Ireland Minister or a Northern Ireland junior Minister or any part of the administration of the National Assembly for Wales providing personal administrative support to the Assembly First Secretary or an Assembly Secretary;

"Northern Ireland junior Minister" means a member of the Northern Ireland Assembly appointed as a junior Minister under section 19 of the Northern Ireland Act 1998.

Prejudice to effective conduct of public affairs

36.—(1) This section applies to—

(a) information which is held by a government department or by the National Assembly for Wales and is not exempt information by virtue of section 35, and
(b) information which is held by any other public authority.

(2) Information to which this section applies is exempt information if, in the reasonable opinion of a qualified person, disclosure of the information under this Act—

(a) would, or would be likely to, prejudice—

(i) the maintenance of the convention of the collective responsibility of Ministers of the Crown, or

(ii) the work of the Executive Committee of the Northern Ireland Assembly, or
(iii) the work of the executive committee of the National Assembly for Wales,

(b) would, or would be likely to, inhibit—
(i) the free and frank provision of advice, or
(ii) the free and frank exchange of views for the purposes of deliberation, or

(c) would otherwise prejudice, or would be likely otherwise to prejudice, the effective conduct of public affairs.

(3) The duty to confirm or deny does not arise in relation to information to which this section applies (or would apply if held by the public authority) if, or to the extent that, in the reasonable opinion of a qualified person, compliance with section 1(1)(a) would, or would be likely to, have any of the effects mentioned in subsection (2).

(4) In relation to statistical information, subsections (2) and (3) shall have effect with the omission of the words "in the reasonable opinion of a qualified person".

(5) In subsections (2) and (3) "qualified person"—

(a) in relation to information held by a government department in the charge of a Minister of the Crown, means any Minister of the Crown,
(b) in relation to information held by a Northern Ireland department, means the Northern Ireland Minister in charge of the department,
(c) in relation to information held by any other government department, means the commissioners or other person in charge of that department,
(d) in relation to information held by the House of Commons, means the Speaker of that House,
(e) in relation to information held by the House of Lords, means the Clerk of the Parliaments,
(f) in relation to information held by the Northern Ireland Assembly, means the Presiding Officer,
(g) in relation to information held by the National Assembly for Wales, means the Assembly First Secretary,
(h) in relation to information held by any Welsh public authority other than the Auditor General for Wales, means—

(i) the public authority, or
(ii) any officer or employee of the authority authorised by the Assembly First Secretary,

(i) in relation to information held by the National Audit Office, means the Comptroller and Auditor General,
(j) in relation to information held by the Northern Ireland Audit Office, means the Comptroller and Auditor General for Northern Ireland,
(k) in relation to information held by the Auditor General for Wales, means the Auditor General for Wales,
(l) in relation to information held by any Northern Ireland public authority other than the Northern Ireland Audit Office, means—

(i) the public authority, or
(ii) any officer or employee of the authority authorised by the First Minister and deputy First Minister in Northern Ireland acting jointly,

(m) in relation to information held by the Greater London Authority, means the Mayor of London,
(n) in relation to information held by a functional body within the meaning of the Greater London Authority Act 1999, means the chairman of that functional body, and

(o) in relation to information held by any public authority not falling within any of paragraphs (a) to (n), means—

(i) a Minister of the Crown,
(ii) the public authority, if authorised for the purposes of this section by a Minister of the Crown, or
(iii) any officer or employee of the public authority who is authorised for the purposes of this section by a Minister of the Crown.

(6) Any authorisation for the purposes of this section—

(a) may relate to a specified person or to persons falling within a specified class,
(b) may be general or limited to particular classes of case, and
(c) may be granted subject to conditions.

(7) A certificate signed by the qualified person referred to in subsection (5)(d)or (e) above certifying that in his reasonable opinion—

(a) disclosure of information held by either House of Parliament, or
(b) compliance with section 1(1)(a) by either House,

would, or would be likely to, have any of the effects mentioned in subsection (2) shall be conclusive evidence of that fact.

Communications with Her Majesty, etc. and honours

37.—(1) Information is exempt information if it relates to—

(a) communications with Her Majesty, with other members of the Royal Family or with the Royal Household, or
(b) the conferring by the Crown of any honour or dignity.

(2) The duty to confirm or deny does not arise in relation to information which is (or if it were held by the public authority would be) exempt information by virtue of subsection (1).

Health and safety

38.—(1) Information is exempt information if its disclosure under this Act would, or would be likely to—

(a) endanger the physical or mental health of any individual, or
(b) endanger the safety of any individual.

(2) The duty to confirm or deny does not arise if, or to the extent that, compliance with section 1(1)(a) would, or would be likely to, have either of the effects mentioned in subsection (1).

Environmental information

39.—(1) Information is exempt information if the public authority holding it—

(a) is obliged by regulations under section 74 to make the information available to the public in accordance with the regulations, or
(b) would be so obliged but for any exemption contained in the regulations.

(2) The duty to confirm or deny does not arise in relation to information which is (or if it were held by the public authority would be) exempt information by virtue of subsection (1).

(3) Subsection (1)(a) does not limit the generality of section 21(1).

Personal information

40.—(1) Any information to which a request for information relates is exempt information if it constitutes personal data of which the applicant is the data subject.

(2) Any information to which a request for information relates is also exempt information if—

(a) it constitutes personal data which do not fall within subsection (1), and
(b) either the first or the second condition below is satisfied.

(3) The first condition is—

(a) in a case where the information falls within any of paragraphs (a) to (d) of the definition of "data" in section 1(1) of the Data Protection Act 1998, that the disclosure of the information to a member of the public otherwise than under this Act would contravene—

(i) any of the data protection principles, or
(ii) section 10 of that Act (right to prevent processing likely to cause damage or distress), and

(b) in any other case, that the disclosure of the information to a member of the public otherwise than under this Act would contravene any of the data protection principles if the exemptions in section 33A(1) of the Data Protection Act 1998 (which relate to manual data held by public authorities) were disregarded.

(4) The second condition is that by virtue of any provision of Part IV of the Data Protection Act 1998 the information is exempt from section 7(1)(c) of that Act (data subject's right of access to personal data).

(5) The duty to confirm or deny—

(a) does not arise in relation to information which is (or if it were held by the public authority would be) exempt information by virtue of subsection (1), and
(b) does not arise in relation to other information if or to the extent that either—

(i) the giving to a member of the public of the confirmation or denial that would have to be given to comply with section 1(1)(a) would (apart from this Act) contravene any of the data protection principles or section 10 of the Data Protection Act 1998 or would do so if the exemptions in section 33A(1) of that Act were disregarded, or
(ii) by virtue of any provision of Part IV of the Data Protection Act 1998 the information is exempt from section 7(1)(a) of that Act (data subject's right to be informed whether personal data being processed).

(6) In determining for the purposes of this section whether anything done before 24th October 2007 would contravene any of the data protection principles, the exemptions in Part III of Schedule 8 to the Data Protection Act 1998 shall be disregarded.

(7) In this section—

"the data protection principles" means the principles set out in Part I of Schedule 1 to the Data Protection Act 1998, as read subject to Part II of that Schedule and section 27(1) of that Act;

"data subject" has the same meaning as in section 1(1) of that Act;

"personal data" has the same meaning as in section 1(1) of that Act.

Information provided in confidence

41.—(1) Information is exempt information if—

(a) it was obtained by the public authority from any other person (including another public authority), and
(b) the disclosure of the information to the public (otherwise than under this Act) by the public authority holding it would constitute a breach of confidence actionable by that or any other person.

(2) The duty to confirm or deny does not arise if, or to the extent that, the confirmation or denial that would have to be given to comply with section 1(1)(a) would (apart from this Act) constitute an actionable breach of confidence.

Legal professional privilege

42.—(1) Information in respect of which a claim to legal professional privilege or, in Scotland, to confidentiality of communications could be maintained in legal proceedings is exempt information.

(2) The duty to confirm or deny does not arise if, or to the extent that, compliance with section 1(1)(a) would involve the disclosure of any information (whether or not already recorded) in respect of which such a claim could be maintained in legal proceedings.

Commercial interests

43.—(1) Information is exempt information if it constitutes a trade secret.

(2) Information is exempt information if its disclosure under this Act would, or would be likely to, prejudice the commercial interests of any person (including the public authority holding it).

(3) The duty to confirm or deny does not arise if, or to the extent that, compliance with section 1(1)(a) would, or would be likely to, prejudice the interests mentioned in subsection (2).

Prohibitions on disclosure

44.—(1) Information is exempt information if its disclosure (otherwise than under this Act) by the public authority holding it—

(a) is prohibited by or under any enactment,
(b) is incompatible with any Community obligation, or
(c) would constitute or be punishable as a contempt of court.

(2) The duty to confirm or deny does not arise if the confirmation or denial that would have to be given to comply with section 1(1)(a) would (apart from this Act) fall within any of paragraphs (a) to (c) of subsection (1).

PART III

GENERAL FUNCTIONS OF SECRETARY OF STATE, LORD CHANCELLOR AND INFORMATION COMMISSIONER

Issue of code of practice by the Secretary of State

45.—(1) The [Secretary of State][16] shall issue, and may from time to time revise, a code of practice providing guidance to public authorities as to the practice which it would, in his opinion, be desirable for them to follow in connection with the discharge of the authorities' functions under Part I.

(2) The code of practice must, in particular, include provision relating to—

(a) the provision of advice and assistance by public authorities to persons who propose to make, or have made, requests for information to them,

(b) the transfer of requests by one public authority to another public authority by which the information requested is or may be held,

(c) consultation with persons to whom the information requested relates or persons whose interests are likely to be affected by the disclosure of information,

(d) the inclusion in contracts entered into by public authorities of terms relating to the disclosure of information, and

(e) the provision by public authorities of procedures for dealing with complaints about the handling by them of requests for information.

(3) The code may make different provision for different public authorities.

(4) Before issuing or revising any code under this section, the [Secretary of State][17] shall consult the Commissioner.

(5) The [Secretary of State][18] shall lay before each House of Parliament any code or revised code made under this section.

Issue of code of practice by Lord Chancellor

46.—(1) The Lord Chancellor shall issue, and may from time to time revise, a code of practice providing guidance to relevant authorities as to the practice which it would, in his opinion, be desirable for them to follow in connection with the keeping, management and destruction of their records.

(2) For the purpose of facilitating the performance by the Public Record Office, the Public Record Office of Northern Ireland and other public authorities of their functions under this Act in relation to records which are public records for the purposes of the Public Records Act 1958 or the Public Records Act (Northern Ireland) 1923, the code may also include guidance as to—

(a) the practice to be adopted in relation to the transfer of records under section 3(4) of the Public Records Act 1958 or section 3 of the Public Records Act (Northern Ireland) 1923, and

(b) the practice of reviewing records before they are transferred under those provisions.

(3) In exercising his functions under this section, the Lord Chancellor shall have regard to the public interest in allowing public access to information held by relevant authorities.

---

[16] Words substituted by SI 2003/1887 (Secretary of State for Constitutional Affairs Order), Sch.2, para.12(1)(a).

[17] *ibid.*

[18] *ibid.*

(4) The code may make different provision for different relevant authorities.

(5) Before issuing or revising any code under this section the Lord Chancellor shall consult—

[(a) the Secretary of State,][19]
(b) the Commissioner, and
(c) in relation to Northern Ireland, the appropriate Northern Ireland Minister.

(6) The Lord Chancellor shall lay before each House of Parliament any code or revised code made under this section.

(7) In this section "relevant authority" means—

(a) any public authority, and
(b) any office or body which is not a public authority but whose administrative and departmental records are public records for the purposes of the Public Records Act 1958 or the Public Records Act (Northern Ireland) 1923.

General functions of Commissioner

47.—(1) It shall be the duty of the Commissioner to promote the following of good practice by public authorities and, in particular, so to perform his functions under this Act as to promote the observance by public authorities of—

(a) the requirements of this Act, and
(b) the provisions of the codes of practice under sections 45 and 46.

(2) The Commissioner shall arrange for the dissemination in such form and manner as he considers appropriate of such information as it may appear to him expedient to give to the public—

(a) about the operation of this Act,
(b) about good practice, and
(c) about other matters within the scope of his functions under this Act,

and may give advice to any person as to any of those matters.

(3) The Commissioner may, with the consent of any public authority, assess whether that authority is following good practice.

(4) The Commissioner may charge such sums as he may with the consent of the [Secretary of State][20] determine for any services provided by the Commissioner under this section.

(5) The Commissioner shall from time to time as he considers appropriate—

(a) consult the Keeper of Public Records about the promotion by the Commissioner of the observance by public authorities of the provisions of the code of practice under section 46 in relation to records which are public records for the purposes of the Public Records Act 1958, and
(b) consult the Deputy Keeper of the Records of Northern Ireland about the promotion by the Commissioner of the observance by public authorities of those provisions in relation to records which are public records for the purposes of the Public Records Act (Northern Ireland) 1923.

(6) In this section "good practice", in relation to a public authority, means such practice in the discharge of its functions under this Act as appears to the Commissioner to be

---

19 Words added by SI 2003/1887 (Secretary of State for Constitutional Affairs Order), Sch.2, para.12(2).

20 Words substituted by SI 2003/1887 (Secretary of State for constitutional Affairs Order), Sch.2, para.12(1)(a).

desirable, and includes (but is not limited to) compliance with the requirements of this Act and the provisions of the codes of practice under sections 45 and 46.

Recommendations as to good practice

48.—(1) If it appears to the Commissioner that the practice of a public authority in relation to the exercise of its functions under this Act does not conform with that proposed in the codes of practice under sections 45 and 46, he may give to the authority a recommendation (in this section referred to as a "practice recommendation") specifying the steps which ought in his opinion to be taken for promoting such conformity.

(2) A practice recommendation must be given in writing and must refer to the particular provisions of the code of practice with which, in the Commissioner's opinion, the public authority's practice does not conform.

(3) Before giving to a public authority other than the Public Record Office a practice recommendation which relates to conformity with the code of practice under section 46 in respect of records which are public records for the purposes of the Public Records Act 1958, the Commissioner shall consult the Keeper of Public Records.

(4) Before giving to a public authority other than the Public Record Office of Northern Ireland a practice recommendation which relates to conformity with the code of practice under section 46 in respect of records which are public records for the purposes of the Public Records Act (Northern Ireland) 1923, the Commissioner shall consult the Deputy Keeper of the Records of Northern Ireland.

Reports to be laid before Parliament

49.—(1) The Commissioner shall lay annually before each House of Parliament a general report on the exercise of his functions under this Act.

(2) The Commissioner may from time to time lay before each House of Parliament such other reports with respect to those functions as he thinks fit.

PART IV

ENFORCEMENT

Application for decision by Commissioner

50.—(1) Any person (in this section referred to as "the complainant") may apply to the Commissioner for a decision whether, in any specified respect, a request for information made by the complainant to a public authority has been dealt with in accordance with the requirements of Part I.

(2) On receiving an application under this section, the Commissioner shall make a decision unless it appears to him—

(a) that the complainant has not exhausted any complaints procedure which is provided by the public authority in conformity with the code of practice under section 45,

(b) that there has been undue delay in making the application,

(c) that the application is frivolous or vexatious, or

(d) that the application has been withdrawn or abandoned.

(3) Where the Commissioner has received an application under this section, he shall either—

(a) notify the complainant that he has not made any decision under this section as a result of the application and of his grounds for not doing so, or
(b) serve notice of his decision (in this Act referred to as a "decision notice") on the complainant and the public authority.

(4) Where the Commissioner decides that a public authority—

(a) has failed to communicate information, or to provide confirmation or denial, in a case where it is required to do so by section 1(1), or
(b) has failed to comply with any of the requirements of sections 11 and 17,

the decision notice must specify the steps which must be taken by the authority for complying with that requirement and the period within which they must be taken.

(5) A decision notice must contain particulars of the right of appeal conferred by section 57.

(6) Where a decision notice requires steps to be taken by the public authority within a specified period, the time specified in the notice must not expire before the end of the period within which an appeal can be brought against the notice and, if such an appeal is brought, no step which is affected by the appeal need be taken pending the determination or withdrawal of the appeal.

(7) This section has effect subject to section 53.

Information notices

51.—(1) If the Commissioner—

(a) has received an application under section 50, or
(b) reasonably requires any information—
    (i) for the purpose of determining whether a public authority has complied or is complying with any of the requirements of Part I, or
    (ii) for the purpose of determining whether the practice of a public authority in relation to the exercise of its functions under this Act conforms with that proposed in the codes of practice under sections 45 and 46,

he may serve the authority with a notice (in this Act referred to as "an information notice") requiring it, within such time as is specified in the notice, to furnish the Commissioner, in such form as may be so specified, with such information relating to the application, to compliance with Part I or to conformity with the code of practice as is so specified.

(2) An information notice must contain—

(a) in a case falling within subsection (1)(a), a statement that the Commissioner has received an application under section 50, or
(b) in a case falling within subsection (1)(b), a statement—
    (i) that the Commissioner regards the specified information as relevant for either of the purposes referred to in subsection (1)(b), and
    (ii) of his reasons for regarding that information as relevant for that purpose.

(3) An information notice must also contain particulars of he right of appeal conferred by section 57.

(4) The time specified in an information notice must not expire before the end of the period within which an appeal can be brought against the notice and, if such an appeal is brought, the information need not be furnished pending the determination or withdrawal of the appeal.

(5) An authority shall not be required by virtue of this section to furnish the Commissioner with any information in respect of—

(a) any communication between a professional legal adviser and his client in connection with the giving of legal advice to the client with respect to his obligations, liabilities or rights under this Act, or
(b) any communication between a professional legal adviser and his client, or between such an adviser or his client and any other person, made in connection with or in contemplation of proceedings under or arising out of this Act (including proceedings before the Tribunal) and for the purposes of such proceedings.

(6) In subsection (5) references to the client of a professional legal adviser include references to any person representing such a client.

(7) The Commissioner may cancel an information notice by written notice to the authority on which it was served.

(8) In this section "information" includes unrecorded information.

Enforcement notices

52.—(1) If the Commissioner is satisfied that a public authority has failed to comply with any of the requirements of Part I, the Commissioner may serve the authority with a notice (in this Act referred to as "an enforcement notice") requiring the authority to take, within such time as may be specified in the notice, such steps as may be so specified for complying with those requirements.

(2) An enforcement notice must contain—

(a) a statement of the requirement or requirements of Part I with which the Commissioner is satisfied that the public authority has failed to comply and his reasons for reaching that conclusion, and
(b) particulars of the right of appeal conferred by section 57.

(3) An enforcement notice must not require any of the provisions of the notice to be complied with before the end of the period within which an appeal can be brought against the notice and, if such an appeal is brought, the notice need not be complied with pending the determination or withdrawal of the appeal.

(4) The Commissioner may cancel an enforcement notice by written notice to the authority on which it was served.

(5) This section has effect subject to section 53.

Exception from duty to comply with decision notice or enforcement notice

53.—(1) This section applies to a decision notice or enforcement notice which—

(a) is served on—

(i) a government department,
(ii) the National Assembly for Wales, or
(iii) any public authority designated for the purposes of this section by an order made by the [Secretary of State],[21] and

(b) relates to a failure, in respect of one or more requests for information—

(i) to comply with section 1(1)(a) in respect of information which falls within any provision of Part II stating that the duty to confirm or deny does not arise, or
(ii) to comply with section 1(1)(b) in respect of exempt information.

(2) A decision notice or enforcement notice to which this section applies shall cease to

[21] Words substituted by SI 2003/1887 (Secretary of State for Constitutional Affairs Order), Sch.2, para.12(1)(a).

have effect if, not later than the twentieth working day following the effective date, the accountable person in relation to that authority gives the Commissioner a certificate signed by him stating that he has on reasonable grounds formed the opinion that, in respect of the request or requests concerned, there was no failure falling within subsection (1)(b).

(3) Where the accountable person gives a certificate to the Commissioner under subsection (2) he shall as soon as practicable thereafter lay a copy of the certificate before—

(a) each House of Parliament,
(b) the Northern Ireland Assembly, in any case where the certificate relates to a decision notice or enforcement notice which has been served on a Northern Ireland department or any Northern Ireland public authority, or
(c) the National Assembly for Wales, in any case where the certificate relates to a decision notice or enforcement notice which has been served on the National Assembly for Wales or any Welsh public authority.

(4) In subsection (2) "the effective date", in relation to a decision notice or enforcement notice, means—

(a) the day on which the notice was given to the public authority, or
(b) where an appeal under section 57 is brought, the day on which that appeal (or any further appeal arising out of it) is determined or withdrawn.

(5) Before making an order under subsection (1)(a)(iii), the [Secretary of State][22] shall—

(a) if the order relates to a Welsh public authority, consult the National Assembly for Wales,
(b) if the order relates to the Northern Ireland Assembly, consult the Presiding Officer of that Assembly, and
(c) if the order relates to a Northern Ireland public authority, consult the First Minister and deputy First Minister in Northern Ireland.

(6) Where the accountable person gives a certificate to the Commissioner under subsection (2) in relation to a decision notice, the accountable person shall, on doing so or as soon as reasonably practicable after doing so, inform the person who is the complainant for the purposes of section 50 of the reasons for his opinion.

(7) The accountable person is not obliged to provide information under subsection (6) if, or to the extent that, compliance with that subsection would involve the disclosure of exempt information.

(8) In this section "the accountable person"—

(a) in relation to a Northern Ireland department or any Northern Ireland public authority, means the First Minister and deputy First Minister in Northern Ireland acting jointly,
(b) in relation to the National Assembly for Wales or any Welsh public authority, means the Assembly First Secretary, and
(c) in relation to any other public authority, means—
    (i) a Minister of the Crown who is a member of the Cabinet, or
    (ii) the Attorney General, the Advocate General for Scotland or the Attorney General for Northern Ireland.

(9) In this section "working day" has the same meaning as in section 10.

---

[22] Words substituted by SI 2003/1887 (Secretary of State for Constitutional Affairs Order), Sch.2, para.12(1)(a).

Failure to comply with notice

54.—(1) If a public authority has failed to comply with—

(a) so much of a decision notice as requires steps to be taken,
(b) an information notice, or
(c) an enforcement notice,

the Commissioner may certify in writing to the court that the public authority has failed to comply with that notice.

(2) For the purposes of this section, a public authority which, in purported compliance with an information notice—

(a) makes a statement which it knows to be false in a material respect, or
(b) recklessly makes a statement which is false in a material respect,

is to be taken to have failed to comply with the notice.

(3) Where a failure to comply is certified under subsection (1), the court may inquire into the matter and, after hearing any witness who may be produced against or on behalf of the public authority, and after hearing any statement that may be offered in defence, deal with the authority as if it had committed a contempt of court.

(4) In this section "the court" means the High Court or, in Scotland, the Court of Session.

Powers of entry and inspection

55.—Schedule 3 (powers of entry and inspection) has effect.

No action against public authority

56.—(1) This Act does not confer any right of action in civil proceedings in respect of any failure to comply with any duty imposed by or under this Act.

(2) Subsection (1) does not affect the powers of the Commissioner under section 54.

PART V

APPEALS

Appeal against notice served under Part IV

57.—(1) Where a decision notice has been served, the complainant or the public authority may appeal to the Tribunal against the notice.

(2) A public authority on which an information notice or an enforcement notice has been served by the Commissioner may appeal to the Tribunal against the notice.

(3) In relation to a decision notice or enforcement notice which relates—

(a) to information to which section 66 applies, and
(b) to a matter which by virtue of subsection (3) or (4) of that section falls to be determined by the responsible authority instead of the appropriate records authority,

subsections (1) and (2) shall have effect as if the reference to the public authority were a reference to the public authority or the responsible authority.

Determination of appeals

58.—(1) If on an appeal under section 57 the Tribunal considers—

(a) that the notice against which the appeal is brought is not in accordance with the law, or
(b) to the extent that the notice involved an exercise of discretion by the Commissioner, that he ought to have exercised his discretion differently,

the Tribunal shall allow the appeal or substitute such other notice as could have been served by the Commissioner; and in any other case the Tribunal shall dismiss the appeal.

(2) On such an appeal, the Tribunal may review any finding of fact on which the notice in question was based.

Appeals from decision of Tribunal

59.—Any party to an appeal to the Tribunal under section 57 may appeal from the decision of the Tribunal on a point of law to the appropriate court; and that court shall be—

(a) the High Court of Justice in England if the address of the public authority is in England or Wales,
(b) the Court of Session if that address is in Scotland, and
(c) the High Court of Justice in Northern Ireland if that address is in Northern Ireland.

Appeals against national security certificate

60.—(1) Where a certificate under section 23(2) or 24(3) has been issued—

(a) the Commissioner, or
(b) any applicant whose request for information is affected by the issue of the certificate,

may appeal to the Tribunal against the certificate.

(2) If on an appeal under subsection (1) relating to a certificate under section 23(2), the Tribunal finds that the information referred to in the certificate was not exempt information by virtue of section 23(1), the Tribunal may allow the appeal and quash the certificate.

(3) If on an appeal under subsection (1) relating to a certificate under section 24(3), the Tribunal finds that, applying the principles applied by the court on an application for judicial review, the Minister did not have reasonable grounds for issuing the certificate, the Tribunal may allow the appeal and quash the certificate.

(4) Where in any proceedings under this Act it is claimed by a public authority that a certificate under section 24(3) which identifies the information to which it applies by means of a general description applies to particular information, any other party to the proceedings may appeal to the Tribunal on the ground that the certificate does not apply to the information in question and, subject to any determination under subsection (5), the certificate shall be conclusively presumed so to apply.

(5) On any appeal under subsection (4), the Tribunal may determine that the certificate does not so apply.

Appeal proceedings

61.—(1) Schedule 4 (which contains amendments of Schedule 6 to the Data Protection Act 1998 relating to appeal proceedings) has effect.

(2) Accordingly, the provisions of Schedule 6 to the Data Protection Act 1998 have effect (so far as applicable) in relation to appeals under this Part.

PART VI

HISTORICAL RECORDS AND RECORDS IN PUBLIC RECORD OFFICE OR PUBLIC RECORD OFFICE OF NORTHERN IRELAND

Interpretation of Part VI

62.—(1) For the purposes of this Part, a record becomes a "historical record" at the end of the period of thirty years beginning with the year following that in which it was created.

(2) Where records created at different dates are for administrative purposes kept together in one file or other assembly, all the records in that file or other assembly are to be treated for the purposes of this Part as having been created when the latest of those records was created.

(3) In this Part "year" means a calendar year.

Removal of exemptions: historical records generally

63.—(1) Information contained in a historical record cannot be exempt information by virtue of section 28, 30(1), 32, 33, 35, 36, 37(1)(a), 42 or 43.

(2) Compliance with section 1(1)(a) in relation to a historical record is not to be taken to be capable of having any of the effects referred to in section 28(3), 33(3), 36(3), 42(2) or 43(3).

(3) Information cannot be exempt information by virtue of section 37(1)(b) after the end of the period of sixty years beginning with the year following that in which the record containing the information was created.

(4) Information cannot be exempt information by virtue of section 31 after the end of the period of one hundred years beginning with the year following that in which the record containing the information was created.

(5) Compliance with section 1(1)(a) in relation to any record is not to be taken, at any time after the end of the period of one hundred years beginning with the year following that in which the record was created, to be capable of prejudicing any of the matters referred to in section 31(1).

Removal of exemptions: historical records in public record offices

64.—(1) Information contained in a historical record in the Public Record Office or the Public Record Office of Northern Ireland cannot be exempt information by virtue of section 21 or 22.

(2) In relation to any information falling within section 23(1) which is contained in a historical record in the Public Record Office or the Public Record Office of Northern Ireland, section 2(3) shall have effect with the omission of the reference to section 23.

Decisions as to refusal of discretionary disclosure of historical records

65.—(1) Before refusing a request for information relating to information which is contained in a historical record and is exempt information only by virtue of a provision not specified in section 2(3), a public authority shall—

(a) if the historical record is a public record within the meaning of the Public Records Act 1958, consult the Lord Chancellor, or

(b) if the historical record is a public record to which the Public Records Act (Northern Ireland) 1923 applies, consult the appropriate Northern Ireland Minister.

(2) This section does not apply to information to which section 66 applies.

Decisions relating to certain transferred public records

66.—(1) This section applies to any information which is (or, if it existed, would be) contained in a transferred public record, other than information which the responsible authority has designated as open information for the purposes of this section.

(2) Before determining whether—

(a) information to which this section applies falls within any provision of Part II relating to the duty to confirm or deny, or
(b) information to which this section applies is exempt information,

the appropriate records authority shall consult the responsible authority.

(3) Where information to which this section applies falls within a provision of Part II relating to the duty to confirm or deny but does not fall within any of the provisions of that Part relating to that duty which are specified in subsection (3) of section 2, any question as to the application of subsection (1)(b) of that section is to be determined by the responsible authority instead of the appropriate records authority.

(4) Where any information to which this section applies is exempt information only by virtue of any provision of Part II not specified in subsection (3) of section 2, any question as to the application of subsection (2)(b) of that section is to be determined by the responsible authority instead of the appropriate records authority.

(5) Before making by virtue of subsection (3) or (4) any determination that subsection (1)(b) or (2)(b) of section 2 applies, the responsible authority shall consult—

(a) where the transferred public record is a public record within the meaning of the Public Records Act 1958, the Lord Chancellor, and
(b) where the transferred public record is a public record to which the Public Records Act (Northern Ireland) 1923 applies, the appropriate Northern Ireland Minister.

(6) Where the responsible authority in relation to information to which this section applies is not (apart from this subsection) a public authority, it shall be treated as being a public authority for the purposes of Parts III, IV and V of this Act so far as relating to—

(a) the duty imposed by section 15(3), and
(b) the imposition of any requirement to furnish information relating to compliance with Part I in connection with the information to which this section applies.

Amendments of public records legislation

67.—Schedule 5 (which amends the Public Records Act 1958 and the Public Records Act (Northern Ireland) 1923) has effect.

PART VII

AMENDMENTS OF DATA PROTECTION ACT 1998

Amendments relating to personal information held by public authorities

Extension of meaning of "data"

68.—(1) Section 1 of the Data Protection Act 1998 (basic interpretative provisions) is amended in accordance with subsections (2) and (3).

(2) In subsection (1)—

(a) in the definition of "data", the word "or" at the end of paragraph (c) is omitted and after paragraph (d) there is inserted

"or

(e) is recorded information held by a public authority and does not fall within any of paragraphs (a) to (d);"

, and

(b) after the definition of "processing" there is inserted—

"'public authority' has the same meaning as in the Freedom of Information Act 2000;".

(3) After subsection (4) there is inserted—

"(5) In paragraph (e) of the definition of "data" in subsection (1); the reference to information "held" by a public authority shall be construed in accordance with section 3(2) of the Freedom of Information Act 2000.

(6) Where section 7 of the Freedom of Information Act 2000 prevents Parts I to V of that Act from applying to certain information held by a public authority, that information is not to be treated for the purposes of paragraph (e) of the definition of "data" in subsection (1) as held by a public authority."

(4) In section 56 of that Act (prohibition of requirement as to production of certain records), after subsection (6) there is inserted—

"(6A) A record is not a relevant record to the extent that it relates, or is to relate, only to personal data falling within paragraph (e) of the definition of "data" in section 1(1)."

(5) In the Table in section 71 of that Act[23] (index of defined expressions) after the entry relating to processing there is inserted—[. . .]

Right of access to unstructured personal data held by public authorities

69.—(1) In section 7(1) of the Data Protection Act 1998 (right of access to personal data), for " sections 8 and 9" there is substituted " sections 8, 9 and 9A".

(2) After section 9 of that Act there is inserted—

"9A.—Unstructured personal data held by public authorities.

(1) In this section "unstructured personal data" means any personal data falling within paragraph (e) of the definition of "data" in section 1(1), other than information which is recorded as part of, or with the intention that it should form part of, any set of information relating to individuals to the extent that the set is structured by reference to individuals or by reference to criteria relating to individuals.

(2) A public authority is not obliged to comply with subsection (1) of section 7 in relation to any unstructured personal data unless the request under that section contains a description of the data.

(3) Even if the data are described by the data subject in his request, a public authority is not obliged to comply with subsection (1) of section 7 in relation to unstructured personal data if the authority estimates that the cost of complying with the request so far as relating to those data would exceed the appropriate limit.

(4) Subsection (3) does not exempt the public authority from its obligation to comply

[23] Table in web format not available via Offline Print. View on *uk.westlaw.com*.

with paragraph (a) of section 7(1) in relation to the unstructured personal data unless the estimated cost of complying with that paragraph alone in relation to those data would exceed the appropriate limit.

(5) In subsections (3) and (4) "the appropriate limit" means such amount as may be prescribed by the [Secretary of State][24] by regulations, and different amounts may be prescribed in relation to different cases.

(6) Any estimate for the purposes of this section must be made in accordance with regulations under section 12(5) of the Freedom of Information Act 2000."

(3) In section 67(5) of that Act (statutory instruments subject to negative resolution procedure), in paragraph (c), for "or 9(3)" there is substituted ", 9(3) or 9A(5)".

Exemptions applicable to certain manual data held by public authorities

70.—(1) After section 33 of the Data Protection Act 1998 there is inserted—

"33A.—Manual data held by public authorities.

(1) Personal data falling within paragraph (e) of the definition of "data" in section 1(1) are exempt from—

(a) the first, second, third, fifth, seventh and eighth data protection principles,

(b) the sixth data protection principle except so far as it relates to the rights conferred on data subjects by sections 7 and 14,

(c) sections 10 to 12,

(d) section 13, except so far as it relates to damage caused by a contravention of section 7 or of the fourth data protection principle and to any distress which is also suffered by reason of that contravention,

(e) Part III, and

(f) section 55.

(2) Personal data which fall within paragraph (e) of the definition of "data" in section 1(1) and relate to appointments or removals, pay, discipline, superannuation or other personnel matters, in relation to—

(a) service in any of the armed forces of the Crown,

(b) service in any office or employment under the Crown or under any public authority, or

(c) service in any office or employment, or under any contract for services, in respect of which power to take action, or to determine or approve the action taken, in such matters is vested in Her Majesty, any Minister of the Crown, the National Assembly for Wales, any Northern Ireland Minister (within the meaning of the Freedom of Information Act 2000) or any public authority,

are also exempt from the remaining data protection principles and the remaining provisions of Part II."

(2) In section 55 of that Act (unlawful obtaining etc. of personal data) in subsection (8) after " section 28" there is inserted "or 33A".

(3) In Part III of Schedule 8 to that Act (exemptions available after 23rd October 2001 but before 24th October 2007) after paragraph 14 there is inserted—

"14A.—

(1) This paragraph applies to personal data which fall within paragraph (e) of the definition of "data" in section 1(1) and do not fall within paragraph 14(1)(a), but does not apply to eligible manual data to which the exemption in paragraph 16 applies.

[24] Words substituted by SI 2003/1887 (Secretary of State for Constitutional Affairs Order), Sch.2, para.12(1)(b).

(2) During the second transitional period, data to which this paragraph applies are exempt from—

(a) the fourth data protection principle, and

(b) section 14(1) to (3)."

(4) In Schedule 13 to that Act (modifications of Act having effect before 24th October 2007) in subsection (4)(b) of section 12A to that Act as set out in paragraph 1, after " paragraph 14" there is inserted "or 14A".

Particulars registrable under Part III of Data Protection Act 1998

71.—In section 16(1) of the Data Protection Act 1998 (the registrable particulars), before the word "and" at the end of paragraph (f) there is inserted—

"(ff) where the data controller is a public authority, a statement of that fact,".

Availability under Act disregarded for purpose of exemption

72.—In section 34 of the Data Protection Act 1998 (information available to the public by or under enactment), after the word "enactment" there is inserted "other than an enactment contained in the Freedom of Information Act 2000".

Other amendments

Further amendments of Data Protection Act 1998

73.—Schedule 6 (which contains further amendments of the Data Protection Act 1998) has effect.

PART VIII

MISCELLANEOUS AND SUPPLEMENTAL

Power to make provision relating to environmental information

74.—(1) In this section "the Aarhus Convention" means the Convention on Access to Information, Public Participation in Decision-making and Access to Justice in Environmental Matters signed at Aarhus on 25th June 1998.

(2) For the purposes of this section "the information provisions" of the Aarhus Convention are Article 4, together with Articles 3 and 9 so far as relating to that Article.

(3) The Secretary of State may by regulations make such provision as he considers appropriate—

(a) for the purpose of implementing the information provisions of the Aarhus Convention or any amendment of those provisions made in accordance with Article 14 of the Convention, and

(b) for the purpose of dealing with matters arising out of or related to the implementation of those provisions or of any such amendment.

(4) Regulations under subsection (3) may in particular—

(a) enable charges to be made for making information available in accordance with the regulations,

(b) provide that any obligation imposed by the regulations in relation to the disclosure of information is to have effect notwithstanding any enactment or rule of law,
(c) make provision for the issue by the Secretary of State of a code of practice,
(d) provide for sections 47 and 48 to apply in relation to such a code with such modifications as may be specified,
(e) provide for any of the provisions of Parts IV and V to apply, with such modifications as may be specified in the regulations, in relation to compliance with any requirement of the regulations, and
(f) contain such transitional or consequential provision (including provision modifying any enactment) as the Secretary of State considers appropriate.

(5) This section has effect subject to section 80.

Power to amend or repeal enactments prohibiting disclosure of information

75.—(1) If, with respect to any enactment which prohibits the disclosure of information held by a public authority, it appears to the [Secretary of State][25] that by virtue of section 44(1)(a) the enactment is capable of preventing the disclosure of information under section 1, he may by order repeal or amend the enactment for the purpose of removing or relaxing the prohibition.

(2) In subsection (1)—

"enactment" means—

(a) any enactment contained in an Act passed before or in the same Session as this Act, or
(b) any enactment contained in Northern Ireland legislation or subordinate legislation passed or made before the passing of this Act;

"information" includes unrecorded information.

(3) An order under this section may do all or any of the following—

(a) make such modifications of enactments as, in the opinion of the [Secretary of State],[26] are consequential upon, or incidental to, the amendment or repeal of the enactment containing the prohibition;
(b) contain such transitional provisions and savings as appear to the [Secretary of State][27] to be appropriate;
(c) make different provision for different cases.

Disclosure of information between Commissioner and ombudsmen

76.—(1) The Commissioner may disclose to a person specified in the first column of the Table below[28] any information obtained by, or furnished to, the Commissioner under or for the purposes of this Act or the Data Protection Act 1998 if it appears to the Commissioner that the information relates to a matter which could be the subject of an investigation by that person under the enactment specified in relation to that person in the second column of that Table.

(2) Schedule 7 (which contains amendments relating to information disclosed to ombudsmen under subsection (1) and to the disclosure of information by ombudsmen to the Commissioner) has effect.

[25] Words substituted by SI 2003/1887 (Secretary of State for Constitutional Affairs Order), Sch.2, para.12(1)(c).
[26] *ibid.*
[27] *ibid.*
[28] Table in web format not available via Offline Print. View on *uk.westlaw.com*.

Offence of altering etc. records with intent to prevent disclosure

77.—(1) Where—

(a) a request for information has been made to a public authority, and
(b) under section 1 of this Act or section 7 of the Data Protection Act 1998, the applicant would have been entitled (subject to payment of any fee) to communication of any information in accordance with that section,

any person to whom this subsection applies is guilty of an offence if he alters, defaces, blocks, erases, destroys or conceals any record held by the public authority, with the intention of preventing the disclosure by that authority of all, or any part, of the information to the communication of which the applicant would have been entitled.

(2) Subsection (1) applies to the public authority and to any person who is employed by, is an officer of, or is subject to the direction of, the public authority.

(3) A person guilty of an offence under this section is liable on summary conviction to a fine not exceeding level 5 on the standard scale.

(4) No proceedings for an offence under this section shall be instituted—

(a) in England or Wales, except by the Commissioner or by or with the consent of the Director of Public Prosecutions;
(b) in Northern Ireland, except by the Commissioner or by or with the consent of the Director of Public Prosecutions for Northern Ireland.

Saving for existing powers

78.—Nothing in this Act is to be taken to limit the powers of a public authority to disclose information held by it.

Defamation

79.—Where any information communicated by a public authority to a person ("the applicant") under section 1 was supplied to the public authority by a third person, the publication to the applicant of any defamatory matter contained in the information shall be privileged unless the publication is shown to have been made with malice.

Scotland

80.—(1) No order may be made under section 4(1) or 5 in relation to any of the bodies specified in subsection (2); and the power conferred by section 74(3) does not include power to make provision in relation to information held by any of those bodies.

(2) The bodies referred to in subsection (1) are—

(a) the Scottish Parliament,
(b) any part of the Scottish Administration,
(c) the Scottish Parliamentary Corporate Body, or
(d) any Scottish public authority with mixed functions or no reserved functions (within the meaning of the Scotland Act 1998).

Application to government departments, etc.

81.—(1) For the purposes of this Act each government department is to be treated as a person separate from any other government department.

(2) Subsection (1) does not enable—

(a) a government department which is not a Northern Ireland department to claim for the purposes of section 41(1)(b) that the disclosure of any information by it would constitute a breach of confidence actionable by any other government department (not being a Northern Ireland department), or

(b) a Northern Ireland department to claim for those purposes that the disclosure of information by it would constitute a breach of confidence actionable by any other Northern Ireland department.

(3) A government department is not liable to prosecution under this Act, but section 77 and paragraph 12 of Schedule 3 apply to a person in the public service of the Crown as they apply to any other person.

(4) The provisions specified in subsection (3) also apply to a person acting on behalf of either House of Parliament or on behalf of the Northern Ireland Assembly as they apply to any other person.

Orders and regulations

82.—(1) Any power of the [. . .][29] Secretary of State to make an order or regulations under this Act shall be exercisable by statutory instrument.

(2) A statutory instrument containing (whether alone or with other provisions)—

(a) an order under section 5, 7(3) or (8), 53(1)(a)(iii) or 75, or
(b) regulations under section 10(4) or 74(3),

shall not be made unless a draft of the instrument has been laid before, and approved by a resolution of, each House of Parliament.

(3) A statutory instrument which contains (whether alone or with other provisions)—

(a) an order under section 4(1), or
(b) regulations under any provision of this Act not specified in subsection (2)(b),

and which is not subject to the requirement in subsection (2) that a draft of the instrument be laid before and approved by a resolution of each House of Parliament, shall be subject to annulment in pursuance of a resolution of either House of Parliament.

(4) An order under section 4(5) shall be laid before Parliament after being made.

(5) If a draft of an order under section 5 or 7(8) would, apart from this subsection, be treated for the purposes of the Standing Orders of either House of Parliament as a hybrid instrument, it shall proceed in that House as if it were not such an instrument.

Meaning of "Welsh public authority"

83.—(1) In this Act "Welsh public authority" means—

(a) any public authority which is listed in Part II, III, IV or VI of Schedule 1 and whose functions are exercisable only or mainly in or as regards Wales, other than an excluded authority, or
(b) any public authority which is an Assembly subsidiary as defined by section 99(4) of the Government of Wales Act 1998.

(2) In paragraph (a) of subsection (1) "excluded authority" means a public authority which is designated by the [Secretary of State][30] by order as an excluded authority for the purposes of that paragraph.

(3) Before making an order under subsection (2), the [Secretary of State][31] shall consult the National Assembly for Wales.

---

[29] Words repealed by SI 2003/1887 (Secretary of State for Constitutional Affairs Order), Sch.2, para.12(3).

[30] Words substituted by SI 2003/1887 (Secretary of State for Constitutional Affairs Order), Sch.2, para.12(1)(c).

[31] *ibid.*

Interpretation

84.—In this Act, unless the context otherwise requires—

"applicant", in relation to a request for information, means the person who made the request;

"appropriate Northern Ireland Minister" means the Northern Ireland Minister in charge of the Department of Culture, Arts and Leisure in Northern Ireland;

"appropriate records authority", in relation to a transferred public record, has the meaning given by section 15(5);

"body" includes an unincorporated association;

"the Commissioner" means the Information Commissioner;

"decision notice" has the meaning given by section 50;

"the duty to confirm or deny" has the meaning given by section 1(6);

"enactment" includes an enactment contained in Northern Ireland legislation;

"enforcement notice" has the meaning given by section 52;

"executive committee", in relation to the National Assembly for Wales, has the same meaning as in the Government of Wales Act 1998;

"exempt information" means information which is exempt information by virtue of any provision of Part II;

"fees notice" has the meaning given by section 9(1);

"government department" includes a Northern Ireland department, the Northern Ireland Court Service and any other body or authority exercising statutory functions on behalf of the Crown, but does not include—

(a) any of the bodies specified in section 80(2),
(b) the Security Service, the Secret Intelligence Service or the Government Communications Headquarters, or
(c) the National Assembly for Wales;

"information" (subject to sections 51(8) and 75(2)) means information recorded in any form;

"information notice" has the meaning given by section 51;

"Minister of the Crown" has the same meaning as in the Ministers of the Crown Act 1975;

"Northern Ireland Minister" includes the First Minister and deputy First Minister in Northern Ireland;

"Northern Ireland public authority" means any public authority, other than the Northern Ireland Assembly or a Northern Ireland department, whose functions are exercisable only or mainly in or as regards Northern Ireland and relate only or mainly to transferred matters;

"prescribed" means prescribed by regulations made by the [Secretary of State][32];

"public authority" has the meaning given by section 3(1);

[32] *ibid.*

"public record" means a public record within the meaning of the Public Records Act 1958 or a public record to which the Public Records Act (Northern Ireland) 1923 applies;

"publication scheme" has the meaning given by section 19;

"request for information" has the meaning given by section 8;

"responsible authority", in relation to a transferred public record, has the meaning given by section 15(5);

"the special forces" means those units of the armed forces of the Crown the maintenance of whose capabilities is the responsibility of the Director of Special Forces or which are for the time being subject to the operational command of that Director;

"subordinate legislation" has the meaning given by subsection (1) of section 21 of the Interpretation Act 1978, except that the definition of that term in that subsection shall have effect as if "Act" included Northern Ireland legislation;

"transferred matter", in relation to Northern Ireland, has the meaning given by section 4(1) of the Northern Ireland Act 1998;

"transferred public record" has the meaning given by section 15(4);

"the Tribunal" means the Information Tribunal;

"Welsh public authority" has the meaning given by section 83.

Expenses

85.—There shall be paid out of money provided by Parliament—

(a) any increase attributable to this Act in the expenses of the [Secretary of State][33] in respect of the Commissioner, the Tribunal or the members of the Tribunal,
(b) any administrative expenses of the [Secretary of State][34] attributable to this Act,
(c) any other expenses incurred in consequence of this Act by a Minister of the Crown or government department or by either House of Parliament, and
(d) any increase attributable to this Act in the sums which under any other Act are payable out of money so provided.

Repeals

86.—Schedule 8 (repeals) has effect.

Commencement

87.—(1) The following provisions of this Act shall come into force on the day on which this Act is passed—

(a) sections 3 to 8 and Schedule 1,
(b) section 19 so far as relating to the approval of publication schemes,
(c) section 20 so far as relating to the approval and preparation by the Commissioner of model publication schemes,
(d) section 47(2) to (6),
(e) section 49,
(f) section 74,
(g) section 75,

33 Words substituted by SI 2003/1887 (Secretary of State for Constitutional Affairs Order), Sch.2, para.12(1)(c).

34 *ibid.*

(h) sections 78 to 85 and this section,
(i) paragraphs 2 and 17 to 22 of Schedule 2 (and section 18(4) so far as relating to those paragraphs),
(j) paragraph 4 of Schedule 5 (and section 67 so far as relating to that paragraph),
(k) paragraph 8 of Schedule 6 (and section 73 so far as relating to that paragraph),
(l) Part I of Schedule 8 (and section 86 so far as relating to that Part), and
(m) so much of any other provision of this Act as confers power to make any order, regulations or code of practice.

(2) The following provisions of this Act shall come into force at the end of the period of two months beginning with the day on which this Act is passed—

(a) section 18(1),
(b) section 76 and Schedule 7,
(c) paragraphs 1(1), 3(1), 4, 6, 7, 8(2), 9(2), 10(a), 13(1) and (2), 14(a) and 15(1) and (2) of Schedule 2 (and section 18(4) so far as relating to those provisions), and
(d) Part II of Schedule 8 (and section 86 so far as relating to that Part).

(3) Except as provided by subsections (1) and (2), this Act shall come into force at the end of the period of five years beginning with the day on which this Act is passed or on such day before the end of that period as the [Secretary of State][35] may by order appoint; and different days may be appointed for different purposes.

(4) An order under subsection (3) may contain such transitional provisions and savings (including provisions capable of having effect after the end of the period referred to in that subsection) as the [Secretary of State][36] considers appropriate.

(5) During the twelve months beginning with the day on which this Act is passed, and during each subsequent complete period of twelve months in the period beginning with that day and ending with the first day on which all the provisions of this Act are fully in force, the [Secretary of State][37] shall—

(a) prepare a report on his proposals for bringing fully into force those provisions of this Act which are not yet fully in force, and
(b) lay a copy of the report before each House of Parliament.

Short title and extent

88.—(1) This Act may be cited as the Freedom of Information Act 2000.

(2) Subject to subsection (3), this Act extends to Northern Ireland.

(3) The amendment or repeal of any enactment by this Act has the same extent as that enactment.

SCHEDULES

SCHEDULE 1

PUBLIC AUTHORITIES

PART I

GENERAL

1.—Any government department.

[35] *ibid.*
[36] *ibid.*
[37] *ibid.*

2.—The House of Commons.

3.—The House of Lords.

4.—The Northern Ireland Assembly.

5.—The National Assembly for Wales.

6.—The armed forces of the Crown, except—
(a) the special forces, and
(b) any unit or part of a unit which is for the time being required by the Secretary of State to assist the Government Communications Headquarters in the exercise of its functions.

PART II

LOCAL GOVERNMENT

England and Wales

7.—A local authority within the meaning of the Local Government Act 1972, namely—
(a) in England, a county council, a London borough council, a district council or a parish council,
(b) in Wales, a county council, a county borough council or a community council.

8.—The Greater London Authority.

9.—The Common Council of the City of London, in respect of information held in its capacity as a local authority, police authority or port health authority.

10.—The Sub-Treasurer of the Inner Temple or the Under-Treasurer of the Middle Temple, in respect of information held in his capacity as a local authority.

11.—The Council of the Isles of Scilly.

12.—A parish meeting constituted under section 13 of the Local Government Act 1972.

13.—Any charter trustees constituted under section 246 of the Local Government Act 1972.

14.—A fire authority constituted by a combination scheme under section 5 or 6 of the Fire Services Act 1947.

15.—A waste disposal authority established by virtue of an order under section 10(1) of the Local Government Act 1985.

16.—A port health authority constituted by an order under section 2 of the Public Health (Control of Disease) Act 1984.

17.—A licensing planning committee constituted under section 119 of the Licensing Act 1964.

18.—An internal drainage board which is continued in being by virtue of section 1 of the Land Drainage Act 1991.

19.—A joint authority established under Part IV of the Local Government Act 1985 (fire services, civil defence and transport).

20.—The London Fire and Emergency Planning Authority.

21.—A joint fire authority established by virtue of an order under section 42(2) of the Local Government Act 1985 (reorganisation of functions).

22.—A body corporate established pursuant to an order under section 67 of the Local Government Act 1985 (transfer of functions to successors of residuary bodies, etc.).

23.—A body corporate established pursuant to an order under section 22 of the Local Government Act 1992 (residuary bodies).

24.—The Broads Authority established by section 1 of the Norfolk and Suffolk Broads Act 1988.

25.—A joint committee constituted in accordance with section 102(1)(b) of the Local Government Act 1972.

26.—A joint board which is continued in being by virtue of section 263(1) of the Local Government Act 1972.

27.—A joint authority established under section 21 of the Local Government Act 1992.

28.—A Passenger Transport Executive for a passenger transport area within the meaning of Part II of the Transport Act 1968.

29.—Transport for London.

30.—The London Transport Users Committee.

31.—A joint board the constituent members of which consist of any of the public authorities described in paragraphs 8, 9, 10, 12, 15, 16, 20 to 31, 57 and 58.

32.—A National Park authority established by an order under section 63 of the Environment Act 1995.

33.—A joint planning board constituted for an area in Wales outside a National Park by an order under section 2(1B) of the Town and Country Planning Act 1990.

34.—A magistrates' court committee established under section 27 of the Justices of the Peace Act 1997.

35.—The London Development Agency.

Northern Ireland

36.—A district council within the meaning of the Local Government Act (Northern Ireland) 1972.

PART III

THE NATIONAL HEALTH SERVICE

England and Wales

36A.—A Strategic Health Authority established under section 8 of the National Health Service Act 1977.[38]

37.—A Health Authority established under section 8 of the National Health Service Act 1977.

38.—A special health authority established under section 11 of the National Health Service Act 1977.

39.—A primary care trust established under section 16A of the National Health Service Act 1977.

39A.—A Local Health Board established under section 16BA of the National Health Service Act 1977.[39,40]

40.—A National Health Service trust established under section 5 of the National Health Service and Community Care Act 1990.

41.—A Community Health Council established under section 20 of the National Health Service Act 1977.[40a]

41A.—A Patients' Forum established under section 15 of the National Health Service Reform and Health Care Professions Act 2002.[40b]

---

[38] Words added by SI 2002/2469 (National Health Service Reform and Health Care Professions Act 2002 (Supplementary, Consequential, etc., Provisions) Regulations), Sch.1(1) para.29.

[39] In relation to Wales: para.39A is inserted.

[40] Words added by National Health Service Reform and Health Care Professions Act (2002, c.17), Sch.5, para.48.

[40a] In relation to Wales:
"41. A Community Health Council continued in existence by or established under section 20A of the National Health Service Act 1977." As substituted by Health (Wales) Act (2003, c.4), Sch.3, para.14.

[40b] Words added by National Health Service Reform and Health Care Professions Act (2002, c.17), s.19(7).

42.—The Dental Practice Board constituted under regulations made under section 37 of the National Health Service Act 1977.

43.—The Public Health Laboratory Service Board constituted under Schedule 3 to the National Health Service Act 1977.

44.—Any person providing general medical services, general dental services, general ophthalmic services or pharmaceutical services under Part II of the National Health Service Act 1977, in respect of information relating to the provision of those services.

45.—Any person providing personal medical services or personal dental services under arrangements made under section 28C of the National Health Service Act 1977, in respect of information relating to the provision of those services.

45A.—Any person providing local pharmaceutical services under—

(a) a pilot scheme established under section 28 of the Health and Social Care Act 2001; or

(b) an LPS scheme established under Schedule 8A to the National Health Service Act 1977 (c. 49),

in respect of information relating to the provision of those services. [. . .][41]

45B.—The Commission for Patient and Public Involvement in Health.[42,43]

Northern Ireland

46.—A Health and Social Services Board established under Article 16 of the Health and Personal Social Services (Northern Ireland) Order 1972.

47.—A Health and Social Services Council established under Article 4 of the Health and Personal Social Services (Northern Ireland) Order 1991.

48.—A Health and Social Services Trust established under Article 10 of the Health and Personal Social Services (Northern Ireland) Order 1991.

49.—A special agency established under Article 3 of the Health and Personal Social Services (Special Agencies) (Northern Ireland) Order 1990.

50.—The Northern Ireland Central Services Agency for the Health and Social Services established under Article 26 of the Health and Personal Social Services (Northern Ireland) Order 1972.

51.—Any person providing general medical services, general dental services, general ophthalmic services or pharmaceutical services under Part VI of the Health and Personal Social Services (Northern Ireland) Order 1972, in respect of information relating to the provision of those services.

PART IV

MAINTAINED SCHOOLS AND OTHER EDUCATIONAL INSTITUTIONS

England and Wales

52.—The governing body of a maintained school, within the meaning of the School Standards and Framework Act 1998.[44,45]

53.—(1) The governing body of—

(a) an institution within the further education sector,

---

[41] Words added by Health and Social Care Act (2001, c.15), Sch.5(1), para.14(1).

[42] In relation to England: para.45B is inserted.

[43] Words added by National Health Service Reform and Health Care Professions Act (2002, c.17), Sch.6, para.19.

[44] In relation to England:

"52. The governing body of—

(a) a maintained school, as defined by section 20(7) of the School Standards and Framework Act 1998, or

(b) a maintained nursery school, as defined by section 22(9) of that Act."

[45] Words substituted by Education Act (2002, c.32), Sch.21, para.127.

(b) a university receiving financial support under section 65 of the Further and Higher Education Act 1992,
(c) an institution conducted by a higher education corporation,
(d) a designated institution for the purposes of Part II of the Further and Higher Education Act 1992 as defined by section 72(3) of that Act, or
(e) any college, school, hall or other institution of a university which falls within paragraph (b).

(2) In sub-paragraph (1)—
(a) "governing body" is to be interpreted in accordance with subsection (1) of section 90 of the Further and Higher Education Act 1992 but without regard to subsection (2) of that section,
(b) in paragraph (a), the reference to an institution within the further education sector is to be construed in accordance with section 91(3) of the Further and Higher Education Act 1992,
(c) in paragraph (c), "higher education corporation" has the meaning given by section 90(1) of that Act, and
(d) in paragraph (e) "college" includes any institution in the nature of a college.

Northern Ireland

54.—(1) The managers of—
(a) a controlled school, voluntary school or grant-maintained integrated school within the meaning of Article 2(2) of the Education and Libraries (Northern Ireland) Order 1986, or
(b) a pupil referral unit as defined by Article 87(1) of the Education (Northern Ireland) Order 1998.

(2) In sub-paragraph (1) "managers" has the meaning given by Article 2(2) of the Education and Libraries (Northern Ireland) Order 1986.

55.—(1) The governing body of—
(a) a university receiving financial support under Article 30 of the Education and Libraries (Northern Ireland) Order 1993,
(b) a college of education maintained in pursuance of arrangements under Article 66(1) or in respect of which grants are paid under Article 66(2) or (3) of the Education and Libraries (Northern Ireland) Order 1986, or
(c) an institution of further education within the meaning of the Further Education (Northern Ireland) Order 1997.

(2) In sub-paragraph (1) "governing body" has the meaning given by Article 30(3) of the Education and Libraries (Northern Ireland) Order 1993.

56.—Any person providing further education to whom grants, loans or other payments are made under Article 5(1)(b) of the Further Education (Northern Ireland) Order 1997.

Part V

Police

England and Wales

57.—A police authority established under section 3 of the Police Act 1996.

58.—The Metropolitan Police Authority established under section 5B of the Police Act 1996.

59.—A chief officer of police of a police force in England or Wales.

Northern Ireland

60.—The Police Authority for Northern Ireland.

61.—The Chief Constable of the Royal Ulster Constabulary.

Miscellaneous

62.—The British Transport Police.

63.—The Ministry of Defence Police established by section 1 of the Ministry of Defence Police Act 1987.

64.—Any person who—

(a) by virtue of any enactment has the function of nominating individuals who may be appointed as special constables by justices of the peace, and

(b) is not a public authority by virtue of any other provision of this Act,

in respect of information relating to the exercise by any person appointed on his nomination of the functions of a special constable.

PART VI

OTHER PUBLIC BODIES AND OFFICES

General

1.—The Adjudication Panel for Wales.
The Adjudicator for the Inland Revenue and Customs and Excise.
The Administration of Radioactive Substances Advisory Committee.
The Adult Learning Inspectorate.
[. . .][46]
The Advisory Board on Restricted Patients.
The Advisory Board on the Registration of Homoeopathic Products.
The Advisory Committee for Cleaner Coal Technology.
The Advisory Committee for Disabled People in Employment and Training.
The Advisory Committee for the Public Lending Right.
[. . .][47]
The Advisory Committee on Advertising.
The Advisory Committee on Animal Feedingstuffs.
The Advisory Committee on Borderline Substances.
The Advisory Committee on Business and the Environment.
The Advisory Committee on Business Appointments.
The Advisory Committee on Conscientious Objectors.
The Advisory Committee on Consumer Products and the Environment.
The Advisory Committee on Dangerous Pathogens.
The Advisory Committee on Distinction Awards.
An Advisory Committee on General Commissioners of Income Tax.
The Advisory Committee on the Government Art Collection
The Advisory Committee on Hazardous Substances.
The Advisory Committee on Historic Wreck Sites.
An Advisory Committee on Justices of the Peace in England and Wales.
The Advisory Committee on the Microbiological Safety of Food.
[. . .][48]
The Advisory Committee on Novel Foods and Processes.
The Advisory Committee on Overseas Economic and Social Research.
The Advisory Committee on Packaging.
The Advisory Committee on Pesticides.
The Advisory Committee on Releases to the Environment.
The Advisory Committee on Telecommunications for the Disabled and Elderly.
The Advisory Council on Historical Manuscripts.
The Advisory Council on Libraries.
The Advisory Council on the Misuse of Drugs.
The Advisory Council on National Records and Archives.
The Advisory Council on Public Records.
The Advisory Group on Hepatitis.
The Advisory Group on Medical Countermeasures.

46 Entries repealed by SI 2003/1883 (Freedom of Information (Removal of References to Public Authorities) Order), Sch.1, para.1.
47 *ibid.*
48 *ibid.*

The Advisory Panel on Beacon Councils.
The Advisory Panel on Standards for the Planning Inspectorate.
The Aerospace Committee.
An Agricultural Dwelling House Advisory Committee.
An Agricultural Wages Board for England and Wales.
An Agricultural Wages Committee.
The Agriculture and Environment Biotechnology Commission.
The Airborne Particles Expert Group.
The Air Quality Expert Group.
The All-Wales Medicines Strategy Group.
The Alcohol Education and Research Council.
The Ancient Monuments Board for Wales.
The Animal Procedures Committee.
The Animal Welfare Advisory Committee.
[. . .][49]
The Armed Forces Pay Review Body.
The Arts Council of England.
The Arts Council of Wales.
The Audit Commission for Local Authorities and the National Health Service in England and Wales.
The Auditor General for Wales.
The Authorised Conveyancing Practitioners Board.
The Bank of England, in respect of information held for purposes other than those of its functions with respect to—

(a) monetary policy,
(b) financial operations intended to support financial institutions for the purposes of maintaining stability, and
(c) the provision of private banking services and related services.

The Better Regulation Task Force.
The Biotechnology and Biological Sciences Research Council.
Any Board of Visitors established under section 6(2) of the Prison Act 1952.
The Britain-Russia Centre and East-West Centre.
The British Association for Central and Eastern Europe.
The British Broadcasting Corporation, in respect of information held for purposes other than those of journalism, art or literature.
The British Coal Corporation.
The British Council.
The British Educational Communications and Technology Agency.
The British Hallmarking Council.
The British Library.
The British Museum.
The British Pharmacopoeia Commission.
The British Potato Council.
The British Railways Board.
British Shipbuilders.
The British Tourist Authority.
The British Waterways Board.
The British Wool Marketing Board.
The Broadcasting Standards Commission.
The Building Regulations Advisory Committee.
The Business Incubation Fund Investment Panel.
The Care Council for Wales.
The Central Advisory Committee on War Pensions.
The Central Police Training and Development Authority.
The Central Rail Users' Consultative Committee.

49 Entries repealed by SI 2003/1883 (Freedom of Information (Removal of References to Public Authorities) Order), Sch.1, para.1.

The Certification Officer.
The Channel Four Television Corporation, in respect of information held for purposes other than those of journalism, art or literature.
The Children and Family Court Advisory and Support Service.
The Children's Commissioner for Wales.
The Civil Aviation Authority.
The Civil Justice Council.
The Civil Procedure Rule Committee.
The Civil Service Appeal Board.
The Civil Service Commissioners.
The Coal Authority.
The Commission for Architecture and the Built Environment.
The Commission for Health Improvement.
The Commission for Local Administration in England.
The Commission for Local Administration in Wales.
The Commission for Racial Equality.
The Commission for the New Towns.
The Commissioner for Integrated Transport.
The Commissioner for Public Appointments.
The Commissioners of Northern Lighthouses.
The Committee for Monitoring Agreements on Tobacco Advertising and Sponsorship.
The Committee of Investigation for Great Britain.
The Committee on Agricultural Valuation.
The Committee on Carcinogenicity of Chemicals in Food, Consumer Products and the Environment.
The Committee on Chemicals and Materials of Construction For Use in Public Water Supply and Swimming Pools.
The Committee on Medical Aspects of Food and Nutrition Policy.
The Committee on Medical Aspects of Radiation in the Environment.
The Committee on Mutagenicity of Chemicals in Food, Consumer Products and the Environment.
The Committee on Safety of Devices.
The Committee on Standards in Public Life.
The Committee on Toxicity of Chemicals in Food, Consumer Products and the Environment.
The Committee on the Medical Effects of Air Pollutants.
The Committee on the Safety of Medicines.
The Commonwealth Scholarship Commission in the United Kingdom.
Communications for Business.
The Community Development Foundation.
The Competition Commission, in relation to information held by it otherwise than as a tribunal.
The Competition Service.
The Construction Industry Training Board.
Consumer Communications for England.
The Consumer Council for Postal Services.
[. . .][50]
The consumers' committee for Great Britain appointed under section 19 of the Agricultural Marketing Act 1958.
The Council for Professions Supplementary to Medicine.
The Council for the Central Laboratory of the Research Councils.
The Council for the Regulation of Health Care Professionals
The Council for Science and Technology.
The Council on Tribunals.
The Countryside Agency.
The Countryside Council for Wales.
The Covent Garden Market Authority.
The Criminal Cases Review Commission.

[50] Entries repealed by SI 2003/1883 (Freedom of Information (Removal of References to Public Authorities) Order), Sch.1, para.1.

The Criminal Injuries Compensation Appeals Panel, in relation to information held by it otherwise than as a tribunal.
The Criminal Injuries Compensation Authority.
The Criminal Justice Consultative Council.
The Crown Court Rule Committee.
The Dartmoor Steering Group and Working Party.
The Darwin Advisory Committee.
The Defence Nuclear Safety Committee.
The Defence Scientific Advisory Council.
The Design Council.
[. . .][51]
The Diplomatic Service Appeal Board.
The Disability Employment Advisory Committee.
The Disability Living Allowance Advisory Board.
The Disability Rights Commission.
The Disabled Persons Transport Advisory Committee.
The Economic and Social Research Council.
[. . .][52]
The Electoral Commission.
[. . .][53]
The Engineering Construction Industry Training Board.
The Engineering and Physical Sciences Research Council.
English Nature.
The English Sports Council.
The English Tourist Board.
The Environment Agency.
The Equal Opportunities Commission.
The Ethnic Minority Business Forum.
The Expert Advisory Group on AIDS.
The Expert Group on Cryptosporidium in Water Supplies.
An Expert Panel on Air Quality Standards.
The Export Guarantees Advisory Council.
The Family Proceedings Rules Committee.
The Farm Animal Welfare Council.
The Financial Reporting Advisory Board.
The Financial Services Authority.
The Fire Services Examination Board.
The Firearms Consultative Committee.
The Food Advisory Committee.
Food from Britain.
The Football Licensing Authority.
The Fuel Cell Advisory Panel.
[. . .][54]
The Gaming Board for Great Britain.
[. . .][55]
The Gas and Electricity Consumer Council.
The Gene Therapy Advisory Committee.
The General Chiropractic Council.
The General Dental Council.
The General Medical Council.
The General Osteopathic Council.

51 Entries repealed by SI 2003/1883 (Freedom of Information (Removal of References to Public Authorities) Order), Sch.1, para.1.
52 *ibid.*
53 *ibid.*
54 *ibid.*
55 *ibid.*

The General Social Care Council.
The General Teaching Council for England.
The General Teaching Council for Wales.
The Genetic Testing and Insurance Committee.
The Government Hospitality Advisory Committee for the Purchase of Wine.
The Government Chemist.
The Government-Industry Forum on Non-Food Use of Crops.
The Great Britain-China Centre.
The Health and Safety Commission.
The Health and Safety Executive.
The Health Service Commissioner for England.
The Health Service Commissioner for Wales.
The Hearing Aid Council.
Her Majesty's Chief Inspector of Education and Training in Wales or Prif Arolygydd Ei Mawrhydi dros Addysg a Hyfforddiant yng Nghymru
The Higher Education Funding Council for England.
The Higher Education Funding Council for Wales.
The Hill Farming Advisory Committee.
The Hill Farming Advisory Sub-committee for Wales.
The Historic Buildings Council for Wales.
The Historic Buildings and Monuments Commission for England.
The Historic Royal Palaces Trust.
The Home-Grown Cereals Authority.
[. . .][56]
The Horserace Betting Levy Board.
The Horserace Totalisator Board.
The Horticultural Development Council.
Horticulture Research International.
The House of Lords Appointments Commission.
Any Housing action trust established under Part III of the Housing Act 1988.
The Housing Corporation.
The Human Fertilisation and Embryology Authority.
The Human Genetics Commission.
The Immigration Services Commissioner.
The Imperial War Museum.
The Independent Advisory Group on Teenage Pregnancy.
The Independent Board of Visitors for Military Corrective Training Centres.
The Independent Case Examiner for the Child Support Agency.
The Independent Living Funds.
The Independent Scientific Group on Cattle Tuberculosis.
The Independent Television Commission.
[. . .][57]
The Industrial Development Advisory Board.
The Industrial Injuries Advisory Council.
The Information Commissioner.
The Inland Waterways Amenity Advisory Council.
The Insolvency Rules Committee.
The Integrated Administration and Controls System Appeals Panel.
The Intellectual Property Advisory Committee.
Investors in People UK.
The Joint Committee on Vaccination and Immunisation.
The Joint Nature Conservation Committee.
The Joint Prison/Probation Accreditation Panel.
The Judicial Studies Board.

[56] Entries repealed by SI 2003/1883 (Freedom of Information (Removal of References to Public Authorities) Order), Sch.1, para.1.
[57] *ibid.*

The Know-How Fund Advisory Board.
The Land Registration Rule Committee.
The Law Commission.
The Learning and Skills Council for England.
The Legal Services Commission.
The Legal Services Consultative Panel.
The Legal Services Ombudsman.
The Library and Information Services Council (Wales).
The Local Government Boundary Commission for Wales.
The Local Government Commission for England.
A local probation board established under section 4 of the Criminal Justice and Court Services Act 2000.
The London Pensions Fund Authority.
The Low Pay Commission.
The Magistrates' Courts Rules Committee.
The Marshall Aid Commemoration Commission.
The Measurement Advisory Committee.
The Meat and Livestock Commission.
[. . .][58]
The Medical Research Council.
[. . .][59]
The Medicines Commission.
The Milk Development Council.
The Millennium Commission.
The Museum of London.
The National Army Museum.
The National Audit Office.
The National Biological Standards Board (UK).
The National Care Standards Commission.
The National Consumer Council.
The National Council for Education and Training for Wales.
The National Crime Squad.
The National Employers' Liaison Committee.
The National Employment Panel.
The National Endowment for Science, Technology and the Arts.
The National Expert Group on Transboundary Air Pollution.
The National Forest Company.
The National Gallery.
The National Heritage Memorial Fund.
The National Library of Wales.
The National Lottery Charities Board.
The National Lottery Commission.
The National Maritime Museum.
The National Museum of Science and Industry.
The National Museums and Galleries of Wales.
The National Museums and Galleries on Merseyside.
The National Portrait Gallery.
The National Radiological Protection Board.
The Natural Environment Research Council.
The Natural History Museum.
The New Deal Task Force.
The New Opportunities Fund.
The Nuclear Research Advisory Council.
The Nursing and Midwifery Council.

[58] Entries repealed by SI 2003/1883 (Freedom of Information (Removal of References to Public Authorities) Order), Sch.1, para.1.
[59] *ibid.*

The Occupational Pensions Regulatory Authority.
The Office of Communications.
The Office of Government Commerce.
The Office of Manpower Economics.
The Oil and Pipelines Agency.
The OSO Board.
The Overseas Service Pensions Scheme Advisory Board.
The Panel on Standards for the Planning Inspectorate.
The Parliamentary Boundary Commission for England.
The Parliamentary Boundary Commission for Scotland.
The Parliamentary Boundary Commission for Wales.
The Parliamentary Commissioner for Administration.
The Parole Board.
The Particle Physics and Astronomy Research Council.
The Patient Information Advisory Group.
The Pensions Compensation Board.
The Pensions Ombudsman.
The Pesticide Residues Committee.
The Pharmacists' Review Panel.
[. . .][60]
The Poisons Board.
The Police Complaints Authority.
The Police Information Technology Organisation.
The Police Negotiating Board.
The Political Honours Scrutiny Committee.
The Post Office.
[. . .][61] [. . .][62]
The Property Advisory Group.
The Qualifications, Curriculum and Assessment Authority for Wales.
The Qualifications Curriculum Authority.
The Race Education and Employment Forum.
The Race Relations Forum.
The Radio Authority.
The Radioactive Waste Management Advisory Committee.
Any Rail Passengers' Committee established under section 2(2) of the Railways Act 1993.[63]
A Regional Cultural Consortium.
Any regional development agency established under the Regional Development Agencies Act 1998, other than the London Development Agency.
Any regional flood defence committee.
The Registrar of Occupational and Personal Pension Schemes.
The Registrar of Public Lending Right.
Remploy Ltd.
The Renewable Energy Advisory Committee.
Resource: The Council for Museums, Archives and Libraries.
The Review Board for Government Contracts.
The Review Body for Nursing Staff, Midwives, Health Visitors and Professions Allied to Medicine.
The Review Body on Doctors and Dentists Remuneration.
The Reviewing Committee on the Export of Works of Art.
The Royal Air Force Museum.
The Royal Armouries.

[60] Entries repealed by SI 2003/1883 (Freedom of Information (Removal of References to Public Authorities) Order), Sch.1, para.1.
[61] *ibid.*
[62] *ibid.*
[63] These bodies were formerly known as Rail Users' Consultative Committees, but were renamed by s.227(1) of the Transport Act 2000 (c.38), and s.2(2) of the Railways Act 1993 was amended accordingly.

The Royal Botanic Gardens, Kew.
The Royal Commission on Ancient and Historical Monuments of Wales.
The Royal Commission on Environmental Pollution.
The Royal Commission on Historical Manuscripts.
The Royal Military College of Science Advisory Council.
The Royal Mint Advisory Committee on the Design of Coins, Medals, Seals and Decorations.
The School Teachers' Review Body.
The Scientific Advisory Committee on Nutrition.
The Scientific Committee on Tobacco and Health.
The Scottish Advisory Committee on Telecommunications.
The Scottish Committee of the Council on Tribunals.
The Sea Fish Industry Authority.
The Security Industry Authority
The Senior Salaries Review Body.
The Sentencing Advisory Panel.
The Service Authority for the National Crime Squad.
Sianel Pedwar Cymru, in respect of information held for purposes other than those of journalism, art or literature.
Sir John Soane's Museum.
The Skills Task Force.
The Small Business Council.
The Small Business Investment Task Force.
The Social Care Institute for Excellence.
The social fund Commissioner appointed under section 65 of the Social Security Administration Act 1992.
The Social Security Advisory Committee.
The Social Services Inspectorate for Wales Advisory Group.
The Specialist Advisory Committee on Antimicrobial Research.
The Spongiform Encephalopathy Advisory Committee.
The Sports Council for Wales.
The Standards Board for England.
The Standing Advisory Committee on Industrial Property.
The Standing Advisory Committee on Trunk Road Assessment.
The Standing Dental Advisory Committee.
The Standing Nursing and Midwifery Advisory Committee.
The Standing Medical Advisory Committee.
The Standing Pharmaceutical Advisory Committee.
The Statistics Commission.
The Steering Committee on Pharmacy Postgraduate Education.
The Strategic Investment Board.
The Strategic Rail Authority.
The subsidence adviser appointed under section 46 of the Coal Industry Act 1994.
The Substance Misuse Advisory Panel.
The Sustainable Development Commission.
[. . .][64]
The Tate Gallery.
The Teacher Training Agency.
The Technical Advisory Board.
The Theatres Trust.
The Traffic Commissioners, in respect of information held by them otherwise than as a tribunal.
The Treasure Valuation Committee.
The UK Advisory Panel for Health Care Workers Infected with Bloodborne Viruses.
The UK Chemicals Stakeholder Forum.
The UK Sports Council.
The United Kingdom Atomic Energy Authority.
The United Kingdom Register of Organic Food Standards.

---

64 Entries repealed by SI 2003/1883 (Freedom of Information (Removal of References to Public Authorities) Order), Sch.1, para.1.

The United Kingdom Xenotransplantation Interim Regulatory Authority.
The Unlinked Anonymous Serosurveys Steering Group.
The Unrelated Live Transplant Regulatory Authority.
The Urban Regeneration Agency.
The Veterinary Products Committee.
The Veterinary Residues Committee.
The Victoria and Albert Museum.
[. . .][65]
The Wales Tourist Board.
The Wallace Collection.
The War Pensions Committees.
The Water Regulations Advisory Committee.
The Welsh Administration Ombudsman.
The Welsh Advisory Committee on Telecommunications.
The Welsh Committee for Professional Development of Pharmacy.
The Welsh Dental Committee.
The Welsh Development Agency.
The Welsh Industrial Development Advisory Board.
The Welsh Language Board.
The Welsh Medical Committee.
The Welsh Nursing and Midwifery Committee.
The Welsh Optometric Committee.
The Welsh Pharmaceutical Committee.
The Welsh Scientific Advisory Committee.
The Westminster Foundation for Democracy.
The Wilton Park Academic Council.
The Wine Standards Board of the Vintners' Company.
The Women's National Commission.
The Youth Justice Board for England and Wales.
The Zoos Forum.

PART VII

OTHER PUBLIC BODIES AND OFFICES

Northern Ireland

1.—An Advisory Committee on General Commissioners of Income Tax (Northern Ireland).
The Advisory Committee on Justices of the Peace in Northern Ireland.
The Advisory Committee on Juvenile Court Lay Panel (Northern Ireland).
The Advisory Committee on Pesticides for Northern Ireland.
The Agricultural Research Institute of Northern Ireland.
The Agricultural Wages Board for Northern Ireland.
The Arts Council of Northern Ireland.
The Assembly Ombudsman for Northern Ireland.
The Belfast Harbour Commissioners.
The Board of Trustees of National Museums and Galleries of Northern Ireland.
Boards of Visitors and Visiting Committees.
The Boundary Commission for Northern Ireland.
The Certification Officer for Northern Ireland.
The Charities Advisory Committee.
The Chief Electoral Officer for Northern Ireland.
The Civil Service Commissioners for Northern Ireland.
[Comhairle na Gaelscolaíochta.][66]

[65] Entries repealed by SI 2003/1883 (Freedom of Information (Removal of References to Public Authorities) Order), Sch.1, para.1.
[66] Entries added by SI 2003/1882 (Freedom of Information (Additional Public Authorities) Order), Sch.2, para.1.

The Commissioner for Public Appointments for Northern Ireland.
The Construction Industry Training Board.
The consultative Civic Forum referred to in section 56(4) of the Northern Ireland Act 1998.
The Council for Catholic Maintained Schools.
The Council for Nature Conservation and the Countryside.
The County Court Rules Committee (Northern Ireland).
[The Criminal Injuries Compensation Appeals Panel for Northern Ireland, in relation to information held by it otherwise than as a tribunal.][67]
The Disability Living Allowance Advisory Board for Northern Ireland.
The Distinction and Meritorious Service Awards Committee.
The Drainage Council for Northern Ireland.
An Education and Library Board established under Article 3 of the Education and Libraries (Northern Ireland) Order 1986.
Enterprise Ulster.
The Equality Commission for Northern Ireland.
The Family Proceedings Rules Committee (Northern Ireland).
The Fire Authority for Northern Ireland.
The Fisheries Conservancy Board for Northern Ireland.
The General Consumer Council for Northern Ireland.
[The General Teaching Council for Northern Ireland.
The Governors of the Armargh Observatory and Planetarium.
The Harbour of Donaghadee Commissioners.][68]
The Health and Safety Agency for Northern Ireland.
The Historic Buildings Council.
The Historic Monuments Council.
The Independent Assessor of Military Complaints Procedures in Northern Ireland.
The Independent Reviewer of the Northern Ireland (Emergency Provisions) Act.
The Independent Commissioner for Holding Centres.
The Industrial Development Board for Northern Ireland.
The Industrial Research and Technology Unit.
The Juvenile Justice Board.
The Labour Relations Agency.
The Laganside Corporation.
The Law Reform Advisory Committee for Northern Ireland.
The Lay Observer for Northern Ireland.
[The Learning and Skills Advisory Board.][69]
The Legal Aid Advisory Committee (Northern Ireland).
The Livestock & Meat Commission for Northern Ireland.
The Local Enterprise Development Unit.
The Local Government Staff Commission.
The Londonderry Port and Harbour Commissioners.
The Magistrates' Courts Rules Committee (Northern Ireland).
The Mental Health Commission for Northern Ireland.
The Northern Ireland Advisory Committee on Telecommunications.
The Northern Ireland Audit Office.
The Northern Ireland Building Regulations Advisory Committee.
The Northern Ireland Civil Service Appeal Board.
The Northern Ireland Commissioner for Complaints.
The Northern Ireland Community Relations Council.
The Northern Ireland Consumer Committee for Electricity.
The Northern Ireland Council for the Curriculum, Examinations and Assessment.
The Northern Ireland Council for Postgraduate Medical and Dental Education.
The Northern Ireland Crown Court Rules Committee.

67 Entries added by SI 2003/1882 (Freedom of Information (Additional Public Authorities) Order), Sch.2, para.1.
68 *ibid.*
69 *ibid.*

The Northern Ireland Economic Council.
The Northern Ireland Fishery Harbour Authority.
The Northern Ireland Higher Education Council.
The Northern Ireland Housing Executive.
The Northern Ireland Human Rights Commission.
The Northern Ireland Insolvency Rules Committee.
The Northern Ireland Local Government Officers' Superannuation Committee.
The Northern Ireland Museums Council.
The Northern Ireland Pig Production Development Committee.
[The Northern Ireland Practice and Education Council for Nursing and Midwifery.
The Northern Ireland Social Care Council.][70]
The Northern Ireland Supreme Court Rules Committee.
The Northern Ireland Tourist Board.
The Northern Ireland Transport Holding Company.
The Northern Ireland Water Council.
The Parades Commission.
The Police Ombudsman for Northern Ireland.
The Probation Board for Northern Ireland.
The Rural Development Council for Northern Ireland.
The Sentence Review Commissioners appointed under section 1 of the Northern Ireland (Sentences) Act 1998.
The social fund Commissioner appointed under Article 37 of the Social Security (Northern Ireland) Order 1998.
The Sports Council for Northern Ireland.
The Staff Commission for Education and Library Boards.
The Statistics Advisory Committee.
The Statute Law Committee for Northern Ireland.
A sub-group established under section 21 of the Police (Northern Ireland) Act 2000.[70a]
The Training and Employment Agency.
Ulster Supported Employment Ltd.
The Warrenpoint Harbour Authority.
[The Waste Management Advisory Board.][71]
The Youth Council for Northern Ireland.

SCHEDULE 2

THE COMMISSIONER AND THE TRIBUNAL

PART I

PROVISION CONSEQUENTIAL ON SECTION 18(1) AND (2)

General

1.—(1) Any reference in any enactment, instrument or document to the Data Protection Commissioner or the Data Protection Registrar shall be construed, in relation to any time after the commencement of section 18(1), as a reference to the Information Commissioner.

(2) Any reference in any enactment, instrument or document to the Data Protection Tribunal shall be construed, in relation to any time after the commencement of section 18(2), as a reference to the Information Tribunal.

2.—(1) Any reference in this Act or in any instrument under this Act to the Commissioner shall be construed, in relation to any time before the commencement of section 18(1), as a reference to the Data Protection Commissioner.

---

70 Entries added by SI 2003/1882 (Freedom of Information (Additional Public Authorities) Order), Sch.2, para.1.
70a Words added by Police (Northern Ireland) Act (2003, c.6), Sch.1, para.15.
71 *ibid.*

(2) Any reference in this Act or in any instrument under this Act to the Tribunal shall be construed, in relation to any time before the commencement of section 18(2), as a reference to the Data Protection Tribunal.

Public Records Act 1958 (c.51)

3.—(1) In Part II of the Table in paragraph 3 of Schedule 1 to the Public Records Act 1958 (definition of public records), the entry relating to the Data Protection Commissioner is omitted and there is inserted at the appropriate place—

"Information Commissioner."

(2) In paragraph 4(1) of that Schedule, for paragraph (nn) there is substituted—

"(nn) records of the Information Tribunal;".

Parliamentary Commissioner Act 1967 (c.13)

4.—In Schedule 2 to the Parliamentary Commissioner Act 1967 (departments etc. subject to investigation), the entry relating to the Data Protection Commissioner is omitted and there is inserted at the appropriate place—

"Information Commissioner".

5.—In Schedule 4 to that Act (tribunals exercising administrative functions), for the entry relating to the Data Protection Tribunal there is substituted—

"Information Tribunal constituted under section 6 of the Data Protection Act 1998."

Superannuation Act 1972 (c.11)

6.—In Schedule 1 to the Superannuation Act 1972 (employment with superannuation scheme), for "Data Protection Commissioner" there is substituted "Information Commissioner".

Consumer Credit Act 1974 (c.39)

7.—In section 159 of the Consumer Credit Act 1974 (correction of wrong information), in subsections (7) and (8)(b), for "Data Protection Commissioner", in both places where it occurs, there is substituted "Information Commissioner".

House of Commons Disqualification Act 1975 (c.24)

8.—(1) In Part II of Schedule 1 to the House of Commons Disqualification Act 1975 (bodies whose members are disqualified), the entry relating to the Data Protection Tribunal is omitted and there is inserted at the appropriate place—

"The Information Tribunal".

(2) In Part III of that Schedule (disqualifying offices), the entry relating to the Data Protection Commissioner is omitted and there is inserted at the appropriate place—

"The Information Commissioner".

Northern Ireland Assembly Disqualification Act 1975 (c.25)

9.—(1) In Part II of Schedule 1 to the Northern Ireland Assembly Disqualification Act 1975 (bodies whose members are disqualified), the entry relating to the Data Protection Tribunal is omitted and there is inserted at the appropriate place—

"The Information Tribunal".

(2) In Part III of that Schedule (disqualifying offices), the entry relating to the Data Protection Commissioner is omitted and there is inserted at the appropriate place—

"The Information Commissioner".

Tribunals and Inquiries Act 1992 (c.53)

10.—In paragraph 14 of Part I of Schedule 1 to the Tribunals and Inquiries Act 1992 (tribunals under direct supervision of Council on Tribunals)—

(a) in sub-paragraph (a), for "The Data Protection Commissioner" there is substituted "The Information Commissioner", and

(b) for sub-paragraph (b) there is substituted—

"(b) the Information Tribunal constituted under that section, in respect of its jurisdiction under—

(i) section 48 of that Act, and

(ii) section 57 of the Freedom of Information Act 2000."

Judicial Pensions and Retirement Act 1993 (c.8)

11.—In Schedule 5 to the Judicial Pensions and Retirement Act 1993 (retirement provisions: the relevant offices), in the entry relating to the chairman and deputy chairman of the Data Protection Tribunal, for "the Data Protection Tribunal" there is substituted "the Information Tribunal".

12.—In Schedule 7 to that Act (retirement dates: transitional provisions), in paragraph 5(5)(xxvi) for "the Data Protection Tribunal" there is substituted "the Information Tribunal".

Data Protection Act 1998 (c.29)

13.—(1) Section 6 of the Data Protection Act 1998 (the Data Protection Commissioner and the Data Protection Tribunal) is amended as follows.

(2) For subsection (1) there is substituted—

"(1) For the purposes of this Act and of the Freedom of Information Act 2000 there shall be an officer known as the Information Commissioner (in this Act referred to as 'the Commissioner')."

(3) For subsection (3) there is substituted—

"(3) For the purposes of this Act and of the Freedom of Information Act 2000 there shall be a tribunal known as the Information Tribunal (in this Act referred to as "the Tribunal")."

14.—In section 70(1) of that Act (supplementary definitions)—

(a) in the definition of "the Commissioner", for "the Data Protection Commissioner" there is substituted "the Information Commissioner", and

(b) in the definition of "the Tribunal", for "the Data Protection Tribunal" there is substituted "the Information Tribunal".

15.—(1) Schedule 5 to that Act (the Data Protection Commissioner and the Data Protection Tribunal) is amended as follows.

(2) In paragraph 1(1), for "Data Protection Commissioner" there is substituted "Information Commissioner".

(3) Part III shall cease to have effect.

PART II

AMENDMENTS RELATING TO EXTENSION OF FUNCTIONS OF COMMISSIONER AND TRIBUNAL

Interests represented by lay members of tribunal

16.—In section 6(6) of the Data Protection Act 1998 (lay members of Tribunal)—

(a) for the word "and" at the end of paragraph (a) there is substituted—

"(aa) persons to represent the interests of those who make requests for information under the Freedom of Information Act 2000,"

, and

(b) after paragraph (b) there is inserted

"and

(bb) persons to represent the interests of public authorities."

Expenses incurred under this act excluded in calculating fees

17.—In section 26(2) of that Act (fees regulations), in paragraph (a)—

(a) after "functions" there is inserted "under this Act", and

(b) after "Tribunal" there is inserted "so far as attributable to their functions under this Act".

Information provided to commissioner or tribunal

18.—In section 58 of that Act (disclosure of information to Commissioner or Tribunal), after "this Act" there is inserted "or the Freedom of Information Act 2000".

19.—(1) Section 59 of that Act (confidentiality of information) is amended as follows.

(2) In subsections (1) and (2), for "this Act", wherever occurring, there is substituted "the information Acts".

(3) After subsection (3) there is inserted—

"(4) In this section "the information Acts" means this Act and the Freedom of Information Act 2000."

Deputy Commissioners

20.—(1) Paragraph 4 of Schedule 5 to that Act (officers and staff) is amended as follows.

(2) In sub-paragraph (1)(a), after "a deputy commissioner" there is inserted "or two deputy commissioners".

(3) After sub-paragraph (1) there is inserted—

"(1A) The Commissioner shall, when appointing any second deputy commissioner, specify which of the Commissioner's functions are to be performed, in the circumstances referred to in paragraph 5(1), by each of the deputy commissioners."

Exercise of commissioner's functions by others

21.—(1) Paragraph 5 of Schedule 5 to that Act (exercise of functions of Commissioner during vacancy etc.) is amended as follows.

(2) In sub-paragraph (1)—

(a) after "deputy commissioner" there is inserted "or deputy commissioners", and

(b) after "this Act" there is inserted "or the Freedom of Information Act 2000".

(3) In sub-paragraph (2) after "this Act" there is inserted "or the Freedom of Information Act 2000".

Money

22.—In paragraph 9(1) of Schedule 5 to that Act (money) for "or section 159 of the Consumer Credit Act 1974" there is substituted ", under section 159 of the Consumer Credit Act 1974 or under the Freedom of Information Act 2000".

SCHEDULE 3

Powers of Entry and Inspection

Issue of Warrants

1.—(1) If a circuit judge is satisfied by information on oath supplied by the Commissioner that there are reasonable grounds for suspecting—

(a) that a public authority has failed or is failing to comply with—

(i) any of the requirements of Part I of this Act,

(ii) so much of a decision notice as requires steps to be taken, or

(iii) an information notice or an enforcement notice, or

(b) that an offence under section 77 has been or is being committed,

and that evidence of such a failure to comply or of the commission of the offence is to be found on any premises specified in the information, he may, subject to paragraph 2, grant a warrant to the Commissioner.

(2) A warrant issued under sub-paragraph (1) shall authorise the Commissioner or any of his officers or staff at any time within seven days of the date of the warrant—

(a) to enter and search the premises,

(b) to inspect and seize any documents or other material found there which may be such evidence as is mentioned in that sub-paragraph, and

(c) to inspect, examine, operate and test any equipment found there in which information held by the public authority may be recorded.

2.—(1) A judge shall not issue a warrant under this Schedule unless he is satisfied—

(a) that the Commissioner has given seven days' notice in writing to the occupier of the premises in question demanding access to the premises, and

(b) that either—

(i) access was demanded at a reasonable hour and was unreasonably refused, or

(ii) although entry to the premises was granted, the occupier unreasonably refused to comply with a request by the Commissioner or any of the Commissioner's officers or staff to permit the Commissioner or the officer or member of staff to do any of the things referred to in paragraph 1(2), and

(c) that the occupier, has, after the refusal, been notified by the Commissioner of the application for the warrant and has had an opportunity of being heard by the judge on the question whether or not it should be issued.

(2) Sub-paragraph (1) shall not apply if the judge is satisfied that the case is one of urgency or that compliance with those provisions would defeat the object of the entry.

3.—A judge who issues a warrant under this Schedule shall also issue two copies of it and certify them clearly as copies.

Execution of Warrants

4.—A person executing a warrant issued under this Schedule may use such reasonable force as may be necessary.

5.—A warrant issued under this Schedule shall be executed at a reasonable hour unless it appears to the person executing it that there are grounds for suspecting that the evidence in question would not be found if it were so executed.

6.—(1) If the premises in respect of which a warrant is issued under this Schedule are occupied by a public authority and any officer or employee of the authority is present when the warrant is executed, he shall be shown the warrant and supplied with a copy of it; and if no such officer or employee is present a copy of the warrant shall be left in a prominent place on the premises.

(2) If the premises in respect of which a warrant is issued under this Schedule are occupied by a person other than a public authority and he is present when the warrant is executed, he shall be shown the warrant and supplied with a copy of it; and if that person is not present a copy of the warrant shall be left in a prominent place on the premises.

7.—(1) A person seizing anything in pursuance of a warrant under this Schedule shall give a receipt for it if asked to do so.

(2) Anything so seized may be retained for so long as is necessary in all the circumstances but the person in occupation of the premises in question shall be given a copy of anything that is seized if he so requests and the person executing the warrant considers that it can be done without undue delay.

Matters exempt from inspection and seizure

8.—The powers of inspection and seizure conferred by a warrant issued under this Schedule shall not be exercisable in respect of information which is exempt information by virtue of section 23(1) or 24(1).

9.—(1) Subject to the provisions of this paragraph, the powers of inspection and seizure conferred by a warrant issued under this Schedule shall not be exercisable in respect of—

(a) any communication between a professional legal adviser and his client in connection with the giving of legal advice to the client with respect to his obligations, liabilities or rights under this Act, or

(b) any communication between a professional legal adviser and his client, or between such an adviser or his client and any other person, made in connection with or in contemplation of proceedings under or arising out of this Act (including proceedings before the Tribunal) and for the purposes of such proceedings.

(2) Sub-paragraph (1) applies also to—

(a) any copy or other record of any such communication as is there mentioned, and

(b) any document or article enclosed with or referred to in any such communication if made in connection with the giving of any advice or, as the case may be, in connection with or in contemplation of and for the purposes of such proceedings as are there mentioned.

(3) This paragraph does not apply to anything in the possession of any person other than the professional legal adviser or his client or to anything held with the intention of furthering a criminal purpose.

(4) In this paragraph references to the client of a professional legal adviser include references to any person representing such a client.

10.—If the person in occupation of any premises in respect of which a warrant is issued under this Schedule objects to the inspection or seizure under the warrant of any material on the grounds that it consists partly of matters in respect of which those powers are not exercisable, he shall, if the person executing the warrant so requests, furnish that person with a copy of so much of the material in relation to which the powers are exercisable.

Return of Warrants

11.—A warrant issued under this Schedule shall be returned to the court from which it was issued—

(a) after being executed, or

(b) if not executed within the time authorised for its execution;

and the person by whom any such warrant is executed shall make an endorsement on it stating what powers have been exercised by him under the warrant.

Offences

12.—Any person who—

(a) intentionally obstructs a person in the execution of a warrant issued under this Schedule, or

(b) fails without reasonable excuse to give any person executing such a warrant such assistance as he may reasonably require for the execution of the warrant,

is guilty of an offence.

Vessels, vehicles, etc.

13.—In this Schedule "premises" includes any vessel, vehicle, aircraft or hovercraft, and references to the occupier of any premises include references to the person in charge of any vessel, vehicle, aircraft or hovercraft.

Scotland and Northern Ireland

14.—In the application of this Schedule to Scotland—

(a) for any reference to a circuit judge there is substituted a reference to the sheriff, and

(b) for any reference to information on oath there is substituted a reference to evidence on oath.

15.—In the application of this Schedule to Northern Ireland—

(a) for any reference to a circuit judge there is substituted a reference to a county court judge, and

(b) for any reference to information on oath there is substituted a reference to a complaint on oath.

SCHEDULE 4
APPEAL PROCEEDINGS

Amendments of Schedule 6 to Data Protection Act 1998

Constitution of tribunal in national security cases

1.—In paragraph 2(1) of Schedule 6 to the Data Protection Act 1998 (constitution of Tribunal in national security cases), at the end there is inserted "or under section 60(1) or (4) of the Freedom of Information Act 2000".

2.—For paragraph 3 of that Schedule there is substituted—

"3. The Tribunal shall be duly constituted—

(a) for an appeal under section 28(4) or (6) in any case where the application of paragraph 6(1) is excluded by rules under paragraph 7, or

(b) for an appeal under section 60(1) or (4) of the Freedom of Information Act 2000,

if it consists of three of the persons designated under paragraph 2(1), of whom one shall be by the Lord Chancellor to preside."

Constitution of tribunal in other cases

3.—(1) Paragraph 4 of that Schedule (constitution of Tribunal in other cases) is amended as follows.

(2) After sub-paragraph (1) there is inserted—

"(1A) Subject to any rules made under paragraph 7, the Tribunal shall be duly constituted for an appeal under section 57(1) or (2) of the Freedom of Information Act 2000 if it consists of—

(a) the chairman or a deputy chairman (who shall preside), and

(b) an equal number of the members appointed respectively in accordance with paragraphs (aa) and (bb) of section 6(6)."

(3) In sub-paragraph (2), after "(1)" there is inserted "or (1A)".

Rules of procedure

4.—(1) Paragraph 7 of that Schedule (rules of procedure) is amended as follows.

(2) In sub-paragraph (1), for the words from "regulating" onwards there is substituted

"regulating—

(a) the exercise of the rights of appeal conferred—

(i) by sections 28(4) and (6) and 48, and

(ii) by sections 57(1) and (2) and section 60(1) and (4) of the Freedom of Information Act 2000, and

(b) the practice and procedure of the Tribunal."

(3) In sub-paragraph (2), after paragraph (a) there is inserted—

"(aa) for the joinder of any other person as a party to any proceedings on an appeal under the Freedom of Information Act 2000,

(ab) for the hearing of an appeal under this Act with an appeal under the Freedom of Information Act 2000,".

SCHEDULE 5

AMENDMENTS OF PUBLIC RECORDS LEGISLATION

PART I

AMENDMENTS OF PUBLIC RECORDS ACT 1958

Functions of Advisory Council on public records

1.—In section 1 of the Public Records Act 1958 (general responsibility of the Lord Chancellor for public records), after subsection (2) there is inserted—

"(2A) The matters on which the Advisory Council on Public Records may advise the Lord Chancellor include matters relating to the application of the Freedom of Information Act 2000 to information contained in public records which are historical records within the meaning of Part VI of that Act."

Access to public records

2.—(1) Section 5 of that Act (access to public records) is amended in accordance with this paragraph.

(2) Subsections (1) and (2) are omitted.

(3) For subsection (3) there is substituted—

"(3) It shall be the duty of the Keeper of Public Records to arrange that reasonable facilities are available to the public for inspecting and obtaining copies of those public records in the Public Record Office which fall to be disclosed in accordance with the Freedom of Information Act 2000."

(4) Subsection (4) and, in subsection (5), the words from "and subject to" to the end are omitted.

3.—Schedule 2 of that Act (enactments prohibiting disclosure of information obtained from the public) is omitted.

Power to extend meaning of "public records"

4.—In Schedule 1 to that Act (definition of public records) after the Table at the end of paragraph 3 there is inserted—

"3A.—

(1) Her Majesty may by Order in Council amend the Table at the end of paragraph 3 of this Schedule by adding to either Part of the Table an entry relating to any body or establishment—

(a) which, at the time when the Order is made, is specified in Schedule 2 to the Parliamentary Commissioner Act 1967 (departments, etc. subject to investigation), or

(b) in respect of which an entry could, at that time, be added to Schedule 2 to that Act by an Order in Council under section 4 of that Act (which confers power to amend that Schedule).

(2) An Order in Council under this paragraph may relate to a specified body or establishment or to bodies or establishments falling within a specified description.

(3) An Order in Council under this paragraph shall be subject to annulment in pursuance of a resolution of either House of Parliament."

PART II

AMENDMENT OF PUBLIC RECORDS ACT (NORTHERN IRELAND) 1923

5.—After section 5 of th Public Records Act (Northern Ireland) 1923 (deposit of documents in Record Office by trustees or other persons) there is inserted—

"5A. Access to public records

It shall be the duty of the Deputy Keeper of the Records of Northern Ireland to arrange that reasonable facilities are available to the public for inspecting and obtaining copies of those public records in the Public Record Office of Northern Ireland which fall to be disclosed in accordance with the Freedom of Information Act 2000."

SCHEDULE 6

FURTHER AMENDMENTS OF DATA PROTECTION ACT 1998

Requests by Data Controller for further information

1.—In section 7 of the Data Protection Act 1998 (right of access to personal data), for subsection (3) there is substituted—

"(3) Where a data controller—

(a) reasonably requires further information in order to satisfy himself as to the identity of the person making a request under this section and to locate the information which that person seeks, and

(b) has informed him of that requirement,

the data controller is not obliged to comply with the request unless he is supplied with that further information."

Parliament

2.—After section 35 of that Act there is inserted—

"35A. Parliamentary privilege.

Personal data are exempt from—

(a) the first data protection principle, except to the extent to which it requires compliance with the conditions in Schedules 2 and 3,

(b) the second, third, fourth and fifth data protection principles,

(c) section 7, and

(d) sections 10 and 14(1) to (3),

if the exemption is required for the purpose of avoiding an infringement of the privileges of either House of Parliament."

3.—After section 63 of that Act there is inserted—

"63A.—Application to Parliament.

(1) Subject to the following provisions of this section and to section 35A, this Act applies to the processing of personal data by or on behalf of either House of Parliament as it applies to the processing of personal data by other persons.

(2) Where the purposes for which and the manner in which any personal data are, or are to be, processed are determined by or on behalf of the House of Commons, the data controller in respect of those data for the purposes of this Act shall be the Corporate Officer of that House.

(3) Where the purposes for which and the manner in which any personal data are, or are to be, processed are determined by or on behalf of the House of Lords, the data controller in respect of those data for the purposes of this Act shall be the Corporate Officer of that House.

(4) Nothing in subsection (2) or (3) is to be taken to render the Corporate Officer of the House of Commons or the Corporate Officer of the House of Lords liable to prosecution under this Act, but section 55 and paragraph 12 of Schedule 9 shall apply to a person acting on behalf of either House as they apply to any other person."

4.—In Schedule 2 to that Act (conditions relevant for the purposes of the first data protection principle: processing of any personal data) in paragraph 5 after paragraph (a) there is inserted—

"(aa) for the exercise of any functions of either House of Parliament,".

5.—In Schedule 3 to that Act (conditions relevant for the purposes of the first data protection principle: processing of sensitive personal data) in paragraph 7 after paragraph (a) there is inserted—

"(aa) for the exercise of any functions of either House of Parliament,".

Honours

6.—In Schedule 7 to that Act (miscellaneous exemptions) in paragraph 3(b) (honours) after "honour" there is inserted "or dignity".

Legal professional privilege

7.—In paragraph 10 of that Schedule (legal professional privilege), for the words "or, in Scotland, to confidentiality as between client and professional legal adviser," there is substituted "or, in Scotland, to confidentiality of communications".

Extension of transitional exemption

8.—In Schedule 14 to that Act (transitional provisions), in paragraph 2(1) (which confers transitional exemption from the prohibition on processing without registration on those registered under the Data Protection Act 1984) the words "or, if earlier, 24th October 2001" are omitted.

SCHEDULE 7

Disclosure of Information by Ombudsmen

The Parliamentary Commissioner for administration

1.—At the end of section 11 of the Parliamentary Commissioner Act 1967 (provision for secrecy of information) there is inserted—

"(5) Information obtained from the Information Commissioner by virtue of section 76(1) of the Freedom of Information Act 2000 shall be treated for the purposes of subsection (2) of this section as obtained for the purposes of an investigation under this Act and, in relation to such information, the reference in paragraph (a) of that subsection to the investigation shall have effect as a reference to any investigation."

2.—After section 11A of that Act there is inserted—

"11AA.—Disclosure of information by Parliamentary Commissioner to Information Commissioner.

(1) The Commissioner may disclose to the Information Commissioner any information obtained by, or furnished to, the Commissioner under or for the purposes of this Act if the information appears to the Commissioner to relate to—

(a) a matter in respect of which the Information Commissioner could exercise any power conferred by—
  (i) Part V of the Data Protection Act 1998 (enforcement),
  (ii) section 48 of the Freedom of Information Act 2000 (practice recommendations), or
  (iii) Part IV of that Act (enforcement), or
(b) the commission of an offence under—
  (i) any provision of the Data Protection Act 1998 other than paragraph 12 of Schedule 9 (obstruction of execution of warrant), or
  (ii) section 77 of the Freedom of Information Act 2000 (offence of altering etc. records with intent to prevent disclosure).

(2) Nothing in section 11(2) of this Act shall apply in relation to the disclosure of information in accordance with this section."

The commissions for local administration in England and Wales

3.—In section 32 of the Local Government Act 1974 (law of defamation, and disclosure of information) after subsection (6) there is inserted—

"(7) Information obtained from the Information Commissioner by virtue of section 76 of the Freedom of Information Act 2000 shall be treated for the purposes of subsection (2) above as obtained for the purposes of an investigation under this Part of this Act and, in relation to such information, the reference in paragraph (a) of that subsection to the investigation shall have effect as a reference to any investigation."

4.—After section 33 of that Act there is inserted—

"33A.—Disclosure of information by Local Commissioner to Information Commissioner.

(1) A Local Commissioner may disclose to the Information Commissioner any information

obtained by, or furnished to, the Local Commissioner under or for the purposes of this Part of this Act if the information appears to the Local Commissioner to relate to—

(a) a matter in respect of which the Information Commissioner could exercise any power conferred by—
 (i) Part V of the Data Protection Act 1998 (enforcement),
 (ii) section 48 of the Freedom of Information Act 2000 (practice recommendations), or
 (iii) Part IV of that Act (enforcement), or
(b) the commission of an offence under—
 (i) any provision of the Data Protection Act 1998 other than paragraph 12 of Schedule 9 (obstruction of execution of warrant), or
 (ii) section 77 of the Freedom of Information Act 2000 (offence of altering etc. records with intent to prevent disclosure).

(2) Nothing in section 32(2) of this Act shall apply in relation to the disclosure of information in accordance with this section."

The Health Service Commissioners

5.—At the end of section 15 of the Health Service Commissioners Act 1993 (confidentiality of information) there is inserted—

"(4) Information obtained from the Information Commissioner by virtue of section 76 of the Freedom of Information Act 2000 shall be treated for the purposes of subsection (1) as obtained for the purposes of an investigation and, in relation to such information, the reference in paragraph (a) of that subsection to the investigation shall have effect as a reference to any investigation."

6.—After section 18 of that Act there is inserted—

"18A.—Disclosure of information to Information Commissioner.

(1) The Health Service Commissioner for England or the Health Service Commissioner for Wales may disclose to the Information Commissioner any information obtained by, or furnished to, the Health Service Commissioner under or for the purposes of this Act if the information appears to the Health Service Commissioner to relate to—

(a) a matter in respect of which the Information Commissioner could exercise any power conferred by—
 (i) Part V of the Data Protection Act 1998 (enforcement),
 (ii) section 48 of the Freedom of Information Act 2000 (practice recommendations), or
 (iii) Part IV of that Act (enforcement), or
(b) the commission of an offence under—
 (i) any provision of the Data Protection Act 1998 other than paragraph 12 of Schedule 9 (obstruction of execution of warrant), or
 (ii) section 77 of the Freedom of Information Act 2000 (offence of altering etc. records with intent to prevent disclosure).

(3) Nothing in section 15 (confidentiality of information) applies in relation to the disclosure of information in accordance with this section."

The Welsh Administration Ombudsman

7.—In Schedule 9 to the Government of Wales Act 1998 (the Welsh Administration Ombudsman), at the end of paragraph 25 (confidentiality of information) there is inserted—

"(5) Information obtained from the Information Commissioner by virtue of section 76 of the Freedom of Information Act 2000 shall be treated for the purposes of sub-paragraph (1) as obtained for the purposes of an investigation and, in relation to such information, the reference in paragraph (a) of that subsection to the investigation shall have effect as a reference to any investigation."

8.—After paragraph 27 of that Schedule there is inserted—

"28.—Disclosure of information to Information Commissioner

(1) The Welsh Administration Ombudsman may disclose to the Information Commissioner any information obtained by, or furnished to, the Welsh Administration Ombudsman under or for the purposes of this Schedule if the information appears to the Welsh Administration Ombudsman to relate to—

(a) a matter in respect of which the Information Commissioner could exercise any power conferred by—
  (i) Part V of the Data Protection Act 1998 (enforcement),
  (ii) section 48 of the Freedom of Information Act 2000 (practice recommendations), or
  (iii) Part IV of that Act (enforcement), or
(b) the commission of an offence under—
  (i) any provision of the Data Protection Act 1998 other than paragraph 12 of Schedule 9 (obstruction of execution of warrant), or
  (ii) section 77 of the Freedom of Information Act 2000 (offence of altering etc. records with intent to prevent disclosure).

(2) Nothing in paragraph 25(1) applies in relation to the disclosure of information in accordance with this paragraph."

The Northern Ireland Commissioner for complaints

9.—At the end of Article 21 of the Commissioner for Complaints (Northern Ireland) Order 1996 (disclosure of information by Commissioner) there is inserted—

"(5) Information obtained from the Information Commissioner by virtue of section 76 of the Freedom of Information Act 2000 shall be treated for the purposes of paragraph (1) as obtained for the purposes of an investigation under this Order and, in relation to such information, the reference in paragraph (1)(a) to the investigation shall have effect as a reference to any investigation."

10.—After that Article there is inserted—

"21A.—Disclosure of information to Information Commissioner

(1) The Commissioner may disclose to the Information Commissioner any information obtained by, or furnished to, the Commissioner under or for the purposes of this Order if the information appears to the Commissioner to relate to—
(a) a matter in respect of which the Information Commissioner could exercise any power conferred by—
  (i) Part V of the Data Protection Act 1998 (enforcement),
  (ii) section 48 of the Freedom of Information Act 2000 (practice recommendations), or
  (iii) Part IV of that Act (enforcement), or
(b) the commission of an offence under—
  (i) any provision of the Data Protection Act 1998 other than paragraph 12 of Schedule 9 (obstruction of execution of warrant), or
  (ii) section 77 of the Freedom of Information Act 2000 (offence of altering etc. records with intent to prevent disclosure).

(2) Nothing in Article 21(1) applies in relation to the disclosure of information in accordance with this Article."

The Assembly Ombudsman for Northern Ireland

11.—At the end of Article 19 of the Ombudsman (Northern Ireland) Order 1996 there is inserted—

"(5) Information obtained from the Information Commissioner by virtue of section 76 of the Freedom of Information Act 2000 shall be treated for the purposes of paragraph (1) as obtained for the purposes of an investigation under this Order and, in relation to such information, the reference in paragraph (1)(a) to the investigation shall have effect as a reference to any investigation."

12.—After that Article there is inserted—

"19A.—Disclosure of information to Information Commissioner

(1) The Ombudsman may disclose to the Information Commissioner any information obtained by, or furnished to, the Ombudsman under or for the purposes of this Order if the information appears to the Ombudsman to relate to—
(a) a matter in respect of which the Information Commissioner could exercise any power conferred by—
  (i) Part V of the Data Protection Act 1998 (enforcement),
  (ii) section 48 of the Freedom of Information Act 2000 (practice recommendations), or
  (iii) Part IV of that Act (enforcement), or

(b) the commission of an offence under—
   (i) any provision of the Data Protection Act 1998 other than paragraph 12 of Schedule 9 (obstruction of execution of warrant), or
   (ii) section 77 of the Freedom of Information Act 2000 (offence of altering etc. records with intent to prevent disclosure).

(2) Nothing in Article 19(1) applies in relation to the disclosure of information in accordance with this Article."

The Commissioner for Local Administration in Scotland

13.—[. . .][72]

SCHEDULE 8

REPEALS

PART I

REPEAL COMING INTO FORCE ON PASSING OF ACT

1.—Not reproduced here: sets out various statutory provisions repealed on the stated date.

PART II

REPEALS COMING INTO FORCE IN ACCORDANCE WITH SECTION 87(2)

1.—Not reproduced here: sets out various statutory provisions repealed on the stated date.

PART III

REPEALS COMING INTO FORCE IN ACCORDANCE WITH SECTION 87(3)

1.—Not reproduced here: sets out various statutory provisions repealed on the stated date.

[72] Repealed by Scottish Public Services Ombudsman Act (2002 ASP.11), Sch.6, para.23(3).

Freedom of Information (Scotland) Act 2002

(2002, asp 13)

ARRANGEMENT OF SECTIONS

PART 1

ACCESS TO INFORMATION HELD BY SCOTTISH PUBLIC AUTHORITIES

Right to information

Section

Review of refusal, etc.

20. Requirement for review of refusal etc.
21. Review by Scottish public authority

Records transferred to the Keeper of the Records of Scotland

22. Special provisions relating to records transferred to Keeper

Publication schemes

23. Publication schemes
24. Model publication schemes

PART 2

EXEMPT INFORMATION

25. Information otherwise accessible
26. Prohibitions on disclosure
27. Information intended for future publication
28. Relations within the United Kingdom
29. Formulation of Scottish Administration policy etc.
30. Prejudice to effective conduct of public affairs
31. National security and defence
32. International relations
33. Commercial interests and the economy
34. Investigations by Scottish public authorities and proceedings arising out of such investigations
35. Law enforcement
36. Confidentiality
37. Court records, etc.
38. Personal information
39. Health, safety and the environment
40. Audit functions
41. Communications with Her Majesty etc. and honours

PART 6

CODES OF PRACTICE

PART 7

MISCELLANEOUS AND SUPPLEMENTAL

SCHEDULES

An Act of the Scottish Parliament to make provision for the disclosure of information held by Scottish public authorities or by persons providing services for them; and for connected purposes. App 1–0

[MAY 28, 2002]

PART 1

ACCESS TO INFORMATION HELD BY SCOTTISH PUBLIC AUTHORITIES

Right to information

General entitlement

1.—(1) A person who requests information from a Scottish public authority which holds it is entitled to be given it by the authority.

(2) The person who makes such a request is in this Part and in Parts 2 and 7 referred to as the "applicant".

(3) If the authority—

(a) requires further information in order to identify and locate the requested information; and

(b) has told the applicant so (specifying what the requirement for further information is),

then, provided that the requirement is reasonable, the authority is not obliged to give the requested information until it has the further information.

(4) The information to be given by the authority is that held by it at the time the request is received, except that, subject to subsection (5), any amendment or deletion which would have been made, regardless of the receipt of the request, between that time and the time it gives the information may be made before the information is given.

(5) The requested information is not, by virtue of subsection (4), to be destroyed before it can be given (unless the circumstances are such that it is not reasonably practicable to prevent such destruction from occurring).

(6) This section is subject to sections 2, 9, 12 and 14.

Effect of exemptions

2.—(1) To information which is exempt information by virtue of any provision of Part 2, section 1 applies only to the extent that—

(a) the provision does not confer absolute exemption; and

(b) in all the circumstances of the case, the public interest in disclosing the information is not outweighed by that in maintaining the exemption.

(2) For the purposes of paragraph (a) of subsection (1), the following provisions of Part 2 (and no others) are to be regarded as conferring absolute exemption—

(a) section 25;
(b) section 26;
(c) section 36(2);
(d) section 37; and
(e) in subsection (1) of section 38—

(i) paragraphs (a), (c) and (d); and
(ii) paragraph (b) where the first condition referred to in that paragraph is satisfied by virtue of subsection (2)(a)(i) or (b) of that section.

Scottish public authorities

3.—(1) In this Act, "Scottish public authority" means—

(a) any body which, any other person who, or the holder of any office which—

(i) is listed in schedule 1; or
(ii) is designated by order under section 5(1); or

(b) a publicly-owned company, as defined by section 6.

(2) For the purposes of this Act but subject to subsection (4), information is held by an authority if it is held—

(a) by the authority otherwise than—

(i) on behalf of another person; or
(ii) in confidence, having been supplied by a Minister of the Crown or by a department of the Government of the United Kingdom; or

(b) by a person other than the authority, on behalf of the authority.

(3) Subsection (1)(a)(i) is subject to any qualification set out in schedule 1.

(4) Information is not held by the Keeper of the Records of Scotland if it is contained in a record transferred to the Keeper by a public authority within the meaning of the Freedom of Information Act 2000 (c.36) unless it is information—

(a) to which subsections (2) to (5) of section 22 apply by virtue of subsection (6) of that section; or
(b) designated by that authority as open information for the purposes of this subsection.

(5) Where the public authority mentioned in subsection (4) is the Secretary of State for Scotland and the information is contained in a record transferred as is mentioned in subsection (6) of section 22 the reference in subsection (4)(b) to "that authority" is to be construed as a reference to the Scottish Ministers.

Amendment of schedule 1

4.—(1) The Scottish Ministers may by order amend Schedule 1 by—

(a) adding to that Schedule a reference to—

(i) any body which; or
(ii) the holder of any office which,

is not for the time being listed there and is either a part of the Scottish Administration or a Scottish public authority with mixed functions or no reserved functions; or

(b) removing from that schedule an entry for the time being listed there.

(2) The reference in paragraph (a) of subsection (1) to an authority with mixed functions or no reserved functions is to be construed in accordance with paragraphs 1(4) and 2 of Part III of Schedule 5 to the Scotland Act 1998 (c.46).

(3) An order under subsection (1) may relate to a specified person or office or to persons or offices falling within a specified description.

Further power to designate Scottish public authorities

5.—(1) The Scottish Ministers may by order designate as a Scottish public authority for the purposes of this Act any person mentioned in subsection (2) who—

(a) is neither for the time being listed in schedule 1 nor capable of being added to that schedule by order under section 4(1); and
(b) is neither a public body nor the holder of any public office.

(2) The persons are those who either—

(a) appear to the Scottish Ministers to exercise functions of a public nature; or
(b) are providing, under a contract made with a Scottish public authority, any service whose provision is a function of that authority.

(3) An order under subsection (1) may designate a specified person or persons falling within a specified description.

(4) An order under subsection (1) made by virtue of—

(a) subsection (2)(a) must specify the functions of a public nature which appear to be exercised;
(b) subsection (2)(b) must specify the service being provided.

(5) Before making an order under subsection (1), the Scottish Ministers must consult—

(a) every person to whom the order relates; or
(b) persons appearing to them to represent such persons.

Publicly-owned companies

6.—(1) A company is a "publicly-owned company" for the purposes of section 3(1)(b) if it is wholly owned—

(a) by the Scottish Ministers; or
(b) by any other Scottish public authority listed in schedule 1, other than an authority so listed only in relation to information of a specified description.

(2) For the purposes of subsection (1), a company is wholly owned—

(a) by the Scottish Ministers if it has no members except—

(i) the Scottish Ministers or companies wholly owned by the Scottish Ministers; or
(ii) persons acting on behalf of the Scottish Ministers or of such companies; and

(b) by any other Scottish public authority if it has no members except—

(i) the authority or companies wholly owned by the authority; or
(ii) persons acting on behalf of the authority or of such companies.

(3) In subsections (1) and (2), "company" includes any body corporate.

Public authorities to which Act has limited application

7.—(1) An order under section 4(1)(a) may, in adding an entry to schedule 1, list the authority only in relation to information of a specified description; and where an authority is so listed nothing in this Act applies to any other information held by the authority.

(2) The Scottish Ministers may by order amend that Schedule—

(a) by limiting the entry relating to an authority to information of a specified description; or

(b) by removing or amending any such limitation for the time being contained in an entry so relating.

(3) Nothing in this Act applies to information held by a person designated as a Scottish public authority by order under subsection (1) of section 5 if the order is made by virtue of—

(a) subsection (2)(a) of that section and the information does not relate to the functions; or

(b) subsection (2)(b) of that section and the information does not relate to the service,

specified in the order.

(4) Nothing in this Act applies in relation to information—

(a) held by a publicly-owned company; and

(b) of a description specified in relation to that company in an order made for the purposes of this subsection by the Scottish Ministers.

Requesting information

8.—(1) Any reference in this Act to "requesting" information is a reference to making a request which—

(a) is in writing or in another form which, by reason of its having some permanency, is capable of being used for subsequent reference (as, for example, a recording made on audio or video tape);

(b) states the name of the applicant and an address for correspondence; and

(c) describes the information requested.

(2) For the purposes of paragraph (a) of subsection (1) (and without prejudice to the generality of that paragraph), a request is to be treated as made in writing where the text of the request is—

(a) transmitted by electronic means;

(b) received in legible form; and

(c) capable of being used for subsequent reference.

Fees

9.—(1) A Scottish public authority receiving a request which requires it to comply with section 1(1) may, within the time allowed by section 10 for so complying, give the applicant a notice in writing (in this Act referred to as a "fees notice") stating that a fee of an amount specified in the notice is to be charged by the authority for so complying.

(2) Subsection (1) is subject to section 19.

(3) If a fees notice is given to the applicant, the authority is not obliged to give the requested information unless the fee is duly paid; and for the purposes of this subsection and section 10(2) due payment is payment within the period of three months beginning with the day on which the notice is given.

(4) Subject to subsection (7), a fee charged under subsection (1) is to be determined by the authority in accordance with regulations made by the Scottish Ministers.

(5) Without prejudice to the generality of subsection (4), the regulations may in particular provide that—

(a) a fee is not to exceed such amount as may be specified in, or determined in accordance with, the regulations;
(b) a fee is to be calculated in such manner as may be so specified; and
(c) no fee is payable in a case so specified.

(6) Before making the regulations, the Scottish Ministers are to consult the Commissioner.

(7) Subsection (4) does not apply where provision is made, by or under any enactment, as to the fee that may be charged by the authority for the disclosure of the information.

Time for compliance

10.—(1) Subject to subsections (2) and (3), a Scottish public authority receiving a request which requires it to comply with section 1(1) must comply promptly; and in any event by not later than the twentieth working day after—

(a) in a case other than that mentioned in paragraph (b), the receipt by the authority of the request; or
(b) in a case where section 1(3) applies, the receipt by it of the further information.

(2) If—

(a) the authority is the Keeper of the Records of Scotland; and
(b) the information is information to which section 22(2) to (5) applies,

subsection (1) applies with the substitution, for the reference to the twentieth working day, of a reference to the thirtieth working day.

(3) Where the authority gives a fees notice to the applicant and the fee is duly paid, the working days in the period—

(a) beginning with the day on which that notice is given; and
(b) ending with the day on which the fee is received by the authority,

are to be disregarded in calculating, for the purposes of subsection (1), the twentieth (or as the case may be the thirtieth) working day mentioned in that subsection.

(4) The Scottish Ministers may by regulations provide that subsections (1) and (3) are to have effect as if references to the twentieth (or as the case may be the thirtieth) working day were references to such other working day, not later than the sixtieth, after receipt by the authority of the request as is specified in, or determined in accordance with, the regulations.

(5) Regulations under subsection (4) may—

(a) prescribe different days in relation to different cases; and
(b) confer a discretion on the Scottish Information Commissioner, exercisable both at the request of the authority and where no such request has been made.

Means of providing information

11.—(1) Where, in requesting information from a Scottish public authority, the applicant expresses a preference for receiving it by any one or more of the means mentioned in subsection (2), the authority must, so far as is reasonably practicable, give effect to that preference.

(2) The means are—

(a) the provision to the applicant, in permanent form or in another form acceptable to the applicant, of a copy of the information;
(b) such provision to the applicant of a digest or summary of the information; and
(c) the provision to the applicant of a reasonable opportunity to inspect a record containing the information.

(3) In determining, for the purposes of subsection (1), what is reasonably practicable, the authority may have regard to all the circumstances, including cost; and where it determines that it is not reasonably practicable to give effect to the preference it must notify the applicant of the reasons for that determination.

(4) Subject to subsection (1), information given in compliance with section 1(1) may be given by any means which are reasonable in the circumstances.

(5) Such tests of reasonable practicability as are imposed by this section are not to be construed as detracting from any duty which a provider of services has under or by virtue of section 21 of the Disability Discrimination Act 1995 (c.50) (duty to make adjustments to practices, policies, procedures or physical features so that use of services by disabled persons is facilitated or made possible).

Excessive cost of compliance

12.—(1) Section 1(1) does not oblige a Scottish public authority to comply with a request for information if the authority estimates that the cost of complying with the request would exceed such amount as may be prescribed in regulations made by the Scottish Ministers; and different amounts may be so prescribed in relation to different cases.

(2) The regulations may provide that, in such circumstances as they may specify, where two or more requests for information are made to the authority—

(a) by one person;
(b) by different persons who appear to it to be acting in concert or whose requests appear to have been instigated wholly or mainly for a purpose other than the obtaining of the information itself; or
(c) by different persons in circumstances where the authority considers it would be reasonable to make the information available to the public at large and elects to do so,

then if the authority estimates that the total cost of complying with both (or all) of the requests exceeds the amount prescribed, in relation to complying with either (or any) of those requests, under subsection (1), section 1(1) does not oblige the authority to comply with either (or any) of those requests.

(3) The regulations may, in respect of an election made as mentioned in subsection (2)(c), make provision as to the means by which and the time within which the information is to be made available to the public at large.

(4) The regulations may make provision as to—

(a) the costs to be estimated; and
(b) the manner in which those costs are to be estimated.

(5) Before making the regulations, the Scottish Ministers are to consult the Commissioner.

(6) References in this section to the cost of complying with a request are not to be construed as including any reference to costs incurred in fulfilling any such duty under or by virtue of the Disability Discrimination Act 1995 (c.50) as is mentioned in section 11(5).

Fees for disclosure in certain circumstances

13.—(1) A Scottish public authority may charge for the communication of any information—

(a) which by virtue of section 12(1) or (2) it is not obliged to communicate; and
(b) which it is not otherwise required by law to communicate,

such fee as may be determined by it in accordance with regulations made by the Scottish Ministers.

(2) Without prejudice to the generality of subsection (1), the regulations may in particular provide that a fee—

(a) is not to exceed such amount as may be specified in, or determined in accordance with, the regulations; and
(b) is to be calculated in such manner as may be so specified.

(3) Before making the regulations, the Scottish Ministers are to consult the Commissioner.

(4) Subsection (1) does not apply where provision is made, by or under any enactment, as to the fee that may be charged by the authority for the disclosure of the information.

Vexatious or repeated requests

14.—(1) Section 1(1) does not oblige a Scottish public authority to comply with a request for information if the request is vexatious.

(2) Where a Scottish public authority has complied with a request from a person for information, it is not obliged to comply with a subsequent request from that person which is identical or substantially similar unless there has been a reasonable period of time between the making of the request complied with and the making of the subsequent request.

Duty to provide advice and assistance

15.—(1) A Scottish public authority must, so far as it is reasonable to expect it to do so, provide advice and assistance to a person who proposes to make, or has made, a request for information to it.

(2) A Scottish public authority which, in relation to the provision of advice or assistance in any case, conforms with the code of practice issued under section 60 is, as respects that case, to be taken to comply with the duty imposed by subsection (1).

Responses to request

Refusal of request

16.—(1) Subject to section 18, a Scottish public authority which, in relation to a request for information which it holds, to any extent claims that, by virtue of any provision of Part 2, the information is exempt information must, within the time allowed by or by virtue of section 10 for complying with the request, give the applicant a notice in writing (in this Act referred to as a "refusal notice") which—

(a) discloses that it holds the information;
(b) states that it so claims;
(c) specifies the exemption in question; and
(d) states (if not otherwise apparent) why the exemption applies.

(2) Where the authority's claim is made only by virtue of a provision of Part 2 which does not confer absolute exemption, the notice must state the authority's reason for claiming that, in all the circumstances of the case, the public interest in maintaining the exemption outweighs that in disclosure of the information.

(3) The authority is not obliged to make a statement under subsection (1)(d) in so far as the statement would disclose information which would itself be exempt information.

(4) A Scottish public authority which, in relation to a request for information, claims that section 12(1) applies must, within the time allowed by or by virtue of section 10 for complying with the request, give the applicant a notice which states that it so claims.

(5) A Scottish public authority which, in relation to such a request, claims that section 14 applies must, within that time, give the applicant a notice which states that it so claims; except that the notice need not be given if—

(a) the authority has, in relation to a previous identical or substantially similar such request, given the applicant a notice under this subsection; and

(b) it would in all the circumstances be unreasonable to expect it to serve a further such notice in relation to the current request.

(6) Subsections (1), (4) and (5) are subject to section 19.

Notice that information is not held

17.—(1) Where—

(a) a Scottish public authority receives a request which would require it either—

(i) to comply with section 1(1); or

(ii) to determine any question arising by virtue of paragraph (a) or (b) of section 2(1) if it held the information to which the request relates; but

(b) the authority does not hold that information,

it must, within the time allowed by or by virtue of section 10 for complying with the request, give the applicant notice in writing that it does not hold it.

(2) Subsection (1) is subject to section 19.

(3) Subsection (1) does not apply if, by virtue of section 18, the authority instead gives the applicant a refusal notice.

Further provision as respects responses to request

18.—(1) Where, if information existed and was held by a Scottish public authority, the authority could give a refusal notice under section 16(1) on the basis that the information was exempt information by virtue of any of sections 28 to 35, 39(1) or 41 but the authority considers that to reveal whether the information exists or is so held would be contrary to the public interest, it may (whether or not the information does exist and is held by it) give the applicant a refusal notice by virtue of this section.

(2) Neither paragraph (a) of subsection (1) of section 16 nor subsection (2) of that section applies as respects a refusal notice given by virtue of this section.

Content of certain notices

Content of certain notices

19.—A notice under section 9(1) or 16(1), (4) or (5) (including a refusal notice given by virtue of section 18(1)) or 17(1) must contain particulars—

(a) of the procedure provided by the authority for dealing with complaints about the handling by it of requests for information; and
(b) about the rights of application to the authority and the Commissioner conferred by sections 20(1) and 47(1).

Review of refusal, etc.

Requirement for review of refusal etc.

20.—(1) An applicant who is dissatisfied with the way in which a Scottish public authority has dealt with a request for information made under this Part of this Act may require the authority to review its actions and decisions in relation to that request.

(2) A requirement under subsection (1) is referred to in this Act as a "requirement for review".

(3) A requirement for review must—

(a) be in writing or in another form which, by reason of its having some permanency, is capable of being used for subsequent reference (as, for example, a recording made on audio or video tape);
(b) state the name of the applicant and an address for correspondence; and
(c) specify—

(i) the request for information to which the requirement for review relates; and
(ii) the matter which gives rise to the applicant's dissatisfaction mentioned in subsection (1).

(4) For the purposes of paragraph (a) of subsection (3) (and without prejudice to the generality of that paragraph), a requirement for review is treated as made in writing where the text of the requirement is as mentioned in paragraphs (a) to (c) of section 8(2).

(5) Subject to subsection (6), a requirement for review must be made by not later than the fortieth working day after—

(a) the expiry of the time allowed by or by virtue of section 10 for complying with the request; or
(b) in a case where the authority purports under this Act—

(i) to comply with a request for information; or
(ii) to give the applicant a fees notice, a refusal notice or a notice under section 17(1) that information is not held,

but does so outwith that time, the receipt by the applicant of the information provided or, as the case may be, the notice.

(6) A Scottish public authority may comply with a requirement for review made after the expiry of the time allowed by subsection (5) for making such a requirement if it considers it appropriate to do so.

(7) The Scottish Ministers may by regulations provide that subsections (5) and (6) are to have effect as if the reference in subsection (5) to the fortieth working day were a reference to such other working day as is specified in (or determined in accordance with) the regulations.

(8) Regulations under subsection (7) may—

(a) prescribe different days in relation to different cases; and
(b) confer a discretion on the Scottish Information Commissioner.

(9) In subsection (1), the reference to "actions" and "decisions" includes inaction and failure to reach a decision.

Review by Scottish public authority

21.—(1) Subject to subsection (2), a Scottish public authority receiving a requirement for review must (unless that requirement is withdrawn or is as mentioned in subsection (8)) comply promptly; and in any event by not later than the twentieth working day after receipt by it of the requirement.

(2) If—

(a) the authority is the Keeper of the Records of Scotland; and
(b) a different authority is, by virtue of section 22(4), to review a decision to which the requirement relates,

subsection (1) applies with the substitution, for the reference to the twentieth working day, of a reference to the thirtieth working day.

(3) A requirement for review may be withdrawn by the applicant who made it, by notice in writing to the authority, at any time before the authority makes its decision on the requirement.

(4) The authority may, as respects the request for information to which the requirement relates—

(a) confirm a decision complained of, with or without such modifications as it considers appropriate;
(b) substitute for any such decision a different decision; or
(c) reach a decision, where the complaint is that no decision had been reached.

(5) Within the time allowed by subsection (1) for complying with the requirement for review, the authority must give the applicant notice in writing of what it has done under subsection (4) and a statement of its reasons for so doing.

(6) The Scottish Ministers may by regulations provide that subsections (1) and (5) and section 47(4)(b) are to have effect as if the reference in subsection (1) to the twentieth (or as the case may be the thirtieth) working day were a reference to such other working day as is specified in (or determined in accordance with) the regulations.

(7) Regulations under subsection (6) may—

(a) prescribe different days in relation to different cases; and
(b) confer a discretion on the Scottish Information Commissioner.

(8) Subsection (1) does not oblige a Scottish public authority to comply with a requirement for review if—

(a) the requirement is vexatious; or
(b) the request for information to which the requirement for review relates was one with which, by virtue of section 14, the authority was not obliged to comply.

(9) Where the authority considers that paragraph (a) or (b) of subsection (8) applies, it must give the applicant who made the requirement for review notice in writing, within the time allowed by subsection (1) for complying with that requirement, that it so claims.

(10) A notice under subsection (5) or (9) must contain particulars about the rights of application to the Commissioner and of appeal conferred by sections 47(1) and 56.

Records transferred to the keeper of the records of Scotland

Special provisions relating to records transferred to Keeper

22.—(1) Subsections (2) to (5) apply to information which—

(a) is contained in a record transferred to the Keeper of the Records of Scotland by a Scottish public authority; and
(b) has not been designated by the authority as open information for the purposes of this section.

(2) The Keeper must, as soon as practicable after receiving a request for information to which this subsection applies, send a copy of that request to the authority which transferred the information; and it is for the authority, instead of the Keeper, to come to a decision as to whether the information is exempt information by virtue of any provision of Part 2 and to determine any question then arising by virtue of paragraph (a) or (b) of section 2(1) as respects the information.

(3) After receiving the copy, the authority must, within such time as will make it practicable for the Keeper to comply with section 10 as respects the request, inform the Keeper of the decision mentioned in subsection (2) and of any determination required by virtue of that decision.

(4) The Keeper must, as soon as practicable after receiving a requirement for review in which the specification under section 20(3)(c)(ii) relates to a decision made by the authority by virtue of subsection (2), send a copy of that requirement to the authority; and it is for the authority, instead of the Keeper, to review the decision and to do anything which is to be done under section 21(4).

(5) After receiving the requirement, the authority must, within such time as will make it practicable for the Keeper to comply with subsection (5) of section 21 as respects the requirement, inform the Keeper of what it has done under subsection (4) of that section and provide a statement of its reasons for so doing; and it is that information and statement which the Keeper shall, in the notice in writing, give in so complying.

(6) Subsections (2) to (5) also apply to information which is contained in a record transferred to the Keeper, before 1st July 1999, by the Secretary of State for Scotland and is not designated by the Scottish Ministers as open information for the purposes of section 3(4); but for the purposes of that application references in subsections (2) to (5) to "the authority" are to be construed as references to the Scottish Ministers.

Publication schemes

Publication schemes

23.—(1) A Scottish public authority must—

(a) adopt and maintain a scheme (in this Act referred to as a "publication scheme") which relates to the publication of information by the authority and is approved by the Commissioner;
(b) publish information in accordance with that scheme; and
(c) from time to time review that scheme.

(2) A publication scheme must specify—

(a) classes of information which the authority publishes or intends to publish;
(b) the manner in which information of each class is, or is intended to be, published; and
(c) whether the published information is, or is intended to be, available to the public free of charge or on payment.

(3) In adopting or reviewing its publication scheme the authority must have regard to the public interest in—

(a) allowing public access to information held by it and in particular to information which—

(i) relates to the provision of services by it, the cost to it of providing them or the standards attained by services so provided; or

(ii) consists of facts, or analyses, on the basis of which decisions of importance to the public have been made by it;

(b) the publication of reasons for decisions made by it.

(4) The authority must publish its publication scheme but may do so in such manner as it thinks fit.

(5) The Commissioner may—

(a) when approving a publication scheme, provide that the approval expires at the end of a specified period; and

(b) at any time give notice to an authority revoking, as from the end of the period of six months beginning at that time, approval of its publication scheme.

(6) The Commissioner, when—

(a) refusing to approve a proposed publication scheme; or

(b) revoking approval of a publication scheme,

must state the reason for doing so.

Model publication schemes

24.—(1) The Commissioner may, in relation to Scottish public authorities falling within particular classes—

(a) prepare and approve model publication schemes; or

(b) approve such schemes prepared by other persons.

(2) If an authority which falls within the class to which an approved model publication scheme relates adopts that scheme without modification, no further approval of the Commissioner is required so long as that model scheme remains approved; but the approval of the Commissioner is required in relation to any modification of the scheme by an authority.

(3) The Commissioner may—

(a) when approving a model publication scheme, provide that the approval expires at the end of a specified period; and

(b) at any time publish, in such manner as the Commissioner thinks fit, a notice revoking, as from the end of the period of six months beginning at that time, approval of such a scheme.

(4) The Commissioner, when—

(a) refusing to approve—

(i) under subsection (1)(b), a proposed model scheme; or

(ii) any such modification as is mentioned in subsection (2),

must state the reason for doing so; or

(b) revoking approval of a model publication scheme, must include in the notice under subsection (3)(b) a statement of the reason for doing so.

Part 2

Exempt Information

Information otherwise accessible

25.—(1) Information which the applicant can reasonably obtain other than by requesting it under section 1(1) is exempt information.

(2) For the purposes of subsection (1), information—

(a) may be reasonably obtainable even if payment is required for access to it;

(b) is to be taken to be reasonably obtainable if—

(i) the Scottish public authority which holds it, or any other person, is obliged by or under any enactment to communicate it (otherwise than by making it available for inspection) to; or

(ii) the Keeper of the Records of Scotland holds it and makes it available for inspection and (in so far as practicable) copying by,

members of the public on request, whether free of charge or on payment.

(3) For the purposes of subsection (1), information which does not fall within paragraph (b) of subsection (2) is not, merely because it is available on request from the Scottish public authority which holds it, reasonably obtainable unless it is made available in accordance with the authority's publication scheme and any payment required is specified in, or determined in accordance with, the scheme.

Prohibitions on disclosure

26.—Information is exempt information if its disclosure by a Scottish public authority (otherwise than under this Act)—

(a) is prohibited by or under an enactment;

(b) is incompatible with a Community obligation; or

(c) would constitute, or be punishable as, a contempt of court.

Information intended for future publication

27.—(1) Information is exempt information if—

(a) it is held with a view to its being published by—

(i) a Scottish public authority; or

(ii) any other person,

at a date not later than twelve weeks after that on which the request for the information is made;

(b) when that request is made the information is already being held with that view; and

(c) it is reasonable in all the circumstances that the information be withheld from disclosure until such date as is mentioned in paragraph (a).

(2) Information obtained in the course of, or derived from, a programme of research is exempt information if—

(a) the programme is continuing with a view to a report of the research (whether or not including a statement of that information) being published by—

(i) a Scottish public authority; or
(ii) any other person; and

(b) disclosure of the information before the date of publication would, or would be likely to, prejudice substantially—

(i) the programme;
(ii) the interests of any individual participating in the programme;
(iii) the interests of the authority which holds the information; or
(iv) the interests of the authority mentioned in sub-paragraph (i) of paragraph (a) (if it is a different authority from that which holds the information).

Relations within the United Kingdom

28.—(1) Information is exempt information if its disclosure under this Act would, or would be likely to, prejudice substantially relations between any administration in the United Kingdom and any other such administration.

(2) In subsection (1), "administration in the United Kingdom" means—

(a) the Government of the United Kingdom;
(b) the Scottish Administration;
(c) the Executive Committee of the Northern Ireland Assembly; or
(d) the National Assembly for Wales.

Formulation of Scottish Administration policy etc.

29.—(1) Information held by the Scottish Administration is exempt information if it relates to—

(a) the formulation or development of government policy;
(b) Ministerial communications;
(c) the provision of advice by any of the Law Officers or any request for the provision of such advice; or
(d) the operation of any Ministerial private office.

(2) Once a decision as to policy has been taken, any statistical information used to provide an informed background to the taking of the decision is not to be regarded, for the purposes of—

(a) paragraph (a) of subsection (1), as relating to the formulation or development of the policy in question; or
(b) paragraph (b) of that subsection, as relating to Ministerial communications.

(3) In determining any question under section 2(1)(b) as respects information which is exempt information by virtue of subsection (1)(a), the Scottish Administration must have regard to the public interest in the disclosure of factual information which has been used, or is intended to be used, to provide an informed background to the taking of a decision.

(4) In this section—

"government policy" means—

(a) the policy of the Scottish Administration; and
(b) in relation to information created before 1st July 1999, the policy of the Government of the United Kingdom;

"the Law Officers" means the Lord Advocate, the Solicitor General for Scotland, the Advocate General for Scotland, the Attorney General, the Solicitor General and the Attorney General for Northern Ireland;

"Ministerial communications" means any communications between Ministers and includes, in particular, communications relating to proceedings of the Scottish Cabinet (or of any committee of that Cabinet); and

"Ministerial private office" means any part of the Scottish Administration which provides personal administrative support to a Minister.

(5) In the definitions of "Ministerial communications" and "Ministerial private office" in subsection (4), "Minister" means a member of the Scottish Executive or a junior Scottish Minister.

Prejudice to effective conduct of public affairs

30.—Information is exempt information if its disclosure under this Act—

(a) would, or would be likely to, prejudice substantially the maintenance of the convention of the collective responsibility of the Scottish Ministers;
(b) would, or would be likely to, inhibit substantially—
  (i) the free and frank provision of advice; or
  (ii) the free and frank exchange of views for the purposes of deliberation; or
(c) would otherwise prejudice substantially, or be likely to prejudice substantially, the effective conduct of public affairs.

National security and defence

31.—(1) Information is exempt information if exemption from section 1(1) is required for the purpose of safeguarding national security.

(2) A certificate signed by a member of the Scottish Executive certifying that such exemption is, or at any time was, required for the purpose of safeguarding national security is conclusive of that fact.

(3) Without prejudice to the generality of subsection (2), a certificate under that subsection may identify the information to which it applies by means of a general description and may be expressed to have prospective effect.

(4) Information is exempt information if its disclosure under this Act would, or would be likely to, prejudice substantially—

(a) the defence of the British Islands or of any colony; or
(b) the capability, effectiveness or security of any relevant forces.

(5) In subsection (4)—

(a) in paragraph (a), "British Islands" and "colony" are to be construed in accordance with Schedule 1 to the Interpretation Act 1978 (c.30); and
(b) in paragraph (b), "relevant forces" means—
  (i) the armed forces of the Crown; and
  (ii) any forces co-operating with those forces,

or any part of the armed forces of the Crown or of any such co-operating forces.

International relations

32.—(1) Information is exempt information if—

(a) its disclosure under this Act would, or would be likely to, prejudice substantially—
  (i) relations between the United Kingdom and any other State;
  (ii) relations between the United Kingdom and any international organisation or international court;

(iii) the interests of the United Kingdom abroad; or
(iv) the promotion or protection by the United Kingdom of its interests abroad; or

(b) it is confidential information obtained from—

(i) a State other than the United Kingdom; or
(ii) an international organisation or international court.

(2) For the purposes of subsection (1), information obtained from a State, organisation or court is confidential at any time while—

(a) the terms on which that information was obtained require it to be held in confidence; or
(b) the circumstances in which it was obtained make it reasonable for the State, organisation or court to expect that it will be so held.

(3) In subsection (1)—
"international court" means an international court which—

(a) is not an international organisation; and
(b) is established—

(i) by a resolution of an international organisation of which the United Kingdom is a member; or
(ii) by an international agreement to which the United Kingdom is a party;

"international organisation" means—

(a) an international organisation whose members include any two or more States; or
(b) an organ of such an international organisation;

"State" includes—

(a) the government of any State; and
(b) any organ of such a government,

and references to a State other than the United Kingdom include references to any territory outwith the United Kingdom.

Commercial interests and the economy

33.—(1) Information is exempt information if—

(a) it constitutes a trade secret; or
(b) its disclosure under this Act would, or would be likely to, prejudice substantially the commercial interests of any person (including, without prejudice to that generality, a Scottish public authority).

(2) Information is exempt information if its disclosure under this Act would, or would be likely to, prejudice substantially—

(a) the economic interests of the whole or part of the United Kingdom; or
(b) the financial interests of an administration in the United Kingdom.

(3) In subsection (2), "administration in the United Kingdom" has the same meaning as in section 28(2).

Investigations by Scottish public authorities and proceedings arising out of such investigations

34.—(1) Information is exempt information if it has at any time been held by a Scottish public authority for the purposes of—

(a) an investigation which the authority has a duty to conduct to ascertain whether a person—

(i) should be prosecuted for an offence; or
(ii) prosecuted for an offence is guilty of it;

(b) an investigation, conducted by the authority, which in the circumstances may lead to a decision by the authority to make a report to the procurator fiscal to enable it to be determined whether criminal proceedings should be instituted; or
(c) criminal proceedings instituted in consequence of a report made by the authority to the procurator fiscal.

(2) Information is exempt information if—

(a) held by a Scottish public authority for the purposes of an inquiry instituted under the Fatal Accidents and Sudden Deaths Inquiry (Scotland) Act 1976 (c.14) but not for the time being concluded; or
(b) held at any time by a Scottish public authority for the purposes of any other investigation being carried out—

(i) by virtue of a duty to ascertain; or
(ii) for the purpose of making a report to the procurator fiscal as respects,

the cause of death of a person.

(3) Information held by a Scottish public authority is exempt information if—

(a) it was obtained or recorded by the authority for the purposes of investigations (other than such investigations as are mentioned in subsection (1)) which are, by virtue either of Her Majesty's prerogative or of powers conferred by or under any enactment, conducted by the authority for any purpose specified in section 35(2); and
(b) it relates to the obtaining of information from confidential sources.

(4) Information is exempt information if obtained or recorded by a Scottish public authority for the purposes of civil proceedings, brought by or on behalf of the authority, which arise out of such investigations as are mentioned in subsection (1) or (3).

Law enforcement

35.–(1) Information is exempt information if its disclosure under this Act would, or would be likely to, prejudice substantially—

(a) prevention or detection of crime;
(b) the apprehension or prosecution of offenders;
(c) the administration of justice;
(d) the assessment or collection of any tax or duty (or of any imposition of a similar nature);
(e) the operation of the immigration controls;
(f) the maintenance of security and good order in prisons or in other institutions where persons are lawfully detained;
(g) the exercise by any public authority (within the meaning of the Freedom of Information Act 2000 (c.36)) or Scottish public authority of its functions for any of the purposes mentioned in subsection (2);

(h) any civil proceedings—

(i) brought; and
(ii) arising out of an investigation conducted, for any such purpose,

by or on behalf of any such authority, by virtue either of Her Majesty's prerogative or of powers conferred by or under any enactment.

(2) The purposes are—

(a) to ascertain whether a person has failed to comply with the law;
(b) to ascertain whether a person is responsible for conduct which is improper;
(c) to ascertain whether circumstances which would justify regulatory action in pursuance of any enactment exist or may arise;
(d) to ascertain a person's fitness or competence in relation to—

(i) the management of bodies corporate; or
(ii) any profession or other activity which the person is, or seeks to become, authorised to carry on;

(e) to ascertain the cause of an accident;
(f) to protect a charity against misconduct or mismanagement (whether by trustees or other persons) in its administration;
(g) to protect the property of a charity from loss or mismanagement;
(h) to recover the property of a charity;
(i) to secure the health, safety and welfare of persons at work; and
(j) to protect persons, other than persons at work, against risk to health or safety where that risk arises out of, or in connection with, the actions of persons at work.

Confidentiality

36.—(1) Information in respect of which a claim to confidentiality of communications could be maintained in legal proceedings is exempt information.

(2) Information is exempt information if—

(a) it was obtained by a Scottish public authority from another person (including another such authority); and
(b) its disclosure by the authority so obtaining it to the public (otherwise than under this Act) would constitute a breach of confidence actionable by that person or any other person.

Court records, etc.

37.—(1) Information is exempt information if it is contained in—

(a) a document—

(i) lodged with, or otherwise placed in the custody of, a court for the purposes of proceedings in a cause or matter;
(ii) served on, or by, a Scottish public authority for the purposes of such proceedings; or
(iii) created by a court or a member of its administrative staff for the purposes of, or in the course of, such proceedings; or

(b) a document—

(i) lodged with, or otherwise placed in the custody of, a person conducting an inquiry or arbitration, for the purposes of that inquiry or arbitration; or
(ii) created by such a person for such purposes,

and a Scottish public authority holds the information solely because it is contained in such a document.

(2) In this section—

"court" includes a tribunal or body exercising the judicial power of the State; and

"inquiry" means an inquiry or hearing held under a provision contained in, or made under, an enactment.

(3) This section does not apply to information held by a Scottish public authority for the purposes of an inquiry instituted under the Fatal Accidents and Sudden Deaths Inquiry (Scotland) Act 1976 (c.14).

Personal information

38.—(1) Information is exempt information if it constitutes—

(a) personal data of which the applicant is the data subject;
(b) personal data and either the condition mentioned in subsection (2) (the "first condition") or that mentioned in subsection (3) (the "second condition") is satisfied;
(c) personal census information; or
(d) a deceased person's health record.

(2) The first condition is—

(a) in a case where the information falls within any of paragraphs (a) to (d) of the definition of "data" in section 1(1) of the Data Protection Act 1998 (c.29), that the disclosure of the information to a member of the public otherwise than under this Act would contravene—
   (i) any of the data protection principles; or
   (ii) section 10 of that Act (right to prevent processing likely to cause damage or distress); and

(b) in any other case, that such disclosure would contravene any of the data protection principles if the exemptions in section 33A(1) of that Act (which relate to manual data held) were disregarded.

(3) The second condition is that, by virtue of any provision of Part IV of that Act, the information is exempt from section 7(1)(c) of that Act (data subject's right of access to personal data).

(4) In determining for the purposes of this section whether anything done before 24th October 2007 would contravene any of the data protection principles, the exemptions in Part III of Schedule 8 to that Act are to be disregarded.

(5) In this section—

"the data protection principles" means the principles set out in Part I of Schedule 1 to that Act, as read subject to Part II of that Schedule and to section 27(1) of that Act;

"data subject" and "personal data" have the meanings respectively assigned to those terms by section 1(1) of that Act;

"health record" has the meaning assigned to that term by section 1(1) of the Access to Health Records Act 1990 (c.23); and

"personal census information" means any census information—

(a) as defined in section 8(7) of the Census Act 1920 (c.41); or

(b) acquired or derived by virtue of sections 1 to 9 of the Census (Great Britain) Act 1910 (c.27),

which relates to an identifiable person or household.

(6) In section 8(7) of the Census Act 1920 (penalties), in the definition of "personal census information", at the end there is added "but does not include information which, by virtue of section 58(2)(b) of the Freedom of Information (Scotland) Act 2002 (asp 13) (falling away of exemptions with time), is not exempt information within the meaning of that Act".

Health, safety and the environment

39.—(1) Information is exempt information if its disclosure under this Act would, or would be likely to, endanger the physical or mental health or the safety of an individual.

(2) Information is exempt information if a Scottish public authority—

(a) is obliged by regulations under section 62 to make it available to the public in accordance with the regulations; or
(b) would be so obliged but for any exemption contained in the regulations.

(3) Subsection (2)(a) is without prejudice to the generality of section 25(1).

Audit functions

40.—Information is exempt information if its disclosure under this Act would, or would be likely to, prejudice substantially the exercise of a Scottish public authority's functions in relation to—

(a) the audit of the accounts of other Scottish public authorities; or
(b) the examination of the economy, efficiency and effectiveness with which such authorities use their resources in discharging their functions.

Communications with Her Majesty etc. and honours

41.—Information is exempt information if it relates to—

(a) communications with Her Majesty, with other members of the Royal Family or with the Royal Household; or
(b) the exercise by Her Majesty of Her prerogative of honour.

PART 3

THE SCOTTISH INFORMATION COMMISSIONER

The Scottish Information Commissioner

42.—(1) For the purposes of this Act there is to be an officer known as the Scottish Information Commissioner (in this Act referred to as the "Commissioner") who is to be an individual appointed by Her Majesty on the nomination of the Parliament.

(2) The Commissioner is entitled to—

(a) a salary of such amount; and
(b) such allowances,

as the Parliamentary corporation may determine.

(3) Subject to subsection (4), the Commissioner is to hold office for such period not exceeding five years as the Parliamentary corporation, at the time of appointment, may determine.

(4) The Commissioner—

(a) may be relieved of office by Her Majesty at that officer's request;
(b) vacates office on 31st December in the year of service in which that officer attains the age of 65;
(c) may be removed from office by Her Majesty in pursuance of a resolution of the Parliament, which, if passed on a division, must be voted for by the number of members equivalent to not less than two thirds of the total number of seats for members of the Parliament; and
(d) in other respects, holds office on such terms and conditions as the Parliamentary corporation may determine.

(5) A person whose term of office as Commissioner expires (other than by virtue of subsection (4)(b)) is eligible for re-appointment; but re-appointment for a third term is competent only if, by reason of special circumstances, such re-appointment is desirable in the public interest.

(6) The validity of any actings of the Commissioner is not affected by a defect in the nomination by the Parliament for that officer's appointment.

(7) The Commissioner, in the exercise of that officer's functions (except the function of preparing accounts), is not subject to the direction or control of the Parliamentary corporation, of any member of the Scottish Executive or of the Parliament; but this subsection is without prejudice to paragraph 3(4) of schedule 2.

(8) Where the office of Commissioner is vacant, the Parliamentary corporation may appoint a person (who may or may not be a member of the Commissioner's staff) to discharge the functions of that office until a new Commissioner is appointed.

(9) A person appointed under subsection (8)—

(a) may be relieved of that appointment at that person's request;
(b) may be removed from office by the Parliamentary corporation by notice in writing given by it;
(c) in other respects, holds office on such terms and conditions as the Parliamentary corporation may determine; and
(d) while holding that appointment, is to be treated for all purposes, except those of subsections (1) to (6) and those of paragraph 2 of schedule 2, as the Commissioner.

(10) Any function of the Commissioner may be exercised on behalf of that officer by any person (whether or not a member of that officer's staff) authorised by the Commissioner to do so (and to the extent so authorised).

(11) The Parliamentary corporation is to pay—

(a) the salary and allowances of the Commissioner;
(b) any expenses incurred by that officer in the exercise of functions under this Act; and
(c) any sums payable by virtue of subsection (9)(a) to (c) to, or in respect of, a person who—
    (i) is appointed under subsection (8); or
    (ii) has ceased to hold office by virtue of having been so appointed.

(12) Schedule 2 to this Act has effect with respect to the Commissioner.

General functions of Commissioner

43.—(1) The Commissioner, with a view in particular to promoting the observance by Scottish public authorities of the provisions of—

(a) this Act; and
(b) the codes of practice issued under sections 60 and 61,

is to promote the following of good practice by those authorities.

(2) The Commissioner—

(a) must determine what information it is expedient to give the public concerning the following matters—

(i) the operation of this Act;
(ii) good practice;
(iii) other matters within the scope of that officer's functions,

and must secure the dissemination of that information in an appropriate form and manner; and

(b) may give advice to any person as to any of those matters.

(3) The Commissioner may assess whether a Scottish public authority is following good practice.

(4) The Commissioner may from time to time make proposals to the Scottish Ministers for the exercise by them of their functions under sections 4 and 5 of this Act.

(5) The Commissioner may determine and charge sums for services provided under this section.

(6) Any sum received by the Commissioner by virtue of subsection (5) is to be retained by that officer and applied to meet expenditure incurred in respect of the services so provided.

(7) The Commissioner must from time to time consult the Keeper of the Records of Scotland about the promotion under subsection (1) of the observance by Scottish public authorities of the provisions of the code of practice issued under section 61.

(8) In this section "good practice", in relation to a Scottish public authority, means such practice in the discharge of its functions under this Act as appears to the Commissioner to be desirable, and includes (but is not limited to) compliance with the requirements of this Act and the provisions of the codes of practice issued under sections 60 and 61.

Recommendations as to good practice

44.—(1) If it appears to the Commissioner that the practice of a Scottish public authority in relation to the exercise of its functions under this Act does not conform with the code of practice issued under section 60 or 61, the Commissioner may give the authority a recommendation (in this Act referred to as a "practice recommendation").

(2) A practice recommendation must—

(a) be in writing and specify the code and the provisions of that code with which, in the Commissioner's opinion, the authority's practice does not conform; and
(b) specify the steps which that officer considers the authority ought to take in order to conform.

(3) The Commissioner must consult the Keeper of the Records of Scotland before giving a practice recommendation to a Scottish public authority (other than the Keeper) in relation to conformity with the code of practice issued under section 61.

Confidentiality of information obtained by or furnished to Commissioner

45.—(1) A person who is or has been the Commissioner, a member of the Commissioner's staff or an agent of the Commissioner must not disclose any information which—

(a) has been obtained by, or furnished to, the Commissioner under or for the purposes of this Act; and
(b) is not at the time of the disclosure, and has not previously been, available to the public from another source,

unless the disclosure is made with lawful authority.

(2) For the purposes of subsection (1), disclosure is made with lawful authority only if, and to the extent that—

(a) the disclosure is made with the consent of the person from whom the information was so obtained or by whom it was so furnished;
(b) the information was provided for the purpose of its being made available to the public (in whatever manner) under a provision of this Act;
(c) the disclosure is made for the purpose of, and is necessary for, the discharge of—
    (i) a function under this Act; or
    (ii) a Community obligation;
(d) the disclosure is made for the purpose of proceedings, whether criminal or civil and whether arising under, or by virtue of, this Act or otherwise; or
(e) either—
    (i) in a case where the person mentioned in paragraph (a) is a Scottish public authority, had that person received on the day of disclosure a request for the information that person; or
    (ii) in any other case, had the Commissioner received on that day such a request the Commissioner,

would, by virtue of section 1(1), have been under an obligation to give it.

(3) A person who knowingly or recklessly discloses information in contravention of subsection (1) is guilty of an offence.

(4) A person guilty of an offence under subsection (3) is liable—

(a) on summary conviction, to a fine not exceeding the statutory maximum; or
(b) on conviction on indictment, to a fine.

Laying of reports

46.—(1) The Commissioner must lay annually before the Parliament a general report on the exercise of the functions conferred on that officer under this Act.

(2) The report mentioned in subsection (1) (without prejudice to the generality of that subsection) must record the number of occasions, during the period covered by the report, on which the Commissioner failed to reach a decision on an application under section 47(1) (being an application on which a decision fell to be made) within the period of four months specified in section 49(3)(b).

(3) The Commissioner may from time to time lay before the Parliament such other reports with respect to the functions conferred on that officer under this Act as that officer thinks fit.

PART 4

ENFORCEMENT

Application for decision by Commissioner

47.—(1) A person who is dissatisfied with—

(a) a notice given under section 21(5) or (9); or
(b) the failure of a Scottish public authority to which a requirement for review was made to give such a notice,

may make application to the Commissioner for a decision whether, in any respect specified in that application, the request for information to which the requirement relates has been dealt with in accordance with Part 1 of this Act.

(2) An application under subsection (1) must—

(a) be in writing or in another form which, by reason of its having some permanency, is capable of being used for subsequent reference (as, for example, a recording made on audio or video tape);
(b) state the name of the applicant and an address for correspondence; and
(c) specify—

(i) the request for information to which the requirement for review relates;
(ii) the matter which was specified under sub-paragraph (ii) of section 20(3)(c); and
(iii) the matter which gives rise to the dissatisfaction mentioned in subsection (1).

(3) For the purposes of paragraph (a) of subsection (2) (and without prejudice to the generality of that paragraph), an application under that subsection is treated as made in writing where the text of the application is as mentioned in paragraphs (a) to (c) of section 8(2).

(4) Subject to subsection (5), an application to the Commissioner under subsection (1) must be made—

(a) where the application concerns a matter mentioned in paragraph (a) of subsection (1), before the expiry of six months after the date of receipt by the applicant of the notice complained of; or
(b) where the application concerns a matter mentioned in paragraph (b) of that subsection, before the expiry of six months after the period allowed in section 21(1) for complying with a requirement for review has elapsed.

(5) The Commissioner may consider an application under subsection (1) made after the expiry of the time allowed by subsection (4) for the making of that application if, in the opinion of the Commissioner, it is appropriate to do so.

(6) The Scottish Ministers may by regulations provide—

(a) that a paragraph of subsection (4) is to have effect as if the reference in that paragraph to six months were a reference to such other period of months (being a period of not less than six months) as is specified in (or determined in accordance with) the regulations; and
(b) that subsection (5) is to have effect accordingly.

(7) Regulations under subsection (6) may—

(a) prescribe different periods of months in relation to different cases; and
(b) confer a discretion on the Commissioner.

(8) This section is subject to section 48.

When application excluded

48.—No application may be made to the Commissioner for a decision under section 47(1) as respects a request for review made to—

(a) the Commissioner;
(b) a procurator fiscal; or
(c) the Lord Advocate, to the extent that the information requested is held by the Lord Advocate as head of the systems of criminal prosecution and investigation of deaths in Scotland.

Commissioner's decision

49.—(1) The Commissioner must make a decision in relation to an application made in accordance with section 47(1) which is not excluded by section 48 unless—

(a) in the opinion of the Commissioner, the application is frivolous or vexatious; or
(b) in the opinion of the Commissioner, the application appears to have been withdrawn or abandoned.

(2) In a case where the Commissioner determines that subsection (1) does not require a decision to be made, that officer must give the applicant and the Scottish public authority in question notice in writing within one month of receipt of the application, or within such other period as is reasonable in the circumstances, specifying—

(a) that no decision falls to be made in relation to the application; and
(b) the reasons why that is the case.

(3) In any other case, the Commissioner must—

(a) give that authority notice in writing of the application and invite its comments; and
(b) if no settlement has in the meantime been effected, reach a decision on the application before the expiry of four months after receiving it, or before the expiry of such other period as is reasonable in the circumstances.

(4) The Commissioner may endeavour to effect a settlement between the applicant and that authority before the expiry of the period allowed by subsection (3) for reaching a decision on the application.

(5) The Commissioner must give the applicant and that authority, within the time allowed by subsection (3), notice in writing (referred to in this Act as a "decision notice") of any decision under paragraph (b) of that subsection.

(6) Where the Commissioner decides that that authority has not dealt with a request for information in accordance with Part 1 of this Act, the notice under subsection (5) must specify—

(a) the provision of that Part with which the authority has failed to comply and the respect in which it has so failed;
(b) the steps which, in the opinion of the Commissioner, the authority must take to comply with the provision; and
(c) the time within which those steps must be taken.

(7) The time specified under subsection (6)(c) must not expire before the end of the period within which an appeal may be brought under section 56 against the decision of the Commissioner and, if such an appeal is brought, no step which is affected by the appeal need be taken before the cause is finally determined.

(8) A notice under subsection (2) or (5) must contain particulars of the right of appeal conferred by section 56.

(9) This section is subject to section 52.

Information notices

50.—(1) Where the Commissioner—

(a) has received an application under section 47(1); or
(b) reasonably requires information—

(i) for the purpose of determining whether a Scottish public authority has complied or is complying with the provisions of this Act; or
(ii) for the purpose of determining whether the practice of a Scottish public authority conforms with the code of practice issued under section 60 or 61,

that officer may give the authority notice in writing (referred to in this Act as "an information notice") requiring it, within such time as is specified in the notice, to give the officer, in such form as may be so specified, such information relating to the application, to compliance with this Act or to conformity with the code of practice as is so specified.

(2) An information notice must contain—

(a) in a case mentioned in paragraph (a) of subsection (1) a statement that the Commissioner has received an application under section 47(1); or
(b) in a case mentioned in paragraph (b) of that subsection, a statement of—

(i) the purpose mentioned in that paragraph for which that officer regards the specified information as relevant;
(ii) the officer's reasons for so regarding the information; and
(iii) the time within which the information is to be given.

(3) An information notice must contain also particulars of the right of appeal conferred by section 56.

(4) The time specified under subsection (2)(b)(iii) in an information notice must not expire before the end of the period within which an appeal may be brought under section 56 against the notice; and, if such an appeal is brought, the information need not be given pending the determination or withdrawal of the appeal.

(5) A Scottish public authority is not obliged by virtue of this section to give the Commissioner information in respect of—

(a) a communication between professional legal adviser and client in connection with the giving of legal advice to the client with respect to that client's obligations under this Act; or
(b) a communication between professional legal adviser and client, or between such adviser or client and another person, made in connection with or in contemplation of proceedings under or arising out of this Act and for the purpose of such proceedings.

(6) In subsection (5), references to the client of a professional legal adviser include references to a person representing such client.

(7) Subject to subsection (5), neither—

(a) an obligation to maintain secrecy; nor
(b) any other restriction on disclosure,

however arising or imposed, affects the duty to comply with an information notice.

(8) The Commissioner may cancel an information notice by notice in writing given to the authority.

(9) In this section, "information" includes unrecorded information.

Enforcement notices

51.—(1) If the Commissioner is satisfied that a Scottish public authority has failed to comply with a provision of Part 1 of this Act, the Commissioner may give the authority a notice (referred to in this Act as "an enforcement notice") requiring the authority to take, within such time as is specified in the notice, such steps as are so specified for so complying.

(2) An enforcement notice must contain—

(a) a statement of the provision with which the Commissioner is satisfied that the authority has failed to comply and the respect in which it has not done so; and
(b) particulars of the right of appeal conferred by section 56.

(3) The time specified under subsection (1) must not expire before the end of the period within which an appeal may be brought under section 56 against the notice and, if such an appeal is brought, the notice need not be complied with before the cause is finally determined.

(4) The Commissioner may cancel an enforcement notice by notice in writing given to the authority.

(5) This section is subject to section 52.

Exception from duty to comply with certain notices

52.—(1) This section applies to a decision notice or enforcement notice which—

(a) is given to the Scottish Administration; and
(b) relates to a perceived failure, in respect of one or more requests for information, to comply with section 1(1) in respect of information which, by virtue of section 29, 31(1), 32(1)(b), 34, 36(1) or 41(b), is exempt information.

(2) A decision notice or enforcement notice to which this section applies ceases to have effect, in so far as it relates to the perceived failure, if, not later than the thirtieth working day following the effective date, the First Minister of the Scottish Executive, after consulting the other members of that Executive, signs and gives the Commissioner a certificate stating that the First Minister has on reasonable grounds formed, after such consultation, the opinion both that—

(a) there was no such failure; and
(b) the information requested is of exceptional sensitivity.

(3) The First Minister is, by not later than the tenth working day after such a certificate—

(a) is given, to lay a copy of it before the Parliament; and
(b) is given in relation to a decision notice, to inform the person to whose application the notice relates of the reasons for the opinion formed,

except that the First Minister is not obliged to provide information under paragraph (b) if, or to the extent that, compliance with that paragraph would necessitate the disclosure of exempt information.

(4) In subsection (2), "the effective date", in relation to a notice, means—

(a) the day on which the notice was given to the Scottish Administration; or
(b) where an appeal under section 56 is brought, the day on which the cause is finally determined.

Failure to comply with notice

53.—(1) If a Scottish public authority has failed to comply with—

(a) so much of a notice given to it by the Commissioner under subsection (5) of section 49 as, by virtue of subsection (6)(b) of that section, requires steps to be taken by the authority;
(b) an information notice; or
(c) an enforcement notice,

the Commissioner may certify in writing to the court that the authority has failed to comply with the notice.

(2) For the purposes of this section, a Scottish public authority which, in purported compliance with an information notice—

(a) makes a statement which it knows to be false in a material respect; or
(b) recklessly makes a statement which is false in a material respect,

is to be taken to have failed to comply with the notice.

(3) Where a failure to comply is certified under subsection (1), the court may inquire into the matter and, after hearing any witness who may be produced against or on behalf of the authority, and after hearing any statement that may be offered in defence, may deal with the authority as if it had committed a contempt of court.

(4) In this section, "the court" means the Court of Session.

Powers of entry and inspection

54.—Schedule 3, which makes provision as to powers of entry and inspection, has effect.

No civil right of action against Scottish public authority

55.—(1) This Act does not confer a right of action in civil proceedings in respect of failure by a Scottish public authority to comply with a duty imposed by, under or by virtue of this Act.

(2) Subsection (1) does not affect the powers of the Commissioner under section 53(1).

Appeal against notices under Part 4

56.—An appeal, on a point of law, to the Court of Session may be made—

(a) against a decision by the Commissioner under subsection (2) of section 49, by the person who applied for that decision;
(b) against a decision by the Commissioner under subsection (3)(b) of that section—
    (i) by that person; or
    (ii) by the Scottish public authority in respect of which the decision was made; or
(c) against the decision which resulted in the giving of—
    (i) an information notice; or
    (ii) an enforcement notice,

to a Scottish public authority, by that authority.

PART 5

HISTORICAL RECORDS

The expression "historical record"

57.—(1) For the purposes of this Part, a record becomes a "historical record" at the end of that period of thirty years which commences at the beginning of the calendar year following that in which the record is created.

(2) Where records created at different dates are for administrative purposes kept together in one file or other assemblage, all the records in that file or assemblage are to be treated for the purposes of this Part as created when the latest of those records is created.

Falling away of exemptions with time

58.—(1) Information contained in a historical record cannot be exempt information by virtue of any of sections 28 to 30, 33(1), 36, 37, 40 and 41(a).

(2) Information cannot be exempt information by virtue of—

(a) section 41(b) after the end of that period of sixty years; or
(b) section 34(2)(b), 35 or 38(1)(c) or (d) after the end of that period of one hundred years,

which commences at the beginning of the calendar year following that in which the record containing the information is created.

Power to vary periods mentioned in sections 57 and 58

59.—(1) The Scottish Ministers may by order amend subsection (1) of section 57 or paragraph (a) or (b) of subsection (2) of section 58 so as to substitute for the number of years for the time being mentioned in the provision in question such other number of years (not being a number which exceeds that mentioned in the provision as originally enacted) as may be specified in the order.

(2) An order under subsection (1) may contain such transitional provisions and savings as the Scottish Ministers think fit.

PART 6

CODES OF PRACTICE

Code of practice as to functions under this Act

60.—(1) The Scottish Ministers are to issue, and may from time to time revise, a code of practice providing guidance to Scottish public authorities as to the practice which it would, in the opinion of the Ministers, be desirable for the authorities to follow in connection with the discharge of the authorities' functions under this Act.

(2) The code must, in particular, include provision relating to—

(a) the provision of advice and assistance by the authorities to persons who propose to make, or have made, requests for information;

(b) the transfer of requests by one of the authorities to another by which the information requested is or may be held;
(c) consultation with persons to whom information requested relates or with persons whose interests are likely to be affected by the disclosure of such information;
(d) the inclusion in contracts entered into by the authorities of terms relating to the disclosure of information;
(e) the provision by the authorities of procedures for dealing with complaints about the handling by the authorities of requests for information; and
(f) the collection and recording by the authorities of statistics as respects the discharge by them of their functions under this Act.

(3) The code may make different provision for different Scottish public authorities.

(4) Before issuing or revising the code, the Scottish Ministers are to consult the Commissioner.

(5) The Scottish Ministers must lay the code, and any revised code made under this section, before the Parliament.

Code of practice as to the keeping, management and destruction of records

61.—(1) The Scottish Ministers are to issue, and may from time to time revise, a code of practice providing guidance to Scottish public authorities as to the practice which it would, in the opinion of the Ministers, be desirable for the authorities to follow in connection with the keeping, management and destruction of the authorities' records.

(2) The code may also include guidance as to the practice—

(a) to be adopted in relation to the transfer of records to the Keeper of the Records of Scotland;
(b) of reviewing records before they are so transferred; and
(c) to be adopted where one Scottish public authority holds records on behalf of another such authority.

(3) In exercising their functions under this section, the Scottish Ministers are to have regard to the public interest in allowing public access to information held by Scottish public authorities.

(4) The code may make different provision for different Scottish public authorities.

(5) Before issuing or revising the code the Scottish Ministers are to consult—

(a) the Commissioner; and
(b) the Keeper of the Records of Scotland.

(6) The Scottish Ministers must lay the code, and any revised code made under this section, before the Parliament.

PART 7

MISCELLANEOUS AND SUPPLEMENTAL

Power to make provision relating to environmental information

62.—(1) In this section "the Aarhus Convention" means the Convention on Access to Information, Public Participation in Decision making and Access to Justice in Environmental Matters signed at Aarhus on 25th June 1998.

(2) For the purposes of this section, "the information provisions" of the Aarhus Convention are Article 4, together with Articles 3 and 9 so far as relating to that Article.

(3) The Scottish Ministers may, in relation to information held by or requested from any Scottish public authority, by regulations make such provision as they consider appropriate—

(a) for the purpose of implementing the information provisions of the Aarhus Convention or any amendment of those provisions made in accordance with Article 14 of the Convention; and

(b) for the purpose of dealing with matters arising out of, or related to, the implementation of those provisions or of any such amendment.

(4) Regulations under subsection (3) may in particular—

(a) enable charges to be made for making information available in accordance with the regulations;

(b) provide that any obligation imposed by the regulations in relation to the disclosure of information is to have effect notwithstanding any enactment or rule of law;

(c) make provision for the issue by the Scottish Ministers of a code of practice;

(d) provide for sections 43 and 44 to apply in relation to such a code with such modifications as may be specified in the regulations;

(e) provide for all or any of the provisions of Part 4 to apply, with such modifications as may be so specified, in relation to compliance with any requirement of the regulations; and

(f) contain such transitional or consequential provision (including provision modifying any enactment) as the Scottish Ministers consider appropriate.

Disclosure of information to Scottish Public Services Ombudsman or to Information Commissioner

63.—The Commissioner may disclose to—

(a) the Scottish Public Services Ombudsman any information obtained by, or furnished to, the Commissioner under or for the purposes of this Act if it appears to the Commissioner that the information relates to a matter which is, or could be, the subject of an investigation by the Ombudsman under the Scottish Public Services Ombudsman Act 2002 (asp 11); or

(b) the Information Commissioner any information so obtained or furnished if it appears to the Commissioner that the information so relates as is mentioned in paragraph (a) or (b) of section 11AA(1) of the Parliamentary Commissioner Act 1967 (c. 13) (disclosure of information by Parliamentary Commissioner to Information Commissioner).

Power to amend or repeal enactments prohibiting disclosure of information

64.—(1) If it appears to the Scottish Ministers that by virtue of section 26(a) a relevant enactment is capable of preventing the disclosure of information under section 1, they may by order repeal or amend that enactment, in so far as it relates to any Scottish public authority, so as to remove or relax the prohibition.

(2) In subsection (1)—

"relevant enactment" means an Act of Parliament, or Act of the Scottish Parliament, which receives Royal Assent before the end of the calendar year in which this Act receives Royal Assent or any subordinate legislation made before the date on which this Act receives Royal Assent; and

"information" includes unrecorded information.

(3) An order under subsection (1) may do all or any of the following—

(a) make such modifications of enactments as, in the opinion of the Scottish Ministers, are consequential upon, or incidental to, the repeal or amendment of the relevant enactment;
(b) contain such transitional provisions and savings as appear to them to be appropriate;
(c) make different provision in relation to different cases.

Offence of altering etc. records with intent to prevent disclosure

65.—(1) Where—

(a) a request for information is made to a Scottish public authority; and
(b) the applicant is, under section 1, entitled to be given the information or any part of it,

a person to whom this subsection applies who, with the intention of preventing the disclosure by the authority of the information, or part, to which the entitlement relates, alters, defaces, blocks, erases, destroys or conceals a record held by the authority, is guilty of an offence.

(2) Subsection (1) applies to the authority and to any person who is employed by, is an officer of, or is subject to the direction of, the authority.

(3) A person guilty of an offence under subsection (1) is liable, on summary conviction, to a fine not exceeding level 5 on the standard scale.

Saving for existing powers of disclosure

66.—Nothing in this Act is to be taken to limit the powers of a Scottish public authority to disclose information held by it.

Protection from actions for defamation

67.—Where, in compliance with a request for information, information supplied to a Scottish public authority by a third party is communicated by the authority, under section 1, to the applicant, the publication to the applicant of any defamatory matter contained in the information so supplied is privileged unless that publication is shown to have been made with malice.

Scottish Parliament and Scottish Administration

68.—Section 65 and paragraph 10 of schedule 3 apply to—

(a) a member of the staff of, or a person acting on behalf of, the Parliament or the Parliamentary corporation; or
(b) a member of the staff of the Scottish Administration,

as they apply to any other person; but none of those bodies is liable to prosecution under this Act.

Exercise of rights by children

69.—(1) Where a question falls to be determined as to the legal capacity of a person who has not attained the age of sixteen years to exercise any right conferred by any provision of this Act, any such person is to be taken to have that capacity who has a general understanding of what it means to exercise the right.

(2) Without prejudice to the generality of subsection (1), a person who has attained the age of twelve years is to be presumed to be of sufficient age and maturity to have such understanding as is mentioned in that subsection.

Amendment of Public Records (Scotland) Act 1937

70.—(1) The Public Records (Scotland) Act 1937 (c.43) is amended as follows.

(2) In section 7 (constitution of Scottish Records Advisory Council), after subsection (3) there is inserted—

"(3A) The matters on which the aforesaid Council may advise the Scottish Ministers include matters relating to the application of the Freedom of Information (Scotland) Act 2002 (asp 13) to information contained in records held by the Keeper.".

(3) After section 12 there is inserted—

"12A Duty to afford facilities for inspection etc. of certain records

It shall be the duty of the Keeper to arrange that reasonable facilities are available to the public for—

(a) inspecting; and
(b) obtaining copies of,

such records held by the Keeper as either fall to be disclosed in accordance with the Freedom of Information (Scotland) Act 2002 (asp 13) or comprise information which is exempt information (within the meaning of that Act) by virtue of section 25(2)(b)(ii) of that Act.".

Amendment of Scottish Public Services Ombudsman Act 2002

71.—(1) In Part 2 of schedule 2 to the Scottish Public Services Ombudsman Act 2002 (asp 11) (persons listed as liable to investigation under that Act), after paragraph 45 there is inserted—

"45A The Scottish Information Commissioner.".

(2) Schedule 4 to this Act, which contains amendments to that Act consequential on the provisions of this Act, has effect.

Orders and regulations

72.—(1) Any power of the Scottish Ministers to make an order or regulations under this Act is exercisable by statutory instrument.

(2) A statutory instrument—

(a) made in exercise of any of the powers conferred by sections 4(1) (except in the case mentioned in subsection (3)), 13(1) or 62(3) is subject to annulment in pursuance of a resolution of the Parliament;
(b) containing an order under section 4(1) (but only in the case so mentioned), 5(1), 7(2) or (4)(b), 59(1) or 64(1) or regulations under section 9(4), 10(4), 12, 20(7), 21(6) or 47(6) is not made unless a draft of the instrument has been—

(i) laid before; and
(ii) approved by resolution of,

the Parliament.

(3) The case is that the instrument contains an order under paragraph (a) of section 4(1) and lists an authority in the way mentioned in section 7(1).

Interpretation

73.—In this Act, unless the context requires a different interpretation—

"the Commissioner" means the Scottish Information Commissioner;

"body" includes an unincorporated association;

"decision notice" has the meaning given by section 49(5);

"enactment" includes an enactment comprised in, or in an instrument made under, an Act of the Scottish Parliament;

"enforcement notice" has the meaning given by section 51(1);

"exempt information" means information which is so described in any provision of Part 2;

"fees notice" has the meaning given by section 9(1);

"information" (subject to sections 50(9) and 64(2)) means information recorded in any form;

"information notice" has the meaning given by section 50(1);

"Minister of the Crown" has the same meaning as in the Ministers of the Crown Act 1975 (c.26);

"the Parliamentary corporation" means the Scottish Parliamentary Corporate Body;

"publication scheme" has the meaning given by section 23(1)(a);

"refusal notice" has the meaning given by section 16(1) (including that section as read with section 18(2));

"requirement for review" has the meaning given by section 20(2);

"Scottish public authority" has the meaning given by section 3(1);

"subordinate legislation" has the same meaning as in the Interpretation Act 1978 (c.30) but includes an instrument made under an Act of the Scottish Parliament; and

"working day" means any day other than a Saturday, a Sunday, Christmas Day or a day which, under the Banking and Financial Dealings Act 1971 (c.80), is a bank holiday in Scotland.

Giving of notice etc.

74.—(1) In this Act, any reference to—

(a) a notice being given is to be construed as a reference to its being—
  (i) delivered; or
  (ii) posted; and

(b) a request for information, a requirement for review or an application being made, or a certificate being given, is to be construed as a reference to its being—
  (i) delivered;
  (ii) posted; or
  (iii) transmitted by electronic means.

(2) For the purposes of any provision of this Act, a thing—

(a) posted is presumed not to be received until the third day after the day of posting; and
(b) transmitted by electronic means is presumed to be received on the day of transmission.

Commencement

75.—(1) This section and sections 72 and 76 come into force on Royal Assent; and the other provisions of this Act come into force—

(a) on such day as the Scottish Ministers may by order appoint, that day being, subject to paragraph (b), a day no later than 31st December 2005; or
(b) if the Commissioner recommends to the Scottish Ministers that a day after 31st December 2005 and specified in the recommendation be so appointed and they accept that recommendation, then on the specified day as so appointed,

and different days may be so appointed (or as the case may be recommended and appointed) for different provisions, for different persons or categories of person and for different purposes.

(2) An order under paragraph (b) of subsection (1) may contain such transitional provisions and savings (including provisions capable of having effect after the coming into force of provisions of this Act other than this section and sections 72 and 76) as the Scottish Ministers consider appropriate.

(3) During—

(a) that period of twelve months which begins with the date of Royal Assent; and
(b) each subsequent period of twelve months until all the provisions of this Act are fully in force,

the Scottish Ministers are to prepare, and lay before the Parliament, a report of their proposals (including their response to any recommendations made under subsection (1)(b)) for bringing fully into force the provisions of this Act.

Short title

76.—This Act may be cited as the Freedom of Information (Scotland) Act 2002.

SCHEDULES

SCHEDULE 1

Scottish Public Authorities

Part 1

Ministers, The Parliament

1.—The Scottish Ministers.

2.—The Scottish Parliament.

3.—The Scottish Parliamentary Corporate Body.

PART 2

NON MINISTERIAL OFFICE HOLDERS IN THE SCOTTISH ADMINISTRATION

4.—The Chief Dental Officer of the Scottish Administration.

5.—The Chief Medical Officer of the Scottish Administration.

6.—Her Majesty's Chief Inspector of Constabulary.

7.—Her Majesty's Chief Inspector of Prisons for Scotland.

8.—Her Majesty's Inspector of Anatomy for Scotland.

9.—Her Majesty's Inspector of Fire Services for Scotland.

10.—Her Majesty's inspectors of schools (that is to say, the inspectors of schools appointed by Her Majesty on the recommendation of the Scottish Ministers under the Education (Scotland) Act 1980 (c.44)).

11.—The Keeper of the Records of Scotland.

12.—The Keeper of the Registers of Scotland.

13.—A procurator fiscal.

14.—The Queen's and Lord Treasurer's Remembrancer.

15.—The Queen's Printer for Scotland.

16.—The Registrar General of Births, Deaths and Marriages for Scotland.

17.—The Registrar of Independent Schools in Scotland.

18.—A rent officer appointed under section 43(3) of the Rent (Scotland) Act 1984 (c.58).

19.—A social work inspector (that is to say, an officer authorised as such an inspector under section 6 of the Social Work (Scotland) Act 1968 (c.49)).

PART 3

LOCAL GOVERNMENT

20.—An assessor appointed under section 27(2) of the Local Government etc. (Scotland) Act 1994 (c.39).

21.—A council constituted by section 2 of that Act.

22.—A joint board, within the meaning of section 235(1) of the Local Government (Scotland) Act 1973 (c.65).

23.—A licensing board constituted in accordance with the provisions of section 1 of the Licensing (Scotland) Act 1976 (c.66).

24.—The Strathclyde Passenger Transport Authority.

PART 4

THE NATIONAL HEALTH SERVICE

25.—The Clinical Standards Board for Scotland.

26.—The Common Services Agency for the Scottish Health Service.

27.—A Health Board, constituted under section 2 of the National Health Service (Scotland) Act 1978.

28.—The Health Education Board for Scotland.

29.—The Health Technology Board for Scotland.

30.—A local health council, established under section 7 of the National Health Service (Scotland) Act 1978.

31.—A National Health Service trust.

32.—NHS 24.

33.—A person providing general medical services, general dental services, general ophthalmic services or pharmaceutical services under Part II of the National Health Service (Scotland) Act 1978, but only in respect of information relating to the provision of those services.

34.—A person providing personal medical services or personal dental services under arrangements made under section 17C of that Act, but only in respect of information relating to the provision of those services.

35.—A person providing, in Scotland, piloted services within the meaning of the National Health Service (Primary Care) Act 1997 (c.46), but only in respect of information relating to the provision of those services.

36.—The Post Qualification Education Board for Health Service Pharmacists in Scotland.

37.—The Scottish Advisory Committee on Distinction Awards.

38.—The Scottish Advisory Committee on the Medical Workforce.

39.—The Scottish Ambulance Service Board.

40.—The Scottish Council for Post Graduate Medical and Dental Education.

41.—The Scottish Dental Practice Board.

42.—The Scottish Health Advisory Service.

43.—The Scottish Hospital Endowments Research Trust.

44.—The Scottish Hospital Trust.

45.—The State Hospitals Board for Scotland.

46.—The Scottish Medical Practices Committee.

PART 5

EDUCATIONAL INSTITUTIONS

47.—The board of management of a college of further education (expressions used in this paragraph having the same meaning as in section 36(1) of the Further and Higher Education (Scotland) Act 1992 (c.37)).

48.—A central institution within the meaning of the Education (Scotland) Act 1980.

49.—An institution in receipt of funding from the Scottish Higher Education Funding Council other than any institution whose activities are principally carried on outwith Scotland.

PART 6

POLICE

50.—A chief constable of a police force in Scotland.

51.—A joint police board constituted by an amalgamation scheme made or approved under the Police (Scotland) Act 1967 (c.77).

52.—The Police Advisory Board for Scotland.

Part 7

Others

53.—The Accounts Commission for Scotland.

54.—The Advisory Committee on Sites of Special Scientific Interest.

55.—[. . .][1]

56.—An area tourist board established by virtue of section 172(1) of the Local Government (Scotland) Act 1994 (c.39).

57.—Audit Scotland.

58.—The Auditor General for Scotland.

59.—The Board of Trustees for the National Galleries of Scotland.

60.—The Board of Trustees of the National Museums of Scotland.

61.—The Board of Trustees of the Royal Botanic Garden, Edinburgh.

62.—The Central Advisory Committee on Justices of the Peace.

63.—The Crofters Commission.

64.—The Deer Commission for Scotland.

65.—The Fisheries Committee continued in existence by paragraph 5 of Schedule 9 to the Electricity Act 1989 (c.29).

66.—The General Teaching Council for Scotland.

67.—Highlands and Islands Enterprise

67A.—[The Historic Environment Advisory Council for Scotland.][2]

68.—[. . .][3]

69.—A justice of the peace advisory committee.

70.—Learning and Teaching Scotland.

71.—The Local Government Boundary Commission for Scotland

72.—The Mental Welfare Commission for Scotland.

73.—A National Park authority, established by virtue of schedule 1 to the National Parks (Scotland) Act 2000 (asp 10).

74.—The Parole Board for Scotland.

75.—A person appointed for Scotland under section 3(1) of the Local Government and Housing Act 1989 (c.42).

76.—The Royal Commission on the Ancient and Historical Monuments of Scotland.

77.—The Scottish Agricultural Wages Board.

78.—The Scottish Arts Council.

79.—The Scottish charities nominee, appointed under section 12 of the Law Reform (Miscellaneous Provisions) (Scotland) Act 1990 (c.40).

---

[1] Words repealed by Public Appointments and Public Bodies, etc., (Scotland) Act 2003 (ASP 4), Sch.4, para.17(b)(i).

[2] Words added by Public Appointments and Public Bodies, etc., (Scotland) Act 2003 (ASP 4), Sch. 4, para. 17(c)(ii).

[3] Words repealed by Public Appointments and Public Bodies, etc., (Scotland) Act 2003 ASP 4), Sch. 4, para 17(b)(ii).

80.—The Scottish Children's Reporter Administration.

81.—The Scottish Commission for the Regulation of Care.

82.—[. . .][4]

83.—The Scottish Criminal Cases Review Commission.

84.—Scottish Enterprise.

85.—The Scottish Environment Protection Agency.

86.—The Scottish Further Education Funding Council.

87.—The Scottish Higher Education Funding Council.

88.—Scottish Homes.

89.—The Scottish Industrial Development Advisory Board.

90.—The Scottish Information Commissioner.

91.—The Scottish Law Commission.

92.—The Scottish Legal Aid Board.

93.—Scottish Natural Heritage.

94.—The Scottish Prison Complaints Commission.

95.—The Scottish Public Services Ombudsman.

96.—The Scottish Qualifications Authority.

97.—The Scottish Records Advisory Council.

98.—Scottish Screen.

99.—The Scottish Social Services Council.

100.—The Scottish Sports Council.

101.—The Scottish Tourist Board.

102.—Scottish Water.

103.—Social Inclusion Partnerships.

104.—The Standards Commission for Scotland.

105.—The Trustees of the National Library of Scotland.

106.—The Water Industry Commissioner for Scotland.

SCHEDULE 2

The Scottish Information Commissioner

Status

1.—The Commissioner and that officer's staff are not to be regarded as servants or agents of the Crown or as having any status, immunity or privilege of the Crown; and the Commissioner's property is not to be regarded as property of, or property held on behalf of, the Crown.

Pensions, allowances, etc.

2.—(1) The Parliamentary corporation may make arrangements for the payment of pensions, allowances or gratuities to, or in respect of, any person who has ceased to hold the office of Commissioner and (without prejudice to that generality) may—

[4] Words repealed by Public Appointments and Public Bodies, etc., (Scotland) Act 2003 (ASP 4), Sch.4, para.17(b)(iii).

(a) make contributions or payments towards provision for such pensions, allowances or gratuities; and
(b) for the purposes of this sub-paragraph, establish and administer one or more pension schemes.

(2) The references in sub-paragraph (1) to pensions, allowances and gratuities include references to, as the case may be, pensions, allowances or gratuities by way of compensation for loss of office.

Staff

3.—(1) The Commissioner may appoint such staff, on such terms and conditions, as that officer may determine.

(2) The Commissioner may make arrangements for the payment of pensions, allowances or gratuities to, or in respect of, any person who has ceased to be a member of such staff and (without prejudice to that generality) may—

(a) make contributions or payments towards provision for such pensions, allowances or gratuities; and
(b) for the purposes of this sub-paragraph, establish and administer one or more pension schemes.

(3) The references in sub-paragraph (2) to pensions, allowances and gratuities include references to, as the case may be, pensions, allowances or gratuities by way of compensation for loss of employment.

(4) A determination under sub-paragraph (1) requires, and arrangements under sub-paragraph (2) require, the approval of the Parliamentary corporation.

Accountable officer

4.—(1) The Parliamentary corporation is to designate the Commissioner or a member of that officer's staff as the accountable officer for the purposes of this paragraph.

(2) The functions of the accountable officer are—

(a) those specified in sub-paragraph (3); and
(b) where the accountable officer is not the Commissioner, the duty set out in sub-paragraph (4),

and the accountable officer is answerable to the Parliament for the exercise of those functions.

(3) The functions referred to in sub-paragraph (2)(a) are—

(a) signing the accounts of the expenditure and receipts of the Commissioner;
(b) ensuring the propriety and regularity of the finances of the Commissioner; and
(c) ensuring that the resources of the Commissioner are used economically, efficiently and effectively.

(4) The duty referred to in sub-paragraph (2)(b) is a duty, where the accountable officer is required to act in some way but considers that to do so would be inconsistent with the proper performance of the functions specified in sub-paragraph (3), to—

(a) obtain written authority from the Commissioner before taking the action; and
(b) send a copy of that authority as soon as possible to the Auditor General.

Accounts

5.—(1) The Commissioner must—

(a) keep accounts; and
(b) prepare annual accounts in respect of each financial year,

in accordance with such directions as the Scottish Ministers may give that officer.

(2) The Commissioner must send a copy of the annual accounts to the Auditor General for Scotland for auditing.

(3) The financial year of the Commissioner is—

(a) the period beginning with the date on which the Commissioner is appointed and ending with 31st March next following that date; and
(b) each successive period of twelve months ending with 31st March.

(4) If requested by any person, the Commissioner must make available at any reasonable time, without charge, in printed or in electronic form, the audited accounts, so that they may be inspected by that person.

General powers

6.—The Commissioner may do anything which appears necessary or expedient for the purpose of, or in connection with, or which appears conducive to, the exercise of that officer's functions; and without prejudice to that generality, may in particular—

(a) acquire and dispose of land and other property; and
(b) enter into contracts.

SCHEDULE 3

Powers of Entry and Inspection

Grant of warrants

1.—(1) If a sheriff is satisfied by evidence on oath supplied by the Commissioner that there are reasonable grounds for suspecting—
(a) that a Scottish public authority has failed or is failing to comply with—
(i) any of the requirements of Part 1 of this Act;
(ii) so much of a notice given to it by the Commissioner under subsection (5) of section 49 as, by virtue of subsection (6)(b) of that section, requires steps to be taken; or
(iii) an information notice or an enforcement notice; or
(b) that an offence under section 65(1) has been or is being committed,
and that evidence of such a failure to comply or of the commission of the offence is to be found on any premises specified as part of that evidence, the sheriff, subject to paragraph 2, may grant to the Commissioner such warrant as is mentioned in sub-paragraph (2).

(2) The warrant is one which authorises the Commissioner, or any member of the Commissioner's staff, at any time within seven days after the date of the warrant—
(a) to enter and search the premises;
(b) to inspect and seize any documents or other material found there which may constitute the evidence in question; and
(c) to inspect, examine, operate and test any equipment found there in which information held by the authority may be recorded.

2.—(1) A sheriff must not grant the warrant unless satisfied—
(a) that the Commissioner has given seven days' notice in writing to the occupier of the premises demanding access to them; and
(b) that either—
(i) access was demanded at a reasonable hour and was unreasonably refused; or
(ii) although entry to the premises was granted, the occupier unreasonably refused to comply with a request by the Commissioner, or any member of the Commissioner's staff, to permit the Commissioner or any such member of staff to do any of the things referred to in paragraph 1(2); and
(c) that the occupier has, after the refusal, been notified by the Commissioner of the application for the warrant and has had an opportunity of being heard by the sheriff on the question of whether or not it should be granted.

(2) Sub-paragraph (1) does not apply if the sheriff is satisfied that the case is one of urgency or that compliance with the provisions of that sub-paragraph would defeat the object of the entry.

Execution of warrants

3.—A person executing the warrant may use such reasonable force as may be necessary.

4.—The warrant must be executed at a reasonable hour, unless it appears to the person executing it that there are grounds for suspecting that the evidence in question would not be found if it were so executed.

5.—(1) If the premises in respect of which the warrant is granted are occupied by a Scottish public authority and any officer or employee of the authority is present when the warrant is executed, that officer or employee must be shown the warrant and supplied with a copy of it; and if no such officer or employee is present a copy of the warrant must be left in a prominent place on the premises.

(2) If the premises in respect of which the warrant is granted are occupied by a person other than a Scottish public authority and that person is present when the warrant is executed, the person must be shown the warrant and supplied with a copy of it; and if the person is not present a copy of the warrant must be left in a prominent place on the premises.

6.—(1) A person seizing anything in pursuance of the warrant must give a receipt for it if asked to do so.

(2) Anything so seized may be retained for so long as is necessary in all the circumstances; but the person in occupation of the premises must be given a copy of anything that is seized if that person so requests and the person executing the warrant considers that it can be done without undue delay.

Matters exempt from inspection and seizure

7.—The powers of inspection and seizure conferred by the warrant are not exercisable in respect of information which is exempt information by virtue of section 31(1).

8.—(1) Subject to the provisions of this paragraph, the powers of inspection and seizure conferred by the warrant are not exercisable in respect of—

(a) a communication between professional legal adviser and client in connection with the giving of legal advice to the client with respect to the client's obligations, liabilities or rights under this Act; or

(b) a communication between professional legal adviser and client, or between such adviser or client and another person, made in connection with or in contemplation of proceedings under or arising out of this Act and for the purpose of such proceedings.

(2) Sub-paragraph (1) applies also to—

(a) a copy or other record of such communication as is there mentioned; and

(b) a document or article enclosed with or referred to in such communication if made in connection with the giving of any advice or, as the case may be, in connection with or in contemplation of and for the purpose of such proceedings as are there mentioned.

(3) This paragraph does not apply to anything in the possession of a person other than the professional legal adviser or client or to anything held with the intention of furthering a criminal purpose.

(4) In this paragraph references to the client of a professional legal adviser include references to a person representing such a client.

9.—If the person in occupation of premises in respect of which the warrant is granted objects to the inspection or seizure under it of any material on the grounds that the material consists partly of matters in respect of which those powers are not exercisable, that person must, if requested, provide in response to the warrant a copy of so much of the material as is material in relation to which the powers are exercisable.

Offences

10.—(1) A person who—

(a) intentionally obstructs a person who is executing the warrant; or

(b) fails, without reasonable excuse, to give the person who is executing the warrant such assistance as that person may reasonably require for executing it,

is guilty of an offence.

(2) A person guilty of an offence under sub-paragraph (1) is liable, on summary conviction, to a fine not exceeding level 5 on the standard scale.

Vessels, vehicles, etc.

11.—In this schedule, "premises" includes vessel, vehicle, aircraft or hovercraft, and references to the occupier of premises include references to the person in charge of a vessel, vehicle, aircraft or hovercraft.

SCHEDULE 4

Consequential Amendments to Scottish Public Services Ombudsman Act 2002

1.—In section 19(8) of the Scottish Public Services Ombudsman Act 2002 (asp 11) (which restricts the purposes for which information obtained by the Ombudsman from the Information Commissioner may be disclosed)—

(a) the words from "the Information Commissioner" to " Freedom of Information Act 2000 (c.36)" become paragraph (a); and

(b) after that paragraph, there is inserted the word "or" and the following paragraph—

"(b) the Scottish Information Commissioner by virtue of section 63 of the Freedom of Information (Scotland) Act 2002 (asp 13),".

2.—In schedule 5 to that Act (which specifies persons or bodies to whom the Ombudsman in certain circumstances may disclose information in relation to certain matters), after the entry relating to the Information Commissioner, there is inserted—[1]

1 Not reproduced here: sets out various statutory provisions repealed on the stated date.

Data Protection Act 1998

(1998, c.29)

ARRANGEMENT OF SECTIONS

PART I

PRELIMINARY

Section

PART II

RIGHTS OF DATA SUBJECTS AND OTHERS

PART IV

EXEMPTIONS

PART V

ENFORCEMENT

PART VI

MISCELLANEOUS AND GENERAL

Functions of Commissioner

Unlawful obtaining etc. of personal data

Records obtained under data subject's right of access

56. Prohibition of requirement as to production of certain records.
57. Avoidance of certain contractual terms relating to health records.

Information provided to Commissioner or Tribunal

58. Disclosure of information.
59. Confidentiality of information.

General provisions relating to offences

60. Prosecutions and penalties.
61. Liability of directors etc.

Amendments of Consumer Credit Act 1974

62. Amendments of Consumer Credit Act 1974.

General

63. Application to Crown.
64. Transmission of notices etc. by electronic or other means.
65. Service of notices by Commissioner.
66. Exercise of rights in Scotland by children.
67. Orders, regulations and rules.
68. Meaning of "accessible record".
69. Meaning of "health professional".
70. Supplementary definitions.
71. Index of defined expressions.
72. Modifications of Act.
73. Transitional provisions and savings.
74. Minor and consequential amendments and repeals and revocations.
75. Short title, commencement and extent.

SCHEDULES

Schedule 1—The data protection principles.

Part I—The principles.
Part II—Interpretation of the principles in Part I.

Schedule 2—Conditions relevant for purposes of the first principle: processing of any personal data.

Schedule 3—Conditions relevant for purposes of the first principle: processing of sensitive personal data.
Schedule 4—Cases where the eighth principle does not apply.
Schedule 5—The Data Protection Commissioner and the Data Protection Tribunal.

Part I—The Commissioner.
Part II—The Tribunal.
Part III—Transitional provisions.

Schedule 6—Appeal proceedings.
Schedule 7—Miscellaneous exemptions.
Schedule 8—Transitional relief.

Part I—Interpretation of Schedule.
Part II—Exemptions available before October 24, 2001.
Part III—Exemptions available after October 23, 2001 but before October 24, 2007.
Part IV—Exemptions after October 23, 2001 for historical research.
Part V—Exemption from section 22.

Schedule 9—Powers of entry and inspection.
Schedule 10—Further provisions relating to assistance under section 53.
Schedule 11—Educational records.
Schedule 12—Accessible public records.
Schedule 13—Modifications of Act having effect before October 24, 2007.
Schedule 14—Transitional provisions and savings.

PART I

PRELIMINARY

Basic interpretative provisions

1.—(1) In this Act, unless the context otherwise requires— App 1–03

"data" means information which—

(a) is being processed by means of equipment operating automatically in response to instructions given for that purpose,
(b) is recorded with the intention that it should be processed by means of such equipment,
(c) is recorded as part of a relevant filing system or with the intention that it should form part of a relevant filing system,
(d) does not fall within paragraph (a), (b) or (c) but forms part of an accessible record as defined by section 68, or
[(e) is recorded information held by a public authority and does not fall within any paragraphs (a) to (d).][1]

"data controller" means, subject to subsection (4), a person who (either alone or jointly or in common with other persons) determines the purposes for which and the manner in which any personal data are, or are to be, processed;

1 Words inserted by Freedom of Information Act 2000, s.68(1) and (2)(a).

"data processor", in relation to personal data, means any person (other than an employee of the data controller) who processes the data on behalf of the data controller;

"data subject" means an individual who is the subject of personal data;

"personal data" means data which relate to a living individual who can be identified—

(a) from those data, or
(b) from those data and other information which is in the possession of, or is likely to come into the possession of, the data controller,

and includes any expression of opinion about the individual and any indication of the intentions of the data controller or any other person in respect of the individual;

"processing", in relation to information or data, means obtaining, recording or holding the information or data or carrying out any operation or set of operations on the information or data, including—

(a) organisation, adaptation or alteration of the information or data,
(b) retrieval, consultation or use of the information or data,
(c) disclosure of the information or data by transmission, dissemination or otherwise making available, or
(d) alignment, combination, blocking, erasure or destruction of the information or data;

"relevant filing system" means any set of information relating to individuals to the extent that, although the information is not processed by means of equipment operating automatically in response to instructions given for that purpose, the set is structured, either by reference to individuals or by reference to criteria relating to individuals, in such a way that specific information relating to a particular individual is readily accessible.

(2) In this Act, unless the context otherwise requires—

(a) "obtaining" or "recording", in relation to personal data, includes obtaining or recording the information to be contained in the data, and
(b) "using" or "disclosing", in relation to personal data, includes using or disclosing the information contained in the data.

(3) In determining for the purposes of this Act whether any information is recorded with the intention—

(a) that it should be processed by means of equipment operating automatically in response to instructions given for that purpose, or
(b) that it should form part of a relevant filing system,

it is immaterial that it is intended to be so processed or to form part of such a system only after being transferred to a country or territory outside the European Economic Area.

(4) Where personal data are processed only for purposes for which they are required by or under any enactment to be processed, the person on whom the obligation to process the data is imposed by or under that enactment is for the purposes of this Act the data controller.

Sensitive personal data

2. In this Act "sensitive personal data" means personal data consisting of information as to—

(a) the racial or ethnic origin of the data subject,
(b) his political opinions,

(c) his religious beliefs or other beliefs of a similar nature,
(d) whether he is a member of a trade union (within the meaning of the Trade Union and Labour Relations (Consolidation) Act 1992),
(e) his physical or mental health or condition,
(f) his sexual life,
(g) the commission or alleged commission by him of any offence, or
(h) any proceedings for any offence committed or alleged to have been committed by him, the disposal of such proceedings or the sentence of any court in such proceedings.

The special purposes

3. In this Act "the special purposes" means any one or more of the following—

(a) the purposes of journalism,
(b) artistic purposes, and
(c) literary purposes.

The data protection principles

4.—(1) References in this Act to the data protection principles are to the principles set out in Part I of Schedule 1.

(2) Those principles are to be interpreted in accordance with Part II of Schedule 1.

(3) Schedule 2 (which applies to all personal data) and Schedule 3 (which applies only to sensitive personal data) set out conditions applying for the purposes of the first principle; and Schedule 4 sets out cases in which the eighth principle does not apply.

(4) Subject to section 27(1), it shall be the duty of a data controller to comply with the data protection principles in relation to all personal data with respect to which he is the data controller.

Application of Act

5.—(1) Except as otherwise provided by or under section 54, this Act applies to a data controller in respect of any data only if—

(a) the data controller is established in the United Kingdom and the data are processed in the context of that establishment, or

(b) the data controller is established neither in the United Kingdom nor in any other EEA State but uses equipment in the United Kingdom for processing the data otherwise than for the purposes of transit through the United Kingdom.

(2) A data controller falling within subsection (1)(b) must nominate for the purposes of this Act a representative established in the United Kingdom.

(3) For the purposes of subsections (1) and (2), each of the following is to be treated as established in the United Kingdom—

(a) an individual who is ordinarily resident in the United Kingdom,
(b) a body incorporated under the law of, or of any part of, the United Kingdom,
(c) a partnership or other unincorporated association formed under the law of any part of the United Kingdom, and
(d) any person who does not fall within paragraph (a), (b) or (c) but maintains in the United Kingdom—

(i) an office, branch or agency through which he carries on any activity, or
(ii) a regular practice;

and the reference to establishment in any other EEA State has a corresponding meaning.

The Commissioner and the Tribunal

6.—(1) For the purposes of this Act and of the Freedom of Information Act 2000 there shall be an officer known as the Information Commissioner (in this Act referred to as "the Commissioner").

(2) The Commissioner shall be appointed by Her Majesty by Letters Patent.

(3) For the purposes of this Act and of the Freedom of Information Act 2000 there shall be a tribunal known as the Information Tribunal (in this Act referred to as "the Tribunal").

(4) The Tribunal shall consist of—

(a) a chairman appointed by the Lord Chancellor after consultation with the Lord Advocate,
(b) such number of deputy chairmen so appointed as the Lord Chancellor may determine, and
(c) such number of other members appointed by the [Secretary of State][1A] as he may determine.

(5) The members of the Tribunal appointed under subsection (4)(a) and (b) shall be—

(a) persons who have a 7 year general qualification, within the meaning of section 71 of the Courts and Legal Services Act 1990,
(b) advocates or solicitors in Scotland of at least 7 years' standing, or
(c) members of the bar of Northern Ireland or solicitors of the Supreme Court of Northern Ireland of at least 7 years' standing.

(6) The members of the Tribunal appointed under subsection (4)(c) shall be—

(a) persons to represent the interests of data subjects,
(aa) persons to represent the interests of those who make requests for information under the Freedom of Information Act 2000,
(b) persons to represent the interests of data controllers. and
(bb) persons to represent the interests of public authorities.

(7) Schedule 5 has effect in relation to the Commissioner and the Tribunal.

PART II

RIGHTS OF DATA SUBJECTS AND OTHERS

Right of access to personal data

7.—(1) Subject to the following provisions of this section and to sections 8, 9 and 9A, an individual is entitled—

(a) to be informed by any data controller whether personal data of which that individual is the data subject are being processed by or on behalf of that data controller,
(b) if that is the case, to be given by the data controller a description of—
    (i) the personal data of which that individual is the data subject,
    (ii) the purposes for which they are being or are to be processed, and
    (iii) the recipients or classes of recipients to whom they are or may be disclosed,

[1A] Words substituted by SI 2003/1887 (Secretary of State for Constitutional Affairs Order), Sch.2, para.9(1)(a).

(c) to have communicated to him in an intelligible form—
   (i) the information constituting any personal data of which that individual is the data subject, and
   (ii) any information available to the data controller as to the source of those data, and

(d) where the processing by automatic means of personal data of which that individual is the data subject for the purpose of evaluating matters relating to him such as, for example, his performance at work, his credit worthiness, his reliability or his conduct, has constituted or is likely to constitute the sole basis for any decision significantly affecting him, to be informed by the data controller of the logic involved in that decision-taking.

(2) A data controller is not obliged to supply any information under subsection (1) unless he has received—

(a) a request in writing, and
(b) except in prescribed cases, such fee (not exceeding the prescribed maximum) as he may require.

(3) Where a data controller—

(a) reasonably requires further information in order to satisfy himself as to the identity of the person making a request under this section and to locate the information which that person seeks, and
(b) has informed him of that requirement,

the data controller is not obliged to comply with the request unless he is supplied with that further information.

(4) Where a data controller cannot comply with the request without disclosing information relating to another individual who can be identified from that information, he is not obliged to comply with the request unless—

(a) the other individual has consented to the disclosure of the information to the person making the request, or
(b) it is reasonable in all the circumstances to comply with the request without the consent of the other individual.

(5) In subsection (4) the reference to information relating to another individual includes a reference to information identifying that individual as the source of the information sought by the request; and that subsection is not to be construed as excusing a data controller from communicating so much of the information sought by the request as can be communicated without disclosing the identity of the other individual concerned, whether by the omission of names or other identifying particulars or otherwise.

(6) In determining for the purposes of subsection (4)(b) whether it is reasonable in all the circumstances to comply with the request without the consent of the other individual concerned, regard shall be had, in particular, to—

(a) any duty of confidentiality owed to the other individual,
(b) any steps taken by the data controller with a view to seeking the consent of the other individual,
(c) whether the other individual is capable of giving consent, and
(d) any express refusal of consent by the other individual.

(7) An individual making a request under this section may, in such cases as may be prescribed, specify that his request is limited to personal data of any prescribed description.

(8) Subject to subsection (4), a data controller shall comply with a request under this section promptly and in any event before the end of the prescribed period beginning with the relevant day.

(9) If a court is satisfied on the application of any person who has made a request under the foregoing provisions of this section that the data controller in question has failed to comply with the request in contravention of those provisions, the court may order him to comply with the request.

(10) In this section—

"prescribed" means prescribed by the [Secretary of State][2] by regulations:

"the prescribed maximum" means such amount as may be prescribed:

"the prescribed period" means forty days or such other period as may be prescribed:

"the relevant day", in relation to a request under this section, means the day on which the data controller receives the request or, if later, the first day on which the data controller has both the required fee and the information referred to in subsection (3).

(11) Different amounts or periods may be prescribed under this section in relation to different cases.

Provisions supplementary to section 7

8.—(1) The [Secretary of State][3] may by regulations provide that, in such cases as may be prescribed, a request for information under any provision of subsection (1) of section 7 is to be treated as extending also to information under other provisions of that subsection.

(2) The obligation imposed by section 7(1)(c)(i) must be complied with by supplying the data subject with a copy of the information in permanent form unless—

(a) the supply of such a copy is not possible or would involve disproportionate effort, or

(b) the data subject agrees otherwise;

and where any of the information referred to in section 7(1)(c)(i) is expressed in terms which are not intelligible without explanation the copy must be accompanied by an explanation of those terms.

(3) Where a data controller has previously complied with a request made under section 7 by an individual, the data controller is not obliged to comply with a subsequent identical or similar request under that section by that individual unless a reasonable interval has elapsed between compliance with the previous request and the making of the current request.

(4) In determining for the purposes of subsection (3) whether requests under section 7 are made at reasonable intervals, regard shall be had to the nature of the data, the purposes for which the data are processed and the frequency with which the data are altered.

(5) Section 7(1)(d) is not to be regarded as requiring the provision of information as to the logic involved in any decision-taking if, and to the extent that, the information constitutes a trade secret.

(6) The information to be supplied pursuant to a request under section 7 must be supplied by reference to the data in question at the time when the request is received, except that it may take account of any amendment or deletion made between that time and the time when the information is supplied, being an amendment or deletion that would have been made regardless of the receipt of the request.

---

2 Words substituted by SI 2003/1887 (Secretary of State for Constitutional Affairs Order), Sch.2, para.9(1)(a).

3 *ibid.*

(7) For the purposes of section 7(4) and (5) another individual can be identified from the information being disclosed if he can be identified from that information, or from that and any other information which, in the reasonable belief of the data controller, is likely to be in, or to come into, the possession of the data subject making the request.

Application of section 7 where data controller is credit reference agency

9.—(1) Where the data controller is a credit reference agency, section 7 has effect subject to the provisions of this section.

(2) An individual making a request under section 7 may limit his request to personal data relevant to his financial standing, and shall be taken to have so limited his request unless the request shows a contrary intention.

(3) Where the data controller receives a request under section 7 in a case where personal data of which the individual making the request is the data subject are being processed by or on behalf of the data controller, the obligation to supply information under that section includes an obligation to give the individual making the request a statement, in such form as may be prescribed by the [Secretary of State][4] by regulations, of the individual's rights—

(a) under section 159 of the Consumer Credit Act 1974, and

(b) to the extent required by the prescribed form, under this Act.

Unstructured personal data held by public authorities

9A.—(1) In this section "unstructured personal data" means any personal data falling within paragraph (e) of the definition of "data" in section 1(1), other than information which is recorded as part of, or with the intention that it should form part of, any set of information relating to individuals to the extent that the set is structured by reference to individuals or by reference to criteria relating to individuals.

(2) A public authority is not obliged to comply with subsection (1) of section 7 in relation to any unstructured personal data unless the request under that section contains a description of the data.

(3) Even if the data are described by the data subject in his request, a public authority is not obliged to comply with subsection (1) of section 7 in relation to unstructured personal data if the authority estimates that the cost of complying with the request so far as relating to those data would exceed the appropriate limit.

(4) Subsection (3) does not exempt the public authority from its obligation to comply with paragraph (a) of section 7(1) in relation to the unstructured personal data unless the estimated cost of complying with that paragraph alone in relation to those data would exceed the appropriate limit.

(5) In subsections (3) and (4) "the appropriate limit" means such amount as may be prescribed by the [Secretary of State][5] by regulations, and different amounts may be prescribed in relation to different cases.

(6) Any estimate for the purposes of this section must be made in accordance with regulations under section 12(5) of the Freedom of Information Act 2000.

Right to prevent processing likely to cause damage or distress

10.—(1) Subject to subsection (2), an individual is entitled at any time by notice in writing to a data controller to require the data controller at the end of such period as is reasonable in the circumstances to cease, or not to begin, processing, or processing for a specified purpose or in a specified manner, any personal data in respect of which he is the data subject, on the ground that, for specified reasons—

[4] *ibid.*

[5] Words substituted by Freedom of Information Act 2000 (c.36), Pt VII, s.69.

(a) the processing of those data or their processing for that purpose or in that manner is causing or is likely to cause substantial damage or substantial distress to him or to another, and
(b) that damage or distress is or would be unwarranted.

(2) Subsection (1) does not apply—

(a) in a case where any of the conditions in paragraphs 1 to 4 of Schedule 2 is met, or
(b) in such other cases as may be prescribed by the [Secretary of State][6] by order.

(3) The data controller must within twenty-one days of receiving a notice under subsection (1) ("the data subject notice") give the individual who gave it a written notice—

(a) stating that he has complied or intends to comply with the data subject notice, or
(b) stating his reasons for regarding the data subject notice as to any extent unjustified and the extent (if any) to which he has complied or intends to comply with it.

(4) If a court is satisfied, on the application of any person who has given a notice under subsection (1) which appears to the court to be justified (or to be justified to any extent), that the data controller in question has failed to comply with the notice, the court may order him to take such steps for complying with the notice (or for complying with it to that extent) as the court thinks fit.

(5) The failure by a data subject to exercise the right conferred by subsection (1) or section 11(1) does not affect any other right conferred on him by this Part.

Right to prevent processing for purposes of direct marketing

11.—(1) An individual is entitled at any time by notice in writing to a data controller to require the data controller at the end of such period as is reasonable in the circumstances to cease, or not to begin, processing for the purposes of direct marketing personal data in respect of which he is the data subject.

(2) If the court is satisfied, on the application of any person who has given a notice under subsection (1), that the data controller has failed to comply with the notice, the court may order him to take such steps for complying with the notice as the court thinks fit.

[(2A) This section shall not apply in relation to the processing of such data as are mentioned in paragraph (1) of regulation 8 of the Telecommunications (Data Protection and Privacy) Regulations 1999 (processing of telecommunications billing data for certain marketing purposes) for the purposes mentioned in paragraph (2) of that regulation.][7]

(3) In this section "direct marketing" means the communication (by whatever means) of any advertising or marketing material which is directed to particular individuals.

Rights in relation to automated decision-taking

12.—(1) An individual is entitled at any time, by notice in writing to any data controller, to require the data controller to ensure that no decision taken by or on behalf of the data controller which significantly affects that individual is based solely on the processing by automatic means of personal data in respect of which that individual is the data subject

6 Words substituted by SI 2003/1887 (Secretary of State for Constitutional Affairs Order), Sch.2, para.9(1)(a).

7 Words added by SI 1999/2093 (Telecommunications (Data Protection and Privacy), Regulations), Sch.1(II), para.3.

for the purpose of evaluating matters relating to him such as, for example, his performance at work, his credit worthiness, his reliability or his conduct.

(2) Where, in a case where no notice under subsection (1) has effect, a decision which significantly affects an individual is based solely on such processing as is mentioned in subsection (1)—

(a) the data controller must as soon as reasonably practicable notify the individual that the decision was taken on that basis, and
(b) the individual is entitled, within twenty-one days of receiving that notification from the data controller, by notice in writing to require the data controller to reconsider the decision or to take a new decision otherwise than on that basis.

(3) The data controller must, within twenty-one days of receiving a notice under subsection (2)(b) ("the data subject notice") give the individual a written notice specifying the steps that he intends to take to comply with the data subject notice.

(4) A notice under subsection (1) does not have effect in relation to an exempt decision; and nothing in subsection (2) applies to an exempt decision.

(5) In subsection (4) "exempt decision" means any decision—

(a) in respect of which the condition in subsection (6) and the condition in subsection (7) are met, or
(b) which is made in such other circumstances as may be prescribed by the [Secretary of State][8] by order.

(6) The condition in this subsection is that the decision—

(a) is taken in the course of steps taken—
 (i) for the purpose of considering whether to enter into a contract with the data subject,
 (ii) with a view to entering into such a contract, or
 (iii) in the course of performing such a contract, or
(b) is authorised or required by or under any enactment.

(7) The condition in this subsection is that either—

(a) the effect of the decision is to grant a request of the data subject, or
(b) steps have been taken to safeguard the legitimate interests of the data subject (for example, by allowing him to make representations).

(8) If a court is satisfied on the application of a data subject that a person taking a decision in respect of him ("the responsible person") has failed to comply with subsection (1) or (2)(b), the court may order the responsible person to reconsider the decision, or to take a new decision which is not based solely on such processing as is mentioned in subsection (1).

(9) An order under subsection (8) shall not affect the rights of any person other than the data subject and the responsible person.

Rights of data subjects in relation to exempt manual data

[**12A.** Rights of data subjects in relation to exempt manual data.

(1) A data subject is entitled at any time by notice in writing—

(a) to require the data controller to rectify, block, erase or destroy exempt manual data which are inaccurate or incomplete, or

[8] Words substituted by SI 2003/1887 (Secretary of State for Constitutional Affairs Order), Sch.2, para.9(1)(a).

(b) to require the data controller to cease holding exempt manual data in a way incompatible with the legitimate purposes pursued by the data controller.

(2) A notice under subsection (1)(a) or (b) must state the data subject's reasons for believing that the data are inaccurate or incomplete or, as the case may be, his reasons for believing that they are held in a way incompatible with the legitimate purposes pursued by the data controller.

(3) If the court is satisfied, on the application of any person who has given a notice under subsection (1) which appears to the court to be justified (or to be justified to any extent) that the data controller in question has failed to comply with the notice, the court may order him to take such steps for complying with the notice (or for complying with it to that extent) as the court thinks fit.

(4) In this section "exempt manual data" means—

(a) in relation to the first transitional period, as defined by paragraph 1(2) of Schedule 8, data to which paragraph 3 or 4 of that Schedule applies, and
(b) in relation to the second transitional period, as so defined, data to which paragraph 14 of that Schedule applies.

(5) For the purposes of this section personal data are incomplete if, and only if, the data, although not inaccurate, are such that their incompleteness would constitute a contravention of the third or fourth data protection principles, if those principles applied to the data.][9]

Compensation for failure to comply with certain requirements

13.—(1) An individual who suffers damage by reason of any contravention by a data controller of any of the requirements of this Act is entitled to compensation from the data controller for that damage.

(2) An individual who suffers distress by reason of any contravention by a data controller of any of the requirements of this Act is entitled to compensation from the data controller for that distress if—

(a) the individual also suffers damage by reason of the contravention, or
(b) the contravention relates to the processing of personal data for the special purposes.

(3) In proceedings brought against a person by virtue of this section it is a defence to prove that he had taken such care as in all the circumstances was reasonably required to comply with the requirement concerned.

Rectification, blocking, erasure and destruction

14.—(1) If a court is satisfied on the application of a data subject that personal data of which the applicant is the subject are inaccurate, the court may order the data controller to rectify, block, erase or destroy those data and any other personal data in respect of which he is the data controller and which contain an expression of opinion which appears to the court to be based on the inaccurate data.

(2) Subsection (1) applies whether or not the data accurately record information received or obtained by the data controller from the data subject or a third party but where the data accurately record such information, then—

(a) if the requirements mentioned in paragraph 7 of Part II of Schedule 1 have been complied with, the court may, instead of making an order under subsection (1), make an order requiring the data to be supplemented by such statement of the

[9] Words added by Data Protection Act 1998 (c.29), Sch.13, para.1.

true facts relating to the matters dealt with by the data as the court may approve, and

(b) if all or any of those requirements have not been complied with, the court may, instead of making an order under that subsection, make such order as it thinks fit for securing compliance with those requirements with or without a further order requiring the data to be supplemented by such a statement as is mentioned in paragraph (a).

(3) Where the court—

(a) makes an order under subsection (1), or
(b) is satisfied on the application of a data subject that personal data of which he was the data subject and which have been rectified, blocked, erased or destroyed were inaccurate,

it may, where it considers it reasonably practicable, order the data controller to notify third parties to whom the data have been disclosed of the rectification, blocking, erasure or destruction.

(4) If a court is satisfied on the application of a data subject—

(a) that he has suffered damage by reason of any contravention by a data controller of any of the requirements of this Act in respect of any personal data, in circumstances entitling him to compensation under section 13, and
(b) that there is a substantial risk of further contravention in respect of those data in such circumstances,

the court may order the rectification, blocking, erasure or destruction of any of those data.

(5) Where the court makes an order under subsection (4) it may, where it considers it reasonably practicable, order the data controller to notify third parties to whom the data have been disclosed of the rectification, blocking, erasure or destruction.

(6) In determining whether it is reasonably practicable to require such notification as is mentioned in subsection (3) or (5) the court shall have regard, in particular, to the number of persons who would have to be notified.

Jurisdiction and procedure

15.—(1) The jurisdiction conferred by sections 7 to 14 is exercisable by the High Court or a county court or, in Scotland, by the Court of Session or the sheriff.

(2) For the purpose of determining any question whether an applicant under subsection (9) of section 7 is entitled to the information which he seeks (including any question whether any relevant data are exempt from that section by virtue of Part IV) a court may require the information constituting any data processed by or on behalf of the data controller and any information as to the logic involved in any decision-taking as mentioned in section 7(1)(d) to be made available for its own inspection but shall not, pending the determination of that question in the applicant's favour, require the information sought by the applicant to be disclosed to him or his representatives whether by discovery (or, in Scotland, recovery) or otherwise.

PART III

NOTIFICATION BY DATA CONTROLLERS

[Not reproduced here.]

Part IV

Exemptions

Preliminary

27.—(1) References in any of the data protection principles or any provision of Parts II and III to personal data or to the processing of personal data do not include references to data or processing which by virtue of this Part are exempt from that principle or other provision.

(2) In this Part "the subject information provisions" means—

(a) the first data protection principle to the extent to which it requires compliance with paragraph 2 of Part II of Schedule 1, and
(b) section 7.

(3) In this Part "the non-disclosure provisions" means the provisions specified in subsection (4) to the extent to which they are inconsistent with the disclosure in question.

(4) The provisions referred to in subsection (3) are—

(a) the first data protection principle, except to the extent to which it requires compliance with the conditions in Schedules 2 and 3,
(b) the second, third, fourth and fifth data protection principles, and
(c) sections 10 and 14(1) to (3).

(5) Except as provided by this Part, the subject information provisions shall have effect notwithstanding any enactment or rule of law prohibiting or restricting the disclosure, or authorising the withholding, of information.

National security

28.—(1) Personal data are exempt from any of the provisions of—

(a) the data protection principles,
(b) Parts II, III and V, and
(c) [sections 54A and][1] 55,

if the exemption from that provision is required for the purpose of safeguarding national security.

(2) Subject to subsection (4), a certificate signed by a Minister of the Crown certifying that exemption from all or any of the provisions mentioned in subsection (1) is or at any time was required for the purpose there mentioned in respect of any personal data shall be conclusive evidence of that fact.

(3) A certificate under subsection (2) may identify the personal data to which it applies by means of a general description and may be expressed to have prospective effect.

(4) Any person directly affected by the issuing of a certificate under subsection (2) may appeal to the Tribunal against the certificate.

(5) If on an appeal under subsection (4), the Tribunal finds that, applying the principles applied by the court on an application for judicial review, the Minister did not have reasonable grounds for issuing the certificate, the Tribunal may allow the appeal and quash the certificate.

---

[1] Words prospectively substituted by Crime (International Co-operation) Act (2003, c.32), Sch.5, paras 68, 69 as from a date to be appointed.

(6) Where in any proceedings under or by virtue of this Act it is claimed by a data controller that a certificate under subsection (2) which identifies the personal data to which it applies by means of a general description applies to any personal data, any other party to the proceedings may appeal to the Tribunal on the ground that the certificate does not apply to the personal data in question and, subject to any determination under subsection (7), the certificate shall be conclusively presumed so to apply.

(7) On any appeal under subsection (6), the Tribunal may determine that the certificate does not so apply.

(8) A document purporting to be a certificate under subsection (2) shall be received in evidence and deemed to be such a certificate unless the contrary is proved.

(9) A document which purports to be certified by or on behalf of a Minister of the Crown as a true copy of a certificate issued by that Minister under subsection (2) shall in any legal proceedings be evidence (or, in Scotland, sufficient evidence) of that certificate.

(10 The power conferred by subsection (2) on a Minister of the Crown shall not be exercisable except by a Minister who is a member of the Cabinet or by the Attorney General or the Lord Advocate.

(11) No power conferred by any provision of Part V may be exercised in relation to personal data which by virtue of this section are exempt from that provision.

(12) Schedule 6 shall have effect in relation to appeals under subsection (4) or (6) and the proceedings of the Tribunal in respect of any such appeal.

Crime and taxation

29.—(1) Personal data processed for any of the following purposes—

(a) the prevention or detection of crime,
(b) the apprehension or prosecution of offenders, or
(c) the assessment or collection of any tax or duty or of any imposition of a similar nature,

are exempt from the first data protection principle (except to the extent to which it requires compliance with the conditions in Schedules 2 and 3) and section 7 in any case to the extent to which the application of those provisions to the data would be likely to prejudice any of the matters mentioned in this subsection.

(2) Personal data which—

(a) are processed for the purpose of discharging statutory functions, and
(b) consist of information obtained for such a purpose from a person who had it in his possession for any of the purposes mentioned in subsection (1),

are exempt from the subject information provisions to the same extent as personal data processed for any of the purposes mentioned in that subsection.

(3) Personal data are exempt from the non-disclosure provisions in any case in which—

(a) the disclosure is for any of the purposes mentioned in subsection (1), and
(b) the application of those provisions in relation to the disclosure would be likely to prejudice any of the matters mentioned in that subsection.

(4) Personal data in respect of which the data controller is a relevant authority and which—

(a) consist of a classification applied to the data subject as part of a system of risk assessment which is operated by that authority for either of the following purposes—

(i) the assessment or collection of any tax or duty or any imposition of a similar nature, or

(ii) the prevention or detection of crime, or apprehension or prosecution of offenders, where the offence concerned involves any unlawful claim for any payment out of, or any unlawful application of, public funds, and

(b) are processed for either of those purposes,

are exempt from section 7 to the extent to which the exemption is required in the interests of the operation of the system.

(5) In subsection (4)—

"public funds" includes funds provided by any Community institution;

"relevant authority" means—

(a) a government department,
(b) a local authority, or
(c) any other authority administering housing benefit or council tax benefit.

Health, education and social work

30.—(1) The [Secretary of State][10] may by order exempt from the subject information provisions, or modify those provisions in relation to, personal data consisting of information as to the physical or mental health or condition of the data subject.

(2) The [Secretary of State][11] may by order exempt from the subject information provisions, or modify those provisions in relation to—

(a) personal data in respect of which the data controller is the proprietor of, or a teacher at, a school, and which consist of information relating to persons who are or have been pupils at the school, or

(b) personal data in respect of which the data controller is an education authority in Scotland, and which consist of information relating to persons who are receiving, or have received, further education provided by the authority.

(3) The [Secretary of State][12] may by order exempt from the subject information provisions, or modify those provisions in relation to, personal data of such other descriptions as may be specified in the order, being information—

(a) processed by government departments or local authorities or by voluntary organisations or other bodies designated by or under the order, and

(b) appearing to him to be processed in the course of, or for the purposes of, carrying out social work in relation to the data subject or other individuals;

but the [Secretary of State][13] shall not under this subsection confer any exemption or make any modification except so far as he considers that the application to the data of those provisions (or of those provisions without modification) would be likely to prejudice the carrying out of social work.

(4) An order under this section may make different provision in relation to data consisting of information of different descriptions.

---

[10] Words substituted by SI 2003/1887 (Secretary of State for Constitutional Affairs Order), Sch.2, para.9(1)(a).
[11] *ibid.*
[12] *ibid.*
[13] *ibid.*

(5) In this section—

"education authority" and "further education" have the same meaning as in the Education (Scotland) Act 1980 ("the 1980 Act"), and

"proprietor"—

(a) in relation to a school in England or Wales, has the same meaning as in the Education Act 1996,
(b) in relation to a school in Scotland, means—
  (i) in the case of a self-governing school, the board of management within the meaning of the Self-Governing Schools etc. (Scotland) Act 1989,
  (ii) in the case of an independent school, the proprietor within the meaning of the 1980 Act,
  (iii) in the case of a grant-aided school, the managers within the meaning of the 1980 Act, and
  (iv) in the case of a public school, the education authority within the meaning of the 1980 Act, and
(c) in relation to a school in Northern Ireland, has the same meaning as in the Education and Libraries (Northern Ireland) Order 1986 and includes, in the case of a controlled school, the Board of Governors of the school.

Regulatory activity

31.—(1) Personal data processed for the purposes of discharging functions to which this subsection applies are exempt from the subject information provisions in any case to the extent to which the application of those provisions to the data would be likely to prejudice the proper discharge of those functions.

(2) Subsection (1) applies to any relevant function which is designed—

(a) for protecting members of the public against—
  (i) financial loss due to dishonesty, malpractice or other seriously improper conduct by, or the unfitness or incompetence of, persons concerned in the provision of banking, insurance, investment or other financial services or in the management of bodies corporate,
  (ii) financial loss due to the conduct of discharged or undischarged bankrupts, or
  (iii) dishonesty, malpractice or other seriously improper conduct by, or the unfitness or incompetence of, persons authorised to carry on any profession or other activity,
(b) for protecting charities against misconduct or mismanagement (whether by trustees or other persons) in their administration,
(c) for protecting the property of charities from loss or misapplication,
(d) for the recovery of the property of charities,
(e) for securing the health, safety and welfare of persons at work, or
(f) for protecting persons other than persons at work against risk to health or safety arising out of or in connection with the actions of persons at work.

(3) In subsection (2) "relevant function" means—

(a) any function conferred on any person by or under any enactment,
(b) any function of the Crown, a Minister of the Crown or a government department, or
(c) any other function which is of a public nature and is exercised in the public interest.

(4) Personal data processed for the purpose of discharging any function which—

(a) is conferred by or under any enactment on—

(i) the Parliamentary Commissioner for Administration,
(ii) the Commission for Local Administration in England, the Commission for Local Administration in Wales or the Commissioner for Local Administration in Scotland,
(iii) the Health Service Commissioner for England, the Health Service Commissioner for Wales or the Health Service Commissioner for Scotland,
(iv) the Welsh Administration Ombudsman,
(v) the Assembly Ombudsman for Northern Ireland, or
(vi) the Northern Ireland Commissioner for Complaints, and

(b) is designed for protecting members of the public against—

(i) maladministration by public bodies,
(ii) failures in services provided by public bodies, or
(iii) a failure of a public body to provide a service which it was a function of the body to provide,

are exempt from the subject information provisions in any case to the extent to which the application of those provisions to the data would be likely to prejudice the proper discharge of that function.

(4A) Personal data processed for the purpose of discharging any function which is conferred by or under Part XVI of the Financial Services and Markets Act 2000 on the body established by the Financial Services Authority for the purposes of that Part are exempt from the subject information provisions in any case to the extent to which the application of those provisions to the data would be likely to prejudice the proper discharge of the function.

(5) Personal data processed for the purpose of discharging any function which—

(a) is conferred by or under any enactment on the [the Office of Fair Trading],[14] and
(b) is designed—

(i) for protecting members of the public against conduct which may adversely affect their interests by persons carrying on a business,
(ii) for regulating agreements or conduct which have as their object or effect the prevention, restriction or distortion of competition in connection with any commercial activity, or
(iii) for regulating conduct on the part of one or more undertakings which amounts to the abuse of a dominant position in a market,

are exempt from the subject information provisions in any case to the extent to which the application of those provisions to the data would be likely to prejudice the proper discharge of that function.

Journalism, literature and art

32.—(1) Personal data which are processed only for the special purposes are exempt from any provision to which this subsection relates if—

(a) the processing is undertaken with a view to the publication by any person of any journalistic, literary or artistic material,

[14] Words substituted by Enterprise Act 2002 (c.40), Sch.25, para.37(2).

(b) the data controller reasonably believes that, having regard in particular to the special importance of the public interest in freedom of expression, publication would be in the public interest, and
(c) the data controller reasonably believes that, in all the circumstances, compliance with that provision is incompatible with the special purposes.

(2) Subsection (1) relates to the provisions of—

(a) the data protection principles except the seventh data protection principle,
(b) section 7,
(c) section 10,
(d) section 12, and
(dd) section 12A,
(e) section 14(1) to (3).

(3) In considering for the purposes of subsection (1)(b) whether the belief of a data controller that publication would be in the public interest was or is a reasonable one, regard may be had to his compliance with any code of practice which—

(a) is relevant to the publication in question, and
(b) is designated by the [Secretary of State][15] by order for the purposes of this subsection.

(4) Where at any time ("the relevant time") in any proceedings against a data controller under section 7(9), 10(4), 12(8), 12A(3) or 14 or by virtue of section 13 the data controller claims, or it appears to the court, that any personal data to which the proceedings relate are being processed—

(a) only for the special purposes, and
(b) with a view to the publication by any person of any journalistic, literary or artistic material which, at the time twenty-four hours immediately before the relevant time, had not previously been published by the data controller,

the court shall stay the proceedings until either of the conditions in subsection (5) is met.

(5) Those conditions are—

(a) that a determination of the Commissioner under section 45 with respect to the data in question takes effect, or
(b) in a case where the proceedings were stayed on the making of a claim, that the claim is withdrawn.

(6) For the purposes of this Act "publish", in relation to journalistic, literary or artistic material, means make available to the public or any section of the public.

Research, history and statistics

33.—(1) In this section—

"research purposes" includes statistical or historical purposes;

"the relevant conditions", in relation to any processing of personal data, means the conditions—

(a) that the data are not processed to support measures or decisions with respect to particular individuals, and

[15] Words substituted by SI 2003/1887 (Secretary of State for Constitutional Affairs Order), Sch.2, para.9(1)(a).

(b) that the data are not processed in such a way that substantial damage or substantial distress is, or is likely to be, caused to any data subject.

(2) For the purposes of the second data protection principle, the further processing of personal data only for research purposes in compliance with the relevant conditions is not to be regarded as incompatible with the purposes for which they were obtained.

(3) Personal data which are processed only for research purposes in compliance with the relevant conditions may, notwithstanding the fifth data protection principle, be kept indefinitely.

(4) Personal data which are processed only for research purposes are exempt from section 7 if—

(a) they are processed in compliance with the relevant conditions, and
(b) the results of the research or any resulting statistics are not made available in a form which identifies data subjects or any of them.

(5) For the purposes of subsections (2) to (4) personal data are not to be treated as processed otherwise than for research purposes merely because the data are disclosed—

(a) to any person, for research purposes only;
(b) to the data subject or a person acting on his behalf,
(c) at the request, or with the consent, of the data subject or a person acting on his behalf, or
(d) in circumstances in which the person making the disclosure has reasonable grounds for believing that the disclosure falls within paragraph (a), (b) or (c).

Information available to the public by or under enactment

34.—Personal data are exempt from—

(a) the subject information provisions,
(b) the fourth data protection principle and sections 12A and 14(1) to (3), and
(c) the non-disclosure provisions,

if the data consist of information which the data controller is obliged by or under any enactment [other than an enactment contained in the Freedom of Information Act 2000][16] to make available to the public, whether by publishing it, by making it available for inspection, or otherwise and whether gratuitously or on payment of a fee.

Disclosures required by law or made in connection with legal proceedings etc.

35.—(1) Personal data are exempt from the non-disclosure provisions where the disclosure is required by or under any enactment, by any rule of law or by the order of a court.

(2) Personal data are exempt from the non-disclosure provisions where the disclosure is necessary—

(a) for the purpose of, or in connection with, any legal proceedings (including prospective legal proceedings), or
(b) for the purpose of obtaining legal advice,

or is otherwise necessary for the purposes of establishing, exercising or defending legal rights.

---

16 Words inserted by Freedom of Information Act 2000 (c.36), Pt VII, s.72.

Domestic purposes

36.—Personal data processed by an individual only for the purposes of that individual's personal, family or household affairs (including recreational purposes) are exempt from the data protection principles and the provisions of Parts II and III.

Miscellaneous exemptions

37.—Schedule 7 (which confers further miscellaneous exemptions) has effect.

Powers to make further exemptions by order

38.—(1) The [Secretary of State][17] may by order exempt from the subject information provisions personal data consisting of information the disclosure of which is prohibited or restricted by or under any enactment if and to the extent that he considers it necessary for the safeguarding of the interests of the data subject or the rights and freedoms of any other individual that the prohibition or restriction ought to prevail over those provisions.

(2) The [Secretary of State][18] may by order exempt from the non- disclosure provisions any disclosures of personal data made in circumstances specified in the order, if he considers the exemption is necessary for the safeguarding of the interests of the data subject or the rights and freedoms of any other individual.

Transitional relief

39.—Schedule 8 (which confers transitional exemptions) has effect.

PART V

ENFORCEMENT

Enforcement notices

40.—(1) If the Commissioner is satisfied that a data controller has contravened or is contravening any of the data protection principles, the Commissioners may serve him with a notice (in this Act referred to as "an enforcement notice") requiring him, for complying with the principle or principles in question, to do either or both of the following—

(a) to take within such time as may be specified in the notice, or to refrain from taking after such time as may be so specified, such steps as are so specified, or
(b) to refrain from processing any personal data, or any personal data of a description specified in the notice, or to refrain from processing them for a purpose so specified or in a manner so specified, after such time as may be so specified.

(2) In deciding whether to serve an enforcement notice, the Commissioner shall consider whether the contravention has caused or is likely to cause any person damage or distress.

---

[17] Words substituted by SI 2003/1887 (Secretary of State for Constitutional Affairs Order), Sch.2, para.9(1)(a).
[18] *ibid.*

(3) An enforcement notice in respect of a contravention of the fourth data protection principle which requires the data controller to rectify, block, erase or destroy any inaccurate data may also require the data controller to rectify, block, erase or destroy any other data held by him and containing an expression of opinion which appears to the Commissioner to be based on the inaccurate data.

(4) An enforcement notice in respect of a contravention of the fourth data protection principle, in the case of data which accurately record information received or obtained by the data controller from the data subject or a third party, may require the data controller either—

(a) to rectify, block, erase or destroy any inaccurate data and any other data held by him and containing an expression of opinion as mentioned in subsection (3), or
(b) to take such steps as are specified in the notice for securing compliance with the requirements specified in paragraph 7 of Part II of Schedule 1 and, if the Commissioner thinks fit, for supplementing the data with such statement of the true facts relating to the matters dealt with by the data as the Commissioner may approve.

(5) Where—

(a) an enforcement notice requires the data controller to rectify, block, erase or destroy any personal data, or
(b) the Commissioner is satisfied that personal data which have been rectified, blocked, erased or destroyed had been processed in contravention of any of the data protection principles,

an enforcement notice may, if reasonably practicable, require the data controller to notify third parties to whom the data have been disclosed of the rectification, blocking, erasure or destruction; and in determining whether it is reasonably practicable to require such notification regard shall be had, in particular, to the number of persons who would have to be notified.

(6) An enforcement notice must contain—

(a) a statement of the data protection principle or principles which the Commissioner is satisfied have been or are being contravened and his reasons for reaching that conclusion, and
(b) particulars of the rights of appeal conferred by section 48.

(7) Subject to subsection (8), an enforcement notice must not require any of the provisions of the notice to be complied with before the end of the period within which an appeal can be brought against the notice and, if such an appeal is brought, the notice need not be complied with pending the determination or withdrawal of the appeal.

(8) If by reason of special circumstances the Commissioner considers that an enforcement notice should be complied with as a matter of urgency he may include in the notice a statement to that effect and a statement of his reasons for reaching that conclusion; and in that event subsection (7) shall not apply but the notice must not require the provisions of the notice to be complied with before the end of the period of seven days beginning with the day on which the notice is served.

(9) Notification regulations (as defined by section 16(2)) may make provision as to the effect of the service of an enforcement notice on any entry in the register maintained under section 19 which relates to the person on whom the notice is served.

(10) This section has effect subject to section 46(1).

Cancellation of enforcement notice

41.—(1) If the Commissioner considers that all or any of the provisions of an enforcement notice need not be complied with in order to ensure compliance with the data protection principle or principles to which it relates, he may cancel or vary the notice by written notice to the person on whom it was served.

(2) A person on whom an enforcement notice has been served may, at any time after the expiry of the period during which an appeal can be brought against that notice, apply in writing to the Commissioner for the cancellation or variation of that notice on the ground that, by reason of a change of circumstances, all or any of the provisions of that notice need not be complied with in order to ensure compliance with the data protection principle or principles to which that notice relates.

Request for assessment

42.—(1) A request may be made to the Commissioner by or on behalf of any person who is, or believes himself to be, directly affected by any processing of personal data for an assessment as to whether it is likely or unlikely that the processing has been or is being carried out in compliance with the provisions of this Act.

(2) On receiving a request under this section, the Commissioner shall make an assessment in such manner as appears to him to be appropriate, unless he has not been supplied with such information as he may reasonably require in order to—

(a) satisfy himself as to the identity of the person making the request, and
(b) enable him to identify the processing in question.

(3) The matters to which the Commissioner may have regard in determining in what manner it is appropriate to make an assessment include—

(a) the extent to which the request appears to him to raise a matter of substance,
(b) any undue delay in making the request, and
(c) whether or not the person making the request is entitled to make an application under section 7 in respect of the personal data in question.

(4) Where the Commissioner has received a request under this section he shall notify the person who made the request—

(a) whether he has made an assessment as a result of the request, and
(b) to the extent that he considers appropriate, having regard in particular to any exemption from section 7 applying in relation to the personal data concerned, of any view formed or action taken as a result of the request.

Information notices

43.—(1) If the Commissioner—

(a) has received a request under section 42 in respect of any processing of personal data, or
(b) reasonably requires any information for the purpose of determining whether the data controller has complied or is complying with the data protection principles,

he may serve the data controller with a notice (in this Act referred to as "an information notice") requiring the data controller, within such time as is specified in the notice, to furnish the Commissioner, in such form as may be so specified, with such information relating to the request or to compliance with the principles as is so specified.

(2) An information notice must contain—

(a) in a case falling within subsection (1)(a), a statement that the Commissioner has received a request under section 42 in relation to the specified processing, or
(b) in a case falling within subsection (1)(b), a statement that the Commissioner regards the specified information as relevant for the purpose of determining

whether the data controller has complied, or is complying, with the data protection principles and his reasons for regarding it as relevant for that purpose.

(3) An information notice must also contain particulars of the rights of appeal conferred by section 48.

(4) Subject to subsection (5), the time specified in an information notice shall not expire before the end of the period within which an appeal can be brought against the notice and, if such an appeal is brought, the information need not be furnished pending the determination or withdrawal of the appeal.

(5) If by reason of special circumstances the Commissioner considers that the information is required as a matter of urgency, he may include in the notice a statement to that effect and a statement of his reasons for reaching that conclusion; and in that event subsection (4) shall not apply, but the notice shall not require the information to be furnished before the end of the period of seven days beginning with the day on which the notice is served.

(6) A person shall not be required by virtue of this section to furnish the Commissioner with any information in respect of—

(a) any communication between a professional legal adviser and his client in connection with the giving of legal advice to the client with respect to his obligations, liabilities or rights under this Act, or

(b) any communication between a professional legal adviser and his client, or between such an adviser or his client and any other person, made in connection with or in contemplation of proceedings under or arising out of this Act (including proceedings before the Tribunal) and for the purposes of such proceedings.

(7) In subsection (6) references to the client of a professional legal adviser include references to any person representing such a client.

(8) A person shall not be required by virtue of this section to furnish the Commissioner with any information if the furnishing of that information would, by revealing evidence of the commission of any offence other than an offence under this Act, expose him to proceedings for that offence.

(9) The Commissioner may cancel an information notice by written notice to the person on whom it was served.

(10) This section has effect subject to section 46(3).

Special information notices

44.—(1) If the Commissioner—

(a) has received a request under section 42 in respect of any processing of personal data, or

(b) has reasonable grounds for suspecting that, in a case in which proceedings have been stayed under section 32, the personal data to which the proceedings relate—

(i) are not being processed only for the special purposes, or

(ii) are not being processed with a view to the publication by any person of any journalistic, literary or artistic material which has not previously been published by the data controller,

he may serve the data controller with a notice (in this Act referred to as a "special information notice") requiring the data controller, within such time as is specified in the notice, to furnish the Commissioner, in such form as may be so specified, with such information as is so specified for the purpose specified in subsection (2).

(2) That purpose is the purpose of ascertaining—

(a) whether the personal data are being processed only for the special purposes, or

(b) whether they are being processed with a view to the publication by any person of any journalistic, literary or artistic material which has not previously been published by the data controller.

(3) A special information notice must contain—

(a) in a case falling within paragraph (a) of subsection (1), a statement that the Commissioner has received a request under section 42 in relation to the specified processing, or
(b) in a case falling within paragraph (b) of that subsection, a statement of the Commissioner's grounds for suspecting that the personal data are not being processed as mentioned in that paragraph.

(4) A special information notice must also contain particulars of the rights of appeal conferred by section 48.

(5) Subject to subsection (6), the time specified in a special information notice shall not expire before the end of the period within which an appeal can be brought against the notice and, if such an appeal is brought, the information need not be furnished pending the determination or withdrawal of the appeal.

(6) If by reason of special circumstances the Commissioner considers that the information is required as a matter of urgency, he may include in the notice a statement to that effect and a statement of his reasons for reaching that conclusion; and in that event subsection (5) shall not apply, but the notice shall not require the information to be furnished before the end of the period of seven days beginning with the day on which the notice is served.

(7) A person shall not be required by virtue of this section to furnish the Commissioner with any information in respect of—

(a) any communication between a professional legal adviser and his client in connection with the giving of legal advice to the client with respect to his obligations, liabilities or rights under this Act, or
(b) any communication between a professional legal adviser and his client, or between such an adviser or his client and any other person, made in connection with or in contemplation of proceedings under or arising out of this Act (including proceedings before the Tribunal) and for the purposes of such proceedings.

(8) In subsection (7) references to the client of a professional legal adviser include references to any person representing such a client.

(9) A person shall not be required by virtue of this section to furnish the Commissioner with any information if the furnishing of that information would, by revealing evidence of the commission of any offence other than an offence under this Act, expose him to proceedings for that offence.

(10) The Commissioner may cancel a special information notice by written notice to the person on whom it was served.

Determination by Commissioner as to the special purposes

45.—(1) Where at any time it appears to the Commissioner (whether as a result of the service of a special information notice or otherwise) that any personal data—

(a) are not being processed only for the special purposes, or
(b) are not being processed with a view to the publication by any person of any journalistic, literary or artistic material which has not previously been published by the data controller,

he may make a determination in writing to that effect.

(2) Notice of the determination shall be given to the data controller; and the notice must contain particulars of the right of appeal conferred by section 48.

(3) A determination under subsection (1) shall not take effect until the end of the period within which an appeal can be brought and, where an appeal is brought, shall not take effect pending the determination or withdrawal of the appeal.

Restriction on enforcement in case of processing for the special purposes

46.—(1) The Commissioner may not at any time serve an enforcement notice on a data controller with respect to the processing of personal data for the special purposes unless—

(a) a determination under section 45(1) with respect to those data has taken effect, and

(b) the court has granted leave for the notice to be served.

(2) The court shall not grant leave for the purposes of subsection (1)(b) unless it is satisfied—

(a) that the Commissioner has reason to suspect a contravention of the data protection principles which is of substantial public importance, and

(b) except where the case is one of urgency, that the data controller has been given notice, in accordance with rules of court, of the application for leave.

(3) The Commissioner may not serve an information notice on a data controller with respect to the processing of personal data for the special purposes unless a determination under section 45(1) with respect to those data has taken effect.

Failure to comply with notice

47.—(1) A person who fails to comply with an enforcement notice, an information notice or a special information notice is guilty of an offence.

(2) A person who, in purported compliance with an information notice or a special information notice—

(a) makes a statement which he knows to be false in a material respect, or

(b) recklessly makes a statement which is false in a material respect,

is guilty of an offence.

(3) It is a defence for a person charged with an offence under subsection (1) to prove that he exercised all due diligence to comply with the notice in question.

Rights of appeal

48.—(1) A person on whom an enforcement notice, an information notice or a special information notice has been served may appeal to the Tribunal against the notice.

(2) A person on whom an enforcement notice has been served may appeal to the Tribunal against the refusal of an application under section 41(2) for cancellation or variation of the notice.

(3) Where an enforcement notice, an information notice or a special information notice contains a statement by the Commissioner in accordance with section 40(8), 43(5) or 44(6) then, whether or not the person appeals against the notice, he may appeal against—

(a) the Commissioner's decision to include the statement in the notice, or

(b) the effect of the inclusion of the statement as respects any part of the notice.

(4) A data controller in respect of whom a determination has been made under section 45 may appeal to the Tribunal against the determination.

(5) Schedule 6 has effect in relation to appeals under this section and the proceedings of the Tribunal in respect of any such appeal.

Determination of appeals

49.—(1) If on an appeal under section 48(1) the Tribunal considers—

(a) that the notice against which the appeal is brought is not in accordance with the law, or
(b) to the extent that the notice involved an exercise of discretion by the Commissioner, that he ought to have exercised his discretion differently,

the Tribunal shall allow the appeal or substitute such other notice or decision as could have been served or made by the Commissioner; and in any other case the Tribunal shall dismiss the appeal.

(2) On such an appeal, the Tribunal may review any determination of fact on which the notice in question was based.

(3) If on an appeal under section 48(2) the Tribunal considers that the enforcement notice ought to be cancelled or varied by reason of a change in circumstances, the Tribunal shall cancel or vary the notice.

(4) On an appeal under subsection (3) of section 48 the Tribunal may direct—

(a) that the notice in question shall have effect as if it did not contain any such statement as is mentioned in that subsection, or
(b) that the inclusion of the statement shall not have effect in relation to any part of the notice,

and may make such modifications in the notice as may be required for giving effect to the direction.

(5) On an appeal under section 48(4), the Tribunal may cancel the determination of the Commissioner.

(6) Any party to an appeal to the Tribunal under section 48 may appeal from the decision of the Tribunal on a point of law to the appropriate court; and that court shall be—

(a) the High Court of Justice in England if the address of the person who was the appellant before the Tribunal is in England or Wales,
(b) the Court of Session if that address is in Scotland, and
(c) the High Court of Justice in Northern Ireland if that address is in Northern Ireland.

(7) For the purposes of subsection (6)—

(a) the address of a registered company is that of its registered office, and
(b) the address of a person (other than a registered company) carrying on a business is that of his principal place of business in the United Kingdom.

Powers of entry and inspection

50.—Schedule 9 (powers of entry and inspection) has effect.

PART VI

MISCELLAEOUS AND GENERAL

Functions of commissioner

General duties of Commissioner

51.—(1) It shall be the duty of the Commissioner to promote the following of good practice by data controllers and, in particular, so to perform his functions under this Act as to promote the observance of the requirements of this Act by data controllers.

(2) The Commissioner shall arrange for the dissemination in such form and manner as he considers appropriate of such information as it may appear to him expedient to give to the public about the operation of this Act, about good practice, and about other matters within the scope of his functions under this Act, and may give advice to any person as to any of those matters.

(3) Where—

(a) the [Secretary of State][19] so directs by order, or
(b) the Commissioner considers it appropriate to do so,

the Commissioner shall, after such consultation with trade associations, data subjects or persons representing data subjects as appears to him to be appropriate, prepare and disseminate to such persons as he considers appropriate codes of practice for guidance as to good practice.

(4) The Commissioner shall also—

(a) Where he considers it appropriate to do so, encourage trade associations to prepare, and to disseminate to their members, such codes of practice, and
(b) where any trade association submits a code of practice to him for his consideration, consider the code and, after such consultation with data subjects or persons representing data subjects as appears to him to be appropriate, notify the trade association whether in his opinion the code promotes the following of good practice.

(5) An order under subsection (3) shall describe the personal data or processing to which the code of practice is to relate, and may also describe the persons or classes of persons to whom it is to relate.

(6) The Commissioner shall arrange for the dissemination in such form and manner as he considers appropriate of—

(a) any Community finding as defined by paragraph 15(2) of Part II of Schedule 1,
(b) any decision of the European Commission, under the procedure provided for in Article 31(2) of the Data Protection Directive, which is made for the purposes of Article 26(3) or (4) of the Directive, and
(c) such other information as it may appear to him to be expedient to give to data controllers in relation to any personal data about the protection of the rights and freedoms of data subjects in relation to the processing of personal data in countries and territories outside the European Economic Area.

(7) The Commissioner may, with the consent of the data controller, assess any pro-

[19] Words substituted by SI 2003/1887 (Secretary of State for Constitutional Affairs Order), Sch.2, para.9(1)(a).

cessing of personal data for the following of good practice and shall inform the data controller of the results of the assessment.

(8) The Commissioner may charge such sums as he may with the consent of the [Secretary of State][20] determine for any services provided by the Commissioner by virtue of this Part.

(9) In this section—

"good practice" means such practice in the processing of personal data as appears to the Commissioner to be desirable having regard to the interests of data subjects and others, and includes (but is not limited to) compliance with the requirements of this Act;

"trade association" includes any body representing data controllers.

Reports and codes of practice to be laid before Parliament

52.—(1) The Commissioner shall lay annually before each House of Parliament a general report on the exercise of his functions under this Act.

(2) The Commissioner may from time to time lay before each House of Parliament such other reports with respect to those functions as he thinks fit.

(3) The Commissioner shall lay before each House of Parliament any code of practice prepared under section 51(3) for complying with a direction of the [Secretary of State],[21] unless the code is included in any report laid under subsection (1) or (2).

Assistance by Commissioner in cases involving processing for the special purposes

53.—(1) An individual who is an actual or prospective party to any proceedings under section 7(9), 10(4), 12(8)[, 12A(3)][22] or 14 or by virtue of section 13 which relate to personal data processed for the special purposes may apply to the Commissioner for assistance in relation to those proceedings.

(2) The Commissioner shall, as soon as reasonably practicable after receiving an application under subsection (1), consider it and decide whether and to what extent to grant it, but he shall not grant the application unless, in his opinion, the case involves a matter of substantial public importance.

(3) If the Commissioner decides to provide assistance, he shall, as soon as reasonably practicable after making the decision, notify the applicant, stating the extent of the assistance to be provided.

(4) If the Commissioner decides not to provide assistance, he shall, as soon as reasonably practicable after making the decision, notify the applicant of his decision and, if he thinks fit, the reasons for it.

(5) In this section—

(a) references to "proceedings" include references to prospective proceedings, and
(b) "applicant", in relation to assistance under this section, means an individual who applies for assistance.

(6) Schedule 10 has effect for supplementing this section.

International co-operation

54.—(1) The Commissioner—

---

20 Words substituted by SI 2003/1887 (Secretary of State for Constitutional Affairs Order), Sch.2, para.9(1)(a).

21 *ibid.*

22 Words inserted by Data Protection Act 1998 (c.29), Sch.13, para.4.

(a) shall continue to be the designated authority in the United Kingdom for the purposes of Article 13 of the Convention, and
(b) shall be the supervisory authority in the United Kingdom for the purposes of the Data Protection Directive.

(2) The [Secretary of State][23] may by order make provision as to the functions to be discharged by the Commissioner as the designated authority in the United Kingdom for the purposes of Article 13 of the Convention.

(3) The [Secretary of State][24] may by order make provision as to co- operation by the Commissioner with the European Commission and with supervisory authorities in other EEA States in connection with the performance of their respective duties and, in particular, as to—

(a) the exchange of information with supervisory authorities in other EEA States or with the European Commission, and
(b) the exercise within the United Kingdom at the request of a supervisory authority in another EEA State, in cases excluded by section 5 from the application of the other provisions of this Act, of functions of the Commissioner specified in the order.

(4) The Commissioner shall also carry out any data protection functions which the [Secretary of State][25] may by order direct him to carry out for the purpose of enabling Her Majesty's Government in the United Kingdom to give effect to any international obligations of the United Kingdom.

(5) The Commissioner shall, if so directed by the [Secretary of State],[26] provide any authority exercising data protection functions under the law of a colony specified in the direction with such assistance in connection with the discharge of those functions as the [Secretary of State][27] may direct or approve, on such terms (including terms as to payment) as the [Secretary of State][28] may direct or approve.

(6) Where the European Commission makes a decision for the purposes of Article 26(3) or (4) of the Data Protection Directive under the procedure provided for in Article 31(2) of the Directive, the Commissioner shall comply with that decision in exercising his functions under paragraph 9 of Schedule 4 or, as the case may be, paragraph 8 of that Schedule.

(7) The Commissioner shall inform the European Commission and the supervisory authorities in other EEA States—

(a) of any approvals granted for the purposes of paragraph 8 of Schedule 4, and
(b) of any authorisations granted for the purposes of paragraph 9 of that Schedule.

(8) In this section—

"the Convention" means the Convention for the Protection of Individuals with regard to Automatic Processing of Personal Data which was opened for signature on 28th January 1981;

"data protection functions" means functions relating to the protection of individuals with respect to the processing of personal information.

---

[23] Words substituted by SI 2003/1887 (Secretary of State for Constitutional Affairs Order), Sch.2, para.9(1)(a).
[24] *ibid.*
[25] *ibid.*
[26] *ibid.*
[27] *ibid.*
[28] *ibid.*

Unlawful obtaining, etc., of personal data

Unlawful obtaining etc. of personal data

55.—(1) A person must not knowingly or recklessly, without the consent of the data controller—

(a) obtain or disclose personal data or the information contained in personal data, or
(b) procure the disclosure to another person of the information contained in personal data.

(2) Subsection (1) does not apply to a person who shows—

(a) that the obtaining, disclosing or procuring—
   (i) was necessary for the purpose of preventing or detecting crime, or
   (ii) was required or authorised by or under any enactment, by any rule of law or by the order of a court,
(b) that he acted in the reasonable belief that he had in law the right to obtain or disclose the data or information or, as the case may be, to procure the disclosure of the information to the other person,
(c) that he acted in the reasonable belief that he would have had the consent of the data controller if the data controller had known of the obtaining, disclosing or procuring and the circumstances of it, or
(d) that in the particular circumstances the obtaining, disclosing or procuring was justified as being in the public interest.

(3) A person who contravenes subsection (1) is guilty of an offence.

(4) A person who sells personal data is guilty of an offence if he has obtained the data in contravention of subsection (1).

(5) A person who offers to sell personal data is guilty of an offence if—

(a) he has obtained the data in contravention of subsection (1), or
(b) he subsequently obtains the data in contravention of that subsection.

(6) For the purposes of subsection (5), an advertisement indicating that personal data are or may be for sale is an offer to sell the data.

(7) Section 1(2) does not apply for the purposes of this section; and for the purposes of subsections (4) to (6), "personal data" includes information extracted from personal data.

(8) References in this section to personal data do not include references to personal data which by virtue of section 28 are exempt from this section.

Records obtained under data subects right of access

Prohibition of requirement as to production of certain records

56.—(1) A person must not, in connection with—

(a) the recruitment of another person as an employee,
(b) the continued employment of another person, or
(c) any contract for the provision of services to him by another person,

require that other person or a third party to supply him with a relevant record or to produce a relevant record to him.

(2) A person concerned with the provision (for payment or not) of goods, facilities or services to the public or a section of the public must not, as a condition of providing or offering to provide any goods, facilities or services to another person, require that other person or a third party to supply him with a relevant record or to produce a relevant record to him.

(3) Subsections (1) and (2) do not apply to a person who shows—

(a) that the imposition of the requirement was required or authorised by or under any enactment, by any rule of law or by the order of a court, or
(b) that in the particular circumstances the imposition of the requirement was justified as being in the public interest.

(4) Having regard to the provisions of Part V of the Police Act 1997 (certificates of criminal records etc.), the imposition of the requirement referred to in subsection (1) or (2) is not to be regarded as being justified as being in the public interest on the ground that it would assist in the prevention or detection of crime.

(5) A person who contravenes subsection (1) or (2) is guilty of an offence.

(6) In this section "a relevant record" means any record which—

(a) has been or is to be obtained by a data subject from any data controller specified in the first column of the Table below in the exercise of the right conferred by section 7, and
(b) contains information relating to any matter specified in relation to that data controller in the second column,

and includes a copy of such a record or a part of such a record.

(7) In the Table in subsection (6)—[29]

"caution" means a caution given to any person in England and Wales or Northern Ireland in respect of an offence which, at the time when the caution is given, is admitted;

"conviction" has the same meaning as in the Rehabilitation of Offenders Act 1974 or the Rehabilitation of Offenders (Northern Ireland) Order 1978.

(8) The [Secretary of State][29a] may by order amend—

(a) the Table in subsection (6), and
(b) subsection (7).

(9) For the purposes of this section a record which states that a data controller is not processing any personal data relating to a particular matter shall be taken to be a record containing information relating to that matter.

(10) In this section "employee" means an individual who—

(a) works under a contract of employment, as defined by section 230(2) of the Employment Rights Act 1996, or
(b) holds any office,

whether or not he is entitled to remuneration;
and "employment" shall be construed accordingly.

---

[29] Table available at *http://www.legislation.hmso.gov.uk/acts/acts1998/80029--h.htm#56* and in Sweet & Maxwell's *Encyclopedia of Data Protection*, Vol.1, para.2–336, Release 26.

[29a] Words substituted by SI 2003/1887 (Secretary of State for Constitutional Affairs Order), Sch.2, para.9(1)(a).

Avoidance of certain contractual terms relating to health records

57.—(1) Any term or condition of a contract is void in so far as it purports to require an individual—

(a) to supply any other person with a record to which this section applies, or with a copy of such a record or a part of such a record, or
(b) to produce to any other person such a record, copy or part.

(2) This section applies to any record which—

(a) has been or is to be obtained by a data subject in the exercise of the right conferred by section 7, and
(b) consists of the information contained in any health record as defined by section 68(2).

Information provided to commissioner or tribunal

Disclosure of information

58.—No enactment or rule of law prohibiting or restricting the disclosure of information shall preclude a person from furnishing the Commissioner or the Tribunal with any information necessary for the discharge of their functions under this Act[or the Freedom of Information Act 2000].[30]

Confidentiality of information

59.—(1) No person who is or has been the Commissioner, a member of the Commissioner's staff or an agent of the Commissioner shall disclose any information which—

(a) has been obtained by, or furnished to, the Commissioner under or for the purposes of the information Acts.
(b) relates to an identified or identifiable individual or business, and
(c) is not at the time of the disclosure, and has not previously been, available to the public from other sources,

unless the disclosure is made with lawful authority.

(2) For the purposes of subsection (1) a disclosure of information is made with lawful authority only if, and to the extent that—

(a) the disclosure is made with the consent of the individual or of the person for the time being carrying on the business,
(b) the information was provided for the purpose of its being made available to the public (in whatever manner) under any provision of the information Acts,
(c) the disclosure is made for the purposes of, and is necessary for, the discharge of—
   (i) any functions under the information Acts, or
   (ii) any Community obligation,
(d) the disclosure is made for the purposes of any proceedings, whether criminal or civil and whether arising under, or by virtue of, the information Acts or otherwise, or

[30] Words added by Freedom of Information Act 2000 (c.36), Sch.2 (II), para.18.

(e) having regard to the rights and freedoms or legitimate interests of any person, the disclosure is necessary in the public interest.

(3) Any person who knowingly or recklessly discloses information in contravention of subsection (1) is guilty of an offence.

[(4) In this section "the information Acts" means this Act and the Freedom of Information Act 2000.][31]

General provisions relating to offences

Prosecutions and penalties

60.—(1) No proceedings for an offence under this Act shall be instituted—

(a) in England or Wales, except by the Commissioner or by or with the consent of the Director of Public Prosecutions;
(b) in Northern Ireland, except by the Commissioner or by or with the consent of the Director of Public Prosecutions for Northern Ireland.

(2) A person guilty of an offence under any provision of this Act other than [section 54A and][31a] paragraph 12 of Schedule 9 is liable—

(a) on summary conviction, to a fine not exceeding the statutory maximum, or
(b) on conviction on indictment, to a fine.

(3) A person guilty of an offence under [section 54A and][31b] paragraph 12 of Schedule 9 is liable on summary conviction to a fine not exceeding level 5 on the standard scale.

(4) Subject to subsection (5), the court by or before which a person is convicted of—

(a) an offence under section 21(1), 22(6), 55 or 56,
(b) an offence under section 21(2) relating to processing which is assessable processing for the purposes of section 22, or
(c) an offence under section 47(1) relating to an enforcement notice,

may order any document or other material used in connection with the processing of personal data and appearing to the court to be connected with the commission of the offence to be forfeited, destroyed or erased.

(5) The court shall not make an order under subsection (4) in relation to any material where a person (other than the offender) claiming to be the owner of or otherwise interested in the material applies to be heard by the court, unless an opportunity is given to him to show cause why the order should not be made.

Liability of directors etc.

61.—(1) Where an offence under this Act has been committed by a body corporate and is proved to have been committed with the consent or connivance of or to be attributable to any neglect on the part of any director, manager, secretary or similar officer of the body corporate or any person who was purporting to act in any such capacity, he as well as the body corporate shall be guilty of that offence and be liable to be proceeded against and punished accordingly.

---

[31] Words added by Freedom of Information Act (2000 c.36), Sch.2(II), para.19(3).
[31a] Words prospectively substituted by Crime (International Co-operation) Act (2003, c.32), Sch.5, paras 68, 70 as from a date to be appointed.
[31b] *ibid.*

(2) Where the affairs of a body corporate are managed by its members subsection (1) shall apply in relation to the acts and defaults of a member in connection with his functions of management as if he were a director of the body corporate.

(3) Where an offence under this Act has been committed by a Scottish partnership and the contravention in question is proved to have occurred with the consent or connivance of, or to be attributable to any neglect on the part of, a partner, he as well as the partnership shall be guilty of that offence and shall be liable to be proceeded against and punished accordingly.

Amendmens of consumer credit act 1974

Amendments of Consumer Credit Act 1974

62.—(1) In section 158 of the Consumer Credit Act 1974 (duty of agency to disclose filed information)—

(a) in subsection (1)—

(i) in paragraph (a) for "individual" there is substituted "partnership or other unincorporated body of persons not consisting entirely of bodies corporate", and

(ii) for "him" there is substituted "it",

(b) in subsection (2), for "his" there is substituted "the consumer's", and

(c) in subsection (3), for "him" there is substituted "the consumer".

(2) In section 159 of that Act (correction of wrong information) for subsection (1) there is substituted—

"(1) Any individual (the "objector") given—

(a) information under section 7 of the Data Protection Act 1998 by a credit reference agency, or

(b) information under section 158,

who considers that an entry in his file is incorrect, and that if it is not corrected he is likely to be prejudiced, may give notice to the agency requiring it either to remove the entry from the file or amend it."

(3) In subsections (2) to (6) of that section—

(a) for "consumer", wherever occurring, there is substituted "objector", and

(b) for "Director", wherever occurring, there is substituted "the relevant authority".

(4) After subsection (6) of that section there is inserted—

"(7) The Data Protection Commissioner may vary or revoke any order made by him under this section.

(8) In this section "the relevant authority" means—

(a) where the objector is a partnership or other unincorporated body of persons, the Director, and

(b) in any other case, the Data Protection Commissioner."

(5) In section 160 of that Act (alternative procedure for business consumers)—

(a) in subsection (4)—

(i) for "him" there is substituted "to the consumer", and

(ii) in paragraphs (a) and (b) for "he" there is substituted "the consumer", and for "his" there is substituted "the consumer's", and

(b) after subsection (6) there is inserted—

"(7) In this section "consumer" has the same meaning as in section 158."

General

Application to Crown

63.—(1) This Act binds the Crown.

(2) For the purposes of this Act each government department shall be treated as a person separate from any other government department.

(3) Where the purposes for which and the manner in which any personal data are, or are to be, processed are determined by any person acting on behalf of the Royal Household, the Duchy of Lancaster or the Duchy of Cornwall, the data controller in respect of those data for the purposes of this Act shall be—

(a) in relation to the Royal Household, the Keeper of the Privy Purse,

(b) in relation to the Duchy of Lancaster, such person as the Chancellor of the Duchy appoints, and

(c) in relation to the Duchy of Cornwall, such person as the Duke of Cornwall, or the possessor for the time being of the Duchy of Cornwall, appoints.

(4) Different persons may be appointed under subsection (3)(b) or (c) for different purposes.

(5) Neither a government department nor a person who is a data controller by virtue of subsection (3) shall be liable to prosecution under this Act, but [section 54A and][31c] 55 and paragraph 12 of Schedule 9 shall apply to a person in the service of the Crown as they apply to any other person.

Transmission of notices etc. by electronic or other means

64.—(1) This section applies to—

(a) a notice or request under any provision of Part II,

(b) a notice under subsection (1) of section 24 or particulars made available under that subsection, or

(c) an application under section 41(2),

but does not apply to anything which is required to be served in accordance with rules of court.

(2) The requirement that any notice, request, particulars or application to which this section applies should be in writing is satisfied where the text of the notice, request, particulars or application—

(a) is transmitted by electronic means,

(b) is received in legible form, and

(c) is capable of being used for subsequent reference.

[31c] Words prospectively substituted by Crime (International Co-operation) Act (2003, c.32), Sch.5, paras 68, 71 as from date to be appointed.

(3) The [Secretary of State][32] may by regulations provide that any requirement that any notice, request, particulars or application to which this section applies should be in writing is not to apply in such circumstances as may be prescribed by the regulations.

Service of notices by Commissioner

65.—(1) Any notice authorised or required by this Act to be served on or given to any person by the Commissioner may—

(a) if that person is an individual, be served on him—

(i) by delivering it to him, or
(ii) by sending it to him by post addressed to him at his usual or last-known place of residence or business, or
(iii) by leaving it for him at that place;

(b) if that person is a body corporate or unincorporate, be served on that body—

(i) by sending it by post to the proper officer of the body at its principal office, or
(ii) by addressing it to the proper officer of the body and leaving it at that office;

(c) if that person is a partnership in Scotland, be served on that partnership—

(i) by sending it by post to the principal office of the partnership, or
(ii) by addressing it to that partnership and leaving it at that office.

(2) In subsection (1)(b) "principal office", in relation to a registered company, means its registered office and "proper officer", in relation to any body, means the secretary or other executive officer charged with the conduct of its general affairs.

(3) This section is without prejudice to any other lawful method of serving or giving a notice.

Exercise of rights in Scotland by children

66.—(1) Where a question falls to be determined in Scotland as to the legal capacity of a person under the age of sixteen years to exercise any right conferred by any provision of this Act, that person shall be taken to have that capacity where he has a general understanding of what it means to exercise that right.

(2) Without prejudice to the generality of subsection (1), a person of twelve years of age or more shall be presumed to be of sufficient age and maturity to have such understanding as is mentioned in that subsection.

Orders, regulations and rules

67.—(1) Any power conferred by this Act on the [Secretary of State][33] to make an order, regulations or rules shall be exercisable by statutory instrument.

(2) Any order, regulations or rules made by the [Secretary of State][34] under this Act may—

(a) make different provision for different cases, and
(b) make such supplemental, incidental, consequential or transitional provision or savings as the [Secretary of State][35] considers appropriate;

32 Words substituted by SI 2003/1887 (Secretary of State for Constitutional Affairs Order), Sch.2, para.9(1)(a).
33 *ibid.*
34 *ibid.*
35 *ibid.*

and nothing in section 7(11), 19(5), 26(1) or 30(4) limits the generality of paragraph (a).

(3) Before making—

(a) an order under any provision of this Act other than section 75(3),
(b) any regulations under this Act other than notification regulations (as defined by section 16(2)),

the [Secretary of State][36] shall consult the Commissioner.

(4) A statutory instrument containing (whether alone or with other provision) an order under—

section 10(2)(b),
section 12(5)(b),
section 22(1),
section 30,
section 32(3),
section 38,
section 56(8),
paragraph 10 of Schedule 3, or
paragraph 4 of Schedule 7,

shall not be made unless a draft of the instrument has been laid before and approved by a resolution of each House of Parliament.

(5) A statutory instrument which contains (whether alone or with other provisions)—

(a) an order under—
section 22(7),
section 23,
section 51(3),
section 54(2), (3) or (4),
paragraph 3, 4 or 14 of Part II of Schedule 1,
paragraph 6 of Schedule 2,
paragraph 2, 7 or 9 of Schedule 3,
paragraph 4 of Schedule 4,
paragraph 6 of Schedule 7,
(b) regulations under section 7 which—
  (i) prescribe cases for the purposes of subsection (2)(b),
  (ii) are made by virtue of subsection (7), or
  (iii) relate to the definition of "the prescribed period",
(c) regulations under section 8(1), 9(3) or 9A(5),
(d) regulations under section 64,
(e) notification regulations (as defined by section 16(2)), or
(f) rules under paragraph 7 of Schedule 6,

and which is not subject to the requirement in subsection (4) that a draft of the instrument be laid before and approved by a resolution of each House of Parliament, shall be subject to annulment in pursuance of a resolution of either House of Parliament.

(6) A statutory instrument which contains only—

(a) regulations prescribing fees for the purposes of any provision of this Act, or
(b) regulations under section 7 prescribing fees for the purposes of any other enactment,

[36] Words substituted by SI 2003/1887 (Secretary of State for Constitutional Affairs Order), Sch.2, para.9(1)(a).

shall be laid before Parliament after being made.

Meaning of "accessible record"

68.—(1) In this Act "accessible record" means—

(a) a health record as defined by subsection (2),
(b) an educational record as defined by Schedule 11, or
(c) an accessible public record as defined by Schedule 12.

(2) In subsection (1)(a) "health record" means any record which—

(a) consists of information relating to the physical or mental health or condition of an individual, and
(b) has been made by or on behalf of a health professional in connection with the care of that individual.

Meaning of "health professional"

69.—(1) In this Act "health professional" means any of the following—

(a) a registered medical practitioner,
(b) a registered dentist as defined by section 53(1) of the Dentists Act 1984,
(c) a registered optician as defined by section 36(1) of the Opticians Act 1989,
(d) a registered pharmaceutical chemist as defined by section 24(1) of the Pharmacy Act 1954 or a registered person as defined by Article 2(2) of the Pharmacy (Northern Ireland) Order 1976,
(e) a registered nurse or midwife,
(f) a registered osteopath as defined by section 41 of the Osteopaths Act 1993,
(g) a registered chiropractor as defined by section 43 of the Chiropractors Act 1994,
(h) any person who is registered as a member of a profession to which the Professions Supplementary to Medicine Act 1960 for the time being extends,
(i) a clinical psychologistor child psychotherapist,
[. . .][37]
(k) a scientist employed by such a body as head of a department.

(2) In subsection (1)(a) "registered medical practitioner" includes any person who is provisionally registered under section 15 or 21 of the Medical Act 1983 and is engaged in such employment as is mentioned in subsection (3) of that section.

(3) In subsection (1) "health service body" means—

(a) a Strategic Health Authority or a Health Authority established under section 8 of the National Health Service Act 1977,
(b) a Special Health Authority established under section 11 of that Act,
(bb) a Primary Care Trust established under section 16A of that Act,
(bbb) a Local Health Board established under section 16BA of that Act,
(c) a Health Board within the meaning of the National Health Service (Scotland) Act 1978,
(d) a Special Health Board within the meaning of that Act,
(e) the managers of a State Hospital provided under section 102 of that Act,
(f) a National Health Service trust first established under section 5 of the National Health Service and Community Care Act 1990 or section 12A of the National Health Service (Scotland) Act 1978,

[37] Words repealed by SI 2003/1590 (Health Professions Order 2001 (Consequential Amendments) Order), Sch.1(1), para.1(b).

(g) a Health and Social Services Board established under Article 16 of the Health and Personal Social Services (Northern Ireland) Order 1972,
(h) a special health and social services agency established under the Health and Personal Social Services (Special Agencies) (Northern Ireland) Order 1990, or
(i) a Health and Social Services trust established under Article 10 of the Health and Personal Social Services (Northern Ireland) Order 1991.

Supplementary definitions

70.—(1) In this Act, unless the context otherwise requires—

"business" includes any trade or profession;

"the Commissioner" means the Information Commissioner;

"credit reference agency" has the same meaning as in the Consumer Credit Act 1974;

"the Data Protection Directive" means Directive 95/46/EC on the protection of individuals with regard to the processing of personal data and on the free movement of such data;

"EEA State" means a State which is a contracting party to the Agreement on the European Economic Area signed at Oporto on 2nd May 1992 as adjusted by the Protocol signed at Brussels on 17th March 1993;

"enactment" includes an enactment passed after this Act and any enactment comprised in, or in any instrument made under, an Act of the Scottish Parliament;

"government department" includes a Northern Ireland department and any body or authority exercising statutory functions on behalf of the Crown;

"Minister of the Crown" has the same meaning as in the Ministers of the Crown Act 1975;

"public register" means any register which pursuant to a requirement imposed—

(a) by or under any enactment, or
(b) in pursuance of any international agreement,

is open to public inspection or open to inspection by any person having a legitimate interest;

"pupil"—

(a) in relation to a school in England and Wales, means a registered pupil within the meaning of the Education Act 1996,
(b) in relation to a school in Scotland, means a pupil within the meaning of the Education (Scotland) Act 1980, and
(c) in relation to a school in Northern Ireland, means a registered pupil within the meaning of the Education and Libraries (Northern Ireland) Order 1986;

"recipient", in relation to any personal data, means any person to whom the data are disclosed, including any person (such as an employee or agent of the data controller, a data processor or an employee or agent of a data processor) to whom they are disclosed in the course of processing the data for the data controller, but does not include any person to whom disclosure is or may be made as a result of, or with a view to, a particular inquiry by or on behalf of that person made in the exercise of any power conferred by law;

"registered company" means a company registered under the enactments relating to companies for the time being in force in the United Kingdom;

"school"—

(a) in relation to England and Wales, has the same meaning as in the Education Act 1996,
(b) in relation to Scotland, has the same meaning as in the Education (Scotland) Act 1980, and
(c) in relation to Northern Ireland, has the same meaning as in the Education and Libraries (Northern Ireland) Order 1986;

"teacher" includes—

(a) in Great Britain, head teacher, and
(b) in Northern Ireland, the principal of a school;

"third party", in relation to personal data, means any person other than—

(a) the data subject,
(b) the data controller, or
(c) any data processor or other person authorised to process data for the data controller or processor;

"the Tribunal" means [the Information Tribunal][38].

(2) For the purposes of this Act data are inaccurate if they are incorrect or misleading as to any matter of fact.

Index of defined expressions

71.—The following Table[39] shows provisions defining or otherwise explaining expressions used in this Act (other than provisions defining or explaining an expression only used in the same section or Schedule).

Modifications of Act

72.—During the period beginning with the commencement of this section and ending with 23rd October 2007, the provisions of this Act shall have effect subject to the modifications set out in Schedule 13.

Transitional provisions and savings

73.—Schedule 14 (which contains transitional provisions and savings) has effect.

Minor and consequential amendments and repeals and revocations

74.—(1) Schedule 15 (which contains minor and consequential amendments) has effect.

(2) The enactments and instruments specified in Schedule 16 are repealed or revoked to the extent specified.

Short title, commencement and extent

75.—(1) This Act may be cited as the Data Protection Act 1998.

(2) The following provisions of this Act—

[38] Words substituted by Freedom of Information Act 2000 (c.36), Sch.2(I), para.14(b).

[39] Table available at *http://www.legislation.hmso.gov.uk/acts/acts1998/80029--k.htm#71* and in Sweet & Maxwell's *Encyclopedia of Data Protection*, Vol.1, para.2–356, Release 26.

(a) sections 1 to 3,
(b) section 25(1) and (4),
(c) section 26,
(d) sections 67 to 71,
(e) this section,
(f) paragraph 17 of Schedule 5,
(g) Schedule 11,
(h) Schedule 12, and
(i) so much of any other provision of this Act as confers any power to make subordinate legislation,

shall come into force on the day on which this Act is passed.

(3) The remaining provisions of this Act shall come into force on such day as the [Secretary of State][40] may by order appoint; and different days may be appointed for different purposes.

(4) The day appointed under subsection (3) for the coming into force of section 56 must not be earlier than the first day on which sections 112, 113 and 115 of the Police Act 1997 (which provide for the issue by the Secretary of State of criminal conviction certificates, criminal record certificates and enhanced criminal record certificates) are all in force.

(5) Subject to subsection (6), this Act extends to Northern Ireland.

(6) Any amendment, repeal or revocation made by Schedule 15 or 16 has the same extent as that of the enactment or instrument to which it relates.

SCHEDULE 1

The Data Protection Principles

Part I

The Principles

1.—Personal data shall be processed fairly and lawfully and, in particular, shall not be processed unless—
(a) at least one of the conditions in Schedule 2 is met, and
(b) in the case of sensitive personal data, at least one of the conditions in Schedule 3 is also met.

2.—Personal data shall be obtained only for one or more specified and lawful purposes, and shall not be further processed in any manner incompatible with that purpose or those purposes.

3.—Personal data shall be adequate, relevant and not excessive in relation to the purpose or purposes for which they are processed.

4.—Personal data shall be accurate and, where necessary, kept up to date.

5.—Personal data processed for any purpose or purposes shall not be kept for longer than is necessary for that purpose or those purposes.

6.—Personal data shall be processed in accordance with the rights of data subjects under this Act.

7.—Appropriate technical and organisational measures shall be taken against unauthorised or unlawful processing of personal data and against accidental loss or destruction of, or damage to, personal data.

8.—Personal data shall not be transferred to a country or territory outside the European Economic Area unless that country or territory ensures an adequate level of protection for the rights and freedoms of data subjects in relation to the processing of personal data.

---

[40] Words substituted by SI 2003/1887 (Secretary of State for Constitutional Affairs Order), Sch.2, para.9(1)(a).

PART II

INTERPRETATION OF THE PRINCIPLES IN PART I

The first principle

1.—(1) In determining for the purposes of the first principle whether personal data are processed fairly, regard is to be had to the method by which they are obtained, including in particular whether any person from whom they are obtained is deceived or misled as to the purpose or purposes for which they are to be processed.

(2) Subject to paragraph 2, for the purposes of the first principle data are to be treated as obtained fairly if they consist of information obtained from a person who—

(a) is authorised by or under any enactment to supply it, or

(b) is required to supply it by or under any enactment or by any convention or other instrument imposing an international obligation on the United Kingdom.

2.—(1) Subject to paragraph 3, for the purposes of the first principle personal data are not to be treated as processed fairly unless—

(a) in the case of data obtained from the data subject, the data controller ensures so far as practicable that the data subject has, is provided with, or has made readily available to him, the information specified in sub- paragraph (3), and

(b) in any other case, the data controller ensures so far as practicable that, before the relevant time or as soon as practicable after that time, the data subject has, is provided with, or has made readily available to him, the information specified in sub-paragraph (3).

(2) In sub-paragraph (1)(b) "the relevant time" means—

(a) the time when the data controller first processes the data, or

(b) in a case where at that time disclosure to a third party within a reasonable period is envisaged—

(i) if the data are in fact disclosed to such a person within that period, the time when the data are first disclosed,

(ii) if within that period the data controller becomes, or ought to become, aware that the data are unlikely to be disclosed to such a person within that period, the time when the data controller does become, or ought to become, so aware, or

(iii) in any other case, the end of that period.

(3) The information referred to in sub-paragraph (1) is as follows, namely—

(a) the identity of the data controller,

(b) if he has nominated a representative for the purposes of this Act, the identity of that representative,

(c) the purpose or purposes for which the data are intended to be processed, and

(d) any further information which is necessary, having regard to the specific circumstances in which the data are or are to be processed, to enable processing in respect of the data subject to be fair.

3.—(1) Paragraph 2(1)(b) does not apply where either of the primary conditions in sub-paragraph (2), together with such further conditions as may be prescribed by the [Secretary of State][41] by order, are met.

(2) The primary conditions referred to in sub-paragraph (1) are—

(a) that the provision of that information would involve a disproportionate effort, or

(b) that the recording of the information to be contained in the data by, or the disclosure of the data by, the data controller is necessary for compliance with any legal obligation to which the data controller is subject, other than an obligation imposed by contract.

4.—(1) Personal data which contain a general identifier falling within a description prescribed by the [Secretary of State][42] by order are not to be treated as processed fairly and lawfully unless they are processed in compliance with any conditions so prescribed in relation to general identifiers of that description.

---

[41] Words substituted by SI 2003/1887 (Secretary of State for Constitutional Affairs Order), Sch. 2, para. 9(1)(b).

[42] *ibid.*

(2) In sub-paragraph (1) "a general identifier" means any identifier (such as, for example, a number or code used for identification purposes) which—

(a) relates to an individual, and
(b) forms part of a set of similar identifiers which is of general application.

The second principle

5.—The purpose or purposes for which personal data are obtained may in particular be specified—

(a) in a notice given for the purposes of paragraph 2 by the data controller to the data subject, or
(b) in a notification given to the Commissioner under Part III of this Act.

6.—In determining whether any disclosure of personal data is compatible with the purpose or purposes for which the data were obtained, regard is to be had to the purpose or purposes for which the personal data are intended to be processed by any person to whom they are disclosed.

The fourth principle

7.—The fourth principle is not to be regarded as being contravened by reason of any inaccuracy in personal data which accurately record information obtained by the data controller from the data subject or a third party in a case where—

(a) having regard to the purpose or purposes for which the data were obtained and further processed, the data controller has taken reasonable steps to ensure the accuracy of the data, and
(b) if the data subject has notified the data controller of the data subject's view that the data are inaccurate, the data indicate that fact.

The six principle

8.—A person is to be regarded as contravening the sixth principle if, but only if—

(a) he contravenes section 7 by failing to supply information in accordance with that section,
(b) he contravenes section 10 by failing to comply with a notice given under subsection (1) of that section to the extent that the notice is justified or by failing to give a notice under subsection (3) of that section,
(c) he contravenes section 11 by failing to comply with a notice given under subsection (1) of that section,
(d) he contravenes section 12 by failing to comply with a notice given under subsection (1) or (2)(b) of that section or by failing to give a notification under subsection (2)(a) of that section or a notice under subsection (3) of that section.

[or (e) he contravenes section 12A by failing to comply with a notice given under subsection (1) of that section to the extent that the notice is justified.][43]

The seventh principle

9.—Having regard to the state of technological development and the cost of implementing any measures, the measures must ensure a level of security appropriate to—

(a) the harm that might result from such unauthorised or unlawful processing or accidental loss, destruction or damage as are mentioned in the seventh principle, and
(b) the nature of the data to be protected.

10.—The data controller must take reasonable steps to ensure the reliability of any employees of his who have access to the personal data.

11.—Where processing of personal data is carried out by a data processor on behalf of a data controller, the data controller must in order to comply with the seventh principle—

(a) choose a data processor providing sufficient guarantees in respect of the technical and organisational security measures governing the processing to be carried out, and
(b) take reasonable steps to ensure compliance with those measures.

---

[43] Para.(e) and the word "or" immediatley preceeding it inserted by Data Protection Act 1998 (c.29), Sch.13, para.5.

12.—Where processing of personal data is carried out by a data processor on behalf of a data controller; the data controller is not to be regarded as complying with the seventh principle unless—
(a) the processing is carried out under a contract—
(i) which is made or evidenced in writing, and
(ii) under which the data processor is to act only on instructions from the data controller, and
(b) the contract requires the data processor to comply with obligations equivalent to those imposed on a data controller by the seventh principle.

The eighth principle

13.—An adequate level of protection is one which is adequate in all the circumstances of the case, having regard in particular to—
(a) the nature of the personal data,
(b) the country or territory of origin of the information contained in the data,
(c) the country or territory of final destination of that information,
(d) the purposes for which and period during which the data are intended to be processed,
(e) the law in force in the country or territory in question,
(f) the international obligations of that country or territory,
(g) any relevant codes of conduct or other rules which are enforceable in that country or territory (whether generally or by arrangement in particular cases), and
(h) any security measures taken in respect of the data in that country or territory.

14.—The eighth principle does not apply to a transfer falling within any paragraph of Schedule 4, except in such circumstances and to such extent as the [Secretary of State][44] may by order provide.

15.—(1) Where—
(a) in any proceedings under this Act any question arises as to whether the requirement of the eighth principle as to an adequate level of protection is met in relation to the transfer of any personal data to a country or territory outside the European Economic Area, and
(b) a Community finding has been made in relation to transfers of the kind in question,
that question is to be determined in accordance with that finding.

(2) In sub-paragraph (1) "Community finding" means a finding of the European Commission, under the procedure provided for in Article 31(2) of the Data Protection Directive, that a country or territory outside the European Economic Area does, or does not, ensure an adequate level of protection within the meaning of Article 25(2) of the Directive.

SCHEDULE 2

Conditions Relevant for Purposes of The First Principle:

Processing of any Personal Data

1.—The data subject has given his consent to the processing.

2.—The processing is necessary—
(a) for the performance of a contract to which the data subject is a party, or
(b) for the taking of steps at the request of the data subject with a view to entering into a contract.

3.—The processing is necessary for compliance with any legal obligation to which the data controller is subject, other than an obligation imposed by contract.

4.—The processing is necessary in order to protect the vital interests of the data subject.

5.—The processing is necessary—

[44] Words substituted by SI 2003/1887 (Secretary of State for Constitutional Affairs Order), Sch.2, para.9(1)(b).

(a) for the administration of justice,
(b) for the exercise of any functions conferred on any person by or under any enactment,
(c) for the exercise of any functions of the Crown, a Minister of the Crown or a government department, or
(d) for the exercise of any other functions of a public nature exercised in the public interest by any person.

6.—(1) The processing is necessary for the purposes of legitimate interests pursued by the data controller or by the third party or parties to whom the data are disclosed, except where the processing is unwarranted in any particular case by reason of prejudice to the rights and freedoms or legitimate interests of the data subject.

(2) The [Secretary of State][45] may by order specify particular circumstances in which this condition is, or is not, to be taken to be satisfied.

SCHEDULE 3

Conditions Relevant for Purposes of the First Principle:

Processing of Sensitive Personal Data

1.—The data subject has given his explicit consent to the processing of the personal data.

2.—(1) The processing is necessary for the purposes of exercising or performing any right or obligation which is conferred or imposed by law on the data controller in connection with employment.

(2) The [Lord Chancellor][46] may by order—
(a) exclude the application of sub-paragraph (1) in such cases as may be specified, or
(b) provide that, in such cases as may be specified, the condition in sub- paragraph (1) is not to be regarded as satisfied unless such further conditions as may be specified in the order are also satisfied.

3.—The processing is necessary—
(a) in order to protect the vital interests of the data subject or another person, in a case where—
(i) consent cannot be given by or on behalf of the data subject, or
(ii) the data controller cannot reasonably be expected to obtain the consent of the data subject, or
(b) in order to protect the vital interests of another person, in a case where consent by or on behalf of the data subject has been unreasonably withheld.

4.—The processing—
(a) is carried out in the course of its legitimate activities by any body or association which—
(i) is not established or conducted for profit, and
(ii) exists for political, philosophical, religious or trade-union purposes,
(b) is carried out with appropriate safeguards for the rights and freedoms of data subjects,
(c) relates only to individuals who either are members of the body or association or have regular contact with it in connection with its purposes, and
(d) does not involve disclosure of the personal data to a third party without the consent of the data subject.

5.—The information contained in the personal data has been made public as a result of steps deliberately taken by the data subject.

6.—The processing—
(a) is necessary for the purpose of, or in connection with, any legal proceedings (including prospective legal proceedings),

---

45 Words substituted by SI 2003/1887 (Secretary of State for Constitutional Affairs Order), Sch.2, para.9(1)(b).

46 Words substituted by SI 2001/3500 (Transfer of Functions (Miscellaneous) Order), Sch.2(I), para.6(1)(z).

(b) is necessary for the purpose of obtaining legal advice, or
(c) is otherwise necessary for the purposes of establishing, exercising or defending legal rights.

7.—(1) The processing is necessary—
(a) for the administration of justice,
(b) for the exercise of any functions conferred on any person by or under an enactment, or
(c) for the exercise of any functions of the Crown, a Minister of the Crown or a government department.

(2) The [Lord Chancellor][47] may by order—
(a) exclude the application of sub-paragraph (1) in such cases as may be specified, or
(b) provide that, in such cases as may be specified, the condition in sub- paragraph (1) is not to be regarded as satisfied unless such further conditions as may be specified in the order are also satisfied.

8.—(1) The processing is necessary for medical purposes and is undertaken by—
(a) a health professional, or
(b) a person who in the circumstances owes a duty of confidentiality which is equivalent to that which would arise if that person were a health professional.

(2) In this paragraph "medical purposes" includes the purposes of preventative medicine, medical diagnosis, medical research, the provision of care and treatment and the management of health care services.

9.—(1) The processing—
(a) is of sensitive personal data consisting of information as to racial or ethnic origin,
(b) is necessary for the purpose of identifying or keeping under review the existence or absence of equality of opportunity or treatment between persons of different racial or ethnic origins, with a view to enabling such equality to be promoted or maintained, and
(c) is carried out with appropriate safeguards for the rights and freedoms of data subjects.

(2) The [Secretary of State][48] may by order specify circumstances in which processing falling within sub-paragraph (1)(a) and (b) is, or is not, to be taken for the purposes of sub-paragraph (1)(c) to be carried out with appropriate safeguards for the rights and freedoms of data subjects.

10.—The personal data are processed in circumstances specified in an order made by the [Lord Chancellor][49] for the purposes of this paragraph.

SCHEDULE 4

Cases Where The Eighth Principle Does Not Apply

1.—The data subject has given his consent to the transfer.

2.—The transfer is necessary—
(a) for the performance of a contract between the data subject and the data controller, or
(b) for the taking of steps at the request of the data subject with a view to his entering into a contract with the data controller.

3.—The transfer is necessary—
(a) for the conclusion of a contract between the data controller and a person other than the data subject which—
  (i) is entered into at the request of the data subject, or
  (ii) is in the interests of the data subject, or
(b) for the performance of such a contract.

[47] *ibid*.
[48] Words substituted by SI 2003/1887 (Secretary of State for Constitutional Affairs Order), Sch.2, para.9(1)(b).
[49] Words substituted by SI 2001/3500 (Transfer of Functions (Miscellaneous) Order), Sch.2(I), para.61(z).

4.—(1) The transfer is necessary for reasons of substantial public interest.

(2) The [Lord Chancellor][50] may by order specify—

(a) circumstances in which a transfer is to be taken for the purposes of sub- paragraph (1) to be necessary for reasons of substantial public interest, and

(b) circumstances in which a transfer which is not required by or under an enactment is not to be taken for the purpose of sub-paragraph (1) to be necessary for reasons of substantial public interest.

5.—The transfer—

(a) is necessary for the purpose of, or in connection with, any legal proceedings (including prospective legal proceedings),

(b) is necessary for the purpose of obtaining legal advice, or

(c) is otherwise necessary for the purposes of establishing, exercising or defending legal rights.

6.—The transfer is necessary in order to protect the vital interests of the data subject.

7.—The transfer is of part of the personal data on a public register and any conditions subject to which the register is open to inspection are complied with by any person to whom the data are or may be disclosed after the transfer.

8.—The transfer is made on terms which are of a kind approved by the Commissioner as ensuring adequate safeguards for the rights and freedoms of data subjects.

9.—The transfer has been authorised by the Commissioner as being made in such a manner as to ensure adequate safeguards for the rights and freedoms of data subjects.

SCHEDULE 5

The Data Protection Commission and the Data Protection Tribunal

Part I

The Commissioner

Status and capacity

1.—(1) The corporation sole by the name of the Data Protection Registrar established by the Data Protection Act 1984 shall continue in existence by the name of the [Information Commissioner][51].

(2) The Commissioner and his officers and staff are not to be regarded as servants or agents of the Crown.

Tenure of office

2.—(1) Subject to the provisions of this paragraph, the Commissioner shall hold office for such term not exceeding five years as may be determined at the time of his appointment.

(2) The Commissioner may be relieved of his office by Her Majesty at his own request.

(3) The Commissioner may be removed from office by Her Majesty in pursuance of an Address from both Houses of Parliament.

(4) The Commissioner shall in any case vacate his office—

(a) on completing the year of service in which he attains the age of sixty- five years, or

(b) if earlier, on completing his fifteenth year of service.

(5) Subject to sub-paragraph (4), a person who ceases to be Commissioner on the expiration of his term of office shall be eligible for re-appointment, but a person may not be re-appointed for a third or subsequent term as Commissioner unless, by reason of special circumstances, the person's re-appointment for such a term is desirable in the public interest.

---

50 Words substituted by SI 2001/3500 (Transfer of Functions (Miscellaneous) Order), Sch.2(I), para.6(1)(aa).

51 Words substituted by Freedom of Information Act 2000 (c.36), Sch.2(I), para.15(2).

Salary, etc.

3.—(1) There shall be paid—

(a) to the Commissioner such salary, and

(b) to or in respect of the Commissioner such pension,

as may be specified by a resolution of the House of Commons.

(2) A resolution for the purposes of this paragraph may—

(a) specify the salary or pension,

(b) provide that the salary or pension is to be the same as, or calculated on the same basis as, that payable to, or to or in respect of, a person employed in a specified office under, or in a specified capacity in the service of, the Crown, or

(c) specify the salary or pension and provide for it to be increased by reference to such variables as may be specified in the resolution.

(3) A resolution for the purposes of this paragraph may take effect from the date on which it is passed or from any earlier or later date specified in the resolution.

(4) A resolution for the purposes of this paragraph may make different provision in relation to the pension payable to or in respect of different holders of the office of Commissioner.

(5) Any salary or pension payable under this paragraph shall be charged on and issued out of the Consolidated Fund.

(6) In this paragraph "pension" includes an allowance or gratuity and any reference to the payment of a pension includes a reference to the making of payments towards the provision of a pension.

Officers and staff

4.—(1) The Commissioner—

(a) shall appoint a deputy commissioner or two deputy commissioners, and

(b) may appoint such number of other officers and staff as he may determine.

(1A) The Commissioner shall, when appointing any second deputy commissioner, specify which of the Commissioner's functions are to be performed, in the circumstances referred to in paragraph 5(1), by each of the deputy commissioners.

(2) The remuneration and other conditions of service of the persons appointed under this paragraph shall be determined by the Commissioner.

(3) The Commissioner may pay such pensions, allowances or gratuities to or in respect of the persons appointed under this paragraph, or make such payments towards the provision of such pensions, allowances or gratuities, as he may determine.

(4) The references in sub-paragraph (3) to pensions, allowances or gratuities to or in respect of the persons appointed under this paragraph include references to pensions, allowances or gratuities by way of compensation to or in respect of any of those persons who suffer loss of office or employment.

(5) Any determination under sub-paragraph (1)(b), (2) or (3) shall require the approval of the [Secretary of State].[52]

(6) The Employers' Liability (Compulsory Insurance) Act 1969 shall not require insurance to be effected by the Commissioner.

5.—(1) The deputy commissioner or deputy commissioners shall perform the functions conferred by this Act or the Freedom of Information Act 2000 on the Commissioner during any vacancy in that office or at any time when the Commissioner is for any reason unable to act.

(2) Without prejudice to sub-paragraph (1), any functions of the Commissioner under this Act[or the Freedom of Information Act 2000][53] may, to the extent authorised by him, be performed by any of his officers or staff.

Authentication of seal of the commissioner

6.—The application of the seal of the Commissioner shall be authenticated by his signature or by the signature of some other person authorised for the purpose.

[52] Words substituted by SI 2003/1887 (Secretary of State for Constitutional Affairs Order), Sch. 2, para. 9(1)(c).

[53] Words added by Freedom of Information Act 2000 (c.36), Sch. 2(II), para. 21(3).

Presumption of authenticity of documents issued by the commissioner

7.—Any document purporting to be an instrument issued by the Commissioner and to be duly executed under the Commissioner's seal or to be signed by or on behalf of the Commissioner shall be received in evidence and shall be deemed to be such an instrument unless the contrary is shown.

Money

8.—The [Secretary of State][54] may make payments to the Commissioner out of money provided by Parliament.

9.—(1) All fees and other sums received by the Commissioner in the exercise of his functions under this Act, under section 159 of the Consumer Credit Act 1974 or under the Freedom of Information Act 2000 shall be paid by him to the [Secretary of State].[55]

(2) Sub-paragraph (1) shall not apply where the [Secretary of State],[56] with the consent of the Treasury, otherwise directs.

(3) Any sums received by the [Secretary of State][57] under sub-paragraph (1) shall be paid into the Consolidated Fund.

Accounts

10.—(1) It shall be the duty of the Commissioner—

(a) to keep proper accounts and other records in relation to the accounts,

(b) to prepare in respect of each financial year a statement of account in such form as the [Secretary of State][58] may direct, and

(c) to send copies of that statement to the Comptroller and Auditor General on or before 31st August next following the end of the year to which the statement relates or on or before such earlier date after the end of that year as the Treasury may direct.

(2) The Comptroller and Auditor General shall examine and certify any statement sent to him under this paragraph and lay copies of it together with his report thereon before each House of Parliament.

(3) In this paragraph "financial year" means a period of twelve months beginning with 1st April.

Application of part I in Scotland

11.—Paragraphs 1(1), 6 and 7 do not extend to Scotland.

PART II

THE TRIBUNAL

Tenure of office

12.—(1) Subject to the following provisions of this paragraph, a member of the Tribunal shall hold and vacate his office in accordance with the terms of his appointment and shall, on ceasing to hold office, be eligible for re- appointment.

(2) Any member of the Tribunal may at any time resign his office by notice in writing to the Lord Chancellor[(in the case of the chairman or a deputy chairman) or to the Secretary of State (in the case of any other member)].[59]

(3) A person who is the chairman or deputy chairman of the Tribunal shall vacate his office on the day on which he attains the age of seventy years; but this sub-paragraph is subject to section

[54] Words substituted by SI 2003/1887 (Secretary of State for Constitutional Affairs Order), Sch.2, para.9(1)(c).

[55] *ibid.*

[56] *ibid.*

[57] *ibid.*

[58] *ibid.*

[59] Words inserted by SI 2003/1887 (Secretary of State for Constitutional Affairs Order), Sch.2, para.9(2).

26(4) to (6) of the Judicial Pensions and Retirement Act 1993 (power to authorise continuance in office up to the age of seventy-five years).

Salary etc.

13.—The [Secretary of State][60] shall pay to the members of the Tribunal out of money provided by Parliament such remuneration and allowances as he may determine.

Officers and staff

14.—The [Secretary of State][61] may provide the Tribunal with such officers and staff as he thinks necessary for the proper discharge of its functions.

Expenses

15.—Such expenses of the Tribunal as the [Secretary of State][62] may determine shall be defrayed by the [Secretary of State][63] out of money provided by Parliament.

PART III

TRANSITIONAL PROVISIONS

16.—[. . .][64]

17.—[. . .][65]

SCHEDULE 6

APPEAL PROCEEDINGS

Hearing of appeals

1.—For the purpose of hearing and determining appeals or any matter preliminary or incidental to an appeal the Tribunal shall sit at such times and in such places as the chairman or a deputy chairman may direct and may sit in two or more divisions.

Constitution of tribunal in national security cases

2.—(1) The Lord Chancellor shall from time to time designate, from among the chairman and deputy chairman appointed by him under section 6(4)(a) and (b), those persons who are to be capable of hearing appeals under section 28(4) or (6)[or under section 60(1) or (4) of the Freedom of Information Act 2000].[66]

(2) A designation under sub-paragraph (1) may at any time be revoked by the Lord Chancellor.

3.—In any case where the application of paragraph 6(1) is excluded by rules under paragraph 7, the Tribunal shall be duly constituted for an appeal under section 28(4) or (6) if it consists of three of the persons designated under paragraph 2(1), of whom one shall be designated by the Lord Chancellor to preside.

60 Words substituted by SI 2003/1887 (Secretary of State for Constitutional Affairs Order), Sch. 2, para. 9(1)(c).
61 *ibid.*
62 *ibid.*
63 *ibid.*
64 Words repealed by Freedom of Information Act 2000 (c.36), Sch. 8(II), para. 1.
65 *ibid.*
66 Words inserted by Freedom of Information Act 2000 (c.36), Sch.4, para.1.

Constitution of tribunal in other cases

4.—(1) Subject to any rules made under paragraph 7, the Tribunal shall be duly constituted for an appeal under section 48(1), (2) or (4) if it consists of—
(a) the chairman or a deputy chairman (who shall preside), and
(b) an equal number of the members appointed respectively in accordance with paragraphs (a) and (b) of section 6(6).

(1A) Subject to any rules made under paragraph 7, the Tribunal shall be duly constituted for an appeal under section 57(1) or (2) of the Freedom of Information Act 2000 if it consists of—
(a) the chairman or a deputy chairman (who shall preside), and
(b) an equal number of the members appointed respectively in accordance with paragraphs (aa) and (bb) of section 6(6).

(2) The members who are to constitute the Tribunal in accordance with sub- paragraph (1) [or (1A)][67] shall be nominated by the chairman or, if he is for any reason unable to act, by a deputy chairman.

Determination of questions by full tribunal

5.—The determination of any question before the Tribunal when constituted in accordance with paragraph 3 or 4 shall be according to the opinion of the majority of the members hearing the appeal.

Ex parte proceedings

6.—(1) Subject to any rules made under paragraph 7, the jurisdiction of the Tribunal in respect of an appeal under section 28(4) or (6) shall be exercised ex parte by one or more persons designated under paragraph 2(1).

(2) Subject to any rules made under paragraph 7, the jurisdiction of the Tribunal in respect of an appeal under section 48(3) shall be exercised ex parte by the chairman or a deputy chairman sitting alone.

Rules of procedure

7.—(1) The [Secretary of State][68] may make rules for regulating—
(a) the exercise of the rights of appeal conferred—
(i) by sections 28(4) and (6) and 48, and
(ii) by sections 57(1) and (2) and section 60(1) and (4) of the Freedom of Information Act 2000, and
(b) the practice and procedure of the Tribunal.

(2) Rules under this paragraph may in particular make provision—
(a) with respect to the period within which an appeal can be brought and the burden of proof on an appeal,
(aa) for the joinder of any other person as a party to any proceedings on an appeal under the Freedom of Information Act 2000,
(ab) for the hearing of an appeal under this Act with an appeal under the Freedom of Information Act 2000,
(b) for the summoning (or, in Scotland, citation) of witnesses and the administration of oaths,
(c) for securing the production of documents and material used for the processing of personal data,
(d) for the inspection, examination, operation and testing of any equipment or material used in connection with the processing of personal data,
(e) for the hearing of an appeal wholly or partly in camera,
(f) for hearing an appeal in the absence of the appellant or for determining an appeal without a hearing,
(g) for enabling an appeal under section 48(1) against an information notice to be determined by the chairman or a deputy chairman,
(h) for enabling any matter preliminary or incidental to an appeal to be dealt with by the chairman or a deputy chairman,

---

[67] Words inserted by Freedom of Information Act (2000 c.36), Sch.4, para.3(3).
[68] Words substituted by SI 2003/1887 (Secretary of State for Constitutional Affairs Order), Sch.2 Para.9(1)(d).

(i) for the awarding of costs or, in Scotland, expenses,
(j) for the publication of reports of the Tribunal's decisions, and
(k) for conferring on the Tribunal such ancillary powers as the [Secretary of State][69] thinks necessary for the proper discharge of its functions.

(3) In making rules under this paragraph which relate to appeals under section 28(4) or (6) the [Secretary of State][70] shall have regard, in particular, to the need to secure that information is not disclosed contrary to the public interest.

Obstruction etc.

8.—(1) If any person is guilty of any act or omission in relation to proceedings before the Tribunal which, if those proceedings were proceedings before a court having power to commit for contempt, would constitute contempt of court, the Tribunal may certify the offence to the High Court or, in Scotland, the Court of Session.

(2) Where an offence is so certified, the court may inquire into the matter and, after hearing any witness who may be produced against or on behalf of the person charged with the offence, and after hearing any statement that may be offered in defence, deal with him in any manner in which it could deal with him if he had committed the like offence in relation to the court.

SCHEDULE 7

Miscellaneous Exemptions

Confidential references given by the data controller

1.—Personal data are exempt from section 7 if they consist of a reference given or to be given in confidence by the data controller for the purposes of—
(a) the education, training or employment, or prospective education, training or employment, of the data subject,
(b) the appointment, or prospective appointment, of the data subject to any office, or
(c) the provision, or prospective provision, by the data subject of any service.

Armed forces

2.—Personal data are exempt from the subject information provisions in any case to the extent to which the application of those provisions would be likely to prejudice the combat effectiveness of any of the armed forces of the Crown.

Judicial appointments and honors

3.—Personal data processed for the purposes of—
(a) assessing any person's suitability for judicial office or the office of Queen's Counsel, or
(b) the conferring by the Crown of any honour[or dignity],[71]
are exempt from the subject information provisions.

Crown employment and crown or ministerial appointments

4.—(1) The [Secretary of State][72] may by order exempt from the subject information provisions personal data processed for the purposes of assessing any person's suitability for—
(a) employment by or under the Crown, or
(b) any office to which appointments are made by Her Majesty, by a Minister of the Crown or by a Northern Ireland authority.

(2) In this paragraph "Northern Ireland authority" means the First Minister, the deputy First Minister, a Northern Ireland Minister or a Northern Ireland department.

[69] *ibid.*
[70] *ibid.*
[71] Words added by Freedom of Information Act 2000 (c.36), Sch.6, para.6.
[72] Words substituted by SI 2003/1887 (Secretary of State for Constitutional Affairs Order), Sch.2, para.9(1)(e).

Management forecasts etc.

5.—Personal data processed for the purposes of management forecasting or management planning to assist the data controller in the conduct of any business or other activity are exempt from the subject information provisions in any case to the extent to which the application of those provisions would be likely to prejudice the conduct of that business or other activity.

Corporate finance

6.—(1) Where personal data are processed for the purposes of, or in connection with, a corporate finance service provided by a relevant person—

(a) the data are exempt from the subject information provisions in any case to the extent to which either—

(i) the application of those provisions to the data could affect the price of any instrument which is already in existence or is to be or may be created, or

(ii) the data controller reasonably believes that the application of those provisions to the data could affect the price of any such instrument, and

(b) to the extent that the data are not exempt from the subject information provisions by virtue of paragraph (a), they are exempt from those provisions if the exemption is required for the purpose of safeguarding an important economic or financial interest of the United Kingdom.

(2) For the purposes of sub-paragraph (1)(b) the [Secretary of State][73] may by order specify—

(a) matters to be taken into account in determining whether exemption from the subject information provisions is required for the purpose of safeguarding an important economic or financial interest of the United Kingdom, or

(b) circumstances in which exemption from those provisions is, or is not, to be taken to be required for that purpose.

(3) In this paragraph—

"corporate finance service" means a service consisting in—

(a) underwriting in respect of issues of, or the placing of issues of, any instrument,

(b) advice to undertakings on capital structure, industrial strategy and related matters and advice and service relating to mergers and the purchase of undertakings, or

(c) services relating to such underwriting as is mentioned in paragraph (a);

"instrument" means any instrument listed in section B of the Annex to the Council Directive on investment services in the securities field (93/22/EEC);

"price" includes value;

"relevant person" means—

(a) any person who, by reason of any permission he has under Part IV of the Financial Services and Markets Act 2000, is able to carry on a corporate finance service without contravening the general prohibition, within the meaning of section 19 of that Act;

(b) an EEA firm of the kind mentioned in paragraph 5(a) or (b) of Schedule 3 to that Act which has qualified for authorisation under paragraph 12 of that Schedule, and may lawfully carry on a corporate finance service;

(c) any person who is exempt from the general prohibition in respect of any corporate finance service—

(i) as a result of an exemption order made under section 38(1) of that Act, or

(ii) by reason of section 39(1) of that Act (appointed representatives);

(cc) any person, not falling within paragraph (a), (b) or (c) who may lawfully carry on a corporate finance service without contravening the general prohibition;

(d) any person who, in the course of his employment, provides to his employer a service falling within paragraph (b) or (c) of the definition of "corporate finance service", or

(e) any partner who provides to other partners in the partnership a service falling within either of those paragraphs.

[73] Words substituted by SI 2003/1887 (Secretary of State for Constitutional Affairs Order), Sch.2, para.9(1)(e).

Negotiations

7.—Personal data which consist of records of the intentions of the data controller in relation to any negotiations with the data subject are exempt from the subject information provisions in any case to the extent to which the application of those provisions would be likely to prejudice those negotiations.

Examination marks

8.—(1) Section 7 shall have effect subject to the provisions of sub- paragraphs (2) to (4) in the case of personal data consisting of marks or other information processed by a data controller—

(a) for the purpose of determining the results of an academic, professional or other examination or of enabling the results of any such examination to be determined, or

(b) in consequence of the determination of any such results.

(2) Where the relevant day falls before the day on which the results of the examination are announced, the period mentioned in section 7(8) shall be extended until—

(a) the end of five months beginning with the relevant day, or

(b) the end of forty days beginning with the date of the announcement,

whichever is the earlier.

(3) Where by virtue of sub-paragraph (2) a period longer than the prescribed period elapses after the relevant day before the request is complied with, the information to be supplied pursuant to the request shall be supplied both by reference to the data in question at the time when the request is received and (if different) by reference to the data as from time to time held in the period beginning when the request is received and ending when it is complied with.

(4) For the purposes of this paragraph the results of an examination shall be treated as announced when they are first published or (if not published) when they are first made available or communicated to the candidate in question.

(5) In this paragraph—

"examination" includes any process for determining the knowledge, intelligence, skill or ability of a candidate by reference to his performance in any test, work or other activity;

"the prescribed period" means forty days or such other period as is for the time being prescribed under section 7 in relation to the personal data in question;

"relevant day" has the same meaning as in section 7.

Examination scripts etc.

9.—(1) Personal data consisting of information recorded by candidates during an academic, professional or other examination are exempt from section 7.

(2) In this paragraph "examination" has the same meaning as in paragraph 8.

Legal professional privilege

10.—Personal data are exempt from the subject information provisions if the data consist of information in respect of which a claim to legal professional privilege [or, in Scotland, to confidentiality of communications][74] could be maintained in legal proceedings.

Self-incrimination

11.—(1) A person need not comply with any request or order under section 7 to the extent that compliance would, by revealing evidence of the commission of any offence other than an offence under this Act, expose him to proceedings for that offence.

(2) Information disclosed by any person in compliance with any request or order under section 7 shall not be admissible against him in proceedings for an offence under this Act.

[74] Words substituted by Freedom of Information Act 2000 (c.36), Sch. 6, para. 7.

SCHEDULE 8

Transitional Relief

Part I

Interpretation of Schedule

1.—(1) For the purposes of this Schedule, personal data are "eligible data" at any time if, and to the extent that, they are at that time subject to processing which was already under way immediately before 24th October 1998.

(2) In this Schedule—

"eligible automated data" means eligible data which fall within paragraph (a) or (b) of the definition of "data" in section 1(1);

"eligible manual data" means eligible data which are not eligible automated data;

"the first transitional period" means the period beginning with the commencement of this Schedule and ending with 23rd October 2001;

"the second transitional period" means the period beginning with 24th October 2001 and ending with 23rd October 2007.

Part II

Exemptions Available Before October 24, 2001

Manual data

2.—(1) Eligible manual data, other than data forming part of an accessible record, are exempt from the data protection principles and Parts II and III of this Act during the first transitional period.

(2) This paragraph does not apply to eligible manual data to which paragraph 4 applies.

3.—(1) This paragraph applies to—

(a) eligible manual data forming part of an accessible record, and

(b) personal data which fall within paragraph (d) of the definition of "data" in section 1(1) but which, because they are not subject to processing which was already under way immediately before 24th October 1998, are not eligible data for the purposes of this Schedule.

(2) During the first transitional period, data to which this paragraph applies are exempt from—

(a) the data protection principles, except the sixth principle so far as relating to sections 7 and 12A,

(b) Part II of this Act, except—

(i) section 7 (as it has effect subject to section 8) and section 12A, and

(ii) section 15 so far as relating to those sections, and

(c) Part III of this Act.

4.—(1) This paragraph applies to eligible manual data which consist of information relevant to the financial standing of the data subject and in respect of which the data controller is a credit reference agency.

(2) During the first transitional period, data to which this paragraph applies are exempt from—

(a) the data protection principles, except the sixth principle so far as relating to sections 7 and 12A,

(b) Part II of this Act, except—

(i) section 7 (as it has effect subject to sections 8 and 9) and section 12A, and

(ii) section 15 so far as relating to those sections, and

(c) Part III of this Act.

Processing otherwise than by reference to the data subject

5.—During the first transitional period, for the purposes of this Act (apart from paragraph 1), eligible automated data are not to be regarded as being "processed" unless the processing is by reference to the data subject.

Payrolls and accounts

6.—(1) Subject to sub-paragraph (2), eligible automated data processed by a data controller for one or more of the following purposes—

(a) calculating amounts payable by way of remuneration or pensions in respect of service in any employment or office or making payments of, or of sums deducted from, such remuneration or pensions, or

(b) keeping accounts relating to any business or other activity carried on by the data controller or keeping records of purchases, sales or other transactions for the purpose of ensuring that the requisite payments are made by or to him in respect of those transactions or for the purpose of making financial or management forecasts to assist him in the conduct of any such business or activity,

are exempt from the data protection principles and Parts II and III of this Act during the first transitional period.

(2) It shall be a condition of the exemption of any eligible automated data under this paragraph that the data are not processed for any other purpose, but the exemption is not lost by any processing of the eligible data for any other purpose if the data controller shows that he had taken such care to prevent it as in all the circumstances was reasonably required.

(3) Data processed only for one or more of the purposes mentioned in sub- paragraph (1)(a) may be disclosed—

(a) to any person, other than the data controller, by whom the remuneration or pensions in question are payable;

(b) for the purpose of obtaining actuarial advice,

(c) for the purpose of giving information as to the persons in any employment or office for use in medical research into the health of, or injuries suffered by, persons engaged in particular occupations or working in particular places or areas,

(d) if the data subject (or a person acting on his behalf) has requested or consented to the disclosure of the data either generally or in the circumstances in which the disclosure in question is made, or

(e) if the person making the disclosure has reasonable grounds for believing that the disclosure falls within paragraph (d).

(4) Data processed for any of the purposes mentioned in sub-paragraph (1) may be disclosed—

(a) for the purpose of audit or where the disclosure is for the purpose only of giving information about the data controller's financial affairs, or

(b) in any case in which disclosure would be permitted by any other provision of this Part of this Act if sub-paragraph (2) were included among the non- disclosure provisions.

(5) In this paragraph "remuneration" includes remuneration in kind and "pensions" includes gratuities or similar benefits.

Unincorporated members' clubs and mailing lists

7.—Eligible automated data processed by an unincorporated members' club and relating only to the members of the club are exempt from the data protection principles and Parts II and III of this Act during the first transitional period.

8.—Eligible automated data processed by a data controller only for the purposes of distributing, or recording the distribution of, articles or information to the data subjects and consisting only of their names, addresses or other particulars necessary for effecting the distribution, are exempt from the data protection principles and Parts II and III of this Act during the first transitional period.

9.—Neither paragraph 7 nor paragraph 8 applies to personal data relating to any data subject unless he has been asked by the club or data controller whether he objects to the data relating to him being processed as mentioned in that paragraph and has not objected.

10.—It shall be a condition of the exemption of any data under paragraph 7 that the data are not disclosed except as permitted by paragraph 11 and of the exemption under paragraph 8 that the data are not processed for any purpose other than that mentioned in that paragraph or as permitted by paragraph 11, but—

(a) the exemption under paragraph 7 shall not be lost by any disclosure in breach of that condition, and

(b) the exemption under paragraph 8 shall not be lost by any processing in breach of that condition,

if the data controller shows that he had taken such care to prevent it as in all the circumstances was reasonably required.

11.—Data to which paragraph 10 applies may be disclosed—

(a) if the data subject (or a person acting on his behalf) has requested or consented to the disclosure of the data either generally or in the circumstances in which the disclosure in question is made,

(b) if the person making the disclosure has reasonable grounds for believing that the disclosure falls within paragraph (a), or

(c) in any case in which disclosure would be permitted by any other provision of this Part of this Act if paragraph 8 were included among the non- disclosure provisions.

Back-up data

12.—Eligible automated data which are processed only for the purpose of replacing other data in the event of the latter being lost, destroyed or impaired are exempt from section 7 during the first transitional period.

Exemption of all eligible automated data from certain requirements

13.—(1) During the first transitional period, eligible automated data are exempt from the following provisions—

(a) the first data protection principle to the extent to which it requires compliance with—
 (i) paragraph 2 of Part II of Schedule 1,
 (ii) the conditions in Schedule 2, and
 (iii) the conditions in Schedule 3,

(b) the seventh data protection principle to the extent to which it requires compliance with paragraph 12 of Part II of Schedule 1;

(c) the eighth data protection principle,

(d) in section 7(1), paragraphs (b), (c)(ii) and (d),

(e) sections 10 and 11,

(f) section 12, and

(g) section 13, except so far as relating to—
 (i) any contravention of the fourth data protection principle,
 (ii) any disclosure without the consent of the data controller,
 (iii) loss or destruction of data without the consent of the data controller, or
 (iv) processing for the special purposes.

(2) The specific exemptions conferred by sub-paragraph (1)(a), (c) and (e) do not limit the data controller's general duty under the first data protection principle to ensure that processing is fair.

PART III

EXEMPTIONS AVAILABLE AFTER OCTOBER 23, 2001 BUT BEFORE OCTOBER 24, 2007

14.—(1) This paragraph applies to—

(a) eligible manual data which were held immediately before 24th October 1998, and

(b) personal data which fall within paragraph (d) of the definition of "data" in section 1(1) but do not fall within paragraph (a) of this sub-paragraph.

but does not apply to eligible manual data to which the exemption in paragraph 16 applies.

(2) During the second transitional period, data to which this paragraph applies are exempt from the following provisions—

(a) the first data protection principle except to the extent to which it requires compliance with paragraph 2 of Part II of Schedule 1,

(b) the second, third, fourth and fifth data protection principles, and

(c) section 14(1) to (3).

Part IV

Exemptions After October 23, 2001 for Historical Research

15.—In this Part of this Schedule "the relevant conditions" has the same meaning as in section 33.

16.—(1) Eligible manual data which are processed only for the purpose of historical research in compliance with the relevant conditions are exempt from the provisions specified in sub-paragraph (2) after 23rd October 2001.

(2) The provisions referred to in sub-paragraph (1) are—

(a) the first data protection principle except in so far as it requires compliance with paragraph 2 of Part II of Schedule 1,

(b) the second, third, fourth and fifth data protection principles, and

(c) section 14(1) to (3).

17.—(1) After 23rd October 2001 eligible automated data which are processed only for the purpose of historical research in compliance with the relevant conditions are exempt from the first data protection principle to the extent to which it requires compliance with the conditions in Schedules 2 and 3.

(2) Eligible automated data which are processed—

(a) only for the purpose of historical research,

(b) in compliance with the relevant conditions, and

(c) otherwise than by reference to the data subject,

are also exempt from the provisions referred to in sub-paragraph (3) after 23rd October 2001.

(3) The provisions referred to in sub-paragraph (2) are—

(a) the first data protection principle except in so far as it requires compliance with paragraph 2 of Part II of Schedule 1,

(b) the second, third, fourth and fifth data protection principles, and

(c) section 14(1) to (3).

18.—For the purposes of this Part of this Schedule personal data are not to be treated as processed otherwise than for the purpose of historical research merely because the data are disclosed—

(a) to any person, for the purpose of historical research only,

(b) to the data subject or a person acting on his behalf,

(c) at the request, or with the consent, of the data subject or a person acting on his behalf, or

(d) in circumstances in which the person making the disclosure has reasonable grounds for believing that the disclosure falls within paragraph (a), (b) or (c).

Part V

Exemption From Section 22

19.—Processing which was already under way immediately before 24th October 1998 is not assessable processing for the purposes of section 22.

SCHEDULE 9

Powers of Entry and Inspection

Issue of warrants

1.—(1) If a circuit judge is satisfied by information on oath supplied by the Commissioner that there are reasonable grounds for suspecting—

(a) that a data controller has contravened or is contravening any of the data protection principles, or

(b) that an offence under this Act has been or is being committed,

and that evidence of the contravention or of the commission of the offence is to be found on any premises specified in the information, he may, subject to sub-paragraph (2) and paragraph 2, grant a warrant to the Commissioner.

(2) A judge shall not issue a warrant under this Schedule in respect of any personal data processed for the special purposes unless a determination by the Commissioner under section 45 with respect to those data has taken effect.

(3) A warrant issued under sub-paragraph (1) shall authorise the Commissioner or any of his officers or staff at any time within seven days of the date of the warrant to enter the premises, to search them, to inspect, examine, operate and test any equipment found there which is used or intended to be used for the processing of personal data and to inspect and seize any documents or other material found there which may be such evidence as is mentioned in that sub- paragraph.

2.—(1) A judge shall not issue a warrant under this Schedule unless he is satisfied—

(a) that the Commissioner has given seven days' notice in writing to the occupier of the premises in question demanding access to the premises, and

(b) that either—

(i) access was demanded at a reasonable hour and was unreasonably refused, or

(ii) although entry to the premises was granted, the occupier unreasonably refused to comply with a request by the Commissioner or any of the Commissioner's officers or staff to permit the Commissioner or the officer or member of staff to do any of the things referred to in paragraph 1(3), and

(c) that the occupier, has, after the refusal, been notified by the Commissioner of the application for the warrant and has had an opportunity of being heard by the judge on the question whether or not it should be issued.

(2) Sub-paragraph (1) shall not apply if the judge is satisfied that the case is one of urgency or that compliance with those provisions would defeat the object of the entry.

3.—A judge who issues a warrant under this Schedule shall also issue two copies of it and certify them clearly as copies.

Execution of warrants

4.—A person executing a warrant issued under this Schedule may use such reasonable force as may be necessary.

5.—A warrant issued under this Schedule shall be executed at a reasonable hour unless it appears to the person executing it that there are grounds for suspecting that the evidence in question would not be found if it were so executed.

6.—If the person who occupies the premises in respect of which a warrant is issued under this Schedule is present when the warrant is executed, he shall be shown the warrant and supplied with a copy of it; and if that person is not present a copy of the warrant shall be left in a prominent place on the premises.

7.—(1) A person seizing anything in pursuance of a warrant under this Schedule shall give a receipt for it if asked to do so.

(2) Anything so seized may be retained for so long as is necessary in all the circumstances but the person in occupation of the premises in question shall be given a copy of anything that is seized if he so requests and the person executing the warrant considers that it can be done without undue delay.

Matters exempt from inspection and seizure

8.—The powers of inspection and seizure conferred by a warrant issued under this Schedule shall not be exercisable in respect of personal data which by virtue of section 28 are exempt from any of the provisions of this Act.

9.—(1) Subject to the provisions of this paragraph, the powers of inspection and seizure conferred by a warrant issued under this Schedule shall not be exercisable in respect of—

(a) any communication between a professional legal adviser and his client in connection with the giving of legal advice to the client with respect to his obligations, liabilities or rights under this Act, or

(b) any communication between a professional legal adviser and his client, or between such an adviser or his client and any other person, made in connection with or in contemplation of proceedings under or arising out of this Act (including proceedings before the Tribunal) and for the purposes of such proceedings.

(2) Sub-paragraph (1) applies also to—

(a) any copy or other record of any such communication as is there mentioned, and
(b) any document or article enclosed with or referred to in any such communication if made in connection with the giving of any advice or, as the case may be, in connection with or in contemplation of and for the purposes of such proceedings as are there mentioned.

(3) This paragraph does not apply to anything in the possession of any person other than the professional legal adviser or his client or to anything held with the intention of furthering a criminal purpose.

(4) In this paragraph references to the client of a professional legal adviser include references to any person representing such a client.

10.—If the person in occupation of any premises in respect of which a warrant is issued under this Schedule objects to the inspection or seizure under the warrant of any material on the grounds that it consists partly of matters in respect of which those powers are not exercisable, he shall, if the person executing the warrant so requests, furnish that person with a copy of so much of the material as is not exempt from those powers.

Return of warrants

11.—A warrant issued under this Schedule shall be returned to the court from which it was issued—
(a) after being executed, or
(b) if not executed within the time authorised for its execution;

and the person by whom any such warrant is executed shall make an endorsement on it stating what powers have been exercised by him under the warrant.

Offences

12.—Any person who—
(a) intentionally obstructs a person in the execution of a warrant issued under this Schedule, or
(b) fails without reasonable excuse to give any person executing such a warrant such assistance as he may reasonably require for the execution of the warrant,

is guilty of an offence.

Vessels, vehicles, etc.

13.—In this Schedule "premises" includes any vessel, vehicle, aircraft or hovercraft, and references to the occupier of any premises include references to the person in charge of any vessel, vehicle, aircraft or hovercraft.

Scotland and Northern Ireland

14.—In the application of this Schedule to Scotland—
(a) for any reference to a circuit judge there is substituted a reference to the sheriff,
(b) for any reference to information on oath there is substituted a reference to evidence on oath, and
(c) for the reference to the court from which the warrant was issued there is substituted a reference to the sheriff clerk.

15.—In the application of this Schedule to Northern Ireland—
(a) for any reference to a circuit judge there is substituted a reference to a county court judge, and
(b) for any reference to information on oath there is substituted a reference to a complaint on oath.

SCHEDULE 10

Further Provisions Relating to Assistance Under Section 53

1.—In this Schedule "applicant" and "proceedings" have the same meaning as in section 53.

2.—The assistance provided under section 53 may include the making of arrangements for, or for the Commissioner to bear the costs of—
(a) the giving of advice or assistance by a solicitor or counsel, and

(b) the representation of the applicant, or the provision to him of such assistance as is usually given by a solicitor or counsel—
(i) in steps preliminary or incidental to the proceedings, or
(ii) in arriving at or giving effect to a compromise to avoid or bring an end to the proceedings.

3.—Where assistance is provided with respect to the conduct of proceedings—
(a) it shall include an agreement by the Commissioner to indemnify the applicant (subject only to any exceptions specified in the notification) in respect of any liability to pay costs or expenses arising by virtue of any judgment or order of the court in the proceedings,
(b) it may include an agreement by the Commissioner to indemnify the applicant in respect of any liability to pay costs or expenses arising by virtue of any compromise or settlement arrived at in order to avoid the proceedings or bring the proceedings to an end, and
(c) it may include an agreement by the Commissioner to indemnify the applicant in respect of any liability to pay damages pursuant to an undertaking given on the grant of interlocutory relief (in Scotland, an interim order) to the applicant.

4.—Where the Commissioner provides assistance in relation to any proceedings, he shall do so on such terms, or make such other arrangements, as will secure that a person against whom the proceedings have been or are commenced is informed that assistance has been or is being provided by the Commissioner in relation to them.

5.—In England and Wales or Northern Ireland, the recovery of expenses incurred by the Commissioner in providing an applicant with assistance (as taxed or assessed in such manner as may be prescribed by rules of court) shall constitute a first charge for the benefit of the Commissioner—
(a) on any costs which, by virtue of any judgment or order of the court, are payable to the applicant by any other person in respect of the matter in connection with which the assistance is provided, and
(b) on any sum payable to the applicant under a compromise or settlement arrived at in connection with that matter to avoid or bring to an end any proceedings.

6.—In Scotland, the recovery of such expenses (as taxed or assessed in such manner as may be prescribed by rules of court) shall be paid to the Commissioner, in priority to other debts—
(a) out of any expenses which, by virtue of any judgment or order of the court, are payable to the applicant by any other person in respect of the matter in connection with which the assistance is provided, and
(b) out of any sum payable to the applicant under a compromise or settlement arrived at in connection with that matter to avoid or bring to an end any proceedings.

SCHEDULE 11

Educational Records

Meaning of "educational record"

1.—For the purposes of section 68 "educational record" means any record to which paragraph 2, 5 or 7 applies.

England and Wales

2.—This paragraph applies to any record of information which—
(a) is processed by or on behalf of the governing body of, or a teacher at, any school in England and Wales specified in paragraph 3,
(b) relates to any person who is or has been a pupil at the school, and
(c) originated from or was supplied by or on behalf of any of the persons specified in paragraph 4,

other than information which is processed by a teacher solely for the teacher's own use.

3.—The schools referred to in paragraph 2(a) are—
(a) a school maintained by a local education authority, and
(b) a special school, as defined by section 6(2) of the Education Act 1996, which is not so maintained.

4.—The persons referred to in paragraph 2(c) are—
(a) an employee of the local education authority which maintains the school,
(b) in the case of—
(i) a voluntary aided, foundation or foundation special school (within the meaning of the School Standards and Framework Act 1998), or
(ii) a special school which is not maintained by a local education authority,
a teacher or other employee at the school (including an educational psychologist engaged by the governing body under a contract for services),
(c) the pupil to whom the record relates, and
(d) a parent, as defined by section 576(1) of the Education Act 1996, of that pupil.

Scotland

5.—This paragraph applies to any record of information which is processed—
(a) by an education authority in Scotland, and
(b) for the purpose of the relevant function of the authority,
other than information which is processed by a teacher solely for the teacher's own use.

6.—For the purposes of paragraph 5—
(a) "education authority" means an education authority within the meaning of the Education (Scotland) Act 1980 ("the 1980 Act") or, in relation to a self-governing school, the board of management within the meaning of the Self-Governing Schools etc. (Scotland) Act 1989 ("the 1989 Act"),
(b) "the relevant function" means, in relation to each of those authorities, their function under section 1 of the 1980 Act and section 7(1) of the 1989 Act, and
(c) information processed by an education authority is processed for the purpose of the relevant function of the authority if the processing relates to the discharge of that function in respect of a person—
(i) who is or has been a pupil in a school provided by the authority, or
(ii) who receives, or has received, further education (within the meaning of the 1980 Act) so provided.

Northern Ireland

7.—(1) This paragraph applies to any record of information which—
(a) is processed by or on behalf of the Board of Governors of, or a teacher at, any grant-aided school in Northern Ireland,
(b) relates to any person who is or has been a pupil at the school, and
(c) originated from or was supplied by or on behalf of any of the persons specified in paragraph 8,
other than information which is processed by a teacher solely for the teacher's own use.

(2) In sub-paragraph (1) "grant-aided school" has the same meaning as in the Education and Libraries (Northern Ireland) Order 1986.

8.—The persons referred to in paragraph 7(1) are—
(a) a teacher at the school,
(b) an employee of an education and library board, other than such a teacher,
(c) the pupil to whom the record relates, and
(d) a parent (as defined by Article 2(2) of the Education and Libraries (Northern Ireland) Order 1986) of that pupil.

England and Wales: transitory provisions

9.—(1) Until the appointed day within the meaning of section 20 of the School Standards and Framework Act 1998, this Schedule shall have effect subject to the following modifications.

(2) Paragraph 3 shall have effect as if for paragraph (b) and the "and" immediately preceding it there were substituted—
"(aa) a grant-maintained school, as defined by section 183(1) of the Education Act 1996,
(ab) a grant-maintained special school, as defined by section 337(4) of that Act, and
(b) a special school, as defined by section 6(2) of that Act, which is neither a maintained special school, as defined by section 337(3) of that Act, nor a grant-maintained special school."

(3) Paragraph 4(b)(i) shall have effect as if for the words from "foundation", in the first place where it occurs, to "1998)" there were substituted "or grant-maintained school".

SCHEDULE 12

Accessible Public Records

Meaning of "accessible public record"

1.—For the purposes of section 68 "accessible public record" means any record which is kept by an authority specified—

(a) as respects England and Wales, in the Table in paragraph 2,
(b) as respects Scotland, in the Table in paragraph 4, or
(c) as respects Northern Ireland, in the Table in paragraph 6,

and is a record of information of a description specified in that Table in relation to that authority.

Housing and social service records: England and Wales

2.—The following is the Table referred to in paragraph 1(a).[74a]

3.—(1) The following provisions apply for the interpretation of the Table in paragraph 2.

(2) Any authority which, by virtue of section 4(e) of the Housing Act 1985, is a local authority for the purpose of any provision of that Act is a "Housing Act local authority" for the purposes of this Schedule, and so is any housing action trust established under Part III of the Housing Act 1988.

(3) Information contained in records kept by a Housing Act local authority is "held for the purpose of any of the authority's tenancies" if it is held for any purpose of the relationship of landlord and tenant of a dwelling which subsists, has substituted or may subsist between the authority and any individual who is, has been or, as the case may be, has applied to be, a tenant of the authority.

(4) Any authority which, by virtue of section 1 or 12 of the Local Authority Social Services Act 1970, is or is treated as a local authority for the purposes of that Act is a "local social services authority" for the purposes of this Schedule; and information contained in records kept by such an authority is "held for any purpose of the authority's social services functions" if it is held for the purpose of any past, current or proposed exercise of such a function in any case.

(5) Any expression used in paragraph 2 or this paragraph and in Part II of the Housing Act 1985 or the Local Authority Social Services Act 1970 has the same meaning as in that Act.

Housing and social services records: Scotland

4.—The following is the Table referred to in paragraph 1(b).[74b]

5.—(1) The following provisions apply for the interpretation of the Table in paragraph 4.

(2) "Local authority" means—

(a) a council constituted under section 2 of the Local Government etc. (Scotland) Act 1994,
(b) a joint board or joint committee of two or more of those councils, or
(c) any trust under the control of such a council.

(3) Information contained in records kept by a local authority or Scottish Homes is held for the purpose of any of their tenancies if it is held for any purpose of the relationship of landlord and tenant of a dwelling-house which subsists, has subsisted or may subsist between the authority or, as the case may be, Scottish Homes and any individual who is, has been or, as the case may be, has applied to be a tenant of theirs.

(4) "Social work authority" means a local authority for the purposes of the Social Work (Scotland) Act 1968; and information contained in records kept by such an authority is held for any purpose of their functions if it is held for the purpose of any past, current or proposed exercise of such a function in any case.

Housing and social services records: Northern Ireland

6.—The following is the Table referred to in paragraph 1(c).[74c]

[74a] Table available at *http://www.legislation.hmso.gov.uk/acts/acts1998/80029-ad.htm#sch12* and in Sweet & Maxwell's *Encyclopedia of Data Protection*, Vol.1, para.2–430, Release 26.

[74b] Table available at *http://www.legislation.hmso.gov.uk/acts/acts1998/80029-ad.htm#sch12* and in Sweet & Maxwell's *Encyclopedia of Data Protection*, Vol.1, para.2–432, Release 26.

[74c] Table available at *http://www.legislation.hmso.gov.uk/acts/acts1998/80029-ad.htm#sch12* and in Sweet & Maxwell's *Encyclopedia of Data Protection*, Vol.1, para.2–434, Release 26.

7.—(1) This paragraph applies for the interpretation of the Table in paragraph 6.

(2) Information contained in records kept by the Northern Ireland Housing Executive is "held for the purpose of any of the Executive's tenancies" if it is held for any purpose of the relationship of landlord and tenant of a dwelling which subsists, has subsisted or may subsist between the Executive and any individual who is, has been or, as the case may be, has applied to be, a tenant of the Executive.

SCHEDULE 13

Modifications of Act Having Effect Before October 24, 2007

1.—After section 12 there is inserted—

"12A.—Rights of data subjects in relation to exempt manual data.

(1) A data subject is entitled at any time by notice in writing—

(a) to require the data controller to rectify, block, erase or destroy exempt manual data which are inaccurate or incomplete, or

(b) to require the data controller to cease holding exempt manual data in a way incompatible with the legitimate purposes pursued by the data controller.

(2) A notice under subsection (1)(a) or (b) must state the data subject's reasons for believing that the data are inaccurate "or incomplete or, as the case may be, his reasons for believing that they are held in a way incompatible with the legitimate purposes pursued by the data controller.

(3) If the court is satisfied, on the application of any person who has given a notice under subsection (1) which appears to the court to be justified (or to be justified to any extent) that the data controller in question has failed to comply with the notice, the court may order him to take such steps for complying with the notice (or for complying with it to that extent) as the court thinks fit.

(4) In this section "exempt manual data" means—

(a) in relation to the first transitional period, as defined by paragraph 1(2) of Schedule 8, data to which paragraph 3 or 4 of that Schedule applies, and

(b) in relation to the second transitional period, as so defined, data to which paragraph 14 of that Schedule applies.

(5) For the purposes of this section personal data are incomplete if, and only if, the data, although not inaccurate, are such that their incompleteness would constitute a contravention of the third or fourth data protection principles, if those principles applied to the data."

2.—In section 32—

(a) in subsection (2) after " section 12" there is inserted—

"(dd) section 12A,"

and

(b) in subsection (4) after "12(8)" there is inserted ", 12A(3)".

3.—In section 34 for " section 14(1) to (3)" there is substituted " sections 12A and 14(1) to (3)."

4.—In section 53(1) after "12(8)" there is inserted ", 12A(3)".

5.—In paragraph 8 of Part II of Schedule 1, the word "or" at the end of paragraph (c) is omitted and after paragraph (d) there is inserted

"or

(e) he contravenes section 12A by failing to comply with a notice given under subsection (1) of that section to the extent that the notice is justified."

SCHEDULE 14

Transitional Provisions and Savings

Interpretation

1.—In this Schedule—

"the 1984 Act" means the Data Protection Act 1984;

"the old principles" means the data protection principles within the meaning of the 1984 Act;

"the new principles" means the data protection principles within the meaning of this Act.

Effect of registration under part II of 1984 Act

2.—(1) Subject to sub-paragraphs (4) and (5) any person who, immediately before the commencement of Part III of this Act—

(a) is registered as a data user under Part II of the 1984 Act, or
(b) is treated by virtue of section 7(6) of the 1984 Act as so registered,

is exempt from section 17(1) of this Act until the end of the registration period[. . .].[75]

(2) In sub-paragraph (1) "the registration period", in relation to a person, means—

(a) where there is a single entry in respect of that person as a data user, the period at the end of which, if section 8 of the 1984 Act had remained in force, that entry would have fallen to be removed unless renewed, and
(b) where there are two or more entries in respect of that person as a data user, the period at the end of which, if that section had remained in force, the last of those entries to expire would have fallen to be removed unless renewed.

(3) Any application for registration as a data user under Part II of the 1984 Act which is received by the Commissioner before the commencement of Part III of this Act (including any appeal against a refusal of registration) shall be determined in accordance with the old principles and the provisions of the 1984 Act.

(4) If a person falling within paragraph (b) of sub-paragraph (1) receives a notification under section 7(1) of the 1984 Act of the refusal of his application, sub-paragraph (1) shall cease to apply to him—

(a) if no appeal is brought, at the end of the period within which an appeal can be brought against the refusal, or
(b) on the withdrawal or dismissal of the appeal.

(5) If a data controller gives a notification under section 18(1) at a time when he is exempt from section 17(1) by virtue of sub-paragraph (1), he shall cease to be so exempt.

(6) The Commissioner shall include in the register maintained under section 19 an entry in respect of each person who is exempt from section 17(1) by virtue of sub-paragraph (1); and each entry shall consist of the particulars which, immediately before the commencement of Part III of this Act, were included (or treated as included) in respect of that person in the register maintained under section 4 of the 1984 Act.

(7) Notification regulations under Part III of this Act may make provision modifying the duty referred to in section 20(1) in its application to any person in respect of whom an entry in the register maintained under section 19 has been made under sub-paragraph (6).

(8) Notification regulations under Part III of this Act may make further transitional provision in connection with the substitution of Part III of this Act for Part II of the 1984 Act (registration), including provision modifying the application of provisions of Part III in transitional cases.

Rights of data subjects

3.—(1) The repeal of section 21 of the 1984 Act (right of access to personal data) does not affect the application of that section in any case in which the request (together with the information referred to in paragraph (a) of subsection (4) of that section and, in a case where it is required, the consent referred to in paragraph (b) of that subsection) was received before the day on which the repeal comes into force.

(2) Sub-paragraph (1) does not apply where the request is made by reference to this Act.

(3) Any fee paid for the purposes of section 21 of the 1984 Act before the commencement of section 7 in a case not falling within sub-paragraph (1) shall be taken to have been paid for the purposes of section 7.

4.—The repeal of section 22 of the 1984 Act (compensation for inaccuracy) and the repeal of section 23 of that Act (compensation for loss or unauthorised disclosure) do not affect the application of those sections in relation to damage or distress suffered at any time by reason of anything done or omitted to be done before the commencement of the repeals.

5.—The repeal of section 24 of the 1984 Act (rectification and erasure) does not affect any case in which the application to the court was made before the day on which the repeal comes into force.

---

[75] Words repealed by Freedom of Information Act 2000 (c.36), Sch. 8(I), para. 1.

6.—Subsection (3)(b) of section 14 does not apply where the rectification, blocking, erasure or destruction occurred before the commencement of that section.

Enforcement and transfer prohibition notices served under part V of 1984 Act

7.—(1) If, immediately before the commencement of section 40—

(a) an enforcement notice under section 10 of the 1984 Act has effect, and

(b) either the time for appealing against the notice has expired or any appeal has been determined,

then, after that commencement, to the extent mentioned in sub-paragraph (3), the notice shall have effect for the purposes of sections 41 and 47 as if it were an enforcement notice under section 40.

(2) Where an enforcement notice has been served under section 10 of the 1984 Act before the commencement of section 40 and immediately before that commencement either—

(a) the time for appealing against the notice has not expired, or

(b) an appeal has not been determined,

the appeal shall be determined in accordance with the provisions of the 1984 Act and the old principles and, unless the notice is quashed on appeal, to the extent mentioned in sub-paragraph (3) the notice shall have effect for the purposes of sections 41 and 47 as if it were an enforcement notice under section 40.

(3) An enforcement notice under section 10 of the 1984 Act has the effect described in sub-paragraph (1) or (2) only to the extent that the steps specified in the notice for complying with the old principles or principles in question are steps which the data controller could be required by an enforcement notice under section 40 to take for complying with the new principles or any of them.

8.—(1) If, immediately before the commencement of section 40—

(a) a transfer prohibition notice under section 12 of the 1984 Act has effect, and

(b) either the time for appealing against the notice has expired or any appeal has been determined,

then, on and after that commencement, to the extent specified in sub- paragraph (3), the notice shall have effect for the purposes of sections 41 and 47 as if it were an enforcement notice under section 40.

(2) Where a transfer prohibition notice has been served under section 12 of the 1984 Act and immediately before the commencement of section 40 either—

(a) the time for appealing against the notice has not expired, or

(b) an appeal has not been determined,

the appeal shall be determined in accordance with the provisions of the 1984 Act and the old principles and, unless the notice is quashed on appeal, to the extent mentioned in sub-paragraph (3) the notice shall have effect for the purposes of sections 41 and 47 as if it were an enforcement notice under section 40.

(3) A transfer prohibition notice under section 12 of the 1984 Act has the effect described in sub-paragraph (1) or (2) only to the extent that the prohibition imposed by the notice is one which could be imposed by an enforcement notice under section 40 for complying with the new principles or any of them.

Notices under new law relating to matters in relation to which 1984 Act had effect

9.—The Commissioner may serve an enforcement notice under section 40 on or after the day on which that section comes into force if he is satisfied that, before that day, the data controller contravened the old principles by reason of any act or omission which would also have constituted a contravention of the new principles if they had applied before that day.

10.—Subsection (5)(b) of section 40 does not apply where the rectification, blocking, erasure or destruction occurred before the commencement of that section.

11.—The Commissioner may serve an information notice under section 43 on or after the day on which that section comes into force if he has reasonable grounds for suspecting that, before that day, the data controller contravened the old principles by reason of any act or omission which would also have constituted a contravention of the new principles if they had applied before that day.

12.—Where by virtue of paragraph 11 an information notice is served on the basis of anything done or omitted to be done before the day on which section 43 comes into force, subsection (2)(b) of that section shall have effect as if the reference to the data controller having complied, or complying, with the new principles were a reference to the data controller having contravened the old principles by reason of any such act or omission as is mentioned in paragraph 11.

Self-incrimination, etc.

13.—(1) In section 43(8), section 44(9) and paragraph 11 of Schedule 7, any reference to an offence under this Act includes a reference to an offence under the 1984 Act.

(2) In section 34(9) of the 1984 Act, any reference to an offence under that Act includes a reference to an offence under this Act.

Warrants issued under 1984 Act

14.—The repeal of Schedule 4 to the 1984 Act does not affect the application of that Schedule in any case where a warrant was issued under that Schedule before the commencement of the repeal.

Complaints under section 36(2) of 1984 Act and requests for assessment under section 42

15.—The repeal of section 36(2) of the 1984 Act does not affect the application of that provision in any case where the complaint was received by the Commissioner before the commencement of the repeal.

16.—In dealing with a complaint under section 36(2) of the 1984 Act or a request for an assessment under section 42 of this Act, the Commissioner shall have regard to the provisions from time to time applicable to the processing, and accordingly—

(a) in section 36(2) of the 1984 Act, the reference to the old principles and the provisions of that Act includes, in relation to any time when the new principles and the provisions of this Act have effect, those principles and provisions, and

(b) in section 42 of this Act, the reference to the provisions of this Act includes, in relation to any time when the old principles and the provisions of the 1984 Act had effect, those principles and provisions.

Applications under Access to Health Records Act 1990 or corresponding Northern Ireland legislation

17.—(1) The repeal of any provision of the Access to Health Records Act 1990 does not affect—

(a) the application of section 3 or 6 of that Act in any case in which the application under that section was received before the day on which the repeal comes into force, or

(b) the application of section 8 of that Act in any case in which the application to the court was made before the day on which the repeal comes into force.

(2) Sub-paragraph (1)(a) does not apply in relation to an application for access to information which was made by reference to this Act.

18.—(1) The revocation of any provision of the Access to Health Records (Northern Ireland) Order 1993 does not affect—

(a) the application of Article 5 or 8 of that Order in any case in which the application under that Article was received before the day on which the repeal comes into force, or

(b) the application of Article 10 of that Order in any case in which the application to the court was made before the day on which the repeal comes into force.

(2) Sub-paragraph (1)(a) does not apply in relation to an application for access to information which was made by reference to this Act.

Applications under regulations under access to personal files act 1987 or corresponding Northern Ireland legislation

19.—(1) The repeal of the personal files enactments does not affect the application of regulations under those enactments in relation to—

(a) any request for information,

(b) any application for rectification or erasure, or

(c) any application for review of a decision,

which was made before the day on which the repeal comes into force.

(2) Sub-paragraph (1)(a) does not apply in relation to a request for information which was made by reference to this Act.

(3) In sub-paragraph (1) "the personal files enactments" means—

(a) in relation to Great Britain, the Access to Personal Files Act 1987, and
(b) in relation to Northern Ireland, Part II of the Access to Personal Files and Medical Reports (Northern Ireland) Order 1991.

Applications under section 158 or Consumer Credit Act 1974

20.—Section 62 does not affect the application of section 158 of the Consumer Credit Act 1974 in any case where the request was received before the commencement of section 62, unless the request is made by reference to this Act.

APPENDIX 2

Related UK Statutory Instruments

Data Protection (Corporate Finance Exemption) Order 2000

(SI 2000/184)

[MADE: JANUARY 31, 2000]

[LAID BEFORE PARLIAMENT: FEBRUARY 7, 2000]

[COMING INTO FORCE: MARCH 1, 2000]

App 2–01 The Secretary of State, in exercise of the powers conferred on him by section 67(2) of, and paragraph 6(2) of Schedule 7 to, the Data Protection Act 1998, and after consultation with the Data Protection Commissioner in accordance with section 67(3) of that Act, hereby makes the following Order:

Citation and commencement

1.—(1) This Order may be cited as the Data Protection (Corporate Finance Exemption) Order 2000 and shall come into force on March 1, 2000.

(2) In this Order, "the Act" means the Data Protection Act 1998.

Matters to be taken into account

2.—(1) The matter set out in paragraph (2) below is hereby specified for the purposes of paragraph 6(1)(b) of Schedule 7 to the Act (matters to be taken into account in determining whether exemption from the subject information provisions is required for the purpose of safeguarding an important economic or financial interest of the United Kingdom).

(2) The matter referred to in paragraph (1) above is the inevitable prejudicial effect on—

(a) the orderly functioning of financial markets, or
(b) the efficient allocation of capital within the economy,

which will result from the application (whether on an occasional or regular basis) of the subject information provisions to data to which paragraph (3) below applies.

(3) This paragraph applies to any personal data to which the application of the subject information provisions could, in the reasonable belief of the relevant person within the meaning of paragraph 6 of Schedule 7 to the Act, affect—

(a) any decision of any person whether or not to—

(i) deal in,
(ii) subscribe for, or
(iii) issue, any instrument which is already in existence or is to be, or may be, created; or

(b) any decision of any person to act or not to act in a way that is likely to have an effect on any business activity including, in particular, an effect on—

(i) the industrial strategy of any person (whether the strategy is, or is to be, pursued independently or in association with others),
(ii) the capital structure of an undertaking, or
(iii) the legal or beneficial ownership of a business or asset.

Signatures

Mike O'Brien

Parliamentary Under-Secretary of State

Home Office

January 31, 2000

Data Protection (Functions of Designated Authority) Order 2000

(SI 2000/186)

[MADE: JANUARY 31, 2000]

[LAID BEFORE PARLIAMENT: FEBRUARY 7, 2000]

[COMING INTO FORCE: MARCH 1, 2000]

App 2–02 The Secretary of State, in exercise of the powers conferred upon him by sections 54(2) and 67(2) of the Data Protection Act 1998 and after consultation with the Data Protection Commissioner in accordance with section 67(3) of that Act, hereby makes the following Order:

Citation and commencement

1.—This Order may be cited as the Data Protection (Functions of Designated Authority) Order 2000 and shall come into force on March 1, 2000.

Interpretation

2.—(1) In this Order:

"the Act" means the Data Protection Act 1998;

"foreign designated authority" means an authority designated for the purposes of Article 13 of the Convention by a party (other than the United Kingdom) which is bound by that Convention;

"register" means the register maintained under section 19(1) of the Act;

"request", except in article 3, means a request for assistance under Article 14 of the Convention which states—

(a) the name and address of the person making the request;
(b) particulars which identify the personal data to which the request relates;
(c) the rights under Article 8 of the Convention to which the request relates;
(d) the reasons why the request has been made;

and "requesting person" means a person making such a request.

(2) In this Order, references to the Commissioner are to the Commissioner as the designated authority in the United Kingdom for the purposes of Article 13 of the Convention.

Co-operation between the Commissioner and foreign designated authorities

3.—(1) The Commissioner shall, at the request of a foreign designated authority, furnish to that foreign designated authority such information referred to in Article 13(3)(a) of the Convention, and in particular the data protection legislation in force in the United Kingdom at the time the request is made, as is the subject of the request.

(2) The Commissioner shall, at the request of a foreign designated authority, take appropriate measures in accordance with Article 13(3)(b) of the Convention, for

furnishing to that foreign designated authority information relating to the processing of personal data in the United Kingdom.

(3) The Commissioner may request a foreign designated authority to furnish to him or, as the case may be, to take appropriate measures for furnishing to him, the information referred to in Article 13(3) of the Convention.

Persons resident outside the United Kingdom

4.—(1) This article applies where a person resident outside the United Kingdom makes a request to the Commissioner under Article 14 of the Convention, including a request forwarded to the Commissioner through the Secretary of State or a foreign designated authority, seeking assistance in exercising any of the rights under Article 8 of the Convention.

(2) If the request—

(a) seeks assistance in exercising the rights under section 7 of the Act; and

(b) does not indicate that the data controller has failed, contrary to section 7 of the Act, to comply with the same request on a previous occasion,

the Commissioner shall notify the requesting person of the data controller's address for the receipt of notices from data subjects exercising their rights under that section and of such other information as the Commissioner considers necessary to enable that person to exercise his rights under that section.

(3) If the request indicates that a data protection principle has been contravened by a data controller the Commissioner shall either—

(a) notify the requesting person of the rights of data subjects and the remedies available to them under Part II of the Act together with such particulars as are contained in the data controller's entry in the register as are necessary to enable the requesting person to avail himself of those remedies; or

(b) if the Commissioner considers that notification in accordance with sub-paragraph (a) would not assist the requesting person or would, for any other reason, be inappropriate, treat the request as if it were a request for an assessment which falls to be dealt with under section 42 of the Act.

(4) The Commissioner shall not be required, in response to any request referred to in paragraphs (2) and (3) above, to supply to the requesting person a duly certified copy in writing of the particulars contained in any entry made in the register other than on payment of such fee as is prescribed for the purposes of section 19(7) of the Act.

Persons resident in the United Kingdom

5.—(1) Where a request for assistance in exercising any of the rights referred to in Article 8 of the Convention in a country or territory (other than the United Kingdom) specified in the request is made by a person resident in the United Kingdom and submitted through the Commissioner under Article 14(2) of the Convention, the Commissioner shall, if he is satisfied that the request contains all necessary particulars referred to in Article 14(3) of the Convention, send it to the foreign designated authority in the specified country or territory.

(2) If the Commissioner decides that he is not required by paragraph (1) above to render assistance to the requesting person he shall, where practicable, notify that person of the reasons for his decision.

Restrictions on use of information

6.—Where the Commissioner receives information from a foreign designated authority as a result of either—

(a) a request made by him under article 3(3) above; or
(b) a request received by him under articles 3(2) or 4 above,

the Commissioner shall use that information only for the purposes specified in the request.

Signatures

Mike O'Brien

Parliamentary Under-Secretary of State

Home Office

January 31, 2000

The Data Protection Tribunal (Enforcement Appeals) Rules 2000

(SI 2000/189)

ARRANGEMENT OF RULES

[MADE: OCTOBER 30, 2002][1]

[LAID BEFORE PARLIAMENT: NOVEMBER 1, 2002][2]

[COMING INTO FORCE: NOVEMBER 30, 2002][3]

[1] As amended by SI 2002/2722.
[2] *ibid*.
[3] *ibid*.

App 2–03 The [Lord Chancellor],[4] in exercise of the powers conferred [upon][5] him by section 67(2) of, and paragraph 7 of Schedule 6 to, the Data Protection Act 1998,[6] and after consultation with the Council on Tribunals in accordance with section 8 of the Tribunals and Inquiries Act 1992, hereby makes the following Rules:

Citation and commencement

1.—These Rules may be cited as the Data Protection Tribunal (Enforcement Appeals) Rules 2000 and shall come into force on [November 30, 2002].[7]

Application and interpretation

2.—[(1) These Rules apply to appeals under section 48 of the 1998 Act and section 57(2) of the 2000 Act, and the provisions of these Rules are to be construed accordingly.

(2) In these Rules, unless the context otherwise requires—

"the 1998 Act" means the Data Protection Act 1998;

"the 2000 Act" means the Freedom of Information Act 2000;

"appeal" means an appeal under—

(a) section 48 of the 1998 Act, or
(b) section 57(2) of the 2000 Act;

"appellant" means—

(a) a person who brings or intends to bring an appeal under section 48 of the 1998 Act, or
(b) a public authority which brings or intends to bring an appeal under section 57(2) of the 2000 Act;

"chairman" means the chairman of the Tribunal, and includes a deputy chairman of the Tribunal presiding or sitting alone;

"costs"—

(a) except in Scotland, including fees, charges, disbursements, expenses and remuneration;
(b) in Scotland means expenses, and including fees, charges, disbursements and remuneration;

"disputed decision" means—

(a) in relation to an appeal under section 48 of the 1998 Act other than an appeal under section 48(3)(b) of that Act, the decision of the Commissioner,
(b) in relation to an appeal under section 48(3)(b) of the 1998 Act, the decision of the Commissioner, and
(c) in relation to an appeal under section 57(2) of the 2000 Act, the decision of the Commissioner,

against which the appellant appeals or intends to appeal to the Tribunal;

[4] As amended by SI 2002/2722.

[5] *ibid.*

[6] Para.7 of Sch.6 was amended by para.4 of Sch.4 to the Freedom of Information Act 2000 (c.36). The functions of the Secretary of State under s.67 of, and Sch.6 to, the Data Protection Act 1998 were transferred to the Lord Chancellor by the Transfer of Functions (Miscellaneous) Order 2001 (SI 2001/3500), which Order amended those provisions accordingly.

[7] As amended by SI 2002/2722.

"party" has the meaning given in paragraph 3 below; and

"proper officer" in relation to a rule means an officer or member of staff provided to the Tribunal under paragraph 14 of Schedule 5 to the 1998 Act and appointed by the chairman to perform the duties of a proper officer under that rule.][8]

(3) In these Rules, "party" means the appellant or the Commissioner, and, except where the context otherwise requires, references in these Rules to a party (including references in rule 12 below) include a person appointed under rule 16 below to represent his interests.

(4) In relation to proceedings before the Tribunal in Scotland, for the words "on the trial of an action" in rules 11(4), 12(8) and 23(2) below there is substituted "in a proof".

Method of appealing

3.—(1) An appeal must be brought by a written notice of appeal served on the Tribunal.

(2) The notice of appeal shall—

(a) identify the disputed decision and the date on which the notice relating to such decision was served on or given to the appellant; and
(b) state—
  (i) the name and address of the appellant;
  (ii) the grounds of the appeal;
  (iii) whether the appellant considers that he is likely to wish a hearing to be held or not;
  (iv) where applicable, the special circumstances which the appellant considers justify the Tribunal's accepting jurisdiction under rule 4(2) below; and
  (v) an address for service of notices and other documents on the appellant.

(3) Where an appeal is brought under section 48(1) of the [1998 Act or section 57(2) of the 2000][9] in relation to an information notice, the notice of appeal shall also contain a statement of any representations the appellant wishes to make as to why it might be necessary in the interests of justice for the appeal to be heard and determined otherwise than by the chairman sitting alone as provided by rule 18(2) below.

(4) A notice of appeal may include a request for an early hearing of the appeal and the reasons for that request.

Time limit for appealing

4.—(1) Subject to paragraph (2) below, a notice of appeal must be served on the Tribunal within 28 days of the date on which the notice relating to the disputed decision was served on or given to the appellant.

(2) The Tribunal may accept a notice of appeal served after the expiry of the period permitted by paragraph (1) above if it is of the opinion that, by reason of special circumstances, it is just and right to do so.

(3) A notice of appeal shall if sent by post in accordance with rule 27(1) below be treated as having been served on the date on which it is received for dispatch by the Post Office.

Acknowledgement of notice of appeal and notification to the Commissioner

5.—(1) Upon receipt of a notice of appeal, the proper officer shall send—

(a) an acknowledgement of the service of a notice of appeal to the appellant, and
(b) subject to paragraph (3) below, a copy of the notice of appeal to the Commissioner.

[8] As amended by SI 2002/2722.
[9] *ibid.*

(2) An acknowledgement of service under paragraph (1)(a) above shall be accompanied by a statement of the Tribunal's powers to award costs against the appellant under rule 25 below.

(3) Paragraph (1)(b) above does not apply to a notice of appeal relating to an appeal under section 48(3) of the [1998][10] Act, but in such a case—

(a) the proper officer shall send a copy of the notice of appeal to the Commissioner if the Tribunal is of the opinion that the interests of justice require the Commissioner to assist it by giving evidence or being heard on any matter relating to the appeal, and

(b) where a copy is sent to the Commissioner under subparagraph (a) above, the jurisdiction referred to in paragraph 6(2) of Schedule 6 to the [1998][11] Act shall not be exercised ex parte.

Reply by Commissioner

6.—(1) The Commissioner shall take the steps specified in paragraph (2) below—

(a) where he receives a copy of a notice of appeal under rule 5(1)(b) above, within 21 days of the date of that receipt, and

(b) where he receives a copy of a notice of appeal under rule 5(3)(a) above, within such time, not exceeding 21 days from the date of that receipt, as the Tribunal may allow.

(2) The steps are that the Commissioner must—

(a) send to the Tribunal a copy of the notice relating to the disputed decision, and

(b) send to the Tribunal and the appellant a written reply acknowledging service upon him of the notice of appeal, and stating—

(i) whether or not he intends to oppose the appeal and, if so,

(ii) the grounds upon which he relies in opposing the appeal.

(3) Before the expiry of the period referred to in paragraph (1) above which is applicable to the case, the Commissioner may apply to the Tribunal for an extension of that period, showing cause why, by reason of special circumstances, it would be just and right to do so, and the Tribunal may grant such extension as it considers appropriate.

(4) Where the appellant's notice of appeal has stated that he is not likely to wish a hearing to be held, the Commissioner shall in his reply inform the Tribunal and the appellant whether he considers that a hearing is likely to be desirable.

(5) Where an appeal is brought under section 48(1) of the [1998 Act or section 57(2) of the 2000][12] in relation to an information notice, the Commissioner may include in his reply a statement of representations as to why it might be necessary in the interests of justice for the appeal to be heard and determined otherwise than by the chairman sitting alone as provided by rule 18(2) below.

(6) A reply under this rule may include a request for an early hearing of the appeal and the reasons for that request.

Application for striking out

7.—(1) Subject to paragraph (3) below, where the Commissioner is of the opinion that an appeal does not lie to, or cannot be entertained by, the Tribunal, or that the notice of appeal discloses no reasonable grounds of appeal, he may include in his reply

---

[10] As amended by SI 2002/2722.
[11] *ibid.*
[12] *ibid.*

under rule 6(2) above a notice to that effect stating the grounds for such contention and applying for the appeal to be struck out.

(2) An application under this rule may be heard as a preliminary issue or at the beginning of the hearing of the substantive appeal.

(3) This rule does not apply in the case of an appeal under section 48(3) of the [1998][13] Act.

Amendment and supplementary grounds

8.—(1) With the leave of the Tribunal, the appellant may amend his notice of appeal or deliver supplementary grounds of appeal.

(2) Paragraphs (1) and (3) of rule 5 above apply to an amended notice of appeal and to supplementary grounds of appeal provided under paragraph (1) above as they do to a notice of appeal.

(3) Upon receipt of a copy of an amended notice of appeal or amended grounds of appeal under rule 5(1)(b) or (3)(a) above, the Commissioner may amend his reply to the notice of appeal, and must send the amended reply to the Tribunal and the appellant—

(a) where he receives a copy of a notice of appeal under rule 5(1)(b) above, within 21 days of the date of that receipt, and

(b) where he receives a copy of a notice of appeal under rule 5(3)(a) above, within such time, not exceeding 21 days from the date of that receipt, as the Tribunal may allow.

(4) Rule 6(3) above applies to the periods referred to in paragraph (3) above.

(5) Without prejudice to paragraph (3) above, the Commissioner may, with the leave of the Tribunal, amend his reply to the notice of appeal, and must send the amended reply to the Tribunal and the appellant.

Withdrawal of appeal

9.—(1) The appellant may at any time withdraw his appeal by sending to the Tribunal a notice of withdrawal signed by him or on his behalf, and the proper officer shall send a copy of that notice to the Commissioner.

(2) A notice of withdrawal shall if sent by post in accordance with rule 27(1) below have effect on the date on which it is received for dispatch by the Post Office.

(3) Where an appeal is withdrawn under this rule a fresh appeal may not be brought by the appellant in relation to the same disputed decision except with the leave of the Tribunal.

Consolidation of appeals

10.—(1) Subject to paragraph (2) below, where in the case of two or more appeals to which these Rules apply it appears to the Tribunal—

(a) that some common question of law or fact arises in both or all of them, or

(b) that for some other reason it is desirable to proceed with the appeals under this rule,

the Tribunal may order that the appeals be consolidated or heard together.

(2) The Tribunal shall not make an order under this rule without giving the parties an opportunity to show cause why such an order should not be made.

[13] As amended by SI 2002/2722.

Directions

11.—(1) Subject to paragraphs (4) and (5) below, the Tribunal may at any time of its own motion or on the application of any party give such directions as it thinks proper to enable the parties to prepare for the hearing of the appeal or to assist the Tribunal to determine the issues.

(2) Such directions may in particular—

(a) provide for a particular matter to be dealt with as a preliminary issue and for a pre-hearing review to be held;

(b) provide for—

(i) the exchange between the parties of lists of documents held by them which are relevant to the appeal,

(ii) the inspection by the parties of the documents so listed,

(iii) the exchange between the parties of statements of evidence, and

(iv) the provision by the parties to the Tribunal of statements or lists of agreed matters;

(c) require any party to send to the Tribunal and to the other party—

(i) statements of facts and statements of the evidence which will be adduced, including such statements provided in a modified or edited form;

(ii) a skeleton argument which summarises the submissions which will be made and cites the authorities which will be relied upon, identifying any particular passages to be relied upon;

(iii) a chronology of events;

(iv) any other particulars or supplementary statements which may reasonably be required for the determination of the appeal;

(v) any document or other material which the Tribunal may require and which it is in the power of that party to deliver;

(vi) an estimate of the time which will be needed for any hearing; and

(vii) a list of the witnesses the party intends to call to give evidence at any hearing;

(d) limit the length of oral submissions and the time allowed for the examination and cross-examination of witnesses; and

(e) limit the number of expert witnesses to be heard on either side.

(3) The Tribunal may, subject to any specific provisions of these Rules, specify time limits for steps to be taken in the proceedings and may extend any time limit.

(4) Nothing in this rule may require the production of any document or other material which the party could not be compelled to produce on the trial of an action in a court of law in that part of the United Kingdom where the appeal is to be determined.

(5) It shall be a condition of the supply of any information or material provided under this rule that any recipient of that information or material may use it only for the purposes of the appeal.

(6) The power to give directions may be exercised in the absence of the parties.

(7) Notice of any directions given under this rule shall be served on the parties, and the Tribunal may, on the application of any party, set aside or vary such directions.

Power to require entry of premises for testing of equipment or material

12.—(1) Subject to paragraph (8) below, the Tribunal may, for the purpose of determining an appeal [under section 48 of the 1998 Act],[14] make an order requiring the occupier of any premises ("the occupier") to permit the Tribunal to enter those premises at a spec-

[14] As amended by SI 2002/2722.

ified time and inspect, examine, operate or test any equipment on those premises used or intended to be used in connection with the processing of personal data, and to inspect, examine or test any documents or other material on those premises connected with the processing of personal data.

(2) An order under paragraph (1) above shall also require the occupier to permit the Tribunal to be accompanied by—

(a) the parties, and
(b) such number of the officers or members of staff provided to the Tribunal under paragraph 14 of Schedule 5 to the [1998][15] Act as it considers necessary.

(3) The Tribunal shall serve a copy of the order on the occupier and the parties.

(4) The time specified in the order shall not be earlier than 7 days after the date of service of the copy.

(5) The Tribunal may upon the application of the occupier set the order aside.

(6) Subject to paragraph (4) above, the Tribunal may upon the application of any person mentioned in paragraph (3) above alter the time specified in the order without being obliged to serve further copies under that paragraph, but shall notify the other persons so mentioned of the revised time.

(7) This rule also applies where the occupier is a party to the appeal.

(8) Documents or other material which the appellant could not be compelled to produce on the trial of an action in that part of the United Kingdom where the appeal is to be determined shall be immune from inspection, examination or testing under this rule.

Power to determine without a hearing

13.—(1) Where either—

(a) the parties so agree in writing, or
(b) it appears to the Tribunal that the issues raised on the appeal have been determined on a previous appeal brought by the appellant on the basis of facts which did not materially differ from those to which the appeal relates and the Tribunal has given the parties an opportunity of making representations to the effect that the appeal ought not to be determined without a hearing,

the Tribunal may determine an appeal, or any particular issue, without a hearing.

(2) Before determining any matter under this rule, the Tribunal may if it thinks fit direct any party to provide in writing further information about any matter relevant to the appeal within such time as the Tribunal may allow.

Time and place of hearings

14.—(1) Except where rule 13 above applies, as soon as practicable after notice of appeal has been given, and with due regard to the convenience of the parties and any request made under rule 3(4) or 6(6) above, the Tribunal shall appoint a time and place for a hearing of the appeal.

(2) The proper officer shall send to each party a notice informing him of the time and place of any hearing.

(3) The reference to a "party" in paragraph (2) above does not include the Commissioner in the case of an appeal under section 48(3) of the [1998][16] Act other than a case to which rule 5(3)(a) above applies.

(4) The time notified under paragraph (1) above shall not be earlier than 14 days after the date on which the notice is sent unless—

[15] As amended by SI 2002/2722.
[16] *ibid.*

(a) the parties agree otherwise, or
(b) the appellant agrees otherwise, and the hearing relates to an appeal under section 48(3) of the [1998][17] Act.

(5) A notice to a party under this rule shall inform him of the effect of rule 17 below.
(6) The Tribunal may—

(a) postpone the time appointed for any hearing;
(b) adjourn a hearing to such time as the Tribunal may determine; or
(c) alter the place appointed for any hearing;

and, if it exercises any of the above powers, it shall notify each party previously notified of that hearing under this rule, and any person summoned under rule 15 below to attend as a witness at that hearing, of the revised arrangements.

Summoning of witnesses

15.—(1) Subject to paragraph (2) below, the Tribunal may by summons require any person in the United Kingdom to attend as a witness at a hearing of an appeal at such time and place as may be specified in the summons and, subject to rule 23(2) and (3) below, at the hearing to answer any questions or produce any documents in his custody or under his control which relate to any matter in question in the appeal.

(2) No person shall be required to attend in obedience to a summons under paragraph (1) above unless he has been given at least 7 days' notice of the hearing or, if less than 7 days, he has informed the Tribunal that he accepts such notice as he has been given.

(3) The Tribunal may upon the application of a person summoned under this rule set the summons aside.

(4) A person who has attended a hearing as a witness in obedience to a summons shall be entitled to such sum as the Tribunal considers reasonable in respect of his attendance at, and his travelling to and from, the hearing; and where the summons was issued at the request of a party such sum shall be paid or tendered to him by that party.

(5) In relation to proceedings before the Tribunal in Scotland, in this rule "summons" means citation and the provisions of this rule are to be construed accordingly.

Representation at a hearing

16.—(1) At any hearing by the Tribunal a party may conduct his case himself or may appear and be represented by any person whom he may appoint for the purpose.

(2) In this rule, references to a "party" do not include the Commissioner in the case of an appeal under section 48(3) of the [1998][18] Act other than a case to which rule 5(3)(a) above applies.

Default of appearance at hearing

17.—If, without furnishing the Tribunal with sufficient reason for his absence, a party fails to appear at a hearing, having been duly notified of the hearing, the Tribunal may, if that party is the appellant, dismiss the appeal or, in any case, hear and determine the appeal, or any particular issue, in the party's absence and may make such order as to costs as it thinks fit.

---

17 As amended by SI 2002/2722.
18 *ibid.*

Hearings and determinations in the case of appeals against an information notice

18.—(1) This rule applies to any appeal under section 48(1) of the [1998 Act or section 57(2) of the 2000][19] in respect of an information notice.

(2) Subject to paragraph (3) below, any hearing of or relating to an appeal to which this rule applies shall be by the chairman sitting alone, and any appeal or issue relating to an appeal to which this rule applies shall be determined by the chairman sitting alone.

(3) Paragraph (2) above does not apply where it appears to the chairman that a hearing or determination by the Tribunal constituted in accordance with paragraph 4 of Schedule 6 to the [1998][20] Act is necessary in the interests of justice, taking into account any representations made under rule 3(3) or 6(5) above.

Hearings in public or in private

19.—(1) All hearings by the Tribunal (including preliminary hearings) shall be in public unless, having regard to the desirability of safeguarding—

(a) the privacy of data subjects or
(b) commercially sensitive information,

the Tribunal directs that the hearing or any part of the hearing shall take place in private.

(2) Without prejudice to paragraph (3) below, the following persons, in addition to the parties, may attend a hearing notwithstanding that it is in private—

(a) the chairman or any deputy chairman or member of the Tribunal in his capacity as such, notwithstanding that they do not constitute the Tribunal for the purpose of the hearing; and
(b) any other person with the leave of the Tribunal and the consent of the parties present.

(3) Whether or not a hearing is held in public, a member of the Council on Tribunals or the Scottish Committee of the Council on Tribunals in his capacity as such may attend the hearing, and may remain present during the deliberations of the Tribunal but must not take part in the deliberations.

Conduct of proceedings at hearing

20.—(1) Subject to rule 17 above, the Tribunal shall at the hearing of an appeal give to each party an opportunity—

(a) to address the Tribunal and to amplify orally written statements previously furnished under these Rules, to give evidence and to call witnesses, and to put questions to any person giving evidence before the Tribunal, and
(b) to make representations on the evidence (if any) and on the subject matter of the appeal generally but, where evidence is taken, such opportunity shall not be given before the completion of the taking of evidence.

(2) Subject to paragraph (3) below, in this rule, references to a "party" do not include the Commissioner in the case of an appeal under section 48(3) of the [1998][21] Act.

(3) In a case to which rule 5(3)(a) above applies, the Tribunal shall give the Commissioner the opportunity referred to in paragraph (1) above to the extent that it is of

---

[19] As amended by SI 2002/2722.
[20] *ibid.*
[21] *ibid.*

the opinion that the interests of justice require the Commissioner to assist it by giving evidence or being heard on any matter relating to the appeal.

(4) Except as provided by these Rules, the Tribunal shall conduct the proceedings in such manner as it considers appropriate in the circumstances for discharging its functions and shall so far as appears to it appropriate seek to avoid formality in its proceedings.

Preliminary and incidental matters

21.—As regards matters preliminary or incidental to an appeal the chairman may act for the Tribunal under rules 4(2), 6(1) and (3), 8 to 12, 14(1) and (6)(a) and (c) and 15.

Burden of proof

22.—In any proceedings before the Tribunal relating to an appeal to which these Rules apply, other than an appeal under section 48(3) of the [1998][22] Act, it shall be for the Commissioner to satisfy the Tribunal that the disputed decision should be upheld.

Evidence

23.—(1) The Tribunal may receive in evidence any document or information notwithstanding that such document or information would be inadmissible in a court of law.

(2) No person shall be compelled to give any evidence or produce any document which he could not be compelled to give or produce on the trial of an action in a court of law in that part of the United Kingdom where the appeal is to be determined.

(3) The Tribunal may require oral evidence of a witness (including a party) to be given on oath or affirmation and for that purpose the chairman or the proper officer shall have power to administer oaths or take affirmations.

Determination of appeal

24.—(1) As soon as practicable after the Tribunal has determined an appeal, the chairman shall certify in writing that determination and sign and date the certificate.

(2) The certificate shall include—

(a) any material finding of fact, and
(b) the reasons for the decision.

(3) The proper officer shall send a copy of the certificate to the parties.

(4) The Tribunal shall make arrangements for the publication of its determination but in doing so shall have regard to the desirability of safeguarding the privacy of data subjects and commercially sensitive information, and for that purpose may make any necessary amendments to the text of the certificate.

Costs

25.—(1) In any appeal before the Tribunal, including one withdrawn under rule 9 above, the Tribunal may make an order awarding costs—

(a) against the appellant and in favour of the Commissioner where it considers that the appeal was manifestly unreasonable;
(b) against the Commissioner and in favour of the appellant where it considers that the disputed decision was manifestly unreasonable;
(c) where it considers that a party has been responsible for frivolous, vexatious, improper or unreasonable action, or for any failure to comply with a direction or

[22] As amended by SI 2002/2722.

any delay which with diligence could have been avoided, against that party and in favour of the other.

(2) The Tribunal shall not make an order under paragraph (1) above awarding costs against a party without first giving that party an opportunity of making representations against the making of the order.

(3) An order under paragraph (1) above may be to the party or parties in question to pay to the other party or parties either a specified sum in respect of the costs incurred by that other party or parties in connection with the proceedings or the whole or part of such costs as taxed (if not otherwise agreed).

(4) Any costs required by an order under this rule to be taxed may be taxed in the county court according to such of the scales prescribed by the county court rules for proceedings in the county court as shall be directed by the order.

(5) In relation to proceedings before the Tribunal in Scotland, for the purposes of the application of paragraph (4) above, for the reference to the county court and the county court rules there shall be substituted references to the sheriff court and the sheriff court rules and for the reference to proceedings there shall be substituted a reference to civil proceedings.

Irregularities

26.—(1) Any irregularity resulting from failure to comply with any provision of these Rules or of any direction of the Tribunal before the Tribunal has reached its decision shall not of itself render the proceedings void, but the Tribunal may, and shall if it considers that any person may have been prejudiced by that irregularity, give such directions or take such steps as it thinks fit before reaching its decision to cure or waive the irregularity, whether by amendment of any document, the giving of notice or otherwise.

(2) Clerical mistakes in any document recording or certifying a direction, decision or determination of the Tribunal or chairman, or errors arising in such a document from an accidental slip or omission, may at any time be corrected by the chairman, by certificate signed by him.

Notices etc.

27.—(1) Any notice or other document required or authorised by these Rules to be served on or sent to any person or authority may be sent by post in a registered letter or by the recorded delivery service—

(a) in the case of the Tribunal, to the proper officer of the Tribunal;
(b) in the case of the Commissioner, to him at his office;
(c) in the case of an appellant, to him at his address for service under these Rules; and
(d) in the case of an occupier within the provisions of rule 12 above, to him at the premises in question.

(2) An appellant may at any time by notice to the Tribunal change his address for service under these Rules.

Signed by the authority of the Lord Chancellor

Yvette Cooper
Parliamentary Secretary

Lord Chancellor's Department
October 30, 2002

The Data Protection (Subject Access) (Fees and Miscellaneous Provisions) Regulations 2000

(SI 2000/191)

ARRANGEMENT OF REGULATIONS

[MADE: SEPTEMBER 23, 2001][1]

[LAID BEFORE PARLIAMENT: SEPTEMBER 25, 2001][2]

[COMING INTO FORCE: OCTOBER 23, 2001][3]

App 2–04 The Secretary of State, in exercise of the powers conferred on him by sections 7(2) [. . .][4] and (11) [. . .][5] of the Data Protection Act 1998[6] [(having regard to the definitions of "prescribed" and "the prescribed maximum" (in section 7(10) and 67(2) of that Act))][7] and having consulted the [Information Commissioner][8] in accordance with section 67(3) of that Act [[9]],[10] hereby makes the following Regulations[—][11]

[1] As amended by SI 2001/3223.
[2] *ibid.*
[3] *ibid.*
[4] Words omitted by SI 2001/3223.
[5] *ibid.*
[6] 1998 c.29.
[7] Words amended by SI 2001/3223.
[8] *ibid.*
[9] The consultation requirement in s.67(3) now refers to the Information Commissioner as s.6(1) has been substituted by the Freedom of Information Act 2000 (c.36).
[10] Words added by SI 2001/3223.
[11] As amended by SI 2001/3223.

Citation, commencement and interpretation

1.—(1) These Regulations may be cited as the Data Protection (Subject Access) (Fees and Miscellaneous Provisions) Regulations 2000 and shall come into force on [October 23, 2001.][12]

(2) In these Regulations "the Act" means the Data Protection Act 1998.

Extent of subject access requests

2.—(1) A request for information under any provision of section 7(1)(a), (b) or (c) of the Act is to be treated as extending also to information under all other provisions of section 7(1)(a), (b) and (c).

(2) A request for information under any provision of section 7(1) of the Act is to be treated as extending to information under the provisions of section 7(1)(d) only where the request shows an express intention to that effect.

(3) A request for information under the provisions of section 7(1)(d) of the Act is to be treated as extending also to information under any other provision of section 7(1) only where the request shows an express intention to that effect.

Maximum subject access fee

3.—Except as otherwise provided by regulations 4, 5 and 6 below, the maximum fee which may be required by a data controller under section 7(2)(b) of the Act is £10.

Limited requests for subject access where data controller is credit reference agency

4.—(1) In any case in which a request under section 7 of the Act has been made to a data controller who is a credit reference agency, and has been limited, or by virtue of section 9(2) of the Act is taken to have been limited, to personal data relevant to an individual's financial standing—

(a) the maximum fee which may be required by a data controller under section 7(2)(b) of the Act is £2, and
(b) the prescribed period for the purposes of section 7(8) of the Act is seven working days.

(2) In this regulation "working day" means any day other than—

(a) Saturday or Sunday,
(b) Christmas Day or Good Friday,
(c) a bank holiday, within the meaning of section 1 of the Banking and Financial Dealings Act 1971,[13] in the part of the United Kingdom in which the data controller's address is situated.

(3) For the purposes of paragraph (2)(c) above—

(a) the address of a registered company is that of its registered office, and
(b) the address of a person (other than a registered company) carrying on a business is that of his principal place of business in the United Kingdom.

Subject access requests in respect of educational records

5.—(1) This regulation applies to any case in which a request made under section 7 of the Act relates wholly or partly to personal data forming part of an accessible record which is an educational record within the meaning of Schedule 11 to the Act.

---

12 As amended by SI 2001/3223
13 1971 c.80.

(2) Except as provided by paragraph (3) below, a data controller may not require a fee under section 7(2)(b) of the Act in any case to which this regulation applies.

(3) Where, in a case to which this regulation applies, the obligation imposed by section 7(1)(c)(i) of the Act is to be complied with by supplying the data subject with a copy of information in permanent form, the maximum fee which may be required by a data controller under section 7(2)(b) of the Act is that applicable to the case under the Schedule to these Regulations.

(4) In any case to which this regulation applies, and in which the address of the data controller to whom the request is made is situated in England and Wales, the prescribed period for the purposes of section 7(8) of the Act is fifteen school days within the meaning of section 579(1) of the Education Act 1996.[14]

Certain subject access requests in respect of health records [. . .][15]

6.—(1) This regulation applies only to cases in which a request made under section 7 of the Act—

(a) relates wholly or partly to personal data forming part of an accessible record which is a health record within the meaning of section 68(2) of the Act, [and][16]

(b) does not relate exclusively to data within paragraphs (a) and (b) of the definition of "data" in section 1(1) of the Act. [. . .][17]

(2) Where in a case to which this regulation applies, the obligation imposed by section 7(1)(c)(i) of the Act is to be complied with by supplying the data subject with a copy of information in permanent form, the maximum fee which may be required by a data controller under section 7(2)(b) of the Act is £50.

(3) Except in a case to which paragraph (2) above applies, a data controller may not require a fee under section 7(2)(b) of the Act where, in a case to which this regulation applies, the request relates solely to personal data which—

(a) form part of an accessible record—

  (i) which is a health record within the meaning of section 68(2) of the Act, and

  (ii) at least some of which was made after the beginning of the period of 40 days immediately preceding the date of the request; and

(b) do not fall within paragraph (a) or (b) of the definition of "data" in section 1(1) of the Act.

(4) For the purposes of paragraph (3) above, an individual making a request in any case to which this regulation applies may specify that his request is limited to personal data of the description set out in that paragraph.

[Alan Milburn

One of Her Majesty's Principal Secretaries of State, Department of Health
September 23, 2001][18]

14 1996 c.56.
15 Words omitted by SI 2001/3223.
16 As amended by SI 2001/3223.
17 Words omitted by SI 2001/3223.
18 As amended by SI 2001/3223.

SCHEDULE

Regulation 5(3)

MAXIMUM SUBJECT ACCESS FEES WHERE A COPY OF INFORMATION CONTAINED IN AN EDUCATIONAL RECORD IS SUPPLIED IN PERMANENT FORM

1.—In any case in which the copy referred to in regulation 5(3) includes material in any form other than a record in writing on paper, the maximum fee applicable for the purposes of regulation 5(3) is £50.

2.—In any case in which the copy referred to in regulation 5(3) consists solely of a record in writing on paper, the maximum fee applicable for the purposes of regulation 5(3) is set out in the table below.[19]

[19] Table available at *http://www.legislation.hmso.gov.uk/si/si2000/20000191.htm* and in Sweet & Maxwell's *Encyclopedia of Data Protection*, Vol.1, para.3–322, Release 25.

The Data Protection Tribunal (National Security Appeals) Rules 2000

(SI 2000/206)

[MADE: FEBRUARY 2, 2000]

[LAID BEFORE PARLIAMENT: FEBRUARY 8, 2000]

[COMING INTO FORCE: MARCH 1, 2000]

ARRANGEMENT OF RULES

The Secretary of State, in exercise of the powers conferred on him by section 67(2) of, and paragraph 7 of Schedule 6 to, the Data Protection Act 1998,[1] hereby makes the following Rules: App 2–05

Citation and commencement

1.—These Rules may be cited as the Data Protection Tribunal (National Security Appeals) Rules 2000 and shall come into force on March 1, 2000.

Application and interpretation

2.—(1) These Rules apply to appeals under section 28 of the Act, and the provisions of these Rules are to be construed accordingly.

(2) In these Rules, unless the context otherwise requires—

"the Act" means the Data Protection Act 1998;

"appeal" means an appeal under section 28 of the Act;

"appellant" means a person who brings or intends to bring an appeal under section 28 of the Act;

"costs"—

(a) except in Scotland, includes fees, charges, disbursements, expenses and remuneration;
(b) in Scotland means expenses, and includes fees, charges, disbursements and remuneration;

"disputed certification" means—

(a) in relation to an appeal under section 28(4) of the Act, the certificate against which the appeal is brought or intended to be brought, and
(b) in relation to an appeal under section 28(6) of the Act, the claim by the data controller, against which the appeal is brought or intended to be brought, that a certificate applies to any personal data;

"party" has the meaning given in paragraph (3) below;

"president" means the person designated by the Lord Chancellor under paragraph 3 of Schedule 6 to the Act to preside when the Tribunal is constituted under that paragraph;

"proper officer" in relation to a rule means an officer or member of staff provided to the Tribunal under paragraph 14 of Schedule 5 to the Act and appointed by the chairman to perform the duties of a proper officer under that rule;

"relevant Minister" means the Minister of the Crown who is responsible for the signing of the certificate under section 28(2) of the Act to which the appeal relates, and except where the context otherwise requires, references in these Rules to the relevant Minister include a person appointed under rule 21 below to represent his interests; and

"respondent data controller" in relation to an appeal under section 28(6) of the Act means the data controller making the claim which constitutes the disputed certification.

(3) In these Rules, except where the context otherwise requires, "party " means the appellant or—

[1] 1998 c.29.back

(a) in relation to an appeal under section 28(4) of the Act, the relevant Minister, and
(b) in relation to an appeal under section 28(6) of the Act, the respondent data controller,

and, except where the context otherwise requires, references in these Rules to a party or to any such party include a person appointed under rule 21 below to represent his interests.

(4) In relation to proceedings before the Tribunal in Scotland, for the words " on the trial of an action" in rules 15(6) and 26(2) below there is substituted " in a proof".

Constitution and general duty of the Tribunal

3.—(1) When exercising its functions under these Rules, the Tribunal shall secure that information is not disclosed contrary to the interests of national security.

(2) Paragraph 6(1) of Schedule 6 to the Act applies only to the exercise of the jurisdiction of the Tribunal in accordance with rule 11 below.

(3) For the purposes of paragraph (1) above, but without prejudice to the application of that paragraph, the disclosure of information is to be regarded as contrary to the interests of national security if it would indicate the existence or otherwise of any material.

Method of appealing

4.—(1) An appeal must be brought by a written notice of appeal served on the Tribunal.

(2) The notice of appeal shall—

(a) identify the disputed certification; and
(b) state—

(i) the name and address of the appellant;
(ii) the grounds of the appeal; and
(iii) an address for service of notices and other documents on the appellant.

(3) In the case of an appeal under section 28(6) of the Act, the notice of appeal shall also state—

(a) the date on which the respondent data controller made the claim constituting the disputed certification;
(b) an address for service of notices and other documents on the respondent data controller; and
(c) where applicable, the special circumstances which the appellant considers justify the Tribunal's accepting jurisdiction under rule 5(3) below.

Time limit for appealing

5.—(1) In the case of an appeal under section 28(4) of the Act, a notice of appeal may be served on the Tribunal at any time during the currency of the disputed certification to which it relates.

(2) In the case of an appeal under section 28(6) of the Act, subject to paragraph (3) below, a notice of appeal must be served on the Tribunal within 28 days of the date on which the claim constituting the disputed certification was made.

(3) The Tribunal may accept a notice of appeal served after the expiry of the period permitted by paragraph (2) above if it is of the opinion that, by reason of special circumstances, it is just and right to do so.

(4) A notice of appeal shall if sent by post in accordance with rule 30(1) below be treated as having been served on the date on which it is received for dispatch by the Post Office.

Acknowledgment of notice of appeal and notification by the Tribunal

6.—(1) Upon receipt of a notice of appeal, the proper officer shall send—

(a) an acknowledgment of the service of a notice of appeal to the appellant, and
(b) a copy of the notice of appeal to—

(i) the relevant Minister,
(ii) the Commissioner, and
(iii) in the case of an appeal under section 28(6) of the Act, the respondent data controller.

(2) An acknowledgment of service under paragraph (1)(a) above shall be accompanied by a statement of the Tribunal's powers to award costs against the appellant under rule 28 below.

Relevant Minister's notice in reply

7.—(1) No later than 42 days after receipt of a copy of a notice of appeal under rule 6(1)(b) above, the relevant Minister shall send to the Tribunal—

(a) a copy of the certificate to which the appeal relates, and
(b) a written notice in accordance with paragraph (2) below.

(2) The notice shall state—

(a) with regard to an appeal under section 28(4) of the Act, whether or not he intends to oppose the appeal and, if so—

(i) a summary of the circumstances relating to the issue of the certificate, and the reasons for the issue of the certificate;
(ii) the grounds upon which he relies in opposing the appeal; and
(iii) a statement of the evidence upon which he relies in support of those grounds; and

(b) with regard to an appeal under section 28(6) of the Act, whether or not he wishes to make representations in relation to the appeal and, if so—

(i) the extent to which he intends to support or oppose the appeal;
(ii) the grounds upon which he relies in supporting or opposing the appeal; and
(iii) a statement of the evidence upon which he relies in support of those grounds.

(3) Except where the Tribunal proposes to determine the appeal in accordance with rule 11 below, and subject to rule 12 below, the proper officer shall send a copy of the notice to—

(a) the appellant,
(b) the Commissioner, and
(c) in the case of an appeal under section 28(6) of the Act, the respondent data controller.

Reply by respondent data controller

8.—(1) A respondent data controller shall, within 42 days of the date on which he receives a copy of a notice of appeal under rule 6(1)(b) above, send to the Tribunal a written reply acknowledging service upon him of the notice of appeal, and stating—

(a) whether or not he intends to oppose the appeal and, if so,
(b) the grounds upon which he relies in opposing the appeal.

(2) Before the expiry of the period of 42 days referred to in paragraph (1) above, the respondent data controller may apply to the Tribunal for an extension of that period, showing cause why, by reason of special circumstances, it would be just and right to do so, and the Tribunal may grant such extension as it considers appropriate.

(3) Except where the Tribunal proposes to determine the appeal in accordance with rule 11 below, the proper officer shall send a copy of the reply to—

(a) the relevant Minister; and
(b) subject to paragraph (4) and rule 12 below, the appellant and the Commissioner.

(4) No copy may be sent under paragraph (3)(b) above before the period of 42 days referred to in 12(2)(b) below has expired, otherwise than in accordance with rule 12, unless the relevant Minister has indicated that he does not object.

Amendment and supplementary grounds

9.—(1) With the leave of the Tribunal, the appellant may amend his notice of appeal or deliver supplementary grounds of appeal.

(2) Rule 6(1) above and rule 11(1)(a) below apply to an amended notice of appeal and to supplementary grounds of appeal provided under paragraph (1) above as they do to a notice of appeal.

(3) Upon receipt of a copy of an amended notice of appeal or amended grounds of appeal under rule 6(1) above, the relevant Minister may amend his notice in reply and, in the case of an appeal under section 28(6) of the Act, the respondent data controller may amend his reply to the notice of appeal.

(4) An amended notice or reply under paragraph (3) above must be sent to the Tribunal within 28 days of the date on which the copy referred to in that paragraph is received.

(5) Without prejudice to paragraph (3) above, and with the leave of the Tribunal—

(a) the relevant Minister may amend a notice in reply, and
(b) the respondent data controller may amend a reply to the notice of appeal.

(6) Rule 7(3) above and rules 11(1)(b) and 12(1)(a) below apply to an amended notice in reply by the relevant Minister provided under paragraph (3) or (5) above as they do to a notice in reply.

(7) Rule 8(3) and (4) above and rules 11(1)(c) and 12(1)(b) below apply to an amended reply by the respondent data controller provided under paragraph (3) or (5) above as they do to a reply.

Application for striking out

10.—(1) Where the relevant Minister or, in the case of an appeal under section 28(6) of the Act, the respondent data controller is of the opinion that an appeal does not lie to, or cannot be entertained by, the Tribunal, or that the notice of appeal discloses no reasonable grounds of appeal, he may include in his notice under rule 7 or, as the case may be, his reply under rule 8 above a notice to that effect stating the grounds for such contention and applying for the appeal to be struck out.

(2) An application under this rule may be heard as a preliminary issue or at the beginning of the hearing of the substantive appeal.

Summary disposal of appeals

11.—(1) Where, having considered—

(a) the notice of appeal,
(b) the relevant Minister's notice in reply and,
(c) in the case of an appeal under section 28(6) of the Act, the respondent data controller's reply,

the Tribunal is of the opinion that the appeal is of such a nature that it can properly be determined by dismissing it forthwith, it may, subject to the provisions of this rule, so determine the appeal.

(2) Where the Tribunal proposes to determine an appeal under paragraph (1) above, it must first notify the appellant and the relevant Minister of the proposal.

(3) A notification to the appellant under paragraph (2) above must contain particulars of the appellant's entitlements set out in paragraph (4) below.

(4) An appellant notified in accordance with paragraph (2) above is entitled, within such time as the Tribunal may reasonably allow—

(a) to make written representations, and
(b) to request the Tribunal to hear oral representations

against the proposal to determine the appeal under paragraph (1) above.

(5) Where an appellant requests a hearing under paragraph (4)(b) above, the Tribunal shall, as soon as practicable and with due regard to the convenience of the appellant, appoint a time and place for a hearing accordingly.

(6) The proper officer shall send to the appellant a notice informing him of—

(a) the time and place of any hearing under paragraph (5) above, which, unless the appellant otherwise agrees, shall not be earlier than 14 days after the date on which the notice is sent, and
(b) the effect of rule 22 below.

(7) The Tribunal must as soon as practicable notify the appellant and the relevant Minister if, having given a notification under paragraph (2) above, it ceases to propose to determine the appeal under paragraph (1) above.

Relevant Minister's objection to disclosure

12.—(1) Where the relevant Minister objects, on grounds of the need to secure that information is not disclosed contrary to the interests of national security, to the disclosure of—

(a) his notice in reply to the appellant, the Commissioner or, in the case of an appeal under section 28(6) of the Act, the respondent data controller; or
(b) the reply of a respondent data controller to the appellant or the Commissioner,

he may send a notice of objection to the Tribunal.

(2) A notice of objection under paragraph (1) above must be sent—

(a) where paragraph (1)(a) above applies, with the notice in reply; and
(b) where paragraph (1)(b) above applies, within 42 days of the date on which he receives the copy mentioned in rule 8(3) above.

(3) A notice of objection under paragraph (1) above shall—

(a) state the reasons for the objection; and
(b) where paragraph (1)(a) above applies, if and to the extent it is possible to do so without disclosing information contrary to the interests of national security, be accompanied by a version of the relevant Minister's notice in a form which can be shown to the appellant, the Commissioner or, as the case may be, the respondent data controller.

(4) Where the relevant Minister sends a notice of objection under paragraph (1) above, the Tribunal must not disclose the material in question otherwise than in accordance with rule 17 below.

Withdrawal of appeal

13.—(1) The appellant may at any time withdraw his appeal by sending to the Tribunal a notice of withdrawal signed by him or on his behalf, and the proper officer shall send a copy of that notice to—

(a) the relevant Minister,
(b) the Commissioner, and
(c) in the case of an appeal under section 28(6) of the Act, the respondent data controller.

(2) A notice of withdrawal shall if sent by post in accordance with rule 30(1) below have effect on the date on which it is received for dispatch by the Post Office.

(3) Where an appeal is withdrawn under this rule a fresh appeal may not be brought by the same appellant in relation to the same disputed certification except with the leave of the Tribunal.

Consolidation of appeals

14.—(1) Subject to paragraph (2) below, where in the case of two or more appeals to which these Rules apply it appears to the Tribunal—

(a) that some common question of law or fact arises in both or all of them, or
(b) that for some other reason it is desirable to proceed with the appeals under this rule,

the Tribunal may order that the appeals be consolidated or heard together.

(2) The Tribunal shall not make an order under this rule without giving the parties and the relevant Minister an opportunity to show cause why such an order should not be made.

Directions

15.—(1) This rule is subject to rule 16 below.

(2) In this rule, references to a "party" include the relevant Minister notwithstanding that he may not be a party to an appeal under section 28(6) of the Act.

(3) Subject to paragraphs (6) and (7) below, the Tribunal may at any time of its own motion or on the application of any party give such directions as it thinks proper to enable the parties to prepare for the hearing of the appeal or to assist the Tribunal to determine the issues.

(4) Such directions may in particular—

(a) provide for a particular matter to be dealt with as a preliminary issue and for a pre-hearing review to be held;
(b) provide for—
    (i) the exchange between the parties of lists of documents held by them which are relevant to the appeal,
    (ii) the inspection by the parties of the documents so listed,
    (iii) the exchange between the parties of statements of evidence, and
    (iv) the provision by the parties to the Tribunal of statements or lists of agreed matters;
(c) require any party to send to the Tribunal and to the other parties—
    (i) statements of facts and statements of the evidence which will be adduced, including such statements provided in a modified or edited form;
    (ii) a skeleton argument which summarises the submissions which will be made and cites the authorities which will be relied upon, identifying any particular passages to be relied upon;

(iii) a chronology of events;
(iv) any other particulars or supplementary statements which may reasonably be required for the determination of the appeal;
(v) any document or other material which the Tribunal may require and which it is in the power of that party to deliver;
(vi) an estimate of the time which will be needed for any hearing; and
(vii) a list of the witnesses he intends to call to give evidence at any hearing;

(d) limit the length of oral submissions and the time allowed for the examination and cross-examination of witnesses; and
(e) limit the number of expert witnesses to be heard on either side.

(5) The Tribunal may, subject to any specific provisions of these Rules, specify time limits for steps to be taken in the proceedings and may extend any time limit.

(6) Nothing in this rule may require the production of any document or other material which the party could not be compelled to produce on the trial of an action in a court of law in that part of the United Kingdom where the appeal is to be determined.

(7) It shall be a condition of the supply of any information or material provided under this rule that any recipient of that information or material may use it only for the purposes of the appeal.

(8) The power to give directions may be exercised in the absence of the parties.

(9) Notice of any directions given under this rule shall be served on all the parties, and the Tribunal may, on the application of any party, set aside or vary such directions.

Applications by relevant Minister

16.—(1) This rule applies in any case where the Tribunal proposes to—

(a) give or vary any direction under rule 15 above or rule 18(2) below,
(b) issue a summons under rule 20 below, or
(c) certify or publish a determination under rule 27 below.

(2) Before the Tribunal proceeds as proposed in any case to which this rule applies, it must first notify the relevant Minister of the proposal.

(3) If the relevant Minister considers that proceeding as proposed by the Tribunal would cause information to be disclosed contrary to the interests of national security, he may make an application to the Tribunal requesting it to reconsider the proposal or reconsider it to any extent.

(4) An application by the relevant Minister under paragraph (3) above must be made within 14 days of receipt of notification under paragraph (2), and the Tribunal must not proceed as proposed in any case to which this rule applies before that period has expired, otherwise than in accordance with rule 17 below, unless the relevant Minister has indicated that he does not object.

(5) Where the relevant Minister makes an application under this rule, the Tribunal must not proceed as proposed otherwise than in accordance with rule 17 below.

Determinations on relevant Minister's objections and applications

17.—(1) Except where rule 11 above applies, the Tribunal shall determine whether to uphold any objection of the relevant Minister under rule 12 above, and any application under rule 16 above, in accordance with this rule.

(2) Subject to paragraph (3) below, proceedings under this rule shall take place in the absence of the parties.

(3) The relevant Minister (or a person authorised to act on his behalf) may attend any proceedings under this rule, whether or not he is a party to the appeal in question.

(4) An objection under rule 12 above must be considered under this rule as a preliminary issue, and an application under rule 16 above may be considered as a preliminary issue or at the hearing of the substantive appeal.

(5) Where, in the case of an objection under rule 12 above, the Tribunal is minded to overrule the relevant Minister's objection, or to require him to provide a version of his notice in a form other than that in which he provided it under rule 12(3)(b) above, the Tribunal must invite the relevant Minister to make oral representations.

(6) Where the Tribunal under paragraph (5) above overrules an objection by the relevant Minister under rule 12 above, or requires him to provide a version of his notice in a form other than that in which he provided it under rule 12(3)(b) above, the Tribunal shall not disclose, and the relevant Minister shall not be required to disclose, any material which was the subject of the unsuccessful objection if the relevant Minister chooses not to rely upon it in opposing the appeal.

(7) Where, in the case of an objection under rule 12 above, the Tribunal upholds the relevant Minister's objection and either—

(a) approves the version of his notice provided under rule 12(3)(b) or
(b) requires him to provide a version of his notice in a form other than that in which he provided it under rule 12(3)(b),

rule 7(3) above applies to that version of the notice.

Power to determine without a hearing

18.—(1) Without prejudice to rule 11 above, where either—

(a) the parties so agree in writing, or
(b) it appears to the Tribunal that the issues raised on the appeal have been determined on a previous appeal brought by the appellant on the basis of facts which did not materially differ from those to which the appeal relates and the Tribunal has given the parties an opportunity of making representations to the effect that the appeal ought not to be determined without a hearing,

the Tribunal may determine an appeal, or any particular issue, without a hearing.

(2) Before determining any matter under this rule, the Tribunal may, subject to rule 16 above, if it thinks fit direct any party to provide in writing further information about any matter relevant to the appeal within such time as the Tribunal may allow.

Time and place of hearings

19.—(1) Except where rule 11 or 18 above applies, as soon as practicable after notice of appeal has been given, and with due regard to the convenience of the parties, the Tribunal shall appoint a time and place for a hearing of the appeal.

(2) Except in relation to a hearing under rule 11(5) above, the proper officer shall send to each party, the Commissioner and the relevant Minister a notice informing him of the time and place of any hearing, which, unless the parties otherwise agree, shall not be earlier than 14 days after the date on which the notice is sent.

(3) A notice to a party under this rule shall inform him of the effect of rule 22 below.

(4) The Tribunal may—

(a) postpone the time appointed for any hearing;
(b) adjourn a hearing to such time as the Tribunal may determine; or
(c) alter the place appointed for any hearing;

and, if it exercises any of the above powers, it shall notify each person previously notified of that hearing under this rule or rule 11(6) above, and any person summoned under rule 20 below to attend as a witness at that hearing, of the revised arrangements.

Summoning of witnesses

20.—(1) This rule is subject to rule 16 above.

(2) Subject to paragraph (3) below, the Tribunal may by summons require any person in the United Kingdom to attend as a witness at a hearing of an appeal at such time and place as may be specified in the summons and, subject to rule 26(2) and (3) below, at the hearing to answer any questions or produce any documents in his custody or under his control which relate to any matter in question in the appeal.

(3) No person shall be required to attend in obedience to a summons under paragraph (2) above unless he has been given at least 7 days' notice of the hearing or, if less than 7 days, he has informed the Tribunal that he accepts such notice as he has been given.

(4) The Tribunal may upon the application of a person summoned under this rule set the summons aside.

(5) A person who has attended a hearing as a witness in obedience to a summons shall be entitled to such sum as the Tribunal considers reasonable in respect of his attendance at, and his travelling to and from, the hearing; and where the summons was issued at the request of a party such sum shall be paid or tendered to him by that party.

(6) In relation to proceedings before the Tribunal in Scotland, in this rule "summons" means citation and the provisions of this rule are to be construed accordingly.

Representation at a hearing

21.—(1) At any hearing by the Tribunal, other than a hearing under rule 11 above—

(a) a party may, subject to rules 17(2) above and 23(3) below, conduct his case himself or may appear and be represented by any person whom he may appoint for the purpose, and

(b) the relevant Minister may appear and be represented by any person whom he may appoint for the purpose.

(2) At any hearing by the Tribunal under rule 11(5) above, the appellant may conduct his case himself or may appear and be represented by any person whom he may appoint for the purpose.

Default of appearance at hearing

22.—If, without furnishing the Tribunal with sufficient reason for his absence, a party fails to appear at a hearing, having been duly notified of the hearing, the Tribunal may, if that party is the appellant, dismiss the appeal or, in any case, hear and determine the appeal, or any particular issue, in the party's absence and may make such order as to costs as it thinks fit.

Hearings to be in private

23.—(1) All hearings by the Tribunal (including preliminary hearings) shall be in private unless the Tribunal, with the consent of the parties and the relevant Minister, directs that the hearing or any part of the hearing shall take place in public.

(2) Where the Tribunal sits in private it may, with the consent of the parties and the relevant Minister, admit to a hearing such persons on such terms and conditions as it considers appropriate.

(3) Where the Tribunal considers it necessary for any party other than the relevant Minister to be excluded from proceedings or any part of them in order to secure that information is not disclosed contrary to the interests of national security, it must—

(a) direct accordingly,

(b) inform the person excluded of its reasons, to the extent that it is possible to do so without disclosing information contrary to the interests of national security, and record those reasons in writing, and
(c) inform the relevant Minister.

(4) The relevant Minister, or a person authorised to act on his behalf, may attend any hearing, other than a hearing under rule 11 above, notwithstanding that it is in private.

Conduct of proceedings at hearing

24.—(1) Subject to rules 22 and 23(3) above, the Tribunal shall at the hearing of an appeal give to each party and the relevant Minister an opportunity—

(a) to address the Tribunal and to amplify orally written statements previously furnished under these Rules, to give evidence and to call witnesses, and to put questions to any person giving evidence before the Tribunal, and
(b) to make representations on the evidence (if any) and on the subject matter of the appeal generally but, where evidence is taken, such opportunity shall not be given before the completion of the taking of evidence.

(2) Except as provided by these Rules, the Tribunal shall conduct the proceedings in such manner as it considers appropriate in the circumstances for discharging its functions and shall so far as appears to it appropriate seek to avoid formality in its proceedings.

Preliminary and incidental matters

25.—As regards matters preliminary or incidental to an appeal the president may act for the Tribunal under rules 5(3), 8(2), 9, 13 to 15, 19(1) and (4)(a) and (c) and 20.

Evidence

26.—(1) The Tribunal may receive in evidence any document or information notwithstanding that such document or information would be inadmissible in a court of law.

(2) No person shall be compelled to give any evidence or produce any document which he could not be compelled to give or produce on the trial of an action in a court of law in that part of the United Kingdom where the appeal is to be determined.

(3) The Tribunal may require oral evidence of a witness (including a party) to be given on oath or affirmation and for that purpose the president or the proper officer shall have power to administer oaths or take affirmations.

Determination of appeal

27.—(1) As soon as practicable after the Tribunal has determined an appeal, the president shall certify in writing that determination and sign and date the certificate.

(2) If and to the extent that it is possible to do so without disclosing information contrary to the interests of national security, and subject to rule 16 above, the certificate shall include—

(a) any material finding of fact, and
(b) the reasons for the decision.

(3) The proper officer shall send a copy of the certificate to—

(a) the parties,
(b) the relevant Minister, and
(c) the Commissioner.

(4) Subject to rule 16 above, the Tribunal shall make arrangements for the publication of its determination but in doing so shall have regard to—

(a) the desirability of safeguarding the privacy of data subjects and commercially sensitive information, and

(b) the need to secure that information is not disclosed contrary to the interests of national security,

and for those purposes may make any necessary amendments to the text of the certificate.

(5) For the purposes of this rule (but without prejudice to its generality), the disclosure of information is to be regarded as contrary to the interests of national security if it would indicate the existence or otherwise of any material.

Costs

28.—(1) In any appeal before the Tribunal, including one withdrawn under rule 13 above, the Tribunal may make an order awarding costs—

(a) in the case of an appeal under section 28(4) of the Act—

(i) against the appellant and in favour of the relevant Minister where it considers that the appeal was manifestly unreasonable;

(ii) against the relevant Minister and in favour of the appellant where it allows the appeal and quashes the disputed certification, or does so to any extent;

(b) in the case of an appeal under section 28(6) of the Act—

(i) against the appellant and in favour of any other party where it dismisses the appeal or dismisses it to any extent;

(ii) in favour of the appellant and against any other party where it allows the appeal or allows it to any extent; and

(c) where it considers that a party has been responsible for frivolous, vexatious, improper or unreasonable action, or for any failure to comply with a direction or any delay which with diligence could have been avoided, against that party and in favour of the other.

(2) The Tribunal shall not make an order under paragraph (1) above awarding costs against a party without first giving that party an opportunity of making representations against the making of the order.

(3) An order under paragraph (1) above may be to the party or parties in question to pay to the other party or parties either a specified sum in respect of the costs incurred by that other party or parties in connection with the proceedings or the whole or part of such costs as taxed (if not otherwise agreed).

(4) Any costs required by an order under this rule to be taxed may be taxed in the county court according to such of the scales prescribed by the county court rules for proceedings in the county court as shall be directed by the order.

(5) In relation to proceedings before the Tribunal in Scotland, for the purpose of the application of paragraph (4) above, for the reference to the county court and the county court rules there shall be substituted references to the sheriff court and the sheriff court rules and for the reference to proceedings there shall be substituted a reference to civil proceedings.

Irregularities

29.—(1) Any irregularity resulting from failure to comply with any provision of these Rules or of any direction of the Tribunal before the Tribunal has reached its decision shall not of itself render the proceedings void, but the Tribunal may, and shall if it considers that any person may have been prejudiced by that irregularity, give such directions or take such steps as it thinks fit before reaching its decision to cure or waive the irregularity, whether by amendment of any document, the giving of notice or otherwise.

(2) Clerical mistakes in any document recording or certifying a direction, decision or determination of the Tribunal or president, or errors arising in such a document from an accidental slip or omission, may at any time be corrected by the president by certificate signed by him.

Notices etc.

30.—(1) Any notice or other document required or authorised by these Rules to be served on or sent to any person or authority may be sent by post in a registered letter or by the recorded delivery service—

(a) in the case of the Tribunal, to the proper officer of the Tribunal;
(b) in the case of an appellant or a respondent data controller, to him at his address for service under these Rules;
(c) in the case of the relevant Minister or the Commissioner, to him at his office.

(2) An appellant or respondent data controller may at any time by notice to the Tribunal change his address for service under these Rules.

Mike O'Brien

Parliamentary Under-Secretary of State
Home Office

February 2, 2000

Data Protection (Subject Access Modification) (Health) Order 2000

(SI 2000/413)

[MADE: FEBRUARY 17, 2000]

[COMING INTO FORCE: MARCH 1, 2000]

Whereas a draft of this Order has been laid before and approved by a resolution of each House of Parliament: App 2–06

Now, therefore, the Secretary of State, in exercise of the powers conferred on him by sections 30(1) and (4) and 67(2) of the Data Protection Act 1998[1] and after consultation with the Data Protection Commissioner in accordance with section 67(3) of that Act, hereby makes the following Order:

Citation and commencement

1.—This Order may be cited as the Data Protection (Subject Access Modification) (Health) Order 2000 and shall come into force on March 1, 2000.

Interpretation

2.—In this Order—

"the Act" means the Data Protection Act 1998;

"the appropriate health professional" means—

(a) the health professional who is currently or was most recently responsible for the clinical care of the data subject in connection with the matters to which the information which is the subject of the request relates; or

(b) where there is more than one such health professional, the health professional who is the most suitable to advise on the matters to which the information which is the subject of the request relates; or

(c) where—

(i) there is no health professional available falling within paragraph (a) or (b), or

(ii) the data controller is the Secretary of State and data to which this Order applies are processed in connection with the exercise of the functions conferred on him by or under the Child Support Act 1991 and the Child Support Act 1995 or his functions in relation to social security or war pensions,

[1] As respects Wales, the functions of the Secretary of State under s.30 were transferred to the National Assembly for Wales by art.2 of, and Sch.1 to, SI 1999/672, but are also exercisable by the Secretary of State by virtue of para.5 of Sch.3 to the Government of Wales Act 1998 (c.38) for the purposes set out in that paragraph.

a health professional who has the necessary experience and qualifications to advise on the matters to which the information which is the subject of the request relates;

"care" includes examination, investigation, diagnosis and treatment;

"section 7" means section 7 of the Act; and

"war pension" has the same meaning as in section 25 of the Social Security Act 1989 (establishment and functions of war pensions committees).

Personal data to which Order applies

3.—(1) Subject to paragraph (2), this Order applies to personal data consisting of information as to the physical or mental health or condition of the data subject.

(2) This Order does not apply to any data which are exempted from section 7 by an order made under section 38(1) of the Act.

Exemption from the subject information provisions

4.—(1) Personal data falling within paragraph (2) and to which this Order applies are exempt from the subject information provisions.

(2) This paragraph applies to personal data processed by a court and consisting of information supplied in a report or other evidence given to the court by a local authority, Health and Social Services Board, Health and Social Services Trust, probation officer or other person in the course of any proceedings to which the Family Proceedings Courts (Children Act 1989) Rules 1991],[2] the Magistrates' Courts (Children and Young Persons) Rules 1992,[3] the Magistrates' Courts (Criminal Justice (Children)) Rules (Northern Ireland) 1999, the Act of Sederunt (Child Care and Maintenance Rules) 1997[4] or the Children's Hearings (Scotland) Rules 1996[5] apply where, in accordance with a provision of any of those Rules, the information may be withheld by the court in whole or in part from the data subject.

Exemptions from section 7

5.—(1) Personal data to which this Order applies are exempt from section 7 in any case to the extent to which the application of that section would be likely to cause serious harm to the physical or mental health or condition of the data subject or any other person.

(2) Subject to article 7(1), a data controller who is not a health professional shall not withhold information constituting data to which this Order applies on the ground that the exemption in paragraph (1) applies with respect to the information unless the data controller has first consulted the person who appears to the data controller to be the appropriate health professional on the question whether or not the exemption in paragraph (1) applies with respect to the information.

(3) Where any person falling within paragraph (4) is enabled by or under any enactment or rule of law to make a request on behalf of a data subject and has made such a request, personal data to which this Order applies are exempt from section 7 in any case to the extent to which the application of that section would disclose information—

(a) provided by the data subject in the expectation that it would not be disclosed to the person making the request;

---

[2] As amended by SI 1991/1991, SI 1992/2068, SI 1994/2166, SI 1994/3156 and SI 1997/1895.

[3] As amended by SI 1997/2420.

[4] SI 1997/291, s.19.

[5] SI 1996/3261, s.251.

(b) obtained as a result of any examination or investigation to which the data subject consented in the expectation that the information would not be so disclosed; or

(c) which the data subject has expressly indicated should not be so disclosed,

provided that sub-paragraphs (a) and (b) shall not prevent disclosure where the data subject has expressly indicated that he no longer has the expectation referred to therein.

(4) A person falls within this paragraph if—

(a) except in relation to Scotland, the data subject is a child, and that person has parental responsibility for that data subject;

(b) in relation to Scotland, the data subject is a person under the age of sixteen, and that person has parental responsibilities for that data subject; or

(c) the data subject is incapable of managing his own affairs and that person has been appointed by a court to manage those affairs.

Modification of section 7 relating to data controllers who are not health professionals

6.—(1) Subject to paragraph (2) and article 7(3), section 7 of the Act is modified so that a data controller who is not a health professional shall not communicate information constituting data to which this Order applies in response to a request unless the data controller has first consulted the person who appears to the data controller to be the appropriate health professional on the question whether or not the exemption in article 5(1) applies with respect to the information.

(2) Paragraph (1) shall not apply to the extent that the request relates to information which the data controller is satisfied has previously been seen by the data subject or is already within the knowledge of the data subject.

Additional provision relating to data controllers who are not health professionals

7.—(1) Subject to paragraph (2), article 5(2) shall not apply in relation to any request where the data controller has consulted the appropriate health professional prior to receiving the request and obtained in writing from that appropriate health professional an opinion that the exemption in article 5(1) applies with respect to all of the information which is the subject of the request.

(2) Paragraph (1) does not apply where the opinion either—

(a) was obtained before the period beginning six months before the relevant day (as defined by section 7(10) of the Act) and ending on that relevant day, or

(b) was obtained within that period and it is reasonable in all the circumstances to re-consult the appropriate health professional.

(3) Article 6(1) shall not apply in relation to any request where the data controller has consulted the appropriate health professional prior to receiving the request and obtained in writing from that appropriate health professional an opinion that the exemption in article 5(1) does not apply with respect to all of the information which is the subject of the request.

Further modifications of section 7

8.—In relation to data to which this Order applies—

(a) section 7(4) of the Act shall have effect as if there were inserted after paragraph (b) of that subsection

"or,

(c) the information is contained in a health record and the other individual is a health professional who has compiled or contributed to the health record or has been involved in the care of the data subject in his capacity as a health professional".

(b) section 7(9) shall have effect as if—

(i) there was substituted—

"(9) If a court is satisfied on the application of—

(a) any person who has made a request under the foregoing provisions of this section, or

(b) any other person to whom serious harm to his physical or mental health or condition would be likely to be caused by compliance with any such request in contravention of those provisions,

that the data controller in question is about to comply with or has failed to comply with the request in contravention of those provisions, the court may order him not to comply or, as the case may be, to comply with the request."

; and

(ii) the reference therein to a contravention of the foregoing provisions of that section included a reference to a contravention of the provisions contained in this Order.

Signatures

Mike O'Brien

Parliamentary Under-Secretary of State

Home Office

February 17, 2000

Data Protection (Subject Access Modification) (Education) Order 2000

(SI 2000/414)

[MADE: FEBRUARY 17, 2000]

[COMING INTO FORCE: MARCH 1, 2000]

Whereas a draft of this Order has been laid before and approved by a resolution of each House of Parliament: **App 2–07**

Now therefore, the Secretary of State, in exercise of powers conferred upon him by sections 30(2) and (4) and 67(2) of the Data Protection Act 1998,[1] and after consultation with the Data Protection Commissioner in accordance with section 67(3) of the Act, hereby makes the following Order:

Citation and commencement

1.—This Order may be cited as the Data Protection (Subject Access Modification) (Education) Order 2000 and shall come into force on March 1, 2000.

Interpretation

2.—In this Order

"the Act" means the Data Protection Act 1998;

"education authority" in article 6 has the same meaning as in paragraph 6 of Schedule 11 to the Act;

"Principal Reporter" means the Principal Reporter appointed under section 127 of the Local Government etc. (Scotland) Act 1994 or any officer of the Scottish Children's Reporter Administration to whom there is delegated under section 131(1) of that Act any function of the Principal Reporter;

"request" means a request made under section 7; and

"section 7" means section 7 of the Act.

Personal data to which the Order applies

3.—(1) Subject to paragraph (2), this Order applies to personal data consisting of information constituting an educational record as defined in paragraph 1 of Schedule 11 to the Act.

(2) This Order does not apply—

---

[1] As respects Wales, the functions of the Secretary of State under s.30 were transferred to the National Assembly for Wales by art.2 of, and Sch.1 to, SI 1999/672, but are also exercisable by the Secretary of State by virtue of para.5 of Sch.3 to the Government of Wales Act 1998 (c.38) for the purposes set out in that paragraph.

(a) to any data consisting of information as to the physical or mental health or condition of the data subject to which the Data Protection (Subject Access Modification) (Health) Order 2000 applies; or
(b) to any data which are exempted from section 7 by an order made under section 38(1) of the Act.

Exemption from the subject information provisions

4.—(1) Personal data falling within paragraph (2) and to which this Order applies are exempt from the subject information provisions.

(2) This paragraph applies to personal data processed by a court and consisting of information supplied in a report or other evidence given to the court in the course of proceedings to which the Magistrates' Courts (Children and Young Persons) Rules 1992,[2] the Magistrates' Courts (Criminal Justice (Children)) Rules (Northern Ireland) 1999, the Act of Sederunt (Child Care and Maintenance Rules) 1997[3] or the Children's Hearings (Scotland) Rules 1996[4] apply where, in accordance with a provision of any of those Rules, the information may be withheld by the court in whole or in part from the data subject.

Exemptions from section 7

5.—(1) Personal data to which this Order applies are exempt from section 7 in any case to the extent to which the application of that section would be likely to cause serious harm to the physical or mental health or condition of the data subject or any other person.

(2) In circumstances where the exemption in paragraph (1) does not apply, where any person falling within paragraph (3) is enabled by or under any enactment or rule of law to make a request on behalf of a data subject and has made such a request, personal data consisting of information as to whether the data subject is or has been the subject of or may be at risk of child abuse are exempt from section 7 in any case to the extent to which the application of that section would not be in the best interests of that data subject.

(3) A person falls within this paragraph if—

(a) the data subject is a child, and that person has parental responsibility for that data subject; or
(b) the data subject is incapable of managing his own affairs and that person has been appointed by a court to manage those affairs.

(4) For the purposes of paragraph (2), "child abuse" includes physical injury (other than accidental injury) to, and physical and emotional neglect, ill- treatment and sexual abuse of, a child.

(5) Paragraph (2) shall not apply in Scotland.

Modification of section 7 relating to Principal Reporter

6.—Where in Scotland a data controller who is an education authority receives a request relating to information constituting data to which this Order applies and which the education authority believes to have originated from or to have been supplied by or on behalf of the Principal Reporter acting in pursuance of his statutory duties, other than information which the data subject is entitled to receive from the Principal Reporter, section 7 shall be modified so that—

[2] As amended by SI 1997/2420.
[3] SI 1997/291, s.19.
[4] SI 1996/3261, s.251.

(a) the data controller shall, within fourteen days of the relevant day (as defined by section 7(10) of the Act), inform the Principal Reporter that a request has been made; and

(b) the data controller shall not communicate information to the data subject pursuant to that section unless the Principal Reporter has informed that data controller that, in his opinion, the exemption specified in article 5(1) does not apply with respect to the information.

Further modifications of section 7

7.—(1) In relation to data to which this Order applies—

(a) section 7(4) of the Act shall have effect as if there were inserted after paragraph (b) of that subsection

"or

(c) the other individual is a relevant person"

;

(b) section 7(9) shall have effect as if—

(i) there was substituted—

"(9) If a court is satisfied on the application of—

(a) any person who has made a request under the foregoing provisions of this section, or

(b) any person to whom serious harm to his physical or mental health or condition would be likely to be caused by compliance with any such request in contravention of those provisions,

that the data controller in question is about to comply with or has failed to comply with the request in contravention of those provisions, the court may order him not to comply or, as the case may be, to comply with the request."

; and

(ii) the reference to a contravention of the foregoing provisions of that section included a reference to a contravention of the provisions contained in this Order.

(2) After section 7(ii) of the Act insert—

"(12) A person is a relevant person for the purposes of subsection (4)(c) if he—

(a) is a person referred to in paragraph 4(a) or (b) or paragraph 8(a) or (b) of Schedule 11;

(b) is employed by an education authority (within the meaning of paragraph 6 of Schedule 11) in pursuance of its functions relating to education and the information relates to him, or he supplied the information in his capacity as such an employee; or

(c) is the person making the request."

Signatures

Mike O'Brien

Parliamentary Under-Secretary of State

Home Office

February 17, 2000

Data Protection (Subject Access Modification) (Social Work) Order 2000

(SI 2000/415)

[MADE: FEBRUARY 17, 2000]

[COMING INTO FORCE: MARCH 1, 2000]

App 2–08 Whereas a draft of this Order has been laid before and approved by a resolution of each House of Parliament:

Whereas the Secretary of State considers that the application of the subject information provisions (or those provisions without modification) in the circumstances and to the extent specified in this Order would be likely to prejudice the carrying out of social work:

Now, therefore, the Secretary of State, in exercise of the powers conferred on him by sections30(3) and (4) and 67(2) of the Data Protection Act 1998,[1] and after consultation with the Data Protection Commissioner in accordance with section 67(3) of that Act, hereby makes the following Order:

Citation and commencement

1.—This Order may be cited as the Data Protection (Subject Access Modification) (Social Work) Order 2000 and shall come into force on March 1, 2000.

Interpretation

2.—(1) In this Order—

"the Act" means the Data Protection Act 1998;

"compulsory school age" in paragraph 1(f) of the Schedule has the same meaning as in section 8 of the Education Act 1996,[2] and in paragraph 1(g) of the Schedule has the same meaning as in Article 46 of the Education and Libraries (Northern Ireland) Order 1986[3];

"Health and Social Services Board" means a Health and Social Services Board established under Article 16 of the Health and Personal Social Services (Northern Ireland) Order 1972;

"Health and Social Services Trust" means a Health and Social Services Trust established under the Health and Personal Social Services (Northern Ireland) Order 1991;

---

[1] As respects Wales, the functions of the Secretary of State under s.30 were transferred to the National Assembly for Wales by art.2 of, and Sch.1 to, SI 1999/672, but are also exercisable by the Secretary of State by virtue of para.5 of Sch.3 to the Government of Wales Act 1998 (c.38) for the purposes set out in that paragraph.

[2] As amended by s.52(1) to (3) of the Education Act 1997 (c.44).

[3] SI 1986/594 (N.I. 3). Art.46 was substituted by Art.156 of SI 1989/2406 (N.I. 20).

"Principal Reporter" means the Principal Reporter appointed under section 127 of the Local Government etc. (Scotland) Act 1994 or any officer of the Scottish Children's Reporter Administration to whom there is delegated under section 131(1) of that Act any function of the Principal Reporter;

"request" means a request made under section 7;

"school age" in paragraph 1(h) of the Schedule has the same meaning as in section 31 of the Education (Scotland) Act 1980;

"section 7" means section 7 of the Act; and

"social work authority" in article 6 means a local authority for the purposes of the Social Work (Scotland) Act 1968.

(2) Any reference in this Order to a local authority in relation to data processed or formerly processed by it includes a reference to the Council of the Isles of Scilly in relation to data processed or formerly processed by the Council in connection with any functions mentioned in paragraph 1(a)(ii) of the Schedule which are or have been conferred upon the Council by or under any enactment.

Personal data to which Order applies

3.—(1) Subject to paragraph (2), this Order applies to personal data falling within any of the descriptions set out in paragraphs 1 and 2 of the Schedule.

(2) This Order does not apply—

(a) to any data consisting of information as to the physical or mental health or condition of the data subject to which the Data Protection (Subject Access Modification) (Health) Order 2000 or the Data Protection (Subject Access Modification) (Education) Order 2000 applies; or

(b) to any data which are exempted from section 7 by an order made under section 38(1) of the Act.

Exemption from subject information provisions

4.—Personal data to which this Order applies by virtue of paragraph 2 of the Schedule are exempt from the subject information provisions.

Exemption from section 7

5.—(1) Personal data to which this Order applies by virtue of paragraph 1 of the Schedule are exempt from the obligations in section 7(1)(b) to (d) of the Act in any case to the extent to which the application of those provisions would be likely to prejudice the carrying out of social work by reason of the fact that serious harm to the physical or mental health or condition of the data subject or any other person would be likely to be caused.

(2) In paragraph (1) the "carrying out of social work" shall be construed as including—

(a) the exercise of any functions mentioned in paragraph 1(a)(i), (d), (f) to (j), (m) or (o) of the Schedule;

(b) the provision of any service mentioned in paragraph 1(b), (c) or (k) of the Schedule; and

(c) the exercise of the functions of any body mentioned in paragraph 1(e) of the Schedule or any person mentioned in paragraph 1(p) or (q) of the Schedule.

(3) Where any person falling within paragraph (4) is enabled by or under any enactment or rule of law to make a request on behalf of a data subject and has made such a

request, personal data to which this Order applies are exempt from section 7 in any case to the extent to which the application of that section would disclose information—

(a) provided by the data subject in the expectation that it would not be disclosed to the person making the request;
(b) obtained as a result of any examination or investigation to which the data subject consented in the expectation that the information would not be so disclosed; or
(c) which the data subject has expressly indicated should not be so disclosed,

provided that sub-paragraphs (a) and (b) shall not prevent disclosure where the data subject has expressly indicated that he no longer has the expectation referred to therein.

(4) A person falls within this paragraph if—

(a) except in relation to Scotland, the data subject is a child, and that person has parental responsibility for that data subject;
(b) in relation to Scotland, the data subject is a person under the age of sixteen, and that person has parental responsibilities for that data subject; or
(c) the data subject is incapable of managing his own affairs and that person has been appointed by a court to manage those affairs.

Modification of section 7 relating to Principal Reporter

6.—Where in Scotland a data controller who is a social work authority receives a request relating to information constituting data to which this Order applies and which originated from or was supplied by the Principal Reporter acting in pursuance of his statutory duties, other than information which the data subject is entitled to receive from the Principal Reporter, section 7 shall be modified so that—

(a) the data controller shall, within fourteen days of the relevant day (within the meaning of section 7(10) of the Act), inform the Principal Reporter that a request has been made; and
(b) the data controller shall not communicate information to the data subject pursuant to that section unless the Principal Reporter has informed that data controller that, in his opinion, the exemption specified in article 5(1) does not apply with respect to the information.

Further modifications of section 7

7.—(1) In relation to data to which this Order applies by virtue of paragraph 1 of the Schedule—

(a) section 7(4) shall have effect as if there were inserted after paragraph (b) of that subsection

"or,

(c) the other individual is a relevant person";

(b) section 7(9) shall have effect as if—

(i) there was substituted—

"(9) If a court is satisfied on the application of—

(a) any person who has made a request under the foregoing provisions of this section, or
(b) any person to whom serious harm to his physical or mental health or condition would be likely to be caused by compliance with any such request in contravention of those provisions,

that the data controller in question is about to comply with or has failed to comply with the request in contravention of those provisions, the court may order him not to comply or, as the case may be, to comply with the request."

; and

(ii) the reference to a contravention of the foregoing provisions of that section included a reference to a contravention of the provisions contained in this Order.

(2) After section 7(11) of the Act insert—

"(12) A person is a relevant person for the purposes of subsection (4)(c) if he—

(a) is a person referred to in paragraph 1(p) or (q) of the Schedule to the Data Protection (Subject Access Modification) (Social Work) Order 2000; or

(b) is or has been employed by any person or body referred to in paragraph 1 of that Schedule in connection with functions which are or have been exercised in relation to the data consisting of the information; or

(c) has provided for reward a service similar to a service provided in the exercise of any functions specified in paragraph 1(a)(i), (b), (c) or (d) of that Schedule,

and the information relates to him or he supplied the information in his official capacity or, as the case may be, in connection with the provision of that service.".

Signatures

Mike O'Brien

Parliamentary Under-Secretary of State

Home Office

February 17, 2000

SCHEDULES

SCHEDULE 1

Personal Data to Which this Order Applies

1.—This paragraph applies to personal data falling within any of the following descriptions—

(a) data processed by a local authority—

(i) in connection with its social services functions within the meaning of the Local Authority Social Services Act 1970 or any functions exercised by local authorities under the Social Work (Scotland) Act 1968 or referred to in section 5(1B) of that Act,[4] or

(ii) in the exercise of other functions but obtained or consisting of information obtained in connection with any of those functions;

(b) data processed by a Health and Social Services Board in connection with the provision of personal social services within the meaning of the Health and Personal Social Services (Northern Ireland) Order 1972 or processed by the Health and Social Services Board in the exercise of other functions but obtained or consisting of information obtained in connection with the provision of those services;

(c) data processed by a Health and Social Services Trust in connection with the provision of personal social services within the meaning of the Health and Personal Social Services (Northern Ireland) Order 1972 on behalf of a Health and Social Services Board by virtue of an authorisation made under Article 3(1) of the Health and Personal Social Services (Northern

[4] s.5(1B) was inserted by para.76(3) of Sch.13 of the Local Government, etc. (Scotland) Act 1994 (c.39), as amended by para.15(4) of Sch.4 and Sch.5 to the Children (Scotland) Act 1995 (c.36).

Ireland) Order 1994 or processed by the Health and Social Services Trust in the exercise of other functions but obtained or consisting of information obtained in connection with the provision of those services;

(d) data processed by a council in the exercise of its functions under Part II of Schedule 9 to the Health and Social Services and Social Security Adjudications Act 1983;

(e) data processed by a probation committee established by section 3 of the Probation Service Act 1993 or the Probation Board for Northern Ireland established by the Probation Board (Northern Ireland) Order

(f) data processed by a local education authority in the exercise of its functions under section 36 of the Children Act 1989 or Chapter II of Part VI of the Education Act 1996 so far as those functions relate to ensuring that children of compulsory school age receive suitable education whether by attendance at school or otherwise;

(g) data processed by an education and library board in the exercise of its functions under article 55 of the Children (Northern Ireland) Order 1995 or article 45 of, and Schedule 13 to, the Education and Libraries (Northern Ireland) Order 1986[5] so far as those functions relate to ensuring that children of compulsory school age receive efficient full-time education suitable to their age, ability and aptitude and to any special educational needs they may have, either by regular attendance at school or otherwise;

(h) data processed by an education authority in the exercise of its functions under sections 35 to 42 of the Education (Scotland) Act 1980 so far as those functions relate to ensuring that children of school age receive efficient education suitable to their age, ability and aptitude, whether by attendance at school or otherwise;

(i) data relating to persons detained in a special hospital provided under section 4 of the National Health Service Act 1977[6] and processed by a special health authority established under section 11 of that Act[7] in the exercise of any functions similar to any social services functions of a local authority;

(j) data relating to persons detained in special accommodation provided under article 110 of the Mental Health (Northern Ireland) Order 1986 and processed by a Health and Social Services Trust in the exercise of any functions similar to any social services functions of a local authority;

(k) data processed by the National Society for the Prevention of Cruelty to Children or by any other voluntary organisation or other body designated under this sub-paragraph by the Secretary of State or the Department of Health, Social Services and Public Safety and appearing to the Secretary of State or the Department, as the case may be, to be processed for the purposes of the provision of any service similar to a service provided in the exercise of any functions specified in sub-paragraphs (a)(i), (b), (c) or (d) above;

(l) data processed by—

(i) a Strategic Health Authority established under section 8 of the National Health Service Act 1977;

(i) a Health Authority established under section 8 of the National Health Service Act 1977.[8]

(ii) an NHS Trust established under section 5 of the National Health Service and Community Care Act 1990[9];

(iia) a Primary Care Trust established under section 16A of the National Health Service Act 1977; or

(iii) a Health Board established under section 2 of the National Health Service (Scotland) Act 1978,

which were obtained or consisted of information which was obtained from any authority or body mentioned above or government department and which, whilst processed by that authority or body or government department, fell within any sub-paragraph of this paragraph;

(m) data processed by an NHS Trust as referred to in sub-paragraph (1)(ii) above in the exercise of any functions similar to any social services functions of a local authority;

[5] SI 1986/594 (N.I. 3), as amended by art.27 of SI 1996/275 (N.I. 1).

[6] As amended by para.2 of Sch.1 to the Health Authorities Act 1995 (c.17).

[7] s.11 was amended by para.6 of Sch.4 to the Health Act 1999 (c.8).

[8] As amended by s.1 of the Health Authorities Act 1995 (c.17) and para.4 of Sch.4 to the Health Act 1999 (c.8).

[9] As amended by para.65 of Sch.1 to the Health Authorities Act 1995 (c.17) and ss 13 and 14 of the Health Act 1999 (c.8).

(n) data processed by a government department and obtained or consisting of information obtained from any authority or body mentioned above and which, whilst processed by that authority or body, fell within any of the preceding sub-paragraphs of this paragraph;
(o) data processed for the purposes of the functions of the Secretary of State pursuant to section 82(5) of the Children Act 1989;
(p) data processed by any guardian ad litem appointed under section 41 of the Children Act 1989, Article 60 of the Children (Northern Ireland) Order 1995 or Article 66 of the Adoption (Northern Ireland) Order 1987.[10] or by a safeguarder appointed under section 41 of the Children (Scotland) Act 1995;
(q) data processed by the Principal Reporter.[11,12]

1. This paragraph applies to personal data falling within any of the following descriptions—
(a) data processed by a local authority—
  (i) in connection with its social services functions within the meaning of the Local Authority Social Services Act 1970 or any functions exercised by local authorities under the Social Work (Scotland) Act 1968 or referred to in section 5(1B) of that Act Section 5 (1B) was inserted by paragraph 76(3) of Schedule 13 of the Local Government etc. (Scotland) Act 1994 (c. 39), as amended by paragraph 15(4) of Schedule 4 and Schedule 5 to the Children (Scotland) Act 1995 (c. 36)., or
  (ii) in the exercise of other functions but obtained or consisting of information obtained in connection with any of those functions;
(b) data processed by a Health and Social Services Board in connection with the provision of personal social services within the meaning of the Health and Personal Social Services (Northern Ireland) Order 1972 or processed by the Health and Social Services Board in the exercise of other functions but obtained or consisting of information obtained in connection with the provision of those services;
(c) data processed by a Health and Social Services Trust in connection with the provision of personal social services within the meaning of the Health and Personal Social Services (Northern Ireland) Order 1972 on behalf of a Health and Social Services Board by virtue of an authorisation made under Article 3(1) of the Health and Personal Social Services (Northern Ireland) Order 1994 or processed by the Health and Social Services Trust in the exercise of other functions but obtained or consisting of information obtained in connection with the provision of those services;
(d) data processed by a council in the exercise of its functions under Part II of Schedule 9 to the Health and Social Services and Social Security Adjudications Act 1983;
(e) data processed by a probation committee established by section 3 of the Probation Service Act 1993 or the Probation Board for Northern Ireland established by the Probation Board (Northern Ireland) Order
(f) data processed by a local education authority in the exercise of its functions under section 36 of the Children Act 1989 or Chapter II of Part VI of the Education Act 1996 so far as those functions relate to ensuring that children of compulsory school age receive suitable education whether by attendance at school or otherwise;
(g) data processed by an education and library board in the exercise of its functions under article 55 of the Children (Northern Ireland) Order 1995 or article 45 of, and Schedule 13 to, the Education and Libraries (Northern Ireland) Order 1986. SI 1986/594 (N.I. 3), as amended by article 27 of SI 1996/274 (N.I. 1). so far as those functions relate to ensuring that children of compulsory school age receive efficient full-time education suitable to their age, ability and aptitude and to any special educational needs they may have, either by regular attendance at school or otherwise;
(h) data processed by an education authority in the exercise of its functions under sections 35 to 42 of the Education (Scotland) Act 1980 so far as those functions relate to ensuring that children of school age receive efficient education suitable to their age, ability and aptitude, whether by attendance at school or otherwise;
(i) data relating to persons detained in a special hospital provided under section 4 of the

---

10 SI 1987/2203 (N.I. 22), as amended by para.166 of Sch.9 to SI 1995/755 (N.I. 2).
11 In relation to England and Wales:
12 Words substituted by SI 2002/3220 (Children and Family Court Advisory and Support Service (Miscellaneous Amendments) Order), Art.3.

National Health Service Act 1977. As amended by paragraph 2 of Schedule 1 to the Health Authorities Act 1995 (c.17). and processed by a special health authority established under section 11 of that Act Section 11 was amended by paragraph 6 of Schedule 4 to the Health Act 1999 (c.8). in the exercise of any functions similar to any social services functions of a local authority;

(j) data relating to persons detained in special accommodation provided under article 110 of the Mental Health (Northern Ireland) Order 1986 and processed by a Health and Social Services Trust in the exercise of any functions similar to any social services functions of a local authority;

(k) data processed by the National Society for the Prevention of Cruelty to Children or by any other voluntary organisation or other body designated under this sub-paragraph by the Secretary of State or the Department of Health, Social Services and Public Safety and appearing to the Secretary of State or the Department, as the case may be, to be processed for the purposes of the provision of any service similar to a service provided in the exercise of any functions specified in sub-paragraphs (a)(i), (b), (c) or (d) above;

(l) data processed by—

(zi) a Strategic Health Authority established under section 8 of the National Health Service Act 1977;

(i) a Health Authority established under section 8 of the National Health Service Act 1977.As amended by section 1 of the Health Authorities Act 1995 (c.17) and paragraph 5 of Schedule 4 to the Health Act 1999 (c.8);

(ii) an NHS Trust established under section 5 of the National Health Service and Community Care Act 1990As amended by paragraph 65 of Schedule 1 to the Health Authorities Act 1995 (c.17) and sections 13 and 14 of the Health Act 1999 (c.8);

(iia) a Primary Care Trust established under section 16A of the National Health Service Act 1977; or

(iii) a Health Board established under section 2 of the National Health Service (Scotland) Act 1978,

which were obtained or consisted of information which was obtained from any authority or body mentioned above or government department and which, whilst processed by that authority or body or government department, fell within any sub-paragraph of this paragraph;

(m) data processed by an NHS Trust as referred to in sub-paragraph (1)(ii) above in the exercise of any functions similar to any social services functions of a local authority;

(n) data processed by a government department and obtained or consisting of information obtained from any authority or body mentioned above and which, whilst processed by that authority or body, fell within any of the preceding sub-paragraphs of this paragraph;

(o) data processed for the purposes of the functions of the Secretary of State pursuant to section 82(5) of the Children Act 1989;

(p) data processed by any children's guardian appointed under section 41 of the Children Act 1989, by any guardian ad litem appointed under Article 60 of the Children (Northern Ireland) Order 1995 or Article 66 of the Adoption (Northern Ireland) Order 1987 or by a safeguarder appointed under section 41 of the Children (Scotland) Act 1995;

(q) data processed by the Principal Reporter.

2.—This paragraph applies to personal data processed by a court and consisting of information supplied in a report or other evidence given to the court by a local authority, Health and Social Services Board, Health and Social Services Trust, probation officer or other person in the course of any proceedings to which the Family Proceedings Courts (Children Act 1989) Rules 1991,[13] the Magistrates' Courts (Children and Young Persons) Rules 1992,[14] the Magistrates' Courts (Criminal Justice (Children)) Rules (Northern Ireland) 1999, the Act of Sederunt (Child Care and Maintenance Rules) 1997[15] or the Children's Hearings (Scotland) Rules 1996[16] apply where, in accordance with a provision of any of those Rules, the information may be withheld by the court in whole or in part from the data subject.

---

13 As amended by SI 1991/1991, SI 1992/2068, SI 1994/2166, SI 1994/1356 and SI 1997/1895.

14 As amended by SI 1997/2420.

15 s.19.

16 s.251.

Data Protection (Crown Appointments) Order 2000

(SI 2000/416)

[MADE: FEBRUARY 17, 2000]

[COMING INTO FORCE: MARCH 1, 2000]

Whereas a draft of this Order has been laid before and approved by a resolution of each House of Parliament: **App 2–0**

Now, therefore, the Secretary of State, in exercise of the powers conferred upon him by paragraph 4 of Schedule 7 to the Data Protection Act 1998, and after consultation with the Data Protection Commissioner in accordance with section 67(3) of that Act, hereby makes the following Order:

1.—This Order may be cited as the Data Protection (Crown Appointments) Order 2000 and shall come into force on March 1, 2000.

2.—There shall be exempted from the subject information provisions of the Data Protection Act 1998 (as defined by section 27(2) of that Act) personal data processed for the purposes of assessing any person's suitability for any of the offices listed in the Schedule to this Order.

Signatures

Mike O'Brien

Parliamentary Under-Secretary of State

Home Office

February 17, 2000

SCHEDULE

SCHEDULE 1

EXEMPTIONS FROM SUBJECT INFORMATION PROVISIONS

1.—Offices to which appointments are made by Her Majesty:

(a) Archbishops, diocesan and suffragan bishops in the Church of England
(b) Deans of cathedrals of the Church of England
(c) Deans and Canons of the two Royal Peculiars
(d) The First and Second Church Estates Commissioners
(e) Lord-Lieutenants
(f) Masters of Trinity College and Churchill College, Cambridge
(g) The Provost of Eton
(h) The Poet Laureate
(i) The Astronomer Royal

Data Protection (Miscellaneous Subject Access Exemptions) Order 2000

(SI 2000/419)

[MADE: FEBRUARY 17, 2000]

[COMING INTO FORCE: MARCH 1, 2000]

App 2–10 Whereas a draft of this Order has been laid before and approved by a resolution of each House of Parliament

Whereas the Secretary of State considers it necessary for the safeguarding of the interests of data subjects or the rights and freedoms of other individuals that the prohibitions or restrictions on disclosure contained in the enactments and instruments listed in the Schedule to this Order ought to prevail over section 7 of the Data Protection Act 1998;

Now, therefore, the Secretary of State, in exercise of the powers conferred on him by sections 38(1) and 67(2) of the Data Protection Act 1998, and after consultation with the Data Protection Commissioner in accordance with section 67(3) of that Act, hereby makes the following Order—

1.—This Order may be cited as the Data Protection (Miscellaneous Subject Access Exemptions) Order 2000 and shall come into force on March 1, 2000.

2.—Personal data consisting of information the disclosure of which is prohibited or restricted by the enactments and instruments listed in the Schedule to this Order are exempt from section 7 of the Data Protection Act 1998.

Signatures

Mike O'Brien

Parliamentary Under-Secretary of State

Home Office

February 17, 2000

SCHEDULE

SCHEDULE 1

EXEMPTIONS FROM SECTION 7

PART I

ENACTMENTS AND INSTRUMENTS EXTENDING TO THE UNITED KINGDOM

1.—Human fertilisation and embryology: information about the provision of treatment services, the keeping or use of gametes or embryos and whether identifiable individuals were born in consequence of treatment services.

Sections 31 and 33 of the Human Fertilisation and Embryology Act 1990.[1]

PART II

ENACTMENTS AND INSTRUMENTS EXTENDING TO ENGLAND AND WALES

1.—(a) Adoption records and reports

Sections 50 and 51 of the Adoption Act 1976.[2]

Regulations 6 and 14 of the Adoption Agencies Regulations 1983[3] [. . .][4]

Rules 5, 6, 9, 17, 18, 21, 22 and 53 of the Adoption Rules 1984.[5]

Rules 5, 6, 9, 17, 18, 21, 22 and 32 of the Magistrates' Courts (Adoption) Rules 1984.[6]

(b) Statement of child's special educational needs

Regulation 19 of the Educational (Special Educational Needs) Regulations 1994.

(c) Parental order records and reports

Sections 50 and 51of the Adoption Act 1976 as modified by paragraphs 4(a) and (b) of Schedule 1 to the Parental Orders (Human Fertilisation and Embryology) Regulations 1994 in relation to parental orders made under section 30 of the Human Fertilisation and Embryology Act 1990.

Rules 4A.5 and 4A.9 of the Family Proceedings Rules 1991.[7]

Rules 21E and 21I of the Family Proceedings Courts (Children Act 1989) Rules 1991.[8]

PART III

ENACTMENTS AND INSTRUMENTS EXTENDING TO SCOTLAND

1.—(a) Adoption records and reports

Section 45 of the Adoption (Scotland) Act 1978.[9]

Regulation 23 of the Adoption Agencies (Scotland) Regulations 1996[10] [. . .].[11]

---

1 s.33 was amended by s.1 of the Human Fertilisation and Embryology (Disclosure of Information) Act 1992 (c.54).

2 s.51 was amended by para.20 of Sch.10 to the Children Act 1989 (c.41).

3 As amended by reg. 2 of SI 1997/2308 and reg. 2 of SI 1997/649.

4 Words ", so far as they relate to records and other information in the possession of local authorities" omitted by SI 2000/1865 (Data Protection (Miscellaneous Subject Access Exemptions) (Amendment) Order), Art.2(2).

5 As amended by SI 1991/1880.

6 As amended by SI 1989/384 (L.7) and para.4 of Sch.2 to SI 1991/1991.

7 As amended by SI 1994/2165.

8 As amended by SI 1994/2166.

9 s.45 was amended by para.41 of Sch.10 to the Children Act 1989 (c.41) and para.22 of Sch.2 to the Children (Scotland) Act 1995 (c.36).

10 s.254.

11 Words ", so far as it relates to records and other information in the possession of locla authorities" omitted by SI 2000/1865 (Data Protection (Miscellaneous Subject Access Exemptions) (Amendment) Order), Art.2(3).

Rule 67.3 of the Act of Sederunt (Rules of the Court of Session 1994) 1994.
Rules 2.12, 2.14, 2.30 and 2.33 of the Act of Sederunt (Child Care and Maintenance Rules) 1997.[12]
Regulation 8 of the Adoption Allowance (Scotland) Regulations 1996.

(b) Information provided by principal reporter for children's hearing
Rules 5 and 21 of the Children's Hearings (Scotland) Rules 1996.

(c) Record of child or young person's special educational needs
Section 60(4) of the Education (Scotland) Act 1980.[13]
Proviso (bb) to regulation 7(2) of the Education (Record of Needs) (Scotland) Regulations 1982.

(d) Parental order records and reports
Section 45 of the Adoption (Scotland) Act 1978 as modified by paragraph 10 of Schedule 1 to the Parental Orders (Human Fertilisation and Embryology) (Scotland) Regulations 1994[14] in relation to parental orders made under section 30 of the Human Fertilisation and Embryology Act 1990.
Rules 2.47 and 2.59 of the Act of Sederunt (Child Care and Maintenance Rules) 1997.
Rules 81.3 and 81.18 of the Act of Sederunt (Rules of the Court of Session 1994) 1994.[15]

PART IV

ENACTMENTS AND INSTRUMENTS EXTENDING TO NORTHERN IRELAND

1.—(a) Adoption records and reports
Articles 50 and 54 of the Adoption (Northern Ireland) Act 1987.[16]
Rule 53 of Order 84 of the Rules of the Supreme Court (Northern Ireland) 1980.[17]
Rule 22 of the County Court (Adoption) Rules (Northern Ireland) 1980.
Rule 32 of Order 50 of the County Court Rules (Northern Ireland) 1981.[18]

(b) Statement of child's special educational needs
Regulation 17 of the Education (Special Educational Needs) Regulations (Northern Ireland) 1997.

(c) Parental order records and reports
Articles 50 and 54 of the Adoption (Northern Ireland) Order 1987 as modified by paragraph 5(a) and (e) of Schedule 2 to the Parental Orders (Human Fertilisation and Embryology) Regulations 1994 in respect of parental orders made under section 30 of the Human Fertilisation and Embryology Act 1990.
Rules 4, 5 and 16 of Order 84A of the Rules of the Supreme Court (Northern Ireland) 1980.[19]
Rules 3, 4 and 15 of Order 50A of the County Court Rules (Northern Ireland) 1981.[20]

---

12 s.19.
13 s.60 was amended by s.4 of the Education (Scotland) Act 1981 (c.58).
14 As amended by SI 1994/2804 s.141.
15 s.143.
16 SI 1987/2203 (N.I. 22). Art.54 was amended by para.158 of Sch.9 to SI 1995/755 (N.I. 2).
17 S.R. (N.I.) 1980 No.346 as amended by S.R. (N.I.) 1989 No.343.
18 S.R. (N.I.) 1981 No.225 as amended by S.R. (N.I.) 1989 No.307.
19 S.R. (N.I.) 1980 No.346, as amended by S.R. (N.I.) 1995 No.2.
20 S.R. (N.I.) 1981 No.225, as amended by S.R. (N.I.) 1995 No.48.

The Data Protection (Processing of Sensitive Personal Data) (Elected Representatives) Order 2002

(SI 2002/2905)

[MADE: NOVEMBER 19, 2002]

[COMING INTO FORCE: DECEMBER 17, 2002]

Whereas a draft of this Order has been laid before and approved by a resolution of each House of Parliament: App 2–11

Now, therefore, the Lord Chancellor, in exercise of the powers conferred upon him by section 67(2) of, and paragraph 10 of Schedule 3 to, the Data Protection Act 1998,[1] and after consultation with the Information Commissioner[2] in accordance with section 67(3) of that Act, hereby makes the following Order:

1. This Order may be cited as the Data Protection (Processing of Sensitive Personal Data) (Elected Representatives) Order 2002 and shall come into force on the twenty-eighth day after the day on which it is made.

2. For the purposes of paragraph 10 of Schedule 3 to the Data Protection Act 1998, the circumstances specified in any of paragraphs 3, 4, 5 or 6 in the Schedule to this Order are circumstances in which sensitive personal data may be processed.[3]

Signed by the authority of the Lord Chancellor

Yvette Cooper

Parliamentary Secretary, Lord Chancellor's Department

19th November 2002

---

1 1998 c. 29. The functions of the Secretary of State under s.67 of, and para.10 of Sch.3 to, the Data Protection Act 1998 were transferred to the Lord Chancellor by Art.3 of, and para.11 of Sch.1 to, the Transfer of Functions (Miscellaneous) Order 2001 (S.I. 2001/3500). Art.8 of, and paras 6(v) and (z) of Sch.2 to, that Order amended s.67 of, and Sch.3 to, the Data Protection Act 1998 so as to refer to the Lord Chancellor.

2 The Data Protection Commissioner became the Information Commissioner on January 30, 2001 by virtue of ss 18(1) and 87(2)(a) of the Freedom of Information Act 2000 (c.36). The consultation requirement in s.67(3) of the Data Protection Act 1998 now refers to the Information Commissioner as the definitions of "the Commissioner" in ss 6(1) and 70(1) of that Act have been amended by paras 13(2) and 14(a) of Sch.2 to the Freedom of Information Act 2000.

3 Additional circumstances in which sensitive personal data may be processed are specified in the Data Protection (Processing of Sensitive Personal Data) Order 2000 (SI 2000/417).

SCHEDULE

Article 2

CIRCUMSTANCES IN WHICH SENSITIVE PERSONAL DATA MAY BE PROCESSED

Interpretation

1.—In this Schedule, "elected representative" means—

(a) a Member of the House of Commons, a Member of the National Assembly for Wales, a Member of the Scottish Parliament or a Member of the Northern Ireland Assembly;
(b) a Member of the European Parliament elected in the United Kingdom;
(c) an elected member of a local authority within the meaning of section 270(1) of the Local Government Act 1972,[4] namely—
  (i) in England, a county council, a district council, a London borough council or a parish council,
  (ii) in Wales, a county council, a county borough council or a community council;
(d) an elected mayor of a local authority within the meaning of Part II of the Local Government Act 2000[5];
(e) the Mayor of London or an elected member of the London Assembly;
(f) an elected member of—
  (i) the Common Council of the City of London, or
  (ii) the Council of the Isles of Scilly;
(g) an elected member of a council constituted under section 2 of the Local Government etc (Scotland) Act 1994[6]; or
(h) an elected member of a district council within the meaning of the Local Government Act (Northern Ireland) 1972.[7]

2.—For the purposes of paragraph 1 above—

(a) a person who is—
  (i) a Member of the House of Commons immediately before Parliament is dissolved,
  (ii) a Member of the Scottish Parliament immediately before that Parliament is dissolved, or
  (iii) a Member of the Northern Ireland Assembly immediately before that Assembly is dissolved,

shall be treated as if he were such a member until the end of the fourth day after the day on which the subsequent general election in relation to that Parliament or Assembly is held;

(b) a person who is a Member of the National Assembly for Wales and whose term of office comes to an end, in accordance with section 2(5)(b) of the Government of Wales Act 1998,[8] at the end of the day preceding an ordinary election (within

4 1972 c. 70.
5 2000 c. 22.
6 1994 c. 39.
7 1972 c. 9 (N. I.).
8 1998 c. 38. S.2(5) provides that "The term of office of an Assembly member—(a) begins when he is declared to be returned as an Assembly member, and (b) continues until the end of the day before the day of the poll at the next ordinary election." By s.2(4), "An ordinary election involves the holding of elections for the return of the entire Assembly."

the meaning of section 2(4) of that Act), shall be treated as if he were such a member until the end of the fourth day after the day on which that ordinary election is held; and

(c) a person who is an elected member of the Common Council of the City of London and whose term of office comes to an end at the end of the day preceding the annual Wardmotes[9] shall be treated as if he were such a member until the end of the fourth day after the day on which those Wardmotes are held.

Processing by elected representatives

3.—The processing—

(a) is carried out by an elected representative or a person acting with his authority;
(b) is in connection with the discharge of his functions as such a representative;
(c) is carried out pursuant to a request made by the data subject to the elected representative to take action on behalf of the data subject or any other individual; and
(d) is necessary for the purposes of, or in connection with, the action reasonably taken by the elected representative pursuant to that request.

4.—The processing—

(a) is carried out by an elected representative or a person acting with his authority;
(b) is in connection with the discharge of his functions as such a representative;
(c) is carried out pursuant to a request made by an individual other than the data subject to the elected representative to take action on behalf of the data subject or any other individual;
(d) is necessary for the purposes of, or in connection with, the action reasonably taken by the elected representative pursuant to that request; and
(e) is carried out without the explicit consent of the data subject because the processing—
    (i) is necessary in a case where explicit consent cannot be given by the data subject,
    (ii) is necessary in a case where the elected representative cannot reasonably be expected to obtain the explicit consent of the data subject,
    (iii) must necessarily be carried out without the explicit consent of the data subject being sought so as not to prejudice the action taken by the elected representative, or
    (iv) is necessary in the interests of another individual in a case where the explicit consent of the data subject has been unreasonably withheld.

Processing limited to disclosures to elected representatives

5.—The disclosure—

(a) is made to an elected representative or a person acting with his authority;
(b) is made in response to a communication to the data controller from the elected representative, or a person acting with his authority, acting pursuant to a request made by the data subject;

---

9 By s.2 of the Act of Common Council made on June 14, 1984, the annual Wardmotes for the election of Common Councilmen to the Common Council of the City of London are held on the first Friday in December each year, and persons elected as Common Councilmen cease to hold office at midnight on the Thursday immediately preceding the day of the next annual Wardmotes. (Copies of the Act of Common Council made on June 14, 1984 can be obtained from the Town Clerk's Department, Corporation of London, PO Box 270, Guildhall, London EC2P 2EJ.)

(c) is of sensitive personal data which are relevant to the subject matter of that communication; and
(d) is necessary for the purpose of responding to that communication.

6.—The disclosure—

(a) is made to an elected representative or a person acting with his authority;
(b) is made in response to a communication to the data controller from the elected representative, or a person acting with his authority, acting pursuant to a request made by an individual other than the data subject;
(c) is of sensitive personal data which are relevant to the subject matter of that communication;
(d) is necessary for the purpose of responding to that communication; and
(e) is carried out without the explicit consent of the data subject because the disclosure—
   (i) is necessary in a case where explicit consent cannot be given by the data subject,
   (ii) is necessary in a case where the data controller cannot reasonably be expected to obtain the explicit consent of the data subject,
   (iii) must necessarily be carried out without the explicit consent of the data subject being sought so as not to prejudice the action taken by the elected representative, or
   (iv) is necessary in the interests of another individual in a case where the explicit consent of the data subject has been unreasonably withheld.

APPENDIX 3

Codes of Practice and Guidance

Lord Chancellor's Code Of Practice on the Discharge of Public Authorities Functions under Part I of the Freedom of Information Act 2000

(ISSUED UNDER SECTION 45 OF THE ACT)

[NOVEMBER 2002]

Foreword

Introduction

1. The Code of Practice, to which this is a foreword, fulfils the duty on the Lord Chancellor set out in section 45 of the Freedom of Information Act 2000, to provide guidance to public authorities as to the practice which it would, in his opinion, be desirable for them to follow in connection with the discharge of their functions under Part I of the Act. It is envisaged that Regulations to be made with respect to environmental information will make provision for the issue by the Secretary of State of a Code of Practice applying to the discharge of authorities' functions under those Regulations. App 3–01

2. This foreword does not form part of the Code itself.

3. The Government is committed to greater openness in the public sector. The Freedom of Information Act will further this aim by helping to transform the culture of the public sector to one of greater openness, enabling members of the public to question the decisions of public authorities more closely and ensuring that services provided by the public sector are more efficiently and properly delivered. Conformity with the Code will assist this.

4. The Code is a supplement to the provisions in the Act. It is not a substitute for legislation. Public authorities should seek legal advice as considered necessary on general issues relating to the implementation of the Act, or its application to individual cases.

Practice Recommendations

5. Under the provisions of section 47 of the Act, the Information Commissioner has a duty to promote the observance of this Code by public authorities. If it appears to the

Commissioner that the practice of a public authority in the exercise of its functions under Part I of the Act does not conform with that proposed in the Code of Practice, he may give to the authority a recommendation, under section 48 (known as a "practice recommendation"), specifying the steps which should, in his opinion, be taken to promote such conformity.

6. A practice recommendation must be given in writing and must refer to the particular provisions of the Code of Practice with which, in the Commissioner's opinion, the public authority's practice does not conform. A practice recommendation is simply a recommendation and cannot be directly enforced by the Information Commissioner. However, a failure to comply with a practice recommendation may lead to a failure to comply with the Act. Further, a failure to take account of a practice recommendation may lead to an adverse comment in a report to Parliament by the Commissioner.

7. It should be noted that because the provisions of the Act relating to the general right of access will not be brought into force until January 1, 2005, the Commissioner's powers to issue practice recommendations in relation to the handling of individual requests for information under the general right of access will not take effect before that date.

Information Notices

8. The Information Commissioner determines whether the practice of a public authority conforms to the Code. Under section 51 of the Act, he may serve an information notice on the authority, requiring it to provide information relating to its conformity with the Code.

9. Under the provisions of section 54 of the Act, if a public authority fails to comply with an information notice, the Commissioner may certify in writing to the court that the public authority has failed to comply with that notice. The court may then inquire into the matter and, after hearing any witnesses who may be produced against or on behalf of, the public authority, and after hearing any statement that may be offered in defence, deal with the authority as if it had committed a contempt of court.

Duty to provide advice and assistance

10. Section 16 of the Act places a duty on public authorities to provide advice and assistance to applicants. A public authority is deemed to have complied with this duty in any particular case if it has conformed with the Code in relation to the provision of advice and assistance in that case. The duty to assist and advise is enforceable by the Information Commissioner. If a public authority fails in its statutory duty, the Commissioner may issue a decision notice under section 50, or an enforcement notice under section 52.

11. Public authorities should not forget that other Acts of Parliament may be relevant to the way in which authorities provide advice and assistance to applicants or potential applicants, e.g. the Disability Discrimination Act 1995 and the Race Relations Act 1976 (as amended by the Race Relations (Amendment) Act 2000).

Main Features of the Act

12. The main features of the Freedom of Information Act 2000 are:

i. a general right of access to recorded information held by public authorities, subject to certain conditions and exemptions;
ii. in cases where information is exempted from disclosure, except where an absolute exemption applies, a duty on public authorities to:

a. inform the applicant whether they hold the information requested, and
b. communicate the information to him or her,

unless the public interest in maintaining the exemption in question outweighs the public interest in disclosure;

iii. a duty on every public authority to adopt and maintain a scheme, approved by the Commissioner, which relates to the publication of information by the authority, and to publish information in accordance with the scheme. An authority may adopt a model scheme approved by the Commissioner, which may have been prepared by the Commissioner or by other persons;

iv. a new office of Information Commissioner with wide powers to enforce the rights created by the Act and to promote good practice, and a new Information Tribunal;

v. a duty on the Lord Chancellor to promulgate Codes of Practice for guidance on specific issues.

Copyright

13. Public authorities should be aware that information which is disclosed under the Act may be subject to copyright protection. If an applicant wishes to use any such information in a way that would infringe copyright, for example by making multiple copies, or issuing copies to the public, he or she would require a licence from the copyright holder. HMSO have issued guidance on this subject in relation to Crown Copyright, which is available on HMSO's website or by contacting HMSO at:

HMSO Licensing Division
St Clements House
2–16 Colegate
Norwich NR3 1BQ
Tel: 01613–621000
Fax: 01603–723000
email: hmsolicensing@cabinet-office.x.gsi.gov.uk

Training

14. All communications in writing to a public authority, including those transmitted by electronic means, potentially amount to a request for information within the meaning of the Act, and if they do, they must be dealt with in accordance with the provisions of the Act. It is therefore essential that everyone working in a public authority who deals with correspondence, or who otherwise may be required to provide information, is familiar with the requirements of the Act and the Codes of Practice issued under its provisions and takes account of any relevant guidance on good practice issued by the Commissioner. Authorities should ensure that proper training is provided in this regard.

15. In planning and delivering training authorities should be aware of other provisions affecting the disclosure of information such as Environmental Information Regulations and the Data Protection Act 1998.

Code of Practice on the Discharge of the Functions of Public Authorities Under Part I of the Freedom of Information Act 2000

The Lord Chancellor, after consulting the Information Commissioner, issues the following Code of Practice pursuant to section 45 of the Act.

Laid before Parliament on November 20, 2002 pursuant to section 45(5) of the Freedom of Information Act 2000.

I Introduction

1. This code of practice outlines to public authorities the practice which it would, in the opinion of the Lord Chancellor, be desirable for them to follow in connection with the discharge of their functions under Part I (Access to information held by public authorities) of the Freedom of Information Act 2000 ("the Act").

2. The aims of the Code are to:

- facilitate the disclosure of information under the Act by setting out good administrative practice that it is desirable for public authorities to follow when handling requests for information, including, where appropriate, the transfer of a request to a different authority;
- protect the interests of applicants by setting out standards for the provision of advice which it would be good practice to make available to them and to encourage the development of effective means of complaining about decisions taken under the Act;
- ensure that the interests of third parties who may be affected by any decision to disclose information are considered by the authority by setting standards for consultation; and
- ensure that authorities consider the implications for Freedom of Information before agreeing to confidentiality provisions in contracts and accepting information in confidence from a third party more generally.

3. Although there is a statutory duty on the Lord Chancellor to issue the Code, the provisions of the Code themselves do not have statutory force. However, authorities are expected to abide by the Code unless there are good reasons, capable of being justified to the Information Commissioner, why it would be inappropriate to do so. The statutory requirements for dealing with requests for information are contained in the Act and regulations made under it and public authorities must comply with these statutory provisions at all times. However, section 47 of the Act places a duty on the Information Commissioner to promote the following of good practice by public authorities ("good practice" includes compliance with the provisions of the Code), and section 48 of the Act enables the Information Commissioner to issue a "practice recommendation" to a public authority if it appears to him that the practice of the authority does not conform with that proposed in the Code. Further, section 16 of the Act places a duty on public authorities to provide advice and assistance to applicants and potential applicants. Authorities will have complied with this duty in any particular case if they have conformed with the Code in relation to the provision of advice or assistance in that case.

4. Words and expressions used in this Code have the same meaning as the same words and expressions used in the Act.

II The provision of advice and assistance to persons making requests for information

5. Every public authority should be ready to provide advice and assistance, including but not necessarily limited to the steps set out below, to those who propose to make, or have made requests to it, in order to facilitate their use of the Act. The duty on the public authority is to provide advice and assistance "so far as it would be reasonable to expect the authority to do so". Any public authority which conforms with this Code in relation to the provision of advice and assistance in any case will be taken to comply with this duty in relation to that case.

6. Public authorities should publish their procedures for dealing with requests for information. These procedures may include what the public authority's usual procedure

will be where it does not hold the information requested. (See also VI — "Transferring requests for information".) It may also alert potential applicants to the fact that the public authority may need to consult other public authorities and/or third parties in order to reach a decision on whether the requested information can be released, and therefore alert potential applicants that they may wish to be notified before any transfer of request or consultation is made and if so, they should say so in their applications. (See also VII — "Consultation with third parties".) The procedures should include an address or addresses (including an e-mail address where possible) to which applicants may direct requests for information or for assistance. A telephone number should also be provided, where possible that of a named individual who can provide assistance. These procedures should be referred to in the authority's publication scheme.

7. Staff working in public authorities in contact with the public should bear in mind that not everyone will be aware of the Act, or Regulations made under it, and they will need to draw these to the attention of potential applicants who appear unaware of them.

8. A request for information under the Act's general right of access must be made in writing (which includes a request transmitted by electronic means which is received in legible form and is capable of being used for subsequent reference). Where a person is unable to frame their request in writing, the public authority should ensure that appropriate assistance is given to enable that person to make a request for information. Depending on the circumstances, appropriate assistance might include:

- advising the person that another person or agency (such as a Citizens Advice Bureau) may be able to assist them with the application, or make the application on their behalf;
- in exceptional circumstances, offering to take a note of the application over the telephone and then send the note to the applicant for confirmation (in which case the written note of the telephone request, once verified by the applicant and returned, would constitute a written request for information and the statutory time limit for reply would begin when the written confirmation was received).

This list is not exhaustive, and public authorities should be flexible in offering advice and assistance most appropriate to the circumstances of the applicant.

9. Where the applicant does not describe the information sought in a way which would enable the public authority to identify or locate it, or the request is ambiguous, the authority should, as far as practicable, provide assistance to the applicant to enable him or her to describe more clearly the information requested. Authorities should be aware that the aim of providing assistance is to clarify the nature of the information sought, not to determine the aims or motivation of the applicant. Care should be taken not to give the applicant the impression that he or she is obliged to disclose the nature of his or her interest or that he or she will be treated differently if he or she does. It is important that the applicant is contacted as soon as possible, preferably by telephone, fax or e-mail, where more information is needed to clarify what is sought.

10. Appropriate assistance in this instance might include:

- providing an outline of the different kinds of information which might meet the terms of the request;
- providing access to detailed catalogues and indexes, where these are available, to help the applicant ascertain the nature and extent of the information held by the authority;
- providing a general response to the request setting out options for further information which could be provided on request;

This list is not exhaustive, and public authorities should be flexible in offering advicc and assistance most appropriate to the circumstances of the applicant.

11. In seeking to clarify what is sought public authorities should bear in mind that applicants cannot reasonably be expected to possess identifiers such as a file reference number, or a description of a particular record, unless this information is made available by the authority for the use of applicants.

12. If, following the provision of such assistance, the applicant still fails to describe the information requested in a way which would enable the authority to identify and locate it, the authority is not expected to seek further clarification. The authority should disclose any information relating to the application which has been successfully identified and found for which it does not wish to claim an exemption. It should also explain to the applicant why it cannot take the request any further and provide details of the authority's complaints procedure and the applicant's rights under section 50 of the Act (see "Complaints Procedure" in section XII below).

13. Where the applicant indicates that he or she is not prepared to pay the fee notified in any fees notice given to the applicant, the authority should consider whether there is any information that may be of interest to the applicant that is available free of charge.

14. Where an authority is not obliged to comply with a request for information because, under section 12(1) and regulations made under section 12(4), the cost of complying would exceed the "appropriate limit" (*i.e* cost threshold), and where the public authority is not prepared to comply on a discretionary basis because of the cost of doing so, the authority should consider providing an indication of what information could be provided within the cost ceiling.

15. An authority is not expected to provide assistance to applicants whose requests are vexatious within the meaning of section 14 of the Act.

III Handling requests for information which appear to be part of an organised campaign

16. Where an authority is not required to comply with a number of related requests because, under section 12(1) and regulations made under section 12(4), the cumulative cost of complying with the requests would exceed the "appropriate limit" (*i.e.* cost threshold) prescribed in Fees Regulations, the authority should consider whether the information could be disclosed in another, more cost-effective, manner. For example, the authority should consider if the information is such that publication on the authority's website, and a brief notification of the website reference to each applicant, would bring the cost within the appropriate limit.

IV Timeliness in dealing with requests for information

17. Public authorities are required to comply with all requests for information promptly and they should not delay responding until the end of the 20 working day period under section 10(1) if the information could reasonably have been provided earlier.

18. Public authorities should aim to make *all* decisions within 20 working days, including in cases where a public authority needs to consider where the public interest lies in respect of an application for exempt information. However, it is recognised there will be some instances where it will not be possible to deal with such an application within 20 working days. Although there is no statutory time limit on the length of time the authority may take to reach a decision where the public interest must be considered, it must, under section 17(2), give an estimate of the date by which it expects to reach such a decision. In these instances, authorities are expected to give estimates which are realistic and reasonable in the circumstances of the particular case, taking account, for example, of the need to consult third parties where this is necessary. Public authorities are expected to comply with their estimates unless there are good reasons not to. If the public authority exceeds its estimate, it should apologise to the applicant and explain the reason(s) for the delay. If a public authority finds, while considering the public interest, that the estimate given

is proving unrealistic, it should keep the applicant informed. Public authorities should keep a record of instances where estimates are exceeded, and where this happens more than occasionally, take steps to identify the problem and rectify it.

V Charging fees

19. The Act does not require charges to be made, but public authorities have discretion to charge applicants a fee in accordance with Fees Regulations made under sections 9, 12 and 13 of the Act in respect of requests made under the general right of access.

20. The Fees Regulations do not apply:

- to material made available under a publication scheme under section 19;
- to information which is reasonably accessible to the applicant by other means within the meaning of the exemption provided for at section 21; or
- where provision is made by or under any enactment as to the fee that may be charged by the public authority for disclosure of the information as provided in sections 9(5) and 13(3) of the Act".

Public authorities should ensure that any charges they make in cases falling outside those covered by the Fees Regulations are in accordance with any relevant legislation and are within the terms of any relevant guidance which has been issued or approved by HM Treasury and which is applicable to the public authority, or any relevant guidance issued or approved by the Northern Ireland Department of Finance and Personnel applicable to devolved public bodies in Northern Ireland.

VI Transferring requests for information

21. A request can only be transferred where a public authority receives a request for information which it does not hold, within the meaning of section 3(2) of the Act, but which is held by another public authority. If a public authority in receipt of a request holds some of the information requested, a transfer can only be made in respect of the information it does not hold (but is held by another public authority).

22. Public authorities should bear in mind that "holding" information includes holding a copy of a record produced or supplied by another person or body (but does not extend to holding a record on behalf of another person or body as provided for in section 3(2)(a) of the Act).

23. The authority receiving the initial request must always process it in accordance with the Act in respect of such information relating to the request as it holds. The authority should also advise the applicant that it does not hold part of the requested information, or all of it, whichever applies. But before doing this, the authority must be certain as to the extent of the information relating to the request which it holds itself.

24. If the authority to whom the original request was made believes that some or all of the information requested is held by another public authority, the authority should consider what would be the most helpful way of assisting the applicant with his or her request. In most cases this is likely to involve:

- contacting the applicant and informing him or her that the information requested may be held by another public authority;
- suggesting that the applicant re-applies to the authority which the original authority believes to hold the information;
- providing him or her with contact details for that authority.

25. However, in some cases the authority to whom the original request is made may consider it to be more appropriate to transfer the request to another authority in respect of the information which it does not hold. In such cases, the authority should consult the other authority with a view to ascertaining whether it does hold the information and, if

so, consider whether it should transfer the request to it. A request (or part of a request) should not be transferred without confirmation by the second authority that it holds the information.

26. Before transferring a request for information to another authority, the authority should consider:

- whether a transfer is appropriate; and if so
- whether the applicant is likely to have any grounds to object to the transfer;

If the authority reasonably concludes that the applicant is not likely to object, it may transfer the request without going back to the applicant, but should tell him or her it has done so.

27. Where there are reasonable grounds to believe an applicant is likely to object, the authority should only transfer the request to another authority with his or her consent. If the authority is in any doubt, it may prefer contact the applicant with a view to suggesting that he or she makes a new request to the other authority, as in paragraph 23 above.

28. Where a request or part of a request is transferred from one public authority to another, the receiving authority must comply with its obligations under Part I of the Act in the same way as it would for a request that is received direct from an applicant. The time for complying with such a request will be measured from the day that the receiving authority receives the request.

29. All transfers of requests should take place as soon as is practicable, and the applicant should be informed as soon as possible once this has been done.

30. Where a public authority is unable either to advise the applicant which public authority holds, or may hold, the requested information or to facilitate the transfer of the request to another authority (or considers it inappropriate to do so) it should consider what advice, if any, it can provide to the applicant to enable him or her to pursue his or her request.

VII Consultation With Third Parties

31. In some cases the disclosure of information pursuant to a request may affect the legal rights of a third party, for example where information is subject to the common law duty of confidence or where it constitutes "personal data" within the meaning of the Data Protection Act 1998 ("the DPA"). Public authorities must always remember that unless an exemption provided for in the Act applies in relation to any particular information, they will be obliged to disclose that information in response to a request.

32. Where a disclosure of information cannot be made without the consent of a third party (for example, where information has been obtained from a third party and in the circumstances the disclosure of the information without their consent would constitute an actionable breach of confidence such that the exemption at section 41 of the Act would apply), the authority should consult that third party with a view to seeking their consent to the disclosure, unless such a consultation is not practicable, for example because the third party cannot be located or because the costs of consulting them would be disproportionate.

33. Where information constitutes "personal data" within the meaning of the DPA, public authorities should have regard to section 40 of the Act which makes detailed provision for cases in which a request relates to such information and the interplay between the Act and the DPA in such cases.

34. Where the interests of the third party which may be affected by a disclosure do not give rise to legal rights, consultation may still be appropriate.

35. Consultation should take place where:

- the views of the third party may assist the authority to determine whether an exemption under the Act applies to the information requested; or

- the views of the third party may assist the authority to determine where the public interest lies under section 2 of the Act.

36. A public authority may consider that consultation is not appropriate where the cost of consulting with third parties would be disproportionate. In such cases, the authority should consider what is the most reasonable course of action for it to take in light of the requirements of the Act and the individual circumstances of the request.

37. Consultation will be unnecessary where:

- the public authority does not intend to disclose the information relying on some other legitimate ground under the terms of the Act;
- the views of the third party can have no effect on the decision of the authority, for example, where there is other legislation preventing or requiring the disclosure of this information;
- no exemption applies and so under the Act's provisions, the information must be provided.

38. Where the interests of a number of third parties may be affected by a disclosure and those parties have a representative organisation which can express views on behalf of those parties, the authority may, if it considers consultation appropriate, consider that it would be sufficient to consult that representative organisation. If there is no representative organisation, the authority may consider that it would be sufficient to consult a representative sample of the third parties in question.

39. The fact that the third party has not responded to consultation does not relieve the authority of its duty to disclose information under the Act, or its duty to reply within the time specified in the Act.

40. In all cases, it is for the public authority, not the third party (or representative of the third party) to determine whether or not information should be disclosed under the Act. A refusal to consent to disclosure by a third party does not, in itself, mean information should be withheld.

VIII Freedom of Information and public sector contracts

41. When entering into contracts public authorities should refuse to include contractual terms which purport to restrict the disclosure of information held by the authority and relating to the contract beyond the restrictions permitted by the Act. Public authorities cannot "contract out" of their obligations under the Act. Unless an exemption provided for under the Act is applicable in relation to any particular information, a public authority will be obliged to disclose that information in response to a request, regardless of the terms of any contract.

42. When entering into contracts with non-public authority contractors, public authorities may be under pressure to accept confidentiality clauses so that information relating to the terms of the contract, its value and performance will be exempt from disclosure. Public authorities should reject such clauses wherever possible. Where, exceptionally, it is necessary to include non-disclosure provisions in a contract, an option could be to agree with the contractor a schedule of the contract which clearly identifies information which should not be disclosed. But authorities will need to take care when drawing up any such schedule, and be aware that any restrictions on disclosure provided for could potentially be overridden by their obligations under the Act, as described in the paragraph above.

43. In any event, public authorities should not agree to hold information 'in confidence' which is not in fact confidential in nature. Authorities should be aware that the exemption provided for in section 41 only applies if information has been obtained by a public authority from another person, and the disclosure of the information to the public, otherwise than under the Act would constitute a breach of confidence actionable by that, or any other person.

44. Any acceptance of such confidentiality provisions must be for good reasons and capable of being justified to the Commissioner.

45. It is for the public authority to disclose information pursuant to the Act, and not the non-public authority contractor. However, the public authority may wish to protect from disclosure by the contractor, by appropriate contractual terms, information which the authority has provided to the contractor which would clearly be exempt from disclosure under the Act, by appropriate contractual terms. In order to avoid unnecessary secrecy, any such constraints should be drawn as narrowly as possible, and according to the individual circumstances of the case. Apart from such cases, public authorities should not impose terms of secrecy on contractors.

46. Section 5(1)(b) of the Act empowers the Lord Chancellor to designate as public authorities for the purposes of the Act, persons (or bodies) who provide under a contract made with a public authority, any service whose provision is a function of that authority. Thus, some non-public authority contractors will be regarded as public authorities within the meaning of the Act, although only in respect of the services provided under the contract. As such, and to that extent, the contractor will be required to comply with the Act like any other public authority.

IX Accepting information in confidence from third parties

47. A public authority should only accept information from third parties in confidence if it is necessary to obtain that information in connection with the exercise of any of the authority's functions and it would not otherwise be provided. In addition, public authorities should not agree to hold information received from third parties "in confidence" which is not confidential in nature. Again, acceptance of any confidentiality provisions must be for good reasons, capable of being justified to the Commissioner.

X Consultation with devolved administrations

48. Public authorities should consult with the relevant devolved administration before disclosing information provided by or directly concerning that administration, except where:

- the views of the devolved administration can have no effect on the decision of the authority (for example where there is other legislation requiring the disclosure of the information), or there is no applicable exemption so the information must be disclosed under the Act; or
- in the circumstances, consultation would be disproportionate.

49. Similarly, the devolved administrations should consult with the relevant non-devolved public authority before disclosing information provided by or directly concerning that authority, except where the views of the public authority can have no effect on the decision whether to disclose, or where consultation would be disproportionate in the circumstances.

XI Refusal of request

50. Where a request for information is refused in reliance on an exemption, the Act requires that the authority notifies the applicant which exemption has been claimed, and if it would otherwise not be apparent, why that exemption applies. Public authorities should not (subject to the proviso in section 17(4), *i.e.* if the statement would involve the disclosure of information which would itself be exempt information) merely paraphrase the wording of the exemption. The Act also requires authorities, when withholding information (other than under an "absolute" exemption), to state the reasons for claiming that the public interest in maintaining the exemption outweighs the public interest in disclosure. Public authorities should specify the public interest factors (for and against

disclosure) which they have taken into account before reaching the decision (again, subject to the proviso in section 17(4)).

51. For monitoring purposes public authorities should keep a record of all applications where either all or part of the requested information is withheld. In addition to a record of the numbers of applications involved where information is withheld, senior managers in each public authority need information on each case to determine whether cases are being properly considered, and whether the reasons for refusals are sound. This could be done by requiring all staff who refuse a request for information to forward the details to a central point in the organisation for collation. Details of information on complaints about applications which have been refused (see XII — "Complaints procedure" below) could be collected at the same central point.

XII Complaints procedure

52. Each public authority should have a complaints procedure in place by the date that its duties in respect of the publication scheme provisions of the Act come into effect. The complaints procedure may then be used by any person who perceives that the authority is not complying with its publication scheme. If the matter cannot be dealt with satisfactorily on an informal basis, the public authority should inform such persons if approached by them of the details of its internal complaints procedure, and how to contact the Information Commissioner, if the complainant wishes to write to him about the matter. The authority should also explain that although the complainant cannot apply to the Commissioner for a decision under section 50 of the Act, the Commissioner may investigate the matter at his discretion.

53. When the provisions of the Act relating to the general right of access come into force, the complaints procedure will also be required for dealing with complaints from people who consider that their request has not been properly handled, or who are otherwise dissatisfied with the outcome of the consideration of their request, and where the issue is such that it cannot be resolved informally in discussion with the official dealing with the request. If a public authority has failed to introduce a complaints procedure, an applicant is entitled, under the Act, to complain directly to the Commissioner.

54. When communicating any decision made in relation to a request under the Act's general right of access, public authorities are obliged, under section 17(7) of the Act notify the applicant of their rights of complaint. They should provide details of their own complaints procedure, including how to make a complaint and inform the applicant of the right to complain to the Commissioner under section 50 if he or she is still dissatisfied following the authority's review.

55. Any written reply from the applicant (including one transmitted by electronic means) expressing dissatisfaction with an authority's response to a valid request for information should be treated as a complaint, as should any written communication from a person who perceives the authority is not complying with its publication scheme. These communications should be handled in accordance with the authority's complaints procedure, even if, in the case of a request for information under the general right of access, the applicant does not state his or her desire for the authority to review their decision or their handling of the application.

56. The complaints procedure should be a fair and impartial means of dealing with handling problems and reviewing decisions taken pursuant to the Act, including decisions taken about where the public interest lies in respect of exempt information. It should be possible to reverse or otherwise amend decisions previously taken. Complaints procedures should be clear and not unnecessarily bureaucratic. They should be capable of producing a prompt determination of the complaint.

57. Where the complaint concerns a request for information under the general right of access, the review should be handled by a person who was not a party to the original decision, where this is practicable. If this is not possible (for example in a very small

public authority), the circumstances should be explained to the applicant. Where the decision on the application was taken by someone in a position where a review cannot realistically be undertaken (*e.g.* a Minister), the public authority may consider whether to waive the internal review procedure (and inform the applicant if this is what is decided), so that the applicant is free to approach the Commissioner.

58. In all cases, complaints should be acknowledged and the complainant should be informed of the authority's target date for determining the complaint. Where it is apparent that determination of the complaint will take longer than the target time (for example because of the complexity of the particular case), the authority should inform the applicant and explain the reason for the delay. The complainant should always be informed of the outcome of his or her complaint.

59. Authorities may set their own target times for dealing with complaints but these should be reasonable, defensible , and subject to regular review. Each public authority should publish its target times for determining complaints and information as to how successful it is with meeting those targets.

60. Records should be kept of all complaints and of their outcome. Authorities should have procedures in place for monitoring complaints and for reviewing, and, if necessary, amending, procedures for dealing with requests for information where such action is indicated by more than occasional reversals of initial decisions.

61. Where the outcome of a complaint is that information should be disclosed which was previously withheld, the information in question should be disclosed as soon as practicable and the applicant should be informed how soon this will be.

62. Where the outcome of a complaint is that the procedures within an authority have not been properly followed by the authority's staff, the authority should apologise to the applicant. The authority should also take appropriate steps to prevent similar errors occurring in future.

63. Where the outcome of a complaint is that an initial decision to withhold information is upheld, or is otherwise in the authority's favour, the applicant should be informed of his or her right to apply to the Commissioner, and be given details of how to make an application, for a decision on whether the request for information has been dealt with in accordance with the requirements of Part I of the Act.

Lord Chancellor's Code of Practice on the Management of Records

(ISSUED UNDER SECTION 46 OF THE FREEDOM OF INFORMATION ACT 2000)

[NOVEMBER 2002]

Foreword

General

i. This Code of Practice (hereafter referred to as "the Code") provides guidance to all public authorities as to the practice which it would, in the opinion of the Lord Chancellor, be desirable for them to follow in connection with the discharge of their functions under the Freedom of Information Act 2000 ("FOIA"). The Code applies also to other bodies that are subject to the Public Records Act 1958 and the Public Records Act (NI) 1923. **App 3–02**

ii. The Code fulfils the duty of the Lord Chancellor under section 46 of the FOIA.

iii. Any freedom of information legislation is only as good as the quality of the records to which it provides access. Such rights are of little use if reliable records are not created in the first place, if they cannot be found when needed or if the arrangements for their eventual archiving or destruction are inadequate. Consequently, all public authorities are strongly encouraged to pay heed to the guidance in the Code.

iv. The Code is a supplement to the provisions in the FOIA. But its adoption will help authorities to comply with their duties under that Act. It is not a substitute for legislation. Public authorities should seek legal advice as appropriate on general issues relating to the implementation of the FOIA, or its application to individual cases. The Code is complemented by the Code of Practice under section 45 of the FOIA and by Memoranda of Understanding setting out how the consultation requirements of section 66 of the FOIA will be put into effect.

v. The Information Commissioner will promote the observance of the Code by public authorities, acting as required by the FOIA. If it appears to the Commissioner that the practice of an authority in relation to the exercise of its functions under the FOIA does not conform with that set out in the Code, he may issue a practice recommendation under section 48 of the Act. A practice recommendation must be in writing and must specify the provisions of the Code which have not been met and the steps which should, in his opinion, be taken to promote conformity with Code.

vi. If the Commissioner reasonably requires any information for the purpose of determining whether the practice of a public authority in relation to the exercise of its functions under the FOIA conforms with that proposed in this Code, he may serve on the authority a notice (known as an "information notice") under the provisions of section 51 of the Act. This requires it, within such time as is specified in the notice, to furnish the Commissioner, in such form as may be so specified, with such information relating to conformity with the Code of Practice as is so specified.

vii. An information notice must contain a statement that the Commissioner regards the specified information as relevant for the purpose of deciding whether the practice of the authority conforms with that proposed in the Code of Practice and of his reasons for regarding that information as relevant for that purpose. It must also contain particulars of the rights of appeal conferred by section 57 of the FOIA.

viii. Authorities should note that if they are failing to comply with the Code, they may also be failing to comply with the Public Records Acts 1958 and 1967, the Local Government (Records) Act 1962, the Local Government Act 1972, the Local Government (Access to Information) Act 1985 or other record-keeping or archives legislation, and they may consequently be in breach of their statutory obligations.

ix. The Public Records Act (NI) 1923 sets out the duties of public record bodies in Northern Ireland in respect of the records they create and requires that records should be transferred to, and preserved by, the Public Record Office of Northern Ireland.

Main features of the FOIA

x. The main features of the FOIA are:

1. a general right of access to recorded information held by a wide range of bodies across the public sector, subject to certain conditions and exemptions. The right includes provisions in respect of historical records which are more than 30 years old.
2. in relation to most exempt information, the information must nonetheless be disclosed unless the public interest in maintaining the exemption in question outweighs the public interest in disclosure.
3. a duty on every public authority to adopt and maintain a scheme which relates to the publication of information by the authority and is approved by the Information Commissioner. Authorities must publish information in accordance with their publication schemes. This scheme must specify:
   a. classes of information which the public authority publishes or intends to publish;
   b. the manner in which information of each class is, or is intended to be, published; and
   c. whether the material is, or is intended to be, available to the public free of charge, or on payment.
4. a new office of Information Commissioner and a new Information Tribunal, with wide powers to enforce the rights created and to promote good practice;
5. a duty on the Lord Chancellor to promulgate Codes of Practice for guidance on specific issues;
6. the amendment of the public records system to integrate it with the new right of access under the FOIA.

Training

xi. All communications in writing (including by electronic means) to a public authority fall within the scope of the FOIA, if they seek information, and must be dealt with in accordance with the provisions of the Act. It is therefore essential that everyone working in a public authority is familiar with the provisions of the FOIA, the Codes of Practice issued under its provisions, any relevant Memoranda of Understanding, and any relevant guidance on good practice issued by the Commissioner. Authorities should ensure that proper training is provided.

xii. In planning and delivering training, authorities should be aware of other provisions affecting the disclosure of information, such as the Environmental Information Regulations 1992 and their successors which, for example, do not require requests to be in writing.

Authorities subject to the Public Records Acts

xiii. The guidance on records management and on the transfer of public records in the Code should be read in the context of existing legislation on record-keeping. In particular, the Public Records Act 1958 (as amended) gives duties to public record bodies in respect of the records they create. It also requires the Keeper of Public Records to supervise the discharge of those duties. Authorities that are subject to the Public Records Acts 1958 and 1967 should note that if they are failing to comply with the Code, they may also be failing to comply with those Acts.

xiv. The Public Records Act (NI) 1923 sets out the duties of public record bodies in Northern Ireland in respect of the records they create and requires that records should be transferred to, and preserved by, the Public Record Office of Northern Ireland.

xv. The Information Commissioner will promote the observance of the Code in consultation with the Keeper of Public Records when dealing with bodies which are subject to the Public Records Acts 1958 and 1967 and with the Deputy Keeper of the Records of Northern Ireland for bodies subject to the Public Records Act (NI) 1923.

xvi. If it appears to the Commissioner that the practice of an authority in relation to the exercise of its functions under the FOIA does not conform with that set out in the Code, he may issue a practice recommendation under section 48 of the Act. Before issuing such a recommendation to a body subject to the Public Records Acts 1958 and 1967 or the Public Records Act (NI) 1923, the Commissioner shall consult the Keeper of Public Records or the Deputy Keeper of the Records of Northern Ireland.

xvii. The content of this Code has been agreed by the Deputy Keeper of Records of Northern Ireland. Part II, in particular, describes the roles which public record bodies should perform to ensure the timely and effective review and transfer of public records to the Public Record Office or to places of deposit (as defined in Section 4 of the Public Records Act 1958) or to the Public Record Office of Northern Ireland (under the Public Records Act 1958 or the Public Records Act (NI) 1923). For the avoidance of doubt the term "public records" includes Welsh public records as defined by sections 116–118 of the Government of Wales Act 1998.

Role of the Lord Chancellor's Advisory Council on Public Records and of the Public Record Office

xviii. To advise authorities on the review of public records, the Lord Chancellor, having received the advice of his Advisory Council on Public Records, (hereafter "the Advisory Council") may prepare and issue guidance. This may include advice on the periods of time for which the Advisory Council considers it appropriate to withhold categories of sensitive records beyond the 30-year period. In Northern Ireland similar guidance shall be issued by the Deputy Keeper of the Records of Northern Ireland following consultation with the Departments responsible for the records affected by the guidance.

xix. The Public Record Office will provide support as appropriate to the Advisory Council in its consideration of applications from authorities in respect of public records and in its preparation of guidance to authorities. In Northern Ireland the Public Record Office of Northern Ireland will provide similar support to the Sensitivity Review Group.

CODE OF PRACTICE ON (1) THE MANAGEMENT OF RECORDS BY PUBLIC AUTHORITIES AND (2) THE TRANSFER AND REVIEW OF PUBLIC RECORDS UNDER THE FREEDOM OF INFORMATION ACT 2000

The Lord Chancellor, after consulting the Information Commissioner and the appropriate Northern Ireland Minister, issues the following Code of Practice pursuant to section 46 of the Freedom of Information Act.

Laid before Parliament on November 20, 2002 pursuant to section 46(6) of the Freedom of Information Act 2000.

Introduction

1. The aims of the Code are:

a. to set out practices which public authorities, and bodies subject to the Public Records Act 1958 and the Public Records Act (NI) 1923, should follow in relation to the creation, keeping, management and destruction of their records (Part I of the Code); and

b. to describe the arrangements which public record bodies should follow in reviewing public records and transferring them to the Public Record Office or to places of deposit or to the Public Record Office of Northern Ireland (Part II of the Code).

2. This Code refers to records in all technical or physical formats.

3. Part One of the Code provides a framework for the management of records of public authorities and of bodies subject to the Public Records Act 1958 and the Public Records Act (NI) 1923, and Part Two deals with the review and transfer of public records. More detailed guidance on both themes may be obtained from published standards. Those which support the objectives of this Code most directly are listed at Annex A.

4. Words and expressions used in this Code have the same meaning as the same words and expressions used in the FOIA.

Part I: Records Management

5 Functional Responsibility

5.1 The records management function should be recognised as a specific corporate programme within an authority and should receive the necessary levels of organisational support to ensure effectiveness. It should bring together responsibilities for records in all formats, including electronic records, throughout their life cycle, from planning and creation through to ultimate disposal. It should have clearly defined responsibilities and objectives, and the resources to achieve them. It is desirable that the person, or persons, responsible for the records management function should also have either direct responsibility or an organisational connection with the person or persons responsible for freedom of information, data protection and other information management issues.

6 Policy

6.1 An authority should have in place an overall policy statement, endorsed by top management and made readily available to staff at all levels of the organisation, on how it manages its records, including electronic records.

6.2 This policy statement should provide a mandate for the performance of all records and information management functions. In particular, it should set out an authority's commitment to create, keep and manage records which document its principal activities. The policy should also outline the role of records management and its relationship to the authority's overall strategy; define roles and responsibilities including the responsibility of individuals to document their actions and decisions in the authority's records, and to dispose of records; provide a framework for supporting standards, procedures and guidelines; and indicate the way in which compliance with the policy and its supporting standards, procedures and guidelines will be monitored.

6.3 The policy statement should be reviewed at regular intervals (at least once every three years) and, if appropriate, amended to maintain its relevance.

7 Human Resources

7.1 A designated member of staff of appropriate seniority should have lead responsibility for records management within the authority. This lead role should be formally acknowledged and made known throughout the authority.

7.2 Staff responsible for records management should have the appropriate skills and knowledge needed to achieve the aims of the records management programme. Responsibility for all aspects of record keeping should be specifically defined and incorporated in the role descriptions or similar documents.

7.3 Human resource policies and practices in organisations should address the need to recruit and retain good quality staff and should accordingly support the records management function in the following areas:

- the provision of appropriate resources to enable the records management function to be maintained across all of its activities;
- the establishment and maintenance of a scheme, such as a competency framework, to identify the knowledge, skills and corporate competencies required in records and information management;
- the regular review of selection criteria for posts with records management duties to ensure currency and compliance with best practice;
- the regular analysis of training needs;
- the establishment of a professional development programme for staff with records management duties;
- the inclusion in induction training programmes for all new staff of an awareness of records issues and practices.

8 Active Records Management

Record Creation

8.1 Each operational/business unit of an authority should have in place an adequate system for documenting its activities. This system should take into account the legislative and regulatory environments in which the authority works.

8.2 Records of a business activity should be complete and accurate enough to allow employees and their successors to undertake appropriate actions in the context of their responsibilities, to

- facilitate an audit or examination of the business by anyone so authorised,
- protect the legal and other rights of the authority, its clients and any other person affected by its actions, and
- provide authenticity of the records so that the evidence derived from them is shown to be credible and authoritative.

8.3 Records created by the authority should be arranged in a record keeping system that will enable the authority to obtain the maximum benefit from the quick and easy retrieval of information.

Record Keeping

8.4 Installing and maintaining an effective records management programme depends on knowledge of what records are held, in what form they are made accessible, and their relationship to organisational functions. An information survey or record audit will meet this requirement, help to promote control over the records, and provide valuable data for developing records appraisal and disposal procedures.

8.5 Paper and electronic record keeping systems should contain metadata (descriptive and technical documentation) to enable the system and the records to be understood and to be operated efficiently, and to provide an administrative context for effective management of the records.

8.6 The record-keeping system, whether paper or electronic, should include a set of rules for referencing, titling, indexing and, if appropriate, security marking of records. These should be easily understood and should enable the efficient retrieval of information.

Record Maintenance

8.7 The movement and location of records should be controlled to ensure that a record can be easily retrieved at any time, that any outstanding issues can be dealt with, and that there is an auditable trail of record transactions.

8.8 Storage accommodation for current records should be clean and tidy, and it should prevent damage to the records. Equipment used for current records should provide storage which is safe from unauthorised access and which meets fire regulations, but which allows maximum accessibility to the information commensurate with its frequency of use. When records are no longer required for the conduct of current business, their placement in a designated records centre rather than in offices may be a more economical and efficient way to store them. Procedures for handling records should take full account of the need to preserve important information.

8.9 A contingency or business recovery plan should be in place to provide protection for records which are vital to the continued functioning of the authority.

9 Disposal Arrangements

9.1 It is particularly important under FOI that the disposal of records — which is here defined as the point in their lifecycle when they are either transferred to an archives or destroyed — is undertaken in accordance with clearly established policies which have been formally adopted by authorities and which are enforced by properly authorised staff.

Record Closure

9.2 Records should be closed as soon as they have ceased to be of active use other than for reference purposes. As a general rule, files should be closed after five years and, if action continues, a further file should be opened. An indication that a file of paper records or folder of electronic records has been closed should be shown on the record itself as well as noted in the index or database of the files/folders. Wherever possible, information on the intended disposal of electronic records should be included in the metadata when the record is created.

9.3 The storage of closed records awaiting disposal should follow accepted standards relating to environment, security and physical organisation.

Appraisal Planning and Documentation

9.4 In order to make their disposal policies work effectively and for those to which the FOIA applies to provide the information required under FOI legislation, authorities need to have in place systems for managing appraisal and for recording the disposal decisions made. An assessment of the volume and nature of records due for disposal, the time taken to appraise records, and the risks associated with destruction or delay in appraisal will provide information to support an authority's resource planning and workflow arrangements.

9.5 An appraisal documentation system will ensure consistency in records appraisal and disposal. It should show what records are designated for destruction, the authority under which they are to be destroyed and when they are to be destroyed. It should also provide background information on the records, such as legislative provisions, functional context and physical arrangement. This information will provide valuable data for placing records selected for preservation into context and will enable future records managers to provide evidence of the operation of their selection policies.

Record Selection

9.6 Each authority should maintain a selection policy which states in broad terms the functions from which records are likely to be selected for permanent preservation and the periods for which other records should be retained. The policy should be supported by or linked to disposal schedules which should cover all records created, including electronic records. Schedules should be arranged on the basis of series or collection and should indicate the appropriate disposal action for all records (*e.g.* review after x years; destroy after y years).

9.7 Records selected for permanent preservation and no longer in regular use by the authority should be transferred as soon as possible to an archival institution that has adequate storage and public access facilities (see Part Two of this Code for arrangements for bodies subject to the Public Records Acts).

9.8 Records not selected for permanent preservation and which have reached the end of their administrative life should be destroyed in as secure a manner as is necessary for the level of confidentiality or security markings they bear. A record of the destruction of records, showing their reference, description and date of destruction should be maintained and preserved by the records manager. Disposal schedules would constitute the basis of such a record.

9.9 If a record due for destruction is known to be the subject of a request for information, destruction should be delayed until disclosure has taken place or, if the authority has decided not to disclose the information, until the complaint and appeal provisions of the FOIA have been exhausted.

10 Management of Electronic Records

10.1 The principal issues for the management of electronic records are the same as those for the management of any record. They include, for example the creation of authentic records, the tracking of records and disposal arrangements. However, the means by which these issues are addressed in the electronic environment will be different.

10.2 Effective electronic record keeping requires:

- a clear understanding of the nature of electronic records;
- the creation of records and metadata necessary to document business processes: this should be part of the systems which hold the records;
- the maintenance of a structure of folders to reflect logical groupings of records;
- the secure maintenance of the integrity of electronic records;
- the accessibility and use of electronic records for as long as required (which may include their migration across systems);
- the application of appropriate disposal procedures, including procedures for archiving; and
- the ability to cross reference electronic records to their paper counterparts in a mixed environment.

10.3 Generic requirements for electronic record management systems are set out in the 1999 Public Record Office statement Functional Requirements and Testing of Electronic Records Management Systems. Authorities are encouraged to use these, and any subsequent versions, as a model when developing their specifications for such systems.

10.4 Audit trails should be provided for all electronic information and documents. They should be kept securely and should be available for inspection by authorised personnel. The BSI document *Principles of Good Practice for Information Management* (PD0010) recommends audits at predetermined intervals for particular aspects of electronic records management.

10.5 Authorities should seek to conform to the provisions of BSI DISC PD0008 — A Code of Practice for Legal Admissibility and Evidential Weight of Information Stored Electronically (2nd edn) — especially for those records likely to be required as evidence.

Part II: Review and Transfer of Public Records

11.1 This part of the Code relates to the arrangements which authorities should follow to ensure the timely and effective review and transfer of public records. Accordingly, it is relevant only to authorities which are subject to the Public Records Acts 1958 and 1967 or to the Public Records Act (NI) 1923. The general purpose of this part of the Code is to facilitate the performance by the Public Record Office, the Public Record Office of Northern Ireland and other public authorities of their functions under the Freedom of Information Act.

11.2 Under the Public Records Acts, records selected for preservation may be transferred either to the Public Record Office or to places of deposit appointed by the Lord Chancellor. This Code applies to all such transfers. For guidance on which records may be transferred to which institution, and on the disposition of UK public records relating to Northern Ireland, see the Public Record Office Acquisition Policy (1998) and the Public Record Office Disposition Policy (2000).

11.3 In reviewing records for public release, authorities should ensure that public records become available to the public at the earliest possible time in accordance with the FOIA.

11.4 Authorities which have created or are otherwise responsible for public records should ensure that they operate effective arrangements to determine

a. which records should be selected for permanent preservation; and
b. which records should be released to the public.

These arrangements should be established and operated under the supervision of the Public Record Office or, in Northern Ireland, in conjunction with the Public Record Office of Northern Ireland. The objectives and arrangements for the review of records for release are described in greater detail below.

11.5 In carrying out their review of records for release to the public, authorities should observe the following points:

11.5.1 transfer to the Public Record Office must take place by the time the records are 30 years old, unless the Lord Chancellor gives authorisation for them to be retained for a longer period of time (see section 3(4) of the Public Records Act 1958). By agreement with the Public Record Office, transfer and release may take place before 30 years;

11.5.2 review — for selection and release — should therefore take place before the records in question are 30 years old.

11.5.3 in Northern Ireland transfer under the Public Records Act (NI) 1923 to the Public Record Office of Northern Ireland is normally at 20 years.

11.6 In the case of records to be transferred to the Public Record Office or to a place of deposit appointed under section 4 of the Public Records Act 1958, or to the Public Record Office of Northern Ireland, the purpose of the review of records for release to the public is to:

- consider which information must be available to the public on transfer because no exemptions under the FOIA apply;
- consider which information must be available to the public at 30 years because relevant exemptions in the FOIA have ceased to apply;
- consider whether the information must be released in the public interest, notwithstanding the application of an exemption under the FOIA; and
- consider which information merits continued protection in accordance with the provisions of the FOIA.

11.7 If the review results in the identification of specified information which the authorities consider ought not to be released under the terms of the FOIA, the authorities should prepare a schedule identifying this information precisely, citing the relevant exemption(s), explaining why the information may not be released and identifying a date at which either release would be appropriate or a date at which the case for release should be reconsidered. Where the information is environmental information to which the exemption at section 39 of the FOIA applies, the schedule should cite the appropriate exception in the Environmental Information Regulations. This schedule must be submitted to the Public Record Office or, in Northern Ireland, to the Public Record Office of Northern Ireland prior to transfer which must be before the records containing the information are 30 years old (in the case of the Public Record Office) or 20 years old (in the case of the Public Record Office of Northern Ireland). Authorities should consider whether parts of records might be released if the sensitive information were blanked out.

11.8 In the first instance, the schedule described in 11.7 is to be submitted to the Public Record Office for review and advice. The case in favour of withholding the records for a period longer than 30 years is then considered by the Advisory Council. The Advisory Council may respond as follows:

a. by accepting that the information may be withheld for longer than 30 years and earmarking the records for release or re-review at the date identified by the authority;
b. by accepting that the information may be withheld for longer than 30 years but asking the authority to reconsider the later date designated for release or re-review;
c. by questioning the basis on which it is deemed that the information may be withheld for longer than 30 years and asking the authority to reconsider the case;
d. by advising the Lord Chancellor if it is not satisfied with the responses it receives from authorities on particular cases;
e. by taking such other action as it deems appropriate within its role as defined in the Public Records Act.

In Northern Ireland there are separate administrative arrangements requiring that schedules are submitted to a Sensitivity Review Group consisting of representatives of different departments. The Sensitivity Review Group has the role of advising public authorities as to the appropriateness or otherwise of releasing records.

11.9 For the avoidance of doubt, none of the actions described in this Code affects the statutory rights of access established under the FOIA. Requests for information in public records transferred to the Public Record Office or to a place of deposit appointed under section 4 of the Public Records Act 1958 or to the Public Record Office of Northern Ireland will be dealt with on a case by case basis in accordance with the provisions of the FOIA.

11.10 Where records are transferred to the Public Record Office or a place of deposit before they are 30 years old, they should be designated by the transferring department or agency for immediate release unless an exemption applies: there will be no formal review of these designations.

11.11 When an exemption has ceased to apply under section 63 of the FOIA the records will become automatically available to members of the public on the day specified in the finalised schedule (*i.e.* the schedule after it has been reviewed by the Advisory Council). In other cases, if the authority concerned wishes further to extend the period during which the information is to be withheld in accordance with the FOIA, it should submit a further schedule explaining the sensitivity of the information. This is to be done before the expiry of the period stated in the earlier schedule. The Public Record Office and Advisory Council will then review the schedule in accordance with the process described in paragraph 11.8 above. In Northern Ireland, Ministerial approval is required for any further extension of the stated period.

11.12 In reviewing records an authority may identify those which are appropriate for retention within the department, after they are 30 years old, under section 3(4) of the Public Records Act 1958. Applications must be submitted to the Public Record Office for review and advice. The case in favour of retention beyond the 30 year period will then be considered by the Advisory Council. The Advisory Council will consider the case for retaining individual records unless there is already in place a standing authorisation by the Lord Chancellor for the retention of a whole category of records. It will consider such applications on the basis of the guidance in chapter 9 of the White Paper *Open Government* (Cm. 2290, 1993) or subsequent revisions of government policy on retention.

ANNEX A

Standards Accepted in Records Management

- British Standards (BSI)

BS 4783	Storage, transportation and maintenance of media for use in data processing and information storage
BS 7799	Code of practice for information security management
BS ISO 15489–1	Information and Documentation — Records Management — Part 1: General
BSI DISC PD 0008	Code of practice for legal admissibility and evidential weight of information stored on electronic document management systems
BSI DISC PD0010	Principles of good practice for information management
BSI DISC PD0012	Guide to the practical implications of the Data Protection Act 1998

- Public Record Office standards for the management of public records

The Public Record Office publishes standards, guidance and toolkits on the management of public records, in whatever format, covering their entire life cycle.

Freedom of Information Act 2000—Publication Schemes

Central Government and Non-Departmental Public Body Guidance

[JULY 2002]

1. The Freedom of Information Act 2000 requires all public authorities to make information available proactively by virtue of the Publication Scheme provisions set out in section 19 of the Act. Publication Schemes give details of the classes of information that an authority makes available proactively and how they are accessible. The plans indicate a commitment to publish proactively as much information as possible and will look at how best to transmit the information to those who need to know more. App 3–03

Introduction

2. This paper sets out Guidance for Government Departments and non-Departmental Public Bodies (NDPBs) as to the issues that they should consider when deciding what information they will commit to make publicly available in their Publication Schemes. This is guidance not instructions; neither is it intended to be a model publication scheme. How the commitments in their Schemes are delivered is a matter for individual Departments and NDPBs. But where Departments or NDPBs depart from the guidance in this paper, they should know why they are doing so and be prepared to justify their approach if asked by the Information Commissioner or other interested parties. Executive agencies are not required to have their own publication schemes, but should be included within the scope of the scheme applied by their parent Department.

The Legal Requirement

Section 19 of the Act places a duty on every public authority to:

a. adopt and maintain a scheme which relates to the publication of information by the authority and to have that scheme approved by the Commissioner;
b. publish information in accordance with that scheme;
c. review the scheme from time to time.

Each authority's Publication Scheme must specify:

a. the classes of information which the public authority publishes or intends to publish;
b. the manner in which information of each class is, or is intended to be, published;
c. whether the material is, or is intended to be, available free of charge or on payment.

In adopting or reviewing a Publication Scheme, the Act requires that a public authority should have regard to the public interest in:

a. allowing public access to information held by the authority, and
b. the publication of reasons for decisions made by the authority.

3. Given the different nature of the business of Departments and NDPBs it is impossible to have prescribed rules on what each one will include in the Publication Scheme. The aim of this guidance is to achieve as much common ground as possible.

4. All central Government Departments and those Non-Departmental Public Bodies covered by the Code of Practice on Access to Government Information, are required to have their Publication Scheme approved and in place by November 30, 2002. The Scheme will have to be submitted to the Information Commissioner for approval between July 1 and September 30, 2002.

Content

5. In deciding the content of their publication scheme, Departments and NDPBs should have regard to the public interest in the information that they hold. Some information held by an organisation will be of particular interest to the public and Departments and NDPBs should consider what information they hold that they could make available proactively to meet this demand. The information included in an organisation's Publication Scheme should focus on the key areas of accountability of the organisation.

6. Departments and NDPBs will also need to consider when the information included in their Publication Scheme will be made available. For example, facts and analysis of the facts relating to policy decisions will normally be made available when policies and decisions are announced. Papers relating to meetings may need to be made available a number of weeks or months before or after the event. Allowance should be made for the time taken to approve minutes or to obtain transcripts. Items will then be held in accordance with the Department's or NDPB's record disposal policy as normal in light of their business needs. The Scheme should specify the usual retention period for each class of information.

7. There are some kinds of information which all Departments and NDPBs should consider for inclusion within their Publication Schemes. These are detailed in paragraphs 7.1 to 7.12 below. The headings are not intended as specific 'classes of information' although Departments and NDPBs may chose to use them as such.

Guidance to Staff

7.1 It is expected that Publication Schemes will provide access to explanatory material on Departments' and NDPBs' dealings with the public and other organisations. This includes such rules, procedures, internal guidance to officials, and similar administrative manuals as will assist better understanding of the organisation's interaction in dealing with the public. It will also include internal guidance to officials on implementing/operating the Code of Practice on Access to Government Information (before 2005), the Freedom of Information Act (after 2005), the Environmental Information Regulations and the Data Protection Act 1998.

Background to Policy

7.2 The Code of Practice on Access to Government information already commits Departments and NDPBs to publishing the facts and analysis of the facts which Government considers relevant and important in framing major policy proposals and decisions. This commitment should be carried forward to the Publication Scheme.

Management Information

7.3.1 The Code of Practice on Access to Government Information requires Departments and NDPBs to publish:

i. full information about how public services are run, how much they cost, who is in charge, and what complaints and redress procedures are available;
ii. full and, where possible, comparable information about what services are being provided , what targets are set, what standards of service are expected and the results achieved.

These commitments should be carried forward to the Publication Scheme.

7.3.2 In addition, Publication Scheme commitments are also likely to provide access to the following in relation to the role, function and management of the public authority:

i. mission, objectives and functions of the authority;
ii. organisation of the authority, including information about who is responsible for which function and how to contact him or her;
iii. information about Board Meetings. This may include the agendas and minutes of the meetings and associated papers or summaries where appropriate;
iv. targets, including those set for standards of service and financial performance, together with results achieved and comparative information;
v. sources of income, and how effectively money is raised and spent, for example, on different aspects of administration.

7.3.3 The information described above often appears in Departmental reports, Management Statements, Financial Memoranda etc. Agency Framework Documents are also useful as they encapsulate the essential management operating arrangements for each agency with regard to its organisation of a Department. For the purpose of this guidance it is the information itself and not the form that it is presented in that is important.

7.3.4 On (ii) above, Departments and NDPBs will want to consider the appropriate level of seniority of the staff about which this kind of information is to be published. It is important that the public can identify a person who can provide the information they require. How this is achieved may well vary between Departments and NDPBs and in some instances requests for information may be channelled through call centres.

7.3.5 Departments and NDPBs should also consider for which formal meetings it is appropriate to publish the agenda, papers and minutes or summaries of these documents. It is likely that Departments and NDPBs will want to specify what information will be made available proactively for which meetings, or type of meetings. Regular formal committees or advisory groups are more likely to be included in the Publication Scheme than ad-hoc or impromptu discussions.

Public Consultation

7.4 The Cabinet Office guidelines on consultation should be followed. Responses submitted in confidence should have that confidence respected if the information submitted is properly confidential. The number of confidential responses should be published.

Departmental Circulars

7.5 There are many different types of circular and they are used to communicate a variety of information. It is probable that some of these circulars will be relevant for inclusion on a publication scheme. Many Departments and NDPBs already have this sort of information on their websites and for some circulars it may be helpful to provide an index to improve accessibility. The scale of this task will therefore vary and Departments and NDPBs may find that some of this information will be subsumed within other commitments within their Scheme.

Information placed in the Libraries of the Houses of Parliament

7.6 Departments and NDPBs should consider whether documents placed in the library of either Houses of Parliament should be included within the Publication Scheme.

Decisions

7.7.1 Decisions of the Information Commissioner in relation to the Freedom of Information Act 2000 and Data Protection Act 1998, and the Parliamentary Ombudsman in relation to the Code of Practice on Access to Government Information, relating to the organisation, are also items to which a Publication Scheme is likely to provide access. Some of these decisions are published by the Ombudsman and if so it may be appropriate simply to provide a link to that information. However, not all of the decisions are published and this information should be considered for inclusion. The public availability of details of departmental infractions under the Environmental Information Regulations should also be considered.

7.7.2 Decisions of other bodies relating to the Department should be accessible where appropriate.

7.7.3 Reasons should be published for decisions made by the Department where the decision affects a significant number of interested parties. An example is the Charity Commission, which is making more information available in relation to its decisions, particularly when there is considerable public interest. The decisions, and reasons, most likely to be appropriate to include in a publication scheme are those which affect a significant number of people. This may sometimes include a decision in relation to an individual, but which sets a precedent or has ramifications for the future handling of similar cases. Personal data relating to individuals should be handled in accordance with the Data Protection principles.

Speeches

7.8 Keynote speeches by Ministers and senior officials are likely to be made available proactively. In practice these are often already made available through a Department's Press Office.

Legislation and Related Information

7.9.1 It is helpful to the public to know more about the legal framework within which Departments and other public authorities operate. Collating a list in a single place and giving a brief description of the relationship between the legislation and the Department's structure and functions should be considered, as should providing details of legislation or Codes of Practice that give rights of access to information.

7.9.2 Her Majesty's Stationery Office in the Cabinet Office have responsibility for the publication of UK legislation including Acts of Parliament, Statutory Instruments (including those made by the National Assembly for Wales), Acts of the Northern Ireland Assembly, Statutory Rules of Northern Ireland, Church of England Measures and Explanatory Notes to Acts of Parliament and Explanatory Notes to Acts of the Northern Ireland Assembly. Details of these categories of publications will be featured on HMSO's Publication Scheme with details of where users can view or purchase the documents. It follows that there is no need for organisations to provide full details of legislation which they have policy responsibility for in their own Publication Schemes. They may, however, wish to feature a reference in their Publication Scheme to the HMSO website where all newly enacted legislation can be viewed.

7.9.3 Parliament is responsible for the publication of Bills before Parliament and Explanatory Notes to Bills. This material can be viewed on the Parliamentary web site. Again, there is no necessity for departments to feature details in their own publication schemes although they may wish to provide a link to the Parliamentary website

7.9.4 HMSO also arranges for the publication of the London, Edinburgh and Belfast Gazettes. Details of these will be featured on HMSO's publication scheme. Organisations should, however, refer in their Publication Schemes to the categories of individual notices which are submitted for publication in the Gazettes.

7.9.5 Departments should provide details of Command Papers, White Papers and Green Papers which they have responsibility for publishing. For reference, a list of all Command Papers is published on HMSO's website.

7.9.6 Texts of international treaties, conventions and agreements should be accessible if not provided elsewhere. Departments may wish to provide cross-references to relevant documents of European Community legislation. It is suggested that details could be supplied of websites where the material can be viewed or from where the information can be obtained.

Procurement, grants, loans and guarantees

7.10.1 Departments and NDPBs are encouraged to be as open as possible when considering making available information in relation to procurement, grants, loans and guarantees.

7.10.2 In particular, the publication of procurement and supplier policies should be considered for publication as should the details of contracts awarded. Departments and NDPBs should also consider the provision of information on specific projects including notification of bidding opportunities, decision criteria, contract performance standards, results of regular performance reviews, and results achieved where appropriate. Good examples of the type of information that can be provided can be found on the websites of Southampton Council and the National Assembly for Wales. The Office of Government Commerce can provide further advice about the provision of information on Government procurement.

7.10.3 Departments and NDPBs should consider including their policies on the awarding of grants, loans and the provision of guarantees in their publication scheme as well as background information on schemes administered by the organisation . Publishing an account of how grants have been dispensed under a particular scheme, including overall funds dispensed and an assessment of the benefit of the scheme in terms of its objectives should be considered. The publication of details of guarantees such as the guarantee recipient, purpose and amount should be considered for inclusion in departmental publication schemes whilst respecting legitimate personal and commercial confidentiality.

7.10.4 Information relating to the items above need not include all such information but could be covered in a generic fashion or include information on projects above a particular cost threshold as decided by the Department or NDPB.

7.10.5 The Lord Chancellor's Code of Practice on the Discharge of the Functions of Public Authorities under Part 1 of the Freedom of Information Act requires that Departments and NDPBs ensure that they consider the implications for Freedom of Information before agreeing to confidentiality provisions in contracts and accepting information in confidence from a third party more generally. In particular, Departments and NDPBs should only accept information from third parties in confidence if it is necessary to obtain that information in connection with the exercise of any of their functions. They should not agree to hold information received from third parties "in confidence" which is not confidential in nature. Acceptance of any confidentiality provisions must be for good reasons and capable of being justified to the Information Commissioner.

Information required to be published under other legislation

7.11 This includes a wide range of information, some of which will be specific to individual organisations. In particular, information relating to the environment that would be accessible under the Environmental Information Regulations such as Estate Management information and Greening Government Reports as well as Environmental Impact Assessments and Departmental Sustainable Development Strategies should be made available where appropriate.

Research Reports; Risk and Impact Assessments, etc.

7.12 Appropriate guidance on the publication of scientific research from the Office of Science and Technology and on risk assessment should be followed when considering the content of a Publication Scheme. Regulatory Impact Assessments are also likely to be accessible.

Information disclosed under the Code of Practice on Access to Government Information

7.13 Where information is disclosed to an individual in response to a request under the Code of Practice or Access to Government Information, or, from January 1, 2005, in response to a request under the Act, Departments and NDPBs should consider whether the information disclosed is of general interest and include released information in the Publication Scheme where appropriate.

Presentation and Delivery

8. Publication Schemes are intended to increase access to government information. Therefore the accessibility of the scheme and the information in it is very important. It is best practice to include:

Copyright

8.1 A general copyright statement should be included at the head of the Publication Scheme. Documents accessible under the scheme should feature an appropriate copyright notice whether published in print or on official websites in accordance with guidance issued by HMSO.

Formats

8.2.1 Details of the formats that the scheme itself and the information accessible under it are available in *e.g.* Braille, Welsh, other languages, electronic, paper etc should be given. The decision to publish information in alternative formats is a result of normal business deliberations and should be considered when a document is produced and is not a matter for a Publication Scheme.

8.2.2 The Scheme itself should be provided on paper and electronically. Consideration of other formats should be in line with the relevant accessibility criteria for publications including the organisation's Welsh Language Scheme.

8.2.3 Departments and NDPBs may not be able to rely wholly on the internet as a means of making information available proactively. There are many ways by which information can be made available proactively.

Access to the Information

8.3 Departments and NDPBs should make clear how information can be obtained by the public under the Scheme. They should publish a guide for users on applying for information and exercising associated rights under the Code of Practice on Access to Government Information (before 2005), under the Freedom of Information Act (after 2005), under the Data Protection Act 1998 and under the Environmental Information Regulations. Links to information that is part of the organisation's commitment to publish but is provided elsewhere should be provided, including an indication of any online resources, such as databases, which can be interrogated directly by requesters where this is reasonable and practicable to do so.

Relationship with Information Asset Register

8.4.1 The Information Asset Register ("IAR") details Government information assets that can be reused under licence. The IAR focuses primarily on unpublished data holdings and thus provides a guide to the unpublished information resources held by Departments. The IAR can help identify what information a Department holds, how useful that information is and how to access it. For further information about the Information Asset register and their links with publication schemes, see HMSO's Guidance Note 18.

8.4.2 The Department's Information Asset Register should be directly referred to in its Publication Scheme and should form an important part of their preparations for Freedom of Information. Each Department is responsible for creating its records within its own departmental asset register.

Archiving

8.5 Archiving of the Publication Scheme for records management purposes should be considered whenever the scheme is updated or otherwise amended. It is suggested that Departments and NDPBs should keep their initial scheme, and subsequent versions of the Scheme that contain significant changes.

UK Official Publications

8.6 Departments and NDPBs are reminded of their responsibilities for providing information relation to maintaining the complete bibliographic record of all United Kingdom Official Publications. For details please see HMSO's Guidance Note 17.

Plain Language

8.7 Publication Schemes should be in plain language. The Cabinet Office Plain Language guide should be followed.

Public Interest and Consultation

9. When having regard to the public interest in the information held by the organisation, it is best practice to consider all the different stakeholders who might be interested in the information and to consult with these groups where possible — this may have to be after the Publication Scheme is in place with initial assessment of the public interest based on information the organisation already holds *e.g.* Minister's Cases, website hits, etc.

10. Consultation can take a variety of forms. These include traditional written consultation, listening events, seminars with, and visits to, representative groups. Having an email address for comments or an online feedback form can encourage user feedback. Internet discussions are also a valid way of consulting with your 'public' as is both quantitative and qualitative research including surveys and focus groups.

Charging

11. A Publication Scheme must state whether documents in the Scheme will be available free of charge or for a charge.

Interpreting the law

11.1.1 The Environmental Information Regulations permit charges in respect of costs reasonably attributable to the supply of information, provided a schedule of the charges that may be levied is made available to all persons requesting environmental information. The EI Regulations apply to both published and unpublished information, including EI supplied under other enactments. (Treasury and DEFRA will let departments have further advice on charges for Environmental Information when the negotiations on the revised EI Regulations have reached a firmer point.) Some organisations may also have legislation on non-environmental matters under which they publish certain information.

11.1.2 The FOI Act does not require that a schedule of charges is included within the publication scheme, but only that the publication scheme specify whether the material is, or is intended to be, available free of charge or on payment. This is important as the Information Commissioner proposes to approve a publication scheme for three to five years. Organisations will therefore be seeking in their classes of information to anticipate the document types or subject areas which the department will be publishing during that period, but it is unlikely to be either practical nor possible to anticipate every future title or charge.

11.1.3 It is suggested that in their Publication Schemes, organisations should therefore set out their charging policy, but indicate that, where charges are made, the charge for each publication will be listed by the title of the publication on the up to date publications list. A link to the up to date list or a note of where it can be obtained is recommended. For information published under another enactment, this may in some cases take the form of a link to the relevant Fees Order.

11.1.4 For the purposes of defining the potential coverage of a publication scheme, we must have regard to both section 19 and section 21 of the FOI Act. The latter indicates that where information is available from the public authority on request, it can be regarded as reasonably accessible to the applicant where it is made available in accordance with the authority's publication scheme, and any payment required is specified in, or determined in accordance with, the scheme.

Definition of charging

11.2.1 For the purposes of charges, HM Treasury is assuming that a publication is material which:

- has appeared on a public website; or
- has been advertised on a public website, or in a commercial publisher's list, as available, and which is already held by, or immediately available in store to, the Department's Public Enquiry Unit in its final format for supply to the public, or similarly by the Department's commercial publisher; or
- is available from book shops, public libraries, etc supplied by the department or the commercial publisher.

Information which is held by an organisation, but which it has not been intended to publish, and has to be extracted specifically for the requestor, is not covered by a publication scheme.

Form of words for use in Publication Schemes

11.3.1 A possible approach is to describe some broad pricing categories which could be applied either to an organisation's publication scheme as a whole or to individual classes. A single pricing category may apply to a particular class, but two or more pricing categories to other classes.

11.3.2 Annex A contains a suggested form of words which assumes that any payment can be requested in advance before a publication is supplied, but this is not yet certain for information supplied under the revised EI Regulations. Square brackets indicate where Departments or NDPBs are most likely to need to adapt the wording to their own circumstances.

Review

12. The Information Commissioner has said in her Publication Scheme Guidance that she will want to review Publication Schemes every three years although this might be

extended slightly for the very first approvals (Central and Local Government) but in any event that period will not exceed five years. The Information Commissioner will require notification of any additions to a Scheme during that period and will require Departments and NDPBs to seek approval of the removal of any commitment made in the publication scheme over the same period.

Conclusion

13. When developing their Publication Scheme, Departments and NDPBs should keep in mind that publication schemes are intended as a tool for openness, to increase transparency and accountability and improve decision-making. All schemes should have the public interest as their driver and should help to promote trust between the Government and the electorate. In developing its Publication Scheme, Departments are encouraged to look at the experience of their counterparts in other countries with Freedom of Information legislation and keep in mind that other openness regimes frequently over-estimated perceived risks associated with openness.

ANNEX A

Suggested form of Words for Charging on Publication Schemes

Is information free of charge or on payment?
We indicate [for each class of information] in our Publication Scheme which of the following categories could apply to information you intend to use for your private research/study:

a. free of charge on website (*i.e.* there is no charge by us, although the user would of course have to meet any charges by their Internet service provider, personal printing costs, etc.). For those without Internet access, a single print-out as on the website would be available by post from [. . .] [or by personal application at . . .]. However, requests for multiple print-outs, or for archived copies of documents which are no longer available on the web, may attract a charge for the cost of retrieval, photocopy, postage, etc. We would let you know this at the time of your request [the charge would be payable in advance];

b. free of charge leaflets or booklets on, *e.g.* services we offer to the public. List available from [. . . . . .], material itself from [. . . . .]

c. free of charge to view at [local office or wherever but charge for [certified] photocopy [a schedule of charges for [. . . . .] is available from [. . . .] [For other items, we would let you know the relevant charge at the time of your request [the charge would be payable in advance];

d. information available via a website, but a charge would have to be paid before the main part of the information could be accessed. [This is the exception.] This may arise, eg where the website is used to deliver a value-added customised service, particularly where the basic data is also available to private sector users who may provide their own value-added service. Where this applies, the reason for the charge and the level of charges would be advertised [where?].

   (Note: some "information" accessible on our website is not published for the information of the general public, but is part of our electronic delivery of services, for example where applications for licences can be made online or where tax returns can be filed online. In that case, access to records bearing details about a named individual or company is limited to the individual or company concerned and other authorised persons. We explain the conditions applying on our website so that you can read them before you begin to use the relevant online service.)

e. "glossy" or other bound paper copies, or in some cases a CD Rom, video or other mediums, are for charge as in our publication lists available at [. . ..] [or those of our publisher available at [. . . . . .].

If you want to re-use or reproduce our publications, eg commercially or for circulation for education, etc, purposes, you will in most cases need to apply for a copyright licence for this. This [Department] [is a Crown body and our information is subject to Crown copyright administered by Her Majesty's Stationery Office]. For HMSO Guidance Notes on a range of copyright issues, see the HMSO website or write to [. . . .].

[We own the copyright in our information. Our charging policy for re-use and reproduction is [. . . .] [Note: this applies only to NDPBs which are non-Crown and other non-Crown public sector bodies.]

More details of the Government's policy on where charges are made and on determining the level of charges is available in *Charges for Information: When and How — Guidance for Government Departments and other Crown Bodies.*

Code of Practice on Access to Government Information

[December 11, 1997]

Part 1

Purpose

1. This Code of Practice supports the Government's policy under the Citizen's Charter of extending access to official information, and responding to reasonable requests for information. The approach to release of information should in all cases be based on the assumption that information should be released except where disclosure would not be in the public interest, as specified in Part II of this Code. **App 3–04**

2. The aims of the Code are:

- to improve policy-making and the democratic process by extending access to the facts and analyses which provide the basis for the consideration of proposed policy;
- to protect the interests of individuals and companies by ensuring that reasons are given for administrative decisions, except where there is statutory authority or established convention to the contrary; and
- to support and extend the principles of public service established under the Citizen's Charter.

These aims are balanced by the need:

- to maintain high standards of care in ensuring the privacy of personal and commercially confidential information; and
- to preserve confidentiality where disclosure would not be in the public interest or would breach personal privacy or the confidences of a third party, in accordance with statutory requirements and Part II of the Code.

Information the Government will release

3. Subject to the exemptions in Part II, the Code commits departments and public bodies under the jurisdiction of the Parliamentary Commissioner for Administration (the Ombudsman):

(i) to publish the facts and analysis of the facts which the Government considers relevant and important in framing major policy proposals and decisions; such information will normally be available when policies and decisions are announced;

(ii) to publish or otherwise make available, as soon as practicable after the Code becomes operational, explanatory material on departments' dealings with the public (including such rules, procedures, internal guidance to officials, and similar administrative manuals as will assist better understanding of departmental action in dealing with the public) except where publication could prejudice any matter which should properly be kept confidential under Part II of the Code;

(iii) to give reasons for administrative decisions to those affected;

(iv) to publish in accordance with the Citizen's Charter:

- full information about how public services are run, how much they cost, who is in charge, and what complaints and redress procedures are available;

- full and, where possible, comparable information about what services are being provided, what targets are set, what standards of service are expected and the results achieved.

(v) to release, in response to specific requests, information relating to their policies, actions and decisions and other matters related to their areas of responsibility.

4. There is no commitment that pre-existing documents, as distinct from information, will be made available in response to requests. The Code does not require departments to acquire information they not possess, to provide information which is already published, or to provide information which is provided as part of an existing charged service other than through that service.

Responses to requests for information

5. Information will be provided as soon as practicable. The target for response to simple requests for information is 20 working days from the date of receipt. This target may need to be extended when significant search or collation of material is required. Where information cannot be provided under the terms of the Code, an explanation will normally be given.

Scope

6. The Code applies to those Government departments and other bodies within the jurisdiction of the Ombudsman (as listed in Schedule 2 to the Parliamentary Commissioner Act 1967). The Code applies to agencies within departments and to functions carried out on behalf of a department or public body by contractors. The Security and Intelligence Services are not within the scope of the Code, nor is information obtained from or relating to them.

Charges

7. Departments, agencies and public bodies will make their own arrangements for charging. Details of charges are available from departments on request. Schemes may include a standard charge for processing simple requests for information. Where a request is complex and would require extensive searches of records or processing or collation of information, an additional charge, reflecting reasonable costs may be notified.

Relationship to statutory access rights

8. This Code is non-statutory and cannot override provisions contained in statutory rights of access to information or records (nor can it override statutory prohibitions on disclosure). Where the information could be sought under an existing statutory right, the terms of the right of access takes precedence over the Code. There are already certain access rights to health, medical and educational records, to personal files held by local authority housing and social services departments, and to personal data held on computer. There is also a right of access to environmental information. It is not envisaged that the Ombudsman will become involved in supervising these statutory rights.

The White Paper on Open Government (Cm 2290) proposed two new statutory rights to information:

an access right to personal records, proposed in Chapter 5;
an access right to health and safety information, proposed in Chapter 6.

Where a statutory right is proposed but has yet to be implemented, access to relevant information may be sought under the Code, but the Code should not be regarded as a means of access to original documents or personal files.

Public records

9. The Code is not intended to override statutory provisions on access to public records, whether over or under thirty years old. Under section 12(3) of the Parliamentary Commissioner Act 1967, the Ombudsman is not required to question the merits of a decision if it is taken without maladministration by a Government department or other body in the exercise of a discretion vested in it. Decisions on public records made in England and Wales by the Lord Chancellor, or in Scotland and Northern Ireland by the Secretary of State, are such discretionary decisions.

Jurisdiction of courts, tribunals or inquiries

10. The Code only applies to Government-held information. It does not apply to or affect information held by courts or contained in court documents. ("Court" includes tribunals, inquiries and the Northern Ireland Enforcement of Judgments Office). The present practice covering disclosure of information before courts, tribunals and inquiries will continue to apply.

Investigation of complaints

11. Complaints that information which should have been provided under the Code has not been provided, or that unreasonable charges have been demanded, should be made first to the department or body concerned. If the applicant remains dissatisfied, complaints may be made through a Member of Parliament to the Ombudsman. Complaints will be investigated at the Ombudsman's discretion in accordance with the procedures provided in the 1967 Act.

Part II

Reasons for Confidentiality

The following categories of information are exempt from the commitments to provide information in this Code. In those categories which refer to harm or prejudice, the presumption remains that information should be disclosed unless the harm likely to arise from disclosure would outweigh the public interest in making the information available.

References to harm or prejudice include both actual harm or prejudice and risk or reasonable expectation of harm or prejudice. In such cases it should be considered whether any harm or prejudice arising from disclosure is outweighed by the public interest in making information available.

The exemptions will not be interpreted in a way which causes injustice to individuals.

1. Defence, security and international relations

(a) Information whose disclosure would harm national security or defence.
(b) Information whose disclosure would harm the conduct of international relations or affairs.
(c) Information received in confidence from foreign governments, foreign courts or international organisations.

2. Internal discussion and advice

Information whose disclosure would harm the frankness and candour of internal discussion, included:

- proceedings of Cabinet and Cabinet committees;
- internal opinion, advice, recommendation, consultation and deliberation;
- projections and assumptions relating to internal policy analysis; analysis of alternative policy options and information relating to rejected policy options;
- confidential communications between departments, public bodies and regulatory bodies.

3. Communications with the Royal Household

Information relating to confidential communications between Ministers and Her Majesty the Queen or other Members of the Royal Household, or relating to confidential proceedings of the Privy Council.

4. Law enforcement and legal proceedings

(a) Information whose disclosure could prejudice the administration of justice (including fair trial), legal proceedings or the proceedings or any tribunal, public inquiry or other formal investigations (whether actual or likely) or whose disclosure is, has been, or is likely to be addressed in the context of such proceedings.

(b) Information whose disclosure could prejudice the enforcement or proper administration of the law, including the prevention, investigation or detection of crime, or the apprehension or prosecution of offenders.

(c) Information relating to legal proceedings or the proceedings of any tribunal, public inquiry or other formal investigation which have been completed or terminated, or relating to investigations which have or might have resulted in proceedings.

(d) Information covered by legal professional privilege.

(e) son, or identify the source of information or assistance given in confidence for law enforcement or security purposes.

(f) Information whose disclosure would increase the likelihood of damage to the environment, or rare or endangered species and their habitats.

5. Immigration and nationality

Information relating to immigration, nationality, consular and entry clearance cases. However, information will be provided, though not through access to personal records, where these is no risk that disclosure would prejudice the effective administration of immigration controls or other statutory provisions.

6. Effective management of the economy and collection of tax

(a) Information whose disclosure would harm the ability of the Government to manage the economy, prejudice the conduct of official market operations, or could lead to improper gain or advantage.

(b) Information whose disclosure would prejudice the assessment or collection of tax, duties or National Insurance contributions, or assist tax avoidance or evasion.

7. Effective management and operations of the public service

(a) Information whose disclosure could lead to improper gain or advantage or would prejudice:

- the competitive position of a department of other public body or authority;
- negotiations or the effective conduct or personnel management, or commercial or contractual activities;
- the awarding of discretionary grants.

(b) Information whose disclosure would harm the proper and efficient conduct of the operations of a department of other public body or authority, including NHS organisations, or of any regulatory body.

8. Public employment, public appointments and honours

(a) Personnel records (relating to public appointments as well as employees of public authorities) including those relating to recruitment, promotion and security vetting.

(b) Information, opinions and assessments given in confidence in relation to public employment and public appointments made by Ministers of the Crown, by the Crown on the advice of Ministers or by statutory office holders.

(c) Information, opinions and assessments given in relation to recommendations for honours.

9. Voluminous or vexatious requests

Requests for information which are vexatious or manifestly unreasonable or are formulated in too general a manner, or which (because of the amount of information to be processed or the need to retrieve information from files not in current use) would require unreasonable diversion of resources.

10. Publication and prematurity in relation to publication

Information which is or will soon be published, or whose disclosure, where the material related to a planned or potential announcement or publication, could cause harm (for example, of a physical or financial nature).

11. Research, statistics and analysis

(a) Information relating to incomplete analysis, research or statistics, where disclosure could be misleading or deprive the holder of priority of publication or commercial value.

(b) Information held only for preparing statistics or carrying out research, or for surveillance for health and safety purposes (including food safety), and which relates to individuals, companies or products which will not be identified in reports of that research or surveillance, or in published statistics.

12. Privacy of an individual

Unwarranted disclosure to a third party of personal information of any person (including a deceased person) or any other disclosure which would constitute or could facilitate an unwarranted invasion of privacy.

13. Third party's commercial confidences

Information including commercial confidences, trade secrets or intellectual property whose unwarranted disclosure would harm the competitive position of a third party.

14. Information given in confidence

(a) Information held in consequence of having been supplied in confidence by a person who:

- gave the information under a statutory guarantee that its confidentiality would be protected; or

- was not under any legal obligation, whether actual or implied, to supply it, and has not consented to its disclose.

(b) Information whose disclosure without the consent of the supplier would prejudice the future supply of such information.

(c) Medical information provided in confidence if disclosure to the subject would harm their physical or mental health, or should only be made by a medical practitioner.

15. Statutory and other restrictions

(a) Information whose disclosure is prohibited by or under any enactment, regulation, European Community law or international agreement.

(b) Information whose release would constitute a breach of Parliamentary Privilege.

APPENDIX 4

Local Government Records

Public Bodies (Admission to Meetings) Act 1960

(1960, c. 67)

ARRANGEMENT OF SECTIONS

Section

An Act to provide for the admission of representatives of the press and other members of the public to the meetings of certain bodies exercising public functions. **App 4–01**

[OCTOBER 27, 1960]

Admission of public to meetings of local authorities and other bodies

1.—(1) Subject to subsection (2) below, any meeting of a [. . .][1] body exercising public functions, being [a body][2] to which this Act applies, shall be open to the public.

(2) A body may, by resolution, exclude the public from a meeting (whether during the whole or part of the proceedings) whenever publicity would be prejudicial to the public interest by reason of the confidential nature of the business to be transacted or for other

[1] Words repealed by Local Government (Access to Information) Act 1985 (c.43), s.3, Sch.2, para.4(2), Sch.3.

[2] Words substituted by Local Government (Access to Information) Act 1985 (c.43), s.3, Sch.2, para.4(2).

special reasons stated in the resolution and arising from the nature of that business or of the proceedings; and where such a resolution is passed, this Act shall not require the meeting to be open to the public during proceedings to which the resolution applies.

(3) A body may under subsection (2) above treat the need to receive or consider recommendations or advice from sources other than members, committees or sub-committees of the body as a special reason why publicity would be prejudicial to the public interest, without regard to the subject or purport of the recommendations or advice; but the making by this subsection of express provision for that case shall not be taken to restrict the generality of subsection (2) above in relation to other cases (including in particular cases where the report of a committee or sub-committee of the body is of a confidential nature).

(4) Where a meeting of a body is required by this Act to be open to the public during the proceedings or any part of them, the following provisions shall apply, that is to say—

(a) public notice of the time and place of the meeting shall be given by posting it at the offices of the body (or, if the body has no offices, then in some central and conspicuous place in the area with which it is concerned) three clear days at least before the meeting or, if the meeting is convened at shorter notice, then at the time it is convened;

(b) there shall, on request and on payment of postage or other necessary charge for transmission, be supplied for the benefit of any newspaper a copy of the agenda for the meeting as supplied to members of the body (but excluding, if thought fit, any item during which the meeting is likely not to be open to the public), together with such further statements or particulars, if any, as are necessary to indicate the nature of the items included or, if thought fit in the case of any item, with copies of any reports or other documents supplied to members of the body in connection with the item;

(c) while the meeting is open to the public, the body shall not have power to exclude members of the public from the meeting and duly accredited representatives of newspapers attending for the purpose of reporting the proceedings for those newspapers shall, so far as practicable, be afforded reasonable facilities for taking their report and, unless the meeting is held in premises not belonging to the body or not on the telephone, for telephoning the report at their own expense.

(5) Where a meeting of a body is required by this Act to be open to the public during the proceedings or any part of them, and there is supplied to a member of the public attending the meeting, or in pursuance of paragraph (b) of subsection (4) above there is supplied for the benefit of a newspaper, any such copy of the agenda as is mentioned in that paragraph, with or without further statements or particulars for the purpose of indicating the nature of any item included in the agenda, the publication thereby of any defamatory matter contained in the agenda or in the further statements or particulars shall be privileged, unless the publication is proved to be made with malice.

(6) When a body to which this Act applies resolves itself into committee, the proceedings in committee shall for the purposes of this Act be treated as forming part of the proceedings of the body at the meeting.

(7) Any reference in this section to a newspaper shall apply also to a news agency which systematically carries on the business of selling and supplying reports or information to newspapers, and to any organisation which is systematically engaged in collecting news for sound or television broadcasts [or for programme services (within the meaning of the Broadcasting Act 1990) other than sound or television broadcasting services][3]; but nothing in this section shall require a body to permit the taking of photographs of any proceedings, or the use of any means to enable persons not present to see

[3] Words substituted by Broadcasting Act 1990 (c.42), ss.4(6), 87(6), 203(1), Sch.20, para.5.

or hear any proceedings (whether at the time or later), or the making of any oral report on any proceedings as they take place.

(8) The provisions of this section shall be without prejudice to any power of exclusion to suppress or prevent disorderly conduct or other misbehaviour at a meeting.

Application of Act, and consequential provisions

2.—(1) This Act shall apply to the bodies specified in the Schedule to this Act, and to such bodies as may for the time being be added to that Schedule by order made under subsection (3) below; and where this Act applies to a body, the foregoing section shall apply in relation to any committee of the body whose members consist of or include all members of the body, as that section applies in relation to the body itself, but so that for the purposes of paragraph (c) of subsection (4) of that section premises belonging to the body shall be treated as belonging to the committee.

(2) [. . .][4]

(3) Any body established by or under any Act may be added to the Schedule to this Act, and any body so added may be removed from the Schedule, by order of the appropriate Minister made by statutory instrument, but a statutory instrument made by a Minister under this section shall be of no effect unless it is approved by resolution of each House of Parliament; and for this purpose the appropriate Minister is, in the case of any body, the Minister of the Crown in charge of the Government department concerned or primarily concerned with the matters dealt with by that body, but an order made under this subsection by any Minister of the Crown shall be effective, whether or not he is the appropriate Minister.

Short title, repeal, extent and commencement.

3.—(1) This Act may be cited as the Public Bodies (Admission to Meetings) Act, 1960.

(2) [. . .][5]

(3) This Act shall not extend to Northern Ireland.

(4) This Act shall come into force on June 1, 1961.

SCHEDULE 1

BODIES TO WHICH THIS ACT APPLIES

1.—The bodies to which in England and Wales this Act applies are—

(a) parish or community councils, the Council of the Isles of Scilly and joint boards or joint committees which discharge functions of any of those bodies (or of any of those bodies and of a principal council, within the meaning of the Local Government Act 1972, or a body falling within paragraph (a), (b) or (c) of section 100J(1) of that Act)

(b) the parish meetings of rural parishes;

(ba) the Welsh Development Agency;

(bc) the Commission for Health Improvement;

(bd) the Care Council for Wales;

[(bd) the Council for the Regulation of Health Care Professionals;][6]

(be) the General Social Care Council;

[4] Words repealed by Local Government (Access to Information) Act 1985 (c.43), s.3, Sch.2, para.4(3), Sch.3.

[5] Words repeals Local Authorities (Admission of the Press to Meetings) Act 1908 (c.43), Local Government Act 1933 (c.51), Sch.3, Pt IV, para.1(4) and Education (Scotland) Act 1946 (c.72), s.84.

[6] Possible drafting error, despite there already being a Sch.1 para.1(bd) in existence, para.1(bd) is inserted by National Health Service Reform and Health Care Professions Act (2002 c.17), Sch.7 para.21

(bf) the National Care Standards Commission;

(f) Health Authorities, except as regards the exercise of functions under the National Health Service (Service Committees and Tribunal) Regulations 1992 or any regulations amending or replacing those Regulations;

(g) if the order establishing a Special Health Authority so provides, the Special Health Authority;

(gh) Local Health Boards;

(h) bodies not mentioned above but having, within the meaning of the Public Works Loans Act, 1875, power to levy a rate (other than bodies to which sections 100A to 100D of the Local Government Act 1972 apply, whether or not by virtue of section 100Eor 100J of that Act).

(i) regional and local flood defence committees;

(j) advisory committees established and maintained under section 12 or 13 of the Environment Act 1995;

(k) customer service committees maintained under section 28 of the Water Industry Act 1991.

(l) National Health Service trusts established under section 5(1) of the National Health Service and Community Care Act 1990.[7]

2.—The bodies to which in Scotland this Act applies are—

(d) Health Boards constituted under the National Health Service (Scotland) Act 1978, but only so far as regards the exercise of their executive functions

[(dd) National Health Service trusts established under section 12A of the National Health Service (Scotland) Act 1978.[8]][9]

---

[7] In relation to England:

1. The bodies to which in England and Wales this Act applies are—

(a) parish or community councils, the Council of the Isles of Scilly and joint boards or joint committees which discharge functions of any of those bodies (or of any of those bodies and of a principal council, within the meaning of the Local Government Act 1972, or a body falling within para.(a), (b) or (c) of s.100J(1) of that Act)

(b) the parish meetings of rural parishes;

(ba) the Welsh Development Agency;

(bc) the Commission for Health Improvement;

(bd) the Care Council for Wales;

(be) the General Social Care Council;

(bf) the National Care Standards Commission;

(ea) Strategic Health Authorities;

(f) Health Authorities, except as regards the exercise of functions under the National Health Service (Service Committees and Tribunal) Regulations 1992 or any regulations amending or replacing those Regulations;

(g) if the order establishing a Special Health Authority so provides, the Special Health Authority;

(gg) Primary Care Trusts, except as regards the exercise of functions under the National Health Service (Service Committees and Tribunal) Regulations 1992 or any regulations amending or replacing those Regulations;

(h) bodies not mentioned above but having, within the meaning of the Public Works Loans Act, 1875, power to levy a rate (other than bodies to which ss 100A to 100D of the Local Government Act 1972 apply, whether or not by virtue of s.100Eor 100J of that Act).

(i) regional and local flood defence committees;

(j) advisory committees established and maintained under s.12 or 13 of the Environment Act 1995;

(k) customer service committees maintained under s.28 of the Water Industry Act 1991.

(l) National Health Service trusts established under s.5(1) of the National Health Service and Community Care Act 1990.

[8] S.12A was inserted by the National Health Service and Community Care Act 1990 (c.19), s.31.

[9] Words added by SI 1997/2763 (Public Bodies (Admission to Meetings) (National Health Service Trusts) Order), Art.2(3).

Local Government Act 1972

(1972, c. 70)

Arrangement of Sections

Part VA

Access to Meetings and Documents of Certain Authorities, Committees and Sub-Committees

Section

Part XI

General Provisions as to Local Authorities

Schedules

Part VA

Access to Meetings and Documents of Certain Authorities, Committees and Sub-Committees

Admission to meetings of principal councils

App 4–02 **100A.**—(1) A meeting of a principal council shall be open to the public except to the extent that they are excluded (whether during the whole or part of the proceedings) under subsection (2) below or by resolution under subsection(4) below.

(2) The public shall be excluded from a meeting of a principal council during an item of business whenever it is likely, in view of the nature of the business to be transacted or the nature of the proceedings, that, if members of the public were present during that item, confidential information would be disclosed to them in breach of the obligation of confidence; and nothing in this Part shall be taken to authorise or require the disclosure of confidential information in breach of the obligation of confidence.

(3) For the purposes of subsection (2) above, "confidential information" means—

(a) information furnished to the council by a Government department upon terms (however expressed) which forbid the disclosure of the information to the public; and
(b) information the disclosure of which to the public is prohibited by or under any enactment or by the order of a court;

and, in either case, the reference to the obligation of confidence is to be construed accordingly.

(4) A principal council may by resolution exclude the public from a meeting during an item of business whenever it is likely, in view of the nature of the business to be transacted or the nature of the proceedings, that if members of the public were present during that item there would be disclosure to them of exempt information, as defined in section 100I below.

(5) A resolution under subsection (4) above shall—

(a) identify the proceedings, or the part of the proceedings, to which it applies, and
(b) state the description, in terms of Schedule 12A to this Act, of the exempt information giving rise to the exclusion of the public,

and where such a resolution is passed this section does not require the meeting to be open to the public during proceedings to which the resolution applies.

(6) The following provisions shall apply in relation to a meeting of a principal council, that is to say—

(a) public notice of the time and place of the meeting shall be given by posting it at the offices of the council three clear days at least before the meeting or, if the meeting is convened at shorter notice, then at the time it is convened;
(b) while the meeting is open to the public, the council shall not have power to exclude members of the public from the meeting; and
(c) while the meeting is open to the public, duly accredited representatives of newspapers attending the meeting for the purpose of reporting the proceedings for those newspapers shall, so far as practicable, be afforded reasonable facilities for taking their report and, unless the meeting is held in premises not belonging to the council or not on the telephone, for telephoning the report at their own expense.

(7) Nothing in this section shall require a principal council to permit the taking of photographs of any proceedings, or the use of any means to enable persons not present to see or hear any proceedings (whether at the time or later), or the making of any oral report on any proceedings as they take place.

(8) This section is without prejudice to any power of exclusion to suppress or prevent disorderly conduct or other misbehaviour at a meeting.[1][2]

---

[1] In relation to England:

"**Admission to meetings of principal councils**

100A.—(1) A meeting of a principal council shall be open to the public except to the extent that they are excluded (whether during the whole or part of the proceedings) under subsection (2) below or by resolution under subsection(4) below.

(2) The public shall be excluded from a meeting of a principal council during an item of business whenever it is likely, in view of the nature of the business to be transacted or the nature of the proceedings, that, if members of the public were present during that item, confidential information would be disclosed to them in breach of the obligation of confidence; and nothing in this Part shall be taken to authorise or require the disclosure of confidential information in breach of the obligation of confidence.

(3) For the purposes of subsection (2) above, "confidential information" means—

(a) information furnished to the council by a Government department upon terms (however expressed) which forbid the disclosure of the information to the public; and

(b) information the disclosure of which to the public is prohibited by or under any enactment or by the order of a court;

and, in either case, the reference to the obligation of confidence is to be construed accordingly.

(4) A principal council may by resolution exclude the public from a meeting during an item of business whenever it is likely, in view of the nature of the business to be transacted or the nature of the proceedings, that if members of the public were present during that item there would be disclosure to them of exempt information, as defined in section 100I below.

(5) A resolution under subsection (4) above shall—

(a) identify the proceedings, or the part of the proceedings, to which it applies, and

(b) state the description, in terms of Schedule 12A to this Act, of the exempt information giving rise to the exclusion of the public,

and where such a resolution is passed this section does not require the meeting to be open to the public during proceedings to which the resolution applies.

(6) The following provisions shall apply in relation to a meeting of a principal council, that is to say—

(a) public notice of the time and place of the meeting shall be given by posting it at the offices of the council five clear days at least before the meeting or, if the meeting is convened at shorter notice, then at the time it is convened;

(b) while the meeting is open to the public, the council shall not have power to exclude members of the public from the meeting; and

(c) while the meeting is open to the public, duly accredited representatives of newspapers attending the meeting for the purpose of reporting the proceedings for those newspapers shall, so far as practicable, be afforded reasonable facilities for taking their report and, unless the meeting is held in premises not belonging to the council or not on the telephone, for telephoning the report at their own expense.

(7) Nothing in this section shall require a principal council to permit the taking of photographs of any proceedings, or the use of any means to enable persons not present to see or hear any proceedings (whether at the time or later), or the making of any oral report on any proceedings as they take place.

(8) This section is without prejudice to any power of exclusion to suppress or prevent disorderly conduct or other misbehaviour at a meeting."

[2] Words substituted by SI 2002/715 (Local Authorities (Access to Meetings and Documents) (Period of Notice) (England) Order), Art.2.

Access to agenda and connected reports

100B.—(1) Copies of the agenda for a meeting of a principal council and, subject to subsection (2) below, copies of any report for the meeting shall be open to inspection by members of the public at the offices of the council in accordance with subsection (3) below.

(2) If the proper officer thinks fit, there may be excluded from the copies of reports provided in pursuance of subsection (1) above the whole of any report which, or any part which, relates only to items during which, in his opinion, the meeting is likely not to be open to the public.

(3) Any document which is required by subsection (1) above to be open to inspection shall be so open at least three clear days before the meeting, except that—

(a) where the meeting is convened at shorter notice, the copies of the agenda and reports shall be open to inspection from the time the meeting is convened, and

(b) where an item is added to an agenda copies of which are open to inspection by the public, copies of the item (or of the revised agenda), and the copies of any report for the meeting relating to the item, shall be open to inspection from the time the item is added to the agenda;

but nothing in this subsection requires copies of any agenda, item or report to be open to inspection by the public until copies are available to members of the council.

(4) An item of business may not be considered at a meeting of a principal council unless either—

(a) a copy of the agenda including the item (or a copy of the item) is open to inspection by members of the public in pursuance of subsection (1) above for at least three clear days before the meeting or, where the meeting is convened at shorter notice, from the time the meeting is convened; or

(b) by reason of special circumstances, which shall be specified in the minutes, the chairman of the meeting is of the opinion that the item should be considered at the meeting as a matter of urgency.

(5) Where by virtue of subsection (2) above the whole or any part of a report for a meeting is not open to inspection by the public under subsection (1) above—

(a) every copy of the report or of the part shall be marked "Not for publication"; and

(b) there shall be stated on every copy of the whole or any part of the report the description, in terms of Schedule 12A to this Act,of the exempt information by virtue of which the council are likely to exclude the public during the item to which the report relates.

(6) Where a meeting of a principal council is required by section 100A above to be open to the public during the proceedings or any part of them, there shall be made available for the use of members of the public present at the meeting a reasonable number of copies of the agenda and, subject to subsection (8) below, of the reports for the meeting.

(7) There shall, on request and on payment of postage or other necessary charge for transmission, be supplied for the benefit of any newspaper—

(a) a copy of the agenda for a meeting of a principal council and, subject to subsection (8) below, a copy of each of the reports for the meeting; (b) such further statements or particulars, if any, as are necessary to indicate the nature of the items included in the agenda; and

(c) if the proper officer thinks fit in the case of any item, copies of any other documents supplied to members of the council in connection with the item.

(8) Subsection (2) above applies in relation to copies of reports provided in pursuance of subsection (6) or (7) above as it applies in relation to copies of reports provided in pursuance of subsection (1) above.[[3]][4]

---

[3] In relation to England:

"Access to agenda and connected reports

100B.—(1) Copies of the agenda for a meeting of a principal council and, subject to subsection (2) below, copies of any report for the meeting shall be open to inspection by members of the public at the offices of the council in accordance with subsection (3) below.

(2) If the proper officer thinks fit, there may be excluded from the copies of reports provided in pursuance of subsection (1) above the whole of any report which, or any part which, relates only to items during which, in his opinion, the meeting is likely not to be open to the public.

(3) Any document which is required by subsection (1) above to be open to inspection shall be so open at least five clear days before the meeting, except that—

(a) where the meeting is convened at shorter notice, the copies of the agenda and reports shall be open to inspection from the time the meeting is convened, and

(b) where an item is added to an agenda copies of which are open to inspection by the public, copies of the item (or of the revised agenda), and the copies of any report for the meeting relating to the item, shall be open to inspection from the time the item is added to the agenda;

but nothing in this subsection requires copies of any agenda, item or report to be open to inspection by the public until copies are available to members of the council.

(4) An item of business may not be considered at a meeting of a principal council unless either—

(a) a copy of the agenda including the item (or a copy of the item) is open to inspection by members of the public in pursuance of subsection (1) above for at least five clear days before the meeting or, where the meeting is convened at shorter notice, from the time the meeting is convened; or

(b) by reason of special circumstances, which shall be specified in the minutes, the chairman of the meeting is of the opinion that the item should be considered at the meeting as a matter of urgency.

(5) Where by virtue of subsection (2) above the whole or any part of a report for a meeting is not open to inspection by the public under subsection (1) above—

(a) every copy of the report or of the part shall be marked "Not for publication"; and

(b) there shall be stated on every copy of the whole or any part of the report the description, in terms of Schedule 12A to this Act,of the exempt information by virtue of which the council are likely to exclude the public during the item to which the report relates.

(6) Where a meeting of a principal council is required by section 100A above to be open to the public during the proceedings or any part of them, there shall be made available for the use of members of the public present at the meeting a reasonable number of copies of the agenda and, subject to subsection (8) below, of the reports for the meeting.

(7) There shall, on request and on payment of postage or other necessary charge for transmission, be supplied for the benefit of any newspaper—

(a) a copy of the agenda for a meeting of a principal council and, subject to subsection (8) below, a copy of each of the reports for the meeting;

(b) such further statements or particulars, if any, as are necessary to indicate the nature of the items included in the agenda; and

(c) if the proper officer thinks fit in the case of any item, copies of any other documents supplied to members of the council in connection with the item.

(8) Subsection (2) above applies in relation to copies of reports provided in pursuance of subsection (6) or (7) above as it applies in relation to copies of reports provided in pursuance of subsection (1) above."

[4] Substituted by SI 2002/715 (Local Authorities (Access to Meetings and Documents) (Period of Notice) (England) Order), Art.3.

Inspection of minutes and other documents after meetings[5]

[**100C.**—(1) After a meeting of a principal council the following documents shall be open to inspection by members of the public at the offices of the council until the expiration of the period of six years beginning with the date of the meeting, namely—

(a) the minutes, or a copy of the minutes, of the meeting, excluding so much of the minutes of proceedings during which the meeting was not open to the public as discloses exempt information;
(b) where applicable, a summary under subsection (2) below;
(c) a copy of the agenda for the meeting; and
(d) a copy of so much of any report for the meeting as relates to any item during which the meeting was open to the public.

(2) Where, in consequence of the exclusion of parts of the minutes which disclose exempt information, the document open to inspection under subsection (1)(a) above does not provide members of the public with a reasonably fair and coherent record of the whole or part of the proceedings, the proper officer shall make a written summary of the proceedings or the part, as the case may be, which provides such a record without disclosing the exempt information.][6]

Inspection of background papers

[**100D.**—(1) Subject, in the case of section 100C(1), to subsection (2) below, if and so long as copies of the whole or part of a report for a meeting of a principal council are required by section 100B(1) or 100C(1) above to be open to inspection by members of the public-

(a) those copies shall each include a copy of a list, compiled by the proper officer, of the background papers for the report or the part of the report, and
(b) at least one copy of each of the documents included in that list shall also be open to inspection at the offices of the council.

(2) Subsection (1) above does not require a copy of any document included in the list, to be open to inspection after the expiration of the period of four years beginning with the date of the meeting.

(3) Where a copy of any of the background papers for a report is required by subsection (1) above to be open to inspection by members of the public, the copy shall be taken for the purposes of this Part to be so open if arrangement sexist for its production to members of the public as soon as is reasonably practicable after the making of a request to inspect the copy.

(4) Nothing in this section—

(a) requires any document which discloses exempt information to be included in the list referred to in subsection (1) above; or
(b) without prejudice to the generality of subsection (2) of section 100A above, requires or authorises the inclusion in the list of any document which, if open to

[5] Act modified by Representation of the People Act 1983 (c.2), s.40(2), SI 1979/1123, arts 4(2), 5, extended by Charlwood and Horley Act 1974 (c.11), s.2. Words of enactment omitted under authority of Statute Law Revision Act 1948 (c.62), s.3. Power to modify Act conferred by Representation of the People Act 1983 (c.2), s.39(6)(7). Pt VA modified by Local Government (Access to Information) Act 1985 (c.43), s.3, Sch.2, para.7. S.100C extended with modifications by Health Services Joint Consultative Committees (Access to Information) Act 1986 (c.24), s.2(1); applied with modifications by Community Health Councils (Access to Information) Act 1986 (c.24), s.1(1)(2).

[6] Pt VA inserted by Local Government (Access to Information) Act 1985 (c.43), s.1(1).

inspection by the public, would disclose confidential information in breach of the obligation of confidence, within the meaning of that subsection.

(5) For the purposes of this section the background papers for a report are those documents relating to the subject matter of the report which—

(a) disclose any facts or which, matters on which, in the opinion of the proper officer, the report or an important part of the report is based, and
(b) have, in his opinion, been relied on to a material extent in preparing the report,

but do not include any published works.][7]

Application to committees and sub-committees

[100E.—(1) Sections100A to 100D above shall apply in relation to a committee or sub-committee of a principle council as they apply in relation to a principal council.

(2) In the application by virtue of this section of sections 100A to100D above in relation to a committee or sub-committee—

(a) section 100A(6)(a) shall be taken to have been complied with if the notice is given by posting it at the time there mentioned at the offices of every constituent principal council and, if the meeting of the committee or sub-committee to which that section so applies is to be held at premises other than the offices of such a council, at those premises;
(b) for the purposes of section 100A(6)(c), premises belonging to a constituent principal council shall be treated as belonging to the committee or sub-committee; and
(c) for the purposes of sections 100B(1), 100C(1) and 100D(1), offices of any constituent principal council shall be treated as offices of the committee or sub-committee.

(3) Any reference in this Part to a committee or sub-committee of a principle council is a reference to—

(a) a committee which is constituted under an enactment specified in section 101(9) below or which is appointed by one or more principal councils under section 102 below; or
(b) a joint committee not falling within paragraph (a) above which is appointed or established under any enactment by two or more principal councils and is not a body corporate; or
[(bb) the Navigation Committee of the Broads Authority; or][8]
(c) a sub-committee appointed or established under any enactment by one or more committees falling within [paragraphs(a) to (bb)][9] above.

(4) Any reference in this Part to a constituent principal council, in relation to a committee or sub-committee, is a reference—

(a) in the case of a committee, to the principal council, or any of the principal councils, of which it is a committee; and

---

7 Words substituted by Local Government Act 2000 (c.22), Pt V, s.97.

8 S.100E(3)(bb) inserted by Norfolk and Suffolk Broads Act 1988 (c.4), ss.21, 23(2), 27(2), Sch.6, para.10(4).

9 Words substituted by Norfolk and Suffolk Broads Act 1988 (c.4), ss.21, 23(2), 27(2), Sch.6 para.10(4).

(b) in the case of a sub-committee, to any principal council which, by virtue of paragraph (a) above, is a constituent principal council in relation to the committee, or any of the committees, which established or appointed the sub-committee.][10]

Additional rights of access to documentsfor members of principal councils

[**100F.**—(1) Any document which is in the possession or under the control of a principal council and contains material relating to any business to be transacted at a meeting of the council or a committee or sub-committee of the council shall, subject to subsection(2) below, be open to inspection by any member of the council.

(2) Where it appears to the proper officer that a document discloses exempt information of a description for the time being falling within any of paragraphs 1 to 6, 9, 11, 12 and 14 of Part I of Schedule 12A to this Act, subsection (1) above does not require the document to be open to inspection.

(3) The Secretary of State may by order amend subsection (2) above—

(a) by adding to the descriptions of exempt information to which that subsection refers for the time being; or

(b) by removing any description of exempt information to which it refers for the time being.

(4) Any statutory instrument containing an order under subsection (3)above shall be subject to annulment in pursuance of a resolution of either House of Parliament.

(5) The rights conferred by this section on a member of a principal council are in addition to any other rights he may have apart from this section.][11]

Principal councils to publish additionalinformation

[**100G.**—(1) A principal council shall maintain a register stating—

(a) the name and address of every member of the council for the time being and the ward or division which he represents; and

(2) A principal council shall maintain a list—

(a) specifying those powers of the council which, for the time being,are exercisable from time to time by officers of the council in pursuance of arrangements made under this Act or any other enactment for their discharge by those officers; and

(b) stating the title of the officer by whom each of the powers so specified is for the time being so exercisable;

but this subsection does not require a power to be specified in the list if the arrangements for its discharge by the officer are made for a specified period not exceeding six months.

(3) There shall be kept at the offices of every principal council a written summary of the rights—

(a) to attend meetings of a principal council and of committees and sub- committees of a principal council, and

(b) to inspect and copy documents and to be furnished with documents,

which are for the time being conferred by this Part, Part XI below and such other enactments as the Secretary of State by order specifies.

---

10 Pt VA inserted by Local Government (Access to Information) Act 1985 (c.43), s.1(1).
11 *ibid.*

(4) The register maintained under subsection (1) above, the list maintained under subsection (2) above and the summary kept under subsection (3) above shall be open to inspection by the public at the offices of the council.][12]

Supplemental provisions and offences

[100H.—(1) A document directed by any provisions of this Part to be open to inspection shall be so open at all reasonable hours and—

(a) in the case of a document open to inspection by virtue of section 100D(1) above, upon payment of such reasonable fee as may be required for the facility;and
(b) in any other case, without payment.

(2) Where a document is open to inspection by a person under any provisions of this Part, the person may, subject to subsection (3) below—

(a) make copies of or extracts from the document, or
(b) require the person having custody of the document to supply to him a photographic copy of or of extracts from the document,

upon payment of such reasonable fee as may be required for the facility.

(3) Subsection (2) above does not require or authorise the doing of any such act which infringes the copyright in any work except that, where the owner of the copyright is a principal council, nothing done in pursuance of that subsection shall constitute an infringement of the copyright.

(4) If, without reasonable excuse, a person having the custody of a document which is required by section 100B(1) or 100C(1) above to be open to inspection by the public—

(a) intentionally obstructs any person exercising a right conferred by this Part to inspect, or to make a copy of or extracts from, the document, or
(b) refuses to furnish copies to any person entitled to obtain them under any provision of this Part,

he shall be liable on summary conviction to a fine not exceeding level 1 on the standard scale.

(5) Where any accessible document for a meeting to which this subsection applies—

(a) is supplied to, or open to inspection by, a member of the public,or
(b) is supplied for the benefit of any newspaper, in pursuance of section 100B(7) above,

the publication thereby of any defamatory matter contained in the document shall be privileged unless the publication is proved to be made with malice.

(6) Subsection (5) above applies to any meeting of a principal council and any meeting of a committee or sub-committee of a principal council; and, for the purposes of that subsection, the "accessible documents"for a meeting are the following—

(a) any copy of the agenda or of any item included in the agenda for the meeting;
(b) any such further statements or particulars for the purpose of indicating the nature of any item included in the agenda as are mentioned in section 100B(7)(b) above;
(c) any copy of a document relating to such an item which is supplied for the benefit of a newspaper in pursuance of section 100B(7)(c) above;
(d) any copy of the whole or part of a report for the meeting;
(e) any copy of the whole or part of any background papers for a report for the meeting, within the meaning of section 100D above.

[12] Pt VA inserted by Local Government (Access to Information) Act 1985 (c.43), s.1(1).

(7) The rights conferred by this Part to inspect, copy and be furnished with documents are in addition, and without prejudice, to any such rights conferred by or under any other enactment.][13]

Exempt information and power to vary Schedule12A

[**100I.**—(1) The descriptions of information which are, for the purposes of this Part, exempt information are those for the time being specified in Part I of Schedule 12A to this Act, but subject to any qualifications contained in Part II of that Schedule; and Part IIIhas effect for the interpretation of that Schedule.

(2) The Secretary of State may by order vary Schedule 12Ato this Act by adding to it any description or other provision or by deleting from it or varying any description or other provision for the time being specified or contained in it.

(3) The Secretary of State may exercise the power conferred by subsection(2) above by amending any Part of Schedule 12A to this Act, with or without amendment of any other Part.

(4) Any statutory instrument containing an order under this section shall be subject to annulment in pursuance of a resolution of either House of Parliament.][14]

Application to new authorities, Common Council, etc

100J.—(1) Except in this section, any reference in this Part to a principal council includes a reference to—

(b) a joint authority;
(bb) the London Fire and Emergency Planning Authority;
(c) the Common Council;
(cc) The Broads Authority;
(cd) a National Park authority;
(d) a joint board or joint committee falling within subsection (2) below;
(e) a police authority established under section 3 of the Police Act 1996;
(eza) the Metropolitan Police Authority;
(f) a combined fire authority.

(2) A joint board or joint committee falls within this subsection if—

(a) it is constituted under any enactment as a body corporate; and
(b) it discharges functions of two or more principal councils;

and for the purposes of this subsection any body falling within paragraph (a), (b), (bb) or (c) of subsection (1) above shall be treated as a principal council.

(3) In its application by virtue of subsection (1) above in relation to a body falling within paragraph (b), (bb), (cc), (cd), (d), (e), (eza) or (f) of that subsection, section 100A (6)(a) above shall have effect with the insertion after the words "council" of the words

[13] S.100H amended by Community Health Councils (Access to Information) Act 1988 (c.24), s.1(4)(a); extended with modifications by Health Services Joint Consultative Committees (Access to Information) Act 1986 (c.24), ss.2(2), 4. S.100H(3) modified by Community Health Councils (Access to Information) Act 1988 (c.24), s.1(4)(c). S.100H(5) applied by Community Health Councils (Access to Information) Act 1988 (c.24), s.1(4)(d). S.100H(2)(b) modified by Community Health Councils (Access to Information) Act 1988 (c.24), s.1(4)(b). Pt VA inserted by Local Government (Access to Information) Act 1985 (c.43), s.1(1).

[14] S.100I(2) extended by Health Services Joint Consultative Committees (Access to Information) Act 1986 (c.24), ss.2(3), 4. S.100I(2) extended by Community Health Councils (Access to Information) Act 1988 (c.24), s.1(5). Pt VA inserted by Local Government (Access to Information) Act 1985 (c.43), s.1(1).

"(and, if the meeting is to be held at premises other than those offices, at those premises)".

(4) In its application by virtue of subsection (1) above, section 100G(1)(a) above shall have effect—

(a) in relation to a joint authority or a police authority established under section 3 of the Police Act 1996 or the Metropolitan Police Authority [. . .][15] with the substitution for the words from ward onwards of the words name or description of the body or other person that appointed him; and

(aa) in relation to the Broads Authority or its Navigation Committee or any National Park authority, with the substitution for the words from "ward" onwards of the words "name of the person who appointed him"; and

(b) in relation to joint board or joint committee falling within subsection (2) above, with the omission of the words from "and the ward" onwards; and

(c) in relation to a combined fire authority, with the substitution for the words "ward or division" of the words "constituent area".

(4A) In its application by virtue of subsection (1)(bb) above in relation to the London Fire and Emergency Planning Authority, section 100G(1)(a) shall have effect with the substitution for the words "the ward or division which he represents" of the words

"whether he is an Assembly representative or a borough representative, and—

(i) if he is an Assembly representative, whether he is a London member or a constituency member and, if a constituency member, the Assembly constituency for which he is a member, or

(ii) if he is a borough representative, the council of which he is a member (whether a London borough council or the Common Council)".

(5) In this section "combined fire authority" means a fire authority constituted by a combination scheme under the Fire Services Act 1947.

Interpretation and application of Part VA

[**100K.**—(1) In this Part—

"committee or sub-committee of a principal council" shall be construed in accordance with section 100E(3) above;

"constituent principal council" shall be construed in accordance with section 100E(4) above;

"copy", in relation to any document, includes a copy made from a copy;

"exempt information" has the meaning given by section 100I above;

"information" includes an expression of opinion, any recommendations and any decision taken;

"newspaper" includes—

(a) a news agency which systematically carries on the business of selling and supplying reports or information to newspapers;and

(b) any organisation which is systematically engaged in collecting news—

(i) for sound or television broadcasts; or

(ii) for inclusion in programmes to be included in any programme service (within the meaning of the Broadcasting Act 1990) other than a sound or television broadcasting service;

[15] Words repealed by Criminal Justice and Police Act 2001 (c.16), Sch.7(5)(1) Para.1.

"principal council" shall be construed in accordance with section 100J above.

(2) Any reference in this Part to a meeting is a reference to a meeting held after 1st April 1986.

(3) The Secretary of State may by order amend sections 100A(6)(a) and 100B(3) and (4)(a) above so as to substitute for each reference to three clear days such greater number of days as may be specified in the order.

(4) Any statutory instrument containing an order under subsection (3) above shall be subject to annulment in pursuance of a resolution of either House of Parliament.][16]

Part XI

General Provisions as to Local Authorities

Documents and notices, etc.

Inspection of documents

228.—(1) The minutes of proceedings of a parish or community council shall be open to the inspection of any local government elector for the area of the authority the council and any such local government elector may make a copy of or extract from the minutes.

(2) A local government elector for the area of a local authority may inspect and make a copy of or extract from an order for the payment of money made by the local authority.

(3) The accounts of a local authority and of any proper officer of a local authority shall be open to the inspection of any member of the authority, and any such member may make a copy of or extract from the accounts.

(5) Subject to any provisions to the contrary in any other enactment or instrument, a person interested in any document deposited as mentioned in section 225 above may, at all reasonable hours, inspect and make copies thereof or extracts therefrom on payment to the person having custody thereof of the sum of 10p for every such inspection, and of the further sum of 10p for every hour during which such inspection continues after the first hour.

(6) A document directed by this section to be open to inspection shall be so open at all reasonable hours and, except where otherwise expressly provided, without payment.

(7) If a person having the custody of any such document—

(a) obstructs any person entitled to inspect the document or to make a copy thereof or extract there from in inspecting the document or making a copy or extract,

(b) refuses to give copies or extracts to any persons entitled to obtain copies or extracts,

he shall be liable on summary conviction to a fine not exceeding level 1 on the standard scale .

(7A) This section shall apply to the minutes of proceedings and the accounts of a joint authority or a police authority established under section 3 of the Police Act 1996 or the Metropolitan Police Authority [. . .][17] as if that authority were a local authority and

---

16 Words added by Local Government Act 2000 (c.22), Pt V, s.98(1).

17 Words repealed by Criminal Justice and Police Act 2001 (c.16), Sch.7(5)(1) Para.1.

as if, references to a local government elector for the area of the authority were a reference to a local government elector for any local government area in the area for which the authority is established.

(8) This section shall apply to the minutes of proceedings and to the accounts of a parish meeting as if that meeting were a parish council.

(9) In relation to the Boards Authority, the references in this section to a local government elector for the area of the authority shall be construed as references to a local government elector for the area of any of the local authorities mentioned in section 1(3)(a) of the Norfolk and Suffolk Broads Act 1988.

SCHEDULE 12A

Access to Information: Exempt Information

Part I

Descriptions of Exempt Information

[1. Information relating to a particular employee, former employee or applicant to become an employee of, or a particular office-holder, former office-holder or applicant to become an office-holder under, the authority.][18]

[2. Information relating to a particular employee, former employee or applicant to become an employee of, or a particular officer, former officer or applicant to become an officer appointed by—

(a) a magistrates' court committee;

(b) a probation committee within the meaning of the Probation Service Act 1993[; or][19]

[(c) a local probation board within the meaning of the Criminal Justice and Court Services Act 2000.][20]

[2A. Information relating to a particular chief officer, former chief officer or applicant to become a chief officer of a local probation board within the meaning of the Criminal Justice and Court Services Act 2000.][21]

---

18 Act modified by Representation of the People Act 1983 (c.2), s.40(2), SI 1979/1123, arts 4(2), 5, extended by Charlwood and Horley Act 1974 (c.11), s.2. Words of enactment omitted under authority of Statute Law Revision Act 1948 (c.62), s.3. Power to modify Act conferred by Representation of the People Act 1983 (c.2), s.39(6)(7). Sch.12A modified by Community Health Councils (Access to Information) Act 1988 (c.24), s.1(6); extended with modifications by Health Service Joint Consultative Committees (Access to Information) Act 1986 (c.24), ss.2(4), 4(2)(3)(4). Sch.12A inserted by Local Government (Access to Information) Act 1985 (c.43), s.1(2), Sch.1, Pt I.

19 Words added by Criminal Justice and Court Services Act 2000 (c.43), Sch.7(II) Para.46(b).

20 *ibid.*

21 Act modified by Representation of the People Act 1983 (c.2), s.40(2), SI 1979/1123, arts 4(2), 5, extended by Charlwood and Horley Act 1974 (c.11), s.2. Words of enactment omitted under authority of Statute Law Revision Act 1948 (c.62), s.3. Power to modify Act conferred by Representation of the People Act 1983 (c.2), s.39(6)(7). Sch.12A modified by Community Health Councils (Access to Information) Act 1988 (c.24), s.1(6); extended with modifications by Health Service Joint Consultative Committees (Access to Information) Act 1986 (c.24), ss.2(4), 4(2)(3)(4). Words added by Criminal Justice and Court Services Act 2000 (c.43), Sch.7(II), para.46(c).

[3. Information relating to any particular occupier or former occupier of, or applicant for, accommodation provided by or at the expense of the authority.][22]

[4. Information relating to any particular applicant for, or recipient or former recipient of, any service provided by the authority.][23]

[5. Information relating to any particular applicant for, or recipient or former recipient of, any financial assistance provided by the authority.][24]

[6. Information relating to the adoption, care, fostering or education of any particular child.][25]

[7. Information relating to the financial or business affairs of any particular person (other than the authority).][26]

[8. The amount of any expenditure proposed to be incurred by the authority under any particular contract for the acquisition of property or the supply of goods or services.][27]

[9. Any terms proposed or to be proposed by or to the authority in the course of negotiations for a contract for the acquisition or disposal of property or the supply of goods or services.][28]

[10. The identity of the authority (as well as of any other person, by virtue of paragraph 7 above) as the person offering any particular tender for a contract for the supply of goods or services.][29]

[11. Information relating to any consultations or negotiations, or contemplated consultations or negotiations, in connection with any labour relations matter arising between the authority or a Minister of the Crown and employees of, or office-holders under, the authority.][30]

[12. Any instructions to counsel and any opinion of counsel (whether or not in connection with any proceedings) and any advice received, information obtained or action to be taken in connection with—

(a) any legal proceedings by or against the authority, or
(b) the determination of any matter affecting the authority,
(whether, in either case, proceedings have been commenced or are in contemplation).][31]

[13. Information which, if disclosed to the public, would reveal that the authority proposes—

(a) to give under any enactment a notice under or by virtue of which requirements are imposed on a person; or
(b) to make an order or direction under any enactment.][32]

22 Sch.12A inserted by Local Government (Access to Information) Act 1985 (c.43), s.1(2), Sch.1, Pt I.
23 *ibid.*
24 *ibid.*
25 *ibid.*
26 *ibid.*
27 *ibid.*
28 *ibid*
29 *ibid.*
30 *ibid.*
31 *ibid.*
32 *ibid.*

[14. Any action taken or to be taken in connection with the prevention, investigation or prosecution of crime.][33]

[15. The identity of a protected informant.][34]

Part II

Qualifications

[1. Information relating to a person of a description specified in any of paragraphs 1 to 5 of Part I above is not exempt information by virtue of that paragraph unless it relates to an individual of that description in the capacity indicated by the description.][35]

[2. Information falling within paragraph 7 of Part I above is not exempt information by virtue of that paragraph if it is required to be registered under—
(a) the Companies Act 1985;
(b) the Friendly Societies Act 1974;
(c) the Industrial and Provident Societies Acts 1965 to 1978;
(d) the Building Societies Act [1986][36]; or
(e) the Charities Act 1960.][37]

[3. Information falling within paragraph 8 of Part I above is exempt information if and so long as disclosure to the public of the amount there referred to would be likely to give an advantage to a person entering into, or seeking to enter into, a contract with the authority in respect of the property, goods or services, whether the advantage would arise as against the authority or as against other such persons.][38]

[4. Information falling within paragraph 9 of Part I above is exempt information if and so long as disclosure to the public of the terms would prejudice the authority in those or any other negotiations concerning the property or goods or services.][39]

[5. Information falling within paragraph 11 of Part I above is exempt information if and so long as disclosure to the public of the information would prejudice the authority in those or any other consultations or negotiations in connection with a labour relations matter arising as mentioned in that paragraph.][40]

[6. Information falling within paragraph 13 of Part I above is exempt information if and so long as disclosure to the public might afford an opportunity to a person affected by the notice, order or direction to defeat the purpose or one of the purposes for which the notice, order or direction is to be given or made.][41]

33 Sch.12A inserted by Local Government (Access to Information) Act 1985 (c.43), s.1(2), Sch.1 Pt I.
34 *ibid.*
35 *ibid.*
36 Words "1986" substituted for words "1962" by Building Societies Act 1986 (c.53), ss.120, 126(3), Sch.18 para.9.
37 Sch.12A inserted by Local Government (Access to Information) Act 1985 (c.43), s.1(2), Sch.1 Pt. I.
38 *ibid.*
39 *ibid.*
40 *ibid.*
41 *ibid.*

[7. Information falling within any paragraph of Part 1 above is not exempt information by virtue of that paragraph if it relates to proposed development for which the local planning authority can grant itself planning permission pursuant to regulation 3 of the Town and Country Planning General Regulations 1992.][42]

PART III

INTERPRETATION

1.—(1) In this Schedule—

"child" means a person under the age of eighteen years and any person who has attained that age and—

(a) is registered as a pupil at a school; or

(b) is the subject of a care order, within the meaning of section 31 of the Children Act 1989;

"disposal" , in relation to property, includes the granting of an interest in or right over it;

"employee" means a person employed under a contract of service;

"financial or business affairs" includes contemplated, as well as past or current, activities;

"labour relations matter" means —

(a) any of the matters specified in paragraphs(a) to (g) of section 29(1) of the Trade Union and Labour Relations Act 1974 (matters which may be the subject of a trade dispute, within the meaning of that Act); or

(b) any dispute about a matter falling within paragraph (a) above;

and for the purposes of this definition the enactments mentioned in paragraph (a) above, with the necessary modifications, shall apply in relation to office-holders under the authority as they apply in relation to employees of the authority;

"office-holder", in relation to the authority, means the holders of any paid office appointments to which are or may be made or confirmed by the authority or by any joint board on which the authority is represented or by any person who holds any such office or is an employee of the authority;

"protected informant" means a person giving the authority information which tends to show that—

(a) a criminal offence,

(b) a breach of statutory duty,

(c) a breach of planning control, as defined in [171A of the Town and Country Planning Act 1990],[43]

or

(d) a nuisance,

has been, is being or is about to be committed;

"registered", in relation to information required to be registered under the Building Societies Act 1986, means recorded in the public file of any building society (within the meaning of that Act);

"tender for a contract" includes a written statement prepared by the authority in pursuance of section 9(2) of the Local Government, Planning and Land Act 1980 (estimated cost of carrying out functional work by direct labour).

(2) Any reference in this Schedule to 'the authority' is a reference to the principal council or, as the case may be, the committee or sub-committee in relation to whose proceedings or documents the question whether information is exempt or not falls to be determined and includes a reference—

(a) in the case of a principal council, to any committee or sub-committee of the council; and

(b) in the case of a committee, to—

(i) any constituent principal council;

(ii) any other principal council by which appointments are made to the committee or whose functions the committee discharges; and

---

42 Words added by SI 1992/1497 (Local Government (Access to Information) (Variation) Order), Art.2

43 Words substituted within definition by Planning and Compensation Act 1991 (c.34), Sch.7 para.2.

(iii) any other committee or sub-committee of a principal council falling within sub-paragraph (i) or (ii) above; and

(c) in the case of a sub-committee, to—

(i) the committee, or any of the committees, of which it is a sub- committee;and

(ii) any principal council which falls within paragraph (b) above in relation to that committee.

Local Government, Planning and Land Act 1980

(1980, c.65)

PART X

LAND HELD BY PUBLIC BODIES

Public access to information

App 4–03 **96.**—(1) The Secretary of State shall send to a council in respect of whose area a register is maintained under section 95 above—

(a) a copy of that register; and
(b) such amendments to it as he may from time to time consider appropriate.

(2) It shall be the duty of a council to whom amendments to a register are sent under subsection (1)(b) above to incorporate the amendments in their copy of the register.

(3) A copy of a register sent to a council under this section shall be available at the council's principal office for inspection by any member of the public at all reasonable hours.

(4) If any member of the public requires a council to supply him with a copy of any information contained in such a copy of a register, the council shall supply him with a copy of that information on payment of such reasonable charge for making it as the council may determine.

Local Government Finance Act 1992

(1992, c.14)

PART I

COUNCIL TAX: ENGLAND AND WALES

CHAPTER II

VALUATION LISTS

Supplemental

Information about lists

28.—(1) A person may require a listing officer to give him access to such information as will enable him to establish what is the state of a list, or has been its state at any time since it came into force, if— **App 4–04**

(a) the officer is maintaining the list; and
(b) the list is in force or has been in force at any time in the preceding five years.

(2) A person may require a billing authority to give him access to such information as will enable him to establish what is the state of a copy of a list, or has been its state at any time since it was deposited, if—

(a) the authority has deposited the copy under [section 22(8) or 22A(10) [or 22B(10)][1a]][1] above; and
(b) the list is in force or has been in force at any time in the preceding five years.

(3) A person may require a billing authority to give him access to such information as will enable him to establish what is the state of a copy of a proposed list if—

(a) the authority has deposited the copy under section 22(6) [or 22B(8)][1b] above; and
(b) the list itself is not yet in force.

(4) A requirement under subsection (1), (2) or (3) above must be complied with at a reasonable time and place and without payment being sought; but the information may be in documentary or other form, as the person or authority of whom the requirement is made thinks fit.

(5) Where access is given under this section to information in documentary form the person to whom access is given may—

(a) make copies of (or of extracts from) the document;
(b) require a person having custody of the document to supply to him a photographic copy of (or of extracts from) the document.

[1] Words inserted by Local Government (Wales) Act 1994 (c.19), Sch.16 para.97.
[1a] Words inserted by Local Government Act 2003 (c.26), Sch.7, para.48(b)
[1b] *ibid.*

(6) Where access is given under this section to information in a form which is not documentary the person to whom access is given may—

(a) make transcripts of (or of extracts from) the information;

(b) require a person having control of access to the information to supply to him a copy in documentary form of (or of extracts from) the information.

(7) If a reasonable charge is required for a facility under subsection (5) or (6) above, the subsection concerned shall not apply unless the person seeking to avail himself of the facility pays the charge.

(8) If without reasonable excuse a person having custody of a document containing, or having control of access to, information access to which is sought under this section—

(a) intentionally obstructs a person in exercising a right under subsection (1), (2), (3), (5)(a) or (6)(a) above; or

(b) refuses to comply with a requirement under subsection (5)(b) or (6)(b) above,

he shall be liable on summary conviction to a fine not exceeding level 2 on the standard scale.

PART II

COUNCIL TAX: SCOTLAND

VALUATION LISTS: SUPPLEMENTAL

Information about lists

91.—(1) A person may require a local assessor to give him access to such information as will enable him to establish what is the state of a list, or has been its state at any time since it came into force, if—

(a) the local assessor is maintaining the list; and

(b) the list is in force or has been in force at any time in the preceding five years.

(2) A person may require a [local][2] authority to give him access to such information as will enable him to establish what is the state of a copy of a list, or has been its state at any time since it was deposited, if—

(a) the authority has deposited the copy under section 85(5) above; and

(b) the list is in force or has been in force at any time in the preceding 5 years.

(3) A person may require a [local][3] authority to give him access to such information as will enable him to establish what is the state of a copy of a proposed list if—

(a) the authority has deposited the copy under section 85(3) above; and

(b) the list itself is not yet in force.

(4) A requirement under subsection (1), (2) or (3) above must be complied with at a reasonable time and place and without payment being sought; but the information may be in documentary or other form, as the person or authority of whom the requirement is made thinks fit.

---

2 Word substituted by Local Government, etc. (Scotland) Act 1994 (c.39), Sch.13, para.176(8).

3 *ibid.*

(5) Where access is given under this section to information in documentary form the person to whom access is given may—

(a) make copies of (or of extracts from) the document;
(b) require a person having custody of the document to supply to him a photographic copy of (or of extracts from) the document.

(6) Where access is given under this section to information in a form which is not documentary the person to whom access is given may—

(a) make transcripts of (or of extracts from) the information;
(b) require a person having control of access to the information to supply to him a copy in documentary form of (or of extracts from) the information.

(7) If a reasonable charge is required for a facility under subsection (5) or (6) above, the subsection concerned shall not apply unless the person seeking to avail himself of the facility pays the charge.

(8) If a person having custody of a document containing, or having control of access to, information access to which is sought under this section—

(a) intentionally obstructs a person in exercising a right under subsection (1), (2), (3), (5)(a) or (6)(a) above; or
(b) refuses to comply with a requirement under subsection (5)(b) or (6)(b) above,

he shall be guilty of an offence and liable on summary conviction to a fine not exceeding level 2 on the standard scale.

(9) It shall be a defence for a person charged with an offence under subsection (8) above to prove that he had a reasonable excuse for acting as he did.

Greater London Authority Act 1999

(1999, c.29)

PART II

GENERAL FUNCTIONS AND PROCEDURE

Meetings and procedure of the assembly

Openness

App 4–05 58.—(1) Part VA of the Local Government Act 1972 (access to meetings and documents of certain authorities, committees and sub-committees) shall have effect as if—

(a) the Assembly were a principal council, and
(b) any committee or sub-committee of the Assembly were a committee or sub-committee of a principal council, within the meaning of that Part,

but with the following modifications

(2) In the application of Part VA of that Act by subsection (1) above—

(a) any information furnished to the Authority and available to the Assembly shall be treated as information furnished to the Assembly;
(b) any offices of, or belonging to, the Authority shall be treated as also being offices of or belonging to the Assembly; and
(c) the proper officer of the Authority shall be taken to be the proper officer in relation to the Assembly.

(3) In the following provisions of that Act, namely—

(a) section 100A(2) (which requires the exclusion of the public from meetings and makes other provision to prevent disclosure of confidential information in breach of the obligation of confidence), and
(b) section 100D(4) (which prevents the inclusion in a list of documents of any document which would so disclose such information),

any reference to the disclosure (or likelihood of disclosure) of confidential information in breach of the obligation of confidence includes a reference to the disclosure of information of any of the descriptions specified in subsection (4) below without the consent of the relevant body concerned.

(4) The descriptions are—

(a) any information relating to the financial or business affairs of any particular person which was acquired in consequence of a relationship between that person and a relevant body;
(b) the amount of any expenditure proposed to be incurred by a relevant body under any particular contract; if and so long as disclosure would be likely to give an advantage to a person entering into, or seeking to enter into, a contract with the relevant body, whether the advantage would arise against the relevant body or another such person;

(c) any terms proposed or to be proposed by or to a relevant body in the course of negotiations for any particular contract, if and so long as disclosure would prejudice the relevant body in those or any other negotiations concerning the subject matter of the contract;
(d) the identity of any person as the person offering any particular tender for a contract for the supply of goods or services to a relevant body;

and in this subsection "relevant body" means Transport for London or the London Development Agency.

(5) In section 100C of that Act (inspection of minutes and other documents after meetings) any reference to the minutes of a meeting shall, in the case of a meeting of the Assembly under section 52(3) above, be taken to include a reference to—

(a) the text of any question put pursuant to section 52(3) above at the meeting, and
(b) the text of the answer given to any such question,

whether the question was put, or the answer given, orally or in writing.

(6) Nothing in section 100D of that Act (inspection of background papers) requires or authorises the inclusion in any such list as is referred to in subsection (1) of that section of any document which discloses anything which, by virtue of subsection (6) of section 45 above, is not required to be disclosed under subsection (3) or (4) of that section.

(7) In section 100E of that Act (application to committees and sub- committees) subsection (3)(a) shall have effect as if section 55 above were included among the enactments specified in section 101(9) of that Act.

(8) For the purposes of section 100F of that Act (additional rights of access to documents for members of principal councils) any document which is in the possession or under the control of the Authority and which is available to the Assembly shall be treated as a document which is in the possession or under the control of the Assembly.

(9) In the case of the Assembly, the register of members required to be maintained under section 100G(1) of that Act shall, instead of stating the ward or division which a member represents, state—

(a) whether the member is a London member or a constituency member; and
(b) if he is a constituency member, the Assembly constituency for which he is the member.

(10) For the purposes of section 100H(3) of that Act (acts which infringe copyright) the Authority shall be treated as a principal council.

(11) In the application in relation to the Assembly of Schedule 12A to that Act (access to information: exempt information) any reference to "the authority" includes a reference to the Authority.

Local Government Act 2000

(2000, c.22)

PART II

ARRANGEMENTS WITH RESPECT TO EXECUTIVES, ETC.

Provisions with respect to executive arrangements

Access to information etc.

App 4–06 22.—(1) Meetings of a local authority executive, or a committee of such an executive, are to be open to the public or held in private.

(2) Subject to regulations under subsection (9), it is for a local authority executive to decide which of its meetings, and which of the meetings of any committee of the executive, are to be open to the public and which of those meetings are to be held in private.

(3) A written record must be kept of prescribed decisions made at meetings of local authorities executives, or committees of such executives, which are held in private.

(4) A written record must be kept of prescribed decisions made by individual members of local authority executives.

(5) Written records under subsection (3) or (4) must include reasons for the decisions to which they relate.

(6) Written records under subsections (3) and (4), together with such reports, background papers or other documents as may be prescribed, must be made available to members of the public in accordance with regulations made by the Secretary of State.

(7) Regulations under subsection (6) may make provision for or in connection with preventing the whole or part of any record or document containing prescribed information from being made available to members of the public.

(8) The Secretary of State may by regulations make provision—

(a) with respect to the access of the public to meetings of joint committees, or sub-committees of such committees, at which decisions are made in connection with the discharge of functions which are the responsibility of executives (including provision enabling such meetings to be held in private),

(b) for or in connection with requiring written records to be kept of decisions made at meetings which by virtue of paragraph (a) are held in private,

(c) for or in connection with requiring written records falling within paragraph (b) to include reasons,

(d) for or in connection with requiring any such written records to be made available to members of the public,

(e) for or in connection with requiring documents connected with decisions to which any such written records relate to be made available to members of the public.

(9) The Secretary of State may by regulations make provision-

(a) as to the circumstances in which meetings mentioned in subsection (2), or particular proceedings at such meetings, must be open to the public,

(b) as to the circumstances in which meetings mentioned in subsection (2), or particular proceedings at such meetings, must be held in private,

(c) with respect to the information which is to be included in written records kept by virtue of this section,
(d) with respect to the reasons which are to be included in any such written records,
(e) with respect to the persons who are to produce, keep or make available any such written records,
(f) for or in connection with requiring any such written records to be made available to members of local authorities or to overview and scrutiny committees or sub-committees,
(g) for or in connection with requiring documents connected with decisions to which any such written records relate to be made available to members of local authorities or to overview and scrutiny committees or sub-committees,
(h) for or in connection with requiring information to be made available by electronic means,
(i) for or in connection with conferring rights on members of the public, members of local authorities or overview and scrutiny committees or sub- committees in relation to records or documents,
(j) for or in connection with the creation of offences in respect of any rights or requirements conferred or imposed by virtue of this section.

(10) The Secretary of State may by regulations make provision for or in connection with requiring prescribed information about prescribed decisions made in connection with the discharge of functions which are the responsibility of a local authority executive to be made available to members of the public or members of the authority.

(11) The provision which may be made under subsection (10) includes provision-

(a) requiring prescribed information to be made available in advance of the prescribed decisions mentioned in that subsection,
(b) as to the way or form in which prescribed information is to be made available.

(12) The Secretary of State may by regulations make provision which, in relation to meetings of—

(a) local authority executives or committees of such executives, or
(b) joint committees, or sub-committees of such committees, falling within subsection (8)(a),

applies or reproduces (with or without modifications) any provisions of Part VA of the Local Government Act 1972.

(13) In this section—

"joint committee" means a joint committee falling within section 101(5)(a) of the Local Government Act 1972,

"prescribed" means prescribed by regulations made by the Secretary of State.

PART V

MISCELLANEOUS

Welfare services

Disclosure of information

94.—(1) Subsection (3) applies to information which is held by, or by a person providing services to, the Secretary of State and which relates to income support[, income-based jobseeker's allowance or state pension credit].[1]

(2) Subsection (3) also applies to information relating to housing benefit which is held by-

(a) an authority administering housing benefit, or
(b) a person authorised to exercise any function of such an authority relating to housing benefit.

(3) Information to which this subsection applies may be supplied to-

(a) a local authority to which any grant is or will be paid under section 93, or
(b) a person authorised to exercise any function of that authority relating to that grant,

for purposes connected with the application of that grant towards expenditure falling within section 93(1) or (2) (as the case may be).

(4) Information which is supplied to an authority or other person under subsection (3) may be supplied by the authority or person to a person who provides qualifying welfare services for purposes connected with the provision of those services.

(5) For the purposes of this section a person is to be regarded as providing qualifying welfare services if-

(a) he provides welfare services,
(b) a local authority contribute or will contribute to the expenditure incurred by him in providing those services, and
(c) that contribution is or will be derived (in whole or in part) from any grant which is or will be paid to the authority under section 93.

(6) In this section "local authority" and "welfare services" have the same meaning as in section 93.

(7) The Secretary of State may by order make such modifications of this section as he considers necessary or expedient in consequence of any provision corresponding to section 93 which is enacted by the Scottish Parliament.

1 Words substituted by State Pension Credit Act 2002 (c.16), Sch.2(3), para.43.

Access to information

Background papers

97.—(1) In section 100D of the Local Government Act 1972 (inspection of background papers) for subsection (1) there is substituted-

"(1) Subject, in the case of section 100C(1), to subsection (2) below, if and so long as copies of the whole or part of a report for a meeting of a principal council are required by section 100B(1) or 100C(1) above to be open to inspection by members of the public-

(a) those copies shall each include a copy of a list, compiled by the proper officer, of the background papers for the report or the part of the report, and

(b) at least one copy of each of the documents included in that list shall also be open to inspection at the offices of the council."

(2) In subsection (2) the words "of the list, or" are omitted.

Local Authorities (Executive Arrangements) (Access to Information) (England) Regulations 2000

(SI 2000/3272)

[MADE: MARCH 14, 2002][1]

[LAID BEFORE PARLIAMENT: MARCH 21, 2002][2]

[COMING INTO FORCE: REGS 1 TO 13: APRIL 15, 2002 AND REG.14: OCTOBER 1, 2002][3]

ARRANGEMENT OF REGULATIONS

PART I

GENERAL

PART II

PROVISIONS FOR AND IN CONNECTION WITH EXECUTIVE DECISIONS

[1] Amended by SI 2000/3272.
[2] *ibid.*
[3] *ibid.*

PART III

ADDITIONAL REQUIREMENTS IN RESPECT OF KEY DECISIONS AND FOR PUBLIC MEETINGS

PART IV

ADDITIONAL RIGHTS OF MEMBERS OF THE LOCAL AUTHORITY AND OF MEMBERS OF OVERVIEW AND SCRUTINY COMMITTEES

PART V

GENERAL PROVISIONS RELATING TO INFORMATION

The Secretary of State for the [Transport, Local Government and the Regions],[4] in exercise of the powers conferred upon him by sections 22 and 105 of the Local Government Act 2000[5] hereby makes the following Regulations: **App 4–07**

---

[4] Amended by SI 2000/3272.

[5] For the application of ss 22 and 105 to Wales, see s.106 of the Local Government Act 2000. See s.22(13) for the definition of "prescribed".

Part I

General

Citation, commencement and application

1.—(1) These Regulations may be cited as the Local Authorities (Executive Arrangements) (Access to Information) (England) Regulations [2000][6] and shall come into force on [October 1, 2002].[7]

(2) These Regulations apply in relation to local authorities in England.

Interpretation

2.—In these Regulations—

"the 1972 Act" means the Local Government Act 1972;

"the 2000 Act" means the Local Government Act 2000;

"background papers", in relation to a report or part of a report, means those documents other than published works, that—

(a) relate to the subject matter of the report or, as the case may be the part of the report; and
(b) in the opinion of the proper officer—
  (i) disclose any facts or matters on which the report or an important part of the report is based; and
  (ii) were relied on to a material extent in preparing the report;

"confidential information" means—

(a) information provided to the local authority by a government department upon terms (however expressed) which forbid the disclosure of the information to the public; or
(b) information the disclosure of which to the public is prohibited by or under any enactment or by the order of a court,

and in either case, a reference to the obligation of confidence is to be construed accordingly;

"copy", in relation to any document, includes a copy made from a copy;

"decision maker" means the decision making body by which, or the individual by whom, an executive decision is made;

"decision making body", in relation to an executive decision, means—

(a) the executive of a local authority;
(b) a committee of a local authority executive;
(c) a joint committee, where all the members of the joint committee are members of a local authority executive; or
(d) a sub-committee of a joint committee where all the members of the joint committee are members of a local authority executive,

---

6 Word substituted by SI 2002/716 (Local Authorities (Executive Arrangements) (Access to Information) (England) Amendment Regulations), reg.3.

7 Amended by SI 2002/716.

which is authorised to discharge the function to which the executive decision relates in accordance with the Local Authorities (Arrangements for the Discharge of Functions) (England) Regulations 2000[8];

"document" means any report or background papers, other than that only in a draft form, taken into consideration in relation to an executive decision;

"executive decision" means a decision made or to be made, by a decision maker, in connection with the discharge of a function which is the responsibility of the executive of a local authority;

"exempt information" has the meaning given by section 100I of the 1972 Act[9] (exempt information and power to vary Schedule 12A);

"information" includes an expression of opinion, any recommendations and any decision made;

"joint committee" means a committee appointed under section 102(1) of the 1972 Act (appointment of committees) in accordance with regulations made under section 20 of the 2000 Act[10];

"key decision" has the meaning given in regulation 8;

"local authority" means a county council, a district council which or a London borough council which is operating executive arrangements;

"newspaper" includes—

(a) a news agency which systematically carries on the business of selling and supplying reports or information to newspapers; and
(b) any organisation which is systematically engaged in collecting news—
  (i) for sound or television broadcasts; or
  (ii) for inclusion in programmes to be included in any programme service within the meaning of the Broadcasting Act 1990 other than a sound or television broadcasting service within the meaning of Part III or Part I of that Act respectively[11];

"political adviser or assistant" means a person appointed pursuant to section 9 of the Local Government and Housing Act 1989 (assistants for political groups) or regulations made under paragraph 6 of Schedule 1 to the 2000 Act (mayor's assistant);

"private meeting", in relation to a local authority executive, means a meeting which is not a public meeting;

"proper officer", has the same meaning as in section 270(3) of the 1972 Act (general provisions as to interpretation);

---

8 The Local Government (Arrangements for the Discharge of Functions) (England) Regulations 2000 (SI 2000/2851).

9 S.100I was inserted by the Local Government (Access to Information) Act 1985 (c.43).

10 See reg.11 of the Local Authorities (Arrangements for the Discharge of Functions) (England) Regulations 2000 (SI 2000/2851).

11 1990 (c.42). The definition of "programme service" is found in s.201. Subsequently, subs.(1)(bb) of that section was inserted by the Broadcasting Act 1996 (c.55), Sch.10, Pt I, para.11. The definition of "sound broadcasting service" is to be found in s.126(1), amended by the Broadcasting Act 1996, Sch.10, Pt I and para.9. The definition of "television broadcasting service" is found in s.2(5), amended by the Broadcasting Act 1996, Sch.10, Pt I para.1.

["public meeting" in relation to a decision making body, means—

(a) a meeting which, in accordance with regulation 7, is required to be held in public; or
(b) any other meeting of a decision making body that the decision making body determines shall be held in public;][12]

"relevant local authority" means the local authority whose executive is responsible for the discharge of the function to which the executive decision relates;

"relevant overview and scrutiny committee" means an overview and scrutiny committee of the relevant local authority which has terms of reference including the power to review or scrutinise decisions made, or other actions taken, in connection with the discharge of the function to which the decision relates;

"report" in relation to an executive decision does not include a report in draft form;

"section 11(2) mayor"[13] means an elected mayor who is a member of a mayor and cabinet executive; and

"standards committee" means the standards committee of the local authority as established under section 53 of the 2000 Act (standards committees).

PART II

PROVISIONS FOR AND IN CONNECTION WITH EXECUIVE DECISIONS

Recording of executive decisions made at meetings

3.—(1) As soon as reasonably practicable after a private meeting or a public meeting of a decision making body at which an executive decision has been made, the proper officer, or in the event that the proper officer is not present at that meeting, the person presiding, shall ensure that a written statement is produced in respect of every executive decision made at that meeting which must include the information specified in paragraph (2).

(2) The statement referred to in paragraph (1) must include;

(a) a record of the decision;
(b) a record of the reasons for the decision;
(c) details of any alternative options considered and rejected by the decision making body at the meeting at which the decision was made;
(d) a record of any conflict of interest in relation to the matter decided which is declared by any member of the decision making body which made the decision; and
(e) in respect of any declared conflict of interest, a note of any dispensation granted by the local authority's standards committee.

(3) For the purposes of paragraph (1) of this regulation "person presiding" means the person actually presiding, or the person nominated to preside, at that meeting.

(4) Executive decisions made by decision making bodies are prescribed decisions for the purposes of section 22(3) of the 2000 Act (duty to keep written records of private meetings).

[12] Definition substituted by SI 2002/716 (Local Authorities (Executive Arrangements) (Access to Information) (England) Amendment Regulations), Reg.4

[13] See s.11(2) of the Local Government Act 2000 (Local Authority Executives).

Recording of executive decisions made by individuals

4.—(1) As soon as is reasonably practicable after an individual member has made any executive decision he shall produce, or if he instructs the proper officer to do so, the proper officer shall produce, a written statement in respect of that executive decision which includes the information specified in paragraph (2).

(2) The statement referred to in paragraph (1) must include—

(a) a record of the decision;
(b) a record of the reasons for the decision;
(c) details of any alternative options considered and rejected at the time by the member when he made the decision;
(d) a record of any conflict of interest declared by any executive member who is consulted by the member, in relation to the decision; and
(e) in respect of any declared conflict of interest a note of any dispensation granted by the local authority's standards committee.

(3) Executive decisions made by individual members of local authority executives are prescribed decisions for the purposes of section 22(4) of the 2000 Act (duty to keep a written record of decisions made by individual members of local authority executives).

(4) As soon as is reasonably practicable after an officer has made a decision which is a key decision, the officer shall produce a written statement which must include—

(a) a record of the decision;
(b) a record of the reasons for the decision;
(c) details of any alternative options considered and rejected by the officer at the time when he made the decision;
(d) a record of any conflict of interest declared, in relation to the decision, by any executive member who was consulted by the officer who made the decision; and
(e) in respect of any declared conflict of interest in relation to the decision a note of any dispensation granted by the local authority's standards committee.

Inspection of documents following executive decisions

5.—(1) Subject to regulation 21, after a private meeting or a public meeting of a decision making body at which an executive decision has been made, after an individual member has made an executive decision or after an officer has made a key decision the proper officer shall ensure that a copy of—

(a) any records prepared in accordance with regulations 3 or 4; and
(b) any report considered at the meeting or, as the case may be, considered by the individual member or officer and relevant to a decision recorded in accordance with regulations 3 or 4 or, where only part of the report is relevant to such a decision, that part,

shall be available for inspection by members of the public, as soon as is reasonably practicable, at the offices of the relevant local authority.

(2) Where a request on behalf of a newspaper is made for a copy of any of the documents available for public inspection under paragraph (1), those documents shall be supplied for the benefit of the newspaper by the local authority on payment by the newspaper to the local authority of postage, copying or other necessary charge for transmission.

Inspection of background papers

6.—Subject to regulation 21, when a copy of the whole or part of a report for a private meeting or a public meeting is made available for inspection by members of the public in accordance with regulation 5 or 11, at the same time—

(a) a copy of a list complied by the proper officer of the background papers to the report or part of the report, must be included in the report or, as the case may be, part of the report; and

(b) at least one copy of each of the documents included in that list,

shall be available for inspection by the public at the offices of the relevant local authority.

PART III

ADDITIONAL REQUIREMENTS IN RESPECT OF KEY DESICIONS AND PUBLIC MEETINGS

Meetings of local authority executives and their committees to be held in public

7.—[(1) Subject to regulation 21, where the executive leader, section 11(2) mayor or council manager (as the case may be) or any other person likely to preside at the meeting reasonably believes that one of the circumstances specified in paragraph (2) below applies in relation to a meeting, or part of a meeting, of a decision making body, that meeting or part of a meeting must be held in public.

(2) The circumstances are—

(a) a decision to be made will be a key decision;

(b) a matter that is included on the forward plan or is the subject of a notice given under regulation 15 is likely to be discussed; and

(i) the decision on that matter is likely to be made within 28 days; and

(ii) an officer who is not a political adviser, assistant or council manager will be present at the discussion.

(2A) For the purposes of paragraph (1), "meeting" does not include a meeting to which the circumstances specified in paragraph (2)(b) apply and the principal purpose of which is for an officer of the local authority to brief a decision maker on matters connected with the making of an executive decision.][14]

(3) In accordance with section 38 of the 2000 Act, in determining the meaning of "principal purpose" for the purposes of paragraph (2), regard shall be had to any guidance for the time being issued by the Secretary of State.

Key decisions

8.—(1) In these regulations a "key decision" means an executive decision which, is likely—

(a) to result in the local authority incurring expenditure which is, or the making of savings which are, significant having regard to the local authority's budget for the service or function to which the decision relates; or

[14] Reg.7(1)–(2A) substituted for reg.7(1)–(2) by SI 2002/716 (Local Authorities (Executive Arrangements) (Access to Information) (England) Amendment Regulations), reg.5.

(b) to be significant in terms of its effects on communities living or working in an area comprising two or more wards or electoral divisions in the area of the local authority.

(2) In accordance with section 38 of the 2000 Act, in determining the meaning of "significant" for the purposes of paragraph (1) regard shall be had to any guidance for the time being issued by the Secretary of State.

Individual executive decisions

9.—(1) Where an executive member or officer receives a report, which he intends to take into consideration when he makes a key decision, he shall not make the that decision until the report has been available for public inspection, pursuant to paragraph (2), for at least [five clear days].[15]

(2) Subject to regulation 21, the member or officer making the decision referred to in paragraph (1) shall ensure that the proper officer makes the report referred to in that paragraph available for inspection by the public as soon as is reasonably practicable after that officer or member receives it.

(3) Where a report has been submitted to an executive member or officer with a view to it being considered by him when he makes a key decision, the person who submitted the report shall, as soon as is reasonably practicable, supply a copy of it to the chairman of every relevant overview and scrutiny committee or where there is no chairman to every member of the relevant overview and scrutiny committee.

(4) The proper officer shall, in any report required by paragraph (2) to be available for inspection by the public include a list of background papers for the report or part of the report, and shall ensure that sufficient copies of the background papers are available, or that facilities exist for the production of sufficient copies of those papers, to meet every reasonable request from members of the public for them.

Procedures prior to public meetings

10.—An item of business shall only be considered at a public meeting—

(a) where a copy of the agenda or part of the agenda, including the item, has been available for inspection by the public as required by regulation 11 for at least [five clear days][16] before the meeting; or

(b) where the meeting is convened at shorter notice in accordance with regulation 15 or 16, a copy of the agenda including the item has been available for inspection by the public from the time that the meeting was convened.

Access to agenda and connected reports

11.—(1) Subject to paragraph (2), a copy of the agenda and every report for a public meeting shall be available for inspection by the public at the offices of the local authority when they are made available to the members of the executive or decision making body responsible for making the decision to which they relate.

(2) If the proper officer thinks fit, there may be excluded from the copy of any report provided pursuant to paragraph (1) the whole, or any part, of the report which relates only to the transaction of an item of business during which, in his opinion, the meeting is likely not to be open to the public.

---

15 Words substituted by SI 2002/716 (Local Authorities (Executive Arrangements) (Access to Information) (England) Amendment Regulations), reg.14.

16 *ibid.*

(3) Subject to paragraph (4), any document which is required by paragraph (1) to be available for inspection by the public shall be available for such inspection for at least [five clear days][17] before the meeting, except that—

(a) where the meeting is convened at shorter notice in accordance with regulation 15 or 16, a copy of the agenda and associated reports shall be available for inspection at the time the meeting is convened; and

(b) where an item which would be available for inspection by the public is added to the agenda, a copy of the revised agenda, and of any report relating to the item for consideration at the meeting, shall be available for inspection by the public when the item is added to the agenda.

(4) Nothing in paragraph (3) shall require a copy of the agenda, item or report to be available for inspection by the public until a copy is available to members of the decision making body concerned.

(5) Where by virtue of paragraph (2) the whole or any part of a report for a public meeting is not available for inspection by the public—

(a) every copy of the whole report or of the part of the report, as the case may be, shall be marked "not for publication"; and

(b) there shall be stated on every copy of the whole or the part of the report—

(i) that it contains confidential information;

(ii) by reference to the descriptions in Schedule 12A to the 1972 Act, the description of exempt information by virtue of which the decision making body discharging the executive function are likely to exclude the public during the item to which the report relates; or

(iii) that the report or the part of the report contains the advice of a political adviser or assistant as the case may be.

(6) Except during any part of a public meeting during which the public are excluded, the local authority shall make available for the use of members of the public present at the meeting a reasonable number of copies of the agenda and of the reports for the meeting.

(7) Subject to regulation 21, a local authority shall, following any request on behalf of a newspaper and on payment being made of postage charges or any other necessary charge for transmission, supply to the newspaper—

(a) a copy of the agenda for a public meeting and a copy of each of the reports for consideration at the meeting;

(b) such further statements or particulars, if any, as are necessary to indicate the nature of the items contained in the agenda; and

(c) if the proper officer thinks fit in the case of any item, a copy of any other document supplied to members of the executive in connection with the item.

(8) Paragraph (3) applies in relation to copies of reports provided pursuant to paragraph (6) or (7) as it applies in relation to copies of reports provided pursuant to paragraph (1).

Publicity in connection with key decisions

12.—(1) The executive leader or, as the case may be, the section 11(2) mayor or the council manager shall instruct the proper officer to publish, in accordance with paragraph (2), a document which states—

[17] Words substituted by SI 2002/716 (Local Authorities (Executive Arrangements) (Access to Information) (England) Amendment Regulations), reg.14.

(a) that key decisions are to be made on behalf of the local authority;
(b) that a plan (to be known as the "forward plan") containing particulars of the matters in respect of which those decisions are to be made, will be prepared on a monthly basis by the local authority;
(c) that a forward plan will contain details of the key decisions likely to be made by the local authority for the four month period following the publication of the forward plan;
(d) that each current forward plan may be inspected at all reasonable hours and free of charge at the local authority's offices;
(e) that each forward plan contains a list of the documents submitted to the decision makers for consideration in relation to the matters in respect of which decisions are to be made;
(f) the address from which, subject to any prohibition or restriction on their disclosure, copies of, or extracts from, any document listed in the forward plan is available;
(g) that other documents relevant to those matters may be submitted to the decision makers;
(h) the procedure for requesting details of those documents (if any) as they become available; and
 (i) the dates in each month in the following twelve months on which each forward plan will be published and available to the public at the local authority's offices.

(2) The document referred to in paragraph (1) shall be published—

(a) in at least one newspaper circulating in the area of the local authority; and
(b) annually, on a date at least 14 days, but not more than 21 days before the first forward plan of that year comes into effect.

Forward plans

13.—[(1) A forward plan shall be prepared, in accordance with this regulation and regulation 14, by the executive leader or, as the case may be, by the section 11(2) mayor or the council manager and the first such forward plan shall be prepared as soon as is reasonably practicable after the authority has adopted executive arrangements.][18]

(2) A forward plan shall contain details of all the matters likely to be the subject of key decisions in the relevant authority for a period of four months; and the first such plan shall have effect from the first working day of any month.

(3) A forward plan shall be updated on a monthly basis, and a new forward plan produced at least 14 days prior to the first day upon which the forward plan will come into effect, with any outstanding matters contained in the previous forward plan being included in the latest forward plan.

(4) The most recent forward plan shall be taken to have superseded any earlier plan or, as the case may be, each earlier plan.

Content of the forward plan

14.—(1) Subject to regulation 15(2), each forward plan shall contain, as regards each matter referred to in regulation 13(1) such of the particulars specified in paragraph (2) as are available when the plan is prepared or which the person preparing it may then reasonably be expected to obtain.

[18] Words substituted by SI 2002/716 (Local Authorities (Executive Arrangements) (Access to Information) (England) Amendment Regulations), reg.6.

(2) The particulars referred to in paragraph (1) are—

(a) the matter in respect of which the decision is to be made;
(b) where the decision maker is an individual his name, his title if any and, where the decision maker is a decision making body, its name and a list of its members;
(c) the date on which, or the period within which, the decision is to be made;
(d) the identity of the principal groups or organisations whom the decision maker proposes to consult before making the decision;
(e) the means by which any such consultation is proposed to be undertaken;
(f) the steps that may be taken by any person who wishes to make representations to the local authority executive or to the decision maker about the matter in respect of which the decision is to be made, and the date by which those steps are to be taken; and
(g) a list of the documents, submitted to the decision maker for consideration in relation to the matter in respect of which the decision is to be made.

(3) Where, in relation to any matter—

(a) the public may be excluded under regulation 21(1) from the meeting at which that matter is to be discussed; or
(b) documents relating to the decision need not, because of regulation 21(5), be disclosed to the public,

the forward plan shall contain particulars of the matter but may not contain any confidential or exempt information or particulars of the advice of a [political adviser or assistant].[19]

General exception

15.—(1) Subject to regulation 16, where the inclusion of a matter on the forward plan is impracticable and the matter would be a key decision, that decision shall only be made—

(a) where the proper officer has informed the chairman of the relevant overview and scrutiny committee or, if there is no such person, each member of the relevant overview and scrutiny committee by notice in writing, of the matter about which the decision is to be made;
(b) where the proper officer has made available at the offices of the local authority for inspection by the public a copy of the notice given pursuant to paragraph (a); and
(c) after [five clear days][20] have elapsed following the day on which the proper officer made available the notice referred to in sub-paragraph (b).

(2) Where paragraph (1) applies to any matter, regulation 14 need not be complied with in relation to that matter.

Cases of special urgency

16.—Where the date by which an executive decision that would be a key decision must be made, makes compliance with regulation 15 impracticable, the decision shall only be made where the decision maker has obtained agreement from—

(a) the chairman of the relevant overview and scrutiny committee; or

---

[19] Words substituted by SI 2002/716 (Local Authorities (Executive Arrangements) (Access to Information) (England) Amendment Regulations), reg.7(2).

[20] Words substituted by SI 2002/716 (Local Authorities (Executive Arrangements) (Access to Information) (England) Amendment Regulations), reg.14.

(b) if there is no such person, or if the chairman of the relevant overview and scrutiny committee is unable to act, the chairman of the relevant local authority; or

(c) where there is no chairman of either the relevant overview and scrutiny committee or of the relevant local authority the vice-chairman of the relevant local authority,

[. . .][21] that the making of the decision is urgent and cannot reasonably be deferred.

PART IV

ADDITIONAL RIGHTS OF MEMBERS OF THE LOCAL AUTHORITY AND OF MEMBERS OF OVERVIEW AND SCRUTINY COMMITTEES

Additional rights of access to documents for members of local authorities

17.—(1) Subject to paragraphs (3) and (4), any document which—

(a) is in the possession, or under the control, of the executive of a local authority; and

(b) contains material relating to any business to be transacted at a public meeting,

shall be available for inspection by any member of the local authority.

(2) Subject to paragraphs (3) and (4) any document which—

(a) is in the possession, or under the control, of the executive of a local authority; and

(b) contains material relating to—

(i) any business transacted at a private meeting;

(ii) any decision made by an individual member in accordance with executive arrangements; or

(iii) any key decision made by an officer in accordance with executive arrangements,

shall be available for inspection by any member of the local authority when the meeting concludes or, where an executive decision is made by an individual member or a key decision made by an officer, immediately after the decision has been made.

(3) Where it appears to the proper officer that compliance with paragraph (1) or (2) in relation to a document or part of a document would involve the disclosure of exempt information of a description falling within any of paragraphs 1 to 6, 9, 11, 12 and 14 of Part I of Schedule 12A to the 1972 Act, paragraph (1) or (2), as the case may be, shall not apply as regards that document or part.

(4) Where it appears to the proper officer that compliance with paragraph (1) or (2) in relation to a document or part of a document would involve the disclosure of advice provided by a political adviser or assistant, that paragraph shall not apply as regards that document or part.

(5) The rights conferred by paragraphs (1) and (2) are in addition to any other rights that a member of a local authority may have.

[21] Words repealed by SI 2002/716 (Local Authorities (Executive Arrangements) (Access to Information) (England) Amendment Regulations), reg.9.

PART IV

ADDITIONAL RIGHTS OF MEMBERS OF THE LOCAL AUTHORITY AND OF MEMBERS OF OVERVIEW AND SCRUTINY COMMITTEES

Additional rights of access to documents for members of overview and scrutiny committees

18.—(1) Subject to paragraph (2), a member of an overview and scrutiny committee of a local authority shall be entitled to a copy of any document which—

(a) is in the possession or under the control of the executive of that authority; and
(b) contains material relating to—

(i) any business that has been transacted at a private meeting or a public meeting of a decision making body of that authority;
(ii) any decision that has been made by an individual member of that executive in accordance with executive arrangements; or
(iii) any key decision that has been made by an officer of the authority in accordance with executive arrangements.

[(2) No member of an overview and scrutiny committee shall be entitled to a copy—

(a) of any such document or part of a document as contains exempt or confidential information unless that information is relevant to—

(i) an action or decision that he is reviewing or scrutinising; or
(ii) any review contained in any programme of work of such a committee or sub-committee of such a committee; or

(b) of a document or part of a document containing advice provided by a political adviser or assistant.][22]

Reports to the local authority where the key decision procedure is not followed

19.—(1) Where an executive decision has been made and—

(a) was not treated as being a key decision; and
(b) a relevant overview and scrutiny committee are of the opinion that the decision should have been treated as a key decision,

that overview and scrutiny committee may require the executive which is responsible for the decision to submit a report to the relevant local authority within such reasonable period as the committee may specify.

(2) A report under paragraph (1) shall include details of—

(a) the decision and the reasons for the decision;
(b) the decision making body by which, or the individual by whom, the decision was made; and
(c) if the executive of the relevant local authority are of the opinion that the decision was not a key decision, the reasons for that opinion.

[22] Words substituted by SI 2002/716 (Local Authorities (Executive Arrangements) (Access to Information) (England) Amendment Regulations), reg.10.

Quarterly reports to the local authority

20.—(1) The executive leader or, as the case may be, the section 11(2) mayor or the council manager shall submit to the local authority at quarterly intervals a report containing details of each executive decision taken during the preceding three months where the making of the decision was agreed as urgent in accordance with regulation 16.

(2) A report submitted for the purposes of paragraph (1) shall include—

(a) particulars of each decision made; and
(b) a summary of the matters in respect of which each decision was made.

PART V

GENERAL PROVISIONS RELATING TO INFORMATION

Confidential information, exempt information and advice of a political adviser or assistant

21.—(1) Subject to paragraph (3), nothing in these Regulations shall prevent the exclusion of the public from a meeting of a decision making body that is exercising an executive function where—

(a) it is likely, in view of the nature of the business to be transacted or of the nature of the proceedings, that if members of the public were present during the transaction of an item of business, confidential information would be disclosed to them in breach of the obligation of confidence;
(b) a resolution has been passed, by the decision making body concerned, excluding the public during the transaction of an item of business where it is likely, in view of the nature of the item of business, that if members of the public were present during the transaction of that item, exempt information would be disclosed to them;
(c) a resolution has been passed, by the decision making body concerned, excluding the public during an item of business where it is likely, in view of the nature of the item, that if members of the public were present during the transaction of that item, the advice of a political adviser or assistant would be disclosed to them; or
(d) a lawful power is used to exclude a member or members of the public in order to maintain orderly conduct or to prevent misbehaviour at a meeting.

(2) A resolution under paragraph (1)(b) shall—

(a) identify the proceedings, or part of the proceedings, to which it applies; and
(b) state by reference to the descriptions in Schedule 12A to the 1972 Act (access to information: exempt information) the description of exempt information giving rise to the exclusion of the public.

(3) An exclusion of the public under sub-paragraph (a), (b) or (c) of paragraph (1) shall apply only to the part or parts of the meeting during which it is likely that confidential information, exempt information or the advice of a political adviser or assistant would be disclosed.

[(4) Nothing in these Regulations shall—

(a) authorise or require a local authority to disclose to the public or make available for public inspection any document or part of a document if, in the opinion of the proper officer, that document or part of a document contains or may contain confidential information; or

(b) require a local authority to disclose to the public or make available for public inspection any document or part of a document if, in the opinion of the proper officer, that document or part of a document contains or is likely to contain exempt information or the advice of a political adviser or assistant.

(5) Where a member of a local authority executive or an officer makes an executive decision in accordance with executive arrangements, nothing in these Regulations shall—

(a) authorise or require documents relating to that decision to be disclosed to the public, or made available for public inspection where, the documents contain confidential information; or

(b) require documents relating to that decision to be disclosed to the public, or made available for public inspection where the disclosure of the documents would, in the opinion of the member or officer making the decision, give rise to the disclosure of exempt information or the advice of a political adviser or assistant.][23]

(6) Nothing in these Regulations shall require a decision making body or decision maker to permit the taking of any photographs of any proceedings, or the use of any means to enable persons not present to see or hear any proceedings (whether at the time or later), or the making of any oral report on any proceedings as they take place.

Documents to be available for inspection at the offices of the local authority

22.—(1) Any document required by regulation 5, 6 or 11 to be available for inspection by members of the public shall be available for inspection—

(a) at all reasonable hours at the offices of the local authority; and

(b) in the case of documents to be available for inspection pursuant to regulation 6, upon payment by the person seeking to inspect the documents of any reasonable fee required by the local authority.

(2) Subject to paragraph (3), where a document is to be available for inspection by a person under any provision in these Regulations, the person may—

(a) make a copy of the whole or part of the document; or

(b) require the person having custody of the document to supply him with a copy of the whole or part of the document,

upon payment by the person requiring the copy of any reasonable fee required by the local authority.

(3) Paragraph (2) does not require or authorise the doing of any act which infringes the copyright in any work except that, where the owner of the copyright is the local authority, nothing done pursuant to that paragraph shall constitute an infringement of the copyright.

(4) Where any document required by these Regulations to be open to inspection by the public—

(a) is supplied to, or available for inspection by members of the public; or

(b) is supplied for the benefit of any newspaper, pursuant to [regulation 5(2) or 11(7)],[24]

[23] Words substituted by SI 2002/716 (Local Authorities (Executive Arrangements) (Access to Information) (England) Amendment Regulations), reg.11.

[24] Words inserted by SI 2002/716 (Local Authorities (Executive Arrangements) (Access to Information) (England) Amendment Regulations), reg.12.

the publication thereby of any defamatory matter contained in the document shall be privileged unless the publication is proved to be made with malice.

(5) Any written record of an executive decision or any report required by regulation 5 to be available for inspection by the members of the public, shall be retained by the local authority and made available for inspection by the public for a period of at least six years beginning on the date on which the decision to which the record or report relates, was made.

(6) Any background papers required by regulation 6 to be available for inspection by members of the public shall be retained by the local authority and be available for inspection by the public for a period of at least four years beginning on the date on which the decision, to which the background papers relate, was made.

(7) The rights conferred on any person by these Regulations to inspect, copy or be supplied with documents are in addition to any such rights that he may have apart from those under these Regulations.

Offences

23.—(1) A person who has custody of a document which is required by regulation 5, 6 or 11 to be available for inspection by members of the public commits an offence if, without reasonable excuse—

(a) he intentionally obstructs any person exercising a right conferred under these Regulations to inspect, or to make a copy of the whole or part of the document; or

(b) he refuses to supply a copy of the whole or part of the document in accordance with [regulation 5(2), 11(7) or 22(2)].[25]

(2) A person who commits an offence under paragraph (1) shall be liable on summary conviction to a fine not exceeding level 1 on the standard scale.

Signatures

Signed by authority of the Secretary of State for the Environment, Transport and the Regions

Hilary Armstrong

Minister of State,

Department for the Environment, Transport and the Regions

December 13, 2000

[25] Words inserted by SI 2002/716 (Local Authorities (Executive Arrangements) (Access to Information) (England) Amendment Regulations), reg.13.

APPENDIX 5

Health, Medical and Case Records

Access to Health Records Act 1990

(1990, c.23)

ARRANGEMENT OF SECTIONS

SECTIONS

App 5–01 An Act to establish a right of access to health records by the individuals to whom they relate and other persons; to provide for the correction of inaccurate health records and for the avoidance of certain contractual obligations; and for connected purposes.

[JULY 13, 1990]

BE IT ENACTED by the Queen's most Excellent Majesty, by and with the advice and consent of the Lords Spiritual and Temporal, and Commons, in this present Parliament assembled, and by the authority of the same, as follows:

"Health record" and related expressions

1.—In this Act "health record" means a record which—

(a) consists of information relating to the physical or mental health of an individual who can be identified from that information, or from that and other information in the possession of the holder of the record; and

(b) has been made by or on behalf of a health professional in connection with the care of that individual;

(2) In this Act "holder", in relation to a health record, means—

"(a) in the case of a record made by a general practitioner (other than an employed practitioner), or by a health professional employed by such a general practitioner—

(i) the general practitioner on whose list the patient is included (or, where the patient is included on the list of a medical practice consisting of two or more partners who are general practitioners, any such partner); or

(ii) where the patient is not on any such list, the Health Authority [Primary Care Trust,][1] or Health Board by arrangement with whom a general practitioner last treated him;"

(b) in the case of a record made by a health professional for purposes connected with the provision of health services by a health service body, the health service body by which or on whose behalf the record is held;

(c) in any other case, the health professional by whom or on whose behalf the record is held.

(3) In this Act "patient", in relation to a health record, means the individual in connection with whose care the record has been made.

Health professionals

[2.—In this Act "health professional" has the same meaning as in the Data Protection Act 1998.][2]

Main provisions

Right of access to health records

3.—(1) An application for access to a health record, or to any part of a health record, may be made to the holder of the record by any of the following, namely—

[(ee) where the record is held in Scotland and the patient is incapable, within the meaning of the Adults with Incapacity (Scotland) Act 2000 (asp 4) in relation to making or authorising the application, any person entitled to act on behalf of the patient under that Act.][3]

(f) where the patient has died, the patient's personal representative and any person who may have a claim arising out of the patient's death.

---

1 Words inserted by National Health Service Reform and Health Care Professions Act (2002 c.17), Sch.2(2) para.59(2).

2 Substituted by Data Protection Act (1998 c.29), Sch.15 para.11.

3 Possible drafting error, intention appears to have been to insert s.3(1)(ee) rather than s.3(3)(ee) by Adults with Incapacity (Scotland) Act (2000 ASP.4), Sch.5 para.21.

(2) Subject to section 4 below, where an application is made under subsection (1) above the holder shall, within the requisite period, give access to the record, or the part of a record, to which the application relates—

(a) in the case of a record, by allowing the applicant to inspect the record or, where section 5 below applies, an extract setting out so much of the record as is not excluded by that section;

(b) in the case of a part of a record, by allowing the applicant to inspect an extract setting out that part or, where that section applies, so much of that part as is not so excluded; or

(c) in either case, if the applicant so requires, by supplying him with a copy of the record or extract.

(3) Where any information contained in a record or extract which is so allowed to be inspected, or a copy of which is so supplied, is expressed in terms which are not intelligible without explanation, an explanation of those terms shall be provided with the record or extract, or supplied with the copy.

(4) No fee shall be required for giving access under subsection (2) above other than the following, namely—

(a) where access is given to a record, or part of a record, none of which was made after the beginning of the period of 40 days immediately preceding the date of the application, a fee not exceeding such maximum as may be prescribed for the purposes of this section by regulations under section 7 of the Data Protection Act 1998; and

(b) where a copy of a record or extract is supplied to the applicant, a fee not exceeding the cost of making the copy and (where applicable) the cost of posting it to him.

(5) For the purposes of subsection (2) above the requisite period is—

(a) where the application relates to a record, or part of a record, none of which was made before the beginning of the period of 40 days immediately preceding the date of the application, the period of 21 days beginning with that date;

(b) in any other case, the period of 40 days beginning with that date.

(6) Where—

(a) an application under subsection (1) above does not contain sufficient information to enable the holder of the record to identify the patient or, to satisfy himself that the applicant is entitled to make the application; and

(b) within the period of 14 days beginning with the date of the application, the holder of the record requests the applicant to furnish him with such further information as he may reasonably require for that purpose,

subsection (5) above shall have effect as if for any reference to that date there were substituted a reference to the date on which that further information is so furnished.

Cases where right of access may be wholly excluded

4.—[. . .][4]

(3) Where an application is made under subsection (1)(f) of section 3 above, access shall not be given under subsection (2) of that section if the record includes a note, made at the patient's request, that he did not wish access to be given on such an application.

4 Repealed by Data Protection Act (1998 c.29), Sch.16(I) para.1.

Cases where right of access may be partially excluded

5.—(1) Access shall not be given under section 3(2) above to any part of a health record—

(a) which, in the opinion of the holder of the record, would disclose—

(i) information likely to cause serious harm to the physical or mental health of any individual; or

(ii) information relating to or provided by an individual, other than the patient, who could be identified from that information; or

(b) which was made before the commencement of this Act.

(2) Subsection (1)(a)(ii) above shall not apply—

(a) where the individual concerned has consented to the application; or

(b) where that individual is a health professional who has been involved in the care of the patient;

and subsection (1)(b) above shall not apply where and to the extent that, in the opinion of the holder of the record, the giving of access is necessary in order to make intelligible any part of the record to which access is required to be given under section 3(2) above.

(3) [Access shall not be given under section 3(2) to any part of a health record][5] which, in the opinion of the holder of the record, would disclose—

(a) information provided by the patient in the expectation that it would not be disclosed to the applicant; or

(b) information obtained as a result of any examination or investigation to which the patient consented in the expectation that the information would not be so disclosed.

(4) Where an application is made under subsection (1)(f) of section 3 above, access shall not be given under subsection (2) of that section to any part of the record which, in the opinion of the holder of the record, would disclose information which is not relevant to any claim which may arise out of the patient's death.

(5) The Secretary of State may by regulations provide that, in such circumstances as may be prescribed by the regulations, access shall not be given under section 3(2) above to any part of a health record which satisfies such conditions as may be so prescribed.

Correction of inaccurate health records

6.—(1) Where a person considers that any information contained in a health record, or any part of a health record, to which he has been given access under section 3(2) above is inaccurate, he may apply to the holder of the record for the necessary correction to be made.

(2) On an application under subsection (1) above, the holder of the record shall—

(a) if he is satisfied that the information is inaccurate, make the necessary correction;

(b) if he is not so satisfied, make in the part of the record in which the information is contained a note of the matters in respect of which the information is considered by the applicant to be inaccurate; and

(c) in either case, without requiring any fee, supply the applicant with a copy of the correction or note.

(3) In this section "inaccurate" means incorrect, misleading or incomplete.

[5] Words substituted by Data Protection Act (1998 c.29), Sch.15 para.13.

Duty of health service bodies etc. to take advice

7.—(1) A health service body shall take advice from the appropriate health professional before they decide whether they are satisfied as to any matter for the purposes of this Act, or form an opinion as to any matter for those purposes.

(2) In this section "the appropriate health professional" in relation to a health service body (other than a [Primary Care Trust,][6] Health Authority or Health Board which is the holder of the record by virtue of section 1(2)(a) above), means—

(a) where, for purposes connected with the provision of health services by the body, one or more medical or dental practitioners are currently responsible for the clinical care of the patient, that practitioner or, as the case may be, such one of those practitioners as is the most suitable to advise the body on the matter in question;

(b) where paragraph (a) above does not apply but one or more medical or dental practitioners are available who, for purposes connected with the provision of such services by the body, have been responsible for the clinical care of the patient, that practitioner or, as the case may be, such one of those practitioners as was most recently so responsible; and

(c) where neither paragraph (a) nor paragraph (b) above applies, a health professional who has the necessary experience and qualifications to advise the body on the matter in question.

(3) In this section "the appropriate health professional" in relation to a [Primary Care Trust,][7] Health Authority or Health Board which is the holder of the record by virtue of section 1(2)(a) above, means—

(a) where the patient's most recent general practitioner is available, that practitioner; and

(b) where that practitioner is not available, a registered medical practitioner who has the necessary experience and qualifications to advise the [Primary Care Trust,][8] Health Authority or Health Board on the matter in question.

Supplemental

Applications to the court

8.—(1) Subject to subsection (2) below, where the court is satisfied, on an application made by the person concerned within such period as may be prescribed by rules of court, that the holder of a health record has failed to comply with any requirement of this Act, the court may order the holder to comply with that requirement.

(2) The court shall not entertain an application under subsection (1) above unless it is satisfied that the applicant has taken all such steps to secure compliance with the requirement as may be prescribed by regulations made by the Secretary of State.

(3) For the purposes of subsection (2) above, the Secretary of State may by regulations require the holders of health records to make such arrangements for dealing with complaints that they have failed to comply with any requirements of this Act as may be prescribed by the regulations.

---

6 Words inserted by National Health Service Reform and Health Care Professions Act (2002 c.17), Sch.2(2), para.59(3).

7 *ibid.*

8 *ibid.*

(4) For the purpose of determining any question whether an applicant is entitled to be given access under section 3(2) above to any health record, or any part of a health record, the court—

(a) may require the record or part to be made available for its own inspection; but
(b) shall not, pending determination of that question in the applicant's favour, require the record or part to be disclosed to him or his representatives whether by discovery (or, in Scotland, recovery) or otherwise.

(5) The jurisdiction conferred by this section shall be exercisable by the High Court or a county court or, in Scotland, by the Court of Session or the sheriff.

Avoidance of certain contractual terms

9.—Any term or condition of a contract shall be void in so far as it purports to require an individual to supply any other person with a copy of a health record, or of an extract from a health record, to which he has been given access under section 3(2) above.

Regulations and orders

10.—(1) Regulations under this Act may make different provision for different cases or classes of cases including, in particular, different provision for different health records or classes of health records.

(2) Any power to make regulations under this Act shall be exercisable by statutory instrument.

(3) Any statutory instrument containing regulations under this Act [. . .][9] above shall be subject to annulment in pursuance of a resolution of either House of Parliament.

Interpretation

11.—In this Act—

"application" means an application in writing and "apply" shall be construed accordingly;

"care" includes examination, investigation, diagnosis and treatment;

"general practitioner" means a medical practitioner who is —

(a) providing general medical services in accordance with arrangements made under section 29 of the National Health Service Act 1977 or section 19 of the National Health Service (Scotland) Act 1978; or
(b) performing personal medical services in accordance with arrangements made under section 28C of the 1977 Act or section 17C of the 1978 Act;

"Health Authority" means a Health Authority established under section 8 of the National Health Service Act 1977;

"Health Board" has the same meaning as in the National Health Service (Scotland) Act 1978;

"health service body" means —

(a) a Strategic Health Authority, Health Authority, Special Health Authority or Primary Care Trust;
(b) a Health Board;
(c) a State Hospital Management Committee constituted under section 91 of the Mental Health (Scotland) Act 1984; or

9 Words repealed by Data Protection Act (1998 c.29), Sch.16(I), para.1.

(d) a National Health Service trust first established under section 5 of the National Health Service and Community Care Act 1990 or section 12A of the National Health Service (Scotland) Act 1978;

"information", in relation to a health record, includes any expression of opinion about the patient;

"make", in relation to such a record, includes compile;

"Primary Care Trust" means a Primary Care Trust established under section 16A of the National Health Service Act 1977;

"Special Health Authority" means a Special Health Authority established under section 11 of the National Health Service Act 1977.

["Strategic Health Authority" means a Strategic Health Authority established under section 8 of the National Health Service Act 1977.][10]

Short title, commencement, and extent

12.—(1) This Act may be cited as the Access to Health Records Act 1990.

(2) This Act shall come into force on 1st November 1991.

(3) This Act does not extend to Northern Ireland.

[10] Definition inserted by SI 2002/2469 (National Health Service Reform and Health Care Professions Act 2002 (Supplementary, Consequential etc. Provisions) Regulations), Sch.1(1), para.17(b).

Access to Medical Reports Act 1988

(1988, c.28)

ARRANGEMENT OF SECTIONS

SECTIONS

An Act to establish a right of access by individuals to reports relating to themselves provided by medical practitioners for employment or insurance purposes and to make provision for related matters. **App 5–02**

[JULY 29, 1988]

BE IT ENACTED by the Queen's most Excellent Majesty, by and with the advice and consent of the Lords Spiritual and Temporal, and Commons, in this present Parliament assembled, and by the authority of the same, as follows:

Right of access

1.—It shall be the right of an individual to have access, in accordance with the provisions of this Act, to any medical report relating to the individual which is to be, or has been, supplied by a medical practitioner for employment purposes or insurance purposes.

Interpretation

2.—(1) In this Act—

"the applicant" means the person referred to in section 3(1) below;

"care" includes examination, investigation or diagnosis for the purposes of, or in connection with, any form of medical treatment;

"employment purposes", in the case of any individual, means the purposes in relation to the individual of any person by whom he is or has been, or is seeking to be, employed (whether under a contract of service or otherwise);

"health professional" has the same meaning as in the Data Protection Act 1998;

"insurance purposes", in a case of any individual who has entered into, or is seeking to enter into, a contract of insurance with an insurer, means the purposes of that insurer in relation to that individual;

"insurer" means—

(a) a person who has permission under Part 4 of the Financial Services and Markets Act 2000 to effect or carry out contracts of insurance;
(b) an EEA firm of the kind mentioned in paragraph 5(d) of Schedule 3 to that Act, which has permission under paragraph 15 of that Schedule (as a result of qualifying for authorisation under paragraph 12 of that Schedule) to effect or carry out relevant contracts of insurance;

"medical practitioner" means a person registered under the Medical Act 1983;

"medical report", in the case of an individual, means a report relating to the physical or mental health of the individual prepared by a medical practitioner who is or has been responsible for the clinical care of the individual.

[(1A) The definitions of "insurance purposes" and "insurer" in subsection (1) must be read with—

(a) section 22 of the Financial Services and Markets Act 2000;
(b) any relevant order under that section; and
(c) Schedule 2 to that Act.][1]

(2) Any reference in this Act to the supply of a medical report for employment or insurance purposes shall be construed—

(a) as a reference to the supply of such a report for employment or insurance purposes which are purposes of the person who is seeking to be supplied with it; or
(b) (in the case of a report that has already been supplied) as a reference to the supply of such a report for employment or insurance purposes which, at the time of its being supplied, were purposes of the person to whom it was supplied.

Consent to applications for medical reports for employment or insurance purposes

3.—(1) A person shall not apply to a medical practitioner for a medical report relating to any individual to be supplied to him for employment or insurance purposes unless—

(a) that person ("the applicant") has notified the individual that he proposes to make the application; and
(b) the individual has notified the applicant that he consents to the making of the application.

(2) Any notification given under subsection (1)(a) above must inform the individual of his right to withhold his consent to the making of the application, and of the following rights under this Act, namely—

(a) the rights arising under sections 4(1) to (3) and 6(2) below with respect to access to the report before or after it is supplied,
(b) the right to withhold consent under subsection (1) of section 5 below, and
(c) the right to request the amendment of the report under subsection (2) of that section,

as well as of the effect of section 7 below.

[1] Words added by SI 2001/3649 (Financial Services and Markets Act 2000 (Consequential Amendments and Repeals) Order), Pt 8, Art.311(3).

Access to reports before they are supplied

4.—(1) An individual who gives his consent under section 3 above to the making of an application shall be entitled, when giving his consent, to state that he wishes to have access to the report to be supplied in response to the application before it is so supplied; and, if he does so, the applicant shall—

(a) notify the medical practitioner of that fact at the time when the application is made, and

(b) at the same time notify the individual of the making of the application;

and each such notification shall contain a statement of the effect of subsection (2) below.

(2) Where a medical practitioner is notified by the applicant under subsection (1) above that the individual in question wishes to have access to the report before it is supplied, the practitioner shall not supply the report unless—

(a) he has given the individual access to it and any requirements of section 5 below have been complied with, or

(b) the period of 21 days beginning with the date of the making of the application has elapsed without his having received any communication from the individual concerning arrangements for the individual to have access to it.

(3) Where a medical practitioner—

(a) receives an application for a medical report to be supplied for employment or insurance purposes without being notified by the applicant as mentioned in subsection (1) above, but

(b) before supplying the report receives a notification from the individual that he wishes to have access to the report before it is supplied,

the practitioner shall not supply the report unless—

(i) he has given the individual access to it and any requirements of section 5 below have been complied with, or

(ii) the period of 21 days beginning with the date of that notification has elapsed without his having received (either with that notification or otherwise) any communication from the individual concerning arrangements for the individual to have access to it.

(4) References in this section and section 5 below to giving an individual access to a medical report are references to—

(a) making the report or a copy of it available for his inspection; or

(b) supplying him with a copy of it;

and where a copy is supplied at the request, or otherwise with the consent, of the individual the practitioner may charge a reasonable fee to cover the costs of supplying it.

Consent to supplying of report and correction of errors

5.—(1) Where an individual has been given access to a report under section 4 above the report shall not be supplied in response to the application in question unless the individual has notified the medical practitioner that he consents to its being so supplied.

(2) The individual shall be entitled, before giving his consent under subsection (1) above, to request the medical practitioner to amend any part of the report which the individual considers to be incorrect or misleading; and, if the individual does so, the practitioner—

(a) if he is to any extent prepared to accede to the individual's request, shall amend the report accordingly;

(b) if he is to any extent not prepared to accede to it but the individual requests him to attach to the report a statement of the individual's views in respect of any part of the report which he is declining to amend, shall attach such a statement to the report.

(3) Any request made by an individual under subsection (2) above shall be made in writing.

Retention of reports

6.—(1) A copy of any medical report which a medical practitioner has supplied for employment or insurance purposes shall be retained by him for at least six months from the date on which it was supplied.

(2) A medical practitioner shall, if so requested by an individual, give the individual access to any medical report relating to him which the practitioner has supplied for employment or insurance purposes in the previous six months.

(3) The reference in subsection (2) above to giving an individual access to a medical report is a reference to—

(a) making a copy of the report available for his inspection; or
(b) supplying him with a copy of it;

and where a copy is supplied at the request, or otherwise with the consent, of the individual the practitioner may charge a reasonable fee to cover the costs of supplying it.

Exemptions

7.—(1) A medical practitioner shall not be obliged to give an individual access, in accordance with the provisions of section 4(4) or 6(3) above, to any part of a medical report whose disclosure would in the opinion of the practitioner be likely to cause serious harm to the physical or mental health of the individual or others or would indicate the intentions of the practitioner in respect of the individual.

(2) A medical practitioner shall not be obliged to give an individual access, in accordance with those provisions, to any part of a medical report whose disclosure would be likely to reveal information about another person, or to reveal the identity of another person who has supplied information to the practitioner about the individual, unless—

(a) that person has consented; or
(b) that person is a health professional who has been involved in the care of the individual and the information relates to or has been provided by the professional in that capacity.

(3) Where it appears to a medical practitioner that subsection (1) or (2) above is applicable to any part (but not the whole) of a medical report—

(a) he shall notify the individual of that fact; and
(b) references in the preceding sections of this Act to the individual being given access to the report shall be construed as references to his being given access to the remainder of it;

and other references to the report in sections 4(4), 5(2) and 6(3) above shall similarly be construed as references to the remainder of the report.

(4) Where it appears to a medical practitioner that subsection (1) or (2) above is applicable to the whole of a medical report—

(a) he shall notify the individual of that fact; but
(b) he shall not supply the report unless he is notified by the individual that the individual consents to its being supplied;

and accordingly, if he is so notified by the individual, the restrictions imposed by section 4(2) and (3) above on the supply of the report shall not have effect in relation to it.

Application to the court

8.—(1) If a court is satisfied on the application of an individual that any person, in connection with a medical report relating to that individual, has failed or is likely to fail to comply with any requirement of this Act, the court may order that person to comply with that requirement.

(2) The jurisdiction conferred by this section shall be exercisable by a county court or, in Scotland, by the sheriff.

Notifications under this Act

9.—Any notification required or authorised to be given under this Act—

(a) shall be given in writing; and
(b) may be given by post.

Short title, commencement and extent

10.—(1) This Act may be cited as the Access to Medical Reports Act 1988.

(2) This Act shall come into force on January 1, 1989.

(3) Nothing in this Act applies to a medical report prepared before the coming into force of this Act.

(4) This Act does not extend to Northern Ireland.

Care Standards Act 2000

(2000, C.14)

PART VII

PROTECTION OF CHILDREN AND VULNERABLE ADULTS

Protection of vulnerable adults

App 5–03 **Basic definitions**

80.—(1) Subsections (2) to (7) apply for the purposes of this Part.

(2) "Care worker" means—

(a) an individual who is or has been employed in a position which is such as to enable him to have regular contact in the course of his duties with adults to whom accommodation is provided at a care home;
(b) an individual who is or has been employed in a position which is such as to enable him to have regular contact in the course of his duties with adults to whom prescribed services are provided by an independent hospital, an independent clinic, an independent medical agency or a National Health Service body;
(c) an individual who is or has been employed in a position which is concerned with the provision of personal care in their own homes for persons who by reason of illness, infirmity or disability are unable to provide it for themselves without assistance.

(3) "Care position", in relation to an individual, means a position such as is mentioned in subsection (2)(a), (b) or (c).

(4) "Employment" has the same meaning as in the Protection of Children Act 1999 (referred to in this Act as "the 1999 Act"); and references to an individual being employed shall be construed accordingly.

(5) "Supply worker"—

(a) in relation to an employment agency, means an individual supplied by the agency for employment in a care position or for whom the agency has found employment in a care position;
(b) in relation to an employment business, means an individual supplied by the business for employment in a care position.

(6) "Vulnerable adult" means-

(a) an adult to whom accommodation and nursing or personal care are provided in a care home;
(b) an adult to whom personal care is provided in their own home under arrangements made by a domiciliary care agency; or
(c) an adult to whom prescribed services are provided by an independent hospital, independent clinic, independent medical agency or National Health Service body.

(7) The persons who provide care for vulnerable adults are—

(a) any person who carries on a care home;

(b) any person who carries on a domiciliary care agency;
(c) any person who carries on an independent hospital, an independent clinic or an independent medical agency, which provides prescribed services; and
(d) a National Health Service body which provides prescribed services.

(8) Regulations for the purposes of this section or section 91, 93 or 103 may only be made by the Secretary of State; and before making any regulations for the purposes of this section or section 93 or 103 the Secretary of State shall consult the Assembly.

Access to list before commencement of section 90

91.—(1) In relation to any time before the commencement of section 90, any person seeking to ascertain whether a relevant individual is included in the list kept under section 81 shall be entitled to that information on making application for the purpose to the Secretary of State.

(2) For the purposes of subsection (1) a relevant individual is—

(a) an individual to whom the person proposes to offer employment in a care position;
(b) an individual for whom the person proposes to find employment, or whom he proposes to supply for employment, in a care position; or
(c) an individual of a prescribed description who does not fall within paragraph (a) or (b).

The list kept under section 1 of the 1999 Act

Employment agencies and businesses

94.—(1) In subsection (9) of section 2 of the 1999 Act (inclusion on reference to Secretary of State in list of individuals who are considered unsuitable to work with children)—

(a) for "This section" there shall be substituted " Subsections (1) to (8) and (10) of this section"; and
(b) for the words from "(a)" to "harm" there shall be substituted—

"(a) in subsection (1), for the words from 'there is' to the end there were substituted the following paragraphs—
"(a) the organisation has decided not to do any further business with the individual on the grounds of misconduct (whether or not in the course of his employment) which harmed a child or placed a child at risk of harm; or
(b) the organisation has decided on such grounds not to find the individual further employment, or supply him for further employment, in a child care position;' "

(2) After subsection (9) of that section there shall be inserted—

"(9A) Subsections (1) to (8) and (10) of this section shall have effect in relation to an organisation which carries on an employment business as if—
(a) in subsection (1)—
(i) for the words from "who" to "position" there were substituted the words "who has been supplied by the organisation for employment in a child care position"; and
(ii) paragraph (b) and the word "or" preceding it were omitted;
(b) for subsection (2)(c) and (d) there were substituted the following paragraph—
"(c) that the organisation has, on such grounds, decided not to supply the individual for further employment in a child care position."
and
(c) subsections (3), (6)(b) and (8) were omitted."

Temporary provision for access to lists

103.—(1) Any person seeking to ascertain whether a relevant individual is included in—

(a) the list kept under section 1 of the 1999 Act;
(b) the list kept for the purposes of regulations made under section 218(6) of the Education Reform Act 1988; or
(c) any list kept by the Secretary of State or the Assembly of persons disqualified under section 470 or 471 of the Education Act 1996,

shall be entitled to that information on making, before the relevant commencement, an application for the purpose to the Secretary of State.

(2) In this section "relevant individual" means—

(a) in relation to a person who carries on an employment agency, an individual with whom he proposes to do business or an individual of any other prescribed description;
(b) in relation to any other person, an individual to whom he proposes to offer, or whom he proposes to supply for employment in, a child care position or an individual of any other prescribed description.

(3) The relevant commencement is—

(a) for applications relating to the list mentioned in subsection (1)(a) or (b), the commencemen of section 8 of the 1999 Act; and
(b) for applications relating to the list mentioned in subsection (1)(c), the commencement of section 102.

(4) Paragraphs (b) and (c) of subsection (1) are without prejudice to any right conferred otherwise than by virtue of those provisions.

Community Health Councils (Access to Information) Act 1988

(1988, C.24)

An Act to provide for access by the public to meetings of, and to certain documents and information relating to, Community Health Councils and committees of those Councils and for related purposes. App 5–04

[JULY 29, 1988]

BE IT ENACTED by the Queen's most Excellent Majesty, by and with the advice and consent of the Lords Spiritual and Temporal, and Commons, in this present Parliament assembled, and by, the authority of the same, as follows—

Access to meetings and documents of Community Health Councils

1.—(1) Sections 100A to 100D of the Local Government Act 1972 (access to meetings and documents of certain authorities) shall apply to a Community Health Council established in accordance with section 20 of the National Health Service Act 1977 as they apply to a principal council within the meaning of Part VA of the said Act of 1972, but subject to the following modifications, namely—

- (a) the reference in section 100A(6)(c) to premises not belonging to a principal council shall be construed as a reference to premises not under the control of the Community Health Council;
- (b) he proper officer for the purposes of sections 100B , 100C and 100D shall be a person appointed for the purpose by the Community Health Council; and
- (c) the references in sections 100C(1) and 100D(2) to the periods of six and four years shall be construed as references to the periods of three years and two years respectively.

(2) Those sections of the said Act of 1972 shall apply also in relation to a community health committee as they apply to a principal council within the meaning of Part VA of that Act but subject to subsection (1)(c) above and to the following further modifications, namely—

- (a) section 100A(6)(a) shall be taken to have been complied with if the notice is given by posting it at the time there mentioned at the offices of every constituent Council and, if the meeting of the committee is to be held at premises other than the offices of such a Council, at those premises;
- (b) for the purposes of section 100A(6)(c), premises under the control of a constituent Council shall be treated as belonging to the committee;
- (c) for the purposes of sections 100B(1), 100C(1) and 100D(1), offices of any constituent Council shall be treated as offices of the committee; and
- (d) the proper officer, for the purposes of sections 100B, 100C and 100D, shall be a person appointed for the purpose by the constituent Council.

(3) In this section "community health committee" means a committee appointed by a Community Health Council or a joint committee appointed by two or more such Councils and "constituent Council", in relation to such a committee, means the Council or Councils by whom the committee was appointed.

(4) In section 100H of the said Act of 1972 (supplemental provisions and offences)—

(a) any reference to any provision of Part VA of that Act or to any right conferred by that Part includes a reference to any such provision as it applies by virtue of this section or, as the case may be, to any right conferred by that Part as it so applies;
(b) in subsection (2)(b) as it so applies the reference to supplying a copy shall be construed as supplying a copy before the end of the period of three days beginning with the day on which the copy is requested;
(c) in subsection (3) as it so applies the reference to a principal council shall be construed as a reference to a Community Health Council; and
(d) subsection (5) shall apply to any meeting of a Community Health Council or a community health committee.

(5) The power conferred on the Secretary of State by section 100I(2) of that Act to vary Schedule 12A to that Act (exempt information) shall include power to vary that Schedule as it applies by virtue of this section.

(6) In that Schedule, as it so applies—

(a) Part I shall have effect with the insertion at the end of paragraph 1 (information concerning employees of the authority) of the words "or any Health Authority[or Primary Care Trust][1] within whose area the authority exercises functions or any National Health Service trust which is established under Part I of the National Health Service and Community Care Act 1990 and carries on any of its activities from premises in the area of the authority or any National Health Service trust which is established under Part I of the National Health Service and Community Care Act 1990 and carries on any of its activities from premises in the area of the authority" and with the insertion after paragraph 6 of the following paragraphs—

"6A. Information relating to the physical or mental health of any particular person.

6B. Information relating to—

(a) any particular person who is or was formerly included in a list of persons undertaking to provide services under Part II of the National Health Service Act 1977 or is an applicant for inclusion in such a list; or
(b) any particular employee of such a person.";

(b) paragraph 1 of Part II shall have effect with the insertion after the words "paragraphs 1 to 5" of the words "or 6B"; and
(c) any reference to "the authority" shall be construed as a reference to the Community Health Council, and to a community health committee (and accordingly paragraph 1(2) of Part III shall not apply).[2]

---

[1] Words inserted by SI 2000/90 (Health Act 1999 (Supplementary, Consequential etc. Provisions) Order), Sch.1, para.21.

[2] In relation to Wales:

[1. Access to meetings and documents of Community Health Councils.

(1) S.100A to 100D of the Local Government Act 1972 (access to meetings and documents of certain authorities) shall apply to a Community Health Council continued in existence by or established under s.20A of the National Health Service Act 1977 as they apply to a principal council within the meaning of Pt VA of the said Act of 1972, but subject to the following modifications, namely—

(a) the reference in s.100A(6)(c) to premises not belonging to a principal council shall be construed as a reference to premises not under the control of the Community Health Council;

Access to information relating to members of Community Health Councils etc.

2.—(1) A Community Health Council shall maintain a register containing the name and address of every member of the Council and of every committee appointed by the Council whether alone or jointly with another Council and stating in the case of each member of the Council—

(a) the name and address of the body which appointed him;
(b) whether or not he is a member of that body; and
(c) in the case of a member appointed by a voluntary organisation (within the meaning of the National Health Service Act 1977), that he has been so appointed.

(b) the proper officer for the purposes of ss.100B, 100C and 100D shall be a person appointed for the purpose by the Community Health Council; and
(c) the references in ss.100C(1) and 100D(2) to the periods of six to four years shall be construed as references to the periods of three and two years respectively.

(2) Those sections of the said Act of 1972 shall apply also in relation to a community health committee as they apply to a principal council within the meaning of Pt VA of that Act but subject to subs.(1)(c) above and to the following further modifications, namely—
(a) s.100A(6)(a) shall be taken to have been complied with if the notice is given by posting it at the time there mentioned at the offices of every constituent Council and, if the meeting of the committee is to be held at premises other than the offices of such a Council, at those premises;
(b) for the purposes of s.100A(6)(c), premises under the control of a constituent Council shall be treated as belonging to the committee;
(c) for the purposes of ss.100B(1), 100C(1) and 100D(1), offices of any constituent Council shall be treated as offices of the committee; and
(d) the proper officer, for the purposes of ss.100B, 100C and 100D, shall be a person appointed for the purpose by the constituent Council.

(3) In this section "community health committee" means a committee appointed by a Community Health Council or a joint committee appointed by two or more such Councils and "constituent Council", in relation to such a committee, means the Council or Councils by whom the committee was appointed.

(4) In s.100H of the said Act of 1972 (supplemental provisions and offences)—
(a) any reference to any provision of Pt VA of that Act or to any right conferred by that Part includes a reference to any such provision as it applies by virtue of this section or, as the case may be, to any right conferred by that Part as it so applies;
(b) in subs.(2)(b) as it so applies the reference to supplying a copy shall be construed as supplying a copy before the end of the period of three days beginning with the day on which the copy is requested;
(c) in subs.(3) as it so applies the reference to a principal council shall be construed as a reference to a Community Health Council; and
(d) subs.(5) shall apply to any meeting of a Community Health Council or a community health committee.

(5) The power conferred on the Secretary of State by s.100I(2) of that Act to vary Sch.12A to that Act (exempt information) shall include power to vary that Schedule as it applies by virtue of this section.

(6) In that Schedule, as it so applies—
(a) Pt I shall have effect with the insertion at the end of para.1 (information concerning employees of the authority) of the words "or any Health Authority or Primary Care Trust within whose area the authority exercises functions or any National Helath Service trust which is established under Part I of the National Health Service and Community Care Act 1990 and carries on any of its activities from the premises in the area of the authority or any National Helath Service trust which is established under Part I of the National Health Service and Community Care Act 1990 and carries on any of its activities from premises in the area of the authority" and with the insertion after para.6 of the following paragraphs—

(2) A written summary of the rights—

(a) to attend meetings of a Community Health Council and community health committee, and
(b) to inspect and copy, and be furnished with, documents relating to such a Council or committee,

which are for the time being conferred by virtue of section 1 above shall be kept at the offices of each such Council.

(3) The register maintained by a Council under subsection (1) above and the summary kept by it under subsection (2) above shall be open to inspection by the public at all reasonable hours and without payment at the offices of the Council; and any person may, on payment of such reasonable fee as the Council may determine—

(a) make copies of or extracts from any such register or summary kept by it; and
(b) require the Council to supply him before the end of the period of three days beginning with the day on which the request is made with a photographic copy of or of extracts from any such register or summary.

Short title, commencement and extent

3.—(1) This Act may be cited as the Community Health Councils (Access to Information) Act 1988.

(2) This Act shall come into force on April 1, 1989.

(3) Nothing in this Act applies in relation to any meeting held before that date.

(4) This Act extends to England and Wales only.

"6A. Information relating to the physical or mental health of any particular person.

6B. Information relating to—

(a) any particular person who is or was formerly included in a list of persons undertaking to provide services under Part II of the National Health Service Act 1977 or is an applicant for inclusion in such a list; or
(b) any particular employee of such a person.";

(b) para.1 of Pt II shall have effect with the insertion after the words "paragraphs 1 to 5" of the words "or 6B"; and
(c) any reference to "the authority" shall be construed as a reference to the Community Health Council, and to a community health committee (and accordingly para.1(2) of Pt III shall not apply).][3]

[3] Words substituted by Health (Wales) Act 2003 (c.4), Sch.3, para.5.

APPENDIX 6

Environmental Information

Convention on Access to Information, Public Participation in Decision-Making and Access to Justice in Environmental Matters

(DONE AT AARHUS, DENMARK)

[JUNE 25, 1998]

THE PARTIES TO THIS CONVENTION, App 6–01

Recalling principle l of the Stockholm Declaration on the Human Environment,

Recalling also principle 10 of the Rio Declaration on Environment and Development,

Recalling further General Assembly resolutions 37/7 of October 28, 1982 on the World Charter for Nature and 45/94 of December 14, 1990 on the need to ensure a healthy environment for the well-being of individuals,

Recalling the European Charter on Environment and Health adopted at the First European Conference on Environment and Health of the World Health Organisation in Frankfurt-am-Main, Germany, on December 8, 1989,

Affirming the need to protect, preserve and improve the state of the environment and to ensure sustainable and environmentally sound development,

Recognising that adequate protection of the environment is essential to human well-being and the enjoyment of basic human rights, including the right to life itself,

Recognising also that every person has the right to live in an environment adequate to his or her health and well-being, and the duty, both individually and in association with others, to protect and improve the environment for the benefit of present and future generations,

Considering that, to be able to assert this right and observe this duty, citizens must have access to information, be entitled to participate in decision-making and have access to justice in environmental matters, and acknowledging in this regard that citizens may need assistance in order to exercise their rights,

Recognising that, in the field of the environment, improved access to information and public participation in decision-making enhance the quality and the implementation of decisions, contribute to public awareness of environmental issues, give the public the opportunity to express its concerns and enable public authorities to take due account of such concerns,

Aiming thereby to further the accountability of and transparency in decision-making and to strengthen public support for decisions on the environment,

Recognising the desirability of transparency in all branches of government and inviting legislative bodies to implement the principles of this Convention in their proceedings,

Recognising also that the public needs to be aware of the procedures for participation in environmental decision-making, have free access to them and know how to use them,

Recognising further the importance of the respective roles that individual citizens, non-governmental organisations and the private sector can play in environmental protection,

Desiring to promote environmental education to further the understanding of the environment and sustainable development and to encourage widespread public awareness of, and participation in, decisions affecting the environment and sustainable development,

Noting, in this context, the importance of making use of the media and of electronic or other, future forms of communication,

Recognising the importance of fully integrating environmental considerations in governmental decision-making and the consequent need for public authorities to be in possession of accurate, comprehensive and up-to-date environmental information,

Acknowledging that public authorities hold environmental information in the public interest,

Concerned that effective judicial mechanisms should be accessible to the public, including organisations, so that its legitimate interests are protected and the law is enforced,

Noting the importance of adequate product information being provided to consumers to enable them to make informed environmental choices,

Recognising the concern of the public about the deliberate release of genetically modified organisms into the environment and the need for increased transparency and greater public participation in decision-making in this field,

Convinced that the implementation of this Convention will contribute to strengthening democracy in the region of the United Nations Economic Commission for Europe ("ECE"),

Conscious of the role played in this respect by ECE and recalling, *inter alia*, the ECE Guidelines on Access to Environmental Information and Public Participation in Environmental Decision-making endorsed in the Ministerial Declaration adopted at the Third Ministerial Conference "Environment for Europe" in Sofia, Bulgaria, on October 25, 1995,

Bearing in mind the relevant provisions in the Convention on Environmental Impact Assessment in a Transboundary Context, done at Espoo, Finland, on February 25, 1991, and the Convention on the Transboundary Effects of Industrial Accidents and the Convention on the Protection and Use of Transboundary Watercourses and International Lakes, both done at Helsinki on March 17, 1992, and other regional conventions,

Conscious that the adoption of this Convention will have contributed to the further strengthening of the "Environment for Europe" process and to the results of the Fourth Ministerial Conference in Aarhus, Denmark, in June 1998,

HAVE AGREED AS FOLLOWS:

OBJECTIVE

1.—In order to contribute to the protection of the right of every person of present and future generations to live in an environment adequate to his or her health and well-being, each Party shall guarantee the rights of access to information, public participation in decision-making, and access to justice in environmental matters in accordance with the provisions of this Convention.

DEFINITIONS

2.—For the purposes of this Convention,

1. "Party" means, unless the text otherwise indicates, a Contracting Party to this Convention;

2. "Public authority" means:

(a) Government at national, regional and other level;
(b) Natural or legal persons performing public administrative functions under national law, including specific duties, activities or services in relation to the environment;
(c) Any other natural or legal persons having public responsibilities or functions, or providing public services, in relation to the environment, under the control of a body or person falling within subparagraphs (a) or (b) above;
(d) The institutions of any regional economic integration organisation referred to in article 17 which is a Party to this Convention.

This definition does not include bodies or institutions acting in a judicial or legislative capacity;

3. "Environmental information" means any information in written, visual, aural, electronic or any other material form on:

(a) The state of elements of the environment, such as air and atmosphere, water, soil, land, landscape and natural sites, biological diversity and its components, including genetically modified organisms, and the interaction among these elements;
(b) Factors, such as substances, energy, noise and radiation, and activities or measures, including administrative measures, environmental agreements, policies, legislation, plans and programmes, affecting or likely to affect the elements of the environment within the scope of subparagraph (a) above, and cost-benefit and other economic analyses and assumptions used in environmental decision-making;
(c) The state of human health and safety, conditions of human life, cultural sites and built structures, inasmuch as they are or may be affected by the state of the elements of the environment or, through these elements, by the factors, activities or measures referred to in subparagraph (b) above;

4. "The public" means one or more natural or legal persons, and, in accordance with national legislation or practice, their associations, organisations or groups;

5. "The public concerned" means the public affected or likely to be affected by, or having an interest in, the environmental decision-making; for the purposes of this definition, non-governmental organisations promoting environmental protection and meeting any requirements under national law shall be deemed to have an interest.

GENERAL PROVISIONS

3.—1. Each Party shall take the necessary legislative, regulatory and other measures, including measures to achieve compatibility between the provisions implementing the information, public participation and access-to-justice provisions in this Convention, as well as proper enforcement measures, to establish and maintain a clear, transparent and consistent framework to implement the provisions of this Convention.

2. Each Party shall endeavour to ensure that officials and authorities assist and provide guidance to the public in seeking access to information, in facilitating participation in decision-making and in seeking access to justice in environmental matters.

3. Each Party shall promote environmental education and environmental awareness among the public, especially on how to obtain access to information, to participate in decision-making and to obtain access to justice in environmental matters.

4. Each Party shall provide for appropriate recognition of and support to associations, organisations or groups promoting environmental protection and ensure that its national legal system is consistent with this obligation.

5. The provisions of this Convention shall not affect the right of a Party to maintain or introduce measures providing for broader access to information, more extensive public participation in decision-making and wider access to justice in environmental matters than required by this Convention.

6. This Convention shall not require any derogation from existing rights of access to information, public participation in decision-making and access to justice in environmental matters.

7. Each Party shall promote the application of the principles of this Convention in international environmental decision-making processes and within the framework of international organisations in matters relating to the environment.

8. Each Party shall ensure that persons exercising their rights in conformity with the provisions of this Convention shall not be penalised, persecuted or harassed in any way for their involvement. This provision shall not affect the powers of national courts to award reasonable costs in judicial proceedings.

9. Within the scope of the relevant provisions of this Convention, the public shall have access to information, have the possibility to participate in decision-making and have access to justice in environmental matters without discrimination as to citizenship, nationality or domicile and, in the case of a legal person, without discrimination as to where it has its registered seat or an effective centre of its activities.

ACCESS TO ENVIRONMENTAL INFORMATION

4.—1. Each Party shall ensure that, subject to the following paragraphs of this article, public authorities, in response to a request for environmental information, make such information available to the public, within the framework of national legislation, including, where requested and subject to subparagraph (b) below, copies of the actual documentation containing or comprising such information:

(a) Without an interest having to be stated;

(b) In the form requested unless:

  (i) It is reasonable for the public authority to make it available in another form, in which case reasons shall be given for making it available in that form; or

  (ii) The information is already publicly available in another form.

2. The environmental information referred to in paragraph 1 above shall be made available as soon as possible and at the latest within one month after the request has been submitted, unless the volume and the complexity of the information justify an extension of this period up to two months after the request. The applicant shall be informed of any extension and of the reasons justifying it.

3. A request for environmental information may be refused if:

(a) The public authority to which the request is addressed does not hold the environmental information requested;

(b) The request is manifestly unreasonable or formulated in too general a manner; or

(c) The request concerns material in the course of completion or concerns internal communications of public authorities where such an exemption is provided for in national law or customary practice, taking into account the public interest served by disclosure.

4. A request for environmental information may be refused if the disclosure would adversely affect:

(a) The confidentiality of the proceedings of public authorities, where such confidentiality is provided for under national law;
(b) International relations, national defence or public security;
(c) The course of justice, the ability of a person to receive a fair trial or the ability of a public authority to conduct an enquiry of a criminal or disciplinary nature;
(d) The confidentiality of commercial and industrial information, where such confidentiality is protected by law in order to protect a legitimate economic interest. Within this framework, information on emissions which is relevant for the protection of the environment shall be disclosed;
(e) Intellectual property rights;
(f) The confidentiality of personal data and/or files relating to a natural person where that person has not consented to the disclosure of the information to the public, where such confidentiality is provided for in national law;
(g) The interests of a third party which has supplied the information requested without that party being under or capable of being put under a legal obligation to do so, and where that party does not consent to the release of the material; or
(h) The environment to which the information relates, such as the breeding sites of rare species.

The aforementioned grounds for refusal shall be interpreted in a restrictive way, taking into account the public interest served by disclosure and taking into account whether the information requested relates to emissions into the environment.

5. Where a public authority does not hold the environmental information requested, this public authority shall, as promptly as possible, inform the applicant of the public authority to which it believes it is possible to apply for the information requested or transfer the request to that authority and inform the applicant accordingly.

6. Each Party shall ensure that, if information exempted from disclosure under paragraphs 3 (c) and 4 above can be separated out without prejudice to the confidentiality of the information exempted, public authorities make available the remainder of the environmental information that has been requested.

7. A refusal of a request shall be in writing if the request was in writing or the applicant so requests. A refusal shall state the reasons for the refusal and give information on access to the review procedure provided for in accordance with Article 9. The refusal shall be made as soon as possible and at the latest within one month, unless the complexity of the information justifies an extension of this period up to two months after the request. The applicant shall be informed of any extension and of the reasons justifying it.

8. Each Party may allow its public authorities to make a charge for supplying information, but such charge shall not exceed a reasonable amount.

Public authorities intending to make such a charge for supplying information shall make available to applicants a schedule of charges which may be levied, indicating the circumstances in which they may be levied or waived and when the supply of information is conditional on the advance payment of such a charge.

COLLECTION AND DISSEMINATION OF ENVIRONMENTAL INFORMATION

5.—1. Each Party shall ensure that:

(a) Public authorities possess and update environmental information which is relevant to their functions;
(b) Mandatory systems are established so that there is an adequate flow of information to public authorities about proposed and existing activities which may significantly affect the environment;
(c) In the event of any imminent threat to human health or the environment, whether caused by human activities or due to natural causes, all information which could

enable the public to take measures to prevent or mitigate harm arising from the threat and is held by a public authority is disseminated immediately and without delay to members of the public who may be affected.

2. Each Party shall ensure that, within the framework of national legislation, the way in which public authorities make environmental information available to the public is transparent and that environmental information is effectively accessible, inter alia, by:

(a) Providing sufficient information to the public about the type and scope of environmental information held by the relevant public authorities, the basic terms and conditions under which such information is made available and accessible, and the process by which it can be obtained;

(b) Establishing and maintaining practical arrangements, such as:

(i) Publicly accessible lists, registers or files;

(ii) Requiring officials to support the public in seeking access to information under this Convention; and

(iii) The identification of points of contact; and

(c) Providing access to the environmental information contained in lists, registers or files as referred to in subparagraph (b)(i) above free of charge.

3. Each Party shall ensure that environmental information progressively becomes available in electronic databases which are easily accessible to the public through public telecommunications networks. Information accessible in this form should include:

(a) Reports on the state of the environment, as referred to in paragraph 4 below;

(b) Texts of legislation on or relating to the environment;

(c) As appropriate, policies, plans and programmes on or relating to the environment, and environmental agreements; and

(d) Other information, to the extent that the availability of such information in this form would facilitate the application of national law implementing this Convention, provided that such information is already available in electronic form.

4. Each Party shall, at regular intervals not exceeding three or four years, publish and disseminate a national report on the state of the environment, including information on the quality of the environment and information on pressures on the environment.

5. Each Party shall take measures within the framework of its legislation for the purpose of disseminating, *inter alia*:

(a) Legislation and policy documents such as documents on strategies, policies, programmes and action plans relating to the environment, and progress reports on their implementation, prepared at various levels of government;

(b) International treaties, conventions and agreements on environmental issues; and

(c) Other significant international documents on environmental issues, as appropriate.

6. Each Party shall encourage operators whose activities have a significant impact on the environment to inform the public regularly of the environmental impact of their activities and products, where appropriate within the framework of voluntary eco-labelling or eco-auditing schemes or by other means.

7. Each Party shall:

(a) Publish the facts and analyses of facts which it considers relevant and important in framing major environmental policy proposals;

(b) Publish, or otherwise make accessible, available explanatory material on its dealings with the public in matters falling within the scope of this Convention; and

(c) Provide in an appropriate form information on the performance of public functions or the provision of public services relating to the environment by government at all levels.

8. Each Party shall develop mechanisms with a view to ensuring that sufficient product information is made available to the public in a manner which enables consumers to make informed environmental choices.

9. Each Party shall take steps to establish progressively, taking into account international processes where appropriate, a coherent, nationwide system of pollution inventories or registers on a structured, computerised and publicly accessible database compiled through standardised reporting. Such a system may include inputs, releases and transfers of a specified range of substances and products, including water, energy and resource use, from a specified range of activities to environmental media and to on-site and offsite treatment and disposal sites.

10. Nothing in this article may prejudice the right of Parties to refuse to disclose certain environmental information in accordance with Article 4, paragraphs 3 and 4.

PUBLIC PARTICIPATION IN DECISIONS ON SPECIFIC ACTIVITIES

6.—1. Each Party:

(a) Shall apply the provisions of this article with respect to decisions on whether to permit proposed activities listed in Annex I;
(b) Shall, in accordance with its national law, also apply the provisions of this article to decisions on proposed activities not listed in Annex I which may have a significant effect on the environment. To this end, Parties shall determine whether such a proposed activity is subject to these provisions; and
(c) May decide, on a case-by-case basis if so provided under national law, not to apply the provisions of this article to proposed activities serving national defence purposes, if that Party deems that such application would have an adverse effect on these purposes.

2. The public concerned shall be informed, either by public notice or individually as appropriate, early in an environmental decision-making procedure, and in an adequate, timely and effective manner, *inter alia*, of:

(a) The proposed activity and the application on which a decision will be taken;
(b) The nature of possible decisions or the draft decision;
(c) The public authority responsible for making the decision;
(d) The envisaged procedure, including, as and when this information can be provided:
    (i) The commencement of the procedure;
    (ii) The opportunities for the public to participate;
    (iii) The time and venue of any envisaged public hearing;
    (iv) An indication of the public authority from which relevant information can be obtained and where the relevant information has been deposited for examination by the public;
    (v) An indication of the relevant public authority or any other official body to which comments or questions can be submitted and of the time schedule for transmittal of comments or questions; and
    (vi) An indication of what environmental information relevant to the proposed activity is available; and
(e) The fact that the activity is subject to a national or transboundary environmental impact assessment procedure.

3. The public participation procedures shall include reasonable time-frames for the different phases, allowing sufficient time for informing the public in accordance with paragraph 2 above and for the public to prepare and participate effectively during the environmental decision-making.

4. Each Party shall provide for early public participation, when all options are open and effective public participation can take place.

5. Each Party should, where appropriate, encourage prospective applicants to identify the public concerned, to enter into discussions, and to provide information regarding the objectives of their application before applying for a permit.

6. Each Party shall require the competent public authorities to give the public concerned access for examination, upon request where so required under national law, free of charge and as soon as it becomes available, to all information relevant to the decision-making referred to in this article that is available at the time of the public participation procedure, without prejudice to the right of Parties to refuse to disclose certain information in accordance with Article 4, paragraphs 3 and 4. The relevant information shall include at least, and without prejudice to the provisions of Article 4:

(a) A description of the site and the physical and technical characteristics of the proposed activity, including an estimate of the expected residues and emissions;
(b) A description of the significant effects of the proposed activity on the environment;
(c) A description of the measures envisaged to prevent and/or reduce the effects, including emissions;
(d) A non-technical summary of the above;
(e) An outline of the main alternatives studied by the applicant; and
(f) In accordance with national legislation, the main reports and advice issued to the public authority at the time when the public concerned shall be informed in accordance with paragraph 2 above.

7. Procedures for public participation shall allow the public to submit, in writing or, as appropriate, at a public hearing or inquiry with the applicant, any comments, information, analyses or opinions that it considers relevant to the proposed activity.

8. Each Party shall ensure that in the decision due account is taken of the outcome of the public participation.

9. Each Party shall ensure that, when the decision has been taken by the public authority, the public is promptly informed of the decision in accordance with the appropriate procedures. Each Party shall make accessible to the public the text of the decision along with the reasons and considerations on which the decision is based.

10. Each Party shall ensure that, when a public authority reconsiders or updates the operating conditions for an activity referred to in paragraph 1, the provisions of paragraphs 2 to 9 of this article are applied mutatis mutandis, and where appropriate.

11. Each Party shall, within the framework of its national law, apply, to the extent feasible and appropriate, provisions of this article to decisions on whether to permit the deliberate release of genetically modified organisms into the environment.

PUBLIC PARTICIPATION CONCERNING PLANS, PROGRAMMES AND POLICIES RELATING TO THE ENVIRONMENT

7.—Each Party shall make appropriate practical and/or other provisions for the public to participate during the preparation of plans and programmes relating to the environment, within a transparent and fair framework, having provided the necessary information to the public. Within this framework, Article 6, paragraphs 3, 4 and 8, shall be applied. The public which may participate shall be identified by the relevant public authority, taking into account the objectives of this Convention. To the extent appropriate, each Party shall endeavour to provide opportunities for public participation in the preparation of policies relating to the environment.

PUBLIC PARTICIPATION DURING THE PREPARATION OF EXECUTIVE REGULATIONS AND/OR GENERALLY APPLICABLE LEGALLY BINDING NORMATIVE INSTRUMENTS

8.—Each Party shall strive to promote effective public participation at an appropriate stage, and while options are still open, during the preparation by public authorities of executive regulations and other generally applicable legally binding rules that may have a significant effect on the environment. To this end, the following steps should be taken:

(a) Time-frames sufficient for effective participation should be fixed;
(b) Draft rules should be published or otherwise made publicly available; and
(c) The public should be given the opportunity to comment, directly or through representative consultative bodies.

The result of the public participation shall be taken into account as far as possible.

ACCESS TO JUSTICE

9.—1. Each Party shall, within the framework of its national legislation, ensure that any person who considers that his or her request for information under Article 4 has been ignored, wrongfully refused, whether in part or in full, inadequately answered, or otherwise not dealt with in accordance with the provisions of that article, has access to a review procedure before a court of law or another independent and impartial body established by law. In the circumstances where a Party provides for such a review by a court of law, it shall ensure that such a person also has access to an expeditious procedure established by law that is free of charge or inexpensive for reconsideration by a public authority or review by an independent and impartial body other than a court of law.

Final decisions under this paragraph 1 shall be binding on the public authority holding the information. Reasons shall be stated in writing, at least where access to information is refused under this paragraph.

2. Each Party shall, within the framework of its national legislation, ensure that members of the public concerned

(a) Having a sufficient interest or, alternatively,
(b) Maintaining impairment of a right, where the administrative procedural law of a Party requires this as a precondition, have access to a review procedure before a court of law and/or another independent and impartial body established by law, to challenge the substantive and procedural legality of any decision, act or omission subject to the provisions of article 6 and, where so provided for under national law and without prejudice to paragraph 3 below, of other relevant provisions of this Convention.

What constitutes a sufficient interest and impairment of a right shall be determined in accordance with the requirements of national law and consistently with the objective of giving the public concerned wide access to justice within the scope of this Convention. To this end, the interest of any non-governmental organisation meeting the requirements referred to in article 2, paragraph 5, shall be deemed sufficient for the purpose of subparagraph (a) above. Such organisations shall also be deemed to have rights capable of being impaired for the purpose of subparagraph (b) above.

The provisions of this paragraph 2 shall not exclude the possibility of a preliminary review procedure before an administrative authority and shall not affect the requirement of exhaustion of administrative review procedures prior to recourse to judicial review procedures, where such a requirement exists under national law.

3. In addition and without prejudice to the review procedures referred to in paragraphs 1 and 2 above, each Party shall ensure that, where they meet the criteria, if any, laid down in its national law, members of the public have access to administrative or judicial procedures to challenge acts and omissions by private persons and public authorities which contravene provisions of its national law relating to the environment.

4. In addition and without prejudice to paragraph 1 above, the procedures referred to in paragraphs 1, 2 and 3 above shall provide adequate and effective remedies, including injunctive relief as appropriate, and be fair, equitable, timely and not prohibitively expensive. Decisions under this article shall be given or recorded in writing. Decisions of courts, and whenever possible of other bodies, shall be publicly accessible.

5. In order to further the effectiveness of the provisions of this article, each Party shall ensure that information is provided to the public on access to administrative and judicial review procedures and shall consider the establishment of appropriate assistance mechanisms to remove or reduce financial and other barriers to access to justice.

MEETING OF THE PARTIES

10.—1. The first meeting of the Parties shall be convened no later than one year after the date of the entry into force of this Convention. Thereafter, an ordinary meeting of the Parties shall be held at least once every two years, unless otherwise decided by the Parties, or at the written request of any Party, provided that, within six months of the request being communicated to all Parties by the Executive Secretary of the Economic Commission for Europe, the said request is supported by at least one third of the Parties.

2. At their meetings, the Parties shall keep under continuous review the implementation of this Convention on the basis of regular reporting by the Parties, and, with this purpose in mind, shall:

(a) Review the policies for and legal and methodological approaches to access to information, public participation in decision-making and access to justice in environmental matters, with a view to further improving them;
(b) Exchange information regarding experience gained in concluding and implementing bilateral and multilateral agreements or other arrangements having relevance to the purposes of this Convention and to which one or more of the Parties are a party;
(c) Seek, where appropriate, the services of relevant ECE bodies and other competent international bodies and specific committees in all aspects pertinent to the achievement of the purposes of this Convention;
(d) Establish any subsidiary bodies as they deem necessary;
(e) Prepare, where appropriate, protocols to this Convention;
(f) Consider and adopt proposals for amendments to this Convention in accordance with the provisions of Article 14;
(g) Consider and undertake any additional action that may be required for the achievement of the purposes of this Convention;
(h) At their first meeting, consider and by consensus adopt rules of procedure for their meetings and the meetings of subsidiary bodies;
(i) At their first meeting, review their experience in implementing the provisions of Article 5, paragraph 9, and consider what steps are necessary to develop further the system referred to in that paragraph, taking into account international processes and developments, including the elaboration of an appropriate instrument concerning pollution release and transfer registers or inventories which could be annexed to this Convention.

3. The Meeting of the Parties may, as necessary, consider establishing financial arrangements on a consensus basis.

4. The United Nations, its specialized agencies and the International Atomic Energy Agency, as well as any State or regional economic integration organisation entitled under Article 17 to sign this Convention but which is not a Party to this Convention, and any intergovernmental organisation qualified in the fields to which this Convention relates, shall be entitled to participate as observers in the meetings of the Parties.

5. Any non-governmental organisation, qualified in the fields to which this Convention relates, which has informed the Executive Secretary of the Economic Commission for Europe of its wish to be represented at a meeting of the Parties shall be entitled to participate as an observer unless at least one third of the Parties present in the meeting raise objections.

6. For the purposes of paragraphs 4 and 5 above, the rules of procedure referred to in

paragraph 2(h) above shall provide for practical arrangements for the admittance procedure and other relevant terms.

RIGHT TO VOTE

11.—1. Except as provided for in paragraph 2 below, each Party to this Convention shall have one vote.

2. Regional economic integration organisations, in matters within their competence, shall exercise their right to vote with a number of votes equal to the number of their member States which are Parties to this Convention. Such organisations shall not exercise their right to vote if their member States exercise theirs, and *vice-versa*.

SECRETARIAT

12.—The Executive Secretary of the Economic Commission for Europe shall carry out the following secretariat functions:

(a) The convening and preparing of meetings of the Parties;
(b) The transmission to the Parties of reports and other information received in accordance with the provisions of this Convention; and
(c) Such other functions as may be determined by the Parties.

ANNEXES

13.—The annexes to this Convention shall constitute an integral part thereof.

AMENDMENTS TO THE CONVENTION

14.—1. Any Party may propose amendments to this Convention.

2. The text of any proposed amendment to this Convention shall be submitted in writing to the Executive Secretary of the Economic Commission for Europe, who shall communicate it to all Parties at least ninety days before the meeting of the Parties at which it is proposed for adoption.

3. The Parties shall make every effort to reach agreement on any proposed amendment to this Convention by consensus. If all efforts at consensus have been exhausted, and no agreement reached, the amendment shall as a last resort be adopted by a three-fourths majority vote of the Parties present and voting at the meeting.

4. Amendments to this Convention adopted in accordance with paragraph 3 above shall be communicated by the Depositary to all Parties for ratification, approval or acceptance. Amendments to this Convention other than those to an annex shall enter into force for Parties having ratified, approved or accepted them on the ninetieth day after the receipt by the Depositary of notification of their ratification, approval or acceptance by at least three fourths of these Parties. Thereafter they shall enter into force for any other Party on the ninetieth day after that Party deposits its instrument of ratification, approval or acceptance of the amendments.

5. Any Party that is unable to approve an amendment to an annex to this Convention shall so notify the Depositary in writing within 12 months from the date of the communication of the adoption. The Depositary shall without delay notify all Parties of any such notification received. A Party may at any time substitute an acceptance for its previous notification and, upon deposit of an instrument of acceptance with the Depositary, the amendments to such an annex shall become effective for that Party.

6. On the expiry of 12 months from the date of its communication by the Depositary as provided for in paragraph 4 above an amendment to an annex shall become effective for those Parties which have not submitted a notification to the Depositary in accordance with the provisions of paragraph 5 above, provided that not more than one third of the Parties have submitted such a notification.

7. For the purposes of this article, "Parties present and voting" means Parties present and casting an affirmative or negative vote.

REVIEW OF COMPLIANCE

15.—The Meeting of the Parties shall establish, on a consensus basis, optional arrangements of a non-confrontational, non-judicial and consultative nature for reviewing compliance with the provisions of this Convention. These arrangements shall allow for appropriate public involvement and may include the option of considering communications from members of the public on matters related to this Convention.

SETTLEMENT OF DISPUTES

16.—1. If a dispute arises between two or more Parties about the interpretation or application of this Convention, they shall seek a solution by negotiation or by any other means of dispute settlement acceptable to the parties to the dispute.

2. When signing, ratifying, accepting, approving or acceding to this Convention, or at any time thereafter, a Party may declare in writing to the Depositary that, for a dispute not resolved in accordance with paragraph 1 above, it accepts one or both of the following means of dispute settlement as compulsory in relation to any Party accepting the same obligation:

(a) Submission of the dispute to the International Court of Justice;
(b) Arbitration in accordance with the procedure set out in Annex II.

3. If the parties to the dispute have accepted both means of dispute settlement referred to in paragraph 2 above, the dispute may be submitted only to the International Court of Justice, unless the parties agree otherwise.

SIGNATURE

17.—This Convention shall be open for signature at Aarhus (Denmark) on June 25, 1998, and thereafter at United Nations Headquarters in New York until December 21, 1998, by States members of the Economic Commission for Europe as well as States having consultative status with the Economic Commission for Europe pursuant to paragraphs 8 and 11 of Economic and Social Council resolution 36 (IV) of March 28, 1947, and by regional economic integration organisations constituted by sovereign States Members of the Economic Commission for Europe to which their Member States have transferred competence over matters governed by this Convention, including the competence to enter into treaties in respect of these matters.

DEPOSITARY

18.—The Secretary-General of the United Nations shall act as the Depositary of this Convention.

RATIFICATION, ACCEPTANCE, APPROVAL AND ACCESSION

19.—1. This Convention shall be subject to ratification, acceptance or approval by signatory States and regional economic integration organisations.

2. This Convention shall be open for accession as from December 22, 1998 by the States and regional economic integration organisations referred to in Article 17.

3. Any other State, not referred to in paragraph 2 above, that is a Member of the United Nations may accede to the Convention upon approval by the Meeting of the Parties.

4. Any organisation referred to in Article 17 which becomes a Party to this

Convention without any of its Member States being a Party shall be bound by all the obligations under this Convention. If one or more of such an organisation's Member

States is a Party to this Convention, the organisation and its Member States shall decide on their respective responsibilities for the performance of their obligations under this Convention. In such cases, the organisation and the Member States shall not be entitled to exercise rights under this Convention concurrently.

5. In their instruments of ratification, acceptance, approval or accession, the regional economic integration organisations referred to in Article 17 shall declare the extent of their competence with respect to the matters governed by this Convention. These organisations shall also inform the Depositary of any substantial modification to the extent of their competence.

ENTRY INTO FORCE

20.—1. This Convention shall enter into force on the ninetieth day after the date of deposit of the sixteenth instrument of ratification, acceptance, approval or accession.

2. For the purposes of paragraph 1 above, any instrument deposited by a regional economic integration organisation shall not be counted as additional to those deposited by States Members of such an organisation.

3. For each State or organisation referred to in Article 17 which ratifies, accepts or approves this Convention or accedes thereto after the deposit of the sixteenth instrument of ratification, acceptance, approval or accession, the Convention shall enter into force on the ninetieth day after the date of deposit by such State or organisation of its instrument of ratification, acceptance, approval or accession.

WITHDRAWAL

21.—At any time after three years from the date on which this Convention has come into force with respect to a Party, that Party may withdraw from the Convention by giving written notification to the Depositary. Any such withdrawal shall take effect on the ninetieth day after the date of its receipt by the Depositary.

AUTHENTIC TEXTS

22.—The original of this Convention, of which the English, French and Russian texts are equally authentic, shall be deposited with the Secretary-General of the United Nations.

IN WITNESS WHEREOF the undersigned, being duly authorised thereto, have signed this Convention.

DONE at Aarhus (Denmark), this twenty-fifth day of June, one thousand nine hundred and ninety-eight.

ANNEXES

ANNEX I

List of Activities Referred to in Article 6, Paragraph 1(a)

1. Energy sector:

— Mineral oil and gas refineries;

— Installations for gasification and liquefaction;

— Thermal power stations and other combustion installations with a heat input of 50 megawatts ("MW")or more;

— Coke ovens;

— Nuclear power stations and other nuclear reactors including the dismantling or decommissioning of such power stations or reactors (see note 1 below) (except research installations for the production and conversion of fissionable and fertile materials whose maximum power does not exceed 1 kW continuous thermal load);

— Installations for the reprocessing of irradiated nuclear fuel;
— Installations designed:
— For the production or enrichment of nuclear fuel;
— For the processing of irradiated nuclear fuel or high-level radioactive waste;
— For the final disposal of irradiated nuclear fuel;
— Solely for the final disposal of radioactive waste;
— Solely for the storage (planned for more than 10 years) of irradiated nuclear fuels or radioactive waste in a different site than the production site.

2. Production and processing of metals:

— Metal ore (including sulphide ore) roasting or sintering installations;
— Installations for the production of pig-iron or steel (primary or secondary fusion) including continuous casting, with a capacity exceeding 2.5 tons per hour;
— Installations for the processing of ferrous metals:
    (i) Hot-rolling mills with a capacity exceeding 20 tons of crude steel per hour;
    (ii) Smitheries with hammers the energy of which exceeds 50 kilojoules per hammer, where the calorific power used exceeds 20 MW;
    (iii) Application of protective fused metal coats with an input exceeding 2 tons of crude steel per hour;

— Ferrous metal foundries with a production capacity exceeding 20 tons per day;
— Installations:
    (i) For the production of non-ferrous crude metals from ore, concentrates or secondary raw materials by metallurgical, chemical or electrolytic processes;
    (ii) For the smelting, including the alloying, of non-ferrous metals, including recovered products (refining, foundry casting, etc.), with a melting capacity exceeding 4 tons per day for lead and cadmium or 20 tons per day for all other metals;
— Installations for surface treatment of metals and plastic materials using an electrolytic or chemical process where the volume of the treatment vats exceeds 30 m^3.

3. Mineral industry:

— Installations for the production of cement clinker in rotary kilns with a production capacity exceeding 500 tons per day or lime in rotary kilns with a production capacity exceeding 50 tons per day or in other furnaces with a production capacity exceeding 50 tons per day;
— Installations for the production of asbestos and the manufacture of asbestos-based products;
— Installations for the manufacture of glass including glass fibre with a melting capacity exceeding 20 tons per day;
— Installations for melting mineral substances including the production of mineral fibres with a melting capacity exceeding 20 tons per day;
— Installations for the manufacture of ceramic products by firing, in particular roofing tiles, bricks, refractory bricks, tiles, stoneware or porcelain, with a production capacity exceeding 75 tons per day, and/or with a kiln capacity exceeding 4 m^3 and with a setting density per kiln exceeding 300 kg/m^3.

4. Chemical industry: Production within the meaning of the categories of activities contained in this paragraph means the production on an industrial scale by chemical processing of substances or groups of substances listed in subparagraphs (a) to (g):

(a) Chemical installations for the production of basic organic chemicals, such as:
   (i) Simple hydrocarbons (linear or cyclic, saturated or unsaturated, aliphatic or aromatic);
   (ii) Oxygen-containing hydrocarbons such as alcohols, aldehydes, ketones, carboxylic acids, esters, acetates, ethers, peroxides, epoxy resins;
   (iii) Sulphurous hydrocarbons;
   (iv) Nitrogenous hydrocarbons such as amines, amides, nitrous compounds, nitro compounds or nitrate compounds, nitriles, cyanates, isocyanates;
   (v) Phosphorus-containing hydrocarbons;
   (vi) Halogenic hydrocarbons;
   (vii) Organometallic compounds;
   (viii) Basic plastic materials (polymers, synthetic fibres and cellulose-based fibres);
   (ix) Synthetic rubbers;
   (x) Dyes and pigments;
   (xi) Surface-active agents and surfactants;

(b) Chemical installations for the production of basic inorganic chemicals, such as:
   (i) Gases, such as ammonia, chlorine or hydrogen chloride, fluorine or hydrogen fluoride, carbon oxides, sulphur compounds, nitrogen oxides, hydrogen, sulphur dioxide, carbonyl chloride;
   (ii) Acids, such as chromic acid, hydrofluoric acid, phosphoric acid, nitric acid, hydrochloric acid, sulphuric acid, oleum, sulphurous acids;
   (iii) Bases, such as ammonium hydroxide, potassium hydroxide, sodium hydroxide;
   (iv) Salts, such as ammonium chloride, potassium chlorate, potassium carbonate, sodium carbonate, perborate, silver nitrate;
   (v) Non-metals, metal oxides or other inorganic compounds such as calcium carbide, silicon, silicon carbide;

(c) Chemical installations for the production of phosphorous-, nitrogen- or potassium-based fertilisers (simple or compound fertilizers);
(d) Chemical installations for the production of basic plant health products and of biocides;
(e) Installations using a chemical or biological process for the production of basic pharmaceutical products;
(f) Chemical installations for the production of explosives;
(g) Chemical installations in which chemical or biological processing is used for the production of protein feed additives, ferments and other protein substances.

5. Waste management:

— Installations for the incineration, recovery, chemical treatment or landfill of hazardous waste;
— Installations for the incineration of municipal waste with a capacity exceeding 3 tons per hour;
— Installations for the disposal of non-hazardous waste with a capacity exceeding 50 tons per day;
— Landfills receiving more than 10 tons per day or with a total capacity exceeding 25,000 tons, excluding landfills of inert waste.

6. Waste-water treatment plants with a capacity exceeding 150,000 population equivalent.

7. Industrial plants for the:

(a) Production of pulp from timber or similar fibrous materials;
(b) Production of paper and board with a production capacity exceeding 20 tons per day.

8.(a) Construction of lines for long-distance railway traffic and of airports (see note 2 below) with a basic runway length of 2,100 m or more;
(b) Construction of motorways and express roads; (see note 3 below)
(c) Construction of a new road of four or more lanes, or realignment and/or widening of an existing road of two lanes or less so as to provide four or more lanes, where such new road, or realigned and/or widened section of road, would be 10 km or more in a continuous length.

9.(a) Inland waterways and ports for inland-waterway traffic which permit the passage of vessels of over 1,350 tons;
(b) Trading ports, piers for loading and unloading connected to land and outside ports (excluding ferry piers) which can take vessels of over 1,350 tons.

10. Groundwater abstraction or artificial groundwater recharge schemes where the annual volume of water abstracted or recharged is equivalent to or exceeds 10 million cubic metres.

11.(a) Works for the transfer of water resources between river basins where this transfer aims at preventing possible shortages of water and where the amount of water transferred exceeds 100 million cubic metres/year;
(b) In all other cases, works for the transfer of water resources between river basins where the multiannual average flow of the basin of abstraction exceeds 2,000 million cubic metres/year and where the amount of water transferred exceeds 5 per cent of this flow.

In both cases transfers of piped drinking water are excluded.

12. Extraction of petroleum and natural gas for commercial purposes where the amount extracted exceeds 500 tons/day in the case of petroleum and 500,000 cubic metres/day in the case of gas.

13. Dams and other installations designed for the holding back or permanent storage of water, where a new or additional amount of water held back or stored exceeds 10 million cubic metres.

14. Pipelines for the transport of gas, oil or chemicals with a diameter of more than 800 mm and a length of more than 40 km.

15. Installations for the intensive rearing of poultry or pigs with more than:
(a) 40,000 places for poultry;
(b) 2,000 places for production pigs (over 30 kg); or
(c) 750 places for sows.

16. Quarries and opencast mining where the surface of the site exceeds 25 hectares, or peat extraction, where the surface of the site exceeds 150 hectares.

17. Construction of overhead electrical power lines with a voltage of 220 kV or more and a length of more than 15 km.

18. Installations for the storage of petroleum, petrochemical, or chemical products with a capacity of 200,000 tons or more.

19. Other activities:

— Plants for the pretreatment (operations such as washing, bleaching, mercerisation) or dyeing of fibres or textiles where the treatment capacity exceeds 10 tons per day;
— Plants for the tanning of hides and skins where the treatment capacity exceeds 12 tons of finished products per day;

(a) Slaughterhouses with a carcass production capacity greater than 50 tons per day;
(b) Treatment and processing intended for the production of food products from:

(i) Animal raw materials (other than milk) with a finished product production capacity greater than 75 tons per day;
(ii) Vegetable raw materials with a finished product production capacity greater than 300 tons per day (average value on a quarterly basis);

(c) Treatment and processing of milk, the quantity of milk received being greater than 200 tons per day (average value on an annual basis);

— Installations for the disposal or recycling of animal carcasses and animal waste with a treatment capacity exceeding 10 tons per day;
— Installations for the surface treatment of substances, objects or products using organic solvents, in particular for dressing, printing, coating, degreasing, waterproofing, sizing, painting, cleaning or impregnating, with a consumption capacity of more than 150 kg per hour or more than 200 tons per year;
— Installations for the production of carbon (hard-burnt coal) or electrographite by means of incineration or graphitisation.

20. Any activity not covered by paragraphs 1–19 above where public participation is provided for under an environmental impact assessment procedure in accordance with national legislation.

21. The provision of Article 6, paragraph 1(a) of this Convention, does not apply to any of the above projects undertaken exclusively or mainly for research, development and testing of new methods or products for less than two years unless they would be likely to cause a significant adverse effect on environment or health.

22. Any change to or extension of activities, where such a change or extension in itself meets the criteria/thresholds set out in this annex, shall be subject to Article 6, paragraph 1(a) of this Convention. Any other change or extension of activities shall be subject to Article 6, paragraph 1(b) of this Convention.

Notes

1. Nuclear power stations and other nuclear reactors cease to be such an installation when all nuclear fuel and other radioactively contaminated elements have been removed permanently from the installation site.

2. For the purposes of this Convention, "airport" means an airport which complies with the definition in the 1944 Chicago Convention setting up the International Civil Aviation Organisation (Annex 14).

3. For the purposes of this Convention, "express road" means a road which complies with the definition in the European Agreement on Main International Traffic Arteries of November 15, 1975.

ANNEX II

Arbitration

1. In the event of a dispute being submitted for arbitration pursuant to Article 16, paragraph 2, of this Convention, a party or parties shall notify the secretariat of the subject matter of arbitration and indicate, in particular, the articles of this Convention whose interpretation or application is at issue. The secretariat shall forward the information received to all Parties to this Convention.

2. The arbitral tribunal shall consist of three members. Both the claimant party or parties and the other party or parties to the dispute shall appoint an arbitrator, and the two arbitrators so appointed shall designate by common agreement the third arbitrator, who shall be the president of the arbitral tribunal. The latter shall not be a national of one of the parties to the dispute, nor have his or her usual place of residence in the territory of one of these parties, nor be employed by any of them, nor have dealt with the case in any other capacity.

3. If the president of the arbitral tribunal has not been designated within two months of the appointment of the second arbitrator, the Executive Secretary of the Economic Commission for Europe shall, at the request of either party to the dispute, designate the president within a further two-month period.

4. If one of the parties to the dispute does not appoint an arbitrator within two months of the receipt of the request, the other party may so inform the Executive Secretary of the Economic Commission for Europe, who shall designate the president of the arbitral tribunal within a further two-month period. Upon designation, the president of the arbitral tribunal shall request the party which has not appointed an arbitrator to do so within two months. If it fails to do so within that period, the president shall so inform the Executive Secretary of the Economic Commission for Europe, who shall make this appointment within a further two-month period.

5. The arbitral tribunal shall render its decision in accordance with international law and the provisions of this Convention.

6. Any arbitral tribunal constituted under the provisions set out in this annex shall draw up its own rules of procedure.

7. The decisions of the arbitral tribunal, both on procedure and on substance, shall be taken by majority vote of its members.

8. The tribunal may take all appropriate measures to establish the facts.

9. The parties to the dispute shall facilitate the work of the arbitral tribunal and, in particular, using all means at their disposal, shall:

(a) Provide it with all relevant documents, facilities and information;
(b) Enable it, where necessary, to call witnesses or experts and receive their evidence.

10. The parties and the arbitrators shall protect the confidentiality of any information that they receive in confidence during the proceedings of the arbitral tribunal.

11. The arbitral tribunal may, at the request of one of the parties, recommend interim measures of protection.

12. If one of the parties to the dispute does not appear before the arbitral tribunal or fails to defend its case, the other party may request the tribunal to continue the proceedings and to render its final decision. Absence of a party or failure of a party to defend its case shall not constitute a bar to the proceedings.

13. The arbitral tribunal may hear and determine counter-claims arising directly out of the subject matter of the dispute.

14. Unless the arbitral tribunal determines otherwise because of the particular circumstances of the case, the expenses of the tribunal, including the remuneration of its members, shall be borne by the parties to the dispute in equal shares. The tribunal shall keep a record of all its expenses, and shall furnish a final statement thereof to the parties.

15. Any Party to this Convention which has an interest of a legal nature in the subject matter of the dispute, and which may be affected by a decision in the case, may intervene in the proceedings with the consent of the tribunal.

16. The arbitral tribunal shall render its award within five months of the date on which it is established, unless it finds it necessary to extend the time limit for a period which should not exceed five months.

17. The award of the arbitral tribunal shall be accompanied by a statement of reasons. It shall be final and binding upon all parties to the dispute. The award will be transmitted by the arbitral tribunal to the parties to the dispute and to the secretariat. The secretariat will forward the information received to all Parties to this Convention.

18. Any dispute which may arise between the parties concerning the interpretation or execution of the award may be submitted by either party to the arbitral tribunal which made the award or, if the latter cannot be seized thereof, to another tribunal constituted for this purpose in the same manner as the first.

Directive 2003/4/EC of the European Parliament and of the Council on Public Access to Environmental Information and Repealing Council Directive 90/313/EEC

[JANUARY 28, 2003]

THE EUROPEAN PARLIAMENT AND THE COUNCIL OF THE EUROPEAN UNION, **App 6–02**

Having regard to the Treaty establishing the European Community, and in particular Article 175(1) thereof,

Having regard to the proposal from the Commission,

Having regard to the opinion of the European Economic and Social Committee,

Having regard to the opinion of the Committee of the Regions,

Acting in accordance with the procedure laid down in Article 251 of the Treaty in the light of the joint text approved by the Conciliation Committee on November 8, 2002,

Whereas:

(1) Increased public access to environmental information and the dissemination of such information contribute to a greater awareness of environmental matters, a free exchange of views, more effective participation by the public in environmental decision-making and, eventually, to a better environment.

(2) Council Directive 90/313/EEC of June 7, 1990 on the freedom of access to information on the environment initiated a process of change in the manner in which public authorities approach the issue of openness and transparency, establishing measures for the exercise of the right of public access to environmental information which should be developed and continued. This Directive expands the existing access granted under Directive 90/313/EEC.

(3) Article 8 of that Directive requires Member States to report to the Commission on the experience gained, in the light of which the Commission is required to make a report to the European Parliament and to the Council together with any proposal for revision of the Directive which it may consider appropriate.

(4) The report produced under Article 8 of that Directive identifies concrete problems encountered in the practical application of the Directive.

(5) On June 25, 1998 the European Community signed the UN/ECE Convention on Access to Information, Public Participation in Decision-Making and Access to Justice in Environmental Matters ("the Aarhus Convention"). Provisions of Community law must be consistent with that Convention with a view to its conclusion by the European Community.

(6) It is appropriate in the interest of increased transparency to replace Directive 90/313/EEC rather than to amend it, so as to provide interested parties with a single, clear and coherent legislative text.

(7) Disparities between the laws in force in the Member States concerning access to environmental information held by public authorities can create inequality within the Community as regards access to such information or as regards conditions of competition.

(8) It is necessary to ensure that any natural and legal person has a right of access to environmental information held by or for public authorities without his having to state an interest.

(9) It is also necessary that public authorities make available and disseminate environmental information to the general public to the widest extent possible, in particular by using information and communication technologies. The future development of these technologies should be taken into account in the reporting on, and reviewing of, this Directive.

(10) The definition of environmental information should be clarified so as to encompass information in any form on the state of the environment, on factors, measures or activities affecting or likely to affect the environment or designed to protect it, on cost-benefit and economic analyses used within the framework of such measures or activities and also information on the state of human health and safety, including the contamination of the food chain, conditions of human life, cultural sites and built structures in as much as they are, or may be, affected by any of those matters.

(11) To take account of the principle in Article 6 of the Treaty, that environmental protection requirements should be integrated into the definition and implementation of Community policies and activities, the definition of public authorities should be expanded so as to encompass government or other public administration at national, regional or local level whether or not they have specific responsibilities for the environment. The definition should likewise be expanded to include other persons or bodies performing public administrative functions in relation to the environment under national law, as well as other persons or bodies acting under their control and having public responsibilities or functions in relation to the environment.

(12) Environmental information which is physically held by other bodies on behalf of public authorities should also fall within the scope of this Directive.

(13) Environmental information should be made available to applicants as soon as possible and within a reasonable time and having regard to any timescale specified by the applicant.

(14) Public authorities should make environmental information available in the form or format requested by an applicant unless it is already publicly available in another form or format or it is reasonable to make it available in another form or format. In addition, public authorities should be required to make all reasonable efforts to maintain the environmental information held by or for them in forms or formats that are readily reproducible and accessible by electronic means.

(15) Member States should determine the practical arrangements under which such information is effectively made available. These arrangements shall guarantee that the information is effectively and easily accessible and progressively becomes available to the public through public telecommunications networks, including publicly accessible lists of public authorities and registers or lists of environmental information held by or for public authorities.

(16) The right to information means that the disclosure of information should be the general rule and that public authorities should be permitted to refuse a request for environmental information in specific and clearly defined cases. Grounds for refusal should be interpreted in a restrictive way, whereby the public interest served by disclosure should be weighed against the interest served by the refusal. The reasons for a refusal should be provided to the applicant within the time limit laid down in this Directive.

(17) Public authorities should make environmental information available in part where it is possible to separate out any information falling within the scope of the exceptions from the rest of the information requested.

(18) Public authorities should be able to make a charge for supplying environmental information but such a charge should be reasonable. This implies that, as a general rule, charges may not exceed actual costs of producing the material in question. Instances where advance payment will be required should be limited. In particular cases, where public authorities make available environmental information on a commercial basis, and where this is necessary in order to guarantee the continuation of collecting and publishing such information, a market-based charge is considered to be reasonable; an advance payment may be required. A schedule of charges should be published and made available to applicants together with information on the circumstances in which a charge may be levied or waived.

(19) Applicants should be able to seek an administrative or judicial review of the acts or omissions of a public authority in relation to a request.

(20) Public authorities should seek to guarantee that when environmental information is compiled by them or on their behalf, the information is comprehensible, accurate and comparable. As this is an important factor in assessing the quality of the information supplied the method used in compiling the information should also be disclosed upon request.

(21) In order to increase public awareness in environmental matters and to improve environmental protection, public authorities should, as appropriate, make available and disseminate information on the environment which is relevant to their functions, in particular by means of computer telecommunication and/or electronic technology, where available.

(22) This Directive should be evaluated every four years, after its entry into force, in the light of experience and after submission of the relevant reports by the Member States, and be subject to revision on that basis. The Commission should submit an evaluation report to the European Parliament and the Council.

(23) Since the objectives of the proposed Directive cannot be sufficiently achieved by the Member States and can therefore be better achieved at Community level, the Community may adopt measures, in accordance with the principle of subsidiarity as set out in Article 5 of the Treaty. In accordance with the principle of proportionality, as set out in that Article, this Directive does not go beyond what is necessary in order to achieve those objectives.

(24) The provisions of this Directive shall not affect the right of a Member State to maintain or introduce measures providing for broader access to information than required by this Directive,

HAVE ADOPTED THIS DIRECTIVE:

Objectives

1.—The objectives of this Directive are:

(a) to guarantee the right of access to environmental information held by or for public authorities and to set out the basic terms and conditions of, and practical arrangements for, its exercise; and

(b) to ensure that, as a matter of course, environmental information is progressively made available and disseminated to the public in order to achieve the widest possible systematic availability and dissemination to the public of environmental information. To this end the use, in particular, of computer telecommunication and/or electronic technology, where available, shall be promoted.

Definitions

2.—For the purposes of this Directive:

1. "Environmental information" shall mean any information in written, visual, aural, electronic or any other material form on:

(a) the state of the elements of the environment, such as air and atmosphere, water, soil, land, landscape and natural sites including wetlands, coastal and marine areas, biological diversity and its components, including genetically modified organisms, and the interaction among these elements;

(b) factors, such as substances, energy, noise, radiation or waste, including radioactive waste, emissions, discharges and other releases into the environment, affecting or likely to affect the elements of the environment referred to in (a);

(c) measures (including administrative measures), such as policies, legislation, plans, programmes, environmental agreements, and activities affecting or likely to affect the elements and factors referred to in (a) and (b) as well as measures or activities designed to protect those elements;

(d) reports on the implementation of environmental legislation;
(e) cost-benefit and other economic analyses and assumptions used within the framework of the measures and activities referred to in (c); and
(f) the state of human health and safety, including the contamination of the food chain, where relevant, conditions of human life, cultural sites and built structures inasmuch as they are or may be affected by the state of the elements of the environment referred to in (a) or, through those elements, by any of the matters referred to in (b) and (c).

2. "Public authority" shall mean:

(a) government or other public administration, including public advisory bodies, at national, regional or local level;
(b) any natural or legal person performing public administrative functions under national law, including specific duties, activities or services in relation to the environment; and
(c) any natural or legal person having public responsibilities or functions, or providing public services, relating to the environment under the control of a body or person falling within (a) or (b).

Member States may provide that this definition shall not include bodies or institutions when acting in a judicial or legislative capacity. If their constitutional provisions at the date of adoption of this Directive make no provision for a review procedure within the meaning of Article 6, Member States may exclude those bodies or institutions from that definition.

3. "Information held by a public authority" shall mean environmental information in its possession which has been produced or received by that authority.

4. "Information held for a public authority" shall mean environmental information which is physically held by a natural or legal person on behalf of a public authority.

5. "Applicant" shall mean any natural or legal person requesting environmental information.

6. "Public" shall mean one or more natural or legal persons, and, in accordance with national legislation or practice, their associations, organisations or groups.

Access to environmental information upon request

3.—1. Member States shall ensure that public authorities are required, in accordance with the provisions of this Directive, to make available environmental information held by or for them to any applicant at his request and without his having to state an interest.

2. Subject to Article 4 and having regard to any timescale specified by the applicant, environmental information shall be made available to an applicant:

(a) as soon as possible or, at the latest, within one month after the receipt by the public authority referred to in paragraph 1 of the applicant's request; or
(b) within two months after the receipt of the request by the public authority if the volume and the complexity of the information is such that the one-month period referred to in (a) cannot be complied with. In such cases, the applicant shall be informed as soon as possible, and in any case before the end of that one-month period, of any such extension and of the reasons for it.

3. If a request is formulated in too general a manner, the public authority shall as soon as possible, and at the latest within the timeframe laid down in paragraph 2(a), ask the applicant to specify the request and shall assist the applicant in doing so, *e.g.* by providing information on the use of the public registers referred to in paragraph 5(c). The public authorities may, where they deem it appropriate, refuse the request under Article 4(1)(c).

4. Where an applicant requests a public authority to make environmental information available in a specific form or format (including in the form of copies), the public authority shall make it so available unless:

(a) it is already publicly available in another form or format, in particular under Article 7, which is easily accessible by applicants; or
(b) it is reasonable for the public authority to make it available in another form or format, in which case reasons shall be given for making it available in that form or format.

For the purposes of this paragraph, public authorities shall make all reasonable efforts to maintain environmental information held by or for them in forms or formats that are readily reproducible and accessible by computer telecommunications or by other electronic means.

The reasons for a refusal to make information available, in full or in part, in the form or format requested shall be provided to the applicant within the time limit referred to in paragraph 2(a).

5. For the purposes of this Article, Member States shall ensure that:

(a) officials are required to support the public in seeking access to information;
(b) lists of public authorities are publicly accessible; and
(c) the practical arrangements are defined for ensuring that the right of access to environmental information can be effectively exercised, such as:

— the designation of information officers;
— the establishment and maintenance of facilities for the examination of the information required,
— registers or lists of the environmental information held by public authorities or information points, with clear indications of where such information can be found.

Member States shall ensure that public authorities inform the public adequately of the rights they enjoy as a result of this Directive and to an appropriate extent provide information, guidance and advice to this end.

Exceptions

4.—1. Member States may provide for a request for environmental information to be refused if:

(a) the information requested is not held by or for the public authority to which the request is addressed. In such a case, where that public authority is aware that the information is held by or for another public authority, it shall, as soon as possible, transfer the request to that other authority and inform the applicant accordingly or inform the applicant of the public authority to which it believes it is possible to apply for the information requested;
(b) the request is manifestly unreasonable;
(c) the request is formulated in too general a manner, taking into account Article 3(3);
(d) the request concerns material in the course of completion or unfinished documents or data;
(e) the request concerns internal communications, taking into account the public interest served by disclosure.

Where a request is refused on the basis that it concerns material in the course of com pletion, the public authority shall state the name of the authority preparing the material and the estimated time needed for completion.

2. Member States may provide for a request for environmental information to be refused if disclosure of the information would adversely affect:

(a) the confidentiality of the proceedings of public authorities, where such confidentiality is provided for by law;
(b) international relations, public security or national defence;
(c) the course of justice, the ability of any person to receive a fair trial or the ability of a public authority to conduct an enquiry of a criminal or disciplinary nature;
(d) the confidentiality of commercial or industrial information where such confidentiality is provided for by national or Community law to protect a legitimate economic interest, including the public interest in maintaining statistical confidentiality and tax secrecy;
(e) intellectual property rights;
(f) the confidentiality of personal data and/or files relating to a natural person where that person has not consented to the disclosure of the information to the public, where such confidentiality is provided for by national or Community law;
(g) the interests or protection of any person who supplied the information requested on a voluntary basis without being under, or capable of being put under, a legal obligation to do so, unless that person has consented to the release of the information concerned;
(h) the protection of the environment to which such information relates, such as the location of rare species.

The grounds for refusal mentioned in paragraphs 1 and 2 shall be interpreted in a restrictive way, taking into account for the particular case the public interest served by disclosure. In every particular case, the public interest served by disclosure shall be weighed against the interest served by the refusal. Member States may not, by virtue of paragraph 2(a), (d), (f), (g) and (h), provide for a request to be refused where the request relates to information on emissions into the environment.

Within this framework, and for the purposes of the application of subparagraph (f), Member States shall ensure that the requirements of Directive 95/46/EC of the European Parliament and of the Council of October 24, 1995 on the protection of individuals with regard to the processing of personal data and on the free movement of such data are complied with(6).

3. Where a Member State provides for exceptions, it may draw up a publicly accessible list of criteria on the basis of which the authority concerned may decide how to handle requests.

4. Environmental information held by or for public authorities which has been requested by an applicant shall be made available in part where it is possible to separate out any information falling within the scope of paragraphs 1(d) and (e) or 2 from the rest of the information requested.

5. A refusal to make available all or part of the information requested shall be notified to the applicant in writing or electronically, if the request was in writing or if the applicant so requests, within the time limits referred to in Article 3(2)(a) or, as the case may be, (b). The notification shall state the reasons for the refusal and include information on the review procedure provided for in accordance with Article 6.

Charges

5.—1. Access to any public registers or lists established and maintained as mentioned in Article 3(5) and examination in situ of the information requested shall be free of charge.

2. Public authorities may make a charge for supplying any environmental information but such charge shall not exceed a reasonable amount.

3. Where charges are made, public authorities shall publish and make available to

applicants a schedule of such charges as well as information on the circumstances in which a charge may be levied or waived.

Access to justice

6.—1. Member States shall ensure that any applicant who considers that his request for information has been ignored, wrongfully refused (whether in full or in part), inadequately answered or otherwise not dealt with in accordance with the provisions of Articles 3, 4 or 5, has access to a procedure in which the acts or omissions of the public authority concerned can be reconsidered by that or another public authority or reviewed administratively by an independent and impartial body established by law. Any such procedure shall be expeditious and either free of charge or inexpensive.

2. In addition to the review procedure referred to in paragraph 1, Member States shall ensure that an applicant has access to a review procedure before a court of law or another independent and impartial body established by law, in which the acts or omissions of the public authority concerned can be reviewed and whose decisions may become final. Member States may furthermore provide that third parties incriminated by the disclosure of information may also have access to legal recourse.

3. Final decisions under paragraph 2 shall be binding on the public authority holding the information. Reasons shall be stated in writing, at least where access to information is refused under this Article.

Dissemination of environmental information

7.—1. Member States shall take the necessary measures to ensure that public authorities organise the environmental information which is relevant to their functions and which is held by or for them, with a view to its active and systematic dissemination to the public, in particular by means of computer telecommunication and/or electronic technology, where available.

The information made available by means of computer telecommunication and/or electronic technology need not include information collected before the entry into force of this Directive unless it is already available in electronic form.

Member States shall ensure that environmental information progressively becomes available in electronic databases which are easily accessible to the public through public telecommunication networks.

2. The information to be made available and disseminated shall be updated as appropriate and shall include at least:

(a) texts of international treaties, conventions or agreements, and of Community, national, regional or local legislation, on the environment or relating to it;
(b) policies, plans and programmes relating to the environment;
(c) progress reports on the implementation of the items referred to in (a) and (b) when prepared or held in electronic form by public authorities;
(d) the reports on the state of the environment referred to in paragraph 3;
(e) data or summaries of data derived from the monitoring of activities affecting, or likely to affect, the environment;
(f) authorisations with a significant impact on the environment and environmental agreements or a reference to the place where such information can be requested or found in the framework of Article 3;
(g) environmental impact studies and risk assessments concerning the environmental elements referred to in Article 2(1)(a) or a reference to the place where the information can be requested or found in the framework of Article 3.

3. Without prejudice to any specific reporting obligations laid down by Community legislation, Member States shall take the necessary measures to ensure that national,

and, where appropriate, regional or local reports on the state of the environment are published at regular intervals not exceeding four years; such reports shall include information on the quality of, and pressures on, the environment.

4. Without prejudice to any specific obligation laid down by Community legislation, Member States shall take the necessary measures to ensure that, in the event of an imminent threat to human health or the environment, whether caused by human activities or due to natural causes, all information held by or for public authorities which could enable the public likely to be affected to take measures to prevent or mitigate harm arising from the threat is disseminated, immediately and without delay.

5. The exceptions in Article 4(1) and (2) may apply in relation to the duties imposed by this Article.

6. Member States may satisfy the requirements of this Article by creating links to Internet sites where the information can be found.

Quality of environmental information

8.—1. Member States shall, so far as is within their power, ensure that any information that is compiled by them or on their behalf is up to date, accurate and comparable.

2. Upon request, public authorities shall reply to requests for information pursuant to Article 2(1)b, reporting to the applicant on the place where information, if available, can be found on the measurement procedures, including methods of analysis, sampling, and pre-treatment of samples, used in compiling the information, or referring to a standardised procedure used.

Review procedure

9.—1. Not later than February 14, 2009, Member States shall report on the experience gained in the application of this Directive.

They shall communicate the report to the Commission not later than August 14, 2009.

No later than February 14, 2004, the Commission shall forward to the Member States a guidance document setting out clearly the manner in which it wishes the Member States to report.

2. In the light of experience and taking into account developments in computer telecommunication and/or electronic technology, the Commission shall make a report to the European Parliament and to the Council together with any proposal for revision, which it may consider appropriate.

Implementation

10.—Member States shall bring into force the laws, regulations and administrative provisions necessary to comply with this Directive by February 14, 2005. They shall forthwith inform the Commission thereof.

When Member States adopt these measures, they shall contain a reference to this Directive or shall be accompanied by such reference on the occasion of their official publication. The methods of making such reference shall be laid down by Member States.

Repeal

11.—Directive 90/313/EEC is hereby repealed with effect from February 14, 2005.

References to the repealed Directive shall be construed as referring to this Directive and shall be read in accordance with the correlation table in the Annex.

Entry into force

12.—This Directive shall enter into force on the day of its publication in the *Official Journal of the European Union.*

Addressees

13.—This Directive is addressed to the Member States.

Done at Brussels, January 28, 2003.

For the European Parliament
The President
P. Cox

For the Council
The President
G. Papandreou

ANNEX

CORRELATON TABLE

Directive 90/313/EEC	This Directive
Article 1	Article 1(a) Article 1(b)
Article 2(a) Article 2(b) — — —	Article 2(1) Article 2(2) Article 2(3) Article 2(4) Article 2(5) Article 2(6)
Article 3(1) Article 3(2) Article 3(3) Article 3(4) — — —	Article 3(1) and Article 3(5) Article 4(2) and Article 4(4) Article 4(1)(b), (c), (d) and (e) Article 3(2) and Article 4(5) Article 4(1)(a) Article 3(3) Article 3(4)
Article 4 —	Article 6(1) and Article 6(2) Article 6(3)
Article 5	Article 5(1) Article 5(2) Article 5(3)
Article 6	Article 2(2)(c), Article 3(1)
Article 7 — — —	Article 7(1), (2), and (3) Article 7(4) Article 7(5) Article 7(6)
—	Article 8
Article 8	Article 9
Article 9	Article 10
Article 10	Article 13
—	Article 11
—	Article 12

Environment Act 1995

(1995, c.25)

SCHEDULE 11

AIR QUALITY: SUPPLEMENTAL PROVISIONS

Consultation requirements

App 6–03 **1.**—(1) A local authority in carrying out its functions in relation to—

(a) any air quality review,
(b) any assessment under section 82 or 84 of this Act, or
(c) the preparation of an action plan or any revision of an action plan,

shall consult such other persons as fall within sub-paragraph (2) below.

(2) Those persons are—

(a) the Secretary of State;
(b) the appropriate new Agency;
(c) in England and Wales, the highway authority for any highway in the area to which the review or, as the case may be, the action plan or revision relates;
(d) every local authority whose area is contiguous to the authority's area;
(e) any county council in England whose area consists of or includes the whole or any part of the authority's area;
(f) any National Park authority for a National Park whose area consists of or includes the whole or any part of the authority's area;
(g) such public authorities exercising functions in, or in the vicinity of, the authority's area as the authority may consider appropriate;
(h) such bodies appearing to the authority to be representative of persons with business interests in the area to which the review or action plan in question relates as the authority may consider appropriate;
(j) such other bodies or persons as the authority considers appropriate.

(2A) A local authority specified in sub-paragraph (2B) below shall in carrying out the functions falling within sub-paragraph (1)(a) to (c) above also consult the Mayor of London.

(2B) The local authorities mentioned in sub-paragraph (2A) above are—

(a) any local authority in Greater London,
(b) any local authority whose area is contiguous to the area of Greater London.

(3) Except in its application to Scotland, In this paragraph "National Park authority", means a National Park authority established under section 63 of this Act which has become the local planning authority for the National Park in question.

[(5) In the application of this paragraph to Scotland "National Park authority" means a National Park authority established by virtue of section 7(1)(b) of the National Parks (Scotland) Act 2000 (asp 10).][1]

---

1 Words added by National Parks (Scotland) Act 2000 (ASP10), Sch.5, para.17(b).

Exchange of information with County Councils in England

2.—(1) This paragraph applies in any case where a district in England for which there is a district council is comprised in an area for which there is a county council; and in this paragraph—

(a) any reference to the county council is a reference to the council of that area; and
(b) any reference to a district council is a reference to the council of a district comprised in that area.

(2) It shall be the duty of the county council to provide a district council with all such information as is reasonably requested by the district council for purposes connected with the carrying out of its functions under or by virtue of this Part.

(3) It shall be the duty of a district council to provide the county council with all such information as is reasonably requested by the county council for purposes connected with the carrying out of any of its functions relating to the assessment or management of the quality of air.

(4) Information provided to a district council or county council under sub-paragraph (2) or (3) above shall be provided in such form and in such manner and at such times as the district council or, as the case may be, the county council may reasonably require.

(5) A council which provides information under sub-paragraph (2) or (3) above shall be entitled to recover the reasonable cost of doing so from the council which requested the information.

(6) The information which a council may be required to provide under this paragraph shall include information which, although it is not in the possession of the council or would not otherwise come into the possession of the council, is information which it is reasonable to require the council to obtain.

Joint exercise of Local Authority functions

3.—(1) The appropriate authority may give directions to any two or more local authorities requiring them to exercise the powers conferred by—

(a) section 101(5) of the Local Government Act 1972 (power of two or more local authorities to discharge functions jointly), or
(b) section 56(5) of the Local Government (Scotland) Act 1973 (which makes similar provision for Scotland),

in relation to functions under or by virtue of this Part in accordance with the directions.

(2) The appropriate authority may give directions to a local authority requiring it—

(a) not to exercise those powers, or
(b) not to exercise those powers in a manner specified in the directions,

in relation to functions under or by virtue of this Part.

(3) Where two or more local authorities have exercised those powers in relation to functions under or by virtue of this Part, the appropriate authority may give them directions requiring them to revoke, or modify in accordance with the directions, the arrangements which they have made.

(4) In this paragraph, "the appropriate authority" means —

(a) in relation to England and Wales, the Secretary of State; and
(b) in relation to Scotland, SEPA acting with the approval of the Secretary of State.

Public access to information about air quality

4.—(1) It shall be the duty of every local authority—

(a) to secure that there is available at all reasonable times for inspection by the public free of charge a copy of each of the documents specified in sub-paragraph (2) below; and

(b) to afford to members of the public facilities for obtaining copies of those documents on payment of a reasonable charge.

(2) The documents mentioned in sub-paragraph (1)(a) above are—

(a) a report of the results of any air quality review which the authority has caused to be conducted;

(b) a report of the results of any assessment which the authority has caused to be made under section 82 or 84 of this Act;

(c) any order made by the authority under section 83 of this Act;

(d) any action plan prepared by the authority;

(e) any proposals or statements submitted to the authority pursuant to subsection (3) or (4) of section 86 of this Act;

(f) any directions given to the authority under this Part;

(g) in a case where section 86 of this Act applies, any directions given to the county council under this Part.

Fixed penalty offences

5.—(1) Without prejudice to the generality of paragraph (o) of subsection (2) of section 87 of this Act, regulations may, in particular, make provision—

(a) for the qualifications, appointment or authorisation of persons who are to issue fixed penalty notices;

(b) for the offences in connection with which, the cases or circumstances in which, the time or period at or within which, or the manner in which fixed penalty notices may be issued;

(c) prohibiting the institution, before the expiration of the period for paying the fixed penalty, of proceedings against a person for an offence in connection with which a fixed penalty notice has been issued;

(d) prohibiting the conviction of a person for an offence in connection with which a fixed penalty notice has been issued if the fixed penalty is paid before the expiration of the period for paying it;

(e) entitling, in prescribed cases, a person to whom a fixed penalty notice is issued to give, within a prescribed period, notice requesting a hearing in respect of the offence to which the fixed penalty notice relates;

(f) for the amount of the fixed penalty to be increased by a prescribed amount in any case where the person liable to pay the fixed penalty fails to pay it before the expiration of the period for paying it, without having given notice requesting a hearing in respect of the offence to which the fixed penalty notice relates;

(g) for or in connection with the recovery of an unpaid fixed penalty as a fine or as a civil debt or as if it were a sum payable under a county court order;

(h) for or in connection with execution or other enforcement in respect of an unpaid fixed penalty by prescribed persons;

(j) for a fixed penalty notice, and any prescribed proceedings or other prescribed steps taken by reference to the notice, to be rendered void in prescribed cases where a person makes a prescribed statutory declaration, and for the consequences of any notice, proceedings or other steps being so rendered void (including extension of any time limit for instituting criminal proceedings);

(k) for or in connection with the extension, in prescribed cases or circumstances, by a prescribed person of the period for paying a fixed penalty;

(l) for or in connection with the withdrawal, in prescribed circumstances, of a fixed penalty notice, including—

(i) repayment of any amount paid by way of fixed penalty in pursuance of a fixed penalty notice which is withdrawn; and

(ii) prohibition of the institution or continuation of proceedings for the offence in connection with which the withdrawn notice was issued;

(m) for or in connection with the disposition of sums received by way of fixed penalty;

(n) for a certificate purporting to be signed by or on behalf of a prescribed person and stating either—

(i) that payment of a fixed penalty was, or (as the case may be) was not, received on or before a date specified in the certificate, or

(ii) that an envelope containing an amount sent by post in payment of a fixed penalty was marked as posted on a date specified in the certificate,

to be received as evidence of the matters so stated and to be treated, without further proof, as being so signed unless the contrary is shown;

(o) requiring a fixed penalty notice to give such reasonable particulars of the circumstances alleged to constitute the fixed penalty offence to which the notice relates as are necessary for giving reasonable information of the offence and to state—

(i) the monetary amount of the fixed penalty which may be paid;

(ii) the person to whom, and the address at which, the fixed penalty may be paid and any correspondence relating to the fixed penalty notice may be sent;

(iii) the method or methods by which payment of the fixed penalty may be made;

(iv) the period for paying the fixed penalty;

(v) the consequences of the fixed penalty not being paid before the expiration of that period;

(p) similar to any provision made by section 79 of the Road Traffic Offenders Act 1988 (statements by constables in fixed penalty cases);

(q) for presuming, in any proceedings, that any document of a prescribed description purporting to have been signed by a person to whom a fixed penalty notice has been issued has been signed by that person;

(r) requiring or authorising a fixed penalty notice to contain prescribed information relating to, or for the purpose of facilitating, the administration of the fixed penalty system;

(s) with respect to the giving of fixed penalty notices, including, in particular, provision with respect to—

(i) the methods by which,

(ii) the officers, servants or agents by, to or on whom, and

(iii) the places at which,

fixed penalty notices may be given by, or served on behalf of, a prescribed person;

(t) prescribing the method or methods by which fixed penalties may be paid;

(u) for or with respect to the issue of prescribed documents to persons to whom fixed penalty notices are or have been given;

(w) for a fixed penalty notice to be treated for prescribed purposes as if it were an information or summons or any other document of a prescribed description.

(2) The provision that may be made by regulations prescribing fixed penalty offences includes provision for an offence to be a fixed penalty offence—

(a) only if it is committed in such circumstances or manner as may be prescribed; or
(b) except if it is committed in such circumstances or manner as may be prescribed.

(3) Regulations may provide for any offence which is a fixed penalty offence to cease to be such an offence.

(4) An offence which, in consequence of regulations made by virtue of sub- paragraph (3) above, has ceased to be a fixed penalty offence shall be eligible to be prescribed as such an offence again.

(5) Regulations may make provision for such exceptions, limitations and conditions as the Secretary of State considers necessary or expedient.

(6) In this paragraph—

"fixed penalty" means a penalty of such amount as may be prescribed (whether by being specified in, or made calculable under, regulations);

"fixed penalty notice" means a notice offering a person an opportunity to discharge any liability to conviction for a fixed penalty offence by payment of a penalty of a prescribed amount;

"fixed penalty offence" means , subject to sub-paragraph (2) above, any offence (whether under or by virtue of this Part or any other enactment) which is for the time being prescribed as a fixed penalty offence;

"the fixed penalty system" means the system implementing regulations made under or by virtue of paragraph (o) of subsection (2) of section 87 of this Act;

"the period for paying", in relation to any fixed penalty, means such period as may be prescribed for the purpose;

"regulations" means regulations under or by virtue of paragraph (o) of subsection (2) of section 87 of this Act.

National Parks and Access to the Countryside Act 1949

(1949, c.97)

PART VI

GENERAL, FINANCIAL AND SUPPLEMENTARY

General powers and duties of commission

General duty of [Agency][1] to advise on questions relating to natural beauty App 6–04

85.—Without prejudice to their respective duties relating to National Parks, it shall be the duty of [the Agency][2] and the Council—

(a) in circumstances where it appears to the Minister and to [the Agency],[3] or, as the case may be, to the Minister and to the Council, desirable that their assistance should be generally available, to inquire into and report on such questions referred to them by any other body of persons or person;

(b) to bring to the attention of the Minister or of local planning authorities the effect on the natural beauty of such areas or places as aforesaid of developments, or developments of any class, which appear to [the Agency][4] (as respects England) or to the Council (as respects Wales) to be likely to be prejudicial thereto.

Information services to be provided by Agency

86.—(1) It shall be the duty of [the Agency][5] to take such steps as appear to them expedient for securing that persons interested—

(a) will be informed of the situation and extent of and means of access to, National Parks, other areas, being areas of outstanding natural beauty, and long-distance routes for which proposals under section fifty-one of this Act have been approved, and the accommodation and facilities available for persons wishing to visit National Parks and such other areas or persons wishing to use such routes;

(b) will be able to learn about the history, natural features, flora and fauna of National Parks and the objects of architectural, archaeological or historical interest therein and the opportunities for recreation available therein,

and that suitable methods of publicity are used for the prevention of damage in National Parks and such other areas as aforesaid and otherwise for encouraging a proper standard of behaviour on the part of persons visiting National Parks and such other areas; and the said methods shall include the preparation and publication of a code of conductor for the guidance of persons visiting the countryside.

---

1 Words substituted by SI 1999/416 (Development Commission (Transfer of Functions and Miscellaneous Provisions) Order), Sch.1 para.1(5).
2 *ibid.*
3 *ibid.*
4 *ibid.*
5 *ibid.*

(2) Without prejudice to the provisions of the last foregoing subsection, [the Agency][6] may for the purposes thereof procure the production and sale to the public of books, guides and maps, the exhibition of posters and other advertisements, the giving of lectures and the provision and exhibition of cinematography films.

(3) For the avoidance of doubt it is hereby declared that the steps mentioned in subsection (1) of this section include the making of contributions towards expenses incurred by other bodies of persons.

[6] Words substituted by SI 1999/416 (Development Commission (Transfer of Functions and Miscellaneous Provisions) Order), Sch.1 para.1(5).

APPENDIX 7

Personal Information

Children Act 1989

(1989, c.41)

PART IV

CARE AND SUPERVISION

Guardians ad litem

Right of officer of the Service to have access to local authority records App 7–01

42.—(1) Where an officer of the Service has been appointed under section 41 he shall have the right at all reasonable times to examine and take copies of—

(a) any records of, or held by, a local authority or an authorised person which were compiled in connection with the making, or proposed making, by any person of any application under this Act with respect to the child concerned;
(b) any records of, or held by, a local authority which were compiled in connection with any functions which stand referred to their social services committee under the Local Authority Social Services Act 1970, so far as those records relate to that child; or
(c) any records of, or held by, an authorised person which were compiled in connection with the activities of that person, so far as those records relate to that child.

(2) Where an officer of the Service takes a copy of any record which he is entitled to examine under this section, that copy or any part of it shall be admissible as evidence of any matter referred to in any—

(a) report which he makes to the court in the proceedings in question; or
(b) evidence which he gives in those proceedings.

(3) Subsection (2) has effect regardless of any enactment or rule of law which would otherwise prevent the record in question being admissible in evidence.

(4) In this section "authorised person" has the same meaning as in section 31.[1]

[1] In relation to England:

"Right of guardian ad litem to have access to local authority records.

42.—(1) Where an officer of the Service has been appointed under section 41 he shall have the right at all reasonable times to examine and take copies of—

(a) any records of, or held by, a local authority or an authorised person which were compiled in connection with the making, or proposed making, by any person of any application under this Act with respect to the child concerned;

(b) any records of, or held by, a local authority which were compiled in connection with any functions which are social services functions within the meaning of the Local Authority Social Services Act 1970, so far as those records relate to that child; or

(c) any records of, or held by, an authorised person which were compiled in connection with the activities of that person, so far as those records relate to that child.

(2) Where an officer of the Service takes a copy of any record which he is entitled to examine under this section, that copy or any part of it shall be admissible as evidence of any matter referred to in any—

(a) report which he makes to the court in the proceedings in question; or

(b) evidence which he gives in those proceedings.

(3) Subsection (2) has effect regardless of any enactment or rule of law which would otherwise prevent the record in question being admissible in evidence.

(4) In this section "authorised person" has the same meaning as in section 31."

Arrangements for Placement of Children (General) Regulations 1991

(SI 1991/890)

Access by guardians *ad litem* to records and register

11.—Each voluntary organisation, where they are not acting as an authorised person,[1] and every person carrying on a registered children's home shall provide a guardian ad litem of a child— App 7–02

(a) such access as may be required to-

(i) case records and registers maintained in accordance with these Regulations; and

(ii) the information from such records or registers held in whatever form (such as by means of computer);

(b) such copies of the records or entries in the registers as he may require.[2,3,4]

---

1 For access by guardians ad litem to local authority and authorised person's records see s.42 of the 1989 Act as amended by para.18 of Sch.16 to the Courts and Legal Services Act 1990 (c.41). "Authorised person" is defined in s.31, of the 1989 Act.

2 In relation to Wales:

"Access by officers of the service to records and register

11. Each voluntary organisation, where they are not acting as an authorised personFor access by officers of the service to local authority and authorised person's records see section 42 of the 1989 Act as amended by paragraph 18 of Schedule 16 to the Courts and Legal Services Act 1990 (c.41). "Authorised person" is defined in section 31, of the 1989 Act, and every person carrying on a private children's home shall provide an officer of the service of a child—

(a) such access as may be required to—

(i) case records and registers maintained in accordance with these Regulations; and

(ii) the information from such records or registers held in whatever form (such as by means of computer);

(b) such copies of the records or entries in the registers as he may require."

3 Words substituted by SI 2002/2935 (Children Act 1989 and the Care Standards Act 2000 (Miscellaneous Regulations) (Amendment) (Wales) (No.2) Regulations), reg.5.

4 In relation to England:

"Access by officers of the service to records and register

11. Each voluntary organisation, where they are not acting as an authorised person for access by officers of the service to local authority and authorised person's records see section 42 of the 1989 Act as amended by paragraph 18 of Schedule 16 to the Courts and Legal Services Act 1990 (c.41). "Authorised person" is defined in section 31, of the 1989 Act., and every person carrying on a private children's home shall provide a officer of the service of a child—

(a) such access as may be required to-

(i) case records and registers maintained in accordance with these Regulations; and

(ii) the information from such records or registers held in whatever form (such as by means of computer);

(b) such copies of the records or entries in the registers as he may require."

Adoption Act 1976

(1976, c.36)

PART V

REGISTRATION AND REVOCATION OF ADOPTION ORDERS AND CONVENTION

Adoptions

Disclosure of birth records of adopted children

App 7–03 **51.**—(1) Subject to what follows, the Registrar General shall on an application made in the prescribed manner by an adopted person a record of whose birth is kept by the Registrar General and who has attained the age of 18 years supply to that person on payment of the prescribed fee (if any) such information as is necessary to enable that person to obtain a certified copy of the record of his birth.

(2) On an application made in the prescribed manner by an adopted person under the age of 18 years, a record of whose birth is kept by the Registrar General and who is intending to be married in England or Wales, and on payment of the prescribed fee (if any), the Registrar General shall inform the applicant whether or not it appears from information contained in the registers of live births or other records that the applicant and the person whom he intends to marry may be within the prohibited degrees of relationship for the purposes of the Marriage Act 1949.

(3) Before supplying any information to an applicant under subsection (1), the Registrar General shall inform the applicant that counselling services are available to him—

(a) if he is in England and Wales—

(i) at the General Register Office;
(ii) from the local authority in whose area he is living;
(iii) where the adoption order relating to him was made in England and Wales, from the local authority in whose area the court which made the order sat; or
(iv) from any other local authority;

(b) if he is in Scotland—

(i) from the regional or islands council in whose area he is living;
(ii) where the adoption order relating to him was made in Scotland, from the council in whose area the court which made the order sat; or
(iii) from any other regional or islands council;

(c) if he is in Northern Ireland—

(i) from the Board in whose area he is living;
(ii) where the adoption order relating to him was made in Northern Ireland, from the Board in whose area the court which made the order sat; or
(iii) from any other Board;

(d) if he is in the United Kingdom and his adoption was arranged by an adoption society—

(i) which is an appropriate voluntary organisation,
(ii) approved under section 3 of the Adoption (Scotland) Act 1978,
(iii) registered under Article 4 of the Adoption (Northern Ireland) Order 1987,
from that society.

(4) Where an adopted person who is in England and Wales—

(a) applies for information under—

(i) subsection (1), or
(ii) Article 54 of the Adoption (Northern Ireland) Order 1987, or

(b) is supplied with information under section 45 of the Adoption (Scotland) Act 1978,

it shall be the duty of the persons and bodies mentioned in subsection (5) to provide counselling for him if asked by him to do so.

(5) The persons and bodies are—

(a) the Registrar General;
(b) any local authority falling within subsection (3)(a)(ii) to (iv);
(c) any adoption society falling within subsection (3)(d) in so far as it is acting as an adoption society in England and Wales.

(6) If the applicant chooses to receive counselling from a person or body falling within subsection (3), the Registrar General shall send to the person or body the information to which the applicant is entitled under subsection (1).

(7) Where a person—

(a) was adopted before 12th November 1975, and
(b) applies for information under subsection (1),

the Registrar General shall not supply the information to him unless he has attended an interview with a counsellor arranged by a person or body from whom counselling services are available as mentioned in subsection (3).

(8) Where the Registrar General is prevented by subsection (7) from supplying information to a person who is not living in the United Kingdom, he may supply the information to any body which—

(a) the Registrar General is satisfied is suitable to provide counselling to that person, and
(b) has notified the Registrar General that it is prepared to provide such counselling.

(9) In this section—

"a Board" means a Health and Social Services Board established under Article 16 of the Health and Personal Social Services (Northern Ireland) Order 1972; and

"prescribed" means prescribed by regulations made by the Registrar General.[1]

[1] Words substituted by Care Standards Act 2000 (c.14), Sch.4, para.5(9).

APPENDIX 8

Economic and Business Information

Industry Act 1975

(1975, c.68)

PART IV

DISCLOSURE OF INFORMATION

Disclosure by Government

Disclosure of information by Government

App 8–01 27.—Ministers of the Crown and the Treasury shall publish, make available and provide access to information and analysis as specified in Schedule 5 to this Act.

SCHEDULE 5

DISCLOSURE OF INFORMATION BY GOVERNMENT

1.—For the purposes of this Schedule the Treasury shall keep a macro-economic model suitable for demonstrating the likely effects on economic events in the United Kingdom of different assumptions about the following matters, namely—

(a) government economic policies;
(b) economic events outside the United Kingdom; and
(c) such (if any) other matters as appear to the Treasury from time to time likely to have a substantial effect on economic events in the United Kingdom.

2.—The model shall enable forecasts to be made—

(a) of any of the following, namely—
  (i) the level of gross domestic product;
  (ii) unemployment;
  (iii) the balance of payments on current account;
  (iv) the general index of retail prices; and
  (v) average earnings; and
(b) of such (if any) other economic variables as are appropriate in the opinion of the Treasury from time to time.

3.—The references to forecasts in paragraph 2 above are references to forecasts relating to successive periods of three months and not to shorter periods.

4.—The model shall be maintained on a computer.

5.—The model shall be available to members of the public to make forecasts based on their own assumptions, using the computer during office hours upon payment of such reasonable fee as the Treasury may determine.

6.—Not less than twice in each year commencing with a date not later than one year from the coming into force of this Act, the Treasury shall publish forecasts produced with the aid of the model as to such matters and based on such alternative assumptions as appear to them to be appropriate.

7.—Any forecast under this Schedule shall indicate, where possible, the margin of error attaching to it.

8.—The Treasury shall from time to time publish an analysis of errors in such forecasts that would have remained even if the assumptions set out in the forecasts and on which they were based had been correct.

9.—[. . .][1]

1 Words Repealed by Industry Act 1980 (c.33), Sch.2.

Radioactive Substances Act 1993

(1993, c.12)

Public Access to Documents and Records

Public access to documents and records

App 8–02 39.—(1) The appropriate Agency shall keep copies of—

(a) all applications made to it under any provision of this Act,
(b) all documents issued by it under any provision of this Act,
(c) all other documents sent by it to any local authority in pursuance of directions of the Secretary of State, and
(d) such records of convictions under section 32, 33, 34 or 35 as may be prescribed in regulations;

and the appropriate Agency shall make copies of those documents available to the public except to the extent that that would involve the disclosure of information relating to any relevant process or trade secret or would involve the disclosure of information as respects which the Secretary of State has directed that knowledge should be restricted on grounds of national security.

(2) Each local authority shall keep and make available to the public copies of all documents sent to the authority under any provision of this Act unless directed by the appropriate Agency[. . .],[1] that all or any part of any such document is not to be available for inspection.

(3) Directions under subsection (2) shall only be given for the purpose of preventing disclosure of relevant processes or trade secrets and may be given generally in respect of all, or any description of, documents or in respect of specific documents.

(4) The copies of documents required to be made available to the public by this section need not be kept in documentary form.

(5) The public shall have the right to inspect the copies of documents required to be made available under this section at all reasonable times and, on payment of a reasonable fee, to be provided with a copy of any such document.

(6) In this section "relevant process" has the same meaning as in section 34.

(7) In the application of this section to Northern Ireland, references to the Secretary of State shall have effect as references to the Department of the Environment for Northern Ireland.

---

1 Words repealed by Environment Act 1995 (c.25), Sch.24, para.1.

Coal Industry Act 1994

(1994, c.21)

PART IV

GENERAL AND SUPPLEMENTAL

Information provisions

Public access to information held by the Authority

57.—(1) This section applies to the information contained in any register maintained by the Authority under section 35 or 56 above and to any of the following information which is for the time being in the possession of the Authority, that is to say— **App 8–03**

(a) information about the geological or physiographical features or characteristics of any land in which any unworked coal or any coal mine is situated or of any other land;
(b) information about the identity of the persons in whom interests and rights in or in relation to any unworked coal or any coal mine have been vested;
(c) the contents of the plans of any coal mines or coal workings;
(d) any other information about proposals for the carrying on by any person of any coal-mining operations;
(e) information about any subsidence or subsidence damage or about claims made under the 1991 Act; and
(f) information about such other matters as the Secretary of State may by regulations prescribe for the purposes of this section.

(2) Subject to subsections (3) and (4) below, it shall be the duty of the Authority to establish and maintain arrangements under which every person is entitled, in such cases, on payment to the Authority of such fee and subject to such other conditions as the Authority may consider appropriate—

(a) to be furnished with any information to which this section applies;
(b) to have the contents of so much of the records maintained by the Authority as contains any information to which this section applies made available to him, at such office of the Authority as it may determine, for inspection at such times as may be reasonable; and
(c) to make or be supplied with copies of, or of extracts from, so much of the records maintained by the Authority as contains any information to which this section applies.

(3) Subject to subsection (5) below, nothing in this section shall require or authorise this disclosure by the Authority of any information which—

(a) relates to the affairs of an individual or specifically to the affairs of any body of persons (whether corporate or unincorporate), including the Authority itself, and
(b) is not contained in a register maintained under section 35 or 56 above,

if the disclosure of that information would or might, in the opinion of the Authority, seriously and prejudicially affect the interests of that individual or, as the case may be, of that body.

(4) Subject to subsection (5) below, nothing in this section shall require or authorise the disclosure by the Authority, without the consent of the person to whom the Authority owes the obligation of confidence, of any information which—

(a) has been furnished to the Authority—

(i) in pursuance of the provisions of a licence under Part II of this Act;

(ii) in pursuance of any provisions of an agreement entered into in connection with, or with any proposals for, the carrying on of any activities in the course of any exploration for coal or of any activities for which a licence under [section 3 of the Petroleum Act 1998][1] is required; or

(iii) for the purposes of any application to the Authority for the grant of a licence under Part II of this Act, for the making of such an agreement or for the transfer or creation of any interests or rights in or in relation to any land; and

(b) under the provisions of the licence under Part II of this Act, of that agreement or of any undertaking given by the Authority to the applicant for the purposes of that application, is to be treated as subject to an obligation of confidence owed by the Authority to any other person.

(5) The information that is to be excluded by virtue of subsections (3) and (4) above from the information which is to be made available to any person in pursuance of arrangements under this section shall not include any information of a description that appears to the Authority to comprise information relating to matters which are or may be relevant to the safety of members of the public or of any particular individual or individuals other than the person whose consent is required for its disclosure.

(6) For the purposes of this section it shall be the duty of the Authority to maintain such records as it considers appropriate of any information which comes into its possession and is information to which this section applies.

(7) The power to make regulations for the purposes of this section shall be exercisable by statutory instrument subject to annulment in pursuance of a resolution of either House of Parliament.

(8) In this section "records" includes registers, maps, plans and accounts, as well as computer records and other records kept otherwise than in documentary form.

[1] Words substituted by Petroleum Act 1998 (c.17), Sch.4, para.38(4).

Land Registration Act 2002

(2002, c.9)

PART VI

REGISTRATION: GENERAL

Information, etc.

Inspection of the registers, etc.

66.—(1) Any person may inspect and make copies of, or of any part of— **App 8–0**

(a) the register of title,
(b) any document kept by the registrar which is referred to in the register of title,
(c) any other document kept by the registrar which relates to an application to him, or
(d) the register of cautions against first registration.

(2) The right under subsection (1) is subject to rules which may, in particular—

(a) provide for exceptions to the right, and
(b) impose conditions on its exercise, including conditions requiring the payment of fees.

Index

68.—(1) The registrar must keep an index for the purpose of enabling the following matters to be ascertained in relation to any parcel of land—

(a) whether any registered estate relates to the land,
(b) how any registered estate which relates to the land is identified for the purposes of the register,
(c) whether the land is affected by any, and, if so what, caution against first registration, and
(d) such other matters as rules may provide.

(2) Rules may—

(a) make provision about how the index is to be kept and may, in particular, make provision about—

(i) the information to be included in the index,
(ii) the form in which information included in the index is to be kept, and
(iii) the arrangement of that information;

(b) make provision about official searches of the index.

Historical information

69.—(1) The registrar may on application provide information about the history of a registered title.

(2) Rules may make provision about applications for the exercise of the power conferred by subsection (1).

(3) The registrar may—

(a) arrange for the provision of information about the history of registered titles, and
(b) authorise anyone who has the function of providing information under paragraph (a) to have access on such terms as the registrar thinks fit to any relevant information kept by him.

APPENDIX 9

Educational Information

Education (No.2) Act 1986

(1986, c.61)

PART IV

MISCELLANEOUS

Access to papers, etc., of governing bodies

62.—(1) The Secretary of State may make regulations requiring the governing body [of every institution of a kind mentioned in section 61 of this Act;][1] [. . .][2] to make available, to such persons or classes of person as may be prescribed, such documents and information relating to the meetings and proceedings of the governing body as may be prescribed. App 9–01

(2) Documents and information required by the regulations to be made available shall be made available in such form and manner, and at such times, as may be prescribed.

1 Words repealed by Education Act 1996 (c.56), Sch.38(I), para.1.

2 The "(b)" immediately following that sub-paragraph is also repealed by Education Act 1996 (c.56), Sch.38(I), para.1.

Learning and Skills Act 2000

(2000, c.21)

Part V

Miscellaneous and General

Support for 13 to 19 year olds: England

Educational institutions: information and access

App 9–02 **117.**—(1) Where a person is involved in the provision of services in pursuance of section 114(1), an educational institution to which this section applies shall, for the purpose of the provision of those services—

(a) provide him on request with the name and address of a pupil or student;
(b) provide him on request with the name and address of a parent of a pupil or student;
(c) provide him on request with information in the institution's possession about a pupil or student;
(d) permit him to have access to a pupil or student on the institution's premises at reasonable times;
(e) make available to him, so far as is reasonably convenient, facilities on the institution's premises for providing services to individual pupils or students or groups of pupils or students.

(2) Information shall not be provided under subsection (1)(c)—

(a) in the case of a pupil or student who has not attained the age of 16, if a parent of his has instructed the institution not to provide information of that kind under this section, or
(b) in the case of a pupil or student who has attained the age of 16, if he has instructed the institution not to provide information of that kind under this section.

(3) This section applies to the following institutions—

(a) community, foundation and voluntary schools,
(b) community or foundation special schools (other than those established in hospitals),
(c) city technology colleges, city colleges for the technology of the arts and [Academies],[1]
(d) pupil referral units,
(e) institutions within the further education sector, and
(f) institutions in receipt of funding from the Learning and Skills Council for England.

1 Words substituted by Education Act 2002 (c.32), Sch.7(2), para.10.

Support for 11 to 25 year olds: Wales

Educational institutions: information and access

126.—(1) Where a person is involved in the provision of services in pursuance of section 123(1)(a) or (b), an educational institution to which this section applies shall, for the purpose of the provision of those services—

(a) provide him on request with the name and address of a pupil or student;
(b) provide him on request with the name and address of a parent of a pupil or student;
(c) provide him on request with information in the institution's possession about a pupil or student;
(d) permit him to have access to a pupil or student on the institution's premises at reasonable times;
(e) make available to him, so far as is reasonably convenient, facilities on the institution's premises for providing services to individual pupils or students or groups of pupils or students.

(2) Information shall not be provided under subsection (1)(c)—

(a) in the case of a pupil or student who has not attained the age of 16, if a parent of his has instructed the institution not to provide information of that kind under this section, or
(b) in the case of a pupil or student who has attained the age of 16, if he has instructed the institution not to provide information of that kind under this section.

(3) This section applies to the following institutions—

(a) community, foundation and voluntary schools,
(b) community or foundation special schools (other than those established in hospitals),
(c) city technology colleges and city colleges for the technology of the arts,
(d) pupil referral units,
(e) institutions within the further education sector, and
(f) institutions in receipt of funding from the National Council for Education and Training for Wales.

Conduct and effect of inspections

128.—(1) This section applies where a service is inspected pursuant to a request under section 127(1)(c) or in accordance with section 127(1)(d).

(2) A person carrying out or participating in the inspection shall have the same powers as an Inspector under the following provisions of the School Inspections Act 1996—

(a) section 6(3)(a) and (b) (right of access), and
(b) section 42 (computer records).

(3) Section 42A of that Act (publication of reports) shall apply.

(4) Where the Chief Inspector arranges for the publication of a report of an inspection, the person who provides the inspected service shall—

(a) prepare a written statement of the action which he proposes to take in the light of the report and the period within which he proposes to take it,
(b) publish the statement within such period, and in such manner, as may be prescribed by regulations made by the National Assembly for Wales, and

(c) send copies of the statement to such persons as may be prescribed by regulations made by the National Assembly.

(5) Where a local authority provides an inspected service, or secures or participates in the provision of an inspected service, the authority—

(a) shall ensure that the action specified in any statement prepared under subsection (4)(a) is sufficient to remedy any weakness mentioned in the report, and
(b) shall take all reasonable steps to ensure that the action specified in the statement is taken within the period specified.

(6) If the National Assembly consider that a local authority is failing to comply with its duties under subsection (5)—

(a) the National Assembly may give directions to the local authority about the performance of those duties, and
(b) the authority shall comply with the directions.

APPENDIX 10

European Material Relevant to UK Public Body Information

Article 255 (ex Article 191a)

1. Any citizen of the Union, and any natural or legal person residing or having its registered office in a Member State, shall have a right of access to European Parliament, Council and Commission documents, subject to the principles and the conditions to be defined in accordance with paragraphs 2 and 3. App 10–01

2. General principles and limits on grounds of public or private interest governing this right of access to documents shall be determined by the Council, acting in accordance with the procedure referred to in Article 251 within two years of the entry into force of the Treaty of Amsterdam.

3. Each institution referred to above shall elaborate in its own Rules of Procedure specific provisions regarding access to its documents.

Directive 95/46/EC of the European Parliament and of the Council on the Protection of Individuals with Regard to the Processing of Personal Data and on the Free Movement of Such Data

[OCTOBER 24, 1995]

App 10–02 THE EUROPEAN PARLIAMENT AND THE COUNCIL OF THE EUROPEAN UNION,

Having regard to the Treaty establishing the European Community, and in particular Article 100a thereof,

Having regard to the proposal from the Commission,

Having regard to the opinion of the Economic and Social Committee,

Acting in accordance with the procedure referred to in Article 189b of the Treaty,

(1) Whereas the objectives of the Community, as laid down in the Treaty, as amended by the Treaty on European Union, include creating an ever closer union among the peoples of Europe, fostering closer relations between the States belonging to the Community, ensuring economic and social progress by common action to eliminate the barriers which divide Europe, encouraging the constant improvement of the living conditions of its peoples, preserving and strengthening peace and liberty and promoting democracy on the basis of the fundamental rights recognised in the constitution and laws of the Member States and in the European Convention for the Protection of Human Rights and Fundamental Freedoms;

(2) Whereas data-processing systems are designed to serve man; whereas they must, whatever the nationality or residence of natural persons, respect their fundamental rights and freedoms, notably the right to privacy, and contribute to economic and social progress, trade expansion and the well-being of individuals;

(3) Whereas the establishment and functioning of an internal market in which, in accordance with Article 7a of the Treaty, the free movement of goods, persons, services and capital is ensured require not only that personal data should be able to flow freely from one Member State to another, but also that the fundamental rights of individuals should be safeguarded;

(4) Whereas increasingly frequent recourse is being had in the Community to the processing of personal data in the various spheres of economic and social activity; whereas the progress made in information technology is making the processing and exchange of such data considerably easier;

(5) Whereas the economic and social integration resulting from the establishment and functioning of the internal market within the meaning of Article 7a of the Treaty will necessarily lead to a substantial increase in cross-border flows of personal data between all those involved in a private or public capacity in economic and social activity in the Member States; whereas the exchange of personal data between undertakings in different Member States is set to increase; whereas the national authorities in the various Member States are being called upon by virtue of Community law to collaborate and exchange personal data so as to be able to perform their duties or carry out tasks on behalf of an authority in another Member State within the context of the area without internal frontiers as constituted by the internal market;

(6) Whereas, furthermore, the increase in scientific and technical co-operation and the coordinated introduction of new telecommunications networks in the Community necessitate and facilitate cross-border flows of personal data;

(7) Whereas the difference in levels of protection of the rights and freedoms of individuals, notably the right to privacy, with regard to the processing of personal data

afforded in the Member States may prevent the transmission of such data from the territory of one Member State to that of another Member State; whereas this difference may therefore constitute an obstacle to the pursuit of a number of economic activities at Community level, distort competition and impede authorities in the discharge of their responsibilities under Community law; whereas this difference in levels of protection is due to the existence of a wide variety of national laws, regulations and administrative provisions;

(8) Whereas, in order to remove the obstacles to flows of personal data, the level of protection of the rights and freedoms of individuals with regard to the processing of such data must be equivalent in all Member States; whereas this objective is vital to the internal market but cannot be achieved by the Member States alone, especially in view of the scale of the divergences which currently exist between the relevant laws in the Member States and the need to coordinate the laws of the Member States so as to ensure that the cross-border flow of personal data is regulated in a consistent manner that is in keeping with the objective of the internal market as provided for in Article 7a of the Treaty; whereas Community action to approximate those laws is therefore needed;

(9) Whereas, given the equivalent protection resulting from the approximation of national laws, the Member States will no longer be able to inhibit the free movement between them of personal data on grounds relating to protection of the rights and freedoms of individuals, and in particular the right to privacy; whereas Member States will be left a margin for manoeuvre, which may, in the context of implementation of the Directive, also be exercised by the business and social partners; whereas Member States will therefore be able to specify in their national law the general conditions governing the lawfulness of data processing; whereas in doing so the Member States shall strive to improve the protection currently provided by their legislation; whereas, within the limits of this margin for manoeuvre and in accordance with Community law, disparities could arise in the implementation of the Directive, and this could have an effect on the movement of data within a Member State as well as within the Community;

(10) Whereas the object of the national laws on the processing of personal data is to protect fundamental rights and freedoms, notably the right to privacy, which is recognised both in Article 8 of the European Convention for the Protection of Human Rights and Fundamental Freedoms and in the general principles of Community law; whereas, for that reason, the approximation of those laws must not result in any lessening of the protection they afford but must, on the contrary, seek to ensure a high level of protection in the Community;

(11) Whereas the principles of the protection of the rights and freedoms of individuals, notably the right to privacy, which are contained in this Directive, give substance to and amplify those contained in the Council of Europe Convention of January 28, 1981 for the Protection of Individuals with regard to Automatic Processing of Personal Data;

(12) Whereas the protection principles must apply to all processing of personal data by any person whose activities are governed by Community law; whereas there should be excluded the processing of data carried out by a natural person in the exercise of activities which are exclusively personal or domestic, such as correspondence and the holding of records of addresses;

(13) Whereas the acitivities referred to in Titles V and VI of the Treaty on European Union regarding public safety, defence, State security or the acitivities of the State in the area of criminal laws fall outside the scope of Community law, without prejudice to the obligations incumbent upon Member States under Article 56 (2), Article 57 or Article 100a of the Treaty establishing the European Community; whereas the processing of personal data that is necessary to safeguard the economic well-being of the State does not fall within the scope of this Directive where such processing relates to State security matters;

(14) Whereas, given the importance of the developments under way, in the framework of the information society, of the techniques used to capture, transmit, manipulate,

record, store or communicate sound and image data relating to natural persons, this Directive should be applicable to processing involving such data;

(15) Whereas the processing of such data is covered by this Directive only if it is automated or if the data processed are contained or are intended to be contained in a filing system structured according to specific criteria relating to individuals, so as to permit easy access to the personal data in question;

(16) Whereas the processing of sound and image data, such as in cases of video surveillance, does not come within the scope of this Directive if it is carried out for the purposes of public security, defence, national security or in the course of State activities relating to the area of criminal law or of other activities which do not come within the scope of Community law;

(17) Whereas, as far as the processing of sound and image data carried out for purposes of journalism or the purposes of literary or artistic expression is concerned, in particular in the audiovisual field, the principles of the Directive are to apply in a restricted manner according to the provisions laid down in Article 9;

(18) Whereas, in order to ensure that individuals are not deprived of the protection to which they are entitled under this Directive, any processing of personal data in the Community must be carried out in accordance with the law of one of the Member States; whereas, in this connection, processing carried out under the responsibility of a controller who is established in a Member State should be governed by the law of that State;

(19) Whereas establishment on the territory of a Member State implies the effective and real exercise of activity through stable arrangements; whereas the legal form of such an establishment, whether simply branch or a subsidiary with a legal personality, is not the determining factor in this respect; whereas, when a single controller is established on the territory of several Member States, particularly by means of subsidiaries, he must ensure, in order to avoid any circumvention of national rules, that each of the establishments fulfils the obligations imposed by the national law applicable to its activities;

(20) Whereas the fact that the processing of data is carried out by a person established in a third country must not stand in the way of the protection of individuals provided for in this Directive; whereas in these cases, the processing should be governed by the law of the Member State in which the means used are located, and there should be guarantees to ensure that the rights and obligations provided for in this Directive are respected in practice;

(21) Whereas this Directive is without prejudice to the rules of territoriality applicable in criminal matters;

(22) Whereas Member States shall more precisely define in the laws they enact or when bringing into force the measures taken under this Directive the general circumstances in which processing is lawful; whereas in particular Article 5, in conjunction with Articles 7 and 8, allows Member States, independently of general rules, to provide for special processing conditions for specific sectors and for the various categories of data covered by Article 8;

(23) Whereas Member States are empowered to ensure the implementation of the protection of individuals both by means of a general law on the protection of individuals as regards the processing of personal data and by sectorial laws such as those relating, for example, to statistical institutes;

(24) Whereas the legislation concerning the protection of legal persons with regard to the processing data which concerns them is not affected by this Directive;

(25) Whereas the principles of protection must be reflected, on the one hand, in the obligations imposed on persons, public authorities, enterprises, agencies or other bodies responsible for processing, in particular regarding data quality, technical security, notification to the supervisory authority, and the circumstances under which processing can be carried out, and, on the other hand, in the right conferred on individuals, the data on

whom are the subject of processing, to be informed that processing is taking place, to consult the data, to request corrections and even to object to processing in certain circumstances;

(26) Whereas the principles of protection must apply to any information concerning an identified or identifiable person; whereas, to determine whether a person is identifiable, account should be taken of all the means likely reasonably to be used either by the controller or by any other person to identify the said person; whereas the principles of protection shall not apply to data rendered anonymous in such a way that the data subject is no longer identifiable; whereas codes of conduct within the meaning of Article 27 may be a useful instrument for providing guidance as to the ways in which data may be rendered anonymous and retained in a form in which identification of the data subject is no longer possible;

(27) Whereas the protection of individuals must apply as much to automatic processing of data as to manual processing; whereas the scope of this protection must not in effect depend on the techniques used, otherwise this would create a serious risk of circumvention; whereas, nonetheless, as regards manual processing, this Directive covers only filing systems, not unstructured files; whereas, in particular, the content of a filing system must be structured according to specific criteria relating to individuals allowing easy access to the personal data; whereas, in line with the definition in Article 2(c), the different criteria for determining the constituents of a structured set of personal data, and the different criteria governing access to such a set, may be laid down by each Member State; whereas files or sets of files as well as their cover pages, which are not structured according to specific criteria, shall under no circumstances fall within the scope of this Directive;

(28) Whereas any processing of personal data must be lawful and fair to the individuals concerned; whereas, in particular, the data must be adequate, relevant and not excessive in relation to the purposes for which they are processed; whereas such purposes must be explicit and legitimate and must be determined at the time of collection of the data; whereas the purposes of processing further to collection shall not be incompatible with the purposes as they were originally specified;

(29) Whereas the further processing of personal data for historical, statistical or scientific purposes is not generally to be considered incompatible with the purposes for which the data have previously been collected provided that Member States furnish suitable safeguards; whereas these safeguards must in particular rule out the use of the data in support of measures or decisions regarding any particular individual;

(30) Whereas, in order to be lawful, the processing of personal data must in addition be carried out with the consent of the data subject or be necessary for the conclusion or performance of a contract binding on the data subject, or as a legal requirement, or for the performance of a task carried out in the public interest or in the exercise of official authority, or in the legitimate interests of a natural or legal person, provided that the interests or the rights and freedoms of the data subject are not overriding; whereas, in particular, in order to maintain a balance between the interests involved while guaranteeing effective competition, Member States may determine the circumstances in which personal data may be used or disclosed to a third party in the context of the legitimate ordinary business activities of companies and other bodies; whereas Member States may similarly specify the conditions under which personal data may be disclosed to a third party for the purposes of marketing whether carried out commercially or by a charitable organisation or by any other association or foundation, of a political nature for example, subject to the provisions allowing a data subject to object to the processing of data regarding him, at no cost and without having to state his reasons;

(31) Whereas the processing of personal data must equally be regarded as lawful where it is carried out in order to protect an interest which is essential for the data subject's life;

(32) Whereas it is for national legislation to determine whether the controller performing a task carried out in the public interest or in the exercise of official authority should be a public administration or another natural or legal person governed by public law, or by private law such as a professional association;

(33) Whereas data which are capable by their nature of infringing fundamental freedoms or privacy should not be processed unless the data subject gives his explicit consent; whereas, however, derogations from this prohibition must be explicitly provided for in respect of specific needs, in particular where the processing of these data is carried out for certain health-related purposes by persons subject to a legal obligation of professional secrecy or in the course of legitimate activities by certain associations or foundations the purpose of which is to permit the exercise of fundamental freedoms;

(34) Whereas Member States must also be authorized, when justified by grounds of important public interest, to derogate from the prohibition on processing sensitive categories of data where important reasons of public interest so justify in areas such as public health and social protection—especially in order to ensure the quality and cost-effectiveness of the procedures used for settling claims for benefits and services in the health insurance system—scientific research and government statistics; whereas it is incumbent on them, however, to provide specific and suitable safeguards so as to protect the fundamental rights and the privacy of individuals;

(35) Whereas, moreover, the processing of personal data by official authorities for achieving aims, laid down in constitutional law or international public law, of officially recognised religious associations is carried out on important grounds of public interest;

(36) Whereas where, in the course of electoral activities, the operation of the democratic system requires in certain Member States that political parties compile data on people's political opinion, the processing of such data may be permitted for reasons of important public interest, provided that appropriate safeguards are established;

(37) Whereas the processing of personal data for purposes of journalism or for purposes of literary of artistic expression, in particular in the audiovisual field, should qualify for exemption from the requirements of certain provisions of this Directive in so far as this is necessary to reconcile the fundamental rights of individuals with freedom of information and notably the right to receive and impart information, as guaranteed in particular in Article 10 of the European Convention for the Protection of Human Rights and Fundamental Freedoms; whereas Member States should therefore lay down exemptions and derogations necessary for the purpose of balance between fundamental rights as regards general measures on the legitimacy of data processing, measures on the transfer of data to third countries and the power of the supervisory authority; whereas this should not, however, lead Member States to lay down exemptions from the measures to ensure security of processing; whereas at least the supervisory authority responsible for this sector should also be provided with certain ex-post powers, *e.g.* to publish a regular report or to refer matters to the judicial authorities;

(38) Whereas, if the processing of data is to be fair, the data subject must be in a position to learn of the existence of a processing operation and, where data are collected from him, must be given accurate and full information, bearing in mind the circumstances of the collection;

(39) Whereas certain processing operations involve data which the controller has not collected directly from the data subject; whereas, furthermore, data can be legitimately disclosed to a third party, even if the disclosure was not anticipated at the time the data were collected from the data subject; whereas, in all these cases, the data subject should be informed when the data are recorded or at the latest when the data are first disclosed to a third party;

(40) Whereas, however, it is not necessary to impose this obligation of the data subject already has the information; whereas, moreover, there will be no such obligation if the recording or disclosure are expressly provided for by law or if the provision of

information to the data subject proves impossible or would involve disproportionate efforts, which could be the case where processing is for historical, statistical or scientific purposes; whereas, in this regard, the number of data subjects, the age of the data, and any compensatory measures adopted may be taken into consideration;

(41) Whereas any person must be able to exercise the right of access to data relating to him which are being processed, in order to verify in particular the accuracy of the data and the lawfulness of the processing; whereas, for the same reasons, every data subject must also have the right to know the logic involved in the automatic processing of data concerning him, at least in the case of the automated decisions referred to in Article 15(1); whereas this right must not adversely affect trade secrets or intellectual property and in particular the copyright protecting the software; whereas these considerations must not, however, result in the data subject being refused all information;

(42) Whereas Member States may, in the interest of the data subject or so as to protect the rights and freedoms of others, restrict rights of access and information; whereas they may, for example, specify that access to medical data may be obtained only through a health professional;

(43) Whereas restrictions on the rights of access and information and on certain obligations of the controller may similarly be imposed by Member States in so far as they are necessary to safeguard, for example, national security, defence, public safety, or important economic or financial interests of a Member State or the Union, as well as criminal investigations and prosecutions and action in respect of breaches of ethics in the regulated professions; whereas the list of exceptions and limitations should include the tasks of monitoring, inspection or regulation necessary in the three last-mentioned areas concerning public security, economic or financial interests and crime prevention; whereas the listing of tasks in these three areas does not affect the legitimacy of exceptions or restrictions for reasons of State security or defence;

(44) Whereas Member States may also be led, by virtue of the provisions of Community law, to derogate from the provisions of this Directive concerning the right of access, the obligation to inform individuals, and the quality of data, in order to secure certain of the purposes referred to above;

(45) Whereas, in cases where data might lawfully be processed on grounds of public interest, official authority or the legitimate interests of a natural or legal person, any data subject should nevertheless be entitled, on legitimate and compelling grounds relating to his particular situation, to object to the processing of any data relating to himself; whereas Member States may nevertheless lay down national provisions to the contrary;

(46) Whereas the protection of the rights and freedoms of data subjects with regard to the processing of personal data requires that appropriate technical and organisational measures be taken, both at the time of the design of the processing system and at the time of the processing itself, particularly in order to maintain security and thereby to prevent any unauthorized processing; whereas it is incumbent on the Member States to ensure that controllers comply with these measures; whereas these measures must ensure an appropriate level of security, taking into account the state of the art and the costs of their implementation in relation to the risks inherent in the processing and the nature of the data to be protected;

(47) Whereas where a message containing personal data is transmitted by means of a telecommunications or electronic mail service, the sole purpose of which is the transmission of such messages, the controller in respect of the personal data contained in the message will normally be considered to be the person from whom the message originates, rather than the person offering the transmission services; whereas, nevertheless, those offering such services will normally be considered controllers in respect of the processing of the additional personal data necessary for the operation of the service;

(48) Whereas the procedures for notifying the supervisory authority are designed to ensure disclosure of the purposes and main features of any processing operation for the

purpose of verification that the operation is in accordance with the national measures taken under this Directive;

(49) Whereas, in order to avoid unsuitable administrative formalities, exemptions from the obligation to notify and simplification of the notification required may be provided for by Member States in cases where processing is unlikely adversely to affect the rights and freedoms of data subjects, provided that it is in accordance with a measure taken by a Member State specifying its limits; whereas exemption or simplification may similarly be provided for by Member States where a person appointed by the controller ensures that the processing carried out is not likely adversely to affect the rights and freedoms of data subjects; whereas such a data protection official, whether or not an employee of the controller, must be in a position to exercise his functions in complete independence;

(50) Whereas exemption or simplification could be provided for in cases of processing operations whose sole purpose is the keeping of a register intended, according to national law, to provide information to the public and open to consultation by the public or by any person demonstrating a legitimate interest;

(51) Whereas, nevertheless, simplification or exemption from the obligation to notify shall not release the controller from any of the other obligations resulting from this Directive;

(52) Whereas, in this context, ex post facto verification by the competent authorities must in general be considered a sufficient measure;

(53) Whereas, however, certain processing operation are likely to pose specific risks to the rights and freedoms of data subjects by virtue of their nature, their scope or their purposes, such as that of excluding individuals from a right, benefit or a contract, or by virtue of the specific use of new technologies; whereas it is for Member States, if they so wish, to specify such risks in their legislation;

(54) Whereas with regard to all the processing undertaken in society, the amount posing such specific risks should be very limited; whereas Member States must provide that the supervisory authority, or the data protection official in cooperation with the authority, check such processing prior to it being carried out; whereas following this prior check, the supervisory authority may, according to its national law, give an opinion or an authorisation regarding the processing; whereas such checking may equally take place in the course of the preparation either of a measure of the national parliament or of a measure based on such a legislative measure, which defines the nature of the processing and lays down appropriate safeguards;

(55) Whereas, if the controller fails to respect the rights of data subjects, national legislation must provide for a judicial remedy; whereas any damage which a person may suffer as a result of unlawful processing must be compensated for by the controller, who may be exempted from liability if he proves that he is not responsible for the damage, in particular in cases where he establishes fault on the part of the data subject or in case of *force majeure*; whereas sanctions must be imposed on any person, whether governed by private of public law, who fails to comply with the national measures taken under this Directive;

(56) Whereas cross-border flows of personal data are necessary to the expansion of international trade; whereas the protection of individuals guaranteed in the Community by this Directive does not stand in the way of transfers of personal data to third countries which ensure an adequate level of protection; whereas the adequacy of the level of protection afforded by a third country must be assessed in the light of all the circumstances surrounding the transfer operation or set of transfer operations;

(57) Whereas, on the other hand, the transfer of personal data to a third country which does not ensure an adequate level of protection must be prohibited;

(58) Whereas provisions should be made for exemptions from this prohibition in certain circumstances where the data subject has given his consent, where the transfer is necessary in relation to a contract or a legal claim, where protection of an important

public interest so requires, for example in cases of international transfers of data between tax or customs administrations or between services competent for social security matters, or where the transfer is made from a register established by law and intended for consultation by the public or persons having a legitimate interest; whereas in this case such a transfer should not involve the entirety of the data or entire categories of the data contained in the register and, when the register is intended for consultation by persons having a legitimate interest, the transfer should be made only at the request of those persons or if they are to be the recipients;

(59) Whereas particular measures may be taken to compensate for the lack of protection in a third country in cases where the controller offers appropriate safeguards; whereas, moreover, provision must be made for procedures for negotiations between the Community and such third countries;

(60) Whereas, in any event, transfers to third countries may be effected only in full compliance with the provisions adopted by the Member States pursuant to this Directive, and in particular Article 8 thereof;

(61) Whereas Member States and the Commission, in their respective spheres of competence, must encourage the trade associations and other representative organisations concerned to draw up codes of conduct so as to facilitate the application of this Directive, taking account of the specific characteristics of the processing carried out in certain sectors, and respecting the national provisions adopted for its implementation;

(62) Whereas the establishment in Member States of supervisory authorities, exercising their functions with complete independence, is an essential component of the protection of individuals with regard to the processing of personal data;

(63) Whereas such authorities must have the necessary means to perform their duties, including powers of investigation and intervention, particularly in cases of complaints from individuals, and powers to engage in legal proceedings; whereas such authorities must help to ensure transparency of processing in the Member States within whose jurisdiction they fall;

(64) Whereas the authorities in the different Member States will need to assist one another in performing their duties so as to ensure that the rules of protection are properly respected throughout the European Union;

(65) Whereas, at Community level, a Working Party on the Protection of Individuals with regard to the Processing of Personal Data must be set up and be completely independent in the performance of its functions; whereas, having regard to its specific nature, it must advise the Commission and, in particular, contribute to the uniform application of the national rules adopted pursuant to this Directive;

(66) Whereas, with regard to the transfer of data to third countries, the application of this Directive calls for the conferment of powers of implementation on the Commission and the establishment of a procedure as laid down in Council Decision 87/373/EEC;

(67) Whereas an agreement on a modus vivendi between the European Parliament, the Council and the Commission concerning the implementing measures for acts adopted in accordance with the procedure laid down in Article 189b of the EC Treaty was reached on December 20, 1994;

(68) Whereas the principles set out in this Directive regarding the protection of the rights and freedoms of individuals, notably their right to privacy, with regard to the processing of personal data may be supplemented or clarified, in particular as far as certain sectors are concerned, by specific rules based on those principles;

(69) Whereas Member States should be allowed a period of not more than three years from the entry into force of the national measures transposing this Directive in which to apply such new national rules progressively to all processing operations already under way; whereas, in order to facilitate their cost-effective implementation, a further period expiring 12 years after the date on which this Directive is adopted will be allowed to Member States to ensure the conformity of existing manual filing systems with certain

of the Directive's provisions; whereas, where data contained in such filing systems are manually processed during this extended transition period, those systems must be brought into conformity with these provisions at the time of such processing;

(70) Whereas it is not necessary for the data subject to give his consent again so as to allow the controller to continue to process, after the national provisions taken pursuant to this Directive enter into force, any sensitive data necessary for the performance of a contract concluded on the basis of free and informed consent before the entry into force of these provisions;

(71) Whereas this Directive does not stand in the way of a Member State's regulating marketing activities aimed at consumers residing in territory in so far as such regulation does not concern the protection of individuals with regard to the processing of personal data;

(72) Whereas this Directive allows the principle of public access to official documents to be taken into account when implementing the principles set out in this Directive,

HAVE ADOPTED THIS DIRECTIVE:

Chapter I

General Provisions

Object of the Directive

1.—1. In accordance with this Directive, Member States shall protect the fundamental rights and freedoms of natural persons, and in particular their right to privacy with respect to the processing of personal data.

2. Member States shall neither restrict nor prohibit the free flow of personal data between Member States for reasons connected with the protection afforded under paragraph 1.

Definitions

2.—For the purposes of this Directive:

(a) "personal data" shall mean any information relating to an identified or identifiable natural person ("data subject"); an identifiable person is one who can be identified, directly or indirectly, in particular by reference to an identification number or to one or more factors specific to his physical, physiological, mental, economic, cultural or social identity;

(b) "processing of personal data" ("processing") shall mean any operation or set of operations which is performed upon personal data, whether or not by automatic means, such as collection, recording, organisation, storage, adaptation or alteration, retrieval, consultation, use, disclosure by transmission, dissemination or otherwise making available, alignment or combination, blocking, erasure or destruction;

(c) "personal data filing system" ("filing system") shall mean any structured set of personal data which are accessible according to specific criteria, whether centralised, decentralised or dispersed on a functional or geographical basis;

(d) "controller" shall mean the natural or legal person, public authority, agency or any other body which alone or jointly with others determines the purposes and means of the processing of personal data; where the purposes and means of processing are determined by national or Community laws or regulations, the controller or the specific criteria for his nomination may be designated by national or Community law;

(e) "processor" shall mean a natural or legal person, public authority, agency or any other body which processes personal data on behalf of the controller;

(f) "third party" shall mean any natural or legal person, public authority, agency or any other body other than the data subject, the controller, the processor and the persons who, under the direct authority of the controller or the processor, are authorised to process the data;

(g) "recipient" shall mean a natural or legal person, public authority, agency or any other body to whom data are disclosed, whether a third party or not; however, authorities which may receive data in the framework of a particular inquiry shall not be regarded as recipients;

(h) "the data subject"s consent" shall mean any freely given specific and informed indication of his wishes by which the data subject signifies his agreement to personal data relating to him being processed.

Scope

3.—1. This Directive shall apply to the processing of personal data wholly or partly by automatic means, and to the processing otherwise than by automatic means of personal data which form part of a filing system or are intended to form part of a filing system.

2. This Directive shall not apply to the processing of personal data:

— in the course of an activity which falls outside the scope of Community law, such as those provided for by Titles V and VI of the Treaty on European Union and in any case to processing operations concerning public security, defence, State security (including the economic well-being of the State when the processing operation relates to State security matters) and the activities of the State in areas of criminal law,

— by a natural person in the course of a purely personal or household activity.

National law applicable

4.—1. Each Member State shall apply the national provisions it adopts pursuant to this Directive to the processing of personal data where:

(a) the processing is carried out in the context of the activities of an establishment of the controller on the territory of the Member State; when the same controller is established on the territory of several Member States, he must take the necessary measures to ensure that each of these establishments complies with the obligations laid down by the national law applicable;

(b) the controller is not established on the Member State's territory, but in a place where its national law applies by virtue of international public law;

(c) the controller is not established on Community territory and, for purposes of processing personal data makes use of equipment, automated or otherwise, situated on the territory of the said Member State, unless such equipment is used only for purposes of transit through the territory of the Community.

2. In the circumstances referred to in paragraph 1(c), the controller must designate a representative established in the territory of that Member State, without prejudice to legal actions which could be initiated against the controller himself.

CHAPTER II

GENERAL RULES ON THE LAWFULNESS OF THE PROCESSING OF PERSONAL DATA

5.—Member States shall, within the limits of the provisions of this Chapter, determine more precisely the conditions under which the processing of personal data is lawful.

Section I—Principles relating to data quality

6.—1. Member States shall provide that personal data must be:

(a) processed fairly and lawfully;
(b) collected for specified, explicit and legitimate purposes and not further processed in a way incompatible with those purposes. Further processing of data for historical, statistical or scientific purposes shall not be considered as incompatible provided that Member States provide appropriate safeguards;
(c) adequate, relevant and not excessive in relation to the purposes for which they are collected and/or further processed;
(d) accurate and, where necessary, kept up to date; every reasonable step must be taken to ensure that data which are inaccurate or incomplete, having regard to the purposes for which they were collected or for which they are further processed, are erased or rectified;
(e) kept in a form which permits identification of data subjects for no longer than is necessary for the purposes for which the data were collected or for which they are further processed. Member States shall lay down appropriate safeguards for personal data stored for longer periods for historical, statistical or scientific use.

2. It shall be for the controller to ensure that paragraph 1 is complied with.

Section II—Criteria for making data processing legitimate

7.—Member States shall provide that personal data may be processed only if:

(a) the data subject has unambiguously given his consent; or
(b) processing is necessary for the performance of a contract to which the data subject is party or in order to take steps at the request of the data subject prior to entering into a contract; or
(c) processing is necessary for compliance with a legal obligation to which the controller is subject; or
(d) processing is necessary in order to protect the vital interests of the data subject; or
(e) processing is necessary for the performance of a task carried out in the public interest or in the exercise of official authority vested in the controller or in a third party to whom the data are disclosed; or
(f) processing is necessary for the purposes of the legitimate interests pursued by the controller or by the third party or parties to whom the data are disclosed, except where such interests are overridden by the interests for fundamental rights and freedoms of the data subject which require protection under Article 1(1).

Section III—Special categories of processing

The processing of special categories of data

8.—1. Member States shall prohibit the processing of personal data revealing racial or ethnic origin, political opinions, religious or philosophical beliefs, trade-union membership, and the processing of data concerning health or sex life.

2. Paragraph 1 shall not apply where:

(a) the data subject has given his explicit consent to the processing of those data, except where the laws of the Member State provide that the prohibition referred to in paragraph 1 may not be lifted by the data subject's giving his consent; or
(b) processing is necessary for the purposes of carrying out the obligations and specific rights of the controller in the field of employment law in so far as it is authorised by national law providing for adequate safeguards; or
(c) processing is necessary to protect the vital interests of the data subject or of another person where the data subject is physically or legally incapable of giving his consent; or
(d) processing is carried out in the course of its legitimate activities with appropriate guarantees by a foundation, association or any other non-profit-seeking body with a political, philosophical, religious or trade-union aim and on condition that the processing relates solely to the members of the body or to persons who have regular contact with it in connection with its purposes and that the data are not disclosed to a third party without the consent of the data subjects; or
(e) the processing relates to data which are manifestly made public by the data subject or is necessary for the establishment, exercise or defence of legal claims.

3. Paragraph 1 shall not apply where processing of the data is required for the purposes of preventive medicine, medical diagnosis, the provision of care or treatment or the management of health-care services, and where those data are processed by a health professional subject under national law or rules established by national competent bodies to the obligation of professional secrecy or by another person also subject to an equivalent obligation of secrecy.

4. Subject to the provision of suitable safeguards, Member States may, for reasons of substantial public interest, lay down exemptions in addition to those laid down in paragraph 2 either by national law or by decision of the supervisory authority.

5. Processing of data relating to offences, criminal convictions or security measures may be carried out only under the control of official authority, or if suitable specific safeguards are provided under national law, subject to derogations which may be granted by the Member State under national provisions providing suitable specific safeguards. However, a complete register of criminal convictions may be kept only under the control of official authority.

Member States may provide that data relating to administrative sanctions or judgements in civil cases shall also be processed under the control of official authority.

6. Derogations from paragraph 1 provided for in paragraphs 4 and 5 shall be notified to the Commission.

7. Member States shall determine the conditions under which a national identification number or any other identifier of general application may be processed.

Processing of personal data and freedom of expression

9.—Member States shall provide for exemptions or derogations from the provisions of this Chapter, Chapter IV and Chapter VI for the processing of personal data carried out solely for journalistic purposes or the purpose of artistic or literary expression only if they are necessary to reconcile the right to privacy with the rules governing freedom of expression.

Section IV—Information to be given to the data subject

Information in cases of collection of data from the data subject

10.—Member States shall provide that the controller or his representative must provide a data subject from whom data relating to himself are collected with at least the following information, except where he already has it:

(a) the identity of the controller and of his representative, if any;
(b) the purposes of the processing for which the data are intended;
(c) any further information such as

— the recipients or categories of recipients of the data,
— whether replies to the questions are obligatory or voluntary, as well as the possible consequences of failure to reply,
— the existence of the right of access to and the right to rectify the data concerning him

in so far as such further information is necessary, having regard to the specific circumstances in which the data are collected, to guarantee fair processing in respect of the data subject.

Information where the data have not been obtained from the data subject

11.—1. Where the data have not been obtained from the data subject, Member States shall provide that the controller or his representative must at the time of undertaking the recording of personal data or if a disclosure to a third party is envisaged, no later than the time when the data are first disclosed provide the data subject with at least the following information, except where he already has it:

(a) the identity of the controller and of his representative, if any;
(b) the purposes of the processing;
(c) any further information such as

— the categories of data concerned,
— the recipients or categories of recipients,
— the existence of the right of access to and the right to rectify the data concerning him

in so far as such further information is necessary, having regard to the specific circumstances in which the data are processed, to guarantee fair processing in respect of the data subject.

2. Paragraph 1 shall not apply where, in particular for processing for statistical purposes or for the purposes of historical or scientific research, the provision of such information proves impossible or would involve a disproportionate effort or if recording or disclosure is expressly laid down by law. In these cases Member States shall provide appropriate safeguards.

Section V—The data subject's right of access to data

Right of access

12.—Member States shall guarantee every data subject the right to obtain from the controller:

(a) without constraint at reasonable intervals and without excessive delay or expense:

— confirmation as to whether or not data relating to him are being processed and information at least as to the purposes of the processing, the categories of data concerned, and the recipients or categories of recipients to whom the data are disclosed,

— communication to him in an intelligible form of the data undergoing processing and of any available information as to their source,

— knowledge of the logic involved in any automatic processing of data concerning him at least in the case of the automated decisions referred to in Article 15(1);

(b) as appropriate the rectification, erasure or blocking of data the processing of which does not comply with the provisions of this Directive, in particular because of the incomplete or inaccurate nature of the data;

(c) notification to third parties to whom the data have been disclosed of any rectification, erasure or blocking carried out in compliance with (b), unless this proves impossible or involves a disproportionate effort.

Section VI—Exemptions and restrictions

Exemptions and restrictions

13.—1. Member States may adopt legislative measures to restrict the scope of the obligations and rights provided for in Articles 6(1), 10, 11 (1), 12 and 21 when such a restriction constitutes a necessary measures to safeguard:

(a) national security;
(b) defence;
(c) public security;
(d) the prevention, investigation, detection and prosecution of criminal offences, or of breaches of ethics for regulated professions;
(e) an important economic or financial interest of a Member State or of the European Union, including monetary, budgetary and taxation matters;
(f) a monitoring, inspection or regulatory function connected, even occasionally, with the exercise of official authority in cases referred to in (c), (d) and (e);
(g) the protection of the data subject or of the rights and freedoms of others.

2. Subject to adequate legal safeguards, in particular that the data are not used for taking measures or decisions regarding any particular individual, Member States may, where there is clearly no risk of breaching the privacy of the data subject, restrict by a legislative measure the rights provided for in Article 12 when data are processed solely for purposes of scientific research or are kept in personal form for a period which does not exceed the period necessary for the sole purpose of creating statistics.

Section VII—The data subject's right ot object

The data subject's right to object

14.—Member States shall grant the data subject the right:

(a) at least in the cases referred to in Article 7(e) and (f), to object at any time on compelling legitimate grounds relating to his particular situation to the processing of data relating to him, save where otherwise provided by national legislation. Where there is a justified objection, the processing instigated by the controller may no longer involve those data;

(b) to object, on request and free of charge, to the processing of personal data relating to him which the controller anticipates being processed for the purposes of direct marketing, or to be informed before personal data are disclosed for the first time to third parties or used on their behalf for the purposes of direct marketing, and to be expressly offered the right to object free of charge to such disclosures or uses.

Member States shall take the necessary measures to ensure that data subjects are aware of the existence of the right referred to in the first subparagraph of (b).

Automated individual decisions

15.—1. Member States shall grant the right to every person not to be subject to a decision which produces legal effects concerning him or significantly affects him and which is based solely on automated processing of data intended to evaluate certain personal aspects relating to him, such as his performance at work, creditworthiness, reliability, conduct, etc.

2. Subject to the other Articles of this Directive, Member States shall provide that a person may be subjected to a decision of the kind referred to in paragraph 1 if that decision:

(a) is taken in the course of the entering into or performance of a contract, provided the request for the entering into or the performance of the contract, lodged by the data subject, has been satisfied or that there are suitable measures to safeguard his legitimate interests, such as arrangements allowing him to put his point of view; or

(b) is authorised by a law which also lays down measures to safeguard the data subject's legitimate interests.

Section VIII—Confidentiality and security of processing

Confidentiality of processing

16.—Any person acting under the authority of the controller or of the processor, including the processor himself, who has access to personal data must not process them except on instructions from the controller, unless he is required to do so by law.

Security of processing

17.—1. Member States shall provide that the controller must implement appropriate technical and organisational measures to protect personal data against accidental or unlawful destruction or accidental loss, alteration, unauthorised disclosure or access, in particular where the processing involves the transmission of data over a network, and against all other unlawful forms of processing.

Having regard to the state of the art and the cost of their implementation, such measures shall ensure a level of security appropriate to the risks represented by the processing and the nature of the data to be protected.

2. The Member States shall provide that the controller must, where processing is carried out on his behalf, choose a processor providing sufficient guarantees in respect of the technical security measures and organisational measures governing the processing to be carried out, and must ensure compliance with those measures.

3. The carrying out of processing by way of a processor must be governed by a contract or legal act binding the processor to the controller and stipulating in particular that:

— the processor shall act only on instructions from the controller,
— the obligations set out in paragraph 1, as defined by the law of the Member State in which the processor is established, shall also be incumbent on the processor.

4. For the purposes of keeping proof, the parts of the contract or the legal act relating to data protection and the requirements relating to the measures referred to in paragraph 1 shall be in writing or in another equivalent form.

Section IX—Notification

Obligation to notify the supervisory authority

18.—1. Member States shall provide that the controller or his representative, if any, must notify the supervisory authority referred to in Article 28 before carrying out any wholly or partly automatic processing operation or set of such operations intended to serve a single purpose or several related purposes.

2. Member States may provide for the simplification of or exemption from notification only in the following cases and under the following conditions:

— where, for categories of processing operations which are unlikely, taking account of the data to be processed, to affect adversely the rights and freedoms of data subjects, they specify the purposes of the processing, the data or categories of data undergoing processing, the category or categories of data subject, the recipients or categories of recipient to whom the data are to be disclosed and the length of time the data are to be stored, and/or
— where the controller, in compliance with the national law which governs him, appoints a personal data protection official, responsible in particular:
— for ensuring in an independent manner the internal application of the national provisions taken pursuant to this Directive
— for keeping the register of processing operations carried out by the controller, containing the items of information referred to in Article 21 (2),

thereby ensuring that the rights and freedoms of the data subjects are unlikely to be adversely affected by the processing operations.

3. Member States may provide that paragraph 1 does not apply to processing whose sole purpose is the keeping of a register which according to laws or regulations is intended to provide information to the public and which is open to consultation either by the public in general or by any person demonstrating a legitimate interest.

4. Member States may provide for an exemption from the obligation to notify or a simplification of the notification in the case of processing operations referred to in Article 8(2)(d).

5. Member States may stipulate that certain or all non-automatic processing operations involving personal data shall be notified, or provide for these processing operations to be subject to simplified notification.

Contents of notification

19.—1. Member States shall specify the information to be given in the notification. It shall include at least:

(a) the name and address of the controller and of his representative, if any;
(b) the purpose or purposes of the processing;
(c) a description of the category or categories of data subject and of the data or categories of data relating to them;
(d) the recipients or categories of recipient to whom the data might be disclosed;
(e) proposed transfers of data to third countries;
(f) a general description allowing a preliminary assessment to be made of the appropriateness of the measures taken pursuant to Article 17 to ensure security of processing.

2. Member States shall specify the procedures under which any change affecting the information referred to in paragraph 1 must be notified to the supervisory authority.

Prior checking

20.—1. Member States shall determine the processing operations likely to present specific risks to the rights and freedoms of data subjects and shall check that these processing operations are examined prior to the start thereof.

2. Such prior checks shall be carried out by the supervisory authority following receipt of a notification from the controller or by the data protection official, who, in cases of doubt, must consult the supervisory authority.

3. Member States may also carry out such checks in the context of preparation either of a measure of the national parliament or of a measure based on such a legislative measure, which define the nature of the processing and lay down appropriate safeguards.

Publicising of processing operations

21.—1. Member States shall take measures to ensure that processing operations are publicised.

2. Member States shall provide that a register of processing operations notified in accordance with Article 18 shall be kept by the supervisory authority.

The register shall contain at least the information listed in Article 19(1)(a) to (e).

The register may be inspected by any person.

3. Member States shall provide, in relation to processing operations not subject to notification, that controllers or another body appointed by the Member States make available at least the information referred to in Article 19(1)(a) to (e) in an appropriate form to any person on request.

Member States may provide that this provision does not apply to processing whose sole purpose is the keeping of a register which according to laws or regulations is intended to provide information to the public and which is open to consultation either by the public in general or by any person who can provide proof of a legitimate interest.

CHAPTER III

JUDICIAL REMEDIES, LIABILITY AND SANCTIONS

Remedies

22.—Without prejudice to any administrative remedy for which provision may be made, inter alia before the supervisory authority referred to in Article 28, prior to referral to the judicial authority, Member States shall provide for the right of every person to a judicial remedy for any breach of the rights guaranteed him by the national law applicable to the processing in question.

Liability

23.—1. Member States shall provide that any person who has suffered damage as a result of an unlawful processing operation or of any act incompatible with the national provisions adopted pursuant to this Directive is entitled to receive compensation from the controller for the damage suffered.

2. The controller may be exempted from this liability, in whole or in part, if he proves that he is not responsible for the event giving rise to the damage.

Sanctions

24.—The Member States shall adopt suitable measures to ensure the full implementation of the provisions of this Directive and shall in particular lay down the sanctions to be imposed in case of infringement of the provisions adopted pursuant to this Directive.

CHAPTER IV

TRANSFER OF PERSONAL DATA TO THIRD COUNTRIES

Principles

25.—1. The Member States shall provide that the transfer to a third country of personal data which are undergoing processing or are intended for processing after transfer may take place only if, without prejudice to compliance with the national provisions adopted pursuant to the other provisions of this Directive, the third country in question ensures an adequate level of protection.

2. The adequacy of the level of protection afforded by a third country shall be assessed in the light of all the circumstances surrounding a data transfer operation or set of data transfer operations; particular consideration shall be given to the nature of the data, the purpose and duration of the proposed processing operation or operations, the country of origin and country of final destination, the rules of law, both general and sectoral, in force in the third country in question and the professional rules and security measures which are complied with in that country.

3. The Member States and the Commission shall inform each other of cases where they consider that a third country does not ensure an adequate level of protection within the meaning of paragraph 2.

4. Where the Commission finds, under the procedure provided for in Article 31(2), that a third country does not ensure an adequate level of protection within the meaning of paragraph 2 of this Article, Member States shall take the measures necessary to prevent any transfer of data of the same type to the third country in question.

5. At the appropriate time, the Commission shall enter into negotiations with a view to remedying the situation resulting from the finding made pursuant to paragraph 4.

6. The Commission may find, in accordance with the procedure referred to in Article 31(2), that a third country ensures an adequate level of protection within the meaning of paragraph 2 of this Article, by reason of its domestic law or of the international commitments it has entered into, particularly upon conclusion of the negotiations referred to in paragraph 5, for the protection of the private lives and basic freedoms and rights of individuals.

Member States shall take the measures necessary to comply with the Commission's decision.

Derogations

26.—1. By way of derogation from Article 25 and save where otherwise provided by domestic law governing particular cases, Member States shall provide that a transfer or a set of transfers of personal data to a third country which does not ensure an adequate level of protection within the meaning of Article 25(2) may take place on condition that:

(a) the data subject has given his consent unambiguously to the proposed transfer; or
(b) the transfer is necessary for the performance of a contract between the data subject and the controller or the implementation of precontractual measures taken in response to the data subject"s request; or
(c) the transfer is necessary for the conclusion or performance of a contract concluded in the interest of the data subject between the controller and a third party; or
(d) the transfer is necessary or legally required on important public interest grounds, or for the establishment, exercise or defence of legal claims; or
(e) the transfer is necessary in order to protect the vital interests of the data subject; or
(f) the transfer is made from a register which according to laws or regulations is intended to provide information to the public and which is open to consultation either by the public in general or by any person who can demonstrate legitimate interest, to the extent that the conditions laid down in law for consultation are fulfilled in the particular case.

2. Without prejudice to paragraph 1, a Member State may authorize a transfer or a set of transfers of personal data to a third country which does not ensure an adequate level of protection within the meaning of Article 25 (2), where the controller adduces adequate safeguards with respect to the protection of the privacy and fundamental rights and freedoms of individuals and as regards the exercise of the corresponding rights; such safeguards may in particular result from appropriate contractual clauses.

3. The Member State shall inform the Commission and the other Member States of the authorisations it grants pursuant to paragraph 2.

If a Member State or the Commission objects on justified grounds involving the protection of the privacy and fundamental rights and freedoms of individuals, the Commission shall take appropriate measures in accordance with the procedure laid down in Article 31(2).

Member States shall take the necessary measures to comply with the Commission's decision.

4. Where the Commission decides, in accordance with the procedure referred to in Article 31(2), that certain standard contractual clauses offer sufficient safeguards as

required by paragraph 2, Member States shall take the necessary measures to comply with the Commission's decision.

CHAPTER V

CODES OF CONDUCT

27.—1. The Member States and the Commission shall encourage the drawing up of codes of conduct intended to contribute to the proper implementation of the national provisions adopted by the Member States pursuant to this Directive, taking account of the specific features of the various sectors.

2. Member States shall make provision for trade associations and other bodies representing other categories of controllers which have drawn up draft national codes or which have the intention of amending or extending existing national codes to be able to submit them to the opinion of the national authority.

Member States shall make provision for this authority to ascertain, among other things, whether the drafts submitted to it are in accordance with the national provisions adopted pursuant to this Directive. If it sees fit, the authority shall seek the views of data subjects or their representatives.

3. Draft Community codes, and amendments or extensions to existing Community codes, may be submitted to the Working Party referred to in Article 29. This Working Party shall determine, among other things, whether the drafts submitted to it are in accordance with the national provisions adopted pursuant to this Directive. If it sees fit, the authority shall seek the views of data subjects or their representatives. The Commission may ensure appropriate publicity for the codes which have been approved by the Working Party.

CHAPTER VI

SUPERVISORY AUTHORITY AND WORKING PARTY ON THE PROTECTION OF INDIVIDUALS WITH REGARD TO THE PROCESSING OF PERSONAL DATA

Supervisory authority

28.—1. Each Member State shall provide that one or more public authorities are responsible for monitoring the application within its territory of the provisions adopted by the Member States pursuant to this Directive.

These authorities shall act with complete independence in exercising the functions entrusted to them.

2. Each Member State shall provide that the supervisory authorities are consulted when drawing up administrative measures or regulations relating to the protection of individuals' rights and freedoms with regard to the processing of personal data.

3. Each authority shall in particular be endowed with:

— investigative powers, such as powers of access to data forming the subject-matter of processing operations and powers to collect all the information necessary for the performance of its supervisory duties,

— effective powers of intervention, such as, for example, that of delivering opinions before processing operations are carried out, in accordance with Article 20, and ensuring appropriate publication of such opinions, of ordering the blocking, erasure or destruction of data, of imposing a temporary or definitive ban on processing, of warning or admonishing the controller, or that of referring the matter to national parliaments or other political institutions,
— the power to engage in legal proceedings where the national provisions adopted pursuant to this Directive have been violated or to bring these violations to the attention of the judicial authorities.

Decisions by the supervisory authority which give rise to complaints may be appealed against through the courts.

4. Each supervisory authority shall hear claims lodged by any person, or by an association representing that person, concerning the protection of his rights and freedoms in regard to the processing of personal data. The person concerned shall be informed of the outcome of the claim.

Each supervisory authority shall, in particular, hear claims for checks on the lawfulness of data processing lodged by any person when the national provisions adopted pursuant to Article 13 of this Directive apply. The person shall at any rate be informed that a check has taken place.

5. Each supervisory authority shall draw up a report on its activities at regular intervals. The report shall be made public.

6. Each supervisory authority is competent, whatever the national law applicable to the processing in question, to exercise, on the territory of its own Member State, the powers conferred on it in accordance with paragraph 3. Each authority may be requested to exercise its powers by an authority of another Member State.

The supervisory authorities shall cooperate with one another to the extent necessary for the performance of their duties, in particular by exchanging all useful information.

7. Member States shall provide that the members and staff of the supervisory authority, even after their employment has ended, are to be subject to a duty of professional secrecy with regard to confidential information to which they have access.

Working Party on the Protection of Individuals with regard to the Processing of Personal Data

29.—1. A Working Party on the Protection of Individuals with regard to the Processing of Personal Data, hereinafter referred to as "the Working Party", is hereby set up.

It shall have advisory status and act independently.

2. The Working Party shall be composed of a representative of the supervisory authority or authorities designated by each Member State and of a representative of the authority or authorities established for the Community institutions and bodies, and of a representative of the Commission.

Each member of the Working Party shall be designated by the institution, authority or authorities which he represents. Where a Member State has designated more than one supervisory authority, they shall nominate a joint representative. The same shall apply to the authorities established for Community institutions and bodies.

3. The Working Party shall take decisions by a simple majority of the representatives of the supervisory authorities.

4. The Working Party shall elect its chairman. The chairman's term of office shall be two years. His appointment shall be renewable.

5. The Working Party's secretariat shall be provided by the Commission.

6. The Working Party shall adopt its own rules of procedure.

7. The Working Party shall consider items placed on its agenda by its chairman, either on his own initiative or at the request of a representative of the supervisory authorities or at the Commission's request.

30.—1. The Working Party shall:

(a) examine any question covering the application of the national measures adopted under this Directive in order to contribute to the uniform application of such measures;
(b) give the Commission an opinion on the level of protection in the Community and in third countries;
(c) advise the Commission on any proposed amendment of this Directive, on any additional or specific measures to safeguard the rights and freedoms of natural persons with regard to the processing of personal data and on any other proposed Community measures affecting such rights and freedoms;
(d) give an opinion on codes of conduct drawn up at Community level.

2. If the Working Party finds that divergences likely to affect the equivalence of protection for persons with regard to the processing of personal data in the Community are arising between the laws or practices of Member States, it shall inform the Commission accordingly.

3. The Working Party may, on its own initiative, make recommendations on all matters relating to the protection of persons with regard to the processing of personal data in the Community.

4. The Working Party's opinions and recommendations shall be forwarded to the Commission and to the committee referred to in Article 31.

5. The Commission shall inform the Working Party of the action it has taken in response to its opinions and recommendations. It shall do so in a report which shall also be forwarded to the European Parliament and the Council. The report shall be made public.

6. The Working Party shall draw up an annual report on the situation regarding the protection of natural persons with regard to the processing of personal data in the Community and in third countries, which it shall transmit to the Commission, the European Parliament and the Council. The report shall be made public.

CHAPTER VII

COMMUNITY IMPLEMENTING MEASURES

Committee

31.—1. The Commission shall be assisted by a committee composed of the representatives of the Member States and chaired by the representative of the Commission.

2. The representative of the Commission shall submit to the committee a draft of the measures to be taken. The committee shall deliver its opinion on the draft within a time limit which the chairman may lay down according to the urgency of the matter.

The opinion shall be delivered by the majority laid down in Article 148(2) of the Treaty. The votes of the representatives of the Member States within the committee shall be weighted in the manner set out in that Article. The chairman shall not vote.

The Commission shall adopt measures which shall apply immediately. However, if these measures are not in accordance with the opinion of the committee, they shall be communicated by the Commission to the Council forthwith. It that event:

— the Commission shall defer application of the measures which it has decided for a period of three months from the date of communication,
— the Council, acting by a qualified majority, may take a different decision within the time limit referred to in the first indent.

FINAL PROVISIONS

32.—1. Member States shall bring into force the laws, regulations and administrative provisions necessary to comply with this Directive at the latest at the end of a period of three years from the date of its adoption.

When Member States adopt these measures, they shall contain a reference to this Directive or be accompanied by such reference on the occasion of their official publication. The methods of making such reference shall be laid down by the Member States.

2. Member States shall ensure that processing already under way on the date the national provisions adopted pursuant to this Directive enter into force, is brought into conformity with these provisions within three years of this date.

By way of derogation from the preceding subparagraph, Member States may provide that the processing of data already held in manual filing systems on the date of entry into force of the national provisions adopted in implementation of this Directive shall be brought into conformity with Articles 6, 7 and 8 of this Directive within 12 years of the date on which it is adopted. Member States shall, however, grant the data subject the right to obtain, at his request and in particular at the time of exercising his right of access, the rectification, erasure or blocking of data which are incomplete, inaccurate or stored in a way incompatible with the legitimate purposes pursued by the controller.

3. By way of derogation from paragraph 2, Member States may provide, subject to suitable safeguards, that data kept for the sole purpose of historical research need not be brought into conformity with Articles 6, 7 and 8 of this Directive.

4. Member States shall communicate to the Commission the text of the provisions of domestic law which they adopt in the field covered by this Directive.

33.—The Commission shall report to the Council and the European Parliament at regular intervals, starting not later than three years after the date referred to in Article 32(1), on the implementation of this Directive, attaching to its report, if necessary, suitable proposals for amendments. The report shall be made public.

The Commission shall examine, in particular, the application of this Directive to the data processing of sound and image data relating to natural persons and shall submit any appropriate proposals which prove to be necessary, taking account of developments in information technology and in the light of the state of progress in the information society.

34.—This Directive is addressed to the Member States.

Done at Luxembourg, October 24, 1995.

For the European Parliament
The President
K. HAENSCH

For the Council
The President
L. ATIENZA SERNA

APPENDIX B

Precedents

APPENDIX B

Precedents

Precedent 1

Standard, simple request under the Freedom of Information Act 2000

Request for information made under the Freedom of Information Act 2000

TO: Department of Environment Food and Rural Affairs
Attention: The Freedom of Information Unit or Officer
Nobel House
17 Smith Square
London
SW1P 3JR

APPLICANT: John Citizen

ADDRESS FOR CORRESPONDENCE:
123 Birdcage Walk
London
SW1A 6BD
Tel: 020–7654 3210
Fax: 020–7654 3201
e-mail: jc@world.co.uk

DESCRIPTION OF THE INFORMATION REQUESTED:

1. All information taken into account by the Minister in making his decision on or about January 1, 2005 under under reg.5(5)(a) of the Control of Pesticides Regulations Act 1986 to suspend the authorisation of ABC Chemical UK Limited for one of its products (dichlorvos)(**"the Decision"**).
2. To the extent not covered by 1., all information taken into account by any person within the Department involved with advising (whether directly or indirectly) the Minister in relation to the Decision.
3. To the extent not covered by 1. or 2., all other information held by the Department relating to the authorisation of ABC Chemical UK Limited for dichlorvos.

PREFERRED MEANS OF COMMUNICATION:
Provision of a copy of the information in printed form.

DATE OF THIS REQUEST:
Tuesday February 1, 2005

FURTHER INFORMATION:

1. In the event that you believe that information or more information answering the terms of this request is held by another public authority, please advise by return but continue to process this request in relation to all information answering the terms of the request held by you.
2. This request is considered to be perfectly clear. In the event, however, that you require further information in order to identify and locate the information requested, please advise by return.

SIGNED:...
John Citizen

Notes:

1. The request illustrates that the applicant does not need to demonstrate any interest in the subject matter of the request. Requests such as this can readily be adapted as a form of pre-action disclosure to consider whether judicial review proceedings should be instituted.
2. Useful addresses can be found at *http://www.tagish.co.uk/links/*.
3. The request should nominate a body which is a public authority within the meaning of the Act. Identification of the most suitable public authority is important as the obligation is upon that public authority to disclose information that it (and not any other public authority) holds. A public authority may transfer the request if it relates to information that it does not hold but which it believes is held by another public authority: see paras 11–032 to 11–033.
4. It is not essential to include telephone or fax numbers nor an e-mail address. However, provision of these may speed up matters where the public authority claims that it requires further information from the Applicant in order to identify and locate the information requested.
5. The description of the information requested is very important. It must be as precise as possible. Although it has not been done in this example, it will often be sensible to limit the information by date in some way. Where various sorts of information is sought, it is prudent to enumerate the information in separate paragraphs, each as precise as possible, as this will help to prevent the whole request being found vexatious and will facilitate severance of its parts in the event that the costs of compliance will involve exceeding the appropriate limit.
6. It is not essential to specify the preferred means of communication, but if it is specified then the public authority must, so far as reasonably practicable, give effect to the preference. Section 11(1) sets out the three means of communication. It is permissible to select more than one means of communication.
7. The Further Information section is entirely optional. It is included in order to maximise the chances of a helpful response.

Precedent 2

Request under the Freedom of Information Act 2000 where a qualified exemption is likely to be relied upon

Request for information made under the Freedom of Information Act 2000

TO: The Attorney-General
c/- The Legal Secretariat to the Law Officers
Attorney General's Chambers
9 Buckingham Gate
London
SW1E 6JP

APPLICANT: John Citizen

ADDRESS FOR CORRESPONDENCE:
123 Birdcage Walk
London
SW1A 6BD
Tel: 020–7654 3210
Fax: 020–7654 3201
e-mail: jc@world.co.uk

DESCRIPTION OF THE INFORMATION REQUESTED:

1. Any legal advice drafted, sent or received in the period September 1, 2002 to April 30, 2003 (inclusive) relating to or dealing with the legal basis for the use of force against Iraq.
2. Any request made in the period September 1, 2002 to April 30, 2003 (inclusive) for the provision of any such advice.

PREFERRED MEANS OF COMMUNICATION:
Provision of a copy of the information in printed form.

DATE OF THIS REQUEST:
Tuesday, February 1, 2005

FURTHER INFORMATION:

1. In the event that you believe that information or more information answering the terms of this request is held by another public authority, please advise by return but continue to process this request in relation to all information answering the terms of the request held by you.
2. This request is considered to be perfectly clear. In the event, however, that you require further information in order to identify and locate the information requested, please advise by return.
3. There is an overwhelming public interest in disclosing the information requested:
   (1) The information will assist in informed discussion on an issue of fundamental public importance.
   (2) In March 2003, the Attorney-General provided a written answer in the House of Lords to the effect that authority to use force against Iraq existed

from the combined effect of three UN Resolutions, each of which was adopted under Chapter VII of the UN Charter. It is in the public interest to see that the answer provided was an accurate summary of the totality of the advice that had been given on the issue.

SIGNED:...
John Citizen

Notes:

1. Any refusal of this request would almost certainly rely on section 35(1) and/or section 42, both of which are qualified exemptions. Although an applicant is not obliged to spell out the public interest in disclosure of the information requested, it is considered that where reliance upon a qualified exemption is predictable and it is possible to identify aspects of the public interest in disclosure, these should be included in order to maximise the prospects of success.

Precedent 3

Request under the Data Protection Act 1998 for personal information relating to the applicant

Request for data made under section 7 of the Data Protection Act 1998

TO: Westminster City Council
Attention: The Data Controller for the purposes of the Data Protection Act 1998
P.O. Box 240
Westminster City Hall
64 Victoria Street
London
SW1E 6QP

APPLICANT: John Citizen

ADDRESS FOR CORRESPONDENCE:
123 Birdcage Walk
London
SW1A 6BD
Tel: 020–7654 3210
Fax: 020–7654 3201
e-mail: jc@world.co.uk

REQUEST:
Pursuant to section 7 of the Data Protection Act 1998, you are hereby required:

(1) to inform me whether personal data of which I am the data subject are being processed by or on behalf of you;
(2) if "yes" to (1), to give me a description of:
    (a) the personal data of which I am the data subject;
    (b) the purposes for which those data are being or are to be processed; and
    (c) the recipients or classes or recipients to whom those data are or may be disclosed;
(3) to communicate to me in an intelligible form:
    (a) the information constituting any personal data of which I am the data subject; and
    (b) any information available to you as to the source of those data; and
(4) to inform me of the logic involved in any decision-taking significantly affecting me.

PREFERRED MEANS OF RECEIPT OF INFORMATION:
Please provide the data in printed form.

DATE OF THIS REQUEST:
Tuesday, February 1, 2005

CHEQUE ENCLOSED:
A cheque in the sum of £10 (ten pounds) made payable to Westminster City Council is enclosed.

FURTHER INFORMATION:

1. I have signed this document and enclosed a personal cheque as proof of my identity. Although I consider that these a perfectly adequate evidence of my identity, should you feel the need for further proof, please advise me by return.
2. This request is considered to be perfectly clear. In the event, however, that you require further information in order to locate the information requested, please advise by return.
3. To the extent that compliance with this request would disclose information relating to another individual and that individual can be identified from that information and that individual has not consented to the disclosure of the information to me, please redact just that part of the information from which that individual can be identified.

SIGNED:...

John Citizen

APPENDIX C

Dealing with a request for information under the *Freedom of Information Act 2000*

TIME LIMITS

APPENDIX C

Dealing with a Request for Information under the Freedom of Information Act 2000

Time limits

1. Step 1 to Step 5 (inclusive) must, as a general rule, be complied with promptly and in any event not later than the twentieth working-day following the "date of receipt" of the request. The time-limit will be deferred in certain circumstances (see 11–022 to 11–027 and 11–029).
2. Step 6 to Step 9 (inclusive), if not already complied with at the same time as Step 5, must as a general rule thereafter be complied with within such time as is reasonable in the circumstances (see 11–028 to 11–029).

Step 1 Determining whether the request is a valid request.

1. The recipient of the request must be a "public authority" to which the FOI Act applies (see 7–016 to 7–028 and 17–009 to 17–025).
2. The request must:

   — be in writing;
   — state the name of the applicant;
   — state an address for correspondence; and
   — describe the information requested (see 11–001 to 11–008).

   If there are formal details missing, the recipient public authority may have to help the applicant as part of its duty to advise and assist (see 8–004(4) and 11–010).
3. The request must be adequately particularised in order to enable the recipient public authority to identify and locate the information. If it is not adequately particularised, the public authority is not obliged to provide the information (see 11–011 to 11–012) nor otherwise to deal with the request (see 13–002(1)). The public authority may be obliged to assist the applicant adequately particularise the request (see 8–004(4) and 11–010).
4. The public authority should determine whether the cost of compliance with the request would be excessive (see 12–001 to 12–007 and 13–002(4)). As to the form of the refusal notice if the cost of compliance is excessive, see 13–008. The public authority may be obliged to assist the applicant in these circumstances (see 8–002 to 8–004).

5. The public authority should determine whether the request is vexatious (see 12–008 to 12–009 and 13–002(2)). As to the form of the refusal notice if the request is vexatious, see 13–007.
6. The public authority should determine whether the request is a repeat request (see 12–011 to 12–014 and 13–002(2)). As to the form of the refusal notice if it is a repeat request, see 13–007. As to the cumulative cost of compliance, see 12–005.
7. The identity and motive of the applicant are generally irrelevant to the validity of a request (see 7–011 to 7–015).

Step 2 Locating the information that answers the terms of the request.

1. The recipient public authority must search for and locate the information held by it that answers the terms of the request (see 11–034). As to:

   — what is "information" for the purposes of the Act, see 7–001 to 7–007;
   — when information is "held" by a public authority, see 7–008 to 7–009;
   — information that may be altered by a public authority after receipt of a request but before answering it, see 7–010.

2. If the recipient public authority believes that another public authority holds the requested information, it may be necessary to transfer the request to that public authority (see 8–002, 8–004(1) and (6) and 11–032 to 11–033).
3. If the recipient public authority locates either no information or only some information answering the terms of the request, some explanation to the applicant may be required (see 11–034 to 11–035).

Step 3 Identifying any exempt information.

1. Although information constitutes exempt information according to whether it falls within one or more of the provisions of Part II of the Act (ss.21–44), where more than one such provision applies to information, a public authority may, in refusing a request, choose the provision or provisions upon which it relies (see 13–009 and 14–013). For each provision relied upon, the public authority must bear in mind whether it is an absolute exemption or a qualified exemption: see paras 2–4 below.
2. In relation to each item of information answering the terms of the request, determine whether that information is exempt by reason of a purely class-based, absolute exemption. That is to say, the public authority must determine whether that information:

   (1) constitutes information that is reasonably accessible to the applicant otherwise than under the FOI Act (see 10–001 and 16–001 to 16–004);
   (2) constitutes information held by the requested public authority that was directly or indirectly supplied to it by, or that relates to, any of the specified security bodies (see 17–009 to 17–032);[1]
   (3) constitutes information held by the requested public authority only by virtue of that information being contained in a formal document filed with a court or tribunal, in a formal document served for the purposes of court or tribunal proceedings, or in a formal document created by a court or by staff of a court (see 20–031);
   (4) constitutes information held by the requested public authority only by virtue of it being contained in a document placed in the custody of a person con-

[1] If there is a conclusive certificate covering the information, that will conclude the determination: see 14–030 to 14–037 and 17–041 to 17–050.

ducting an inquiry or arbitration, or in a document created by a person conducting an inquiry or arbitration, for the purposes of the inquiry or arbitration (see 20–031);

(5) constitutes information for which exemption is required for the purpose of avoiding an infringement of the privileges of either House of Parliament (see 21–01 to 21–009);[2]

(6) constitutes personal data of which the applicant is the data subject (see 4–010, 4–017 to 4–022 and 24–005);

(7) constitutes personal data of which the applicant is not the data subject, that is not manual data and the disclosure of which would contravene one of the data protection principles (see 4–010 to 4–022 and 24–007 to 24–016);

(8) constitutes personal data of which the applicant is not the data subject and the disclosure of which would contravene one of the data protection principles (in the case of manual data, disregarding the exemptions from the data protection principles granted by s.33A of the Data Protection Act 1998) (see 4–010 to 4–022 and 24–007 to 24–016);

(9) constitutes information obtained by the public authority from any other person (including another public authority) the disclosure of which would constitute an actionable breach of confidence by the public authority (see 25–001 to 25–027); or

(10) constitutes information the disclosure of which is prohibited by or under an enactment, is incompatible with any Community obligation or would constitute a contempt of court (see 26–015 to 26–033).

3. In relation to each item of information answering the terms of the request, determine whether that information is exempt by reason of a prejudice-based, absolute exemption.[3] That is to say, the public authority must determine whether it constitutes information held by the House of Commons or the House of Lords that, in the reasonable opinion of the Speaker of the House of Commons or the Clerk of the Parliaments respectively, if disclosed under the FOI Act, would or would be likely to:

(i) prejudice the convention of the collective responsibility of Ministers of the Crown etc;

(ii) inhibit the free and frank provision of advice or exchange of views for the purposes of deliberation; or

(iii) otherwise prejudice the effective conduct of public affairs (see 22–018 to 22–024);

4. In relation to each item of information answering the terms of the request, determine whether that information is exempt by reason of a purely class-based, qualified exemption. That is to say, the public authority must determine whether that information:

(1) constitutes information intended for future publication (see 10–001 and 16–006 to 16–007);

(2) constitutes confidential information obtained from a foreign state or from an international organisation or court (see 25–039 to 25–040);

(3) constitutes information held by a public authority for the purposes of a criminal investigation or proceedings (see 20–004 to 20–005 and 20–014);

[2] If there is a Parliamentary certificate covering the information, that will conclude the determination: see 14–039 to 14–040.

[3] In relation to "prejudice" and the required degree of likelihood, see generally 15–012 to 15–020.

(4) constitutes information relating to the formulation of government policy (see 22–007 to 22–016);
(5) constitutes communications with Her Majesty or the Royal Household (see 26–001 to 26–013);
(6) constitutes environmental information (see 16–009 to 16–012); or
(7) constitutes information in respect of which a claim to legal professional privilege could be maintained (see 21–011 to 21–014);

5. In relation to each item of information answering the terms of the request, determine whether that information is exempt by reason of a prejudice-based, qualified exemption.[4] That is to say, the public authority must determine whether that information:
(1) constitutes information whose exemption is required for the purpose of safeguarding national security (see 17–033 to 17–040);[5]
(2) constitutes information whose disclosure would or would be likely to prejudice the defence of the British Islands or colonies or the armed forces (see 17–051 to 17–058);
(3) constitutes information whose disclosure would or would be likely to prejudice relations between the United Kingdom and any other State or international organisation or to prejudice the interests of the United Kingdom abroad (see 18–001 to 18–009);
(4) constitutes information whose disclosure would or would be likely to prejudice relations between administrations within the United Kingdom (see 18–014 to 18–018);
(5) constitutes information the disclosure of which would or would be likely to prejudice the economic or financial interests of the United Kingdom or any part of it (see 19–001 to 19–008);
(6) constitutes information the disclosure of which would or would be likely to prejudice the prevention or detection of crime, etc. (see 20–004 to 20–032);
(7) constitutes information the disclosure of which would or would be likely to endanger the physical or mental health of an individual or endanger an individual's safety (see 23–001 to 23–003);
(8) constitutes information that would or would be likely to prejudice an auditing body's audit functions (see 20–035);
(9) constitutes information, other than that held by the House of Commons or the House of Lords that, in the reasonable opinion of a qualified person, if disclosed under the FOI Act, would or would be likely to:
   (i) prejudice the convention of the collective responsibility of Ministers of the Crown, etc;
   (ii) inhibit the free and frank provision of advice or exchange of views for the purposes of deliberation; or
   (iii) otherwise prejudice the effective conduct of public affairs (see 22–001 to 22–024);[6] or
(10) constitutes a trade secret or constitutes information the disclosure of which would or would be likely to prejudice the commercial interests of any person (see 25–028 to 25–036).

[4] In relation to "prejudice" and the required degree of likelihood, see generally 15–012 to 15–020.
[5] If there is a conclusive certificate covering the information, that will conclude the determination: see 14–030 to 14–037 and 17–041 to 17–050.
[6] If there is a conclusive certificate covering the information, that will conclude the determination: see 14–030 to 14–037.

6. Where:
   (1) either:
      (a) it appears to a public authority that information is not exempt information; or
      (b) although the information is exempt information, the public authority does not intend to rely on a particular provision in Part II (ss. 21–44) of the Act,

   and
   (2) disclosure of the information, or of the existence of the information, will have implications for a third party,

   then the public authority should, as a matter of good practice, give consideration to consulting with that third party before concluding Step 3 (see 11–042 to 11–047).

Step 4 In relation to exempt information, determining whether under Part II of the FOI Act the existence duty does not arise.

1. This Step need not be complied with in relation to exempt information that has been (or within the time-limit will be) communicated to the applicant in accordance with s.1(1)(b) of the Act. In other words, it need not be complied with in relation to information rendered exempt information only by one or more qualified exemptions, where the public authority has, within the time-limit (see 11–022 to 11–029), reached a decision that, in all the circumstances of the case, the public interest in maintaining the exemption does not outweigh the public interest in disclosing the information and has communicated the information to the applicant: see 11–040.
2. In relation to other exempt information, the public authority must determine if the duty on it to inform the applicant whether it holds information of the description specified in the request does not arise by reason of a provision in Pt II (ss.21–44) of the FOI Act. Subject to the public interest weighing exercise (Step 7), the duty to confirm or deny will not arise:
   (1) Where the information sought:
      (a) has at any time been held for the purposes of a criminal investigation or is confidential information obtained for the purposes of the authority's functions relating to such an investigation;
      (b) has at any time been held as part of court or arbitral proceedings;
      (c) is held by a government department and relates to the formulation of policy or to Ministerial communications;
      (d) relates to communications with the Royal Family or the conferring of honours or dignities;
      (e) is required to be made available under the access to environmental information provisions; or
      (f) constitutes personal data of which the applicant is the data subject,

      then the public authority is excused from the duty to confirm or deny that such information is held.
   (2) Where, or to the extent that, exclusion from confirmation or denial of a holding of the information sought is required:
      (a) to safeguard national security;
      (b) to avoid an infringement of the privileges of either House of Parliament;
      (c) to avoid an actionable breach of confidence;

(d) to maintain the possibility of a claim of legal professional privilege; or
(e) to avoid contravention of an enactment or of a community obligation, or to avoid a contempt of court,

then the public authority is excused from the duty to confirm or deny that any information answering the request is held.

(3) Where the information sought:

(a) is intended for future publication;
(b) is supplied by, or relates to, bodies dealing with security matters; or
(c) is confidential information obtained from the Government of any State other than the United Kingdom or from an international organisation or court,

then the duty to confirm or deny does not arise if, or to the extent that, confirmation or denial that the requested public authority holds the information sought would itself involve the disclosure of any information so exempted from disclosure.

(4) Where confirmation or denial that the public authority holds the information sought would, or would be likely to, prejudice:

(a) the defence of the nation or the effectiveness of the armed forces;
(b) relations between the United Kingdom and another state or an international organisation or the interests of the United Kingdom abroad;
(c) governmental relations within the United Kingdom;
(d) the economic interests of the United Kingdom or the financial interests of any administration within the United Kingdom;
(e) the efficacy of law enforcement;
(f) the exercise of an auditing body's functions;
(g) Cabinet confidentiality, the frank provision of advice or the effective conduct of public affairs;
(h) the physical or mental health or safety of an individual; or
(i) the commercial interests of a person,

then the duty to confirm or deny is, to that extent, disapplied.

(5) Where the information sought constitutes personal data of which the applicant is not the data subject and where confirmation or denial that the public authority holds the information requested would contravene one of the data protection principles or s.10 of the Data Protection Act 1998 or the information is exempt from s.7(1)(a) of that Act, then the duty to confirm or deny is, to that extent, disapplied.

3. In relation to:

(1) information accessible to a applicant by other means; and
(2) information that constitutes a trade secret,

there is no disapplication of the duty to confirm or deny the existence of such information (see 14–004(6)).

Step 5 The first part of the response.

1. Having carried out Step 1 to Step 4, the public authority must respond promptly and in any event within specified time-limits (see 11–022 to 11–029).
2. The public authority may decide to give the applicant a fees notice (see 11–014 to 11–021). If a fees notice is given, this will defer the date for compliance with Step 5 for the period during which the fees notice is unsatisfied (see 11–027). In relation to the fees that may be sought, see 12–006 to 12–007. If the public authority

has not received the fee within 3 months of the fees notice having been given to the applicant, the public authority is thereafter not obliged to comply with the request (see 13–002(3)).

The duty to communicate

3. Where information is required to be communicated to the applicant, the means by which the recipient public authority does so may need to be in accordance with a preference expressed by the applicant (see 11–036 to 11–039). By communicating the information, the public authority is excused from compliance with the duty to confirm or deny in relation to that information (see 11–040) and, so far as that information is concerned, that concludes the public authority's duties under s.1(1).
4. Where the public authority is not obliged to communicate information on the basis that it is exempted by an absolute exemption, the public authority must, within the required time, give a refusal notice that includes all the details required by s.17(1) (see 13–009). The public authority may also be required to confirm or deny the existence of information (see paras 6–8 below).
5. Where the information is rendered exempt information by a qualified exemption,[7] then:

(1) If the public authority has, within the time specified in s.10(1) (see 11–028), reached a decision that in all the circumstances of the case, the public interest in maintaining the exemption outweighs the public interest in disclosing the information, then the public authority must within the specified period give a notice that includes:

— all the details required by s.17(1) (see 13–009); and
— a statement of the reasons for the claim that, in all the circumstances of the case, the public interest in maintaining the exemption outweighs the public interest in disclosing the information.

(2) If the public authority has not, within the time specified in s.10(1) (see 11–028), reached a decision that, in all the circumstances of the case, the public interest in maintaining the exemption outweighs the public interest in disclosing the information, then the public authority must within the specified period give a notice that includes:

— all the details required by s.17(1) (see 13–009);
— an indication that no decision as to the application of s.2(2)(b) has yet been reached; and
— an estimate of the date by which the public authority expects the public interest weighing decision to have been reached.

The public authority will then have to deal with Step 6 and Step 8 (*i.e.* weighing the public interest and informing the applicant of the outcome of that process).

In either case, the public authority may also be required to confirm or deny the existence of information (see paras 6–8 below).

[7] And not by an absolute exemption as well, unless the public authority seeks to rely only on the qualified exemption.

The duty to confirm or deny

6. Where, or to the extent that, under Step 4, a public authority is not obliged to inform the applicant that it holds information of the description specified in the request on the basis that the duty to confirm or deny is excluded by an absolute exclusion, the public authority must, within the time-limit, give a refusal notice that includes all the details required by s.17(1) (see 13–009). So far as that information is concerned, that concludes the public authority's duties under s.1(1) of the Act.
7. Where, or to the extent that, under Step 4, a public authority is not obliged to inform the applicant that it holds information of the description specified in the request on the basis that the duty to confirm or deny is excluded by a qualified exclusion[8] and:

   (1) The public authority has, within the time specified in s.10(1), reached a decision that in all the circumstances of the case, the public interest in maintaining the exclusion of the duty to confirm or deny outweighs the public interest in disclosing whether the public authority holds the information, then the public authority must within the time-limit give a notice that includes:

   — all the details required by s.17(1)(see 13–009); and
   — a statement of the reasons for the claim that, in all the circumstances of the case, the public interest in maintaining the exclusion outweighs the public interest in disclosing whether the public authority holds the information.

   So far as that information is concerned, that concludes the public authority's duties under s.1(1) of the Act.

   (2) The public authority has not, within the time specified in s.10(1), reached a decision that, in all the circumstances of the case, the public interest in maintaining the exclusion of the duty to confirm or deny outweighs the public interest in disclosing whether the public authority holds the information, then the public authority must within the time-limit give a notice that includes:

   — all the details required by s.17(1)(see 13–009);
   — an indication that no decision as to the application of s.2(1)(b) has yet been reached; and
   — an estimate of the date by which the public authority expects the public interest weighing decision to have been reached.

   So far as this information is concerned, the public authority will then have to deal with Step 7 and Step 8.

8. Where, or to the extent that, under Step 4, a public authority is obliged to inform the applicant that it holds information of the description specified in the request but is not, under Step 3, obliged to communicate that information to the applicant, the public authority must inform the applicant in writing that it holds information of the description specified in the request. So far as that information is concerned, that concludes the public authority's duties under s.1(1) of the Act.

---

[8] And not by an absolute exclusion as well, unless the public authority seeks to rely only on the qualified exclusion.

Step 6 In relation to each item of information to which para.5(2) in Step 5 applies, determining whether the public interest in maintaining the exemption outweighs the public interest in disclosing the information.

1. As to the manner in which the public interest is to be weighed, see 15–005 to 15–009.
2. Where information relates to a third party, it may be prudent to consult the third party before making the public interest determination (see 11–042 to 11–049).

Step 7 Where para.7(2) in Step 5 applies, determining whether the public interest in maintaining the exclusion of the duty to confirm or deny outweighs the public interest in disclosing whether the public authority holds the information.

1. As to the manner in which the public interest is to be weighed, see 15–010 to 15–011.

Step 8 The second part of the response.

1. The second part of the response is only required where the public authority, having to any extent relied upon a claim that s.2(1)(b) or 2(2)(b) applies (*i.e.* that the public interests weighed in favour of exemption/exclusion), did not in the first part of the response (Step 5) state that it was so relying on s.2 and state the reasons for that claim.
2. The public authority must respond within such time as is reasonable in the circumstances (see 11–028).

The duty to communicate

3. Where the public interest in maintaining the exemption outweighs the public interest in disclosing the information, the public authority must within the reasonable time, give a separate notice that states the reasons for the claim that, in all the circumstances of the case, the public interest in maintaining the exemption outweighs the public interest in disclosing the information (see 13–010).
4. Where the public interest in maintaining the exemption does not outweigh the public interest in disclosing the information, the public authority must communicate the information to the applicant. So far as that information is concerned, that concludes the public authority's duties under s.1(1).
5. Where information is required to be communicated to the applicant, the means by which the recipient public authority does so may need to be in accordance with a preference expressed by the applicant (see 11–036 to 11–039).

The duty to confirm or deny

6. Where, or to the extent that, under Step 5, a public authority is not obliged to inform the applicant that it holds information of the description specified in the request on the basis that the public interest in maintaining the exclusion of the duty to confirm or deny outweighs the public interest in disclosing that the public authority holds the information, the public authority must, within the reasonable time, give a separate notice that states the reasons for the claim that, in all the circumstances of the case, the public interest in maintaining the exemption outweighs the public interest in disclosing the information (see 13–010). So far as

that information is concerned, that concludes the public authority's duties under s.1(1) of the Act.

Step 9 Discretionary disclosure and assisting the applicant.

1. Where, as a result of the exercise in Step 5 or Step 8, the information requested by the applicant is not required to be disclosed, the public authority should as a matter of good practice:

   (1) Consider whether as a matter of discretion the information should be disclosed (see 5–001 to 5–010 and 14–006 to 14–012); and
   (2) Otherwise offer the applicant assistance (see 8–001 to 8–005). In particular, where the applicant has another statutory means of access to some or all the information requested (e.g. under the Data Protection Act 1998), the public authority should so advise the applicant (see Ch.4 and 5–011 to 5–072).
   (3) Where a public authority has, in part or in whole, refused a request for information, it should, as a matter of good practice, advise the applicant of his rights of appeal (see 28–001 to 28–012).

INDEX

all references are to paragraph number